55

R... EN... AND
and
WALES

Scale 1 : 1.500.000

0 5 10 15 20 25 30 35 40 45 50

English Miles.

0 10 20 30 40 50 60 70 80 90 100

Kilomètres.

French Steamers.

2°

Casquets
Southampton
Alderney
St. Anne
Race of Alderney
Cape de la Hague
Southampton
Cherbourg
Guernsey
Little Russel
Herm
Great Russel
St. Peter Port
Sark
40°
30'
La Déroute
Carteret
Jersey
La Corbière
Gorey
St Heliers
St Malo
Granville
2.° W. f. Gr.

borough Head
O
R
G
E
R
M
A
Withernsea
trington
Spurn Head
Humber
imsby
ethorpes
Thoresby
udboro

54

Railways
in use
in construction
Canals
Steamboat R...

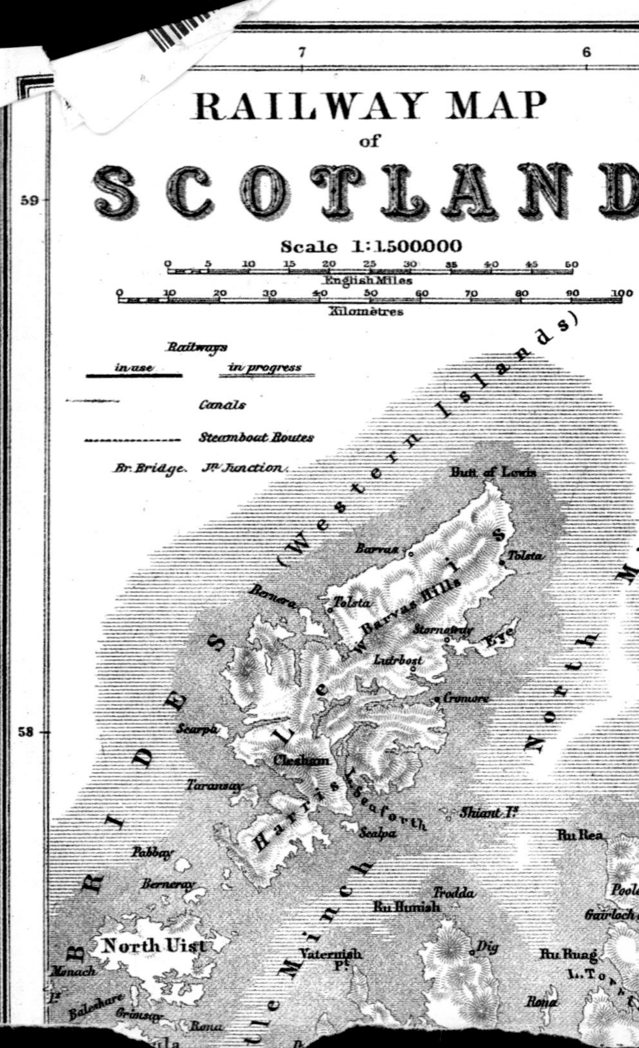

7
6
RAILWAY MAP
of
SCOTLAND
Scale 1:1.500.000
English Miles
Kilomètres
Railways
in use
in progress
Canals
Steamboat Routes
Br. Bridge. Jn. Junction.
59
58
(Western Islands)
Butt of Lewis
Barvas
Tolsta
Bernera
Tolsta
Barvas Hills
Stornoway
Eye
Lurbost
Crimore
Scarpa
Clesham
Taransay
Harris
Shiant Is.
Scalpa
Ru Rea
Pabbay
Berneray
Trodda
Ru Hunish
Poolewe
Gairloch
North Uist
Dig
Vaternish Pt.
Ru Ruag
Monach
Rona
Baleshare
Grimsay
Rona
North Minch

Baedeker's

GREAT BRITAIN

1890

A HANDBOOK FOR TRAVELLERS

WITH FOLD OUT MAPS, BUILDING PLANS,
STREET PLANS AND REGIONAL MAPS.

OLD HOUSE BOOKS
MORETONHAMPSTEAD DEVON
www.OldHouseBooks.co.uk

'Go, little book, God send thee good passage,
and specially let this be thy prayere
Unto them all that thee will read or hear,
Where thou art wrong, after their help to call,
Thee to correct in any part or all.'

PREFACE.

The *Handbook to Great Britain*, which was published in response to repeated requests from English and American tourists, and now appears in a second edition, is intended to help the traveller in planning his tour and disposing of his time to the best advantage, and thus to enable him the more thoroughly to enjoy and appreciate the objects of interest he meets with. The writer is *Mr. J. F. Muirhead, M. A.*, who has for several years taken part in the preparation of the English editions of Baedeker's Handbooks, and has personally visited the greater part of the districts described.

No one is better aware than the Editor himself of the imperfections almost inseparable from the early editions of a guide-book. For the improvement of this work, however, he confidently and gratefully looks forward to a continuance of those valuable corrections and suggestions with which travellers have long been in the habit of favouring him. Hotel-bills, with annotations showing the traveller's opinion as to his treatment and accommodation, are particularly useful.

The second edition of the Handbook to Great Britain has been carefully revised and brought down to date. The section devoted to Scotland has, in particular, been considerably extended and improved, but it is still so condensed as to form merely a stop-gap for the special Scottish volume which the Editor hopes to publish on some future occasion. A Handbook to Ireland is also contemplated.

In the preparation of the Handbook the Editor has received most material aid from numerous English friends. In particular he cannot refrain from expressing his acknowledgments to the Deans of the English and Welsh cathedrals; to several resident members of the Universities of Oxford and Cambridge; to *Professor Kirkpatrick* of Edinburgh; to the *Rev. Robert Gwynne, B. A.;* to the *Rev. W. S. Lach-Szyrma* (for data on Cornwall); to *Professor Tout* of Manchester; to *Professor Campbell Brown* of Liverpool; to the superior officials of most of the leading Railway Companies; and to *Messrs. Baddeley* and *Ward*, whose 'Thorough Guides' may be recommended to those in search of more detailed information regarding any particular district. The Introductory

Sketch of Architecture in England, from the pen of *Professor Edward A. Freeman*, will also materially enhance the value of the Handbook.

On the Maps and Plans, the number of which has been considerably increased in this edition, the Editor has bestowed special care, and he believes that they will often render material service to the traveller, and enable him at a glance to ascertain his bearings and select the best routes.

Hotels. The Editor has endeavoured to enumerate, not only the first-class hotels, but others also of more modest pretensions, which may be safely selected by the 'voyageur en garçon', with little sacrifice of comfort and great saving of expenditure. Although changes frequently take place, and prices generally have an upward tendency, the average charges stated in the Handbook will enable the traveller to form a fair estimate of his expenditure. The value of the asterisks, which are used as marks of commendation, is relative only; those prefixed to town-hotels and village-inns signifying respectively that the houses are good of their kind.

To hotel-proprietors, tradesmen, and others the Editor begs to intimate that a character for fair dealing and courtesy towards travellers forms the sole passport to his commendation, and that advertisements of every kind are strictly excluded from his Handbooks. Hotel-keepers are also warned against persons representing themselves as agents for Baedeker's Handbooks.

CONTENTS.

Scotland.

Railways

Cathedral Plans

Castle Plan

Street Plans

Maps

Panorama

Abbreviations

R = Room; A = Attendance; B = Breakfast; D = Dinner; L = Luncheon; N = North, Northern etc; S = South etc; E = East etc; W = West etc; M = English mile; ft = English foot; min = minute; hr = hour; L.N.W.R = London & North West Railway; G.W.R = Great Western Railway; N.B.R = North British Railway; and so on. E.E. = Early English (architecture); Dec = Decorated; Perp = Perpendicular;

The letter *d* with a date, after the name of a person, indicates the year of his death. The number of feet given after the name of a place shows its height above sea-level. The number of miles placed before the principal places on railway-routes indicates their distance from the starting-point of the route.

ASTERISKS are used as marks of commendation.

INTRODUCTION.

I. Money. Expenses. Passports. Custom House. Time.

Money. In Great Britain alone of the more important states of Europe the currency is arranged without much reference to the decimal system. The English *Gold* coins are the sovereign or pound (*l.* = livre) equal to 20 shillings, and the half-sovereign. The *Silver* coins are the crown (5 shillings), the half-crown, the double florin (4 shillings), the florin (2 shillings), the shilling (*s.*), and the sixpenny and threepenny pieces. The *Bronze* coinage consists of the penny (*d.*, Lat. denarius), of which 12 make a shilling, the halfpenny, and the farthing ($^1/_4$ *d.*). The *Guinea*, a sum of 21 *s.*, though still used in popular reckoning, is no longer in circulation as a coin. A sovereign is approximately equal to 5 American dollars, 25 francs, 20 German marks, or 10 Austrian florins (gold). The *Bank of England* issues notes for 5, 10, 20, 50, and 100 pounds, and upwards. These are useful in paying large sums; but for ordinary use, as change is not always readily procured, gold is preferable. The number of each note should be taken down in a pocket-book, for the purpose, in the event of its being lost or stolen, of stopping payment of it at the Bank, and thus possibly recovering it. The notes of certain provincial banks circulate locally, and in Scotland the place of the sovereign is very generally taken by the one-pound notes of several privileged banks, which circulate freely throughout the country. *Foreign Money* does not circulate in England, and it should always be exchanged on arrival. A convenient and safe mode of carrying money from America or the Continent is in the shape of letters of credit, or circular notes, which are readily procurable at the principal banks. A larger sum than will suffice for the day's expenses should never be carried on the person, and gold and silver coins of a similar size (*e.g.* sovereigns and shillings) should not be kept in the same pocket.

Expenses. The cost of a visit to Great Britain depends of course on the habits and tastes of the traveller. If he frequents first-class hotels, travels first-class on the railways, and systematically prefers driving to walking, he must be prepared to spend 30-40*s.* a day or upwards. Persons of moderate requirements, however, will have little difficulty, with the aid of the information in the Handbook, in travelling comfortably with a daily expenditure of 20-25*s.*, while the pedestrian of moderate requirements may reduce his expenses to 10-15*s.* per diem, or even less in some of the remoter districts.

Passports. These documents are not necessary in England, though occasionally useful in procuring delivery of registered and *poste restante* letters. A *visa* is quite needless.

Custom House. Almost the only articles likely to be in the possession of ordinary travellers on which duty is charged are spirits and tobacco, but a flask of the former and 1/2lb. of the latter are allowed for private use. Three pounds of tobacco may be passed on payment of a duty of 5*s.* per pound, with the addition (in the case of cigars) of a slight fine for the contravention of the law forbidding the importation of cigars in chests of fewer than 10,000. Foreign reprints of copyright English books are liable to confiscation. The custom-house examination is generally lenient.

Time. Uniformity of time throughout the country is maintained by telegraphic communication with Greenwich Observatory.

II. Routes to and from England.

It may not be out of place here to furnish a list of the principal oceanic routes between the New World and England, and also to indicate how Transatlantic visitors may continue their European travels by passing from London to the Continent. An enumeration of the routes between the Continent of Europe and London may also prove serviceable to foreigners coming in the reverse direction. It should, however, be borne in mind that the times and fares mentioned in our list are liable to alteration.

Routes to England from the United States of America and from Canada. The traveller has abundant room for choice in the matter of his oceanic passage, the steamers of any of the following companies affording comfortable accommodation and speedy transit.

Inman Line. Every Wed. from New York to Liverpool; cabin 60-650 dollars. From Liverpool also every Wed.; fare 12-135*l.* Return-tickets (available for 12 months) issued at reduced rates.

Cunard Line. A steamer of this company starts every Sat. and every second Tues. from New York and every Thurs. from Boston for Queenstown and Liverpool. Cabin fare 60, 80, 100, or 125 dollars, according to accommodation; return-ticket (available for 12 months) 120, 144, 180, or 220 dollars. Steamers from Liverpool for New York every Sat. and every second Tues., for Boston every Thursday. Fare 12, 15, 18, or 21 guineas, or 26*l.*; return-ticket, 25, 30, or 35 guineas, or 45*l.*

White Star Line. Steamer every alternate Wed. from New York to Queenstown and Liverpool. Cabin 60-140 dollars; steerage 20 dollars. From Liverpool to New York every Wednesday. Cabin 12-22*l.*, return (available for one year) 24-40*l.*; intermediate 7-8*l.*

American Steamship Company. From Philadelphia to Liverpool every Thurs., and from Liverpool to Philadelphia every Wednesday. Cabin 10 to 18*gs.*; return-ticket 20 to 30*gs.*; intermediate 6*l.*

National Steamship Company. Steamers from Liverpool, and also from London direct, to New York every week. From New York to Liverpool and from New York to London weekly.

North German Lloyd Line. Between New York and Southampton twice weekly (from Southampton on Thurs. and Sun.); first saloon 16-23*l.*, second saloon 10*l.* 10*s.* and 13*l.*

Anchor Line. Steamer between Liverpool and New York monthly. Saloon 12-25*l.*; return 22-44*l.* Also weekly mail-steamer between New York and Glasgow. Saloon from 9*gs.*, second cabin 6*gs.*, steerage 4*l.*

Allan Line. From Liverpool every Thurs. and from London fortnightly to Quebec and Montreal, and every alternate Tues. from Liverpool to St. John's, Halifax, and Baltimore. Saloon 10-20*gs.*; intermediate 6*gs.* Also to New York weekly (Wilson-Hill Line).

Guion Line. Weekly steamers between New York and Liverpool. Cabin fare 10-26*l.*; children under 12 years, half-fare.

State Line. Weekly steamers between New York and Glasgow. Saloon 6 to 8*gs.*

Dominion Line. From Liverpool weekly and from Bristol fortnightly in summer to Quebec and Montreal; in winter from Liverpool fortnightly to Halifax and Portland. Saloon 10-18*gs.*; intermediate 6-8*gs.*

The average duration of the passage across the Atlantic is 8-10$^1/_2$ days. The best time for crossing is in summer. Passengers should pack clothing and other necessaries for the voyage in small flat boxes or portmanteaus, such as can lie easily in the cabin, as all bulky luggage is stowed away in the hold. State-room trunks should not exceed 3 ft. in length, 2 ft. in breadth, and 1$^1/_2$ ft. in height. Dress for the voyage should be of a plain and serviceable description, and it is advisable, even in midsummer, to be provided with warm clothing. A deck-chair, which may be purchased at the dock or on the steamer before sailing (from 7*s.* upwards), is a luxury that may almost be called a necessary (comp. p. 324). It may be left in charge of the Steamship Co.'s agents until the return-journey. On going on board, the traveller should apply to the purser or chief steward for seats at table, as the same seats are retained throughout the voyage. It is usual to give a fee of 10*s.* (2$^1/_2$ dollars) to the table-steward and to the state-room steward, and small gratuities are also expected by the boot-cleaner, the bath-steward, etc. The state-room steward should not be 'tipped' until he has brought all the passenger's small baggage safely on to the landing-stage or tender. — Landing at Liverpool, see pp. 324, 330.

Routes from England to the Continent. The following are the favourite routes between London and the Continent: —

From *Dover to Calais*, thrice daily, in 1$^1/_4$-1$^1/_2$ hr.; cabin 8*s.* 6*d.*, steerage 6*s.* 6*d.* (Railway from London to Dover, or *vice versâ*, in 2-4 hrs.; fares 20*s.* or 18*s.* 6*d.*, 15*s.* or 13*s.* 6*d.*, 6*s.* 9*d.* or 6*s.* 2$^1/_2$*d.*)

From *Folkestone* to *Boulogne*, twice daily, in 1$^1/_2$-2 hrs.; cabin 8*s.*, steerage 6*s.* (Railway from London to Folkestone in 2-4 hrs.; fares same as to Dover, except 3rd class, which is 6*s.*)

From *Dover* to *Ostend*, thrice daily, in 4-5 hrs.; cabin 15*s.*, fore-cabin 10*s.*

From *London* to *Ostend*, twice weekly, in 12 hrs. (6 hrs. at sea); 10*s.*, 7*s.* 6*d.*

From *London* to *Rotterdam*, twice a week, in 18-20 hrs. (9-10 hrs. at sea); 20*s.* or 16*s.*

From *Harwich* to *Rotterdam*, daily (Sundays excepted), in 11-12 hrs.; railway from London to Harwich in 2-3 hrs. (fares 13*s.* 3*d.*, 10*s.*, 5*s.* 11$^1/_2$*d.*); fare from London to Rotterdam, 26*s.* or 15*s.*

From *London* to *Antwerp*, every Sat., in 16 hrs. (8-9 hrs. of which are on the open sea); 15*s.* or 11*s.*

From *Harwich* to *Antwerp*, daily (Sundays excepted), in 12-13 hrs. (train from London to Harwich in 2-3 hrs.); 26*s.* or 15*s.* (from London).

From *Harwich* to *Hamburg*, twice weekly (train from London to Harwich in 2-3 hrs.); fares from London 1*l.* 17*s.* 6*d.*, 1*l.* 15*s.* 9*d.*, 1*l.* 5*s.* 9*d.*

From *London* to *Bremen*, twice a week, in 36-40 hrs.; 1*l.* 10*s.*, 15*s.*, or 10*s.*

From *London* to *Hamburg*, thrice weekly, in 36-40 hrs.; 1*l.* 10*s.* or 1*l.*

From *Queenborough* to *Flushing*, twice daily (Sundays excepted), in 8 hrs. (5 hrs. at sea); train from London to Queenborough in 1$^1/_2$ hr., from Flushing to Amsterdam in 6-9 hrs.; through-fare 33*s.* 6*d.* or 20*s.* 11*d.*

From *Newhaven* to *Dieppe*, daily, in 6-8 hrs.; 17*s.* 7*d.* or 13*s.* 1*d.* (Rail from London to Newhaven, or *vice versâ*, in 2-3 hrs.; fares 11*s.* 3*d.*, 7*s.* 10*d.*, and 4*s.* 8$^1/_2$*d.*)

On the longer voyages (10 hrs. and upwards), or when special attention has been required, the steward expects a gratuity of 1*s.* or more, according to circumstances. Food and liquors are supplied on board all the steamboats at fixed charges, but the viands are often not very inviting. An official *Interpreter* accompanies the chief trains on the Dover and Folkestone routes.

III. Railways. Coaches. Steamboats.

Railways. In proportion to area and population, the railway-system of Great Britain is more extensive than that of any other country in Europe, Belgium excepted. The length of lines in operation amounts to fully 17,000 M., of which 14,000 M. are in England and Wales and 3000 M. in Scotland. The lines are all in private hands, by far the greater part of the traffic being monopolised by ten or twelve large railway-companies (see table). The carriages (1st, 2nd, and 3rd class) of the more important companies are generally clean and comfortable, but those of some of the lines

Company	Miles	Gross Revenue	Train-Miles run	No. of Passengers
Great Western	2477	8,468,637*l.*	33,046,892	55,098,300
London & North Western	1875½	11,207,008*l.*	40,543,888	59,333,417
Midland	1800	8,331,120*l.*	37,638,022	34,581,522
North Eastern	1578	6,837,870*l.*	25,360,992	38,211,572
Great Eastern	1112	3,965,047*l.*	17,016,845	73,654,253
Great Northern	936	4,185,030*l.*	18,977,560	28,475,387
London & South Western	815	3,305,669*l.*	12,390,762	39,718,347
Lancashire & Yorkshire	524	4,181,040*l.*	15,535,741	42,571,329
London, Brighton, & South Coast	476	2,382,209*l.*	8,849,261	40,679,783
South Eastern	392½	2,291,790*l.*	7,222,604	28,656,417
Manchester, Sheffield, & Lincolnshire	290	2,140,853*l.*	11,605,553	—
London, Chatham, & Dover	194	1,419,458*l.*	4,104,277	28,776,962

to the S. of London, as well as of most of the minor railways still surviving throughout the country, leave much to be desired. The Midland Railway Co. discontinued the use of second-class carriages some years ago, an example that has lately been followed by the Great Northern Railway on the part of its system not near London and by other companies. This action has had the effect of improving the third-class accommodation throughout the country, and of inducing a superior class of travellers to use it, especially on long journeys. Each company is bound by Act of Parliament to run at least one train daily ('parliamentary train') at a fare (3rd cl.) not exceeding 1*d.* per mile; but the 3rd class fares in many of the fast trains are considerably in excess of this rate. Return-tickets are usually granted on very liberal terms; and circular tour tickets

See foldout Railway Map of England and Wales at front of book are issued in all the districts chiefly frequented by tourists (comp. pp. 277, 451). Smoking is not permitted except in the compartments provided for the purpose. The speed of British trains is usually much higher than that of Continental railways, and a rate of 40-50 M. an hour is not uncommon (comp. pp. 106, 455).

On all the English lines the first-class passenger is entitled to carry 112*lb.* of luggage free, second-class 80*lb.*, and third-class 60*lb.* The companies, however, rarely make any charge for overweight, unless the excess is exorbitant. On all inland routes the traveller should see that his luggage is duly labelled for his destination, and put into the right van, as otherwise the railways are not responsible for its transport. Travellers to the Continent require to book their luggage and obtain a ticket for it, after which it gives them no farther trouble. The railway porters are nominally forbidden to accept gratuities, but it is a common custom to give 2*d*-6*d*. to the porter who transfers the luggage from the cab to the train or vice versâ.

Travellers accustomed to the formalities of Continental railway officials may perhaps consider that in England they are too much left to themselves. Tickets are not invariably checked at the beginning of a journey, and travellers should therefore make sure that they are in the proper compartment. The names of the stations are not always so conspicuous as they should be (especially at night); and the way in which the porters call them out, laying all the stress on the last syllable, is seldom of much assistance. The officials, however, are generally civil in answering questions and giving information. In winter foot-warmers with hot water are usually provided. It is 'good form' for a passenger quitting a railway-carriage where there are other travellers to close the door behind him, and to pull up the window if he has had to let it down to reach the door-handle.

The figures in the accompanying table refer to 1889; the number of passengers is exclusive of season-ticket holders.

Bradshaw's Railway Guide (monthly; 6*d.*) is the most complete; but numerous others (the *ABC Railway Guide*, etc.), claiming to be easier of reference, are also published. Each of the great railway-companies publishes a monthly guide to its own system (price 1-2*d.*).

Coaches. There is now practically nothing in England or Wales corresponding to the diligence of the Continent, as the railway net has substantially covered the entire island. In some of the most frequented tourist-districts, however, such as Wales, the Lakes, Devon, and Cornwall, coaches with two or four horses run regularly in the season, affording a very pleasant mode of locomotion in fine weather. In some places (*e.g.* between New Quay and Bideford; R. 19) coaches afford the only regular communication. Coaches also ply from London to various points in the vicinity. The coaches are generally well-horsed and the fares reasonable. The best places are on the box-seat, beside the driver, who usually expects a small gratuity. — The regular charge for one-horse carriages is 1*s.* per mile, carriage-and-pair 1*s.* 6*d.*-2*s.* per mile (half-fare in returning; *i.e.* the one-horse carr. fare to a point 10 M. off, and back, should be about 15*s.*); driver extra.

Steamboats. Steamboats play by no means so important a part in the tourist-districts of England and Wales as they do in those of Scotland (see p. 452); but lovers of the sea will find no difficulty in indulging their taste, as the coasts of England are alive with steamers plying between the various ports. In summer steamers run between the chief sea-bathing resorts and the nearest large towns, and small pleasure-steamers ply on some of the lakes in the Lake District and on a few of the prettier rivers, particularly in the S. of England (comp. pp. 133, 142, 145, 448).

Steamers to the *Isle of Man*, see p. 340; to *Scotland*, see p. 462; to the *Isle of Wight*, see p. 67; to the *Channel Islands*, see p. 84.

IV. Plan of Tour.

The plan of tour must depend entirely on the traveller's taste and the time he has at his disposal. It may, however, be stated here that all the attractions of the island cannot possibly be visited in the course of a single summer. Among the most attractive districts are the English Lakes (R. 48); Edinburgh and the Scottish Highlands (RR. 64, 66-69); North Wales (R. 40); Devon and Cornwall (RR. 17-21); South Wales (RR. 25-29) and the Valley of the Wye (R. 22); the Shakespeare Country (RR. 33, 34); the Derbyshire Peak (R. 45); Surrey (R. 8); the Isle of Wight (R. 10); and the Channel Islands (R. 12). A glance at the map will show which groups can be most easily combined; but it should be remembered that even the most widely separated districts are brought comparatively near each other by the admirable and speedy service of the railway-system. One of the most characteristic and interesting features of England consists in its cathedral cities, a round of which alone makes a most delightful tour, while a visit to two or three can easily be added to an excursion in any of the districts above named, the map again helping to decide. Among the more important cathedrals may be mentioned those of Canterbury (p. 25), Lincoln (p. 426), York (p. 406), Salisbury (p. 99), Durham (p. 411), Ely (p. 440), Gloucester (p. 170), Norwich (p. 445), Lichfield (p. 347), Peterborough (p. 362), Winchester (p. 77), and Wells (p. 123); but many of the others are of nearly equal interest. Those who can manage it should not omit a visit to either Oxford (R. 32) or Cambridge (R. 56), or both.

The pedestrian is unquestionably the most independent of travellers, and in exploring the Scottish and Welsh mountains he will have many advantages over the traveller by rail or coach. For a short tour a couple of flannel shirts, a pair of worsted stockings, slippers, the articles of the toilet, a light waterproof, and a stout umbrella will generally be found a sufficient equipment. Strong and well-tried boots are essential to comfort. Heavy and complicated knapsacks should be avoided; a light pouch or game-bag is far less irksome, and its position may be shifted at pleasure. A more extensive reserve of clothing should not exceed the limits of a small portmanteau, which may be forwarded from town to town by railway. The sheets of the Ordnance Survey, published at a very moderate price, will be found invaluable for the pedestrian (see p. xxxii). — For hints to cyclists, see p. xxv.

V. Hotels.

The first-class hotels in the principal towns, fashionable watering places, and most frequented tourist-resorts throughout England and Wales are generally good and somewhat expensive; but in many of the large commercial and industrial centres the requirements of the 'uncommercial traveller' are very inadequately met. When ladies are of the party, it is advisable to frequent the best hotels, as the charges of the second-best are often not appreciably lower, while the comforts are considerably less. Gentlemen travelling alone, however, will often find comfortable accommodation at a moderate rate in smaller inns of quite unassuming appearance. — *Temperance Hotels*, *i.e.* houses in which no intoxicating liquors are supplied, abound throughout the country. Their charges are moderate, but as a general rule their cuisine and fitting up do not entitle them to rank higher than second-class.

The average charges in a first-class hotel are as follows: room 2*s.* 6*d.*-4*s.*; attendance 1*s.* 6*d.*; plain breakfast 1*s.* 6*d.*, with ham and eggs or meat 2*s.*-2*s.* 6*d.*, with fish 2*s.* 6*d.*-3*s.*; table d'hôte dinner 4-5*s.*; tea, same charges as for breakfast; hot bath 1*s.*, cold bath in bedroom 6*d.* As a rule the price of dinner, whether table d'hôte or a coffee-room dinner of 3-6 courses, may be approximately stated as equal to the charge for room and attendance. No charge is made for lights. 'Pension' as used throughout the Handbook includes board, lodging, and attendance; D. means table d'hôte dinner. At many hotels in watering-places, it is customary to supply breakfast also on the table-d'hôte system, at a charge of 2*s.* 6*d.*-3s. Luncheon is generally ordered *à la carte;* for bread and cheese the ordinary charge is 1*s.* The head-waiter, who presents the bill, and the 'boots' expect a gratuity when the visitor leaves; but the services of the former are, strictly speaking, included in 'attendance'.

As compared with Continental hotels, English hotels may be said as a rule to excel in beds, cleanliness, and sanitary arrangements, while their cuisine is on the whole inferior. The English table d'hôte dinner is usually dear and seldom so good as its prototype on the Continent; while the culinary art of hotels off the beaten track of tourists scarcely soars beyond the preparation of plain joints, steaks, chops, vegetables, and puddings. Those, however, who are content with simple but substantial fare will find little to complain of. Beer is the customary beverage (2-3*d.* per glass, 4-6*d.* per pint or tankard), but wine is more usual at fashionable tables d'hôte, where beer is sometimes not supplied except in bottles and at higher rates. Restaurants are not nearly so common in England as on the Continent, and in most provincial places it is better to go to a hotel for meals. The dining-room is called the *Coffee Room.* Smoking is not permitted except in the *Smoking Room* and the *Billiard Room.* Refreshments ordered in either of the last are generally paid for on the spot. Billiard-rooms are not usually found at second-class hotels except in large towns; the charge is 6*d.* per game of 50 points.

In all first-class hotels the visitor has a right to expect a high degree of comfort; and he need have no hesitation in requiring such small conveniences as hot water in the morning and before table d'hôte, an abundant supply of towels, pen and ink in his bedroom, etc. In hotels not lighted throughout with gas there should be a supply of bedroom-candles on every floor, and not merely at the foot of the staircase. Station hotels are sometimes convenient, but often noisy. At some of the fashionable spas (Harrogate, Buxton, etc.) it is usual to make a fixed charge per day, covering everything; and if visitors do not wish to be tied down to the hotel-meals they should make a special agreement.

The **Hydropathic Establishments**, now so numerous in the popular tourist-districts of England, Wales, and Scotland, are frequented by pleasure-seekers as much as by patients, and may almost be described as large temperance hotels, in which the guests take their meals in common at prescribed hours and submit to various other general regulations. The hydropathic treatment may be followed or not, as the visitor pleases. The usual charge is about 8-10*s.* a day or 2½-3 guineas a week.

VI. Sports and Pastimes

by

W. Blew.

Although there are few places in Great Britain which do not offer the visitor more or less facility for sport and pastime, the stranger will find the most varied programme when he locates himself in some large town. The tendency of the time is to bring as many amusements as possible within the limits of enclosed grounds. These enclosures are, almost without exception, the property of a club, for the members of which the best accommodation is reserved. The public, however, can obtain admission by payment to the grounds and to stands not set apart for members. Forth-coming events are advertised in the papers, and any information on sporting matters may be obtained by addressing a letter to the editor of one of the sporting journals, such as the *Field* or the *Sporting News*.

Horse Racing. The chief Race Meetings held in enclosed grounds are those at Sandown and Kempton Park (see *Baedeker's London)*, Manchester, Leicester, Derby, Four Oaks (near Birmingham), and Gosforth Park (near Newcastle-on-Tyne). There are several annual meetings at each of these places; and owing to the large sums raced for, and the superior nature of the arrangements, these 'Gate-money' meetings are very popular. Many of the old-fashioned 'open' meetings, however, still survive. There is no charge for going on the course at Newmarket (p. 449), Epsom, Ascot (see *Baedeker's London)*, Goodwood (p. 56), and many other places, though, of course, payment must be made for entrance to the stands and paddocks. When the racing season closes, towards the end of November, the enclosed grounds are used for steeplechases and coursing meetings, the hares being kept in a pen and 'enlarged' as required. The chief steeplechase of the year is the *Liverpool Grand National*, run for in March; the course is upwards of 4½ M. long and the value of the stakes is about 1000*l.* The *Grand National Hunters' Steeplechase* is for horses coming under the definition of hunters, and takes place on a different course each year. Hunt Steeplechases, confined for the most part to horses which have been ridden with specified packs of hounds, are frequent in March and April, and are growing more and more popular.

Hunting. Nearly the whole of England is hunted over by hounds of some kind or another, and no difficulty need be experienced in seeing a pack at work. In most counties hunters may be hired at a charge of 2-3 guineas a day. — The *Devon and Somerset Staghounds* hunt over Exmoor (p. 164) and the Quantocks, pursuing the wild red deer which is found by the 'tufters.' Horses may be hired at Dulverton (p. 128), Taunton (p. 127), etc. With the exception of the *New Forest Pack*, all other packs of staghounds hunt the carted deer. Fox-hunting, however, is the most popular branch of this sport, and is seen in its glory in the so-called 'Shires', including Leicestershire (the chief), Northamptonshire, and parts of Rutland and Warwickshire. Most packs are maintained by subscription; and though anyone may hunt with them for a day or two without giving anything, more frequent visitors are expected to contribute to the support of the hounds. The packs of harriers are very numerous. The hunting season is opened by the Devon and Somerset Staghounds in the second week in August; cub-hunting begins in September; and the *Royal Buckhounds* meet for forest-hunting at Ascot on the first Tuesday in October. Regular hunting begins on Nov. 1st, and lasts till about the middle of April, though in some counties a May fox is killed.

Fishing. Wherever there is a river in England and Wales, some kind of fishing may be had; and full information as to the conditions may generally be obtained at the local fishing-tackle shops. A good deal of the water is free, but in some cases a charge is made to anglers, while in others fishing is granted as a favour only, and the general public are entirely excluded. Slapton Lea (p. 133) merits notice, as the lake is close to the sea, and salt and fresh water fishing can be had within a stone's throw of each other. Deep-sea fishing can be indulged in at any of the seaside resorts, but it is useless for the stranger to try it without a fisherman.

Shooting. Though a few hotels advertise the right of shooting over a considerable area as open to their visitors, this is seldom of much account; and this pastime is practically confined to the owners and hirers of shootings and their friends.

Aquatics. *Boating* is practised on all rivers wide and deep enough. The beauties of the Thames are well-known, and a favourite trip is to descend from Oxford to London by boat (see p. 218). The chief rowing fixture of the year is Henley Regatta (p. 220). — The *Yachting* season begins on the Thames and ends with the regattas on the Devonshire Coast in September. Comp. pp. 75, 131. — Sailing on the Norfolk Broads, see p. 449.

Cricket is played everywhere, and the visitor who makes a prolonged stay will find no difficulty in joining a club. The best cricket is to be seen at Lord's and the Oval in London (see *Baedeker's London*), on the grounds of the 'first-class' counties, and at Oxford and Cambridge. The leading counties are Nottingham, Surrey, York, Lancashire, Middlesex, Kent, Sussex, and Gloucester. The cricket weeks at Canterbury (p. 25; in Aug.) and at Scarborough (p. 419; Sept.) also deserve notice. The Marylebone Club (at Lord's) is the chief governing body in the cricket world.

Lawn Tennis. Courts open to strangers on payment are found here and there in old skating-rinks, drill-halls, public gardens, etc., but as a rule this game cannot be seen to perfection except in the grounds of clubs or private persons. Tournaments, open to visitors on payment, take place in London, Buxton, Leamington, Torquay, and many other centres. Tennis lawns are often attached to the large hotels in fashionable resorts.

Lack of space forbids more than a mere mention of the following sports and pastimes, all more or less popular in England: *Polo*, *Archery*, *Football*, *Hockey*, *Otter-hunting*, *Golf*, and *La Crosse*.

Cycling (communicated by *Mr. E. R. Shipton*). Cycling prospers to an amazing degree in Britain, where it is estimated that there are about 500,000 cyclists, men and women, while about 50,000 hands derive employment, directly or indirectly, from the manufacture and sale of bicycles and tricycles. The English roads, though inferior to some of the 'chaussées' of the Continent, are upon the whole above the average; and the American cyclist will probably find them far better adapted to his requirements than the ordinary highways of the United States. Speaking roughly, cycling in Britain is circumscribed only by the area of the island; but as a general rule the gradients of the roads inland will be found less severe than those along the coast, while their surfaces are also generally better. The roads of England and Scotland are usually preferable to those of Wales and Ireland. The tourist, however, should not plan his route without regard to the configuration of the country, a knowledge of which is best attained by consulting a good map. [Black's map on the scale of 4 miles to an inch, mounted on linen, is portable and well adapted to the cyclist's use; it may be obtained in sections (at 2*s*. 6*d*. per sheet) from Messrs. Collins, New Bridge St., Blackfriars, London, S.E., or from any bookseller.]

The American traveller who lands at Liverpool and has either brought his machine with him or has arranged to have one sent to meet him may profitably begin riding at once. If he turn to the S., he may proceed viâ *Chester*, *Stafford*, and *Birmingham* to *Coventry*, whence he may diverge to take in *Stratford-on-Avon*, *Kenilworth*, and *Leamington*, continuing the journey to *London* either direct or viâ *Oxford*. Should time admit, the run may be continued to *Reading*, *Bristol*, and through *Mid-Devon* to the *Land's End;* or in shorter stages, as befits the roads, along the beautiful coast of *North Devon*. From Cornwall he may return to London viâ *Plymouth* and *Exeter;* or he may skirt the S. coast to *Southampton*, *Brighton*, and *Ramsgate*, running thence to London through *Canterbury* and *Maid-*

stone. Should the traveller elect to go northward from Liverpool, he may visit the *English Lakes*, *Carlisle*, the *Land of Burns*, the *Scottish Lakes*, the *Highlands*, and so to *John o' Groat's House;* returning by *Aberdeen*, *Perth*, *Edinburgh*, *Newcastle*, *York*, *Cambridge*, etc. The Continental cyclist, landing at Dover, Harwich, or any of the other usual steamboat harbours, may also begin his riding at once.

The cyclist who contemplates even the shortest tour in Great Britain will find it decidedly advantageous to become a member of the *Cyclists' Touring Club*, which now possesses nearly 25,000 members. It has a resident Chief Consul in the United States (*Mr. F. W. Weston*, Savin Hill, Boston) and also a Chief Consul for Continental Europe (*Mr. S. A. Stead*, 30 St. George's Avenue, Tufnell Park, London, N.). The entrance fee of this club is 1*s*., and the annual subscription 2*s*. 6*d*. American cyclists who wish to become members may apply to Mr. Weston. Should they arrive in England without having been enrolled, they should communicate with the secretary (*Mr. E. R. Shipton*, 139 Fleet St., London, E.C.), who, should their credentials be satisfactory, will send them a provisional certificate of membership on payment of an additional fee of 2*s*. 6*d*. The new member should then at once buy the Handbook of the C. T. C. (1*s*.; sold to members only). This contains a list of 2000 hotels throughout the country, which charge members of the Club a reduced tariff; the addresses of nearly 1000 consuls (*i.e.* local resident wheelmen, who are pledged to help their fellow-members by information and advice); the names of over 2000 cycle repairers; and much other useful information. The Club has published a Road Book of the Continent, and is preparing one of Great Britain.

VII. Outline of English History.

The following sketch of English history may prove useful for reference in connection with the interesting historical associations which crowd upon the traveller at every step.

Roman Period (B. C. 55–A. D. 445).

B. C. 55-54. Of Britain before its first invasion by **Julius Cæsar** in B. C. 55 there is no authentic history. Cæsar repeats his invasion in B. C. 54, but makes no permanent settlement.

43 A. D. Emp. **Claudius** undertakes the subjugation of Britain.

78-85. Britain, with part of Caledonia, is overrun by the Roman general **Agricola**, and reduced to the form of a province.

412. Roman legions recalled from Britain by **Honorius.**

445. The Britons, deprived of their Roman protectors, are unable to resist the attacks of the *Picts*, and summon the *Saxons*, under *Hengist* and *Horsa*, to their aid.

Anglo-Saxon Period (445-1066).

445-577. The Saxons, re-inforced by the *Angles*, *Jutes*, and other Germanic tribes, gradually overrun Britain and thus lay the foundations of the kingdom of *England*. To this period belong the semi-mythical exploits of *King Arthur* and his knights.

588-685. The Northumbrian Kingdom. Christianity re-introduced by *St. Augustine* (597). *Caedmon* (about 665).

685-828. The Three Kingdoms (Northumbria, Mercia, Wessex). The *Venerable Bede* (d. 735).

828. **Egbert** of Wessex recognized as overlord of all English kingdoms.

835-871. Contests with the *Danes*, who repeatedly invade England.

871-901. **Alfred the Great** defeats the Danes, and compels them to make peace. Creates navy, establishes militia, revises laws, re-organises institutions, is a patron of learning, and himself an author.

979-1016. **Ethelred the Unready** draws down upon England the vengeance of the Danes by a massacre of those who had settled in England.

1013. The Danish king **Sweyn** conquers England.

1016-1035. **Canute the Great,** the son of Sweyn, reigns over England.

1035-1040. **Harold Harefoot,** illegitimate son of Canute, usurps the throne.

1040-1042. **Hardicanute,** son of Canute. — The Saxon line is restored in the person of —

1042-1066. **Edward the Confessor,** who makes London the capital of England, and builds Westminster Abbey. His brother-in-law and successor —

1066. **Harold,** son of Earl Godwin, loses his kingdom and his life at the *Battle of Hastings*, where he opposed the invasion of the Normans, under William the Conqueror.

NORMAN DYNASTY (1066-1154).

1066-1087. **William the Conqueror,** of Normandy, establishes himself as King of the English. Introduction of Norman (French) language and customs.

1087-1100. **William II.,** surnamed *Rufus*, after a tyrannical reign, is accidentally shot by Sir Walter Tyrrell while hunting (p. 83).

1100-1135. **Henry I.,** *Beauclerc*, defeats his elder brother Robert, Duke of Normandy, at the battle of *Tenchebrai* (1106), and adds Normandy to the possessions of the English crown. He leaves his kingdom to his daughter *Matilda*, who however, is unable to wrest it from —

1135-1154. **Stephen,** *of Blois*, grandson of the Conqueror. David, King of Scotland, and uncle of Matilda, is defeated and taken prisoner at the *Battle of the Standard* (1138). Stephen appoints as his successor Matilda's son, Henry of Anjou or Plantagenet (from the *planta genista* or broom, the badge of this family).

HOUSE OF PLANTAGENET (1154-1399).

1154-1189. **Henry II.** Strife with *Thomas Becket*, Archbishop of Canterbury, regarding the respective spheres of the civil and ecclesiastical powers. The Archbishop excommunicates the King's followers, and is murdered by four knights at Canterbury (1170). Conquest of Ireland (1170-72). *Robin Hood*, the forest outlaw, flourishes.

1189-1199. **Richard I.,** *Coeur de Lion*, takes a prominent part in the Third Crusade, but is captured on his way home, and imprisoned in Germany for upwards of a year. He carries on war with Philip II. of France.

1199-1216. **John,** surnamed *Lackland*, is defeated at *Bouvines* (1214) by Philip II. of France, and loses Normandy. *Magna Charta*, the groundwork of the English constitution, is extorted from him by his Barons (1215).

1216-1272. **Henry III.,** by his misrule, becomes involved in a war with his Barons, headed by *Simon de Montfort*, and is defeated at *Lewes*. His son Edward gains the battle of *Evesham*, where De Montfort is slain. *Hubert de Burgh* defeats the French at sea. Provisions of Oxford (1258). Commons summoned to Parliament (1265). *Roger Bacon*, the philosopher.

1272-1307. **Edward I.,** *Longshanks*, overcomes the Welsh under *Llewellyn*, and completes the conquest of Wales. The heir-apparent to the English throne thenceforward bears the title of *Prince of Wales*. *Robert Bruce* and *John Baliol* struggle for the crown of Scotland. Edward espouses the cause of the latter (who swears fealty to England), and overruns Scotland. The Scots, led by *Sir William Wallace*, offer a determined resistance. Wallace executed at London (1305). The Scots defeated at *Falkirk* and *Methuen*, and the country subdued. Establishment of the English Parliament substantially in its modern form (1295).

1307-1327. **Edward II.** is signally defeated at *Bannockburn* by the Scots under *Robert Bruce* the younger, and is forced to retire to England (1314). The Queen and her paramour *Mortimer* join with the Barons in taking up arms against the King, who is deposed, and shortly afterwards murdered in prison.

1327-1377. **Edward III.** defeats the Scots at *Halidon Hill* and *Neville's Cross*. Lays claim to the throne of France, and invades that country, thus beginning the Hundred Years' War between France and England. Victories of *Sluys* (naval; 1340), *Crécy* (1346), and *Poitiers* (1356). John the

Good of France, taken prisoner by the *Black Prince*, dies in captivity (1364). After the death of the Black Prince, England loses all her French possessions, except Calais. Order of the Garter founded. Movement against the corruption of the clergy, headed by the reformer *John Wycliffe*. House of Commons holds its meetings apart from the House of Lords.

1377-1399. **Richard II.** Rebellion of *Wat Tyler*, occasioned by increase of taxation. Victory over the Scots at *Otterburn* or *Chevy Chase*. *Henry of Bolingbroke*, *Duke of Lancaster*, leads an army against the King, takes him captive, and according to popular tradition, starves him to death in Pontefract Castle. *Geoffrey Chaucer*, the father of English poetry.

House of Lancaster (1399-1461).

1399-1413. **Henry IV.**, *Bolingbroke*, now secures his election to the crown, in right of his descent from Henry III. Outbreak of the nobility, under the *Earl of Northumberland* and his son *Percy Hotspur*, is quelled by the victory of *Shrewsbury*, at which the latter is slain (1403).

1413-1422. **Henry V.** renews the claims of England to the French crown, wins the battle of *Agincourt* (1415), and subdues the N. of France. Persecution of the *Lollards*, or followers of Wycliffe.

1422-1461. **Henry VI.** is proclaimed King of France at Paris. The *Maid of Orleans* defeats the English and recovers French possessions. Outbreak of the civil contest called the '*Wars of the Roses*', between the houses of Lancaster (red rose) and York (white rose). Henry becomes insane. *Richard*, *Duke of York*, grandson of Edward III., lays claim to the throne, joins himself with *Warwick*, the 'King-Maker', and wins the battle of *Northampton*, but is defeated and slain at *Wakefield*. His son *Edward*, however, is appointed King. Rebellion of *Jack Cade*.

House of York (1461-1485).

1461-1483. **Edward IV.** wins the battles of *Towton*, *Hedgley Moor*, and *Hexham*. Warwick takes the part of *Margaret of Anjou*, wife of Henry VI., and forces Edward to flee to Holland, whence, however, he soon returns and wins the victories of *Barnet* and *Tewkesbury*. Henry VI. dies suddenly in the Tower (1471). Edward's brother, the *Duke of Clarence*, is said to have been drowned in a butt of malmsey.

1483. **Edward V.**, the youthful son of Edward IV., is declared illegitimate, and murdered in the Tower, along with his brother, by his uncle, the *Duke of Gloucester*, who takes possession of the throne as —

1483-1485. **Richard III.**, but is defeated and slain at *Bosworth* by *Henry Tudor*, *Earl of Richmond*, a scion of the House of Lancaster.

House of Tudor (1485-1603).

1485-1509. **Henry VII.** marries *Elizabeth*, daughter of Edward IV., and so puts an end to the Wars of the Roses. The pretenders *Lambert Simnel* and *Perkin Warbeck*.

1509-1547. **Henry VIII.**, married six times (to *Catherine of Aragon*, *Anne Boleyn*, *Jane Seymour*, *Anne of Cleves*, *Catherine Howard*, and *Catherine Parr*). Battles of the *Spurs* and *Flodden*. Separation of the Church of England from that of Rome. Dissolution of monasteries and persecution of the Papists. *Cardinal Wolsey* and *Thomas Cromwell*, all-powerful ministers. Whitehall and St. James's Palace built.

1547-1553. **Edward VI.** encourages the Reformed faith.

1553-1558. **Mary I.** causes *Lady Jane Grey*, whom Edward had appointed his successor, to be executed, and imprisons her own sister *Elizabeth*. Marries *Philip of Spain*, and restores Roman Catholicism. Persecution of the Protestants. Calais taken by the French (1558).

1558-1603. **Elizabeth.** Protestantism re-established. Flourishing state of commerce. *Mary, Queen of Scots*, executed after a long confinement in England (1587). Destruction of the Spanish 'Invincible Armada' (1588). *Sir Francis Drake*, the celebrated circumnavigator. Foundation of the East India Company. Golden age of English literature: *Shakespeare*, *Bacon*, *Spenser*, *Jonson*, *Beaumont*, *Fletcher*, *Marlowe*, *Drayton*.

HOUSE OF STUART (1603-1714).

1603-1625. **James I.**, King of Scots, and son of **Mary Stuart**, unites by his accession the two kingdoms of England and Scotland. Persecution of the Puritans and Roman Catholics. Influence of ***Buckingham.*** Gunpowder Plot (1605). Execution of ***Sir Walter Raleigh*** (1618).

1625-1649. **Charles I.** imitates his father in the arbitrary nature of his rule, quarrels with **Parliament** on questions of taxation, dissolves it repeatedly, and tyrannically arrests five leading members of the House of Commons (*Hampden*, *Pym*, etc.). Rise of the ***Covenanters*** in Scotland. *Long Parliament.* Outbreak of civil war between the King and his adherents *(Cavaliers)* on the one side, and the Parliament and its friends *(Roundheads)* on the other. The King defeated by ***Oliver Cromwell*** at ***Marston Moor*** and *Naseby*. He takes refuge in the Scottish camp, but is betrayed to the Parliamentary leaders, tried, and executed at Whitehall.

1649-1653. **Commonwealth.** The Scots rise in favour of Charles II., but are defeated at *Dunbar* and *Worcester* by Cromwell.

1653-1660. **Protectorate. Oliver Cromwell** now becomes Lord Protector of England, and by his vigorous and wise government makes England prosperous at home and respected abroad. On Cromwell's death (1658), he is succeeded by his son **Richard**, who soon resigns, whereupon Charles II. is restored by ***General Monk. John Milton***, the poet; ***Thomas Hobbes***, the philosopher; *George Fox*, the founder of the Quakers.

1660-1685. **Charles II.** General amnesty proclaimed, a few of the regicides only being excepted. Arbitrary government. The ***Cabal.*** Wars with Holland. Persecution of the Papists after the pretended discovery of a *Popish Plot.* Passing of the ***Habeas Corpus Act*** (1679). Wars with the Covenanters. Battle of ***Bothwell Bridge. Rye House Plot.*** Charles a pensioner of France. Names ***Whig*** and ***Tory*** come into use. ***Dryden*** and *Butler*, the poets; *Locke*, the philosopher; ***John Bunyan.***

1685-1688. **James II.**, a Roman Catholic, soon alienates the people by his love for that form of religion, is quite unable to resist the invasion of *William of Orange*, escapes to France, and spends his last years at St. Germain. *Sir Isaac Newton* ('Principia', 1687).

1688-1702. **William III. and Mary II.** William of Orange, with his wife, the eldest daughter of James II., now ascends the throne. The Declaration of Rights. Battles of ***Killiecrankie*** and ***The Boyne.*** Grand Alliance against Louis XIV. Peace of Ryswick (1697). First Partition Treaty (1698). Second Partition Treaty (1700). Act of Settlement (1701).

1702-1714. **Anne**, younger daughter of James II., completes the fusion of England and Scotland by the union of their parliaments. ***Marlborough's*** victories of ***Blenheim***, ***Ramilies***, ***Oudenarde***, and ***Malplaquet***, in the Spanish War of Succession. Capture of ***Gibraltar.*** The poets *Pope*, ***Addison***, ***Swift***, *Prior*, and ***Allan Ramsay.***

HANOVERIAN DYNASTY (1714 et seq.).

1714-1727. **George I.** succeeds in right of his descent from James I. Rebellion in Scotland (in favour of the *Pretender*) quelled. ***Sir Robert Walpole***, prime minister. *Daniel Defoe.*

1727-1760. **George II.** Rebellion in favour of the Young Pretender, ***Charles Edward Stuart***, crushed at ***Culloden*** (1746). ***Canada*** taken from the French. *William Pitt*, *Lord Chatham*, prime minister; ***Richardson***, ***Fielding***, ***Smollett***, ***Sterne***, novelists; *Thomson*, *Young*, *Gray*, *Collins*, *Gay*, poets.

1760-1820. **George III.** American War of Independence. War with France. Victories of ***Nelson*** at *Aboukir* and ***Trafalgar***, and of ***Wellington*** in ***Spain*** and at ***Waterloo.*** British conquests in India. The younger *Pitt*, prime minister; ***Edmund Burke; Charles Fox; Shelley*** and ***Keats***, poets; ***Adam Smith's*** 'Wealth of Nations' (1776).

1820-1830. **George IV.** Roman Catholic Emancipation Bill. ***Daniel O'Connell.*** The English aid the Greeks in the War of Independence. Victory of ***Navarino. Byron***, ***Sir Walter Scott***, ***Wordsworth***, ***Coleridge***, ***Southey.***

1830-1837. **William IV.** Abolition of slavery. Reform Bill.

The present sovereign of Great Britain is —

Queen Victoria, born 24th May, 1819; ascended the throne in 1837; married, on 10th Feb., 1840, her cousin, Prince Albert of Saxe-Coburg-Gotha (d. 14th Dec., 1861).

The children of this marriage are: —

(1) Victoria, born 21st Nov., 1840; married to the Crown Prince of Germany (afterwards Emp. Frederick), 25th Jan., 1858.

(2) Albert Edward, Prince of Wales, Heir Apparent to the throne, born 9th Nov., 1841; married Alexandra, Princess of Denmark, 10th March, 1863.

(3) Alice, born 25th April, 1843; married to the Grand-Duke of Hessen-Darmstadt, 1st July, 1862; died 14th Dec., 1878.

(4) Alfred, Duke of Edinburgh, born 6th Aug., 1844; married the Grand Duchess Marie of Russia, 23rd Jan., 1874.

(5) Helena, born 25th May, 1846; married to Prince Christian of Schleswig-Holstein-Sonderburg-Augustenburg, 5th July, 1866.

(6) Louise, born 18th March, 1848; married to the Marquis of Lorne, eldest son of the Duke of Argyll, 21st March, 1871.

(7) Arthur, Duke of Connaught, born 1st May, 1850; married Princess Louise Margaret, daughter of Prince Frederick Charles, nephew of the German Emperor, 13th March, 1879.

(8) Leopold, Duke of Albany, born 7th April, 1853; married Princess Helen of Waldeck-Pyrmont, 27th April, 1882; died 28th March, 1884.

(9) Beatrice, born 14th April, 1857; married Prince Henry of Battenberg, 23rd July, 1885.

VIII. Wales and the Welsh Language.

The formerly independent *Principality of Wales* (Welsh *Cymru*), with an area of 7363 sq. M. and (1881) 1,360,513 inhab., has been an integral and undisputed part of the British monarchy since 1535. South Wales was conquered by the Norman French in the reigns of William II. (1087-1100) and Henry I. (1100-1135), and North Wales was subdued by Edward I. (1276-84). Wales is by far the most mountainous part of South Britain, fully one-quarter of its surface being incapable of cultivation, and it contains, especially in its N. half, a great abundance of picturesque scenery (comp. R. 40). In all essential particulars travelling in Wales is similar to travelling in England, and the tourist requires no special directions. Except in the remoter districts English is everywhere understood, but a few data in regard to the Welsh language are given below to aid in the pronunciation of proper names. — The national Welsh costume is now rare.

LANGUAGE. Welsh *(Cymraeg)* is a branch of the great family of Celtic languages to which the Armoric of Brittany, Cornish, Manx, and the Gaelic of Scotland and Ireland also belong. Its orthography is at first somewhat startling to Saxon eyes, but with the exception of one or two characteristic sounds, the difficulty is not so formidable as it appears on the surface.

Most of the consonants of the Welsh alphabet are pronounced as in English; but *f* is pronounced like *v*, while *c* and *g* are always hard. *Dd* is pronounced like *th* in thus, *th* like *th* in think, *ff* like *f*, and *ch* like the German *ch* (guttural). The sound of *ll*, perhaps the most difficult for a stranger, is produced by forming the mouth as if to pronounce *l* and then blowing. This sound bears the same relation to *l* as *f* does to *v*.

A passable imitation of it is *thl* (*e.g.* Llangollen = Thlangothlen). The vowels *a*, *e*, *i* are pronounced as in the Continental languages (*ah*, *eh*, *ee*), *o* almost as in English, and *u* is a kind of wide sound, the nearest approach to it in English being ĭ as in *fit*. When used as a vowel (more often than not) *w* is pronounced *oo*; *y* is invariably a vowel and is equivalent to the Welsh *u* in the last syllable of a word and to *u* (as in but) in other positions. The circumflex (^) is often used to denote a long vowel. The letters j, k, q, x, and z do not occur in Welsh. In combination the initial letter of a word is often transmuted; thus d and t interchange; also f and b, and f and m. This change of letter often corresponds to a change of gender. In pronunciation the accent is always on the penultimate, except in a few cases when it is on the last syllable.

The following list of Welsh words occurring in the names of places will be useful. *Aber*, mouth of a river, confluence of rivers; *afon*, river; *bach*, *bychan* (fem. *fach*, *fechan*), small; *bedd*, a grave; *bod*, a dwelling; *bryn (fryn)*, hill; *bwlch*, pass, defile; *caer (gaer)*, fort; *carn*, *carnedd*, cairn, heap of stones, rocky mountain; *cefn*, back, ridge; *clogwyn*, precipice; *crib* (pl. *cribau*), comb, crest; *cwm*, valley (comp. *combe*); *din*, *dinas*, a fortified post; *drws*, door, passage; *du (ddu)*, black; *dwr*, *dwfr*, water; *eglwys*, church; *ffynnon*, a well or source; *glyn*, glen; *gwy*, water; *gwyn*, *wyn* (fem. *gwen*, *wen*), white, fair; *llan*, church or church-village (lit. enclosure); *llyn* (pl. *llynnau*), lake; *maen*, *faen*, *vaen* (pl. *meini*), a stone; *maes*, *faes*, a field; *mawr*, *fawr*, *vawr*, great; *moel*, *foel*, bare, bald; *mynach*, monk; *mynydd*, mountain; *nant*, brook, valley (also common in this sense in French Switzerland); *newydd*, new; *pant*, a hollow; *pen*, top, head; *pistyll*, spout, cataract; *plâs*, palace, mansion; *pont*, *bont*, bridge; *porth*, *borth*, port, harbour; *pwll*, pool; *rhaiadr*, waterfall; *rhiw*, steep, slope; *rhos*, moor; *rhudd*, red; *rhyd*, a ford; *sych*, dry; *tal*, front, high, head; *tan*, under; *tomen*, a mound; *traeth*, beach; *trwyn*, a point (lit. nose); *twll*, a pit; *ty*, a house; *tyddyn*, a farm; *uchaf*, highest, upper; *y*, *yr*, the; *yn*, in, into; *ynys*, island; *ystrad*, vale.

If an opportunity presents itself, the traveller in Wales should not fail to attend an Eisteddfod (pron. eistéthvod; lit. a 'sitting'), or gathering for competition in music, literature, etc. The best is the National Eisteddfod, held once a year; but the local 'Eisteddfodau' are also interesting.

IX. Bibliography.

The following is a small selection of the most recent, the most interesting, and the most easily accessible topographical and other books relating to England and Wales. Bulky works, such as county histories, and older books of which the value is mainly antiquarian have been purposely omitted. Numerous other works of local interest are referred to throughout the text of the Handbook.

A full list of British topographical works will be found in the 'Book of British Topography' by *John P. Anderson* (Satchell & Co., London, 1881), and a judicious selection of accessible books is given in 'The Best Books' by *W. Swan Sonnenschein*, which contains 50,000 titles (2nd ed., 1890). The asterisks indicate publications of special interest and importance.

*England: its People, Polity, and Pursuits, by *T. H. Escott* (new ed., 1885).

Our Own Country, with 1200 illus., published by *Cassell & Co.* (6 vols.; 1879-83).

The Land We Live In, by *Wm. Howitt* (3 vols., 1854-56).

The British Isles, translated from the French of *J. J. E. Reclus* and edited by *E. G. Ravenstein* (1887).

Notes on England, by *H. A. Taine* (from the French; 1872).

English Traits, by *R. W. Emerson*.

One Hundred Days in Europe, by *O. W. Holmes* (1887).

England, Without and Within, by *R. G. White* (Boston, 1881).

Passages from the English Note-Books of *Nathaniel Hawthorne* (2 vols.; Boston, 1870).

*English Towns and Districts, by *E. A. Freeman* (London, 1883).
Gilpin's Forest Scenery, edited by *Francis G. Heath* (London, 1879).
The Strange Adventures of a Phaeton, by *Wm. Black* (3rd ed.; Lon., 1872).
Rural Rides in the Counties of Surrey, etc., during the years 1821-1832, by *Wm. Cobbett* (new ed., 2 vols.; London, 1885).
Rambles by *Patricius Walker* (London, 1873).
Old England and its Scenery (6th ed.; Boston, 1879).
England, Picturesque and Descriptive, by *J. Cook* (Philadelphia, 1882).
Portraits of Places, by *Henry James* (1883).
Visits to Remarkable Places, by *Wm. Howitt* (new ed., 1888).
Bicycle Tour in England, by *A. D. Chandler* (Boston, 1881).
**Pennant's* Tour in Wales; new ed., by *Rhys*, 1883 (kept in many of the Welsh hotels).
Wild Wales, by *Geo. Borrow* (3 vols.; 2nd ed., 1865).
*Handbook to the Cathedrals of England and Wales, by *R. J. King;* 6 vols., illus. (new ed., 1876 et seq.; London, Murray). This is the standard work on English cathedrals.
English Cathedrals, by *Mrs. Van Rensselaer*, with illustrations by *Joseph Pennell* (Century Magazine, 1889-90; soon to be published in book form).
Cathedral Churches of England and Wales; illus.; *Cassell & Co.* (1884).
Abbeys and Churches of England and Wales; illus.; *Cassell & Co.* (1887).
*History of Architecture, by *James Fergusson* (2nd ed., 1873-6; see vols. II. and IV.).
*Introduction to the Study of Gothic Architecture, by *J. H. Parker* (6th ed., 1881). See the same author's edition of Rickman, his Architectural Glossary, etc.
*Mediæval Military Architecture in England, by *G. T. Clark* (2 vols.; 1884).
The Monumental Effigies of Great Britain, by *C. A. Stothard* (new ed., 1876).
Treasures of Art in Great Britain, by *G. F. Waagen* (translated from the German by *Lady Eastlake;* 1854-7).
Anecdotes of Painting in England, by *Horace Walpole* (new ed., in 3 vols., edited by R.N. Wornum; 1887).
*The Norman Conquest, by *E. A. Freeman* (6 vols.; London, 1867-79). See, in particular, chap. 26, vol. V.
The Making of England, by *J. R. Green* (London, 1881).
The Conquest of England, by *J. R. Green* (London, 1883).
*The Historic Towns Series, edited by *E. A. Freeman* and the *Rev. W. Hunt* (Longmans; 1886 et seq.)
Popular County Histories, a series now publishing by *Elliot Stock.*
The Races of Britain, by *J. Beddoe* (1886).
Contributions to the Physical History of the British Isles, by *Ed. Hull* (1883).
Physical Geology and Geography of Great Britain, by *Sir A. C. Ramsay* (last ed., 1878; 15*s*.).
Topographical Botany, by *H. C. Watson* (2nd ed.; 1883).
British Manufacturing Industries, by *G. P. Bevan* (14 vols., 1876-8).
Industries of Great Britain, published by *Cassell*; illus. (3 vols.; 1880).
The Railways of England, by *W. M. Acworth;* illus. (1889).
Among the numerous comprehensive works of the older English topographers may be mentioned *Brayley and Britton's* Beauties of England and Wales (1801-15; 18 vols.), *Camden's* Britannia (orig. Latin ed., 1586; 2nd Eng. ed., 1806), and *Lysons*' Magna Britannia (6 vols.; 1813).

Ordnance Survey Maps. The whole of *England and Wales* has been published on the scale of one inch to a mile, partly in full sheets (40 x 27 inches; 2*s.* 6*d.*) and partly in quarter sheets (20 x 15 inches; 1*s.*). A new survey on this scale is in progress, of which 178 quarter sheets have been published. The whole of *Scotland* has been issued on the same scale (each sheet 30 x 22 inches; 1*s.* 9*d.*). Indexes to show the divisions of sheets sent post-free on application to *Edward Stanford*, 26 Cockspur St., Charing Cross, London, S.W., agent for the sale of the Ordnance Maps.

Historical Sketch of Architecture in England

by

Edward A. Freeman.

It follows from the peculiar history of Britain that the history of English architecture takes a different course from that of the same art in Gaul and Italy. In these lands it is possible to trace an unbroken succession of buildings from the time of Roman dominion down to our own day. There is no sudden break in architecture any more than in anything else; the earliest Romanesque grows out of the later Roman. Direct Roman influences, the imitation of Roman buildings, the use of Roman materials, go on for ages; in Italy a strongly classical Romanesque survives to meet the earliest Renaissance, which is hardly to be distinguished from it. In Britain on the other hand, the complete severance from the Roman world which followed on the settlement of the Angles and Saxons hindered any such continuity. But few Roman buildings lived through the havoc of the English conquest, and those that did certainly did not supply the Teutonic conquerors with architectural models. The continuous history of architecture in England begins with the mission of Augustine in 597, or perhaps a few years earlier, with the marriage of Æthelberht.

The existing Roman Remains in Britain are works of engineering rather than of architecture. No building, perfect or nearly so, remains, like the temples and amphitheatres of Arles, Nîmes, and Vienne, no monument like those of Igel near Treves and of Saint Remy in Provence. It may be safely said that not a single Roman column is now standing in its own place anywhere in Britain. Even the using up again of Roman columns in later buildings, so common in southern lands, may be said to be unknown; an example in the doorway of Saint Woollos' church in Monmouthshire (p. 187) seems to be unique. The greatest of all Roman works in Britain is purely military, the Great Wall, built to defend the Roman province of Britain against the independent barbarians to the North (see p. 376). This is wholly of stone. Most of the surviving Roman works in Britain are in the late Roman manner of building, where rows of small stones alternate with courses of narrow bricks. This construction, common in Gaul and in other Roman lands, but unknown in Rome itself, may be seen at Leicester, Lincoln, and above all, York; at Lincoln too is one arch of a Roman gateway, besides the bases and stumps of a row of columns. The nearest approach to a perfect Roman building is to be found in the *Pharos* in Dover castle. Large Roman remains are also to be seen at Bath,

Silchester, Aldborough in Yorkshire, Wroxeter, Saint Albans, and above all Colchester. At the two last places the Roman bricks were largely used in later buildings and were imitated down to a late time. Remains of Roman country houses are frequently brought to light by digging, as a very remarkable one lately at Brading in the Isle of Wight. The mass of Roman remains underground in England is undoubtedly very large; it is the rarity of whole buildings or large parts of buildings which forms the contrast with more southern lands.

The art of architecture in England began with the first building of churches. A church of the Roman time at Canterbury was repaired for the use of Æthelberht's Christian queen, and new churches were built by Augustine at Canterbury, by Paulinus at York and Lincoln, and by others of the early bishops and of the kings who favoured them. They naturally built in the Roman fashion of the time, '*more Romano*' is the phrase often used of these early buildings; but the earliest examples were necessarily small and rude. None is actually standing, unless we accept the church in Dover castle as the work of Eadbald. But there is little doubt that some of the masonry of King Edwin's church at York may be seen in the crypt of the minster. Indeed during the whole five hundred years between the conversion and the Norman Conquest, we have comparatively few churches — we have no other buildings — left, and those for the most part small and plain. The great cathedral and monastic churches were all but universally rebuilt soon after the Norman Conquest; the buildings of earlier date that remain were mostly preserved by their own obscurity. But there is no greater mistake than to suppose that Englishmen before the Norman Conquest were incapable of building or incapable of building in stone. The use of wood was common, more common than in later times; but then, as in later times, its use was largely a question of district. In the eleventh century a church of 'stone and lime' is mentioned as remarkable in Essex, while a wooden church is mentioned as remarkable in Somerset. The last was the ancient church of Glastonbury, the only church of the Britons of which we have any distinct record which lived on through the English conquest. In the eighth century a stone church was built to the east of it; in the twelfth the wooden structure was itself replaced by a stone one. And though the surviving churches older than the Conquest are all small and plain, we have distinct evidence from contemporary descriptions, as of Wilfrith at York and Ripon in the seventh century and of Æthelwald at Winchester in the tenth, that large, rich, and elaborate buildings were perfectly well known.

The style of building doubtless varied in the space of five hundred years; but it varied very much less than in the five hundred years that followed. The buildings of this date belong to one general type of ROMANESQUE, one that differs widely from the Norman type of Romanesque that followed it. But it is misleading to talk of a 'Saxon' or 'Anglo-Saxon' style. English buildings may well have had their local peculiarities even then, but there is nothing about these early buildings which entitles them to be classed as belonging to a distinct style from the contemporary buildings on the continent. Down to the middle of the eleventh century, all Western Europe had a common style; in the course of that century, several countries struck out local types, as in Northern and Southern Gaul and in Northern Italy; Germany clave to the older style and improved and developed it. The small and plain 'Saxon' buildings of England are simply ruder examples of the same style as the great German churches of the twelfth century. But the style is as little of German as of English origin; it is the common heritage which the whole West received from the common centre at Rome.

As no great church earlier than the Norman Conquest remains in England, and not many perfect churches of any scale, our account of our early buildings is necessarily fragmentary. Small pieces of work either actually older than the Norman Conquest or at all events belonging to the fashion of building which prevailed before the Norman Conquest, are common enough, specially in particular districts, as Northamptonshire. We have to compare what little we have left with contemporary descriptions, and with analogous work in other lands. If the church in Dover castle attached to the Roman Pharos is really Eadbald's work, it must be the oldest surviving church in England. The large and strange church of Brixworth in Northamptonshire was either a Roman building turned into a church or a church built out of Roman materials in the seventh century. But the most perfect examples of very early churches in England are two on a very small scale, in Northern and Southern England severally, the old church at Bradford-on-Avon in Wiltshire, built by Saint Ealdhelm between 675 and 709, and the church of Escomb in Durham. Jarrow and Monkwearmouth, also in Durham, the former the dwelling-place of Bæda, contain large portions as old as his day (674-735). On a larger scale and probably later is the church of Worth in Sussex, a cruciform building. To reckon up all the examples of small portions of work of this type would be endless. In all there is a closer tradition of Roman work than we see in the later Norman form of Romanesque. There is a tendency to large stones, to flat jambs, to windows with a double splay (as in the German churches of the twelfth century), to the fashion of covering walls with horizontal and vertical strips, and to a peculiar arrangement of masonry at the angles, known as *long and short work*. This last too is a Roman feature; it may be seen on a vast scale in the amphitheatre at Verona. As we have no aisled church of this date surviving, it is not easy to speak of the interiors. That columns were used is plain from descriptions; they are still standing in the crypt at Repton in Derbyshire, where some other columns remain moved from their places. They belong to the same general type as those in some of the earlier churches of Germany, as at Hildesheim. The straight- sided arch is often used, as in Auvergne and in the gateway at Lorsch, which last has very much the character of these early buildings in England.

But the distinguishing feature is the towers. Still there is in these too nothing peculiar to England. They are simply smaller and ruder examples of a type which went on in use in Germany and Italy to a much later date and in much more artistic shapes. They are tall, slender, unbuttressed, with small round-headed windows, with shafts (sometimes balusters) set in the middle of the wall, whence the name of *midwall shafts*. The windows are set in groups of two or more, but they are never grouped under a containing arch, as in the Norman style that followed. The towers seldom keep their finish at the top; but an original capping may be seen at Sompting in Sussex, the low four-sided spire so common in Germany, as at Coblenz. This type of tower, plain and stern, loftier than the ordinary Norman type, has a singular dignity of its own which caused it to remain in use for some while after the Norman Conquest, sometimes even into the twelfth century. The evidence of Domesday proves that the towers of this style in the lower town of Lincoln were built between 1068 and 1085, while the minster and the castle were rising on the hill, in the wholly different Norman style. It is plain that, while the new fashion prevailed in other respects, men still often built towers of the elder type by choice. In Lindsey (North Lincolnshire) towers of this kind may be almost called common; there are several in Northumberland and Northamptonshire; in some districts, as Somerset, they are quite unknown. Among the finest, and those which have the most distinctive character of their own, are those of Earls Barton in Northamptonshire and Barton-on-Humber in Lincolnshire, loaded with rude enrichment, Saint Bene't at Cambridge, and Saint Michael at Oxford. This last, there is every reason to believe, belongs to the reign of William the Conqueror, and is contemporary with the work in the castle of somewhat the same kind. That this Primitive Romanesque style, common to England with all Western Europe, is something quite distinct from the later Norman Romanesque is best shown by these examples of the two fashions used side by side.

Of this *Primitive Romanesque* there is a good deal in some parts of Gaul, specially towers in the Pyrenees, and buildings in those parts of Western Switzerland which formed part of the kingdom of Burgundy. The great church of Romainmotier in Vaud is plainly kindred with the smaller and fragmentary English buildings. In Normandy there is exceedingly little work of this kind, perhaps not a single tower with midwalls. One cause is this, that in the middle of the eleventh century, there arose in Normandy, perhaps under influences from North Italy, a very distinctyped of

Romanesque, just as other types arose in Auvergne and elsewhere. This NORMAN VARIETY OF ROMANESQUE was first brought into England by the Norman tastes of Edward the Confessor, whose great church at Westminster, consecrated in 1065, was distinctly said by William of Malmesbury in the next century to have been built in a new style of building which continued in fashion in his own day; that is of course the style known as Norman. Introduced under Edward, its use was confirmed by the actual Conquest under William, and it gradually displaced the earlier mode of building. By the end of the eleventh century, most of the great churches of England had been rebuilt in the new style. The reason seems to have been mainly that their size was not great enough for the taste of the Norman prelates, who took in England to building churches on a gigantic scale, such as they certainly had not been used to in their own country. It would almost seem that Edward's church, which was of vast size, set the example. It could hardly have been that the English churches were condemned for lack of ornament, as the early Norman buildings are remarkably plain, even more so than those that went before them. And throughout the prevalence of the Norman style the greatest amount of ornament is to be found in the smallest buildings. And in truth no style can better dispense with ornament; none can better trust to sheer stateliness and solemnity of general effect. In this it recalls the old Doric of Greece.

The Norman form of Romanesque prevailed in England from the middle of the eleventh century to the end of the twelfth; but it went through several changes during that time, mostly in the direction of increased lightness and ornament. The earliest Norman minsters are of vast size, very massive and very plain, and they sometimes keep about them some traces of the earlier style. So it is in Saint Albans abbey, the vastest of all and the plainest of all, being chiefly built out of Roman bricks from Verulam. The transepts of Winchester cathedral (1079-1093) are of the same date, and also keep some Primitive traces, but the effect of the stone church is very different from that of the brick. Norwich cathedral is a little later (1096-1109) and rather more advanced in style; but it belongs on the whole to the early Norman type of church with low massive piers and triforium as large or nearly so as the pier-arch. Gloucester abbey (1089-1100) shows another type, in which the piers, though massive, are very lofty, and the triforium and clerestory small; this is carried yet further in the abbey of Tewkesbury (1102-1121). The usual arrangement among the great churches of this time was the cross shape with a central tower, and most commonly two towers at the west end, a long western limb — the choir being under the tower or even west of it — and a short eastern limb with an apse. The style is easily distinguished from the earlier style by its use of shafts in the jambs of doors and windows, by the single splay of the windows, by the coupling of belfry windows under an arch, and by the beginning of a system of surface mouldings which gradually increased in richness. The strips and long-and-short work of the Primitive style go out of use, and we get instead flat pilaster buttresses. Two forms of capital are very characteristic of the Norman style, the *cushion* capital, an imitation of the Doric which lasted through the whole Norman period, and a rude imitation of the Ionic, which is used only in its earlier stages. The piers are sometimes square, with shafts in the angles, sometimes round, but far too heavy to be called columns; the genuine column is hardly found, except in crypts. The relation to Roman architecture is quite different in the Primitive style and in the Norman. In the older style it is not so much that Roman forms are imitated as that survivals of them are kept on by unbroken tradition. The Norman style (like the other contemporary forms of Romanesque) shows a conscious and eclectic imitation of particular Roman details, as we have just seen in the shafts; but in its spirit and feeling it departs much further from Roman work. But the comparison can hardly be made in England, where no great Primitive church survives. The difference is well seen by comparing a Norman minster with an early German one, as at Hildesheim.

The beginning of a new variety of Norman is seen in Durham abbey, begun in 1093 by Bishop William of Saint Calais. He died in 1096, having finished only the eastern part of the church. Here we get a less massive proportion; the round pillars are not so extravagantly lofty as at Gloucester and Tewkesbury, while they give a much higher pier-arch and a much lower triforium than Winchester and Norwich. They are fluted in various forms, a peculiarity found elsewhere (as in a few at Norwich), but chiefly in churches coæval with Durham, as Waltham, Dunfermline, and Lindisfarne — the last much later in the style. Durham in short has hit on the most perfect proportions that the style allows; it is as distinctly the head of Norman Romanesque as Pisa is the head of the Italian and Saint Sernin at Toulouse of the Aquitanian variety of the style. The work is more finished than in the earlier buildings, and more of ornament comes in; but the building cannot be called rich. It shows how architecture was affected by the genius of particular men, and how independent style sometimes is of date, that after Bishop William's death the transepts were continued by the monks in a much plainer and ruder style which anybody would take to be twenty or thirty years older than the work which is really earlier than itself. Then came Bishop Randolf Flambard and continued the nave from Bishop William's general design, but with a certain increase of ornament.

The work of William of Saint-Calais marks a stage intermediate between the very early and plain and the very late and rich Norman. The beginning of the latter is due to Bishop Roger of

Salisbury, the minister of Henry the First, a great builder both of churches and castles. He brought in both great enrichment in detail and the use of more finely-jointed masonry. Men said that his buildings looked as if they were all of one stone. This style and the early Norman can be well compared in the west front of Lincoln minster, where the plain work of the original founder Bishop Remigius (1085-1092) is contrasted in a marked way with the more elaborate detail of the parts built by Bishop Alexander (1146), the nephew of Roger of Salisbury. This middle Norman style of Roger is perhaps hardly to be found in the whole of any church of great size; but we may assign to it many buildings and parts of buildings which show a certain increase of lightness, but without either the excessive ornament or the classical tendency of the next stage. Saint Peter's at Northampton may perhaps pass as an example. In truth the development of art which was started by Roger was thrown back by the anarchy of Stephen's day, and took life again under Henry the Second. The Norman style of his day grows richer and richer, lighter and lighter; the appropriate surface ornament of the style is now wrought into most elaborate shapes; columns are used wherever the weight to be borne was not too heavy for them; the capitals forsake the ruder types of the earlier Norman, either for more elaborate forms of the old cushion or even for foliage almost reproducing the richness of the ancient Corinthian. Of this late Norman style we have many examples; of course all do not reach the same measure of richness; but the feeling is essentially the same throughout. Such are the nave of Saint David's cathedral, Selby abbey, Worksop priory, the western church at Glastonbury (commonly known as Saint Joseph's chapel), the hall of Oakham castle, the church of Iffley near Oxford, and many others. None departs so widely from the idea of Norman Romanesque as a massive style as the Galilee or Western chapel of Durham abbey. There the arches originally rested on two slender shafts under a single abacus, a feature found in some Roman buildings and specially adopted by the Saracens. It is common in cloisters in Aquitaine, Italy, and Sicily, but it seems a strange shape for the piers of a considerable building. At a later time it was clearly deemed unsafe, and two other shafts were added for strength. Through all this time the rule still holds that, the greater the building, the plainer it is. Very few churches on the scale of Saint David's are so rich, and Saint David's is one of the smaller cathedral churches. Throughout the Norman style, both early and late, special attention was paid to the doorways. Small and otherwise plain churches often have a doorway of considerable richness, and Norman doorways have often been preserved when the rest of the building has been rebuilt in a later style. The reason doubtless is that a doorway has more of separate existence than most other features. This is specially true where the doorway is under a porch; but porches are rare in Norman churches, though there is a fine one at Southwell minster.

During the Norman period we are no longer confined to churches and their appurtenances as subjects of architectural study. We have a store of castles and some houses to refer to. It is perhaps hardly needful to say that at no period of good art was there any special *style* for churches or for any other class of buildings. The different purposes of a church, a castle, a house, a barn, will cause great differences of form, outline, proportion, among the different classes of buildings: but the *style*, strictly so-called, the details, the ornamental forms, are always the same. A military building is likely to have less ornament than an ecclesiastical one; but those parts of it which are enriched will be enriched in the same way. Thus we have mentioned the hall of Oakham castle. This, like many other early halls and monastic infirmaries, has columns and arches which might just as well have stood in a church. The castle, a novelty of Norman introduction, now became a chief feature in the architecture of England as of other countries. The usual type of the Norman castle has for its main feature the massive rectangular keep, which, without changing its essential character, may either swell into such vast buildings as those of London and Colchester or sink into the peel-tower of the borders of England and Scotland, which are simply the Norman keep on a very small scale. Pre-eminent among the Norman castles of England is the Conqueror's own fortress planted to keep London in awe. The Tower of London, built by Gundulf, Bishop of Rochester, shows how the plain and early Norman style could be wrought into perfectly finished forms in military as well as in ecclesiastical work. Its most interesting part, the chapel, unites both characters. It is plain but not rude, with columns and an apse in the thickness of the wall. This great building may be compared with the small tower which Gundulf built for himself at Malling in Kent. The castle of Rochester is not his work, but that of Archbishop William Corbeil (1126-1139); it is an excellent example of much the same style as Bishop Roger, a great advance in ornament, but with much of the massiveness of the elder style living on. And it is now in a castle rather than a church, in the remains of his castle at Sherborne that we can best study the work of Roger himself. Another type of castle, less usual during this period than the square tower, and less easily lending itself to architectural forms, was the *Shell kepe*, a single wall, commonly polygonal. This is chiefly found when the castle was built on a mound of earth which might not have borne the weight of the heavy square tower.

Houses, strictly so called, are still rare, but there are a few examples. Some of the best are in towns, as at Lincoln and Bury Saint Edmunds, where they bear the name of Jews, and some have thought that stone houses in towns at this date were first built by

Jews. A contemporary writer speaks of their 'houses like the palaces of kings'. There is some other domestic Norman work at Lincoln, namely Saint Mary's Guild, commonly called John of Gaunt's stables. There is also a house of very late Norman just outside Cambridge, called Pythagoras' School. And there are a few others elsewhere. But for the best examples of domestic architecture at this time, we must look, not so much to houses strictly so called, as to those parts of castles and monasteries which were not military or religious. Of monastic buildings of this date a good deal is left, as very largely at Christ Church, Canterbury. The great hall of the palace of Westminster, as built by William Rufus, must have been a wonderful specimen of early Norman work, with two rows of pillars and arches, as in the later hall at Oakham (1175-1191). But it was recast in the fourteenth century, and the architectural features are lost. Of Romanesque applied in municipal buildings, in which Italy is so rich, England has now perhaps nothing to show; but examples survived not so long ago at Exeter and Colchester.

We now come to the great change by which the style known as Gothic or Pointed gradually took the place of Romanesque. This style, it must be remembered, in England supplanted the Norman variety of Romanesque; in Germany it supplanted a developed form of that earlier Romanesque which in England died out before the Norman. This change implies a great deal more than the mere introduction of the pointed arch. The pointed arch is really as old as the round, and its shape is actually found in some of the earliest attempts at the arch in Greece and Italy. It was used by the Saracens for some centuries before the time to which we have come, and from them it was brought into the Christian buildings of Sicily and Southern Gaul at least as early as the eleventh century. In those countries the pointed arch by itself is no sign of approaching Gothic, and the buildings in which it is used show no other mark of approach to that style. In England, France, and Germany, the mere use of the pointed arch was most likely brought in from the East by the crusaders; so that it is in a sense of Saracen origin in those countries also. But the Saracens, while using the pointed arch, had never developed a system of ornament which thoroughly suited it. This last is exactly what the architects of northern countries did, and, in so doing, produced the style called Gothic, a name absurd enough in itself, as it had nothing whatever to do with any Goths, but which may be accepted, as being commonly understood. The process by which the new style was developed out of the old, followed somewhat different stages in England, France, and Germany, but the general result was the same in all. Each country produced its own characteristic form of Gothic. Thus in England mouldings developed faster than they did in France, while in France windows developed faster than they did in England. We have here to do with the process of change, the *Transitional* style between Romanesque and Gothic, as it went on in England. First of all, the pointed arch came in as a constructive feature, without any new system of ornament; the arches are either plain or have Romanesque ornaments. It is not uncommon to see the great constructive arches of a church, the pier-arches and those of the vault, pointed, while all the smaller arches are still round. There can be no better example than the nave of Malmesbury abbey, a grand massive design, Romanesque in everything, except the form of the pier-arches. Gradually the pointed arch came in in other places besides the main arches; gradually too the ornament changes, from the flat surface of the Romanesque to a system of deep mouldings, rounds and hollows, affecting the section. As a general rule, the constructive lines become Gothic, while the mouldings are still largely Romanesque; but sometimes things take the opposite course, and we find round arches with Gothic mouldings nearly or wholly developed. This is a local fashion in Northamptonshire; as the Norman doorways were so much admired and often preserved, so something in the Norman fashion went on in doorways when it had gone out of use in other features. The Norman ornaments went on longer in this district than elsewhere, and the round arch went on longer than the ornaments. This Transitional period is a most interesting study, and there are many fine examples of it. Such are the whole eastern part of Canterbury cathedral (1175-84), part of the nave of Worcester, Glastonbury abbey, both the eastern and the western church, while a plain type will be found among the Cistercians, as at Kirkstall. But the most instructive examples are to be found at Peterborough and Ely, examples of the way in which, while the Transition was fast going on, men sometimes followed an earlier type for some particular reason. Both these naves were built quite late in the twelfth century, but, being adapted to earlier Romanesque work, they keep the proportions and general effect of the earlier style, though a narrow examination will show that the mouldings are considerably advanced in the new fashion. But, as soon as the west front was reached, where adaptation to an earlier model was no longer held needful, later outlines as well as details came in freely.

The earliest type of English Gothic, called by different writers *Early English* and *Lancet*, had pretty well reached perfection by the last years of the twelfth century. Saint Hugh's work at Lincoln must be reckoned as belonging to it, though it is perhaps not quite clear of Romanesque traces. The perfect English form of this style is all but peculiar to England; one or two examples may perhaps be found in Normandy. We may define it as the style which combines the use of the simple lancet in windows with the use of the round abacus in shafts. This distinguishes it from contemporary French work, where fully developed tracery in the windows is constantly found along with the square abacus. The English work also has much bolder mouldings; it deals much more in detached shafts — a favourite kind of pillar is a column with small banded shafts round it; the foliage of its capitals is freer, and departs farther from classical models. On the other hand, the French style is far richer in sculpture, above all in the magnificent doorways which have hardly any fellows in England. The difference between the two countries may be best seen by comparing (as has often been done) the two churches of Amiens and Salisbury, which were building at the same time. The French church has as much the advantage in the windows and doorways as the English has in all the smaller details. But there is a local variety of the English Early Gothic which comes far nearer to the French style, having square or octagonal abaci, less bold mouldings, and few or no detached shafts; the capitals of the shafts too are far more like French work. This style is found in the West of England and South Wales; that it is strictly a lingering of Romanesque feeling is shown by several of the details showing themselves in the late Romanesque of Saint David's and the Transitional work at Glastonbury. It is continued in more fully developed Gothic at Llandaff cathedral, and it may be best studied at Wells, where it can be compared with work of the more usual English kind in the same church. This style is also to be found in several smaller buildings in the district to which it belongs; the inner porch of Saint Mary Redcliff at Bristol, the church of Slymbridge in Gloucestershire, and the small churches of Whitchurch in Somerset and Cheriton in Gower will supply good examples.

It was in the thirteenth century, during the prevalence of this Early Gothic style, that English churches, great and small, put on those peculiar features which distinguish them from those of the continent, especially from those of France†. Even in the twelfth century, the English churches began to throw out much longer choirs, a practice which perhaps began at Canterbury under Saint Anselm, and which in the thirteenth century became the rule. The next stage was to leave off the apse and to use a square east end, either with a single large window or group of windows, or

† The words *France* and *French* in these comparisons must be understood of France in the strictest sense, or at all events only of the lands north of the Loire. Southern Gaul, which gradually became French in a political sense, had nothing to do with France architecturally, save that some grand French churches were here and there built in those lands as something quite foreign. But the native style at all times is so different that, widely as French and English buildings differ from each other, we may put them together as a single Northern manner of building, as distinguished from the national architecture of Aquitaine and Provence.

with a lower Lady chapel beyond it. Even in the Norman period, though the apse was all but universal in the great English churches — it remains at Peterborough and Norwich — it was the exception in the small churches, and from the thirteenth century onwards an apse in an English parish church is most rare, and the few that there are are mostly much later than this time. Indeed even in cathedral and other great churches the apse is very rare, being of course, where it is found, polygonal and not round. So we see at Westminster abbey, great part of which is really French work on English soil, and in the smaller abbeys of Tewkesbury and Pershore. The central tower remained the almost universal rule for great churches — Exeter and Llandaff are the only real exceptions — while in France (save in Normandy) it went out of use in the great churches, and remained far more common in smaller ones than it is in England. A great English church is usually much longer and lower than a French one; the English church has the better external grouping, while the French church has the grander internal effect; Saint Ouen at Rouen alone contrives to combine the merits of both. Again in England there grew up a type of parish church, wholly different from the minster, but just as good in its own way, while in France, where a small church has any architectural merit, it is commonly (not always) by way of reproducing the minster on a small scale. A French church was always vaulted whenever it could be; a wooden roof, whenever there is one, is a mere shift. But in England the vault is rare indeed in small churches and is not altogether universal in minsters. It was clearly omitted by preference, and various forms of enriched wooden roofs were used instead, not as shifts but as approved substitutes. And the absence of the vault of course enabled the pillars to be lighter than when they had to bear such a much greater weight. All these tendencies reach their fullest development in the latest form of English Gothic; it is there that they are thoroughly wrought into an artistic shape: but they begin from the beginning. We do not see in England, in the thirteenth century any more than in the fifteenth, the small minster-like churches which we see in France. New Shoreham is perhaps the only English parish church of this date which affects the type of the minster, and that might be a minster in scale as well as in style. These two points of difference, the absence of the apse and the vault are enough of themselves to distinguish an English and a French church, and it is perhaps worth noting that in Ireland the English peculiarities appear in a more marked shape still. In short the differences between insular and continental buildings begin in the Early Gothic of the thirteenth century, and they go on widening as long as Gothic architecture lasts.

Of this English style of the thirteenth century the most distinctive feature of all is the Lancet window, from which it has been well called the Lancet style. These long narrow windows are used alone, or in groups of twos, threes, and greater numbers. Sometimes two or three are grouped under an arch. There we get the first approach to window tracery. The space above the openings was pierced with some figure, a circle or quatrefoil; this is already usual in openings which are not meant to be glazed, as in triforia and belfry-windows; but it does not as yet grow into actual tracery. The triforium is now commonly lower and the pier-arch higher than it was in the Norman style; only at Ely, the same feeling of adaptation to older work which gave the nave its peculiar character, affected also the work of this date, and the triforium is unusually large. The work of this date at Ely, including the east end, is the very finest example of the style in point of detail. All the characteristic features come in, and with a remarkable degree of richness. For, while this style can be very simple, it can also put on an almost lavish amount of ornament. Sculpture too, in the stricter sense, the carving of the human figure, takes a sudden leap; in the twelfth century attempts of this kind were still very rude; in the thirteenth we have admirable sculptures on the west front of Wells, not the less admirable as sculptures because the front, as an architectural design, is sacrificed to them. On the whole, at no period of mediæval architecture was there so much richness and freedom of detail as in the days of the earliest fully developed English Gothic.

Of this style we have many examples in our great churches. The nave of Lincoln, the choir of Southwell, the whole eastern part of Beverley, much of Worcester, the eastern transept at Durham, the transepts of York (with their very strange wooden vaulting), and specially the whole church of Salisbury, except the tower and spire, belong to this style. Salisbury is naturally often quoted as the model of the style, as it is so rare to find a great church all in one style from one end to the other. But it is surely far surpassed by the contemporary parts of Lincoln in proportion and by that of Ely in detail. A crowd of smaller churches might be quoted; two remarkable ones are the church of Warmington in Northamptonshire (with a wooden vault to the nave) and the very small church of Skelton near York.

Two features which may be traced back to the twelfth century reached their full development in the thirteenth. The earliest and the latest chapter-houses are rectangular. That at Worcester in the twelfth century was round; just as in the case of the apse, the round form naturally became polygonal, and from the thirteenth century onwards we get a remarkable class of polygonal chapter-houses, usually with a single central pillar, a form of singular beauty. The earliest is that at Lincoln, which belongs to our present period; the rest belong to a time a little later. The other feature was the tendency to finish the west end of a great church with something other than either the mere ends of the nave and aisles (as at Norwich) or the aisles ending in towers, as in most large Romanesque churches. Sometimes, as at Ely and Peterborough, this took the shape of an actual western transept. In the magnificent Transitional part of Ely, a single vast western tower rises in the middle of the transept, a fashion which, on a smaller scale and in a ruder form, is the rule in Auvergne. At Peterborough the transept was combined with two small western towers, only one of which was ever finished. But here a second addition was made in the shape of a magnificent portico of three lofty arches, in the best work of this style, perhaps the grandest conception for a single feature which mediæval architecture has produced. It is in fact the Greek portico translated into Gothic language. But in other cases all that is done is to disguise the real shape of the front, whether with or without towers, by a mere wall, a sheer piece of pretence. So it was in Malmesbury abbey even in the twelfth century; so it is in different shapes, at Lincoln (where there is a kind of western transept), at Wells (where the western towers stand beyond the aisles), at Salisbury (where there are no western towers). In these, and in some other cases, the shape of the front is not the real constructive shape. This fashion afterwards went out; the later fronts are either the mere ends of the nave and aisles, or else there are western towers, sometimes, as at Beverley, with an unreal wall built between them, but with no screen in front.

Church towers now begin to be taller than they were in the Norman time; that is, in truth, they fell back on the older Primitive type. And now their roofs begin to shoot up into tall spires, first of wood, then of stone. But these are in their first stage to be mainly studied in parish churches, specially in a district which takes in North Northamptonshire, the southern part of Lincolnshire called Holland, and parts of other counties. These early spires (known as *broach* spires) keep their character as roofs by hanging over the tower, and they are more massive than spires become afterwards. But there are very few of this kind to be seen in the great English churches; the low spire of Saint Frideswide at Oxford (now the cathedral church) stands almost alone.

In the latter part of the thirteenth century another change comes in. Tracery now begins to be used in the windows, as had been the case long before in France. Tracery grew very naturally out of the figures pierced in the head of a window of two or more lights under an arch. Bring the circles, or other figures, close to the arches, and pierce the spandrils or spaces between them, and we at once have the simplest form of tracery, that which uses only a few simple geometrical figures, circles, quatrefoils, trefoils, sometimes the spherical triangle, and even the spherical square, which last is very common is Germany and very rare in England. Windows of this kind may be formed of any size; the arches supporting circles may be repeated over and over again on different planes, so that a window of eight lights shall be made up of two windows of four lights, and those again each of two windows of two. Such is the great east window of Lincoln minster, the finest example of this stage; the whole eastern part of the church, called the Angels' choir (1255-1280) is of this date, and is as perfect in its way as the Lancet work at Ely is in its way. The nave of Lichfield, the chapter-house at Salisbury, the staircase to the chapter-house at Wells, the north transept at Hereford, the church of Winchelsea, the ruined abbeys of Tintern and Netley, are other examples of this style. The earlier among these have fallen away but very little from the perfect beauty of detail which belonged to the style in use just before; but even in the Angels' choir the mouldings are not so deep nor the foliage so bold as in the eastern parts of Ely. By those who have divided the mediæval styles according to their windows, this style is called the *Geometrical.*

The next form in idea is where the lines of tracery cease to be Geometrical and become *Flowing;* that is, the figures no longer merely rest on the arches, but the mullions themselves are actually continued in the lines of tracery, but always in various forms of curves. But the change from the Geometrical forms to these was very gradual. There is a style of window, of which those in the choir of Merton College chapel at Oxford are among the very best, in which the tracery is Geometrical and not Flowing, but which still differs a good deal from the simple Geometrical of Lincoln. The design of the tracery is far more elaborate and brings in a much greater choice of figures. We see these forms again in the nave (1291-1329) and chapter-house at York — a chapter-house without a central pillar — while the great west window, the pride of the nave (1338) has fully developed Flowing tracery. Of this last the two grandest examples are those at the east ends of Carlisle cathedral and Selby abbey, the latter of which has a Geometrical window alongside of it. Heckington church, Lincolnshire, and Snettisham, Norfolk, are fine examples on a smaller scale; but the building of all others in which to study the developement of tracery is Exeter cathedral (1280-1370). Here it starts from the simple Geometrical in the eastern Lady chapel, and advances westward.

The truth is that there is in idea a very wide gap between the styles which are marked by the use of Geometrical and Flowing tracery, but that it is by no means easy always to divide them in practice. All the forms of window-tracery, English, French, and German, fall into two great classes, admitting of further divisions according to periods and countries. There is, first, the *Geometrical,* the forms of which in the different countries differ less from each other than the later forms do. There are, secondly, all those forms in which the mullions are continued in the tracery, whether in straight or in curved lines, which have ben grouped together under the common head of *Continuous.* This will take in both the Flowing and Perpendicular forms in England, as also the Flamboyant of France, and the contemporary late Gothic of Germany, forms which differ far more widely from one another than the various forms of Geometrical, but which agree in carrying on the mullion into the tracery. And in England the Perpendicular line came in so very early that its first examples are actually contemporary, not only with Flowing but with Geometrical forms. In all times of transition earlier and later forms cannot fail to be used side by side, and the details which accompany the purely Geometrical and the purely Flowing tracery differ less from each other than each does from the details used immediately before and after it. Hence the Geometrical and the Flowing forms have often been, with some degree of practical convenience, grouped together under the somewhat unmeaning name of *Decorated.* But during the whole period from the time when the simple Lancet windows went out of use till confirmed Perpendicular became dominant, detail was ever changing in the direction of the later type of Gothic. The sections of mouldings and of clustered pillars became less and less bold; so does foliage, though it now more commonly, as conspicuously in the chapter-house at Southwell, directly copies natural forms. Ornamental arcades with distinct shafts gradually sink into mere panelling; the triforium gets smaller and smaller; there is a constantly increasing tendency to carry lines straight upwards. The naves of York and Exeter have much in common; but Exeter, both in proportion and detail, keeps on a good deal of earlier feeling, while York is an advance in the direction of what was coming. Exeter is very English; York has more in common with some of the great French churches. But the most remarkable example of all is the work of this date at Ely. The proportions impressed on the building by the Norman architects, as they influenced the work of the thirteenth century, influenced that of the fourteenth also. There is a triforium on a scale such as no architect of the time would have designed if he had been left to himself; but the details are very far advanced, and have altogether lost the boldness of the earlier work to which the fourteenth century reconstruction is adapted. At Beverley again the nave of the fourteenth century is in many things adapted to the choir of the thirteenth.

In the matter of towers, some of the very grandest in England belong to this time. Several of the great central towers were now carried up, as at Salisbury, Hereford, Wells, and above all Lincoln, where the western towers were carried up at the same time. Of these Salisbury alone had a stone spire; but that at Hereford, and all three at Lincoln, once had spires of wood covered with lead. Lichfield alone among English churches, had three stone spires.

At Ely something different from a tower and quite unique in England arose. The central tower, which had hitherto stood in fellowship with the single western tower, fell, and was replaced by a vast octagonal lantern, not exactly a tower, not exactly a cupola, but coming nearer to a domical effect than anything else in the Gothic architecture of England.

The origin of the *Perpendicular* style, a style peculiar to England, is to be found in the abbey of Gloucester. This was made out beyond doubt by Professor Willis in his examination of that church in the year 1860. The distinguishing feature of the style in the matter of windows is that the mullions are continued in the tracery, in the shape, not of curved but of right lines. Such right lines are now and then found in earlier tracery: but only incidentally: they now become dominant, and give the character to the style. But the straight line came in first, not in windows, but in panelling; it arose out of a special need in the works carried on at Gloucester by Abbot Wigmore (1329-1337); it is there fully developed in the panelling, not quite so much so in the window-tracery. When this date, which is perfectly certain from documents, was first ascertained by Professor Willis, it showed that the Perpendicular style was used many years before the date commonly given to its beginning; and there can be no doubt that it remained for a long time a local style at Gloucester, used there both in the abbey and in other buildings, but making no way elsewhere. Its general prevalence began when it was taken up at Winchester, first by Bishop William of Edington (before 1366) and then by his successor William of Wykeham (1394-1404). In Edington's work the style still keeps some slight trace of the earlier style; that of Wykeham is fully developed, and clearly set the fashion throughout the country. Other work of his is to be seen in his two colleges at Winchester and Oxford, where his chapel and hall at New College became models for others. In tracing out the growth of this style we can again, just as we could in the Norman time, mark the personal action of particular men, which we have been less able to do in the intermediate styles.

The English Perpendicular style, like the French Flamboyant which grew up about the same time, was the latest form of Gothic in England, that which gradually gave way to the introduction of Italian forms in the sixteenth century. The earlier and the later examples differ a good deal, but the main principles of the style remain the same throughout, and the difference between early and late Perpendicular is certainly not greater than the difference between the plain Norman of the days of the Conquest and the enriched Norman of Henry the Second's reign. The leading principle of the style is the prominence given to the vertical line in every thing, a prominence which is often made yet more thorough by the presenco of strengly marked horizontal lines. This comes out in panelling and window-tracery; the windows reach a vast size, as the great windows at Winchester, Bath, Beverley, York, and above all Gloucester. There is not so much scope for transitional forms between the Flowing and the Perpendicular lines as there was between the Geometrical and the Flowing; still examples are not wanting; windows in which curved and straight lines are intermingled are seen, as has been said, in the earliest Perpendicular at Gloucester and also at York. Indeed the growth of the Continuous style can nowhere be better studied than in the successive works at York: the nave (1291-1329), the presbytery (1361-1370), and the choir (1380-1400).

In the style which now came in, mouldings lose still more of their depth; capitals are less commonly floriated, and with less of depth when they are; ornamental arcades altogether give way to panellings. On the other hand, the richer buildings become more loaded with ornament of various kinds than ever. But it is rather ornament added to the constructive features than the constructive features themselves brought into ornamental shapes. It is otherwise however with one very important feature which now for the first time puts on its full importance. This is that specially English feature, the wooden roof. This is no longer a mere substitute for a vault, but a form of equal dignity which is often chosen by preference. It puts on various shapes. There are the grand hammer-beam roofs of East-Anglia, which after all seem better suited to halls than churches; there are the roofs which in a large district on the borders of Wales are used in churches, but which in the West of England are used only in halls, a variety which uses a vast deal of wood with trefoils and other figures cut in the solid. Then there are the characteristic coved or cradle roofs of the West of England, which modern architects are commonly bent on destroying. And lastly there is the low-pitched tie-beam roof, which is common everywhere, except perhaps in East-Anglia. This last form is connected with one of the features of the style which has been already mentioned, the prominence given to the horizontal line in contrast with the vertical. This tendency, it should be remembered, came in before Perpendicular tracery was at all dominant in the windows; it begins while the Flowing forms of tracery are still in use, sometimes even earlier. The roofs and gables became low-pitched, as in one of the classes of wooden roofs already spoken of; the low gable may be seen over the grand Flowing west window of York minster. Outside, instead of the high roof, the parapet, pierced or embattled, becomes a main feature. So with the towers; magnificent spires were still built, sometimes in Northamptonshire keeping to the so-called *broach* form, but more usually with parapets, pinnacles, and flying-buttresses. But, as the spire is one form of the high roof, the tendency of the style is to leave out the spire, and to finish the tower itself with a parapet and pinnacles. Most commonly the square tower itself is all; but sometimes the square is finished with an octagonal; sometimes the octagon again supports a spire. In churches again the arches of doors and windows had commonly been pointed. But all through the fourteenth century, even while Geometrical tracery is still in use, other alternative forms come in, and become more usual as Perpendicular advances. A square-headed window is often convenient in churches, and constantly so in houses. The form was therefore used very early, whenever it was wanted, as also was the segmental arch, most commonly round. The square-headed form becomes more usual in the Perpendicular style, but the segmental gives way to the four-centred arch (answering to the elliptic, three-centred, or flat-topped arch in France and Sicily), which is used all through the style, but becomes more common towards the end.

In all these ways the horizontal line comes in after a fashion in which it does not in the earlier Gothic styles. But the vertical line is still dominant, all the more dominant. The great work of the Perpendicular style, as applied to ecclesiastical purposes, was to bring out the distinctive type of the great English parish church as distinguished from the minster. In the interior of such a church, if the wooden roof is of lower pitch than of old, it is a substitute for the vault and not a make-shift, and it far more commonly rests on shafts rising from the ground. Nothing can be more truly vertical than some of the West of England churches that follow this type. Even when the shafts do not rise from the ground, the tall slender pillars, commonly with narrow arches, have an upward tendency which the flatter lines of the roof help to bring out more strongly. The great Perpendicular parish church has commonly a western tower; the central tower is rather avoided, and it sometimes gives way to a western one; the distinction between nave and chancel becomes less strong, and is sometimes made wholly by wood work; aisles to the chancel are more common than before, and chapels are often added beyond the aisles. The apse is still very rare, but it is found at Saint Michael's at Coventry, and, as an addition, at Mold and Wrexham in North Wales. Vaulting is common over small parts of the building, as porches and chapels, but it is all but unknown over a main body. Examples are found everywhere; but there are two districts, Somerset and East-Anglia, where fine examples of two distinct types are specially thick on the ground. The differences in the two types of roof have been already mentioned. The towers also are widely different, though singularly stately in both; in the East-Anglian churches both the towers and other parts are greatly affected by their material, which is chiefly flint; cut flint arranged so as to make forms of panelling is a very distinctive feature. They are also distinguished for the vast number of small windows in the clerestory, two in each bay, while in Somerset the large churches commonly have one large window in each bay, while in the smaller ones with coved roofs the clerestory is often left out. In Yorkshire there is a third type of tower, which evidently follows the western towers of the minster, having a single large belfry-window, where in Somerset there would be two or more. In Northamptonshire, rich in spires and octagons, there is perhaps only one square tower of great merit, at Titchmarsh. Gloucestershire and Worcestershire have another type of tower, continued from the beginnings of the Perpendicular style in Gloucester abbey; the panelling looks as if it were nailed on, which it never does either in Somerset or in East-Anglia. Of large parish churches in this style (out of the special districts) the two University churches of Oxford and Cambridge may supply good examples: also the collegiate (now cathedral) church of Manchester, which is purely parochial in its architecture; Fairford in Gloucestershire, which has a central tower without transepts and which comes within the sixteenth century; and, among very small churches, Whiston in Northamptonshire, (near Castle Ashby, p. 252), from its extraordinary grace and its extremely late date, 1534. But a full list would be endless; all that can be done is to pick out a few examples here and there.

In minsters the style is on the whole less happy than in parish churches. The stateliest example is doubtless to be found in the Perpendicular parts of York; but here, though the feeling, as in the earlier nave, is thoroughly Continuous, it is hardly thoroughly Perpendicular. The shafts of the clustered pillars have a prominence unusual in the style, and which gives the building an effect of its own. And another building which belongs to this period by date can still less be said to belong to it by style. The nave of Westminster abbey was built in the fifteenth century, and a near examination will show that the details are of that date; but the proportions and general effect are utterly unlike anything in the Perpendicular style; everything is closely adapted to the adjoining work of the thirteenth century. And, just as in the case of the nave of Ely, where, in the west front, the architect got free of his model, he built in the usual fashion of his own time. The series of genuine Perpendicular buildings begins, as we have seen, at Gloucester and goes on at Winchester. The work of Wykeham at Winchester keeps all the massiveness and solemnity of earlier style, because it is in truth not a rebuilding from the ground, but the Norman nave cased in the new style. This should be compared with the eastern parts of Gloucester, where the Norman work is not *cased* but merely *overlaid* in the peculiar local style, and with the nave at Canterbury which was rebuilt from the ground. Here we cannot but feel that there is the same fault as in the Romanesque naves of Gloucester and Tewkesbury; the pier-arches are too high and the clerestory too low; the triforium has of course vanished. The style perhaps comes out better in a type of building which has a very lofty clerestory. We see this in Sherborne minster and in parts of Christchurch in Hampshire. Saint Mary Redcliff at Bristol also comes here, a parish church, but — like Shoreham in earlier times — ranking architecturally as a minster, and the only English parish church which is vaulted throughout. It is well to compare it with great churches of the purely parochial type, as Boston, Newark, Saint Michael at Coventry, and Trinity church at Hull, one of the greatest parish churches in England, supplying a noble study of tracery, and so far minster-like as to have a central tower, but having all the lightness — an enemy might say flimsiness — of the parochial type, with the slender pillars and wooden roof. Saint Mary Redcliff was designed for a central tower which would have been of an oblong shape, the transepts being narrower than the nave and choir, as at Limoges and some other French churches. This form was actually carried out in Bath abbey (1500-1539), the only cathedral church altogether in the Perpendicular style, which it shows in a late and for the most part a poor form. The mouldings are coarse, and the four-centred arch, often very useful in doorways, windows, and even small chapels, has thrust itself into the main pier-arches, where it is quite out of place. The tower is ungraceful, and it was great perversity to make the belfry-windows and the great east window square-headed.

The one good feature at Bath is the fan-tracery vault of the choir, imitated in modern times over the nave. This form of roof is the great contribution of the Perpendicular style to the art of vaulting. It begins early in the style, as in the cloister at Gloucester (1351-77), one of the most perfect examples; but it did not come into use over large spaces till much later. The earlier Perpendicular vaults forsake the simpler arrangements of earlier times and do not bring in the compact magnificence of the fan-roof. In the wooden roofs at York and in many stone roofs, the ribs seem to run over the vault without much meaning. The flat pier-arches at Bath point to another tendency of the latest form of the style, where there almost seems a wish to get rid of piers and arches. In the two most elaborate examples of late Perpendicular, Saint George's chapel at Windsor and Henry the Seventh's chapel at Westminster, the arcades are of very little importance. The Westminster chapel is a wonderful work, but it must be allowed to be overcharged with ornament; minute enrichment has taken the place of boldness of design. The really grandest building in late Perpendicular is the chapel of King's College, Cambridge. Here the windows and the fan-tracery roof are of the very best kind, and the ornament throughout, though rich, is not overdone. And the design is as bold and simple as a Greek temple. In the choir of a college chapel pier-arches are not needed; the type of chapel brought in by William of Wykeham has a short nave of two bays with of course two arches and one pillar on each side. King's chapel consists of twelve bays, with no architectural distinction between nave and choir. There are no aisles, therefore no pier-arches; but there are chapels between the buttresses, as in many French churches.

These three famous chapels, at Westminster, Windsor, and Cambridge, have no towers. King's could not have any but a detached campanile, like Magdalen at Oxford. Otherwise, the Perpendicular style which, in the parish church, tends to sacrifice the central to the western tower, tends in the minster to make the central tower more predominant than ever. At Winchester, Gloucester, and Saint Albans, western towers were pulled down, clearly to give greater predominance to the central one; and this at Winchester and Saint Albans, without ever actually rebuilding (whatever may have been designed), the old central towers in the new style. At Gloucester the central tower was rebuilt in the stateliest guise of the local style, and it set the fashion to Worcester, Malvern, and some smaller examples. On the other hand, at York the western towers were finished in the new style, while the central tower kept its Norman massiveness even with Perpendicular details. It was seemingly designed to carry some farther finish, perhaps an imperial crown, like those at Newcastle-on-Tyne, Edinburgh, and Aberdeen. The York tower may be said to be in some sort repeated at Beverley, where the mid-tower was never carried up. The great towers of Durham and its dependency Howden were carried up with the finish of a smaller square stage, answering to the octagon in some other cases, which was itself to receive a crown. At Durham, as at York, the western towers were spared, and carried up in the new style. In some cases, both of larger and smaller churches, a western tower was added to a building which already had a central tower. So it was at Hereford cathedral, Malmesbury abbey, Wimborne minster (where the tower of this date is said to have succeeded an earlier one), Christchurch, Hampshire, and the parish churches of Purton in Wiltshire and Saint Cuthberht at Wells. These in fact, except in the absence of the western transept, repeat the outline of Ely as it stood before the substitution of the octagon for the square central tower. The strange thing is that this grouping of a central and a western tower, common in France, was in England not only rare but hardly ever destined to last when it was used. In most cases either the western or the central tower has fallen, and it is only at Wimborne and Purton that this grouping can now be studied.

Meanwhile domestic architecture was fast advancing. In England, it should be noticed, nearly all mediæval architecture that is not strictly ecclesiastical or military is domestic. The history of England gave no room for such developments of municipal independence, and thereby of municipal architecture, as were to be seen in Italy, Germany, and the Netherlands. There are some fine guild-halls in England, as those of London, York, Exeter, and Coventry; but the hall itself does not differ essentially from the hall of a palace or great monastery, and the whole municipal building nowhere becomes, as often on the continent, a rival to the minster and the castle. Another thing to be noticed in England is that country-houses, great and small, manor-houses, parsonages, houses in villages and open towns, put on an artistic character much sooner than they did in lands where safety could be had only either in a castle or in a walled town. The French *château* commonly belongs to the last days of Gothic architecture, and commonly supplants an actual castle. In England the simple manor-house, quite distinct from the castle, existed at least from the thirteenth century, and grew with every developement of art up to the sixteenth. The mere architectural style is of course the same in a house and in a church of the same date; but some features are more convenient in domestic buildings; thus in houses the square-headed window is more convenient than the pointed, except in rooms of special dignity, as the hall and chapel. Again the projecting *oriel* or bay-window is a specially domestic feature, for which there is no place in a church. The hall is the main feature of a mediæval house, great or small; at first it was almost the whole house; gradually the number of rooms increased; the *solar* opening into the hall grew into the (with) drawing-room; towards the end of the fifteenth century the dining-room, as distinct from the hall, began to creep in. The hall is commonly of the full height and width of the house, with an open roof; as the art of making such roofs grew, the old fashion of building halls with pillars and arches died out. Thus Richard the Second, in rebuilding Westminster hall, the grandest of the class, took away the arches of William Rufus, and threw the whole into one body, under one vast timber roof. But sometimes in halls, and more commonly in barns, the wooden roof is a construction independent of the walls, and rests on wooden pillars, as in the Bishop's hall at Hereford. The great oriel window at the upper end of the hall is commonly a marked feature. The materials of houses depended more on the district than those of churches, for, though there were wooden churches, even down to quite late times, especially in Essex and East-Anglia, yet stone was the usual material. In houses stone was constantly used in stone districts like Somerset and Northamptonshire, while in the western midland counties, timber or timber and brick, prevailed even in houses of great size (as Speke Hall near Liverpool), and in the eastern counties brick came into use very early. Examples of houses of all kinds become more common as we go on. In the fourteenth century Clevedon Court in Somerset is one of the finest; in the fifteenth examples are very common, and at the beginning of the sixteenth English domestic architecture reaches its perfection in buildings like Cowdray in Sussex — unluckily damaged by fire — and Thornbury castle in Gloucestershire — unluckily never finished. Cowdray is perhaps the grandest actual example of a manor-house on a vast scale, keeping nothing of the character of a castle beyond the gate-house. Thornbury is a mere fragment; but the oriels, round, and not, as usual, polygonal, are of the most magnificent kind. Both these buildings, of the reign of Henry the Eighth, belong to the very last days of Gothic architecture, just before Italian influences came in. The work of Wolsey at Hampton Court is of the same kind. Of the same date too are many of the college buildings at Oxford and Cambridge; the colleges indeed were originally built after the type of large houses; there is hardly any difference in ground-plan between Haddon Hall in Derbyshire and Queens' College, Cambridge, buildings of the fifteenth century. Some of the gateways of the Cambridge colleges are specially fine; and one of the grandest pieces of Perpendicular architecture is the Divinity school at Oxford, with its vast windows and rich vaulted roof. It is a building by itself, having a design and proportion of its own, quite unlike that of either a church or a hall.

Barns too, as has been casually implied, were at this time works of architecture; they were plain but not rude, exactly suiting their purpose. The windows are commonly mere slits, but the gables and doorways are artistically treated, and the roofs are often wonders of carpentry. Very fine ones may be seen at Glastonbury, Wells, Bradford-on-Avon, Frocester in Gloucestershire, and elsewhere.

In the middle of the sixteenth century Gothic architecture began in England, as it had already begun in France, to give way to the Revived Italian. The change of taste began in the accessory arts before it touched architecture proper. Thus, at Westminster — to say nothing of the tomb of Henry the Third and the shrine of Edward the Confessor, Italian work of the thirteenth century — while Henry the Seventh's chapel is of pure Gothic, though of the very latest type, his tomb is Italian. So a new taste in woodwork, *cinque-cento* or whatever we may choose to call it, begins in King's College chapel. The change of style in France may be studied in a very remarkable class of churches of the sixteenth and the first half of the seventeenth century of which Saint Eustace at Paris is the head; the general idea, the proportions and the main lines of the building are still strictly Gothic, but the minuter details are Italian. In England, where at this time more churches were pulled down than built up, the progress of this age of transition mainly has to be traced in houses. The general conception remains Gothic; indeed no outline can be more picturesque than that of an Elizabethan house, with its great windows and endless gables. But the Gothic detail loses its purity, and gets mixed up with Italian features. The Italian details, however, are used after a Gothic fashion; classical or *quasi*-classical columns come in again; but they are used just as the mediæval builders used their windows and blank arcades, many ranges are placed one over the other. The earliest house of this kind was most likely Longleat, in the reign of Edward the Sixth; but this, the work of an Italian architect, though still *cinque-cento* and by no means fully developed Revived Italian, was too advanced for English taste, and the struggle of styles may be looked on as going on quite to the time of the Civil Wars. Indeed in the first half of the seventeenth century, there is, specially in Oxford, what has been called *After-Gothic*, a distinct return to purer designs. Thus the chapel of Wadham college, built by builders from Somerset, is known to be a work of the seventeenth century, otherwise any one would have assigned it to the fifteenth. The staircase of Christ Church, with its single central pillar and fan-tracery, a most bold and original design, is later still, about 1640. In some cases the tracery of this date forsook the Perpendicular line and fell back upon Flowing forms.

But meanwhile the more strictly Italian taste was coming in. Inigo Jones added a classical portico to Saint Paul's, and Archbishop Laud added a porch with twisted columns to Saint Mary's at Oxford. After the Restoration the Italian taste decidedly prevailed, and any traces of the mediæval styles are now mere survivals. But in some districts and under some circumstances the survivals lasted a long while. Small houses with very good outlines and with mullioned windows were built into the eighteenth century; in Somerset indeed, perhaps in Northamptonshire, the two great districts of domestic architecture in stone, the survival may be said to have met the modern revival; the mullioned window never quite went out of use, though it often put on very poor and meagre forms. But from the time when St. Paul's cathedral was rebuilt in Italian (1675-1710) till the time when the Houses of Parliament were rebuilt in Perpendicular (1840-1850), Italian architecture, varied now and then by attempts at reproducing strictly Greek fashions, must be looked on as the received style in England.

From the middle of the sixteenth century onwards, the relations between ecclesiastical and secular architecture become the exact opposite to what they had been in earlier times. Churches were now comparatively seldom built, while secular public buildings of all kinds became of more and more importance. Here is a marked contrast between England and Italy, to some extent between England and either Germany or France. In all those countries there was a greater or less tendency, far more prevalent in Italy than in the other two countries, to build new churches and to rebuild or recast the old ones in the style which had become fashionable. In England there is far less of this. There is nothing in England answering to the Jesuits' churches on the continent, to great abbeys like Fulda and Einsiedeln wholly rebuilt in Italian, or to churches like Würzburg transformed as far as might be into Italian from Romanesque or Gothic. The French fashion of rebuilding the domestic buildings of a monastery in Italian, but leaving the ancient church, has its parallel in the designs, sometimes not getting beyond designs but sometimes more or less fully carried out, for rebuilding various colleges in Oxford in the prevalent fashion. The rebuilding of London after the fire caused the building of a good many churches there in the new style. But on the whole, there is, compared with other countries, but little in England of ecclesiastical work of this kind. Saint Paul's stands alone as an Italian church of the first class. And it should be noticed that Wren, though he despised Gothic architecture and knew nothing of its details, was quite able, when he chose, to catch a Gothic outline, as he showed at Westminster and at Warwick. For at least a hundred years mediæval architecture was, as the name *Gothic* shows, an object of fashionable and literary contempt, as is nowhere better shown than by several passages of Addison in the Spectator. A few however, antiquaries or poets, ventured always to cherish some admiration for the older fashion, and attention was again drawn to it as part of the revival of the romantic taste late in the last century. We do owe something to Horace Walpole after all. The call for a number of new churches in the first half of the eighteenth century largely helped on the Gothic revival. There was a very general belief that Gothic was the right style for a church, but not for any other building. This would have seemed a strange doctrine to the architects of any earlier period, pagan or Christian, as they all built their religious and their secular buildings in the same style. The earlier attempts at the revived Gothic were naturally very bad in point of detail, and still worse in point of ecclesiastical arrangement; but in point of mere outline we now and then meet with buildings, specially spires in the midland counties, which have really caught more of the spirit of earlier design, than many more recent buildings whose detail is immeasureably better.

Along with the practical revival of mediæval architecture came the revival of its study. But with this we are hardly concerned, except so far as it practically influenced buildings. It is clear that older styles could not be revived till their succession and the nature of their characteristic detail had been made out, otherwise details of the thirteenth and the sixteenth century might be jumbled together. The first at all successful attempt to distinguish the varieties of English Gothic was made by George Millers, a minor canon of Ely, in his History of that cathedral. After him came Rickman, whose useful labours did much to spread knowledge on the subject. Since the middle of the present century few churches have been built in England in any style but some form of Gothic, though there has been endless diversity of taste and opinion as to the form of Gothic to be chosen. The style was slower in making its way into houses and other secular buildings. The building of the New Houses of Parliament in the latest form of English Gothic was in one sense the greatest victory of the revival; in another way it did it great mischief. For faults which belonged to the building itself, and which would have been just as keenly felt if the details had been Italian, were vulgarly attributed to the style chosen. Since then we have had an Italian Foreign Office, but the latest great public buildings have again been Gothic, though of another form.

The history of the Gothic revival can be nowhere better traced than in the University and College buildings at Oxford. The last Italian building (if it can be called Italian) was the Taylor Building in 1842. Before that there had been many attempts at Gothic, the most successful of which in point of detail was the Martyrs' Memorial in 1839. Between 1840 and 1850 it seemed established that the revival was to start from the last days of English Gothic. This was surely a reasonable doctrine; no one can wish architecture to remain imitative; but a revived art must start from some point, and the last period of good work in past times is surely the most natural point to start from. From that it may develope afresh in any direction. But chiefly owing to the writings of Mr. Ruskin, a new fashion set in. Everything was to be Gothic; only it must not be any form of English Gothic. We were to go to Venice and Verona for details which suited Venice and Verona, but which did not suit England; we were not to learn anything from Cowdray, Thornbury, or Wells. Lastly there has come a stranger fashion still; of all the styles in the world the one last picked out for imitation has been the corrupt jumble of Gothic and Italian detail which prevailed in the time of James the First. This style, if style it can be called, marks a very interesting stage in the history of art; but surely, for a style to build in, any pure style of any kind would be better. It is like the macaronic verses, with one line in one language and the next in another. On the other hand, some colleges, like Magdalen and New College, have withstood all these strange fashions, and have steadily built in the latest form of national art.

A modern architect is placed in a position in which no architect of any other age ever was placed. In all earlier times, Greek, Roman, Saracen, Mediæval, Revived Italian, there has been some one prevalent style in which men built as a matter of course. Even in periods of transition the only choice lay between the style that was going out and the style that was coming in, and the result for a season commonly was a mixture of the two. But now there is no one acknowledged style. We can hardly say that Gothic is now so fully acknowledged as it was a little time ago, and as to the form of Gothic there is still no agreement at all. Each architect practically chooses his own style. That is, he sits down and considers of what past age he shall try and reproduce the architecture. Such a state of things is altogether new; there has been nothing like it at any earlier time. The nineteenth century stands alone in having no one characteristic style. The fact is at least worth notice in an attempt to sketch the succession of the characteristic styles of earlier centuries.

Table of the Architectural Styles in England.

I. Romanesque	Primitive or Pre-Norman Romanesque (pp. xxxiv-xxxvii)	Before 1066
	Norman	1066—1195
II. Gothic or Pointed	Early English or Lancet	1189—1300
	Decorated (Geometrical, Flowing)	1300—1377
	Perpendicular	1377—1547
III. Renaissance or Revived Italian, including *Jacobean* (see p. lix), *Georgian*, *Palladian*, etc.		1547 et seq.

The last thirty years or so of each period may be described as a time of Transition from one style to the following. The *Elizabethan* or *Tudor* style marks the transition from Gothic to Renaissance.

Glossary of Architectural Terms used in the Handbook.

Abacus, the tablet or slab above the capital of a column.

Aisle, the side-building of a church (or hall), attached to the main body, commonly at a lower height.

Apse, the circular or polygonal ending of a church or its main body, commonly of the E. limb, in Germany often at both ends.

Arcade, a series of arches supported by piers or columns, either open or backed by masonry.

Arches may be *Round* (semicircular, etc.) or *Pointed* (Lancet, etc.). A *Stilted Arch* is one in which the curve begins above the impost (q. v.). The *Four-centred* or *Tudor Arch* is a depressed form, in which the curves must be referred to four different centres. A *Containing Arch* is the outer arch of a window, enclosing the smaller arches at the top of the lights (q. v.). *Segmental Arch*, one forming a segment of a circle.

Architrave, the lowest member of the entablature, resting on the abacus (see above) and connecting one column with another.

Ashlar, hewn or squared stone used in building.

Bailey, court-yard of a castle.

Bay, the part of the building between two pillars in the nave of a church, or any similar individual of a series of repetitions.

Bay-window, a projecting window of any shape, built up from the ground, often called *Bow-window*.

Boss, a mass of carving at the intersection of the ribs of a vault, etc.

Broach Spire, a spire springing from a tower without the intervention of a parapet or other architectural feature to mark the transition.

Buttress, an external support to the wall of a building; *Flying Buttress*, one supporting an upper wall with which it is connected by an arch above a lower part of the building (as the aisle of a church).

Campanile, bell tower (Ital.).

Cathedral Church, a church containing the *cathedra* or seat of a bishop. A *Conventual Church* is a church served by monks or regular clergy; a *Collegiate Church* is one served by a body of canons or other secular clergy. A *Minster* is a great church, commonly cathedral, conventual, or collegiate.

Chancel, the same as Choir (q. v.).

Chantry, a small chapel over or near the tomb of the founder, used for the chanting of masses for his soul.

Chapter-house, the place of meeting of a chapter or monastery.

Chevron, zigzag moulding or ornamentation.

Choir, the part of a church set apart for the clergy and other officials, commonly the E. part, but in Germany often at both ends.

Clerestory, the uppermost of the three stages of a great church, standing clear above the aisles.

Cloister, a covered court in a monastery or college, commonly attached to the church.

Column, the support of an arch or entablature, keeping somewhat of classical style and proportion.

Corbel, an ornamented projection or bracket supporting a weight.

Cornice, the highest member of the entablature.

Crocket, a conventional tuft of foliage used in the ornamentation of gables, etc.

Crypt, a vault beneath a building, wholly or partly under ground.

Diaper, a uniform ornamental pattern covering a flat surface.

Dormer-window, a window rising from a sloping roof and covered by a small gable.

Dormitory, the sleeping-place of a monastery.

Entablature, the horizontal mass supported by the columns in Greek architecture, divided into Architrave, Frieze, and Cornice (q. v.).

Flamboyant Style, the late-Gothic style of France, so called from the flame-like form of its tracery, occasionally met with in England.

Frieze, the middle member of the entablature, often enriched with sculpture.

Galilee, a porch or chapel at the entrance to a church; see foot-note at p. 412.

Gargoyle, a projecting carved water-spout, usually in the form of a grotesque animal.

Groin, the curve or edge formed by the intersection of two vaults.

Half-timbered or *Timbered Buildings*, buildings consisting of wooden beams and posts, with the intervening spaces filled up with plaster, clay, or brick-work.

Hammer-beam, a large projecting beam used to support the rafters of a roof in place of a tie-beam.

Herring-bone Work, masonry in which the stones are laid aslant instead of flat.

Impost, the point where the arch rises from its piers.

Jamb, the side of a door, window, or archway.

Lady Chapel, a chapel dedicated to the Virgin Mary.

Lich Gate, a covered gateway at the entrance to a churchyard, through which the bodies of the dead are carried (A. S. lic, a corpse).

Lierne-ribs, the smaller intermediate ribs in a vault, not rising from the impost.

Light, a window-opening, compartment of a window.

Moulding, a general term applied to all the varieties of outline or contour given to the angles of the various subordinate parts and features of buildings, whether projections or cavities, such as cornices, capitals, bases, etc. (Parker).

Mullion, an upright bar of stone dividing a window into compartments (lights).

Nave, the main body of a church, occupied by the general congregation.

Ogee, a curved line or moulding partly concave and partly convex (adjec. *Ogival*).

Oriel, a window like a bay-window, but supported by corbels and not resting on the ground.

Panelling, ornamentation of a flat surface by recessed compartments.

Pargeted, adorned with plaster ornamentation.

Pier, the support of an arch, whether taking the form of a column or not.

Presbytery, the part of a church containing the high-altar.

Refectory, the dining-hall of a monastery.

Reredos, the screen at the back of an altar.

Ribs, the raised bars of masonry marking the joints or intersections of a vault.

Rusticated Masonry, masonry marked by deeply grooved joints round each stone, the faces of the stones being generally left rough.

Sedilia, the seats for the officiating clergy on the S. side of the choir, near the altar.

Solar, upper room or loft, withdrawing room.

Spandrel, the space (usually triangular) between the span or curve of an arch and the right angle enclosing it.
Splay, the embrasure, or sloping side of a window-opening.
Tie-beam, a transverse beam holding together the sides of a roof or wall.
Tracery, the ornamental work in the heads of windows, etc., formed by the crossing or interweaving of bars of stone. *Plate Tracery*, the simplest form, consists, as it were, of openings punched or pierced in a stone surface. In *Geometrical Tracery* the forms are those of regular geometrical figures, while in the later *Flowing Tracery* great irregularity of outline prevails.
Transept, the cross-limb of a church (or barn).
Triforium ('thoroughfare'), the second stage or story of a church, between the nave-arcade and the clerestory (q, v.). In its fully developed form a passage runs round it.
Vault, *Vaulting*, the arched ceiling of a building, of stone or brick. The simplest and most ancient form of vault over a rectangular area is the *Cylindrical*, *Barrel*, or *Waggon Vault*, which springs from two parallel walls. *Groined Vaulting* is formed by the intersection of vaults crossing each other at right angles. *Fan Tracery Vaulting*, which seems to be peculiar to English Perp. architecture, is a form in which all the ribs have the same curve and produce an effect somewhat resembling the sticks of a fan.

Ancient Monuments

by

General Pitt Rivers, Government Inspector of Ancient Monuments.

The Ancient Monuments Act of 1882 is purely permissive. It enables the owners of pre-historic and other ancient monuments, who desire to do so, to place them under the guardianship of H. M. Commissioners of Works, after which it becomes illegal to destroy them. They continue to be the property of their owners, as before, but subject to their being preserved as National Monuments, and these provisions are binding on future owners. The fact of a monument being under the Act is consequently no criterion of its historic value; it merely represents a voluntary arrangement between the Government and the owner. Some of the most important are not included, whilst those that are under the Act, amounting to some 40 in all, are not in all cases those which would have been selected as the best examples. They afford, however, a very fair sample of the class to which they belong. In the following brief notice of some of the principal Ancient Monuments of Great Britain, the letter (I) is appended to those which are included under the Act.

Stone Circles and Collections of Standing Stones. The majority of these appear to have been sepulchral, but their uses probably varied in different localities. Amongst these, Stonehenge (p. 101) stands pre-eminent. Its date has never been ascertained, nor is it likely that much light will be thrown upon it, until the ground around has been carefully excavated and examined. It has suffered chiefly from the elements, and is liable to further injury from the same cause. Amongst other monuments of the same class, the most important are: The Ring of Brogar, in the Orkneys, 15 M. from Kirkwall (p. 511); Callernish (I), in the Island of Lewis, 16 M. from Stornoway; the Stone Circle on Castle Rigg (I), near Keswick, Cumberland; Long Meg and her Daughters (p. 374); the Rollrich or Rollright Stones (I; p. 187); and the Circle at Stanton Drew (I; p. 121). — *Cromlechs.* These consist of upright stones, surmounted by one or more cap-stones, and they have generally formed chambers for the reception of the dead, covered by long or round mounds, which have been destroyed, leaving the chambers bare. They belonged for the most part to the Stone Age. Amongst them may be mentioned: Kits Coty House (I; p. 34); Plas Newydd, in Anglesey (p. 289); and the Pentre Evan (I) in Pembrokeshire. — *Chambered Tumuli.* Among the best examples are the burial places of the Stone Age folk at Stoney Littleton (I), near Wellow, Somersetshire, 5 M. from Bath; the

Tumulus at Uley (I), 6 M. to the N.W. of Stroud, Gloucestershire; and the Chambered Mound at Maeshowe. Long Barrows, of the same period, but without chambers, are to be seen in various parts of Great Britain. — *Round Barrows.* The graves of the Bronze Age people are to be seen spread over the greater part of Great Britain. Some of the best, including the so-called *Bowl Barrows*, *Bell Barrows*, and *Disc Barrows*, are to be seen on Salisbury Plain, near Stonehenge, or on the road from Salisbury to Blandford, near Woodyates, about 12 M. from Salisbury. — *British Camps.* These usually occupy commanding positions, on the tops of hills, and are surrounded by one or more banks and ditches. They were probably used as places of refuge for the inhabitants of the districts surrounding them, when attacked by neighbouring tribes, and many are known to have been subsequently occupied in Roman times. Maiden Castle (p. 97) is one of the most elaborate examples of these structures. The entrance to the main entrenchment is covered by a series of earthworks, resembling the *Demi-Lunes* of a modern fortification. Old Sarum (Sorbiodunum; p. 101) was probably originally a British Camp, though much altered in Saxon and Norman times. From its historical associations it is one of the most interesting monuments of this class in the country. Cadbury Camp (p. 122); Worlebury, on the hill above Weston-super-Mare (p. 127); Cisbury (p. 53); Barbury Castle, between Swindon and Marlborough; and the Black and White Catherthuns (I), 5 M. from Brechin, Forfarshire, may also be mentioned as some of the most interesting. — *Places of Worship and Assembly.* These differ from the Camps in having their ditches inside of the ramparts, instead of outside, or in having banks without ditches. The most important, on account of its great size, is undoubtedly Avebury (p. 108). This has a circle of large stones within the ditch, and other smaller circles of stones formerly existed in the interior, which are now partly destroyed. Arbor Low (I; p. 372) is another structure of the same character, having a circle of 32 stones in the interior, all of which have fallen; the Circle on Eyam Moor (I; p. 368) is a smaller example of the same class; Arthur's Round Table, near Penrith, has a bank and ditch, but no stone circle; Mayborough, close to it, has a bank constructed of carried stone; the Circles at Thornborough, near Tanfield, Yorkshire, are of the same class; the Circle at Knowlton, 7 M. to the N. of Wimborne, completes the list of these structures. The latter, though of small relief and little known, is interesting from having an early Norman church in the centre, which in all probability replaced some earlier pagan place of worship. — *Dykes and Continuous Entrenchments.* The Wall of Antoninus, between the Firth of Forth and Firth of Clyde, marking, as it does, the most northern boundary of the Roman Empire, is a monument of interest, not only to Scotchmen, but to the whole civilized world. It is now almost entirely destroyed, with the exception of a well-preserved portion near Falkirk. The Roman Wall between Carlisle and Newcastle is comparatively well-preserved. One of the most interesting of the several Camps, along the line, is that at Chesters (Cilurnum), near Hexham. Traces of the great entrenchment called Wansdyke, having its ditch to the N., may be seen in several places, running from the Severn on the W., to Savernake Forest on the E. The best position for seeing this dyke is at Shepherd's Shore, 4 M. to the N. of Devizes. Bokerly Dyke (p. 102), 11 M. to the W. of Salisbury, on the Roman Road to Badbury Rings, is an entrenchment of high relief, 4 M. in length, with a ditch to the N. E. It is of special interest, on account of its having lately been proved to have been constructed subsequently to the reign of Honorius, 600 Roman coins having been found in the rampart, dating up to that period. It probably formed part of the defensive arrangements of the Romanized Britons against their Saxon invaders. Offa's Dyke (p. 203), running from the Severn northwards to the mouth of the Dee, and several dykes in Norfolk and Suffolk may also be noted. — *Ancient Flint Mines of the Stone Age.* The people of the Stone Age were in the habit of sinking shafts, 30 or 40 feet deep, in chalk districts, to obtain the kind of flint, suitable for the construction of their implements, and wen the proper vein of flints was reached, galleries were driven along it in all directions.

The best example of these is to be seen within the Camp at Cisbury (p. 53), near Worthing. Another similar collection of flint mines is at Grimes Graves, near Brandon, Suffolk. — *Vitrified Forts.* Examples of this class of fortification may be seen at the Hill of Noath, 7 M. to the S. of Huntly, Aberdeenshire; at Knockfarrel, near Strathpeffer, Rossshire; at Craig-Phadrig, near Inverness (p.493); at Finhaven, near Aberlemno, Forfarshire; and Bun Mac Uisneachan, in Loch Ective. — *Cup-marked Stones.* At Ilkley Moor, in Yorkshire; at Drumtroddan (I), 2 M. from Port William, Wigtonshire; at Aberfeldy, Fortingale, and elsewhere in Perthshire; at Blackshore, West Kilbride, Argyleshire, and many other places. — *Pictish Towers.* The most perfect example of this class of structure is at Mousa (I), in Shetland (p. 512); others are at Carloway (I), 15 M. to the W. of Stornoway, in the Island of Lewis; at Glenelg (I), on the W. coast of Invernessshire; at Golspie, Sutherlandshire; and the Dun of Dornadilla, Durness, Sutherlandshire. The most southern monument of this class, somewhat enlarged and modified in form, is Edin's Hall, near Dunse, Berwickshire. — *Sculptured Stones.* These are perhaps the most remarkable monuments in Scotland, Wales, and the north of England, belonging to the period of the Celtic Church. Many of them are elaborately carved with the interlaced patterns and symbols that are peculiar to this period, and by examining a large series of them, the peculiar forms of the Celtic Cross may be traced in their development from the Chi-Rho Monogram of the Catacombs at Rome. Of these, the Pillars at Kirkmadrine (I), 5 M. to the S. of Stranraer, Wigtonshire, are inscribed with the monogram, and are reputed to be the oldest monuments of this class in Scotland. Others of early type may be seen in the ruined Priory at Whithorn in the same county. Amongst the most interesting in other parts of Scotland and Wales are the High Cross at Ruthwell (p. 462), remarkable for its runic inscription; Fowlis Wester, 5 M. to the N.E. of Crieff; St. Madoes, near Glencarse Station, 7 M. to the E. of Perth; Rossie Priory, 3 M. to the N. of Inchture Station, in Perthshire; Glamis, 5 M. to the S.E. of Forfar, and Eassie, not far from it; three at Aberlemno, 6 M. to the N.E. of Forfar; a large number from the neighbourhood of Meigle, in Perthshire, collected in the old school-house there; Dyce and Monymusk, in Aberdeenshire; and many others. The largest monument of this class in Scotland is the Suenos Stone, 1 M. to the E. of Forres, which is elaborately carved with figures on both sides. In Wales, monuments of a similar character are in the church at Llantwit Major (p. 196); several crosses in the grounds at Margam, Glamorganshire (p. 196); an inscribed cross, with a Chi-Rho Monogram, at Penmachno, 4½ M. from Bettws-y-Coed (p. 308); and elsewhere. — *Ogham Stones.* Stones with Ogham Inscriptions may be seen at Hackness, 5 M. to the N. W. of Scarborough, in Yorkshire. In Scotland at Logie Elphinstone, in Aberdeenshire; at Newton, in the New House, near Inverurie, Aberdeenshire; in the Museum at Golspie, Sutherlandshire, and in the Museum of the Society of Antiquaries of Scotland, in Edinburgh. In Wales, at Eglwys Cymmyn, 6 M. from Whitland; at Carreg Fyrddyn, near Abergwili, and in the churchyard of Llandawke, Carmarthenshire; at St. Dogmael; Dugoed, near Clydai, and in Clydai Churchyard, 6 M. to the S.W. of Newcastle-Emlyn (p. 202); near Margam (p. 196), and elsewhere. — *Round Belfry Towers.* Of these structures, of which such a number are to be seen in Ireland, Scotland possesses two examples: *viz.* at Brechin (p. 499), und Abernethy, in Perthshire. Both are in good preservation. — *Romano-British Villages.* The two most interesting villages of this period are those at Woodcuts and Rotherly (p. 102). They are instructive, on account of having been thoroughly explored, and the excavations in them, illustrated by means of a series of upwards of 30 models, which are exhibited in the Museum at Farnham (p. 102), not far from their sites.

The above has no pretension to being a complete list of even the most important pre-historic and ancient Monuments of Great Britain. It may however serve to direct the traveller to some of the most accessible specimens of each class.

1. London.†

Arrival. *Cabs* (see p. 3) are in waiting at the railway-stations and landing-stages, and *Private Omnibuses*, holding 6-10 persons, may be obtained at the chief stations on previous application to the Railway Co. (fare 1*s*. per mile, with a minimum of 3*s*.). Those who arrive by water have sometimes to land in small boats (6*d*. for each person, 3*d*. for each trunk). The watermen with badges are alone bound by the tariff.

Railway Stations. There are in all about 200 railway-stations in London, including those of the Underground Railway (see below) and the suburban stations of the ordinary lines. The following are the terminal stations of the chief lines. 1. *Euston Square Station*, near Euston Road and Tottenham Court Road, for the trains of the London and North Western Railway to Rugby, Chester, N. Wales, Holyhead (for Ireland), Birmingham, Liverpool, Manchester, Carlisle, and Scotland. 2. *St. Pancras Station*, Euston Road, for the trains of the Midland Railway to Bedford, Derby, Nottingham, Leeds, Manchester, Liverpool, Newcastle, and Scotland. 3. *King's Cross Station*, Euston Road, adjoining the last, for the trains of the Great Northern Co. to Peterborough, Sheffield, York, Hull, Lincoln, Manchester, Liverpool, Newcastle, and Scotland. 4. *Paddington Station*, for the trains of the Great Western Railway to the West and South-West of England, Windsor, Oxford, Birmingham, Liverpool, Manchester, and Wales. 5. *Victoria Station*, Victoria Street, S. W., a double station for the trains of the London, Chatham, and Dover Railway, the London, Brighton, and South Coast Railway, and various suburban lines. 6. *Waterloo Station*, Waterloo Road, for the trains of the London and South Western Railway to Reading, Windsor, and the South-West of England. 7. *London Bridge Station*, for the Brighton and South Coast Railway. 8. *Charing Cross Station*, close to Trafalgar Square, for the trains of the South Eastern Railway to Tunbridge, Canterbury, Folkestone, Dover, etc., and of local lines. 9. *Cannon Street Station*, the City terminus for the same lines as Charing Cross. 10. *Ludgate Hill*, and 11. *Holborn Viaduct*, City termini of the London, Chatham, and Dover Railway, and of local lines. 12. *Liverpool Street Station*, for the trains of the Great Eastern Railway to Cambridge, Lincoln, the Eastern Counties, and local stations. 13. *Broad Street Station*, adjoining the last, for the local trains of the North London Railway. 15. *Fenchurch Street Station*, near the Bank, for Blackwall, Gravesend, Southend, etc.

Steamers. Steamers ply from London to all parts of the world. Those from the Continent of Europe, Scotland, etc., land their passengers at wharves below London Bridge (landing, see above), while the large Oceanic liners enter the docks lower down the river, the passengers, when necessary, being sent on to London by special trains. American visitors to England usually land at Liverpool (p. 323) or Southampton (p. 80). The custom-house formalities are similar to those described at p. xix. — Numerous *River Steamboats* ply on the Thames between Hampton Court on the W. and Southend and Sheerness on the E., calling at about 45 intermediate piers, most of which are on the N. bank. Between London Bridge, Chelsea, and intermediate stations the steamers ply at intervals of 10 min. in summer (fares 1/2-2*d*.), between Westminster and Greenwich every 1/2 hr. (3*d*.), and between Chelsea and Kew every 1/2 hr. (6*d*.).

Hotels. The following are large hotels, with rooms at various rates, adjoining the principal railway-stations: GRAND MIDLAND, St. Pancras Station; EUSTON, Euston Square Station; GREAT NORTHERN, King's Cross;

For a coloured Railway Plan of London see pages 556 & 557

For a detailed description of London the traveller is referred to *Baedeker's Handbook for London* as nothing more is attempted here than a bare outline of the principal sights and a small selection of practical information. ***Baedeker's Handbook for London 1900.*** A facsimile edition of this volume was published by Old House Books in 2002. Available from all good book shops or, in case of difficulty, direct from the publisher. For further details see page 602

GREAT WESTERN, Paddington Station; CHARING CROSS, Charing Cross Station, Strand; GROSVENOR, Victoria Station; HOLBORN VIADUCT, Holborn Viaduct Station; CANNON STREET, Cannon St. Station; GREAT EASTERN, Liverpool St.; TERMINUS, London Bridge Station. — Other large hotels belonging to companies: MÉTROPOLE, VICTORIA, GRAND, Northumberland Avenue, Charing Cross; SAVOY, Thames Embankment, overlooking the river; BUCKINGHAM PALACE, Buckingham Palace Gate; WESTMINSTER PALACE, WINDSOR, Victoria St., Westminster; LANGHAM, Portland Place; FIRST AVENUE, Holborn; INNS OF COURT, High Holborn; ALEXANDRA, 16 St. George's Place, Hyde Park Corner. R. & A. at these generally from 4*s.* 6*d.* or 5*s.* upwards, table d'hôte D. 5-6*s.* — At the W. End: CLARIDGE'S, 49 Brook St., Grosvenor Sq., aristocratic and expensive; ALBEMARLE, Albemarle St.; BUCKLAND'S, 42 Brook St.; BERKELEY, 77 Piccadilly; BRISTOL, Burlington Gardens; THOMAS'S, 25 Berkeley Sq.; CONTINENTAL, 1 Regent St.; LIMMER'S, 2 George St., Hanover Sq.; QUEEN'S GATE, 98 Queen's Gate; SOUTH KENSINGTON, Queen's Gate Terrace; CADOGAN, 75 Sloane St.; NORRIS'S, 48 Russell Road, Addison Road Station; BAILEY'S, Gloucester Road; and many others in the streets leading out of Piccadilly, Regent St., and Bond St. The accommodation at these West End hotels is generally good and the terms high: R. & A. 5*s.*, D. 5-10*s.* — In or near Trafalgar Sq. and the Strand: MORLEY'S, Trafalgar Sq.; GOLDEN CROSS, SOMERSET, HAXELL'S, Strand (Nos. 452, 162, 371); PREVITALI, 14 Arundel St., Haymarket; HUMMUMS, TAVISTOCK, (R., B., & A. 7*s.* 6*d.*), COVENT GARDEN, BEDFORD, Covent Garden; ARUNDEL, 19 Arundel St., on the Thames Embankment. There are also numerous quiet family hotels in the streets leading from the Strand to the Thames. Charges at these somewhat less: R. & A. from 3*s.* 6*d.*, D. from 3*s.* — In Bloomsbury: BURR'S (R. 2*s.* 6*d.*), ROWLAND'S, Queen Sq. (Nos. 11, 14), less pretending; BEDFORD, 93 Southampton Row; HORSESHOE, BEDFORD HEAD, Tottenham Court Road (Nos. 264, 235), commercial. — In Holborn: RIDLER'S, WOOD'S, Furnival's Inn (quiet); IMPERIAL, Holborn Viaduct; COCKER'S, 19 Charterhouse Sq. (quiet). — In Fleet Street and the City: ANDERTON'S, PEELE'S, Fleet St. (Nos. 162, 177); CATHEDRAL, 48 St. Paul's Churchyard; DE KEYSER'S ROYAL, Embankment, Blackfriars, a large house (R. & A. from 5*s.*, D. 4*s.*); ALBION, 172 Aldersgate St.; GREEN DRAGON, 188 Bishopsgate Without; CITY OF LONDON, 11 Bishopsgate St. Within; SEYD'S, 39 Finsbury Sq. (R. & B. 5*s.* 6*d.*), etc. — *Temperance Hotels:* WEST CENTRAL, 97 Southampton Row; ARMFIELD'S, South Place, Finsbury; WILD'S, 30 Ludgate Hill; INSULL'S, Burton Crescent, Brunswick Sq., W. C.

BOARDING HOUSES and PRIVATE LODGINGS are generally easily obtainable in London, through application to a respectable house-agent or by advertisement. The dearest and best are in the West End: *e.g.* in the streets leading out of Piccadilly and St. James's St. The neigbbourhood of the British Museum is another convenient quarter for boarding and lodging houses at more moderate prices (R. from 15*s.*, R. with board from 30*s.* a week).

Restaurants. **Holborn*, 218 High Holborn; *Criterion*, Regent Circus, two of the largest and best-known restaurants in London; **St. James's Hall*, 69 Regent St. and 25 Piccadilly; **Verrey*, **Café Royal*, **Burlington*, *Kühn*, Regent St., first-class and expensive; **Gatti*, Adelaide St. and 436 Strand; *Simpson's*, *Gaiety*, *Romano*, Strand (Nos. 101, 343, 399); *Savoy Hotel* (see above), with open-air restaurant, high charges; *Cavour*, 20 Leicester Sq.; **Kettner*, 29 Church St., Soho (French; somewhat expensive); **Monico*, 15 Tichborne St.; *Frascati*, 26 Oxford St.; **Rainbow*, *Cock*, Fleet St. (Nos. 15, 22); *Old Cheshire Cheese*, 16 Wine Office Court, Fleet St. (quaint old rooms); *Lake & Turner*, 49 Cheapside; *Pimm's*, 3 Poultry; **London Tavern*, 53 Fenchurch St.; **Crosby Hall*, Bishopsgate (an interesting mediæval building, handsomely fitted up); *White Hart*, 63 Borough High St., Southwark; *Three Tuns Tavern*, Billingsgate Fish Market, Lower Thames St. (fish-dinner, from 4 to 5 p. m., 2*s.*). — OYSTERS: *Scott*, 18 Coventry St., Haymarket; *Rule*, 38 Maiden Lane, Covent Garden; *Pimm*, 3 Poultry; *Lightfoot*, 22 Lime St.; *Smith*, 357 Strand.

Cafés. *Simpson*, *Gatti*, *Criterion*, *Kühn*, *Verrey*, *Café Royal*, *Monico*, see above; * *Vienna Café*, corner of Oxford St. and Hart St., near the British Museum; *Café de Paris*, Ludgate Hill; *Baker's*, 1 Change Alley, Cornhill.

Cabs. The '*Four-wheelers*' have seats for four persons inside, and the *Hansoms*, or two-wheeled cabs, have seats for two persons, though often used by three. The latter are the faster and more comfortable. The fares are reckoned by distance, unless the cab is expressly hired by time, the rate being 6*d.* per mile or fraction of a mile, with a minimum of 1*s.* Each pers. above two 6*d.* extra for the whole hiring. Beyond the 4-mile radius from Charing Cross the fare is 1*s.* per mile. Per hour 2*s.* for four-wheelers and 2*s.* 6*d.* for hansoms; each addit. 1/4 hr. 6*d.* or 8*d.* For each article of luggage carried outside 2*d.* Each driver is bound to produce the authorised Book of Distances if required. In cases of attempted imposition the passenger should demand the cabman's number, or order him to drive to the nearest police court or station. A rough-and-ready means of calculating fares is to allow 1*d.* per minute in a hansom (less for four-wheelers).

Omnibuses, of which there are at least 200 lines, traverse the streets in all directions from about 8 a.m. till midnight. The destination of each 'bus and the principal streets through which it passes are painted on the outside. 'Buses keep to the *left* in driving along the street, and stop when hailed. To prevent mistakes, the passenger should mention his destination to the conductor on entering. The fares are very low, generally ranging from 1/2*d.* to 4*d.*

Tramways. Several lines are in operation in the outlying districts. The cars are comfortable and the fares moderate (1-4*d.*).

Coaches. During summer well-appointed stage-coaches, generally starting from Northumberland Avenue, ply to various places of interest round London, affording, in fine weather, a very pleasant way of seeing the scenery.

Theatres. London contains about 65 theatres, most of which are in or near the Strand. Opera is performed at *Her Majesty's Theatre* or *Opera House*, Haymarket, and the *Royal Italian Opera* or *Covent Garden Theatre.* The largest theatre is *Drury Lane Theatre*, for spectacular plays, pantomimes, etc. Among the other leading theatres are the *Lyceum* (Mr. Henry Irving and Miss Ellen Terry), the *Haymarket*, *St. James's*, *Savoy* (Gilbert and Sullivan's operas), *Princess's*, *Adelphi*, *Strand*, *Gaiety*, *Vaudeville*, *Globe*, *Royal Court*, *Toole's*, *Garrick*, *Shaftesbury*, *Lyric*, *Terry's*, *Olympic*, *Comedy*, and *Royalty*.

Music Halls. *Alhambra*, *Empire*, Leicester Square (with elaborate ballets); *London Pavilion*, Piccadilly Circus; *Tivoli*, Strand; *Trocadero*, Shaftesbury Avenue; *Oxford*, 14 Oxford St., and many others. — **Concerts** of high-class music are given at *St. James's Hall*, the *Royal Albert Hall*, the *Crystal Palace*, *St. George's Hall*, *Prince's Hall*, etc.

Places of Entertainment. *Tussaud's Waxworks*, Marylebone Road; *German Reed's Dramatic Entertainment*, St. George's Hall; *Egyptian Hall*, Piccadilly; *Moore and Burgess Minstrels* (Christy Minstrels), St. James's Hall; *Royal Aquarium*, Westminster; *Olympia*, near the Addison Road Station, Kensington (a large skating-rink); *Panorama of Niagara*, York St., Westminster (adm. 1*s.*).

Exhibitions of Pictures. *Royal Academy of Fine Arts*, Burlington House, Piccadilly (exhibition of works of modern British artists in summer; adm. 1*s.*); *Grosvenor Gallery*, 137 New Bond St. (1*s.*); *New Gallery*, 121 Regent St. (1*s.*); *Royal Society of Painters in Water-Colours*, 5 Pall Mall East (1*s.*); *Royal Institute of Painters in Water-Colours*, 191 Piccadilly (1*s.*); *Dudley Gallery*, Egyptian Hall; *Royal Society of British Artists*, Suffolk St., Pall Mall; *Doré Gallery*, 35 New Bond St. (1*s.*)

United States Minster, *Hon. Robert T. Lincoln*, 123 Victoria St., S.W. (11-3); **Consul,** *John C. New, Esq.*, 12 St. Helen's Place, Bishopsgate, E. C.

The **Lady Guide Association,** 16 Cockspur St., Charing Cross, gives information of all kinds to travellers.

The accompanying table shows the principal sights of London, with the hours and other conditions of admission.

Museums, Exhibitions, etc.	Sunday	Monday	Tuesday	Wednesday	Thursday	Friday	Saturday	Remarks
Bethnal Green Museum & National Portrait Gallery	—	10-10	10-10	10 to 4, 5, or 6	10-10	10-10	10-10	1
British Museum	—	10 to 4, 5, or 6 and 8-10	10 to 4, 5, or 6 and 8-10	10 to 4, 5, or 6 and 8-10	10 to 4, 5, or 6 and 8-10	10 to 4, 5, or 6 and 8-10	10 to 4, 5, or 6 and 8-10	2
Chelsea Hospital	—	10-1 & 2-7	10-1 & 2-7	10-1 & 2-7	10-1 & 2-7	10-1 & 2-7	10-1 & 2-7	
Crystal Palace	—	From 10a.m.	From 10a.m.	From 10a.m.	From 10a.m.	From 10a.m.	From 10a.m.	3
Dulwich Gallery	—	10 to 4 or 5	10 to 4 or 5	10 to 4 or 5	10 to 4 or 5	10 to 4 or 5	10 to 4 or 5	
Foundling Hospital	After morning service	10-4	—	—	—	—	—	
Geological Museum	—	10-10	10-5	10-5	10-5	—	10-10	
Greenwich Hospital	2 to 4, 5, or 6	10 to 4, 5, or 6	10 to 4, 5, or 6	10 to 4, 5, or 6	10 to 4, 5, or 6	10 to 4, 5, or 6	10 to 4, 5, or 6	
Guildhall Museum	—	10 to 4 or 5	10 to 4 or 5	10 to 4 or 5	10 to 4 or 5	10 to 4 or 5	10 to 4 or 5	
Hampton Court	2-4 or 2-6	10 to 4 or 6	10 to 4 or 6	10 to 4 or 6	10 to 4 or 6	—	10 to 4 or 6	
India Museum	—	10 to 4, 5, or 6	10 to 4, 5, or 6	10 to 4, 5, or 6	10 to 4, 5, or 6	10 to 4, 5 or 6	10 to 4, 5, or 6	
Kew Gardens	1-6	12-6	12-6	12-6	12-6	12-6	12-6	
National Gallery	—	10 to 4, 5, 6, or 7	10 to 4, 5, 6, or 7	10 to 4, 5, 6, or 7	11 to 4, 5, 6, or 7	11 to 4, 5, 6, or 7	10 to 4, 5, 6, or 7	4
Natural History Museum	—	10 to 4, 5, or 6	10 to 4, 5, or 6	10 to 4, 5, or 6	10 to 4, 5, or 6	10 to 4, 5, or 6	10 to 4, 5. or 6	
Parliament, Houses of	—	—	—	—	—	—	10-4	5
Royal College of Surgeons	—	12 to 4 or 5	12 to 4 or 5	12 to 4 or 5	12 to 4 or 5	—	—	
St. Paul's Cathedral	—	9-5	9-5	9-5	9-5	9-5	9-5	6
Soane Museum	—	—	11-5	11-5	11-5	—	11-5	7
South Kensington Museum	—	10-10	10-10	10 to 4, 5, or 6	10 to 4, 5, or 6	10 to 4, 5, or 6	10-10	8
Temple Church	—	10-1 & 2-4	10-1 & 2-4	10-1 & 2-4	10-1 & 2-4	10-1 & 2-4	10-1 & 2-4	9
Tower	—	10-4	10-4	10-4	10-4	10-4	10-4	10
United Service Museum	—	11-4 or 11-5	11-4 or 11-5	11-4 or 11-5	11-4 or 11-5	—	—	
Westminster Abbey	—	9 till dusk	9 till dusk	9 till dusk	9 till dusk	9 till dusk	9 till dusk	11
Zoological Garden	—	9 to sunset	9 to sunset	9 to sunset	9 to sunset	9 to sunset	9 to sunset	12

Remarks: 1. 6*d.* on Wed. — 2. Different sections closed on different days for cleaning: one-half of the galleries only in the evening. — 3. Adm. 1*s.*; sometimes 2*s.* 6*d.* on Sat.; special occasions dearer. — 4. 6*d.* on Thurs. & Frid. — 5. By ticket obtained gratis at the entrance. — 6. Galleries 6*d.*, Crypt 6*d.* — 7. Tues. & Thurs. only in Feb. & Mar.; closed Sept.-Jan. — 8. 6*d.* on Wed., Thurs., & Frid. — 9. Rotunda open on Sun. during service. — 10. Armoury 6*d.*, regalia 6*d.*; free on Mon. & Sat. — 11. Chapels 6*d.*; on Mon. & Tues. free. — 12. Adm. 1*s.*, on Mon. 6*d.*

London, the metropolis of the British Empire and the largest city in the world, lies in the S.E. of England, on both banks of the river Thames, and embraces parts of the four counties of Middlesex, Essex, Kent, and Surrey. At the census of 1881 the aggregate population of the metropolitan parliamentary boroughs (conterminous with the new County of the City of London) was 3,963,307; it is now about 4$^1/_2$ millions. The city has doubled in size within the last half-century, being now about 15 M. long from E. to W., and 9 M. wide from N. to S., and covering 122 sq. M. of ground. The area included in the Metropolitan Police District, extending for a radius of 15 M. from Charing Cross, amounts to 690 sq. M. and contains considerably over 5 million inhabitants.

The principal and larger part of London lies on the N. bank of the Thames, and includes the *City*, or commercial and money-making quarter on the E., and the fashionable *West End*, with the palaces of the Queen and the nobility and most of the sights frequented by visitors. The manufacturing quarters on the right bank of the Thames, and also the outlying districts to the N. and E. are comparatively uninteresting to strangers.

At what period the Britons settled on the spot now occupied by London, we have no means of knowing; but the British settlement became a Roman station in the reign of the Emp. Claudius (41-54 A. D.) and received the name of *Londinium*, evidently an adaptation of the British name *Llyndun* (from *Llyn*, a pool, and *Din* or *Dun*, a hill-fort). Under the Romans London became a commercial city of no little importance, and afterwards, as capital of one of the Saxon kingdoms, it continued to advance rapidly. It became practically the capital of England in the time of Canute, and received a charter from William the Conqueror. The present form of its Corporation dates from the close of the 12th century. In the 13-15th cent. the city suffered severely from fires, pestilences, and the outbreaks of Wat Tyler (1380) and Jack Cade (1450). The Great Plague of 1664-66 carried off about 100,000 of its citizens, and the Great Fire of 1666 destroyed 13,000 houses. Since then its history has been in the main one of constant progress and growth, the stages of which are best marked by the erection of its principal public buildings and by public improvements of all kinds.

Charing Cross, which is the official centre of London, from which the cab-radius, etc., are measured, and also practically the centre of the London of the sight-seer, is the open space to the S. of Trafalgar Square, between the Strand and Whitehall. The name is probably derived from the ancient village of *Cherringe*. ***Trafalgar Square**, one of the finest open spaces in London, contains the *Nelson Column* and statues of *Sir Henry Havelock*, *Sir Chas. Napier*, *George IV.*, and *Gen. Gordon*. To the N.E. is the church of *St. Martin's in the Fields*, by Gibbs.

On the N. side of Trafalgar Square stands the ****National Gallery**, erected in 1832-38 and enlarged in 1860, 1876, and 1887 (adm., see p. 4; catalogues 1*s.* and 6*d.*). From the large number of artists represented, the collections it contains are of the highest value to the student of art, and there is no lack of masterpieces of the first rank. The *Italian* and *Netherlandish Schools* are admirably represented, the *French* and *Spanish* less fully. The *Older British Masters* are well illustrated, and the large collection of *Turner's* landscapes is unrivalled, but the English water-colourists are almost unrepresented. About 1100 pictures in all are exhibited.

Rooms I-IX., reached by the central staircase, contain the Italian pictures; RR. X-XII. the Flemish and Dutch; R. XIII. the late Italian; R. XIV. the French; R. XV. the Spanish; RR. XVI-XVII. (at the head of the staircase to the right) the old British; RR. XIX-XXI. the modern British; and R. XXII. the Turner Collection. In the basement are a collection of water-colours by *Turner* and others, some monochrome drawings by *Rubens* and *Van Dyck*, several paintings belonging to the National Portrait Gallery (right), water-colour copies of early Italian painters, and copies of *Velazquez* and *Rembrandt* (left).

Among the chief treasures of the Gallery are *Raphael's* 'Madonna degli Ansidei' (No. 1171, R. VI.; bought in 1884 for 70,000*l.*), Pope Julius II. (27, R. VI), 'Garvagh Madonna' (744, VI), Vision of a Knight (213, VI), and St. Catharine (168, VI); *Titian's* Bacchus and Ariadne (35, VII), Holy Family (635, VII), and 'Noli me tangere' (270, VII); *Veronese's* Family of Darius (294, VII); portraits by *Moroni* (697, 1022, VII) and *Moretto* (299, VII); good specimens of *Giov. Bellini* (280, 189, 808, VII); the Raising of Lazarus, by *Sebastian del Piombo* (1, VII); Madonna and Child, by *Leon. da Vinci* (1093, I); a portrait by *Andrea del Sarto* (690, I); *Fra Angelico's* Christ with the banner of the Resurrection (663, II); *Botticelli's* Nativity (1034, III); a Madonna by *Perugino* (288, VI); works by *Correggio* (23, 15, 10, IX); portraits and other works by *Rembrandt* (775, 672, 243, 757, 45, X); Charles I., by *Van Dyck* (1172, X; bought for 17,500*l.*); the Idle Servant, by *Maas* (207, X); Triumph of Julius Cæsar and the 'Chapeau de Paille', by *Rubens* (278, X, and 852, XII); Peace of Münster, by *Terburg* (896, X); three beautiful little works by *Jan van Eyck* (222, 186, 290, XI); good specimens of *De Hooghe* (834, 835, XII), *Cuyp*, *Hobbema*, *Hals*, *Van der Helst*, *I. van Ostade*, etc.; landscapes by *Claude Lorrain* (R. XIV); characteristic examples of *Velazquez* and *Murillo* (R. XV); numerous works of *Hogarth*, *Reynolds*, *Gainsborough* (XVI, XVII), *Constable* (XIX), *Turner* (XXII), etc.; two works by *Rossetti* (XIX).

From Trafalgar Square Pall Mall, with the principal *Clubs*, *Marlborough House* (Prince of Wales), and *St. James's Palace*, leads to the S.W. towards the *Green Park*. A little to the S. of Pall Mall lies *St. James's Park*, at the W. end of which is *Buckingham Palace*, the London residence of the Queen, containing a fine picture-gallery (access difficult to obtain).

Northumberland Avenue, leading to the S.E. from Trafalgar Square to the Thames, contains three huge hotels and the *Constitutional Club*. On the Embankment is the *National Liberal Club*.

Whitehall, leading to the S. from Trafalgar Square, passes the *Admiralty*, the *Horse Guards* (headquarters of the military authorities), and the various *Government Offices* (all to the right). On the other side are *Scotland Yard* (headquarters of the police), the *United Service Museum* (adm., see p. 4), and the palace of ***Whitehall**, the only relic of which is the fine Palladian *Banqueting Hall*, now a *Royal Chapel* (adm. on application to the keeper). Whitehall is continued by *Parliament Street*, leading to Parliament Square, which is embellished with statues of *Peel*, *Palmerston*, *Derby*, *Beaconsfield*, and *Canning*. To the left rise the ***Houses of Parliament**, a huge building in the richest late-Gothic (Tudor) style, by *Sir Charles Barry*. The exterior is adorned with innumerable statues, and the interior is fitted up with great taste and splendour (adm., see p. 4; adm. to sittings of the House of Lords or House of Commons through a member; the former open to the public when sitting as a Court of Appeal). The *Victoria Tower*, the largest of the three which adorn the building, is 340 ft. high. — **Westminster Hall,** adjoining the Houses of Parliament on the W. and forming a kind of public entrance-hall, is part of the ancient palace of Westminster and dates mainly from the 14th century. The fine oaken ceiling is a masterpiece of timber architecture.

To the S. of Parliament Square, opposite the Houses of Parliament, stands ****Westminster Abbey,** said to have been founded in the 7th cent., rebuilt by Edward the Confessor (1049-65), and dating in its present form mainly from the latter half of the 13th cent., with numerous important additions and alterations. The chapel of Henry VII. dates from the beginning of the 16th cent., and the towers from 1722-40. With its royal burial-vaults and long series of monuments to celebrated men, Westminster Abbey may claim to be the British Walhalla or Temple of Fame. Admission, see p. 4.

The ***Interior** produces a very fine and imposing effect, though this is somewhat marred by the egregiously bad taste of many of the monuments with which nave, aisles, and transepts are filled. The most interesting monuments are, perhaps, those in the *Poets' Corner* (S. transept). Of the chapels at the E. end of the church (adm., see p. 4) the most noteworthy are those of *Edward the Confessor* and the beautiful Perp. ***Chapel of Henry VII.;* but all contain interesting tombs. The *Cloisters* and *Chapter House* should also be visited.

To the N. of the abbey stands *St. Margaret's Church*, with some interesting monuments and stained-glass windows. On the S. it is adjoined by *Westminster School*, one of the oldest and most important schools in the country. The *Westminster Column*, to the W. of the Abbey, commemorates former pupils killed in war.

From *Westminster Bridge*, which crosses the Thames here, the *VICTORIA EMBANKMENT runs to the N. along the left bank of the river to Blackfriars, while the ALBERT EMBANKMENT extends to the S., on the opposite bank, to Vauxhall Bridge. The former is embellished with *Cleopatra's Needle* (an obelisk brought from Egypt), several *Statues*, and pleasantly laid out gardens. Among the chief buildings adjoining the Victoria Embankment are *Montague House* (Duke of Buccleuch), the *National Liberal Club* (p. 6), the *Savoy Hotel* (p. 2), the *Medical Examination Hall*, *Somerset House* (p. 11), the *School Board Office*, the *Temple* (p. 11), *Sion College*, the *City of London School*, and the *Royal Hotel* (p. 2).

We may now return to Trafalgar Square and proceed to the N.W. to PICCADILLY, a handsome street extending to the W. from Haymarket. The E. portion of the street contains handsome shops, business-houses, and concert-halls. To the right is **Burlington House,** the headquarters of the *Royal Academy*, *Royal Society*, and several other learned bodies. To the left is the *Museum of Practical Geology* (adm., see p. 4; entr. from Jermyn St.). The W. half of

Piccadilly, skirting the *Green Park*, contains many aristocratic residences and clubs.

Piccadilly ends at *Hyde Park Corner*, the S.E. entrance of ***Hyde Park,** the most fashionable of the London parks, covering an area of nearly 400 acres. The favourite drive extends along its S. side from Hyde Park Corner to Kensington Gate and is thronged with carriages from 5 to 7 p. m. in the season. Parallel to the drive is *Rotten Row,* the chief resort of equestrians. The large piece of artificial water is named the *Serpentine.* To the W. Hyde Park is adjoined by *Kensington Gardens,* with their fine old trees, containing *Kensington Palace,* now occupied by the Duke of Teck and various royal pensioners.

The line of Piccadilly is prolonged towards the W. by *Knightsbridge* (with large cavalry barracks) and *Kensington Gore,* skirting the S. side of Hyde Park. To the right, within the park, rises the **Albert Memorial**, a magnificent Gothic monument to the late Prince Consort. Opposite is the **Albert Hall,** a huge circular structure in brick and terracotta, used for concerts and oratorios and accommodating about 10,000 people. At the back of the Albert Hall is the new **Imperial Institute,** situated in what used to be the gardens of the Horticultural Society. Of the *Exhibition Galleries* surrounding these gardens, one (to the E.) contains the ***India Museum** (adm., see p. 4), a fine collection of Oriental works of industry and art, and the others collections connected with South Kensington Museum (see below).

****South Kensington Museum,** situated at the corner of Exhibition Road (leading S. from Kensington Gore) and Cromwell Road, includes a museum of ornamental or applied art, a national gallery of British art, an art library, an art training school, and a school of science (adm., see p. 4).

The ****Art Collection,** one of the largest and finest in the world, is exhibited in three large glass-roofed courts and in the galleries adjoining them. We first enter the ARCHITECTURAL COURT, chiefly containing casts, but also a few fine original works. The SOUTH COURT contains small works of art in metal, ivory, amber, porcelain, etc., many of which are on loan. The NORTH COURT is devoted to Italian art, comprising numerous original sculptures of the Renaissance. — The NATIONAL GALLERY OF BRITISH ART, on the upper floor, contains an extensive and representative **Collection of British Water-Colours*, the *Sheepshanks Collection* of modern paintings, the famous ***Cartoons of Raphael*, etc. On the same floor are the **Ceramic Gallery*, the **Jones Collection of French Furniture*, a **Collection of Enamels* (Prince Consort Gallery), and other valuable works of art.

To the W. of this museum is the ***Natural History Museum,** a handsome and most convenient structure, containing the extensive natural history collections of the British Museum.

On the N. Hyde Park is bounded by the *Uxbridge Road,* the prolongation of which to the E. forms perhaps the most important line of thoroughfare in London. OXFORD STREET, the first of th s magnificent series of streets, begins at the *Marble Arch,* or N.E entrance of Hyde Park, and is about $1^1/_2$ M. in length. The square near its W. half contain many of the most aristocratic houses in London, while its E. half is an unbroken series of attractive shops. Among the chief streets diverging from it are *Edgware Road*, *Bond Street* (with fashionable shops and picture-galleries), *Regent Street* (see below), *Tottenham Court Road*, and *Charing Cross Road* (leading to Charing Cross). *Oxford Circus*, where Oxford St. intersects Regent St., is one of the chief centres of the omnibus traffic.

Regent Street, one of the finest streets in London, containing many of the best shops, extends from Waterloo Place, Pall Mall, to *Portland Place*, which ends at the Regent's Park. ***Regent's Park,** 470 acres in extent, is well worthy of a visit and contains the gardens of the **Zoological Society* (adm., see p. 4), the *Botanical Society*, and the *Toxophilite Society*. On the S. the park is bounded by MARYLEBONE ROAD, with *Tussaud's Waxworks* (adm., see p. 4; close to the Baker St. station of the Metropolitan Railway). Both park and street take their name from the Prince Regent, afterwards George IV. To the N. of Regent's Park rises *Primrose Hill*, beyond which lies *Hampstead*.

From New Oxford St., beyond Tottenham Court Road (see above), two short streets lead to the left (N.) to the ****British Museum** (adm., see p. 4), a huge building with an Ionic portico, containing a series of extensive and highly valuable collections.

GROUND FLOOR. To the right of the entrance is the section for **Printed Books and Manuscripts**, containing numerous incunabula, autographs, and other objects of the greatest interest and value. — The galleries to the left contain the **Greek and Roman Sculptures**, including the famous ***Elgin Marbles*. — Other galleries on this side (W.) contain the almost equally important **Egyptian and Assyrian Collections.** — The door immediately opposite the main entrance leads to the huge circular ***Reading Room**, which is shown to visitors, on application to the official at the entrance.

UPPER FLOOR. The W. wing contains the **Ethnological Department**, the **Mediæval Antiquities**, the **Glass and Ceramic Gallery**, and the **Collection of Prints.** — In the E. wing are the **Vases, Bronzes, Terra Cotta Works,** and **Gold Ornaments.** — The N. galleries are devoted to the smaller **Etruscan, Egyptian, and Assyrian Antiquities**, including an extensive collection of mummies.

Oxford Street is continued by *Holborn*, **Holborn Viaduct* (a clever piece of engineering), *Newgate St.*, and *Cheapside*. To the left diverges the wide *Charterhouse Street*, leading to the extensive **Smithfield Markets** and to the **Charterhouse**, an interesting old building used as an asylum for old men (adm. on application to the porter). Adjoining Smithfield are *St. Bartholomew's Hospital* and the ***Church of St. Bartholomew,** with a fine Norman interior, recently restored.

In Newgate Street, to the left, is **Christ's Hospital** ('Blue-coat School'), a school for 1200 boys and 100 girls, founded by Edward VI. The boys still wear their curious original dress. Just beyond it are the large buildings of the **General Post Office,** the W. section containing the telegraph department.

A few yards to the S. of Newgate Street rises ***St. Paul's Cathedral** (adm., see p. 4), an imposing Romanesque building with a beautifully proportioned dome, erected by *Sir Christopher Wren* in 1675-1710 on the site of the older building destroyed by the Great Fire (1666).

The **Interior,** though somewhat bare and dark, is imposing from the beauty and vastness of its proportions. It is second to Westminster Abbey alone as the burial-place of eminent men, particularly naval and military officers. As in the Abbey, the monuments are seldom of artistic value, but a prominent exception is the monument of the **Duke of Wellington*, by Stevens, in a chapel of the S. aisle. The Duke and *Lord Nelson* are buried in the *Crypt.* The visitor may ascend to the *Whispering Gallery*, with its curious acoustic properties, and to the *Stone Gallery*, which affords an excellent view of the city.

Cheapside, containing the church of *St. Mary-le-Bow*, is prolonged by the *Poultry*, leading to the Bank, the space in front of which is in business-hours the scene of a traffic probably unrivalled elsewhere. The **Bank of England**, an irregular and low edifice by Sir John Soane, is open daily, as far as its business offices are concerned, from 10 to 3. The printing, weighing, and bullion offices are shown by the special order of the Governor or Deputy Governor. — The **Royal Exchange**, to the S. of the Bank, dates from 1842-44 (chief business hour 3.30-4.30 p.m. on Tues. & Frid.). — Opposite the Bank, at the end of the Poultry, rises the **Mansion House**, or official residence of the Lord Mayor, erected in 1739-52. The Lord Mayor's police-court is open daily, 12-2, but the state and reception rooms are shown only by special permission. — In Walbrook, behind the Mansion House, is the church of *St. Stephen's*, with one of Wren's best interiors. — The **Guildhall**, or council-hall of the City, to the N. of Cheapside, was originally built in the 15th cent., but was restored after the Great Fire and provided with a new façade in 1789. Visitors are admitted to the *Great Hall*, with its fine timber roof, and the *Museum* and *Art Gallery* also deserve a visit. The *Free Library* is open to all.

Bethnal Green Museum (adm., see p. 4), with the **National Portrait Gallery*, about 1½ M. to the N.E. of the Bank, may be reached by an Old Ford omnibus from the Bank, by a tramway-car from the Aldgate station of the Metropolitan Railway, or by train from Liverpool St. Station to *Cambridge Heath.*

We may now proceed to the S., through King William Street, to London Bridge, passing the *Monument*, a lofty column (202 ft.) erected in commemoration of the Great Fire (p. 5). **London Bridge**, erected in 1825-31, is the most important of the bridges over the Thames and is the scene of an immense traffic. The oldest bridge at this point was erected by the Saxons, or, perhaps, by the Romans. The bridge commands a good view of the busy river.

From the N. end of London Bridge Lower Thames Street runs along the left bank of the Thames, passing the *Coal Exchange*, *Billingsgate Fish-Market*, and the *Custom House.* The street ends at Great Tower Hill, opposite the ***Tower**, the ancient fortress and state-prison of London (adm., see p. 4).

It is possible that a Roman fort stood here, but the Tower of London properly originated with William the Conqueror, who in 1078 erected the *White Tower, forming the centre of the mass of buildings. It contains a Norman **Chapel*, extensive collections of arms and armour, etc., and, like many of the other small towers, is full of historical interest. The *Crown Jewels* are kept in the *Record* or *Wakefield Tower.*

On the E. side of Tower Hill stands the *Royal Mint* (adm. by order procured by previous written application to the Deputy-Master of the Mint), and on the N. is *Trinity House*, concerned with the regulation of lighthouses and other matters pertaining to navigation. — Below the Thames here are the *Tower Subway* (1/2*d.*) and (a little higher up) the new *City of London and Southwark Subway*, to be traversed by an electric railway. The *Thames Tunnel*, about 2 M. below London Bridge, is now used for railway traffic only. The **Docks,** which begin just below the Tower and extend for several miles down the river, are described in the *Handbook for London.*

From St. Paul's we may return to Charing Cross by Fleet Street and the Strand. Fleet Street, deriving its name from the old Fleet Brook, is one of the busiest thoroughfares in London and contains many newspaper and printing offices. To the S. of it lies the **Temple,** originally a lodge of the Knights Templar, but now belonging to the legal corporations (barristers) of the *Inner* and the *Middle Temple.* The *Temple Gardens* are frequently open.

The ***Temple Church**, in the Inner Temple, consists of a *Round Church* in the Norman style, completed in 1185, and an E.E. choir (1240). — The fine Gothic **Hall* of the Middle Temple should also be visited.

On the N. side of Fleet St., at the corner of *Chancery Lane*, are the **Royal Courts of Justice,** a huge Gothic pile by *Street.* At the back of the Law Courts lies *Lincoln's Inn*, a corporation similar to the Temple, with a valuable old library. [*Gray's Inn*, another Inn of Court, lies to the N. of Holborn, p. 9.]

The Strand, which begins here, was formerly entered from Fleet St. by *Temple Bar*, removed in 1878. It contains numerous theatres and newspaper offices. Adjoining the Law Courts is the church of *St. Clement Danes*, and a little farther on is *St. Mary-le-Strand's.* **Somerset House**, to the left, a large quadrangular building on the site of an old palace of the Protector Somerset, is devoted to various public offices. The E. wing is occupied by *King's College.* Savoy Street, a little farther on, leads to the left to the *Savoy Chapel*, a Perp. building of 1505-11, on the site of the ancient Savoy Palace. — Covent Garden Market lies to the N. of this part of the Strand.

Among the chief points of interest on the S. or Surrey side of the Thames are ***Lambeth Palace,** for 600 years the residence of the Archbishops of Canterbury (the chapel dating from 1245, the 'Lollard's Tower' from 1434, etc.), with a fine library (adm. by special permission); *St. Thomas's Hospital*, on the 'pavilion' system, adjoining Westminster Bridge; *Bethlehem Hospital*, a large lunatic asylum ('Bedlam'); *St. George's Roman Catholic Cathedral; Battersea Park;* ***St. Saviour's Church** (13-16th cent.), near London Bridge; *Barclay and Perkins' Brewery; Spurgeon's Tabernacle;* and *Guy's Hospital.*

The numerous other places of interest in and near London, such as *Chelsea Hospital*, *Greenwich Hospital*, the *Crystal Palace*, *Hampton Court*, *Dulwich*, *Woolwich*, *Richmond*, *Kew*, and *Epping Forest*, are described in *Baedeker's Handbook for London.*

2. From London to Dover.

a. South Eastern Railway viâ Tunbridge and Folkestone.

77 M. Railway in $1^3/_4$-$3^1/_4$ hrs. from *Charing Cross*, *Cannon Street*, and *London Bridge* (fares 18*s.* 6*d.*, 13*s.* 6*d.*, 6*s.* $2^1/_2$*d.*, return 31*s.*, 22*s.* 6*d.*, 12*s.* 5*d.*; mail train 20*s.*, 15*s.*, return 33*s.* 6*d.*, 25*s.*). On Sat. cheap return-tickets, available till the following Mon., are issued at 22*s.* 6*d.*, 17*s.* 6*d.*, and 10*s.* 6*d.* Some of the ordinary trains run viâ *Redhill* and rejoin the direct line at *Tunbridge* (p. 13). — Passengers starting from Charing Cross should remember in choosing their seats, that after backing into Cannon Street the locomotive will be at the other end of the train.

Crossing the Thames and leaving London Bridge Station, the train passes (5 M.) *New Cross* (p. 32), *St. John's*, and ($8^3/_4$ M.) *Grove Park*, beyond which the Crystal Palace is visible in the distance to the right. We then thread a tunnel more than $^1/_2$ M. long.

11 M. **Chislehurst** (A. S. 'Gravel Wood'; comp. Ger. *Kiesel*; *Bickley Arms Hotel*), beautifully situated on a height in a well-wooded district. Not far from the station (turn to the right and then ascend the hill to the left) is *Camden Place*, formerly the residence of Camden the antiquary (d. 1623), but perhaps better known as the retreat of Napoleon III. and the Empress Eugénie after the Franco-German War. Napoleon died here in 1873, and his remains, with those of his son the Prince Imperial (killed in S. Africa in 1879), lay in the Roman Catholic church till their removal to Farnborough (see p. 76). — 14 M. *Orpington* is known chiefly as the place where Mr. Ruskin's works have hitherto been published. — *Downe*, 3 M. to the S.W. of ($15^1/_2$ M.) *Chelsfield*, was for 40 years the home of Charles Darwin (d. 1882). Tunnel. Beyond ($16^1/_2$ M.) *Halstead*, $2^1/_2$ M. to the S.W. of which are the Knockholt Beeches (see below), we traverse another tunnel, $1^3/_4$ M. long, and, passing through rich park-like scenery, reach ($20^1/_2$ M.) *Dunton Green*, the junction of a short branch to *Westerham* (King's Arms; Crown), ascending the valley of the *Darent*. Westerham was the birthplace of General Wolfe (1727-59), to whom there is a memorial in the church.

22 M. **Sevenoaks** (**Crown; Royal Oak*), a prettily situated town with 6300 inhab., may also be reached from London by the London, Chatham, and Dover Railway viâ *Swanley* (comp. p. 18).

To the S. E. lies ***Knole**, the seat of Lord Sackville (minister at Washington, 1881-88), one of the noblest baronial mansions in England, almost unchanged both inside and outside since the times of James I. and Charles I. Visitors are admitted on Frid. by order obtained from Messrs. Glasier & Son, 6 Spring Gardens, London, S.W. (1 pers. 2*s.*, 4 pers. 6*s.*, 7 pers. 10*s.*). The rooms shown to visitors include the *Great Hall*, the *Brown Gallery* with portraits by Holbein and others), the *Spangled Bedroom & Dressing-Room* (portraits by Lely), the *Leicester Gallery* (portraits by Van Dyck, Mytens, etc.), the *Ball Room*, the *Crimson Drawing Room* (portraits by Reynolds), and the *Cartoon Gallery* (with copies, by Mytens, of six of Raphael's cartoons). The magnificent park, with fine beeches, is open to visitors. — Sevenoaks is also a good centre for many other pleasant walks, one of the most interesting being that to the N.W. to the famous *Knockholt Beeches* (*View) and ($3^1/_2$ M.) **Chevening**, the beautiful seat of Earl Stanhope (son of the historian), with a fine park open to the public. — About 3½ M. to the E. is **Ightham Mote*, one of the best specimens of a moated manor-house in England, with a fine domestic chapel of the time of Henry VIII.

Beyond Sevenoaks the train penetrates a range of low hills by a tunnel, 2½ M. long. — 27 M. *Hildenborough.*

29½ M. **Tunbridge** *(Rose & Crown; Rail. Rfmt. Rooms)*, a market-town with 9340 inhab., an old *Castle* (adm. by permission of the owner), and a grammar-school dating from 1553, now in a large modern building, is the junction of the S.E. line from London viâ Redhill and of the main line to *Tunbridge Wells* and *Hastings* (R. 4).

The railway from London to (22 M.) *Redhill Junction* is described in R. 6. The stations between Redhill and (43 M.) *Tunbridge* are *Nutfield*, *Godstone*, (33 M.) *Edenbridge* (Crown), also a station on the L. B. S. C. R. (p. 37), and (38 M.) *Penshurst* (Leicester Arms, in the village, 2 M. from the station). The walk from Edenbridge to Penshurst, viâ Hever (5½ M.) and through the quaint and pretty village of *Chiddingstone*, is very picturesque. *Hever* (rail. stat., p. 37) is an old embattled mansion-house (14th cent.; shown on Wed.), where Henry VIII. often visited Anne Boleyn, and afterwards occupied by Anne of Cleves, who is said to have died here; it is now a farm-house. The church of Hever contains several monuments of the Boleyn family. ***Penshurst Place**, the lovely seat of Lord de Lisle and Dudley, contains a fine picture-gallery, to which visitors are admitted on Mon., Wed., and Frid. (12-1 and 3-6). Its chief historical interest lies in having once belonged to the Sidneys, portraits of many of whom hang on the walls, including two of Sir Philip Sidney (who was born here). The trees in the park are very fine; one avenue is known as 'Sacharissa Walk', from Dorothy Sidney, the 'Sacharissa' of Waller. Good pedestrians may prolong their walk to (5 M.) Tunbridge or to (6 M.) Tunbridge Wells, viâ *Bidborough* (fine views).

The next station beyond Tunbridge is (34½ M.) *Paddock Wood*, whence a branch-line diverges on the left to (10 M.) Maidstone (p. 35), traversing the best hop-district in the kingdom. — From (42 M.) *Staplehurst* omnibuses ply to (6 M.) *Cranbrook* (George; Bull), a small town, formerly of importance for its broadcloth factories, with a Perp. church and an old grammar-school.

56 M. **Ashford** *(Saracen's Head; Royal Oak; Rail. Refreshmt. Rooms)*, with 10,000 inhab., is the site of the large workshops of the S. E. Railway. The parish-church has a good Perp. tower. Lines diverge here on the left to Canterbury (see below), and on the right to Hastings (p. 42). About 3½ M. to the N. of Ashford is *Eastwell*, occupied for some years by the Duke of Edinburgh, with a beautiful park.

From Ashford to Canterbury, 12 M., railway in ½ hr. (fares 3*s.* 6*d.*, 2*s.* 4*d.*, 1*s.* 2½*d.*). — This line descends the valley of the *Stour*, parts of which are very picturesque. — 2 M. *Wye;* 7 M. *Chilham* (Inn), with a ruined Norman castle; 9 M. *Chartham*, with an interesting E. E. and Dec. church, containing some fine brasses and old stained glass. The pretty tracery in the windows of the chancel is of the pattern known *par excellence* as 'Kentish'. — 12 M. *Canterbury*, see p. 25.

60 M. *Smeeth*, with the seat of Lord Brabourne (Knatchbull-Hugessen). At (64½ M.) *Westenhanger* is a farm-house incorporating the remains of an old royal manor-house, said to have been the bower of Fair Rosamond. — 65½ M. *Sandling Junction*, for (2 M.) *Hythe* and (3½ M.) *Sandgate.*

Hythe (*Seabrook Hotel; Swan*), a town with 4470 inhab., has lost ist significance as one of the Cinque Ports, but is now an important military station, with the chief *School of Musketry* of the British army. It possesses an interesting E.E. *Church*, with a raised chancel and a remarkable groined crypt, containing a huge collection of bones and skulls, the origin of which is doubtful. Either from Westenhanger or Hythe a visit may be paid to the ruins of *Saltwood Castle*, formerly belonging to the Archbishops of Canterbury. Near West Hythe is *Studfall Castle*, an ancient Roman camp. — *Sandgate* (Royal Kent; Royal Norfolk) is a small watering-place, with one of the coast-castles built by Henry VIII. It was the birthplace of J. B. Gough, the well-known temperance advocate.

Beyond Westenhanger *Saltwood Castle* (see above) comes into view to the right. At (69 M.) *Shorncliffe* is a permanent military camp, with accommodation for 5000 men; the huts are visible to the right. Line to Canterbury, see p. 25. — Beyond (70 M.) *Radnor Park* the train crosses a lofty viaduct and reaches ($71^1/_2$ M.) *Folkestone*, whence a short branch-line leads to *Folkestone Harbour*.

Folkestone (**Pavilion*, near the harbour, with a winter-garden; *West Cliff; King's Arms*; **Clarendon*, R. & A. 3*s.* 6*d.; Kentish Temperance; Queen's; Longford, Bates, Norfolk House*, private; *Central Café*, Sandgate Road), a cheerful and thriving seaport and watering-place, is an ancient town with 19,000 inhab., in a romantic and sheltered situation. Mail-packets start here daily for Boulogne. Folkestone was the birthplace of *Dr. Thomas Harvey* (1578-1658), discoverer of the circulation of the blood, to whom a monument was erected here in 1881. The *Parish Church* occupies the site of the old priory church of St. Eanswith, founded in 1095, but has been to a great extent rebuilt. The old *Castle* has almost entirely vanished. The favourite promenades are the *Lees*, a grassy expanse on the top of the cliff (fine views; band; hydraulic lift from the beach); the *New* or *Victoria Pier* (band); and the *Pleasure Gardens*, with the large glass pavilion of the exhibition of 1886. The walk along the beach to ($1^3/_4$ M.) *Sandgate* (see above) is very pleasant, and longer excursions may be made to Dover, Hythe, Saltwood Castle, etc. The *Sugar Loaf* and other chalk hills to the N. also afford pleasant objects for a walk. Facilities are also afforded for circular trips to Boulogne, Calais, etc.

The most interesting part of the line is between Folkestone and Dover, where it is carried through the chalk cliffs by numerous cuttings and tunnels. We penetrate the *Martello Tunnel*, 766 yds. long, pass through a long cutting, and enter the *Abbot's Cliff Tunnel*, upwards of 1 M. in length. The line then runs along a terrace, supported by a sea-wall, and passes under the *Shakespeare Cliff* (p. 16) by another tunnel, $^3/_4$ M. long.

77 M. **Dover.** — **Hotels.** Lord Warden Hotel, near the Pier and Railway Station, a large house with a view of the sea, high charges; *Dover Castle, King's Head, both in Clarence St., with a view of the harbour; Shakespeare Hotel, Beach St., well spoken of; Harp, near the harbour, R. & A. 3*s.* 6*d.*; Esplanade, facing the sea; Antwerp, Market Place, commercial; Royal, Clarence St.; *Royal Oak, near the rail. stat., commercial.

Porter from the station to the steamer or the town, each package under 14lbs. 2*d*., over 14lbs. 4*d*.; from the steamer to the station or town, including detention at the custom-house, under 56lbs. 6*d*., over 56lbs. 1*s*.

Steamers to *Calais* thrice daily and to *Ostend* twice daily (p. xix).

Cabs. To or from any part of the town, for 1st class cabs (drawn by horses) 1*s*. 6*d*., for 2nd class cabs (drawn by ponies, mules, or asses) 1*s*.; to or from the Castle or Heights 2*s*. 6*d*.; per hour 2*s*. 6*d*. or 1*s*. 8*d*., each addit. 1/2 hr. 1*s*. 3*d*. or 10*d*.; for each article of luggage 4*d*.

Post Office, Northampton St., on the N. side of the inner harbour.

Sea-Baths, at the E. end of the Marine Parade.

Dover, the Roman *Dubrae*, and the first of the Cinque Ports, is finely situated on a small bay, bounded by lofty chalk cliffs, which are crowned with barracks and fortifications. Near the centre of the bay the line of cliffs is broken by the narrow valley of the *Dour* (Welsh *Dwr* or *Dwfr*, 'water'), on the slopes of which great part of the town is built. Its sheltered situation and mild climate render Dover a favourite bathing-place and winter-resort. The population, including the garrison, is about 35,000.

In the Roman and Saxon periods Dover was a place of comparative insignificance, but after the Norman Conquest it became a harbour and fortress of considerable importance. In the reign of King John (1216) Dover Castle offered a long, obstinate, and successful resistance, under Hubert de Burgh, to the combined forces of the Dauphin Louis and the revolted barons. It was off Dover that the Armada received its first serious check in July, 1588. At the opening of the Civil War Dover Castle was garrisoned by the Royalists, but it fell into the hands of the Parliamentarians by stratagem in 1642. Charles II. landed here in 1660, and both before and since that period Dover has been frequently visited by monarchs and princes on their way to or from the Continent.

On the height to the E. of the town rises *Dover Castle (320 ft. above the sea), to which visitors are freely admitted, except to the underground works, for which a special pass is necessary. This fastness, originally founded by the Romans and afterwards strengthened and enlarged by the Saxons and Normans, is still kept in repair as a fortress. The remains of the Roman *Pharos* and the *Church of St. Mary de Castro*, an almost unique specimen of a Roman-British edifice (restored; roof modern), are interesting. Splendid view of the town and harbour, especially from the top of the *Keep*, built by Henry II. (92 ft. high; walls 23 ft. thick). The coast of France, 21 M. distant, is visible in clear weather. The old towers of the castle bear the names of the various Norman Governors. See 'The Church and Fortress of Dover Castle', by *Rev. John Puckle* (illus., 1*s*.).

Among the smaller objects of interest in the Castle are 'Queen Elizabeth's Pocket Pistol' (near the edge of the cliff), a brass cannon, 24 ft. long, cast at Utrecht in 1544, and presented by Charles V. to Henry VIII.; a Norman loophole in the ground-floor of the keep; a well in the top of the keep, 300 ft. deep; and an old clock, dating from 1348.

The principal feature of the new fortifications connected with the old castle is *Fort Burgoyne*, which stands on the hill to the N.W., beyond the Deal road, and commands the landward approaches. — On the cliffs to the E. of the castle is a large *Convict Prison*.

The Harbour of Dover consists of a large outer tidal basin and two spacious docks. From the W. side projects the *Admiralty Pier*, whence the continental mail-packets depart. This huge structure is

780 yds. long and forms one arm of a harbour of refuge, intended to be one of the most extensive in the kingdom. The pier is a favourite promenade. The fort at the end mounts two 81-ton guns.

The *Western Heights* are also strongly fortified and afford extensive views. They are conveniently reached from Snargate St. by the so-called 'Shaft', which is ascended by a spiral staircase with 480 steps. On the Heights are large *Barracks*, the foundations of a *Pharos,* and an old circular church, known as the *Knights Templar Church.* — Farther to the W., separated from the Western Heights by a deep valley, is *Shakespeare Cliff*, rising sheer to a height of 350 ft.; it takes its name from the well-known passage in 'King Lear' (IV. 6). — Still farther on are the works in connection with the projected Channel Tunnel. A vertical shaft has been sunk here, and the tunnel excavated for some distance under the sea in the direction of the Admiralty Pier.

The *Maison Dieu Hall*, erected by Hubert de Burgh (p. 15) in the first half of the 13th cent. as a pilgrims' hospital, has recently been restored, and is now incorporated with the new *Town Hall* in Biggin St., on the N. side of the town, near the Dour. The modern stained-glass windows illustrate scenes in the history of Dover. — The churches of **St. Mary* and *Old St. James* are both ancient and exhibit some features of interest. In Strond St., near the Pier, is *Trinity Church.* — Near the Priory Station (see p. 32) are some remains of the old Benedictine *Priory of St. Martin* (1132), now incorporated in the buildings of Dover College; they include the Refectory, a good example of plain Norman work, and a Gatehouse. The *Museum* (daily, 10-4, except Thurs. and Sun.), in Market Square, contains antiquities and objects of natural history.

Pleasant walks may be taken along the shore from Dover in both directions, either westward to (6 M.) *Folkestone*, viâ the Shakespeare Cliff (see above), or eastward by *St. Margaret's Bay* (Granville Arms), with a fine Norman church, and the *South Foreland* to (9 M.) *Deal* (comp. p. 25). The geologist will find much to interest him in the formation of the cliffs. The *North Fall Footpath*, a path leading through a tunnel from the E. end of the town to the top of the cliff, is closed when rifle-shooting is being practised in the North Fall Meadow. — Another walk may be taken to *St. Radegund's Abbey*, 3 M. to the N.W.; the ruins are those of a Præmonstratensian foundation dating from the end of the 12th century. — During summer numerous cheap excursions are arranged to Canterbury, Hastings, Ramsgate, etc.; also a circular tour to Calais, Boulogne, and Folkestone.

b. London, Chatham, and Dover Railway viâ Canterbury.

78 M. RAILWAY in 2-3½ hrs. (fares the same as by the South Eastern Railway, p. 12). The trains start from Victoria, Holborn Viaduct, Ludgate Hill, and St. Paul's.

Leaving *Victoria* (see *Baedeker's London*) the train crosses the Thames, with a view of *Battersea Park* to the right, and passes the stations of *Clapham* and *Brixton.* The train from *Holborn Viaduct, Ludgate Hill*, and *St. Paul's* crosses the Thames to Blackfriars, passing the *Elephant and Castle* and *Loughborough Junction*, and unites with the Victoria branch at ($3^1/_2$ M.) *Herne Hill.* Then follow *Dulwich* and *Sydenham Hill*, beyond which the train passes through a long tunnel below the grounds of the Crystal Palace (see *Baedeker's London*). 7 M. *Penge;* $8^3/_4$ M. *Beckenham.*

$10^3/_4$ M. **Bromley** (*White Hart; Bell*), a town of 15,155 inhab., pleasantly situated on the *Ravensbourne*, derives its name from the broom that still flourishes in the neighbourhood. It contains an old palace of the Bishops of Rochester, now a private residence, and a college, or alms-house, founded 200 years ago for the widows of clergymen. In the church is the tomb of Dr. Johnson's wife ('Tetty'), with a Latin inscription by her husband. A pleasant walk may be taken to (3 M.) Chislehurst (p. 12) and ($6^1/_2$ M.) Eltham (p. 33).

About $2^1/_2$ M. to the S. of Bromley and 1 M. from the railway (to the right) is *Hayes Place*, where Lord Chatham died (1778) and William Pitt (1759-1806) was born. It was here that Benjamin Franklin visited Lord Chatham in 1775 before the latter's famous speech on the American question. Visitors to Hayes should prolong their walk to (2 M.) *Keston Common*, where there are the remains of an extensive Roman settlement, known as *Caesar's Camp* and now believed to be the station of *Noviomagus.*

From Beckenham onwards the line traverses the fair and fertile county of *Kent* †, where the extensive *Hop Gardens* soon become one of the characteristic features of the scenery, presenting an especially picturesque appearance in August and September, when thousands of hop-pickers are employed in gathering the beautiful golden blossoms. Kent is also famed for its fruit, especially for its apples and cherries. A curious distinction between the 'Men of Kent', to the W. of the Medway (who claim the superiority), and the 'Kentish Men', to the E. of it, has been maintained down to the present day; and is generally referred to the belief that the former were the original inhabitants of the country, or to the determined resistance they offered to William the Conqueror on his march to London after the battle of Hastings. The S. E. part of the county, known as the *Weald of Kent*, is particularly fertile.

The hop-picking season is very short and requires the employment of far more labour than the local resources can supply. Large numbers of men, women, and children therefore come down from London and other towns to help, and 'hopping' affords a much prized annual outing to thousands of dwellers in the slums. These visitors are generally accommodated in tents, the gleaming white canvas of which contrasts pleasantly with the rich green of the hop-bines. The men cut the hop-bines close to the ground, pull up the long poles to which they are attached, and lay them across the 'binns' at a suitable angle for the women and children to pluck off the hops. The farmer or his representative ('tallyman') comes at intervals to measure the amount of hops in the binns, as payment is made by results. A good picker can earn 3-4*s.* per day. The stripped poles are piled in stacks for future use, and the despoiled bines are left to dry and then either burned or used as manure. The hops are taken to dry in the 'oast-houses' (A.S. *ast*, a kiln), the curious, extinguisher-like ventilators (or cowls) of which are so conspicuous among the gardens. A

† A knight of Cales, a gentleman of Wales, and a laird of the North Countree:
A yeoman of Kent, with his yearly rent, will buy them out all three.
— *Old Rhyme.*

small quantity of sulphur is used in the drying-process to help in purifying the hops. When cool the dried hops are packed in large sacks, technically known as 'pockets', holding $1^1/_2$-2 cwt. each. Hops are singularly sensitive to differences of soil and other conditions and vary greatly in value even in limited districts. The best gardens are round Maidstone, and the most delicate variety of hop is the 'golding' of E. Kent. Hops were introduced into England from Flanders about the beginning of the 15th cent. and now occupy about 60,000 acres of English soil, nearly two-thirds of which are in Kent.

12 M. *Bickley.* — $14^3/_4$ M. *St. Mary Cray*, with a large paper-mill and a Perp. church containing some good brasses. This is one of four contiguous parishes taking their surname from the small river *Cray*. At *St. Paul's Cray*, $^3/_4$ M. to the N., is an interesting E. E. church, with a shingle spire. — From ($17^1/_2$ M.) *Swanley Junction* a branch-line diverges on the right to (8 M.) Sevenoaks (p. 12) and Maidstone (p. 35). Within easy reach of ($20^1/_2$ M.) *Farningham Road* are the interesting old churches of *Horton Kirby* ($^3/_4$ M. to the S.E.; E. E.), *Farningham* (Lion Inn; $1^1/_2$ M. to the S.), *Sutton-at-Hone* ($1^1/_4$ M. to the N.), and *Darent* (2 M. to the N.; early-Norman, with Roman bricks).

Beyond Farningham Road a branch-line diverges to ($4^1/_2$ M.) *Southfleet*, ($6^1/_2$ M.) *Rosherville*, and (7 M.) *Gravesend* (see *Baedeker's London*).

23 M. *Fawkham*; $25^1/_2$ M. *Meopham*, with a large Decorated church (to the left); 27 M. *Sole Street*. The castle and cathedral of Rochester now soon come into view on the right, beyond the Medway. — 33 M. *Rochester and Strood*. The station lies in Strood, a suburb of Rochester, on the left bank of the *Medway* and close to the station of the S. E. Railway (p. 34). There is no railway-station at Rochester itself, which we reach by a handsome iron bridge, contructed in 1850-56 on the site of a much earlier bridge of stone. Readers of Dickens will recall the description of Mr. Pickwick's view. from Rochester bridge, as he leant over the balustrades, 'contemplating nature and waiting for breakfast'. Above is the railway-bridge.

Rochester (*Crown*, near the bridge; *Victoria & Bull*, commended in 'Pickwick'; *King's Head*, all three in the High St.) is a very ancient city, with a pop. of 21,590, inhabited successively by the Britons, under whom its name was *Doubris;* by the Romans, who called it *Durobrivae;* by the Saxons, whose name for it, *Hroff's-ceastre* (perhaps a corruption of Rufus?), is the rugged prototype of its modern form; and by the Normans. It was made a bishop's see early in the 7th century. Rochester was destroyed by the Saxon Ethelbert, was twice pillaged by the Danes, and was besieged by William Rufus, son of the Conqueror; and the castle changed hands more than once during the dissensions of King John and his barons. It was at Rochester that James II. embarked in disguise on his flight in 1688. On crossing the bridge we turn to the right into the *Esplanade*, from which we enter the castle-grounds, now laid out as a public garden. The present *CASTLE, standing conspicuously on an eminence, was built in 1126-39 by William Corbeil, Archbishop of Canterbury. The square Keep, 104 ft. in height,

For a coloured street plan of Rochester and Chatham see page 555 which now alone remains, along with the outer walls, is a fine specimen of Norman architecture, and commands an extensive view (adm. 3*d.*). The castle now belongs to the corporation of Rochester.

To the E. of the castle rises the CATHEDRAL, which, though not pre-eminent among the minsters of England for either size or architecture, is a building of considerable interest. St. Augustine founded a missionary church on this site about the year 600 and consecrated the first Bishop of Rochester in 604. At the time of the Conquest, however, this church was in a completely ruinous condition, and Gundulf, the second Norman bishop, architect of the White Tower at London, undertook the erection of a new church, which was completed and consecrated in 1130. Gundulf also replaced the secular clergy of the old foundation by a colony of Benedictines. This church was afterwards partly destroyed by fire, and the choir and transepts were rebuilt in the E. E. style by *Prior William de Hoo* (1201-27), who is, perhaps, identical with English William of Canterbury (p. 28). The Cathedral was restored in 1825 and again (by Sir G. G. Scott) in 1871-75. The internal length of the Cathedral is 306 ft., breadth of nave and choir 68 ft., across the W. transepts 120 ft. In plan it resembles Canterbury Cathedral, having double transepts, a raised choir, and a spacious crypt. The chief external features are the W. front (Norman), with its fine recessed doorway; the so-called Gundulf's tower, in the angle formed by the N.W. transept and the choir; and the mean central tower, erected by Cottingham in 1825. The figures of Henry I. and Queen Matilda (or Henry II. and Queen Margaret) at the sides of the W. doorway are two of the oldest English statues now extant.

Interior (daily services at 10 a.m. and 3 p.m. in winter and 5.30 p.m. in summer; crypt and choir shown by the verger, small fee). The NAVE is Norman in style, except the two easternmost bays, where the junction between the Norman and later work is effected in a way more curious than beautiful. The triforium arches are elaborately adorned with diaper patterns and have the peculiarity of opening to the aisles as well as to the nave. The W. window and the clerestory are Perpendicular. The W. TRANSEPTS are in the E. E. style, the N. being the earlier and richer. In the S. transept are the quaint monument of *Richard Watts* (see p. 20) and a brass tablet to the memory of *Charles Dickens* (d. 1870), who lived at Gad's Hill, near Rochester (p. 20). The chapel adjoining this transept on the W. was built as a Lady Chapel in the Perp. period.

From the transepts we ascend by a flight of steps to the CHOIR, which is a few feet longer than the nave. It is in the E. E. style and has been skilfully restored by Sir G. G. Scott. The stalls and throne are new, but some of the old misereres have been preserved. The tiled pavement was constructed after old patterns still visible in different parts of the church. Above the pulpit is the fragment of an old mural painting of the Wheel of Fortune. In the N. E. Transept is the tomb of *St. William of Perth* (13th cent.), a Scottish baker, murdered near Rochester when on a pilgrimage to Canterbury; this tomb afterwards became a frequented pilgrim-resort and a source of great wealth to the cathedral. Adjacent is the tomb of *Bishop Walter de Merton* (d. 1277), founder of Merton College, Oxford (p. 229). To the E. of this transept is *Bishop Warner's Chapel*, in the archway between which and the presbytery is the beautiful coloured effigy of *Bishop John de Sheppey* (14th cent.), discovered behind the masonry here in 1825. The windows in the S. E. Transept are memorials of *Gen.*

Gordon, *Capt. Gill* (Professor Palmer's companion in his ill-fated expedition to the Sinaitic Desert in 1882), and other officers of the Royal Engineers. A plain stone coffin in the Sacrarium, or E. end of the choir, is shown as that of *Bishop Gundulf* (p. 19). The great glory of the choir, however, is the beautiful Dec. **Doorway* in the S. E. angle, leading to the CHAPTER HOUSE (copy in the Crystal Palace; see *Baedeker's London*). The figures at the side represent the Synagogue and the Church; originally both were female figures, but the latter was mistakenly restored as a bishop in 1830!

The *CRYPT, reached by a flight of steps adjoining *St. Edmund's Chapel*, on the S. side of the choir, is one of the most extensive in England. The W. end belonged to Bishop Gundulf's church and is very plain in style.

A fragment of the old *Priory of St. Andrew*, coeval with the Cathedral, is preserved in the garden of the Deanery, to the E. Three of the old gateways of the cathedral-precincts still remain, the most important of which is the *Prior's Gate* to the S.

Turning to the S. (left) on leaving the Cathedral, passing through the Prior's Gate (see above), and again turning to the left, we have to the right the wall enclosing the old *Grammar School*, founded by Henry VIII. We next turn to the right and pass through a small gate into the *Vines Recreation Ground*, formerly a vineyard attached to the priory. On the N. (left) side of this are some remains of the old city wall, and at its S.E. end is *Restoration House*, a picturesque red brick mansion, with many windows, owing its name to the fact that Charles II. passed a night here on his return to England in May, 1660.

From this point Crow Lane leads to the left to Eastgate, reaching it a little to the left of *Eastgate House*, an interesting Elizabethan structure, now occupied as a Working-Men's Institute It has been identified with the 'Nun's House' in 'Edwin Drood', which Dickens describes as standing in the midst of the ancient and drowsy city of 'Cloisterham'. Proceeding to the W. along the High Street we soon pass (on the right) the *Watts' Charity House*, founded in 1579 by Richard Watts for 'six poor travellers, not being rogues or proctors', and widely known from the description of it in Dickens's 'Tale of the Seven Poor Travellers'. — On the other side of High St., nearer the bridge, is the old *Bull Inn* (re-christened the *Victoria & Bull*), extolled by Mr. Alfred Jingle ('good house - nice beds'). — *Satis House*, the residence of Richard Watts, situated to the S. of the castle, is said to owe its name to the gracious praise of its accommodation by Queen Elizabeth, who stayed here on her visit to Rochester; the house has, however, since been rebuilt.

In summer pleasant steamboat-excursions on the Medway (pier just above the bridge) may be made from Rochester to (11 M.) *Sheerness* (p. 22) and (18 M.) *Southend* (p. 450), at the mouth of the Thames, affording good views of Upnor Castle, Chatham Dockyards, etc. Small boats may be hired at the Esplanade; charge to (3 M.) Upnor Castle (p. 22), about 3*s*.

About $2^1/_2$ M. to the N. W. of Strood, on the road to Gravesend, is *Gad's Hill* (Falstaff Inn), the scene of Falstaff's encounter with the 'men in buckram' (Henry IV., Part I., ii,4) and also mentioned by Chaucer. It commands an extensive view. *Gad's Hill Place*, the residence of Charles

Dickens, is an old-fashioned red-brick house near the inn. In the 'Wilderness', reached by a tunnel below the road, are some magnificent cedars. About 4 M. to the N. are the ruins of *Coolin, Castle*, the home of Sir John Oldcastle, the supposed prototype of Falstaff; *Cooling Marshes* are the scene of the opening incidents in Dickens's 'Great Expectations'.

A very favourite excursion from Rochester is that to *Cobham Hall*, which lies about 5 M. to the W. of the town and $1^1/_2$ M. to the N. of *Sole Street* station (p. 18). Walkers ascend Strood Hill and turn to the left at the top, into Woodstock Road; at the end of Woodstock Road the field-path to Cobham diverges to the right. ***Cobham Hall**, the fine seat of the Earl of Darnley, lies in the midst of a magnificent park, 7 M. in circumference. (Tickets of admission to the house, which is open to visitors on Fridays from 11 to 4 only, may be obtained at Caddel's Library, King Street, Gravesend, and High Street, Rochester, price 1*s.*; the proceeds are devoted to charitable purposes.) The central portion of this fine mansion was built by *Inigo Jones* (d. 1653); the wings date from the 16th century. The interior was restored during the present century. The fine collection of pictures includes a *Portrait of Ariosto and *Europa and the Bull by *Titian*, *Tomyris with the head of Cyrus by *Rubens*, and examples of *Van Dyck*, *Lely*, *Kneller*, etc. — The church of the village of *Cobham*, at the entrance to the park, is celebrated for its splendid array of brasses (14-16th cent.). The village inn is the 'Leather Bottel', in which Mr. Tracy Tupman sought solitude and solace after the unhappy issue of his *affaire de coeur*.

A good view is obtained from **Windmill Hill*, the path to the top of which is reached by crossing the bridge, turning to the right, passing the S. E. Railway Station on the left, and crossing the canal locks.

Walkers may reach *Maidstone* (p. 35), 8 M. to the S., by a road leading through luxuriant hop-gardens (railway, see R. 3). About $4^1/_2$ M. from Rochester we pass *Kits Coty House* (p. 34); those who do not dread a slight detour should descend thence to ($1^1/_2$ M.) *Aylesford* (p. 34) and follow the Medway to (3 M.) Maidstone.

34 M. **Chatham** (*Sun*, close to the pier; *Mitre; Rail. Refreshment Rooms*) is continuous with Rochester, though its bustling and noisy streets form a striking contrast to the old-fashioned quiet of the latter. It contains 46,800 inhab., and is one of the principal naval arsenals and military stations in Great Britain. Much of the town is irregularly and badly built. It is defended by strongly-fortified lines, as well as by forts on the Medway. These lines are often the scene of military manœuvres, reviews, and sham-fights, which attract numerous visitors from London. In 1667 the Dutch fleet under De Ruyter ascended the Medway as far as Chatham, doing, however, no harm to the town. A *Statue of Lieut. Waghorn* (1800-50), one of the chief advocates and promoters of the overland route to India, a native of Chatham, was erected here in 1888.

The **Royal Dockyard* (adm. 10-1.30; special permission necessary for the ropery, machine-shops, and foundries; foreigners only through their ambassadors), founded by Queen Elizabeth, extend along the Medway for more than 2 M., and embrace an area of about 500 acres. The wet-docks, graving-docks, building-slips, wharves, etc., are all on a most extensive scale, one immense basin having a width of 800 ft. and a quay frontage of 6000 ft. The largest vessels in the navy can be built and fully equipped here. The metal mill, for making copper sheets, bolts, etc., is particularly interesting. About 3000 workmen, besides convicts, are regularly employed in the dockyard. The *Prison* contains 2000 convicts. The *Melville Hospital* has accommodation for a large number of patients. The barracks for the Royal Marines here are very spacious.

The military features of Chatham are nearly as conspicuous as the naval. It is the depôt for a large number of infantry regiments, and about 6000 soldiers are usually in quarters here. The artillery barracks are very extensive, accommodating 1000 men, while there are also large barracks at the suburb of Brompton. It is also the headquarters of the Royal Engineers, attached to whose barracks is a small museum. In front of the Royal Engineers' Institute is a bronze *Statue of Gen. Gordon* (d. 1885), seated on a camel, by E. Onslow Ford, erected in 1890. Troops bound for India usually embark at Chatham.

The best view of Chatham is obtained from *Fort Pitt*, above the railway-station, which contains a large military hospital and an interesting museum. On the opposite side of the Medway, farther down, stands **Upnor Castle**, built in the reign of Elizabeth, and afterwards used as a powder-magazine.

Two tunnels. $35^1/_2$ M. *New Brompton.* To the left are seen the Brompton Lines. On the same side is *Gillingham*, with an old hall of a palace which once belonged to the Archbishops of Canterbury, now used as a barn, and a handsome Perp. church, with a very fine E. window. Gillingham Fort dates from the time of Charles I. This district is famous for its cherry-orchards. — 39 M. *Rainham;* $1^1/_2$ M. to the N.E. is *Upchurch*, known for its deposits of Roman pottery. The line now runs parallel with the high-road, the Roman *Watling Street.* — $41^1/_2$ M. *Newington*, with a church containing mediæval brasses. — $44^1/_2$ M. *Sittingbourne* (Bull; Lion; Rail. Refreshment Rooms), a brick-making town, formerly visited by pilgrims on their way to Canterbury and by kings on their way to the Continent.

Sittingbourne is the junction of a branch-line to ($4^1/_2$ M.) *Queenborough*, the starting-point of the steamers to Flushing, and (7 M.) *Sheerness* (Fountain, well spoken of; Wellington), an uninteresting town (14,000 inhab.) at the mouth of the Medway, with strong fortifications and a dockyard established in the reign of Charles II. Queenborough was so named in honour of Queen Philippa, wife of Edward III., but a castle built here by that monarch has vanished. A walk may be taken along the cliffs from Sheerness to (3 M.) *Minster*, with a church containing the tomb of Sir Robert Shurland, a lord of the manor, whose story has been commemorated in the 'Ingoldsby Legends' ('Grey Dolphin').

52 M. **Faversham**, pronounced *Fevversham (Ship; Rail. Refmt. Rooms)*, a small and ancient town with 7200 inhab., once the seat of a famous abbey, where King Stephen, his wife Matilda, and his son Eustace were buried. The parish-church is a fine E. E. building, with curious old paintings and carvings. Faversham is the junction of the branch-line to Margate and Ramsgate (see below).

From Faversham to Margate, 22 M., railway in $^3/_4$ hr. (fares 5*s*., 3*s*., 1*s*. 10*d*.); to Ramsgate, 27 M., in 1 hr. (fares 6*s*., 4*s*., 2*s*. 3*d*.). Fares from London to *Margate* or *Ramsgate* 15*s*., 10*s*. 6*d*.,

6*s.* 2*d.*; returns 22*s.* 6*d.*, 16*s.*, 10*s.*; special cheap fares in summer. — This line runs to the E. along the coast. The firs. station is (6½ M.) *Whitstable*, celebrated for its 'natives', considered the finest oysters in England. — 10½ M. *Herne Bay* (Dolphin; Pier), a small watering-place with a pier and a fine esplanade.

An excursion may be made to the E. along the cliffs to (3 M.) **Reculver** (*King Ethelbert Inn*), the Roman *Regulbium*, one of the fortresses erected to defend the channel then separating the district known as the *Isle of Thanet* from the mainland. Some remains of the castrum still exist. King Ethelbert afterwards had a palace here, and still later a Christian church rose on its site. The church was taken down in 1804, but its two towers, known as 'The Sisters' and originally erected, according to tradition, by an Abbess of Faversham, to commemorate the escape of herself and her sister from drowning, were restored by the Trinity Board as a landmark for seamen. The sea is here steadily encroaching on the land. — Coaches ply from Herne Bay to (7½ M.) *Canterbury* (p. 25).

At (18½ M.) *Birchington* is the grave of *Dante Gabriel Rossetti* (d. 1882), to whom a memorial window has been placed in the church. Birchington and (20 M.) *Westgate-on-Sea* (Beach House Hotel; St. Mildred's) are also frequented for sea-bathing, affording greater quiet than Margate.

22 M. **Margate** (*York; Cliftonville; Nayland Rock; White Hart; Elephant*, D. 3-4*s.*; numerous private hotels, boarding-houses, and lodgings; *Railway Refreshment Rooms*), one of the most popular, though not one of the most fashionable watering-places in England, is situated on the N. coast of the Isle of Thanet. Pop. 16,000. Its sandy beach is admirably adapted for bathers, and the *Jetty* (1240 ft. long), the *Pier* (900 ft.), and the *Marine Parade* afford excellent promenades. Its other attractions include a *Hall-by-the-Sea* (concerts), a *Grotto* (adm. 6*d.*), etc. On Saturdays and Sundays, in the season, both Margate and Ramsgate (see p. 24) are uncomfortably crowded with excursionists from London, brought in thousands by railway and steamer. The *Church of St. John* is a Norman edifice restored. On the cliffs a little to the W. is the *Royal Sea-Bathing Infirmary.*

In summer steamers ply daily from Margate to *Ramsgate* and *London*, and coaches to (4½ M.) *Ramsgate* and (16 M.) *Canterbury* (p. 25), while numerous special trains (S. E. R.) run to Canterbury in time for the daily services. The walk to Ramsgate along the cliffs (about 6 M.) is a very pleasant one. On the way we pass (3 M.) *Kingsgate* (Inn), so named because Charles II. and the Duke of York landed here in 1683, with a modern castle. About ½ M. farther to the S. is the *North Foreland*, the *Promontorium Acantium* of the Romans, off which the English fleet was defeated by the Dutch in 1666. Visitors are admitted to the *Lighthouse* (small gratuity). Broadstairs (see below) is 1¼ M. farther on. — Other walks may be taken to the old mansion of *Dandelion* and the village of *Garlinge*, 2 M. to the W.; to *Westgate* (see above); to *Quex*, *Acol*, *Minster* (5½ M.), *Salmstone Grange* (¾ M.), etc.

The railway now crosses the isthmus, at some distance from the sea, reaching the coast again at (25 M.) *Broadstairs* (Grand; Ballard's; Victoria; Albion), a quieter watering-place than Ramsgate orMargate, named from the breadth of its 'stair', or gap in the cliffs, affording access to the sea. The old flint arch in Harbour St., called *York Gate*, was erected to protect this passage. Broadstairs was a favourite resort of George Eliot and Charles Dickens; the residence of the latter is named *Bleak House.* About 1 M. inland is the pretty little village of *St. Peter's*, containing a church of the 12th cent., with a fine flint tower added in the 16th century. — Tunnel.

27 M. **Ramsgate** (**Granville*, East Cliff, with good Turkish and other baths, R. & A. 4*s.* 6*d.*-9*s.*, D. 5*s.* 6*d.*, B. 2*s.*-3*s.* 6*d.*; *Albion; Royal; Royal Oak; Bull; Railway Refreshment Rooms)*, a bathing-place and seaport with 22,600 inhab., which may be described as a somewhat less Cockneyfied edition of Margate. In the height of the season (July and Aug.), however, it is overrun by nearly as many excursionists, and George Eliot calls it 'a strip of London come out for an airing'. The N. sands, extending towards Broadstairs, are beautifully firm and smooth. The port is formed by two stone piers, with a joint length of 3000 ft., and is of great importance as a harbour of refuge. At the head of the W. pier is a lighthouse. The Roman Catholic church of **St. Augustine*, on the W. cliff, is, perhaps, the masterpiece of the elder Pugin, whose house, the *Grange*, also designed by him, is close by. The *Granville Hotel* was built by his son E. W. Pugin. Farther to the E. is *East Cliff House*, the residence of the late Sir Moses Montefiore (d. 1885), the Hebrew philanthropist, who erected the Synagogue, Mausoleum, and Alms Houses near *St. Lawrence* (see below).

About 1½ M. to the W. of Ramsgate is *Pegwell Bay* (Inns), famous for picnics and shrimps. It may be reached either on foot or by an excursion-brake. *Ebbsfleet*, near the centre of the bay and about 3 M. from Ramsgate, was the actual landing-place of St. Augustine and his monks, and traditionally that of Hengist and Horsa.

Steamers ply regularly in summer from Ramsgate to *London* and *Margate*, and coaches and excursion-brakes run to *Margate*, (17 M.) *Canterbury*, *Pegwell Bay*, *Richborough* (p. 25), etc. Special trains run to Canterbury in summer, in time for the daily services in the cathedral. — The dangerous quicksands called the **Goodwin Sands,** on which several ships are still lost every year in spite of the light-ships, lie about 7 M. from Ramsgate and may be visited by sailing-boat. At low water the sands become quite firm, and cricket-matches are sometimes played on them. According to tradition these sands were once a fertile island, with a mansion belonging to Earl Godwin, which totally disappeared during a tremendous gale. The saying that Tenterden Steeple caused the Goodwin Sands is generally cited as a striking example of popular haziness on the relations of cause and effect; but an ingenious theory suggests that the statement may mean that the disaster arose through the misappropriation of funds, intended to maintain a sea-wall, for the erection of the church. See '*Memorials of the Goodwin Sands*', by *A. B. Gattie* (1890).

From Ramsgate to Deal, 15 M., railway (S. E. R.) in ¾ hr. (fares 2*s.* 2*d.*, 1*s.* 8*d.*, 1*s.* 1*d.*). — The first station is (1 M.) *St. Lawrence* (see above) and the next (4 M.) *Minster* (not to be confounded with the place of the same name near Sheerness, p. 22; Rail. Rfmt. Rooms), where the Deal line diverges to the right from that to Canterbury (see p. 25). The handsome parish-church of Minster (St. Mary's), with a Norman nave and E. E. chancel and transepts, contains some interesting old stalls and miserere carvings. The nunnery of Minster, founded by King Egbert of Kent in the 8th cent. in expiation of the murder of his cousins, was at one time of considerable importance. The high ground above Minster affords a splendid *View.

Soon after leaving Minster the train crosses the *Stour* and passes *****Richborough** (to the right), the Roman fortress of *Rutupiae*, constructed to command the S. entrance of the channel, the N. end of which was guarded by Regulbium (p. 23), and the principal landing-place of the Roman troops from Gaul. Incredible as it now seems, there is no doubt that Richborough was formerly close to the sea, and that a broad channel, forming the regular water-route from Northern France to London, extended from Sandwich to Reculver. Ebbsfleet (p. 24) also is now at a considerable distance from the sea. The deep channel made by the *Stour* in the otherwise shallow Pegwell Bay is a relic of this ancient waterway. The remains at Richborough are among the most interesting survivals of the Roman period in Britain and should certainly be visited either from Ramsgate (5 M.) or Sandwich (2 M.). The best-preserved portion is the N. wall of the fortress, 460 ft. in length. Near the N.E. corner of the enclosure is '*St. Augustine's Cross*', a cruciform basement of rubble, resting on foundations of solid masonry and now believed to have supported a lighthouse. Many thousands of Roman coins have been found at Richborough, and also Saxon coins and other relics.

9 M. **Sandwich** *(Bell; King's Head; Fleur-de-Lis)*, one of the oldest of the Cinque Ports (p. 41), was formerly one of the most important harbours and naval stations on the S. coast, described in the 11th cent. as '*omnium Anglorum portuum famosissimus*', but it is now 2 M. from the sea in a direct line, and accessible only by small river-craft. The singular cognisance of the Cinque Ports, a half-lion and a half-boat, is still everywhere visible at Sandwich. It was surrounded by walls, the site of which is now occupied by a public promenade; one of the old gates, the *Fisher Gate*, and a Tudor tower, called the *Barbican*, still exist. A colony of Flemish artizans settled here in the time of Queen Elizabeth and have left their mark in the names of the present inhabitants. The most interesting buildings are *St. Clement's Church*, with its Norman tower; the *Hospital of St. Bartholomew*, of the 12th cent.; the *Grammar School*, 1564; and *St. Thomas's Hospital*, founded in 1392 but rebuilt in 1864. Queen Elizabeth visited the town in 1572, and the house she occupied is pointed out in Strand Street. To the S.E. of Sandwich are excellent golfing-links.

15 M. **Deal** *(Victoria; Royal; Black Horse; Walmer Castle; Beach House Temperance)*, another of the Cinque Ports, is also frequented for sea-bathing. *Deal Castle*, now the private residence of Lord Clanwilliam, was built by Henry VIII., like those of Sandown and Walmer, as a coast defence. Sandown Castle, however, where Col. Hutchinson, the Parliamentary leader (p. 430), died in 1664, has been demolished; it stood at the N. end of the town. The '*Downs*', between the Goodwin Sands (p. 24) and the mainland, form an excellent harbour of refuge in stormy weather; but the Deal boatmen have still no lack of opportunity of displaying the courage and skill in aiding distressed mariners for which they have so long been famous. On the S. Deal is adjoined by *Walmer*, with *Walmer Castle*, the official residence of the Lord Warden of the Cinque Ports. The Duke of Wellington died here in 1852, and the rooms occupied by him, as well as that in which William Pitt, another Lord Warden, held consultation with Nelson, are shown in the absence of the present Warden, Earl Granville. *Lower Walmer* is an important military depot, with large barracks and a naval hospital. The low shore near Deal is generally believed to have been the first landing-place of Julius Cæsar in Britain. — Deal is connected with (9 M.) *Dover* (p. 14) by a joint line of the S. E. R. and L. C. D. R.; but fair walkers will find it pleasant to go by the cliffs, passing *Kingsdown*, *St. Margaret's* (p. 16), and the *South Foreland Lighthouses*.

Continuation of Main Line. Beyond Faversham the train turns to the S. E., passes ($55^1/_2$ M.) *Selling*, and soon reaches —

62 M. **Canterbury** *(Fountain; Rose; Fleur-de-Lys; Railway Refreshment Rooms)*, the ecclesiastical metropolis of England,

containing 21,700 inhabitants, and pleasantly situated on the *Stour*, which runs through it in two main branches. It is an ancient city, with numerous quaint old houses, and has been the seat of an archbishop since the 6th century. St. Augustine was appointed Archbishop of all England, but Archbp. Theodore (668-693) was the first who obtained the practical recognition of his primacy from the English bishops, and it was not till after the murder of Thomas Becket (1170) that Canterbury became the undisputed centre of the religious life of England.

The site of Canterbury was occupied in pre-Roman times by the British village of *Durwhern* (*'dwr'*, water), which the Romans converted into one of the first military stations on the high-road to London, Latinizing the name as *Durovernum*. When the Saxons or Jutes invaded England they named it *Cantwarabyrig*, or burgh of the men of Kent, whence its present name is derived. Towards the end of the 6th cent. Queen Bertha established a small Christian church on St. Martin's Hill, and in A.D. 597 St. Augustine arrived here from Rome to convert heathen England. King Ethelbert received him with great friendliness, and embraced Christianity with 10,000 of his people, while Augustine became the first Archbishop of Canterbury. The subsequent history of Canterbury merges, through the archbishops, to a great extent in that of the country at large. The names of *Dunstan* (960-988), *Lanfranc* (1070-93), *Anselm* (1093-1114), *Thomas Becket* (1162-1170), *Stephen Langton* (1207-1229), *Cranmer* (1533-56), *Pole* (1556-9), *Laud* (1633-60), and many others are inseparably connected with English political and social history. Since the Revolution, however, the attention of the primates has been more strictly confined to ecclesiastical affairs. — The present archbishop is the *Most Rev. Edward Benson, D. D.*, created in 1883. The income of the see is 15,000*l*.

The Cathedral, which is naturally the great centre of attraction at Canterbury, lies near the middle of the town, about 1/2 M. from each of the railway-stations. Emerging from the *London, Chatham, & Dover Station*, on the S. side of the town, we see in front of us the pleasure-grounds of the *Dane John* (Donjon), bounded on one side by part of the old city-wall; the Dane John itself is a tumulus 80 ft. high, surmounted by an obelisk and commanding a good view. We turn to the left and then enter Castle St. to the right, where the Norman keep of the *Castle*, now used as gas-works, rises on the left. (At the back of the Castle, on the river Stour, stands *St. Mildred's Church*, containing some Roman work.) At the end of Castle St. we cross *Watling Street* (p. 22), which runs through Canterbury, and then follow St. Margaret's St., passing *St. Margaret's Church*, to High Street, which we reach opposite Mercery Lane, leading to the Cathedral.

The *South Eastern Station* is on the W. side of the town. We first follow Station St. to the right for about 100 yds., to the point where it joins the line of streets leading straight (to the left) to High Street. We may first, however, follow St. Dunstan St. to the right, which leads in 3 min. to *St. Dunstan's Church*, an edifice of the 14th cent., with a square and a semicircular tower. It contains the burial-vault of the Roper family, in which the head of Sir Thomas More (d. 1535) is said to lie, placed here by his daughter, Margaret Roper. On the other side of the street is the gateway of the Ropers' mansion. Returning to the end of Station St., we now follow the street called Westgate Without to the *West Gate*, a handsome embattled structure, built at the end of the 14th cent. on the site of a more ancient one, and the only city-gate now remaining. To the left, just outside the gate, is the quaint little *Falstaff Inn*, with its sign hung from an iron standard. Just inside the gate, to the right, is the venerable-looking *Church of the Holy Cross* (rebuilt at the same time as the gate), containing an ancient font, an old panelled ceiling (chancel), and some 'miserere' carvings. A little farther on we cross the Stour and enter the High Street, in which, immediately to the right, is *St. Bartholomew's Hospital*, originally erected by Thomas Becket for the accommodation of poor pilgrims (visitors admitted). On the opposite side of the street, farther on, is the *Guildhall*, which contains some ancient arms and portraits of local notabilities. In Guildhall St., here diverging to the left, is the *Museum* (open 10-11, free), with interesting collections of Roman and Anglo-Saxon antiquities, natural history, and geology. We have now again reached *Mercery Lane* (see p. 26), so called because it used to be devoted to the sale of small wares to the pilgrims (medallions of St. Thomas, phials of holy water, etc.). At the S. W. (left) corner stood the *Chequers Inn*, the regular hostelry of the pilgrims (comp. *Chaucer's* 'Canterbury Tales'); some remains of the old inn may be traced in the court-yard entered from High Street.

From the end of Mercery Lane we enter the cathedral-precincts by *Christchurch Gate*, a fine late-Perpendicular structure, erected by Prior Goldstone in 1517. From the gateway we obtain a good general view of the Cathedral, with its W. towers, its noble central tower, and its double set of transepts. The present ***Cathedral** *(Christchurch)*, which is the third church on the same site, represents architectural history extending over four centuries (1070-1495), but its general external appearance, at least when viewed from the W., is that of a magnificent building in the Perpendicular style. 'The history of Canterbury Cathedral has been so carefully preserved by contemporary records, and these have been so thoroughly investigated by Professor Willis, and compared with the existing structure, that we may almost put a date upon every stone of this magnificent fabric; it is therefore our best and safest guide in the study of the architecture of that period in England' *(Parker)*. It is said that a Christian church, afterwards used as a pagan temple, was built here in Roman-British times by King Lucius; and that this was presented by Ethelbert, along with his palace, to St. Augustine (p. 26), who converted the buildings into a cathedral and monastery. Augustine's cathedral afterwards fell into decay and became more than once the prey of the flames and of the pillaging Danes, who carried off and murdered Archbp. Alphege in 1011; and at the time of the Norman Conquest it had almost

For a plan of Canterbury Cathedral see page 541

entirely disappeared. *Lanfranc* (1070-89), the first Norman archbishop, accordingly undertook the erection of a completely new cathedral, a work which was continued by his successor *Anselm* and the *Priors Ernulph* and *Conrad*, and finished in 1130. The last-named completed the choir in such a magnificent style, that it was known as the 'Glorious Choir of Conrad'. The choir of this second or Norman cathedral (the church in which Becket was murdered) was burned down in 1174; and the present choir, in the Transition style from Norman to Early English, was erected in its place by the architect, *William of Sens*, who may almost be said to have introduced the Pointed style into England, and his successor *William the Englishman* (1174-1180). The old Norman nave and transepts remained intact for 200 years more, when they were replaced by the present Perpendicular structure (1378-1410), the main credit for which is generally given to *Prior Chillenden* (1390-1421). The great central tower, called the *Bell Harry Tower*, was added by *Prior Goldstone* in 1495. The N. W. tower is modern, the older one having been pulled down, with doubtful wisdom, to make one to match its S. W. neighbour. The principal dimensions of the cathedral are: total length 514 ft., length of choir 180 ft.; breadth of nave and aisles 71 ft.; height of the nave 80 ft., of choir 71 ft., of central tower 235 ft., of W. towers 152 ft.

The Cathedral is open to visitors from 9.30 a. m. to the close of the evening service, except during the daily services at 10 a. m. and 3 p. m. (4 p. m. in Nov., Dec., Jan., Feb.); a fee of 6*d*. is charged for admission to the choir and crypt. The principal entrance is by the *South Porch*, built by Prior Chillenden in 1400, above which is a panel with a curious old sculpture representing the altar of Becket's Martyrdom, and a sword lying in front of it. The figures of the murderers have long since been removed from the niches, which are now, like those on the W. front, filled with modern figures of kings, archbishops, and other dignitaries connected with the history of the cathedral. Comp. *Dean Stanley's* 'Historical Memorials of Canterbury' and *Willis's* 'Architectural History of Canterbury Cathedral'.

Interior. The Nave produces an effect of wonderful lightness in spite of its huge proportions. It is mainly the work of Prior Chillenden (see above). The stained glass is modern, except the great W. window, which is put together from fragments of old glass, pieced out where necessary by modern additions. The monuments are of little general interest. On the arches of the piers of the great central tower may be seen the rebus of its builder, Prior Goldstone.

The Nave Transepts are similar in style to the nave, though differing from it and from each other in details. Parts of Lanfranc's masonry seem to have been retained as the kernel of the walls and of the piers supporting the tower. The N.W. transept is of special interest as the scene of Thomas Becket's murder on Dec. 29th, 1170. The four barons approached by the door on the W. side of the transept, leading from the cloisters, through which the Archbishop with his clerks had previously entered the church, where Vespers were being sung. Becket refused to take refuge either in the vaults or roof of the cathedral and was cut down by the murderers, standing in front of the wall (still *in situ*) between the chapel of St. Benedict and the passage to the crypt. What is believed to be the exact spot where he fell is still pointed out and is marked by a small square incision in the pavement. The large window of this transept contains figures of Edward IV. (1461-83) and his queen, Elizabeth Woodville, who presented the window to the cathedral. Another window represents the life and death of Becket. To the E. of the transept, and separated from it by an open screen, is the *Lady Chapel* (1449-68), also called the *Deans' Chapel*, from the number of these dignitaries buried in it. It occupies the place of the Norman chapel of St. Benedict, mentioned above, and has a rich fan-vaulted roof. The corresponding chapel, opening from the S.W. transept, is dedicated to *St. Michael* and known as the *Warriors' Chapel*. It contains the tomb of *Archbp. Stephen Langton* (1207-29), the champion of national liberty against King John. Here also is the monument of *Margaret Holland*, daughter of the Earl of Kent, with her two husbands, the Earl of Somerset and the Duke of Clarence (son of Henry IV.).

The *Choir, one of the longest in England (180 ft.), is elevated several feet above the nave, a peculiarity which occurs elsewhere among English cathedrals only at Rochester, the cathedral of which is evidently an imitation of Canterbury (comp. p. 9). The beautiful *Screen* between the nave and the choir is a work of the 15th cent., and is adorned with statues of six English kings. The grand Norman arches, supported by circular and octagonal piers alternately, here furnish a striking contrast to those of the nave. The triforium arcade with its combination of circular and pointed arches is an excellent example of the transition from Romanesque to Gothic, and recalls, in some respects, the cathedral of Sens, with which the architect must have been familiar. The visitor will note the singular curved outline of the choir, caused by the manner in which the walls trend inward at the E. end. This is due to the fact that William of Sens, wishing to preserve the towers of St. Anselm and St. Andrew, which had survived the fire that destroyed the earlier buildings, narrowed his choir here so as to pass between them. The screens separating the choir from its aisles were executed by Prior Estria in 1304-5; they are broken at intervals by the canopied tombs of archbishosp, the most conspicuous of which is that of *Archbp. Chichele* (1414-43), founder of All Souls College (p. 235). Nearly opposite is a memorial of *Archbp. Tait* (d. 1883). The reredos, altar, and archbishop's throne are modern. The organ is ingeniously concealed in the triforium, and nothing of it is visible below except the manuals. Part of the stained glass of the choir-aisles dates from the 13th century. At the W. end is a painting of Becket's Death, by *Cross*. This aisle incorporates some remains of the earlier Norman choir, and the triforium windows of the N.E. Transept are also by Prior Ernulph. At the E. end of the N. aisle is the entrance to St. Andrew's Tower (see above), the ground-floor of which is now used as a vestry. At the E. end of the S. aisle of the choir is the corresponding Tower of St. Anselm, also a survival from the older church, with a Decorated window inserted about 1335. The chapel contains the tombs of Archbps. *Anselm* (d. 1108; no monument), *Bradwardine* (d. 1319), and *Meopham* (d. 1333). Above it is a small room, with a grating looking into Trinity Chapel, used by the guardian of the treasures at Becket's shrine (see below). Among the monuents in the aisle are those of Archbishops *Simon of Sudbury* (1375-81; beheaded by Wat Tyler), *Stratford* (1333-69), *Kempe* (1452-54), *Fitz-Walter* (1193-1207), and *Reynolds* (1313-28).

From the E. end of the choir-aisles flights of steps ascend to the Trinity Chapel, which, with the 'Corona' behind it, is the work of *William the Englishman*, 'small in body, but in workmanship of many kinds acute and honest', who succeeded William of Sens, when that unfortunate architect crippled himself by a fall from the clerestory. This was the site of the *Shrine of Thomas Becket*, who was canonized soon after his death and became the most popular of English saints. It was, indeed, the fame of St. Thomas that made Canterbury Cathedral, which had previously been overshadowed by the adjoining Monastery of St. Augustine, the greatest centre of interest among the ecclesiastical establishments of England. His body was interred here in 1220, and the shrine was adorned with such magnificence that Erasmus, who visited it in 1512, tells us 'gold was the meanest thing to be seen'. The shrine was destroyed, its treasures confiscated, and the body of St. Thomas burned by Henry VIII. (1538); and the only remaining trace of the shrine is the pavement that surrounded it, worn away by the knees of thousands of pious pilgrims. [According to one version of the story, however, the relics were not burned but re-interred; and some remains found here in a stone coffin in 1888 are believed by many to be those of Thomas Becket.] The *Stained Glass Windows* of the chapel, of the 13th cent., depict the miracles of St. Thomas. On the N. side of this chapel is the handsome marble *Monument of Henry IV.* (1399-1413), the only king buried in the cathedral. His tomb is shared by his second wife, *Joan of Navarre*. Behind the tomb is the *Chantry of Henry IV.* On the opposite side of Trinity Chapel is the Monument of *Edward, the Black Prince* (d. 1376), with a brazen effigy; above hang the prince's gauntlets, helmet, and shield. *St. Dunstan's Shrine* used to be in the Black Prince's Chantry, where the head of the effigy has lately been discovered. Some remarkable diaper work and other remains of it are incorporated in the S. E. screen, near Archbp. Stratford's memorial.

The extreme E. part of the Cathedral is formed by the beautiful chapel called the *Corona, which formerly contained an altar with a fragment of Becket's skull. On the N. side stands the *Monument of Cardinal Pole* (d. 1559), the last Roman Catholic Archbishop and the last Archbishop interred in the Cathedral. The Corona also contains the so-called *Chair of St. Augustine* (13th cent.), in which the archbishops sit at their installation.

The entrance to the *Crypt, which is very spacious, is from the W. transept. This is the crypt of the early Norman church, and it has been supposed that some of its pillars may even have belonged to the original Roman church on this site. In 1561 Queen Elizabeth placed the crypt at the disposal of the French and Flemish refugees in England, who long carried on their silk manufacture here; and part of it is still occupied as a French church by their descendants. The E. part of the crypt formed the *Chapel of Our Lady Undercroft* and was formerly very richly decorated. The body of Thomas Becket lay here for 50 years after his death, and this was the scene of Henry II.'s penance. Traces of interesting old painting have lately been brought to light in a chapel on the N. side of the crypt. It is also worth noticing that some of the capitals in the crypt are only half-carved, their execution having probably been stopped by the fire of 1174.

We now quit the cathedral and enter the precincts, which contain some interesting remains of the monastery, originally founded by St. Augustine and re-established by Lanfranc.

The Cloisters, in the late-Perpendicular style, are entered from the N.W. transept and are in good preservation. The coats-of-arms at the intersections of the arches are those of benefactors of the cathedral. On the N. side are two fine doorways, and in the N.W. corner is a curious hatch communicating with the cellarer's lodgings. — To the E. of the cloisters is the Chapter House, or *Sermon House*, to which the congregation retired after prayers; the lower part is E.E, the upper part was built at the beginning of the 15th century. The panelled ceiling is of Irish oak. The Chapter House is adjoined on the N. by the Library, an old Norman structure (restored), containing a collection of Bibles, Prayer-Books, and MSS. Farther to the E. is the Norman Baptistery. — A passage called the '*Dark Entry*' (see the 'Ingoldsby Legends'), reached by steps descending from the N.E. transept, leads from the cathedral to the *Prior's Gateway* and the *Green Court*, which was formerly surrounded by monastic buildings. To the E. of it now lies the *Deanery*, and on the N. is the old *Strangers' Hall*. The gate in the N.E. corner of the Green Court was formerly the entrance to this hall. — To the N. of the E. end of the cathedral is a passage called the *Brick Walk*, on the right side of which is a row of arches in an early-Norman style, belonging to the *Monks' Infirmary*. At the end of the Brick Walk is an old house called the *Maister Honours*, formerly the state-room of the priory.

To the N.W. are the remains of the old *Archbishop's Palace*, including a fine arched gateway in Palace Street. — Visitors who wish to enjoy the view from the top of the *Bell Harry* or *Central Tower* (235 ft.) must obtain permission from the Dean or one of the Canons in residence.

At the N. W. corner of the Green Court (p. 30) is the *King's School*, founded by Archbp. Theodore (7th cent.), 'for the study of Greek', and refounded by Henry VIII.; it numbers Christ. Marlowe, Thurlow, Harvey (discoverer of the circulation of the blood), and Robert Boyle among former pupils, and still enjoys a considerable reputation among English schools. The approach to the upper hall is by a beautiful external *Staircase, with open arcades at the sides, the only Norman structure of the kind in the country.

Next to the Cathedral, perhaps the most interesting object in Canterbury is the quaint little **Church of St. Martin*, the 'Mother Church of England'. It lies on the hill to the E., 3/4 M. from the Cathedral, and is reached from Mercery Lane by Burgate St., Church St., and Longport St. The keys are kept at No. 26 in the last, but during the day the verger is generally at the church.

There is little doubt that there was a Christian church here in pre-Saxon days, which had been fitted up as a chapel for Queen Bertha, wife of Ethelbert (p. 26), prior to the arrival of St. Augustine. King Ethelbert is said to have been baptized here in the old font, the lower part of which is probably of Saxon date. An old stone coffin is shown as that of Queen Bertha. Part of the walls, which contain numerous Roman bricks, may belong to the original church; the chancel was rebuilt in the E. E. period. The stained glass is modern. — The churchyard commands a fine view of the city. On the tomb of *Dean Alford* (d. 1871), is the touching epitaph: 'Deversorium Viatoris Hierosolymam Proficiscentis' ('the inn of a traveller on his way to Jerusalem').

On the way to St. Martin's we pass, at the corner of Longport St., one of the gates of the old *Monastery of St. Augustine, now restored and occupied as a *Missionary College* (adm. free after 3 p.m.; all day in vacation). It is, however, better to diverge here to the left and enter by the main **Gate* (1300), a little farther down.

The monastery, a Benedictine house, was established by St. Augustine soon after the foundation of the Cathedral and Christchurch Monastery. At the Reformation it was seized by Henry VIII. for a palace, and afterwards passed through various private hands, being finally used as a brewery. In 1844 the ruins were bought by Mr. Beresford Hope, who caused a Missionary College for about 50 students to be erected, incorporating as much as possible of the old monastery. — On passing through the main gateway we find ourselves in a fine court, with the tasteful modern buildings of the College to the left. These include a large *Library*, with a valuable Oriental collection (below, an ancient crypt); a *Chapel;* picturesque *Cloisters*; and a *Hall*, being the Guest Hall of the old monastery, with its original oaken roof. To the right are the remains of the old *Church*. Within the grounds is the *Kent and Canterbury Hospital*.

Among the remaining points of interest in Canterbury may be enumerated *St. John's Hospital*, founded by Lanfranc, in Northgate St., to the N. of the Cathedral; *St. Alphege's Church*, near the W. end of the Cathedral, dedicated to the martyred archbishop (p. 27) and containing some old brasses; *St. Stephen's*, with some Norman work, near the S. E. Station; the ruins of *St. Sepulchre's Nunnery*, where Elizabeth Barton, the 'Holy Maid of Kent', was a nun (temp.

Henry VIII.), to the S. of the city; the modern Roman Catholic *Church of St. Thomas*, with an elaborately adorned interior; the large *Open-Air Swimming Bath*, on the Stour, to the S.W. of the town, and the extensive *Barracks*, to the N. E. Parts of the old *City Wall* are visible in Broad St., to the E. of the Cathedral.

About 1½ M. to the W. of Canterbury, on the London road, is the village of *Harbledown* (the 'Bob up-and-down' of Chaucer), with the *Hospital of St. Nicholas*, originally founded for lepers by Archbp. Lanfranc. No part of the present buildings is ancient, except portions of the church. Fine view of Canterbury. — *Barfreston Church* (see below) is 10 M. to the S.W. — Coaches to *Margate* and *Ramsgate*, see pp. 23, 24.

From Canterbury to Ramsgate, 15 M., S. E. Railway in ½-¾ hr. (fares 3*s.* 9*d.*, 2*s.* 6*d.*, 1*s.* 4*d.*). — 2½ M. *Sturry;* 6½ M. *Grove Ferry*, 5 M. to the S. of Reculver (p. 23). At (11 M.) *Minster* we join the Ramsgate and Deal railway (see p. 24).

From Canterbury to Shorncliffe, 18 M., railway (S. E. R.) in ¾ hr. The first station is (1 M.) *South Canterbury*, close to the county cricket-ground. The line runs through the *Elham Valley*. At (18 M.) *Shorncliffe* we join the line mentioned at p. 14 (for Folkestone and Dover).

A short line runs from Canterbury to (6 M.) *Whitstable* (p. 23).

Canterbury may also be reached from London by the S. E. Railway viâ *Ashford* (see p. 13), a somewhat longer route (70 M.; same fares).

Beyond Canterbury the train passes (65 M.) *Bekesbourne* and (68 M.) *Adisham*, with an E. E. church. From (72 M.) *Shepherd's Well* or *Siebertswold* the ecclesiologist should pay a visit to *Barfreston Church* (pronounced 'Barson'), a small but highly interesting Norman building, situated 1½ M. to the N. E. The walk may be continued to the S. to *Waldershare*, the Earl of Guildford's house and park, 2 M. to the E. of Shepherd's Well. — The train then penetrates a long tunnel and reaches (75 M.) *Kearsney*, the junction of the line to Deal (see p. 25). *Kearsney Abbey*, the residence of the Marquis of Ely, is modern. To the N.E., ½ M. from the station, is the village of *Ewell*, where King John had his first interview with Pandulf, the Pope's Legate, before resigning his crown at Dover (1213). — We now thread another tunnel, pass (77 M.) *Dover Priory*, and reach 78 M. *Dover Town.* Passengers for the Continent keep their seats and are carried on to the *Admiralty Pier*, where the steamers start.

Dover, see p. 14.

3. From London to Maidstone.

42½ M. South Eastern Railway from *Charing Cross*, *Cannon Street*, and *London Bridge* in 1½-2 hrs. (fares 8*s.*, 5*s.* 6*d.*, 3*s.* 3*d.*; return 12*s.* 6*d.*, 8*s.* 6*d.*, 5*s.*). — The London, Chatham, and Dover Line to Maidstone (41 M.; same times and fares) from *Victoria* and *Holborn* diverges from the Rochester line at (17½ M.) *Swanley* (see p. 18) and runs thence viâ *Otford* (for *Sevenoaks*, p. 12), *Wrotham* (31 M.), and *Malling* (p. 35).

As far as Dartford the South Eastern Railway has two lines, one running viâ *Woolwich* and the other viâ *Eltham.*

1. To Dartford viâ Woolwich. On quitting London Bridge station the train first traverses the busy manufacturing districts of *Bermondsey* and *Rotherhithe*. It then stops at (3 M.) *New Cross*,

St. John's, and (6 M.) *Lewisham Junction*. The train next passes through a tunnel, about 1 M. in length, and arrives at (7 M.) *Blackheath* (see *Baedeker's London*). Then (9 M.) *Charlton*, close to the station of which is the old manor-house of the same name. We next pass through two tunnels, and reach (10 M.) *Woolwich Dockyard*, followed immediately by *Woolwich Arsenal* (see *Baedeker's London*). — 11¼ M. *Plumstead*, with Plumstead Marshes on the left. — 13 M. *Abbey Wood*, a small village of recent origin, with pleasant surroundings, and some scanty remains of *Lesnes Abbey*, an Augustine foundation of the 12th century. To the left is *Crossness*, with the pumping-station of the Main London Sewerage. — Close to (14 M.) *Belvedere* lies *Belvedere House*, an asylum for aged seamen. — 15½ M. *Erith*, pleasantly situated on the *Thames*, at the base of a wooded hill, with a picturesque ivy-clad church. The train crosses the *Cray* and reaches (17 M.) *Dartford* (see below).

2. To Dartford viâ Eltham. Beyond (5½ M.) *St. John's* (see above) the train passes (7½) *Lee*, in the churchyard of which lies Halley, the astronomer (d. 1741).

9 M. **Eltham** *(Greyhound; Chequers)* is prettily situated among trees, with the villas of numerous London merchants. About ¼ M. to the N. of the station lie the remains of **Eltham Palace*, a favourite royal residence from Henry III. (1216-72) to Henry VIII. (1509-1547). Queen Elizabeth often lived here in her childhood. The palace is popularly known as 'King John's Barn', perhaps because the king has been confounded with John of Eltham, son of Edward II., who was born here.

Part of the moat surrounding the palace is still filled with water, and we cross it by a picturesque old bridge. Almost the only relic of the building is the fine **Banqueting Hall* (key kept in the adjacent lodge), somewhat resembling Crosby Hall in London in general style and dating like it from the reign of Edward IV. (1461-83). The hall was long used as a barn, and some of its windows are still bricked up. The *Roof is of chestnut. Adjoining the hall on the left is the *Court House*, a picturesque gabled building, formerly the buttery of the Palace.

There were originally three parks attached to Eltham Palace, one of which, the *Middle Park*, has attained some celebrity in modern days as the home of the Blenkiron stud of race-horses. The *Great Park* has been built over. — The *Church* of Eltham was rebuilt in 1874; in the churchyard are buried *Bishop Horne* (d. 1792), the commentator of the Psalms, and *Doggett*, the comedian, founder of 'Doggett's Coat and Badge', an annual prize for Thames watermen (see *Baedeker's London*). *Van Dyck* had summer-quarters at Eltham during his stay in England (1632-41), probably in the palace.

Pleasant walks may be taken from Eltham to (4 M.) *Woolwich*, across *Shooter's Hill;* to (4 M.) *Greenwich*, crossing *Blackheath* and *Greenwich Park*; and to (3 M.) *Chislehurst* (p. 12).

13½ M. *Bexley*. The train now crosses the *Cray* to (15¼ M.) *Crayford* and (17 M.) *Dartford*.

Dartford *(Bull; Victoria)* is a busy town of 11,000 inhab., with a large paper-mill, the drug-factory of Messrs. Burroughs & Welcome, a gunpowder-factory, and the City of London Lunatic Asylum. The first paper-mill in England was erected here in the reign of Elizabeth (1558-1603). The tomb of the founder is in the church, and from his crest (a fool's cap) foolscap paper derives its name. Dartford was the abode of Wat Tyler, who began his revolt here by killing the poll-tax collector (1381). — We now cross the *Darent* and skirt the bank of the *Thames*. 20 M. *Greenhithe*, with villas and chalk-quarries. In the river here are moored two or three training-ships. Near Greenhithe are *Stone Church*, supposed to have been built by the architect of Westminster Abbey, and *Ingress Abbey*, at one time occupied by the father of Sir Henry Havelock.

22 M. *Northfleet*, with chalk-pits, cement-factories, a fine old church containing some monuments of the 14th cent., a college for indigent ladies and gentlemen, and a working-man's club (a conspicuous red and white brick building).

24 M. **Gravesend** (*Clarendon; New* and *Old Falcon; Talbot; Rosherville*), a favourite river-resort of the Londoners, with the popular *Rosherville Gardens*, is described with more detail in *Baedeker's London*. A steam-ferry plies to *Tilbury* (p. 450).

A branch-line runs hence through the *Hoo District* to (16 M.) *Port Victoria*, in the *Isle of Grain* and at the mouth of the *Medway*, opposite Sheerness (p. 22). — One of the most popular excursions from Gravesend is that to *Cobham Hall* (p. 21), which lies about 4 M. to the S. (tickets obtained at Caddel's Library, King St., price 1*s*.).

28½ M. *Higham*, 1½ M. to the S. of which is *Gad's Hill* (p. 20). We then pass through a long tunnel (2 M.), with a break in the middle, and reach (31 M.) *Strood and Rochester* (see p. 18).

The train now runs along the left bank of the *Medway*, affording a fine view of the cathedral and castle as we leave Rochester. Beyond the river are the chalk hills forming the 'backbone of Kent'. Near (34 M.) *Cuxton* and (36 M.) *Snodland* the beauty of the valley is seriously marred by the numerous chalk-quarries and lime and cement works. The scenery, however, improves greatly at —

39 M. *Aylesford* (George Inn), charmingly situated on the river, with its church rising high above the red-roofed cottages.

Aylesford is the traditional site of a great battle between the British prince Vortigern and the Saxons under Hengist and Horsa, whose direct northward march seems to have been deflected to the E. at Rochester (comp. Green's 'Making of England', p. 35). The name, derived from the Saxon *Eglesford*, is supposed to be connected with the Celtic *Eglwys*, a church. Aylesford was the birthplace of *Sir Charles Sedley*, the poet (1639-1701), one of whose family founded an alms-house here in the time of James I., still existing in an altered form. On the right bank of the Medway, ¾ M. below the village, is the *Friars*, a seat of Lord Aylesford, taking its name from an old Carmelite monastery. On the other side of the river is *Preston Hall*, a modern Tudor mansion on the site of the ancient seat of the Colepeppers. The *Church*, partly of Norman workmanship, contains some interesting monuments of the Colepepper family.

Aylesford is the best starting-point for a visit to the interesting cromlech called ***Kits Coty House**, which lies on the chalk hills, 1½ M. to the N.E., close to the road from Rochester to Maidstone. The cromlech consists of three upright stones of 'Sarsen' sandstone, each about 8 ft. high, with a fourth, 12 ft. long, lying transversely across them. Each stone weighs from 8 to $10^1/_2$ tons. Tradition makes this monument the tomb of a British chief, and the name may mean simply the 'tomb in the wood' (Welsh *coed*, 'wood'). Recent investigation seems to indicate that this was the site of a British cemetery and that the whole district was consecrated to religious uses. In a field between Kits Coty House and Aylesford is another group of monoliths known as the 'Countless Stones', from the superstition, frequently met with elsewhere, that they cannot be counted twice with the same result; and there would seem to have been a complete avenue of similar stones extending from Kits Coty House to the village of *Addington*, 6 M. to the W.

Aylesford is about 3 M. from Maidstone, the walk to which along the river is very attractive, especially in the hop-picking season. At ($1^1/_2$ M.) *Allington* we cross the river by the lock-gates and reach the *Castle*, which once belonged to Sir Thomas Wyatt, the poet, who was born here in 1503. From the castle we ascend to the little *Church*, and proceed thence by a footpath through the hop-gardens to Maidstone.

Beyond Aylesford the train passes *Allington Castle* (see above; to the left) and ($41^1/_2$ M.) *Maidstone Barracks* station.

$42^1/_2$ M. **Maidstone.** — **Hotels.** Star, Mitre, in the High St.; Bell, Week St., an old-fashioned house, commended in 'Pepys's Diary'; *Railway Hotel*, adjoining the S.E. Station, R., A., & B. 5*s*. 3*d*. — *Rail. Refreshment Rooms.*

Railway Stations. The *S. E. R. Station* is at the W. end of the town, beyond the bridge; the *L. C. & D. Station* is at the N. end of Week St.

Maidstone (the 'town on the Medway'), the county-town of Kent, a prosperous-looking place with upwards of 30,000 inhab., is pleasantly situated on both banks of the Medway, which is here crossed by a substantial modern bridge. The chief object of interest is the formerly collegiate **Church of All Saints*, a fine Perp. structure, of which a striking view is obtained from the bridge. It was mainly built by *Archbp. Courtenay*, who died here in 1396, and contains good stalls and sedilia, the interesting tomb of Wootton, first Master of the College (1417), some old monuments of county families, and an arcaded screen between the nave and chancel. Adjoining the church is the *College of All Saints*, established by Archbp. Courtenay and dissolved by Henry VIII. The buildings, which include a fine arched gateway and two towers, are interesting specimens of 14th cent. architecture. To the N. of the church is the former *Palace* of the Archbishops of Canterbury, now a school of art and science; and opposite, to the E. of the church, is a range of out-buildings, with a singular external staircase, probably older than any part of the palace itself.

The *Maidstone Museum, in Faith St., installed in *Chillington House*, a well-preserved specimen of a town-mansion of the 16th cent., contains very interesting collections of pictures, antiquities, and objects of natural history.

Environs. Maidstone lies in the midst of a very attractive country, and numerous pleasant excursions may be made from it.

1. The walk to *Allington*, (3 M.) *Aylesford*, and ($1^1/_2$ M.) *Kits Coty House* has been described in the reverse direction above. From the cromlech the walk may be extended to ($4^1/_2$ M.) *Rochester* (see p. 21), whence we may return by train.

2. At **West** or **Town Malling**, a station on the L.C.D. Railway, 6 M. to the W. of Maidstone, are the remains of a Benedictine abbey founded

by Bishop Gundulf of Rochester (p. 19). To the S. is the so-called *St. Leonard's Tower*, the keep of a castle also erected by Gundulf (ca. 1070), the architecture of which is, according to Parker, of earlier character than that of any keep in Normandy. *Addington*, with some British remains (see p. 35), lies about $2^1/_2$ M. to the N.W. of Town Malling.

3. About 2 M. to the N. E. of Maidstone is *Boxley Abbey*, a Cistercian establishment of the 12th cent., now incorporated with a modern mansion. To reach it we follow the Rochester road to a point a little beyond ($1^1/_2$ M.) *Sandling*, where we diverge to the right by a footpath skirting a small affluent of the Medway. We may return to Maidstone across *Penenden Heath*, famous for its ancient folkmotes and modern political meetings.

4. The Ashford road, leading E. from Maidstone, passes (1 M.) *Mote Park* (to the right) and ($1^1/_2$ M.) *Bearsted*, with a Perp. church-tower, and soon reaches (2 M.) the park of ***Leeds Castle**, one of the finest country-seats in Kent, dating mainly from the 13th cent., though other parts of it are more ancient and more modern. It stands in the midst of a lake, and its defences were very strong. The castle was given by William the Conqueror to the family of Crevecœur, but it reverted to the crown about 1300, and has since passed through many hands, its present proprietors being the Wykeham-Martins.

From Maidstone, travellers may continue their journey by the S. E. R. branch to its junction with the main line at ($9^1/_2$ M.) *Paddock Wood*, running through a rich hop-district and passing ($1^1/_2$ M.) *East Farleigh*, ($4^1/_2$ M.) *Wateringbury*, and ($6^1/_2$ M.) *Yalding;* or they may take the L. C. D. line to (17 M.) *Ashford* (p. 21). The intermediate stations on the latter line, which traverses one of the prettiest parts of Kent, are: $2^1/_2$ M. *Bearsted* (see above); 5 M. *Hollingbourne*, the station for Leeds Castle (see above); 8 M. *Harrietsham;* 10 M. *Lenham*, with an interesting E. E. and Perp. church; 13 M. *Charing*, with a ruined palace of the Archbishops of Canterbury; $15^1/_2$ M. *Hothfield.*

4. From London to Hastings.

62 M. South Eastern Railway from *Charing Cross*, *London Bridge*, and *Cannon St.* in $1^3/_4$-3 hrs. (fares 14*s*., 10*s*., 5*s*. $0^1/_2$*d*.; return, available for 8 days, 21*s*., 15*s*. 6*d*., available from Sat. to Mon. 18*s*., 13*s*., 9*s*.).

There is also another and longer route (76 M. in $2^1/_2$-4 hrs.) by the *London, Brighton, & South Coast Railway* from *Victoria* and *London Bridge* viâ *Lewes* and *Polegate*.

From London to ($29^1/_2$ M.) *Tunbridge*, see R. 2a. The Ashford and Folkestone trains here turn to the E., while the Hastings train runs due south.

$34^1/_2$ M. **Tunbridge Wells.** — **Hotels.** Calverley, near the S.E. Railway Station, overlooking Calverley Park; Wellington, Mount Ephraim, on Mount Ephraim, with view of the Common; Royal Kentish, facing the Common, and about equidistant from both railway-stations, 'pens'. from 12*s*.; Swan, Castle, commercial. — In the vicinity: Camden, at *Pembury*, 3 M. to the N.; Hand & Sceptre, at *Southborough* (p. 38). — Bishop's Down Spa, a hydropathic establishment. — Numerous *Boarding Houses* and *Lodgings*.

Railway Stations. *S. E. R. Station*, near the top of High St.; *L. B. S. C. Station*, Eridge Road, near the Pantiles.

Cabs. Per mile, 1st class (1-5 pers.) 1*s*., 2nd class (1-4 pers.) 10*d*., 3rd class (1-2 pers.) 8*d*.; each addit. $^1/_2$ M. 6*d*., 5*d*., 4*d*.; per hour 3*s*., 2*s*., 1*s*. 6*d*. Between midnight and 6 a.m. fare and a half. Luggage free.

Baths in the New Parade and at the Bishop's Down Spa; *Open-Air Swimming Baths*, at the foot of Quarry Road.

Post Office in the Pantiles; numerous pillar letter-boxes.

Music. A band plays in the Pantiles every day at 11 a. m., and either there or in some other part of the town in the afternoon and evening.

Tunbridge Wells, one of the most popular inland watering-places in England, with 25,000 inhab., is finely situated in a hilly district on the borders of Kent and Sussex, and owes its present favour rather to its pretty surroundings and invigorating air than to its somewhat weak chalybeate springs, the want of any appreciable quantity of free carbonic acid in which puts them out of competition with Spa or Schwalbach. The springs were discovered by Lord North about 1606, and Tunbridge soon became a fashionable watering-place. Somewhat later it seems to have been a favourite resort of the Puritans, who have left traces of their partiality in such names as Mount Ephraim and Mount Zion; and it is still specially affected by adherents of the Evangelical school. The season is at its height in August and September.

The most prominent architectural feature of the town is the **Pantiles, or Parade,** deriving its name from the earlier style of pavement. Many of the houses in the Parade are very quaint and picturesque; and it is still, as in the days of Queen Anne and the Georges, the favourite promenade of the visitors. It also contains many of the best shops, including several for the sale of 'Tunbridge Ware', or small articles in wood-mosaic. The *Assembly Rooms* and the *Pump Room*, with the chief mineral spring, are at the lower end of the Pantiles (water 2*d.* per glass, 2*s.* per week).

Tunbridge Wells is adjoined on the E. by a breezy *Common*, with an area of about 170 acres; and *Calverley Park* is a pleasant open-air resort within the town.

The **Environs** of Tunbridge Wells are undulating and beautifully wooded, affording charming rambles in every direction. The soil dries quickly after rain. The favourite short walks are to the *Toad Rock*, on *Rusthall Common*, 1 M. to the W., and to the *High Rocks* (adm. 6*d.*), 1¼ M. to the S. W., both good examples of the fantastic shapes assumed by sandstone rocks in the process of unequal disintegration. A round of about 3½ M. will include both.

One of the most popular of the longer excursions is that to *Penshurst Place* (p. 13), 6 M. to the N. W., which may be reached by railway viâ Tunbridge (comp. p. 13). Walkers, however, will find the route viâ *Bidborough* very pleasant: and they may extend their excursion to *Hever* (p. 13) and *Edenbridge* (p. 13), returning from the last by train. — About 6 M. to the S. E. lies *Bayham Abbey*, the seat of the Marquis Camden, comprising a mansion in the Elizabethan style and the picturesque remains of a Præmonstratensian Abbey of the 13th cent. (shown on Tues. and Frid.). About 2 M. farther on is *Lamberhurst* (*Chequers Inn), described by Cobbett in his 'Rural Rides' as 'one of the most beautiful villages that man ever set his eyes upon'. In former times this district was the scene of a busy manufacture of iron, which continued as long as the forest furnished charcoal enough for smelting; almost the only trace of it is now preserved in names such as *Forge* and *Furnace Wood*. The return walk may be shortened by taking the train from *Frant* (see below). — A very pleasant round may be made as follows. We follow the road leading S. from the Wells to (2 M.) *Frant*, and walk thence to the W. across

**Eridge Park* (Earl of Abergavenny; castle not shown), and past the **Eridge Rocks* (open to visitors on Thurs.) at *Eridge Green*, to ($2^1/_2$ M.) *Eridge* station. Or we may turn to the N. W. at Eridge Green and cross *Broadwater Wood*, either to (2 M.) *Groombridge* (see below), another railway station, 3 M. nearer Tunbridge Wells, or to the (2 M.) *High Rocks* (p. 37). — Excursion to *Bodiam Castle*, either from Etchingham or Robertsbridge, see below.

The little town of *Southborough*, halfway between Tunbridge Wells and Tunbridge, also possesses a chalybeate spring and is frequented by those who wish quieter and somewhat cheaper quarters.

From Tunbridge Wells to Eastbourne, 30 M., railway in $1^1/_4$ hr. (fares 5*s*. 10*d*., 4*s*. 6*d*., 2*s*. 6*d*.). — 3 M. *Groombridge*, the junction of lines to Three Bridges (p. 47), Lewes (p. 43), and Edenbridge (p. 37), Croydon, and London. — 11 M. *Mayfield*, a village with some quaint timbered houses and an old **Palace* of the Archbishops of Canterbury, now a nunnery (adm. 3-4). This was a favourite residence of the archbishops from Dunstan (d. 988) to Cranmer (d. 1556) and dates mainly from about 1350, with later additions. The Great Hall, now the Chapel, is nearly 70 ft. long. — $22^1/_2$ M. *Hailsham*, 4 M. to the W. of Hurstmonceaux (p. 44); 25 M. *Polegate Junction* (p. 43). — 30 M. *Eastbourne*, see p. 44.

Beyond Tunbridge Wells the train enters Sussex. 37 M. *Frant;* the village (*Inn) lies on a hill 1 M. to the W., on the E. edge of *Eridge Park* (see above). — 39 M. *Wadhurst*, with curious iron tombstones in the church and churchyard; $44^1/_2$ M. *Ticehurst Road*, 3 M. to the S. W. of the village of *Ticehurst;* $47^1/_2$ M. *Etchingham*, with a fine Dec. church. — $49^1/_4$ *Robertsbridge* (George), with the scanty remains of a Cistercian abbey of the 12th cent., 1 M. to the E. of the station.

Robertsbridge is the nearest station to *Bodiam Castle*, which by road is about $4^1/_2$ M. off, but by the following route only $2^1/_2$ M. We follow the cart-track passing the abbey, pass through a gate at the end of it, and take the path along the right bank of the *Rother*. After about 1 M. we reach the high-road, which we follow to the N. for some distance, and then finish the walk by a path on the left (N.) bank of the stream. ***Bodiam Castle** (adm. 6*d*., on Frid. 1*s*., by tickets obtained at the National School, near the gate) is a splendid example of a 14th cent. fortress (ca. 1396), surrounded by a broad moat and possessing fine gateways, machicholated parapets, a portcullis, etc. It is nearly square in groundplan, with circular towers at the corners and rectangular ones between them. A good echo may be awakened on the N. side. Bodiam is a favourite excursion from Hastings (see p. 42).

$55^1/_2$ M. **Battle** *(Star; George)*, an old town with 3500 inhab., famous for the abbey founded here by William the Conqueror (p. 39). To reach the ($^1/_2$ M.) abbey we turn to the left on leaving the station and then to the right, soon skirting the wall enclosing the abbey precincts. To the right lies the *Parish Church* of Battle, a building in the transition style between Norman and E. E., with Dec. and Perp. additions (restored). It contains a few brasses and the fine tomb of *Sir Anthony Browne* (p. 39), with effigies of him and his wife. In the churchyard, close to the E. end of the church, is the grave of *Isaac Ingall*, a servant of one of the owners of the abbey, stated on his tombstone to have died in 1798 at the age of 120. — A little beyond the church we come in sight of the abbey gateway, in the open space in front of which still remains the old ring used in bull-baiting (50 yds. from the gate).

***Battle Abbey**, one of the most interesting and venerable historical monuments in England, was founded by William the Conqueror in fulfilment of a vow made by him during the battle fought here with Harold, the English king, in 1066. Though generally known as the 'Battle of Hastings', the battle is more accurately named after the heights of *Senlac*, on which William found the Saxons entrenched behind a stockade on his march from Pevensey (p. 52), and which lie a short distance to the S.E. of the town of Battle. The abbey, indeed, stands on the very spot where Harold fell. The abbey was entrusted to the care of the Benedictine Order, and the minster was consecrated in 1095. At the Reformation (1538) it was presented to *Sir Anthony Browne*, Henry VIII.'s Master of the Horse, who converted the monastic buildings into a private dwelling-house and added the banqueting hall. Since then it has passed through various hands, and it now belongs to the Duke of Cleveland.

The abbey is open on Tues, from 12 to 4, to visitors provided with tickets (free) obtained from Ticehurst, the bookseller, in the main street near the gateway. Visitors are conducted through the ruins in parties by a guide (who expects a small gratuity), and in the summer months the crowds of excursionists from Hastings are so great that the tourist may deem himself fortunate if he have fewer than 50 companions. The part fitted up as a dwelling-house is not shown.

We enter the precincts of the abbey by a fine late-Decorated **Gatehouse* (1338), described by Nathaniel Hawthorne ('English Note-Books'), as 'the perfect reality of a Gothic battlement and gateway, just as solid and massive as when it was first built, though hoary and venerable with the many intervening centuries'. The longer (E.) wing was formerly the almonry, while the W. wing is now fitted up as a porter's lodge. On entering the gateway we find ourselves in a large grassy court, on the E. (left) side of which stand the abbey-buildings, the portions visible to us (named from left to right) being the *Abbot's Lodge*, the *Porch*, the *Abbot's Hall*, and the *Library* (modern). We pass the front of the building and make our way to the *Terrace*, at the S. end, where we await our cicerone, and in the meantime enjoy a fine view of the battle-field, with the heights of *Telham*, whence the Normans first caught sight of their foe, on the other side of the valley. This terrace marks the site of the old *Guest House*, afterwards replaced by Sir Anthony Browne's *Banqueting Hall*, itself pulled down about 1750. Two turrets at the W. end and some traces of the windows and fireplaces are the only remains. From the terrace we are conducted past the W. front of the abbey and round the N. end of it to the old *Cloisters*, one fine arcade of which is still visible, forming the E. external wall of the present edifice. Farther to the E., on somewhat higher ground than the rest of the abbey, lie the picturesque E. E. ruins of the **Refectory* (wrongly described as the dormitory), with interesting vaulted chambers below, described as the *Day Room*, the *Monks' Parlour*, and the *Kitchen* (perhaps the *Calefactory* or *Scriptorium?*). The last part of the ruins shown on ordinary occasions is the *Abbey Church of St. Martin*, which extended from the N. side of the Abbot's Lodge on the W. to a point opposite the Parish Church (outside the wall) on the E., a distance of fully 300 ft. The remains of this large edifice are, however, of the most scanty nature, consisting merely of a few piers and stones at the E. end; and nearly the whole area is now a garden, containing some fine old yews and cedars. The guide points out the site of the High Altar, supposed to be the spot on which the body of Harold was found after the battle. — The *Abbot's Hall*, shown only in the absenec of the family, contains relics of the Battle of Hastings, some good tapestry, and portraits of the Duke and Duchess of Cleveland. — The so-called 'Roll of Battle Abbey', containing a list of the Norman nobles who came over with the Conqueror, is a forgery composed at a time when a Norman lineage had become fashionable.

On leaving the abbey-gateway the tourist will find vehicles ready to take him to ***Normanhurst**, the handsome modern residence of Lord Brassey, which lies 3 M. to the W. (fare there and back 2*s.* each; adm., on Tues., 1*s.*, by ticket obtained at the Battle booksellers' or at Dorman's Library, St. Leonards). The house is finely situated, commanding a most extensive *View. — Those who prefer it will also generally find an opportunity of driving to Hastings instead of taking the train.

Beyond Battle the train descends towards the sea and soon reaches the ($61^1/_2$ M.) *Warrior Square Station* of *St. Leonards* (see below).

62 M. **Hastings.** — **Railway Stations.** *Central* or *Hastings Station* of the S. E. R., at the top of Havelock Road, Hastings, also used by the L. B. S. C. trains; *Warrior Square Station*, the St. Leonards Station of the S. E. R.; *Bopeep* or *West Marina Station*, the L. B. S. C. R. Station for St. Leonards, situated at the extreme W. end of the town, nearly 1 M. from the Victoria Hotel. — The hotels send *Flys* to meet the principal trains; *Cab* to most of the hotels 1*s.* 6*d.* (first-class) or 1*s.* (second-class).

Hotels. *Queen's, Carlisle Parade, facing the sea, $^1/_4$ M. from the railway station and the pier; Marine, Albion (R. from 2*s.* 6*d.*), on the Marine Parade, farther to the E.; Albany, Robertson Terrace, near the Queen's; Palace, a new house, to the W. of the Pier, with lifts and electric light; Castle, Wellington Square, a little back from the sea; Royal Oak, Castle St., commercial: Grosvenor, White Rock, 'pens'. 8*s.* — At St. Leonards: Royal Victoria, Marina, a large establishment facing the sea, well spoken of; Grand, Verulam Place, opposite the Pier; Eversfield, Alexandra, Eversfield Place; Royal Saxon, Grand Parade, all these close to the sea; Warrior House, Edinburgh, Gifford's ('pens'. from 7*s.* 6*d.*), three private hotels in Warrior Square. — Hydropathic Establishment, Old London Road, Hastings. — *Furnished Apartments* and *Boarding Houses* in all parts of the town.

Restaurants. At the *Queen's Hotel*, see above; *Ballard*, 17 Castle St.; *Addison*, 32 Rock Place; *Buffet* at the Hastings Station.

Omnibuses ply at frequent intervals from the Albert Memorial to the Victoria Hotel, Bopeep, the Alexandra Park, the top of High St., Ore, and Silverhill (fares 1*d.*, 2*d.*, 3*d.*).

Cabs. First-class cabs for 1-5 pers. 3*s.* per hr., each addit. $^1/_4$ hr. 9*d.*; per mile 1*s.* 6*d.*, each addit. $^1/_2$ M. 9*d.*; second-class cabs for 1-4 pers. 2*s.* 6*d.*, $7^1/_2$*d.*, 1*s.*, 6*d.*; no extra charge for luggage. Carriage drawn by hand or by donkey or mule, 1*s.* per hr. for 1 pers., each addit. $^1/_4$ hr. 3*d.*

Pleasure Boats. *Rowing Boat*, per hr. 2*s.* 6*d.*, each addit. $^1/_2$ hr. 1*s.*; *Sailing Boat*, 5-10*s.* per hr. according to size. Excursion in *Sailing Yachts*, 1*s.* each person. — An *Excursion Steamer* also plies in summer to *Eastbourne*, *Brighton*, *Dover*, etc.

Baths. *Hastings Baths*, White Rock Place, with a very large swimming basin, baths 1*s.*-2*s.* 6*d.*; *Faulkner's Turkish Baths*, adjacent, bath 2*s.* 6*d.*, after 5 p. m. 1*s.* 9*d.*; *Royal Baths*, at St. Leonards, opposite the Victoria Hotel; *Pelham Baths*, Pelham Place, Hastings; *Public Corporation Baths*, Bourne St.

Bathing Places for ladies and gentlemen at several points along the beach, indicated by notice-boards. In rough weather the bathers are advised not to quit their hold of the rope attached to the bathing-machines.

Hastings and *St. Leonards* are now virtually one town with about 50,000 inhab., in great repute as a bathing resort and winter residence. St. Leonards, which forms the W. end of the double town, is purely a watering-place, consisting mainly of rows of well-built lodging-houses, while the easternmost part of Hastings retains the picturesque appearance of an old-fashioned fishing-town and seaport.

The sea-front of 3 M., along which runs a fine esplanade, is very striking, and in many respects more than holds its own with any other watering-place on the S. coast. The best view of it, with the hills behind and the ruins of the castle, is obtained from the end of the **Promenade Pier** (adm. 2*d.*), which runs out into the sea for more than 900 ft. The pier may be said to indicate approximately the border line between Hastings and St. Leonards, though nominally the latter is not reached before the *Archway*, farther to the W.

Other suburbs are growing up on the hills at the back of the town, the most important of which is *Ore*, a group of pleasant villas on St. Helen's Down (stat., see p. 42).

The name of Hastings is indissolubly connected with the battle by which the government of England passed from the Saxons to the Normans, though it was fought at a spot 7 M. distant (p. 39). Hastings was also one of the *Cinque Ports* (*i. e.* the 'five' great ports on the S. E. coast; originally, Hastings, Dover, Sandwich, Romney, and Hythe), but its harbour has now practically disappeared. Traces of an early settlement here have been discovered submerged in the sea, which seems to have made great encroachments on this part of the coast.

On the *West Cliff*, above Hastings, are the ruins of the old ***Castle** (adm. 3*d.*), of the history of which little is known, though it claims William the Conqueror as its founder or restorer. The ruins are, to use Hawthorne's phrase, 'somewhat scanty and scraggling', but the grounds in which they stand command a splendid view of the town and sea, extending on the W. to *Beachy Head*. A tunnel is being driven through the cliff from the sea-front, and a lift is to be constructed for easy access to the castle.

A little to the E. of the Castle the hill is partly undermined by *St. Clement's Caves* (adm. 6*d.*; illuminated on Mon. and Thurs. after 2 p.m.), originally excavated for obtaining sand, and afterwards a resort of smugglers. Near the entrance to the caves is *St. Clement's Church*, one of the oldest in Hastings (Perp.; restored), whence we may proceed to the left (N.) along High Street. At the upper end of this street is the Roman Catholic church of *St. Mary Star of the Sea*. Close by is the old *Church of All Saints*, a Perp. edifice with a fine W. window. We may return hence to the beach through All Saints' St. and visit the quaint fishing quarter of *Old Hastings*, with its boats drawn up on the beach and its lofty black sheds for holding the nets. The fish are sometimes sold on the beach here by 'Dutch Auction', and there is also a covered *Fish Market*.

The W. part of Hastings and St. Leonards contain little calling for special mention. In the centre of the town is the *Albert Memorial*, a Gothic clock-tower erected in honour of the late Prince Consort, and in Queen's Road are the *Municipal Buildings*. A little to the W., in Claremont, is a *Public Institution*, presented to the town by Lord Brassey. — At St. Leonards are two handsome modern churches: *Christchurch*, London Road, in the E.E. style, and *St. Paul's*, Church Road, in the Dec. style (elaborate interior, with marble pillars). A new pier is now in course of construction here.

Walks. The prettiest short walk from Hastings is that to *Ecclesbourne Glen*, *Fairlight Glen*, and the *Lovers' Seat* (3½ M.). The best route is the path crossing the *East Hill* (250 ft.; reached by steps from the Fish Market; fine view of Hastings) and then descending to (1 M.) the prettily-wooded *Ecclesbourne Glen*. Crossing this little valley, we ascend again on its E. side and follow the path along the top of the cliffs to (1½ M.) *Fairlight Glen*, another little wooded valley. Here we turn to the left and ascend along the W. side, rounding the head of the valley and passing the (½ M.) 'Dripping Well', now almost dry, beyond which we continue to follow the path leading along the side of the glen towards the S.E. This soon brings us out again to the open cliff and (½ M.) the **Lovers' Seat*, a rocky ledge commanding a splendid view. Good walkers may vary the return-route by turning landward from the Dripping Well, at the head of Fairlight Glen, and ascending past a farm to (¼ M.) the high-road. Here we may turn to the left (below, to the right, the Hall, Fairlight) and make our way to '*North's Seat*', on the top of Fairlight Down (600 ft.), occupying the circular site of *Old Fairlight Mill*, burned down some years ago. The *View from this point is very extensive, including the coast of France; the tower of *Fairlight Church* is conspicuous to the E. We now descend viâ *Ore* (p. 41) to Hastings. — Excursion-waggonettes ply at intervals to the farm above Fairlight Glen, allowing 1 hr. for a visit to the glen and the Lovers' Seat (return-fare 1*s*. 6*d*.).

Excursion Brakes ply daily in summer to (7 M.) *Battle* and (9 M.) *Normanhurst* (see pp. 39, 40; fare for the round 4*s*. 6*d*.), and this drive may be extended to *Ashburnham House* (not shown), the seat of the Earl of Ashburnham, containing some relics of Charles I. (shirt worn at his execution, etc.). For some distance the road runs along the top of a ridge, commanding fine views. — Another lovely drive may be taken to (12 M.) *Bodiam Castle* (p. 38), viâ the charming village of (6 M.) *Sedlescombe*, with its interesting church, and back by *Northiam* (near which is an old timbered house) and *Brede*. — *Crowhurst*, 6 M. to the N.W. and 3 M. from Battle, is another good point for a walk or a drive; it possesses the remains of an old manor-house and a gigantic churchyard-yew. — Other excursions may be made (usually by railway) to *Hurstmonceaux Castle* (p. 52), *Pevensey* (p. 52), *Winchelsea* (see below), *Rye* (see below), etc.

From Hastings to Rye and Ashford, 27 M., South Eastern Railway in 1 hr. (fares 6*s*. 7*d*., 4*s*. 5*d*., 2*s*. 2½*d*.). — The district traversed by this line has no great scenic beauty, but the towns of Winchelsea and Rye will repay a visit. — 1½ M. *Ore* (p. 41).

9 M. **Winchelsea** (*New Inn*), an ancient but decayed town, formerly attached to the Cinque Port of Hastings, possesses various memorials of its former importance, the most immediately striking of which are the width and regularity o fits streets. The **Church of St Thomas* (Becket), an important early-Decorated structure (ca. 1300), of which the nave has long since been destroyed, contains some good monuments. A little to the S.E. of the church is the *Friars*, a modern mansion built with the materials of an old Franciscan monastery, of which part of the chapel remains (adm. on Mon.). Winchelsea was formerly a walled town, and three of the old gates are still standing: *Pipe Well Gate*, *Strand Gate*, and *Land Gate*. — Near the sea, about halfway between Winchelsea and Rye, is *Camber Castle*, one of the coast-defences erected by Henry VIII.; it commands a good view of the picturesque, red-tiled town of Rye (see below). About 1½ M. to the W. is *Icklesham*, with a Norman church.

11 M. **Rye** (*George; Cinque Ports*) is another decayed seaport, ruined, like Winchelsea, by the retirement of the sea; it was also one of the secondary Cinque Ports. Its harbour is still frequented by a few vessels. The large *Church*, restored in 1883, is partly Norman and partly E. E., with windows inserted at a later date. The *Ypres Tower*, at the S.E. corner of the town, now the police-station, was erected as a watch-tower in the 12th cent. and is said to derive its name from William de Ypres, Earl of Kent. The only town-gate remaining is the *Land Gate*, on the London road. *Mermaid Street* is one of the most quaintly picturesque streets in England. After the Revocation of the Edict of Nantes many French refugees settled in

Rye, and have left their mark on the names of the present inhabitants. At a later date it was a great resort of smugglers. — An omnibus plies from Rye to (10 M.) *Tenterden* (White Lion), with a fine church, the Perp. tower of which has been held responsible for the Goodwin Sands (see p. 24).

Beyond Rye the train traverses *Romney Marsh*, an extensive level tract with rich pastures. From (18 M.) *Appledore* a branch-line diverges on the right to *Lydd*, *Dungeness*, and *New Romney* (Ship), formerly one of the Cinque Ports. There is a lighthouse on Dungeness Point. — 21 M. *Ham Street*.

27 M. *Ashford*, see p. 13.

5. From London to Eastbourne. Newhaven.

65 M. London, Brighton, and South Coast Railway, from *Victoria* or *London Bridge*, in $1^3/_4$-$3^1/_4$ hrs. (fares 13*s*., 9*s*. 6*d*., 5*s*.; return, available for 8 days, 19*s*., 14*s*.). — To *Newhaven*, 57 M., in $1^3/_4$-$2^1/_2$ hrs. (fares 11*s*. 3*d*., 7*s*. 10*d*., 4*s*. $8^1/_2$*d*.; Sat. to Mon. return-tickets 14*s*., 9*s*. 6*d*., 7*s*.). Cheap day-tickets are issued in the season at greatly reduced fares.

From London to ($37^1/_2$ M.) *Hayward's Heath*, see R. 6. Our line here diverges to the left. — 44 M. *Plumpton*: 47 M. *Cooksbridge*.

50 M. **Lewes** (*Star*, with a fine staircase of carved oak; *White Hart*, opposite the County Hall; *Rail. Refreshmt. Rooms*), the county-town of Sussex, with 11,200 inhab., is a quaint old place, situated in the heart of the *South Downs*. It is the junction of lines to *Brighton* on the W. (see p. 52), *Newhaven* and *Seaford* (see below) on the S., and *Barcombe*, *East Grinstead*, *Groombridge*, etc., on the N.

The old *Castle* dates from the Norman period, and has a good gateway and a well-preserved keep containing a small museum (adm. 6 *d*.); fine view from the top of the tower. The *Priory of St. Pancras*, a picturesque ruin to the S. of the town (adm. 4*d*.), was founded by Gundrada, daughter of William the Conqueror. Adjacent is *Southover Church*, with a Norman chapel, containing the tombs of Gundrada and her husband, William de Warrenne. The *Fitzroy Memorial Library* was designed by Sir G. G. Scott. About $2^1/_2$ M. to the W. is *Mt. Harry*, where Henry III. was defeated by Simon de Montfort in 1264.

From Lewes to Newhaven, 7 M., railway in 15-20 min. The trains go on to *Newhaven Wharf*, whence steam-packets ply twice daily to Dieppe in 4-5 hrs. (through-tickets from London to Paris issued by this route). **Newhaven** (*London & Paris Hotel; Bridge Inn*), at the mouth of the *Ouse*, possesses a modern fort and an interesting Norman church of the 12th cent., with an apse. — About 2 M. to the E. is *Seaford* (Seaford Bay Hotel), frequented as a sea-bathing place.

The line now skirts **Mount Caburn** and **Firle Beacon** (820 ft.), both of which command extensive views. 53 M. *Glynde*; $57^1/_2$ M. *Berwick*. To the right is the '*Long Man of Wilmington*', a figure, 240 ft. high, cut out on the side of the hill (comp. p. 44); it is supposed to be of Celtic origin, perhaps the 'God of Journeying' mentioned by Cæsar, and has recently been restored.

61 M. **Polegate Junction** (*Rail. Refreshmt. Rooms*), the point of divergence for lines to Hailsham and Tunbridge Wells (p. 36), Hastings (p. 40), and Eastbourne.

65 M. **Eastbourne.** — **Hotels.** *Queen's, Albion, *Anchor, Marine Parade; *Cavendish, *Burlington (R. & A. from 5*s*., D. 5*s*. 6*d*.), Grand Parade; Grand, Cliff ('pens'. in winter 10*s*. 6*d*.); these all first class, facing the sea. — Sussex, Devonshire Park; Gildredge, commercial, close to the station; Southdown, 'pens'. 9*s*. per day. — Numerous *Boarding Houses* and *Lodgings*. — *Railway Refreshment Rooms*.

Cabs, for 1-5 pers., 1*s.* per mile, 6*d.* each addit. 1/2 M.; per hr. 3*s.*, or each 1/4 hr. addit. 9*d.*; 2nd and 3rd class vehicles at lower rates. — **Omnibus** between the town and the station 2*d.*

Bathing. Use of *Bathing Machines* (not compulsory before 8 a.m.) 9*d.*, per doz. tickets 8*s.* — **Baths** at Devonshire Park, with swimming-basins, etc.

Eastbourne, a watering-place which of late has been rapidly growing in popularity, lies near the S. E. end of the *South Downs*, and consists of the new town on the sea and the old town 1 1/2 M. inland. Pop. 30,000. The sea-front, about 2 M. in length, is flanked with a substantial *Esplanade*, at the E. end of which is the *Great Redoubt*, a circular battery mounting 11 guns, while in the middle is a martello tower (see p. 52) known as the '*Wish*'. Near Splash Point, in the centre of the E. half of the Esplanade, an iron *Pier* juts out into the sea for a distance of 1000 ft., forming a favourite resort of visitors. Another rallying-point is *Devonshire Park*, at the W. end of the Esplanade, with its gardens (bands), large pavilion, and lawn-tennis courts. The *Church of All Souls* is a handsome modern Byzantine structure; and *Old Eastbourne Church* is an interesting E.E. edifice, with a Norman chancel-arch. Opposite is the *Lamb Inn*, below which is a vaulted crypt, also of the E. E. period. A handsome new *Town Hall*, with a tower 130 ft. high, was opened in Oct., 1886. Golf-links have been laid out on the Downs behind the town.

About 3 M. to the S. W. of Eastbourne the South Downs terminate in ***Beachy Head** ('Beauchef'), a bold chalk headland, rising to a height of 575 ft. above the sea (fine view). It may be reached either by road or by a footpath along the cliffs. The *Beachy Head* or *Belle Toute Lighthouse* is 2 M. farther to the W.

Excursions. The immediate environs of Eastbourne afford few interesting walks, and the favourite excursions are those made by carriage or by rail, such as *Hurstmonceaux* (p. 52; from Hailsham or Pevensey) and *Pevensey Castle* (p. 52). An excursion-brake also runs to (16 M.) *Battle* (p. 38; return-fare 5*s.*). Pedestrians may walk across the Downs to the N.W. to (7 M.) the scanty remains of *Wilmington Priory*, an offshoot of a Benedictine abbey in Normandy. The 'Wilmington Giant,' (p. 43) is a little to the S. This walk may be extended to *Michelham Priory*, an Augustine foundation of the 13th cent., 4 M. to the N. It was once fortified and is now a farm-house, but there are many interesting remains of the old buildings. Michelham is 3 M. from Berwick (p. 43) and 2 1/2 M. from Hailsham (p. 52).

6. From London to Brighton.

Railway (London, Brighton, and South Coast) from *London Bridge* and *Victoria* stations (51 M.) in 1 1/4-3 hrs.; from *Kensington*, 1/4 hr. longer. Fares 10*s.*, 6*s.* 6*d.*, 4*s.* 2 1/2*d.* Return-tickets available for 7 days are issued at about a fare and a half, and cheap day return-tickets are often issued at little more than single fares, sometimes including admission to the Pavilion and Aquarium (p. 45). The 'Pullman Limited Express', leaving London at 10 a.m. and 3.50 p.m., and Brighton at 1.20 and 5.45 p.m., consists of Pullman day-cars and ordinary first-class carriages only (lighted by electricity; return-fare, for the same day, 12*s.* 6*d.*). The lines from Victoria and Kensington unite with the line from London Bridge at *Croydon*.

Coach from London (Hôtel Métropole) to Brighton (Old Ship) daily in summer in 6 hrs. (fare 10*s.*, inside 7*s.* 6*d.*; box-seat 2*s.* 6*d.* extra). The district traversed is fertile and picturesque.

Leaving London Bridge, the train traverses, by means of a lofty viaduct, $2^1/_2$ M. in length, the manufacturing and unattractive district of *Bermondsey*. There was formerly an abbey here, where Queen Katherine, widow of Henry V., died in 1437, and Queen Elizabeth, widow of Edward IV., in 1492. The red brick building at (3 M.) *New Cross* is the *Royal Naval School*, founded in 1843. The line next passes through a deep cutting in the 'London clay', and arrives at (4 M.) *Brockley* and ($5^1/_2$ M.) *Forest Hill*, prettily situated amid numerous pleasant country-residences. Close to the railway is a German church. Beyond ($6^1/_4$ M.) *Sydenham* we see the *Crystal Palace* (see *Baedeker's Handbook for London*) on our right, 200 ft. above us. 7 M. *Penge*; $7^1/_2$ M. *Anerley*. To the left stands the dark-red *Freemasons' Asylum*. Beyond Anerley, on an eminence to the right, is the *Surrey County Industrial School*, where upwards of 1000 poor children are brought up.

At ($8^1/_2$ M.) **Norwood Junction**, the station for the pretty and growing suburb of *South Norwood*, the line is joined by one of the West End branches of the same company from Victoria. Just before joining the main line this branch traverses **Upper Norwood** *(Queen's Hotel; Crystal Palace)*, one of the chief residential suburbs on the S. side of London (station at *Gipsy Hill*).

In a wooded vale about 1 M. to the S. of Upper Norwood lay *Beulah Spa*, once much frequented, but now built over. Near it is *Streatham*, where Dr. Johnson often visited Mr. and Mrs. Thrale. — From Norwood diverges a branch to *Epsom* and *Dorking* (comp. p. 62).

$10^1/_4$ M. *East Croydon*, one of the five stations at **Croydon** *(*Greyhound; Crown; Rail. Refreshmt. Rooms)*, a very ancient town with 80,000 inhab., now practically forming a suburb of London. The main line from Victoria here joins that from London Bridge. The scenery of the surrounding district, which is thickly dotted with country-houses, is very pleasing. The lower part of the town contains the remains of an *Archiepiscopal Palace*, formerly the country-residence of the Archbishops of Canterbury. The extensive remains of the old building include the lofty dining-hall and the chapel (16th cent.). The *Church of St. John the Baptist*, originally built at the beginning of the 15th cent., destroyed by fire in 1867, and re-erected by Sir G. G. Scott, contains the tombs of several archbishops. Near the middle of the town is *Whitgift's Hospital*, an Elizabethan institution, connected with which there is a large grammar-school.

Pedestrians will find that the following round of 10 to 12 M., with its numerous views of characteristic English scenery, will amply repay the fatigue (comp. Map, p. 12). Starting from Croydon, we proceed first to the S. to ($2^1/_2$ M.) *Sanderstead*, a pretty village, with an interesting church and park, which we reach by following the Brighton road (tramway) to the Red Deer Inn and then turning to the left. [A slight detour to the left will take us by picturesque footpaths to *Crohamhurst* (pron. Croomhurst).] At Sanderstead we turn to the left (E.) and walk to ($2^1/_2$ M.) *Addington*, where the present country-house of the Archbishop of Canterbury is situated; the church, of which the interior is Norman, is interesting to antiquarians. Archbp. Tait (d. 1883) is buried in the churchyard. From Addington we proceed to the N. (left) to (1½ M.) *West Wickham*, with an ancient church, ¾ M. to the S. of which is the picturesque ivy-clad country-seat of *Wickham Court*. From Wickham we may return to Croydon direct, across the *Addington Hills*, in 1¼ hr. — A railway runs from Croydon to Sanderstead, *Warlingham*, and *Oxted* (for *East Grinstead* and *Tunbridge Wells*).

On the left, beyond (10½ M.) *South Croydon*, is *Purley House*, where John Horne Tooke wrote his 'Diversions of Purley'. On a hill to the right are the large and handsome *Warehousemen and Clerks' Schools.*

13 M. *Purley*, whence a branch-line diverges to *Caterham*, 4½ M. to the S.E. To the left is the *Reedham Orphan Asylum*, founded by the *Rev. Andrew Reed;* and to the right, farther on, is the *Surrey County Lunatic Asylum.* The train now passes through a long cutting, and penetrates the *North Downs* by a tunnel upwards of 1 M. long. At the end of the tunnel lies (18 M.) *Merstham*, with a church of the end of the 12th cent. (still interesting in spite of 'restoration'). Near the village is found the so-called 'firestone', which, originally soft, becomes hard and fire-proof on exposure to the air, and is accordingly of great value for building purposes. On the right we obtain a view of *Gatton Park*, the seat of Lord Oxenbridge; the Great Hall (adm. on week-days) is very fine.

From Merstham to Chipstead, a pleasant walk of about 4 M.; to Reigate (see below), through *Gatton Park*, another interesting route, 5 M. The rich carvings in the church at Gatton are of Belgian workmanship; the beautiful altar and pulpit came from Nuremberg, and are ascribed to Albert Dürer. Gatton is notorious for having been among the rottenest of rotten boroughs, seven electors at one time sending two members to parliament.

Just before reaching Redhill we pass *St. Anne's Asylum*, accommodating 400 children. — 20¾ M. **Redhill** (*Warwick Arms; Laker's; Rail. Refreshmt. Rooms*), or *Warwicktown*, with about 10,000 inhab., the junction of the lines to Dover on the E. (see p. 12), and Reigate, Dorking, Guildford, and Reading on the W. (see p. 59). To the left, ¾ M. distant, is the admirably organised Agricultural School of the *Philanthropic Society*, a reformatory for young criminals (about 300). This society was founded in 1788, and is the parent of about 100 similar institutions in England. The white sand of this district is much used in the manufacture o porcelain.

Nutfield, a village with a picturesque church, 2½ M. to the left of the railway, possesses several pits of fuller's earth. Not far off there are distinct traces of a Roman military road leading into Kent, and Roman coins have frequently been found here. — For other walks in this neighbourhood, see p. 59 (Reigate).

21½ M. *Earlswood*, beyond which, on the left, is the handsome and well-known *Asylum for Idiots* (600 inmates), also founded by the *Rev. Andrew Reed* (see above; open to visitors on Mon.). The train now crosses two tributaries of the small river *Mole*, and beyond (25½ M.) *Horley* (Chequers) enters Sussex.

29 M. **Three Bridges** *(Refreshment Rooms)*, the junction of lines to *East Grinstead* (p. 43) and *Tunbridge Wells* (p. 13) on the E., and to *Horsham* and *Ford Junction* (see p. 53) on the W.

At Worth, a small village about $1^1/_2$ M. from Three Bridges, there is a diminutive **Church*, dating certainly from before the Conquest, but spoiled by modern restoration. The beautiful **Forest of Worth* is a favourite resort of painters. Fossil plants are found in great abundance in a sandstone-quarry near the village. — *Field Place*, the birthplace of Shelley (1792-1822), lies 2 M. to the N.W. of Horsham.

The line next traverses a portion of the very ancient *Tilgate Forest*, crosses another branch of the Mole, and, threading a tunnel $^3/_4$ M. in length, reaches ($5^1/_2$ M.) *Balcombe* (Inn), in a picturesque district containing much to interest the botanist and geologist. Beyond Balcombe the train crosses the valley of the *Ouse* by means of an imposing viaduct of 37 arches, 1400 ft. long and 100 ft. high in the middle. To the left we obtain a view of *Ardingley College*, a school for 450 boys. — $37^1/_2$ M. *Hayward's Heath* (Station Hotel).

To the W. ($2^1/_2$ M.) is the pleasing little town of *Cuckfield* (King's Head; Talbot), with *Cuckfield Place*, a mansion in a fine park, in the vicinity. — Branch-lines diverge from Hayward's Heath to *Horsted Keynes* and *East Grinstead* (p. 43) and to *Lewes* (Newhaven, Eastbourne, Hastings; see p. 43). Horsted Keynes was the retirement and burial-place of Archbp. Leighton (d. 1684), whose house, Broadhurst, may still be seen. — About 5 M. to the S.E. of Horsted Keynes (1 M. from *Sheffield Park* station) is *Fletching*, in the church of which Edward Gibbon (d. 1794) is interred.

To the left lies the *Sussex Lunatic Asylum*. $40^1/_2$ M. *Keymer Junction*, for Lewes, Newhaven, Hastings, etc.; $41^1/_2$ M. *Burgess Hill*; $43^1/_2$ M. *Hassocks* ('hassock', Anglo-Saxon, small wood). *Ditchling Beacon* (856 ft.), 3 M. to the E. of Hassocks, is the highest point in Sussex. On the top, which commands a wide view, are remains of an ancient entrenchment, probably of Roman origin.

Hurstpierpoint Park, $2^1/_2$ M. to the W. of Hassocks, deserves a visit for the sake of its noble old oaks. *Wolstonbury Beacon*, in the neighbourhood, shows traces of a cruciform camp, probably British. The walk across the *Downs*, past the *Devil's Dyke* (p. 51), to Brighton, a distance of about 8 M., is very interesting. On the Downs graze about half a million sheep, yielding the famous 'South Down mutton'.

The line passes through the range of the South Down Hills by means of the *Clayton Tunnel*, which is 2240 yds. in length, and takes 2 min. to traverse. Beyond it is a short tunnel. On the left we see a portion of *Stanmer Park*, belonging to the Earl of Chichester. The line next passes ($49^1/_2$ M.) *Preston Park* (Pl. B, 2), whence a branch-line diverges to *West Brighton* (Sussex Hotel) and *Worthing* (p. 52), and it then descends to —

51 M. **Brighton.** — **Railway Stations.** The *Central Station* (Pl. D, E, 4) is at the N. end of Queen's Road and is connected with the suburban stations of *Preston Park* (Pl. B, 2; see above), *West Brighton* (Pl. A, 4; p. 51), *London Road* (Pl. E, 3; p. 52), *Lewes Road* (Pl. F, 3), and *Kemp Town* (Pl. G, 5; p. 50; train to the last in 10 min.).

Hotels. In *Queen's Road*, leading S. from the station to the beach, are several small second-class houses, suitable for single gentlemen only (R. 1*s.* 6*d.* to 2*s.*, D. 1*s.* 6*d.* to 2*s.* 6*d.*). — On the *Esplanade*, facing the sea: to the W. of West Street, the prolongation of Queen's Road, Grand Hotel (Pl. a; D. 6), near the W. Pier, 'pens'. 10*s.* 6*d.*, more in the season; MÉTROPOLE (Pl. b; D, 6), a huge new establishment; BEDFORD (Pl. c; C, 6); NORFOLK (Pl. d; C, 6); to the E. of West Street, HAMBLIN'S (Pl. e; D, E, 6); *OLD SHIP (Pl. f); HARRISON'S (Pl. g; E, 6); MARKWELL'S ROYAL (Pl. i); QUEEN'S, a large and handsome building (Pl. k); CLARENDON (Pl. l), 'pens'. from 3*l.* 3*s.* per week; ROYAL YORK (Pl. m; E, 6); *ALBION (Pl. n); ALBEMARLE (Pl. o); HAXELL'S (Pl. r; E, 6); NEW STEINE HOTEL (Pl. s; F, 6), at the chain pier, 'pens'. 3*l.* 10*s.* per week; ROYAL CRESCENT (Pl. w; F, 6), farther to the E., on the Marine Parade; BRISTOL (Pl. z; G, 6), at Kemp Town; all these are of the first class: R. from 2*s.* 6*d.*, B. 2*s.* 6*d.* to 3*s.*, D. from 3*s.* 6*d.*, A. 1*s.* 6*d.* to 2*s.* 6*d.* The hotels in the streets to the N. of the Esplanade are cheaper, and some of them are quite near the sea: NEW SHIP (Pl. t; E, 6), Ship Street; GLOUCESTER (Pl. u; E, 5), North Steine; KING'S ARMS, George St., R. & A. from 3*s.* 6*d.*; FIFTH AVENUE HOTEL, Manchester St., 'pens'. 9*s.* 6*d.*; PAVILION, Castle Sq.; WHITE LION (Pl. v; D, 5), Queen's Road, commercial. — The numerous BOARDING HOUSES are usually comfortable, and, except during the height of the season, not exorbitant (5*s.* 6*d.*-10*s.* 6*d.* per day).

Restaurants. *Concert Hall (Melisoni)*, West Street, near the Esplanade; *Sweeting's Oyster & Luncheon Rooms*, on the ground-floor of the Orleans Club, at the corner of West St. and King's Road. On the Esplanade: **Mutton's; Grand Hotel Restaurant; Markwell's* (see above); at the *Albemarle Hotel*. In East Street, near the Esplanade: *Booth; The Bristol; Café Royal*, D. 3*s.* *Continental*, King's Road, opposite the W. Pier; *Aquarium Restaurant*. — *Bodega*, 10 Ship St. — CONFECTIONERS: *Maynard*, West St.; *Reynard*, North Street; *Booth*, East Street. — ICES: *La Crêmerie*, 18 East Street; *Mikado*, Esplanade.

Baths. The *Sea-bathing Stations* are in front of the Esplanade; the beach is stony. Bathing-machines (with towels, etc.) for gentlemen 6*d.*, for ladies 9*d.* Swimmers may bathe from either of the pier-heads before 11 a.m., and gentlemen may bathe without a machine at the public bathing-places to the E. and W. of the piers, indicated by notice-boards, between 8 p.m. and 8 a.m. The bathing-machines are lowered to the sea by windlasses. — **Turkish Baths*, 59 West Street, bath 2*s.* 6*d.*, after 6 p.m. 1*s.* 6*d.* (reserved for ladies on Tues. and Frid. forenoon); **Warm, Vapour, Swimming, and other Baths* at *Brill's*, 77 and 78 East Street, near the Esplanade; *Hobden's*, adjoining the Grand Hotel; *Brunswick Baths*, 2 Western Street. — *Electric & Galvanic Baths*, 11 York Place.

Theatres. *Royal* (Pl. E, 6), New Road, for operas and dramas. *Aquarium Theatre*. — *Brighton Alhambra*, King's Road, near the Grand Hotel (music hall).

Music. A band plays two or three times daily on the *Piers*, in the *Esplanade Gardens* to the W., on the roof of the *Aquarium* (p. 50), and in some of the 'steines'. — Promenade and other *Concerts* are frequently given in the grounds of the Pavilion (p. 49).

Post Office, Ship Street. — The *Principal Telegraph Office* is at the Old Steine; sub-offices also at the Head Post Office, the New Pier, the Railway Station, etc.

Cabs. *First-class* (1-4 pers.), per hr. 3*s.*, per mile 1*s.*; to the hotels on the Parade 1*s.* 6*d.*-2*s.* *Second-class* (1-2 pers.), per hr. 2*s.*, per mile and a half 1*s.*; to the nearer hotels 1*s.* and to the more distant 1*s.* 6*d.* Pony-chaises, goat-carriages, etc., cheaper. — Fare and a half between 12 and 2 a.m., double fare from 2 to 6 a.m. — For each article of luggage carried outside, when there are more than 2 passengers, 3*d.* — *Donkeys*, 9*d.* per hr. — *Bicycles* and *Tricycles*, 1*s.* per hr. — *Porter* to the nearer hotels, 3*d.* per package.

Omnibuses run at frequent intervals through the principal thoroughfares to *Hove*, *Kemp Town*, *Preston*, *Lewes Road*, *Rottingdean*, and *Portslade*. — **Marine Electric Railway** from the Aquarium to *Kemp Town* (2*d.*, return 3*d.*).

Boats. *Sailing-boats*, 5-10*s.* per hr., according to size; *Rowing-boats*, 2*s.* 6*d.* per hr. Without boatmen, cheaper. Sailing parties are organirsd by the boatmen in summer, each passenger paying 1*s.* — In summeea *Steamer* makes excursions to Hastings, Eastbourne, the Isle of Wight, etc.

For a coloured street plan of Brighton see pages 558 & 559

Sussex County Cricket Ground, at Hove. — *Hove Rink & Lawn Tennis Courts*, Selborne Road, 1/4 M. from West Brighton Station (adm. 6*d*.). *Lawn Tennis Courts* also in Preston Road (Pl. D, 3; 3*d*.) and in the Pavilion grounds.

Brighton Races in Aug. and Nov., on the race-course on White Hawk Down, to the E. of the town (p. 52). — Good *Hunting* in the neighbourhood.

Brighton, with a population of 140,400 souls (including Hove), and an annual influx of over 50,000 tourists and visitors, lies on the slope of a hill, in the middle of a broad and shallow bay, which is terminated on the W. by the point called *Selsea Bill*, and on the E. by *Beachy Head*. Its original name was *Brighthelmston*, from *Brighthelm*, an Anglo-Saxon bishop, who is reputed to have founded it in the 10th century, and *tun*, a town. That the Romans had a settlement here is proved by the numerous coins and other antiquities of the Roman period which have been found from time to time. The lord of the soil in the 11th cent. was the powerful Earl Godwin, father of the last Anglo-Saxon king, Harold, who lost his kingdom and his life at the battle of Hastings (14th Oct., 1066). The chief attractions of the place are its clear and bracing air, the fine expanse of sea bordered by white chalk cliffs, its bathing facilities, and its gay crowds of visitors. Thackeray highly appreciated these advantages and has sung the praises of 'Dr. Brighton' in '*The Newcomes*'.

Brighton, now by far the most frequented seaside resort in the British Islands, was a poor fishing-village down to 1753. After that year, owing to the commendations of Dr. Russell, a fashionable physician who had experienced the beneficial effects of sea-bathing here, the place began to grow in importance. In 1782 George IV., then Prince of Wales, first took up his residence at Brighton, and the result of his royal patronage was the speedy advance of the town to its present imposing dimensions. The Prince laid out 250,000*l*. on the construction of the Royal Pavilion (Pl. E, 5), an extensive and tasteless building in the Oriental style (*Nash*, architect), where he afterwards spent several months of each year. William IV. and Queen Victoria, however, rarely occupied it, chiefly because the view of the sea is nearly excluded by houses. It now belongs to the town. The royal stables and riding-school with their immense dome (80ft. in diameter), to the N.W. of the Pavilion, have been converted into a ball and concert room (organ-recital on the 1st Mon. of each month). The handsome and well-shaded grounds are open to the public; adm. to the Pavilion 6*d*.

Passing through the Entrance Hall, which contains busts of eminent citizens and natives of Brighton, we enter a long *Corridor*, decorated in the Chinese manner. From this gallery all the rooms of the ground-floor may be entered. The *Banqueting* and *Music Rooms*, at opposite extremities of the corridor, are the most handsomely painted and adorned. The principal chandeliers cost upwards of 2000*l*. each. The rooms are used for lectures, concerts, balls, scientific assemblies, and other public gatherings. The apartments in the upper story contain various collections of no great interest.

The building on the N.W. side of the grounds, near the Dome, contains the *Town Museum* (entrance from Church Street), which boasts of a well-arranged geological and zoological collection, a *Free Library*, and a *Picture Gallery* (adm. daily from 10 a.m.; free).

The Picture Gallery contains a few pictures belonging to the municipality, but is chiefly devoted to loan-collections, which are frequently changed. Among the permanent works are: *Jan Victor* (pupil of Rembrandt), The marriage-contract; *West*, Rejection of Christ; *Downard*, Reading the news, and The naughty child; portraits of George IV., William IV., and Queen Adelaide, by *Lawrence;* and works by *West*, *Armitage*, and *Leatham*. The collection of *English Porcelain*, lent by *Mr. Willet*, is one of the most complete in England.

Contiguous to the Pavilion on the E. is the *Old Steine*, a square with a grass plot and fountains, named from a reef (Ger. *Stein*, Flem. *Steen*, a stone or rock), which jutted into the sea here. On the N. side is a bronze *Statue of George IV.*, by Chantrey.

The *Esplanade*, or sea-front, forms a handsome road about 4 M. in length, in or near which most of the visitors reside. The W. part is called the *King's Road* (Pl. C, D, E, 6). The E. part, called the *Marine Parade* (Pl. F, G, 6), and extending from the Old Steine to Kemp Town, is protected by a sea-wall constructed at a cost of 100,000*l*. Few occupations are more entertaining than to walk or drive here, watching the motley crowds on the beach and piers. The sunsets in spring and autumn are often very gorgeous. Large vessels are often seen sailing past, but none of them touch here, there being insufficient depth of water.

The most popular promenade is the **New*, or *West Pier* (Pl. D, 6; pier-toll 2*d.*), completed in 1866, 1150 ft. in length, at the end of which a band performs morning and evening. On a fine day the scene here is of a most lively and attractive character. The old **Chain Pier* (Pl. F, 6; adm. 2*d.*), constructed in 1823, and extending from the Marine Parade into the sea to a distance of 1130 ft., was formerly the chief resort of visitors, but is now almost entirely supplanted by the W. Pier. The end of the Chain Pier commands a fine view of the sea, the handsome buildings of the town, the long rows of bathing-machines, and the New Pier.

The finest rows of houses, such as *Queen's Mansions*, *Brunswick Square*, and *Adelaide Crescent* (Pl. B, C, 6), are chiefly situated on the *West Cliff*. On the *East Cliff* lies *Kemp Town* (Pl. H, 6), which also contains many handsome dwellings. The *Madeira Road*, at the foot of this cliff, is a favourite resort of invalids (electric railway, see p. 48).

The extensive and admirably-appointed *Aquarium (Pl. E, 6), near the Chain Pier (adm. 1*s.*; after 7 p. m. 6*d.*), is well worthy of a visit. Externally it makes no great show, being built on a site below the level of the road. The entrance is surmounted by a low clock-tower.

The forty large tanks in the interior contain great numbers of fish, including specimens of the octopus or devil-fish, dolphins, porpoises, sharks, etc. There are also turtle, seal, and sea-lion ponds, alligators, and stuffed specimens of fish and reptiles. Attached to the aquarium are a good restaurant, a café, an orchestra, smoking and billiard rooms, reading-rooms supplied with newspapers and periodicals, a skating-rink, and a theatre. The flat roof is laid out with flower-beds and used as a promenade (music, see p. 48).

The old parish-church of *St. Nicholas* (Pl. D, 5), founded in the 14th cent., and occupying an elevated site in the centre of the town, contains a very ancient circular *Font*, ornamented with curious carving. In the graveyard, to the S. of the chancel, is the tomb of Nicholas Tettersell, captain of the vessel that carried Charles II. to France after the battle of Worcester. The present parish-church of Brighton is *St. Peter's* (Pl. E, 4), a handsome modern Gothic edifice in an open space to the N. of the Grand Parade. — Several new churches (*St. Paul's*, West Street; *St. Martin's*, Lewes Road, with a fine pulpit, etc.,) have been built by the Rev. A. D. Wagner, Vicar of St. Paul's. *Trinity Chapel*, of which the *Rev. Fred. W. Robertson* (d. 1853) was incumbent, is in Ship St. [Robertson is buried in the *Extra-Mural Cemetery* (Pl. G, 3), a few paces from Macaulay's victim, 'Satan' Montgomery (d. 1855).] *St. Bartholomew's* is remarkable for its height. — The **Dyke Road Museum* (Pl. C, 3) contains one of the finest collections of birds in England. — Brighton is noted for its colleges and high-class schools for girls and boys.

Brighton is unfortunately so ill-provided with shade that this 'London-by-the-Sea' has been cynically described as made up of 'wind, glare, and fashion'. Numerous young trees have been planted in different parts of the town to remedy this defect. Shelter from the sun may, however, be obtained in the grounds of the Pavilion (p. 49), or in the *Queen's Park* (Pl. F, 5), situated in a small depression farther to the E. Adjacent to the Queen's Park is the so-called *German Spa*, where Dr. Struve's mineral waters are retailed.

Excursions. Pleasant walks do not abound, either in Brighton or its environs. The most attractive are to the W., through the suburb of *Hove* or *West Brighton* (Pl. B, 5, 6), with its handsome town-hall in red brick and terracotta, and to the N. to *Preston* (Pl. C, D, 2, 3), a quiet and picturesquely-situated little place, with an E.E. church and a pretty public park and cricket-ground. A little to the N. rises *Hollingsbury Hill*, with remains of a Roman entrenchment, where Roman coins have frequently been discovered. Beyond it, and about 6 M. from Brighton, is the **Devil's Dyke**, a kind of natural amphitheatre, looking like a huge entrenchment (railway from the central station in 20 min.; also excursion-cars, there and back 1*s.* 6*d.*) The route ascends West Street to the White Lion Hotel, and then turns to the left, past the church; it afterwards leads direct towards the N.W., without deflection either to the right or left. At the top of the Dyke, where there are traces of a Roman camp, we obtain one of the most diversified views in the whole county, seeing immediately below us the rich expanse of the 'Wealden' formation, once a primæval forest called *Coit Andred* by the Britons, *Anderida* by the Romans, and *Andredswald* by the Saxons. To the S. is the far-reaching sea, to the N. the chain of the North Down Hills, to the W. numerous villages, and to the E. busy Brighton itself. At the summit is Thacker's *Dyke Hotel*. At the foot of the Dyke is the village of *Poynings*, with an interesting old church.

To the E. we may drive viâ *Rottingdean* (excursion-cars there and back 1*s*.), which contains mineral springs, to (7½ M.) *Newhaven* (p. 43). The cliffs, which the road skirts, are rich in fossil formations. — To the N.E., at a high level, is the *Race Course* (view).

From Brighton to Hastings, 33 M., railway in 1¼-2 hrs. (fares 6*s*. 8*d*., 4*s*. 8*d*., 2*s*. 10*d*.). Soon after leaving the station the train crosses the London road by a fine curved viaduct of 27 arches, 73 ft. high and 400 yds. long. Afterwards it passes through a tunnel and several deep cuttings in the chalk hills. To the right, beyond (1 M.) *London Road* station, are the Brighton *Cavalry Barracks* (Pl. F, 2); to the left, farther on, *Stanmer Park*, seat of the Earl of Chichester. Near (4 M.) *Falmer* another long tunnel is passed through. At (8 M.) *Lewes* (p. 43) we join the line from London to Eastbourne (see p. 43). The line now skirts *Mt. Caburn* and *Firle Beacon* (820 ft.) and passes *Glynde* and *Berwick*. On the hills to the right, beyond Berwick, is seen the 'Wilmington Giant' (p. 44). 20 M. *Polegate* is the junction for *Hailsham* and *Tunbridge Wells* to the N. (comp. p. 43) and *Eastbourne* (see p. 43) to the S.

Close to (23 M.) *Pevensey & Westham* (Royal Oak Inn) is *Westham Church*, a fine building, partly Norman. ***Pevensey Castle** consists of two distinct parts, an outer fortress of Roman origin and an inner late-Norman one of the 12th century. The Roman wall, still about 20 ft. high at places, encloses a space of about 10 acres and is strengthened at intervals by round towers; this was the Roman *Anderida*. The Norman castle occupies the S. E. corner of this enclosure. Pevensey is the reputed landing-place of William the Conqueror. *Pevensey Church*, to the E. of the Castle, is Early English. — About 4⅓ M. to the N. of Pevensey is ***Hurstmonceaux Castle**, an interesting and beautiful example of a fortified mansion of the 15th cent., constructed of brick (now roofless). *Hurstmonceaux Church*, ¼ M. to the W., is also interesting for its monuments. *Archdeacon Hare* (d. 1855) is buried beneath the great yew in the churchyard.

This part of the coast of Sussex is lined with *Martello Towers*, small forts, each mounting one gun and intended to be garrisoned by about 10 men; they were erected at the time of the last war with France, and their name is said to be derived from a small fort of the same kind in Martella Bay, Corsica, which offered an obstinate resistance to the British forces. — 29 M. *Bexhill* (Devonshire Hotel), a small watering-place; 32 M. *St. Leonards* (*West Marina* station). — 33 M. *Hastings*, see p. 40.

7. From Brighton to Chichester and Portsmouth.

44 M. Brighton and South Coast Railway, in 1¾-2¼ hrs. (fares 8*s*. 10*d*., 6*s*., 3*s*. 8½*d*.). — View of the English Channel on the left, and of a chain of hills on the right. On both sides are pleasant meadow-land and trees, with numerous windmills.

The first station is (1½ M.) *West Brighton*, just before which our line is joined by the branch from Preston Park (p. 47), while beyond diverges the branch to the Devil's Dyke (p. 51). 3 M. *Portslade;* 4¼ M. *Southwick.* — 6 M. *Shoreham* (Royal George; Buckingham Arms), which carries on a considerable trade with the opposite coast of France. The antiquarian will be repaid by a visit to the churches of *Old* and *New Shoreham*, in the Norman and Early English styles, dating from the time of the Crusades. There is a popular resort here called the *Swiss Gardens*. A branch-line to *Horsham* (p. 52) diverges here. Beyond Shoreham the train crosses the wide estuary of the *Adur*, which is also crossed by a fine suspension-bridge (left). — At (8 M.) *Lancing* is a large public school, the buildings of which are seen on a hill to the right.

$10^1/_2$ M. **Worthing** *(Marine; Steyne Hotel; *Royal Sea House; West Worthing; Albion)*, a favourite watering-place (13,000 inhab.), with a fine sandy beach and a long iron pier, frequented by those who like quieter quarters than Brighton. At *West Worthing* (stat.) are large baths and tennis-courts. Excursions may be made to the N. to the interesting churches of (1 M.) *Broadwater* and (2 M.) *Sompting*, and to the N.W. to ($1^1/_2$ M.) *West Tarring*, with fig-gardens and an E.E. church. *Cisbury Hill*, $2^1/_2$ M. distant, is the site of a British or Roman encampment. *Chanctonbury Ring* (814 ft.), 5 M. to the N., and *Highdown Hill*, $4^1/_2$ M. to the N.W., command extensive and beautiful views. On the summit of the latter is the tomb of a miller (d. 1793), buried here at his own request.

13 M. *Goring* and ($15^1/_2$ M.) *Angmering*. Near the latter is a handsome park, belonging to the Duke of Norfolk.

$19^1/_2$ M. **Ford Junction**, with a branch-line to the S.E. to (2 M.) *Littlehampton* (Norfolk; Terminus; Beach), a small watering-place at the mouth of the *Arun*. Another branch runs N. to ($2^1/_2$ M.) *Arundel*, *Amberley* (p. 56), and ($21^1/_2$ M.) *Horsham* (p. 47).

The small town of *Arundel* (Norfolk Arms; Bridge) is situated on the river Arun, $2^1/_2$ M. to the N. of Ford Junction. In the vicinity is ***Arundel Castle,** the magnificent seat of the Duke of Norfolk, which was founded as early as the 10th century. In 1102 it was besieged by Henry I., and afterwards by Stephen, and it was again attacked in 1644 by the Parliamentary troops and left in ruins. The portion of the building now used as a residence was begun in 1791. The ancient **Keep*, dating from the 12th cent., and the *Dairy* (to the E.) are shown on Mon. & Frid. (12-4) by tickets obtained gratis at the Norfolk Arms. Entrance by the principal gateway at the upper end of the town; the top commands a fine prospect of the surrounding country. The tower is tenanted by a colony of owls (bubo maximus), originally brought from America. The **Park* is open to the public. — The **Parish Church*, erected in 1380, with the adjoining chapel of a Benedictine Abbey which once stood here, is worthy of notice. The Fitz-Alan Chapel, or chancel (no admission), contains old monuments of the Arundel family. The *Park* affords several charming walks. The fine modern *Roman Catholic Church* was built by the Duke of Norfolk at a cost of 100,000*l*. The Arun is noted for its mullet, a dish of which may be obtained at the hotel.

22 M. *Barnham*, the junction for a short line to ($3^1/_2$ M.) **Bognor** *(Norfolk; Pier; Bedford; Victoria Park)*, a quiet bathing-place, with a pier and esplanade. — $26^1/_2$ M. *Drayton*, the nearest station for ($3^1/_4$ M.) Goodwood (p. 56).

The train now traverses a level and fertile tract of country, and reaches (in 1-$1^1/_4$ hr. from Brighton) —

$28^1/_2$ M. **Chichester** (**Dolphin*, *Anchor*, *Eagle*, all in West St., facing the cathedral; omn. from the station), a town of great antiquity (8092 inhab.), the *Regnum* of the Romans, the *Cissa's Ceaster* of the Saxons (whence the present name). It became the seat of a bishop after the Norman Conquest, when William transferred the ancient see of Selsey (founded in the 7th cent.) to this place. The diocese of Chichester is conterminous with the county of Sussex, the only instance of such identity in England. As at Chester, the characteristic square ground-plan of the Romans is marked by the four principal streets, which are named after the points of the compass and meet each other at right angles in the centre of the town. At the point of intersection is the handsome **Market Cross*, erected in 1500, but much damaged by the Puritans. The line of the town-walls (date unknown) can still be traced throughout almost their whole circuit: and on the N. and E. sides of the town portions of them have been converted into public promenades.

From the station we approach the centre of the town through *South Street.* On the left we soon reach the *Canon Gate* (15th cent), leading to the cathedral-precincts. Immediately to the right, within the archway, is the small *Vicars' Close*, with its fine *Hall* of the 14th cent., now used by the *Chichester Theological College.* Going straight past the Vicars' Close, we reach St. Richard's Walk, named after Bishop Richard de la Wych (p. 55), a narrow passage on the right leading to the *Cloisters* (Perp.; 16th cent.), which it reaches opposite the S. door of the cathedral. It is better, however, to pass through the cloisters (good view of the Cathedral), turn to the left, and enter the Cathedral by the E. E. *Galilee Porch* on the W.

The ***Cathedral**, originally begun about 1085, completed in 1108, and burned down in 1114, is in its present form substantially a transitional Norman building of the 12th cent., with some pointed details introduced after a second fire in 1186. The Lady Chapel dates from 1288-1304; the spire (277 ft.), erected in the 15th cent., collapsed in 1861 and was rebuilt in 1861-66. The detached Bell Tower, a feature peculiar to Chichester among English cathedrals, is, despite its weather-worn appearance, one of the most recent parts of the building, dating from the 15th century. The absence of the N. W. tower, which fell in 1634, gives a somewhat lop-sided appearance to the W. façade. The whole edifice has been restored since 1848. The total length of the church is 410 ft.; nave 172 ft.; width of nave and aisles 91 ft.; across transepts 131 ft.; height of nave 62 ft., of choir 65 ft. Comp. 'Architectural History of Chichester Cathedral', by *R. Willis.*

The **Interior** (services at 10 and 4; adm. to choir 6*d.*), which was sadly defaced by the iconoclasts in 1643, shows in many respects a strong resemblance to the early French Gothic style, particularly in the superstructure of the choir, the arcades and detached shafts of the presbytery, and the double aisles of the nave. The outer aisles (E. E.), a peculiarity which Chichester shares with Manchester alone among English cathedrals, consisted originally of a series of chapels, afterwards thrown into one. The Nave proper, with its eight bays, is somewhat narrow in proportion to its height. The stained glass is all modern. Among the most interesting monuments are effigies of an Earl and Countess of Arundel (14th cent.; restored) and of a lady (13th cent.?), a *Tablet to Collins the poet, a native of Chichester (1719-59), by *Flaxman*, and a statue of Huskisson, all in the N. aisle; and the monuments of Agnes Cromwell and Jane Smith, in the S. aisle, both by *Flaxman.* Near the N. porch is an ancient wooden *Chest*, brought from Selsey Cathedral (see p. 53). The only old brass now left hangs against one of the buttresses in the S. aisle. The modern

For a plan of Chichester Cathedral see page 542

Pulpit is a memorial of Dean Hook (d. 1875), author of 'Lives of the Arch bishops of Canterbury'. — The N. Transept, formerly used as a parish church, contains a worthless series of portraits of the bishops, from St. Wilfrid (680) to Sherburne (1508-36), painted in the 16th cent. by an Italian named Bernardi. This transept is adjoined by the *Chapel of the Four Virgins* (entered from the N. aisle of the choir), now used as the *Cathedral Library*, and containing some interesting relics. Among the manuscripts is a copy of the prayer-book of Hermann, Archbishop of Cologne, with the autograph of the martyr Cranmer, Archbishop of Canterbury. The S. Transept possesses a fine Dec. window, filled with execrable Munich glass, and two other paintings by Bernardi (see above), representing the foundation of the see at Selsey (680) and the confirmation, by Henry VIII., of Bishop Sherburne's gifts to the Cathedral. Below is the tomb of *Bishop Moleyns* (1446-50).

The Choir, elevated by four steps above the nave, extends three bays eastward from the tower. The carving of the *Choir Stalls* and misereres is very fine. The modern *Reredos*, with its carved group of the Ascension, has been left unfinished on the score of its excessive bulk. The mosaic pavement in front of the altar deserves attention. The choir is divided from its aisles by beautiful hammered iron screens in imitation of ancient work. In the S. aisle are two very interesting and well-preserved *Saxon Sculptures, brought from Selsey, representing Christ at the house of Lazarus and the Raising of Lazarus (the latter inaccurately pieced together), with hollows left by the abstraction of the jewelled eyes. This aisle also contains the *Cenotaph of Dean Hook* (see above), and the tomb of *Bishop Sherburne* (d. 1536). — Behind the reredos, where formerly stood the famous shrine of St. Richard (da la Wych; 1245-53), is the Presbytery, with its interesting triforium, showing the transition to the pointed style. The detached shafts of the piers are placed much farther from the central columns than is usual in other instances when this construction is adopted (comp. ante). — The long and narrow Lady Chapel, forming the E. termination of the cathedral, was restored in 1876. On the vaulting are some remains of the paintings with which the entire roof of the cathedral was adorned by Bernardi (see above).

In the Cloisters (p. 54) is a tablet to *Wm. Chillingworth*, the Protestant controversialist, who died at Chichester in 1643. — A fine view may be obtained from the top of the *Bell Tower* (open 11-12 and 2-4), but an order from the Dean is necessary for an ascent of the *Central Tower.* The spire is said to be the only cathedral spire in England that is visible from the sea.

The Episcopal Palace, adjoining the cathedral on the S. W., contains a fine old mediæval kitchen, now used as a washhouse. The private chapel of the bishops has been restored.

We now return to the Market Cross, proceed down *North Street*, and take the first turning to the right. This brings us to a small archway leading to **St. Mary's Hospital*, originally founded in the 12th cent. as a nunnery, and afterwards refounded as an asylum for old women. It consists of a large hall, with a small chapel (13th cent.) at its E. end. The interesting old windows of the latter were 'restored' in 1878-86. The misereres here resemble those in the cathedral. — Not far from this point, at the N.E. angle of the town, is the *Priory Cricket Ground* (adm. 6*d*.), containing part of the church of an old Franciscan Monastery, now used as the *Guildhall.* — The restored *Church of St. Olave*, in North Street, probably the oldest in Chichester, stands on the foundations of a Roman building. — The *Museum* of the Philosophical Society (open 11-2; adm. 3*d*.), in South Street, contains some Roman antiquities and natural history specimens.

Excursions from Chichester. *Bosham*, a fishing-village, 4 M. to the W., on a bay of the same name, possesses an interesting church, partly Saxon, which figures in the Bayeux Tapestry and contains the tomb of a daughter of King Canute. Harold is said to have here set sail for his ill-omened visit to Normandy. — To the S. the country is flat and uninteresting On the N. it is more attractive, and affords a number of pleasant walks, particularly that to (3½ M.) **Goodwood**, the seat of the Duke of Richmond, with its fine collection of paintings, including specimens of Van Dyck, Rembrandt, Rubens, Kneller, Reynolds, Lely, Lawrence, and Gainsborough (open to visitors in the absence of the family). The **Park*, which is open to the public, contains herds of deer and some fine cedars. A Roman relief of Neptune and Minerva, found at Chichester, is preserved in a kind of temple here. The picturesque **Race Course*, close at hand, is crowded every July with the members of the sporting world. The stables, kennels, pheasantry, and tennis-court also deserve notice. — **Boxgove**, 1½ M. from Goodwood, contains an Early English **Priory Church*, with richly decorated and painted vaulting. The curious external elevation of the presbytery should be noticed. — A pleasant walk may also be taken to *Bignor*, 10½ M. to the N.E. (4 M. from Amberley, p. 53), with the remains of a **Roman Villa* (adm. 1*s.*)

Beyond Chichester the train passes (31½ M.) *Bosham* (1 M. to the N. of the village, see above), and enters the county of *Hampshire*, or *Hants*. Then (35½ M.) *Emsworth*. The Isle of Wight is visible in the distance (left). From (37½ M.) *Havant* (Bear; Albany), a small market-town, where we join the L. S. W. direct line from London (R. 9), a short branch-line diverges to *Hayling Island*, with the favourite bathing-resorts of *North* and *South Hayling* (Royal Hotel). Beyond Havant the hills to the right are crowned with the forts protecting Portsmouth on the land-side. The train crosses a narrow arm of the sea and enters the island of *Portsea*. — 43½ M. *Fratton Junction* (for Southsea, p. 58); 44 M. *Portsmouth Town*; 45 M. *Portsmouth Harbour*, the starting-place of the Isle of Wight steamers (see p. 67).

Portsmouth. — **Hotels.** George (Pl. a; C, 4), 29 High St.; Star & Garter (Pl. b; C, 4), adjoining the floating bridge; Bedford, Sussex (Pl. c; E, 3), close to the Town Station, unpretending, R. & A. 4*s.*; Totterdell's (Pl. d; C, 3), St. George's Sq., Portsea; Keppel's Head (Pl. e; C, 3), on the Hard, Portsea. — At Southsea: Cawte's (Pl. f; D, 5), adjoining the Esplanade Pier, well spoken of; Queen's, Grosvenor (Pl. i; D, 5), Pier (Pl. k; D, 5), fronting the Common and the sea; Beach Mansions (Pl. g; F, 6), opposite the Parade Pier, East Southsea; Portland. — *Refreshment Rooms* at the Town and Harbour stations.

Cabs. From the station to any part of Portsmouth proper and Portsea, to the Dockyard and the Harbour, and to Southsea Pier 1*s.*; to other parts of Southsea 1*s.* 6*d.*, to East Southsea and Southsea Castle 2*s.*

Tramway-Cars ply at frequent intervals from *Portsea* to *Southsea*, from *Southsea* to *North End*, Landport (passing the railway-station), from *Portsmouth Point* to *North End*, etc. — **Omnibuses** from the *Railway Station* to the *Dockyard* (1*d.*) and from *King's Road* to *Havelock Park*.

Steamers to *Southampton* (several times a day), *Ryde* (about every hr.), *Cowes*, etc. — *Steam Floating Bridge* to *Gosport* from Portsmouth Point every 10 min. (1*d.*), and *Steam Launches* from Portsea Pier to Gosport every 5 min. (½*d.*).

Theatre Royal (Pl. D, 3), Commercial Road, near the railway station. — **Military Music** in summer on Governor's Green. Guard-mounting on the Grand Parade (Pl. C, 5) at 11 a.m.

Baths in Park Road (Pl. D, 3), Landport.

U. S. Consular Agent, *Thos. McCheane, Esq.*, 66 St. Thomas St.

For a coloured street plan of Portsmouth see pages 560 & 561

Chief Attractions. After visiting *St. Thomas's Church* we may cross by the floating bridge to *Gosport*, visit *Haslar Hospital* and the *Victualling Yard*, and cross by one of the steam-launches to *Portsea*. Here the *Dockyard* will occupy us for 1½ hr., after which we may take the tramway to Southsea. This, however, would necessitate a very early start to reach the Dockyard before 12 (see below), and many will prefer to begin with the Dockyard at 10 a.m. and cross thence to Gosport, recrossing by the floating bridge to Portsmouth and walking or driving on to Southsea. A visit to the 'Victory' should not be omitted, and a boat may be hired to do this in crossing the harbour.

Portsmouth, a strongly fortified seaport and the chief naval station of England, includes the contiguous towns of *Portsea*, *Southsea*, and *Landport*, with a joint population of about 140,000, Portsmouth proper being the central but smallest part. It is also an important garrison, and one of the few places in England where the soldier is as conspicuous a factor of the population as in most Continental towns. The largest and handsomest of the numerous barracks are the *Eastney Barracks* for marine artillerymen, to the E. of Southsea. The fortifications include a series of 'lines' and a number of detached forts, both to seaward and landward.

Portsmouth owes its importance partly to its magnificent harbour (4½ M. long), and partly to the sheltered roadstead of *Spithead*, between the town and the Isle of Wight. Of architectural beauty or historical remains the town can make little boast, but its extensive nautical establishments are extremely interesting. The ***Dockyard** (Pl. C, D, 1, 2; open 10-12 a.m. and 1.15-3 p.m.; to foreigners with permission from the Admiralty only) is a gigantic establishment, where everything appertaining to the building and equipment of a fleet is constructed. It covers an area of 300 acres, and includes several large fitting and repairing basins with an aggregate area of 60 acres, besides four spacious dry-docks, and several building-slips, where men-of-war of the largest size are constructed. Among the many interesting sights may be noticed the machinery which supplies the whole navy with block-sheaves. The *Gun-Wharf* or arsenal, with its extensive stores of marine ordnance and ammunition, also deserves a visit (adm. 9.30-12 and 2-4). Adjoining the Dockyard is a *Convict Prison*, with space for 1300 inmates.

The **Church of St. Thomas Becket** (Pl. C, 4), in the High Street, is an interesting old building, said to have been originally built in the 13th cent.; it contains a monument to the second Duke of Buckingham, who was assassinated by Felton in a house at the head of the street, now marked 'Buckingham House' (on the E. side, just below the barracks). Charles II. was married on May 22nd, 1662, to Catharine of Braganza in the *Garrison Chapel*, which belonged to a religious institution founded in the time of Henry III. A *Roman Catholic Cathedral* (Pl. D, 3) has been built in Edinburgh Road. The house of *John Pounds*, the cobbler who founded the ragged-school system (1819), is in Oyster Street (Pl. C, 4).

The forts on the hills to the N. of Portsmouth should be visited for the sake of the views they afford of Hampshire and the Isle of Wight. A boat should also be hired for an excursion in the harbour, where a visit may be paid to the old 'Victory', Nelson's flag-ship at the battle of Trafalgar; and on Sunday divine service (10 a.m.) may be attended in the 'Wellington', the flag-ship of the Port Admiral. Off Southsea is a red buoy marking the spot where the 'Royal George' sank in 1782, with 'twice four hundred men'. Philanthropists will find it interesting to visit the *Soldiers' and Sailors' Institute*, founded by Miss Robinson, at the foot of High St. (Pl. C, 4).

Landport, to the E. of Portsea and Portsmouth and N. of Southsea, was the birthplace of *Charles Dickens* (1812), whose father was a clerk in the Dockyard. The *Town Railway Station* (Pl. E, 3) lies here, opposite the *Victoria Park*, formed on the glacis of the old fortifications.

Southsea (hotels, see p. 56), the S. suburb of Portsmouth, with an esplanade, a canoe lake (E. Southsea), two piers, and other attractions, is now a fashionable watering-place and decidedly the pleasantest of the joint towns for a prolonged stay. It is easily reached by tramway, or by the short new railway from Portsmouth Town to East Southsea. *Southsea Castle*, now converted into a modern fort, was built by Henry VIII.

Gosport (*India Arms*, *Star*, both unpretending), with about 8000 inhabitants, lies opposite Portsmouth, on the other side of the harbour (ferry, see p. 56). It contains the provision-magazines and bakehouses (*Royal Clarence Victualling Yard;* open to visitors under the same conditions as the Dockyard), which were formerly a part of Portsmouth Dockyard. The steam corn-mill alone cost more than 75,000*l*. The *Ship-Biscuit Machinery*, by which 2000 cwt. of biscuit can be baked in 1 hr., is extremely interesting. The government establishments here also include a clothes-making department, a brewery, etc., all on a most extensive scale. — A little to the S.E. of Gosport is *Haslar Hospital*, a spacious building, with accommodation for 2000 sick or wounded sailors. At the extremity of Haslar Point is the *Blockhouse Fort*, commanding the narrow entrance to Portsmouth Harbour. — To the W. of the Hospital is the small watering-place of *Anglesey* (Anglesey Hotel), forming an outlying suburb of Gosport. — *Stokes Bay* (stat., see p. 67) contains the 'measured mile' for testing the speed of new government steamships.

A pleasant excursion may be made to **Porchester** (by rail in 1/4 hr.), the earliest seaport on this inlet ('portus castra'). The **Castle*, founded by the Romans, affords an extensive view. The *Keep* is of Norman origin. The outer court is still surrounded by the ancient Roman walls. The church situated within the castle-walls was founded in 1133; some remains of the original Norman edifice are still *in situ*.

Railway from Portsmouth or Gosport to Southampton, 26 M., in 1 hr. (fares 4*s*. 6*d*., 3*s*., 2*s*. 3*d*.). Steamboat from Portsmouth to Southampton in 1 1/2 hr., preferable in fine weather (fares 3*s*. and 2*s*. 6*d*.). — Scenery between Portsmouth and Southampton attractive.

After quitting the island of Portsea, the train skirts the base of Portsdown Hill. 7 M. *Porchester*, see above. To the right, on the top of of the hill, stands *Nelson's Monument*, erected by his comrades at the Battle of Trafalgar, a useful landmark for shipping.

9 M. **Fareham** *(Red Lion)*, a busy little town, is the station for (2½ M.) *Titchfield* (omn. twice daily), which possesses a handsome Early English church and the remains of *Titchfield House*, erected in the 16th cent. for the Earl of Southampton. An omnibus also runs from Fareham to *Lee-on-the-Solent* (Hotels), a small seaside resort of recent origin, with an iron pier. *Boarhunt*, 3 M. to the N.E. of Fareham, has a partly pre-Norman church. A new line from Fareham to *Netley* (p. 82) affords an alternative route to Southampton. — The train now passes through a tunnel 600 yds. in length, and shortly afterwards another, about 200 yds. long. Near *Botley* the line crosses the small river *Hamble*. About 6 M. to the E. lies *Bishop's Waltham* (branch-line), with the ruined castle of the Bishops of Winchester.

20 M. *Bishopstoke*, pleasantly situated on the *Itchen*, is the junction for the lines to Winchester and Salisbury. The train here turns sharply to the S., and soon reaches (26 M.) *Southampton* (see p. 80).

8. From London to Dorking and Guildford.

South Eastern Railway to (30½ M.) *Dorking* in 1¼-1½ hr. (fares 4*s.*, 3*s.*, 2*s.* 1*d.*); to (43 M.) *Guildford* in 1¾-2¼ hrs. (fares 5*s.*, 3*s.* 6*d.*, 2*s.* 6*d.*). The trains start from *Charing Cross*, *Cannon Street*, and *London Bridge*.

[The shortest route to *Dorking* is by the London, Brighton, and South Coast Railway from *London Bridge* and *Victoria* (25 M. from London Bridge, 23½ M. from Victoria, in 1 hr. 7 min. to 1¾ hr.; fares as above); and the most direct route to *Guildford* is by the South Western Railway, described at p. 64 (31 M., in ¾-1½ hr.; fares as above).]

From (5 M.) *New Cross* (pp. 12, 32) to (22¼ M.) *Redhill Junction*, the line coincides with the L. B. S. C. railway to Brighton (R. 6). At Redhill the Reading, Guildford, and Reigate Branch of the S. E. R. diverges to the right.

24 M. **Reigate** *(White Hart*, well spoken of; *Crown)*, a pleasant-looking old town with 19,000 inhab., lying in the midst of very attractive scenery, is a favourite residence of London merchants. 'Reigate Sand' is much in request for florists and glass-makers. Below the remains of the old *Castle* is the *Barons' Cave*, in which, according to a baseless tradition, the barons met to concert the terms of Magna Charta. The castle grounds are prettily laid out. The *Parish Church*, restored by Sir G. G. Scott, contains curious monuments and some early pillars in the nave.

To the S. of the town are *Reigate Priory* (Lady Henry Somerset), with pleasant grounds, and *Reigate Park*, commanding a beautiful view. — To the W., on the way to Dorking, lies *Reigate Heath*, a pleasant spot for a ramble. — From (1½ M.) *Reigate Hill*, to the N. of the town, is obtained a charming *View of the Weald of Sussex, enclosed between the North and South Downs. The descent may be made on the N. side to (1½ M.) *Gatton* (p. 46). — Pedestrians will find themselves repaid by walking from Reigate to (6 M.) *Dorking* (p. 60), either by the high-road across Reigate Heath (see above) and through Betchworth, or by following the ridge of the North Downs to Box Hill (p. 60) and then descending to the left.

Beyond Reigate the train continues to skirt the S. base of the *North Downs*. 27 M. *Betchworth*, a pretty village on the *Mole*, the banks of which between this and Dorking are very picturesque.

For a coloured map of The Environs of Dorking & Guildford see page 562

Betchworth Park lies $1^1/_2$ M. farther to the W., and may be crossed by those approaching Dorking on foot. — $29^1/_2$ M. *Boxhill* lies at the foot of the hill (590 ft.) so named from the box-plants with which it is covered. The top of the hill is easily reached and commands a charming view. The descent may be made on the W. side to *Burford Bridge*, with a good inn, in which Keats wrote his 'Endymion' (room shown).

$30^1/_2$ M. **Dorking** (*White Horse*, R. & A. 4*s*.; *Red Lion*, High St.; *Star & Garter*, near the L. B. S. C. station; **Burford Bridge Hotel*, 1 M. to the N., see above, better than the Dorking inns for any stay), an old-fashioned little town with 6330 inhab., is delightfully situated in a valley at the foot of the *North Downs*, amid some of the most pleasing scenery in England. It is an admirable centre for the pedestrian, who will find charming walks in all directions. The five-toed breed of fowls that takes its name from this place is well-known to poultry-fanciers. Others will know the name from the 'Battle of Dorking', a clever little book by Col. Chesney, who depicts the imaginary overthrow here of the British forces by the invading Teuton. The old custom of playing football in the streets of the town on Shrove Tuesday is still kept up.

The only object of special interest in the town itself is the handsome modern *Church of St. Martin*, with a lofty spire erected as a memorial of Bishop Wilberforce. The large house on the hill opposite, beyond the railway, is *Denbies*, the seat of Geo. Cubitt, Esq., M.P.

To the E. of the town lies the ***Deepdene**, the lovely country-seat of Lord Clinton, containing a fine gallery of pictures and sculptures, including works by Raphael, Correggio, Veronese, Rubens, Reynolds, Beechey, Lawrence, Martin ('Fall of Babylon'), Thorvaldsen, and Flaxman, and also collections of enamels, gems, and other objects of art (not shown). The **Grounds*, including the beautifully-kept Italian gardens and one of the finest shows of rhododendrons and tulips in England, are always open to the public (10-4). In the preface to 'Coningsby', Disraeli records that the work 'was conceived and partly executed amid the glades and galleries of the Deepdene'. One of the finest points of the park is the group of Scottish firs known as the '*Glory*'. The Deepdene is adjoined on the E. by **Betchworth Park*, also belonging to Lord Clinton, with some noble chestnut trees and a famous avenue of limes.

Environs (comp. Map, p. 64). The neighbourhood of Dorking is so rich in pleasant walks and drives that it is impossible to do more than indicate a few of the most attractive. The pedestrian will often feel surprised at the comparative wildness and solitude of the scenery, and will find it difficult to realize that he is within so short a distance of London. The farm-houses near Dorking, and in Surrey generally, are often extremely picturesque.

Travellers bound for Guildford (12 M.) are recommended to leave the railway at Dorking and perform the rest of the journey on foot. The most attractive direct route leads along the ridge of the *North Downs*, coinciding to some extent with the old Pilgrims' Way to Canterbury (p. 25) and affording a constant series of delightful views. The following round (18-20 M.), preferable to the direct route from Dorking to Gomshall, gives as good an idea of the varied scenery in this district as can be obtained in a day.

FROM DORKING TO GUILDFORD VIÂ LEITH HILL, a walk of 18-20 M. We leave the town by South Street, and in 5 min. reach a bifurcation, where we follow the right branch, leading to Coldharbour. We turn again to the left almost immediately, and reach a finger-post indicating our way to Coldharbour. We keep straight up the hill, and at (6 min.) the top choose the right branch of the road. 3 min. Entrance to *Bury Hill Park Farm*, with a 'No Footpath' board. About 1 M. farther on, the road, here running between lofty banks of sand, enters *Redlands Wood*, apparently so called from the colour of the soil. At (1½ M.) some cottages, a lane to the left leads to *Anstiebury Camp*, while our road descends to the right to the pretty village of *Coldharbour* (Plough Inn), where the rugged E. escarpment of Coldharbour Common rises to the right. Beyond Coldharbour it is better to avoid the steep road ascending to the right and to follow the level road in a straight direction, which leads through a succession of beautiful trees. (A branch to the left leads to the white gate of *Kitlands*, with its fine woods, which are open to the public.) We keep to the right, pass the church and vicarage (left), and reach (4 min.) a gate across the road. In ½ M. more we reach a second gate, where we find ourselves just below the tower on Leith Hill, to which we may ascend either by the direct but very steep path (5 min.), or by making a detour to the right. The *View from **Leith Hill** (965 ft.; tower generally open after 12, adm. 1*d.*) is beautiful and extensive, reaching in clear weather from the South Downs and the English Channel on the S. to the dome of St. Paul's on the N. It is said that 12 or 13 counties are visible. So many paths radiate from the heath-clad top of Leith Hill that it is practically impossible to give accurate directions for the next part of the route. With the aid of the Ordnance Map and a pocket compass we shall probably find little difficulty in descending across Wotton Common and through the woods, in a direction a little to the W. of N., to the Swiss-looking little village of (½ hr.) *Friday Street* ('street or way of Friga'), picturesquely situated among trees on a large pond. A path along the E. bank of the stream descends hence to (1 M.) **Wotton House**, the home of *John Evelyn* (d. 1706), the Diarist and author of 'Sylva', to whose love for trees, inherited by his descendants, is owing much of the rich variety of the woods in the district. The house, an extensive red edifice (no admission), contains the MS. of Evelyn's Diary, the prayer-book used by Charles I. at his execution, and other relics; it is now occupied by W. J. Evelyn, Esq., a collateral descendant of the Diarist. There is a pleasing account of a visit to Wotton House in '*Passages from the English Note-Books of Nathaniel Hawthorne*' (Vol. I, p. 399; Boston, 1870). The path keeps to the right of the house and debouches on a private road, which we follow to the left, passing the front gate of Wotton House. At the (5 min.) lodge-gate we may turn either to the right to reach the high-road from Guildford to Dorking, or to the left (better), crossing the stream and taking a path to the right through the wood. On leaving the wood (½ M.) we follow the road to the right for a little and then take a field-path to the left, which joins the high-road at a (¼ M.) cottage known as *Evershed's*. [A little to the E. is the picturesque *Crossways Farm.*] Continuing our way to Guildford, we follow the high-road to (½ M.) *Abinger Hammer* and (½ M.) *Gomshall* (p. 62), where those who are fatigued may rejoin the railway. Beyond Gomshall we soon reach (1 M.) *Shere* (p. 62), on quitting which (at the sign-post) we choose the upper road to the right, leaving *Albury* (p. 62) below us to the left. (Another short digression may be made from the cross-roads to the *Silent Pool*, lying a little to the right of the road; key kept at an adjoining cottage.) This road ascends the *Albury Downs* to (1 M.) **Newlands Corner*, a spot famous for the beautiful view it commands. A finger-post here indicates our way to Guildford across the short turf of the Downs (fine views), passing several ancient yews. The *Church of St. Martha* (see below) is a conspicuous object to the left, on the other side of the valley, along which the pilgrims' path is supposed to have run. After 1 M. we reach a road, which we follow, to the right, to (1/2 M) a finger-post, where we take the field-path leading in a straight direction to (1/2 M.) *Guildford* (see below).

To the N. a pleasant walk may be taken from Dorking past *Denbies* (p. 60) and across *Ranmore Common* to (6 M.) *Leatherhead* (see below). The church of Ranmore is a modern edifice by Sir G. G. Scott, with a spire conspicuous in many views of the district. — About 2 1/2 M. to the N. by the London road is *Mickleham*, where Madame d'Arblay (Fanny Burney) lived and wrote at *Camilla Lacey*, a house named after one of her novels; her husband was one of a little colony of French refugees settled in the neighbouring *Juniper Hall*. The excursion to Mickleham may be easily combined with an ascent of *Boxhill* (p. 60) and may be extended across *Norbury Park* (fine yews in the 'Druids' Walk') to *Leatherhead* (see below). — The walk from Dorking to (6 M.) *Reigate* through Betchworth Park and Betchworth has been mentioned at p. 59.

The direct line of the London, Brighton, and South Coast Railway to Dorking (see p. 59) also traverses a beautiful district. The principal stations are (8 1/2 M. from Victoria) *Mitcham*, (12 M.) *Sutton*, (16 M.) *Epsom* (see *Baedeker's London*), and (20 M.) **Leatherhead** (*Swan; Duke's Head*), pleasantly situated on the right bank of the *Mole* (see also above). The last station before (23 1/2 M.) Dorking is (22 1/2 M.) *Boxhill & Burford Bridge* (comp. p. 60; not to be confounded with the Boxhill stat. of the S.E.R.).

The train still follows the line of the hills, with a pretty wooded country to the right. — 35 M. *Gomshall* is the station for the villages of *Gomshall* (Black Horse) and *Shere* (White Horse), the latter a charming little place, 1 M. to the W. of the station, with a picturesque church and a timber-built parsonage. About 2 1/2 M. to the S. E. of the station is *Abinger* (Abinger Hatch), a small village with an interesting and very early church and the old stocks and whipping-post. Gomshall is also the nearest station to (2 1/4 M.) *Wotton* (p. 61).

Beyond Gomshall the line bends to the left (S.), passing to the S. of *Albury Park*. 38 1/2 M. *Chilworth* is the station for *Albury*, a village about 1 M. to the N. E., the most prominent feature in which is the large *Irvingite Church* in the Perp. style, built by the late Mr. Drummond. The old *Church*, said to be the most ancient in the county, has been converted into a mortuary chapel (no adm.). Both churches are in *Albury Park*, which now belongs to the Duke of Northumberland, son-in-law of Mr. Drummond. Mr. Martin Tupper (d. 1889), of 'Proverbial Philosophy' fame, lived at Albury.

The village of *Chilworth*, a little to the W. of the station, is the best starting-point for a visit to (1/2 hr.) **St. Martha's Church**, which occupies an isolated and conspicuous position on the hill above it. This interesting Norman edifice is supposed to have been erected for the use of pilgrims on their way to Canterbury; and a trace of its old purpose remains in the quasi-pilgrimage still made to it on Good Friday by the people of the neighbourhood. The *View from the church is very extensive.

Beyond (40 1/2 M.) *Shalford* the train crosses the Wey, turns to the right through a tunnel, and reaches —

43 M. **Guildford** (*White Lion; White Hart; Angel; Rail. Refreshmt. Rooms*), the county-town of Surrey, with about 12,000 inhab., pleasantly situated on the *Wey*, and well deserving Cob-

bett's description of it as the most 'happy-looking' town he ever saw. It consists chiefly of one main street, many of the buildings in which are most quaint and picturesque. Guildford is a place of great antiquity, its records extending back to the 10th cent., while there is also some reason to think that there was a Roman station on the same site. According to some historians the massacre here in 1036 of the Norman attendants of Alfred the Atheling, was among the chief links in the chain of events leading to Duke William's invasion of England. The town was formerly the centre of a considerable cloth-making industry, and its corn-market is still one of the most important in the S. of England.

The most prominent building is the keep of the old Norman Castle, which stands a little to the S. of the High St., rising to a height of 70 ft., with walls 10 ft. in thickness; the grounds are now a public garden. Below the castle are large caverns in the chalk, which are supposed to have been connected with the crypt under the Angel Hotel. — Near the top of the High St., on the N. side, is Archbishop Abbot's Hospital, a picturesque Tudor building founded in 1619 for decayed tradesmen and their widows. It contains some interesting portraits (Wycliffe, Calvin, etc.) and two good stained-glass windows (in the chapel). — Opposite the hospital is *Trinity Church*, with monument to Archbp. Abbot (d. 1633; in the S. aisle), who was born at Guildford, and Speaker Onslow. — The *Church of St. Mary*, in Quarry St., to the S. of High St., is more interesting, dating in great part from the Norman period. Visitors should notice the grotesque carvings of the roof and the paintings in the Baptist's Chapel, attributed to William of Florence (ca. 1250).

Other more or less noteworthy buildings are the *Guildhall* (High St.), a brick and timber edifice of 1682, with some historical portraits; the *Grammar School*, at the head of the High St., dating from the 16th cent.; and the *Royal Surrey County Hospital*, on the Farnham Road, near the railway-station.

Guildford is a railway-centre of some importance, being the junction of the Reading and Reigate branch of the S. E. R. with the line of the S. W. R. to Portsmouth and Farnham (see p. 66) and the L. B. S. C. line to Horsham (p. 53).

Environs. Visitors to Guildford had better begin their excursions by an ascent of *St. Catharine's Hill*, a small height 1¼ M. to the S., between the high-road and the river, commanding a good view of the surrounding district. At the top is a small ruined chapel, dating from the beginning of the 14th century. — This walk may be made part of a pleasant round of about 6-7 M. by proceeding to the S.W., viâ *Arlington* and *Littleton*, to (2 M.) *Loseley*, a fine Elizabethan mansion (no admission) in a well-wooded park. Hence we keep due W. to (1 M.) the village of *Compton*, with a very interesting Norman church, with an almost unique double-storied chancel. From Compton we ascend to the top of the (1 M.) *Hog's Back* (p. 64) and follow the ridge eastwards (views) back to (1½ M.) Guildford.

To reach (2½ M.) **St. Martha's Church** (see p. 62) from Guildford, we leave the town by Quarry St. and the Portsmouth (S.) road, and on passing the (½ M.) old toll-house, near *Shalford Park*, take the shady lane to the left. Near the end of the lane we follow a footpath to the right, crossing a small plantation of firs, and reach a cottage at the foot of *Chantry Downs*, along which lies the rest of our route. To vary the return-route we may descend the N.E. side of St Martha's Hill and make for (1½ M.) *Newlands Corner* (p. 61), whence we follow the ridge to (2¾ M.) Guildford as described at pp. 61, 62.

A breezy walk of 10 M., with unimpeded views on either side, may be enjoyed by following the road which leads along the curious chalk ridge called the *Hog's Back* (350-500 ft.) to *Farnham* (p. 75). On reaching (8 M.) the end of the ridge, *Waverley Abbey* (p. 66) may be included in the walk by a digression of 1½ M. to the S. (in all 11½ M.). — Other points of interest within easy walking distance of Guildford are **Sutton Place* (3½ M. to the N.), a Renaissance mansion of the Tudor period, with highly interesting terracotta decorations; *Clandon Park*, 2 M. to the N.E., on the road to (12 M.) *Leatherhead* (p. 62); and *Godalming* (p. 65), 4 M. to the S. A favourite excursion is the ascent of the *Hindhead* (p. 66), 12 M to the S.W., but this is usually accomplished by taking the train to *Haslemere* (p. 65).

From Guildford this branch of the S. E. R. is continued to *Ash* (the junction of a short branch to *Aldershot Town*), *Aldershot* (N. Camp.; comp. p. 75), *Farnborough* (p. 76), *Blackwater* (the station for *Sandhurst Military College*), *Wellington College* (a well known public school), *Wokingham*, *Earley*, and (67 M.) *Reading* (see p. 106).

9. From London to Portsmouth.

74 M. London and South Western Railway from *Waterloo* in 2½-3 hrs. (fares 15*s*., 10*s*. 6*d*., 6*s*. 1½*d*.). — This is the direct route, but Portsmouth may also be reached by the London, Brighton, and South Coast Railway, viâ *Ford Junction* (comp. p. 53), from *London Bridge* and *Victoria* (same times and fares).

The train runs at first on a viaduct above the streets of London. *Vauxhall*, the first station, is still within the town; but we emerge into the country near (4½ M.) *Clapham Junction*, through which 1200 trains pass daily. The first glimpse of the pretty scenery traversed by the line is obtained after passing through the long cutting beyond that station. The landscape, bordered on the N. by gently-sloping hills, and dotted with groups of trees and numerous comfortable-looking country-houses, affords a charming and thoroughly English picture. — 7½ M. *Wimbledon* lies a little to the S. of *Wimbledon Common*, a favourite golfing-ground for Londoners and formerly the scene of the annual meeting of the National Rifle Association (comp. p. 75). Beyond Wimbledon a line diverges to *Epsom* (see *Baedeker's London*). Near (10 M.) *Coombe-Malden*, to the right, is *Coombe House*. About 2 M. beyond (12 M.) *Surbiton* the branch-line to *Hampton Court* (see *Baedeker's London*) diverges on the right. — 14½ M. *Esher* (Bear), a picturesque village, celebrated in the verse of Pope and Thomson. *Esher Place*, once the palace of Cardinal Wolsey, has been rebuilt. In the vicinity stands *Claremont*, at one time the property of Lord Clive, inhabited at a later period by the Princess Charlotte (who died here in 1817) and her husband, Leopold, late King of the Belgians. It was afterwards assigned as a residence to Louis Philippe and his wife, both of whom died here, and is now occupied by the Duchess of Albany. The Sandown Races are run near Esher. — 17 M. *Walton* is the station for *Walton-on-Thames*, 1 M. to the N. (p. 222).

19 M. **Weybridge** (*Hand & Spear; Lincoln Arms; *Oatlands Park*, see below), prettily situated near the Thames, 1 M. from the station. The Roman Catholic church formerly contained the remains of Louis Philippe, King of France, his consort, and his daughter-in-law the Duchess of Orleans, which were removed to France in 1876. To the N. is *Oatlands Park*, formerly a royal demesne, and afterwards the property of the Duke of Newcastle. The house, rebuilt in 1794, is now a favourite hotel. In the neighbourhood rises **St. George's Hill* (500 ft.), commanding a beautiful view, which includes on the N. Windsor Castle and Hampton Court. A little farther on, a branch diverges to *Addlestone*, *Chertsey*, and *Virginia Water* (see *Baedeker's London*).

$24^1/_2$ M. **Woking** (*Albion*, *Railway Hotel*, near the station; *White Hart*, in the village, $1^1/_2$ M. to the S.; *Rail. Refreshmt. Rooms)*, where our line diverges from the line to Basingstoke (Winchester, Southampton; see p. 75). The floriculturist should visit **Waterer's Nursery* at *Knaphill* ($2^1/_2$ M.; turning to the left at the station), especially in June, when the rhododendrons are in bloom. The old church, in the E.E. and Dec. styles, was restored in 1878. The ruins of *Newark Abbey* lie on the *Wey*, $2^1/_2$ M. to the E. of Woking. *Woking Cemetery*, see p. 75.

The Guildford and Portsmouth line now turns to the left and runs due S. — 31 M. *Guildford*, see p. 62. — The train then passes through a tunnel and soon reaches —

35 M. **Godalming** (*King's Arms; Angel)*, a quaint little country-town (accent on the first syllable), with many old-fashioned timber-houses (17th cent.). The *Church* near the station is a large building with a Norman tower. On the hill to the N. is the imposing new building of the *Charterhouse School*, removed from London to Godalming in 1872; it has room for 500 boys. The library contains the MS. of 'The Newcomes' by Thackeray and many of the original 'Punch' drawings by Leech, both novelist and artist having been educated at the Charterhouse. The country round Godalming affords abundance of charming walks. — $36^1/_2$ M. *Milford;* $38^1/_2$ M. *Witley*, with an E. E. church containing some brasses.

43 M. **Haslemere** (*White Horse*, R. & A. 3*s.* 6*d.*; *Railway Inn)* is the best starting-point for a visit to Blackdown and the Hindhead, two fine points of view, and the centre of a district that has become classic as the residence of many celebrities in literature and art. Among these are George Eliot, who lived at Brookbank in *Shotter Mill*, a little to the W. of the station, and Tennyson, who has built himself a house (Aldworth) on the S. side of *Blackdown Hill*, which rises about 2 M. to the S.

From Haslemere to the Hindhead, $2^1/_2$ M. On leaving the station we turn to the left, soon afterwards turning to the left again, crossing the railway, and passing to the right of the church. At the ($^1/_2$ M.) bifurcation we descend to the left, passing a red, gabled house. The long dark ridge of the Hindhead is now in full view ahead of us. In 5 min. more we reach a gate on the left, leading to a villa, the garden of which we cross. Beyond the villa we go diagonally across the field to the right, on the other side of which is a cart-track ascending the hill (to the left). After following this track for 10-12 min. and passing through half-a-dozen gates, we reach the open common near some cottages. To reach Gibbet Hill, the W. extremity and the highest part of the Hindhead, we ascend to the right, the track to it leading nearly straight across the moor. [Another route leads at once under the railway, to the right (S.) of the station, and turns to the right a little way up the hill. The lane thus entered runs right up to (2 M.) the Hindhead.] The highest point of the **Hindhead** (903 ft.), marked by a granite cross, commands a most beautiful and extensive view, including the Hampshire Downs on the S. W. and Leith Hill (p. 61) on the E. The cross and the name *(Gibbet Hill)* attached to this spot commemorate the murder of a sailor in 1786 at a point (marked by a stone) on the old Portsmouth road, on the N. side of the hill, and the fact that the murderers were afterwards captured and hanged on the scene of their crime. The romantic and lonely hollow round which the road here runs, mentioned by Dickens in 'Nicholas Nickleby', is called the **Devil's Punch Bowl;* and the tourist should make his way along it, either by the old coach-road or by the road on the ridge of the Hindhead, to the W., to ($^3/_4$ M.) the *Huts Hotel*, which lies a little beyond the point where the roads meet.

From the Hindhead to Farnham viâ Frensham Ponds and Waverley Abbey, 9-10 M. Tolerable walkers, who do not wish to return to Haslemere, may extend the Hindhead excursion very agreeably as follows. From the Royal Huts Inn we follow the Farnham road to the N. W. and after $^1/_3$ M. diverge from it to the left by the road indicated by the sign-post as leading to Churt and Frensham. This leads across a wide expanse of moor to *Churt* and (4 M.) *Frensham Great Pond*, a small lake in the middle of Frensham Common, a sandy heath, with three curiously-shaped mounds known as the *Devil's Jumps*. We keep to the road, which skirts the E. (right) side of the pond. At the ($^1/_2$ M.) cross-roads, where there is a school, we keep to the right, soon reaching ($^1/_4$ M.) a bridge over the *Wey*. To the right is *Pierrepont House*, a pleasing example of Norman Shaw's modern-antique style. Ascending the hill for a few minutes more, we reach *Millbridge*, where we keep straight on if bound for Farnham direct ($3^1/_2$ M.), or turn to the right at the post-office if going to Waverley Abbey. In the latter case we turn to the left at ($1^1/_4$ M.) *Tilford*, and after $^1/_3$ M. more to the right. $^1/_4$ M. Bridge, where we keep straight on up the hill. At the (5 min.) top we diverge to the left and follow the cart-track through the wood, which rejoins the road $^1/_2$ M. farther on, a little above the entrance to *Waverley Abbey*, to which visitors are admitted on application to the lodge-keeper. The remains of this Cistercian monastery, of the 12th cent., which is said to have suggested to Walter Scott the title of his first novel, are fragmentary, but they are very prettily situated on the bank of the Wey. — Waverley Abbey is 2 M. from Farnham by the direct road. — *Farnham*, see p. 75.

Beyond Haslemere are (47 M.) *Liphook* (Royal Anchor) and ($51^1/_2$ M.) *Liss* (Spread Eagle), both good centres for pedestrians.

About 5 M. to the N.W. of Liss is **Selborne** *(Queen)*, the home of Gilbert White (d. 1793), who has left a full and loving description of the district in his 'Natural History of Selborne'. Walkers to Selborne may go on to (5 M.) *Alton* (Swan), a station on the Aldershot, Farnham, and Winchester branch of the S. W. Railway.

55 M. **Petersfield** *(Red Lion; Dolphin)*, a small town with 6500 inhab. and a large grammar-school, is the junction of a branch-line to ($9^1/_2$ M.) *Midhurst* (Angel), a place frequently visited for

the sake of the fine ruins of **Cowdray*, a magnificent 16th cent. mansion, burned down in 1793.

Beyond Petersfield the train penetrates the chalky South Downs by a tunnel, passes ($63\frac{1}{2}$ M.) *Rowland's Castle*, and reaches (66 M.) *Havant*. — Thence to (74 M.) *Portsmouth*, see R. 7.

10. Isle of Wight.

Railway from London (*South Western Railway* from Waterloo Station, comp. R. 9; or *London, Brighton, and South Coast Railway* from Victoria or London Bridge, see R. 7) to Portsmouth Harbour in $2\frac{1}{2}$-4 hrs. (fares 15*s.* 6*d*, 10*s.* 10*d.*, 6*s.* 2*d.*); to Ryde, Isle of Wight, in 3-5 hrs. (fares 17*s.* 1*d.*, 12*s.*, 7*s.* 4*d.*; return, available for a month, 29*s.* 11*d.*, 21*s.* 4*d.*, 14*s.* 1*d.*). Another direct route from London to the Isle of Wight is by the *South Western Railway* to *Stokes Bay*, to the W. of Portsmouth, and thence by steamer in $\frac{1}{4}$ hr. to Ryde (same time and fares). Through-tickets viâ Stokes Bay are also available viâ Portsmouth. — Steamboat from Portsmouth to *Ryde* in 25 min., at frequent intervals during the day, fares 1*s.* and 8*d.*; return-fares 1*s.* 6*d.*, 1*s.* Steamers from *Southampton*, see p. 74; from *Lymington*, p. 73. Steamers also ply from Portsmouth and Southsea to *Sea View* and *Bembridge* in 1-$1\frac{1}{4}$ hr.

In favourable weather the finest points of the island may be visited in Three Days: — 1st Day. From Ryde to Shanklin by rail (fares 2*s.*, 1*s.* 4*d.*, 7*d.*) in 25 min.; thence on foot to Shanklin Chine, and to Ventnor viâ Bonchurch, in $1\frac{1}{2}$ hr.; in the afternoon to Blackgang and back in $4\frac{1}{2}$ hrs. by coach (comp. p. 70). — 2nd Day. From Ventnor to Freshwater and Alum Bay by coach in $3\frac{1}{2}$ hrs., visiting the Needles, and returning by coach to Freshwater (fare about 7*s.*); from Freshwater to Newport by train in $\frac{3}{4}$ hr. — 3rd Day. Excursions from Newport; from Newport to Cowes, rail in $\frac{1}{4}$ hr. — Alternative routes for the second and third days: — 2nd Day. From Ventnor to Newport (10 M.) by coach (p. 70); excursions from Newport. — 3rd Day. From Newport to Yarmouth and Freshwater by train (p. 73), in $\frac{3}{4}$ hr., visiting Alum Bay and the Needles; in the afternoon back to Newport, and thence to Cowes. — Three days spent in this manner will show the chief beauties of the island, but those who have time to spare will prefer to spend at least 7-10 days here. — To see as much as possible in One Day, take an early train from Ryde to Ventnor, arriving at the latter place in time for the coach (10 a.m.) to Freshwater and Alum Bay, and back to Freshwater (as above); in the afternoon proceed by train from Freshwater to Newport, and visit Carisbrooke Castle; then to Ryde or Cowes by late train. — Two Days: — 1st Day. From Ryde to Newport by train; to Carisbrooke Castle on foot; from Newport to Shanklin by rail; from Shanklin to Ventnor on foot; spend night at Ventnor. — 2nd Day. Coach (as above) to Freshwater and Alum Bay (visiting the Needles), and back to Freshwater; train from Freshwater to Newport; railway to Cowes; steamboat to Portsmouth or Southampton.

The fares of the Isle of Wight railway are very high, and third-class carriages are generally provided only on one or two trains daily, running at an inconveniently early hour. As, however, the distances are short, the traveller will find that the numerous coaches, supplemented by a little walking, will make him comparatively independent of the railway. — In the height of the season the island is crowded with visitors, and accommodation is often difficult to obtain unless previously ordered.

A trip round the island (occupying 5-7 hrs.), for which an opportunity is usually afforded thrice a week in summer by steamers from Ryde and Cowes, is very pleasant in fine weather.

The ***Isle of Wight,** the *Vectis* of the Romans, lying from 3 to 6 M. distant from the S. coast of England, contains within a com-

For a coloured map of The Isle of Wight see page 563

paratively narrow compass a remarkable variety of charming scenery. In circumference it measures about 65 M.; from E. to W. it is 22 M. long, and from N. to S. 13 M. broad. Pop. (1881) 73,652. The highest points are St. Catherine's Hill (p. 71) to the S.W., which is 830 ft. high, and Shanklin Down to the S.E., 795 ft. in height. The Undercliff on the S., and Alum Bay and Freshwater Cliffs on the W. are the finest points.

Ryde. — *PIER HOTEL, R. & A. from 4*s.* 6*d.*, D. 5*s.*; *ESPLANADE; SIVIER'S; EAGLE, all on the beach, with a fine view. In Union Street, reached by turning to the right at the end of the pier, and then taking the first street to the left: KENT; YELF'S. All these are first-class hotels, the Pier and the Esplanade being the most expensive: R. & A. 4*s.* 6*d.*, D. 3*s.* 6*d.* to 5*s.* — Higher up (beyond Yelf's), about 1/3 M. from the Pier, CROWN, R. & A. 3*s.* 6*d.*, commercial. — **Young's Restaurant*, 30 Union Street; *Albany*, on the Esplanade. — Private lodgings not exorbitant. — *Post Office*, Union Street. — *Regattas* in Aug. and Sept. — *Theatre*, at the top of Union St. — *Baths* at the end of the short pier (adm. 6*d.*).

The railway at Ryde runs out to the end of the pier (*Pier Head Station*), and travellers with through-tickets to Ryde are conveyed without extra charge to the *Pier Gates* or *St. John's Road* (town) stations. Passengers for other parts of the island are taken on without change of carriage.

Coaches run from Ryde in summer to Ventnor, Shanklin, Osborne, Newport, and other places of interest.

Ryde, an agreeable and thriving watering-place (11,422 inhab.), surrounded by numberless villas, affords many pleasant walks. The *Promenade Pier* (adm. 2*d.*), 1/2 M. in length, is a favourite and fashionable promenade (*Restaurant); along one side run an electric tramway-line and the pier railway (see above). The *Museum*, in George St., contains objects of local interest. To the W. of the pier is the building of the *Royal Victoria Yacht Club*. To the S.E. of Ryde lie a number of picturesque country-seats, and the pleasant villages of *Spring Vale*, *Sea View* (Crown), with a long pier (steamers to Portsmouth), and *St. Helen's* (p. 69). The surrounding district is finely wooded.

To QUARR ABBEY AND FISHBOURNE, a pleasant walk of 2 hrs. (there and back). Starting from the Crown Hotel, we descend Thomas Street to the N., and take the first turning to the left (Spencer Road; over one of the gates in which we observe the figure of a stag); we then walk straight on till we reach (10 min.) a small gate. To the right, on the other side, is a second gate, opening on a footpath, which leads in 10 min. to *Binstead Church*. The figure of a man on a ram's head over the gateway here is said to have been a Saxon idol. We next turn to the right, and reach a point where we see a road on the left, a narrow wood-path on the right, and another road between the two. We take the last or intermediate track, arriving after a few paces opposite the gate of a private dwelling, where we take the path to the left. Emerging from this on to the high-road we turn to the right, and in 10 min. reach the inconsiderable, but prettily-situated ruin of ***Quarr Abbey**, an old Cistercian monastery, founded in 1132. The name is derived from the neighbouring quarries, which are rich in fossils and much visited by geologists. — From the ruin we proceed in a straight direction, passing through the gate and archway, to (1/4 hr.) **Fishbourne** or *Fishhouse* (Inn, well spoken of), picturesquely situated amid luxuriant wood at the entrance of *Wootton Creek*. Charming view. We return to Ryde by the same road.

FROM RYDE TO NEWPORT. The direct railway route is by *Smallbrook*, *Ashey*, *Haven Street*, *Wootton*, and *Whippingham* (20-25 min.; fares 2*s.*, 1*s.* 5*d.*, 1*s.* or 8 1/2*d.*; comp. Map). Whippingham is the station for

Osborne (see p. 75). In *Whippingham Church*, designed by the late Prince Consort, the Princess Beatrice was married to Prince Henry of Battenberg, in 1885. It contains a medallion of the Prince Consort by Theed and a font designed by Princesses Christian and Louise. The Queen attends the service here when she is residing at Osborne. — Newport may also be reached by railway from Ryde or Ventnor viâ *Sandown* (see below).

From Ryde to Ventnor, 12 M., railway in 1/2-3/4 hr. (fares from St. John's Road 3*s.*, 2*s.*, 11 1/2*d.*, from the Pier Head 4*s.*, 2*s.* 10*d.*, 1*s.* 4 1/2*d.*). — From the *Pier Head* the train runs along the pier, stopping at the *Pier Gates* at its landward end, to *St. John's Road*, in the upper part of the town of Ryde. The railway then runs S. to (4 M. from St. John's Road) **Brading** *(Bugle; Wheatsheaf)*, a small and ancient town at the foot of *Brading Down*. The ancient stocks and bull-baiting ring are still preserved here. The *Church* contains the burial-chapel of the *Oglanders*, a family which came over to England with William the Conqueror; their ancestral seat of *Nunwell*, in the midst of a handsome park, is in the neighbourhood. Near Brading the remains of a large *Roman Villa, with tesselated floors, were discovered in 1880; it is supposed to have been the residence of the Roman governor of the district. A series of Roman coins (A.D. 222-350), numerous tiles, window-glass, and a human skeleton have been found among the ruins.

A branch-line runs from Brading to *St. Helen's* and (3 M.) *Bembridge*, at the mouth of *Brading Harbour* or estuary of the *Yar*, part of which has lately been reclaimed. **Bembridge** *(Royal Spithead Hotel)* is frequented for sea-bathing and has direct steamboat communication with Portsmouth (see p. 67). Adjoining it are excellent golfing links. — About 1 M. to the S.E. of Brading, at the foot of *Bembridge Down* (355 ft.), is the church of *Yaverland*, with a Norman door and chancel-arch. Towards the sea Bembridge Down ends in the fine *Culver Cliffs*.

6 M. **Sandown** (*Sandown Hotel; Pier; King's Head; York*, well spoken of, R. & A. 4*s.*), the junction for *Newchurch*, *Horringford*, and *Newport* (p. 72), a thriving town and frequented bathing-place with 3100 inhab., a pier, and an esplanade.

8 1/2 M. **Shanklin.** — *Daish's, in the town, with pleasant garden; *Hollier's; *Hinton's Royal Spa, on the Esplanade; Marine Hotel, near the station; Clarendon. — Numerous boarding-houses on the Esplanade.

Coaches ply from Shanklin to Blackgang, Carisbrooke, and Newport, to Cowes and Osborne, and to Freshwater and Alum Bay. — **Cab** from the station to the village or cliffs, for 1-2 pers., with one horse 1*s.*, with two horses 1*s.* 6*d.*, to the shore 2*s.* 6*d.* or 3*s.* 6*d.*; each addit. pers. 6*d.* or 9*d.*

Shanklin, situated in a pleasant valley about 300 ft. above the level of the sea, has grown with extraordinary rapidity from a little village to an extensive watering-place. Its population, which was 355 in 1861, had increased to 2764 at the census of 1881. The beach is good, and there is a handsome new pier. The picturesque old *Rectory* is completely overgrown with unusually fine myrtles. Close to Shanklin is **Shanklin Chine* ('ravine', or 'cleft', from the Anglo-Saxon *cinan*, German *gähnen*, to yawn or gape; Inn), a deep fissure in the cliffs, opening towards the sea. To reach it we proceed straight from the station, in an easterly direction, for about 5 min.; then turn to the right through the village, and, about 100 paces beyond Daish's Hotel, descend to the left. A little farther on, a footpath descends, to the right, to the seaward entrance of the Chine (20 min.), closed by a gate (adm. 3*d.*). The ravine, with its luxuriant vegetation, precipitous sides, and small brook, presents a beautiful picture. On a shield over a small fountain are some lines written by Longfellow when staying here in 1868. We traverse the chine in about 10 minutes. Quitting the upper end, we take the footpath to the left, which soon crosses the carriage-road, and leads us in 20 min. (with beautiful retrospective views) to *Luccombe Chine*, another, but less attractive ravine. Without descending (left), we go straight on through the gate. About $^1/_3$ M. farther on, the path descends through wood to the 'Landslip', which it traverses to ($^1/_4$ hr.) —

Bonchurch (**Ribband's Hotel*), lying picturesquely at the E. extremity of the **Undercliff*, a curious rocky plateau or row of cliffs, $^1/_4$-$1^1/_2$ M. in width, owing its position and appearance to a succession of landslips, and extending to Blackgang Chine (p. 71), a distance of 6-7 M. (To reach the village and hotel we ascend to the right.) The old churchyard (gate opened by attendant) contains the graves of John Sterling (a plain stone in the S.W. corner), whose life was written by Carlyle, and of the Rev. W. Adams, author of the 'Shadow of the Cross'. The tiny church is of Norman origin. The lovely *Churchyard of the new church, a little farther up the hill, should also be seen. The *Pulpit Rock* and *Hadfield's Lookout* or *Flagstaff Rock*, in the grounds of *Undermount* (not open to the public), and **St. Boniface Down* (785 ft.), command magnificent views. Either continuing to follow the road, or returning to the path along the cliffs, we reach, in 20 min. more —

Ventnor. — **Hotels.** *Marine, board 3*l.* 3*s.* per week, R. extra; Royal; Queen's, 'pens'. 10*s.* 6*d.* a day; Esplanade, all admirably situated, with view of the sea. In the town, high up, *Crab & Lobster, with a pretty garden, R. & A. from 3*s.* 9*d.*, 'pens'. 10*s.* 6*d.* per day. — Second class: *Commercial, D. 3*s.*; Globe; Crown & Rose, moderate; Terminus Hotel, at the station, unpretending, R. & A. 3*s.* — Solent Temperance Hotel, high up, with fine view. In the vicinity are various other hotels and numerous lodging-houses.

Coaches. In summer the following excursion-coaches ply regularly from Ventnor: 1. To *Freshwater Bay*, the *Needles*, *Alum Bay*, and back, starting about 10 a.m. and reaching Ventnor again at 7 p.m. (fare to Freshwater and back 6*s.*, to Alum Bay and back 7*s.* 6*d.*). A stoppage for luncheon is made at the Freshwater Bay Hotel. — 2. To *Blackgang Chine*, *Carisbrooke Castle*, the *Roman Villa*, and *Newport*, returning viâ *Rookley*, *Appuldurcombe Park*, and *Wroxall* (11 a.m. to 6 p.m.; fare 5*s.*; luncheon at the Blackgang Chine Hotel or at the Red Lion Hotel, Carisbrooke). — 3. To *Arreton*, *Osborne*, and *Cowes*, returning by *Newport* and *Godshill* (11 a.m. to 6 p.m.; fare 5*s.*; luncheon at Cowes). — 4. To *Bonchurch*, *Shanklin*, *Sandown*, *Brading*, and *Ryde* (11 a.m. to 5.30 p.m.; 5*s.*, to Shanklin and back 3*s.*; luncheon at Sandown Hotel). — 5. To *Blackgang*, every morning and afternoon (fare 1*s.* 6*d.*, there and back 2*s.*).

Ventnor, beautifully situated on *Ventnor Cove*, is much frequented, like many other parts of the island, by persons suffering from complaints of the chest. In winter the climate is almost Italian in its mildness, frost and snow being of rare occurrence, while in summer the heat is tempered by sea-breezes. Pop. (1881) 5493. The *Royal Victoria Pier* was opened in 1887. About 1 M. to the W. is *Steephill Castle*, once occupied by the Empress of Austria, with a beautiful garden, which, however, is rarely open to the public. Opposite is **Ventnor Public Park*, commanding a beautiful view of the whole of the Undercliff from its highest point.

Excursions. The principal excursion is to *Blackgang* (coach, see p. 70). The road runs at a high level, passing the Royal Hotel, Ventnor Park, Steephill, and the *Ventnor Consumptive Hospital*, to (2 M.) *St. Lawrence*, a neat little village, the old church of which is the most ancient in the island, and was long the smallest in Great Britain. On the left side of the road stands the new church, beyond which, on the same side, but far below the road, are the ivy-clad remains of a small Roman Catholic chapel. [About $1^1/_2$ M. to the N. of this point is *Whitwell*, with an interesting Norman and E. E. church.] Farther on we pass the prettily-environed villa of *Mirables*, and the fishing-village of *Puckaster*, near which is *Lloyd's Signal Station* (left), and reach ($4^1/_2$ M.) *Sandrock* (*Royal Sandrock Hotel), with a mineral spring, being the modern part of the village of *Niton* (White Lion), which lies a little to the landward. Below the village, on the southernmost point of the island, is *St. Catherine's Lighthouse.* About 1 M. beyond Sandrock is *Blackgang* (*Blackgang Chine Hotel), up to which point the road has wound along the foot of the Undercliff. The fine marine views, with the bright green of the trees and bushes, here recall the scenery of the Mediterranean. Around are numerous country-houses and villas, standing in the midst of tasteful pleasure-grounds and gardens.

Adjoining the hotel is the ravine called ***Blackgang Chine**, to which a steep path, partly cut into steps, descends; the rocks here reach a height of 500 ft. We enter through a bazaar, where we are expected either to purchase something or make a trifling payment (6*d*.). Below is a fine stretch of beach. We return to the top leisurely in $^1/_2$ hr. — Above Blackgang is *St. Catherine's Hill* (830 ft.), commanding a most extensive view over land and sea.

From Ventnor to Freshwater Bay and Alum Bay (22 M.; coach in $3^1/_2$ hrs.; fare 5*s*. or 6*s*.). As far as ($5^1/_2$ m.) Blackgang the route is the same as above. Beyond Blackgang a new military road runs straight along the coast to Freshwater Bay, but the coaches usually follow the more picturesque old road described below. This diverges to the right beyond the village of *Chale* (Clarendon Hotel), and enters a flatter and less attractive district, destitute of the luxuriant vegetation through which we have just passed. *Kingston*, a little farther on, has a small church picturesquely situated on the roadside. Near ($10^1/_2$ M.) *Shorwell* is the fine old mansion of *Northcourt*, the seat of Lady Gordon, lying in the midst of beautiful woods. About $2^1/_2$ M. farther on is *Brixton*, with a picturesque old church, restored in 1852. Next come (15 M.) *Mottistone* and (16 M.) *Brooke*; the manor-house of the latter, on the left, is pleasantly embowered in groves of noble trees. Opposite is a small new church. Above us, on the right, is *Mottistone Down*, 700 ft. above the level of the sea. About 1 M. before reaching Freshwater Bay we obtain a view of Yarmouth (p. 73), the Solent, and the mainland to the right. From (20 M.) *Freshwater Bay* (p. 74) we may proceed to (2 M.) *Alum Bay* (p. 74), where the coach waits long enough to allow of a visit to the *Needles* (p. 74).

From Ventnor to Newport, 15 M., railway in 35 min. (fares 3*s.* 6*d.*, 2*s.* 8*d.*, 1*s.* 3*d.*), passing *Wroxall*, *Sandown* (p. 69), *Alverstone*, *Newchurch*, *Horringford*, *Merstone*, *Blackwater*, and *Shide*. The coaches, which are preferable to the railway, generally run viâ Blackgang (comp. p. 71). The direct road viâ Godshill (10 M.) ascends between *Wroxall Down* (right) and *Rew Down* (left) to (2 M.) *Wroxall* (rail. stat., see above). To the left lies the noble **Park of Appuldurcombe*, containing the magnificent mansion of that name, now used as a school. On the highest point in the park stands a granite obelisk, 70 ft. high, and partly destroyed by lightning, erected in memory of Sir Robert Worsley, author of a complete history of the Isle of Wight, and a former owner of this estate. Splendid *View.

$4^1/_2$ M. *Godshill* (Griffin), with a large and interesting church situated picturesquely on the top of a knoll. Beyond ($6^1/_2$ M.) *Rookley* the road passes near *Gatcombe Park*. — 8 M. *Blackwater*; $9^1/_4$ M. *Shide* (railway stations, see above).

10 M. **Newport.** — Bugle; Warburton; Star. — Wheatsheaf, good second-class house, ordinary at 1.15 o'clock, 1*s.* 6*d.*; Rose & Crown, quite unpretending. — *Coaches* ply in summer to Ventnor (comp. p. 70), Ryde, etc.

Newport, the capital of the Isle of Wight, with 9430 inhab., lies on the river *Medina*, which is navigable up to this point. The Medina divides the island into two portions, or *hundreds*, called the *East* and *West Medina*, each comprising 16 parishes. Newport was once the 'new port' of Carisbrooke (see below), whence the name. The imposing *Church* contains a tasteful *Monument to the memory of the Princess Elizabeth, daughter of Charles I. (see p. 73), by *Marochetti*, erected by Queen Victoria. In Sept., 1648, Charles I. was brought from Carisbrooke to take part in the negotiations for the so-called 'Treaty of Newport', and was lodged in the *Grammar School*. On the fruitless issue of the negotiations Charles was removed (Nov. 30th) to Hurst Castle in Hampshire (p. 95), which he soon left for Whitehall and his death (Jan. 30th, 1649). — About 1 M. to the W. of Newport rises —

***Carisbrooke Castle.** (It is reached by ascending the High Street to the monumental cross, where we turn to the left; at the cross-roads we descend the road bearing slightly to the right, which almost immediately begins to ascend and leads to the castle.) This ancient, ivy-clad stronghold of the lord of the island is picturesquely placed on the top of a steep eminence (admission 4*d.*, no gratuity).

The earliest building was Saxon, but the *Keep*, the oldest existing portion, is of Norman origin. The other parts date chiefly from the 13th cent., while the outworks were added by Queen Elizabeth. Charles I. was detained captive here for a considerable time before his execution; and his son Henry, Duke of Gloucester, and his daughter, Princess Elizabeth, were afterwards imprisoned here. The princess died in the castle 19 months after her father's death, and the young prince was released two years later. The remains of the rooms where Charles was imprisoned, and of the chamber in which his daughter breathed her last, may still be seen. The castle-well, 200 ft. deep, from which the water is drawn by a donkey inside a large windlass wheel, is always an object of interest to visitors. We may ascend to the top, and walk round the walls of the castle, the view from which embraces an extensive and thoroughly English landscape, with numerous houses and villages: close by is the village of Carisbrooke, farther off Newport and the River Medina, and in the distance the Solent and the coast of Hampshire. — The restored *Church* of *Carisbrooke* (Red Lion; Waverley), contemporaneous with the castle, possesses a simple, but handsome and well-proportioned tower. A *Roman Villa*, with a tesselated floor, was discovered at Carisbrooke, near the castle, in 1859 (adm. 6*d*.).

Another very pleasant excursion may be made to the S. E. to the village of (3 M.) **Arreton,** lying in a picturesque valley, the dwelling-place of Legh Richmond's 'Dairyman's Daughter', whose remains repose in the churchyard. A walk of 1/2 hr. from this point will bring us to the summit of ***Arreton Down,** which commands one of the finest and most varied prospects in the island. To the N.E. the view is terminated by Portsmouth and Gosport, while to the S. the eye rests on the fertile valley of the *Yar*, which separates the central chain of hills from the southern. At the top are two large barrows, in which some ancient armour has been discovered. — Arreton and Arreton Down may also be conveniently visited from Ryde or Ventnor, by taking the train to *Horringford* (p. 72), which is 1 M. from Arreton.

From Newport to Yarmouth and Freshwater, 12 M., railway in 35-40 min. (fares 3*s*., 2*s*., 1*s*.). The first station is (1 1/4 M.) *Carisbrooke* (see above). To the right extends *Parkhurst Forest*. — 5 1/2 M. *Calborne* is the station for *Shalfleet* (with a Norman church) and for the fishing-village of *Newtown*, with its large salt-works, on *Newtown Bay*. — 7 M. *Ningwood*.

9 1/2 M. **Yarmouth** *(*George Hotel; Bugle; King's Head)*, a small town in a flat district at the mouth of the *Yar* (not to be confounded with the stream of the same name in the E. part of the island). The church of *St. James* contains the monument of Sir Robert Holmes, governor of the island in 1667-92. The *Castle* was erected by Henry VIII. Good boating and bathing are enjoyed here.

From Yarmouth to Southampton. When time is limited, we may save ourselves the return-journey to Newport by taking one of the steamers which ply 3-4 times a day from Yarmouth to *Lymington* (fare 1*s*. 9*d*. or 1*s*. 2*d*.). The passage occupies about 1/2 hr. From Lymington to Bishopstoke (Southampton), by train in 1 hr. Passengers may book through from Yarmouth to London (Waterloo). — Excursion steamers ply from Yarmouth to Ryde, Cowes, Bournemouth, etc.

12 M. *Freshwater*, the terminus of the line aad the station for (1 M.) Freshwater Gate, (2 M.) Totland Bay, and (3 M.) Alum Bay, to all of which omnibuses ply in connection with the trains.

Freshwater Gate *(*Freshwater Bay Hotel*, R. & A. 4*s*. 6*d*., D. 5*s*., finely situated; *Albion*, well spoken of; *Temperance Hotel)*, taking its name from a cleft in the rocky coast-line, opposite Freshwater

Bay, is now a rising little sea-bathing resort and a good starting-point for boating expeditions and other excursions. In the neighbourhood are '*Lord Holmes' Parlour and Kitchen*' and other remarkable caves. *Farringford*, the marine residence of Lord Tennyson, the Poet Laureate, lies about 1 M. to the W. The bay contains two isolated rocks resembling the Needles. Coach to Ventnor, see p. 70.

The *WALK along the cliffs from Freshwater Bay to Alum Bay is one of the most enjoyable excursions in the island. From the Freshwater Bay Hotel we ascend along the edge of the downs, overlooking the sea, to (1/2 hr.) *High Down* (485 ft.), which is marked by a beacon and affords a splendid *View of the sea to the S., the Solent and the Hampshire coast to the N., and of the W. part of the island. Totland Bay (see below) lies below us on the N. Continuing to follow the edge of the chalk cliffs for 2-2 1/2 M. more, we come in sight of Alum Bay and the Needles. (The best view is obtained from the fort at the point, but visitors are not always admitted.) At the point we are about 1 M. from the Needles Hotel (see below), which lies a little inland from the bay.

In fine weather it is, perhaps, preferable to make the excursion from Freshwater Bay to Alum Bay by boat, as this affords a better view of the Needles and the fine cliffs (boat with boatmen 10-15*s*. or more). The perpendicular **Freshwater Cliffs,** 400-500 ft. high, consist of chalk with clearly defined layers or ribbons of flint. The finest are those of ***Main Bench**, where numerous sea-fowl breed in spring. Before reaching the Needles we pass the entrance of ***Scratchell's Bay**, a small but imposing recess, where the action of the water on the lower strata of the chalk-cliffs has formed a magnificent natural arch, 200 ft. in height.

***Alum Bay** (**Royal Needles Hotel*, R. & A. 4*s*., luncheon 2*s*. 6*d*.), so named because alum is found here, is remarkable for the curious and pleasing effect produced by the vertical stripes of red, yellow, green, and grey sandstone, contrasting with the white chalk of the rest of the cliffs. The ***Needles** are three white, pointed rocks of chalk, resting on dark-coloured bases, and rising abruptly from the sea to a height of 100 ft. On the outermost is a lighthouse. A new pier has been built in the bay, and numerous excursion-steamers call here in summer.

Totland Bay *(Totland Bay Hotel)*, about 1 1/2 M. to the N. of Alum Bay, is another charming little watering-place, with a pier and good boating and bathing. Steamers ply to Lymington, etc.

FROM NEWPORT TO COWES, 4 M., railway in 15-20 min. (fares 1*s*., 9*d*., 4*d*.). — The road (4 1/2 M.) passes the *Union Workhouse* (right) and (left) *Albany Barracks* and *Parkhurst Prison*. Those who prefer it may descend the Medina in a rowing-boat.

West Cowes. — *MARINE; *GLOSTER; FOUNTAIN; VINE; PIER; GLOBE. — STEAMBOATS to Southampton and to Ryde and Portsmouth several times daily.

West Cowes, a busy little town, prettily situated, containing 6500 inhab., and possessing the best harbour in the island, is the headquarters of the *Royal Yacht Squadron*, the 150 members of which are the owners of craft varying in size from 40 to 500 tons, and employ 1500 of the best English sailors as crews. Regattas take place frequently in summer and autumn, the chief one in August. There is a good bathing-beach to the W. of the pier.

Opposite West Cowes, on the other side of the estuary of the Medina, which is about 1/2 M. broad, lies the quiet and pleasant little town of *East Cowes* (Medina Hotel; Prince of Wales); steam-ferry (1/2*d.*) every few minutes. In the environs are the fine country-seats of *East Cowes Castle* and *Norris Castle* (Duke of Bedford). The grounds of the latter are bounded by those of the royal marine residence of *Osborne*, which is beautifully situated and fitted up with great magnificence (not shown to visitors).

Travellers intending to return to London may now take the steamboat from Cowes to *Portsmouth* (40 min.; fares 2*s.* 1*d.* and 1*s.* 7*d.*), which calls at Ryde on its way. The passage along the coast from Cowes to Ryde is picturesque; the shores are luxuriantly wooded, and good views are obtained of Norris Castle and Osborne. — Travellers bound for *Southampton* may either go direct by steamer (1 hr.; fares 2*s.* 1*d.* and 1*s.* 7*d.*) or to Portsmouth by steamer, and thence by railway. In the former case they enjoy a pleasant sail up *Southampton Water*, the mouth of which is protected by *Calshot Castle*, one of the forts built by Henry VIII. About 2 1/2 M. farther up, to the left, lies *Hythe* (Drummond Arms), and on the opposite shore is seen *Netley Hospital* (p. 82; abbey not visible). In mid-stream lies the guard-ship 'Invincible'.

11. From London to Winchester and Southampton.
New Forest.

South Western Railway from *Waterloo* to (66 1/2 M.) *Winchester* in 1 3/4-2 1/2 hrs. (fares 13*s.* 9*d.*, 9*s.* 8*d.*, 5*s.* 6*d.*); to (79 M.) *Southampton* in 2 1/4-3 1/4 hrs. (fares 15*s.* 6*d.*, 11*s.*, 6*s.* 6*d.*).

From London to (24 1/2 M.) *Woking*, see R. 9. Beyond Woking the train passes *Woking Convict Prison* for invalid prisoners and the *Brookwood Lunatic Asylum* (both to the right), and reaches (27 1/2 M.) *Brookwood*. To the left lies *Woking Necropolis*, an immense cemetery, 2000 acres in extent, to which a special funeral train runs daily from London (private station in Westminster Bridge Road). In one corner is a crematorium. — About 1/2 M. to the S. of Brookwood station is *Bisley Common*, the new meeting-place of the National Rifle Association (comp. p. 64).

About 1 1/2 M. beyond Brookwood, on the left (S.), diverges the loop-line to (7 1/2 M.) *Aldershot*, (10 1/2 M.) *Farnham*, (19 M.) *Alton*, and (35 M.) *Winchester*.

Aldershot (*Royal; Imperial*), now a busy town with 20,000 inhab. (including the soldiers), has grown to its present size through the establishment here in 1854 of a large Military Camp, 9 sq. M. in extent, and capable of accommodating 20,000 men. The military manœuvres which take place here from time to time are on an extensive scale and well worth seeing. The most commanding point of view is the eminence called *Caesar's Camp*, on which stands the equestrian statue of the *Duke of Wellington*, formerly on the top of the Green Park Arch in London.

Farnham (*Bush*, well spoken of; *Lion & Lamb*) is a pleasant little town with 4500 inhab., situated in the midst of a hop-district second in importance to Kent alone. The *Castle*, now the palace of the Bishop of Winchester, was originally built in the 12th cent., but dates in its present form mainly from 1662-84; the Keep is probably of the 13th century, *William Cobbett* (d. 1835) was born at Farnham in the 'Jolly Farmers', Bridge Sq. — About 1½ M. to the E. of Farnham is *Moor Park*, where Swift acted as secretary to Sir William Temple (d. 1699) and made the acquaintance of 'Stella'. *Waverley Abbey*, see p. 66.

From *Alton* (Swan) a visit may be paid to *Selborne* (p. 66), which lies 5 M. to the S.E. — Near (33½ M.) *Alresford* is *Tichborne House*, a name well known from the notorious law-suit, which is said to have saddled the estate with a debt of 90,000*l.* — 35 M. *Winchester*, see below.

The train now passes between the *Chobham Ridges* on the right and the *Fox Hills* on the left, and crosses the Guildford and Reading railway (p. 64). — 33 M. *Farnborough* (Queen's, at the North Camp), one of the stations for Aldershot Camp, which begins a little to the S. of it. To the right lies *Farnborough Hill*, the present home of the Empress Eugénie, who has built a chapel (to the left of the railway) for the remains of her husband and son (comp. p. 12). About 250 acres of ground in the environs of Farnborough are occupied by strawberries, cultivated for the London market. — Near (36½ M.) *Fleet* the line skirts a small lake; on the right (¾ M.) is *Elvetham House*, where Queen Elizabeth was entertained in 1591 by the Earl of Hertford. — 39 M. *Winchfield*, with a fine church partly Norman, partly Gothic. About 2 M. to the S.W. (omn.) is *Odiham* (George), with an old castle where King David of Scotland was imprisoned after his capture at Neville's Cross (p. 414). To the N. lies *Eversley*, the home of Charles Kingsley (d. 1875) for 33 years.

The line now passes through (41 M.) *Hook* and the village of *Old Basing*, where a battle took place between the Saxons and Danes in 871. It contains the scanty ruins of *Basing House*, built by the first Marquis of Winchester in the reign of Edward VI., which resisted the Parliamentary troops for four years and was finally stormed by Cromwell himself (1645).

48 M. **Basingstoke** *(Red Lion; Rail. Rfmt. Rooms)*, with 6680 inhab., is the junction of lines to Salisbury (R. 14) and Reading (p. 106). Close to the station, on the right, is a ruined chapel of the 16th century. The *Parish Church* is a Perp. building, restored.

To the N.W. is (6 M.) **Strathfieldsaye,** the seat of the Duke of Wellington, with the camp-bed and other memorials of the Iron Duke, of whom a bronze statue has been erected here. His charger 'Copenhagen', which he rode at the battle of Waterloo, is buried in the garden. — *Silchester*, 4 M. to the W. of Strathfieldsaye, is a very ancient place, with interesting and extensive Roman remains.

The remainder of the route to Winchester traverses the chalk downs and presents no features of special interest.

66½ M. **Winchester.** — **Hotels.** George, corner of High St. and Jewry St., well spoken of; *Royal, St. Peter St., with a garden, quiet; Black Swan, R. & A. 4*s.* 6*d.*; Eagle, near the S.W. station, unpretending.

Cabs. From either of the stations to most of the hotels 1*s.*; from station to station 1*s.* 6*d.*; per hr. 3*s.*, each addit. ½ hr. 1*s.* 3*d.* Each article of luggage carried outside 2*d.*

Railway Stations. *South Western Station*, at the upper end of the town; *Great Western Station* (for Oxford, London viâ Reading, etc.), at the lower end of the town, near the river.

Fishing in the Itchen; apply to *Mr. Chalkley*, fishing-tackle maker, near the Cathedral.

Winchester, a city of great antiquity and the seat of a bishop, with 19,500 inhab., is pleasantly situated on the slope of a chalk-hill on the W. bank of the *Itchen*.

Before the Roman invasions Winchester was known under the name of *Caer Gwent* (white castle), which was Latinised as *Venta Belgarum*, the *Belgae* being the British tribe which had its settlement here. In 495 the Saxons took possession of the town, and named it *Winteceaster* (ceaster = castrum). Winchester was the capital of the Saxon kingdom of Wessex, was converted to Christianity by Birinus, the Apostle of the West of England, in 635, and was afterwards the seat of government of Alfred the Great and Canute the Dane. After the Norman Conquest Winchester for a time rivalled London in commercial importance, but soon lost its pre-eminence, especially after its visitation by a serious fire in 1141. Down to the Reformation, however, it maintained a position of great ecclesiastical dignity. Now-a-days the city has that quiet and venerable appearance which we are wont to associate with the seat of a cathedral; and the woollen manufacture for which it was once famous has entirely died out. See *Dean Kitchin's* 'Winchester' ('Historic Towns' series; 1890).

To reach the Cathedral we descend the High Street, with its curious old pent-house, and turn to the right by a narrow passage close to the *City Cross*, a monument of the 15th cent. (restored).

The ***Cathedral** (daily service at 10 and 4, with fair music), a stately edifice, incorporating every style of English architecture from the Norman to the Perpendicular, was founded by Bp. Walkelin in 1079, close to the site of a Saxon church of the 7th century. The choir and transepts were finished in 1093, the conversion of the nave from Norman to Perpendicular was begun by Bishop Edington before 1366, and the whole was completed in 1486. The builder (or transformer) of by far the greater part of the nave was *Bishop William of Wykeham*, the renowned architect, ecclesiastic, and statesman, who occupied the see from 1366 to 1404. The church is the longest in England, measuring 560 ft. in all; the breadth across the transepts is 208 ft. The arms of the transept are flanked with aisles, and still retain the form of a pillared basilica with arcades. The first employment of Pointed architecture is seen in the addition to the choir on the E. The **W. Façade*, with its spacious portal, was begun in 1350 by Bishop Edington, finished in the 15th cent., and restored in 1860; the statue of William of Wykeham is modern. The general effect of the exterior is somewhat heavy and unimposing, and the stunted proportions of the only tower detract considerably from its dignity. The Dec. and Perp. work at the E. end is, however, very fine. The Cathedral is dedicated to SS. Peter and Paul and the Holy Trinity; the choir is also popularly supposed to be dedicated to St. Swithin (Suetonius; day, July 15th), whose traditionary connection with the weather is ascribed to the legend that the removal of his body to the shrine prepared for it was delayed for 40 days by rain.

For a plan of Winchester Cathedral see page 543

The **Interior** of the church is very impressive owing to the beauty of its proportions, the great length (250 ft.) of the Nave, and the fine groining. Visitors should notice the remaining traces of Walkelin's Norman nave, such as the arches in the triforium. The fact that the core of the piers is also Norman perhaps accounts for their unusual massiveness. One of the most characteristic features of Winchester is its fine **Chantry Chapels*, most of which were founded by Bishops of Winchester between 1350 and 1486. The most interesting of all is that of *Bishop William of Wykeham*, designed by himself (1366-1404), in one of the bays on the S. side of the nave; and the nave also contains that of *Bishop Edington* (p. 77). On the wall of the N. aisle, nearly opposite the chantry of William of Wykeham, is a brass tablet to the memory of *Jane Austen* (1775-1817), the novelist. Above it is a curious old epitaph. Also in the N. aisle, not far off, is the ancient sculptured *Font*, in black marble, dating from the 12th century. At the W. end of the N. aisle is a *Cantoria*, or singing gallery. Much of the old stained glass was destroyed by the Puritans, but that in the **W. Window* dates in part from 1350.

The Transepts are the oldest part of the church as it now stands, and show the Norman work of Bishop Walkelin almost untouched (1079-1093). The later Norman work, necessitated by the fall of the tower early in the 12th cent., is easily recognized by its finer jointing. The S. arm contains memorials of *Bishop Wilberforce* (d. 1873) and of *Izaak Walton* (d. 1683; in the Silkstede Chapel), whose memory is indissolubly associated with the Itchen and other streams of the neighbourhood. The mural paintings in the *Chapel of the Holy Sepulchre*, in the N. transept, are curious, though much damaged by neglect (13th cent.).

The Choir is separated from the nave by an oaken screen, designed by Sir G. G. Scott. On passing it we are struck with the immense thickness of the piers supporting the tower, which owe their unusual solidity to a desire to prevent a repetition of the fate of the first tower, which fell soon after its erection. Under the tower is the ancient tomb which is said by a dubious tradition to hold the bones of *William Rufus* (d. 1100). The oaken **Stalls* of 1296, darkened with age, are richly carved. The pulpit was presented by Prior Silkstede in 1498, but the bishop's throne is modern. The painted glass of the **E. Window* dates from about 1520. Prolonging the choir towards the E. is the *Presbytery*, containing a fine reredos of the 15th cent. (restored) and an altarpiece (Raising of Lazarus) by *West*. The presbytery is enclosed at the sides by handsome stone screens (1500-25), above which lie six richly coloured wooden mortuary chests, containing the bones of Ethelwolf, Egbert, Canute, and other kings, preserved from the old cathedral. The identity of the different skeletons, however, has long been lost.

Behind the reredos is the *Feretory*, a raised platform for the shrines of the patron saints of the cathedral. The E. end of the feretory is adorned with fine tabernacle-work, and in the middle is the entrance to a vault called the *Holy Hole*, probably a receptacle for relics. To the right and left (N. and S.) of the feretory are the chantries of *Bishops Gardiner* (1555) and *Fox* (1528), and farther to the E. those of *Bishop Waynflete* (1447-86) and *Cardinal Beaufort* (d. 1447). Between the last two is the site of the once famous *Shrine of St. Swithin* (p. 77).

The part of the Cathedral to the E. of the feretory, including the aisles, is mostly in the E.E. style, and the work of *Bishop Lucy* (1189-1204). To the E. it terminates in the Lady Chapel, flanked by two smaller ones. The *Lady Chapel*, one bay of which is E.E. and the other Perp. (15th cent.), is adorned with mural paintings ascribed to Flemish or German artists of the 15th century. The marriage of Queen Mary with Philip of Spain was celebrated here in 1554, and the chair preserved in the adjoining chapel to the N. is supposed by some to be that in which she sat during that ceremony. The statue of *Bishop North* (d. 1820) in the Lady Chapel is by Chantrey. The chapel to the S. was fitted up as a chantry by *Bishop Langton* (d. 1501), who is buried here, and that to the N., the *Chapel of the Guardian Angels* (12th cent.), contains the monuments of two bishops and of the Earl of Portland (d. 1634), Lord High Treasurer of Charles I.

In the N. transept is the entrance to the CRYPT, the W. part of which, recently cleared out, shows Walkelin's original plan and is a fine specimen of early-Norman substructure. The E. part is the work of Bp. Lucy (p. 78), and the easternmost bay was added by Prior Silkstede (p. 78).

The *Close* to the S. of the church, with its smooth turf and abundant foliage, forms a striking contrast to the grey and venerable Cathedral. The entrance to the *Deanery*, which contains some remains of the old priory, is distinguished by its three pointed arches of the 13th cent., and some Norman arches of the old chapter-house are also visible. The passage between these and the S. Transept leads to the *Library*, which contains a fine copy of the Vulgate and some relics taken from the coffin of William Rufus.

We quit the Close by a gate in the S. E. corner, pass through the handsome *King's Gate* and by *St. Swithin's Church*, and turn to the left into *College Street*, which soon brings us to the College, the second lion of Winchester. (We apply for admission at the porter's lodge at the second gateway to the right; fee.) ***Winchester School**, or **St. Mary's College**, which is connected with New College, Oxford, was also built by William of Wykeham in 1373-96, and, though extensive new buildings have become necessary, the older parts remain nearly unaltered. It has ranked for centuries among the leading public schools of England, and is attended by 400-500 boys.

The parts shown to visitors include two quadrangles, surrounded by the picturesque old *School Buildings;* the entrance to the *Kitchen*, with a singular picture of a 'Trusty Servant'; the *Chapel*, containing a carved oak pulpit from New College, Oxford; the *Cloisters*, with the names of Bishop Ken (1646) and other eminent Wykhamists cut in the stone; the *Dining Hall;* and the old lavatory, known by the boys as '*Moab*', while they call the shoe-blacking place '*Edom*' (Ps. lx. 8). — The new buildings, also in the form of a quadrangle, lie to the W. of the old. — At the back are the **Cricket Fields*, prettily situated on the river, and affording a good view of the College.

If we continue our way along College Street, we reach, after a short distance, on the opposite side of the street and beyond the river, the ruins of *Wolvesey Palace*, a Norman structure built by Bishop Henri de Blois in 1138. Here, in 1554, Queen Mary received her bridegroom Philip of Spain, a short time before the celebration of their marriage in the Cathedral. The present Episcopal Palace is at Farnham (p. 76).

From Wolvesey Palace the visitor may skirt the river to *Soke Bridge*, at the foot of High St. If time allow, he should cross the bridge and ascend to ($^1/_4$ hr.) the top of *St. Giles's Hill*, which affords an admirable *View of the city. — At one time Winchester is said to have possessed no fewer than ninety churches. Of the eleven now in existence the most interesting, after the Cathedral, is *St. John's Church*, in St. John St., at the foot of St. Giles's Hill, the aisles of which are considerably wider than the nave. The style is partly Norman, and partly E.E.

At the foot of High St., a little above the bridge, is the *Guildhall*, a modern building by Sir G. G. Scott, containing a small museum (open on week-days, 10-4). — Ascending to the top of the High St., passing the City Cross and the Pent House (see p. 77), we reach the *West Gate*, a fortified gateway of the 13th century. — Adjacent (left) is the *County Court*, with a fine hall, belonging to a castle erected here by William the Conqueror, but afterwards altered and heightened (13th cent.). On the wall hangs a curious relic known as 'King Arthur's Round Table', said to date from the 6th cent. but repainted in the time of Henry VIII. — King Alfred is said to be buried in *Hyde Abbey*, Jewry St., part of which is now a barn.

About 1 M. to the S.W. of the town lies the ***Hospital of St. Cross** (adm. for 1-3 pers., 1*s.*), which may be reached either through Southgate Street, or by a path along the bank of the Itchen. This peculiar institution was founded in 1136 by Bishop Henri de Blois for the maintenance of 13 poor men, unable to work, and for the partial support of 100 others. A remnant of the ancient hospitality is still maintained, any one who applies at the porter's lodge being entitled to the refreshment of a horn of ale and a slice of bread, unless the daily quantum has already been distributed. The **Church*, completed before the year 1200, and lately restored, is a beautiful example of the transition from the Norman to the E.E. style of architecture. Among the most interesting features are the exquisitely delicate late-Norman mouldings, a curious triple arch at the S. transept (external), and the modern polychrome painting in the supposed original style. The quadrangle and its surroundings also form a most delightful picture. Visitors are conducted to the Refectory, with its fine open roof, and to the Kitchen. The former contains an ancient triptych, attributed to Dürer (Flemish?).

On the opposite bank of the Itchen, not far from the hospital, is **St. Catherine's Hill*, crowned by a group of trees and a labyrinth cut in the turf, and affording an admirable view of the ancient town.

From St. Cross we may continue our walk along the Itchen to (2 M.) the pretty village of *Twyford* (see below). — Admirers of the 'Christian Year' may combine in one excursion from Winchester a visit to (4½ M.) *Hursley* and (5½ M.) *Otterbourne*, livings held by the *Rev. John Keble* (d. 1866), who is buried in the churchyard of the former. The church was rebuilt by him with the profits of the 'Christian Year'. *Hursley House* occupies the site of the house of Richard Cromwell, many of whose family are buried in the church.

Beyond Winchester the Railway continues to descend the valley of the Itchen. — In the village of *Twyford*, near (70 M.) *Shawford*, Franklin wrote part of his autobiography. — 73 M. *Bishopstoke* (Junction Hotel), the junction of lines to Portsmouth on the left and Salisbury on the right, with Dear's large factory for food for horses, dogs, and cattle. — 76 M. *Swathling*; 77 M. *St. Denys*; 78 M. *Northam*.

79 M. **Southampton.** — **Hotels.** *South Western Railway Hotel, a large house at the terminus; Radley's, opposite the station, R. & A. 5*s.*, high charges for porterage of luggage; Matcham's Dolphin, Royal, Star, Crown, all in High St.; Pier, on the Quay. — *Flower's Temperance, Queen's Terrace; Goodridge's, Railway, near the station. — *Rail. Refreshment Rooms.*

Cabs. Per mile 1*s.*, for each addit. ¼ M. 3*d.*; per ½ hr. 1*s.* 6*d.*, ¾ hr. 2*s.*, 1 hr. 2*s.* 6*d.*, each addit. ¼ hr. 6*d.* With 2 horses 1*s.* 6*d.*, 4*d.*, 2*s.*, 2*s.* 6*d.*, 3*s.*, 8*d.*

Boat to *Netley Abbey* with one man 3*s.*, with two men 4*s.*; there and back, including stay of 2 hrs., 7*s.* By time: first hr. 2*s.*, each addit. hr. 1*s.* — Small boats at the West Quay, without rower, 6*d.* per hr.

Tramway from the Terminus through High St. and Above Bar to the *Park*, and thence on the left to *Shirley* and on the right to *Portswood* (2*d*. or 3*d*.). — **Omnibuses** from the Bar Gate to *Bitterne*, *Totton*, etc.

Steamers to the *Channel Islands*, see R. 12; to the *Isle of Wight*, see R. 10. Steamers also run from Southampton to *Hythe*, *Portsmouth*, *Havre*, *Cherbourg*, and *St. Malo*; and it is the starting-point of the mail-packets to the *West Indies* and the *Cape of Good Hope*. The steamers of the *North German Lloyd* also call here on their way to and from America (for New York on Thurs. & Sun.).

Post and **Telegraph Office**, Oxford St., close to the Railway Terminus.

Swimming Baths on the W. shore, at the foot of Manchester St.

Railway Stations. The *Terminus* or *Docks Station* is near the Docks and about 1/4 M. from the High St.; and there are suburban stations at *Southampton West*, *Northam*, and *St. Denys*.

Southampton, the second town of Hampshire, with 60,235 inhab., is beautifully situated on *Southampton Water*, between two rivers flowing into that arm of the sea, the *Itchen* on the E., and the *Test* or *Anton* on the W. The town was already in existence at the time of the Saxons, and it is said that here Canute the Dane gave the famous rebuke to his flattering courtiers. After the Conquest the town carried on a considerable traffic with Venice, Bordeaux, and Bayonne. In 1189 Southampton was the place of embarkation of the Crusaders under Richard Cœur-de-Lion; and later, in 1345 and 1415 respectively, it saw the armies of Edward III. and Henry V. take ship for the invasion of France. Philip of Spain, consort of Queen Mary, landed here in 1554, and Charles I. resided here for a considerable time.

The main body of the Pilgrim Fathers, who had been living in Holland, left Delfthaven, in July, 1620, in the 'Speedwell', which brought them to Southampton. Here they found the 'Mayflower', a ship hired for their voyage, and a small body of co-religionists from London. The two ships proceeded to Plymouth, where the 'Speedwell' was pronounced unseaworthy, and the whole of the voyagers were crowded into the 'Mayflower'. Comp. p. 139.

Southampton owes its importance to its admirably-sheltered harbour, and to the phenomenon of double tides, which prolong high water for two hours. The **Docks**, including four large dry docks two tidal basins (16 & 18 acres in area), and a closed dock, often contain several steamers of very large size (2000-4000 tons burden), the fitting up and arrangements of which will repay a thorough inspection. About 2000 vessels, with an aggregate tonnage of two millions, enter the port yearly (steamers, see above).

The chief relic of the ancient fortifications of the town is the *Bar Gate* in the High Street, erected in the 11th cent. as the N. city gate, and lately restored, but still exhibiting the original Norman arch. The part above the archway is used as the *Guildhall*. Here are preserved the rude paintings of Sir Bevis of Southampton and the giant Ascupart, whom he overcame in single combat, formerly on the buttresses of the gate. (*View of the town from the roof.) The *South Gate* and the *West Gate* also formed part of the old circumvallation. The former, with a tower once used as a prison, is near the **Town* or *Victoria Pier* (toll 1*d*.). Among the guns of the *Saluting Battery* on the adjoining Platform, or Parade, is one dating from 1542. Adjacent is a *Statue of Prince Albert.* Considerable remains of the old walls and towers still exist on the W. side of the town. The old castle has, however, been destroyed, except part of the foundations. In Queen's Park is a monument to *Gen. Gordon.*

The picturesque *High Street*, with many old houses, runs to the N. from the Town Pier. The *Church of St. Michael* (St. Michael's Square, to the W. of the High Street) contains a good *Font (12th cent.). In Winkle Street, near the quay, is the small hospital called *Domus Dei*, or *God's House*, erected in the 12th cent., and little altered in appearance since then; the *Chapel is now used for religious services by the French residents of Southampton. A tablet commemorates the fact that the Earl of Cambridge, Lord Scrope, and Sir Thomas Grey, who were executed for a conspiracy against the life of Henry V. in 1415, are interred here. The *Hartley Institution*, founded for educational and literary purposes, in the High Street, has an imposing façade in the Italian style. It contains a small picture-gallery and museum. — Near the West Shore, in Blue Anchor Lane, to the W. of the High St., are some remains of an ancient Norman dwelling known as *King John's House.*

The *Ordnance Survey & Map Office*, a Government establishment of great interest and importance, has its seat at Southampton, in a large building on the W. side of the prolongation of the High Street towards the N. About 400 men are employed in it.

At the end of Above Bar St. is the *Park*, containing statues of Dr. Watts (1674-1748), who was a native of Southampton, and Lord Palmerston (d. 1865). Farther on are *Southampton Common* and *Bevois Mount*, the latter (now built over) taking its name from Sir Bevis of Southampton, the legendary hero of the town.

The Environs afford many interesting walks. About 2½ M. to the N. lies the prettily-situated *Priory of St. Denys*, of which the remains are now very scanty. On the other side of the Itchen (to reach which we must return from the Priory to the bridge) stands *Bitterne*, the *Clausentum* of the Romans, where, in the grounds round *Bitterne Manor*, some Roman remains still exist. — To the S.E. lies (3 M.) ***Netley Abbey** (adm. 2*d.*), a Cistercian monastery founded by Henry III. in the 13th cent., and situated in a spot of singular loveliness. Interesting and picturesque remains of the E.E. church and other buildings. [The excursion to the abbey may be made by steamer or small boat (p. 80) the whole way; by railway (to within 1 M.) in 18-27 min.; by floating-bridge across the Itchen, near the docks, to *Woolston*, in 5 min., and thence by railway, in 8-10 min., or on foot; or, lastly, by carriage (fare 5-7*s.*).] A mile to the S. lies the large *Netley Military Hospital*, with accommodation for upwards of 1000 patients.

**Beaulieu Abbey* (p. 84) may be reached directly from Southampton by crossing Southampton Water by steamer (6*d.*) to (20 min.) *Hythe* (Drummond Arms), and walking thence to (4½ M.) the Abbey. The Abbey lies on the borders of the *New Forest* (see p. 83), and may also be easily visited from Brockenhurst or Lyndhurst (p. 83).

From Southampton to Salisbury, 28½ M., railway in 1-1¼ hr. (fares 5*s.*, 3*s.* 6*d.*, 2*s.* 5*d.*). — This line diverges at (6 M.) *Bishopstoke* (p. 80) from the main line to Winchester and London. — 13 M. **Romsey** (*White*

Horse; Dolphin), the junction of a line to Andover (p. 98). The prettily situated little town, with a Norman **Priory Church*, lies about 2½ M. from the station. In the neighbourhood is *Broadlands*, the country-seat of Lord Palmerston (d. 1865). — 28½ M. *Salisbury*, see p. 99.

From Southampton to *Portsmouth*, see p. 58.

To the S.W. of Southampton, stretching westwards from Southampton Water, lies the so-called ***New Forest**, an ancient royal hunting demesne, containing some of the most characteristic woodland scenery in England. The extent of the district included in the name is about 140 square miles, but little more than two-thirds of this now belongs to the crown. Many of the oaks and other trees are very fine, but there are also large tracts of heath and cultivated land; the comparative absence of water will, however, strike most visitors as a drawback. The deer with which the Forest was formerly stocked have almost entirely disappeared, but it contains large numbers of hogs and small, rough-looking horses. The naturalist will also find much to interest him in its fauna and flora, and for entomologists it is a particularly happy hunting-ground. The most convenient centre from which to explore the Forest is Lyndhurst (see below), but the pedestrian may also fix his headquarters at Brockenhurst (p. 95).

Lyndhurst (**Crown*, R. & A. 4*s.*, an unpretending country hotel, often full in summer; numerous lodgings), the capital of the New Forest, is a pleasantly situated village, 2½ M. from *Lyndhurst Road Station* (p. 95; omn. several times a day, 1*s* inside, 6*d.* outside). The church, rebuilt in 1863, contains a fine fresco of the 'Ten Virgins' by *Sir Fred. Leighton* (E. wall) and a piece of very realistic sculpture by *Cockerell* (under the tower). Near the church is the *Queen's House*, the residence of the Deputy Surveyor of the Forest; in the Verderers' Hall (open to visitors) is an old stirrup, which one absurd tradition calls that of William Rufus, while another relates that dogs small enough to pass through it were exempt from the 'expeditation', or removal of the middle claw, formerly inflicted on dogs of private persons living in the Forest.

The pedestrian alone can thoroughly explore the New Forest, but the hurried traveller may see its chief beauties in the course of a single day's drive (or walk) from Lyndhurst by taking the following round of about 15 M. (one-horse carr. about 15*s.* and gratuity). — We first drive to the N. to (2¾ M.) *Minstead* (Trusty Servant Inn), stopping on the way to visit (1 M.) the Kennels of the New Forest Hunt (fee to keeper). For Minstead we turn to the left about ⅓ M. farther on, the road in a straight direction leading to (2 M.) *Cadnam.* Beyond Minstead we pass between *Castle Malwood* on the left and *Castle Malwood Lodge* (Sir Wm. Vernon Harcourt) on the right, and after about 1 M. turn to the left and follow the road crossing the high-lying *Stoney Cross Plain.* In the pretty wooded valley below us to the right is the *Rufus Stone*, erected last century by the Earl of Delaware, a descendant of the founder of the State of Delaware, on the supposed spot of the death of the king (see inscription). [We may send the carriage on to the (1 M.) *Stoney Cross Inn (Compton Arms)*, while we make the short digression to the monument.] At Stoney Cross we bend to the left and begin our homeward journey by making for (3½ M.) **Boldrewood*, where we inspect the 'King' and 'Queen' oaks and other magnificent trees. About 1½ M. farther on is the **Mark Ash Wood*, an imposing forest sanctuary with hundreds of noble beeches. We then proceed by a new road through *Knight Wood*, with its famous oak (about 20 ft. in girth), to the (2 M.) main road, and then follow the latter to the N.E. (left) to (1½ M.) *Bank*, where the red house of Miss Braddon (Mrs. Maxwell) is conspicuous on the hill to the right. Thence to Lyndhurst, 1 M. — Walkers may shorten some of the above distances by footpaths. A map of the New Forest from the Ordnance Survey (1 inch to the mile) may be obtained at Southampton or Lyndhurst for 6*d*.

By the direct road **Beaulieu Abbey** (see p. 82) is 7 M. from Lyndhurst, but a pleasant detour may be made viâ *Brockenhurst* (p. 95), which lies 4 M. to the S. of Lyndhurst and 5 M. to the W. of the abbey. — Beaulieu, pronounced *Bewley* (Montagu Arms), is picturesquely situated at the head of *Beaulieu Creek*, where the little river *Exe* flows into it. The Cistercian abbey of Beaulieu was founded by King John in 1204, and possessed the privilege of a sanctuary down to the dissolution of the monasteries. Margaret of Anjou and her son Prince Edward found shelter here shortly before the battle of Tewkesbury, so fatal to the red rose of Lancaster. Passing under an ivy-clad portal, we reach the Abbot's House, now used as a residence by Baron Montagu. The *Church of the village, in the E. E. style, was the refectory of the Abbey. On the E. wall is a curious monument with an inscription in the form of an acrostic, the name being formed by the initial letters of the lines.

12. The Channel Islands.

The Channel Islands are usually visited by steamboat from *Southampton* or *Weymouth*, as mentioned below; but as the hours are sometimes changed, the traveller should consult the railway and steamboat time-tables. Steamers also ply from *Plymouth*. In all cases the sea-passage is frequently lengthened through fog.

1. From Southampton (p. 80). Mail-steamers ply daily (except Sun.) from Southampton to (8 hrs.) *Guernsey* and (10 hrs.) *Jersey*, usually starting at midnight (Sat. at 10.30 p.m., for Jersey only). They sail in connection with the *London & South Western Railway*, the mail-trains of which leave London (Waterloo) at 9.45 p.m. (Sat. 7.45 p.m.) and run alongside the boats. Through-fares from London 33*s*., 28*s*., 25*s*.; return-tickets, available for one month, 48*s*., 38*s*., 30*s*.; 2nd and 3rd class passengers may travel in the saloon for 5*s*. extra. Fares from Southampton 20*s*., 14*s*.; return 33*s*., 23*s*.

2. From Weymouth (p. 98). Steamers daily (except Mon.; in connection with the trains of the *Great Western Railway;* shortest sea-passage), starting at 2.15 a.m., and reaching Guernsey in 4½, and Jersey in 6¾ hrs. Fares the same as the above. Travellers from London (Paddington) leave at 9.15 p.m., so that the whole journey occupies 9½-11¾ hrs.

3. From Plymouth (Sutton Pool; p. 139). Steamers start for the Channel Islands every Mon. and Thurs. at 8 p.m.; fares to Guernsey 16*s*., 12*s*., 9*s*.; return 27*s*. 6*d*., 20*s*., 15*s*.; to Jersey 18*s*., 14*s*., 10*s*.; return 30*s*., 22*s*., 16*s*.

September is the best month for a visit to the Channel Islands. Few travellers will care to make this trip unless they can spend a week at least among the Islands, but a fortnight, a month, or more may be pleasantly passed in exploring them. The following Plan for a Week's Tour will be found convenient. 1st Day: *St. Peter Port*, in Guernsey, and excursion to *St. Sampson*, *Bordeaux Harbour*, and *L'Ancresse Bay.* — 2nd Day: From St. Peter Port to *Moulin Huet*, the *Creux Mahie*, *Lihou Island*, and other points on the S. and S.W. coast of Guernsey. — 3rd & 4th Days: Visits to *Alderney* and to *Sark* (note the days on which steamers ply to these islands, p. 89). — 5th Day: From Guernsey to Jersey. *St. Helier's.* Excursion to *Gorey* and *Mt. Orgueil.* — 6th Day: From St. Helier's to *St. Aubin's*, *St. Brelade's Bay*, the *Corbière*, the *Etac*, the *Grève au Lançon*, the *Grève au Lecq*, and back through the interior of the island. — 7th Day: Excursion from St. Helier's to *Bouley Bay and the N. Coast.* — The only adequate method of exploring these Islands is on foot. But

For a coloured map of The Channel Islands see page 564

Excursion-Brakes (fare 2*s.* 6*d.*), plying daily (including Sun.) from St. Peter Port in Guernsey and from St. Helier's in Jersey, afford a convenient means of visiting the principal points of interest, which, in the case of each island, are included in the course of three drives. Programmes of the routes may be obtained at the livery-stables or from the guides that accompany the cars. *Carriages*, 20-25*s.* per day.

Jersey and Guernsey have each a local copper coinage, exactly corresponding to British pence and half-pence. With this exception British money alone is legally current in Jersey, but both in that island, and to a greater extent in Guernsey and Alderney, French gold and silver coins and local 1*l.* notes are also in circulation. In many shops in Guernsey a premium of 1*s.* per 1*l.* is given for British money. The custom-dues are light. Tobacco, cigars, and tea are cheap, so are the inferior spirits and cordials used in the Islands. High-class wines and spirits are, however, little cheaper than in England, and provisions generally are quite as dear.

Those who desire a longer account of the Islands are referred to the special histories by ***Falle***, ***Duncan***, ***Tupper***, and ***Hoskins***, to the account of *Inglis*, and to 'The Channel Islands', by *Ansted* and *Latham*. *Victor Hugo's* 'Toilers of the Sea' should be read by visitors to Guernsey; *Miss Hesba Stretton's* 'The Doctor's Dilemma' by visitors to Sark.

The group usually known as the **Channel Islands** consists of *Jersey*, *Guernsey*, *Alderney*, and *Sark*, together with a number of islets and rocks. Their joint area amounts to about 75 sq. M., and in 1881 they contained 87,731 inhabitants. Geographically they belong to France, lying in the bay of St. Malo, within a distance of 10-30 M. from the coast of Normandy, while Alderney, the most northerly of the group, is fully 50 M. from England. They have, however, belonged to England for seven centuries, being a remnant of its Norman possessions lost in 1204. The beautiful scenery of the Islands comprises views of wild grandeur and pleasing rural landscapes within a very limited space. The rocky coasts of the larger islands, indeed, vie with the finest scenery of the kind in Great Britain. The strategic position of the Islands is so important that the British government has spent vast sums on their defences. St. Peter Port, St. Helier's, and other points are defended by strong forts; while the numerous martello-towers, watch-houses, etc. — now left to decay — are relics of an obsolete system of defence. The good roads in the larger islands are also military works.

History. The early history of the Islands is wrapped in obscurity. The original inhabitants, who have left traces of their presence in the cromlechs, were probably of Celtic (Breton) race. The Roman occupation of Gaul extended to these islands, and Jersey is mentioned under the name of ***Caesarea*** in the Itinerary of Antonine. Christianity seems to have been introduced in the 6th cent. by two missionaries from the Continent, whose names have been perpetuated in St. Helier's, in Jersey, and St. Sampson, in Guernsey. At a later date they were occupied by Rollo and his Northmen, and they became part of the duchy of Normandy in 932. Under the first four Norman kings of England the Islands were alternately under English and Norman rule, but since the accession of Henry II. (1154) they have been permanently united with England. They remained, however, under the ecclesiastical jurisdiction of the Bishop of Coutances down to the Reformation, when they were annexed to the see of Winchester. King John is said to have granted a charter to Guernsey, and it seems at least certain that the Islands have enjoyed a distinct political existence since his reign. In the Civil War Jersey espoused the cause of the King, and Guernsey that of the Parliament, a divergence of which traces are still noticeable. During the French and American wars the islanders reaped a rich harvest by privateering and smuggling. Since then their legitimate trade, and with it their prosperity, has steadily increased.

The *Geological Formation* of the Islands is almost entirely granitic, stratified rocks occurring only in Jersey and Alderney. The granite is generally of the syenite variety, and is much quarried for building purposes. The coasts are generally very rugged, forming numerous bold headlands and capacious bays. The Islands contain no hills of great elevation, the highest being about 365 ft. (in Sark). Jersey is well wooded. The *Climate* is very mild and equable, the mean annual temperature being about 51° Fahr., and is admirably adapted for persons with weak chests. The rain-fall, amounting to 30-35 inches, is rather high, but the rapid evaporation prevents undue humidity. Snow and frost are rare. The so-called 'Summer of St. Martin', resembling the Indian Summer of America, usually sets in about the middle of October. The *Soil* is fertile, producing good crops of fruit, wheat, and turnips; and in Jersey potatoes are extensively cultivated for exportation. Large quantities of grapes and tomatoes, ripened under glass but generally without artificial heat, are exported from Guernsey. Figs, medlars, etc. also reach maturity in the open air; and American aloes, palms, magnolias, and similar plants flourish. The chief manure used is *Vraic*, or sea-weed, the regular gathering of which forms one of the most characteristic sights in the Islands. The small and finely-shaped cattle peculiar to the Channel Islands are widely known and highly prized under the name of Alderneys; they are remarkable for the quantity and quality of the milk they yield, and make dairy-farming a very profitable pursuit. The chief varieties of fish are the turbot, mullet, John Dory, lobsters, crabs, conger-eels, oysters, and a kind of sand-eel called the '*lançon*'. The vegetation of the Islands is very rich and varied, and the naturalist will also find much to interest him in the birds of Guernsey and the zoophytes of Sark (p. 91).

The vernacular *Language* is the old Norman French, varying considerably in the different islands †; and commoner in Guernsey than in Jersey. English, however, is very generally spoken in the towns, where there is a large admixture of English residents attracted by the climate and scenery. French is the official language of the courts. The inhabitants have preserved many of their old laws and customs, and are in several respects different both from their English and their French neighbours. In matters of government the Islands form two divisions or bailiwicks, one consisting of Jersey alone, the other of Guernsey and the smaller islands. Freeman styles them 'distinct commonwealths'. Each bailiwick is presided over by a lieutenant-governor and a bailiff, or judge, appointed by the Crown and assisted by a 'States Assembly'. The latter body includes the 'jurats' (see below), the rectors of the parishes, and a number of elected deputies. Judicial affairs are managed by a Royal Court, consisting of the bailiff and twelve 'jurats', or magistrates. The laws relating to property are very peculiar, those of succession being specially elaborate. All male inhabitants are bound to serve in the local militia.

In approaching the Channel Islands from Southampton or Weymouth, the steamer first comes in sight of the dangerous rocks called the *Casquets*, where the only son of Henry I. perished by shipwreck in 1120 ††, and where the Victory, a man-of-war, was lost with 1100 men in 1744. They are now marked by a triple flashing light.

---

† Students of the *patois* will find excellent material in the poems and texts published in the Guille-Allès Library Series, edited by *J. L. Pitts*, with English translations and notes (Bichard, Guernsey).

†† Such is the tradition, but as a matter of fact the catastrophe seems to have taken place upon *Les Cattes Razes* reef near Barfleur. William of Malmesbury, writing in the year of the accident, says: 'the king's son set sail from Barfleur and the ship was driven on a rock *not far from the shore*'.

Alderney (p. 89) lies about 8 M. to the E. The first stopping-place is *St. Peter Port*, the capital of Guernsey, where cabs and porters await the arrival of the steamer.

Guernsey ('green isle'; Latin, *Sarnia*), the second in size of the Channel Islands, is triangular in form, and measures 9½ M. in length from S.E. to N.W. and about 6 M. in breadth at its widest part. The S. coast consists of a bold and almost uninterrupted cliff, rising perpendicularly to a height of 270 ft., from which the land slopes gradually down to the flat beach on the N. The climate of Guernsey is one of the most equable in Europe, the summer being cool and the winter mild, and hence it is the chief resort of the invalid visitors to the Channel Islands. The coast-scenery is finer than that of Jersey, but the interior is thinly wooded and less attractive. Pop. (1881) 32,659.

St. Peter Port. — **Hotels.** *Old Government House, on the hill, R. from 2*s.* 6*d.*, 'pens'. 8*s.* 6*d.*-10*s.*; *Royal, facing the sea, 'pens'. 8*s.* 6*d.*; Carlton or Plaiderie, Pollet Str., R. & A. from 2*s.*, 'pens'. 7*s.*; Victoria, High St., with windows on the Esplanade, commercial, with baths, 'pens'. 7-8*s.*; Channel Islands Hotel, facing the sea; Crown, facing the harbour, plain, 'pens'. 5*s.* — Numerous private lodgings.

Cab from the pier to the hotels 2*s.*; *Porter* from pier 6*d.*

Excursion-Cars, see p. 85. — *Carriage*, 20*s.* per day.

Boats. Small rowing-boats, 6*d.* per hour. Sailing-boat, with man, to *Herm* 10*s.*; to *Sark* (1½ hr. with good wind), 20*s.*

Bathing Places, on the S. side of the bay; adm. 3*d.* *Public Bathing Places* adjoining.

St. Peter Port, a town of 16,500 inhab., is picturesquely situated on a rising ground in a shallow bay on the E. side. The old town next to the sea is somewhat poorly built, though quaint and picturesque, but the modern quarters beyond and on each side contain numerous substantial edifices. At the S. end of the broad *Esplanade* which skirts the harbour is the Gothic *Town Church (St. Peter's)*, perhaps the most important specimen of mediæval architecture (early 14th cent.) in the Islands, lately restored and decorated. Behind the church is the commodious *Market*, 200 ft. in length, where fine displays of fish, flowers, and vegetables are usually to be seen. The arcades to the right are known as the *French Market*, because the fruit and vegetables sold there come chiefly from France. At the E. end of the latter is the entrance to the *Guille-Allés Library and Reading Room*, founded by two natives of the town (open daily, except Sun., 10-9; tourists are invited to use the place without charge). From the S. side of the church the steep Cornet St. ascends to Hauteville St., No 38 in which is **Hauteville House*, a large house of gloomy exterior, the former residence of Victor Hugo, whose 'Toilers of the Sea' has its scene in Guernsey. The house (shown daily; small fee) contains numerous interesting memorials of the poet. The glass-covered room at the top, the floor of which is also a massive slab of glass, admitting light to the house below, was Hugo's study, and commands a beautiful view of the port and neighbouring islands.

From the N. or White Rock Pier, at which the steamers lie, the Avenue St. Julien ascends to the fashionable quarter of the town, near *Cambridge Park*, at one end of which is *Castle Cary*, the residence of several of the governors, and conspicuous from the sea. Near the other end is the *Candie Library*, for which visitors may obtain a ticket on written application. Farther S. is the prominent *Victoria Tower* (view; key at the Militia Arsenal opposite; small fee), built to commemorate the visit of Queen Victoria and Prince Albert in 1846. Still farther to the S. are the *Grange Club* (visitors admitted on introduction) and the large but unattractive building of *Elizabeth College*. In Manor St. is the *Royal Court House*, where the States meet, with several portraits.

On a rocky islet in the harbour, connected with the shore by a long breakwater, rises *Castle Cornet* (no admission), the old residence of the governor, and formerly considered a strong fortress. Part of it is said to be of Roman workmanship. In 1672 it was blown up by an explosion of gunpowder. The infant daughter of the governor, Viscount Hatton, was discovered next day unhurt and asleep amid the ruins, and lived to be the Countess of Winchelsea and mother of 30 children. Farther to the S., on the cliff overlooking the bathing-places (p. 87), is *Fort George*, one of the strongest fortresses in the Islands.

The chief attraction of Guernsey consists in the coast-scenery on the S.E. and S. There are inns at various points of the coast, but the best plan is to fix our headquarters at St. Peter Port.

About 1$^1/_2$ M. to the S. of St. Peter Port is *Fermain Bay*, with a sandy beach backed by walls of rock. On the height, $^1/_2$ M. to the S., rises the *Doyle Column*, 150 ft. high (key at first cottage to the W.), erected in honour of Sir John Doyle, a former governor of the island, and commanding an extensive view. The view from the promontory of *Jerbourg*, $^1/_2$ M. to the S., is, however, quite as fine. **Moulin Huet Bay*, to the W. of the point, and 2$^1/_2$ M. from St. Peter Port, is one of the finest spots in Guernsey. The cliffs here, 200-300 ft. in height, are very imposing. Farther on is the charming *Saints' Bay*. Round the next point is *Icart Bay*, with the picturesque cove of *Petit Bot* (Rfmts.) in its N.W. angle. The most interesting points farther on are the *Gouffre* (Hotel), a kind of rocky cauldron at the mouth of a small gorge, 4$^1/_2$ M. from the harbour; the *Corbière* (5 M.), a headland remarkable for the green veins intersecting its pink and gray granite; and the *Creux Mahie* (6$^1/_2$ M.), a cavern 200 ft. long, accessible by a steep and difficult descent from the cliffs above. The points from Fermain Bay to the Gouffre may be visited in the course of a fatiguing but interesting walk (2-3 hrs.) along a narrow path skirting the slopes and tops of the cliffs.

The church of *St. Martin*, 2$^1/_2$ M. to the S.W. of St. Peter Port, has a pretty porch; and the *Chapel of St. Apolline*, near St.

Saviour's, 4 M. to the W., is a curious example of very early architecture (ascribed to the 5th cent.).

At the S. W. angle of the island are (7½ M. from St. Peter Port) *Pleinmont Point* and *Caves*, and off the coast the *Hanois Rocks* and lighthouse. The deserted watch-house on the cliff, above the *Gull Rock* (echo), is identified with the 'Haunted House' in the 'Toilers of the Sea'. A good road skirts the low N. W. coast, with its picturesque wide bays, defended by forts and batteries. Near the village of *L'Erée* (Inn) is a well-preserved dolmen, known as the *Creux des Fées*. Off the coast here is the small island of *Lihou*, with some picturesque rocks, once the seat of an old priory (12th cent.).

Omnibuses (2*d.*) run to the N. from St. Peter Port to *St. Sampson*, the second town of the island, with important quarries of blue granite, which is largely exported to London. About halfway we pass, ½ M. to the left, *Ivy Castle*, a picturesque Norman ruin; and a little farther on an *Obelisk* in memory of Admiral Lord Saumarez (1757-1836), a native of St. Peter Port. Beyond St. Sampson is *Vale Castle*, or St. Michael's Castle, above the small bay known as *Bordeaux Harbour*, noted for its fine zoophytes. A pleasant walk may be taken thence to *L'Ancresse Bay* and *Common* (with numerous Celtic remains), at the N. extremity of the island, returning to St. Peter Port by *Vale Church* (1117) and 'Doyle's Road'.

About 3 M. to the E. of Guernsey lie the islets of **Herm and Jethou** (occasional excursion-steamers; boat, see p. 87), both overrun by immense numbers of rabbits. Herm possesses a small 'creux' like that in Sark (p. 91); but the only part of the island now open to visitors is the 'Shell-beach', one of the happiest hunting-grounds for the conchologist in Great Britain. The channels to the E. and W. of these islets are known as the *Great* and *Little Russel*.

The islands of *Alderney* and *Sark* should be visited from Guernsey before we go on to Jersey.

Steamers leave St Peter Port for *Alderney* and *Cherbourg* on Tues., Thurs., and Sat. at 9 or 9.30 a.m., returning on Wed., Thurs., and Sat. or Sun. (fares to Alderney 4*s.*; to Cherbourg 8*s.* and 12*s.*, return, available for a month, 12*s.* and 16*s.*); for *Sark*, several times weekly (return-fare 2*s.*); for *Granville* on Mon. (fare 8*s.*); for *St. Malo* on Tues. (fare 8*s.*). The above data refer to the summer months. — Steamers from Guernsey to Jersey, see p. 84 (fares 5*s.*, 3*s.* 6*d.*).

Alderney (French *Aurigny*, Latin *Aurinia*), the third in size of the Channel Islands, lies 20 M. to the N. of Guernsey, and is 4 M. in length and 1½ M. in breadth. In 1881 it contained 2039 inhabitants, most of whom are English. Of great military importance, it is defended by a series of strong forts and batteries, the most important being *Fort Albert*, on the N. side, the guns of which command the harbour of *Braye*, where the steamer lands its passengers. The costly but ill-designed breakwater is often damaged by the violence of the sea. About 1 M. from the pier, in the centre of the island, is the small town of *St. Anne* (Scott's Hotel, 'pens'. 8*s.* 6*d.*; several small Inns; lodgings), with a new church in the E.E. style, designed by Sir G. G. Scott, and erected to the memory of John Le Mesurier, the last of the hereditary governors. As in Guernsey, the S. and S.E. coast of Alderney consists of a range of almost perpendicular cliffs, from the top of which the land slopes gradually down to the flat but rocky shore on the N. The scenery of the granite and porphyry cliffs is very grand and varied, but it is generally difficult to reach the beach at their base either by land or water. Among the finest points are the *Lovers' Chair* and the *Hanging Rock (Roche Pendante)*, the latter a curious isolated column of sandstone, 60 ft. high. The geological veinings of the rocks are often singular. Alderney is separated from the islet of *Burhou* by the channel called *The Swinge*, and from Normandy by the *Race of Alderney*, 7 M. wide, which is very dangerous in rough weather. Through this channel the remnant of the French fleet escaped after the Battle of La Hogue in 1693.

Sark *(Dixcart Hotel*, 7*s*. 6*d*. per day, luncheon 2*s*.; *Victoria*, 6*s*. per day; *Royal)*, also called *Serk* or *Sercq*, 3$^1/_2$ M. long and 1$^3/_4$ M. wide in the middle, with 578 inhab. (in 1881), lies 6 M. to the E. of Guernsey. A visit to this most picturesque island should on no account be omitted. Those who devote to it only the interval between the arrival and departure of the steamer from Guernsey should visit the Coupée, the Gouliot Caves (at low water), Dixcart Bay (lunching at Dixcart Hotel), the Creux Derrible, and, if time and energy permit, the Seigneurie.

The steamer which rounds the S. end of Sark in going, the N. end in returning, lands passengers at the picturesque *Creux Harbour*, on the W. side, to the N. of the *Buron Islets*, whence a tunnel leads through the high cliffs to the interior of the island (boat from the steamer at low water 5*d*. each). The road from the harbour ascends to the Victoria Hotel. Keeping straight on past the hotel, we pass through a gate into a pretty avenue of elms, at the end of which, near the school, we bear to the left. A few yards farther on we turn to the right, and passing a conspicuous windmill, reach the hamlet of *Vaurocque*. Hence the main road leads to the left (S.) direct to (40 min. from the harbour) the **Coupée* †, a natural causeway, 100 yds. long and only from 5 to 8 ft. broad, with a nearly vertical descent of 290 ft. on one side, uniting the N. and S. parts of the island, known as *Great* and *Little Sark*. A little beyond the Coupée a faintly-marked path leads off to the left, across the common, to the curious 'creux', called the *Pot* (steep and difficult descent). We may follow the cliffs to the S. end of Little Sark, where there are some abandoned silver-mines, returning by the road. — The road leading due W. from Vaurocque (see above) soon forks, near a farm. The path to the right (pass through the

† An amusing story is told of an inhabitant of Little Sark, who, on returning home in the evening, used to judge of his ability to cross the Coupée by walking along a dismounted cannon by the side of the path. If his potations had in any degree impaired his equilibrium, he judged it safer to lie down and sleep off the effects before 'trying the pass'.

gate, skirt the wall, and bear to the right at the ruined cottage) leads to the *Gouliot Caves*, which are extraordinarily rich in brilliantly coloured zoophytes. The final descent to the Caves, accessible only at low water, requires caution. Opposite lies *Brecqhou* or *Ile des Marchands*, separated from Sark by a narrow channel noted for its irregular and powerful currents. A frigate is said once to have safely navigated the channel, which it had entered through an error. The path to the left at the farm (see above) leads past a *Monument* to Mr. F. Pilcher and others, drowned off the coast in 1862, to the fisherman's port of *Havre Gosselin*, where a ladder affords the only means of embarking or disembarking. — A road diverging to the left (sign-post) from that between Vaurocque and the Coupée leads to the prettily situated *Dixcart Hotel*, beneath which is the charming *Dixcart Bay*. Farther to the N. is *Derrible Bay*, with the **Creux Derrible*, a natural shaft or funnel in the cliff, nearly 180 ft. high, the bottom of which may be entered at low water. Thence we return to the Victoria Hotel. — The *Seigneurie*, or manor of the 'Lord of Sark', is reached by the road running N. from the W. end of the avenue of elms (p. 90). The well-kept grounds are open to the public on Mon. and Thurs.; the house occupies the site of a church founded by St. Maglorius in the 6th century. On the N.W. coast of the island are the interesting *Boutiques Caverns*, probably once used by smugglers, and a picturesque group of detached rocks called *Les Autelets*.

Jersey ('grass isle'), the largest and most important of the Channel Islands, lies 18 M. to the S.E. of Guernsey and 16 M. from the French coast. It is 10 M. long from E. to W. and 5-6 M. wide from N. to S. The land is high on the N. side, and slopes down to the S. and E. The N. coast consists of a lofty and picturesque wall of cliff, penetrated by numerous small inlets, while the other coasts expand in large and open bays, with fine sandy beaches. The interior, which is intersected by several streams, is also picturesque, especially the small valleys and the old roads, almost concealed by hedgerows and trees. In 1881 the island contained 52,455 inhabitants, who carry on an active trade with England, France, Holland, India, and Newfoundland. Large quantities of potatoes, pears, and apples are annually exported to Covent Garden. Among the vegetable curiosities of the island is the 'Cow Cabbage', which grows to a height of 8-10 ft. and is made into walking-sticks. English is much more generally spoken than in Guernsey.

The steamer (see p. 84) from St. Peter Port takes about 2 hrs. to reach (30 M.) *St. Helier's*, the capital of Jersey, picturesquely situated in the beautiful *Bay of St. Aubin*, on the S. of the island.

St. Helier's. — **Hotels.** Brée's Stopford Hotel, David Place, at some distance from the harbour, 'pens'. 8*s.* 6*d.*-12*s.*, R. & A. from 3*s.* United Service Hotel, David Place, near Brée's, 'pens'. 7*s.*; Yacht Club near the pier, 'pens'. 8*s.* 9*d.*, R. & A. from 2*s.* 3*d.*; Marine, commercial, 'pens'. 8*s.* 3*d.*, with swimming and Turkish baths, Minor's Private Hotel, 'pens'. 8*s*. 6*d*., these both facing the sea, at the W. end of the Esplanade; BRITISH, Broad St., 'pens'. 8*s*.; STAR, near the Pier, unpretending, 'pens'. 6*s*. — French Houses: POMME D'OR, facing the sea, 'pens'. from 7*s*.; PALAIS DE CRISTAL, 62 King St., 'pens'. 8 fr.; HÔTEL DE L'EUROPE, Mulcaster St., 8 fr. — *Boarding Houses* and *Lodgings* numerous, but often full in the season.

Restaurants at most of the hotels; *Café Parisien*, at the Palais de Cristal, see above.

Theatre, Gloucester St., adm. 6*d*.-3*s*. — **Pavilion,** Springfield Road, concerts several evenings weekly. — *Band* on the pier and in the People's Park, each once a week in summer.

Post Office, Grove Place. — **Baths,** *Victoria Baths*, George Town; at the *Marine Hotel*, see p. 91.

Steamers from Jersey to *Granville* and *St. Malo* (fares 10 fr., 6 fr. 25 c.; return, available for a month, 15 fr., 9 fr. 40 c.). The days of starting vary with the season, and are announced in the daily papers. — To *Guernsey*, daily, comp. p. 84. — The Southampton steamers start from the Victoria Pier, the farthest from the town, the Weymouth steamers from the Albert or S. Pier. At low water passengers land in small boats (9*d*. each).

Cabs. For the first mile 1*s*., each additional mile or fraction 6*d*.; from the harbour to the town 1*s*. 6*d*.; per hour 2*s*. 6*d*., each addit. 1/2 hr. 1*s*. — *Omnibus* from the harbour to the town 6*d*.

Excursion Cars, see p. 85. — *Carriages*, 25*s*. per day.

Railway to *Corbière*, 7 1/2 M., in 1/2 hr.; to *Gorey*, 6 M., in 22 min. Trains several times daily. Return-tickets entitle the holders to break the journey at any intermediate station.

St. Helier's, a well-built and flourishing town with 31,000 inhab., combines the character of a busy seaport with that of a fashionable watering-place. It is a favourite residence for retired officers of the army and navy and it contains many schools, the chief of which is *Victoria College*, a handsome building on the E. side of the town (1852).

The harbour is enclosed by substantial piers, but is dry at low water. To the N. is the *Town Church*, a Gothic edifice of the 14th cent., lately restored. Opposite the E. end is *Royal Square*, the former market-place, with a curious gilt statue of George II. The square was the scene of the death of Major Pierson at the Battle of Jersey in 1781, when an attempt by the French to seize the town was successfully repulsed. On the S.E. side of the square is a block of buildings containing the *Cohue Royal* or court-house, the *Salle des Etats*, or parliament-house, and the *Public Library* (17,000 vols.). The two former are shown by an usher (small fee); in the Cohue Royal is a copy of Copley's 'Death of Major Pierson' (see above), and a portrait of Gen. Conway, by Gainsborough. Broad St., leading W. from Royal Square, contains an obelisk in memory of *Pierre Le Sueur* (1811-1853), five times mayor of St. Helier's, and is continued by York St., with the *Hôtel de Ville*, to the *Parade*, an open space planted with trees and embellished with a monument to *Gen. Don*, a former governor. Farther to the W. is the *People's Park*, above which rises the *Gallows Hill*. — To the N.E. of the town is the *Maison St. Louis*, a house of the Jesuits.

On a ridge to the E. of the harbour rises *Fort Regent* (no adm.), a strong and massive modern fortress, erected at a cost of nearly

1,000,000*l.* In size, and as a defence, this stronghold eclipses the picturesque old *Elizabeth Castle*, situated on a rock in the middle of the harbour (permit for the latter on application at the Governor's Office, No. 8, Stopford Road). On an adjoining rock are the ruins of a very ancient structure, which tradition names the *Hermitage* of St. Helier or Elericus (p. 85).

The excursions from St. Helier's may be conveniently grouped into the following three sections, which comprise all the most interesting parts of the island. They may be made by the excursion-cars (p. 85), or partly by rail (p. 92) and partly on foot. The pedestrian, however, may perform the circuit of the island without returning at night to St. Helier's, as there are fair inns at many different points (comp. below and p. 94).

1. From St. Helier's to Gorey and E. Jersey. Eastern Railway to Gorey in 22 min., skirting the flat coast most of the way, affording a view of the wide *Grouville Bay* with Fort Henry in the centre. Near the first station, *George Town*, are the Victoria Baths. *Pontac* (10 min.) is the station for the village of *St. Clement*, with an old church containing some curious frescoes. — The small village of *Gorey* (British Hotel; Hôtel de France; steamer to Cartaret and Port Bail, every second day, fare 5*s.* 4*d.*) is the seat of the Jersey oyster-fishery, which, however, is not so productive as formerly. It lies near a lofty headland crowned with **Mont Orgueil Castle*, an imposing and picturesque ruin, part of which is said to date from the Roman period. The *Chapel of St. George*, with short thick piers and colonettes, is interesting. Charles II. resided here for some time during his exile, and for three years (1637-40) it was the prison of William Prynne, the pamphleteer, who wrote here a poem on the castle. On a clear day the spires of Coutances Cathedral can be seen from the battlements.

Beyond Gorey we proceed on foot along the coast to the N. Beyond *Anne Port* and *St. Catharine's Harbour* is (1 hr. from Gorey) the breakwater of *Pierre Mouillée*. This massive work, 800 yds. long, was constructed in 1843-55 at a cost of 250,000*l.* as the beginning of a harbour of refuge, before it was discovered that the set of the tides, etc., rendered the enterprise entirely useless. Beyond *Verclut Point* is *Flicquet Bay*, bounded on the N. by an almost detached headland called *La Coupe*. On the next headland, the *Couperon*, is a dolmen; and beyond it is the secluded little bay of **Rozel* (Hotel), a favourite point for picnics from St. Helier's. From this point we may return by the road leading to the S. through the interior of the island, passing first *St. Martin's Church* (12th cent.), with an elegant tower disastrously 'restored'. Farther on is *La Hogue Bie*, or the Prince's Tower (adm. 6*d.*), a modern structure erected on an interesting ancient tumulus. [The name, from *Hougue*, a low hill of artificial origin, may be related to the A.S. *hoga* and *howe*, Norse *höge*, and German *hoch.*] The *View from the top is very fine, embracing the whole island, with its park-like interior and indented coasts; to the E. the coast of Normandy is visible. About 1 M. farther on is the hamlet of *Five Oaks*, beyond which we pass *St. Saviour's Church*, the *Government House*, and Victoria College (p. 92), reaching St. Helier's after about 10 M. walking from Gorey.

Those who have less time to spare may proceed from Gorey direct to St. Martin's Church or to La Hogue Bie, reaching St. Helier's after a walk in the former case of 6 M., in the latter of about $4^1/_2$ M. The direct road from Gorey to St. Helier's viâ Grouville is about 3 M.

2. From St. Helier's to St. Aubin's, Corbière, and W. Jersey. The Western Railway (p. 92) and the road skirt the edge of the broad, flat *St. Aubin's Bay*. At low tide the sands may be crossed on foot.

St. Aubin's (*Nicolle's*, near the station, 6*s*. per day; *Sommerville*, 8*s*. 6*d*.-10*s*. 6*d*.) is a small town with a harbour and an old castle built on a detached rock like Elizabeth Castle at St. Helier's.

Beyond St. Aubin's the road leads to the W. to ($1^1/_2$ M.) *St. Brelade's Church*, one of the oldest churches in the Channel Islands (1111), situated on the W. shore of the attractive bay of the same name. Adjoining the church is the *Fisherman's Chapel*, a still earlier structure. At high tide the sea washes over the churchyard. The little inlet of *Beauport*, on the W. side of the bay, contains some very picturesque rock-scenery. About 2 M. beyond the church is La Corbière (see below), which may also be reached by the cliffs.

To the S. of St. Aubin's are the pretty grounds of *Noirmont Manor* (admission usually granted on application at the lodge). The avenue leads to *Noirmont Point*, to the W. of which is *Portelet Bay*, with granite quarries. *Janvrin Island* in this bay (accessible at low water) derives its name from a sea-captain who, with his whole crew, died here of plague in 1721, while in quarantine.

The railway runs inland from St. Aubin's (only 3-4 trains daily beyond St. Aubin's), crossing the sandy plateau of *Le Quenvais*. *La Moye*, the fourth station from St. Aubin's, is the most convenient for those desiring to explore St. Ouen's Bay, etc. (see below), on foot. The terminus of the railway is at ($7^1/_2$ M.) *La Corbière*, the S.W. extremity of the island, where there is a lighthouse (permit obtained at the Hôtel de Ville in St. Helier's). Fantastic rocky scenery.

La Corbière forms the S. headland of the wide and open *Bay of St. Ouen*, which occupies almost the whole of the W. coast. At the opposite end of the bay, $5^1/_2$ M. to the N., is the *Etac*, another detached mass of rock. Accommodation may be obtained at the inn in the adjoining village. About $^3/_4$ M. farther on is a detached pinnacle of rock, 160 ft. high, known as *La Pule*, and $^3/_4$ M. beyond is *Cape Grosnez*, the N.W. point of the island, marked by a picturesque ruined arch. The adjoining **Grève au Lançon* is frequently visited for its curious caverns and fissures, which, however, are most easily reached from *Plemont Point*, on the opposite side. A good view is obtained here of the other Channel Islands. A walk of $1^1/_2$ M. along the coast brings us to the **Grève de Lecq* (Hotel and Inn), another fine bay, with some curious caves and a ruined breakwater. The return to ($7^1/_2$ M.) St. Helier's may be made hence through the heart of the island, passing *St. Mary's Church* (1320), the hamlet of *Six Roads*, and *St. Lawrence's Church* (1199); or the excursion may be continued along the N. coast to join the following.

3. From St. Helier's to Bouley Bay and the N. Coast. This excursion affords a good idea of the luxuriant woods and rich pastures of the interior of the island. The first part of the route lies through the picturesque *Val des Vaux*, the birthplace of Lemprière (1750-1824). A little beyond the ($3^1/_2$ M.) *Church of the Trinity* (1163), a striking *View is disclosed of the bay, the azure sea, and the coast of Normandy in the background. The scenery of ($4^1/_2$ M.) **Bouley Bay* is very bold, the cliffs rising at one point to a height of 250 ft. About $^1/_2$ M. to the E. is Rozel (p. 93). About $1^1/_2$ M. in the opposite direction is *Bonne Nuit Harbour*, behind which are the pink granite quarries of *Mont Mado*. About 2-$2^1/_2$ M. farther on are the curious cove of *La Houle*, *Sorel Point*, the *Les Mouriers Waterfall*, and the cavern of *Creux de Vis* or Devil's Hole (2*d.*), all well worthy of a visit. They are almost immediately followed by the *Crabbé*, a deep and narrow gorge, about 1 M. from the Grève de Lecq (see above).

13. From Southampton to Bournemouth, Dorchester, and Weymouth.

Railway from Southampton to (30 M.) *Bournemouth East* in 1-$1^1/_2$ hr. (fares 6*s.* 3*d.*, 4*s.* 3*d.*, 2*s.* 6*d.*); to ($60^1/_2$ M.) *Dorchester* in $2^1/_4$-$2^3/_4$ hrs. (fares 12*s.* 6*d.*, 8*s.* 9*d.*, 5*s.* 1*d.*); to (68 M.) *Weymouth* in $2^1/_2$-$3^1/_4$ hrs. (14*s.*, 9*s.* 9*d.*, 5*s.* 8*d.*). — The line traverses the New Forest (p. 83), affording charming views of that district and afterwards of the sea (to the left).

Travellers by this line start from the station at *Southampton West*, as the through-trains from London (Waterloo) pass to the N. of the town without running in to the Terminus at the Docks (comp. p. 81). — At ($3^1/_2$ M.) *Redbridge*, whence a branch runs to Romsey (p. 82), the train crosses the head of *Southampton Water* (view to the left) and turns to the S. — 4 M. *Totton*. At (7 M.) *Lyndhurst Road* (New Forest Hotel) we reach the borders of the New Forest (omn. to Lyndhurst, see p. 83). — 14 M. **Brockenhurst** *(Rose & Crown)*, i. e. 'Badgers' Wood', the nearest station to Beaulieu Abbey, and a good starting-point for excursions in the New Forest (comp. p. 83). Part of the interesting church is believed to be Saxon. On *Balmer Lawn*, near Brockenhurst, the annual Races for the ponies of the New Forest take place in August.

From Brockenhurst diverges the line to (5 M.) **Lymington** *(Londesborough Arms; Angel)*, the starting-point of the steamers to Yarmouth and Totland Bay in the Isle of Wight (comp. p. 73). Lymington is celebrated for its yacht-building yards. — About 6 M. to the S., at the mouth of the Solent and best reached by water, is *Hurst Castle*, one of Henry VIII.s coast-defences, and for a time the prison of Charles I. (comp. p. 72).

From Brockenhurst to *Dorchester* and *Weymouth*, see p. 97.

The new Bournemouth line, opened in 1888, passes *Sway*, *Milton* (for *Milford-on-Sea*), and *Hinton Admiral*. — $26^1/_2$ M. **Christchurch** (*King's Arms*, well spoken of) is a seaport with an ancient **Priory Church*, a beautiful Norman and E. E. edifice, possessing a remarkable North Porch. The lack of a central tower is, however, severely felt. The screen separating the nave and choir is a fine Perp. work of 1502. Below the cross is a monument to the poet *Shelley* (d. 1822). Some of the other monuments, the Lady Chapel, and the Salisbury Chapel, built by Margaret, Countess of Salisbury, about 1535, are also interesting. — Near the river *Avon* is *Constable House*, a Norman building; and in the grounds of the hotel are the very scanty remains of an old *Castle*. — About 2 M. to the S. is **Hengistbury Head*, which commands a magnificent sea-view, including the Isle of Wight.

$28^1/_2$ M. *Boscombe*, with the house of Lady Shelley, widow of the poet's son (see above). — 30 M. *Bournemouth East;* $33^1/_2$ M. *Bournemouth West*.

Bournemouth. — Hotels. *Royal Bath, East Cliff, with good sea-view; Highcliffe, West Cliff; Mont Dore, a combination of hotel, sanatorium, and bath-house, in the style of the Mont Dore of Auvergne; Royal Exeter (Newlyn's), Exeter Park; Stewart's, Richmond Hill; Boscombe Chine, 2 M. to the E.; Grand, East Cliff; Pembroke; Lansdowne, East Cliff; Bellevue, opposite the Pier; Bourne Hall; Imperial; Central; Branksome Temperance; Waverley Temperance. — Hydropathic Establishment, West Cliff. — Numerous *Boarding Houses* (5-8*s*. per day) and *Lodgings*. — *Lockyer's Restaurant*, Quadrant.

Steamers ply in summer from Bournemouth to *Swanage*, *Poole*, the *Isle of Wight*, *Portsmouth*, *Weymouth*, etc.

Excursion Brakes run to ($6^1/_2$ M.) *Heron Court*, (18 M.) *Corfe Castle*, the *New Forest* (ca. 20 M.), (19 M.) *Blandford*, etc.

Music. *Bands* perform daily on the Pier and in the Public Gardens.

Bournemouth, a fashionable watering-place and winter-resort of recent growth, on *Poole Bay*, with 17,000 inhab., owes much of its salubrity to the luxuriant pine-woods in which it is embosomed. It lies mainly on two small hills, flanking the sheltered valley of the *Bourne*, the banks of which are laid out as public gardens, with pleasant walks. The sandy beach affords excellent bathing, and the *Pier* provides an agreeable marine promenade. Several of the churches are handsome modern buildings with lofty spires.

Pleasant walks may be taken along the coast in both directions. Among the chief features of interest are the '*Chines*' (comp. p. 69) in the sandstone cliffs (particularly to the W.), the most picturesque being *Boscombe Chine* (2 M. to the E.), *Alum Chine*, (3 M.) **Branksome Chine*, and *Durley Chine*. Rhododendrons grow very luxuriantly in and about Bournemouth; and at the blossoming season (June) a visit should be paid to the magnificent plantations of these shrubs at ($6^1/_2$ M.) *Heron Court*.

From Bournemouth to *Poole* and *Broadstone* (with direct connection with the Midlands and North of England), see p. 97.

Through-trains perform the direct journey from *London* (Waterloo) to *Bournemouth East* in $2^1/_2$-$3^1/_4$ hrs. (fares 22*s*., 15*s*. 5*d*., 9*s*.).

Beyond Brockenhurst (p. 95) the DORCHESTER LINE traverses the S. margin of the New Forest, passing (19 M.) *Holmesley* and reaching the extremity of the Forest at (25½ M.) **Ringwood** *(White Hart; Rail. Refreshmt. Rooms)*, the junction of a branch-line to (8 M.) *Christchurch* and (12½ M.) *Bournemouth East* (p. 96). The train then crosses the *Avon* and enters *Dorsetshire*, one of the many counties claiming the title 'Garden of England' on the score of the richness of their vegetation. At (30 M.) *West Moors* a branch-line diverges on the N. to Salisbury (p. 99). — At (35 M.) **Wimborne** *(Crown; King's Head)* there is a fine old **Minster* or collegiate church, illustrating all the styles from Norman to Perp., and possessing a perhaps unique library, in which the volumes are still chained to the shelves. Near Wimborne are *Cranborne Manor*, a seat of the Marquis of Salisbury, and *Canford House* (Lord Wimborne), containing Assyrian antiquities brought home by Sir A. H. Layard. The railway forks here, the right branch leading into Somerset (Bath, Wells), while our line keeps to the left. — 41 M. *Broadstone & New Poole Junction* is the diverging point of a short line to (5½ M.) *Poole* (Antelope; London), a brisk little seaport, with 12,300 inhab. and a good harbour, *Parkstone*, and 10 M. *Bournemouth West* (p. 96). — The train then skirts *Poole Harbour* to (43 M.) *Hamworthy Junction* and (46 M.) *Wareham* (Red Lion; Bear), an ancient and decayed town with earthen ramparts.

Wareham is the junction of a branch-line to (6 M.) *Corfe Castle* and (11 M.) *Swanage*. — ***Corfe Castle,** erected on the *Purbeck Downs* soon after the Norman Conquest, occupies the site of the hunting-lodge where Edward the Martyr was assassinated in 979. It was a frequent residence of King John, and in the Civil War was stoutly defended against the Parliamentarians by Lady Bankes. — **Swanage** *(Royal Victoria*, well spoken of; *Ship)* is a pleasant little watering-place with a good beach.

Purbeck Island, the peninsula on which both these places lie, is famous for its potter's clay and a stone resembling marble. The coast scenery is interesting *(Tilly Whim, St. Alban's Head, Studland*, with its tiny Norman church, etc.).

The train now follows the valley of the *Frome*. Near (51 M.) *Wool* are the ruins of *Bindon Abbey* (12th cent.), and about 3 M. to the S. is *Lulworth Castle* (16th cent.). 55½ M. *Moreton.*

60½ M. **Dorchester** *(King's Arms; Antelope)*, the county-town of Dorsetshire, an ancient place with 7570 inhab., was the *Durnovaria* of the Romans. The *Dorset Museum* contains one of the best provincial collections of antiquities in England. A statue, by Roscoe Mullins, of the *Rev. Wm. Barnes* (d. 1886), author of poems in the Dorset dialect, was erected in St. Peter's Churchyard in 1889.

To the S. of Dorchester are the *Maumbury Rings*, the most perfect Roman amphitheatre in England, 220 ft. long and 165 ft. wide. In the neighbourhood are *Poundbury* and *Maiden Castle*, two large entrenched camps, the origin of the first being doubtful, while the second is almost certainly British. Huge flocks of South Down sheep graze on the surrounding hills. — Dorchester is the junction of lines to *Bridport* and *Yeovil* (p. 102).

68 M. **Weymouth** *(Burdon; Gloucester; Royal; Victoria; Great Western; Crown)*, a thriving watering-place with 13,700 inhab., situated at the mouth of the *Wey*, in the centre of a beautiful bay. It was a favourite resort of George III., whose visits brought it into fashion. The beach is admirably adapted for bathing, and the bay for boating. The *Nothe*, a promontory dividing the town into two parts, is a fine point of view.

Excursions may be made by steamer from Weymouth to *Lulworth Cove*, *Swanage*, *Bournemouth*, *Lyme Regis*, etc., and on land to the *Fort* (fine view), *Osmington* (with an equestrian figure of George III. cut in the chalk), *Corfe Castle* (p. 97), and *Abbotsbury*, with a ruined monastery and a large swannery.

The chief object of interest in the neighbourhood, however, is **Portland Island**, 4 M. to the S. (branch-railway, fares 6*d*., 4*d*,, 3*d*.), with its convict-prison (1600 inmates), its quarries, and its *Breakwaters*. The last, consisting of two huge stone causeways (the larger $1^3/_4$ M. long and 100 ft. broad), enclosing an immense harbour of refuge, were constructed by convict labour in 1847-72., contain 6,000,000 tons of stone, and cost more than 1,000,000*l*. *Portland Castle* was built by Henry VIII. Portland Island, the S. point of which is called the *Portland Bill*, is really a peninsula, united with the mainland by a curious strip of shingle called the *Chesil Bank* (comp. German '*Kiesel*'), extending to (10 M.) Abbotsbury, and full of interest for the geologist (see Damon's 'Geology of Weymouth and Portland'). The chief villages in the island are *Chesilton* (Royal Victoria), the terminus of the railway, and *Castleton* (Royal Breakwater Hotel). — From Weymouth to the *Channel Islands*, see R. 12.

From London Weymouth is reached either by the G. W. R. (160 M.) or the L. S. W. R. (145 M.) in $4^1/_4$-6 hrs. (fares 29*s*. 6*d*., 20*s*., 12*s*. $1^1/_2$*d*.).

14. From London to Salisbury and Exeter.

$171^1/_2$ M. Railway (South Western, from Waterloo) in $4^1/_2$-$6^3/_4$ hrs. (fares 35*s*., 25*s*., 14*s*. $3^1/_2$*d*.). From London to *Salisbury* ($83^1/_2$ M.) in 2-3 hrs. (17*s*. 5*d*., 12*s*. 3*d*., 6*s*. $11^1/_2$*d*.); from Salisbury to *Exeter* ($87^1/_2$ M.) in 2-$3^1/_2$ hrs. (17*s*. 5*d*., 12*s*. 3*d*., 6*s*. 11*d*.). — Exeter may also be reached by the Great Western Railway viâ Taunton (194 M., in $4^1/_4$-$6^1/_4$ hrs.; fares as above; comp. R. 16).

From London to (48 M.) *Basingstoke*, see R. 11. — About 3 M. farther on the Winchester line diverges to the left. The district now traversed is somewhat unattractive. 59 M. *Whitchurch* (White Hart). About 2 M. to the E. is the paper manufactory of the Bank of England, and 6 M. to the N. is *Kingsclere*, with training-stables for race-horses. — 60 M. *Hurstbourne*, the station for *Hurstbourne Priors*, the seat of the Earl of Portsmouth, surrounded by a picturesque park.

66 M. **Andover** *(Star & Garter; White Hart)*, an agricultural town with 5870 inhab., is the junction of lines to *Savernake* and *Swindon* (N.) and *Romsey* (S.; for Southampton). About $1^1/_2$ M. to the S. is *Bury Hill*, with an extensive and well-defined British camp (view). An important annual fair, chiefly for sheep and hops, is held at *Weyhill*, 3 M. to the N.W. — Near ($72^1/_2$ M.) *Grately* rises **Quarley Hill*, crowned with an ancient and extensive entrenchment, and commanding a fine view. A little beyond (78 M.) *Porton* (right) is seen the fortified hill of *Old Sarum* (comp. p. 101).

$83^1/_2$ M. **Salisbury.** — **Hotels.** *White Hart, St. John's St., R. & A. 4*s.* 6*d.*; Red Lion, Cathedral, Milford St.; *Angel, near the station, R. & A. 4*s.*; Three Swans, Winchester St. — *Rail. Rfmt. Rooms.*

Salisbury, the county-town of Wiltshire, with 15,660 inhab., is pleasantly situated at the confluence of the three small rivers *Wiley*, *Avon*, and *Bourne*. It owes its existence to the transference of the episcopal see from Old Sarum to this site (1220), and has had a peaceful and comparatively uneventful history.

The lofty spire of the Cathedral dominates all views of the town. We may enter the cathedral-precincts by *St. Anne's Gate*, near the White Hart Hotel, or by the similar archway at the end of High St. The beautiful **Close* consists of a large expanse of velvety sward, shaded by lofty trees and affording an unimpeded view of the most graceful and symmetrical of English cathedrals. On the turf of the Close, to the N. of the Cathedral, are the foundations of the old *Campanile*, pulled down by Wyatt (see below). Another old archway *(Harnham Gate)* is still standing at the S. W. corner of the Close.

***Salisbury Cathedral**, a splendid example of pure Early English, enjoyed the rare advantage of having been begun and finished within a period of 40 years (1220-1260), and is remarkable for the uniformity, harmony, and perspicuity of its construction. Mr. Fergusson has well pointed out that there is scarcely a trace of foreign influence in the building, the square E. end in particular taking the place of the apse of the Norman churches and fixing the future character of English choirs; and he adds that it is 'one of the best proportioned and, at the same time, most poetic designs of the Middle Ages' ('History of Architecture', Vol. II).

The various parts of the building all unite to lead the eye to the central point, the richly-adorned **Spire* (1250), which is the loftiest in England (406 ft.). The ground-plan of the Cathedral is cruciform, with two sets of transepts. The sculptures on the W. front were nearly all destroyed by the Puritans, but have been replaced. The chief dimensions of the Cathedral are as follows: length 473 ft., breadth across the W. transepts 230 ft., breadth of nave and aisles 99 ft., height of nave 81 ft. The usual entrance is by the *N. Porch*, which is open 9-6 in summer, 9.30-4 in winter; daily services at 7.30 a. m., 10 a. m., and 4p.m. (3 p.m. in summer).

The ***Interior** is finely proportioned and impressive, but produces a somewhat cold and bare effect, due in part to the want of stained glass and in part to the ruthless manner in which *Wyatt* swept away screens, monuments, and chapels in his 'restoration' at the close of last century. The restoration carried out more recently by *Sir G. G. Scott* was fortunately characterised by a more modest and judicious spirit. The columns throughout are adorned with slender shafts of Purbeck marble. The Nave, consisting of ten bays, is somewhat narrow in proportion to its height. It contains several monuments, few, however, left in their original positions. Among the most interesting are the following (beginning at the W. end of the S. aisle and returning by the N. aisle): *Herman* (? 11th cent.); tombstones of two *Bishops of Old Sarum* (see p. 101; 11-12th cent.), the first of which is believed to be the oldest monument

For a plan of Salisbury Cathedral see page 544

in the church; *Robert, Lord Hungerford* (d. 1459), with effigy in alabaster; *William Longespée* (d. 1226), first Earl of Salisbury, son of Henry II. and Fair Rosamond, one of the founders of the Cathedral, with effigy in marble; *Sir John Cheyney* (d. 1509; N. aisle), the standard-bearer of Henry VII. at Bosworth, with a fine alabaster effigy; *Sir John de Muntacute* (d. 1389); **William Longespée*, 2nd Earl of Salisbury, killed in the Holy Land in 1250; tomb of a '*Boy Bishop*', *i.e.* a choir-boy elected as bishop, according to an old custom, on St. Nicholas Day (Dec. 6th) and bearing the title till Holy Innocents' Day (Dec. 28th). The modern *Pulpit* is by Sir G. G. Scott. The *Stained Glass in the W. window is from Dijon. — In the N.W. Transept are three monuments by *Flaxman*.

The Choir (adm. 6*d.*) is separated from the nave by a modern metal screen by *Skidmore*. The vaulting has been coloured in accordance with the index afforded by a few traces of the original decorations. The stalls, pulpit, and reredos are modern. On the N. side of the choir is the fine Perpendicular *Chantry of Bishop Audley* (1520), and on the S. the *Hungerford Chantry*, a good example of 15th cent. iron-work (1430). — The E. extremity of the Cathedral is occupied by the *Lady Chapel, with five lancets filled with modern stained glass. Adjacent, at the E. end of the N. choir aisle, is the monument of *Sir Thomas Gorges* (d. 1610) and his wife (d. 1635), the builders of Longford Castle (p. 101). — Before leaving this part of the building we should visit the N. E. Transept, with the interesting and curious brass of *Bishop Wyville* (d. 1375). From the S.E. Transept, containing the monument of *Bp. Bridport* (d. 1262), a door leads to the Vestry and Muniment Room.

We enter the beautiful *Cloisters, with their smooth green sward and two old cedars, from the S. W. Transept. They are of somewhat later date than the body of the Cathedral and are in excellent preservation. — On the E. side of the Cloisters is the *Chapter House, an octagonal building of the end of the 13th cent. (52 ft. high). It is adorned with quaint carvings, but those on the *Doorway by which it is entered are finer.

Fine view from the battlements of the Tower, 212 ft. above the ground (entr. from the Great Transept). The W. piers of the tower have settled a little, and the apex of the spire is 2 ft. out of the perpendicular.

Opposite the W. front of the cathedral is the *Deanery*, to the S. of which is the so-called '*King's House*', an interesting mansion of the 14-15th cent. with a projecting porch, now used as a training-college for school-mistresses. To the N. of the Deanery is another dwelling of the 15th cent. called the '*King's Wardrobe*'. — A gate at the S. E. angle of the Cathedral leads into the lovely grounds of the **Bishop's Palace*, an irregular building of various dates.

Among the most interesting secular buildings is the *Halle of John Halle*, with a fine timber front, in Canal St., built as a dwelling by a rich wool-merchant in 1470, restored in 1834, and now used as a shop. Not far off is the late-Gothic *Poultry Cross*, also restored.

In St. Ann St., leading to the E. from the White Hart Hotel, is the *Salisbury and South Wilts Museum* (open free, Mon. 8-9 p. m., other days 2-5, to strangers at other times also), containing geological, ornithological, and antiquarian collections. Attached to it is the *Blackmore Museum*, the chief feature of which is a collection of American antiquities. — In St. John's St., below the White Hart, is the old *King's Arms*, the secret rendezvous of the Royalists after the battle of Worcester. A bronze statue of *Prof. Fawcett* (d. 1884), a native of Salisbury, was erected in the market-place in 1887.

Philip Massinger, the dramatist (d. 1640), *Joseph Addison* (d. 1719), and

Henry Field ng, the novelist (d. 1754), all resided at Salisbury. The 'Vicar of Wakefield', by *Oliver Goldsmith* (d. 1774), issued from the press here.

ENVIRONS. Interesting excursion to *Stonehenge*, lying 9 M. to the N. (carriage there and back, with one horse 13-15*s.*, with two horses 21*s.*, and fee; excursion-brakes sometimes make the trip in summer, fare 5*s.*). The road usually selected leads by (1 M.) *Old Sarum*, the largest entrenched camp in the kingdom, once the site of a Roman fort, and afterwards of a Saxon town. It stands on a high mound affording an admirable view of Salisbury. The cathedral, removed to Salisbury in 1258, originally stood here, and a fragment of the old building still remains. The 'Ordinal of Offices for the Use of Sarum' became the ritual of all S. England. At the neighbouring village of *Stratford* is a house once inhabited by the elder Pitt, who was first returned to parliament in 1735 as member for the rotten borough of Old Sarum. 8 M. *Amesbury* (George), prettily situated in a slight depression on the Avon. In the neighbourhood are the picturesque seat of *Amesbury Abbey*, so named from a former religious house, and *Vespasian's Camp*, of British origin, but afterwards turned to account by the Romans. The old abbey-church deserves a visit. Gay wrote the 'Beggar's Opera' at Amesbury Abbey, when on a visit to the Duke and Duchess of Queensberry. — About 1½ M. to the W. lies ***Stonehenge** (called by the Saxons *Stanhengest*, *i. e.* 'hanging stones'; formerly *Choir Gaur* or *Côr Gawr*, Giant's circle or temple), the imposing ruins of an ancient sanctuary, the origin and object of which are unknown. When complete it seems to have consisted of two concentric circles enclosing two ellipses. Of the outer circle 17 stones are still standing, partly connected with each other by flat slabs lying across their tops. In the middle is the so-called *Altar*, a slab of blue marble. The sacred road leading to the circles can be traced by its banks of earth. The isolated stone at some distance from the rest is known as the 'Friar's Heel'. Most of the larger stones are of 'Sarsen' sandstone, and the others are of granite. — *Salisbury Plain*, an undulating plateau in the midst of which Stonehenge lies, formerly a sterile tract, has been converted into a fertile district by the advance of agriculture. All around are barrows and tumuli. — We may return to Salisbury through the beautiful valley of the *Avon*, passing (2½ M.) *Great Durnford*, with the British camp of *Ogbury Hill*, and (2½ M.) *Heale House*, where Charles II. spent some days after the Battle of Worcester (1651).

Wilton *(Pembroke Arms)*, a small town with 8600 inhab. and important carpet-manufactories, 3 M. to the W. of Salisbury, possesses a handsome modern **Church*, in the Lombard style, elaborately embellished with marble. — Near the town stands **Wilton House** (shown on Wed., 10-4; fee 6*d.*), the seat of the Earl of Pembroke, famed for its valuable Greek and Roman Sculptures, and its *Collection of pictures by Van Dyck, Holbein, Dürer, Poussin, Reynolds, and other masters. The first earl, the friend of Shakspeare, died in 1600; almost all the subsequent earls have been eminent as lovers of art. The drawing-room is adorned with paintings of scenes from Sir Philip Sidney's 'Arcadia', which was written here. The grounds are also worth seeing. The *Italian Garden* contains a pavilion designed by Holbein. — The road to Wilton passes (1½ M.) *Bemerton*, where George Herbert was rector from 1630 to his death in 1635.

***Longford Castle**, the seat of the Earl of Radnor, lies on the *Avon*, 3 M. to the S.E. of Salisbury. The *Collection of pictures (shown on Tues. and Frid.) is fine, but the best three (by Holbein, Velazquez, and Moroni) were sold to the National Gallery in 1890 for 55,000*l.* There is also an exquisite specimen of metal-work in the shape of a steel chair presented by the town of Augsburg to Emp. Rudolf II. in 1574.

From Salisbury to *Bath*, see p. 113.

Beyond Salisbury the train passes through a tunnel, 450 yds. long. 86 M. *Wilton*, see above; the church-tower is visible to the left. — 92 M. *Dinton* (Wyndham Arms), the birthplace of the first Lord Clarendon (1609-1674). About 2 M. to the S.W. of (96 M.) *Tisbury* (Benett Arms) is *Wardour Castle*, the seat of Lord

Arundel, with a fine collection of paintings and antiquities (daily, 11-4). — 101½ M. *Semley*, the station for Hindon and Shaftesbury.

Near *Hindon*, a small town 3 M. to the N., is *Fonthill Abbey*, where Beckford, the author of 'Vathek', lived in complete seclusion; the princely mansion he erected has given place to a less pretentious structure. — **Shaftesbury** (*Grosvenor Arms*), with 8500 inhab., lies 3 M. to the S. (omn. 1*s.*) and is said to be one of the oldest towns in England. A nunnery was founded here by King Alfred in 880. In the neighbourhood is *St. Giles*, the seat of the Earl of Shaftesbury. — About 10 M. to the S. of Semley, in *Cranborne Chase*, lies *Rushmore*, the seat of the well-known archæologist, Gen. Pitt-Rivers, with a small collection of paintings (including some Græco-Egyptian mummy-portraits from the Fayoum), some 13th cent. windows, etc. (shown to visitors). Near it are *King John's House*, traditionally a hunting-seat of King John, and the *Wych Elm* (in the *Larmer Grounds;* band on Sun., 3-5 p.m.). At *Farnham*, 2 M. to the S.E., is an interesting Museum, and near it are the sites of the Romano-British villages of *Woodcuts*, *Rotherly*, and the ancient *Vindogladia* (in *Bokerly Dyke;* 6 M. from the museum). Pleasant drives and walks in *Rushmore Park* and the *Chase Wood* (apply at the lodges).

Beyond (105 M.) *Gillingham* (Phœnix), with large bacon-curing factories, we pass through a tunnel 715 yds. long. — 112 M. *Templecombe Junction* (Royal Hotel; Rfmt. Rooms), where lines diverge to *Bath* and *Wells* (see p. 112) and to *Burnham* on the N.W., and to *Wimborne* (p. 97), *Broadstone* (p. 97), and *Bournemouth* (p. 96) on the S. — 118 M. **Sherborne** (**Digby; Antelope*), with 5000 inhab., pleasantly situated on the *Yeo*. In the 8th cent. it became the seat of a bishopric, transferred to Old Sarum in 1078.

The old **Minster* is a fine Norman structure, afterwards converted into the Perp. style and recently restored. The vaulting and the choir are specially noteworthy. The *Grammar School* dates from about 1550. *Sherborne Castle*, part of which was built by Sir Walter Raleigh, is situated in a beautiful park, open to the public. Near it are the remains of the old castle (12th cent.).

123 M. *Yeovil Junction*, for (3 M.) **Yeovil** (*Three Choughs; Mermaid*), an ancient glove-making town of 8480 inhab., situated in a pretty and diversified district. Fine Perp. church. Yeovil is the junction of lines to *Dorchester* (p. 97), *Durston* (for *Taunton*, p. 127), and *Chippenham* (p. 108). — 125 M. *Sutton Bingham;* 131½ M. *Crewkerne* (George), with a Perp. church (15th cent.) with a fine W. front. Just short of (139½ M.) *Chard Junction*, whence a branch runs to (3 M.) *Chard* (George) and (15 M.) *Taunton* (p. 127), we see to the left **Ford Abbey*, a Cistercian foundation of the 12th cent., now a private mansion. — 144½ M. *Axminster* (George; Three Cups), formerly noted for its carpets.

From Axminster a coach runs several times daily to (5 M.) **Lyme Regis** (*Cups; Lion*), a picturesquely-situated seaport, where the Duke of Monmouth landed in 1685. It is now frequented as a bathing-place. About 1½ M. to the E. is the pretty village of *Charmouth* (Coach & Horses; George), visited for sea-bathing. — *Whitchurch Canonicorum*, 3 M. to the N.E. of Charmouth, has an interesting church (Norman to Perp.). A visit should be paid to the **Dowlands Landslip* (6*d.*), 3 M. to the W. of Lyme.

148 M. *Seaton Junction*, where carriages are changed for *Colyton* and the small watering-place of (4 M.) *Seaton* (Beach; Clarence; Pole Arms), with admirable cricket and lawn-tennis grounds. —

155 M. *Honiton* (Dolphin; Angel), with an old church; the fine lace to which it has given name, first introduced by Dutch refugees, is now chiefly made at the neighbouring villages. — From (159 M.) *Sidmouth Junction* a branch diverges to (3 M.) *Ottery St. Mary* (King's Arms), with a fine church (a reduced copy of Exeter Cathedral, with the only other pair of transeptal towers in England; see p. 104), and (9 M.) *Sidmouth* (Knowle; Bedford; York), a favourite watering-place, with a fine old Gothic church and an esplanade. — 163 M. *Whimple;* 166 M. *Broad Clyst;* 169 M. *Pinhoe.*

$171^1/_2$ M. **Exeter.** — **Arrival.** There are three railway-stations in Exeter: 1. *Queen Street Station*, near the centre of the town, for the South Western Railway; 2. *St. David's*, to the W. of the town, near the river, for the Great Western Railway, but connected with the Queen St. Station; 3. *St. Thomas's Station*, a second station of the G. W. R., on the other side of the Exe. — The hotel-omnibuses meet the trains.

Hotels. *Rougemont, a large and well-equipped establishment, close to the Queen St. Station, R. & A. 4*s.* 6*d.*, table d'hôte at 7 p.m. 5*s.*; *Clarence, quietly situated in the Cathedral Yard, R. & A. 4*s.* 6*d.*, D. 5*s.*; Queen's, Queen St.; New London, Half Moon, High Street; Globe, Cathedral Yard; Museum, unpretending, R. & A. 2*s.* 3*d.* — *Rail. Rfmt. Rooms.*

Tramways from the end of High St. to St. David's Station and to the suburbs. — **Cabs.** Drive within the town 1*s.*; to Heavitree 1*s.* 6*d.*; to Mt. Radford 1*s.* 6*d.*; beyond the municipal boundaries 1*s.* per mile.

Exeter, the capital of Devonshire and one of the chief places in the W. of England, an ancient town with 47,000 inhab., is pleasantly situated on the left bank of the *Exe* and forms a good starting-point for exploring the beautiful scenery of S. Devonshire. It has been described ('Escott's England') as being 'as good a specimen of an English county-town, at once prosperous in business, and with a quiet air of aristocratic distinction about it, as could be found within the four seas'.

The origin of Exeter is very ancient. The Romans Latinized the name of the British town of *Caerwisc* into *Isca*, while the modern form is derived from the Anglo-Saxon *Exanceaster*. It is the one English city in which it is certain that human habitation has never ceased from the Roman period to the present day; and it is the one city which did not fall into the hands of the Anglo-Saxons before their conversion to Christianity. It was repeatedly besieged during the various civil contests that have raged in England, and was the scene of many interesting historical events. William of Orange remained several days at Exeter after his landing at Torbay, and was joined here by many men of rank. The episcopal see has existed here since 1050, when it was transferred from Crediton. Comp. *Freeman's* 'Exeter' ('Historic Towns Series'; 1887).

Exeter carries on a considerable foreign trade, and vessels of 150 tons can ascend to the town by means of a ship-canal first constructed in the 12th century. The chief industrial products are gloves and agricultural machinery, and the city is the principal market for the 'Honiton lace' made in the neighbourhood.

Close to the Queen Street Station rise the ruins of *Rougemont Castle*, founded by William the Conqueror and situated within the grounds of *Rougemont Lodge*. The castle is mentioned in 'Richard III.', iv. 2. Part of the hill above the old moat has been converted into a promenade called the *Northernhay*, shaded with fine elms (views) and containing a statue of *Lord Iddesleigh* (d. 1886), by Boehm.

From the station Queen St. leads to the S. towards High St. and the centre of the city. In it, to the left, is the *Albert Memorial Museum*, containing Devonshire antiquities, a cabinet of natural history, a library, and a school of art (daily, except Thurs., free). On the staircase is a statue of Prince Albert, by *Stephens*.

On reaching the High St. we cross it, and continuing in the same direction reach the Cathedral Yard. The ***Cathedral** (services at 10.30 and 3; adm. to choir 6*d.*), though comparatively small and unimposing, is in virtue of its details one of the most admirable examples in England of the Geometrical Decorated style.

Nothing now remains of the church used as a cathedral on the transference of the see to Exeter in 1050 (see p. 103); and the oldest parts of the present building are the massive transeptal towers, dating from the early part of the 12th cent. and an almost unique feature in English churches (see p. 103). The rest of the cathedral was built (or altered from Norman to Dec.) between 1280 and 1370, mainly from the designs of *Bishop Quivil* (d. 1291). The elaborate W. façade was added by *Bishop Brantyngham* (1370-1394); and the whole was lately restored under the superintendence of Sir G. G. Scott. One of the chief characteristics of the exterior is the large size and number of the buttresses. The Cathedral is 408 ft. long, 76 ft. wide, and 66 ft. high; width across transepts 140 ft.; height of towers 166 ft. — We enter by the *North Porch*.

The ***Interior** (open 10-3) is distinguished by great lightness and elegance, due in part to the absence of a central tower, though the full effect is marred by the obtrusive position of the organ. The long unbroken line of vaulting is particularly fine. The perfect symmetry of the building has often been pointed out. 'Not only does aisle answer to aisle, and pillar to pillar, and window tracery to window tracery, but also chapel to chapel, screen to screen, and even tomb to tomb, and canopy to canopy' ('Architectural History of Exeter Cathedral', by *Archdeacon Freeman*). The triforium here has not the dignity of a distinct story, but is simply a low blank arcade. Most of the stained glass is poor. The **Minstrels' Gallery* on the N. side of the Nave, with figures of angels playing on musical instruments, dates from 1400. On the S. side of the great W. door is the *Chantry of Bishop Grandisson* (d. 1369), formerly *St. Radegunde's Chapel;* and at the W. end of the N. aisle is another small chapel dedicated to *St. Edmund*. The modern *Pulpit*, at the W. end of the nave, is a memorial of *Bishop Patteson* (d. 1871), the missionary bishop. The N. Transept contains a curious clock of the 14th cent. and a statue of Northcote, the painter (d. 1831), by *Chantrey*. It is adjoined by the *Sylke Chantry* (16th cent.) and *St. Paul's Chapel*. Corresponding to the latter is *St. John's Chapel* in the S. Transept, opposite the entrance to which is the monument of *Hugh Courtenay, Earl of Devon* (d. 1377). From the corner of this transept we enter the narrow *Chapel of the Holy Ghost*, beyond which is the E.E. Chapter House, containing the cathedral-library.

The Choir is separated from the body of the church by a stone screen of the first half of the 14th cent., lately restored. It is surrounded by various small chapels and chantries, and contains the tombs of several bishops. The reredos and choir-stalls are modern, but the misereres (1194-1206) and sedilia are old, and also the beautiful **Episcopal Throne* (1308-26). Part of the glass in the Perp. E. window is ancient. — The Lady Chapel contains the interesting monuments of *Bishop Simon de Apulia* (d. 1223), *Bartholomeus Iscanus* (d. 1184), and two other bishops.

Visitors should ascend the N. tower (entr. in N. transept) for the sake of the view. The large bell here, called 'Great Peter', weighs 6 tons.

The CLOISTERS are now being rebuilt on the old foundations, with an attempted reproduction of the old vaulting and tracery (Dec.).

Within the Cathedral Close are the *Episcopal Palace* and the *Deanery*. One of the houses on the N. side has a good bay-window, dating from the end of the 15th century. The pretty grounds of the Palace (shown in the absence of the family) are reached by following the road to the S. of the cathedral (entr. by arched door), of the E. end of which they command a good view.

In the High Street, not far from the Cathedral, is the *Guildhall*, a quaint-looking building of the 15-16th cent., containing some interesting portraits. The upper part projects over the footway, and forms a kind of arcade supported by columns. Some of the private houses in the High Street, and the *College of Priest Vicars* in South St., are also interesting old buildings. Several of the *Churches* of Exeter (e. g. *St. Pancras*) are of considerable interest, and the handsome *Training College for Schoolmasters* may also be mentioned.

A good view of the town is obtained from *Mt. Dinham*, a small hill on the left bank of the Exe, crowned with the handsome modern *Church of St. Michael*. — A still better view is obtained from the *Reservoir*, at the (1/2 hr.) top of the long hill leading through the pleasant suburb of *Pennsylvania*, on the N. W. side of the town (apply at the keeper's cottage). The walk may be extended to (3/4 M.) *Duryard Park* (adm. 1*d.*), whence we may return by a drive leading down to the valley of the Exe.

Excursions. Coaches leave the chief Exeter hotels every Sat. in summer for *Chudleigh* (p. 130), *Dawlish* (p. 129), *Budleigh* (see below), or *Tiverton* (p. 129), all pleasant drives of 20-25 M. (there and back); return fare in each case 3*s.* 6*d.* — An opportunity is afforded of a visit to **Dartmoor** (p. 137) from Exeter by trains leaving Exeter (G. W. R.) at 10.50 a. m., and running (viâ *Newton Abbot*) in connection with the coach starting from *Bovey Tracy* (p. 130) at 12.30 p. m. The coach varies its route daily, visiting *Haytor Rocks*, *Hound Tor*, *Bowerman's Nose*, *Manaton*, the *Becky Falls*, *Moreton*, *Dunsford Bridge*, *Ashburton*, *Holne Chase*, *Buckland*, etc. The train for Exeter leaves at 7.24 p.m., arriving at 9.26 p.m. Fares for the round 4*s.*, box-seat 5*s.* (1*s.* less on Tues.). The above data are subject to alteration; enquiry should be made on the spot.

FROM EXETER TO EXMOUTH, 10$^1/_2$ M., South Western Railway in $^1/_2$ hr. (fares 1*s.* 9*d.*, 1*s.* 4*d.*, 10$^1/_2$*d.*). This short branch descends along the E. bank of the *Exe*. — 5$^1/_2$ M. *Topsham* (Globe), formerly the port of Exeter. — 10$^1/_2$ M. **Exmouth** (**Imperial; Beacon; London*), a pleasant little watering-place, at the mouth of the Exe, with a fair beach and an esplanade. The hill called the *Beacon*, rising above the town, affords good views. — From Exmouth an omnibus runs to *Budleigh Salterton* (Rolle Arms), another charming little watering-place, 4$^1/_2$ M. to the E.

FROM EXETER TO BARNSTAPLE, 39$^1/_2$ M., S. W. Railway in 1$^3/_4$ hr. (fares 8*s.* 2*d.*, 5*s.* 9*d.*, 3*s.* 4*d.*). The scenery on this line is pretty and thoroughly Devonian. — 7$^1/_2$ M. *Crediton* (Angel; Ship) was once the seat of the bishopric of Devonshire, now centred in Exeter (comp. p. 103). At (11$^1/_2$ M.) *Yeoford* the railway to Tavistock and Plymouth diverges to the left, skirting Dartmoor (see p. 137). At (13$^3/_4$ M.) *Copplestone* is an ancient cross. Beyond (18 M.) *Lapford* we enter the valley of the *Taw*, which we follow all the way to Barnstaple. The scenery becomes more open. Fine view of Barnstaple as we approach. — 39$^1/_2$ M. *Barnstaple*, and thence to *Bideford* and *Torrington* (left) and *Ilfracombe* (right), see R. 20.

From Exeter to *Barnstaple* by the *Exe Valley*, see p. 128; to *Torquay*, *Tavistock*, *Launceston*, and *Plymouth*, see R. 17a and R. 17b; to *Bristol*, see R. 16.

15. From London to Bath and Bristol.

118$\frac{1}{2}$ M. Great Western Railway *(Paddington Station)* in 2$\frac{1}{2}$-4$\frac{3}{4}$ hrs. (fares 20*s.* 10*d.*, 15*s.* 7*d.*, 9*s.* 10$\frac{1}{2}$*d.*). From *Bath* to *Bristol*, 11$\frac{1}{2}$ M., in $\frac{1}{3}$-$\frac{1}{2}$ hr. — This line (London to Penzance) is now the only line in England on the 'broad gauge' system, the rails being 7 ft. apart; the carriages are very comfortable and the rate of speed attained is very high. The 77$\frac{1}{4}$ M. between London and Swindon are traversed by the 'Flying Dutchman' in rather less than 1$\frac{1}{2}$ hr., or an average of 53 miles per hour. The 'narrow gauge' is also laid as far as Exeter.

In quitting London the train passes *Kensal Green Cemetery* on the right, near *Westbourne Park*. The first stations beyond the precincts of London are (4$\frac{1}{4}$ M.) *Acton* and (5$\frac{3}{4}$ M.) *Ealing*. At (7$\frac{1}{2}$ M.) *Hanwell*, to the left, is the large *Middlesex Lunatic Asylum*, with room for 1000 inmates. From (9 M.) *Southall*, where we cross the Grand Junction Canal, a line diverges to the left to *Brentford*. 13$\frac{1}{4}$ M. *West Drayton* (branch to *Uxbridge*).

18$\frac{1}{2}$ M. **Slough** *(Crown; Royal)* is the junction of the line to *Eton* and *Windsor*, for a description of which, as well as of *Stoke Poges*, *Burnham Beeches*, and other places in this neighbourhood, see *Baedeker's Handbook for London*. A view of *Windsor Castle* is obtained to the left. The scenery of the Thames Valley between Slough and Goring (see below) is very pleasing.

24 M. *Maidenhead* (p. 221), prettily situated on the Thames, is the junction of a line to *Wycombe* and *Oxford* (see p. 223). From (31 M.) *Twyford* a branch diverges to *Henley-on-Thames* (p. 220).

36 M. **Reading** (*Great Western*, at the station; *Queen's; Vastern Temperance; George*, unpretending, R. & A. 3*s.*), the county-town of Berkshire, is an ancient and flourishing town with 42,000 inhabitants. The *Benedictine Abbey*, founded by Henry I. in 1121, and containing his grave, was once one of the wealthiest in England; a few ruins now alone remain. The gateway has, however, been restored. Several parliaments were held in the great hall of the abbey. Archbishop Laud, beheaded in 1645, was the son of a tailor of Reading. *Huntley & Palmer's* well-known biscuit manufactory employs 3000 hands. The churches of *St. Mary* (16th cent.), *St. Lawrence*, and *Greyfriars* are interesting. The nursery gardens and seed-farms of Sutton & Sons cover 3000 acres of ground.

Reading may also be reached from London by the S. W. Railway viâ *Ascot* (43$\frac{1}{2}$ M.), or by the circuitous route of the S. E. R. viâ *Reigate* and *Guildford* (67 M.; comp. p. 64).

Another branch of the G.W.R., traversed by slow trains only, runs from Reading to Bath viâ Devizes (70 M. in 4-5 hrs.; fares 12*s.* 5*d.*, 9*s.* 4*d.*, 5*s.* 11*d.*). The following are the principal stations. — 17 M. **Newbury** *(Queen; Chequers)*, with 8000 inhab., formerly the seat of an important cloth-trade, and the scene of two battles in the Civil War (1643 and 1644), in the first of which Lord Falkland fell (monument on the battle-field). Branch-lines run hence to Didcot (p. 107) to the N. and Winchester (p. 76) to the S. — 25$\frac{1}{2}$ M. *Hungerford* (Bear; Three Swans), on the *Kennet*, a favourite angling resort. April 15th, called '*Tuttiday*', is celebrated with curious old-fashioned ceremonies. About 4 M. to the N.W. is *Littlecote Hall*, a good specimen of a 16th cent. manor-house, containing numerous family portraits and other objects of interest (not shown). — 34 M. *Savernake*, the junction of a line to (5½ M.) *Marlborough* and (19½ M.) *Swindon* (see p. 108). *Savernake Forest* contains a splendid avenue of beeches and some gigantic oaks. Another line runs S. to *Andover Junction* (p. 98). — 50 M. **Devizes** (**Bear; Castle*), a busy town with an active trade in grain. The name is derived from its Roman name, *Castrum Divisarum* or *Ad Divisas.* The old *Castle*, erected in the reign of Henry I. and destroyed in the 17th cent., has almost completely disappeared. The churches of *St. John* and *St. Mary* have vaulted Norman choirs, and the *Museum* (adm. 6*d.*) contains a fair collection of Wiltshire antiquities. — At (58 M.) *Holt Junction* we cross the Chippenham and Frome line. — 61 M. **Bradford-on-Avon** (*Swan*), with the highly interesting little Saxon **Church of St. Lawrence*, which is believed to date from early in the 8th cent. (comp. p. xxxv). The *Bridge* is also noteworthy. — 63½ M. *Limpley Stoke*. — 70 M. *Bath*, see p. 109.

Reading is also the junction of a line to *Basingstoke* (p. 76).

Near (41½ M.) *Pangbourne* (p. 220) is *Basildon Park*, with a good collection of pictures. Beyond (44¾ M.) *Goring* (p. 219), with an interesting church, the train crosses the Thames for the last time. From (47¾ M.) *Moulsford* (p. 219) a branch diverges to *Wallingford* (Lamb), a small town founded by the ancient Britons, and surrounded by a Roman entrenchment.

53 M. *Didcot Junction* (Junction Hotel; Rail. Rfmt. Rooms), whence the line to *Oxford* (R. 30a) and *Birmingham* (p. 254) diverges to the N. and one to *Newbury* (p. 106) to the S.

60½ M. *Wantage Road* is united by a steam-tramway (fare 6*d.*) with (3 M.) **Wantage** (*Bear*, R. & A. 3s. 6*d.*), the birthplace of Alfred the Great (849-901) and of Bishop Butler (1692-1752), with a handsome church of the 14th century. A statue of King Alfred, by Count Gleichen, was erected in the market-place in 1877.

From Wantage a very pleasant walk (about 10 M.) may be taken by the *Ridgeway* or *Ickleton Street*, a grass-grown Roman road, along the breezy top of the chalk downs, and then down to *Uffington* (see below). About 1½ M. on this side of Uffington, near the little village of *Kingston Lisle*, is the famous 'Blowing Stone' of King Alfred, described in '*Tom Brown's School-Days*', and supposed to have been anciently used as a military signal. It lies below a tree, in front of some cottages on the road descending from the Ridgeway to Kingston Lisle. Various ancient entrenchments are visible on the Downs. Instead of descending to the Blowing Stone we may follow the ridge to the 'White Horse Hill' (see below).

64 M. *Challow*. From (66½ M.) *Uffington*, the home of 'Tom Brown', with a most interesting E. E. *Church, a branch-line runs to (3½ M.) **Faringdon** (*Bell; Crown*), once a residence of the Saxon kings, now famous for its ham and bacon (40-50,000 swine slaughtered here annually).

About 2½ M. to the S. of Uffington is **White Horse Hill** (890 ft.), so called from the huge figure of a horse cut in the turf, 370 ft. in length (visible from the railway); it has existed here for over 1000 years and is said to have been made by Alfred the Great to commemorate his victory over the Danes at Ashdown (873). At the top of the hill, which commands an extensive view, is *Uffington Castle*, an entrenchment probably of Danish origin. "Right down below the White Horse is a curious deep and broad gully called the 'Manger', into one side of which the hills fall with a series of the most lovely sweeping curves, known as the 'Giants' Stairs'; they are not a bit like stairs, but I never saw anything like them anywhere else, with their short green turf, and tender blue-bells, and gossamer and thistle-down gleaming in the sun, and the sheep-paths running along their sides like ruled lines" (Tom Brown's School-Days). — On the other side of the Manger is the *Dragon's Hill*, where St. George is said to have slain the dragon; and the cromlech known as *Wayland Smith's Forge*, immortalized in 'Kenilworth', lies on the Ridgeway about 1 M. farther to the W.

Beyond (71½ M.) *Shrivenham* the train enters *Wiltshire.* — 77¼ M. **Swindon** *(Goddard Arms*, in Old Swindon, 1 M. from the station; *Railway Refreshment Rooms)*, where the line reaches its highest point (300 ft.) and most trains stop for 10 min., is the junction of lines to *Gloucester* (p. 170), *Highworth*, *Marlborough*, and *Cirencester* (direct). About 200 trains pass through the station daily. Swindon, with a population of 22,500, consists of an old town, 1 M. from the station, and the new town, a creation of the Great Western Railway, occupied almost exclusively by railway artificers and employés, who are said to draw nearly 300,000*l.* a year in wages. The extensive works of the railway-company are open to visitors on Wed. afternoon. About 50 locomotives are generally kept here in readiness for service.

About 2 M. to the E. of Highworth (see above), on the road to Faringdon, and 8 M. to the N. E. of Swindon, is *Coleshill House* (Earl of Radnor), a good example of Inigo Jones (1550).

From Swindon to Marlborough and Savernake, 19½ M., railway in ¾-1 hr. — 14 M. **Marlborough** *(Ailesbury Arms; Castle & Ball)* is known for its large *College*, established in 1845 and now one of the great public schools of England. The oldest part of the college was formerly the mansion of Lord Seymour, where Thomson wrote part of his 'Seasons' while the guest of the Countess of Hertford. A handsome new chapel was opened in 1886. — About 6 M. to the W. is ***Avebury Circle**, one of the most extensive and interesting monuments of the kind in existence, and generally looked upon as older than Stonehenge. To the S. of it is *Silbury Hill*, a large artificial mound 170 ft. high, supposed to be of British origin. — 19½ M. *Savernake*, see p. 106.

83 M. *Wootton Bassett*. From (88 M.) *Dauntsey* a short branch diverges to (6 M.) **Malmesbury** *(King's Arms)*, the birthplace of Thomas Hobbes (1588-1679), with the ruins of a fine *Abbey Church (12th cent.) and a Gothic town-cross. William of Malmesbury, the chronicler (d. ca. 1143), was a monk in the abbey. About 2 M. to the S. of Dauntsey station is *Bredenstoke* or *Clack Abbey*, incorporating the remains of an Augustine priory of the 12th century.

94 M. **Chippenham** *(Angel; George)*, an ancient town with 6766 inhab., deriving its name from A. S. *ceapian*, 'to buy', is well known for its corn and cheese markets. It also possesses an iron-foundry and manufactures silk and cloth. Fine old Norman church.

About 3½ M. to the S. E. of Chippenham (2 M. from Calne) is **Bowood**, the handsome seat of the Marquis of Lansdowne, with a fine collection of paintings of all schools. The park is open to the public. To the S. of Chippenham (3 M.) lies *Lacock Abbey*, founded in 1232 as a nunnery, but now a private residence.

Chippenham is the junction of lines to *Calne* (5¼ M. to the E.; Lansdowne Arms), with important pig-killing and bacon-curing industry, and to *Trowbridge*, *Westbury* (for *Weymouth*, *Salisbury*, etc.), *Frome*, *Witham* (*Wells*, etc.), and *Yeovil* (p. 102).

Beyond Chippenham the train follows the pretty valley of the *Avon*. Near (98¼ M) *Corsham* (Methuen Arms) is *Corsham Court*, the seat of Lord Methuen, containing a valuable collection of pictures (upwards of 220, exclusive of family portraits), to which strangers are admitted on written application. The train then enters the *Box Tunnel*, 1 3/4 M. in length, constructed at a cost of 500,000 *l.*, and near (102 M.) *Box*, famous for its stone quarries, passes into *Somersetshire* and re-enters the Avon Valley.—104 1/2 M. *Bathampton.*

107 M. **Bath.** — **Railway Stations.** *Great Western Station*, at the end of Manvers St., on the S. side of the town; *Midland Station* (for Gloucester, Worcester, Birmingham, the Somerset and Dorset line, etc.), in Green Park, to the W. of the town. — Hotel omnibuses meet the chief trains.

Hotels. *Grand Pump Room Hotel (Pl. a; C, 2), a large establishment adjoining the baths; York House (Pl. b; C, 2), York Buildings, quiet; White Lion (Pl. d; C, 3), High St.; Castle (Pl. c; C, 2), Northgate St.; *Christopher (Pl. e; C, 3), near the Abbey, commercial, R. & A. 3*s.* 6*d.*; Royal (Pl. f; B, 3), Railway (Pl. g; B, 3), both opposite the G. W. R. Station; Fernley's Temperance (Pl. h; B, C, 3), near the Abbey.

Cabs. For 2 pers., with 2 horses, 1*s.* 6*d.* per mile, 3*s.* per hr.; with 1 horse or 2 ponies or mules 1*s.* or 2*s.*; with 1 pony or mule or 2 donkeys 6*d.* or 1*s.* 6*d.* Each addit. pers. 6*d.* per mile. Fare and a half between midnight and 6 a.m. Ordinary luggage free. — *Bath Chairs*, 1*s.* per mile or hr.

Tramways starting from the G. W. R. station run through some of the principal streets to *Grosvenor*, on the N. side of the town (fares 2*d.* and 1*d.*).

Music. Band twice daily in the *Victoria Park*, *Sydney Gardens*, or *Institution Gardens* (season-ticket 7*s.*); thrice a week in the *Pump Room*, where vocal concerts are also given (season-ticket 5*s.*). — High-class concerts take place in the *Assembly Rooms.*

Theatre Royal (Pl. C, 2), Beaufort St.; closed in June, July, and August.

Post Office (Pl. D, 2), York Buildings, close to the top of Milsom St.

Bath, the chief place in Somerset, is a handsome town of 53,761 inhab., beautifully situated in the valley of the *Avon* and on the slopes of the surrounding hills, and is perhaps unrivalled among provincial English towns for its combination of archæological, historic, scenic, and social interest. It is a city of crescents and terraces, built in a very substantial manner of a fine grey limestone (oolite), and rising tier above tier to a height of about 600 ft. Among the most characteristic streets are the Royal, Lansdown, and Camden Crescents, the Circus, and Pulteney Street, all of which recall similar streets in Edinburgh. Milsom Street is the fashionable shopping resort.

Tradition ascribes the discovery of the springs of Bath to an ancient British prince named *Bladud*, who was afflicted with leprosy and observed their beneficial effects on a herd of swine suffering from a similar disease. The therapeutic value of the waters did not escape the keen eyes of the bath-loving Romans, who built here a large city, with extensive baths and temples, of which numerous remains have been discovered (comp. p. 110). Their name for it, *Aquae Sulis*, was taken from a local deity *Sul*, whom they identified with Minerva. For a century and a half after the departure of the Romans, Bath remained in possession of the Britons, but about 577 it was taken and destroyed by the Saxons, whose name for it was *Akemanceaster* (from a local corruption of *Aquae*, and *man* = place). At a later date it reappears in history under the name of *Aet Bathum* ('at the bath'), and after the Norman Conquest it became the seat of a bishop. The beginning of its modern reputation as a watering-place may be placed about 1650, but it did not reach the zenith of its prosperity till the following cent., when it became for a time the most fashionable watering-place in England. This was mainly due to the indefatigable exertions of the famous master of the ceremonies, *Beau Nash* (d. 1761),

For a coloured street plan of Bath see page 565

who introduced order and method into the amusements and customs of the place. Among the innumerable visitors of eminence in the 18th and early 19th cent. may be mentioned Chatham, Pitt, Canning, and Burke, Nelson, Wolfe, and Sir Sidney Smith, Gainsborough and Lawrence, Smollett, Fielding, Sheridan, Miss Burney, Goldsmith, Southey, Landor, Miss Austen, Wordsworth, Cowper, Scott, and Moore. Perhaps no other English town of the size has oftener been the theme of literary allusion — from 'Humphrey Clinker' and the 'School for Scandal' down to the 'Papers of the Pickwick Club'. The competition of the Continental Spas and other causes afterwards diverted a great part of the stream of guests, and the 'Queen of all the Spas' subsided into a quiet and aristocratic-looking place, patronised as a residence by retired officers and visited by numerous invalids. Of late years, however, Bath has shown marked signs of revival as a fashionable resort. For some time it was an important cloth-making centre, and it is mentioned in connection with this industry in Chaucer's 'Wife of Bath's Tale'.

The hot MINERAL SPRINGS to which Bath owes its name are what is known as a 'lime sulphated water', and are efficacious in rheumatism, gout, dyspepsia, biliary and liver complaints, and skin-diseases. The daily yield of the springs is upwards of half-a-million gallons. The water, used both for bathing and drinking, rises at a temperature of from 116 to 120° Fahr., which is reduced, when required, by means of cooled mineral water. The **Pump Room** (Pl. C, 2), close to the W. end of the Abbey Church (p. 111), is a large edifice in the classical style, with a motto from Pindar (Αριστον μὲν ὕδωρ) on the portico. Visitors are admitted free to the Pump Room, as well as to inspect the various baths, etc. The charge for a single glass of the mineral water is 2*d*. At one end of the room is a statue of *Beau Nash* (p. 109). — Below is a list of the baths, all of which are within a stone's throw of the Pump Room.

New Royal Baths, adjoining the Grand Hotel (bath 2*s*.-3*s*. 6*d*., fee 3*d*.; swimming bath 6*d*.-1*s*., reserved for ladies on Mon., Wed., and Frid.); *King's and Queen's Baths*, Stall St., adjoining the Pump Room (1st class bath 1*s*. 6*d*.-3*s*. 6*d*., 2nd class 6*d*.-1*s*. 6*d*., fee 1-3*d*.); *Royal Private Baths*, Bath St. (1st class 2*s*., fee 3*d*.; 2nd class 1*s*. 6*d*., fee 2*d*.); *Tepid Swimming Bath* (88° Fahr.), Bath St. (6*d*. and 9*d*.); *Cross Public Swimming Bath* (73°), at the end of Bath St. (1*d*., with towel 2*d*.); *Hot Bath* (120°), Bath St., for the poor; *Kingston Baths*, Church St. The new King's Baths are, perhaps, the most perfectly equipped baths in Europe.

Th King's Baths stand on the site of the Roman Baths, first discovered in 1775, which are supposed to have been founded by Emp. Claudius and to have occupied an area 900 ft. long and 350 ft. wide. Recently more important discoveries were made, and the splendid ***Roman Baths** (Pl. C, 2, 3; adm. free, 11-1 and 3-5) now shown include five large baths (one in a hall 110 ft. long and 68 ft. wide), besides several smaller ones, with the hypocausts for heating the different chambers. One of these baths is still coated with the Roman lead (for details, see Davis's 'Guide to the Roman Baths'). In 1886 the corner-stone of the new King's Baths (opened 1889) was laid on 'Roman masonry 1700 years old, thus connecting in work and object the modern and the ancient world'. — A little to the N. of the baths is the large *General Hospital*, a national institution for poor patients under treatment with the waters, and to the S. is the *United Hospital,* used by local patients.

The **Abbey Church** (Pl. C, 3) is a handsome Perp. edifice of the 16th cent., sometimes called the 'Lantern of England' from the number and size of its windows. The central tower, 162 ft. high, is oblong in form owing to the narrowness of the transepts. The church, 225 ft. in length, is the third which has occupied the same site. The first was that of a nunnery said to have been erected here in the 7th century. The second was a Norman cathedral, begun on the transference of the see of Wells to Bath (1090), and completed in 1160. After the return of the bishop to Wells in the beginning of the 13th cent., this church, the nave of which alone was as large as the present building, was suffered to fall into a state of complete ruin, and *Bishop Oliver King* (1495-1503) undertook the erection of a new one. The ladders on the W. front refer to a dream of this prelate in connection with the building. The church was finally consecrated in 1616. In 1864-1875 a judicious restoration was carried out by Sir G. G. Scott, chiefly at the cost of the *Rev. Prebendary Kemble.* Bath Abbey Church is still the secondary cathedral of the diocese of Bath and Wells, though since 1542 the chapter of Wells has had the sole right of electing the bishops, formerly shared with the monks of Bath.

Interior. The most noteworthy features are the fine W. window, the fan-vaulted roof (added by Scott in accordance with the original design), and the small chantry of *Prior Bird* (c. 1500), on the S. side of the chancel, with its fine carving. Among the numerous monuments, most of them tasteless, are those of *Waller*, the Parliamentary general (d. 1668; S. transept); *Beau Nash* (d. 1761; on wall of S. aisle, E. end); *Quin*, the actor (d. 1766; at E. end of N. aisle of choir, just by the door, with inscription by Garrick; grave-stone in the middle of the nave, also with a rhymed inscription); *Malthus* (d. 1834), the political economist (in the porch of N. door in W. front); *Bishop Montague* (d. 1618), an altar-tomb in the nave; *Mary Frampton*, with an epitaph by Dryden, on the S.E. wall; and *W. Hoare, R. A.*, by Chantrey, to the E. of Prior Bird's chapel.

Among the many other churches of Bath the only one demanding mention is the Roman Catholic *Church of St. John* (Pl. B, 3), in the South Parade, near the G. W. R. Station, with its graceful spire.

The *Royal Literary and Scientific Institution* (Pl. C, 3; open 11-4; 6*d.* on Tues. and Frid., free on other days), in the North Parade, near the Abbey, contains an interesting collection of Roman antiquities found in or near Bath, and also cabinets of geology and natural history. — The *Guildhall* (Pl. C, 3), in High St., to the N. of the Abbey, has a fine banqueting-room with some portraits of historical interest. — Among the numerous schools of Bath are the *New Kingswood School*, for the sons of Wesleyan ministers, and the *Officers' Daughters' College*, two conspicuous buildings, nearly opposite each other, on the ascent to Lansdown.

The ***Victoria Park**, on the N.W. side of the town, is a well-kept pleasure-ground, 50 acres in extent. It is open free, but when the band plays, 6*d.* is charged to non-subscribers for admission to the inner circle. To the E., at the end of Great Pulteney St., are the *Sydney Gardens* (Pl. D, 4; adm. 3*d.*; when the band plays, 6*d.*).

An admirable view of the town, though somewhat circumscribed by foliage, is obtained from (1/4 hr.) **Beechen Cliff* (Pl. A, 3; 390 ft. above the Avon), on the S. side of the town. To reach it we cross the foot-bridge (1/2*d.*) behind the G. W. R. Station and ascend straight on, soon coming to notices which point out the way. At the top we follow the path along the ridge towards the W., and regain the town by the Holloway and the Old Bridge. — Another good point of view is *Sham Castle*, on the hill about 1 1/2 M. to the E. of the G.W.R. Station, and best reached by *Pulteney Street* and the so-called *North Road*.

Bath is surrounded with **'Downs'**, softly rounded hills, the tops of which afford charming views. The most important are *Lansdown* (800 ft., 2 M. to the N.), *Claverton* and *Coombe Down* (550 ft.; 2-3 M. to the S.), and *Hampton Down* (600 ft.; 1 1/2 M. to the E.), with Sham Castle (see above). *Little Solbury* (ca. 600 ft.; 3 M. to the N.E.) is a flat-topped hill with clearly defined earthworks. A walk or drive over Lansdown as far as the third milestone, and thence (for walkers only) across the race-course to (1 M.) *Prospect Stile*, will afford the visitor one of the finest views in the W. of England. On the way we pass (2 M.) *Lansdown Cemetery*, with the tomb of Beckford of Fonthill (p. 102) and a tower built by him, the top of which commands an extensive view (Bath not visible). This walk may be lengthened by returning through *North Stoke* (with an ancient church), and thence through *Upton* or *Bitton* to the railway.

About 2 M. to the S. E. of Bath, beyond *Widcombe* (with an old church and manor-house), is **Prior Park**, now a Roman Catholic college, but formerly the seat of *Ralph Allen* (d. 1764), the original of Squire Allworthy in 'Tom Jones'. Through his building enterprise and sturdy belief in the good qualities of the Bath stone, Mr. Allen justly shares with Beau Nash and the architect Wood the credit of creating modern Bath. Near Prior Park is *Pope's Tower*, erected to commemorate Pope's connection with the district. W. S. Landor (d. 1864) is buried in Old Widcombe Churchyard. — The village of *Claverton*, in the charming *Warleigh Valley*, 3 M. to the E., is best reached by train to *Bathampton* (p. 109) or *Limpley Stoke* (p. 107). — *Farley Castle*, reduced to a ruin in the Parliamentary Wars, lies 7 M. to the E. and may be reached by train to *Freshford* and thence by a field-path (2 M.). — The old manor-houses of *South Wraxall* and *Chadfield* (near *Box*, p. 109), in the Tudor style, are also worth a visit. — The church and manor-house of *St. Catherine's* (5 M. to the N. E., beyond Batheaston), in a pretty valley, both date from about 1500. — In a hollow to the E. of Lansdown, 1 1/2 M. from the town, is *Charlcombe*, traditionally the mother-church of Bath.

From Bath to Wells (fares 5*s.* 6*d.*, 4*s.*, 2*s.* 2 1/2*d.*). The quickest railway-route from Bath to Wells is by the Somerset and Dorset line viâ *Evercreech* and *Glastonbury* (see below; 1 1/2-2 hrs.), but Wells may also be reached by the G. W. R. viâ *Bristol* and *Yatton* (see R. 16; 2-2 1/2 hrs.) or viâ *Westbury*, *Witham*, and *Shepton Mallet* (see below; 2 1/4-3 1/2 hrs.). For those who do not object to a little walking, perhaps the pleasantest way of making this excursion is to take the train to (18 1/2 M.) *Masbury* (see below) and walk thence to (3 M.) Wells. — *Wells*, see p. 123.

From Bath to Gloucester, 41 M., railway in 1 1/2-2 hrs. (fares 7*s.* 6*d.*, 5*s.* 8*d.*, 3*s.* 6*d.*). The trains start from the Midland Railway Station, and join the main line from Bristol at (10 M.) *Mangotsfield Junction* (p. 121).

From Bath to Templecombe, 37 M., Somerset and Dorset railway in 1 1/4-2 hrs. (fares 7*s.* 8*d.*, 5*s.* 4*d.*, 3*s.* 1*d.*). The trains leave Bath from the Midland Station. — The first part of the route is very pretty. At (10 1/2 M.) *Radstock* (Waldegrave Arms) we cross the G. W. R. line from Bristol to Frome. — At (18 1/2 M.) *Masbury*, whence Wells may be reached by a pleasant walk of 3 M., we cross the *Mendip Hills*. Beyond Masbury we have a fine view to the right, including Wells Cathedral and Glastonbury Tor (p. 126). — 21½ M. *Shepton Mallet* (George; Hare & Hounds), the church of which has a fine panelled roof. This is the junction for the G. W. R. line from Yatton (p. 122) to Witham (p. 126). — 26½ M. *Evercreech Junction* is the junction for *Glastonbury (Wells)* and *Burnham* (see p. 127). — 29 M. *Cole*, for Yeovil to the right and Bruton and Westbury to the left. — From (33 M.) *Wincanton* (Greyhound; Bear) excursions may be made to (3½ M.) *Penselwood* and the curious '*Pen Pits*', the object of which is still a bone of antiquarian contention, and to (3½ M.) *Stavordale Priory*. The whole district is rich in early historical interest. — At (37 M.) *Templecombe* (p. 102) we connect with the main S. W. line from London to Exeter (R. 14), though the Somerset & Dorset trains run on to Broadstone and Bournemouth (p. 96).

From Bath to Salisbury, 41 M., Great Western Railway in 1½-2¾ hrs. (fares 8*s*. 6*d*., 5*s*. 8*d*., 3*s*. 5*d*.). — From Bath to (12¾ M.) *Holt Junction*, see p. 107. — Our line here turns to the right (S.). 15¾ M. *Trowbridge* (George), an ugly factory-town, with a good Perp. church (end of 15th cent.). *Crabbe*, the poet, was rector here for 19 years (1813-32), and is buried in the chancel of the church. — From (17 M.) *Westbury* (Lopes Arms) a line diverges on the right to *Frome* (p. 121). There is a fine church at *Edington*, 4½ M. to the W. — 21½ M. *Warminster* (Bath Arms; Lamb) is the station for ***Longleat** (4½ M. to the S. W.), the magnificent seat of the Marquis of Bath, considered the finest Elizabethan mansion in England (shown on Wed. and Frid., 11-4). It contains an interesting collection of portraits. — Beyond Warminster we pass two British camps, *Battlesbury* and *Scratchbury*, on the left, and reach (25¼ M.) *Heytesbury* (Angel), where *Heytesbury Park*, the seat of Lord Heytesbury, contains some good Italian and Spanish pictures. — At (38½ M.) *Wilton* we join the line from Salisbury to Exeter (see p. 101). — 41 M. *Salisbury*, see p. 99.

Continuation of the Railway to Bristol. The first station beyond Bath is (108 M.) *Twerton*, with a large cloth-manufactory and a cottage in which Fielding is said to have written 'Tom Jones'. The train now runs parallel with the Bath branch of the Midland Railway. 111 M. *Saltford*. — At (114 M.) *Keynsham* (Lamb & Lark), a Roman mosaic (Orpheus and the beasts), now at Bristol, was found during the construction of the railway. A little to the N. lies *Bitton*, with an interesting church, parts of which are supposed to be of ante-Norman date. The difficulties overcome in making the railway from Keynsham to Bristol will interest engineers. Beyond *Brislington* the train threads two tunnels and crosses the *Avon*.

118½ M. **Bristol.** — **Hotels.** *Royal (Pl. a; E, 4), pleasantly situated in College Green, close to the Cathedral and nearly 1 M. from the station, with postal telegraph office, R. & A. 4*s*. 6*d*., table-d'hôte 4*s*. 6*d*.; Grand (Pl. b; F, 3), Broad St., well spoken of, R. & A. from 4*s*.; *Royal Talbot (Pl. c; G, 4), Victoria St. — George (Pl. d; H, 5), near the station; Cathedral (Pl. f; E, 4), near the College Green; Colston Temperance (Pl. e; E, 4), College Green, well spoken of. — At *Clifton:* *Clifton Down (Pl. g; B, 4), a large establishment, with fine view of the Suspension Bridge, etc.; *St. Vincent's Rocks (Pl. h; B, 4), with a similar view, suitable for a prolonged stay; Imperial (Pl. i; C, 1), near the Clifton Down Station, well spoken of; Montague Hotel, Kingsdown Parade.

Restaurants. *Grand Hotel Restaurant*, Wine St.; *Dunlop*, Baldwin St.; *Miller (Nattris)*, Wine St.; *The Rummer*, in the Market, adjoining the Exchange; *Refreshment Rooms* at the Railway Station.

Cabs with one horse 1*s*. per mile, 6*d*. each ½ M. addit.; with two horses 1*s*. 6*d*. and 9*d*. Per hour 2*s*. 6*d*. and 4*s*.; each addit. ¼ hr. 6*d*. and

For a coloured street plan of Bristol see pages 566 & 567

9*d*. For each passenger beyond two, 6*d*. extra. Each package carried outside 2*d*. Double fares between midnight and 6 a.m.

Tramways. 1. From the *Railway Station* (Pl. H, 4), to the *Drawbridge* (Pl. F, 4), and to *Hotwells*, below *Clifton Suspension Bridge* (Pl. A, 4), every 12 min. (fares 1*d*., 2*d*.). — 2. From the *Drawbridge* to *Redland*, every 12 min. (2*d*., 3*d*.). — 3. From *Eastville* to *Redland* every 12 min. (2*d*., 3*d*.). — 4, 5, 6. From *Bristol Bridge* (Pl. G, 4), to *St. George's* every 1/4 hr. (2*d*.), to *Totterdown* every 6 min. (1*d*.), and to *Bedminster* (Pl. G, 6) every 10 min. (1*d*.). — 7. From the *Drawbridge* (Pl. F, 4) to *Horfield* (2*d*.).

Steamers ply from Bristol to *Ilfracombe*, *Cardiff*, *London*, *Liverpool*, *Glasgow*, *Plymouth*, *Penzance*, *Torquay*, *Milford*, *Swansea*, *Chepstow* (in summer), *Belfast*, *Dublin*, *Cork*, *Waterford*, *Amsterdam*, *Antwerp*, *Bordeaux*, etc.

Boats. Small boat up and down the *Floating Harbour* 6*d*., more than 1 pers. 3*d*. each; across the *Avon* below the Feeder 4*d*. and 2*d*.; across the *Feeder* 4*d*. and 2*d*.; ferry across the *Frome* 1*d*.

Post Office (Pl. F, 3), Small St., opposite the Assize Courts.

Theatres. *Prince's Theatre* (Pl. E, 4), Park Row; *Old Theatre Royal* (Pl. F, 4), King St.

U. S. Consul, *John D. Delille, Esq.*

Principal Attractions. **Cathedral* (p. 117); **St. Mary Redcliffe* (p. 115); **Clifton Down*, **Durdham Down*, and **Suspension Bridge* (p. 120); *St. Peter's Church & Hospital* (p. 116); *Mayor's Chapel* (p. 118).

Bristol, an ancient and interesting commercial town, the see of a bishop, and at one time the chief seaport of West England, is situated at the junction of the *Avon* and the *Frome*, 7 miles above the point where their united waters reach the *Bristol Channel*. It lies partly in Somerset and partly in Gloucester, but forms a city and county of itself. Its trade, chiefly with the West Indies, America, and Ireland, is still very important, though it has been outstripped in the commercial race by Liverpool and other places. Among the chief of its numerous manufactures are soap, tobacco, leather, boots and shoes, glass, brass and copper wares, chocolate, cotton, and sugar (formerly the staple). It possesses a large harbour and docks, and the Avon has been made navigable for vessels of large tonnage. The population in 1881, including that of Clifton, was 206,503. The spring tides rise to a height of 40 ft.

Bristol (Anglo-Saxon, *Bright-Stow* or *Brig-Stow*) has no certified history earlier than the Norman Conquest, but by the 12th cent. it had attained considerable wealth and importance. The old castle, in which King Stephen was imprisoned by Queen Matilda, was razed by Cromwell, and few traces are left of it (p. 116). In the 15-16th cent. Bristol was the second city of England and carried on a lucrative trade with all parts of the world. Among the numerous naval expeditions it sent out were those of the great explorer *Sebastian Cabot* (1498, etc.), who was probably born at Bristol. The fair fame of the city was sullied by the practice of kidnapping, extensively carried on here to provide labourers for the American Colonies; and Bristol was also one of the British towns principally concerned in the slave-trade. In the Civil War the town was besieged and taken, first by the Royalists (1643), and then by Gen. Fairfax (1645), to whom it was surrendered by Prince Rupert with almost no resistance. In 1831 the discussion of the Reform Bill was accompanied at Bristol by serious riots, in which numerous lives were lost and an immense amount of property destroyed. The 'Great Western', one of the first two British steamers to cross the Atlantic Ocean, was built at Bristol and started from this port for its first Oceanic voyage in 1838. In 1888 the port of Bristol was entered by 815 vessels with an aggregate burden of 577,524 tons.

According to Macaulay ('History of England', chap. iii) the streets of Bristol in 1685 were so narrow, that a coach or cart was in danger of being wedged between the houses or breaking into the cellars. 'Goods were therefore conveyed about the town almost exclusively in trucks drawn by dogs, and the richer inhabitants exhibited their wealth not by riding in gilded carriages but by walking the streets with trains of servants in rich liveries, and by keeping tables loaded with good cheer'. The hospitality of its wealthy sugar-boilers was famous, and one of their favourite beverages, made of Solera sherry, was widely known as 'Bristol milk'. Fuller relates that this concoction was the first 'moisture' given to infant Bristolians, and it is mentioned with approval in Pepys's Diary (13th June, 1668). Comp. 'Bristol Past and Present' by *Nicholls* and *Taylor* (1881-2) and 'Bristol' ('Historic Towns Series'), by the *Rev. W. Hunt* (1887).

From the *Railway Station* (Pl. H, 4), a handsome modern structure in the joint occupation of the Great Western and Midland companies, Victoria Street, traversed by a tramway and passing a more curious than beautiful *Statue of Neptune* (16th cent.), leads direct to the (1/2 M.) centre of the town. [To the right diverges Temple Street, with the *Temple Church*, originally erected for the Knights Templar about 1145, but dating in its present form chiefly from the 14-15th centuries. The tower is 5 ft. out of the perpendicular.] We may, however, diverge at once to the left, down Pile Street, to (5 min.) the church of ***St. Mary Redcliffe** (Pl. G, 5), the lofty spire of which is visible as soon as the station is quitted. This church (usually entered from the S. side) is unquestionably as nearly faultless an example of its kind (rich Perp.) as exists in the country, and justifies Queen Elizabeth's description of it as 'the fairest, the goodliest, and most famous parish-church in England'. It was founded in the 13th cent., but by degrees rebuilt, mainly by the Canynges, grandfather and grandson, each 5-6 times Mayor of Bristol, in the 14-15th centuries. The most noteworthy features of the exterior are the **N. Porch* (earlier than the body of the church, but recently restored), the tower, and the spire (285 ft.; top half modern). The church is 240 ft. long, and 117 ft. wide across the transepts.

Interior (open to visitors free). The narrowness of the nave and transepts is remarkable, and the latter have the rare addition of side aisles. The reredos of Caen stone is also very beautiful, while the Lady Chapel is a blaze of rich colouring. The visitor should also notice the groined roof and a window in the lower belfry (N.W. corner of church), in which most of the old coloured glass has been collected and arranged. There is an effigy of William Canynges the Elder (d. 1396) in the S. aisle of the nave, and one of the Younger (d. after 1467) in the S. transept. On one of the piers of the tower, at the W. end of the nave, hangs the armour of Sir William Penn (d. 1670), father of the founder of Pennsylvania; and in the adjoining belfry we are shown a rib of the famous Dun Cow slain by Guy, Earl of Warwick (comp. p. 243; really a bone of a whale, said to have been brought home by Sebastian Cabot). — Above the N. porch is the muniment room in which *Thomas Chatterton* (d. 1770), 'the marvellous boy, the sleepless soul that perished in his pride', professed to have discovered the Rowley MSS. (shown by the verger on application). His uncle was sexton of the church. Within the enclosure to the N.E. of the church is a memorial of *Chatterton*, who was born in an adjoining street. — A long-established annual event at this church is the Rush-Bearing, which takes places on Whitsunday, when the Mayor and Corporation attend in state and the floor is strewn with rushes.

We now follow Redcliffe Street, which leads northwards to (7 min.) *Bristol Bridge* (Pl. G, 4), crossing the 'Floating Harbour' formed by the diversion of the course of the Avon. A statue of *Samuel Morley, M. P.* (d. 1886), adjoins the bridge. On the left in Redcliffe St., at the corner of Ferry Lane, is *Canynges' House* (see p. 115), now forming part of the premises of Messrs. Jefferies and Sons, publishers, who are always ready to show the Canynges rooms to strangers. Beyond Bristol Bridge, High St. leads to the centre of the town, reaching at the end of Corn St. the long line of streets running N.E. from the Drawbridge (p. 117), which form perhaps the chief artery of traffic and contain the handsomest shops and public buildings. In the meantime, however, we leave High St. to the right by **Mary-le-Port Street* (Pl. F, 3), still consisting to a great extent of quaint houses of the 14-15th centuries. At the end of the street is **St. Peter's Hospital* (Pl. G, 3), one of the most perfect specimens of domestic architecture of its kind in the W. of England, originally erected in the 12th cent. and partly rebuilt in 1608. Visitors are admitted to the handsome court-room. The building was formerly used as a mint, and afterwards as a hospital. Close by is *St. Peter's Church*, the mother-church of Bristol, the tower of which (except the upper story) is early-Norman. The poet *Savage* (d. 1743) is buried at the back of St. Peter's Church.

Beyond Mary-le-Port St. we pass through Peter Street into *Castle Street* (Pl. G, 3), taking name from the extensive feudal fortress, founded probably at the end of the 11th cent., which formerly stood on this site (p. 114). Scarcely any relic of the castle remains except the entrance to the banqueting hall, now incorporated in a private house (in Tower St.). Parts of the outer walls may also be seen amid the modern buildings on the N. and E.

We may now return through Dolphin St. into *Wine Street* (Pl. F, 3), at No. 9 in which (right) *Robert Southey* was born in 1774.

To the right diverges the narrow *Pithay* (Norman *puit*, a well, and *haie*, an enclosure), a genuine though dingy relic of Old Bristol, to which Macaulay's remarks, quoted at p. 114, still apply literally. *Old Tower Lane*, diverging to the left from the Pithay, leads along the line of the old City Walls, some remains of which are visible, to St. John's Church (see below). — In Union Street, a little to the N. of Dolphin St., is *St. James's Church* (Pl. G, 3), one of the oldest in Bristol, still retaining much of the ancient Norman work. The small circular window is a good example of a feature more common in foreign than in English Romanesque churches of the same period.

Wine St. ends at the junction with High St. (see above), opposite which *Broad Street* diverges to the W., containing, to the left, the *Guildhall* (Pl. F, 3), a modern building in the Elizabethan style. At the end is a gateway arch of the old *City Wall*, strangely surmounted by the spire of *St. John's Church* (Pl. F, 3; 15th cent.), the body of which was itself part of the wall. Beyond the archway is *Christmas Street*, leading to the quaint and steep lane called *Christmas Steps*, at the top of which are some curious stone seats and the chapel of a 16th cent. alms-house (1504; dedicated to the Magi).

Returning to Wine St. we next enter Corn Street (Pl. F, 4), mainly consisting of substantial banks and insurance-offices, among which the elaborate façade of the *Wilts & Dorset Bank* (1858) is conspicuous. The bank occupies the site of the '*Bush Inn*', where Mr. Pickwick and Mr. Winkle took up their quarters on their search for Miss Arabella Allen. Adjoining the bank is the *Council House*, containing a valuable collection of old plate and a fine portrait by Van Dyck. On the other side (left) is the *Exchange* (Pl. F, 4; 1740), in front of which are four singular metal tables, known as the '*Nails*'. These belonged to the *Tolsey* (mentioned in Scott's 'Pirate'), the forerunner of the Exchange, and were used by the merchants for making payments (hence, it is said, the phrase 'pay on the nail'). Three of them bear dates (1594, 1625, 1631).

Nearly opposite the Exchange diverges *Small Street* (Pl. F, 3), containing the *Post Office* and the *Assize Courts*. The latter, forming the back of the Guildhall (p. 116), incorporate *Colston's House* (p. 119), of which some interesting remains are pointed out to visitors.

Corn St. is prolonged by *Clare Street*, from which a short street on the right leads to *St. Stephen's Church* (Pl. F, 4), a late-Gothic building of 1470, with a fine restored tower, of which Mr. Freeman notes that it 'is remarkable for having æsthetically dispensed with buttresses'. Tradition says St. Augustine preached here.

Marsh Street, to the left (S.), leads to the *Central Free Library* (Pl. F, 4), the earliest Protestant free library in England (1613), containing a fine sculptured mantel-piece by Grinling Gibbons. Farther on, beyond the *Custom House*, is *Queen's Square* (Pl. F, 4, 5), the principal scene of the riots of 1831, with an equestrian statue of William III. by Rysbrack. David Hume was a clerk at No. 16 Queen's Sq. (S. side) in 1734.

Clare Street ends at the *Drawbridge* over the Floating Harbour, across or past which nearly all the tramway-lines run. Crossing the bridge and turning to the left, we soon reach the pretty, open space named College Green (Pl. E, 4), originally the burial-ground of the abbey (see below); among the buildings round it are the Cathedral, *St. Augustine's Church*, the Mayor's Chapel, and the *Royal Hotel*. Immediately in front is a *Statue of Queen Victoria*, by Boehm.

The **Cathedral** (Pl. E, 4) was originally erected in the 12th cent. (begun in 1142), as the church of an Augustine abbey, by Robert Fitzhardinge, a Bristol merchant, and progenitor of the Berkeley family. It was, however, rebuilt two centuries later, while the nave, destroyed in the 14th cent., was rebuilt by *Street* in harmony with the choir and transept in 1868. The main body of the structure is of the Dec. order, resembling in many respects the German Gothic of the period (13-14th cent.), but the *Chapter House* (1155-1170), a remnant of the original church, is a fine example of late-Norman. The *Elder Lady Chapel* (c. 1210) is good E.E., and the *Cloisters* (incomplete) are Perpendicular. The W. front has a deeply recessed doorway and two towers (1888). The *Tower*, 127 ft. high, is a Perp. addition of the 16th century. The Cathedral is 300 ft. long, 68 ft. wide, and 56 ft. high. — The bishopric of Bristol was founded by Henry VIII. in 1542, and refounded by Pope Paul IV. in 1551. Since 1836 it has been linked with the diocese of Gloucester (the *congé d'élire* being addressed to the two chapters alternately). Daily choral services at 10 and 4.

Interior. The absence of clerestory and triforium makes this church unique among English cathedrals, the aisles being of the same height as the nave, and the arches rising clear up to the spring of the vaulting. The singular flying arches across the aisles, resembling timber-work, take the place of the usual flying buttresses. The arches in the aisles of the NAVE are a clever imitation of those in the choir, but the architect (Street) has allowed himself a few slight deviations from his model, which do not seem to be improvements.

At the E. end of the N. aisle of the nave are two modern brass tablets of good design, and the remains of an old reredos, destroyed to make room for a large monument. The NORTH TRANSEPT contains tablets to the memory of *Southey*, *Hugh Conway* (d. 1885), and *Mary Carpenter* (d. 1877), all natives of Bristol. — On the E. this transept is adjoined by the ELDER LADY CHAPEL, a pure E.E. structure (ca. 1210), containing some grotesque carvings.

The most striking feature in the CHOIR is the fine Dec. *East Window* (a so-called Jesse window), most of the stained glass in which dates from the beginning of the 14th cent.; the arrangement of its tracery symbolises the Trinity. The choir also contains some interesting monuments of the Berkeley family (p. 117) and of the old abbots. Several of these occupy the singular recesses in the walls, which are characteristic of this cathedral. A tablet below Abbot Newland's tomb points out the grave of Bishop Butler (see below). Some of the old miserere carvings deserve attention. — At the E. end of the S. choir-aisle is the BERKELEY CHAPEL, added about 1340; it is entered by a vestibule containing some unique work of this period (Perp.). The SOUTH TRANSEPT contains a monument to *Joseph Butler* (1692-1752), author of the 'Analogy', who was Bishop of Bristol from 1738 to 1750. From this transept we enter the CLOISTERS, from the E. side of which we obtain access to the gem of the cathedral, the *CHAPTER HOUSE, perhaps the most beautiful Norman chamber in the kingdom. Its rich mouldings and interlaced arcade are of the most exquisite workmanship. Like other early chapter-houses in England it is rectangular in shape. It contains a curious old carving in stone (the 'Harrowing of Hell'), somewhat similar to the sculptures at Chichester Cathedral (p. 55) and believed by some to be of Saxon origin.

The body of the church is open free to visitors, but the sub-sacristan (gratuity optional) keeps the keys of the Chapter House, Elder Lady Chapel, and Berkeley Chapel.

To the W. of the Cathedral is **College Gate*, an admirably-preserved Norman archway, with a smaller one by its side, belonging to the old abbey-buildings. The mouldings are very elaborate. The superstructure, with restored oriel windows, is Perpendicular. — To the S. of the Cathedral is a fragment of the old *Bishop's Palace*, burned by the rioters in 1831, when the Cathedral was saved by the vigour and determination of a Nonconformist lawyer. — On the other (N.) side of College Green, nearly opposite the Cathedral, is the **Church of St. Mark* (Pl. E, 4), known as the '*Mayor's Chapel*', a little gem of Gothic (E.E. to Perp.) architecture, containing some curious old monuments and some old stained glass. [The key is kept by Mr. Jarret, 9 Lodge St.; comp. Pl. E, 3.] In Unity St. is the large new *School* (Pl. E, 4) of the ancient and still existing company of the *Merchant Venturers*, incorporated in 1551, of which Sebastian Cabot was the first governor.

Bristol occupies a leading position among English cities for the extent and number of its charitable institutions; and the first place among its philanthropists is unanimously accorded to *Edward Colston* (1636-1721), whose memory is kept green by the annual 'Colston Banquets' on Nov. 13th, now utilised for a display of political oratory. The *Colston Hall* (Pl. F, 4), in Colston St., with a fine organ, is used for public meetings and popular concerts; it can accommodate an audience of 2-3000 persons. Colston is buried in the church of *All Saints* (Pl. F, 3), where a statue of him has been erected. — The well-known **Müller Orphanages**, originally established in 1836, and now containing upwards of 2000 children, are at Ashley Down on the N. side of the town (cab 2*s.* 6*d.*). The Orphanages are still conducted on the principle of trusting to the voluntary and unsolicited contributions of the charitable, and possess no endowments or regular income of any kind. About 1,250,000*l.* have been received in this way since the scheme was started, and about 110,000 pupils have been supported. Visitors are admitted to the different houses on weekdays (Mon. excepted) at 2.30 and 3 p.m. (also 3.30 p.m. in summer); the most interesting is the oldest, the day for which is Wednesday.

From a visitor's point of view, *Fry's Chocolate and Cocoa Works* (1100 hands), in Union St. (Pl. F, 3), and *W. D. & H. O. Wills's Tobacco Factory* in East Street, Bedminster (Pl. G, 6), are among the most interesting of the large manufactories of Bristol. — The charming little **Arno's Vale Cemetery*, at the S.E. corner of the town, contains the grave of *Robert Hall* (d. 1831).

The pleasantest approach to the high-lying and beautiful suburb of **Clifton** (Hotels, see p. 113) is from College Green, either through *Park Street* (Pl. E, 4) or over *Brandon Hill* (Pl. D, 4; 260 ft.; *View). — We may also reach the foot of the Suspension Bridge by tramway (see p. 114).

Park Street ascends from the N. W. angle of the Green. No. 10 is the house in which *Hannah More* and her sisters kept a school. To the left diverges Great George St.. Farther up, to the right, stands the large and handsome *Blind Asylum* (Pl. E, 3; open to visitors on Mon., Wed., & Thurs., 11-12 & 2-4; concert on the first Mon. of each month at 3 p.m.). Adjacent is the *Bristol Museum* (Pl. D, 3; adm. 6*d.*; on Sat. and Mon. 2*d.*), containing a fine statue of Eve by Baily, collections of natural history, geology, industrial products, and antiquities, and a library of 50,000 volumes.

Behind the Museum, in Tyndall's Park, is **Bristol University College** (Pl. D, 3), opened in 1876, and attended by students of both sexes. There is a *Medical School* affiliated to it. — To the N. of the College is *Bristol Grammar School*, founded in 1531.

Beyond the museum, Park St. is prolonged by Queen's Road, in which, straight in front of us, we soon see the *Victoria Rooms* (Pl. D, 3), a handsome building in a Grecian style, with Egyptian details. Opposite it (to the right) is the *Fine Arts Academy* (Pl. D, 3), containing a collection of modern paintings. An annual Exhibition is held here in spring (adm. 1*s.*; 6*d.* on holidays).

From this point *White Ladies Road*, to the right, leads straight to *Durdham Down* (nearly 1 M.), passing near *Clifton Down Station*

(p. 121; Pl. C, 2) and the mouth of the long tunnel (1 M.) extending hence below the Downs to the Avon. The nearest way to (1/2 M.) Clifton Down and the Suspension Bridge is to the left, through Queen's Road (Pl. C, 3), and then, at Victoria Square (Pl. C, 4), to the right. The lofty spire of *Christ Church* (Pl. B, 4), situated at the E. end of Clifton Down, now serves as our land-mark.

*__Clifton Down__ (Pl. A, 1-4; 235 ft.) is an elevated grass-grown plateau of limestone formation, dotted with fine trees and fringed with the villas of well-to-do Bristolians. On the W. it is bounded by the *Avon*, here flowing through a deep and highly picturesque gorge, the rocky wall of which is named **St. Vincent's Rocks.* In the face of the rocks is the *Giant's Cave* (view), formerly used as an oratory, now approached from the observatory (tunnel 6*d.*, observatory 6*d.*). The gorge is crossed by a noble **Suspension Bridge* (Pl. A, 4; toll 1*d.*), with a single span of 700 ft. and 250 ft. above the surface of the water; it originally spanned the Thames at Hungerford near Charing Cross, but was re-erected in its present position in 1864. On the height adjoining the bridge is an *Observatory* (315 ft.), containing a camera obscura and commanding a lovely view. On the W. bank, a little below the bridge, a deep wooded hollow known as **Nightingale Valley* descends to the river-gorge, and both here and on the Observatory hill are extensive traces of British earthworks, with later Roman modifications. A zigzag path descends to the *Hotwells*, which have been known for 400 years but have now completely outlived the reputation they enjoyed in the days of 'Humphrey Clinker' and Miss Burney's 'Evelina'. All that now remains is a pump erected by the Merchant Venturers.

Those whose time is limited may return to Bristol from the Hotwells by tramway; but even the most hurried visitor should at least go as far as the centre of the bridge in order to enjoy the view up and down stream. [The Avon is a tidal river, and it is very desirable to visit the bridge at high water, when its ugly, muddy bed is covered.] Those who have more time should either cross the bridge to the beautiful *Leigh Woods* on the other side of the Avon, or continue to follow the route described below.

To the N., Clifton Down is continued by **Durdham Down* (310 ft.), which has been secured for public use. By crossing Durdham Down on the river side we reach the (3/4 M.) *Sea Wall*, which commands a fine view. A little farther on is a picturesque tower, known as *Cook's Folly*, now forming part of a villa. On the landward side of Durdham Down are the **Zoological Gardens* (Pl. B, 2; adm. 6*d.*). Nearer Clifton is *Clifton College* (Pl. B, 2), founded in 1862, now attended by 650 pupils, and ranking among the chief public schools of England. Its close forms one of the prettiest cricket-grounds in the country. Near the College stands *All Saints* (Pl. C, 2), a modern church by Street, noticeable for the unusual design of its nave and aisles. — We may return to Bristol by the tramway starting from *St. John's Church* (Pl. C, 1) and traversing White Ladies Road, or by train from Clifton Down Station (Pl. C, 2).

Excursions. About $3^1/_2$ M. to the N.W. of Clifton lies ***King's Weston***, a country-house on the Avon, with a beautiful park. Adjacent, to the E., is ***King's Weston Down***, with a well-defined British camp, and to the W., *Penpole Point*, commanding a charming view. At the S.W. base of the latter, near the mouth of the Avon, is the village of *Shirehampton* (see below). About $1^1/_2$ M. to the N. of King's Weston, in a pleasant dale, is *Blaize Castle*, containing a fine collection of paintings. The grounds (visitors admitted on Thurs. after previous application) command excellent views of the Bristol Channel and the coast of S. Wales. On *Blaize Hill* is another of the numerous ancient entrenchments round Bristol. — *Dundry Church*, with its fine tower, 4 M. to the S.E., on the top of a lofty down (790 ft.), is a fine point of view and itself a conspicuous object in the view from *Clifton Down* (p. 120). — Among the more distant points of interest within the limits of a day's excursion from Bristol are *Chepstow* and *Tintern Abbey* (p. 176), *Wells* (p. 123), *Glastonbury* (p. 126), the *Cheddar Cliffs* (p. 122), *Bath* (p. 109), *Weston* (p. 126), and *Clevedon* (p. 122).

From Bristol to Portishead, $11^1/_2$ M., railway in $^1/_2$-$^3/_4$ hr. (fares 2*s*., 1*s*. 4*d*., $11^1/_2$*d*.). The line skirts the S. bank of the Avon, passing *Clifton Bridge*, *Pill*, and *Portbury*. — *Portishead* (Royal Pier Hotel) is a small watering-place and residential suburb on the Severn estuary.

From Bristol to Avonmouth, $9^3/_4$ M., railway in $^1/_2$ hr. (fares 1*s*. 6*d*., 1*s*. 4*d*., 9*d*.). — This line passes the suburban stations of *Lawrence Hill*, *Stapleton Road*, *Montpellier*, and *Clifton Down* (p. 120), penetrates the Downs by a tunnel 1740 yds. long, and emerges on the E. bank of the Avon near *Cook's Folly* (p. 120). $6^1/_4$ M. *Sea Mills;* $7^3/_4$ M. *Shirehampton* (see above). — $9^3/_4$ M. *Avonmouth* (Hotel) has a pier and extensive docks (now belonging to the city of Bristol).

From Bristol to Severn Tunnel Junction (for S. Wales), 17 M., G. W. Railway in $^3/_4$ hr. (fares 5*s*., 3*s*. 8*d*., 2*s*. 6*d*. or 2*s*.). — The first stations are *Lawrence Hill* and *Stapleton Road*, the birthplace of Hannah More (d. 1833). Near *Ashley Hill* are the Orphan Asylums of George Müller (see p. 119). Beyond *Filton* and *Patchway* the train passes through a tunnel $^3/_4$ M. long and reaches *Pilning*. At *New Passage* passengers formerly left the train to cross the estuary of the *Severn* by steamer. In Dec., 1886, however, the ***Severn Tunnel**, one of the greatest triumphs of railway engineering, was opened for passenger traffic, and travellers keep their seats. The estuary here is upwards of $2^1/_4$ M. wide, but the total length of the tunnel is $4^1/_3$ M. The crown of the arch is at a depth below the bed of the river varying from 40 ft. to 100 ft. The tunnel is 26 ft. wide and 20 ft. high, and is traversed by two lines of rails. The difficulty of construction was greatly increased by the frequent flooding of the tunnel by land-springs tapped in the progress of the work, and the total cost was nearly two millions sterling. The tunnel shortens the direct railway journey from London to Newport by 14 M. and that from Bristol to Newport by 55 M.; and it has led to the opening of an important new railway route from the W. of England to the N. of England and Scotland. — We join the South Wales Railway at (17 M.) *Severn Tunnel Junction* (comp. p. 192), on the other side of the Severn.

From Bristol to Frome, $24^1/_4$ M., G. W. Railway in 1-$1^1/_4$ hr. (fares 5*s*. 6*d*., 3*s*. 9*d*., 2*s*. 3*d*.). — The most important intermediate stations are (7 M.) *Pensford* (interesting on account of the great stone circles of *Stanton Drew*, 1 M. to the W.) and (16 M.) *Radstock* (Waldegrave Arms). — $24^1/_2$ M. **Frome** *(Crown; George)*, a thriving agricultural and woollen-manufacturing town, possesses a noble Dec. church, splendidly restored by the Rev. W. J. E. Bennett, the late incumbent (d. 1886). Bishop Ken (d. 1711) is buried in the graveyard, under the chancel-window. At the W. end of the church, outside, is the Bennett Memorial Cross. The church is approached by a set of stone 'Stations of the Cross', erected by Mr. Bennett. We here join the line from Chippenham and Westbury to Yeovil (comp. pp. 108, 102). *Longleat* (p. 113) lies 3 M. to the S.E.

From Bristol to Gloucester, $37^1/_2$ M., railway in 1-$1^1/_2$ hr. (fares 5*s*., 3*s*. $1^1/_2$*d*.). 3 M. *Fish Ponds*. At ($6^1/_2$ M.) *Mangotsfield* our line unites with that from Bath. From (11 M.) *Yate* a branch-line diverges to

Iron Acton and (8 M.) *Thornbury* (Swan), the latter with a fine cruciform church and a large Tudor castle, built by the Duke of Buckingham in 1511 but never finished (p. lvi). To the right, 6 M. off, lies *Badminton*, the large house and park of the Duke of Beaufort. — 15 M. *Wickwar*. Near (17 M.) *Charfield*, to the left, lies *Tortworth Court*, the seat of the Earl of Ducie; the park contains the largest chestnut in England, 50 ft. in circumference, and mentioned in a document of the 13th century. — From (22 M.) *Berkeley Road* a branch-line diverges to *Lydney* (p. 192) and the *Dean Forest* (p. 177), crossing the Severn by a magnificent bridge at *Sharpness* (p. 192). The first station on this branch is (2 M.) Berkeley (*Berkeley Arms*), a small town with 1200 inhab., the birthplace of Edward Jenner (1749-1823), the discoverer of vaccination. **Berkeley Castle* is an ancient baronial castle, with a moat and keep, still occupied as a dwelling (Lord Fitzhardinge; open on Tues. and Frid., 2-4). It contains some portraits of the Berkeley family, the cabin furniture of Admiral Drake, and other interesting relics. It was in this castle that Edward II. was murdered in 1327. — 24 M. *Coaley Junction* is the station for *Dursley* (Old Bell), a small wool-manufacturing town, with a Dec. church. — 27 M. *Frocester* (p. lvi); 28½ M. *Stonehouse*, the junction for *Nailsworth* and *Stroud*. — 37½ M. *Gloucester*, see p. 170.

From Bristol to *Taunton* and *Exeter*, see R. 16

16. From Bristol to Exeter.

Wells.

75½ M. Great Western Railway in 1¾-4 hrs. (16*s.* 6*d.*, 12*s.* 8*d.*, 6*s.* 3½*d.*). — The train passes through a flat country, with few views of the sea.

Beyond the suburban station of (1 M.) *Bedminster* the train affords a view of the *Suspension Bridge* (p. 120) to the right and passes between *Dundry Hill* (790 ft.; p. 121) on the left and *Leigh Down* on the right. 5 M. *Flax-Bourton;* 8 M. *Nailsea;* 12 M. *Yatton*, the junction for Clevedon and Wells, with an interesting church, visible to the left of the line.

Clevedon (*Royal; Rock; Pier*, R. & A. from 3*s.* 6*d.*; *Bristol*), a small watering-place 4 M. to the N.W., is much frequented by the Bristolians. Henry Hallam (d. 1859), the historian, and his son Arthur, the subject of Tennyson's 'In Memoriam', are buried in Clevedon parish-church (St. Andrew's). Coleridge lived at Myrtle Cottage here for some time after his marriage and the abandonment of his Susquehanna scheme (1795). **Clevedon Court*, the 'Castlewood' of 'Esmond', a fine old baronial mansion, with a façade of the 14th cent., was seriously injured by fire in 1882; visitors are admitted to the grounds on Thurs., 12-3. Above Clevedon rises *Dial Hill*, an excellent point of view; at its base are the ruins of *Walton Church* and *Walton Castle*. About 4 M. to the N.W. is a British entrenchment named *Cadbury Camp*.

From Yatton to Wells, 18 M., railway in 1 hr. (fares 3*s.* 5*d.*, 2*s.* 8*d.*, 1*s.* 8*d.* or 1*s.* 5½*d.*). The first station is (1½ M.) *Congresbury*, 2 M. to the E. of which is *Wrington*, the birthplace of John Locke (1632; cottage still standing), with a fine church-tower. — 8 M. *Axbridge* (Lamb), an ancient little town, with interesting brasses in its church. — Near (9½ M.) *Cheddar* (Cheddar Cliffs Hotel; Bath Arms) are **Cheddar Cliffs* (400-500 ft.), the highest limestone cliffs in the country, and the **Cheddar Caverns*, containing interesting stalactites (adm. to each of the two principal caves 1*s.*; *Cox's* by far the finer).

The environs of Cheddar comprise many other charming points for excursions, among which may be mentioned *Black Down* (1065 ft.), the highest of the *Mendip Hills*, 3 M. to the N. The pastures of the district are very rich, and 'Cheddar Cheese' has long been famous. — About $3^1/_2$ M. to the S. of Cheddar station is *Wedmore*, where King Alfred made peace with the Danes in 878. The interesting church dates from the 13-15th centuries.

$16^1/_2$ M. *Wookey* is the station for the *Wookey Hole*, a curious cavern, near which large quantities of bones (elephant, hyæna, etc.) have been found.

18 M. **Wells.** — **Hotels.** SWAN, Sadler St., near the cathedral, well spoken of; STAR, High St.; MITRE, Sadler St., R. & A. 4*s*. — There are two **Railway Stations** at Wells, the *Great Western*, and that of the *Somerset & Dorset Line* (comp. p. 112).

Wells, a small and ancient city with 4600 inhab., is prettily situated at the foot of the Mendip Hills. It has been the see of a bishop since the 10th cent. (see below) and is perhaps the most characteristic cathedral-city in England (Plan, see p. 115).

In Wells the interest of 'the cathedral church and its appurtenances is not only primary but absorbing. They are not only the chief ornament of the place; they are the place itself. The whole history of Wells is the history of the bishoprick and of its church. It was never a royal dwelling-place; it was never a place of commercial importance; it was never a place of military strength. The whole interest of the city is ecclesiastical' (*Freeman's* 'History of the Cathedral Church of Wells').

The ***Cathedral**, dedicated to St. Andrew, is, in its present condition, predominantly an E.E. building of the first half of the 13th cent., and *Bishop Joceline* (1206-1242) is commonly called the 'Fundator Alter', though recent researches assign a considerable share in the work to *Bishop Fitz-Joceline* (1174-91), one of his predecessors (comp. p. xlv). It is the third church on the same site. The first (perhaps of wood) was erected in the 8th cent. by the Saxon king Ina, as a collegiate church for a body of secular clergy. This was afterwards replaced by a Norman cathedral (1135-66), some fragments of the masonry of which still remain. The bishopric was founded in 909 by Edward the Elder, as the bishopric of Somerset, and for a time the see was afterwards removed to Bath (comp. p. 111). The church as designed by Bishop Joceline was finished by the erection of the *Chapter House* at the end of the 13th century. Thereafter a complete transformation of the E. part of the church seems to have been taken in hand, beginning with the *Lady Chapel* (ca. 1320), while the *Presbytery*, as it now stands, dates from about 1350. The upper part of the *Central Tower*, 165 ft. high, also belongs to the early part of the 14th century. The *Vicars' Close* was added in the 14th cent. and partly altered in the 15th. The upper part of the *W. Towers* and *Cloisters* are Perpendicular. — Though comparatively small in size (383 ft. long; 82 ft. wide across the nave and aisles; 67-73 ft. high), Wells Cathedral takes rank among the finest churches in England, and some authorities do not hesitate to give it the first place of all. The best general *View of it is obtained from the Shepton Mallet road, about $^1/_4$ M. from the city.

For a plan of Wells Cathedral see page 545

Mr. Freeman asserts that the group of ecclesiastical buildings at Wells has no rival either in its own island or beyond the sea. 'To most of these objects, taken singly, it would be easy to find rivals which would equal or surpass them. The church itself cannot from mere lack of bulk hold its ground against the soaring apse of Amiens, or against the windows ranging, tier above tier, in the mighty eastern gable of Ely. The cloister cannot measure itself with Gloucester or Salisbury; the chapter-house lacks the soaring roofs of York and Lincoln; the palace itself finds its rival in the ruined pile of St. David's. The peculiar charm and glory of Wells lies in the union and harmonious grouping of all'. It has preserved its ancient buildings and arrangements more perfectly than any other English cathedral; and it has been uninterruptedly in the possession of a chapter of secular canons. Comp. the Introduction, p. xliii.

We enter the *Cathedral Close* by *Browne's Gate* (the 'Dean's Eye'), in Sadler St., or by the *Penniless Porch* ('Palace Eye'), in the market-place, built by Bishop Beckington (1443-1464). The chief exterior glory of the Cathedral is the beautiful *West Façade*, 147 ft. wide, and most elaborately adorned with arcading and sculptures (600 figures in all). It was the first part of the present church to be completed, and has lately been restored with great care and tact. The sculptures, which are believed to be the work of native artists, were added about 1280, almost at the same time that Niccolò Pisano was reviving the art of sculpture in Italy. Beautiful as this façade is, it shares with the W. fronts of Lincoln and Rouen the reproach of being architecturally a mere mask, since the towers are really placed outside of the aisles of which they affect to form the ends. The *North Porch*, with its fine mouldings, is a noteworthy example of the beginning of the E.E. period. Before entering the Cathedral we should also notice the exterior of the Chapter House and the curious gallery running along the Chain Gate and connecting the church with the Vicars' Close.

Interior (services at 10 a. m. and 3 p. m.; adm. to choir 6*d*.). The best view of the interior, which has been restored, is obtained from the W. end, and the general effect is rich and imposing. The Nave, which is 192 ft. long, is somewhat narrow in proportion to its height, and it has the distinct character (according to Mr. Freeman) of having its main lines horizontal rather than vertical. Among the first features to strike the eye are the curious inverted arches inserted in 1338 to prop up the central tower, and forming the general outline of a St. Andrew's Cross. The foliage of the capitals is very elaborate, and is interspersed with birds and animals. The triforium is carried backwards over the aisles. At the E. end of the nave are two interesting *Chantries* of the 15th cent. (Bishop Bubwith, d. 1424; Hugh Sugar, d. 1489), and on the S. side, in the centre, is a *Minstrels' Gallery*, also of the Perp. period. The stained glass in the W. window dates from the beginning of the 16th cent., and was mainly brought from abroad. The colouring on the vault is a modern reproduction from traces of the original design. The stone pulpit was erected in 1541-47. — The Transepts resemble the nave in general character and are flanked with aisles. The capitals of the piers here are very rich and quaint. The fan-vaulting above the cross is fine. The S. transept contains some interesting monuments, including the remains of the Perp. chantry of *Bishop Beckington* (d. 1464). In the N. transept, the W. aisle of which is shut off by a Perp. screen and divided into two chapels, is a curious old *Clock*, with figures set in motion at the hours, originally constructed by a monk of Glastonbury about 1325 (works modern; original in S. Kensington Museum).

The *Choir, which is separated from the nave by a Perp. screen surmounted by the organ, forms with the Presbytery and Lady Chapel one of the most beautiful ecclesiastical interiors in this country. The general style is Early or Geometrical Decorated. The stalls are modern, but the old misericords have been preserved. The fine window at the E. end and the adjoining windows in the clerestory are filled with ancient glass; and a memorial window to *Bishop Ken* (d. 1711) was inserted in the N. aisle in 1885. At the back of the altar is a low *Screen*, forming the end of the choir proper. The *Presbytery*, in a rich Dec. style, is connected with the Lady Chapel by a small transept containing four chapels. *Bishop Joceline* (p. 123) is interred in the centre of the choir, though his tomb has been destroyed; and there are several interesting monuments of bishops and others in the aisles and chapels.

The apsidal termination of the cathedral is formed by the *Lady Chapel, with its 'matchless grouping of slender pillars and no less matchless harmony of colour'. It also belongs to the early Dec. period, and the stained glass, made up chiefly of fragments from other parts of the church, is of contemporary date. The *Chapel of St. John*, or S.E. transept, contains a brass of 1618 with a curious Latin epitaph.

The octagonal *Chapter House, with its beautiful Geometrical window-tracery, dates from about the year 1300, and is a fine example of the period. The ribs of the vaulting radiate from a large shafted column in the centre. The Chapter House is reached from the Cathedral by a beautiful **Staircase*, with admirable details, ascending from the E. aisle of the N. Transept and leading also to the bridge above the Chain Gate (p. 124). The separation of the Chapter House from the Cloisters is not unusual in churches of the old or secular foundation. Below the Chapter House is a curious *Undercroft* or *Crypt* (entered from the N. choir-aisle), containing various antiquarian relics.

The Central Tower, ascended by a staircase from the S. Transept, affords an extensive *View. — From the S.W. corner of the same transept we enter the spacious Perp. Cloisters, which have no walk on the N. side. The Chapter Library is over the E. alley of the cloisters.

To the S. of the Cathedral, beyond the cloisters, is the picturesque ***Episcopal Palace**, built by Bishop Joceline (p. 123) and surrounded with a moat and bastioned wall by Bishop Ralph of Shrewsbury (1329-63). The most interesting features are the ruins of the *Great Hall*, added in 1274-92, and the Dec. *Chapel*. The actual residence of the bishop is on the E. side of the quadrangle. The vaulted lower floor, originally used for cellars, has been converted into a dining-room and entrance-hall. The grounds are shown by the lodge-keeper on application (sometimes also the crypt). — On the N. side of the Cathedral stands the *Deanery*, a good example of a mansion of the 15th cent., with turrets, buttresses, and battlements. It has suffered considerably from modern restoration, but not so much as the *Archdeaconry* (late 13th cent.), a little farther to the E., opposite the N. porch. Some of the *Canons' Houses* are also interesting 15th cent. buildings. Another important member of the group of ecclesiastical buildings at Wells is the ***Vicars' Close**, a highly picturesque enclosure, containing a chapel, a library, a common hall, and residences for several priest and lay vicars (originally 42). One house has been restored to its original condition as in the 16th century. The Vicars' Close communicates with the Cathedral by a unique *Gallery* or *Bridge* (1460), passing above the Chain Gate (comp. p. 124).

After the cathedral group the most interesting building in Wells is *St. Cuthbert's Church*, near the G.W.R. station, originally an E.E. edifice, but transformed in the Perp. period. The W. tower is particularly fine. Near this church are *Bishop Bubwith's Almshouses*. — A good view of the city is obtained from the *Tor Hill*, on the way to which we pass the copious *Springs of St. Andrew*, the chief of the 'wells' that give name to the city. They feed the moat of the Episcopal Palace.

Among the short excursions in the neighbourhood of Wells the most popular is that to *Wookey* (see p. 123), 2 M. to the W.

A branch-line runs S. from Wells to ($5^1/_2$ M.) **Glastonbury** (*George*, a quaint 15th cent. structure; *Crown; Red Lion*), an ancient town, renowned in fable as the spot where Joseph of Arimathæa founded the first Christian church in England, and as the Isle of Avalon, where King Arthur and Queen Guinevere were buried. In sober fact **Glastonbury Abbey*† can trace its foundation back to the 6th cent. and is 'the one great institution which bore up untouched through the storm of English Conquest, the one great tie which binds our race to the race which went before us, and which binds the church of the last 1300 years to the earlier days of Christianity in Britain' (Freeman; comp. p. xxxiv). King Ina founded a monastery here in the 8th cent. and dedicated it to SS. Peter and Paul; and in the 10th cent. *St. Dunstan*, who was born and educated at Glastonbury, built a church of stone to the E. of the primitive British church of wattles and timber. These two churches stood side by side till the 12th cent., when both were pulled down to make way for a Norman edifice on a larger and grander scale. Scarcely was this finished, however, when it was burned down by a fire, which also destroyed the '*Vetusta Ecclesia*', or little wicker chapel of the early missionaries, carefully kept as a sacred relic. Henry II. immediately began to rebuild the church on a yet larger scale, and it was finished about a century after his death. Its length when completed was 528 ft., and it covered the entire area occupied by the two earlier churches. The Abbey was suppressed and dismantled by Henry VIII., who hanged the last abbot on Glastonbury Tor. The ruins, now in the grounds of a private house (adm. 6*d.*), were long used as the stone quarry of the district and are thus comparatively scanty. The most interesting are those of the **Chapel of the Virgin* or *St. Joseph*, erected by Henry II. on the exact site of the Vetusta Ecclesia, at the W. end of the great church which he began. There also exist a transeptal chapel, parts of the S. wall of the nave and choir, two piers of the great tower, and some traces of the cloisters. Nearly all are in the transition Norman style, but the crypt below St. Joseph's Chapel is a 15th cent. addition. The most important relic of the secular buildings of the abbey is the massive stone *Kitchen*, with four large fire-places, probably dating from the 14th century. Among the buildings which led Mr. Parker to describe Glastonbury as 'a perfect store of domestic antiquities' are the *George Inn* (see above), originally erected as an inn for pilgrims to the abbey; the so-called *Tribunal*, also in the High St.; and the *Abbot's Barn*, in Chilkwell St. The church of *St. John the Baptist* has a fine Perp. tower. An *Archaeological Museum* was founded at Glastonbury in 1837. The site of the *Glastonbury Thorn*, which sprang miraculously from Joseph of Arimathæa's staff, and always blossomed on Christmas Day, is marked by a stone inscribed 'I. A. *A. D.* XXXI'. (on *Wearyall Hill*, to the right of the road from the station to the town). The tree was cut down by a Puritan fanatic. — A good view of the abbey and district is obtained from the top of *Glastonbury Tor* (500 ft.). The tower is a relic of an old pilgrims' chapel. — Close to Glastonbury is *Shapwich Moss*, a happy hunting-ground for botanists. — From Glastonbury to *Highbridge* and *Templecombe*, see p. 113.

Beyond Wells the railway from Yatton runs on to *Shepton Mallet* (p. 113) and *Witham* (p. 112).

Beyond Yatton (p. 122) the *Mendip Hills* come into sight on the left. At ($16^3/_4$ M.) *Worle* a short loop-line diverges to (2 M.) **Weston-super-Mare** (*Royal*, 'pens'. from 10*s.* 6*d.*; *Imperial; York; Pier; Claremont; Railway; Plough*), a fashionable and well-sheltered watering-place with 12,885 inhab., situated on the Bristol

† See *Willis's* 'Architectural History of Glastonbury Abbey'.

Channel opposite the islands of *Steep* and *Flat Holm*. The beach is marred by the muddy deposits of the Severn, but the bay affords abundant opportunity for rowing and sailing. One of the favourite promenades is the iron pier connecting the mainland with the rocky islet of *Bearnback*. There is also a long esplanade.

Among the numerous pleasant points near Weston-super-Mare are *Worle Hill* (306 ft.), $1^1/_2$ M. to the N., crowned by an old camp and commanding a magnificent view; *Uphill Old Church*, 2 M. to the S., on a rocky promontory affording an extensive view; *Woodspring Priory* (adm. 6*d*.), 4 M. to the N.; *Brean Down*, projecting into the sea to the S., beyond Uphill.

$21^1/_4$ M. *Bleadon-Uphill*. At ($24^1/_4$ M.) *Brent Knoll* the conical green hill of that name rises to the left. — We now cross the *Axe* and reach (27 M.) *Highbridge*, where the G. W. Railway intersects the Somerset and Dorset line from *Burnham* (Queen's; Clarence), a small watering-place $1^1/_2$ M. to the W., to (12 M.) *Glastonbury* (p. 126; fares 2*s*. 7*d*., 1*s*. 8*d*., 1*s*.), *Evercreech Junction* (p. 112), and *Templecombe* (p. 102). — $30^3/_4$ M. *Dunball*.

$33^1/_4$ M. **Bridgwater** *(Royal Clarence; Bristol; Railway)*, an ancient town of 12,000 inhab., on the *Parrett*, 6 M. from the sea. It was taken by storm by Gen. Fairfax in 1645. The handsome *Church of St. Mary*, dating from 1420, possesses a slender spire, 175 ft. high, and contains a valuable altar-piece ('Descent from the Cross') of the Italian School. *St. John's* is a tasteful modern edifice. The 'Bath Bricks' manufactured here are made of the peculiar slime deposited by the river. During spring-tides the Parrett is subject to a 'Bore', or tidal wave, 6-9 ft. in height; similar phenomena are observed on the Severn and a few other narrow rivers where the rise of the tide is considerable. Bridgwater was the birthplace of *Admiral Blake* (1599-1657), the house still standing near the iron bridge.

About 5 M. to the S.E. of Bridgwater lies *Sedgemoor*, where the Duke of Monmouth was defeated in 1685: the last fight deserving the name of battle that has been fought on English ground. — At *Nether Stowey*, 8 M. to the W., Coleridge lived in 1796-98 and wrote his 'Ancient Mariner'. In 1797 Wordsworth was his neighbour at Alfoxden House. Nether Stowey lies near the *Quantock Hills*, among which numerous pleasant excursions may be made.

The train now follows the valley of the *Tone* to (39 M.) *Durston*, whence a branch-line diverges to Yeovil (p. 102). [The first station on this branch is *Athelney*, the reputed scene of King Alfred's legendary adventure with the cakes.] To the right rise the *Quantock Hills* (see above). The fine church-towers of Taunton soon come into sight on the left.

45 M. **Taunton** (**London; Castle;* **Railway; Clarke's; Nag's Head*, plain, R. & A. 2*s*. 3*d*.), the county-town of Somersetshire, is an ancient and well-built town with 16,610 inhab., situated in the picturesque and fertile vale of *Taunton Deane*. The church of **St. Mary Magdalene* is a large and good example of the Perp. style, with double aisles, a finely carved roof, and a fine modern pulpit. The tower, 155 ft. high, is elaborately embellished with pinnacles, battlements, and carvings. *St. James's Church* has also a good tower.

The *Castle*, originally founded about 700 A.D., dates in its present form from the 11th cent., with additions of the 13th and 15th centuries. It now contains the interesting museum of the *Somersetshire Archaeological Society* (adm. 2*d*.). The Great Hall, entered from the inner ward, was formerly the *Assize Court;* and it was here that Judge Jeffreys held the 'Bloody Assizes' of 1685, when hundreds of prisoners were condemned to death or the plantations. The other most prominent event in the history of the town is its memorable defence by Adm. Blake against the Royalists in 1645. Among the other chief buildings are the large *Independent* and *Wesleyan Colleges* (visible to the right and left as we continue our journey; see below), the *Barracks*, the *Shire Hall*, and the *Somerset County Club*.

From Taunton to Minehead, 24$^3/_4$ M., G. W. Railway in 1$^1/_4$ hr. (fares 5*s*. 3*d*., 4*s*., 2*s*. 3*d*. or 2*s*. $^1/_2$*d*.). This line forms the direct railway-route to *Exmoor* and *Lynton* (see R. 21) from the N. — The train diverges from the main-line at (2 M.) *Norton Fitzwarren* and follows a beautiful valley between the *Quantock Hills* on the E. and the *Brendon Hills* on the W. 5 M. *Bishop's Lydeard*, with a Perp. church; 9 M. *Crowcombe Heathfield;* 11$^3/_4$ M. *Stogumber;* 15 M. *Williton;* 16$^3/_4$ M. *Watchet* (West Somerset Hotel), a pretty little seaport. — 19 M. *Washford* (Inn) is the station for **Cleeve Abbey*, an interesting Cistercian ruin, $^1/_2$ M. to the S. (adm. 1*s*.), the chief features of which are the gate-house (13th cent.), part of the cloisters (15th cent.), the dormitory, the refectory (15th cent.), the common room, and the foundations of the church. — 21$^1/_4$ M. *Blue Anchor*. — 23 M. *Dunster* (Luttrell Arms, a quaint 16th cent. house), with a majestic Elizabethan castle (seen to the left of the railway), situated in a large park, to which visitors are admitted on Tues. and Frid. (tickets at the inn). Adjacent is *Conegar Hill*, surmounted by a tower. The *Church* is a Perp. (nave) and E.E. (choir) edifice, with a fine Perp. screen.

24$^3/_4$ M. **Minehead** (*Beach Hotel*, close to the station and the shore, R. & A. 4*s*.; *Feathers*, in the town, $^1/_2$ M. from the station, well spoken of) is a rising little watering-place at the E. base of *North Hill*, with a fair beach, an esplanade, golf-links, etc. It is a good starting-point for exploring *Exmoor* (see p. 164), and the Exmoor Stag Hounds hold some of their meets in the vicinity. In summer coaches ply twice daily to (7 M.) *Porlock* and (19 M.) *Lynmouth* (see p. 166). Among the pleasantest points in the vicinity are *Dunster* (2$^1/_2$ M.; see above), *Cleeve Abbey* (6 M.; see above), *Greenaley Point* (1$^1/_2$ M.), *Bossington Beacon* (5$^1/_2$ M.), *Selworthy* (5 M.; on the way to Porlock), *Grabhurst Hill*, near Dunster, and the *Brendon Hills* (see above).

From Taunton to Barnstaple, 44$^1/_2$ M., railway in 1$^3/_4$ hr. (8*s*. 6*d*., 6*s*. 7*d*., 4*s*. 3*d*. or 3*s*. 9*d*.). This line, skirting the S. slopes of *Exmoor Forest* (p. 164), forms the direct railway approach to *Ilfracombe* (p. 161). — The first stations are *Norton Fitzwarren* (see above), *Milverton*, (9 M.) *Wiveliscombe*, *Venn Cross*, and *Morebath*. — From (21 M.) *Dulverton* (Carnarvon Arms, at the station; Red Lion, in the village), which lies 2 M. to the N. of the line, a visit may be paid to (5$^1/_2$ M.) the *Tor Steps*, a rude stone bridge over the *Barle*, whence the pedestrian may go on to (19 M.) *Lynton* (p. 166). From Dulverton a branch-line descends the valley of the *Exe* to *Bampton*, (12 M.) *Tiverton* (see p. 129), and (26 M.) *Exeter* (p. 103). — The next important station is (34 M.) *South Molton* (George), a small market-town, whence there is a fine drive over Exmoor, viâ *Simonsbath* (p. 168), to (20 M.) *Lynton* (p. 166). — Farther on the train passes *Castle Hill*, the seat of Earl Fortescue, and crosses the *Bray* by a viaduct 100 ft. high. — 41 M. *Swimbridge*. — 44$^1/_2$ M. *Barnstaple*, see p. 163. From Barnstaple we may go on by railway to *Ilfracombe* (p. 161; through-carriages from Taunton) or *Bideford* (p. 159), or by coach to (18 M.) *Lynton* (p. 166; 5*s*.).

From Taunton a branch-line also runs to *Ilminster* (George) and (15 M.) *Chard* (p. 102) in $^3/_4$ hr.

52 M. *Wellington* (Squirrel; King's Arms), a small town from which the Duke of Wellington takes his title. It lies at the foot of the *Black Down Hills*, one of which is crowned with the (1 hr.) *Wellington Monument.* The train now passes through the *White Ball Tunnel*, 5/8 M. in length, and enters the county of *Devon*, renowned for its leafy lanes and wooded 'combes' or hollows (Welsh *cwm*), for its clotted cream and its cider. — From (60 3/4 M.) *Tiverton Junction* a branch diverges on the right to (7 M.) **Tiverton** *(Palmerston; Angel)*, a town of 10,500 inhab., pleasantly situated at the confluence of the *Exe* and the *Leman*, and long represented in Parliament by Lord Palmerston. It contains a large *Church* of the 15th cent., the remains of an old *Castle*, *Blundell's Grammar School* (an old foundation), and a *Lace Factory* employing 1500 workpeople. To Dulverton and Exeter, see p. 128.

63 M. *Collumpton* (White Hart), a small town of great antiquity, has an interesting church of the 16th century. The line now follows the valley of the *Culm.*

75 1/2 M. **Exeter,** see p. 103.

17. From Exeter to Plymouth.

a. Great Western Railway.

53 M. Railway in **1 3/4-3 hrs.** (fares 11*s.* 6*d.*, 7*s.* 10*d.*, 4*s.* 4 1/2*d.*).

The Great Western Railway from Exeter to Plymouth traverses a picturesque district, and affords a constant succession of charming views. Soon after leaving Exeter (p. 103) we obtain a fine view, to the left, of the mouth of the *Exe.* Beyond (4 1/2 M.) *Exminster*, to the right, is *Powderham Castle*, seat of the Earl of Devon (visitors admitted 11-5, in the absence of the family, on previous written application to the steward). 8 1/2 M. *Starcross* (Courtenay Arms), the station for Powderham, lies opposite Exmouth (p. 105).

12 M. **Dawlish** *(London; Albert; Royal)*, a favourite little sea-bathing resort, under the lee of the *Great Haldon* (818 ft.). The bathing arrangements here are much better than those at most English watering-places, a comfortable dressing-pavilion, connected with the sea by a small tram-car, being substituted for the usual miserable bathing-machines. — Near Dawlish the train reaches the coast and trends to the right. To the left is the curious detached rock known as the '*Parson*'; the 'Clerk' and other similar rocks, which formerly stood close by, have been washed away.

15 M. **Teignmouth** *(Royal*, on the Den, facing the sea; *London; Queen's)*, a large watering-place, prettily situated at the mouth of the *Teign*, which is here spanned by a long bridge of 34 arches, 1670 ft. long. From the middle of the grassy promenade called the *Den* a handsome pier runs out into the sea. Numerous pleasant walks and drives in every direction, one of the pleasantest being to the top of the *Little Haldon* (800 ft.).

The line now skirts the estuary of the Teign, commanding a good view of the Haytor and Rippon Tor on Dartmoor (p. 137), as it bends round t —

20 M. **Newton Abbot** (**Globe, Commercial*, in the town, 1/2 M. from the station; *Queen's*, near the station), a pleasant little town in the valley of the *Leman*, the junction of lines to Moreton Hampstead and to Torquay and Dartmouth. Its two lions are *Ford House* (on the Torquay road), a good specimen of the Tudor style, and the *Stone* on which William III. was first proclaimed king of England in 1688 (in the centre of the town). The *Grammar School* is celebrated. A little to the W. is *Bradley House*, parts of which date from the 14th century.

From Newton Abbot to Moreton Hampstead, 12 M., railway in 1/2-3/4 hr. (fares 2*s*., 1*s*. 6*d*., 1*s*. 2*d*.). This line affords the most convenient approach to the E. side of Dartmoor (p. 137). The first part of it follows the valley of the *Teign* (pron. *Teen*). — 2 1/2 M. *Teigngrace;* 4 M. *Heathfield*, the junction for (2 1/2 M.) *Chudleigh*, *Trusham*, and (6 1/2 M.) *Ashton*.

[**Chudleigh** (*Clifford Arms*) is frequently visited for the sake of **Chudleigh Rock* (fine view from the top), a bod limestone crag rising abruptly from a wooded ravine, which is traversed by a small stream. In the rock are two interesting caverns: *Chudleigh Cavern* (with stalactites; adm. 6*d*.) and the *Pixies' Hole*. Other pleasant excursions may be made from Chudleigh.]

6 M. **Bovey Tracey** (*Union; Dolphin*) is a good centre for excursions to (3 M.) *Haytor*, (4 M.) *Manaton*, etc. The coach mentioned at p. 105 starts here. Bovey Tracey was long the demesne of the Tracey family, and the parish-church is said to have been built and dedicated to St. Thomas of Canterbury by Sir William Tracey, one of the archbishop's murderers.

8 1/2 M. **Lustleigh** (*Cleave Hotel*), a romantically-situated little village, is the station for visitors to (1 M.) **Lustleigh Cleave*, a rock-girt and boulder-strewn upland valley. On one of the enclosing hills is a pile of rocks known as the *Nutcrackers*, from a logan stone so delicately poised as to crack a nut in its oscillation. Lustleigh is also the nearest station for *Manaton* (Half Moon), a beautiful little village 2 1/2 M. to the W., surrounded by tors (views). *Bowerman's Nose*, 1 M. from Manaton, is a curious natural formation, bearing some resemblance to a man, seated. A walk may also be taken to (1 M.) the *Becky Falls* and *Horsham Steps*.

12 M. **Moreton Hampstead** (*White Hart; White Horse*), a small town with 2000 inhab., on the E. skirts of Dartmoor, is visited by tourists mainly as a stepping-stone to the more suitable headquarters at *Chagford* (p. 138), 5 M. to the N.W. (omn.). A good road leads from Moreton Hampstead across Dartmoor to (12 M.) *Two Bridges* (p. 138), whence we may go on to (8 1/2) *Tavistock* (p. 137), to (9 M). *Horrabridge* (p. 136), or to (6 M.) *Princetown* (p. 136).

From Newton Abbot to Torquay and Dartmouth, 15 M., G. W. Railway in 1-1 1/4 hr. (fares 3*s*. 7*d*., 2*s*. 4*d*., 1*s*. 6*d*.) — 2 1/2 M. *Kingskerswell*; 5 M. *Torre*, the station for the N. part of Torquay. Torquay station is on the W. margin of the town.

6 M. **Torquay** (Plan, see p. 138). — **Hotels.** *Imperial (Pl. a; C, 4), a large establishment, finely situated in grounds overlooking the sea, 1 1/2 M. from the station (cab 2*s*.); R. 2*s*. 6*d*.-7*s*., A. 1*s*. 6*d*., table d'hôte 5*s*. 6*d*., B. 2-3*s*., toilet lights 1*s*. 6*d*., board (R. & A. extra) 10*s*. 6*d*. — *Torbay (Pl. d; C, 3), to the W. of the harbour, with sea-view, R. & A. from 4*s*. 6*d*.; Victoria & Albert (Pl. e; B, 3), Belgrave Road; Royal (Pl. b), Queen's (Pl. c), in the centre of the town, overlooking the harbour (Pl. C, 3), commercial and family hotels; Western (Pl. f; A, 3), at the railway-station; Jordan's Temperance, unpretending. — Numerous *Private Hotels*,

For a coloured street plan of Torquay see pages 568

Boarding Houses, and *Lodgings*. — The hotel omnibuses meet the principal trains.

Cab with one horse for 1-3 pers., for 1/2 M. 6*d*., 1 M. 1*s*., 2 M. 1*s*. 6*d*., each addit. 1/2 M. 6*d*.; for more than 3 pers. 1*s*., 1*s*. 6*d*., 2*s*. 6*d*. By time: 2*s*. or 3*s*. per hr., 1*s*. or 1*s*. 3*d*. for each addit. 1/2 hr.; after 9 p.m. (7 p.m. in winter) minimum fares 1*s*. 6*d*. or 2*s*. Luggage up to 112 lbs. free (for the station-cabs, 2*d*. for each package carried outside).

Steamers and **Sailing Yachts** make excursions in summer. — **Rowing Boat** 1*s*. per hr.; with boatman, 1*s*. 6*d*. for the 1st, 1*s*. for each addit. hr.

Bathing Machine 6*d*. — **Public Baths** at the head of the Pier (Pl. C, 4).

Theatre in Abbey Road; performances daily in the winter season. — A *Band* plays daily (12-1) on the Strand.

Torquay, a town of modern growth, with 30,000 inhab., beautifully situated at the N. W. angle of *Tor Bay*, is a favourite resort of persons with delicate chests, on account of its mild and equable climate; and it contests with Brighton and Scarborough the title of Queen of English watering-places. In winter the thermometer seldom descends to 36° Fahr., while in summer the maximum heat is about 77°. The town occupies a considerable space of ground, spreading over a number of small hills, which rise in terraces above the sea, and are dotted with well-built villas embosomed in a luxuriant semi-tropical vegetation scarcely paralleled elsewhere in England. 'It reminds one of Newport', says an American writer, 'in the luxuriousness of its foliage, the elasticity of its lawns, and its masses of flowers'. The bathing and boating are excellent, and the environs abound in charming walks and drives. An admirable view of the town is obtained as we approach it from the railway-station, but it is seen to greatest advantage from a boat in the bay. In the town itself almost the only points calling for notice are the *Harbour* and *Pier* (adm. 1*d*.; Pl. C, 4), the ruins of *Tor Abbey* (Pl. A, 3; 12-14th cent.; not open to the public), and *St. Michael's Chapel* (Pl. A, 1; E.E.), on a commanding site near Torre station. The **Museum* (Pl. D, 3; adm. 1*s*., or by member's order), in the Babbacombe road, chiefly contains a well-arranged collection of the bones found in Kent's Cavern (p. 132). The *Church of St. John* (Pl. C, 3), a modern Gothic edifice, is a handsome and prominent feature of the town. The industrial specialty of Torquay is the manufacture of articles in terracotta; visitors are admitted to the works of the *Torquay Terracotta Co.* at Hele Cross, near Torre station (Pl. A, 1), and the *Watcombe Terracotta Co.* (p. 132). Torquay is an important yachting station, and an annual regatta is held here in Aug. or Sept., while good packs of fox-hounds and harriers are within easy reach. Beyond the Imperial Hotel a public walk, commanding a good view of the bay, leads to a spot called the *Land's End*, in the rocks beyond which is a natural arch known as '*London Bridge*' (Pl. D, 4). *Daddy Hole Plain* (Pl. D, 4), the elevated plateau above, is another good point of view; we reach it by retracing our steps to the Parkhill Road (comp. Pl. C, D, 4).

Excursions. The following *Walk need not take more than a short half-day, unless prolonged by boating or bathing. Starting from the harbour we pass through Torwood St. and ascend the Babbacombe road (Pl. D, E, 3) till we reach a point where a notice-board indicates the way to Kent's Cavern. Here we turn to the right and soon diverge from the road to the right (sign-post) to visit **Kent's Cavern** (Pl. E, 2; open 10-5; 1-3 pers. 1*s.* 6*d.*, each addit. pers. 6*d.*), a limestone cave less interesting for its extent or stalagmites than for the extraordinary quantity of bones and flint implements found here, and their important testimony to the antiquity of man (comp. p. 131) — We then return to the road and follow it to the foot of the hill, where a sign-post shows the uphill way to the left to (1/2 M.) ***Anstey's Cove** (Pl. F, 1). A notice-board to the right, with an inscription in verse, marks the point where we leave the road to descend to this pretty little bay, where boats and bathing-machines may be hired. — We may now either cross the ravine and take a path along the cliffs, or return to the road and follow it to (1 M.) *Babbacombe* (Pl. D, 1; Royal Hotel), where we descend to the right (sign-post) to ***Babbacombe Bay**, another rock-girt bay, where beautiful effects of colouring are produced by the white beach, the red cliffs, the green trees, and the blue sea. Boats may be hired here, but bathers must go on to *Oddicombe Beach*, forming an additional wing of Babbacombe Bay. Simple refreshments may be obtained in the quaint little *Cary Arms Inn*. The *View from Babbacombe Down embraces a long line of coast in both directions. At *Mary Church*, adjoining Babbacombe, is a handsome modern Roman Catholic Church. From Babbacombe we may go on by boat or by road to (1 1/4 M.) *Watcombe*, with its imposing *Giant Rock* and its terracotta works; or we may return direct across *Warberry Hill* (Pl. D, 2; view) to (2 M.) Torquay. — With the above excursion may be combined a visit to *Ilsham Grange* (Pl. F, 2), a farm-house of the 15th cent., formerly belonging to Tor Abbey, and situated at the head of a beautiful combe.

To the W. a pleasant walk may be taken through typical Devonshire lanes to (1 3/4 M.) *Cockington*, with its ivy-clad church; (4 M.) *Marldon*, the church of which (14-15th cent.) contains several monuments of the Gilberts of Compton (see below); and (5 M.) **Compton Castle** (now a farm), erected in the first half of the 15th century. Longer excursions may be made to (8 M.) *Berry Pomeroy Castle* (p. 134), *Dartmouth* and the *Dart* (see below), *Teignmouth* (p. 129; by the coast), *Dartmoor* (p. 137), etc.

On resuming the railway-route to Dartmouth we soon reach (8 M.) **Paignton** (*Esplanade*, table d'hôte 4*s.* 6*d.*; *Gerston*; *Commercial)*, with an interesting church and an excellent sandy beach. — From (10 1/2 M.) *Churston* a branch diverges on the left to (2 M.) **Brixham** (*Bolton*; *Globe)*, a small fishing-town with a statue of William III., erected to commemorate the two hundreth anniversary of his landing here in 1688. About 1 1/4 M. to the E. is *Berry Head*, with traces of Roman occupation; and in the other direction, not far from the Bolton Hotel, is *Brixham Cavern*, second to Kent's alone in the interest and extent of its bone relics.

The railway ends at (14 1/2 M.) *Kingswear* (Royal Dart), whence passengers are ferried across the *Dart* to —

Dartmouth (*Castle*, opposite the landing-stage; *King's Arms*, *Commercial*, unpretending), a quaint little seaport of 5600 inhab., with a roomy and very picturesque harbour, formerly of much greater importance than at present. It is mentioned by Chaucer in the Prologue to the 'Canterbury Tales' ('Dertemouthe'). Steamers for the Cape of Good Hope leave Dartmouth once a fortnight. The interesting old **Church of St. Saviour's* (14th cent.), on the way to which we pass the quaintly-carved arcade of the so-called *Butter Walk* (1640), contains a coloured wooden screen, galleries with the carved and gilt arms of the merchant families of Dartmouth, a curiously carved stone pulpit, a massive oaken frame round the altar-piece, a fine brass slab to John Hawley (in front of the altar), and oaken pews for the Corporation. — A pretty tree-shaded road leads along the Dart to the (1 M.) *Castle* at its mouth, now fitted up as a coast battery (fine view from the top of the castle-mound). Adjacent is *St. Petrock's Church*.

From Dartmouth a charming excursion may be made up the river *Dart* to (10 M.) *Totnes* (see below) by a small steamer plying daily in summer (1¼ hr.; fare 1*s*. 6*d*., 1*s*. 3*d*.). As we leave Dartmouth we pass the Britannia training-ship. Our first stopping-place is (3 M.) *Dittisham*, opposite which is *Greenway House*, at one time the residence of Sir Walter Raleigh, who is said to have been in the habit of smoking his pipe on the 'Anchor Rock' in mid-stream (marked by an iron 'anchor'). Beyond (6½ M.) *Duncannon* we enter the prettiest part of the course, the winding reaches of *Sharpham*, wooded down to the water's edge. — The landing-place at Totnes is about ¼ M. below the bridge (see below).

A coach runs daily from Dartmouth to (15 M.) Kingsbridge (fare 3*s*.). The route follows the coast past (2½ M.) *Stoke Fleming* (old church) to (6 M.) *Slapton Sands* (Sands Hotel) and (8 M.) *Torcross Hotel* ('pens'. 6*s*. 6*d*.) and then leads inland (to the right) to *Charlton* and Kingsbridge. *Slapton Lea* is a small lake, affording excellent perch, pike, and roach fishing. Pedestrians may follow the coast to (4 M.) *Start Point* (Lighthouse), (5 M.) *Prawle Point* (Inn), and (6 M.; in all 15 M.) **Salcombe** (**Marine Hotel*, on the estuary, with gardens, 3-3½ gs. per week; *Victoria; King's Arms*), a charming little watering-place on the W. side of the estuary (ferry), whence a small steamer plies to (6 M.) **Kingsbridge** (*King's Arms; Albion*), a pleasant-looking little town at the head of a small arm of the sea. The climate in this corner of Devonshire is so mild that oranges, citrons, myrtles, and aloes flourish in the open air all the year round. — From Kingsbridge coaches run to (10 M.) *Kingsbridge Road* (p. 134; fare 2*s*.), the nearest railway-station, and to (20 M.) *Plymouth* (p. 139; thrice a week, 2*s*. 6*d*.) viâ *Modbury*. Kingsbridge also communicates with Plymouth by steamer.

Continuation of Railway to Plymouth. Beyond Newton Abbot the train leaves the valley of the Teign, threads a tunnel, and descends into the valley of the *Dart*, which it crosses at Totnes.

29 M. **Totnes** (*Seymour*, *Seven Stars*, near the bridge; *Castle*, at the head of the main street) is an ancient little town of 4100 inhab., 'hanging from E. to W. on the side of a hill' (Camden) and containing numerous quaint old houses with piazzas and projecting gables. From the station we ascend to the castle (p. 134) by the road passing a sign-board which indicates the way to the Castle Hotel and leading through an old gateway (*North Gate*).

Arriving by water (see above) we cross the bridge and ascend the steep main street (*Fore Street*), passing a road leading to the right to the station. Farther up, also to the right (in the pavement), is the so-called '*Brutus Stone*', the very stone, according to hoary tradition, on which Brutus of Troy first set foot on landing in Britain! Beyond this we pass through the old *East Gate*, spanning the street, and reach the **Church* (key at a cottage on the N. side), a good Perp. building (15th cent.), with a fine tower. The interior (restored) contains a carved stone rood-screen, a good W. window, and a curious monument (W. end) of Kit Blackhall and his four wives.

At the Castle Hotel, a little farther up the main street, we turn to the right and reach the entrance to the ***Castle**, the grounds enclosing which are open to the public (free; ring). The only relic of the Castle, a Norman foundation ascribed to a follower of the Conqueror, is the keep, consisting of two circular stages placed one on the top of the other, like a larger and smaller cheese. Fine view from the top (to the W. two curiously-clipped yews). A shady walk skirts the moat on the W. side of the castle-enclosure.

Totnes is the nearest railway-station to ***Berry Pomeroy Castle** (adm. 6*d.*), a picturesque ivy-clad ruin, $2^1/_4$ M. to the E. The castle was originally erected in the Norman epoch, but the oldest existing parts date from the 13th century. In its prime the mansion was so extensive that it 'was a good day's work for a servant but to open and shut the casements'.

About 2 M. to the N. of Totnes is *Dartington*, with an old Hall. The Dart above Totnes is also pretty. At *Little Hempston* is a well-preserved quadrangular rectory of the age of Richard II. (1377-99), with a great hall.

From Totnes to Ashburton, $9^1/_2$ M., railway in $^1/_2$ hr. (fares 1*s.* 11*d.*, 1*s.* 5*d.*, $9^1/_2$*d.*). This pretty little line ascends the valley of the Dart and forms an easy approach to the S. part of Dartmoor. — 3 M. *Staverton*, with a picturesque bridge across the Dart. — 7 M. *Buckfastleigh* (King's Arms), a small serge-making town, with an old Cistercian abbey ($^3/_4$ M. to the N., on the river), lately rebuilt by French monks.

$9^1/_2$ M. **Ashburton** *(London; Golden Lion)*, a 'Stannary' town (see p. 137), with a handsome church, is a starting-point for various Dartmoor excursions. The favourite is that through the **Buckland Drive* and *Holne Chase* (open on Tues., Thurs., and Sat.), to the N., a round of about 10 M. (carr. and pair 15*s.*). About 1 M. above Holne Bridge, on the Dart, is a fine piece of rock scenery called the *Lover's Leap*. Another pleasant walk or drive is that to (3 M.) *Buckland Beacon*, (2 M.) *Rippon Tor*, ($1^1/_4$ M.) *Haytor*, and ($^3/_4$ M.) *Rock Inn*, whence we may go on to (3 M.) *Bovey Tracey* (p. 130) or (5 M.) *Lustleigh* (p. 130). — *Widdecombe in the Moors*, with a handsome Perp. church (the 'Cathedral of Dartmoor'), lies 6 M. to the N., near the centre of the moor. *Two Bridges* (p. 138) is 12 M. to the W. *Holne* (Inn), the birthplace of *Charles Kingsley* (1819-75), lies 3 M. to the W. of Ashburton.

Beyond Totnes the line, skirting the S. base of Dartmoor, passes through a very pretty district. Before reaching (36 M.) *Brent* (Carew Arms) we penetrate a long tunnel. — 38 M. *Kingsbridge Road*, the station for (10 M.) *Kingsbridge* (p. 133). — As we approach ($41^1/_2$ M.) **Ivy Bridge** *(*London; King's Arms)*, the pleasantest headquarters for exploring S. Dartmoor (see p. 137), we cross a lofty viaduct (110 ft. high), from which we enjoy a charming glimpse to the right up the valley of the *Erme*. The view to the left is also attractive. From the *Blatchford Viaduct*, 2 M. father on, another fine view is obtained to the right. Beyond ($43^1/_2$ M.) *Cornwood* the train crosses another viaduct and descends to ($47^1/_2$ M.) *Plympton* (George), the birthplace of Sir Joshua Reynolds, with an old grammar-school (17th cent.) which he attended. We then cross the *Plym*, come in sight of the fortifications of Plymouth, pass the suburban stations of *Mutley* and *North Road*, and enter the *Mill Bay Terminus* at (53 M.) *Plymouth* (see p. 139).

b. South Western Railway.

59 M. Railway in 2-3 hrs. (fares 11*s.* 6*d.*, 7*s.* 10*d.*, 4*s.* 4*d.*). This line skirts the N. side of Dartmoor (p. 137).

From Exeter to (11 1/2 M.) *Yeoford*, see p. 105. Our line here diverges to the left (S.) from the line to Ilfracombe. An omnibus plies regularly from Yeoford to (11 M.) *Chagford* (p. 138). — 17 M. *Bow*, beyond which *Cawsand Beacon* (1800 ft.), an outlying spur of Dartmoor, is visible to the left. Beyond (19 1/2 M.) *North Tawton* we cross the *Taw* and pass (22 1/2 M.) *Sampford Courtney.*

26 M. **Okehampton** (*White Hart*; *Plume of Feathers*), a small town on the N. margin of Dartmoor, with the remains of a partly Norman castle (3/4 M. to the W.). *Yes Tor* (see p.138) may be ascended hence without difficulty in about 2 hrs.

From Okehampton to Holsworthy, 20 M., railway in 3/4 hr. (fares 4*s.*, 2*s.* 10*d.*, 1*s.* 8*d*). — This branch-line is the most direct route to *Bude* (p. 156). 6 1/2 M. *Ashbury* (820 ft.; Eastacombe Hotel), in a breezy situation. — From (10 M.) *Halwill* a branch diverges to (13 1/2 M.) *Launceston* (see below; 1/2 hr.; fares 2*s.* 9*d.*, 2*s.*, 1*s.* 1 1/2*d.*).

20 M. **Holsworthy** (*Stanhope*; *White Hart*), with a church possessing a lofty Perp. tower. A coach plies hence twice daily in summer to (9 1/2 M.) *Bude* (p. 156; fare 2*s.* 6*d.*), passing *Stratton* (p. 156). The *Holsworthy & Bude Canal*, constructed in 1819-26, is interesting for its inclined planes, ingenious substitutes for the ordinary locks.

Beyond Okehampton we obtain a view of its castle to the right, and cross the *Okement* by the *Meldon Viaduct*. From (32 1/2 M.) *Bridestowe* ('Briddystow') we may ascend *Great Links Tor*, 2 M. to the E. of the station. (The village is 1 1/2 M. to the W. of the railway.) A good Dartmoor walk may be taken from Bridestowe along *Tavy Cleave*, skirting 'a magnificent range of castellated tors', to Lidford.

36 M. **Lidford** (*Manor Hotel*; *Castle*, in the village; *Rail. Refreshment Rooms*), which is also a station on the G. W. R. system (see below), is an ancient place with the remains of a castle and was formerly a Stannary town. The old Stannary Court here was notorious for its abuses, and 'Lidford Law', like 'Jeddart Justice' (p. 456), hanged a man first and tried him afterwards. About 1/2 M. to the W. of the G. W. R. station is *Lidford Cascade*, 100 ft. in total height (fee 2*d.*); its volume may be much increased by letting off the water in the mill- pond above (fee). The (1 M.) **Lidford Gorge* (bridge) is among the finest ravines of its kind in England (path open on Mon.).

From Lidford to Launceston, 12 1/2 M., G. W. Railway in 1/2 hr. (fares 2*s.* 5*d.*, 1*s.* 9*d.*, 1*s.*). The intermediate stations are (4 1/2 M.) *Coryton*, with the fine Elizabethan mansion of *Sydenham* and its noble trees (1/2 M. to the W. of the station), and (8 M.) *Lifton*. Beyond the latter we enter Cornwall and follow the winding course of the *Tamar*.

12 1/2 M. **Launceston** (*King's Arms*; *White Hart*; *Railway*), an ancient town with 5500 inhab., situated on the slope of a steep hill, from which it derived its original name of *Dunheved* ('hill top'). The hill is crowned with the circular keep and parts of the walls (12 ft. thick) of a *Castle*, at one time supposed to be of British origin, but now recognised as a Norman work (view). In a small dungeon, near the E. gate, George Fox, the Quaker, was imprisoned in 1656. The church of *St. Mary Mag-*

dalene, lately restored, is a handsome granite edifice in the Perp. style, with curious carvings on the outside of the walls. At the White Hart Hotel is a fine Norman gateway, forming the sole relic of an old Augustine priory; and near the King's Arms is another gateway of later date, which originally belonged to the town-walls.

Launceston is the nearest railway-station to *Tintagel*, *Boscastle*, and *Camelford* (see R. 19), and has become of greater importance as an access to this part of the Cornish coast since the opening of the new S.W. line from *Halwill* (1886; see p. 135), which enables the company to run through-carriages from London to Launceston (223½ M., in 6½-7 hrs.; fares 44*s.* 1*d.*, 31*s.* 7*d.*, 18*s.* 3½*d.*). Coaches ply daily from Launceston, in connection with the morning-express from Waterloo (reaching Launceston about 4 p.m.), to *Camelford* (p. 153; 16 M., 2¼ hrs., 4*s.*), *Wadebridge* (p. 153; 27 M., 4 hrs., 6*s.* 6*d.*), and *Padstow* (p. 153; 35 M., 5 hrs., 8*s.* 6*d.*), connecting on Mon., Wed., & Frid. with the coach to New Quay (p. 144), and on Tues., Thurs., & Sat. with that to *Bude* (p. 156; 20 M., 4¼ hrs., 6*s.* and 5*s.*). None of these routes repay the pedestrian.

The ascent of *Brown Willy* (see p. 153) is sometimes made from Launceston (4 hrs.). We follow the road to Camelford for 3 M., then diverge to the left and pass (4 M.) *Five Lanes* (Inn). About 2 M. farther on we leave the road and cross the moors to the W. (right), reaching the top in 1 hr. more. View from Brown Willy and ascent of *Row Tor*, see p. 154. The descent may be made to Camelford or Bodmin (p. 144).

From Lidford to Plymouth by the G. W. R., 23 M., in 1 hr. (fares 4*s.* 10*d.*, 3*s.* 3*d.*, 1*s.* 11*d.*). — To the right rises *Brentor* (see below). Beyond (3 M.) *Mary-Tavy*, also to the right, is *Kelly College*, for the sons of naval officers. — 6 M. *Tavistock*, see p. 137.

Beyond Tavistock the train threads a tunnel and passes the village of *Whitchurch* on the left. Fine views of the W. slopes of Dartmoor. — 10 M. *Horrabridge* (Roborough Arms) is the station for *Buckland Abbey*, a Cistercian foundation of the 13th cent., wich lies 1½ M. to the S.W. There are few remains of the old buildings, but the mansion, which belongs to the representatives of the Drake family, contains some relics of Sir Francis. The village, *Buckland Monachorum*, has an interesting church. — 11½ M. *Yelverton* (Rock Hotel), the junction of the line to Princetown.

[From Yelverton to Princetown, 10½ M., railway *(Dartmoor Railway)* in ½ hr. (fares 2*s.*, 1*s.* 8*d.*, 10½*d.*). This line ascends rapidly in a series of sharp curves, the average gradient being 1:65. The views in all directions are charming, and the construction of the railway itself is an object of interest. — 1½ M. *Dousland*, the station for *Walkhampton*, with its conspicuous Perp. church. The 'Tors' of Dartmoor are visible on both sides, while behind us the hills of Cornwall form the background. — 10½ M. **Princetown** (1400 ft. above the sea; **Duchy Hotel*), a small town of modern origin, forms a convenient starting-point for excursions in Dartmoor Forest (p. 137), near the centre of which it lies. The large *Convict Prison* here was erected at the beginning of the present century for French prisoners-of-war, of whom it is said to have contained 9000 in 1811. In the war of 1812-14 upwards of 2000 American seamen, who refused to serve in the British navy against their country, were also confined here. Part of the adjoining moorland has been reclaimed by convict labour. Princetown is about 15 M. from Chagford or Moreton Hampstead (see p. 130).]

Sheep's Tor now comes into view on the left. The line follows the windings of the *Plym*. Near (15 M.) *Bickleigh* (p. 143), to the left, is the *Dewerstone*, rising above the confluence of the *Meavy* and the Plym. We now descend the pretty *Bickleigh Vale* (p. 143) to (19 M.) *Marsh Mills*. — 22 M. *Mutley*. — 22½ M. *Plymouth* (*North Road;* see p. 139). 23 M. *Mill Bay*, the G. W. R. terminus.

Beyond Lidford the S.W.R. runs parallel for some distance with the G. W. R. To the right of (37¼ M.) *Brentor* station rises *Brentor* (1114 ft.), an isolated volcanic cone surmounted by the small church of *St. Michael de Rupe*, dating from the 13th cent. (fine view from the churchyard; key of the church kept at the Stag's Head Inn). Farther on the line crosses the G. W. R. The train then enters the valley of the *Tavy*, which it descends to —

$42^1/_2$ M. **Tavistock** *(Bedford*, well spoken of; *Queen's Head; Temperance)*, a pleasant-looking town on the *Tavy*, which flows into the *Tamar* close by. The scanty remains of *Tavistock Abbey*, originally founded in the 10th cent. and once an institution of considerable importance, are close to the Bedford Hotel, which incorporates some parts of the old edifice. Adjacent is the *Parish Church*, a fine Perp. edifice, restored in 1846. In the vicarage-garden are three inscribed stones of the Romano-British period. Tavistock is the centre of an important mining district, in which lead, silver, copper, tin, and manganese are found. It was one of the Stannary Towns (Latin *Stannum*, tin), or towns in which were held the Tin Parliaments for deciding all questions connected with the tin-mining of the district. *Sir Francis Drake* (p. 139) was the son of a mariner of Tavistock, and a statue of the famous admiral, by Boehm, has been erected at his birthplace *Fitzford*, 1 M. to the W. — Tavistock is also a station on the G. W. R. (see p. 136).

A coach plies daily in summer from Tavistock to (18 M.; 3 hrs.) *Liskeard* (p. 144; fare 3*s*.), passing *Gunnislake* (near the Morwell Rocks, p. 142), *St. Ann's Chapel* (near Calstock, p. 142), and *Callington*. Near the road, about 4 M. from Tavistock, is the *Devon Great Consols Mine*, which formerly yielded 1000-1200 tons of copper ore per month, but is now worked mainly for arsenic.

Tavistock is one of the chief starting-points for excursions in *Dartmoor Forest*, a few of the most interesting points in which are described below, while others have been already mentioned.

Dartmoor Forest, so named from the river *Dart*, is a high-lying moorland district, about 25 M. long from N. to S., and 12 M. wide from E. to W. The mean elevation is about 1500 ft. It has been described as 'a monstrous lump of granite covered with a sponge of peaty soil', and one of its most characteristic features are the 'Tors', or huge blocks of granite that crown most of the hills. Numerous small streams rise on Dartmoor, and their pretty wooded valleys often afford a pleasing contrast to the barren scenery of the higher parts of the Forest. These streams, with their numerous little falls and 'stickles' (rapids), are generally well stocked with trout. The moor also offers much to interest the antiquarian, as it abounds in menhirs, stone circles, and other relics of the ancient Britons, though many supposed ancient monuments are now regarded as cattle-pens and deserted mining-shafts of no great age. The air is bracing and the climate in summer is often pleasant and invigorating; but rain is very prevalent at all seasons. Dartmoor ponies are a sturdy and sure-footed race. The pedestrian will find abundant opportunity for his prowess, but should be on his guard against bogs and mists. It is prudent to keep pretty closely to the beaten tracks, and a good map and pocket compass are indispensable to all who are not accompanied by a guide. The best carriage-roads are those from Tavistock to Ivy Bridge, and from Horrabridge to Chagford, Moreton Hampstead, and Ashburton, intersecting each other at Two Bridges (see p. 138). The visitor to Dartmoor will find good headquarters at Princetown (p. 136), Two Bridges (p. 138), and Chagford (p. 138), while Okehampton (p. 135) and Ashburton (p. 134) or Ivy Bridge (p. 134) are conveniently placed for its N. and S. districts respectively.

One of the commoner excursions from Tavistock is to the top of *Brentor* (p. 136), which lies about 4 M. to the N.; but this ascent is better made from Lidford (p. 135). — Walkers may follow the ridge from (3 M.) *Mary-Tavy* (p. 136) to ($5^1/_2$ M.) *Hare Tor* and ($2^1/_2$ M.) the *Great Links Tor* (p. 135), whence they may descend to the W. to (2 M.) *Bridestowe* (p. 135), or go on over *Yes Tor* (see below) to (6 M.) *Okehampton* (p. 135).

From Tavistock a road leads due E. through Dartmoor, soon passing a number of tors. The first on the left is *Cock's Tor* (1470 ft.), beyond which are the *Staple Tors*. Opposite are *Feather Tor* and the curiously-shaped *Vixen Tor*. About 1 M. beyond ($4^1/_4$ M.) *Merrivale* (Inn), to the S. (right) of the road, are some interesting stone circles and avenues. About this point, too, we may turn to the left to visit the ($1^1/_2$ M.) *Great Mis Tor* (1760 ft.), which commands an admirable view. The road to *Princetown* (8 M. from Tavistock) diverges on the right after $^3/_4$ M. more and passes the prison (see p. 136). Our road leads in a straight direction to ($2^1/_4$ M.) *Two Bridges* (Saracen's Head), a pleasant stopping-place for the pedestrian or angler. A little to the N. is *Crockern Tor*, on which the Stannary Parliaments (p. 135) were originally held. Not far off is *Wistman's Wood*, a singular group of ancient dwarf-oaks, the only relic of the 'Forest'. The road here forks, the N. arm leading to Chagford and Moreton Hampstead, the S. arm to (12 M.) *Ashburton* (p. 134), on the S. E. margin of the Forest. The latter coincides to some extent with the course of the *Dart*, the wooded scenery of which is very fine at places. The road to Moreton Hampstead maintains a N.E. direction and crosses some of the highest ground in the Forest. Near ($3^1/_2$ M.) *Post Bridge* (Temperance Hotel) is *Clapper Bridge*, a picturesque old structure of granite slabs over the Dart. At *Merripit*, 1 M. beyond Post Bridge, a road diverges on the right to (5 M.) *Widdecombe* (p. 134). About $1^3/_4$ M. farther on a track on the right leads to the *Vitifer Tin Mine* and (2 M.) *Grimspound*, a curious enclosure, the object of which is uncertain. After 3 M. more we reach *Bector*, where the road to ($2^1/_2$ M.) *Chagford* diverges to the left, while that to (3 M.) *Moreton Hampstead* (p. 130) continues in the same direction.

Chagford *(Moor Park; Globe; Three Crowns; King's Arms)* is a small town with 1500 inhab., conveniently situated for various interesting excursions in Dartmoor (information given by Mr. James Perrott). Among the most attractive spots in the vicinity are *Holy Street Mill* (1 M. to the W.), *Rushford Castle* ($1^1/_2$ M. to the N.), *Gidleigh Castle* ($2^1/_2$ M. to the N.W.), and *Cranbrook Castle* (a British camp) and *Fingle Bridge* ($3^1/_2$ and 4 M. to the N. E.). A longer excursion may be made to *Castor Rock*, the *Gidleigh Antiquities*, and *Cranmere Pool*, a round of about 18 M. (7-8 hrs.; guide desirable). The antiquities are spread over a wide area, and include several curious stone circles and avenues, a British slab-bridge, cromlechs, etc. Cranmere Pool (drained) is a lonely hollow surrounded with morasses, and not easily found without help. The ascent of *Cawsand Beacon* (p. 135) may be combined with this excursion; and those who do not wish to return to Chagford may make their way from Cranmere Pool to (8 M.) Lidford, (9 M.) Two Bridges, or ($6^1/_2$ M.) Okehampton.

From Two Bridges (see above) the active pedestrian may explore much of the most characteristic scenery of Dartmoor by walking due N. to (16 M.; 7 hrs.) *Okehampton* (p. 135). The route leads by (6 M.) *Cut Hill* (1970 ft.; top marked by a turf mound) and (2 M.) *Cranmere Pool* (see above); and *Yes Tor* (2050 ft.; p. 135), the highest point in Dartmoor, may be included by a digression to the left. No inn is passed on the way.

From Princetown (p. 136) a pleasant route for walkers leads through the S. part of Dartmoor to (14 M.) *Ivy Bridge* (p. 134). The most interesting points passed on the way are the ($2^1/_2$ M.) *Nun's Cross*, a granite cross, $7^1/_2$ ft. high, (5 M.) *Erme Pound*, and the ($2^1/_2$ M.) *Three Barrows* (1524 ft.), a fine point of view.

Beyond Tavistock the L. S. W. R. runs considerably to the W. of the G. W. R. — 49 M. *Beer Alston*. Beyond ($51^1/_2$ M.) *Beer Ferris* we cross the *Tavy* and skirt the E. bank of the *Tamar* (p. 142).

To the right is the *Royal Albert Bridge* (p. 142). $55^3/_4$ M. *St. Budeaux* (for *Saltash*, p. 142); 57 M. *Ford;* 58 M. *Devonport* (see p. 141). — 59 M. *Plymouth (North Road Station)*, see below.

Plymouth. — **Hotels.** Duke of Cornwall (Pl. a; D, 3), opposite Mill Bay Terminus; Royal (Pl. b; D, 3), Millbay Road, near the station; *Grand (Pl. c; D, 3), finely situated on the Hoe, the only hotel with a view of the Sound, R. & A. 5*s.*; Harvey's (Pl. d; E, 2), a quiet family hotel, Lockyer St.; Albion (Pl. e; D, 3), Millbay Road; Globe (Pl. m; E, 2), Bedford St.; Mount Pleasant (Pl. f; D, 3), adjoining the Duke of Cornwall, unpretending; *Chubb's (Pl. g; E, 2), Old Town St.; Farley's (Pl. h; D, 2), Union St. — In *Devonport:* Royal (Pl. j), Thomas's (Pl. k), both in Fore St. (Pl. A, 2). — In *Stonehouse:* Brunswick. — *Matthew's Restaurant*, Bedford St.; *Railway Refreshment Rooms* at the principal stations.

Cabs. Under 1 M., 1-2 pers. 8*d.*, 3-4 pers. 1*s.*; each additional $^1/_2$ M. 4*d.* or 6*d.*

Tramway from the E. end of Union St., Plymouth (Pl. C, 2), to Stonehouse and Devonport; fares $1^1/_2$*d.*, 2*d.*

Theatre (Pl. D, 3), in the same building as the Royal Hotel.

Railway Stations. 1. *Millbay Station* (Pl. D, 3), terminus of the G. W. R., near the Docks and the Hoe; 2. *Devonport and Stonehouse Station* (Pl. B, 2), belonging to the L.S.W.R.; 3. *North Road Station* (Pl. E, 1), in the N. suburb, 1 M. from the sea, a joint station of both lines; 4. *Cornwall Station* (Pl. B, 1), of the G.W.R., at Devonport; 5. *Mutley Station* (Pl. E, 1), see above.

Excursion Steamers (*Rowe's*, etc.) ply in summer at frequent intervals, and at moderate fares, to the *Breakwater*, *Mt. Edgcumbe*, *Eddystone Lighthouse*, the *Tamar*, the *Yealm*, etc. See advertisements in the daily papers. — **Deep Sea Steamers** also ply regularly from Plymouth to various British, European, and other ports. — **Ferries** from the *Admiral's Hard*, Stonehouse, to *Cremill (Mt. Edgcumbe);* from *Mutton Cove*, Devonport, to *Cremill;* from the *Barbican* to *Turn Chapel;* from *Ferry Road*, Devonport, to *Torpoint.* Fares 1*d.* or 2*d.*

Post Office, in Guildhall Sq.

Chief Attractions. The *Hoe* (p. 140); *Devonport Dockyard* (p. 141); *Breakwater* (p. 140); *Mt. Edgcumbe* (p. 142); trip up the *Tamar* (p. 142); *Eddystone Lighthouse* (p. 143; for good sailors only); *Barbican* (p. 140); *Municipal Buildings* and *Guildhall* (p. 141); the *Museum* (p. 141); the collection of drawings in *Plymouth Library* (p. 141).

Plymouth, *Stonehouse*, and *Devonport*, the 'Three Towns', with a joint population of 170,000 souls, together form one of the most important seaports in England, thanks to the *Sound*, in which the largest vessels can ride safely at anchor, and to the excellent harbours afforded by its arms, the *Cattewater*, or mouth of the *Plym*, *Sutton Pool*, and the *Hamoaze*, or estuary of the *Tamar*. Plymouth was first fortified in the 14th cent., and it is now a stronghold of the first class, its defences including a girdle of outlying forts. The various barracks can accommodate a garrison of 5000 men.

Plymouth has long been known as one of the chief naval and mercantile harbours of Great Britain, and it witnessed the departure of many of the most noted expeditions of Drake, Hawkins, Cook, and other famous mariners. It was from Plymouth that the English fleet under Lord Howard of Effingham issued to encounter the Armada (1588), and here also the Mayflower set sail for its Transatlantic destination on Sept. 6th, 1620 (comp. p. 81). In the Civil War Plymouth held out for the Parliamentarians when all the rest of Devon and Cornwall was in the hands of the Royalists, and defended itself successfully during a siege of four years. It was also the first large town to proclaim William of Orange king. The

For a coloured street plan of Plymouth see pages 569

town now carries on a considerable trade with the West Indies, South America, Australia, the Cape, the Baltic, and the Mediterranean, and numerous large merchant vessels are almost always to be seen in the Cattewater. The chief exports are copper, lead, tin, granite, marble, china-clay, bricks, and fish. Many of the emigrant ships for Australia, New Zealand, and British North America start from Plymouth. The Hamoaze is reserved for men-of-war.

On the sea-front of the town is the ***Hoe** (Pl. D, E, 3), an elevated promenade commanding an admirable view of the Sound. In the middle of it rises a *Statue of Sir Francis Drake* (p. 137), who is said to have been playing bowls here when news was brought him that the Armada was in sight (see Kingsley's '*Westward Ho!*', chap. xxx). The statue, erected in 1884, is a replica of that at Tavistock (p. 137). To the E. is Smeaton's original *Eddystone Lighthouse* (adm. 1*d.*), re-erected here when replaced by a new one on the rock (p. 143). The *View from the top is very extensive, including (on a clear day) the Eddystone Lighthouse, 14 M. to the S. Beyond Smeaton's Tower is the *Citadel* (Pl. E, 3), erected in 1670, and now somewhat out of date as a fortress (view from the ramparts). Outside its walls is a *Marine Laboratory*, opened in 1888, with an aquarium below. Below the Hoe are a fine *Promenade Pier* (adm. 2*d.*; band) and the *Bathing Places* for ladies and gentlemen.

The ***Sound**, or roadstead of Plymouth, about 3 sq. M. in extent, is one of the finest bays on the S. coast of England, and is generally alive with shipping of the most varied description. In the middle lies the small fortified *St. Nicholas* or *Drake's Island* (Pl. C, D, 4). To the W. rises *Mount Edgcumbe* (p. 142). To the E. is the rocky islet of *Mewstone*. On the S. side the entrance to the Sound is defended by the **Breakwater*, a stupendous piece of granite masonry, 1 M. in length, constructed in 1812-40 at a cost of 1,580,000*l.* The top forms a pleasant promenade, and it may be reached from Plymouth by an excursion-steamer (6*d.*; landing in boat 1*d.*) or by small boat (about 2*s.*). At the W. end is a small *Lighthouse*, the top of which affords a good view (small gratuity to the keeper). Just inside the Breakwater is a circular fort like those at Portsmouth (p. 56). The entrance to the *Cattewater* (Pl. F, 4) is also sheltered by a breakwater, 1000 ft. long, projecting from *Mount Batten Point*. 'Kitchen Middens' found here prove the existence of a prehistoric population near Plymouth. — Visit to *Mt. Edgcumbe*, see p. 142.

From the back of the Citadel we may descend to the quaint bit of old Plymouth known as the *Barbican*, which lies on the edge of *Sutton Pool* (Pl. E, F, 3). The 'Dutch auctions' of fish here are amusing. — Ferry across the Cattewater, see p. 139.

We next make our way through *Southside St.*, *Notte St.*, and *St. Andrew's St.* to the **Church of St. Andrew** (Pl. E, 2), dating from the 15th cent., and restored by Sir G. G. Scott in 1874-75. It contains some interesting monuments. Adjoining the church is a Perp. building named the *Prysten House.* — The church faces

Guildhall Sq., on the right side of which are the **Municipal Offices** and on the left the **Guildhall**, two handsome modern Gothic edifices. The fine hall in the latter, 148 ft. long, is adorned with stained-glass windows representing scenes from the town's history. The *Mayor's Parlour*, on the other side, contains a portrait (with quaint inscriptions) of *Sir Francis Drake* (1545-96), 'fellow traveller of the Sunn', who once sat for Plymouth in Parliament and presented the town with the aqueduct, which supplies it with water from Dartmoor, 24 M. distant. — The fourth side of the square is occupied by the new *Post Office* (Pl. E, 2).

Among the other objects of interest in Plymouth are the building comprising the *Royal Hotel* and the *Theatre* (Pl. D, 3), with an Ionic portico; the Roman Catholic *Cathedral* (Pl. D, 2); the *Home of the Sisters of Mercy*, North Road; the *Clock Tower*, at the junction of George St. and Lockyer St.; the *Athenaeum* (Pl. D, 3), containing a museum and a gallery of art; the *Plymouth Library*, Cornwall Str., near the Market (Pl. E, 2), with a fine collection of prints and drawings (Da Vinci, Rubens, Ruysdael, Correggio, etc.) and three paintings by Reynolds (open on Mon.; at other times on application to the librarian).

Stonehouse (Pl. C, 3, 4) is the seat of the **Royal William Victualling Yard*, a huge establishment for the victualling of the navy, constructed in 1835 at an outlay of 1,500,000*l.* and covering 14 acres of ground. The gateway (Durnford St.) is surmounted by a colossal figure of William IV. The bakehouse and the cooperage are of special interest. From two to three million pounds of salt-meat are always kept on hand in this yard, and the other stores are in like proportions. — To the N. stands the *Royal Naval Hospital* (Pl. C, 2), which has accommodation for 1200 patients. In Durnford St. are the *Royal Marine Barracks* (Pl C, 3), with room for 1500 men (handsome mess-room); and at the back of them are the *Great Western Docks*.

Devonport (Pl. A, B, 2, 3), situated to the W. of Plymouth, and at a considerably higher elevation, is the headquarters of the naval and military officials, and is the most fashionable part of the town for residences. (Tramway, see p. 139, ending close to the entrance to the Dockyard; boat from the *Admiral's Hard*, Pl. B, 3, 2*d.* or 3*d.*) The **Dockyard* (Pl. A, 2, 3) resembles that at Portsmouth (p. 56), but is not so large (visitors admitted 10-11.30 and 2-4; special order requisite for the Ropery); it affords regular employment to about 3000 workpeople. To the N. of the Dockyard is the *Gun Wharf* (Pl. A, 2), and beyond that is the *Keyham Steam Yard* (Pl. A, 1), a most imposing establishment with huge steam-docks and a steam-hammer capable of striking with a force of 100 tons. The finest private houses are in *Higher Stoke*. The blockhouse at the top of *Stoke Hill* commands an excellent view, and so does the top of the *Devonport Column* (Pl. A, 2; 125 ft.). *Mt. Wise* is a fine promenade, with parade-ground and batteries.

Excursions from Plymouth.

Numerous pleasant excursions may be made from Plymouth both by sea and land. The town lies in the S.W. angle of *Devonshire*, one of the most attractive counties in England; and the adjoining parts of *Cornwall* are scarcely less interesting.

1. Strangers should not omit a visit to ***Mount Edgcumbe,** the seat of the Earl of Mount Edgcumbe, which is reached by the ferry from Admiral's Hard (fare 2*d.* or 3*d.*) to *Cremill* (Pl. A, 4; Mt. Edgcumbe Arms); excursion-steamers also ply to *Cawsand* (King's Arms), in Cawsand Bay, opposite the Breakwater. The house itself is not shown, but the park is open to the public on Wed. (on other days by special permission obtained at the Manor Office, Emma Place, Stonehouse). The **Park*, which occupies the whole peninsula between the Sound and the Hamoaze, contains magnificent trees and is traversed by beautiful walks. Camellias and palms grow here in the open air. The *Gardens* (special order necessary) are tastefully laid out in the Italian, the French, and the English style, and include a large orangery. A visit to Mt. Edgcumbe requires at least 2 hrs.; guide to the chief points 2*s.* 6*d.*

2. *By the Tamar to Weir Head.* This excursion may be accomplished by steamer (return-fare 1*s.* 6*d.*; half-a-day) or by a boat chartered for the occasion (a day). The Tamar ('great water') separates Devon from Cornwall. Passing through the *Hamoaze*, we reach the actual mouth of the *Tamar*, 3 M. to the N.W., which is crossed by the ***Royal Albert Bridge** of the G.W.R. line to Cornwall. This gigantic iron structure, 750 yds. long, 10 yds. wide, and 100 ft. above the water, was built by Brunel in 1859 and cost 250,000*l.* The two chief arches have each a span of 450 ft. The tubular principle (comp. p. 288) has also been adopted here, but the train runs on a roadway suspended from the tubes. Considerable difficulty was experienced in its construction owing to the depth of the water (65 ft.), and the foundations of the piers are 20 ft. below the bottom. At the W. end of the bridge lies **Saltash** *(Green Dragon)*, a quaint-looking fishing-town, whence visitors may walk on to the bridge (3*d.*). The women of Saltash are famous for their rowing, often beating the men at regattas. Beyond the bridge the Tamar again expands, and at high water resembles a beautiful lake. To the N.W. the *Great Mis Tor* (p. 137) is visible. The second branch to the right is the *Tavy.* To the left, opposite the mouth of the Tavy, is *Landulph*, in the church of which is buried *Theodore Paleologus* (d. 1637), a scion of a famous race. On the left, 4 M. above Saltash, is *Pentillie Castle*, with beautiful grounds. At *Cotehele*, 2½ M. farther on, the river is very narrow. **Cotehele House,** a Tudor mansion, with a fine baronial hall and interesting old tapestry and furniture, is generally open to visitors. The river now makes a bend to the right and reaches **Calstock** *(Ashburton Hotel)* and *Morwellham Quay.* Time for tea is generally allowed at Calstock by the steamers. Fine view from Calstock church. The most picturesque part of the river begins here, the ***Morwell Rocks** rising precipitously to a height of 300 ft. The steamers rarely get quite so far as *Weir Head* (about 20 M. from Plymouth), but there is much fine river-scenery farther on, which may be visited by small boat.

3. To *St. Germans and Port Eliot*, 10 M. This excursion is made by boat on the *St. Germans River* or *Lynher Creek*, which diverges from the Hamoaze to the left, below Saltash. On the right, 2 M. from Saltash, is *Trematon Castle*, the grounds of which are open to the public on Wednesdays. Opposite is *Antony House*, situated in a fine park, and containing a good collection of pictures (special permission necessary). Farther up, the river is luxuriantly wooded. **St. Germans** (Eliot Arms), a station on the G. W. R., possesses a *Church* showing an interesting mixture of the Norman, E. E., and Perp. styles. St. Germans was the seat of the old Cornish bishopric, and the names of 12 bishops are preserved in the church. Close by is **Port Eliot,** the seat of Earl St. Germans, with a park to which visitors are admitted by the gardener.

4. *To Oreston Quarries and Saltram*, 4 M., a charming small-boat trip on the *Cattewater.* **Saltram House,** the seat of the Earl of Morley, contains a fine collection of pictures, including 16 portraits by Sir Joshua Reynolds and specimens of Titian, Rubens, and Correggio. Visitors require an order from the Earl. The finely-wooded park is open to the

public on Mondays. This excursion may be combined with the following by walking from Saltram to *Plym Bridge* and *Marsh Mills* (see below).

5. *To the Vale of Bickleigh.* This excursion is most conveniently begun at *Marsh Mills* (p. 138), whence we may walk through the narrow wooded valley to (4½ M.) **Bickleigh** (p. 138). The road through the vale is not open except on Mon., Wed., and Saturdays. To the right is *Boringdon House*, lying high and commanding a wide view. Beyond Bickleigh the walk may be extended to *Shaugh Prior*, the valley of the *Cad*, and the villages of *Meavy* and *Sheepstor* (comp. p. 138).

6. *To Rame Head and Whitesand Bay.* This excursion is best made by taking the excursion-steamer to *Cawsand* (p. 141), which is about 2 M. from **Rame Head,** the southernmost promontory of the peninsula on which Mt. Edgcumbe stands. **Whitesand Bay**, with its fine sandy beach and background of cliffs (bathing dangerous), extends in a beautiful curve from Rame Head to *Looe Island.* Walkers may return viâ *Millbrook* to (4 M.) *Cremill* (p. 141).

7. *To Eddystone Lighthouse*, 14 M. Excursion-steamers ply frequently to the lighthouse in summer, but passengers are seldom landed. The first lighthouse erected here in 1697 was washed away six years after its completion; the second, of wood, was burned down in 1755. The third, or Smeaton's Lighthouse, a tower of masonry, 95 ft. high, stood here from 1757 to 1882. It had then to be removed, owing to the insecurity of its base, and has been re-erected on the Hoe at Plymouth (p. 140). The present lighthouse, 135 ft. in height, was built by Sir J. N. Douglass, at a cost of 80,000*l.* The light-keepers are three in number, each of whom has a month's holiday in summer.

From Plymouth to *Truro* and *Penzance*, see R. 18. — *Dartmoor*, see p. 137.

18. From Plymouth to Truro and Penzance. Falmouth.

80 M. G.W. Railway in 3-4 hrs. (fares 17*s.*, 11*s.* 8*d.*, 7*s.* 3*d.*). Trains start from Millbay Station (p. 138) and stop again at the Devonport Station. The line is remarkable for its numerous lofty viaducts. — Steamboats also ply at intervals from Plymouth to Falmouth and Penzance.

The county of **Cornwall,** which this railway traverses, offers much to interest, the chief attraction being the grand rocky scenery of the coast near the Land's End. The climate is exceedingly mild; myrtles and certain kinds of palms thrive luxuriantly in the open air, while orange-trees and vines only require the protection of matting in winter. The average temperature in winter is 50°, in summer 60° Fahr. The great economical importance of Cornwall arose from its rich mines of copper, tin, lead, and silver; but foreign competition has for some years past closed many mines. The tin-mines of Cornwall were worked by the Phœnicians long before the Christian era. The maximum production of copper ore in Cornwall and Devon was reached in 1861, when 180,000 tons, worth upwards of 1,000,000*l.*, were brought to the surface. Nowadays, it has been said, one must go to Nevada to see Cornish miners. The pilchard and other fisheries are also important. The Celtic origin of the inhabitants is still often perceptible in their dark hair and complexions. Their ancient language, closely akin to Breton and Welsh, is now extinct; the last person who spoke it is said to have died in 1777 (see p. 146). The prefixes 'Tre', 'Pol', and 'Pen', which occur so frequently in names, mean 'dwelling', 'pool', and 'summit' or 'head'. Several books in Cornish are extant. Cornwall is famous for its 'squab' and other pasties, made out of such heterogeneous materials that the devil, according to a local proverb, will not enter the county for fear of being put into a pie. The Prince of Wales bears the title of Duke of Cornwall, and has valuable estates in the county. — Geological travellers should procure *Sir Henry de la Beche's* 'Geology of Cornwall, Devon, and West Somerset'.

Soon after leaving Devonport (p. 141) the train crosses the *Tamar* by the Royal Albert Bridge (p. 142; *View), and reaches

($4^1/_2$ M.) *Saltash* (p. 142). The line skirts the *Lynher*, a scene of great beauty at high tide. $9^1/_2$ M. *St. Germans* (p. 142); $14^1/_2$ M. *Menheniot* (omn. to Looe).

18 M. **Liskeard** *(Webb's*, on the Parade; *Stag)*, a small town with 4500 inhab., is a good centre for a few pleasant excursions.

On the coast, 7 M. to the S. (railway in 1 hr.), is **Looe** *(Ship)*, a small seaport, embowered in myrtles and other exotics. The road to it (9 M.) skirts a canal and passes *St. Keyne's Well*, the subject of a ballad by Southey. About 4 M. to the W. of Looe, also on the coast, lies **Polperro** *(*Oliver's Tourist; Ship)*, perhaps the quaintest and most characteristic of Cornish fishing-villages, tightly wedged into a narrow ravine. — To the N. a picturesque walk of about 7 M. may be taken from Liskeard to ($2^3/_4$ M.) *St. Cleer* (with remains interesting to the antiquarian), the ($3^1/_4$ M.) *Hurlers*, three stone circles, and the (1 M.) *Devil's Cheesewring* (*i.e.* cheese-press), a curious pile of granite rocks, 30 ft. high. About 1 M. to the E. of St. Cleer is *Trevethy's Cromlech*. — At *St. Neot's* (Carlyon Arms), $5^1/_2$ M. to the N.W. of Liskeard, is a fine Perp. church of 1480, with celebrated stained-glass windows of the 14-15th cent (comp. p. 144). Between St. Neot's and the Cheesewring is *Dozmare Pool*, the lake into which King Arthur is said to have thrown Excalibur (p. 155). The Cornish man-demon Tregeagle is condemned to empty the pool with a limpet-shell, a penalty for unjust stewardship when in his human form. — Coach from Liskeard to (18 M.) *Tavistock*, see p. 136.

Beyond Liskeard the train crosses the lofty *Moorswater Viaduct* and reaches (21 M.) *Doublebois*. Several viaducts. 27 M. *Bodmin Road*, on the *Fowey*, is the junction of a branch-line to ($3^1/_2$ M.) Bodmin and ($10^1/_2$ M.) Wadebridge.

Bodmin *(Royal; Town Arms)*, the county-town of Cornwall, is an ancient little place with 5000 inhab. and a large church of the 12-15th cent (restored), accounted the finest specimen of a Cornish mediæval church. — From *Wadebridge* (Molesworth Arms) a coach runs to *Padstow* (see p. 153).

The train now turns to the S., passes, on the right, *Restormel Castle*, built in the reign of Henry III., and reaches ($30^1/_2$ M.) *Lostwithiel* (Royal Talbot), a small town on the *Fowey*, which was once represented in parliament by Addison (1704). It is a good trout-fishing centre and possesses a fine church-steeple, surmounted by an open-work lantern. The so-called '*Palace of the Dukes of Cornwall*' is interesting to antiquarians. — 35 M. *Par* (Royal), with silver smelting-works and pilchard-fishery, is the junction of railways to *New Quay* on the N., and to (4 M.) *Fowey* on the S.

From Par to New Quay, 21 M., railway in 1 hr. (fares 3*s.* 9*d.*, 3*s.* 2*d.*, 1*s.* 9*d.*). The intermediate stations are *St. Blazey*, *Bridges* (the starting-point for a visit to the **Luxulion Valley*), *Bugle*, *Victoria*, and *St. Columb Road*. — **New Quay** (*Red Lion*, well spoken of; *Great Western*, R. & A. 5*s.*; *Cocks's Hotel; Prout's Private Hotel; Commercial*, unpretending) is a rising little watering-place. Its bathing-beach, or rather its beaches, consists of several small sandy coves, surrounded with tall cliffs and separated from each other at high-water by rocky bluffs. Good views are obtained from the cliffs at the back of the Great Western Hotel and from the high ground above the harbour (at the W. end of the town). The rock-bound coast both to the N. and S. is fine, particularly at **Bedruthan Steps*, $6^1/_2$ M. to the N. From Bedruthan we may go on to (7 M.) *Padstow* (p. 153), and cross thence (ferry) to *Rock* (Inn), 15 M. from *Tintagel* (p. 154). The cliff-walk southwards, to (23 M.) *Gwithian* (p. 145), on *St. Ives Bay* (p. 148), is also very fine and easy; inns at (7 M.) *Perran Porth*, (4 M.) *St. Agnes*, and (6 M.) *Portreath*. — Coach from New Quay to *Camelford*, etc., see R. 19.

Fowey *(Fowey Hotel; Ship)*, pron 'Foy', which has been described as a 'miniature Dartmouth', is a small seaport, with a picturesque harbour, at the mouth of the river of the same name. The 'Gallants of Fowey' in the 14th cent. are said to have helped largely in the foundation of England's naval greatness before the time of Drake and the other 'Sea-dogs of Devon'.

The beauty of the district now traversed is marred by numerous mines and the white refuse of kaoline, or china-clay, which is found here in great abundance. 40 M. *St. Austell* (White Hart; Globe) is a busy little mining-town. The handsome church is in good preservation; and its exterior, together with the interior of St. Neot's (p. 144), affords a good idea of a Cornish mediæval church. About 3 M. to the N. rises *Hensbarrow Beacon* (1030 ft.; view), which Carew (1602) calls the 'Archbeacon of Cornwall' ('Survey of Cornwall'; p. 138). — 47 M. *Grampound Road*, the station for (2½ M.) *Probus*, with a fine church-tower, and (4 M.) *Tregony*. Near Truro we cross two long viaducts.

54 M. **Truro** *(*Red Lion*, R. & A. 3*s.* 6*d.*; **Royal)*, the mining capital of Cornwall, is an ancient town with 10,700 inhab., situated at the head of a pretty creek of the *Fal*. In 1877 it became the seat of the resuscitated bishopric of Cornwall, and a handsome E. E. *Cathedral* (consecrated in 1887), by Pearson, has been erected on the site of the old church of St. Mary, a part of which (Perp.) has been incorporated in the new building (S. side of choir). The interior (300 ft. long) is very imposing. The *Baptistery* is a memorial of *Henry Martyn* (1781-1812), the missionary, a native of Truro. — The **Museum* (adm. 6*d.*; free on Wed. after 2 p.m.) contains Cornu-British antiquities and Cornish birds. The *Red Lion Hotel*, dating from 1671, formerly belonged to the Foote family, and was the birthplace of Samuel Foote (1720-77), the actor and playwright.

Among the interesting points near Truro are the grounds of (3 M.) *Tregothnan*, on the opposite bank of the Fal; the ancient ruined church of *St. Piran*, 8 M. to the N.W., long hidden by the sand which had been blown over it, and believed to be the oratory where St. Piranus officiated in the 6th cent.; and the *Isnioc Cross*, at *St. Clement's*, 1½ M. to the S.E. Numerous pleasant excursions may be made on the Fal (to Falmouth, see below), and omnibuses ply to *Probus*, *St. Agnes*, etc.

From Truro to Falmouth, 11½ M., railway in 20-30 min. (fares 2*s.* 6*d.*, 1*s.* 9*d.*, 1*s.* 1*d.*). After passing through a series of cuttings and tunnels, we reach (5 M.) *Perranwell*, near which is the country-seat of *Carclew*, with fine gardens containing many exotic plants. — 9 M. *Penryn* (King's Arms), at the head of *Penryn Creek* (view to the left), carries on an extensive trade in granite and contains some traces of the once famous *Glasney Abbey*.

[A much pleasanter way of proceeding from Truro to Falmouth is by the little steamer which plies up and down the *Fal* every day in summer (10 M., in 1 hr.; fare 1*s.*, 9*d.*). For the first 2 M. we descend what is known as *Truro Lake* or *River*, a ramification of the Fal. On entering the Fal proper we have *Tregothnan* (see above) to the left, while farther on the woods of *Trelissick* cover the bank to the right. The steamer then reaches the *Carrick Road*, or wider part of the Fal estuary, passes the mouth of *Restronguet Creek* (to the right), and enters *Penryn Creek*, at the mouth of which Falmouth lies.]

Falmouth (*Falmouth*, on the neck of the peninsula, near the station, with a sea-view both to the back and front; **Green Bank*, $1^1/_2$ M. to the N.W. of the station and $^3/_4$ M. from the landing-stage, with a view of the harbour, R. & A. 4*s*., table d'hôte 4*s*. 6*d*.; *Royal*, in the town, well spoken of), a small and somewhat foreign-looking seaport with about 6000 inhab., was formerly an important mail-packet station, but is now chiefly known as a watering-place. It is still, however, a port of call for vessels waiting for orders and for yachts. The scenery of the estuary of the Fal is very picturesque, and charming water-excursions may be taken in Falmouth Harbour (sailing boat 2*s*., row-boats 1*s*. per hr.). In fine weather excursion-steamers ply to the Lizard, Penzance, etc., and trips are also made by sailing-yachts. Falmouth has bi-weekly steamboat communication with London ($1^1/_2$ day), Dublin, etc. The bathing is good. Palms and other tropical plants grow here in the open air without protection, and the visitor should try to obtain access to one of the lovely private gardens.

The chief object of interest at Falmouth is **Pendennis Castle**, an old Tudor fastness at the E. extremity of the peninsula on which the town stands ($^3/_4$ M. from the station). It is celebrated for its siege in the Civil War and is still maintained as a fortress. The *View from it is very fine. A pleasant drive has been constructed round the promontory, passing below the castle. On the opposite side of the estuary (steam-ferry; return-fare $6^1/_2$*d*.) is *St. Mawes Castle*, another coast-defence erected by Henry VIII. — On the way to Pendennis we pass the remains of *Arwenack House*, the seat of the once powerful but now extinct family of the Killigrews (memorial obelisk in front). Excursions may also be made to (2 M.) *Penryn* (p. 145), at the head of Penryn Creek, and to *Flushing* (ferry $^1/_2$*d*., starting behind the Green Bank Hotel) on its N. bank, whence we may walk across the hill to *Mylor*, on Carrick Road (p. 145).

A coach plies daily in summer from Falmouth to *Penryn* and ($12^1/_2$ M.; fare 2*s*. 6*d*.) *Helston* (see below), where it corresponds with coaches for the (11 M.) *Lizard* and (13 M.) *Penzance* (see below). The direct road from Falmouth to the Lizard (18 M.) leads by *Gweek*, at the head of the *Helford Estuary*, and through *Trelowarren Park* (carr. and pair 30*s*.; driver 5*s*.); in the season a four-horse brake runs by this route from Falmouth to Lizard Town and Kynance Cove (see p. 147). Near Trelowarren House is a very singular series of underground chambers, a standing puzzle to archæologists. The coast-route (for pedestrians; about 25 M.) leads viâ (2 M.) *Maenporth*, (2 M.) *Mawnan Smith*, (2 M.) *Helford Passage* (ferry), (1 M.) *Manaccan*, and (4 M.) *St. Keverne* (Inn), and thence by the cliffs to ($3^1/_2$ M.) *Coverack*, (2 M.) *Black Head*, (4 M.) *Poltesco* (serpentine works), (1 M.) *Cadgwith* (p. 148), and (3 M.) *Lizard Town* (p. 148). The direct walking distance from Helford Passage to Lizard Town, viâ *Newtown*, is 10 M.

Beyond Truro numerous mines are passed, many of which have been abandoned owing to the low price of metals. At (59 M.) *Chacewater* we cross the valley by a high wooden viaduct. In the distance, to the N.W., rises *St. Agnes's Beacon* (630 ft.).

63 M. **Redruth** *(Tabb's; London)*, a market-town with 9335 inhab., formerly important from the numerous copper-mines in the neighbourhood. The *Hunt Memorial Museum* contains minerals. About 3 M. to the S. E. is *Gwennap*, where Wesley used to preach to the miners; open-air meetings of 20-30,000 Wesleyans still occasionally take place here. — Farther on, *Carnbrea Hill* (750 ft.), with British remains and a curious old castle or house perched on the top, rises to the left. 66 M. *Camborne* (Abraham's; Commercial), a mining-town with 13,610 inhabitants. The *Dolcoath Copper Mine* here is upwards of 2000 ft. deep. — From ($68^1/_2$ M.) *Gwinear Road* a branch-line runs to (8 M.) **Helston** *(Angel; Star)*, the usual starting-point for a visit to the interesting

coast-scenery of the Lizard (see below). Coaches run hence to Falmouth (p. 145), to (11 M.) the Lizard (see below; fare 2*s.*), and to (13 M.) Penzance (p. 149; fare 2*s.* 6*d.*). The road to Lizard Town calls for no special remark. About halfway the prettily-situated mansion of *Bochym* is passed on the right.

The name ***Lizard** (Cornish, *Mencage*) is given to the whole peninsula S. of a line drawn from *Gweek*, at the head of Helford River, to *Looe Pool*, but is more specially applied to the town and headland at its S. extremity. The peninsula is an elevated plateau, descending in cliffs to the sea, and its interior is as unattractive as its coast scenery is the reverse. The charms of the latter are chiefly owing to the varied colours and forms of the serpentine rock. Botanists will be interested in the fact that the rare and beautiful Cornish heath, *Erica Vagans*, grows here in abundance. Tourists usually proceed direct from Helston to Lizard Town, and make the latter the centre of their excursions, but those with leisure should spend a night both at Mullyon on the W. and Cadgwith on the E. — The road from Helston to (11 M.) Lizard Town is uninteresting. Good walkers, with time to spare, will prefer to follow the coast, the chief points of interest on which are (3/4 M.) *Looe Pool;* 2 M. *Looe Bar*, formed of pebbles cast up by the sea (supposed to be caused by Tregeagle, p. 144); 3 1/2 M. *Gunwalloe*, with a church of the 15th cent. Then (2 1/2 M.) **Mullyon Cove* and *Cave;* the cave, which is entered by a beautiful natural archway, may be penetrated at low tide for 200 ft. (fine view from within). It was once a great resort of smugglers. The village of *Mullyon* (Old Inn; King's Arms) lies about 1 M. inland. The Perp. church has some features of interest, including some remarkable carved oaken pews. The comfortable but unpretending Old Inn is kept by Mary Munday, a Cornish character whose praises have been sung by Professor Blackie in a poem inscribed in her visitors' book. Continuing to follow the cliff-walk (coast-guard route marked by white paint) beyond Mullyon Cove, we pass the bold headlands of *Pradanack Head* and *Vellan Head* and reach (5 M.) ***Kynance Cove** (small lodging-houses; refreshments), one of the most celebrated points on the Cornish coast. The serpent ine cliffs here are beautifully veined and coloured, and numerous picturesque rocks are scattered about the little bay, with its floor of silvery sand. Various more or less appropriate names have been given to the different features of the Cove, such as *Steeple Rock* and *Gull Rock*. On *Asparagus Island*, the semi-detached promontory on the W. side of the Cove, is the *Devil's Bellows*, a narrow interstice formed by one rock overlying another, through which the water is propelled in clouds of spray (seen to advantage at low tide only). Adjacent is the *Letter Box*, a curious fissure in the rock. The cave in Asparagus Island is known as the *Devil's Throat;* those on the mainland are called the *Kitchen* and

Parlour. Geologists will notice that the action of the sea causes the granite to cleave in cubes, while the serpentine assumes the most varied forms. From Kynance Cove we may either proceed direct to (1¼ M.) Lizard Town, on the E. side of the promontory, or continue our walk round the coast to the (2½ M.) *Lighthouses* (open to visitors, except on Mon. and after the lamps are lit; fine view), on *Lizard Head*, the most southerly point in England (49° 57′ 39″ N. lat.). On the way we pass *Pistol Meadow*, so called from the weapons cast up by the sea after the wreck of a man-of-war at the beginning of last century, and the little harbour of *Polpeor*. Farther on are the columnar *Bumble Rock* and the *Lion's Den*, formed by the falling in of the roof of a cavern in the cliffs. The Lighthouses are about ½ M. from Lizard Town.

Lizard Town (*Hill's Lizard Hotel*, R. & A. 2*s.* 6*d.*; *Lugg's; Mrs. Rowe's Boarding House*, and several others, on the promontory, with sea-view), a small village, frequented as summer-quarters, is 11 M. from Helston by the road and 15 M. by the shore. The bathing-place is at *Housel Cove*, to the E. of the Lighthouses. Part of the ordinary path between Lizard Town and the shore runs along the top of the low walls of turf and stone which form the fences in this part of Cornwall. The church of the Lizard, the southernmost church in England, is at *Landewednack*, a little to the E. Serpentine is freely used here as building material. The *Raven Hugo* (or *Ogo*), *Dolor Hugo*, and other caverns on the E. coast are best explored by boat. — *Cadgwith* (*Star), 2½ M. to the E. of Lizard Town, is chiefly visited for the sake of the *Devil's Frying Pan*, a singular natural amphitheatre somewhat resembling the Lion's Den. The coast between Cadgwith and Helford River is also very fine, though not so much frequented by tourists (comp. p. 147).

Those who have come to Lizard Town by the E. coast, and have not time to follow the whole of the W. coast of the peninsula, are recommended to visit the Lighthouses and go on thence to Kynance Cove, Mullyon Cove, and Mullyon, in time to catch the afternoon coach from Lizard Town to Helston, which passes the cross-roads 1½ to the E. (inland) of Mullyon. This will be in all a walk of 9½ M. The coast-guard path all round the coast is clearly marked by whitewash on stones and rocks, at intervals of 50 yds. or less.

The Coach Route from Helston to (13 M.) *Penzance* (p. 149; fare 2*s.* 6*d.*) calls for little remark, except that a good view of St. Michael's Mt. (p. 149) is enjoyed towards the end. Walkers, however, will find the coast-route (20 M.) interesting.

Continuation of the Railway. 71 M. *Hayle*, with large engine-works. 73 M. *St. Erth* is the junction of a line to (4 M.) *St. Ives*, passing *Lelant* and *Carbis Bay*, the latter a popular picnic resort.

St. Ives (**Tregenna Castle*, charmingly situated above the station, with view, R. & A. 4*s.* 6*d.*, D. 4*s.* 6*d.*; *Western*, *Queen's*, in the town), a quaint little fishing-town, situated on perhaps the most beautiful bay in Cornwall, with a splendid sandy beach. It is said to owe its name to *St. Ia*, an Irish princess who was martyred here about A. D. 450. The best views are obtained from the Tregenna Hotel and the Battery Rocks.

The mean temperature of St. Ives in winter is said to be only 4° Fahr. less than that of Rome, and it has become a favourite bathing and winter resort. The pilchard fishery is prosecuted here with great success. The church is an interesting Perp. building, with carved bench-ends. A visit should be paid to the very ancient church (?5th cent.) of (4½ M.) *Gwithian*, on the other side of the bay, formerly buried in the sand. Good walkers may follow the coast from St. Ives to (15 M.) *St. Just* (p. 152) and (7 M.) the *Land's End* (p. 151), or cross the country to (8 M.) *Penzance* (see below).

The churchyard of *St. Hilary*, near St. Erth, contains tombstones from the time of Constantine the Great down to the present day.

From St. Erth the train runs nearly due S. to (77 M.) *Marazion* or *Market Jew* (Godolphin; Marazion), a prosaic little town, not answering the expectations aroused by the ascription of its name ('bitter Zion') to an early colony of Jews, who traded with the Phœnician miners (see *Max Müller's* 'Are there Jews in Cornwall'; comp. p. 143).

Marazion is the station for ***St. Michael's Mount**, the *Ictis* of the ancients, a curious rocky islet, rising precipitously to a height of 230 ft., and connected with the shore by a natural causeway, ½ M. long, uncovered for about 3 hrs. at low water. It may be described as a miniature copy of Mont St. Michel in Normandy. Its earliest occupant, according to the legend, was the Giant Cormoran, slain by the redoubtable Jack. The priory at the top was dedicated to St. Michael, who is said to have appeared to some hermits here very early in the Christian era, and St. Keyne (A. D. 490) was the first of a long series of pilgrims. The castle, which has for many years been the seat of the St. Aubin family, contains an interesting hall and chapel. Fine *View from the square church-tower. There is a small fishing-village (Inn) at the foot of the Mount.

80 M. **Penzance.** — **Hotels.** QUEEN'S, on the Esplanade, R. & A. from 4*s.* 6*d.*, D. 5*s.*; *UNION, Chapel St., comfortable, but with no view of the sea, R. & A. 4*s.*; WESTERN, Alverton St., R., A., & B. 6*s.*; MOUNT'S BAY, private hotel, next door to the Queen's; RAILWAY, STAR, unpretending.

Penzance, i. e. 'Holy Headland', is a seaport with 11,700 inhab., beautifully situated on the N.W. shore of *Mount's Bay.* It is one of the headquarters of the pilchard and mackerel fisheries, and also trades in copper, tin, china, and granite. Potatoes are extensively cultivated in the environs and sent in large quantities to London. The climate of the district is extremely mild, and frost and snow are rare phenomena; but the annual rainfall (43 inches) is much above the average. The handsome new *Public Buildings* in Alverton St., include the large 'St. John's Hall', the guildhall, a library, and a museum. The *Library* contains rare Cornish books and a valuable collection of prints and autographs. The Esplanade, to the S., is the pleasantest part of the town, and the Pier (near the station) affords good promenades and views. Another fine point of view is *Lescudjack Castle*, a British earthwork on a hill near the railway-station. *Sir Humphrey Davy*, the natural philosopher, was born at Penzance in 1778, and a statue has been erected to him in front of the Market Hall.

Perhaps the pleasantest short walk in the neighbourhood of Penzance is that to 1½ M. *Bleu Bridge*, a small slab-bridge with an ancient inscribed stone. To reach it we turn to the left at the Three Tuns Hotel, near the railway-station, and then immediately to the right. The third turning to the right (¼ hr. from the hotel; the fourth turning if we count a narrow footpath) descends to the bridge. — A visit may also be paid on foot to (3 M.) *Marazion* and *St. Michael's Mt.* (p. 149), but the latter may also be reached in summer by a small steamer (fare each way 6*d.*) — *Gulwal Church*, 1 M. to the N.E., has a curious inscribed 'menhir'.

Excursions from Penzance.

Penzance may be made the traveller's headquarters for several days, as the district of the 'Land's End' affords numerous attractive excursions, in which the lover of natural beauty and the antiquarian will each find his reward. Many of the most important copper and tin mines in Cornwall are also within easy reach, and the traveller should not neglect an opportunity to explore one of these. Comp., however, p. 143.

1. To Lamorna and the Logan Rock by the Coast, 11 M. This excursion may be recommended to good walkers, though the cliff-scenery is not so fine as that nearer the Land's End. We leave the town by the Esplanade and pass the deserted *Wherry Tin Mine* and (1 M.) *Newlyn.* The *Church of St. Peter* at Newlyn contains a reredos after Leon. da Vinci and a memorial window to *Lord Iddesleigh* (d. 1886). At (3 M.) *Mousehole* is a large cavern, and a little inland, in *Paul Church*, is the tomb of Dolly Pentreath (d. 1777), usually said to be the last person who spoke Cornish. The Rev. W. S. Lach-Szyrma, however, in his 'Short History of Penzance' states that he had found two or three persons in Mousehole who could count up to 20 in old Cornish. *Lamorna Cove*, 5 1/2 M. from Penzance, has been somewhat spoiled in appearance by the granite quarries. About 1 1/2 M. inland, near *Boleit*, are the remains of a stone circle known as the *Pipers & Merry Maidens*, said to have been turned into stone for dancing on Sunday. Lamorna is 5 1/2 M. from the Logan Rock (see below) by the coast.

2. To St. Buryan and the Logan Rock, 9 M. (carr. about 10*s.*). The road passes (3/4 M.) *Alverton* and diverges (1/2 M.) to the left from the road to St. Just (see below). It then passes through the beautiful avenue of *Trereife* (pronounced 'treeve') and crosses *Buryas Bridge.* On the left is *Tresvennick Pillar*, a British monument, popularly known as the 'Blind Fiddler'. The road to *Sancreed* (and St. Just) diverges to the right, 1 1/2 M. farther on, and after 3/4 M. more our road quits the direct route to Penzance and leads to the left. 2 M. *St. Buryan* (Ship), a village with an interesting church of the 15th cent., the tower of which is conspicuous far and wide. The interior contains a fine carved screen and the churchyard an interesting old cross. The next village is (3 M.) *Trereen* (Logan Inn), where tourists quit their vehicles to visit (3/4 M.) the ***Trereen Dinas,** a bold and fantastic rocky headland, with the *Logan Rock.* (A guide, useful when time is limited, may be obtained here; fee 1*s.*; more for a party.)

The **Logan Rock** is a mass of granite weighing 70 tons, but so poised that it can be rocked ('logged'), though with some difficulty since Lieut. Goldsmith's exploit (see below). A little climbing is necessary to reach the rocking stone, and those whose heads are not perfectly steady may leave the guide to show how it moves. The guide, too, will relate how Lieutenant Goldsmith, a young naval officer, a nephew of the poet, had the folly to upset the rock in 1824 with the aid of a boat's crew; and how the task of replacing it, which he had to undertake by order of the Admiralty, cost him 2000*l.*, though he had merely succeeded in canting it over, not moving it more than a couple of feet or so. There is another rocking-stone on the promontory, called the '*Logan Lady*'.

The *__Cliff Scenery__ between the Logan Rock and (6 M.) the Land's End is unsurpassed in England, and walkers are recommended to prolong their excursion in this direction and return to Penzance by the road described below. The finest points are the two bold promontories of *Tol Pedn Penwith* ('holed headland of Penwith') and *Pardenick.* The cliffs are 100-250 ft. high.

3. To THE LAND'S END, 10 M. (carr. 10*s.* 6*d.*, with a fee of 2*s.*). The road diverges to the right from that to St. Buryan (p. 150) at a point $3^1/_2$ M. from Penzance. To the right rises *Carn Bran* (690 ft.), on the top of which Wesley is said to have frequently preached to huge crowds of miners. Farther on, $^1/_4$ M. to the left, is the circle of *Boscawen*, about 5 M. from Penzance, which consists of 19 stones, a number constantly recurring in these circles. At the village of *Crows-an-Wra*, $2^1/_2$ M. from the fork, are a curious old circular dwelling (to the right) and a stone cross (to the left). Alongside our road runs the old pack-horse track. The small enclosure to the right, 1 M. beyond Crows-an-Wra, is a disused Friends' Burial Ground. At the ($2^1/_2$ M.) village of *Sennen* (interesting church) the Inn still has for its sign the 'First and Last Hotel in England', though there is now a Hotel (R. & A. from 3*s.*) at the Land's End itself, 1 M. farther on, while the very last house in England is a small cottage near the Land's End Hotel, where tea and other refreshments may be obtained. The ***Land's End,** the ancient *Bolerium*, the most westerly point in England (long. 5° 41′ 31″ W.) is a granite promontory, 60-100 ft. in height. It commands a fine sea-view, including the Scilly Islands (p. 152), 20 M. to the S.W. The *Longship Rocks*, $^1/_2$ M. from the point, are marked by a lighthouse. The cliff scenery on both sides is varied and imposing. Among the numerous detached rocks to which names have been given are the *Armed Knight* to the S. of the Land's End and the *Irish Lady* to the N., by the S. horn of *Whitesand Bay* (numerous shells). The view in this direction is bounded by the bold promontory of *Cape Cornwall* and the *Brisons.*

The last two routes are combined by the great majority of tourists, who take one of the BRAKES which start daily in summer from Penzance for the Land's End, going viâ the Logan Rock (13 M.) and returning by the direct route. They start about 9 a.m. and regain Penzance about 6 p.m., allowing $1^1/_2$-2 hrs. at the Logan Rock and 2-$2^1/_2$ hrs. at the Land's End, and also a few minutes at St. Buryan (p. 150). The return-fare is 3*s.* 6*d.*; single journey 2*s.* — Those who take the coach miss the fine cliff-scenery between the Logan and the Land's End (see above). A good plan is to drive from Penzance to the Logan Rock, send the carriage on to Sennen (see above), walk along the cliffs to the Land's End, and drive back to Penzance direct from Sennen (in all 8-10 hrs). Those who can should arrange to spend a night at the Land's End for the sake of the sunset and sunrise.

4. To St. Just, $6^1/_2$ M., omnibus twice daily in 1 hr. (fare 6*d.*). The road itself is uninteresting, but it passes within a mile or so of the hut-village of *Crellas*, the hill-fort of *Chûn Castle*, and a large *Cromlech*, all of which are among the most interesting antiquities in Cornwall. The omnibus, however, does not allow time for a visit to these, and will therefore be of little use to the tourist. — **St. Just in Penwith** *(Commercial Inn)*, a small market town, has an Early Perp. church, with interesting Irish tracery and one of the oldest Christian tombs in England. Near it is an open-air amphitheatre in which Cornish miracle-plays were represented.

St. Just is the best starting-point for a visit to *Bottallack Mine*, 2 M. to the N.W., which extends for 400 ft. under the sea (permission must be obtained beforehand; make enquiry at the Penzance hotels). *Cape Cornwall* (p. 151), $1^1/_2$ M. to the W., is a fine point of view. The cliff-walk from St. Just to the Land's End (7 M.) is fine, though scarcely equal to that between the Land's End and the Logan.

5. To St. Ives. This excursion may be made either by railway as already described (p. 148) or by road. The direct distance is about 8 M., but tourists will probably prefer a more circuitous route, so as to include a visit to some of the interesting British remains in the district between Penzance and St. Ives.

Among these are *Chysawster*, a hut-village, 4 M. to the N. of Penzance; *Mulfra Cromlech* or *Quoit*, 5 M. to the N.W.; *Zennor Cromlech*, 5 M. to the S.W. of St. Ives, said to be the largest monument of the kind known; the *Lanyon Cromlech*, $2^1/_2$ M. to the S.W. of the Mulfra Cromlech; the *Nine Maidens*, part of a stone circle, near *Morvah*, 2 M. beyond Lanyon; the *Holed Stone* ('Men-an-tol'; prob. used for initiations) and the *Written Stone* ('Men scryfa'), also near Lanyon; and the beehive-hut at *Bosphrennis*, near Mulfra. To the S. of the Nine Maidens is the *Ding Dong Mine*, said to have been worked long before the Christian era.

6. To the Scilly Isles, 40 M., steamer thrice weekly in 4 hrs. (fares 7*s.*, 5*s.*; return 10*s.* 6*d.*, 7*s.* 6*d.*). This sail affords a good view of the Cornish coast, but the sea is often rough. About halfway we pass the *Wolf Lighthouse*. The shadowy land of *Lyonnesse* —

'A land of old upheaven from the abyss
'By fire, to sink into the abyss again' —

stretched from the Scilly Isles to the mainland, and now lies submerged with all the 140 parishes, which the matter-of-fact old chroniclers assign to it.

The **Scilly Isles**, the *Cassiterides* of the ancients, are about 50 in number, but only five are inhabited (pop. 4200). The largest is **St. Mary's**, with a circumference of 9 M. and a population of 1500. On this lies the capital, *Hugh Town* (Hugh House Hotel; Tregarthen's Inn), with *Star Castle*, a fortress erected in the reign of Elizabeth. The churchyard contains the graves of those drowned in the 'Schiller' in 1875. The rocky coast-scenery is fine, the chief points being *Peninis*, *Old Town Bay*, and *Giant's Castle*. *Holy Vale* is picturesque. A good view of the group is obtained from *Telegraph Tower*. **Tresco** *(Canteen Inn)*, the second of the group in size, is the most interesting. Near the ruins of *Tresco Abbey* is the splendid **Mansion* of the proprietor of the islands (Mr. T. A. Dorrien-Smith), picturesquely placed on a rocky height. Its sub-tropical gardens are the finest in the British Isles (fee to gardener). There is also a large cave in this island, named the *Piper's Hole*, shown by the landlord of the Canteen Inn (fee for a party 5*s.*). *Dolphin Church* is pretty. One of the most profitable occupations in the islands is the growing of the narcissus for Covent Garden, to which hundreds of thousands of this beautiful flower are sent every spring.

Travellers who have reached Penzance and the Land's End viâ Plymouth, and wish to return by the N. coast, are recommended to go by railway from Penzance to New Quay, the starting-point for 75 M. of the finest coaching in England (to *Bideford;* see R. 19). Pedestrians may follow the coast the whole way; but if their time is limited they should reserve their walking for the coast to the N. of New Quay, especially from Ilfracombe to Lynmouth and Porlock (pp. 164, 168). Those who have already visited the intermediate points of interest may take the steamer from *Hayle* (p. 148) to *Ilfracombe.*

19. From New Quay to Bideford.

75 M. Coaching Route. The stages are: 1. From New Quay to (29 M.) *Camelford* (fare 6*s.* 6*d.*), thrice weekly (Tues., Thurs., and Sat.), starting about 8 a.m. and connecting at Camelford with the coach to Bude (through-fare 16*s.*). — 2. From Camelford to *Tintagel*, *Boscastle*, and (20 M.) *Bude* (9*s.* 6*d.*) thrice a week, starting about 11.30 a.m. — 3. From Bude to (16 M.) *Clovelly Cross* (6*s.*) and (26 M.) *Bideford* (8*s.*), thrice weekly (Mon., Wed., and Frid.).

Travellers by this fine route may make their first halt at Tintagel, after which they should also visit at least Boscastle and Clovelly. Tintagel and Boscastle are only a few miles apart, and those who spend a night at either may easily visit the other on foot. Bude is not so interesting, but the present coaching arrangements almost necessitate the spending of a night there. From Clovelly there is daily communication with Bideford, while steamers ply frequently to Ilfracombe.

New Quay, see p. 144. The first part of the road is comparatively uninteresting, though there is some fine cliff-scenery, accessible to the pedestrian alone, between New Quay and Padstow (comp. p. 144). 3 M. *St. Columb Minor*, with a lofty church-tower. 8 M. *St. Columb Major* (Red Lion), with an interesting church. St. Columb Road Station (p. 144) lies $2^3/_4$ M. to the S. (omn.). A little to the S. E. of St. Columb Major is *Castle Dinas*, the legendary site of a hunting-seat of King Arthur and residence of the old Cornish kings. The road now turns to the N. and traverses a somewhat bleak district. At (17 M.) *Wadebridge* (Molesworth Arms), a pleasantly-situated little town, the junction of a line to Bodmin (p. 144), we cross the head of the *Camel* estuary by a bridge that was in Carew's time 'the longest, strongest, and fayrest that the Shire could muster'. To the left (W.) we obtain a view of Padstow, at the mouth of the river.

A coach runs 3-4 times daily along the pretty estuary of the *Camel* to (8 M.) **Padstow** *(Commercial Inn)*, a place of no interest in itself, but a good starting-point for a boating excursion along the fine rocky coast.

Part of the road from Wadebridge to Camelford is finely wooded.

29 M. **Camelford** *(Queen's Arms; Darlington Arms)*, the Camelot of Arthurian legend, is the nearest starting-point for an ascent of *Brown Willy* (1370 ft.; 2-3 hrs.), the highest summit in Cornwall, commanding an extensive but monotonous view. Along with its N.

neighbour, *Row Tor* (1296 ft.), it rises about 5 M. to the S.E. The name is a corruption of *Bryn Uhella*, i.e. highest hill.

The coach by which we have travelled thus far goes on to Launceston (see p. 135), while we now take our places in that which runs to Tintagel and Bude. The road passes the extensive *Delabole Slate Quarries* (2 M. to the W. of Camelford), which have been worked since the days of Queen Elizabeth and produce 150,000 tons of slate per annum. 6 M. (from Camelford) **Tintagel**, or more correctly **Trevena** (**Wharncliffe Arms)*, a small village 1/2 M. from the sea, in the very heart of the district consecrated to Arthurian legend. The coach stops here to allow of a hurried visit to the castle, but the traveller should spend at least one day here or at Boscastle. *Tintagel Church*, to the W. of the village, is partly of Saxon origin. To reach the sea we descend a small valley, at the bottom of which is a cottage (refreshments), where we obtain the key for the enclosure on the 'Island'. The remains of the **Castle**, 'Dundagil by the Cornish Sea', are here above us to the left, on the mainland portion of *Tintagel Head*, and are most easily reached by a grassy track ascending from the valley at a point a little above the cottage. The keep, the oldest part of the existing ruins, is probably of Norman construction, though it is not unlikely that a Saxon, if not also a British, stronghold once occupied the same site. Between this part of the promontory and the so-called 'Island' is a deep chasm, which is supposed to be of comparatively recent origin, or is at least much wider than of old. On the other side we see the rough path ascending to the top of the Island, to reach which we must again descend to the little cove in which the cottage stands, with apparatus used in loading boats with slates. The path leads to the locked gate, for which we obtained the key (not required for the castle itself). The whole Island seems to have been included in the fortified area, and there are some ruins near this doorway. On the top of the plateau are the remains of the foundation-walls of a small chapel, an old well, and a so-called hermit's cave. The *View of the grand rocky coast from the extreme point of the headland is very imposing, extending from Trevose Head on the S. to Hartland Point on the N. There is a curious 'pillar rock' on the S. side of the point.

Among the sea-birds flocking round the promontory the visitor may chance to see a specimen of the red-legged Cornish chough, a rare bird, in the form of which, says the legend, King Arthur still haunts the scene of his Round Table.

Familiar as the Arthurian Legend is, the following brief abstract of it, taken from 'An Unsentimental Journey through Cornwall', by *Mrs. Craik*, may not be unwelcome. 'Uther Pendragon, King of Britain, falling in love with Ygrayne, wife of the duke of Cornwall, besieged them in their twin castles of Tintagel and Terrabil, slew the husband, and the same day married the wife. Unto whom a boy was born, and by advice of the enchanter Merlin, carried away from the sea-shore beneath Tintagel, and confided to a good knight, Sir Ector, to be brought up as his own son, and christened Arthur. On the death of the king, Merlin produced the youth, who was recognized by his mother Ygrayne, and proclaimed king in the stead of Uther Pendragon. He instituted the Order of Knights of the Round Table, who were to go everywhere, punishing vice and rescuing oppressed virtue, for the love of God and of some noble lady. He married Guinivere, daughter of King Leodegrance, who forsook him for the love of Sir Launcelot, his bravest knight and dearest friend. One by one, his best knights fell away into sin, and his nephew Mordred raised a rebellion, fought with him, and conquered him at Camelford. Seeing his end was near, Arthur bade his last faithful knight, Sir Bedevere, carry him to the shore of a mere (supposed to be Dozmare Pool) and throw in there his sword Excalibur, when appeared a boat with three queens, who lifted him in, mourning over him. He sailed away with them to be healed of his grievous wound. Some say that he was afterwards buried in a chapel near, others declare that he still lives in fairy land, and will reappear in latter days, to reinstate the Order of Knights of the Round Table, and rule his beloved England, perfect as he once tried to make it, but in vain.' — The reader will scarcely need to be referred to *Sir Thomas Malory's* 'Morte d'Arthur' and *Tennyson's* 'Idylls of the King'.

From Tintagel to Boscastle by the *Cliffs, 4½-5 M. (2-3 hrs.), a charming walk. There is a kind of path for most of the way, but there is a good deal of 'up and down' on the walk, and the crossing of the 'Rocky Valley' (see below) is rather rough. Beyond *Barras Nose*, the headland to the N. of Tintagel Head, we reach *Bossiney Cove*. The detached rocks off *Willapark Point* are called the *Sisters* and *Lye Rock*, and farther on are *Long Island* and *Short Island*. Beyond Bossiney Cove we reach the so-called *Rocky Valley*, the picturesque and somewhat chaotic channel of a little stream, which here enters the sea. Our path deserts us here and we are left to choose our own line in crossing the valley; but the scenery is pretty enough to make a slight detour acceptable and may even tempt to an exploration of the valley up to the *Mill*, about ½ M. inland. Beyond the next promontory we skirt two small bays, cross another depression, and pass a slate-quarry. To the left lies the island of *Growar*. We then reach the deep and gloomy *Blackpit*, the bottom of which may be reached by an easy path. The promontory beyond this, also named *Willapark*, and crowned by a tower, forms the S. buttress of Boscastle Harbour. To reach the village we turn to the right.

Another favourite coast walk from Tintagel is to *Trebarwith Sands*, 1½ M. to the S. Not far off is a fine cave, accessible by boat only.

The road from Tintagel to Boscastle (about 3 M.) affords only occasional views of the sea. After about 1 M., beyond *Bossiney*, we have a good view to the left of the **Rocky Valley*, stretching down to the shore. About ¼ M. farther on, to the right, is a board indicating the way to *St. Nighton's Kieve*, a small waterfall of the stream which lower down flows through the Rocky Valley.

After obtaining the key we follow the lane which here diverges to the right, and after passing four gates on the right, we come to (12 min.) a grassy lane on the same side. On reaching the fields we bend to the left, still following the track, cross a stile, and pass two white gates, below the second of which is the padlocked entrance to the *Fall, prettily embowered in wood. In returning we vary the route by crossing a stile between the padlocked gate and the second white door mentioned above and following the path that descends along the stream.

To the left, ½ M. farther on, is the hamlet of *Trevalga*, beyond which we next reach (¾ M.) *Forrabury*. Another ½ M. brings us to Boscastle (9 M. from Camelford).

Boscastle, *i.e. 'Bottreaux Castle'* (*Wellington*, R. & A. 4*s.* 6*d.*, table d'hôte B. 2*s.* 6*d.*, table d'hôte D. 3*s.* 6*d.*) is a quaint little place, which improves on acquaintance. Though quite near, the sea is not visible; but a walk down either side of the curiously tortuous little harbour soon brings it into sight. The entrance to the harbour is singularly picturesque, and should be viewed from the promontories on both sides. To the right we obtain a distant view of *Lundy* (p. 159), made conspicuous at night by its lighthouse. The coach stops here long enough for a visit to the harbour.

To *Tintagel* and *St. Nighton's Kieve*, see above. — About $1^1/_2$ M. to the E., reached viâ Forrabury (p. 155), is *Minster*, with an interesting little church (key at Boscastle), formerly the chancel of an 'alien' priory of Angevin monks. — To reach **Pentargain Cove*, with its tiny waterfall, we cross the bridge (starting from the hotel) and ascend the steep road to the right. In $^1/_2$ M. we reach a board, on the right, indicating the way to a farm-house, where the key is obtained (small fee expected). The gate to unlock is on the other side of the road, opposite the notice-board, and the path down to the cove is unmistakable.

☞ Pentargain Cove may also be taken in as part of the interesting but somewhat long and fatiguing cliff-walk to *Bude*, a distance of 14 M. (6-7 hrs.). Some of the finest points to the N. of Pentargain are *High Cliff* (700 ft.), *Cambeak*, *Crackington Cove*, *Dazard Point*, *Mill-hook Mouth*, and the *Black Rock*. Refreshments may be obtained at a farm-house at *St. Genny's* (no inn), not quite halfway. All but very energetic pedestrians will take various opportunities of cutting off the sinuosities of the coast.

The road from Boscastle to Bude (16 M.; coach thrice weekly, 6*s.*; carr. and pair about 30*s.*) passes nothing calling for special description. The view as we approach Bude, passing *Marhamchurch* on the right, is attractive. **Bude** or **Bude Haven** *(Falcon; Bude)*, a rising little watering-place, is a convenient starting-point for exploring a fine coast, and is connected by coaches with Boscastle, Tintagel, Camelford, Clovelly, Bideford, Holsworthy, and Launceston. *Bude Castle*, on the left bank of the stream, is a modern mansion.

The finest bits of the coast in the immediate vicinity of Bude are *Compass Point* (with its tower), the S. arm of the haven, and *Efford Beacon* (view), a little farther to the S. — In the opposite direction the favourite excursion is to follow the cliffs to (4 M.) the *Duck Pool*, and then to proceed inland, through the *Combe Valley*, to ($3^1/_2$ M.) *Kilkhampton* (see below), whence we return to (5 M.) Bude *viâ* ($3^1/_2$ M.) *Stratton* (see below). Near the point where we turn inland is *Stow*, the site of Sir Richard Grenville's house (see '*Westward Ho*'). — Following the coast from the Duck Pool (see above), we pass (1 M.) the *Lower Sharpnose*, (1 M.) *Stanbury Mouth*, and (1 M.) the *Upper Sharpnose*, and reach ($^3/_4$ M.) **Morwenstow** *(Inn)*, now a well-known place through its late vicar, the *Rev. R. S. Hawker* (d. 1875), whose Cornish ballads should be familiar to all visitors to this iron-bound coast (see the interesting *Life* of him, by the *Rev. S. Baring-Gould;* also *Hawker's* 'Footprints of Former Men in Cornwall'). The church of Morwenstow is a most interesting building, said to have been originally founded by *St. Morwenna*, a Welsh princess of the 5th century. The oldest parts of the present structure are Norman. Over the door of the vicarage is a curious rhymed inscripton. A little to the S. is *Tonacombe*, a fine example of a manor-house of the 16th century. — On the coast, just to the N. of Morwenstow, is the lofty *Hennacliff*, whence the walk may be prolonged to (7 M.) *Hartland Quay* and ($2^1/_2$ M.) *Hartland Point* (see p. 159).

The road from Bude to Bideford passes ($1^1/_2$ M.) **Stratton** *(Tree Inn)*, a little to the N. W. of which is *Stamford Hill*, where Sir Beville Grenville (tomb in Kilkhampton Church) defeated the

Parliamentarians in 1643. One of the curious inclined planes on the *Bude & Holsworthy Canal* (p. 135) is within 1½ M. (S. E.) of Stratton. — About 3½ M. beyond Stratton we reach **Kilkhampton** *(Inn)*, with a partly Norman, partly Perp. **Church*, containing some fine carved benches. The halfway house is *West Country Inn*, 5½ M. farther on. At (4½ M.) *Clovelly Cross*, 16 M. from Bude, the coach is met by a waggonette, which receives passengers for (1½ M.) Clovelly (no extra charge).

Those who prefer to walk should take the second turning to the right, following the telegraph wires, and so reach the New Road Gate (see below) and the village. Carriages cannot go farther than the New Road Gate, and luggage is taken thence to the village on sledges or on donkey-back.

Clovelly (**New Inn*, halfway down the street, R. & A. 3*s.*, table d'hôte 3*s.* 6*d.*; **Red Lion*, small, at the pier, R. & A. 3*s.*), decidedly the quaintest and perhaps the most beautiful little village in all Devon, lies in a narrow and richly-wooded combe, descending abruptly to the sea. It consists of one main street, or rather a main staircase, with a few houses climbing on each side of the combe so far as the narrow space allows. The houses, each standing on a higher or lower level than its neighbour, are all whitewashed, with gay green doors and lattices, and the general effect is curiously foreign-looking, though, perhaps, Amalfi is almost the only foreign parallel that can be suggested. Clovelly is a Paradise for artists, and exquisite subjects for sketches present themselves at every corner. One of the most characteristic views is that looking down the main street, with the sea far below and in the background. The views from the quaint little pier and (better still) from the sea, with the pier in the foreground, are also very striking. The foundations of the cottages at the lower end of the village are hewn out of the living rock. The New Inn, which contains an interesting collection of china, is often full in summer and it is advisable to telegraph for rooms beforehand. Otherwise visitors may have to put up with the clean but lowly accommodation of a fisherman's cottage.

The following is Dickens's description of this wonderful little village, taken from '*A Message by the Sea*'.

"'And a mighty sing'lar and pretty place it is, as ever I saw in all the days of my life', said Captain Jorgan, looking up at it. Captain Jorgan had to look high to look up at it, for the village was built sheer up the face of a steep and lofty cliff. There was no road in it, there was no wheeled vehicle in it, there was not a level yard in it. From the sea-beach to the cliff top, two irregular rows of white houses, placed opposite to one another, and twisting here and there, and there and here, rose like the sides of a long succession of stages of crooked ladders, and you climbed up the village or climbed down the village by the staves between, some six feet wide or so, and made of sharp irregular stones. The old pack-saddle, long laid aside in most parts of England as one of the appendages of its infancy, flourished here intact. Strings of pack-horses and pack-donkeys toiled slowly up the staves of the ladders, bearing fish and coal, and such other cargo as was unshipping at the pier from the dancing fleet of village boats, and from two or three little coasting traders. As the beasts of burden ascended laden, or descended light, they got so lost at intervals in the floating clouds of village smoke, that they seemed to dive down some of the village chimneys, and come to the surface again far off, high above others. No two houses in the village were alike in chimney, size, shape, door, window, gable, roof-tree, anything. The sides of the ladders were musical with water, running clear and bright. The staves were musical with the clattering feet of the pack-horses and pack-donkeys, and the voices of the fishermen urging them up, mingled with the voices of the fishermen's wives, and their many children. The pier was musical with the wash of the sea, the creaking of capstans and windlasses, and the airy fluttering of little vanes and sails. The rough sea-bleached boulders of which the pier was made, and the whiter boulders of the shore, were brown with drying nets. The red-brown cliffs, richly wooded to their extremest verge, had their softened and beautiful forms reflected in the bluest water, under the clear North Devonshire sky of a November day, without a cloud. The village itself was so steeped in autumnal foliage, from the houses giving on the pier, to the topmost round of the topmost ladder, that one might have fancied it was out a-bird's-nesting, and was (as indeed it was) a wonderful climber".

Clovelly, being the only harbour in Bideford Bay, W. of the Taw, has long been an important herring-fishing place. Its name occurs in Domesday, and some authorities even maintain that there was a Roman station here and that the name is a corruption of 'Clausa Vallis'.

After familiarising himself with the quaint beauties of Clovelly, not forgetting to explore the 'back-staircases', the tourist makes his way to the ***Hobby Drive,** an avenue 3 M. in length, affording at intervals charming views of land and sea, including the coast of South Wales (adm. 4*d*., weekly ticket 1*s*.; carr. 1*s*., with two horses 1*s*. 6*d*.; closed on Sun.). We enter the drive by the New Road Gate (p. 157) and emerge at the other end on the Bideford road, near the 8th milestone from Bideford. We may vary the route in returning by following this road to (3/4 M.) *Clovelly Cross* (p. 157), and visiting the adjacent circular earth-works known as *Clovelly Dikes* or *Ditchen Hills* (extensive view).

Hobby Drive belongs to the owner of *Clovelly Court*, the grounds immediately surrounding which are entered by *Yellery Gate*, opposite the New Road Gate and a little farther to the W. (adm. 6*d*.; closed on Tues. and Sat., but open free on Sun.). The walk along the seaward side of the park to (1 1/4 M.) *Gallantry Bower* (390 ft.), affords, perhaps, the most perfect combination of sea and woodland scenery in England. The *View from the lofty bluff is magnificent. From Gallantry Bower we descend to (1/2 M.) **Mouth Mill*, a romantic, rock-strewn little cove at the end of a wooded combe, through which we may return to the road a little to the W. of Clovelly. Perhaps the best plan is to take the higher of the two tracks on the E. side of the cove; this leads back through part of the grounds of Clovelly Court (fine trees) and brings us out (bending to the left) on a road near the house and church. But we can scarcely go wrong in following the general direction of the stream. The whole round is about 5 M.

In calm weather Mouth Mill may be reached by small boat (about 2*s*. 6*d*.), an excursion which reveals Gallantry Bower to full advantage.

Those who are equal to a very rough and uncomfortable walk may at low water scramble along the shingle to the E. of Clovelly as far as (2½ M.) *Bucks Mill*, whence a lane ascends to the Bideford Road. On the way we pass a curious natural archway of rock and one or two small waterfalls descending from the cliffs (apt to disappear in dry weather), the first of which is the Freshwater of 'Westward Ho!' (chap. v.). According to a local tradition the inhabitants of Bucks are the descendants of ship-wrecked Spaniards.

The road running due W. from Clovelly Cross leads to (4 M.) Hartland Town *(King's Arms)*, and thence to (2 M.) *Stoke* and (1 M.) *Hartland Quay*. [A mail-brake runs daily from Clovelly to Hartland Town; fare 1*s*.] The church at Stoke, sometimes called the 'Cathedral of North Devon', is a handsome edifice with a lofty Perpendicular tower and a fine rood-screen. *Hartland Abbey*, ½ M. to the N. E. of Stoke, is a modern mansion, built on the site of an Augustine monastery and incorporating some remains of the E.E. cloisters. The cliff-scenery at *Hartland Point*, the extreme N.W. angle of Devon, 2 M. to the N. of Hartland Quay and 4 M. by road from Hartland Town, is very imposing. There is a lighthouse here. A pleasant drive may also be made to *Blackmouth Mill*, on the coast ¾ M. to the N. of Hartland Quay, by a private road through the grounds of Hartland Abbey (permission obtained at the King's Arms).

Clovelly is the nearest point for a visit to (17 M.) Lundy † (sailing-boat 20-30*s*.), which should not be attempted except in calm weather, Mail-skiff from Instow, see p. 160; steamer from Ilfracombe, see p. 161. The island, which was formerly a great resort of pirates and smugglers. is 3½ M. long and ½-¾ M. broad. It belongs to a family named Heaven, and contains about threescore inhab., who occupy themselves in farming and in the lobster and other fisheries. A walk round the island reveals much fantastic rock scenery, to many points of which appropriate names have been given. Probably the best-known is the towering *Shutter Rock* at the S. end of the island, which plays a prominent part in one of the most powerful scenes in 'Westward Ho!' (chap. XXXII). A good view is obtained from the top of the *Lighthouse*, about 2½ M. from the Shutter.

In summer Clovelly is frequently visited by an excursion-steamer from Ilfracombe, by which some may prefer to continue their journey; but it is not convenient for the transport of luggage, as passengers embark in small boats. — Besides the tri-weekly coach from Bude, passing Clovelly Cross, Clovelly has daily direct communication with (11 M.) *Bideford* by a mail-brake (fare 3*s*.), starting from New Road Gate.

From Clovelly to Bideford. For this part of the route even pedestrians may follow the road; but whether walking or driving the traveller should go by the lovely *Hobby Drive* (p. 158) for the first 3 M. The mail-brake takes this route in summer, and it is as easy to catch the Bude coach at the London Lodge of the Hobby as at Clovelly Cross. The road for 5 M. or so beyond the Hobby Gate lacks interest, though relieved by views of the sea. It passes the hamlets of *West* and *East Bucks* (comp. above). Refreshments may be obtained at the *Hoops Inn*, halfway between Clovelly and Bideford. Beyond (2 M.) *Fairy Cross* and (¾ M.) *Ford* the road becomes pleasantly shaded. Those who have time should diverge to the left at a point about 1 M. beyond Ford and follow the somewhat longer road viâ *Abbotsham*, a village with a small but interesting church. As we approach Bideford we have a view to the left of the estuary of the *Taw*.

Bideford (*Royal*, new, on the right bank of the river, near the station; *New Inn*, in the highest part of the town, with view; *Tan-*

† 'Island' is a pleonasm, as the 'y', *i. e.* 'ey', in Lundy means island.

ton's, on the river, near the bridge; *Newfoundland*, unpretending; *Rail. Buffet*), a small but busy port and fishing-town, is pleasantly situated on the *Torridge*, about 3 M. above its estuary. The 'little white town of Bideford' (pron. 'Biddyford'), well known from the description in 'Westward Ho!', contains little to arrest the tourist; but before leaving it he should ascend to (1/4 hr.) *Chudleigh's Fort* for the sake of the view. We cross the long bridge (24 arches), originally built in the 14th cent. but afterwards widened, and ascend past the station, soon turning to the left and passing through a farm-gate (2*d.*). The fort, a small modern earthwork on the site of an earlier fortification, commands an extensive view up and down the Torridge.

Omnibuses (fare 1*s.*) and mail-brakes (6*d.*) run daily from Bideford Station to **Westward Ho** (*Royal Hotel; Pebble Ridge Hotel*), a rising little watering-place, 2½ M. to the N.W., named from Kingsley's well-known novel. To the N. are the *Northam Burrows*, one of the best golfing-grounds in England. They are separated from the sea by the *Pebble Ridge*, resembling Chesil Bank at Portland (p. 98). — Still farther to the N. (2½ M.), at the point where the Torridge flows into the estuary of the *Taw*, lies **Appledore** (*Inn*), the busy little foreport of Bideford.

From Bideford to Torrington, 5 M., railway in 12 min., passing (left) *Wear Gifford*, a village with a Perp. church and a 15th cent. manor-house (fine hall). Near Bideford lies **Torrington** (*Globe*), a small and ancient town, where General Fairfax won a decisive battle over the Royalists in 1646.

From Bideford to *Barnstaple* and *Ilfracombe*, see R. 20.

20. From Bideford to Barnstaple and Ilfracombe.

24 M. Railway in 1¼-1¾ hr. (fares 4*s.* 6*d.*, 3*s.*, 1*s.* 11½*d.*).

Bideford, see above. The train descends the E. bank of the Torridge to (3 M.) *Instow Quay* (Marine Inn), a small watering-place and port at the mouth of the river, opposite Appledore (see above). A mail-skiff plies hence every alternate Thurs. to *Lundy* (p. 159; fare 5*s.*, return 7*s.* 6*d.*). — The train now turns to the right and ascends the S. bank of the estuary of the *Taw*. 6 M. *Fremington.*

9 M. **Barnstaple** (*Golden Lion; Fortescue Arms; Rail. Rfmt. Rooms*), locally *Barum*, a thriving and well-built town with 12,500 inhab., is situated on the N. bank of the Taw, about 8 M. from the sea. It was an important seaport at an early period in English history, and still carries on a considerable trade. It possesses three railway-stations, all connected with each other: *Barnstaple Junction (L. S. W. R.)*, for London viâ Exeter and Salisbury, and for Bideford and Ilfracombe; *Barnstaple (G. W. R.)*, 3/4 M. from the first, for London viâ Taunton and Bristol, and for Ilfracombe; and *Barnstaple Town Station*, 1/2 M. from the first, on the N. side of the Taw. The only buildings of interest in the town are the *Parish Church*, dating in part from the 14th cent., but freely restored; the *Grammar School*, formerly *St. Anne's Chapel; Queen Anne's Walk*, a colonnade of last century; and the new *Literary Institute*. There is also an interesting church at *Pilton*, 1/2 M. to the N., and another at

(4 M.) *Swimbridge*, a station on the railway to Taunton (p. 128). A pleasant *Promenade* skirts the river on the E. side of the town, and the *Rock Park* may also be mentioned.

From Barnstaple to *Taunton*, see p. 128; to *Exeter*, see p. 105. — Coaches also run from Barnstaple to (18 M.) *Lynton* (fare 5*s*.).

The Ilfracombe train crosses the Taw to the *Town Station* (see p. 160), and runs along the N. bank of the river. It then turns to the right (N.) and stops at (14 M.) *Wrafton* and (15 M.) *Braunton*, the church of which has an E.E. chancel, a Perp. tower, and some good carved pews. *Braunton Burrows* lie to the S.W. — 21 M. *Morthoe & Lee* (Fortescue Inn). The village of *Morthoe* (see p. 162) lies 2 M. to the W., and *Lee* (p. 162) about the same distance to the N. The train then descends the E. side of the *Slade Valley* to —

24 M. **Ilfracombe.** — **Hotels.** Ilfracombe Hotel, an extensive building facing the sea, with large swimming and other baths, etc., R. & A. from 4*s*., table d'hôte B. 2*s*. 6*d*., D. 5*s*., 'pens'. in winter 3*l*. 3*s*. per week; *Royal Clarence, High St., R. & A. from 3*s*. 6*d*., table d'hôte D. 4*s*. 6*d*., table d'hôte B. 2*s*. 6*d*.; *Belgrave Private Hotel, near the Ilfracombe Hotel; Britannia, at the Pier; Queen's, Great Western, Victoria, all in High St. — Hotel and railway omnibuses meet the principal trains.

Cabs. With 1 horse (for 1-2 pers.) 1*s*. per mile; each addit. 1/2 M. 6*d*.; each addit. pers. 3*d*.; with 2 horses 1*s*. 6*d*., 9*d*., 6*d*.; by time (1-4 pers.) 2*s*. 6*d*. per hr. and 1*s*. each addit. 1/2 hr. for one-horse cabs; 3*s*. 9*d*. and 1*s*. 6*d*. for two-horse cabs. To *Watermouth Castle* and back (1-4 pers.) 4*s*., with stay of 1 hr. 5*s*.; to *Lee Beach* and back, with stay of 1 hr., 1-2 pers. 6*s*., 3-4 pers. 7*s*.; to *Morthoe Church* and back (1-4 pers.), with 2 hrs. stay, 8*s*.; to *Combe Martin*, with stay of 1 hr., 7*s*. Donkey-carriages, 1/2 M. 6*d*., 1 M. 8*d*., each addit. 1/2 M. 4*d*.; per hr. 1*s*., each addit. 1/2 hr. 6*d*. (bargaining desirable for the longer excursions, to the Downs, etc.).

Sailing Boats per hr. for 1-5 pers. 2*s*. 6*d*., each addit. pers. 6*d*. — **Rowing Boats** 10*s*. 6*d*. per day, 1*s*. 6*d*. per hr. (1-4 pers.), each pers. beyond four 6*d*. extra. Boat to or from a steamer 3*d*. each pers.

Steamers ply regularly to *Swansea* (6*s*., 4*s*.) and *Bristol*, and excursion-steamers also ply occasionally to *Clovelly* (return-fares 4*s*. 6*d*., 3*s*.), *Lundy* (4*s*. 6*d*., 3*s*.), and *Lynmouth* (single 2*s*. 6*d*., return 3*s*. 6*d*.).

Coach to *Lynton*, see p. 166.

Bathing Coves for ladies and gentlemen in *Wildersmouth Bay*, below the Tor Walks and approached by tunnels through the rock.

Ilfracombe, picturesquely situated at the mouth of the Bristol Channel, is one of the most fashionable watering-places in Devon, with about 7000 residents. Its chief attractions are its fine air (which, *teste* Charles Kingsley, 'combines the soft warmth of South Devon with the bracing freshness of the Welsh mountains'), the picturesque rock-bound coast, and the numerous pleasant excursions that may be made in all directions. Formerly it was a seaport of some consideration, and it contributed six vessels to the English fleet at a time (14th cent.) when Liverpool sent only one.

The only building calling for mention is the prominently-situated *Parish Church*, a Perp. structure with Norman and E.E. features. Two memorial stones outside the S. aisle of the chancel record the names of seven local centenarians. — The top of *Capstone Hill* (180 ft.), the conical turf-clad bluff to the E. of Wildersmouth Bay, commands an excellent view of the town. At its foot is the

For a coloured map of The Coast of North Devon see page 570

Victoria Promenade, a covered arcade where a band plays and concerts are given. To the E., on the outer side of the harbour, is *Lantern Hill*, a similar knoll, crowned with the ruins of an ancient chapel, now converted into a harbour-light. A pleasant walk may also be enjoyed on the *Pier* (1*d.*), after which we may skirt the S. side of the harbour to *Rapparee Cove* and ascend the lofty *Helesborough* (450 ft.; extensive view; donkey nearly to the top, 1*s.*).

The most frequented resort near Ilfracombe is the ***Tor Walks,** a promenade running along the seaward side of the hills to the W. of the town, and almost challenging comparison with the Great Orme Drive at Llandudno (p. 282). The entrance (adm. 1*d.*) is near the *Baths*, Northfield Road. From the middle of the Tor Walks we may descend to the pretty little *White Pebble Bay*, on the W. side of *Tor Point*. By climbing the fence at the end of the Tor Walks and keeping to the left (inland) across the downs, we can join the path to Lee described below.

Environs. Walk to Lee and Morthoe, 5-6 M. Starting from High St. we follow Church St. and proceed in a straight direction, passing to the left of the church, to a narrow lane ascending to the open cliffs *(Lee Downs)*. Or we may ascend Church Hill, pass to the right of the church, and climb a zigzag path, at the top of which we turn to the left and soon reach the above-mentioned lane (to the right). The walk along the Downs to (2½ M.) *Lee* is very pleasant. A little way down the descent to Lee Beach we pass a stile and notice-board on the left, indicating the nearest way to **Lee Hotel*, which lies in the valley about ½ M. from the sea. We may return from Lee by the road, which passes through *Slade Valley*. — Those who wish to prolong the walk to Morthoe ascend the steep track to the W. of Lee Beach, and soon reach (½ M.) a sign-post pointing the way on the left to (2 M.) Morthoe station (p. 161). We keep straight on, however, and pass through two gates, beyond the second of which is a sign-post showing the way to Bull Point. At the gate which we next pass we descend to the left along the hedgerow and soon strike the path again. On crossing the brook at the bottom of the combe we take the higher path, ascending to the left, which soon brings us to the (1 M.) road, close to a white gate. To visit (½ M.) *Bull Point Lighthouse* we pass through this gate, to which we have to return in any case to pursue our route to Morthoe. For the latter we follow the road towards the left, passing through several other gates, to (1½ M.) **Morthoe** *(Chichester Inn)*, with an E.E. church (restored), containing the interesting tomb of William de Tracey (1322), generally confounded with Thomas Becket's murderer (see pp. 28, 130). About ½ M. farther on is *Barracane Bay*, the beach of which is composed almost wholly of shell-debris; and adjoining this on the W. are the extensive sands of *Wollacombe Bay*. (Donkey from Barracane Bay to Morthoe 3-6*d.*; seat in a vehicle from Morthoe to Morthoe station 6*d.*) About 1 M. due W. of Morthoe is *Morte Point*, a savage rocky promontory that does not belie its name, commanding a fine view. It is reached by passing across the land of a farmer who charges 2*d.* for the privilege. There is a local saying to the effect that 'Morte is the place on earth which Heaven made last and the Devil will take first'. We may now return to Ilfracombe by coast, road, or railway (see p. 161).

Another popular short walk is to *Two Pots* (730 ft.), 2½ M. to the S. We may go by the old Barnstaple road along the ridge, leading S. from Church St., and return by the new road through the valley.

A third favourite excursion is the walk or drive to (4¾ M.) *Combe Martin*, which is described below as part of the charming route to Lynton and Lynmouth (R. 21). *Hele*, *Berry Narbor*, and *Watermouth*, see below. Excursions may also be made to *Chambercombe*, to (7 M.) *Braunton* and *Braunton Burrows* (p. 161), to (6 M.) *Georgeham*, *Bideford*, *Barnstaple* (coach viâ Braunton 3*s*., return-fare 4*s*. 6*d*.), etc.

No one should leave Ilfracombe on his return towards the E. without having seen *Clovelly* (p. 157).

21. From Ilfracombe to Lynton (Lynmouth) and Minehead.

Comp. Map, p. 160.

37 M. This route may be accomplished either by road or by cliff-path along the coast. All tolerable pedestrians are strongly advised to choose the latter, which is one of the most charming walks in England. In either case the journey should be broken for at least a night or two at *Lynton* or *Lynmouth* (p. 166). — During summer Coaches ply daily from Ilfracombe to (17 M.) *Lynton* (fare 4-5*s*.; return 7*s*.), and from Lynton to (20 M.) *Minehead* (6*s*. 6*d*.); and it is possible to make the entire journey in one day. Walkers may obtain night-quarters at *Combe Martin*, *Hunter's Inn*, *Lynton*, and *Porlock*.

a. By Road.

We leave Ilfracombe by Larkstone Terrace and skirt the S. base of *Helesborough* (p. 162) to (1½ M.) *Hele*, below which, to the left, is the pretty little *Hele Bay*. The old road to Lynton here diverges to the right, passing (2 M.) *Berry Narbor*, the birthplace of *Bishop Jewell* (1522-71), a village with a Perp. church and an old manor-house (now a farm), and rejoins the new road at (1½ M.) Combe Martin (see below). We continue to follow the coast-road. 1¼ M. (2¾ M. from Ilfracombe) *Watermouth*, a picturesque little harbour, with a large modern castle. By crossing a small stone bridge to the left we may visit the *Smallmouth Caves*, in a rocky little glen descending to the sea. Opposite the castle is an iron gate admitting to a path by which the foot-passenger may cut off about ½ M. After about 1 M. more we reach *Sandabay*, and ½ M. farther we find ourselves at the seaward end of the long village of **Combe Martin** *(King's Arms)*, which stretches inland for a distance of 1¼ M. The church, partly E.E. and partly Perp., has a beautiful Perp. tower, 100 ft. high. The hill to the left is named the *Little Hangman* (755 ft.); and beyond it, farther to the E., is the *Great Hangman* or *Gurt Down* (1080 ft.). At the end of Combe Martin a rough cross-country road diverges to the left to Trentishoe (p. 165) and so to Lynton, but the coach-road ascends to the right (inland), affording good retrospects of the coast. At (4¼ M.) *Blackmore Gate* (formerly a toll-bar) we turn to the left and descend to (1¾ M.) *Parracombe* (Inn), 6 M. from Lynton, beyond which we again ascend and soon obtain a view of the sea near Heddon's Mouth. The last part of the route descends through the valley of the *West Lyn*, which beyond (4 M.) *Barbrook Mill* is very picturesque. From (¾ M.) *Lyn Bridge* (Inn) the descent to Lynton is rather steep. At the (¾ M.) fork those bound for *Lynton* (p. 166) keep to the left, while those for *Lynmouth* (p. 166) descend to the right.

To continue our journey to Minehead we cross the bridge at *Lynmouth* and ascend the long and steep hill (fine retrospects) to the right to (2 M.) *Countisbury* (Blue Ball Inn). About halfway up, a path on the left diverges to *Sillery Sands*.

Beyond Countisbury the road skirts the N. margin of **Exmoor Forest**, a tract of hilly moorland, about 30 sq. M. in extent, and in many respects resembling a miniature Dartmoor (see p. 137), though the granite tors of the latter are here replaced by the less rugged outlines of slate and sandstone formations. It is known for its ponies, of which the genuine breed is now rare, its red cattle, and its sheep. It is the only part of England where the red deer still occurs in a wild state, and the Exmoor stag-hounds attract numerous visitors (comp. p. 128). Good fishing is afforded by the numerous streamlets traversing the Forest. The highest point of Exmoor is *Dunkery Beacon* (1707 ft.; p. 164), and many of its other hills attain an elevation of 1200-1600 ft. For excursions into or across Exmoor, see pp. 167, 168.

About 1 M. from Countisbury a road on the right descends to the valley of the *Brendon* (p. 167). To the left we have fine views over the Bristol Channel, with the Welsh coast in the background. Farther on we pass, on the left, the *Old Barrow* (1135 ft.) and the entrance to *Glenthorne* (p. 168; seen below, to the left), and then at ($2^1/_2$ M.) *County Gate* (1060 ft.) we leave Devon and enter Somerset. To the right are *Malmsmead* and the *Badgeworthy Glen* (p. 167). A road on the same side diverges to ($^1/_2$ M.) *Oare Church* and the *Exmoor Kennels* (seen below, to the right). On the right, $3^1/_2$ M. farther on, a road diverges to *Oareford*, and at the so-called (1 M.) *White Stones* another on the same side leads to (5 M.) *Exford* (White Horse), an angling resort on the *Exe*. The old road to West Porlock and Porlock (good views) diverges to the left about $^1/_4$ M. farther on, while the easier but less attractive new road leads in a straight direction to ($2^1/_2$ M.; 13 M. from Lynmouth) —

Porlock *(Lorna Doone; *Ship*, unpretending; *Castle)*, a picturesque little village about $^1/_2$ M. from the sea, between *Porlock Hill* and *Bossington Beacon.* About 1 M. to the W., on the old road, is *West Porlock*, and $^1/_2$ M. beyond it, on the coast, is the little harbour of *Porlock Weir* (*Anchor Inn).

Porlock is the best starting-point for an ascent (2-3 hrs.) of **Dunkery Beacon** (1707 ft.), which rises about 4 M. to the S. Driving is practicable, viâ *Luckham*, to a point within easy reach of the top, but the best pedestrian route is by *Horner Woods* and *Cloutsham.* The summit, which is marked by a cairn, commands an extensive view, including Brown Willy (p. 153), Dartmoor, the Bristol Channel, and the S. Welsh coast. — The descent may be made on the S.W. side to ($3^1/_2$ M.) *Exford* (see above), whence we may go on to ($4^1/_2$ M.) *Simonsbath* (p. 168).

Beyond Porlock the road leads somewhat circuitously to (2 M.) *Holnicote*, where it skirts the park of Sir Thomas Acland (to the right). The coach goes straight on to ($4^1/_2$ M.) Minehead, but carriages should diverge to the left and follow the much prettier road through *Selworthy Green.* The two roads reunite at a point about $2^1/_2$ M. from *Minehead* (see p. 168).

b. By the Coast.

As far as ($4^1/_4$ M.) *Combe Martin* this route coincides with that just described. Instead, however, of traversing the whole length of this village, we turn to the left at the fountain, nearly opposite the King's Arms Hotel and ascend towards *Holstone Down* (1185 ft.). [We may, however, go on to the end of the village before turning to the left. The roads unite on the top of the Down, and sign-posts keep us right.] The steep ascent from *Combe Martin* is the worst bit of the walk, and the view is limited. After about 2 M., however, we reach the top of the moor, beyond which we have easy walking and views of increasing attractiveness. As we descend to (3 M.; 5 M. from Combe Martin) *Trentishoe*, we have a good view of the sea in front of us. From Trentishoe we descend rapidly to a beautifully-wooded little combe, through which we proceed to ($^3/_4$ M.) **Hunter's Inn* (unpretending), charmingly situated in a valley about 1 M. from the sea (angling-ticket 1*s.* per day). From this point we may go on to (5 M.) Lynton by road, joining the coach-road (p. 163) after 3 M. Walkers, however, turn to the left and follow the path along the side of the combe in which the inn lies. This is finely wooded at first, but changes its character completely before reaching the sea at (1 M.) **Heddon's Mouth*, where the scene is one of singular wildness. From Heddon's Mouth a path has been cut along the cliffs to ($1^1/_2$ M.) **Wooda Bay*, one of the finest walks in England. Here our path merges in a cart-track, and at the fork we take the lower branch to the left, soon, however, again ascending. Beyond Wooda Bay we reach *Lee Bay*, and at its farther side we pass through ($1^1/_2$ M.) a gate opening on a private road across the grounds of *Lee Abbey*, a modern mansion, which we pass on the left.

The promontory to the N. of the Abbey is called ***Duty Point**, and permission to visit it may be obtained at the house. A legend relates that a lady of the family of Whichchalse, the former owners of Lee Abbey, here put an end to her grief by throwing herself into the sea. — To continue our walk to Lynton we need not return to the Abbey, but may make our way along the cliffs to the Valley of Rocks (see below).

We leave Lee Abbey grounds by another lodge-gate and enter the so-called ($^1/_2$ M.) ***Valley of Rocks**, with the *Castle Rock* (good view from the top) to the left and the *Cheesewring* to the right. The road through the valley leads to ($1^1/_2$ M.) Lynton, but it is better to follow the cliff-path (the **North Walk*), which diverges to the left and leads round the rocky mass known as *Ragged Jack*, beyond the Castle Rock. This path brings us out about halfway between Lynmouth and Lynton, the one lying below us to the left and the other above us to the right.

Continuation of the route to Minehead, see p. 168.

Lynton and **Lynmouth.** — **Hotels** at *Lynton:* *Valley of Rocks, table d'hôte 5*s.*, R. & A. 4*s.* 6*d.*; *Castle, R. & A. 4*s.* 6*d.*, D. 4*s.* 6*d.*, these two with fine views; Lynton Cottage, an annexe of the Castle, in pretty grounds; Crown. — At *Lynmouth:* Bath, well spoken of; Lyndale Hotel, R. & A. 3*s.* 6*d.*, table d'hôte B. 2*s.*, D. 3*s.*; *Tors Park Hotel, a dépendance of the last, on a hill overlooking the sea, R. 2*s.* 6*d.*, D. 3*s.*; Lynmouth Private Hotel, with restaurant.

A **Cliff Railway** (gradient 1 : 1¾), opened in 1890, now connects Lynmouth and Lynton, beginning near the pier and ending near the Valley of Rocks Hotel (½ min.; return-fare 4*d.*). The railway is worked by water-power, and the cars are drawn by steel ropes.

Lynton and *Lynmouth*, though actually as well as nominally distinct, are in so many ways complementary to each other that it would be inconvenient to treat of them separately. Lynmouth, one of the loveliest villages in England, lies below, at the mouth of the *East Lyn* and *West Lyn*, two little streams which unite their waters just before reaching the sea. Lynton stands 400 ft. higher, at the top of the steep cliff enclosing the narrow little valley. Lynmouth has the advantage of being close to the sea (though the bathing is not good), and is the natural starting-point for many of the pleasantest valley-excursions. Lynton, on the other hand, enjoys finer views and a much more open and bracing situation. There is a small pier at Lynmouth, with a tower at the end of it; it commands a good view of the place.

Shelley stayed at Lynmouth for some time in 1812, soon after his marriage with Harriet Westbrook. The 'myrtle-twined' cottage he occupied was the last on the left, looking towards the sea; but it has been rebuilt since his time.

The streams near Lynmouth afford excellent trout, salmon-peel, and salmon fishing. Tickets are issued for various districts at charges ranging from 1*s.* for a day to 30-40*s.* for the season (information at the hotels).

The prettiest way from Lynton to Lynmouth, or vice versâ (about ½ M.), is through the grounds of the Lynton Cottage Hotel. Close to the Lyndale Hotel is the gate of **Glenlyn* (adm. 6*d.*; 1-3 pers. 1*s.*; closed on Sun.), in the grounds of which is a pretty walk (½ M.) along the lower course of the *West Lyn*. The mingled rock, wood, and water scenery recalls the Torrent Walk at Dolgelley (p. 298). — Perhaps the best view of the two villages and their immediate surroundings is obtained from *Summerhouse Hill* or *Lyn Cliff*, 'eight hundred feet of upright wall, which seem ready to topple down into the nest of be-myrtled cottages at its foot'; the top is reached in ½ hr. by a path ascending from Lynmouth.

Excursions from Lynmouth and Lynton.

1. To Watersmeet, Rockford, and the Doone Valley, 10 M. We leave Lynmouth by the road leading to the E., between the Lyndale Hotel and a chapel, and beyond the last house take the path to the left. This soon brings us to (½ M.) a small bridge over the *East Lyn*, which we cross. We then follow the path on the right bank of the stream, which

here runs through a narrow and richly wooded glen, with lofty wood-clad or rocky hills on either side (fine views). After about 1¼ M. we cross the river by a stone bridge, and in ¼ M. more reach a wooden bridge, just below the confluence of the East Lyn and *Combe Park Water*, which is known as the ***Watersmeet.** The best plan is to continue to ascend on the left bank as far as the actual junction (just opposite a cottage-villa on the other side) and pursue the path a few yards farther to the rustic bridge over the Coombe Park stream. [Those who do not wish to walk farther may now return to Lynmouth by the road, on the left bank.] We then retrace our steps to the wooden bridge mentioned above, cross to the right bank of the E. Lyn, and follow the path, which continues to ascend the stream, passing at the back of the above-mentioned cottage. Farther on, the path runs high above the river, passes through *Nutcombe Wood*, crosses an open hillside, and re-enters the woods by a wooden gate. A little farther on, a path diverges to the right to the so-called **Long Pool*, a dark and gloomy stretch of the river, at the end of which is a small waterfall. Returning to the main path we soon reach a bridge crossing to (2 M. from Watersmeet) *Rockford* (Inn). We now follow the road, also leading along the left bank of the East Lyn, or, as it is here called, *Brendon Water*, to (1 M.) *Millslade* (Abbey Inn). The walking part of the excursion may be conveniently shortened by hiring a pony-carriage (either at the inn or at a house at the other end of the village) from Millslade to Malmsmead and back (5*s.*; to Malmsmead, and back to Lynmouth 8*s.*; waiting at Malmsmead included). — As we leave Millslade the road from Countisbury (see p. 164) joins ours on the left, while opposite begins the direct pedestrian route over the moors to the (2¾ M.) Doone Valley. 2 M. *Malmsmead* consists of a group of two or three small farmhouses, at which tea and plain refreshments may be obtained. Carriages must be left here and the rest of the way pursued on foot. We ascend the valley of the *Badgeworthy Water* by a cart-track for about ½ M., and then follow a footpath which runs along the stream. After about ½ M. more a stream descending from the right into the Badgeworthy Water is said to be that which suggested the 'Waterslide' in Mr. Blackmore's well-known novel. Readers of 'Lorna Doone' will be disappointed if they expect to find a close resemblance between the descriptions of the book and the actual facts of nature. The 'Waterslide' is a very mild edition of the one up which little John Ridd struggled so painfully; and the ***Doone Valley** itself, instead of being defended by a 'fence of sheer rock' and approached by 'three rough arches, jagged, black, and terrible', is enclosed by rounded though somewhat bleak moorland hills. The home of the Doones is a side-valley opening to the right about ½ M. beyond the Waterslide; and remains of the foundations of their huts may be observed on each side of the mound which divides it into two branches. Towards the close of the 17th cent. this valley was the stronghold of the Doones, a band of outlaws, who lived here, like a Highland clan on the Lowland borders, by levying black-mail on the country round. The tradition of their terrible strength and cruelty is said to linger still in the neighbourhood; particularly the story of their fiendish cruelty in wantonly murdering a sleeping infant, an act which finally roused the country to exterminate the entire nest of vipers. But see 'Lorna Doone'.

By the direct road-route viâ Countisbury (comp. p. 164), Millslade, and Malmsmead, the Doone Valley is 8½ M. from Lynmouth, and walkers may make it 1 M. shorter by passing direct from Millslade over the moor to Badgeworthy (see above). We may now return by any of the routes above indicated; or we may farther vary the route by following the road from Rockford (see above) to (½ M.) *Brendon Church* and (¾ M.) *Ilford Bridges*, near *Combe Park Gate*. We are here about 2½ M. from Lynton or Lynmouth. The road straight on leads to *Lyn Bridge* (p. 163) and *Lynton;* that to the right descends by the Combe Park Water to a point above the *Watersmeet* (see above) and so to *Lynmouth*. *Summerhouse Hill* may be included by a digression from either road (sign-posts). — Walkers, who wish to see some of the wildest parts of Exmoor, may proceed to the W. over the hill between the Badgeworthy valley and the (3½ M.) *Chalk Water* valley and descend (left) along the latter stream to (1½ M.) *Careford* (p. 164), which is 2 M. by road (viâ *Oare*) from Malmsmead.

2. To Simonsbath, 10 M. For this excursion, which takes us into the heart of Exmoor, we may start from either Lynton or Lynmouth. From the former we proceed by *Lyn Bridge* to (2½ M.) *Ilford Bridges* (p. 167), while from the latter we reach the same point by the road by which we began our walk to Watersmeet. From Ilford Bridges we follow the road leading due S. (to the E. the road to Brendon, see above), and after ½ M. turn to the left, passing *Bridge Ball*. We next (¼ M.) turn to the right, beyond the gate of Brendon Parsonage, and thence follow the road which leads to the S., straight across Exmoor (p. 164), to (6½ M.) Simonsbath. The Forest proper is entered at (2½ M.) the so-called *Two Gates* (now one only), where we pass into Somerset. To the left is the head of the *Doone Valley* (p. 167); to the right rise *Chapman Barrows* (1570 ft.) and *Exe Head Hill*. About 1¼ M. farther on we cross the *Exe*. — 2½ M. **Simonsbath** *(Inn)*, on the *Barle*, is named from a pool a little higher up, which tradition connects with Sigismund, the dragon-slayer. From Simonsbath we go on (S.E.) by the *Tor Steps* to (16 M.) *Dulverton* (see p. 128) or (due S.) to (10 M.) *South Molton* (p. 128). The return-route to Lynmouth may be varied by proceeding to the E. to (4½ M.) *Exford*, and thence to the N. to (5 M.) the *White Stones* (p. 164; 10 M. from Lynmouth). — A coach plies from Lynmouth to *Dulverton* (p. 128; fare 6*s*. 6*d*.).

Other excursions which no visitor to Lynton-Lynmouth should fail to make are those to the (1 M.) *Valley of Rocks*, (1 M.) *Lee*, and (4 M.) *Heddon's Mouth*, and to (7 M.) *Glenthorne* by the cliff-path (see below). These should be preferred to the Simonsbath route. Short walks may be taken to (2 M.) *Countisbury* viâ the Tors, to *Hollardy Hill*, at the E. end of the *North Walk* (p. 165), to *Sillery Sands* (p. 164), etc.

Coaches to *Ilfracombe*, see p. 163; to *Minehead*, see p. 163; to *Barnstaple*, see p. 161. — Excursion Steamers ply in summer between *Lynmouth*, *Ilfracombe*, and *Bristol* (p. 113).

Continuation of Coast Route to Minehead. From Lynmouth to (2 M.) *Countisbury* we follow the road described at p. 164. Instead of continuing in a straight direction through the village, we turn to the left, pass to the right of the church, and follow an obvious cliff-path, affording lovely views. To the left is the promontory called the *Foreland*. This path ends after less than 1 M., near the edge of a wide and deep combe. We must choose our own line in crossing this, and perhaps the easiest, though not the shortest way, is to keep up the side of the combe to a point where it becomes a good deal shallower. On the other side of the combe we strike a cart-track, which we descend to the left (towards the sea) as far as a (½ M.) gate. Beyond this the cart-track continues to descend to *Countisbury Cove*, but we follow the higher path to the right. At the next fork we take the lower path and follow it, avoiding all divergences either up or down. After passing numerous combes, some wooded and some bare, we reach a small iron gate (4 M. from Countisbury), marking the entrance to the grounds of Glenthorne, and a little later the footpath passes through an archway and joins the avenue. This brings us in sight of (½ M.) ***Glenthorne House** (not shown), picturesquely situated on a small plateau overlooking the sea. Visitors are admitted to all parts of the beautiful little glen, and those who do not fear a small addition to the walk should follow part at least of the winding avenue leading to the road (3 M.; $1^1/_2$ M. only in a straight line).

In continuing our coast-walk from Glenthorne House we cross a small paddock, a road, and another field, and reach a gate leading into the woods, where the coast-path proper is resumed. At first it is sometimes not clear which of numerous diverging paths we should follow, but as a rule we avoid descending and keep to the right. In a short time we reach a deep wooded combe, which we have to ascend towards the right for a considerable distance (partly in zigzags) before we reach a feasible point for crossing. On the other side we descend to the left, and reach a cart-track leading to the right along the face of the cliffs, here mostly clothed with wood. We keep as much as possible at the same level, avoiding side-paths up and down, till we reach (4 M. from Glenthorne) *Culbone*, in a narrow little combe containing what is said to be the smallest church in England (33 ft. long and 12 ft. wide); refreshments at a cottage. Until lately pedestrians were allowed to continue their walk by a pleasant road leading through the grounds of *Ashley Combe*, the seat of Lord Lovelace, whose first wife was Lord Byron's daughter Ada (d. 1852). The house stands on an artificial plateau, with a tunnel below it. This road, however, is now closed, and we have to follow the old road, which runs a little lower down through the luxuriant woods here clothing the steep slopes descending to the sea. $1^1/_2$ M. *Porlock Weir* (*Anchor), $^1/_2$ M. beyond which are *West Porlock* and (1 M. farther) *Porlock* (p. 164). This is the end of the finest part of the coast walk, and the traveller will not lose much by completing his journey to ($6^1/_2$ M.) Minehead by coach (comp. p. 165). Those, however, who prefer to continue walking proceed N. E. from Porlock to (1 M.) *Bossington Beacon.* They then follow the top of the ridge, passing (1 M.) a cairn marking the highest part of *North Hill.* About 2 M. farther on they may diverge to the left to visit ($^1/_2$ M.) *Greenaley*, and make their way thence by the coast to ($1^1/_2$ M.) Minehead; or they may proceed to ($1^1/_2$ M.) Minehead direct along the ridge. *Minehead*, see p. 128.

22. From London to Gloucester and Hereford.

Valley of the Wye.

144 M. Great Western Railway in $4^1/_4$-$6^1/_2$ hrs. (fares 25*s.* 6*d.*, 19*s.* 3*d.*, 12*s.* $8^1/_2$*d.*; return 42*s.* 6*d.*, 32*s.* 3*d.*); to *Gloucester* (114 M.) in 3-$4^1/_4$ hrs. (fares 20*s.*, 15*s.*, 9*s.* 6*d.*; return 34*s.*, 26*s.*).

From London (Paddington) to ($77^1/_4$ M.) *Swindon*, see R. 15. The Gloucester line now runs towards the N.W. and passes (81 M.) *Purton* (p. liv) and ($85^1/_2$ M.) *Minety.* — 91 M. *Kemble Junction.*

From Kemble to Cirencester, $4^1/_2$ M., railway in 10-15 minutes. — **Cirencester** *(Fleece; King's Head)*, pronounced *Cisseter*, the *Corinium* of the Romans, is an ancient town with 8500 inhab., situated on the *Churn*, amid the *Cotswold Hills.* 'Our town of Cicester in Gloucestershire' is mentioned by Shakespeare (Richard II., v. 6). It possesses one of the chief wool-markets of England, and is also a hunting-centre of some reputation. The *Parish Church*, which has been carefully restored, is a handsome Perp. building; it has a chapel with a beautiful fan-vaulted roof, numerous brasses, and a tower 134 ft. high. The **Corinium Museum* contains a good collection of Roman antiquities found in the neighbourhood. About 1 M. to the S.W. of the town is the well-known *Royal Agricultural College*, A pleasant drive may be taken in *Oakley Park*, belonging to Earl Bathurst, an ancestor of whom ('who plants like Bathurst') was frequently the host of Alexander Pope; Swift also writes of his visits to Oakley. — About 3 M. to the W. is *Thames Head*, the reputed source of the Thames. — An omnibus runs from Cirencester to (8 M.) *Fairford* (p. 187; 1*s*. 6*d*.).

Another branch-line runs from Kemble Junction to (7 M.) *Tetbury* (White Hart).

We now enter Gloucestershire. Beyond the long *Sapperton Tunnel* we emerge in the picturesque valley of the *Stroudwater*. — 99 M. *Brimscombe*. — 102 M. **Stroud** *(Imperial; George; Railway)*, a cloth-manufacturing town with 7535 inhab., picturesquely situated on the side of a hill. — 105 M. *Stonehouse*, which is also a station on the Midland line from Bath to Gloucester (see p. 112). Beyond Stonehouse the line runs side by side with the Midland Railway for a short distance, and affords fine views to the left of the Welsh hills beyond the valley of the *Severn*. To the right rise the *Cotswolds*.

114 M. **Gloucester**. — **Hotels.** *BELL, Southgate St., R. & A. 4*s*.; SPREAD EAGLE, Foregate St.; NEW INN, Northgate (see p. 171); RAM, Southgate St.; WELLINGTON, opposite the stations; FOWLER'S TEMPERANCE. — *Railway Refreshment Rooms.*

American Consular Agent, *Mr. Charles E. Portlock.*

Cabs for 1-2 pers. 1*s*. per mile, each addit. pers. 6*d*.; per hour 2*s*. 6*d*. — **Tramways** traverse some of the principal streets.

Railway Stations. The stations of the *G. W. Railway* (for London, Hereford, Cheltenham, South Wales, etc.) and the *Mid. Railway* (for Cheltenham, Birmingham, Bristol, etc.) adjoin each other in Station Road.

Steamers (small and crowded) ply in summer to *Tewkesbury* (p. 182), calling near *Deerhurst* (p. 183), and through the ship-canal to *Sharpness* (p. 170).

Gloucester, a city and county of itself, the capital of Gloucestershire, and the see of a bishop (see p. 118), contains 36,550 inhab. and is pleasantly situated on the left bank of the *Severn*, on the site of the British *Caer Glowe* ('fair city') and the Roman *Glevum*. It carries on a considerable trade in agricultural produce and in the minerals of the *Forest of Dean* (p. 177) and also imports large quantities of corn and timber for Birmingham and the Midlands. Its trade is facilitated by the Gloucester and Berkeley Ship Canal, which joins the estuary of the Severn at *Sharpness*, 17 M. lower down, where the river is crossed by a bridge 3/4 M. long. The most outstanding event in the history of the city is the siege of 1643, when it successfully resisted the Royalists for a month and compelled them to retire. In consequence of this 'malignity' its fortifications were dismantled at the Restoration. The ground-plan of the Roman settlement is still preserved in the four main streets, which meet at right angles in the centre of the town and are named after the points of the compass (*Northgate*, *Southgate*, etc.).

The ***Cathedral** *(Holy Trinity)*, a very handsome and elaborately adorned building, occupies a site that has been consecrated to religious purposes since the 7th century. A nunnery was founded here by Wulphere, the first Christian king of Mercia, about 670, and was followed by a monastery (821), which was transferred from secular canons to Benedictine monks in 1022. In its present form the body of the church is the work of Abbot Serlo, at the end of the 11th cent.; but this Norman core was most skilfully altered and recased, chiefly in the 14th cent., and the general external appearance of the edifice is thoroughly Perpendicular. The interior of the *Nave*, the *Crypt*, and the *Chapter House* are Norman; the *Cloisters* date from 1351-1412; the *W. Façade* and the beautiful *S. Porch* were added in 1421-1437; the stately **Tower* (225 ft. high), with its beautiful tracery and pinnacles, and the *Lady Chapel* belong to the second half of the 15th century. The Cathedral suffered considerably in the Civil Wars, when the Parliamentarians are said to have stabled their horses in the cloisters (1641). The whole edifice has undergone a careful restoration under the superintendence of Sir G. G. Scott and Mr. Waller. The ogee arch is one of the leading features of the later work (14-15th cent.). The Cathedral is 420 ft. long and 144 ft. wide; height of nave 68 ft., of choir 86 ft. The nave is open free; the E. part, including the crypt, chapter-house, and cloisters, on payment of 6*d.*; the daily services are at 10.30 a. m. and 3 p. m. The church was raised to cathedral dignity in 1541, having previously been included in the diocese of Worcester. It is now associated with Bristol, the two chapters receiving the *congé d'élire* alternately (comp. p. 118). Comp. the handbook by *Waller* and the illustrated account by *Moore* (1*s.*).

Interior. With the exception of the two westernmost bays, the arches of the Nave are all Norman. The massive circular piers are unusually lofty (30½ ft.), while the triforium (perhaps in consequence of this) is very low (comp. p. xxxvii). The vaulting is E.E. (ca. 1240). Most of the stained glass is modern, but there are two ancient windows (easily distinguishable) in the N. aisle. In this aisle is a good monument to Mrs. Morley (d. 1784), by Flaxman; and there is a statue of *Dr. Jenner* (1749-1823), a native of the county (comp. p. 122), at the W. end of the nave. The Dec. tracery of the windows in the S. aisle dates from about 1318. — In the Transepts, we meet, according to Mr. Willis, the earliest known approach to the Perp. style, engrafted on the Norman frame-work. The vaulting under the tower is apparently supported by curious flying arches, which are perhaps unique. The reliquary in the N. transept is one of the few pieces of E.E. work in the church (13th cent.).

The *Choir, which begins one bay to the W. of the central tower, is a magnificent example of pure Perp. character. The form of the tracery, the elaborate vaulting, the panelled walls, the vast E. window, the rich stalls, taken all together, produce an effect unsurpassed perhaps by any other choir in England. Even the most unobservant visitor will see at a glance how the choir proper forms a kind of Perp. 'cage' inside the original Norman frame, the screen enclosing it being carried on all sides up to the roof. Or it may be compared to a veil or film of tracery thrown over the original walls. Mr. Willis believes that some of the Norman columns were pared down to harmonise with the new design.

For a plan of Gloucester Cathedral see page 546

The date of this (ca. 1351) shows that the Perp. style was originated and completed by the masons of Gloucester. In the ambulatory of the choir the original Norman arches and piers are left undisguised. The E. *Window of the choir, the largest in England (72 ft. by 38 ft.), is filled with fine stained glass of the 14th century. The window is actually wider than the side-walls that contain it. The somewhat unusual feature of a window at the W. end of the choir is due to the fact that the latter is much higher than the nave. The *Stalls*, with grotesque miserere carvings, date from the 14th cent.; the *Reredos* is modern. The beautiful lierne vaulting of the choir should also be noticed. Between the Presbytery and the N. ambulatory is the **Tomb of Edward II.* (murdered at Berkeley Castle in 1327), surmounted by a beautiful canopy. The possession of the body of this unfortunate monarch proved a source of great wealth to the cathedral, and the small pulpit, or desk, at which the priest stood to receive the contributions of the pious pilgrims, still stands at the W. end of the ambulatory. From the N.E. angle of the ambulatory projects *Abbot Boteler's Chapel* (ca. 1445), containing the **Tomb of Robert Curthose* (d. 1135), Duke of Normandy, eldest son of the Conqueror, with a curious effigy in Irish bog-oak. The corresponding chapel (both chapels are polygonal) at the S.E. angle is dedicated to *St. Philip*, and there are also chapels at the ends of the ambulatory adjoining the transepts. The one to the S., dedicated to *St. Andrew*, has been restored and adorned with elaborate coloured decorations by Mr. Gambier Parry (comp. p. 440). — We now ascend to the *Triforium* of the choir, reached by winding stairs in the W. turrets of the transepts, which occupies the whole width of the choir-aisles, and affords access to five small chapels corresponding to those below. The passage at its E. end, just above the entrance to the Lady Chapel (see below), is known as the 'Whispering Gallery', as a whisper uttered close to the wall at one extremity is distinctly audible at the other.

The E. termination of the cathedral is formed by the *Lady Chapel (ca. 1490), a fine Perp. structure with old stained glass (15th cent.) and good lierne vaulting. It has been narrowed at the W. end so as not to obstruct the light of the great E. window of the choir. There is a small chapel on each side, containing the tombs of two bishops. Above the chapels are small galleries, which may have been used by choristers.

The *Cloisters (1350-1410), which have no rival in England, are entered by a door at the E. end of the N. aisle of the nave. The exquisite fan-vaulting is the first known instance of its kind in the country. The S. walk of the cloisters contained the Scriptorium of the monks, and the N. walk their Lavatory. — From the E. walk of the cloisters we enter the Chapter House, which is Norman, except at the E. end, where a large Perp. window has been inserted. A staircase ascends from it to the *Cathedral Library, which contains a copy of Coverdale's Bible (1535) and an Anglo-Saxon MS. of the 10th century.

The Crypt, entered from the S. Transept, is mainly of Norman workmanship, though probably including relics of the Saxon abbey (p. 171), and preserves the original plan of the E. end of the church.

The top of the Tower (225 ft.; visitors seldom admitted) commands a very extensive view. In the lower part of it hangs 'Great Peter', a bell weighing nearly 3 tons. The chimes play at 1, 5, and 8 p.m.

The triennial musical festivals held alternately in the cathedrals of Gloucester, Hereford, and Worcester, for the performance of oratorios and other pieces of sacred music, are very numerously attended.

To the N. of the Cathedral lie some remains of the *Monastic Buildings* of the Benedictine abbey in which the see took its rise (see p. 171). These include the so-called 'Little Cloisters' (Perp.) and several E.E. arches. Three or four ancient *Gateways* to the cathedral-precincts still remain, the most interesting being the *West Gate* (12th cent.), in St. Mary's Square. The modern cross opposite the latter is a memorial to *Bishop Hooper*, who suffered martyrdom on this spot in 1555. The new *Episcopal Palace* adjoins the monastic remains. The picturesque *Deanery, to the N. of the W. front of the cathedral, carefully restored by Sir G. G. Scott, is the old Prior's Lodge. The E. end of the fine room now used as the Dean's Library, and once probably the Prior's Chapel, is pure Norman of the 11th or early 12th cent.; and the curious 'slype' beneath it is of the same period. The back part of the Deanery is of timber and dates from the 12th or 13th cent.; it contains a large room in which the Gloucester Parliament of Richard II. (1377-99) was held.

Gloucester contains about 12 other churches, of which the most interesting are *St. Mary le Crypt* (Perp.), *St. Nicholas* (Perp.), *St. Mary de Lode*, and *St. Michael*, from the tower of which the curfew is still sounded every evening. Near the docks are the scanty remains of *Llanthony Priory*, originally an offshoot from the priory of that name in Monmouthshire (p. 191). The *New Inn* is an interesting brick and timber edifice, erected about 1450 for the accommodation of pilgrims to the shrine of Edward II. (p. 172). — On the S.E. side of the town is a *Public Park*, with a chalybeate spring. The *Museum*, in Brunswick St., contains Roman antiquities found in the neighbourhood, the horns of the cow from which Dr. Jenner (p. 171) procured his original stock of lymph, etc. (adm. on Mon. & Wed., 11-1 and 2-4, 2*d.*; Sat. 11 to 6 or to dusk, 1*d.*). In Southgate St. is a timber-framed house once occupied by *Robert Raikes* (1735-1811), a native of Gloucester and the founder of the first Sunday School in England; and there is another interesting old house in a passage opposite the Fleece Inn in Westgate St. — Numerous pleasant walks and drives may be taken in the environs.

From Gloucester to *Bristol* and to *Bath*, see R. 15; to *Cheltenham* and *Birmingham*, see R. 23. Excursions may easily be made to the *Forest of Dean* (p. 177) and the *Valley of the Wye* (p. 174).

Passengers for Ross and Hereford sometimes change carriages at Gloucester and proceed by the *South Wales Railway* (G.W.R.). On quitting the town we obtain a good retrospect of the cathedral, and afterwards enjoy a succession of fine views of the valley of the Severn. About 2 M. from Gloucester we pass (on the right) *Highnam Church*, the interior of which was elaborately painted by the late Mr. Gambier Parry (p. 172), whose house, *Highnam Court*, is seen on the same side farther on. — At ($121^1/_2$ M.) *Grange Court* our line diverges to the right from the line to South Wales (R. 24). Farther on we pass *Blaisdon Hill* on the right, while 1 M. to the left is *Flaxley Abbey*, the residence of Sir Roger de Coverley's 'Widow' (Mrs. Boevy). To the right, at (125 M.) *Longhope*, rises *May Hill* (1000 ft.). $127^1/_2$ M. *Micheldean Road*, the station for ($1^1/_2$ M.) *Micheldean*, a small town on the N. margin of the Forest of Dean, with a church containing a fine oaken roof. The train now enters *Herefordshire*, a pleasant cattle-grazing district, which, according to Camden (*'Britannia'*) 'would scorne to be considered seconde to any other county throughout all England for fertilite of soile', adding 'that for three W.W.W. — wheat, wool, water — it yieldeth to no shire in England'. The traveller should not omit to taste its perry and cider. To the left, in front of us, rises the *Penyard*.

132 M. **Ross** (**Royal*, near the church, with a fine view, R. & A.

from 4*s.* 6*d.*, B. 2-3*s.*, D. 3*s.* 6*d.*-5*s.*; *Swan; King's Head)*, a pretty little town with 3725 inhab., stands on a hill overlooking the *Wye*, which is here crossed by a picturesque bridge. The **Church*, a handsome Dec. and Perp. building, with a lofty spire, conspicuous in all views of the town, contains the tomb (in the chancel) of *John Kyrle* (d. 1724), the 'Man of Ross' immortalized in Pope's well-known poem, as well as some interesting monuments of the Redhall family. Kyrle also planted the elms in the churchyard, and inside the church are two offshoots from one of these (now dead), which forced their way below the wall. The house of this eminent philanthropist on 500*l.* a year is in the market-place and is marked by his bust. Opposite is the *Town Hall*, a quaint little building, supported by pillars of red sandstone. A lovely view of the Wye is obtained from the *Prospect Walk*, adjoining the churchyard.

***Valley of the Wye.** Ross is the starting-point for a visit to the *Lower Wye*, the 'devious Vaga' of the poet, which presents some of the finest river-scenery in the country. The river also flows past Tintern Abbey, one of the most beautiful of England's ecclesiastical ruins, while Raglan, one of the most interesting of English castles, is within easy reach of its banks. The Wye flows to the S. from Ross, passing Monmouth, and joins the Severn near Chepstow (p. 177), which is 27 M. distant as the crow flies, but about 40 M. by the windings of the river.

The traveller has his choice of road, rail, and river; the last route is preferable, and it may be combined with digressions on foot. A boat with one boatman from Ross to Goodrich Castle costs 6*s.*, to Symond's Yat 10*s.*, to Monmouth 15*s.*, to Tintern 25*s.*, to Chepstow 30*s.*; with two men about one-half more. For boats apply at the Hope & Anchor Inn. Boats may also be hired at (10½ M.) Monmouth. Perhaps the best plan is to go by boat to Tintern and to walk thence to (5¼ M.) Chepstow, as the lower (tidal) part of the Wye, except at high tide, is disfigured by ugly mudbanks. This walk also includes the Wyndcliff (p. 176), considered the finest single point in the valley. Those who have only one day at their disposal should visit Symond's Yat and Tintern by rail, and walk from the latter to Chepstow by the Wyndcliff. Monmouth is the best stopping-place for those who devote two days to the trip. The railway skirts the river nearly the whole way, and most of the stations are close to its banks. The times and fares from Ross are as follows: to (7½ M.) *Symond's Yat* in 25 min. (fares 1*s.* 6*d.*, 1*s.*, 9½*d.* or 7½*d.*); to (13 M.) *Monmouth* in 35 min. (2*s.* 10*d.*, 2*s.* 2*d.*, 1*s.* 4*d.* or 1*s.* 1*d.*); to (22 M.) *Tintern* in 1 hr. (4*s.* 6*d.*, 3*s.* 3*d.*, 2*s.* 4*d.* or 1*s.* 10*d.*); to (27½ M.) *Chepstow* in 1½-1¾ hr. (6*s.*, 4*s.* 4*d.*, 3*s.* or 2*s.* 3½*d.*). Like the Severn, the Wye is famed for its salmon ('there is salmons in both'), and the fishery brings in a yearly rental of 20,000*l.* The lower Wye forms the boundary between Gloucestershire and Monmouthshire. The 'coracle', a primitive British boat made of hides or canvas stretched over a frame of timber or wickerwork, may still be seen on the Wye; and Gilpin ('The Wye Tour') tells of an adventurous boatman who went from the Wye to Lundy (p. 159) and back in one of these frail craft.

Leaving Ross by boat we obtain a good view of *Wilton Castle* (12-16th cent.), on the right bank, and beyond it we pass under *Wilton Bridge.* Wilton Castle at one time belonged to Thomas

Guy, who bequeathed it to the London hospital that bears his name. About $4^1/_2$ M. farther on, on the same bank, are *Goodrich Court*, a modern imitation of a mediæval mansion, and **Goodrich Castle*, a fine ruin dating partly from the 12th cent. (adm. 6*d*.). It was at Goodrich Castle (in 1793) that Wordsworth met the little heroine of 'We are Seven'. Below Goodrich we pass under (1 M.) *Kerne Bridge* (rail. stat.; Inn), beyond which the river makes an immense loop, and the scenery becomes more varied. To the E. lies the *Forest of Dean* (p. 177). At the end of the loop, near ($3^1/_2$ M.) *Lydbrook* (stat.; Queen's Head), we again pass under the railway. Farther on, at ($^3/_4$ M.) the **Coldwell Rocks*, the Wye doubles back upon itself, flowing towards the N. for $2^1/_2$ M. and then returning to within 600 yds. of its former channel. The tourist may leave the boat to navigate this bend, while he ascends ***Symond's Yat** (650 ft.), the hill at the neck of the loop, commanding an exquisite view of rocks, and woods, and meadows, not unlike the view from the Marienburg at Alf, on the Moselle. Close by is *Symond's Yat Station* (Saracen's Head; Prospect House; Rocklea Temperance Inn). Boats may be hired at the Rocklea Inn for excursions to *Lady Park Cave* (adm. 6*d*.), etc. Symond's Yat is separated from the *Great Doward* by a defile named the '*Slaughter*', and both hills are crowned with ancient encampments. The river then flows through the richly-wooded park of the *Leys*, and the valley becomes more open. Monmouth is $10^1/_2$ M. from Ross in a direct line, and about twice as far by the river. The road misses a great part of the scenery.

Monmouth (*Beaufort Arms*, high charges; *King's Head; Bridge; Angel*), a town with 6115 inhab., which Gray calls 'the delight of the eye and the very seat of pleasure', is beautifully situated on a rising ground at the confluence of the *Monnow* and the Wye. The old *Castle*, of which some remains still exist, was the birthplace of Henry V. (1388-1422), the 'Prince Hal' of Shakespeare. The room in which he was born is still pointed out. On the old bridge crossing the Monnow is an interesting *Gateway* of the 13th cent., adjoining which is a small Norman chapel. The romancing chronicler Geoffrey of Monmouth (d. 1154) was born here, and a building (of much later date) is known as 'Geoffrey's Study'. The caps for which Monmouth was formerly celebrated ('wearing leeks in their Monmouth caps', Henry V., IV. 7), are no longer made here. — There are two railway-stations at Monmouth: *May Hill*, near the bridge, and *Monmouth Troy*, to the S. of the town. Passengers for Tintern and Chepstow sometimes have to change carriages at the latter, the train going on to Raglan, Usk, and Pontypool Road (see p. 176).

The *View from ($2^1/_2$ M.) **Kymin Hill** (700 ft. above the river; ascent 1 hr.), on the opposite bank of the Wye, is very extensive and beautiful. About 1 M. to the S.E. of this hill is the *Buckstone*, a rocking-stone, or 'Logan Stone' (*View). The silly exploit of Lieut. Goldsmith with the

For a coloured map of The Valley of the Wye see page 571

famous 'Logan' near the Land's End (p. 147) was emulated here in 1885 by a party of excursionists; but the stone has since been replaced with great cost and labour.

Monmouth is a good centre for numerous charming excursions, and the tourist is advised to interrupt his descent of the Wye long enough at least for a visit to *Raglan* (Beaufort Arms), 7 M. to the S.W.; railway (G. W. R.) in 1/4 hr.; fares 1*s*. 6*d*., 10*d*., 8*d*. ***Raglan Castle** (adm. 6*d*.), now a picturesque ruin, was built in the 14-15th cent., and in 1646 was gallantly defended against the Parliamentarians for 10 weeks by the Marquis of Worcester, then in his 84th year. It was the last fortress to hold out for the king. The second marquis, the son of the heroic royalist, is distinguished for having invented and constructed the first steam-engine, which was set up at Raglan as a pumping engine. Lord Raglan, the English commander in the Crimean War, took his title from this spot. — Beyond Raglan the train goes on to (12 M.) **Usk** *(Three Salmons)*, an ancient place with an old church and castle and a noted salmon-fishery, and (18 M.) *Pontypool Road* (p. 191). — Other interesting places near Monmouth are (8 M.) *Skenfrith Castle*, (13 1/2 M.) *Grosmont Castle*, and (9 1/2 M.) *White Castle*.

Below Monmouth the valley of the Wye soon again contracts, and is enclosed by steep wooded hills. The railway from Monmouth to Chepstow skirts the river nearly the whole way. On the right bank, 2 M. from Monmouth, lies *Pennalt*, near which is *Troy House*, a seat of the Duke of Beaufort. On the opposite bank are various traces of the industries carried on in the Forest of Dean. At (4 M.) *Bigsweir* we reach the highest point where the flow of the tide is perceptible. About 2 M. to the E. is *St. Briavels* (p. 177). The train next passes (3 1/2 M.) *Tintern Parva* and *Tintern Station*, both on the right, and after rounding another loop reaches (1 1/2 M.) the ivy-clad ***Tintern Abbey**, one of the most romantic ruins in England, lying in a green meadow on the right bank of the Wye (adm. 6*d*.).

The abbey was founded by Cistercian monks in 1131, but the church, the chief feature of the ruins, dates from the end of the following century. The building, which is 228 ft. long, is a fine specimen of Dec. Gothic. The roof and central tower are gone, but the rest of the structure is still well preserved. The window-tracery and other decorations are very beautiful. The secular buildings are much smaller and less important than those of Fountains Abbey (p. 423). The village of *Tintern* (Beaufort Arms, R. & A. 4*s*., sometimes over-crowded in summer; George; Rose & Crown) is close to the abbey. The railway-station (see above) is 1 M. distant by road.

The river-scenery between Tintern and (7 M.) Chepstow is very charming, though it loses much of its attraction at low tide (see p. 174). We skirt the base of the wooded Wyndcliff (see below), and farther on pass the fine rocks known as the **Twelve Apostles* (to the right). As we approach Chepstow we have a good view of the castle.

As, however, the Wyndcliff is one of the points that no visitor to the Wye should miss, many will prefer to walk from Tintern to (5 1/4 M.) Chepstow. We follow the road leading to the S. from the Abbey to (2 1/4 M.) the 'Moss Cottage', and pass through the cottage (fee 6*d*.) to a winding path which ascends, partly in steps, to the top of the ***Wyndcliff** (900 ft.). At the top we turn to the right and descend a little to reach the small out-look platform, which commands one of the finest views of river-scenery in Europe, remarkable for the beauty and variety of its foliage. The Severn is seen in the distance. In descending we do not return to the Moss Cottage, but keep to the S. (left) at the point on the summit where we turned to the right, and regain the road at a point 1/3 M. nearer Chepstow. After 1/2 M. more we turn to the left, and then follow the main road to (2 1/4 M.) Chepstow. On a Tuesday, however, we may walk through **Piercefield Park*, from near the point where we regain the road to within 3/4 M. of Chepstow.

In summer a coach plies daily between Tintern Abbey and Chepstow (fares 1*s.* 6*d.*, return 2*s.* 6*d.*), starting from the latter about 11 a.m.

Chepstow *(*Beaufort Arms*, R. & A. 4*s.*; *George)*, a town with 3600 inhab., is picturesquely situated on the W. bank of the Wye, which is here crossed by two bridges, 2 1/2 M. above its junction with the Severn. It is a station on the S. Wales line from Gloucester to Cardiff (see p. 192). **Chepstow Castle* (adm. 6*d.*), on a height commanding the river, dates mainly from the 13-14th cent. and is an extensive and interesting ruin, enclosing four courts. The third court, known as the Chapel, seems to have been the original Norman keep. *Martin's Tower* was for 20 years the prison of the regicide of that name (d. 1680; buried in the church), and Jeremy Taylor was also confined here in 1656. A good view of the castle is obtained from the bridge. The *Church of St. Mary*, near the bridge, has a Norman nave and a fine Norman W. doorway. Some parts of the town-walls and an old gateway are still *in situ*.

From Chepstow an excursion may be made to **Caldicot Castle** (adm. on previous written application), 5 1/2 M. to the S.W., and to *Caerwent*, a Roman camp *(Venta Silurum)*, 1 1/2 M. to the N. of the castle. Freeman describes Caldicot as surpassing in masonry and details every military building he had seen, being fully equal to the best ecclesiastical work.

The **Forest of Dean**, the triangular district between the Wye and the Severn, as far N. as a line drawn from Ross to Gloucester, was formerly a royal domain like the New Forest (see p. 83); and the crown land still amounts to about 25,000 acres. It is now in great part a busy mining district, producing large quantities of coal and iron; but there are also extensive tracts of picturesque woodland, which repay exploration. It is traversed from N. to S. by the railway from *Berkeley Road* to *Lydbrook;* and visitors may conveniently alight at *Speech House Station* and make the *Speech House Inn* (well spoken of) their headquarters. The Speech House contains the *Verderers' Court* (comp. p. 83). The trees of the Forest are chiefly oaks and beeches. Among the pleasantest points are the *Holly Wood*, close to the Speech House; the *High Beeches*, 2 M. to the N.W.; the *Spruce Drive* and *Danby Beeches*, 3 1/2 M. to the S.E.; the *Great Oak*, 4 M. to the W.; *Pleasant Stile*, *Langham Place*, the *Ruardean Hill* (855 ft.), the highest point in the Forest, and *St. Briavels* (p. 176), with a ruined castle and an interesting church. Visitors interested will easily find an opportunity of inspecting a colliery or an iron-mine.

Beyond Ross the Hereford line passes several country-seats. Stations *Fawley* and *Holme Lacy*. The grounds of *Holme Lacy House*, a large red mansion to the right, are open to the public in summer; the fine gardens on Tues. forenoon. The *Wye* is crossed several times.

144 M. **Hereford** *(*Green Dragon; City Arms*, commercial; *Mitre*, R. & A. 3*s*. 9*d*., these three in Broad St.; *Greyhound, Merton*, unpretending; *Railway Refreshment Rooms)*, an episcopal city with 19,825 inhab., pleasantly situated on the left bank of the Wye, is of very ancient origin. It was at one time strongly fortified, and remains of the old walls are still traceable. The see dates from 673, when it was detached from that of Lichfield. The *Castle*, built to hold the Welsh in check, and described by Leland as 'one of the fayrest, largest, and strongest castles in England', has almost wholly disappeared; but its name survives in *Castle Green*, a pleasant promenade on the river near the cathedral. In the centre of the Green, which occupies the site of the outer ward of the Castle, is a Column to the memory of *Lord Nelson*. Hereford carries on an extensive trade in the agricultural produce of the district. The cattle and sheep of Herefordshire are highly valued. Hereford was the birthplace of *David Garrick* (1716-1779) and *Nell Gwynne* (d. 1687).

The *Cathedral *(SS. Mary & Ethelbert)*, the fourth church on the same site, begun in 1079 on the destruction of its predecessor by the Welsh (1055), and not finished till 1530, naturally shows an interesting mixture of architectural styles. The nave, S. transept, choir, and piers of the tower are Norman; the Lady Chapel is E.E. (1226-46); the N. transept was rebuilt in 1250-88; the N. porch was erected about 1290. The central tower dates from the 14th, and the cloisters from the 15th century. The addition of the outer N. porch (about 1530) completed the building as it now stands. The W. façade was marred at the end of last century during the 'renovation' undertaken by *Wyatt* (p. 99) in consequence of the fall of the W. tower (1786), but the whole building was afterwards restored with success by Sir G. G. Scott (1856-63).

The daily services of the cathedral are held at 10 a.m. and 4.30 p.m. Visitors are requested to inscribe their names in a book and contribute 6*d*. to the building expenses. The usual entrance is by the **North Porch*, the outer portion of which is Perp. and the inner E. E. (see above). The principal dimensions of the Cathedral are: length 342 ft., breadth of nave and aisles 73 ft., length of transepts 146 ft., height 64 ft.

Interior. The first thing to strike the visitor on entering the Nave is the contrast presented by its severe and massive piers and arches to the Dec. features of the exterior. The arches are adorned with chevron mouldings. The clerestory and triforium are poor, dating only from the restoration of last cent. (see above), and the unsuitable ornamentation of the ceiling is also modern. The oak pulpit is Jacobean. Among the monuments in this part of the church are those of *Bishop Booth* (1516-35), in the N. aisle, and *Sir Richard Pembridge* (d. 1375), in the S. aisle. Near the latter is the Norman *Font*, of the 12th century. — The N.W. Transept, perhaps the most beautiful part of the edifice, is a fine specimen of the Early Dec. style, with tall, narrow windows, arches of unusual form, and elaborate diaper ornamentation. The modern stained-glass window in memory of Archdeacon Freer, by *Hardman*, is very rich. The transept contains numerous monuments, of which the most interesting are those of *Bishops Peter de Aquablanca* (1240-68), and **Thomas de Cantilupe* (1275-82;

the last Englishman canonized before the Reformation). The exterior of this transept should also be examined. — The S.W. Transept is Norman, with later alterations, and some authorities believe it contains part of the oldest work in the building. On its W. side is a curious old fireplace, an unusual feature in a church. Its E. aisle, now used as a *Vestry*, contains a glass-case, with various interesting objects, including the 'Hereford Use' of about 1270. — Above the crossing rises the *Great Central Tower* (165 ft.), the curious work in the lantern of which resembles a large cage with bars of stone. The *Choir is separated from the nave by an elaborate *Metal Screen*, executed by Skidmore from a design by Sir G. G. Scott, and there are also good metal gates at the ends of the choir-aisles. The main arches and triforium of the choir are Norman, the clerestory E. E. The E. extremity was rebuilt in the present century. The *Episcopal Throne* and the *Stalls* date from the 14th cent.; the *Altar*, *Sedilia*, *Reredos*, *Stained Glass Windows*, and *Tiled Pavement* are modern. To the left of the altar is an interesting old *Bishop's Chair*, dating from the 11th century. Opening off the N. choir-aisle is *Bishop Stanbury's Chantry*, a small chapel of the end of the 15th century. To the W. of it is a door leading into the *Cathedral Library*, which was formerly accessible only by the gangway across the large window in the N.W. transept (see above). The library contains many volumes of great interest and value, nearly all of which are chained to the shelves. In the S. choir-aisle the famous **Hereford Mappa Mundi*, a quaint map of the world executed at the end of the 13th cent., is hung in its original frame, protected by modern doors of oak. Both aisles contain the monuments of several bishops. — The choir ends at the E. Transepts, which date in their present form mainly from the 14th century. From the S.E. transept a passage called the Vicars' Cloister, with a carved wooden roof, leads to the Vicars' College (see below).

The easternmost arm of the cathedral is the Lady Chapel, a good example of E.E., containing, among others, the fine tomb of *Baron de Grandison* (d. 1358). On the S. side, behind a lofty stone screen, is the *Chantry of Bishop Audley* (1492-1502), who, however, is buried in the chantry he built at Salisbury after his translation to that see (p. 99). A door at the N.W. angle of the Lady Chapel leads to the Crypt, said to be the only one in England of later date than the 11th century. — The Cloisters (15th cent.) are entered from the S. side of the nave. In the E. walk is the doorway of the old Chapter House, of which little else remains. The tower at the S.E. angle of the cloisters is traditionally known as the 'Ladye Arbour'.

The *College of Vicars Choral*, to the S. of the cathedral, is an interesting Perp. edifice (1475-1500). The *Episcopal Palace*, between the cathedral and the river, contains a Norman hall. The *Cathedral Grammar School*, at the E. end of the Cathedral, was founded in the 14th century.

After the cathedral the most interesting building is probably the so-named **Old House*, in the square called the High Town, a picturesque example of a half-timbered dwelling (16th or early 17th cent.), now used as a bank. In St. Peter's Sq., a little to the E., is *St. Peter's Church*, containing 14 oaken stalls of the 15th century. The *Church of All Saints*, in High St., to the W., contains similar stalls of somewhat later date. Both churches have lofty spires.

From High Town (see above) Widemarsh St. leads to the N. to (1/3 M.) *Coningsby Hospital*, a neat little building (1614) for old soldiers and servants, on the site of a commandery of the Knights Templar, of which a Norman archway still remains. It is also known as the *Black Cross Hospital*, from the ruins of a priory of

Black Friars in the garden. The most striking of these relics is the *Preaching Cross.— Another walk may be taken westwards from High Town through High St. and Eign St., across the railway bridge, and along Whitecross St. and Whitecross Road to (1¼ M.) the *White Cross*, erected in the 14th cent. to commemorate the cessation of the Black Death (1349). To the left, about 200 yds. from the road, are the *Kennels of the North Herefordshire Hunt.* — A good view is obtained from the *Town Waterworks*, 1 M. to the S.W., reached from High St. by Broad St., King St., Nicholas St., Barton St., and Broomy Hill. — The *Museum*, in Broad St., contains local antiquities, fossils, and birds. — There are two railway-stations at Hereford: the *Barr's Court Station* of the G.W. and L.N.W. railways, on the N.E. side of the town, and the *Barton Station* of the Midland Railway, adjoining the above-mentioned bridge.

Hereford is a fairly good centre for excursions, of which those up and down the *Wye* are the first to suggest themselves. In both directions the pedestrian or cyclist will meet with much characteristic English river-scenery, and numerous small but comfortable inns make it a comparatively easy matter to extend the walk in the one direction to Ross, Monmouth, or Chepstow (comp. p. 174 *et seq.*), or in the other to Hay, Builth, or Rhayader (comp. p. 203). — Among other places of interest within the compass of a day's excursion are *Leominster* (see below); *Malvern* (p. 189); the *Black Mts.* (p. 191); *Dinedor Hill*, a Roman camp 3 M. to the S. (view); *Holme Lacy*, 4 M. to the S.E. (p. 177); *Kilpeck Church*, 7½ M. to the S.W., with grotesque Norman sculptures (see p. 190); *St. Ethelbert's Camp*, 6 M. to the E.; and *Tewkesbury* (p. 182).

From Hereford to Shrewsbury, 51 M., railway in 1½-2⅓ hrs. (10*s.* 6*d.*, 7*s.* 5*d.*, 5*s.* 5*d.* or 4*s.* 3*d.*). — The train traverses rich pasture-land, and penetrates *Dinmore Hill*, 'a specula to see all the country about' (Leland), by a tunnel ¾ M. long. — The first station of importance is (13 M.) **Leominster**, pronounced *Lemster (Royal Oak; Talbot; Rail. Refreshmt. Rooms)*, an ancient town with 6000 inhab., deriving its name from a priory founded here in the 7th century. The *Church of SS. Peter and Paul*, one of the finest parish-churches in the country, contains features of all the principal architectural styles from Norman to Perpendicular. It is adjoined on the N. by an older Norman church. Other interesting buildings are *Dutton House* and the *Clarke Alms Houses* (18th cent.). [From Leominster a branch-line diverges on the left to *New Radnor*.] — From (18 M.) *Wooferton* (Refreshmt. Rooms) a branch-line runs to the E. to *Tenbury*, *Stourbridge*, and *Birmingham*. To the right rises *Titterstone Clee* (1780 ft.).

23 M. **Ludlow** *(Feathers; Angel)*, a very interesting town with 5100 inhab. and many fine old wooden houses, is prettily situated at the confluence of the *Teme* and the *Corve*. It was formerly the seat of the Lords President of Wales and retains many signs of its former importance. Their **Castle*, which is still magnificent in decay (adm. 6*d.*), was built in the 12th cent. and played an important rôle in many historical events. Milton here wrote his '*Comus*', to celebrate the appointment of the Earl of Bridgewater to the office of Lord Marcher; and a great part of Butler's '*Hudibras*' was also written within its walls. The hall in which 'Comus' was 'presented' is still *in situ*, and there are remains of a circular Norman chapel. The **Collegiate Church of St. Lawrence*, the stately Perp. tower of which is conspicuous from the railway (to the left), contains good stained glass and many interesting monuments. Near the castle is a *Museum*, with an extensive collection of Silurian fossils. — Pleasant excursions may be made from Ludlow to the *Vignals* (4 M.; view), *Bringewood Chase* (3 M.; view), *Hay Wood*, *Downton Castle*, *Wigmore Castle*, *Staunton Lacey* (with a pre-Norman church; 2½ M. to the N.), etc.

31 M. **Craven Arms** *(Craven Arms; Rail. Refreshmt. Rooms)* is the

junction for the *Central Wales Railway* to *Llandrindod*, *Swansea*, *Carmarthen*, and *Pembroke*. To the N. E. (right) another branch runs to (18 M.) *Much Wenlock* (Gaskell Arms; Raven), a small town with the fine ruins of a Cluniac **Priory*, which was founded in 1080 and exhibits an interesting mixture of Norman and Gothic architecture. A third branch runs to the left to *Bishop's Castle*. About 1 M. to the S. of Craven Arms is **Stokesay Castle* (13th cent.), surrounded by a moat, one of the finest castellated mansions in England.

Farther on, the line runs parallel with *Watling Street*. To the right are the *Stretton Hills* (1675 ft.). Beyond (38 M.) *Church Stretton* (Church Stretton Hotel) we pass three unimportant stations and reach —

51 M. **Shrewsbury**, see p. 262.

From Hereford to *Malvern* and *Worcester* and to *Newport* and *Cardiff*, see R. 24; to *Brecon* and *Swansea*, see R. 26.

23. From Bristol to Gloucester, Cheltenham, Worcester, Birmingham, and Derby.

Midland Railway (no second class) to (37½ M.) *Gloucester* in ¾-1¼ hr. (fares 5*s*., 3*s*. 1½*d*.); to (43½ M.) *Cheltenham* in 1 hr. 5 min.-2 hrs. (fares 5*s*. 10*d*., 3*s*. 7*d*.); to (65½ M.) *Worcester* in 1¾-3 hrs. (fares 8*s*. 8*d*., 5*s*. 6*d*.); to (90½ M.) *Birmingham* in 2¼-4½ hrs. (fares 12*s*. 4*d*., 7*s*. 8*d*.); to (130 M.) *Derby* in 3¼-4¾ hrs. (fares 18*s*., 10*s*. 4*d*.). — Travellers by this line may also book through to *Manchester* (5¼-6½ hrs.; 24*s*. 1*d*., 13*s*. 7*d*.), *Liverpool* (5¾-7 hrs.; 24*s*. 7*d*., 13*s*. 9*d*.), *Edinburgh* (11¼ hrs.; 56*s*., 30*s*. 5½*d*.), and *Glasgow* (11¾ hrs.; 56*s*. 6*d*., 30*s*. 5½*d*.).

From Bristol to (37½ M.) *Gloucester*, see p. 121. Beyond Gloucester, the cathedral tower of which is well seen to the left, we pass *Churchdown* and soon reach —

43½ M. **Cheltenham.** — **Hotels.** *Plough, High St., an old and very comfortable house, with the largest stable-yard in England, R. & A. 4*s*., D. 4*s*.; Queen's, in the Promenade; Royal; Fleece, commercial; Bellevue, Lansdown, private hotels; Walter's Temperance.

Restaurants. *George's*, High St.; *Lock's*, Clarence St.; *Bayley's*, High St.; *Railway Refreshmt. Rooms.*

Cabs. For 1 pers. 1*s*. per mile, 2 pers. 1*s*. 6*d*., 3 or more pers. 2*s*.; for each addit. ½ M. 6*d*. — **Omnibuses** ply from the railway-stations into the town, and the hotels send omnibuses to meet the principal trains.

Coach daily in summer to (16 M.) *Broadway* (p. 187).

Railway Stations. *Great Western Station*, St. James Sq., for London (3½-4¾ hrs.; fares 20*s*., 15*s*., 10*s*. 1*d*.), Oxford, etc.; *Midland Railway Station*, Queen's Road, for Gloucester, Bristol, Birmingham, and the North.

Theatre Royal, Montpellier St. — **Assembly Rooms**, High St., for balls, concerts, etc. Visitors apply to the Committee. — **Music.** The *Town Band* performs in the morning and afternoon in the Montpellier Gardens and other parts of the town.

Cheltenham, a frequented and well-built inland watering-place with about 50,000 inhab., is pleasantly situated on the *Chelt*, in a fertile plain, bounded on the S. E. by the *Cotswold Hills*. Its springs were discovered at the beginning of last cent., but it was not till after the visit of George III. in 1788 that it became a fashionable resort. The waters are chalybeate and saline, and are considered efficacious for dyspepsia and affections of the liver. The *Pump Room* is in the *Pittville Gardens*, a large recreation-ground to the N. of the High St., and there is also a spa in the *Montpellier Gardens*. Among the residents are numerous retired civil servants and officers, while in winter the town is crowded with fox-hunters.

Anglo-Indians form so large a part of its society, that the town has been called 'Asia Minor'. The *Cricket Week*, held in August in the College Grounds, is a source of attraction to many visitors. Cheltenham is a renowned educational centre, and its *College*, a large building in the Bath Road, ranks high among the public schools of England (600-700 pupils). It possesses a *Museum*, to which visitors are admitted on application. There is also a *Ladies' College*, attended by upwards of 500 pupils.

The principal business-street of the town is the *High Street*, nearly 2 M. long, which intersects it from E. to W. The *Promenade*, a shady avenue leading to the S. from the High St., contains a large *Winter Garden*, and is adjoined by the *Montpellier Gardens*, with the *Montpellier Rotunda*, used in winter for balls and concerts. — The parish-church of *St. Mary* was erected in the 14th cent and has been restored. It possesses a fine rose-window and contains a brass of the Greville family. In the churchyard is a mutilated cross of the 13th century. — Among modern buildings may be mentioned the *Public Library and School of Art*, near the G. W. R. station, and the *Grammar School*, in the High Street.

The environs of Cheltenham, including the *Cotswold Hills*, afford many pleasant excursions. Among the places most visited are *Leckhampton Hill* (980 ft.; view), 2 M. to the S.; *Charlton Kings*, 1½ M. to the E.; *Southam de la Bere*, a manor-house of the 15th cent., 2½ M. to the N. E., on the road to Evesham; *Winchcombe* (fine church) and **Sudeley Castle* (with the grave of Katherine Parr), 4½ M. beyond Southam; *Andoversford* (Frog Mill Inn), 7 M. to the E., on the line to Chipping Norton (p. 187); the *Seven Springs*, another claimant to be the source of the Thames (see p. 174), 3½ to the S.; and the *Roman Villa* at *Chedworth*, 9 M. to the S. E. — Railway-excursions may be made to *Berkeley Castle* (p. 122), *Tewkesbury* (see below), *Gloucester* (p. 170), *Evesham* (p. 187), and *Worcester* (p. 183).

Beyond Cheltenham the train next reaches (47 M.) *Cleeve*, the station for *Bishop's Cleeve*, with a large church, 1 M. to the N. E. — 51 M. *Ashchurch* is the junction of a line to (2 M.) *Tewkesbury* (see below) and (13 M.) *Malvern* (p. 189), and of another to *Evesham* (p. 187) and *Stratford-on-Avon* (see p. 245).

Tewkesbury (*Swan; Bell*), the *Etocessa* of the Romans and *Theocsbyrig* of the Saxons, a small and ancient town with 5000 inhab., at the confluence of the *Severn* and *Avon*, is frequently visited for the sake of its noble abbey-church. It is no longer famous for its mustard as in the days when Falstaff averred that Poins's wit was 'as thick as Tewkesbury mustard' (*Henry IV.*, Part II. II. 4). **Tewkesbury Abbey** was founded in 715, and its **Church*, dating mainly from the early part of the 12th cent., ranks among the most important Norman edifices in the country. It has been restored and is still used. [Visitors are admitted from 9.30 a. m. till dusk or 6.30 p.m., and are expected to contribute 6*d.* towards the Restoration Fund; adm. to the roof, triforium, or tower 6*d.* extra for 1 pers., 3*d.* each for a party.] The hexagonal choir, with its radiating chapels, is in the Dec. style; and many of the windows, chantries, vaults, and other details are either Dec. or Perpendicular. The chief features of the exterior are the massive Norman Tower (132 ft. high), an E. E. chapel on the E. side of the N. transept, the chevet of chapels at the E. end, and the curious recessed *Porch* and *Window* of the W. façade, the composition of which is probably unique. The interior, both of nave and choir, is very impressive. The vaulting of the nave has been coloured by **Mr. Gambier Parry** (p. 440), who has been much more successful than the decorators of the ceiling of the choir. The handsome tiled flooring of the choir is copied from ancient patterns found during the restoration. Among the most important of the numerous interesting monuments are the ***Despenser Tomb** (14th cent.), on the N. side of the choir; the ***Founder's Chapel***, at the E. end of the choir, erected over the tomb of ***Robert Fitz-Hamon*** (d. 1107), the builder of the original Norman church; the brass below the central tower, marking the supposed grave of ***Prince Edward of Wales***, killed at the battle of Tewkesbury (see below); the ****Warwick Chapel***, on the N. side of the choir, erected by Isabel Despenser about 1425; and the tombs of numerous *Abbots*. The stained glass in the choir dates mainly from the 14th century. The remains of the secular buildings are, with the exception of the *Gate House*, comparatively uninteresting. The town contains numerous timber houses of the 16-17th centuries. — The so-called '*Bloody Meadow*', 1/2 M. to the S. of the town, was the scene of the battle of Tewkesbury in 1471, at which the Yorkists gained a decisive victory (see above).

Tewkesbury is the nearest railway-station to **Deerhurst**, situated on the *Severn* (a pleasant trip by boat), 2½ M. to the S., and possessing a fine pre-Norman **Church*. The tower is an excellent specimen of pre-Norman architecture. An interesting pre-Norman **Chapel* has also been brought to light at an old farm-house, near the church. A stone found here, bearing the date 1056 (now in the Ashmolean Museum at Oxford; p. 231) makes either the church or chapel (for authorities differ as to which it belonged to) the earliest dated ecclesiastical building in England.

The train to Worcester now enters Worcestershire, passes (53 M.) *Bredon* (with a fine Dec. church) and (55½ M.) *Eckington*, and crosses the *Avon* close to (56 M.) *Defford*. Beyond (60 M.) *Wadborough* we cross the railway from Worcester to Evesham.

65½ M. **Worcester.** — **Hotels.** Star (Pl. a; C, 3), Foregate St., near the Foregate station, R. & A. 5*s.*; Bell (Pl. b), Unicorn (Pl. c), Crown, all in Broad St. (Pl. C, 4); Hop Market (Pl. d; C, 3), Foregate St.; Great Western (Pl. h; D, 3), close to the joint railway-station.

Cabs. For 1-2 pers., per drive 1*s.*, 3 pers. 1*s.* 6*d.*, 4 pers. 2*s.*; luggage up to 56lbs. free, beyond 56lbs. 1*s.* per cwt. — **Tramways** traverse some of the streets. — In summer a small **Steamer** plies to *Holt* and other places on the Severn.

Railway Stations. 1. *Joint Station* (Pl. D, 3) of the Great Western Railway and the Midland Railway, at Shrub Hill, 1/2 M. to the E. of the centre of the city; 2, 3. *Foregate Street Station* (Pl. C, 3) and *Henwick* (Pl. A, 4), for the G. W. R. trains to Hereford and South Wales.

Race-Course (Pl. A, 2, 3), by the river; races in March, July, and Nov.

Worcester, an episcopal city with 42,000 inhab., is pleasantly situated on a height on the left bank of the *Severn*, in a fertile and picturesque district. Its principal industrial products are gloves, of which 500,000 pairs are made annually, porcelain, boots and shoes, vinegar, and Worcester sauce. Its hop-market is very important.

Worcester is a place of great antiquity. It seems to have been already a British town of some importance *(Caer Guorangon?)* when the Romans captured it and made it one of their military stations. The Saxons called it *Wigorna Ceaster*, of which the present name is a softened form. At first the town was included in the bishopric of Lichfield, but it was elevated to the position of an independent see in 680. The castle was built in the 11th cent., and was occupied by several of the earlier English sovereigns. Worcester was frequently besieged and burned during the wars of the middle ages, and indeed no other English town of equal importance has had a more checquered history. The last and most celebrated siege was that of 1651, when Charles II. and his Scottish troops were defeated by Cromwell before the town after a very

For a coloured street plan of Worcester see pages 572

severe struggle, and the young prince narrowly escaped capture. The city motto, 'Civitas in Bello in Pace Fidelis', refers to this period of loyalty.

A good general view of Worcester and its Cathedral is obtained from the *Bridge* over the Severn (Pl. B, 4). The slender spire, which is so prominent on the E. bank, belongs to the *Church of St. Andrew* (Pl. C, 4), and was erected in the middle of last century.

The *Cathedral (Pl. C, 5), dedicated to Christ and the Blessed Virgin Mary, lies on the river, at the S. end of the main thoroughfare formed by Foregate St., the Cross, and High St. In plan it is a double cross with very short transepts, and with a chapter-house and spacious cloisters on the S. side. Its length is 450 ft.; its width in the nave 78 ft., and across the W. transepts 126 ft.; and its height 60-67 ft. In general characteristics it is E. E. and Dec., but it includes specimens of all styles from the Norman down to the latest Perpendicular. The present church occupies the site of one built by *St. Wulfstan* in the 11th cent., of which the crypt, the two W. bays of the nave, the interior of the chapter-house, and some portions of the walls now alone remain. The oldest parts of the church as re-erected are the choir and lady-chapel, which date from the first quarter of the 13th century. The N. side of the nave belongs to the Dec., and the S. side to the early Perp. period; but they are very similar in general appearance. The central tower, 196 ft. high, was completed in 1374, and shows traces of the transition from Dec. to Perpendicular. The whole edifice was restored under the superintendence of *Sir G. G. Scott*, and this restoration, though urgently needed and carried out with great taste, has somewhat impaired the interest of the exterior by depriving it of its air of venerable antiquity. Visitors are admitted from 9 to 6 in summer, and from 9.30 to 5 in winter; 6*d.* is charged for adm. to the choir and crypt, and 6*d.* extra for the ascent of the tower (week-day services at 10.15 a.m. and 4.15 p.m.). The most famous bishops of Worcester were *Wulfstan II.* (1062-95), *Hugh Latimer* (1535-39), and *Stillingfleet* (1689-99; see p. 185). The usual entrance to the Cathedral is by the *N. Porch* (1386).

The imposing ***Interior** has, in its magnificent groined roof, extending in an unbroken line for 420 ft., a feature that perhaps no other English cathedral can match. The modern decoration has been carried out with great skill and judgment, the tiled flooring being particularly worthy of notice. The stained glass is modern. With the exception of its W. end, the Nave in its present form is later than the choir, and there are differences of detail between its N. and S. sides (see above), the advantage lying with the older work on the N. The unusual arrangement of the triforium and clerestory of the two Transitional Norman bays at the W. end should be noticed. The arched recesses in the wall of the S. aisle (resembling those at Winchester) prove that the lower part of it is a relic of the Norman cathedral. The W. end of the nave was completely altered, and the W. entrance was blocked up towards the close of the 14th century. At the W. end of the S. aisle is a mural monument to *Bishop Gauden* (d. 1662), believed to be the real author of the '*Eikon Basilike*', ascribed to Charles I. The handsome modern *Pulpit* is the gift of the late Lord Dudley, who bore a great part of the expense of the restoration.

For a plan of Worcester Cathedral see page 547

The W. TRANSEPTS contain a good deal of Norman masonry, partly concealed by later work, of which the Perp. veil of tracery in the S. arm is noteworthy. The difference between the Norman and later masonry is easily recognised. In the E. wall of the N. arm is a Norman arch, below which has been placed the monument of *Bishop Hough* (d. 1743), a master-piece of *Roubiliac. Bishop Stillingfleet* (d. 1699) is also buried here. The S. arm is almost entirely filled by the *Organ*, another gift of the Earl of Dudley.

The *CHOIR is separated from the nave by one of these elaborate screens which may be looked upon as the signs-manual of Sir G. G. Scott's restorations; and there are also metal gates at the ends of the aisles. The choir dates from the purest E. E. period, and impresses by its richness and uniformity. As at Salisbury (p. 99), slender shafts of Purbeck marble play an important part in the general design. The carving of the bosses and capitals is very delicate, and the modern painting of the groined roof is effective. The **Stalls* date from 1379, and have been restored and supplemented by modern work; the misereres are very quaint. The *Episcopal Throne* and the *Reredos* are modern; the *Pulpit* dates from 1504. Near the centre of the choir is the *Monument of King John* (d. 1216), who died at Newark (p. 361) and was buried here at his own request; the monument consists of a sarcophagus-tomb of the 16th cent., surmounted by an effigy of the 13th, said to be the earliest existing effigy of an English monarch. To the right of the altar is the *Chantry of Prince Arthur*, elder brother of Henry VIII., who died at Ludlow Castle (p. 180) in 1502 and was interred here; the chantry is a good specimen of the Tudor style. Adjacent are the monuments of *Lord Dudley* (d. 1885) and *Lord Lyttelton* (d. 1876). The S. aisle of the choir is adjoined by an E. E. chapel.

Beyond the sanctuary, forming the E. termination of the Cathedral, is the LADY CHAPEL, erected before the choir, which was built to harmonize with it in structural and ornamental treatment. On the S. wall is a tablet to the memory of Izaak Walton's wife, a sister of Bishop Ken, with a quaint epitaph, doubtless written by her husband; and near it is a fine effigy of the 14th century. The episcopal effigies in front of the altar are those of *Bishops de Blois* (d. 1236) and *de Cantilupe* (d. 1266). The sculptured *Arcade* running round the Lady Chapel and the E. TRANSEPTS is of considerable interest. In the N.E. Transept is the *Monument of Mrs. Digby* (d. 1820), by *Chantrey*.

The *CRYPT, entered from the S.W. Transept, resembles that of Gloucester in preserving the apsidal termination of the earlier Norman church. It differs, however, from that and other Norman crypts in the lightness and elegance of its supporting columns. The groined roof is also fine.

The Perp. CLOISTERS, entered from the S. aisle of the nave, have been carefully restored. In the N. walk of the Cloisters is a tombstone bearing the single word 'Miserrimus'. The somewhat prosaic explanation is that it marks the grave of a Minor Canon, who was deprived of his preferments on refusing to take the oath of supremacy on the accession of William III. Wordsworth's well-known sonnet takes a more romantic view.

From the E. side of the Cloisters we enter the decagonal *CHAPTER HOUSE, one of the earliest examples of vaulting borne by a single column in the centre. The masonry of the walls is mainly Norman, while the windows are of later insertion.

From the top of the TOWER (adm. 6*d.*), which contains a set of chimes, a fine view, extending to the Malvern Hills, is enjoyed.

The CHAPTER LIBRARY, now housed in the triforium of the S. aisle of the nave, contains about 4000 printed vols. and some interesting MSS. — Triennial Musical Festivals, see p. 172.

Among the remains of the Benedictine Priory, with which the Cathedral was originally connected, the most important is the **Refectory*, to the S. of the Cloisters, a fine hall of the 14th cent., 120 ft. long, with a Norman crypt below. It is used for the Cathedral Grammar School, and has lately been restored. The present ceiling is an imitation of the original. To the W. of the Cloisters are some fragments of the *Dormitory*, and to the E., on the N. side of College Green, are the ruins of the *Guesten Hall* (1320). — The principal entrance to the College Green is the so-called *Edgar's Tower* or *St. Mary's Gate*, at the S. E. angle of the Cathedral; it perhaps dates from about 1500. To the S. of the College Green stood Worcester Castle, of which no trace has been left. *View of the Severn, with its two bridges, and of the suburbs on the left bank, from the S.W. side of the close. The Malvern Hills form the background.

A little to the N.W. of the Cathedral, on the river, is the old *Episcopal Palace*, now the *Deanery* (Pl. C, 4). The present residence of the Bishop is *Hartlebury Castle*, 11 M. to the N. of Worcester.

A little to the S. of the Cathedral, in Diglis St., are the Royal Porcelain Works (Pl. C, 5), established in 1751, which cover five acres of ground and employ over 600 hands (visitors admitted from 10 a.m. till dusk; 6*d.*). The various processes of manufacture and the collection of old Worcester are very interesting. Worcester china is noted for its hard enamel finish, and a high pitch of artistic excellence has been attained both in form and decoration.

Following the High Street, which leads to the N. from the neighbourhood of the Cathedral, we soon reach, on the left, the Guildhall (Pl. C, 4; open 10-6 in summer, 10-4 in winter), a substantial building in the Queen Anne style. It is adorned with statues of various monarchs and with allegorical figures of Justice, Plenty, Chastisement, Peace, and Industry. The hall, 110 ft. long, contains two brass cannon, one of which was used at the battle of Worcester. Opposite the Guildhall is the *Market House*.

The High Street is prolonged towards the N. by the *Cross*, a street so named from the old *City Cross*, long since removed, and this in turn is prolonged by *Foregate Street*, the principal street in the town. To the right is the *Hop Market* (Pl. C, 3), which presents a busy scene in the hop-season. The *Public Library & Museum* (Pl. C, 3), also in Foregate Street, contains a good collection of natural history specimens (open daily, 10-8).

Among the other churches of Worcester the most noteworthy are *St. Stephen's* (beyond Pl. B, 1), with a good interior, and *Holy Trinity* (Pl. D, 3), near the railway-station, with the fine timber-roof (14th cent.) from the Guesten Hall (see above). — The *Commandery* (Pl. C, 4), in Sidbury, originally a hospital, but now a college for the blind, is a fine specimen of domestic architecture of the time of Henry VIII. — The house from which Charles II. escaped by the back-door, as his enemies were entering at the front (comp. p. 182), is pointed out, opposite the *Corn Market* (Pl. C, 4). — A visit may also be paid to *Lea & Perrins' Manufactory* of 'Worcester Sauce', to the *Vinegar Works of Hill, Evans, & Co.* (with a cask holding 114,600 gallons), and to the *Glove Manufactories* of *Messrs. Dent* and *Fownes Brothers*.

The immediate environs of Worcester offer little to interest the tourist but excursions may be made to *Droitwich* (p. 187), *Evesham* (p. 187),

Malvern (p. 189), *Warwick* (p. 241), and *Stratford* (p. 245). — From Worcester to *Hereford*, see R. 24.

From Worcester to Oxford, 57 M., G. W. R. in 2-3½ hrs. (12*s.* 6*d.*, 9*s.* 6*d.*, 5*s.* 10*d.* or 4*s.* 9*d.*). — 8 M. *Pershore* (Coventry Arms; Three Tuns), with a handsome abbey-church, with a square tower of the 14th cent.; 11½ M. *Fladbury*, also with a fine church (Perp.). We then cross the *Avon.*

14 M. **Evesham** *(Crown; Northwick Arms; Railway)*, a small town with 5115 inhab., in a fertile valley, celebrated for its orchards and market-gardens. The little town is historically noteworthy as the scene of the battle in which Prince Edward, afterwards Edward I., defeated and slew Simon de Montfort in 1265. Of *Evesham Abbey*, founded in the 8th cent., nothing now remains except the fine *Bell Tower (1533) and a Norman Gateway; the former is visible from the train, above the trees to the left, as we enter the station. Simon de Montfort was buried in the abbey. Within the churchyard are the churches of *St. Lawrence* (fine fan-vaulting) and *All Saints*, both erected by the monks of the abbey. — About 2 M. to the S. E. of Evesham is the village of *Wickhamford*, the church of which contains the flat tomb (near the altar) of Penelope Washington (d. 1697), bearing the Washington coat-of-arms. **Broadway** *(Lyngon Arms)*, a quaint little place 3 M. farther on in the same direction, with interesting Elizabethan houses, is a favourite resort of American artists and authors. Coaches daily in summer to (5 M.) *Evesham* (1*s.*) and (16 M.) *Cheltenham* (p. 181; a beautiful drive over the *Cotswolds;* 5*s.*).

19 M. *Honeybourne* is the junction of a line to Stratford-on-Avon (p. 245) and Warwick (p. 241). — 25 M. *Campden*, with the ruins of a large mansion of the 17th cent., which was burned down to prevent its falling into the hands of the Parliamentarians. Near the town is *Campden House*, belonging to the Earl of Gainsborough. — The small hospital of (29 M.) *Moreton-in-the-Marsh* (White Hart) claims to possess the chair used by Charles I. at his trial. Near (34 M.) *Adlestrop* we pass, on the right, *Daylesford House*, once the seat of Warren Hastings, who died here in 1818 and is buried in the churchyard. The mansion-house at Adlestrop, a fine Tudor edifice, belongs to Lord Leigh.

36 M. *Chipping Norton Junction*, the station for a branch to (4 M.) **Chipping Norton** *(White Hart; Blue Boar)*, a small town with woollen cloth and glove factories and a fine Perp. church. The first part of the name is said to be derived from the Saxon word 'ceapian', to bargain (comp. 'Köping' in Sweden). About 2 M. to the N. are the *Rollright Stones*, the scanty remains of a stone circle like Stonehenge. The branch goes on to *Banbury* (p. 240). — From the same junction another line leads to the W. to Cheltenham and Gloucester (see p. 182). From (39 M.) *Shipton*, (40 M.) *Ascott-under-Wychwood*, or (44 M.) *Charlbury*, with a finely-situated church, a visit may be paid to *Wychwood Forest*, a fine woodland district.

Beyond *Charlbury*, to the left, lies *Blenheim Park*, but little is seen of it owing to the numerous cuttings through which the train here passes. Near (50 M.) *Handborough* the train crosses the *Evenlode*, a tributary of the Isis, the course of which has been followed from Moreton. From (54½ M.) *Yarnton Junction* a branch-line runs to *Witney* and *Fairford* (Bull); the latter contains a fine church, with exquisite stained-glass *Windows, ascribed (wrongly) to Albrecht Dürer. — We now join the main G. W. line, and soon reach (57 M.) *Oxford* (p. 223).

On leaving Worcester the train threads a tunnel and passes (67½ M.) *Fernhill Heath.* To the right is *Westwood House*, the seat of Lord Hampton. — 71 M. **Droitwich** *(Royal Brine Baths Hotel; Raven*, well spoken of; *George)*, a town with 4000 inhab., famous for its brine springs, which have their source 170 ft. below the surface of the earth and contain 35-40 per cent of pure salt. The springs were known to the Romans, and are now again frequented by bathers, while many thousand tons of salt are also produced for commercial use. Droitwich is the junction of the G. W. R. line to Kidderminster (p. 260) and Wolverhampton (p. 260). — 75 M. *Stoke Works*, with rock-salt deposits and copious brine-springs. Beyond (78 M.) *Bromsgrove* (Golden Cross), a nail-making town, with 15,000 inhab. and quaint gabled houses, the train ascends one of the steepest railway-inclines in England (1 : 37). — 81½ M. *Barnt Green* is the junction of a line to *Alcester*, *Redditch* (famous for needles), *Broom* (for *Stratford*), and *Evesham* (p. 187).

93 M. **Birmingham** (New St. Station; *Rail. Rfmt. Rooms*), see p. 254.

The first stations beyond Birmingham are *Saltley*, *Castle Bromwich*, and (96 M.) *Water Orton*, the junction of a line to Walsall and Wolverhampton (see p. 260). From (101 M.) *Whitacre* a line runs to the right to Nuneaton and Leicester (p. 352).

111½ M. **Tamworth** *(Castle; Peel Arms)*, a town with 5000 inhab., on the *Tame*, lies partly in Staffordshire and partly in Warwickshire. The old *Castle*, the relics of which are scanty, was erected by Robert Marmion, a celebrated Norman baron, whose name and description were appropriated by Scott for his well-known hero. The *Church*, also an ancient building, contains effigies of the Marmion family and a monument to Sir Robert Peel. The curious double winding staircase in the tower also deserves notice. In the market-place is a bronze statue, by Noble, of *Sir Robert Peel* (d. 1850), who represented Tamworth in parliament. *Drayton Manor*, the family-seat of the Peels, lies 2 M. to the S. and the great minister is interred in the church of the village of *Drayton Bassett*. — Tamworth is also a station on the Trent Valley Line of the L. N. W. R. (p. 349).

124½ M. **Burton-on-Trent** *(Queen; White Hart; Bowling Green; George)*, famous for its breweries of pale ale and other kinds of beer, is situated on the left bank of the Trent, here crossed by a long bridge. Pop. (1881) 39,285. It is a place of ancient origin, and the churchyard contains some relics of an *Abbey* founded at the beginning of the 11th century. The lions of the place are the huge breweries of *Bass & Co.* and *Allsopp & Co.* The former covers 130 acres of ground, employs 2000 men, brews annually 800,000 barrels of ale and stout, uses 60,000 railway trucks, and pays 300,000*l.* a year for malt tax and excise duty. Permission to visit either of these may be obtained on application at the office, where the traveller inscribes his name in a book kept for the purpose (gratuity of 1*s.*, more for a party, to the attendant).

From Burton branch-lines diverge on the left to *Uttoxeter* (p. 346), the *Potteries* (p. 345), and *Crewe* (p. 345), and on the right to *Ashby-de-la-Zouche* (p. 354), *Leicester* (p. 352), etc.

Near (129 M.) *Repton-Willington* we cross the *Dove. Repton*, 1 M. to the E., possesses a well-known grammar-school, established in an old priory. Below the chancel of St. Wystan is a pre-Norman *Crypt, approached by two staircases of similar date.

On the Dove, 4½ M. higher up, lies *Tutbury* (Castle Inn), with a castle partly built by John of Gaunt, and used as one of the numerous prisons of Mary, Queen of Scots. The parish-church of Tutbury has a Norman façade, which has been spoiled by restoration. Near Tutbury alabaster quarries are worked.

$135^1/_2$ M. **Derby**, see p. 350.

24. From Worcester to Hereford and Newport.

Great Western Railway to (30 M.) *Hereford* in $1^1/_4$-$1^1/_2$ hr. (fares 6*s*. 3*d*., 4*s*. 4*d*., 2*s*. 11*d*. or 2*s*. $5^1/_2$*d*.); to ($71^1/_4$ M.) *Newport* in 3-$4^1/_4$ hrs. (fares 12*s*. 10*d*., 9*s*. 10*d*., 6*s*. $^1/_2$*d*.).

The train crosses the *Severn* and stops again at (1 M.) *Henwick* (p. 183). Beyond (4 M.) *Bransford Road* the Malvern Hills come into view on the right. — $7^1/_2$ M. *Malvern Link*; $8^3/_4$ M. *Great Malvern*; $9^3/_4$ M. *Malvern Wells*.

Malvern. — **Hotels.** At *Great Malvern:* Imperial, near the station, with pleasant grounds and brine baths, 'pens'. from 3*l*. 3*s*. per week; *Abbey, *Bellevue, *Foley Arms, all on the hill; Tudor Private Hotel; Beauchamp, commercial, R. & A. 4*s*. 6*d*., 'pens'. 3*l*. 3*s*. per week; Rayner's Hydropathic; Leicester House Hydropathic, patients 42*s*., boarders 30*s*. a week. Also numerous *Boarding Houses* (5-10*s*. per day) and *Lodgings*. — At *Malvern Wells:* Essington Hotel; Hornyold Arms. — At *North Malvern:* North Malvern Hotel. — At *West Malvern*: Westminster Arms Hotel.

Assembly Rooms and Gardens in Great Malvern, with concerts (adm. 6*d*.). *Spa and Pump Room* on the W. side of Worcester Beacon (adm. 6*d*.).

Cabs, 1*s*. per mile or fraction of a mile for 1-2 pers.; each addit. pers. 6*d*. *Carriage & Pair* 4*s*. per hr., 1*s*. 6*d*. for each addit. $^1/_2$ hr., 21*s*. per day; to *Worcester* and back 8*s*.; to the *British Camp* and back by the *Wyche* 8*s*.; to *Eastnor Castle* and back 12*s*.

Malvern, an inland health-resort, famous for its bracing air and pleasant situation, includes the town of *Great Malvern* (pop. 8000) and the villages of *Malvern Link*, *Malvern Wells*, *Little Malvern*, *North Malvern*, and *West Malvern*, all consisting mainly of villas, hotels, and hydropathic establishments. The first four lie at the E. base of the *Malvern Hills*, a small chain 10 M. long and 1000-1450 ft. high, forming the watershed between the Severn and the Wye; while the other two are on the N. and W. slopes of the same range. The chief centre is Great Malvern, which contains the *Assembly Rooms* and *Gardens*, the best hotels and boarding-houses, and the principal shops; but visitors in search of quiet or economy will probably prefer one of the villages. The principal springs are the *Chalybeate Well* and *St. Ann's Well* (756 ft), at Great Malvern, and the *Holy Well* (680 ft.), above Malvern Wells. Malvern is a great educational centre, the chief school being *Malvern College*.

The beautiful **Priory Church*, belonging to a priory founded in the 11th cent., is externally a Perp. edifice, with a tower apparently modelled on that of Gloucester Cathedral. The nave, however, and part of the rest of the interior are Norman.

Among the points of interest are *St. Anne's Chapel* (13th cent.); the tiles at the back of the choir; the old stained-glass windows (the finest in St. Anne's Chapel); the miserere carvings; the mosaic in the reredos;

and some of the monuments. — The only other relic of the priory is the *Gateway*, a little to the N. To students of early English literature Malvern Priory is of interest as claiming to be the monastery of William Langland, author of 'Piers Plowman's Vision', which begins on a 'May mornynge on Maluerne hulles'. Organ recitals are given in the church on Wed. afternoons.

Little Malvern or *Malvern Parva*, 1 M. to the S. of Malvern Wells, also contains the interesting remains of a Norman church, consisting of the tower and chancel.

Excursions. The **Worcester Beacon** (1444 ft.), the highest of the Malvern Hills, rises immediately above Great Malvern and may be ascended by easy paths in 1/2 hr. (pony or mule, about 1*s.*). The route passes the Priory Church and St. Ann's Well. The *View is very extensive, reaching on the W. to the hills of Brecknock and stretching on the E. over an apparently boundless plain. Hereford, Worcester, Gloucester, Cheltenham, and Tewkesbury are all within sight.

'Twelve fair counties saw the blaze
From Malvern's lonely height.'

The *North Hill* (1326 ft.; 1/2 hr.), to the N. of the Worcester Beacon, may also be ascended; and we may follow the ridge to the S., along an old fosse dividing Worcestershire and Herefordshire, to the (1 M.) *Wyche* (see below). Beyond the Wyche the walk may be continued along the ridge to *Wind's Point* (830 ft.; British Camp Inn) and (3 M.) the **Herefordshire Beacon* (1370 ft.), the top of which has been converted into a strong *British Camp*, capable of holding 20,000 men. According to tradition, this was the scene of the capture of Caractacus by the Romans in A. D. 75.

The Round of the Hills is a favourite drive from Great Malvern, and may be made in an excursion-brake plying from the Bellevue Hotel (1*s.*). We skirt the E. slope of the hills, pass through the (1 1/2 M.) *Wyche Pass* (900 ft.), to the S. of the Worcestershire Beacon, and return along the W. side of the range viâ (1 1/2 M.) *West Malvern* and (1 M.) *North Malvern*.

Excursion-brakes also ply to (8 M.) *Eastnor Park*, the collection of paintings and armour in which is shown to visitors on Tues. and Fridays. The road to it leads by Malvern Wells, Malvern Parva, and Wind's Point (see above), the last part traversing the beautiful park surrounding the castle.

Excursions may also be made to *Worcester*, *Evesham*, *Gloucester*, *Stoke Edith Park* (tickets obtained at the booksellers'), *Ledbury*, *Tewkesbury*, etc.

Beyond Malvern Wells the train penetrates the Malvern Hills by a long tunnel. 11 M. *Colwall*, with an old church. Farther on, *Eastnor Castle* (see above) and an obelisk in Eastnor Park are seen to the right. Another tunnel, nearly 1 M. long, is then threaded. — 16 M. **Ledbury** *(Feathers)*, a busy little town, manufactures cider, perry, sacking, and cordage. The large *Church* is an interesting study in architectural styles, from Norman to Perpendicular.

From Ledbury to Gloucester, 19 M., railway in 3/4-1 1/4 hr. (3*s.* 5*d.*, 2*s.* 9*d.*, 1*s.* 11*d.* or 1*s.* 7*d.*). This line traverses a park-like district, with numerous orchards. The intermediate stations are *Dymock*, with a massive church-tower (to the left), *Newent*, and *Barber's Bridge*. — 19 M. *Gloucester*, see p. 170.

19 M. *Ashperton;* 22 M. *Stoke Edith*, with the beautiful park of Lady Foley; 25 M. *Withington*, with encaustic tile works.

30 M. **Hereford**, see p. 178. — 34 1/2 M. *Tram Inn*. About 1/2 M. from (37 M.) *St. Devereux* is the interesting late-Norman *Church of (1/2 M.) *Kilpeck*, with its elaborate sculptures, which has been described as '*facile princeps* amongs its fellows of the same type'. — From (40 1/2 M.) *Pontrilas* a branch-line runs through the 'Golden Valley' to (11 M.) *Dorstone* and (16 M.) *Hay*. The

scenery now improves. To the right rise the *Black Mountains*. — 47½ M. *Pandy* is the nearest railway-station for **Llanthony Abbey**, 5 M. to the N. W. The ruins consist of the church and chapter-house, and afford an interesting example of Transition Norman (12th cent.), though part is as late as the 14th century. The *Prior's Lodge* is now an inn. Walter Savage Landor (d. 1864) lived here for some years. *Llanthony Monastery*, the home of Father Ignatius, lies about 4 M. farther up the valley. — 48½ M. *Llanvihangel* is 6½ M. from Llanthony Abbey.

Beyond Llanvihangel the *Sugarloaf* (1955 ft.), a spur of the Black Mts., comes into view on the right. From (51 M.) *Abergavenny Junction* a line (L. N. W.) diverges on the right to *Rhymney Bridge* (for *Cardiff*), *Merthyr Tydvil* (p. 194), *Dowlais*, etc. Good view to the right up the valley of the *Usk*.

52 M. **Abergavenny** *(*Angel; *Greyhound; Swan)* is an ancient town with 8000 inhab., situated at the junction of the *Usk* and the *Gavenny*, and enclosed by the *Sugarloaf* (1955 ft.), the *Blorenge* (1908 ft.), *Skyrrid-Vawr* (1600 ft.), and other well-wooded hills (see below). It occupies the site of the Roman *Gobannium* and possesses the remains of a Norman castle (adm. 1*d.*) and a modernized Benedictine priory-church of the 14th cent., with several ancient monuments. Good fishing may be obtained in the Usk (day-tickets for trout 2*s.* 6*d.*, for salmon 5*s.*).

The **Sugarloaf** (1955 ft.) may be easily ascended from Abergavenny in 1½-2 hrs. (pony 5*s.*); *View fine and extensive. The descent may be made on the W. side to Crickhowell (see below). — The **Blorenge** (1908 ft.; 1½ hr.) commands an even finer view of the valley of the Usk, and *Skyrrid-Vawr* (1600 ft.), 4 M. to the N. E., is also a good point of view.

Abergavenny is a good starting-point for a visit to *Llanthony Abbey* (see above), which may be reached direct by road (10½ M.; carr. & pair there and back 25*s.*) or partly by rail viâ Llanvihangel or Pandy (see above). — Another pleasant excursion may be taken up the finest part of the valley of the *Usk* to (6½ M.; omn. 1*s.* 6*d.*) **Crickhowell** *(Bear)*, a village with the remains of an old castle. Above Crickhowell the Usk valley is also picturesque, and walkers or drivers will be repaid by following it to (20 M.) *Brecon* (p. 204). — Tolerable walkers, who have one day at Abergavenny, should ascend the Sugarloaf and return viâ Crickhowell.

From Abergavenny to *Cardiff* by the L. N. W. R. route, see above and p. 194.

Beyond (54½ M.) *Penpergwm* we cross the Usk. — 61½ M. **Pontypool Road** *(Rail. Rfmt. Rooms)*, the junction of lines to *Merthyr* and *Swansea* (p. 193) and to *Raglan* and *Monmouth* (p. 176). The manufacturing town of *Pontypool* (Crown; Clarence) lies 1½ M. to the W. — 68 M. **Caerleon** *(Angel)*, on the Usk, the *Isca Silurum* of the Romans, and the traditional residence of King Arthur.

Near the church is an interesting *Museum* of Roman antiquities (adm. 6*d.*), the road opposite which leads to the well-defined *Amphitheatre* and a mound known as *King Arthur's Round Table*. Caerleon was at a very early period the seat of an archbishop, whose see was transferred in the 11th cent. to St. David's (p. 214).

At (71¼ M.) *Newport* we join the railway described in R. 25.

25. From Gloucester to Cardiff, Swansea, and Milford.

Great Western Railway to (56 M.) *Cardiff* in 1½-2¼ hrs. (fares 11*s.*, 8*s.*, 5*s.* 9*d.*); to (102 M.) *Swansea* in 3-4 hrs. (fares 20*s.*, 14*s.* 3*d.*, 10*s.* 6*d.* or 8*s.* 6*d.*), to (170 M.) *Milford Haven* in 5-7¾ hrs. (fares 33*s.*, 24*s.*, 17*s.* 9*d.* or 14*s.* 2½*d.*). This line traverses the S. part of *Wales* (see p. xxx).

From Gloucester to (7½ M.) *Grange Court*, see p. 173. Our line here diverges to the left (S.) from that to Ross (see R. 22), follows the right bank of the *Severn*, and skirts the E. margin of the *Forest of Dean* (p. 177). 11 M. *Newnham* (Victoria). To the left we have a good view of the Severn bridge mentioned at p. 122. Beyond (14¼ M.) *Awre* we cross the line from Bristol to *Sharpness* and *Lydbrook*, in the heart of the Forest of Dean; and at (19 M.) *Lydney* those who wish to explore the Forest change carriages. — The train then crosses the *Wye* by a tubular bridge, 630 ft. long, and reaches (27½ M.) *Chepstow* (see p. 177). Excursion through the valley of the *Wye*, see pp. 174-177. — Beyond (32 M.) *Portskewett*, the ruins of Caldicott Castle (p. 177) are seen to the right. At (35¼ M.) *Severn Tunnel Junction* our line unites with that from Bristol (see p. 121).

44½ M. **Newport** (**Westgate ; King's Head ; Rail. Rfmt. Rooms*), a flourishing seaport at the mouth of the *Usk*, with 35,385 inhab., extensive docks, and a large export-trade in iron and coal, is also an important railway-centre for the mining district of S. Wales. The remains of the old *Castle* date from the 11th century. The *Church of St. Woollos* has a good Norman interior and a massive square tower (comp. p. xxxiii). Newport was the scene of Frost's abortive Chartist rising in 1839. *Caerleon* (see above) lies about 3 M. above Newport. — Railway to *Pontypool* and *Hereford*, see R. 24.

Beyond (49¾ M.) *Marshfield* the train crosses the *Rhymney* and enters *Glamorganshire*, the southernmost county in Wales.

56 M. **Cardiff.** — **Hotels.** Royal, 65 St. Mary St., R. & A. 4*s.*; Park, Crockherbtown (Queen St.), R. & A. from 4*s.*, D. 2*s.* 6*d.*-7*s.*, board 10*s.* 6*d.*; *Angel, Castle St., near the castle; Great Western, at the E. end of St. Mary St., near the G. W. R. station. — Queen's, 84 St. Mary St., commercial; Alexandra, near the Taff Vale Station; Raper's Temperance, Westgate St., behind the Royal; Dock Hotel, unpretending. — *Philharmonic Restaurant*, St. Mary St.; *Refreshment Rooms*, at the G. W. R. station.

Tramways traverse some of the main streets. — **Omnibus** from the E. end of St. Mary St. to the *Docks* (fare 1*d.*) and *Penarth* (4*d.*), from High St. to *Llandaff* (3*d.*), etc.

Post Office in St. Mary St., not far from the Royal Hotel.

U. S. Consul, *Major Evan Jones*, 52 Mount Stuart Sq.

Royal Theatre, St. Mary St. — *Philharmonic Hall*, St. Mary St.

Steamers ply from Cardiff daily to *Bristol;* 1-3 times weekly to *Cork*, *Swansea*, *Belfast*, and *Glasgow;* also in summer, at irregular intervals to *Ilfracombe*, *Weston*, and *Burnham*. A small steamer also plies from the Docks to *Penarth.*

Railway Stations. *Great Western Railway Station*, at the E. end of St. Mary St.; *Taff Vale Station*, in Queen Street (Crockherbtown), nearly 1 M. to the W.; *Rhymney Station*, adjoining the last; *Docks Station* of the Taff Vale Co.

Cardiff (the 'Caer', or castle, on the Taff), a well-built and rapidly growing town with 105,000 inhab., is situated on the *Taff*, 2 M. above its mouth, and is the principal outlet for the coal and iron of the surrounding district. The magnificent docks (see below) were built by the late Marquis of Bute, the lord of the manor, to whose spirit and energy the town owes much of its importance. At the beginning of the present cent. the population of Cardiff was little over 1000; and its recent growth may be estimated by the fact that it was the only town of any considerable size that doubled its population between 1871 and 1881. Cardiff, with an export of 8 million tons, now more than rivals Newcastle (p. 414) in the extent of its coal-trade. The annual number of vessels clearing the port is about 13,000, of upwards of 5 million tons burden, a total exceeded by Liverpool and London alone among English ports.

The main thoroughfare is *St. Mary Street*, which is prolonged by *High St.*†, leading to the castle and the bridge over the *Taff*. **Cardiff Castle** (adm. by order obtained at the Bute Estate Office), originally erected in the 11th cent., has been elaborately restored, and is occasionally occupied by the Marquis of Bute. The castle was the prison of Robert Curthose, eldest son of the Conqueror, who died here after nearly 30 years' captivity. The ancient keep (14th cent.) is still preserved; but the lofty clock-tower and other prominent features of the exterior are modern, and most of the inhabited rooms are quite new. The most interesting of the frescoes are those in the Banquet Hall, illustrating the history of the Castle. — A good view of the Castle is obtained from the prettily laid-out *Sophia Gardens*, on the opposite bank of the river, which contain the scanty ruins of an old *Grey Friars Monastery*. The *Church of St. John*, in Church St., to the E. of High St., was built in the 13th cent., but the fine Perp. tower is a later addition. — The *Free Library*, in Working St., is well fitted up; upstairs is an *Art Gallery*, with a few modern paintings (open 10-5, on Wed. & Sat. 10-9).

The ***Docks**, reached by crossing the canal at the E. end of St. Mary St., consist of four main basins, with ample accommodation for large vessels, and 5 M. of quays. Additional docks were opened in 1889 at *Barry*, 8 M. to the S. W. (railway in 35-40 min.).

The *South Wales College*, established in the former Infirmary in Newport Road, is attended by about 150 students.

The most interesting excursion from Cardiff is to *Llandaff Cathedral* (see p. 195), reached by railway, by road, or by a pretty field-path (2 M.).

At the mouth of the Taff estuary, 4 M. from Cardiff, lies **Penarth** (*Penarth Hotel*, on Penarth Head; *Marine Inn*, in the town), the marine residence and bathing-resort of the Cardiffians, now containing about 10,000 inhabitants. It may be reached by railway, omnibus, or steamer (comp. p. 192). The commercial part of the town lies on the N. side of the Head, adjoining the extensive *Penarth Docks;* while the other side is occupied by comfortable-looking villas, separated from the sea by an Esplanade. The water is muddy and the beach covered with large pebbles; but fine salt-water swimming-baths have been erected. Above the

† The name High St. is now officially extended to St. Mary St.

Esplanade are the *Windsor Gardens* (adm. 1*d.*), affording pleasant walks and views. A more extensive view is obtained from *Penarth Head* (200 ft.), near the foreign-looking church. Geologists will find much to interest them in the stratification of the cliffs at the E. end of the Esplanade.

FROM CARDIFF TO CAERPHILLY AND RHYMNEY BRIDGE, 24 M., Rhymney Railway in 1 hr. (fares 4*s.* 2*d.*, 2*s.* 10*d.*, 2*s.*). This line, which starts from the Rhymney Station (p. 192), forms part of the L. N. W. route to S. Wales (comp. p. 191). The whole of this district is covered with a dense network of railways, constructed chiefly for the mineral traffic and of comparatively little importance to tourists. — 8 M. *Caerphilly* (Castle Inn), on the *Rhymney*, is often visited for the sake of its ***Castle**, a picturesque and extensive ruin of the 13th cent. (adm. 3*d.*). Its system of fortification is very elaborate, and seems to have included arrangements by which the surrounding country could be laid under water. Soon after its erection it came into the possession of the Despensers, the notorious favourites of Edward II. (1307-1327), and that monarch once found shelter here, just before his fall. The date of the destruction of the castle is unknown. The 'Leaning Tower', at the S. E. corner (60 ft. high), seems to owe its inclination to an attempt to blow it up with gunpowder. The castle now belongs to the Marquis of Bute. — 15 M. *Ystrad*, prettily situated in the valley of the *Rhymney*, which contracts above Caerphilly. — 16 M. *Hengoed* is the junction for the G. W. R. line from Pontypool to Swansea. — 22 M. *Rhymney*, with large iron-works, employing 7000 men. — At (24 M.) *Rhymney Bridge* we join the line from Abergavenny to Merthyr Tydvil (see p. 191).

FROM CARDIFF TO MERTHYR TYDVIL, 24½ M., Taff Vale Railway in ¾-1 hr. (fares 4*s.*, 3*s.*, 1*s.* 11½*d.*). This line ascends the valley of the *Taff*, the natural charms of which have to a great extent disappeared before the steady advance of iron-works and coal-pits. — 4½ M. *Llandaff Station*, 1¼ M. to the E. of the town (see p. 195). — From (7 M.) *Walnut Tree Junction Bridge* (junction of line to *Llantrissant*, p. 197) we may visit (¾ M.) *Castell Coch* ('red castle'), a finely-situated feudal château (13th cent.; restored) belonging to the Marquis of Bute. Wine is made every year from the small vineyard below the castle. — At (13 M.) *Newbridge* or *Pontypridd Junction* a line, diverging to the left, ascends the valley of the *Rhondda*, the most important of the Glamorganshire colliery districts, to (10½ M.) *Treherbert*, while another, to the right, leads to Caerphilly (see above) and Newport (p. 192) The **Bridge* from which Pontypridd takes its name is a singularly graceful stone bridge spanning the Taff in a single arch, 140 ft. wide and forming a perfect segment of a circle. It was constructed in 1755 by a stone-mason named Edwards, after two unsuccessful attempts. The cylindrical tunnels in the 'haunches' of the bridge were made to lighten the masonry and so diminish the inward thrust. — From (16 M.) *Aberdare Junction* a line runs to (7½ M.) *Aberdare* (with large iron-works) and (10½) *Hirwain Junction* (p. 197). — At (18 M.) *Quaker's Yard Junction* we cross the G. W. R. line from Pontypool to Hirwain. — Farther on we pass under the Neath Valley Railway (p. 197).

24½ M. **Merthyr Tydvil** (*Castle*, R. & A. 4*s.*; *Bush*, near the station, both commercial), a busy but mean-looking and uninviting town with about 50,000 inhabitants. It is of ancient origin, taking its name from the virgin saint, Tydvil the Martyr (5th cent.); but its importance is wholly of modern growth, and three-quarters of a century ago it was an inconsiderable village. It is the great centre of the iron-working district of S. Wales, and the night aspect of the valley in which it lies, lit up by the lurid glare of innumerable furnaces, is very impressive. At the *Cyfarthfa Iron Works*, about 1 M. from the station, the newest and best processes for smelting iron and converting it into steel may be seen. Above the works is *Cyfarthfa Castle*, the residence of the senior partner. — An omnibus runs from Merthyr to (2 M.) *Dowlais*, with the *Dowlais Iron & Steel Works*, wich are on a still more extensive scale. Within their precincts are some remains of the old castle of *Morlais*, formerly the residence of the Welsh princes of Brecon. Visitors are courteously admitted to either establishment on application at the office.

Travellers who do not wish to return to Cardiff may go on from Merthyr eastwards to *Abergavenny* (p. 191), northwards to *Brecon* (p. 204), or westwards to *Swansea* (p. 197).

About 5 min. after leaving Cardiff the train stops at (58 M.) *Ely*, the station for **Llandaff** *(Red Lion)*, 1 M. to the right, the smallest city in England (700 inhab.), now practically a suburb of Cardiff and a favourite residence of rich Cardiffians. It is interesting as the seat of perhaps the oldest episcopal see in Great Britain, established by SS. Dubritius and Teilo at the end of the 6th century. On our way from the station to the cathedral we pass the large castellated gateway of the old *Bishop's Palace* (destroyed by Owen Glendower). Near the gateway is a *Cross*, on an ancient base.

The ***Cathedral,** pleasantly situated amid trees, at the foot of a slope rising above the river *Taff*, occupies the same spot as the earliest church of SS. Dubritius and Teilo. This, however, which seems to have been a very small edifice, was removed by Bishop Urban (1107-1133), who undertook the erection of an entirely new church. In the E.E. period Urban's church was extended westwards as far as the present W. front, and the only remains of it are the Norman arch between the Presbytery and Lady Chapel, part of the S. wall of the former, and the Norman doorways incorporated in the aisle-walls. The Chapter House is also E.E., of a somewhat later date; the Lady Chapel is early Dec.; the Presbytery and the walls of the aisles both in nave and choir were rebuilt in the late Dec. period; and the N.W. tower was built by Jasper Tudor, uncle of Henry VII., while the S. W. tower (E. E.) seems to have been left standing. At a later date the building was completely neglected; the W. end of the nave collapsed at the beginning of last cent., and the cathedral became an absolute ruin. About 1735-40 a sort of Italian temple was made within the walls, occupying the presbytery, choir, and E. end of the nave; and this absurd erection remained till 1843, when the restoration which culminated in the present church was begun. The architect was Mr. Prichard, to whom is due also the S.W. tower (195 ft.), replacing the original E. E. tower, pulled down in 1786. — The cathedral is 175 ft. long from E. to W., and 72 ft. wide across the nave and aisles. The daily services are at 10 a. m. and 5 p. m., the latter choral.

'There may be other churches which, in some points, come nearer to ideal perfection, but then there is none which has in the same way risen to a new life out of a state of such seemingly hopeless ruin'.

The **Exterior** of the building, owing to the lack of transepts, suggests a large parish-church rather than a cathedral. The W. façade, however, the central part of which belongs to the E. E. edifice, is fine, and has been compared to those of Ripon Cathedral and St. Remi at Rheims. Mr. Freeman comments on the satisfactory effect produced by the perspicuity of its construction, which is in no way disguised by the ornamentation.

The ***Interior**, being open from end to end, is very impressive. Among the chief points of interest are the grand late-Norman **Arch* between the presbytery and the Lady Chapel; the *Altar-piece by *Rossetti;* the *Lady Chapel;* the *Chapter House*, which is of very unusual form (square, with a central pillar); the monuments of *Sir David Matthew*, standard-bearer of Edward IV. (N. aisle of presbytery) and *Sir William Matthew* (d. 1528; N. aisle of nave); and the supposed tomb of *St. Teilo*, on the S. side of the presbytery. The way in which the E. bays of the ritual choir are blocked up is supposed to be due to the former existence of a pair of small transeptal towers. The roof throughout is modern; so also is the stained glass, which includes some good specimens of *Morris*. — In the churchyard is a Memorial Cross to *Dean Conybeare* (d. 1857), an eminent geologist. — The group of neat modern buildings on the slope above the cathedral include the *Deanery* and the *Canonry*. Adjacent is the *Cathedral School*, founded by Dr. Vaughan, Dean of Llandaff.

Between Cardiff and Llantrissant the train crosses the *Ely* sixteen times. 60 M. *St. Fagans*, with the seat of Lord Windsor, takes its name from an early missionary, said to have been sent from Rome in A. D. 180. — 67 M. *Llantrissant* (Windsor Arms), picturesquely situated on a hill at some distance to the N. of the station, is the junction of a branch-line to (6 M.) *Cowbridge* (Bear), a small town with the remains of some old fortifications.

Cowbridge is the nearest railway-station to (5½ M.) *Llantwit Major*, with an interesting double church, dating in its present form from the 13-14th centuries. It represents, however, a monastic foundation of the 5th cent., to which was attached a famous College ('the first Christian school of learning in Britain'), where Gildas, Taliesin, and other eminent Welshmen were educated. The epithet of 'New Church', generally applied to the E. part of the structure, which is really the older, is supposed to have come into use at the Reformation, when the old monastic church became the 'new' parish-church. — Near Llantwit is a ruined castle locally known as the *Old Place*.

On the coast, about 2 M. to the W. of Llantwit, is *St. Donat's Castle*, a picturesque castellated mansion of the 16th cent., containing some fine wood-carving by Grinling Gibbons. A room is shown in which Archbishop Usher found shelter in 1645-46.

75½ M. **Bridgend** (**Wyndham Arms; Bear, Castle* plain), the junction for the Llynfi Valley Railway (to *Maesteg*), is a small town, with 7000 inhab. and the scanty remains of a Norman castle.

Visits may be paid to *Ogmore Castle*, a Norman fragment, 2½ M. to the S. W.; to the (2 M.) ruins of *Ewenny Priory*, founded in 1146 and (according to Mr. Freeman) 'perhaps the best specimen of a fortified ecclesiastical building, the union of castle and monastery in the same structure'; to *Coity Castle* (13-14th cent.) and *Coity Church* (good window tracery), 2 M. to the N. E.; and to *Southerndown* (Marine), a small watering-place, and *Dunraven Castle*, a modern mansion finely situated on a rocky promontory, 5-6 M. to the S. Dunraven is believed to occupy the site of a royal residence of Caractacus. Near it are the *Nash Cliffs*, a fine bit of coast-scenery.

Near (88 M.) *Port Talbot*, the outlet for the copper, coal, and iron of the Vale of Afon, are the fine mansion and grounds of *Margam Abbey*, with the ruins of a Cistercian monastery of the 12th century. The orangery contains a collection of orange-trees, raised from a cargo that was wrecked here on its way to London for the use of Queen Mary, wife of William III. — 91½ M. *Briton Ferry*, the port of Neath.

94 M. **Neath** (**Castle; *Mackworth; Vale of Neath Arms*), a town with 10,450 inhab., situated at the mouth of the *Neath* and surrounded by coal, iron, tin, and copper works. About 1 M. to the N. are the

ruins of *Neath Abbey*, founded in 1111. The *Castle*, of which only the entrance-gate and towers remain, lies to the right of the station.

From Neath to Merthyr Tydvil, 24 M., railway in 1¼ hr. (fares 4*s.* 9*d.*, 3*s.*, 1*s.* 11*d.*). This railway ascends the beautiful *Vale of Neath, with numerous waterfalls, wooded ravines, and picturesque crags. The finest falls are near *Pont Neath Vaughan* (Dinas Hotel; Angel), where the ravines of the *Neath*, the *Hepste*, the *Mellte*, and the *Perddyn*, each containing a series of falls, converge. Pont Neath lies 3 M. above (7 M.) *Glyn Neath* (Lamb & Flag, ¾ M. from the station), the nearest railway-station. — 16½ M. *Hirwain* (p. 194). — 24 M. *Merthyr Tydvil*, see p. 194.

From Neath to *Brecon*, see R. 26.

On leaving Neath we pass the ruins of the castle on the right, and those of the abbey (a little farther on) on the left. — 101 M. *Landore* (Rail. Refreshmt. Rooms), the junction of the short line to (1 M.) *Swansea*, lies in the middle of a district blackened and desolated by the smoke of innumerable copper-works.

Swansea *(Mackworth Arms*, high charges; **Longlands Temperance*, R. & A. from 3*s.*; *Cameron Arms; Castle; Great Western Temperance)*, Welsh *Abertawe*, a busy town of about 100,000 inhab., situated at the mouth of the *Tawe*, in the N.W. angle of *Swansea Bay*, is the chief seat of the copper trade of England, and perhaps the most important copper-smelting centre in the world.

About 20,000 tons of copper (valued at 3-4 millions sterling) are annually produced by its foundries. No copper is found in this part of Wales, but the ore is brought hither from Cornwall and foreign countries owing to the abundance and cheapness of fuel, there being about 250 coal-pits within a radius of 15 M. This abundance has also led to the erection of numerous iron, zinc, lead, tin-plate, and other manufactories, while the docks are entered annually by 5000 vessels with a burden of upwards of 2,000,000 tons. About 2,000,000 tons of tin-plates, value 3,000,000*l*, are exported annually, while the total value of the trade of Swansea (import and export) is estimated at 8-10 millions sterling. In certain states of the wind Swansea is completely enveloped in the smoke of the copper-works, which, however, is said to be less unhealthy than one would suppose.

In Swansea itself, the name of which may be a corruption of 'Sweyn's Ey', or island, there is little to detain the traveller, and visitors to the Gower Peninsula (p. 198) are advised to proceed at once to the Mumbles. The scanty remains of the *Castle*, dating from the 14th cent., are hidden among the buildings adjoining the *Post Office*, in Castle St.; but a view of the fine arcaded parapet (comp. p. 212) round the keep may be obtained by descending the narrow lane to the right. — Near the *Victoria Station* (L. N. W.) and the extensive *Docks* is the *Royal Institute of South Wales*, containing a small museum of local antiquities (adm. 1*d.*). — In the Alexandra Road, not far from the *G. W. R. Station*, is the *Free Library and Institute of Science and Art*. The nave of the *Parish Church of St. Mary* is ugly and featureless, but the Dec. chancel, the reputed work of Bishop Gower (p. 212), is interesting, and contains a few old brasses and monuments. — Permission to visit one of the large *Copper Works*, or the *Siemens Steel Works* (with 1300 men), at Landore, is generally obtainable on previous application. The 'tapping' of a blast-furnace at night is an imposing sight.

A good general view of Swansea is obtained from the hill named the *Graig*, which rises a little to the W. of the G. W. R. Station. To reach the top we may follow the steep road named Mount Pleasant, bearing to the right beyond the *Grammar School* and leaving the *Work House* to the left. — *Kilvey Hill*, on the opposite (E.) side of the river, is also a good point of view. — A fine view of *Swansea Bay* is obtained from the end of the *W. Pier*, which is 2000 ft. long.

Steamers ply regularly from Swansea to *Bristol*, *Glasgow*, *Liverpool*, and *Belfast*, and in summer to *Ilfracombe* (2 hrs.) and *Padstow*.

From Swansea to *Brecon*, see p. 205.

From Swansea to the Mumbles *(Oystermouth)*, 5 M., Steam Tramway, starting near the Victoria Station (p. 197), hourly during the day (fare 4*d.*; in 'reserved car' 8*d.*). — The pleasant road skirts the sands of *Swansea Bay*, the natural beauty of which triumphs over many disadvantages. For the first 3 M. the L. N. W. Railway (see p. 199) runs between the sea and the road. At *Swansea Bay Station*, St. Helen's Road, the steam-tramway unites with the horse-tramway from Gower St. Farther on we pass (on the right) the *Swansea Cricket Ground* and *Park Wern*, the latter containing a large colony of wild white rabbits. At (3 M.) *Black Pill* is the *Mumbles Road Station* of the L. N. W. Railway. To the left are the remains of a submerged forest. — The tramway-terminus at the Mumbles is about 1/2 M. from the hotels.

The Mumbles *(*Ship & Castle; George; Mermaid; Lodgings)* is a small watering-place which has developed out of the fishing-village of *Oystermouth* and has assumed the name that in strict parlance belongs to the detached rocks off the S. horn of Swansea Bay. The name is supposed to be derived from the resemblance of these rocks to projecting breasts *(mammae)*. The oyster-beds here are nearly exhausted. The bathing is tolerable, and a good view of Swansea is enjoyed across the bay; but, as there is nothing of special interest, the traveller had better sleep at *Langland Bay* or *Caswell Bay* (see below; pony chaise 1*s.* 6*d.*-2*s.* 6*d.*), visiting Oystermouth Castle on the way. A visit may also be paid to the Lighthouse on Mumbles Head.

The Mumbles forms the usual and most convenient portal to the ***Gower Peninsula**, which projects from the S.W. corner of Glamorganshire, and is about 15 M. long and 5-6 M. broad. Though comparatively little known, the whole of this peninsula is picturesque enough to repay a stay of several days; but the finest scenery, that of the S. coast, may be fairly explored in one day's walk. It is emphatically a district for the pedestrian, as beyond the railway-termini there is no convenient transport for visitors (omnibuses, see p. 199), while many of the finest points are inaccessible except on foot. Inns are few and far between, and those who explore the district thoroughly must now and again be content with farm-house or coast-guard accommodation. Two-thirds of Gower are occupied by the English-speaking descendants of Flemish or Norman colonists, who have cooped up the original Welsh inhabitants in the N. W. corner (comp. p. 208). The churches, though rudely built, possess various features of interest; their towers, resembling those of Pembrokeshire (p. 209), combine the character of a campanile and a stronghold. The student of mediæval architecture should provide himself with *Freeman's* 'Notes on the Architectural Antiquities of Gower' (1850). The antiquarian will also find much to interest him in the peninsula.

The railway-stations nearest to the centre of the Peninsula are *Llanmorlais*, to the N., and *Killay*, on the E., both on the ramification of the L. N. W. Railway which extends hence to Craven Arms and Shrewsbury (comp. pp. 201, 205). Omnibuses also ply between Swansea and several of the villages in Gower, generally leaving Gower early in the morning and returning about 6 p.m.

The following round of about 25 M. from the Mumbles, or 20 M. from Caswell Bay, will give a fairly adequate idea of Gower scenery. Ample time (9-10 hrs.) should be allowed for the excursion, as some of the walking is rather rough. — From the tramway-terminus at the Mumbles (see above) we follow the road for 150 yds. farther and take the road leading inland (to the right), past *Oystermouth Castle*, a picturesque and extensive ruin of the 14th cent. (small fee to the keeper). At the top of the hill, a few hundred yards farther, just beyond the school, we diverge to the left from the direct road to Caswell Bay, in order to visit the pretty little (3/4 M.) **Langland Bay** (**Langland Bay Hotel*, D. 4*s*.), where there are a few villas. From Langland a steep lane leads us back to the (1/2 M.) main road, where we turn to the left. 1 M. **Caswell Bay** (**Hotel*, unpretending, R., B., & A. 5*s*.) is a charming little sandy cove, flanked with rocks and enlivened with one or two private residences in addition to the hotel. The bathing here and at Langland Bay is, however, rather dangerous on account of the strong outward currents. From the hotel we follow the road for 5 min. more; then diverge to the left through the bracken and gorse, cross a stile, and descend to (5 min.) *Brandy Cove*, a small green inlet owing its name to smuggling traditions. We cross this cove and follow the path leading round the cliffs (easier than the cart-track over the top of the promontory) to (1/4 hr.) *Pwll-du Bay* ('Poolth-dee'; Beaufort Arms, small), with its curious banks of pebbles. Fine view of the *Pwll-du Head*, a bold mass of limestone on the other side of the bay. [From Pwll-du a path leads inland through the well-wooded *Bishopston Valley* to (2 M.) *Bishopston* (p. 201).] From the inn we ascend a rough and steep track to (8-10 min.) the hamlet of *High Pennard*, where we take a lane to the right (inland), following it to the left when it bends and regaining the cliff-track near (8 min.) a farmhouse, with a pond in front of it. About 4 min. beyond the farm is a ruinous stone cattle-shed, opposite which begins a faintly marked path, descending deviously to the left to *Bacon Hole*, a cave on this side of the W. promontory of the bay, almost in a straight line below the shed. The cave is interesting to scientific visitors owing to the fact that large deposits of prehistoric bones were found here in 1850, but its appearance is insignificant. The limestone cliffs, however, along this part of the coast are very fine, though scarcely so grand or varied as those near Tenby (see p. 209). We now return to the track on the top of the cliffs (though experts, who think it worth while, may follow a difficult and even dangerous path along their face to two other caves) and in about 10 min. reach another stone hut, in a line with which, to the left, is *Minchin Head*, easily recognised by the knob of white limestone at the top. Below this knob is *Minchin Hole*, a cave extending into the rock for a distance of 170 ft. The descent to it, over slippery turf, requires caution and a steady head, but those who do not care for this scramble should not miss the *View of the coast from the top of the promontory.

Continuing to follow the track over the head of the cliffs, we cross the elastic turf of *Pennard Burrows* and soon come in sight of the large *Union Workhouse*, on the slope of *Cefn Bryn*. In 1/4 hr. we see the hamlet of *James Green* to the right, and in 5 min. more the ruin of *Pennard Castle*. To the left the cliffs here recede, leaving room for the sandy bay of *Shire Combe*. At low tide we may descend to the beach and pass through the natural archway at the W. end of this bay, but at high tide we must cross the neck to reach **Three Cliffs Bay*. The origin of the name appears when we look back at the rocks separating it from Shire Combe Bay. A small stream here enters the sea. Three Cliffs Bay is bounded on the W. by a fine promontory called the *High Tor*, which may be rounded at low water. On the other side extend the beautiful sands of *Oxwich Bay*, along which we can walk all the way to (2 M.) the church (a typical example of a Gower church) and parsonage of Oxwich, nestling under the cliffs at the W. extremity. Here also is a coastguard's cottage, where refreshments and a bed may be obtained. Amid the woods to the right, as we cross the bay, are visible the village, church, and old castle of *Penrice*. The village of *Oxwich* lies a little inland (to the N.) of the church, while *Oxwich Castle* (16th cent.), now incorporated with a farm-house, stands on the top of the cliffs.

[Those who do not care to see the Culver Hole (see below), or to go on to the Worms Head, may turn inland at Oxwich and proceed viâ *Pen-y-hitch* and *Reynoldston* to ($5^1/_2$ M.) *Arthur's Stone* (see below).]

From Oxwich we may ascend the rough road passing to the right of the castle, and then descend through the village of *Slade*, to *Port Eynon Bay*, another level expanse of sand. A walk of $^3/_4$ hr. from Oxwich brings us to *Port Eynon* (Inn, small) where primitive summer-quarters and good bathing may be had. Here a boy may be engaged to show the way to *Culver Hole*, an interesting cavern on the other side of the promontory bounding Port Eynon Bay on the W. The cave consists of a spacious chamber in the limestone rock, the lofty and narrow opening of which is filled with solid masonry, leaving only a small and low entrance. This work is usually ascribed to smugglers of byegone days, though it is difficult to see how they could have approached it by sea except in very calm weather. From a point on the top of the cliff an easy zigzag path winds down the grassy slope to the cave, but the last part of the descent is unpleasant for ladies.

[The walk along the cliffs from Port Eynon to (8-9 M.) the Worms Head, passing the *Paviland Caves* and **Mewslade Bay*, is very fine, but would necessitate another day in Gower. The ***Worms Head**, perhaps the grandest piece of rock-scenery in the peninsula, consists of a long narrow promontory, stretching into the sea for about 1 M. and quite detached from the mainland at high-water. Near the point is a curious 'Blow Hole', resembling the Devil's Bellows at Kynance Cove (p. 147), and making a sharp whistling sound when the wind or sea is high. — Visitors to the Worms may obtain accommodation at a farm-house at *Rhossily*, a village about 1 M. from the neck of the headland. Rhossily is 6 M. by road from *Reynoldston* (see below), at which is the nearest decent inn.]

Starting from Port Eynon on our return-journey, we walk across the sand-hills to ($^3/_4$ M.) the village of *Horton*, which we see in front of us. Thence we follow the road in a straight (N.E.) direction to (2 M.) *Penrice* (comp. above), with its church, and beyond it make a rapid descent, at the foot of which is the iron gate of the avenue to *Penrice House*. To visit the ivy-clad ruins of *Penrice Castle* (permission necessary), dating in part from the 12th cent., we pass through this gate, leaving the grounds at the other end of the avenue by the lodge on the main road to Swansea.

[Those who wish to visit *Arthur's Stone*, the best-known cromlech in Gower, here turn to the left, and then, at ($^1/_4$ M.) the cross-roads, where there is a building curiously supported on stone props, to the right. Our road crosses the ridge of Cefn Bryn and leads to (1 M.) the road from Reynoldston to *Killay* (p. 199), at a point near a so-called 'Holy Well'. Hence we proceed to the left for $^1/_3$ M., and then leave the road by a grass-track to visit *Arthur's Stone*, which lies on the moor about $^1/_3$ M. to the right. The cap-stone of this large cromlech is 14 ft. long, and weighs 25 tons. Arthur's Stone is about $4^1/_2$ M. from *Llanmorlais* (p. 199). — In returning we may vary the route by proceeding to the W. to (1 M.) *Reynoldston* (*Arthur's Stone Hotel, unpretending), where the road turns to the S. and soon reaches ($^3/_4$ M.) the Swansea road, at a point about $1^1/_2$ M. to the W. of that at which we quitted it.]

For Caswell Bay we turn to the right on reaching the Swansea road (see p. 200). After about 1 M. we pass the church of *Nicholaston* on the right, and 1 M. farther on reach the houses of *Penmaen*, with the West Gower Workhouse (p. 199) above us on the left. At (1/4 M.) *Penmaen Church*, now of no interest through unskilful restoration, a road diverging to the left leads to the summit of *Cefn Bryn* (690 ft.; *View). Our road descends to (1 M.) the village of *Park Mill*, 1/2 M. beyond which are the new *Schools*, the mouth of the *Ilston Valley*, and the small *Gower Inn*, a convenient centre for several excursions. Pennard Castle (p. 199) lies about 1 M. to the S. Beyond the Gower Inn the road ascends past *Kilvrough House* to (1 1/2 M.) a lime-kiln (on the left). Here we quit the road by a gate on the right and follow a path, which crosses fields, stiles, and another road, to (3/4 M.) *Kittle*. At Kittle we join the road which descends to the bottom of the valley and then ascends steeply to (1/4 M.) *Bishopston* (Inn). (Walk through the valley to the sea, see p. 199.) Passing through Bishopston, we follow the road for 1 M. farther, and turn to the left at the foot of the hill, where it strikes another road at right angles. A few hundred yards farther on, by a stone wall, we turn to the right and follow the road to (3/4 M.) *Caswell Bay* (p. 199).

From the point at which we quitted it (see above), the road to (7 M.) Swansea runs to the N.E. to (3 M.) *Killay Station*, and then almost due E. to (2 M.) *Sketty* and (2 M.) *Swansea* (p. 197).

After leaving Landore (p. 197) the train penetrates a tunnel and near (105 M.) *Gowerton* intersects the L.N.W. line from Craven Arms to Swansea (comp. p. 199). — To the right, at (107 1/2 M.) *Loughor*, are the ruins of a Norman castle. We then cross the estuary of the *Llwchwr (Loughor)*, or *Burry*.

111 1/2 M. **Llanelly** *(Stepney Arms)*, a manufacturing town and mineral port, with 20,000 inhabitants. Large quantities of coal are exported hence to France, Spain, and the Mediterranean. Llanelly is the junction of a line to *Llandilo* (p. 207) and *Llandovery* (comp. p. 206). — Beyond Llanelly the train quits the mineral district, and the scenery improves. The line is carried along the shore on an embankment. — 115 1/2 M. *Pembrey and Burry Port*, with large copper-works. — 120 M. *Kidwelly* (Pelican), pleasantly situated on Carmarthen Bay, with a picturesque ruined castle (14th cent.) and an interesting church (Dec.). — The train now ascends the left bank of the estuary of the *Towy*. From (124 1/2 M.) *Ferryside* (White Lion), a small seaside resort, we have a good view of the ruins of *Llanstephan Castle*, on the opposite side of the estuary.

Walkers may follow the coast from Llanstephan (ferry 3*d*.) to (19 M.) *Tenby* (p. 209), viâ (3 1/2 M.) *Laugharne* (pron. 'Larne'), with an old castle, still inhabited, (4 1/2 M.) *Pendine*, (5 1/2 M.) *Amroth*, and (3 M.) *Saundersfoot*.

From Ferryside the train ascends along the Towy (views) to (130 M.) *Carmarthen Junction* (Rail. Refreshment Rooms), the junction for (1 M.) Carmarthen, Lampeter, and Aberystwith (see p. 208). We have a good view, to the right, of the Vale of Towy and the town of Carmarthen. — The train crosses the Towy. 139 M. *St. Clears* (Station Hotel) was the centre of the 'Rebecca Riots' of 1843, the object of which was the abolition of turnpike-gates. (The name is an allusion to Gen. xxiv. 60.)

145 M. *Whitland* (Yelverton Arms) is the junction of lines to Tenby and Pembroke (see R. 28) and to Cardigan.

FROM WHITLAND TO CARDIGAN, 27½ M., in 1½ hr. (5*s.* 10*d.*, 4*s.* 1*d.*, 2*s.* 11*d.* or 2*s.* 3½*d.*). This line ascends the prettily-wooded valley of the *Afon Taf*. — 16½ M. *Crymmych Arms* is the nearest railway-station for (11 M.) *Newport* (Llwyngair Arms; Commercial), to which a coach plies daily (fare 2*s.* 6*d.*). Crymmych Arms is also the starting-point for a walk along the *Precely Hills* to (6½ M.) *Precely Top* (1735 ft.), the highest point in Pembrokeshire. — Beyond Crymmych Arms the train crosses the culminating point of the line (690 ft.) and descends (fine views of the coast) to (20½ M.) *Boncath* and (24 M.) *Kilgerran*, the latter with a ruined castle (13th cent.), on a high cliff overlooking the most picturesque part of the narrow valley of the *Teifi*. — 27½ M. **Cardigan** *(Black Lion)*, a small and dull town, at the mouth of the *Teifi*, with 4000 inhab. and the scanty remains of an old castle. A coach runs hence through the pretty valley of the Teifi, passing the picturesque ravine at the *Henllan Falls*, to (10 M.) *Newcastle Emlyn* (Salutation Hotel), a good fishing-station, and (19 M.) *Llandyssil* (p. 208). The road running northwards to (20 M.) *New Quay* (p. 208) and (23 M.) *Aberayron* (p. 208) offers few attractions to the tourist, but some of the coast scenery is fine.

Beyond Whitland the *Precely Hills* (see above) are visible to the right. — 162 M. **Haverfordwest** (**Castle*; *Salutation*, commercial), a small town on the *Cleddau*, with 6000 inhab. and the shell of an old castle prominently situated in its midst. The interesting *Church of St. Mary* contains a good effigy of a pilgrim (16th cent.). Near the river are the ruins of an *Augustine Priory* (E.E.). Haverfordwest was the capital of the Flemish colony settled in Pembroke at the beginning of the 12th cent. (see p. 208).

About 4½ M. to the S. E. is ***Picton Castle** (order obtained at the estate-office in Haverfordwest), an admirable specimen of the fastness of a Norman baron of the 11th cent., though somewhat marred by modern additions. It lies in the midst of a beautiful park. — Coaches ply from Haverfordwest to (16 M.) *St. David's* (see p. 214), to (15 M.) *Fishguard* (fare 2*s.* 6*d.*; see p. 216), and to (7 M.) *Little Haven.*

As the train leaves Haverfordwest we obtain good views of the castle and priory to the right. At (167 M.) *Johnston Junction* the line forks, one branch going to (170 M.) *Milford* and the other to (171 M.) *New Milford.* As we approach the former we see the scanty ruins of *Pill Priory* in a valley to the right.

Milford *(Lord Nelson)*, a town with 4000 inhab., lies about 6 M. above the mouth of *Milford Haven*, a splendid harbour, in which the whole English navy could ride securely at anchor. It was formerly a considerable seaport, and it is frequently mentioned in Shakespeare's 'Cymbeline'; but the attempts of modern enterprise and capital to revive its importance have hitherto resulted only in a conglomeration of large but deserted docks, quays, and lines of railway. On a building near the station is a tablet recording, in amusingly pompous language, the visit of George IV. in 1821. Henry VII. landed here in 1485, as Earl of Richmond, on his way to claim the crown.

New Milford or *Neyland* (**South Wales Hotel*, R. & A. from 3*s.* 6*d.*), which lies a little farther up the Haven, directly opposite Pembroke Dock (p. 213), is the terminus of the G. W. Railway and the starting-point of steamers to Waterford and Cork. Steam Ferry to Pembroke Dock (Hobbes Point, p. 213) 2*d.*, return-fare 3*d.*

Pleasant boating-excursions may be made in ***Milford Haven**, and its various ramifications explored. In fine weather a boat is the best means of passing from the one Milford to the other; but the road (5 M.) is also not unattractive. The Haven is protected by fortifications.

26. From Hereford to Brecon and Swansea.

Midland Railway from Hereford to (38 M.) *Brecon* in 1¾ hr. (fares 5*s.*, 3*s.* 1½*d.*); to (78 M.) *Swansea* in 4 hrs. (fares 11*s.* 4*d.*, 6*s.* 5½*d.*). This route traverses much of the finest scenery in South Wales, and a visit to the *Upper Valley of the Wye* (see below) may be combined with it.

The train starts from the *Barton Station* (see p. 180). The first few stations are unimportant. Near (9 M.) *Moorhampton* a well-preserved portion of *Offa's Dyke* (p. 264) is visible. At (13½ M.) *Eardisley* a line diverges to *Kington*, *Presteign*, and *New Radnor*. Beyond (17 M.) *Whitney* we cross the *Wye* and pass *Clifford Castle* (to the left), the traditional birthplace of 'Fair Rosamond'.

21 M. **Hay** *(Crown; Blue Boar)*, an old Norman border-town, with 2000 inhab. and the scanty remains of a castle. The name, like the Hague in Holland, means a hedge or enclosure (French *haie*). The station here is in England (Herefordshire) and the town in Wales (Breconshire). Those who wish to explore the Upper Wye (see below) on foot may begin at Hay; and a pleasant walk may also be taken to the S. across the Black Mts. to (12 M.) Llanthony (p. 191). — 24½ M. *Glasbury.* Good view of the Wye Valley.

26 M. *Three Cocks Junction* (Rail. Refreshmt. Rooms; Three Cocks Inn, ½ M. to the E.) is the junction for the Mid-Wales Railway (Cambrian) through the *Upper Valley of the Wye.* To the left rise the *Black Mountains* (p. 191).

From Three Cocks Junction to Moat Lane, 48 M., railway in 2-3 hrs. (fares 9*s.* 11*d.*, 6*s.* 11*d.*, 4*s.*). This line follows the upper course of the *Wye*, the beautiful scenery of which is, however, best explored by the pedestrian. — From (7 M.) *Boughrood* a visit may be paid to *Craig Pwll Du*, or rock of the black pit, below which is a waterfall 25 ft. high. — 9½ M. *Aberedw*, at the mouth of the romantic glen of the *Edw*, with an old church. — 14 M. **Builth** or *Builth Wells (Lion; Crown)*, a small town with chalybeate and sulphur springs and the earthworks of a castle. About 2½ M. to the W. is *Cwm Llewelyn*, where Llewelyn, the last native Prince of Wales, was defeated and slain by the English in 1282. — At (16 M.) *Llechryd Junction* (Rail. Refreshmt. Rooms) our line intersects the Central Wales Railway (L. N. W.; *Builth Road* station; not to be confounded with the Mid-Wales Railway) from *Craven Arms* to *Carmarthen* and *Swansea* (comp. p. 205). — 20 M. *Newbridge-on-Wye* (New Inn); 24 M. *Doldowlod.*

26½ M. **Rhayader** *(Lion)*, a small town beautifully situated on the Wye and surrounded by lofty hills. **Cwm Elan*, or valley of the *Elan*, 5 M. to the S. W., is a beautiful little glen; 1 M. farther on is *Nant Gwyllt*, occupied by Shelley after his marriage with Harriet Westbrook. — The train now leaves the Wye and runs towards the N., passing the flannel-making town of (30½ M.) **Llanidloes** *(Trewythan Arms)*, to (48 M.) *Moat Lane*, where it reaches the line from Shrewsbury to Aberystwith (see p. 265).

From Rhayader the walker may follow up the *Wye* to its (18 M.) source on the slopes of *Plinlimmon* (2460 ft.), halfway to Aberystwith (p. 267). There are few pleasanter walking-tours of a week's duration in England than that afforded by a descent of the Wye from the source to the mouth, a distance of 130 M. The lower course, from Ross to Chepstow, is described at p. 174 et seq.

29 M. *Talgarth* (Ashburnham Arms). The finely-shaped Brecon Beacons (see below) now come into view on the left. On the same side is *Llyn Safadden* or *Llangorse Pool.* — 33½ M. *Talyllyn* (Rail. Refreshmt. Rooms) is the junction of a line to *Dowlais* and *Merthyr Tydvil* (p. 194). The train now passes through a tunnel, on emerging from which we have a fine view of the *Usk*, with the Brecon Beacons in the background. To the right, as we enter Brecon station, is the *Memorial College*, erected in commemoration of the Nonconforming clergy of 1662.

38 M. **Brecon** (*Castle*, R. & A. 4*s.*; *Wellington*), the capital of *Breconshire* or *Brecknockshire*, is a town of 6623 inhab., charmingly situated in a depression at the confluence of the *Usk* and the *Honddu*. In the *Ely Tower*, a fragment of the old castle, in the garden of the Castle Hotel, took place the famous conference between the Bishop of Ely and the Duke of Buckingham which resulted in the overthrow of Richard III. The top commands a good view of the Beacons. — The **Priory Church of St. John* (keys kept in a white cottage to the left of the entrance; fee 6*d.*), a good E. E. and Dec. edifice, with a massive tower, has been well restored by Sir G. G. Scott. Mr. Freeman considers it the noblest specimen of a class of churches not uncommon in Wales, where massiveness of effect is produced by simplicity of construction. It is reached by the bridge over the Honddu, and on the way to it we pass part of the embattled wall of the old priory. — About ½ M. beyond the *Llanfaes Bridge*, crossing the Usk, is *Christ College*, with a good E. E. chapel, formerly belonging to a Dominican priory. The house in the High St. in which Mrs. Siddons (1755-1831) was born bears an appropriate tablet. The *Priory Walk*, on the Honddu, and the *Captain's Walk*, on the Usk, are two pleasantly shaded promenades.

An admirable view of Brecon and the Beacons is obtained from the top of **Pen-y-Crug**, a hill 1½ M. to the N.W. of the town. To reach it we turn to the right beyond the Castle Hotel and pass the (¼ M.) *Cemetery*. About ½ M. farther on, a little beyond the milestone, we take a path leading across a field to *Pen-y-Crug Farm;* passing through the farm-yard, we reach the open hillside and in 10 min. more gain the top, where there are distinct remains of an ancient camp. — Another good point of view is *Slwch Tump*, on the E. side of the town, reached by following Free St. from the station and passing under the line.

Another pleasant object for a short walk is afforded by the **Frwdgrech Waterfalls.** We cross the *Llanfaes Bridge* (see above), at the S. end of the town, and continue in a straight direction, along the Llandovery Road, passing a toll-gate, to (⅓ M.) a point where the road forks. We take the branch to the left, which is lined with numerous holly and other trees and leads to (⅔ M.) *Frwdgrech Lodge* (on the left). Just beyond this we cross a bridge, on the other side of which are three roads. We follow that in the centre and reach (¾ M.) the bridge crossing the stream which forms the falls, one immediately below and the other a little above the bridge. The falls are small, but their setting is pretty.

The twin peaks of the ***Brecknock** or **Brecon Beacons**, rising 5 M. to the S. of Brecon, are the highest peaks in S. Wales, and among the most gracefully-shaped mountains in the kingdom. The direct route from Brecon to the top takes walkers 3-4 hrs., but driving is practicable to Blaengwdi Farm (see p. 205). As far as (1¼ M.) the bridge beyond Frwdgrech Lodge, see above. Here we take the road to the left and ascend to (1½ M.) *Blaengwdi Farm.* Beyond the farm we turn to the right, and ⅓ M. farther on follow a narrow lane to the left, which brings us to the W. part of a shoulder extending to the (1½-2 hrs.) top of **Pen-y-Fan* (2910 ft.), the loftier peak. — An alternative route from Brecon is the following. We turn to the left at the turnpike-gate, ⅓ M. beyond the Llanfaes Bridge (see p. 204), and follow the high-road, which is steep at first, to (2½ M.) *Pant Farm.* Beyond the farm we turn to the right and pass through a gate leading to the E. arm of the shoulder above mentioned. — Many, however, prefer to ascend from (14 M.) *Torpantau*, a station on the line to Merthyr (see p. 194), on the S. side of the Beacons, and to descend by one of the above routes. The Beacons, however, do not show to advantage from the S., and the pleasantest part of this route is the descent. — The *View from the top includes the Black Mts. on the E., the Carmarthen Van on the W., and the Valley of the Usk and Llangorse Pool to the N. In clear weather Cader Idris is sometimes visible to the N.W. and the Bristol Channel to the S.

Among other points for easy excursions from Brecon are (6 M.) *Llangorse Pool* (see p. 204), a great resort of anglers; *Y Caer Bannau*, the old Roman camp of *Bannium*, 2½ M. to the W.; and (9 M.) *Bwlch*, reached by a beautiful walk or drive through the Usk valley, or from (7 M.) *Talybont* station, on the Merthyr line (p. 194).

As the train leaves Brecon we have another beautiful view of the Beacons and the Usk. 40½ M. *Cradoc*, ¾ M. to the N. of Y Caer Bannau (see above); 42 M. *Aberbran.* — 46½ M. *Devynock* (Usk and Railway; Pont Senny; Bull), a pleasantly-situated village at the confluence of the *Senny* and the Usk.

A very picturesque drive may be taken from Devynock to (12½ M.) *Llandovery* (see p. 206), but there is no public conveyance. The road traverses some of the prettiest scenery in South Wales, passing from the valley of the *Usk* to that of the *Towy.* The chief place on the way is (3 M.) *Trecastle* (Black Horse; Three Horseshoes). Farther on, the road winds through the romantic pass of *Cwm Dwr*, and near Llandovery it crosses the little river *Bran.*

The train now turns to the S. and begins to ascend through a bleak and wild valley. The *Carmarthen Van* rises to the right. Just beyond (56½ M.) *Penwyllt*, in the valley below us to the right, lies *Craig-y-Nos*, the Welsh home of Adelina Patti (Mme. Nicolini), with a large winter-garden and a theatre. Near Penwyllt we cross the watershed and begin the descent into the valley of the *Tawe*, the beauty of which is marred by many signs of metallurgical industry. — At (60 M.) *Colbren Junction* the line to Neath (p. 196) diverges to the left. Farther on we have a retrospect of the Carmarthen Van on the right. — 78 M. *Swansea* (Midland Stat.), see p. 197.

27. From Craven Arms to Llandrindod, Llandovery, and Carmarthen.

84 M. Central Wales Railway (L.N.W.) in 3-4¼ hrs. (fares 17*s.* 12*s.* 3*d.*, 7*s.* ½*d*). — Through-carriages run by this route, parts of which are very picturesque, from Manchester and Liverpool to Swansea, and from London to Tenby.

Craven Arms, see p. 180. — 12½ *Knighton* (Norton Arms; Swan), a small town, 6½ M. to the N. of *Presteign* (p. 203), the county-town of Radnorshire. *Offa's Dyke* (p. 264) passes through

Knighton. — At (15 M.) *Knucklas* we quit the valley of the *Teme*, and near (19 M.) *Llangunllo* we cross the watershed (975 ft.) between that river and the Wye.

32 M. **Llandrindod Wells** (*Rock House*, 'pens'. 8*s*. 6*d*.; *Old Pump House; Llanerch; Bridge; Rail. Rfmt. Rooms)*, a pleasant inland watering-place on the *Ithon*, with chalybeate and saline springs. *Spa Grounds* have been laid out adjoining the springs, and there is a small lake for boating. The Ithon affords fair angling.

Fine view from the top of the *Little Hill* (850 ft.), to the E. of the village. Drives may be taken to (10 M.) *Cwmhir Abbey* (Cistercian; 12th cent.), to (12 M.) *Rhayader* (p. 203), to (8 M.) *Builth* (p. 203), etc.

Beyond Llandrindod the train descends to ($37^1/_2$ M.) *Builth Road*, where the line intersects the Mid-Wales Railway from Three Cocks to Llanidloes (p. 203). For *Builth Wells*, see p. 203. — Farther on the train crosses the Wye and begins again to ascend. Just beyond ($39^1/_2$ M.) *Cilmery* we pass the glen of *Cwm Llewelyn* (p. 203). $44^1/_2$ M. *Llangammarch Wells* (Epynt House), with a mineral spring.

48 M. **Llanwrtyd Wells** (*Dol-y-Coed*, at the Wells, 1 M. from the station, 'pens'. 7-8*s*.; *Neuadd Arms*, *Bellevue* in the village, $^2/_3$ M. from the station; *Askomel Arms*, at the station), another prettily-situated little spa, with sulphur and chalybeate springs.

Excursions may be made to the top of the *Sugar Loaf* (1000 ft.); to ($5^1/_2$ M.) *Abergwessin* (Grouse Inn), with a handsome modern church; to *Twm Shon Catti's Cave;* to the *Nanthir Ravine;* and to numerous other points in the picturesque environs.

The next bit of the route, as the train ascends to the watershed (830 ft.) between the Wye and Towy, is somewhat bleak and uninteresting, but beyond the *Sugar Loaf Tunnel* (1000 yds. long) we obtain a fine view towards the S. — 55 M. *Cynghordy.*

$59^1/_2$ M. **Llandovery** (*Castle*, in the town; *North Western*, at the station), a small town on the *Towy*, with 2050 inhab. and the insignificant remains of an old castle. The largest building is the *Welsh Collegiate Institute.* Llandovery is a good centre for excursions in the valleys of the Towy and the *Bran.*

The finest part of the ***Vale of Towy** is above Llandovery, and may be enjoyed by walking or driving to (10 M.) *Ystradffin*, though walkers may with advantage extend their explorations a few miles farther. Near Ystradffin is *Twm Shon Catti's Cave.* — The **Carmarthen Van** (2630 ft.), a mountain second in height and interest among those of South Wales to the Brecknock Beacons alone, may be ascended from Llandovery in 4-5 hrs. A carriage may be taken to (9 M.) *Blaenau*, a farm 4 M. from the top. — From Llandovery to *Devynock*, see p. 205.

From ($63^1/_2$ M.) *Llanwrda* a picturesque drive may be taken to ($16^1/_2$ M.) Lampeter (p. 208), passing (8 M.) *Pumpsaint* and *Dolaucothie*, with remarkable caves, said to be the remains of Roman gold-mines. — 65 M. *Llangadock* (Red Lion) is another starting-point for an ascent of the Carmarthen Van.

70 M. **Llandilo** (*Cawdor Arms; Castle; Rail. Refreshmt. Rooms)*, a picturesquely-situated little town with 1600 inhab., is a good

centre for excursions. It is one of the three places where, according to tradition, the miraculously multiplied body of St. Teilo was buried. Our line here diverges to the right from the main line to Llanelly and Swansea (see below). The town has given its name to a slate formation well known as the 'Llandilo Flags'.

About $1^1/_2$ M. to the W. of the town is **Dynevor Castle**, an interesting Norman ruin in a beautiful park (keys kept by the head-gardener.) The modern mansion is the residence of Lord Dynevor. The park begins $^1/_4$ M. from the town. Spenser places the cave of Merlin 'amongst the woody hills of Dinevowr', 'a little space from the swift Barry' (*'Faëry Queene', iii. 3*).—Excursions may also be made to *Grongar Hill* (see below), *Golden Grove* (see below), *Talley Abbey* (a picturesquely situated ruin, $7^1/_2$ M. to the N.), and *Castell Carreg Cennen* (a finely-placed ruined castle of the end of the 14th cent., 4 M. to the E.).

From Llandilo to Llanelly and Swansea, 25 M., railway in 1-$1^1/_2$ hr. Most of the stations are unimportant. — 13 M. *Pontardulais* is the junction for the line (G.W.R.) to (7 M.) *Llanelly* (p. 201). The Swansea line (L.N.W.) keeps to the left bank of the Llwchwr estuary and crosses the S. Wales main line at (17 M.) *Gowerton*, whence a branch runs to *Penclawdd* and *Llanmorlais* (p. 199). 20 M. *Killay* (p. 199). From (22 M.) *Mumbles Road* the line runs along Swansea Bay to (26 M.) *Swansea* (Victoria Station; p. 197).

Beyond Llandilo the train continues to descend the Vale of Towy. Dynevor Castle is seen to the right. To the left, near (73 M.) *Golden Grove*, is the mansion of that name, the seat of the Earl of Cawdor, where Jeremy Taylor wrote several of his works. The present house is, however, quite modern. To the N. rises *Grongar Hill*, the subject of the well-known poem by *Dyer* (d. 1758), who was born at its foot.

Farther on we pass the ruins of *Drysllwyn Castle*, to the right. 83 M. *Abergwili*, with the palace of the Bishop of St. David's.

84 M. **Carmarthen** (**Ivy Bush; Boar's Head; Rail. Refreshmt. Rooms*), the county-town of Carmarthenshire, is an ancient place with 10,500 inhab., on the Towy. It occupies the site of the Roman *Maridunum*. The battlemented wall near the station forms part of the *County Gaol*, which incorporates the remains of the old castle. On the river, near the station, is the *Parade Walk* (reached from Spilman St. by Parade Road), an esplanade commanding a good view of 'winding Towy, Merlin's fabled haunt'. Coracles (see p. 174) may still frequently be seen on the river. — At the end of Spilman St. is the *Church of St. Peter*, a large and handsome Dec. building, recently restored.

The interior contains some interesting monuments, among which may be mentioned the altar-tomb of *Sir Rhys-ap-Thomas* (d. 1527) and his wife, on the S. side of the chancel; the memorial of *Lady Anne Vaughan*, with a curious inscription; the monument (near the S. door) of *Bishop Farrar*, who was burned in the market-place under Queen Mary (1555); and the modern tablet to *Sir Richard Steele*, who is buried in the chapel at the E. end of the S. aisle (see also p. 208).

On the W. side of the town are the *County Lunatic Asylum*, the *South Wales Training College*, and an obelisk to *General Picton* (d. 1815).

From the Parade a pretty walk known as **Pond Side** leads to the (2 M.) *Gwili* river. We may return by the Conwil road, or go on to *Bron-*

wydd Arms Station (see below). — Another pleasant walk may be taken to (2 M.) *Llangunnor*, on a lofty site overlooking the Vale of Towy. We cross the bridge, follow the Llandilo road, keep to the left at (1/2 M.) the fork, and then ascend the (1/3 M.) lane to the right. The 'White House' of Llangunnor was the scene of Sir Richard Steele's death in 1729. — Excursions may also be made from Carmarthen to *Grongar Hill* (p. 207), *Dynevor Castle* (p. 207), and other places in the Towy valley.

From Carmarthen Junction (p. 201) to *Swansea*, *Whitland* (for *Tenby*), etc., see R. 25.

From Carmarthen to Aberystwith, 56 M., railway in 4 hrs. (fares 11*s.* 5*d.*, 8*s.* 3*d.*, 4*s.* 8*d.*). This line traverses an uninteresting district, but it forms the most direct route from Swansea, Tenby, etc., to Aberystwith. As far as (15 M.) Pencader it belongs to the G. W. Railway, but beyond that to the Manchester and Milford Railway, which derives its name from its original conception as a link in a direct through-line from Manchester to Milford. The carriages are poor, and the pace slow. — The line diverges to the left from the railway to Llandovery and ascends the pretty valley of the *Gwili*. From (15 M.) *Pencader* the G.W.R. line runs to (3 1/2 M.) *Llandyssil* (Porth Hotel; Rail. Refreshmt. Rooms), whence a coach plies to Newcastle Emlyn and Cardigan (see p. 202) and a car to New Quay (p. 202). — At (16 1/2 M.) *New Quay Road* we enter the valley of the *Teifi*.

27 M. **Lampeter** (**Black Lion*, unpretending, R. & A. 2*s.* 9*d.*), a clean little agricultural town with 1500 inhab., owes much of its prosperity to *St. David's College*, the oldest and largest of the Welsh colleges and the only one with the right of granting degrees (B.A. and B.D.). It is now attended by 150 students, and there is a school in connection with it for 100 boys. The library of 40,000 vols. is rich in theological, historical, and classical works, and contains some MSS. A large horse-fair is held at Lampeter annually on May 8th. — There is a British Camp 1 1/2 M. from Lampeter, and a Roman camp a little farther on. — A good road leads to the W. from Lampeter to (13 M.) *Aberayron* (p. 202), and one to the E. to (8 1/2 M.) *Pumpsaint* and (21 M.) *Llandovery* (p. 206).

To the left, at (29 M.) *Derry Ormond*, is a lofty view-tower on a hill. About 12 M. to the S.E. of (34 M.) *Pont Llanio* is *Llanddewi-Brefi*, with an interesting church, where St. David is said to have held a synod in the 6th cent. to take measures for checking the Pelagian heresy.

42 M. *Strata Florida*, the station for **Strata Florida Abbey** (12th cent.), which lies 3 M. to the E. The Abbey, the name of which is a Latinised form of *Ystrad Fflûr*, or plain of the Fflûr, is an almost effaced ruin, with only one late-Norman arch remaining. Recent excavations have laid bare the ground-plan and brought to light some fine pavements, tombs, and other interesting architectural details. About 3 M. beyond the Abbey, in a hollow amid bleak and desolate moorland, are the *Teifi Pools*, where the Teifi takes its rise.

The train now crosses the watershed between the Teifi and the *Ystwith*, and descends into the prettily wooded valley of the latter. 50 M. *Llanilar*, with an interesting church. As we approach Aberystwith we have a view of the sea and town to the left.

56 M. *Aberystwith*, see p. 267.

28. From Whitland to Tenby and Pembroke.

27 M. Tenby and Pembroke Railway to (16 M.) *Tenby* in 3/4 hr. (fares 3*s.* 4*d.*, 2*s.* 4*d.*, 1*s.* 4*d.*); to (27 M.) *Pembroke Dock* in 1 1/4-1 3/4 hr. (fares 5*s.*, 3*s.* 9*d.*, 2*s.* 3 1/2*d.*). — Through-carriages from London to Tenby and Pembroke are attached to the morning-express from Paddington.

Whitland Junction, see p. 201. The train now enters *Pembrokeshire*, a county which has acquired the name of a 'Little England beyond Wales' owing to the fact that it is mainly peopled by the descendants of a colony of Flemings settled here by Henry I. (in 1107; comp. p. 198). To this day they have preserved their distinctive character, and little or no Welsh is spoken in the county to the S. of Haverfordwest. Visitors should also note the peculiarly massive church-towers that are characteristic of Pembrokeshire, and they will find much to interest them in its numerous fine castles. So many 'Ogham' inscriptions have been found in Pembrokeshire (on Caldy, p. 208; at Treffgarne, etc.) that it has been supposed that this character originated here. — 5 M. *Narberth* (Rutzen Arms), a small market-town with a ruined castle.

About 4 M. to the N.W. of Narberth is **Llawhaden Castle,**, long a residence of the Bishops of St. David's. It owes its ruinous condition to Bishop Barlow, who stripped the lead from its roof (1536-49). The chief feature of the picturesque ruins is the gateway. — *Llawhaden Church* is also interesting.

12 M. *Saundersfoot* (Cambrian Hotel; Hean Castle), a little seaport $1^3/_4$ M. to the S. of the station (omn. 6*d.*), is frequented as a bathing-resort and has a good sandy beach. The environs are picturesque and full of pleasant objects for excursions. On the way from the station to the village is the interesting old *Church of St. Issel.*

16 M. **Tenby.** — **Hotels.** *Royal Gate House, R. & A. 4*s.*, D. 4*s.*; White Lion; Coburg, a comfortable family house; these three near each other, with views of the sea. — Tudor Temperance, in the centre of the town. — *Boarding Houses* and *Lodgings.* — Hotel omnibuses meet the trains.

Steamers ply in summer from Tenby to *Bristol* once weekly, and to *Ilfracombe* and to *Milford* (fine view of the grand-rock-bound coast) occasionally. — *Rowing Boat* with one man, 1*s.* 6*d.* per hr.; 9*d.* each addit. $^1/_2$ hr.; *Sailing Boat*, with two men, 2*s.* and 1*s.*

Cab with one horse, first hour 2*s.* 6*d.*; each addit. $^1/_4$ hr. 6*d.*; with two horses 3*s.* and $7^1/_2$*d.*; per mile 1*s.* or 1*s.* 6*d.*; each addit. $^1/_2$ M. 6*d.* or 9*d.*

Tenby, a small town with about 5000 inhab., is finely placed upon a bold rocky promontory, jutting out between two beautiful sandy bays and towering to a considerable height above them. The sands are smooth, firm, and extensive, the climate is mild and equable, and the coast-scenery in the neighbourhood is of a high order. Indeed, in many respects, Tenby is one of the pleasantest seaside-resorts in the kingdom. The neighbourhood of Tenby is 'the prince of places for a naturalist', and even those who have no claim to this title will find much to interest them in Mr. Gosse's 'Tenby: a Seaside Holiday'. George Eliot and Mr. Lewes lived and worked here for some time in 1856.

The long and lofty wall, with its towers and gateways, known as the 'Arches' and passed on the way from the railway-station, is a remnant of the town-fortifications as strengthened to resist the threatened attack of the Armada in 1588.

The *Parish Church of St. Mary*, in the principal street, is an E.E. edifice (1256), with Perp. and modern alterations. Its chief external feature is the lofty spire (150 ft.).

The interior contains some interesting monuments, of which may be mentioned the old tombs, with effigies, to the E. and W. of the N. door (14th and 15th cent.); that of the wife of *Thomas ap Rhys*, in the N. aisle of the chancel; and that of *Thomas White* (d. 1482), mayor of Tenby, who helped the Earl of Richmond (Henry VII.) to escape after the battle of Tewkesbury. A good effect is produced by the singular elevation of the chancel above the rest of the church.

At the end of the headland on which the town lies are the insignificant ruins of *Tenby Castle* and a *Statue of Prince Albert.* A band plays here in summer, and the promenade affords a good view. Here, too, is the *Tenby Museum* (adm. 6*d.*), with a collection illustrating the natural history (fine shells) and geology of the neighbourhood, and containing some mementoes of the French landing at Fishguard (p. 216). — The real geological ending of the promontory is the detached *St. Catharine's Rock,* on which is mounted a small battery. The coast on both sides is still defended by martello towers (p. 52).

The charming little cove to the N. of the point is known as *Tenby Bay*, while the larger sweep to the S. is called the *South Sands.* The fine rocky promontory that bounds the latter on the S. is named *Giltar Point*, and commands a splendid view of the bold rocky coast to the W. and of the island of *Caldy* (lighthouse). The direct route to it across the sands is $1^1/_4$ M. long; but for the sake of a gentler ascent we may approach from the landward by following the railway as far as the *Black Rock* (at the bridge) and then bearing to the left across *Penally Burrows*, leaving the village of *Penally* to the right. — Tenby is the best headquarters for exploring the S. W. corner of Wales, and a few of the favourite excursions are given below. Good walkers should visit a part at least of the fine coast between Tenby and St. Gowan's Head.

From Tenby to Penally. By the path along the railway the distance is about $1^1/_4$ M., by the road 2 M. The latter, the 'Marsh Road', runs to the W. at first for about $1^1/_4$ M., and then ascends to the S. (left) past a white farm-house. At the next fork we also keep to the left. **Penally** (*Crown Inn*), a pretty little village, with a restored church containing an altar-tomb of the 13th cent. and a Norman font, is one of the three alleged burial-places of St. Teilo (see p. 207). — On the way to Penally we may digress to visit the cave called **Hoyle's Mouth** (a light desirable). We diverge from the road to the right $^1/_4$ M. beyond the Marsh Bridge, pass through the ($^1/_3$ M.) second gate on the left, and ascend by the indistinct path straight up (*not* the well-marked track to the left) to the (1 min.) cave, the mouth of which is hidden among the trees.

From Tenby to Saundersfoot, 3-4 M. Good walkers should go by road and return by the cliffs; the walk may be shortened by taking the railway (p. 209). By Road. Just outside the town, walkers may save $^1/_4$ M. by following the old road to the right, which rejoins the new road about 1 M. from Tenby. After 1 M. more we keep to the right. — By the Cliffs. We follow the path from the Gas-works to (1 M.) *Waterwinch*, and then skirt the top of the cliffs. The best view is obtained from the high ground at the base of the *Monkstone Promontory*, $1^1/_4$ M. beyond Waterwinch.

To Carew Castle, $6^1/_2$-$8^1/_2$ M. The shortest road ($6^1/_2$ M.) leads viâ ($1^3/_4$ M.) *Gumfreston*, with an interesting church, but the pleasantest ($8^1/_2$ M.) follows the *Ridgeway*, a range of low hills running parallel with the railway from Penally to Pembroke. ***Carew Castle** (pron. *Carey;* adm. 3*d.*) is a picturesque and fairly-preserved ruin, on a creek of Milford Haven. It is of different dates, the oldest part being apparently that adjoining the gate-house (early 12th cent.). In the village (*Carew Inn; Castle Inn*), near the castle-entrance, is an ancient *Cross*, 14 ft.

high, supposed to be Saxon or Danish. The *Church*, 1/2 M. to the S., is a Dec. structure, with a Perp. tower. The nearest railway-station is (4 M.) *Lamphey* (see below). — On the opposite bank of the creek on which Carew stands is *Upton Castle*, a smaller and less interesting ruin.

Cliff Walk from Tenby to Lydstep Caverns and Manorbier, 8 M. — Those who have already visited Giltar Point (p. 210) may save a little by following the road to Lydstep, though the walk over the cliffs, passing another bold headland named *Proud Giltar*, is fine. By road we pass through (2 M.) *Penally* (see p. 210) and continue to follow the main (lower) road, passing (1/3 M.) the *Hut Barracks* of a body of soldiers belonging to the garrison of Pembroke. Shortly before reaching (1 3/4 M.) the village of *Lydstep*, some of the old cottages in which have evidently seen better days, we have a fine view of the coast to the left, with the lofty rocks at the W. end of Lydstep Bay, and Lydstep House nestling among the trees in the corner. At the far end of the village we turn to the left and descend to (3 min.) the lodge of Lydstep House. Passing through the gate, we turn to the right over the grassy hill, and almost immediately come in sight of *Lydstep Cove*, with a cottage where light refreshments may be obtained in summer. The **Caverns* are to the right and left of this cove; with the exception of the 'Smugglers' Cave', which has a landward entrance, they are inaccessible except at low water (see tide-tables in the 'Tenby Observer'). — We now make our way to the top of the cliffs, and follow them to (3 M.) Manorbier. There is a more or less distinct path nearly all the way, and stiles over the walls and fences. The cliff formations are very fine, and the transition from the limestone to old red sandstone is well marked, On (1 3/4 M.) *Old Castle Head* is a clearly-defined cliff-castle. Beyond this we continue to follow the shore-line, passing some curious *Fissures* in the cliffs, formed by the falling in of caves, and finally descend past a *Cromlech* to (1 1/4 M.) *Manorbier Bay*. On the left side of the cove, at a little distance from the sea, stands ***Manorbier Castle** (adm. 3*d.*; when two flags are flying, 6*d.*), a large and good example of a feudal stronghold, dating chiefly from the 12-14th centuries. The ruined tower adjoining the gate-house and the square building with the large hall are supposed to be early Norman. Part of it has been fitted up as a modern residence. *Giraldus Cambrensis*, the chronicler, born in the castle in 1146, was a member of the De Barri family to which it then belonged. *Manorbier Church*, on the opposite slope of the bay, is a curiously irregular building, with a Norman nave. It contains a monument of the De Barri family (see above). The village of *Manorbier* (Lion Hotel) lies above the castle, a little more inland. — From Manorbier good walkers may continue their route along the coast to (8 M.) *Stackpole* and (3 M.) *St. Gowan's Head* (see p. 212). The railway-station of Manorbier (see below) lies 1 M. to the N. of the village.

Excursion-brakes ply in summer from Tenby to (14 M.) *Stackpole Court*, (17 1/2 M) *St. Gowan's Chapel*, and (20 1/2 M.) the *Stack Rocks* (fare 5*s.* 6*d.*), but these places may be more easily visited from Pembroke. — *Lamphey Palace* (see below) may be reached by railway or by driving along the Ridgeway (8 M.). — A boating excursion may be made to *Caldy Island* (p. 210). — Other places of interest within easy reach are *Narberth Castle* (p. 209), *Llawhaden Castle* (p. 209), *Pembroke* (p. 212), and *Milford Haven* (p. 213), while *St. David's* (p. 214) may be visited by spending one night there and taking the mail-cart (see p. 213).

As the train leaves Tenby we have a view to the left of Giltar and Caldy Island. Beyond (17 M.) *Penally* (p. 210) the line runs through an unattractive district, bounded on the N. by the Ridgeway. 20 M. *Manorbier*; the village (see above) lies 1 M. to the S. — At (24 M.) *Lamphey* we may alight to visit the ruins of Lamphey Palace (see below), a former residence of the Bishops of St. David's, which lies a little to the N.

On leaving the station we turn to the left, and after 100 yds. reach an iron swing-gate admitting to the grounds of *Lamphey Court*, in which the ruins lie. We follow the path, which soon joins the drive, and pass through (5 min.) an old archway, beyond which we have a lofty garden-wall to our right. At the end of this is a gate to the right (*not* the door in the wall), through which we pass and proceed to another gate, admitting to the ivy-clad ruin. The principal remains are the *Chapel*, with a good Perp. window, and the *Hall*, with an arcade like those at Swansea Castle and St. David's Palace, all three being ascribed to Bishop Gower (1335). — About 1½ M. to the S.E. of Lamphey station is *Hodgeston Church*, the Dec. chancel of which is also said to have been built by Bishop Gower.

25¼ M. **Pembroke** (*Lion; King's Arms*, both near the castle), a meanly-built town with about 10,000 inhab., consists mainly of one street, upwards of ½ M. long, with the railway-station at one end and the castle at the other.

The ***Castle** (adm. 6*d.*; key kept by the saddler nearly opposite the Lion) is externally one of the finest ruins in Wales. The interior is extensive, but it is surpassed by Beaumaris in picturesqueness, and by Carnarvon in magnificence of domestic arrangements. The castle was originally built by Arnulf de Montgomery at the end of the 11th cent., but the buildings of the outer ward were not added till the 14th century. In the Civil War the Castle was taken by Cromwell after a siege of six weeks. The *Gateway*, with its slender flanking turrets, is very imposing as seen from the inside; and the *Great Hall* has a fine roof. At the other end is the massive and lofty Norman *Keep*, with a domed roof, which is still in good preservation, except that the floors are gone. Climbers may ascend the staircase with the aid of a rope, and will be repaid by the *View from the top. From the hall a flight of steps descends to a huge cavern in the living rock, one of the most striking features of the castle. Henry VII. was born at Pembroke Castle in 1456. A good view of the ivy-draped ruins is obtained from the bridge, on the road to Pembroke Dock. A walk has also been formed round the exterior of the castle, skirting the inlet of Milford Haven on which it stands and passing the mouth of the above-mentioned cavern.

Monkton Priory, an ancient Norman structure on the hill opposite the Castle, somewhat resembles Dorchester Abbey (p. 219). The Dec. choir, now roofless, formed the monks' church. To reach the priory from the castle we cross Monkton Bridge (to the S.) and ascend to the right.

Pembroke is the nearest railway-station to *Stackpole Court*, *St. Gowan's Head*, and the *Stack Rocks* (comp. p. 211). The total round, returning by the direct road from the last, is about 17 M. Parties should take luncheon with them, as no inns are passed. — From the station the road leads to the S., passing *St. Daniel's Church*, on the top of the ridge, to (3 M.) the entrance to the park of **Stackpole Court**, the seat of Earl Cawdor, containing a few good pictures and a 'hirlas horn' (p. 288). The house is not shown, but the well-timbered park and fine gardens are open to visitors. [A slight detour may be made, before the park is entered, to *Cheriton Church*, which lies a little to the N.] Beyond the house our road turns to the right, and then, 1 M. farther on, to the left. 1 M. *Bosherston Church*, with an old cross in the churchyard. — About 1 M. to the S. of Bosherston, and 7½ M. from Pembroke, is ***St. Gowan's** or **St. Govan's**

Head, a bold limestone promontory rising 160 ft. above the sea. In a narrow chasm by which the headland is intersected is perched *St. Gowan's Chapel*, which tradition connects with the Arthurian knight Gawain. The present chapel can scarcely be earlier than the 13th century. About 1/3 M. to the W. of St. Gowan's is the *Huntsman's Leap*, a deep and narrow fissure in the cliff, which gets its name from having been cleared by a fox-hunter, who, as the story goes, died of retrospective alarm! A little farther on is *Bosherston Mere*. — The ***Stack Rocks**, two columnar masses of limestone, standing about a stone's throw from the mainland, are 2½ M. farther to the W. Just on this side of them is the ***Cauldron**, a huge and magnificent chasm, which the sea enters by a natural arch. In summer the Stacks are covered with myriads of eligugs (a species of auk), puffins, and other sea-birds. The whole of this part of the coast is fine, and good pedestrians may follow the line of the cliffs to (8 M.) *Angle*, on Milford Haven. All are recommended to go as far the *Wash*, an inlet ½ M. to the W. of the Stacks. — The direct road from the Stack Rocks to (6½ M.) Pembroke leads by *Warren* and *Monkton* (see p. 212).

The road from Pembroke to (2 M.) *Pembroke Dock* (see below) crosses the bridge on the N. side of the castle and runs in a N.W. direction.

From Pembroke excursions may also be made to *Carew*, *Lamphey*, *Milford Haven*, etc.

On leaving Pembroke we have a good view of the castle to the left just before the train plunges into a tunnel. 27 M. **Pembroke Dock** or **Pater** (*Bush*, not far from the station), a Philistine-looking town with 8-10,000 inhab., depends solely on its dockyard for interest as well as existence. From the station we reach the (½ M.) entrance by following the street leading to the main street and then turning to the left. Visitors are conducted over the **Dockyard*, which covers 90 acres and employs 2-3000 men, by a policeman (fee discretionary), but are allowed more time than at Portsmouth or Plymouth; it is closed from 12 to 1.15 p.m.

Those who wish to cross to Milford Haven turn to the left on leaving the dockyard and walk along the wall, passing a *Hut Encampment*, to *Hobbes Point* (ferry 2*d*.).

A fine view of the beautiful ***Milford Haven**, the 'blessed Milford' of Imogen ('Cymbeline', iii. 2), is obtained from the *Barrack Hill*, at the top of which is a fort. Comp. p. 203.

29. From Haverfordwest to St. David's.

16 M. Coach between St. David's and Haverfordwest thrice a week (Tues., Thurs., and Sat.), leaving the former about 6.30 a.m. and the latter about 4 p.m. (fare 2*s*. 6*d*., outside 2*s*.). A Mail-Cart also runs daily in connection with the London mails (fare 5*s*.; return 7*s*. 6*d*.).

The road from Haverfordwest (p. 202) to St. David's traverses a hilly, bleak, and somewhat uninteresting district. 4 M. *Keeston Hill* (Inn). On a hill 1 M. to the right is *Keeston Castle*, an insignificant ruin. — 2½ M. *Roch Castle*, a conspicuous ruined tower, ½ M. to the right of the road; it was built in the 13th cent. by Adam de Rupe. The deep valley which it overlooks forms the W. boundary of 'Little England' (p. 208); beyond this we are again in a purely Celtic district. We now enjoy a good view of *St. Bride's Bay*, while the retrospect is also fine. — From (2½ M.) *Newgate Bridge* (Inn) the road skirts the coast nearly all the way to St. David's. About 1½ M. farther, to the left, is a tumulus marking the site of

Poyntz Castle, a moated grange of St. David's. — 2 M. *Solva* (Cambrian Hotel), a pretty little seaport at the mouth of the *Solva* river.

16 M. **St. David's** (*Grove*, at the E. entrance to the city; **City*, to the N.), the ancient *Menapia* or *Menevia*, is situated on the brook *Alan*, 1$^1/_2$ M. from the sea, at the extreme W. point of the S. Welsh peninsula, and in the midst of a strikingly desolate and out-of-the-world district. It has been the seat of an episcopal see from the 6th cent., and is thus nominally a city, though in fact it is merely an irregularly-built village with 1000 inhabitants.

A lane known as the 'Popples' leads from the centre of the village to the main gateway of the *Cathedral Close*, flanked by an octagonal tower and a round bastion, beyond which we suddenly obtain a *View of the Cathedral and its associated buildings, situated, like other Welsh cathedrals (see pp. 195, 286), in a hollow†.

The ***Cathedral of St. David**, the most important and interesting church in Wales, is in its present form substantially a Transitional Norman building (comp. Introd.), though subsequent additions and alterations have stamped a late Dec. character on its exterior. The foundation of the see is ascribed to St. David, the patron saint of Wales, who is sometimes said to have been born among the cliffs of St. Bride's Bay (p. 213), towards the close of the 5th century. The church he erected has, however, completely disappeared. In 1180 *Bishop Peter de Leia* began to rebuild the cathedral after it had 'beene often destroyed in former times by Danes and other pyrats, and in his time was almost quite ruinated'. The transepts and choir of Leia's church were destroyed by the fall of the tower in 1220 and rebuilt between that date and 1250. The E. E. Lady Chapel, completing the present ground-plan, was added in 1290-1328. Various alterations were made in the Dec. period by *Bishop Gower* (1328-47; comp. pp. 216, 212), the 'Menevian Wykeham' (comp. p. 77), who raised the walls of the aisles, inserted Dec. windows, and added a stage to the tower, the uppermost story of which is Perp. (ca. 1520). The W. front was rebuilt with little judgment at the end of last cent., but has, with the rest of the edifice, been skilfully restored by Sir G. G. Scott (1862-78) and his son. The Lady Chapel, however, is still roofless. — *Archbishop Laud* was Bishop of St. David's from 1621 to 1626, and *Connop Thirwall*, the historian of Greece, from 1840 to 1874.

As a whole the **Exterior** is not very imposing, though considerable variety of outline is given by the chapels at the E. end and the lofty erection adjoining the N.E. transept. The S. side, with its porch, is superior to the N. side, which is somewhat disfigured by heavy buttresses, rendered needful by the unsafe condition of the walls. The principal dimensions are as follows: total length 290 ft.; length of transepts 120 ft.; breadth across nave and aisles 70 ft.; height of nave 46 ft.; height of tower 126 ft. English services are held on Sun. at 11 a.m. and 4 p.m.

---

† *Fenton's* 'Pembrokeshire' and the large work on St. David's Cathedral, by the *Rev. W. B. Jones* (now Bishop of St. David's) and *Mr. E. A. Freeman*, will be found at the Grove Hotel.

and on week-days at 8.30 a.m. and 4 p.m.; Welsh services on Sun. at 9 a.m. and 6 p.m. and on Wed. at 7 p.m. We enter by the *South Porch.*

The *Interior is much more richly decorated than the exterior, and the predominant reddish colour of the stone produces a warm and pleasing effect. The general effect of the Nave (1176-98) 'is extremely striking from the remarkable richness of the architecture, and especially from its great multiplicity of parts; characters sufficiently marked to have been conspicuous anywhere, but which are the more strongly forced on the eye from their utter contrast with the rugged and weather-beaten aspect of the church without' *(Jones & Freeman).* In this respect it differs strongly from any other Norman nave in the country, and some of the massive solemnity characteristic of a Norman interior has been sacrificed to the desire for variety. The arrangement of the triforium and clerestory is unusual, and their ornamentation very rich and varied. The fret-work **Roof*, added in the Perp. period (ca. 1500), harmonizes wonderfully well with the Norman work below. The original builders contemplated a vaulted roof, and the shafts to support it are still *in situ.*

From the aisles we enter the Transepts by Norman doorways instead of arches. The W. walls of the transepts seem to be part of the original church, while the rest dates from after the accident of 1220 (p. 214), with later alterations. They offer a good exhibition of 'a peculiar form of incipient Gothic, found in this church and several others in South Wales and the West of England.' In the N. transepts is the *Shrine of St. Caradoc* (d. 1124). — Attached to the E. face of the N. transept is a singular building, originally erected after 1220 as a *Chapel of St. Thomas*, and now used as the *Chapter House* and *Vestry*. It contains a beautiful E. E. piscina. It is in three stories, the second and third having been originally the chapter-house and the treasury.

The *Lantern* in the interior of the *Tower* is formed by four fine Transitional arches, of which three are pointed and one (to the W.) circular. The roof is Decorated. The space below the tower forms the greater part of the ritual Choir, which is separated from the nave by an elaborate *Rood Screen*, erected by Bishop Gower (1328-47), who is buried in one of its canopied recesses. The *Stalls* and *Bishop's Throne* date from the second half of the 15th century.

To the E. of the ritual choir, and separated from by it by a wooden parclose or screen, is the Presbytery (1220-1248), which is similar in general style to the nave, except that the advance towards the E.E. style is indicated by the substitution of pointed for circular arches. The E. end contains two tiers of lancet windows, the lower of which are filled with mosaics, by Salviati of Murano. On the N. side of the presbytery is the *Shrine of St. David* (d. 601), an E.E. monument which may mark his burial-place. Opposite is the monument of *Bishop Anselm* (d. 1247), and in the middle that of *Edmund Tudor* (d. 1456), father of Henry VII.

Adjoining the presbytery on the E. is *Bishop Vaughan's Chapel*, a good Perp. structure of the beginning of the 16th century. In its W. wall, at the back of the high-altar, is a curious recess with a pierced cross (also visible from the presbytery). Beneath this is an equal-armed cross, in relief, which may be a relic of the church that preceded Bp. de Leia's (see p. 214). The chapel is bounded on the E. by a solid wall, and is entered from the aisles of the presbytery. It would seem that the space between the E. end of the presbytery and the vestibule of the Lady Chapel (see below) was open to the sky, until appropriated by Bishop Vaughan for this chapel. It is obvious that the aisles of the presbytery have also been lengthened towards the E.

The *Lady Chapel* (1290-1328), which has not yet been restored, is approached by a vestibule with a fan-vaulted roof. On the S. side of it is the tomb of its founder, *Bishop Martyn* (d. 1328).

To the N. of the nave of the cathedral are the ruins of *St. Mary's College*, built by Bishop Houghton (1362-89), the most prominent feature being the tall slender tower of its chapel. The space between the college and the cathedral was occupied by a cloister attached to the former. — To the W. of the cathedral, on the opposite bank of the Alan, are the picturesque and extensive remains of the ***Episcopal Palace**, built by *Bishop Gower* (p. 214) about 1347. The most prominent feature is the beautiful arcaded parapet, of which we have already seen foreshadowings at Swansea (p. 197) and Lamphey (p. 212). The *Great Hall* has a fine porch and rose-window, and the *Chapel* also remains. The chief *Domestic Apartments* are on the E. side of the quadrangle. The whole place stands on a series of vaulted crypts. Mr. Freeman considers it to be altogether unsurpassed by any existing English edifice of its own kind. — The fortified *Wall*, enclosing the cathedral-precincts, is also attributed to Bishop Gower, and may be traced throughout nearly its whole extent. The only remaining gateway is mentioned at p. 214.

The **Cliffs** near St. David's, though not remarkable for their height, are picturesque and varied in outline. Among the most interesting points are *St. David's Head* (100 ft. above the sea), a spur of *Carn Llidi*, 2½ M. to the N.W., cut off from the mainland by an ancient stone fortification; the ruined *Chapel of St. Non*, the mother of St. David, due S. of the city; and *Capel Stinan* (2 M. due W.), built by Bishop Vaughan (1509-22), on the site of an ancient pilgrimage-chapel dedicated to St. Justinian, the confessor of St. David. — Off the coast lies the island of *Ramsey*, a great resort of woodcocks in October. To the W. lie the *Bishop and his Clerks*, a group of rocks of which Fenton ('History of Pembrokeshire', p. 126), quoting George Owen (16th cent.), says that they 'preache deadly doctrine to their winter audience, such poor seafaring men as are forcyd thether by tempest; onlie in one thing they are to be commended, they keepe residence better than the rest of the canons of that see are wont to do'.

On the coast, 16 M. to the N.E. of St. David's, is **Fishguard** (*Commercial; Great Western*), a small town in a land-locked bay, near *Strumble Head*, on which a French force of 1400 men landed in 1797, only to be captured by the local militia. *Goodwic*, 1 M. from Fishguard, is a small watering-place. The neighbourhood abounds in meinihirion, cromlechs, crosses, and other antiquities. Coach from Fishguard to *Haverfordwest*, see p. 202. From Fishguard we may continue our northward progress along the coast to (7 M.) *Newport* (p. 202), *Cardigan* (p. 202), etc.

30. From London to Oxford.

a. Great Western Railway viâ Didcot.

63½ M. Railway from *Paddington Station* in 1¾-3 hrs. (fares 11*s*., 8*s*. 4*d*., 5*s*. 3½*d*.; return 18*s*. 6*d*., 14*s*.). This is the quickest route to Oxford.

From London to (53 M.) *Didcot*, see R. 15. The Oxford branch here diverges to the right from the main line of the G.W.R., traverses a fertile and pleasing district, and crosses the *Thames* (or *Isis*), of which many beautiful views are obtained. From (56 M.) *Culham*, with a training-college for schoolmasters, a visit may be paid to Dorchester (see p. 219). We now recross the Isis, pass *Nuneham Park* (p. 218), and once more cross the river. — 58½ M. *Radley*, with an interesting church.

Radley is the junction of a line to (2½ M.) **Abingdon** (*Crown & Thistle*, *Queen's*), a town of 6600 inhab., with a busy trade in corn. Few remains are left of the *Abbey*, once of considerable importance. *St. Helen's Church* is a large edifice, with a fine spire; and *Christ's Hospital*, an old almshouse, has interesting features. *Cumnor Hall* (p. 239), 5 M. to the N., was originally a seat of the Abbots of Abingdon.

Beyond Radley the train again crosses the Isis. *Bagley Woods* are seen to the left, and farther on *Iffley* is passed on the right. As we approach Oxford we have a fine view of the city, with its towers and spires, to the right. — 63 1/2 M. *Oxford*, see p. 223.

b. Great Western Railway viâ Maidenhead and High Wycombe.

63 M. Railway from *Paddington Station* in 3 hrs. (same fares as above).

From London to (24 M.) *Maidenhead*, see p. 106. The Oxford line now turns to the N. The next stations are *Cookham* (with a picturesque church; p. 221) and (29 M.) *Bourne End*, where a short branch diverges on the left to *Great Marlow* (p. 221). — 30 M. *Wooburn Green*, with an interesting church; 31 1/2 M. *Loudwater*.

34 1/2 M. **High Wycombe** *(Red Lion; Falcon)*, a town with 6000 inhab. and manufactories of lace and beechwood-chairs. The *Parish Church* is a large and handsome building.

About 2 M. to the N. lies *Hughenden Manor*, seat of the late Earl of Beaconsfield (d. 1881), who is buried in the village-church.

42 1/2 M. *Prince's Risborough* (George), a small town amid the *Chiltern Hills*, named from an old castle of the Black Prince, of which no trace remains. On one of the hills is a curious old *Cross*, cut in the turf, and said to a commemorate a victory of the Christian Saxons over the Danes.

Branch-lines diverge from Risborough to (9 M.; left) *Watlington* and to (7 M.; right) **Aylesbury** (George; Crown), the latter the county-town of Buckinghamshire and a great agricultural centre, famous for its ducks and milk. *Waddesdon*, a magnificent modern mansion, 6 M. to the N.W., is the seat of Baron Ferd. de Rothschild.

48 M. *Thame* (Spread Eagle), with an old church, where John Hampden died in 1643. Near (56 M.) *Wheatley* is *Cuddesden Palace*, the residence of the Bishop of Oxford. — 63 M. *Oxford*, see p. 223.

c. London and North Western Railway.

78 M. Railway from *Euston Station* in 2 1/3-2 3/4 hrs. (fares as above).

From London to (47 M.) *Bletchley*, see R. 36. The Oxford line here diverges to the left from the main line. — 55 1/2 M. *Verney Junction*.

From Verney Junction to Banbury, 22 M., railway in 50 min. (fares 3*s*. 9*d*., 2*s*. 6*d*., 1*s*. 10*d*.). The chief intermediate station is (17 M.) **Buckingham** *(White Hart; Swan)*, a lace-making town with 4000 inhabitants. Near the town begins a magnificent avenue of elms, 2 M. long, leading to *Stowe*, the princely seat of Earl Temple. Stowe formerly contained one of the finest art-collections in the country, but was dismantled in 1848. The pleasure-gardens, in the taste of last century, have been deservedly commemorated by Pope (no admittance). — 22 M. **Banbury**, see p. 240.

Another line runs from Verney Junction to *Aylesbury* (see above).

65 1/2 M. *Bicester* (King's Arms), a small town with an old priory-church; 72 M. *Islip*. — 78 M. *Oxford*, see p. 223.

31. From Oxford to London by the Thames.

A trip by rowing-boat on the Thames between Oxford and London has now become quite a popular institution, and in fine weather is cordially recommended to oarsmen. The scenery all the way is full of charm and interest. From London Bridge to Oxford the distance is 112 M., but this may be advantageously shortened to 96 M. or to 69 M. by beginning or ending the river-excursion at Richmond or Windsor. With proper precautions the trip is quite safe for practised oarsmen, and even for ladies; but a wide berth should be given to all mill-streams, weirs, and 'lashers'.

Boats may be hired from Salter, Timms, or Crissal, of Oxford, who let boats specially for these excursions, at rates varying from 30*s.* for a canoe or skiff up to 5*l.* for an eight-oared boat and 6*l.* for a large four-oared shallop. These charges are for one week (after which an extra sum is paid for each day), and include the sending of the boat to London or bringing it back from London. — *Steam* and *Electric Launches* may also be hired; and eight charging-stations for the latter have been established between Caversham and Strand-on-the-Green.

Locks. There are 32 locks between Oxford and Richmond, at each of which a charge of 3*d.* is made for pair-oared boats, 6*d.* for four-oared boats, and 1*s.* 6*d.* for launches, the payment entitling the boat to repass the same day without farther toll. When the gates are closed the attention of the lock-keeper is attracted by shouts of 'lock! lock!' Care should be taken in the locks to keep the gunwale from catching on the side-walls. At several of the locks there are inclined planes with rollers for small boats.

Steamers. In summer a small steamer plies between Oxford and Kingston, when the state of the water allows, taking two days in each direction.

Inns. There are good hotels on the banks at frequent intervals, but equally comfortable accommodation at much more moderate charges may often be obtained at the inns a little way back from the river. When ladies are of the party, and at popular holiday-seasons, accommodation should be secured beforehand by letter or telegram. Those who prefer to 'camp out' may hire tents, mattresses, and ground-sheets from the above-mentioned boat-owners, and also at various places in London. Heavy luggage should be sent by rail, as there are many railway-stations close to the river.

The following description is necessarily little more than a note of a few of the chief places of interest passed on the way. Those who wish more details are advised to purchase *Taunt's Map and Guide to the Thames* (2*s.* 6*d.*; cheap edition 1*s.*, illus. edit. 15*s.*), Reynold's *Oarsman's and Angler's Map of the Thames* (1*s.* 6*d.*, coloured 2*s.*, mounted on cloth in case 4*s.* 6*d.*), or *Dickens's Dictionary of the Thames* (1*s.*). The first is most readily obtained by direct application to Taunt & Co., 9 Broad St., Oxford. The words 'right' and 'left' (r., l.) are here used with reference to boats descending the river.

Among common sights on the Thames below Henley are *House Boats*, in which whole families sometimes find summer-quarters, while on the banks and islands are often seen the tents of camping-out parties.

The start is usually made from one of the boat-builders' yards close to *Folly Bridge*. On the left are the College Barges, and the mouth of the *Cherwell*. The straight reach from here to (2 M.) the lock at *Iffley*, with its interesting church and mill (p. 239), is the scene of the university boat-races.

3 M. (l.) *Sandford* (King's Arms), with a Norman church. A little farther on, to the left, are the beautiful woods of ***Nuneham Courtenay** (Col. Harcourt), a favourite spot for picnics from Oxford, and (*teste* Hawthorne) 'as perfect as anything earthly can be'.

On a small eminence in the park is a picturesque *Conduit*, which formerly stood at Carfax in Oxford. The avenues on the river-bank, affording views of Oxford, Radley, and Abingdon, were laid out by 'Capability Brown'. Visitors are admitted to the park on Tues. and Thurs. afternoons, by tickets obtained on written application to the steward; but may land at any time on a portion of the bank reserved for the purpose.

The Thames now runs through flat meadows. $7^3/_4$ M. (r.) *Abingdon*, see p. 216. — 10 M. *Culham Lock*, whence a bridge with arches of four different shapes, leads to *Sutton Courtney*, on the right. To the right of the following straight reach, between low meadows, is a tree-crowned hill, known as Wittenham Clump; a little farther on the church-spire of *Appleford* rises among the trees on the right. About $^1/_2$ M. below (13 M.) *Clifton Lock* is (l.) *Clifton Hampden* (Barley Mow), with a picturesque church and vicarage, embosomed in trees.

16 M. *Day's Lock*, whence there is a pretty view, embracing *Sinodun Hill* (r.), on which there is a Roman camp.

To the left is the small river *Thame*, about 1 M. from the mouth of which lies **Dorchester** (*Fleur de Lys; George*, well spoken of), a village with about 1200 inhab., not to be confounded with Dorchester in Dorsetshire (p. 97). This now unimportant village was the seat of a bishop (of Mercia) from the 7th cent. till after the Norman Conquest, when the see was removed to Lincoln. An Augustine abbey was founded here in 1140. The **Abbey Church*, which Mr. Freeman describes as 'a church of the very rudest and meanest order, as far as outline and ground-plan are concerned, developed to abbatial magnitude, and adorned with all the magnificence that architecture can lavish upon individual features', dates in its present form mainly from the close of the 13th cent., but also comprises much earlier (Norman) and later work. It has lately been restored. The fine 'Jesse' window of the chancel, with stone effigies of the descendants of David, is interesting. Visitors to Dorchester are recommended to leave their boat at Day's Lock, as the Thame is not very suitable for rowing.

Beyond Day's Lock the low banks are picturesquely wooded at a little distance from the river. A pretty retrospect of Dorchester church is obtained just after the houses of *Shillingford* (l.) come in sight in front. The Swan Inn, at the Berkshire (r.) end of ($18^1/_2$ M.) *Shillingford Bridge*, is a favourite resort, often full.

20 M. *Benson* or *Bensington Lock*. The village (White Hart, moderate) lies out of sight, on the left.

21 M. (r.) **Wallingford** (*Lamb; George; Town Arms*, unpretending), an ancient town of 3000 inhab., with the remains of an old castle. *Sir William Blackstone* (d. 1780), the eminent jurist, is interred in St. Peter's Church. — 25 M. *Moulsford* (Beetle and Wedge) is an angling resort. The trial eights of Oxford University are rowed in the reach between this point and ($26^1/_2$ M.) *Cleeve Lock*.

At 27 M.; l.) *Goring* (Miller of Mansfeld) and (r.) *Streatley* (Bull; Swan), two pretty villages united by a long bridge, one of the most picturesque parts of the course of the Thames is reached, extending beyond Mapledurdam (p. 220). Below Goring the Thames Valley is crossed by a range of chalk-hills, and the banks are thickly wooded.

$31^1/_2$ M. (r.) *Pangbourne* (Elephant & Castle; George), a picturesque little village, opposite which lies *Whitchurch*, with an old church containing several good brasses. A little farther down, on the left bank, is *Hardwick House*. Opposite is *Purley* (*not* Horne Tooke's; comp. p. 46).

$33^1/_2$ M. (l.) *Mapledurham* (Roebuck, on the right bank, 1 M. below the lock), with *Mapledurham House*, a fine Elizabethan mansion, the home of Pope's friend, Martha Blount.

38 M. (r.) **Reading**, see p. 106. Oarsmen making a stoppage here should leave their boats at *Caversham Bridge* (Hotel), just above the town, or at *Caversham Lock*, just below it. The Queen's Hotel, Friar St., is the most easily accessible from the river.

41 M. (r.) *Sonning* (White Hart; French Horn), a delightful little village, with an ancient stone bridge. The church contains some interesting brasses. At the islands a mile below Sonning, we keep to the left. — At *Shiplake* (l.), $^1/_2$ M. above ($43^1/_2$ M.) Shiplake Lock, is the church in which Tennyson was married.

44 M. (r.) *Wargrave* (George & Dragon; White Hart; Bull), a resort of artists, with a church containing a monument to Thomas Day, author of 'Sandford and Merton'. The humorous sign-board of the first-named inn, painted by G. D. Leslie, R. A., and J. E. Hodgson, A. R. A., is now kept indoors.

47 M. (l.) **Henley** *(Red Lion; Angel; Royal; Catherine Wheel; White Hart)*, the 'Mecca' of boating men, and also much frequented by anglers, is a well-built town of 4600 inhab., surrounded with wooded heights. The famous regatta, which attracts many thousands of visitors from London, usually takes place about the beginning of July.

It was on a window at the 'Red Lion' that Shenstone wrote his famous lines:

'Whoe'er has travelled life's dull round,
Where'er his stages may have been,
May sigh to think he still has found
The warmest welcome at an inn'.

About 2 M. below Henley, on the left bank, is *Greenlands*, the residence of the Rt. Hon. W. H. Smith, M. P. — 49 M. *Hambledon Lock* (Flower Pot).

51 M. (l.) *Medmenham* (*Ferry Boat, near the abbey), another convenient halting-place for the night. The *Abbey* was founded at the beginning of the 13th cent., but little of the old building now remains. About a century ago it acquired some notoriety from its connection with the so-called 'Medmenham Monks' of John Wilkes and Francis Dashwood, a club or society which was popularly believed to extend its motto, 'Fay ce que voudras', to the wildest extremes of licence.

To the right, at (53 M.) *Hurley Lock*, is *Lady Place*, the residence of the Lord Lovelace who played so conspicuous a part in the Revolution of 1688. Farther on, on the same bank, is *Bisham*

Abbey, in the Tudor style, originally a priory, but now a private residence. Queen Elizabeth lived here for three years in the reign of her sister Mary. *Bisham Church* is an interesting Norman structure.

55 M. (l.) **Great Marlow** (**Anglers; Crown; George & Dragon; Greyhound; Railway*, at the station), with 4730 inhab., a well-known fishing-station, with a graceful suspension-bridge and a lofty church-spire. One of the houses bears an inscription recording that Shelley lived in it in 1817; his 'Revolt of Islam' was composed partly in his boat on the Thames and partly during walks in the neighbouring woods. A regatta is held here every two years, alternating with Maidenhead. The *Quarry Woods* (r.), just below Marlow, are a favourite spot for camping-out parties (permission necessary). — Passing *Bourne End* (p. 217), on the left, we now soon reach (59 M.; r.) *Cookham* (Ferry; King's Arms; Bel & Dragon), one of the most picturesque villages on the Thames, with good fishing (perch, pike, roach) and a favourite pool for bathing.

l. **Clieveden*, the seat of the Duke of Westminster, charmingly situated amid rocks and hanging woods (visitors admitted to the grounds, during the absence of the family, on application to the head-gardener). A little to the E. is *Dropmore*, the beautiful grounds of which (open daily, except Sun.) contain some magnificent pines, the largest araucaria in England, and other fine trees. The next part of the river is unsurpassed for quiet loveliness.

62 M. (r.) **Maidenhead** (**Ray Mead*, near the river; *Lewis's*, well spoken of; *Bear; New Thames*, R. & A. from 3*s.* 6*d.*, B. 2*s.*-2*s.* 6*d.*, D. from 4*s.*), a small town with 8200 inhab., is a convenient place for passing the night. The Thames is here crossed by two bridges. Nearly opposite is the pretty village of *Taplow* (Orkney Arms).

64 M. (r.) *Bray* (George), with a large church, containing some excellent brasses.

The famous 'Vicar of Bray' is said to have been Simon Aleyn (d. 1588), who lived in the reigns of Henry VIII., Edward VI., Mary, and Elizabeth, and thrice changed his creed. Other authorities maintain that the 'Bray' of the song is in Ireland. — Near Bray is ***Ockwells**, a fine specimen of a timbered manor-house (15th cent.), with an interesting interior.

On *Monkey Island*, where the stream is very swift, is an inn, frequented by anglers. Numerous country-houses on both banks. — 67 M. *Boveney Lock*, $1^1/_2$ M. beyond which lie *Eton* (left) and —

69 M. (r.) **Windsor** (**White Hart, Castle*, High St.; *Bridge House Hotel*, near the bridge on the N. bank; *Christopher*, at Eton), a town with 19,000 inhab., well-known as the ancestral residence of the English sovereigns. A detailed description of Windsor, Windsor Castle, and Eton is given in *Baedeker's London*. The best scenery on the Thames lies between Oxford and Windsor, and many tourists begin or end the excursion here (boat-charges $^1/_5$-$^1/_6$ less).

Rounding the next bend, we pass under the *Victoria Bridge*.

$70^1/_2$ M. (l.) *Datchet* (Manor House; Royal Stag), the scene of Sir John Falstaff's unpleasant experiences at the hands of the 'Merry Wives of Windsor'. It is a favourite haunt of anglers. Beyond the (71 M.) *Albert Bridge*, the next bend is avoided by means of a 'cut', rejoining the river at (72 M.) *Old Windsor Lock*, with waterworks for supplying Windsor Castle. A little farther down is the (r.) *Bells of Ouseley Inn*, noted for its ale; and about $^3/_4$ M. farther on is *Magna Charta Island*, where King John signed the charter; the little house is said to cover the very stone that served him for a table. Opposite (l.) rises *Cooper's Hill*, with a well-known military engineering college and the *Holloway College* (for ladies); below it is the famous field of *Runnimede*, where the Barons encamped in 1215.

76 M. (l.) *Staines* (Angel; Pack Horse), with a substantial granite bridge. — 78 M. *Penton Hook Lock*, with a somewhat dangerous weir. — A little farther down, on the left, is *Laleham*, where Dr. Thomas Arnold lived before he became headmaster of Rugby. Matthew Arnold (d. 1888) is buried in Laleham church yard. About 1 M. to the N.W. of the station is *St. Anne's Hill* (view), with the summer residence of Charles James Fox.

$79^1/_2$ M. (r.) **Chertsey** *(Bridge; Crown; Swan)*, a small town with 7800 inhab., $^1/_2$ M. from the river, which is here crossed by a bridge. Scanty remains of the old abbey still exist, and the house in which Cowley the poet died in 1667 is marked by an inscription.

82 M. *Shepperton Lock*, opposite which, at the mouth of the *Wey*, is (r.) *Weybridge* (see p. 65), with a Roman Catholic chapel in which Louis Philippe (d. 1850) was interred. *Shepperton* (Anchor) and *Halliford* (*Ship; Red Lion), lie on the left bank.

To the right is the *Oatlands Park Hotel*, between which and London a coach plies in summer.

$84^1/_2$ M. (r.) *Walton-on-Thames* (Angler; Swan).

$85^1/_2$ M. (l.) *Sunbury* (*Magpie; Flower Pot), with a lock.

$87^1/_2$ M. (l.) *Hampton* (Lion), 1 M. from Hampton Court Palace. On the opposite bank is *Garrick's Villa*, where the famous actor lived from 1754 till his death in 1779. Then ($88^1/_2$ M.) *Moulsey Lock* and *Hampton Court Bridge*, beyond which the river makes a wide bend, skirting *Hampton Court Park* (see *Baedeker's London*), on the left, and *Thames Ditton* (Swan) and *Surbiton* on the right.

$91^1/_2$ M. (r.) *Kingston* (Sun; Griffin; Southampton), a town with 20,000 inhab. (see *Baedeker's London*). The river is crossed here by a bridge with five arches.

93 M. (l.) *Teddington*. Here we pass the last lock. An almost unbroken line of villas extends hence to (l.) *Twickenham* (see *Baedeker's London*), opposite *Eel Pie Island*. Then on the right appears *Richmond Hill*, with the Star and Garter Hotel.

96 M. *Richmond Bridge*. For a description of the Thames hence to (112 M.) *London Bridge*, see *Baedeker's London*.

32. Oxford.

Railway Stations. The stations of the *London & North Western* and *Great Western Railways* lie near each other, on the W. side of the town. — The principal hotels send omnibuses to meet the trains.

Hotels. *Randolph Hotel, Beaumont St., near the Martyrs' Memorial; Clarendon, Cornmarket St.; Mitre, High St., an old-fashioned house. Charges at these: R. 2*s.* 6*d.*-3*s.*, B. 1*s.* 6*d.*-2*s.* 6*d.*, D. 3-5*s.*, A. 1*s.* 6*d.* — Second class: King's Arms, at the corner of Park St. and Holywell St.; *Roebuck, *Golden Cross, George, Cornmarket St.; Railway; Wilberforce Temperance, Queen St. — *Lodgings* easily procurable, especially 'out of term'. The charges of hotels and lodgings are raised in 'Commemoration' and 'Eights Week' (p. 227).

Restaurants. *The Queen*, Queen St.; *Boffin*, *Horn*, High St. (Nos. 107, 142); *The Grill; Boffin*, at the N. end of St. Aldate's St. — **Confectioners.** *Boffin*, *Horn*, see above.

Photographs. *Hills & Saunders*, Cornmarket St., opposite the Clarendon Hotel; *Taunt & Co.*, 9 Broad St.; *Gillman*, 107 St. Aldate's St.

Post Office (Pl. 34; B, C, 3), St. Aldate's St., near Carfax.

Tramways. 1. From the *Railway Station* to *Carfax* (1*d.*), and thence over *Magdalen Bridge* (1*d.* from Carfax) to the cricket-grounds at *Cowley* (3*d.*). — 2. From Carfax to the *Corn Market*, whence one branch leads to a point near *Medley Lock* (where the 'Upper River' begins; fare 2*d.*), another to *Summertown*. — 3. From Carfax, past Christ Church and over Folly Bridge, to *New Hinksey* (fare 1*d.*).

Cab for not exceeding 1¼ M., for 1 pers. 1*s*, each addit. pers. 6*d.*; for each addit. ½ M. 6*d.* for each pers.; from the stations to the town, 2 pers., 1*s.* 6*d.*; per hour for 1-2 pers. 2*s.* 6*d.*, each addit. pers. 6*d.* Fare and a half between midnight and 6 a.m. Luggage up to 112 lbs. free.

Guides, 1*s.* per hour, are of little use.

Boats may be hired on the Isis, for the 'Lower River' at Christ Church Meadow (p. 229) and for the 'Upper River' at Medley Lock (see above). The latter is frequented mainly by the less serious oarsman and the votary of 'centre-boarding' (sailing), while the lower river is left to those in training for the races. The *Cherwell* is also available for boating. The course where all the college-races are decided extends from *Iffley* (p. 239) to the *College Barges*, which are moored to the bank at Christchurch Meadow. The principal races (the 'Eights') are rowed in the middle of the summer term; the 'Torpids' in the Lent term.

Baths. *Turkish Baths*, Merton St. (2*s.* 6*d.*; swimming-bath 1*s.*); *Hot and Cold Baths* (6*d.*) at the Racquet Courts, Holywell, and Museum Terrace. — **River Baths:** *University Bathing Place*, on the Isis, near Clasper's Boat House (towels 3*d.*); on the *Cherwell*, near the Parks (towels 6*d.*).

Principal Attractions. *Christ Church* (p. 227); *Merton College* (p. 229); *Christ Church Meadow* (p. 229); *Broad Walk* (p. 229); *St. Mary's Church* (p. 230); *Radcliffe Library* (p. 230) and view from the top; *Bodleian Library* (p. 230); *Divinity School* (p. 231); *Theatre* (p. 231); *University Museum* (p. 232); *Taylorian Institute* (p. 236); *New College* (p. 232); *Magdalen College* (p. 233), with its beautiful grounds; *Balliol College* (p. 236); *All Souls College* (p. 235); *Exeter College* (p. 235), with its garden; *St. John's College* (p. 236), with its gardens; gardens of *Worcester*, *Wadham*, and *Trinity Colleges* (pp. 237, 232, 236). A college-chapel service should be attended at New College, Magdalen, or Christ Church; and the visitor should also see a boat-race and a cricket or football match in the Parks. The 'Procession of Boats' on the Mon. of Commemoration Week (p. 227) is a highly characteristic sight. Visitors may wander at will about the colleges and college-gardens. The chapels are generally open for 2 hrs. in the forenoon and 2 hrs. in the afternoon, and admission to them when closed, as well as to the halls and libraries, may be obtained on application to the porter (small fee).

Oxford, with 40,862 inhab., the county-town of Oxfordshire, an episcopal see, and the seat of one of the most ancient and cele-

For a coloured street plan of Oxford see pages 574 & 575

brated universities in Europe, is situated amid picturesque environs at the confluence of the *Cherwell* and the *Thames* (often called in its upper course the *Isis*). It is surrounded by an amphitheatre of gentle hills, the tops of which command a fine view of the city, with its domes and towers. Oxford is on the whole more attractive than Cambridge to the ordinary visitor, who should therefore visit Cambridge first, or omit it altogether if he cannot visit both.

Oxford (called *Oxeneford* in Domesday Book, but possibly a corruption of *Ousenford*, or ford over the Ouse or water) is a town of some antiquity, the nucleus of which seems to have been the nunnery of St. Frideswide, established on the site of the present cathedral, probably in the 8th century. The earliest documentary occurrence of the name Oxford is in the Anglo-Saxon Chronicle under the year 912. In the 11th cent. the town was a place of military importance and the scene of several meetings of the Witenagemot. The foundation of the University is popularly ascribed to King Alfred in 972, but this story may be dismissed as entirely apocryphal. The first gathering of masters and scholars, not attached to monastic establishments, took place in the 12th cent., while it was not till the following cent. that anything like colleges in the modern meaning of the word — *i.e.* endowed and incorporated bodies of masters and students within the University — came into existence (comp. below). We first hear of theological lectures about 1130, and of legal studies a little later (but both of these are doubtful); while by the beginning of the 13th cent. Oxford ranked with the most important universities of Europe. About this period the University seems to have been at times attended by as many as 3000 students, but during the religious troubles of the reign of Henry VIII. the number fell to 1000. During the Civil War Oxford was the headquarters of the Royalists, and the colleges loyally devoted their plate to the King's service. Since then the history of the town has been blended with that of the University, which in turn connects itself by a thousand links with the intellectual and moral development of England. It is impossible here to enter into detail, but a reminder may be given of the 'Methodist Movement' of 1729-35 and the 'Tractarian Movement' of 1833-45. — The old 'Town and Gown Riots', of which the most serious (in 1354) resulted in the death of fifty students, are now practically things of the past.

'The world, surely, has not another place like Oxford; it is a despair to see such a place and ever to leave it, for it would take a lifetime and more than one, to comprehend and enjoy it satisfactorily' (*Nat. Hawthorne*). — Comp. *Maxwell Lyte's* excellent 'History of the University of Oxford' (1887), *Boase's* 'Oxford' ('Historic Towns Series'; 1887), *Brodrick's* short 'History of Oxford' (1886), or *Andrew Lang's* 'Oxford' (1890).

The universities of Oxford and Cambridge (see p. 431) have preserved so many of their mediæval institutions unaltered, and differ so materially from the other universities of Great Britain, as well as from those in Continental Europe and America, that a short account of their constitutions and position will, perhaps, not be out of place.

Each of the sister-universities is composed of a number of independent *Colleges* and *Halls*, of which Oxford now possesses twenty-four and Cambridge nineteen. The germ of these colleges, which are an institution now peculiar to England, is found in the 'hostels', 'inns', or 'halls', in which at an early period the students combined to obtain the services of a common teacher (comp. above). Many of the colleges have been richly endowed by kings and private persons; the halls differ mainly in being smaller, poorer, and unincorporated. The government of each university consists in the last resort of the entire body of graduates who have kept their names on the university registers, which is called the *Senate* at Cambridge and *Convocation* at Oxford. Proposals or statutes are, however, in the first instance brought before a small representative Council (called at Oxford the *Hebdomadal Council*, at Cambridge the *Council of the Senate*), consisting of the chief university officials, a few heads of colleges, and some senior members of Senate or Convocation. At Oxford the measures, before being submitted to Convocation, must receive the approval of *Congregation*, which consists of the officials and resident members of Convocation. Corresponding to this at Cambridge is the *Electoral Roll*, the function of which is to elect the Council of the Senate. The principal executive officials are the *Chancellor*, elected by the Senate and Convocation, and the *Vice-Chancellor*, who at Oxford is nominated from the number of the heads of colleges by the Chancellor, while at Cambridge he is elected by the Senate. The former is a person of royal blood or a nobleman of high rank and reputation, while the duties of the office are performed by the Vice-Chancellor. The *Proctors* are two officers selected from the different colleges in rotation to preserve order among the students; they are aided by four pro-proctors and a number of subordinate officials, popularly known as Bull-dogs. The internal affairs of each college are managed by a *Head*, who bears the title of *Master*, *Principal*, *Provost*, *Warden*, *Rector*, or *President* (at Christ Church, *Dean*). He is assisted by *Fellows*, who are selected from the most distinguished *Graduates* and have the right to elect the Head. It is not generally necessary that the Fellows should have been students of the college in which they obtain their fellowships, though at Cambridge this is usual. The Fellows and Tutors are colloquially known as *Dons*.

The *Undergraduates*, or students, now live either in one of the colleges, where two or more rooms are assigned to each, or in private lodgings in the town, approved by the university authorities. They dine together in the college-halls, attend service in the college-chapels on Sundays and several times during the week (except those who have conscientious scruples), and are not allowed to remain out beyond midnight without special reason. The 'Non-Collegiate Students', *i.e.* students of the University, not members of a college, who live in lodgings in the town, now form about 1/12th of the whole number of undergraduates. At lectures, dinner, and chapel, throughout the day on Sundays (at Cambridge), and after dark on other days, the undergraduates are supposed to wear an academical costume, consisting of a black (or dark-blue) gown and a curious square cap known as a 'trencher' or 'mortar-board'. The Bachelors and Masters of Arts also wear an academical dress, differing in some details from that of the students, while Doctors, on state occasions, are resplendent in robes of scarlet and other brilliant hues. At the services on Sundays, festivals, and the eves of festivals, Cambridge graduates and undergraduates wear white surplices instead of their black gowns. At Oxford, while Christ Church and Keble follow the Cambridge practice, the use of the surplice is generally restricted to the Heads, Fellows, and Scholars.

The chief subjects taught at Oxford and Cambridge include ancient languages, mathematics, philosophy, history, theology, law, medicine, and natural science. The university year is divided into four 'terms' at Oxford and three at Cambridge, and does not include much more than half of the calendar year. At Oxford all students, who have not previously passed an equivalent examination, have to present themselves at latest after one year of residence for 'Responsions' (in student parlance, 'Smalls'), an examination in classics and elementary mathematics, entitling them to continue their studies for a degree. The corresponding examination at Cambridge is called the Previous Examination (vulgo 'Little-go'). These are followed by the first Public Examination or 'Moderations' at Oxford and by the General Examination at Cambridge. The subjects are classics, mathematics of a somewhat more advanced character, and the Greek New Testament, to which Cambridge has recently added English history and an English essay. The pass examination for the ordinary degree of *Bachelor of Arts* (B.A.) takes place at the end of the third year of residence. At Cambridge it consists of a special examination in one of several specified branches of study at the option of the candidate. At Oxford the candidate for the ordinary degree is examined in three selected subjects from the following groups: (1) Greek and Roman history and philosophy (in the original languages); (2) English, Modern Languages,

Political Economy, and Law; (3) Geometry, Mechanics, Chemistry, and Physics; (4) Scriptural and Theological Subjects. One of the selected subjects must be either ancient philosophy and history, or a modern language (French or German). Those students, however, who desire to distinguish themselves in their academical career are not content to take merely the ordinary 'pass' degree ('poll' at Cambridge; Greek, οἱ πολλοί), but proceed to the 'Honours' examination. At Oxford honours may be taken in any one of eight 'schools': Literae Humaniores (including classics, ancient history, and philosophy), Modern History, Jurisprudence, Natural Science, Mathematics, Oriental (Indian or Semitic) Subjects, Theology, and Modern Languages and Literature. Successful candidates are placed in four classes according to the position they attain, and it requires a very high standard of scholarship to obtain a 'first'. The highest prestige attaches to those who have obtained a first-class in Literæ Humaniores. At Cambridge the honour-degrees are obtained in a similar manner, ten 'Triposes' taking the place of the Oxford 'Schools'. The greatest interest centres in the examination for mathematical honours, where the successful candidates in the earlier parts of the examinations are arranged in a 'Tripos', of three classes, called respectively Wranglers, Senior Optimes, and Junior Optimes. The first man in the examination is named the Senior Wrangler. There is a farther examination for which only high wranglers ever enter. Bachelors of Arts who have paid all the requisite dues and fees become Masters of Arts (M.A.) after three years, and are thenceforth entitled to a vote in the University Convocation or Senate. Both universities also confer the degrees of Bachelor and Doctor of Medicine, Law, Theology, and Music.

The system of teaching at Oxford and Cambridge differs from that of most other universities in the practically subordinate position occupied by professorial lectures, which in most cases stand practically out of all relation to the general studies of the undergraduates. Professorial teaching is, however, beginning to be more highly valued. The teaching functions of the colleges were formerly confined to the preparation of their own students by tuition for the examinations; but now most of the Honours Lectures given by colleges are open to all members of the University. Most of the *Fellowships*, generally ranging from 200*l.* to 300*l.* a year, were formerly granted for life, provided the holder remained unmarried and took holy orders. Now, however, they are of two kinds, some ('Prize' Fellowships) being held for 6-7 years and without restriction as to marriage, residence, or profession; while the tenure of others is conditional on the performance of tutorial or other college work. There are also numerous *Scholarships* for undergraduates, varying in value from 30*l.* to 120*l.*, with free rooms. Some of the colleges are extremely wealthy, such as Trinity College at Cambridge (p. 436), and Christ Church and Magdalen at Oxford (pp. 227, 233). The total revenue of Oxford University and Colleges is upwards of 400,000*l.*, and that of Cambridge about 250,000*l.* Oxford has in its gift 450 ecclesiastical livings (value 190,000*l.*), and Cambridge 370 livings (value upwards of 100,000*l.*). The number of students at each college or hall varies from 12-20 to 600 (Trinity College, Cambridge).

Oxford and Cambridge are the most aristocratic universities of Great Britain, and the cost of living is higher than at any of the others. From 150*l.* to 200*l.* may be taken as the rate per annum at which a resident undergraduate may live at either university with comfort, though some have been known to confine their expenses to 100*l.* Non-collegiate students in private lodgings can, of course, live more cheaply, and a few colleges (such as Keble at Oxford and Selwyn at Cambridge) make a special point of economy. The number of student-clubs is legion, including associations for all kinds of athletic sports, gymnastics, music, theatricals, whist, chess, and various scientific pursuits. The most important institution of the kind at each university is the Union Debating Society (pp. 237, 437). The well-known annual boat-race between the sister-universities is described in ***Baedeker's London***, and the inter-university cricket-match excites scarcely less interest. Both universities possess volunteer rifle-corps. The best time for a visit to either university is the week at the end of the summer term, when thousands of visitors flock to see the degrees conferred and enjoy the hospitality of the colleges. This period of mingled work and play (the latter predominating) is named *Commemoration* or the *Encaenia* at Oxford, and *Commencement* or the *May Week* (so called, though held in June) at Cambridge. Another pleasant time for a visit is the '*Eights Week*', in the middle of the same term, when the principal college cricket-matches and boat-races are held. The visitor should avoid the vacations at Christmas, at Easter, and in summer; the last, known as the 'Long', extends from June to the beginning of October. It is almost needless to add that an introduction to a 'Don' will add greatly to the visitor's pleasure and profit.

Details about the inner arrangements of the colleges and daily life of the undergraduates will be most easily found in the *Student's Handbooks to the Universities*, *Dickens's Dictionaries of Oxford* and *Cambridge* (1*s.* each), or the *University Calendars*.

Oxford contains 21 colleges and 3 halls, with about 50 professors, 30 readers or lecturers, numerous tutors and fellows, and 3000 students. As the railway-stations lie in the least attractive part of the town, the visitor should drive at once, by omnibus or cab, passing the Castle (p. 238), to Christ Church, with which a round of sight-seeing is conveniently begun.

***Christ Church** (Pl. 14; C, 4), known among its own members as the 'House' *(Ædes Christi)*, was founded by Card. Wolsey in 1525, on the site of a nunnery of the 8th cent. (comp. p. 224), and was renewed by Henry VIII. in 1546. It is one of the largest and most fashionable colleges in Oxford, and is attended by 250-300 undergraduates. The 'Fellows' are here called 'Students'. The handsome gateway, called *Tom Gate*, was begun by Wolsey, but the upper part of the tower was added by Wren in 1682. The bell ('Great Tom') in the latter weighs $7^1/_2$ tons, and every night at five minutes past nine it peals a curfew of 101 strokes, indicating the number of students on the foundation. The *Great Quadrangle*, or *Tom Quad*, is the largest and most imposing in Oxford.

In the S.E. corner is the fine fan-vaulted entrance to the **Hall* (adm. 2*d.*), a beautiful room with a ceiling of carved oak, 115 ft. long, 40 ft. wide, and 50 ft. high. It contains numerous good portraits, including those of Wolsey and Henry VIII. by *Holbein*, Queen Elizabeth by *Zucchero*, John Locke by *Lely*, Gladstone by *Millais*, two by *Gainsborough*, and three by *Reynolds*. Good old glass in the S. oriel window. — The *Kitchen* (small fee to the cook), the oldest part of Wolsey's building, is an interesting specimen of an old English kitchen; it is reached by a staircase descending from the door of the hall.

The ***Cathedral** (Pl. 4) of the diocese of Oxford, originally the church of the priory of St. Frideswide (p. 224), serves at the same time as the chapel of Christ Church. In its present form it is mainly a late-Norman or Transitional building of the second half of the 12th century. The Lady Chapel was added in the 13th, and the Latin Chapel in the 14th century. The lower part of the tower (144 ft. high) is Norman, but the belfry-stage and the octagonal spire (perhaps the oldest in England) are E. E. Wolsey removed half of the nave to make room for his college quadrangle; and the cathedral as it now stands is the smallest in England. Daily services are held at 10 a.m. and 5 p.m.; adm., free, 10-1 and 2.30-4.30. The building has been skilfully restored by Sir G. G. Scott.

Interior. The most striking feature in the Nave is the curious arrangement of the arches, which are double, the lower ones springing from corbels attached to the massive piers. These last are alternately circular and octagonal. The pointed arches of the clerestory are the nearest approach to the E.E. style in the main part of the church. The timber roof is generally ascribed to Wolsey. The pulpit and organ-screen are Jacobean. The most interesting tombs in the nave those of *Bishop Berkeley* (d. 1753) and *Dr. Pusey* (d. 1882). The beautiful W. window of the S. aisle was executed by *Morris*, from the design of *Burne Jones*. — A good general view of the interior is obtained from the platform in the S. Transept. In the E. wall of the aisle of this transept is an old stained-glass window, from which the head of St. Thomas of Canterbury, now replaced by plain white glass, is said to have been struck by a Puritan trooper. — The Choir resembles the nave in general character, though probably of somewhat earlier date. The beautiful groined roof, with its graceful pendants, is also attributed to Wolsey, but Sir G. G. Scott considers it still earlier. The E. end is intended to reproduce as far as possible the original Norman arrangement. The *Windows at the E. ends of the choir-aisles are also by *Burne Jones*. The Stalls and the elaborate Episcopal Throne (a memorial of Bishop Wilberforce) are modern. The S. choir-aisle contains a bust of the late *Duke of Albany* (d. 1884).

Adjoining the N. aisle of the choir is the Lady Chapel, an E.E. addition of the middle of the 13th cent., occupying a very unusual position. The E. window is by *Burne Jones*. On the N. side are a series of interesting monuments: *Sir George Nowers* (d. 1425) and *Lady Montacute* (d. 1353), with fine effigies; the *Prior's Tomb* (ca. 1300); and the so-called *Shrine of St. Frideswide* (15th or 16th cent.), more probably a watching-chamber. On the pier at the foot of the monument of Sir George Nowers is the tablet of *Robert Burton* (d. 1639), author of the 'Anatomy of Melancholy', with an inscription by himself. — To the N. of the Lady Chapel is the Dec. Latin Chapel (14th cent.), so called from the daily reading of the college-prayers in Latin. The flowing tracery of the windows and the vault-bosses deserve attention. The new E. window has poor tracery, but good stained glass (by *Burne Jones;* St. Frideswide). — The E.E. Chapter House is entered by a fine late-Norman door in the E. side of the Cloisters (Perp.), to the S. of the Nave (canon's order necessary).

We now return through the Great Quadrangle, passing the Dean's house on the right, and enter *Peckwater Quadrangle* (1705).

On the S. side is the *Library* (1761), containing a valuable collection of books and a few paintings and drawings by Italian masters (Raphael, etc.; 11-1 and 2-4, in vacation 9-6; adm. 3*d*.). The pictures include a Nativity by Titian and a curious Butcher's Shop by A. Carracci. In the entrance-hall is a statue by *Chantrey*, and on the staircase are a bust of Persephone by *Hiram Powers* and a statue of John Locke by *Rysbrack*. The curiosities of the library (upstairs) include a letter of Charles II. and a Latin exercise book of the Duke of Gloucester, son of Queen Anne, with corrections by his tutor Bishop Burnet (1700).

To the S. of Tom Quad are the modern *Christ Church Meadow Buildings*, the great gate of which forms one of the chief approaches to the Broad Walk and the river (comp. p. 229).

To the N. is *Canterbury Quad*. Here we leave the college by *Canterbury Gate*, on the site of *Canterbury College*, an extinct corporation of which Wycliffe (d. 1384) was once Warden, and which numbered Sir Thomas More (beheaded 1535) among its students.

Among the most distinguished members of Christ Church are Sir Philip Sidney, Locke, Camden, Ben Jonson, the Wesleys, Wellington, Peel, Pusey, Ruskin, and Gladstone. This was also the Prince of Wales's college.

From Canterbury Gate, King Street leads to the E., with the side of Oriel College to the left. To the right is the entrance to —

Corpus Christi College (Pl. 15; C, 4), founded in 1516 by Fox, Bishop of Winchester.

The vaulted roof of the gateway leading to the quadrangle is fine, and the latter contains a curious old sun-dial with a perpetual calendar. In the S.E. corner is the *Chapel* (with an altar-piece by Rubens), and beside it is the passage to the cloisters and to the newer part of the college, added in 1706. The *Library* is rich in illuminated MSS. and incunabula. Bishop Hooker was a student of Corpus, and his rooms are still pointed out; other eminent members are Cardinal Pole, Bishop Jewell, Keble, and Thomas Day, author of 'Sandford and Merton'.

On leaving Corpus we turn to the right (E.), and, passing the chapel, reach the entrance (to the right) of —

***Merton College** (Pl. 21; C, 4), the oldest in the University, founded by Walter de Merton in 1264 and intended by him exclusively for the education of parish-priests.

The **Chapel* (10-5) is one of the finest in Oxford; the choir was built by the founder and consecrated in 1276, while the ante-chapel and tower date from 1417-24 (college services on Sun. at 8 a.m. and 5 p.m., 5.45 in summer term; parish-service at 3 p.m.). The massive tower is one of the landmarks of Oxford. The windows of the ante-chapel are excellent examples of early-Perpendicular. The chapel contains two very fine brasses of the 14th and 15th cent., and *Anthony à Wood* (d. 1695), the chronicler of Oxford, is buried in the ante-chapel. The *Library*, built at the end of the 14th cent., is the most ancient in England and contains many rare books and MSS. The *Inner Quadrangle* is a good example of the Jacobean style. Duns Scotus, Steele, and Bodley (founder of the Bodleian Library) are among the most distinguished alumni of Merton, which has also contributed six archbishops to the see of Canterbury. Harvey (discoverer of the circulation of the blood; comp. p. 436) was Master. The garden commands a fine view: to the E. is Magdalen Tower, to the W. the Cathedral, in front *Christ Church Meadow* (Pl. C, 4, 5). The latter, which is intersected by the **Broad Walk*, an avenue of noble elms, may be reached by the lane between Merton and Corpus. The Broad Walk is the scene of '*Show Sunday*', formerly a fashionable promenade on the evening of the Sunday in Commemoration Week (p. 227), but now almost wholly resigned by 'Gown' to 'Town'. A delightful walk may be taken from Christ Church Meadow along the Isis, passing the *College Barges* (p. 223), to the Cherwell and Magdalen College (comp. p. 233).

Incorporated with Merton is **St. Alban Hall** (Pl. 37), founded in 1230, with a façade of 1600. Among the eminent names connected with this small institution are Massinger, Whateley, and Speaker Lenthall. — We now return to the W. end of Merton St., where Oriel St. diverges to the right. In it, to the right, stands —

Oriel College (Pl. 23; C, 4), founded by Edward II. in 1326. The present buildings date mainly from 1630-37, and though destitute of marked architectural merit form a picturesque and pleasing whole. The library was erected in 1788. Sir Walter Raleigh, Bishop Butler, John Henry Newman, Abp. Whateley, Keble, Dr. Thomas Arnold, Bishop Wilberforce, Thomas Hughes, and Pusey were members of Oriel. — In the same street, a little farther on, is **St. Mary Hall** (Pl. 38; C, 3), established in 1333; it is known in the undergraduate world as 'Skimmery'. Opposite, on the N. side of High St., is **St. Mary's** (Pl. C, 3), the University Church (sacristan, Swan Court, High St.). The handsome spire dates from 1300, the choir from 1460, the nave from 1488, and the S. porch with its curious twisted pillars (p. lvii), added by Dr. Owen, chaplain of Abp. Laud, from 1637. A slab in the chancel pavement records that Amy Robsart was buried in the choir in 1560. The University Sermons, preached here on Sun. forenoon and afternoon, are preceded by the special 'Bidding Prayer' for the University. — At the back (to the N.) of this church rises the —

***Radcliffe Library** (Pl. 36; C, 3), founded in 1737 by Dr. Radcliffe, court-physician to William III. and Mary II. The building is a handsome rotunda, embellished with columns, and surmounted by a dome resting on an octagonal base; Mr. Freeman considers it 'the grandest of all English-Italian designs'. The books have been removed to the University Museum, and the building is now used as part of the Bodleian (10 a.m. to 10 p.m.; adm. 3*d.*). In clear weather an admirable *View of Oxford and the country round is obtained from the foot of the dome. — Opposite the W. gate of the Radcliffe Library rises the old gate-tower of —

Brasenose College (Pl. 13; C, 3), or the *King's Hall*, founded in 1509. The site of this college was originally occupied by a much older institution, called Brasenose Hall, possibly because it was built on the site of a brewery ('Brasenhus'), though there is no evidence to support this conjecture. The form 'brazenose' appears in a document of 1278, and is perpetuated by a large brazen nose affixed to the college-gate and by the Latin phrase ('Collegium Aenei Nasi') in the official documents of the college.

The gate and the *Hall* have preserved their original character unaltered. A new quadrangle was added in 1888, entered by a gateway in the 'High' adjoining St. Mary's (p. 229). The *Library* and the *Chapel*, completed in 1663 and 1666, show an unpleasing medley of Gothic and classic forms. The books of Brasenose contain the names of Foxe ('Book of Martyrs'), Burton ('Anatomy of Melancholy'), Bishop Heber, Rev. F. W. Robertson, Dean Milman, and the Rev. H. Barham ('Ingoldsby Legends').

The large quadrangular block of buildings to the N. of the Radcliffe Library contains the **Old Examination Schools** (comp. p. 234), begun in 1439 and completed in 1613-18. The principal entrance is by a Gothic gateway on the E. side. The side of the tower facing the court is adorned with columns of all the five Roman architectural orders, and with a statue of James I., supported by figures of Religion and Fame. The tower is crowned with an open parapet and pinnacles. — Since the erection of the New Schools (p. 234), however, the whole of this quadrangle has been absorbed by the ***Bodleian Library** (Pl. 2, C 3; open 9 to 3, 4, or 5, according to the season; adm. for a visitor 3*d.*, unless accompanied by a member of the university in academic dress), which was originally established in 1445, opened as a libray in 1488, and practically refounded and rebuilt by Sir Thomas Bodley in 1597-1602. The entrance is in the S.W. corner of the quadrangle.

The library contains about 460,000 printed volumes, 27,000 vols. of MSS., drawings, and 50,000 coins. It also possesses a collection of models of ancient temples and other buildings and a *Gallery of Portraits.* In the part of the reading-room open to visitors are glass-cases containing autographs of celebrated persons, antiquities, curiosities of writing, remarkable early printed books, MSS. distinguished for their age or their illumination, and beautiful or singular bindings. In the portrait gallery are Sir Thomas Bodley's chest and various historical relics.

We quit the Schools by the *Proscholium* or *Pig Market*, 'a rarg example of an original ambulatory', the latter name commemoratine the unworthy use to which the adjoining building was put in the reign of Charles I., and find ourselves opposite the —

***Divinity School** (Pl. 31; C, 3), built in 1445-80 on a scale of great magnificence (see p. lvi). The groined ceiling is remarkable for its beautiful tracery and pendants. In this hall the trial of Cranmer, Latimer, and Ridley was held in 1555. During the Civil Wars and the Commonwealth it was, like the other Schools, used as a storehouse for corn, but at the end of the 17th cent it was restored by Sir Christopher Wren. — To the W. is the **Convocation House,** used for the conferring of degrees, the election of professors, meetings of Convocation, and other university purposes.

To the N. of the Schools rises the **Sheldonian Theatre** (Pl. 40, C, 3; porter generally at hand, 3*d.*), built by Sir Christopher Wren in 1664-69 at the expense of Archbishop Sheldon. This handsome edifice, which can accommodate upwards of 3000 persons, is used for the Encænia, or annual commemoration of founders, when prize-poems and essays are recited and honorary degrees conferred. On this occasion the undergraduates occupy the upper gallery and express their opinions frankly as to the different recipients of degrees.

The ceiling is adorned with paintings by Streater, court-painter to Charles II., representing the triumph of Religion, the Arts, and the Sciences over Envy, Rapine, and Ignorance. Among the portraits are those of George IV., Sir Christopher Wren, Alexander I. of Russia, and Frederick William IV. of Prussia, the last two by Gérard. The view from the cupola, which was added in 1838, resembles that from the dome of the Radcliffe Library (p. 230).

The Theatre abuts on Broad St. and is adjoined on the W. by the **Ashmolean Museum** (Pl. 1; adm. 11-4, 3*d.* unless accompanied by a member of the University), established by Elias Ashmole in 1682.

The original collection, formed by a Dutchman named Tradescant, is partly in the University Museum, while the books have been placed in the Bodleian Library. The collection of antiquities formed by Ashmole himself is, however, still kept in this building; among these are 'King Alfred's Jewell', watches which belonged to Queen Elizabeth and Oliver Cromwell, and other interesting historical relics. In the sunk floor are some of the *Arundel Marbles*, a collection of ancient sculptural fragments and inscriptions, formed by an Earl of Arundel in the 17th century. [Most of the inscriptions are in a room on the ground-floor of the Old Schools, and the rest of the sculptures are in the University Galleries.]

Also in Broad St., to the E. of the Theatre, is the **Clarendon Building** (Pl. 10; C, 3), built in 1713, in part with the profits of the sale of Lord Clarendon's History of the Rebellion, the copyright of which was presented to the University by his son. The Clarendon was long occupied by the University printing-press, but now contains offices of the governing body of the University.

To the E. of the Clarendon buildings, at the end of Broad St. and

Holywell St., is the **Indian Institute**, a building in an Oriental style, intended for students qualifying for the Indian Civil Service. Its museum is open 10-4 in winter and 10-6 in summer. — In *Holywell St.*, a little to the E. of the Indian Institute, is a *Music Room.*

From the end of Broad St., Park St. leads N. to **Wadham College** (Pl. 29, C 3; on the right), founded in 1613, and built in a uniform and pleasing style.

The *Gate-Tower* and the timber-ceiling of the *Hall* deserve inspection, and the *Chapel* (see p. lvii), with some stained glass of 1622, is also fine. The **Gardens* are among the prettiest in Oxford. Among the alumni of Wadham are Sir Christopher Wren, Lord Chancellor Westbury, and Admiral Blake. The Royal Society (see *Baedeker's London*) grew out of meetings for scientific discussion held here in the time of the Commonwealth (ca. 1648). Most of the leaders of the English Positivists (Congreve, Frederic Harrison, Beesly) came from Wadham.

A little to the E. of Wadham is **Mansfield College** (Pl. D, 2; buildings finished in 1889), a theological college in connection with the Congregationalist body, and intended to serve as a centre for the more orthodox Nonconformists in Oxford. — Adjacent is the site of *Manchester New College*, a similar institution connected with the Unitarians, recently transferred from London to Oxford.

Farther to the N., at the beginning of the Parks, is the ***University Museum** (Pl. 43; C, D, 2), a modern Gothic building (1857-60), containing valuable geological, chemical, anatomical, zoological, and other collections (open daily, 2-4). The chemical laboratory is well equipped.

Nearly opposite the Museum is **Keble College** (Pl. 18; C, 1, 2), built in 1868-70 as a memorial of the Rev. John Keble, author of the 'Christian Year', and intended to afford the opportunity of a university career to those whose means do not permit them to study at the older and more expensive colleges. The buildings are of variegated brick, and the *Chapel*, entered from the archway at its W. end (open 10-12 and 2-4, in summer till 5.30), is gorgeously adorned with mosaics. Keble resembles the Halls in having no Fellows. The library (2-4) contains Holman Hunt's 'Light of the World'.

In front of Keble is the **University Park** (Pl. D, 1, 2), one of the most charming recreation-grounds in England. The scene during an important cricket-match is very bright and varied. The *University Observatory* stands in the Park.

From Keble we now return, passing Wadham College, to the end of Broad St., and follow Catherine St., which leads hence in a straight direction towards the S. To the left stands **Hertford College** (Pl. 32; C, 3), on the site of *Hart* or *Hertford Hall*, which was founded about 1282. In 1822 the buildings were occupied by *Magdalen Hall*, which was dissolved in 1874, but immediately refounded as Hertford College. Among the members of Magdalen Hall and Hertford College were Thomas Hobbes, Lord Chancellor Clarendon, and Dean Swift. — New College St. leads hence to —

***New College** (Pl. 22; D, 3), which in spite of its name is one of the oldest and most interesting buildings in Oxford. It was founded by William of Wykeham, Bishop of Winchester (p. 77), in 1386, and a great part of the building still retains its original appearance. The upper story of the principal quadrangle dates, however, from 1678, the garden-wing was added in 1684, and new buildings were added in 1880 by Sir G. G. Scott.

The **Chapel*, which is, perhaps, the earliest building in England erected from the foundations entirely in the Perp. style, contains the silver-gilt crozier of the founder. The stained-glass windows in the ante-chapel and the upper lights of the other windows are old (14th cent.), the lower lights in the chapel itself are partly by Flemish (S. side) and partly by English (N. side) masters. The large W. window was executed in 1777 from designs by Reynolds. The fine altar-screen was restored in 1789. The organ is said to be one of the best in England. [Divine service is held daily at 8 a.m. (7.30 a.m. in summer) and 5 p.m.; adm. 11-1 and 2-4 free, at other times 1s.] The smaller quadrangle, adjoining the chapel, with its **Cloisters* and *Tower*, was not built till the rest of the college was completed. A manifold echo may be awakened here. The tower, the last work of William of Wykeham, seems to have been meant partly as a fortification. The beautiful **Gardens*, 'a sweet, quiet, sacred, stately seclusion' *(Hawthorne)*, afford a good view of the bastions of the old city-wall. A gate in the city-wall leads to the 'Slype' (good view of the outside of the wall and of the tower) and to the range of new buildings facing Holywell. Sydney Smith, Augustus Hare, and numerous bishops and archbishops were students of New College.

On quitting New College we turn to the left, pass beneath an archway, and reach the ancient church of **St. Peter in the East** (Pl. 9; D, 3), with a Norman **Crypt* and *Choir* of the middle of the 12th century. The S. wall of the nave and its fine doorway date from the same period; the pillars and arches are of the 13th cent., the N. windows of the 14th cent., the W. and S. windows and the porch of the 15th century. — A few paces to the S. is —

St. Edmund Hall (Pl. D, 3, 4), a small institution founded in 1226 and rebuilt in 1559. Its quadrangle contains a remarkably fine wisteria. Bishop Wilson, the Metropolitan of India, was a student here. — We now regain the High Street, where we turn to the left (E.) and soon reach, at the end of the street —

***St. Mary Magdalen College** (Pl. 20, D 4; pronounced *Maudlin*), founded by Bishop Waynflete in 1457, but not built till 1474-81. This college has perhaps the best claim to be regarded as the most beautiful in Oxford.

We enter the quadrangle by a new gateway erected in 1885. In the corner to the right, on a level with the first-floor windows, is an old stone pulpit, from which a University sermon used to be preached on the festival of St. John the Baptist. To the left are part of old Magdalen Hall and the newly-built '*St. Swithin's Quad*' (Bodley & Garner); immediately opposite is the *President's House*. In a small court to the right is the so-called '*Founder's Tower*', a graceful ivy-clad structure. The chambers occupied by the founder were carefully restored in 1857 and contain some valuable old tapestry, representing the marriage of Prince Arthur, elder brother of Henry VIII., with Catherine of Aragon. The *Chapel* (service daily at 10 a. m. and 6 p. m., adm. to choir by ticket from a Fellow; adm. to the ante-chapel, 11-12.30, free) was successfully restored in 1833 and contains an elaborate reredos with numerous statues. The *First Quadrangle* is surrounded with cloisters, one side of which is modern. In the S. E. corner is a flight of steps leading to the *Hall*, a fine room with carved oak panelling of 1541. A small passage connects the cloister with the *Chaplain's Quadrangle*, a small court affording a good view of **Magdalen*

Tower. The latter, erected in the Perp. style in 1492-1505, is one of the chief architectural glories of the city; it is said to have been built under the superintendence of Wolsey, when Bursar of the College. The choir sings a Latin hymn on the top of this tower at 5 a.m. on May Day, a custom supposed (but without sufficient reason) to have originated as an annual requiem for Henry VII. (d. 1509). The *Library* contains some valuable MSS. (including Wolsey's copy of the Gospels) and early printed books. The tasteless *Fellows' Buildings* harmonize very badly with the older parts of the college. — The college **Grounds* should also be visited; *Addison's Walk* is said to have been a favourite resort of the essayist when an undergraduate, and the *Water Walks* along the Cherwell, of which it forms a part, are very beautiful (reached by turning to the right in the inner quadrangle). Behind the inner quadrangle is a paddock containing deer. — The names of Wolsey, Hampden, Addison, Professor John Wilson, Charles Reade, Collins, and Gibbon are among the most eminent on the books of Magdalen. The Fellows of Magdalen in 1688 earned a memorable place in history by their courageous resistance to James II.'s unconstitutional interference in the election of the president of the college.

On leaving Magdalen we see almost opposite us the gate (built in 1632) of the *Botanic Garden.* To the left is *Magdalen Bridge*, the regular approach to Oxford from the E. A little to the right we enjoy a capital view of the whole length of the **High Street** or **'The High'**, the principal street of the city, flanked on both sides with a long array of picturesque and interesting buildings. Wordsworth has devoted a sonnet to the 'stream-like windings of that glorious street', Hawthorne calls it 'the noblest old street in England', and Sir Walter Scott admits that it rivals the High St. of Edinburgh. We now follow it towards the W., passing the back of St. Edmund's Hall, nearly opposite which, to the left, are the **New Examination Schools** (Pl. D, 4), a handsome building by Jackson, with a fine entrance-hall. Visitors (3*d.* each, if unaccompanied by a member of the University) may enter any of the *Vivâ Voce* rooms and witness the examination. Next door are the *Buildings of the Non-Collegiate Students.*

A little farther on, to the right, is **Queen's College** (Pl. 25; D, 3), founded in 1340 by Robert de Eglesfield, confessor of Philippa, consort of Edward III., and named by him in honour of his royal mistress. No part of the original building now remains; the present college dates from 1692, and its chapel from 1714.

The *Hall*, a well-proportioned room designed by Wren, is adorned with portraits of the founder and various benefactors of the college. The buttery contains an old drinking-horn, presented by Queen Philippa. The *Library*, which inherited a bequest of 30,000*l.* in 1841, is the largest collegiate library in Oxford. Queen's was the college of the Black Prince, Henry V., Cardinal Beaufort, Addison, Wycherley, and Jeremy Bentham.

Opposite, on the S. side of the High St., is **University College** (Pl. 28; C, 3), which pretends to have been founded by King Alfred, but has no substantial proof of an earlier origin than 1249, when William, Archdeacon of Durham, left a sum of money for the support of a number of masters, who, however, were not incorporated till 1280. University College is thus younger than Merton (p. 229) as an incorporated college, though it represents the earliest endowment for scholastic purposes in Oxford.

The present buildings date from 1634-74 and 1850. The imposing Gothic front, with two tower-gateways, is one of the most conspicuous ornaments of the High Street. On the W. gateway are statues of Queen Anne (outside) and James II. (inside), on the E. gateway are Queen Mary and Dr. Radcliffe. Shelley was an undergraduate at University College and the names of Lord Chancellor Eldon, Lord Herbert of Cherbury, the hymn-writer Faber, Robert Lowe (Lord Sherbrooke), and Dr. Radcliffe are also on the books.

A few paces farther on, on the N. side of High St., is —

***All Souls College** (Pl. 11; C, 3), founded in 1437 by Archbishop Chichele, to provide masses for the souls of those who died in the Hundred Years' War with France. The second quadrangle, with its two towers, was added in 1720.

The *Gateway*, with its fine vaulted roof, and the *First Quadrangle* are in the state in which they were left by the founder. The entrance to the *Chapel* (open 12-1 and 2-4), under the E. turret, has some exquisite fan-tracery in the roof; inside is a very handsome reredos. The *New Quadrangle*, on the N. side of which is the *Library*, makes a somewhat imposing impression in spite of its questionable taste; it commands a good view of the Radcliffe (p. 230). The library contains Wren's original designs for St. Paul's. All Souls is singular in having practically no undergraduates, though it has 50 fellowships, mostly held by lawyers. Jeremy Taylor, Herrick, and Blackstone were members of All Souls.

All Souls is adjoined by the church of St. Mary, already mentioned at p. 230. On the same side, a little farther on, is *All Saints' Church*, built in 1705-8. At this point *Turl Street*, so named from an old entrance to the town at the N. end (A. S. *thyrl*, a hole), diverges to the right. In it, on the right, is —

Lincoln College (Pl. 19; C, 3), founded by a Bishop of Lincoln in 1427. The chapel, dating from 1631, contains some good stained glass brought from Italy at that period. In the quadrangle to the right are two luxuriant vines. John Wesley was a fellow of Lincoln, and Mark Pattison was Rector.

In the same street, separated from Lincoln College by a lane, is **Exeter College** (Pl. 16; C, 3), founded by Walter of Stapleton, Bishop of Exeter, in 1314. All the buildings have been repeatedly restored, and several of them were erected in the present century.

The **Chapel* is a very successful modern revival of 13th cent. Gothic (adm. 10-12 and 2-4, free). The *Hall*, built in 1618 and restored in 1818, is also noteworthy. The new buildings next the 'High', including the *Principal's House*, are by Jackson (1889). The *Fellows' Garden*, to which visitors are admitted after 1 p.m. affords a good view of the Bodleian Library and the Divinity School. The large chestnut at the foot of the garden is known as 'Heber's Tree', because it overhung Heber's rooms in Brasenose (see p. 230). Among the famous alumni of Exeter are Lyell, Dyce (the Shakespearian commentator), F. D. Maurice, and J. A. Froude.

Opposite Exeter College stands **Jesus College** (Pl. 17; C, 3), founded by Queen Elizabeth and Dr. Hugh Price in 1571, rebuilt in 1621-67, and restored in 1856.

The *Chapel* dates from 1621, and contains some oaken wainscoting of that period. The *Hall* contains a fine Jacobean screen and some portraits, including one of Charles I., ascribed to Van Dyck, and there is a fine portrait of Queen Elizabeth by Zucchero in one of the common-rooms. The valuable Welsh MSS. belonging to Jesus College have been deposited in the Bodleian (p. 230). In the *Bursary* is a huge silver punch-bowl, holding eight gallons. This college was originally intended for Welsh students only, and divine service is still held in the chapel in Welsh twice a week. It has been prolific of Welsh bishops.

We now proceed to the N. end of Turl Street and cross *Broad Street.* Here, facing us, is the gateway leading to **Trinity College** (Pl. 27; C, 2), established in 1554 on the site of a Benedictine college suppressed by Henry VIII. The *Chapel*, built in 1694 in the classical style, contains a beautiful carved screen and altar-piece by Grinling Gibbons. The new buildings are by Jackson. In the *Garden* is a celebrated avenue of limes. Chillingworth, Selden, Landor, the elder Pitt, Lord Selborne, Cardinal Newman, and E. A. Freeman are among the members of Trinity. — In Broad St., to the W. of Trinity College, lies —

Balliol College (Pl. 12; C, 3), commonly said to have been founded in 1263 by John Balliol, whose son was for a short time King of Scotland. None of the present buildings are older than the 15th cent., and the S. front, with its massive tower, has lately been rebuilt.

The Gothic *Chapel*, built by Butterfield in 1858, supplants one of the most perfect architectural groups in Oxford, consisting of the old chapel and library. The new *Hall* is by Waterhouse (1876). Balliol is one of the largest colleges in Oxford, and its standard of scholarship is very high. It is much frequented by Scottish students. The library contains some ancient Bibles and valuable MSS. Wycliffe was for a time Master of Balliol, an office now held by Mr. Jowett. Besides several Archbishops of Canterbury, the books of the college contain the names of Adam Smith, Sir William Hamilton (the metaphysician), Southey, Lockhart, Cardinal Manning, Dean Stanley, Matthew Arnold, and Swinburne.

To the W. of Balliol rises the church of **St. Mary Magdalen** (Pl. 7; C, 2, 3), founded in 1320. The tower dates from 1511-31, but the rest of the building has been so frequently altered and restored that almost nothing remains of the original structure. To the N. of the church stands the **Martyrs' Memorial** (Pl. 33; C, 2), designed by Sir G. G. Scott and erected in 1841 to the memory of Cranmer, Latimer, and Ridley, who were burned in front of Balliol College in 1555 and 1556. The monument is in the richest Gothic style, and is adorned with statues of the three martyrs, by Weekes. — To the N.W. of the Memorial, at the corner of St. Giles Street and Beaumont Street, is the **Taylor Institution** (Pl. 39; B, 2), erected as a building for the teaching of modern languages, and also accommodating the **University Galleries** (Pl. 42; B, 2).

The galleries contain a collection of paintings and sculptures, casts from the antique, the original models of Chantrey's busts and statues, some fine water-colours by Turner, and a very valuable series of drawings, including 157 by Raphael and 53 by Michael Angelo (open daily, 12-4, except for a few weeks in the Long Vacation; adm. to visitors, unaccompanied by a member of the University in academic gown, 2*d*.). On the ground-floor of the S.W. wing is the *Ruskin Drawing School* (open, Mon. & Thurs. 2-4, Wed. and Sat. 12-4).

Nearly opposite, in St. Giles St., is **St. John's College** (Pl. 26; C, 2), founded in 1555.

The old quadrangle belonged to the College of St. Bernard, founded by Archbishop Chichele about 1440; the Hall is of the same period, but has been restored. The *Chapel*, consecrated in 1530, was restored in 1843. From the first quadrangle a vaulted passage with delicate fan-tracery leads to the second quadrangle, built mainly by Archbishop Laud (1631), President of St. John's, who is buried in the chapel. The S. and E. sides are occupied by the library. The oriel windows on the garden-side are very picturesque. The **Gardens* of St. John's, with their beautiful lawns, are among the finest in Oxford. The *Library* contains several relics of Abp. Laud, including the skull-cap in which he was executed; also some fine MSS. and early printed works. Among eminent members of St. John's are Abp. Juxon, Dean Mansel, and the poet Shirley.

Beyond St. John's the road forks, the right branch, Banbury Road, leading past *St. Giles's Church* (Pl. 6; C, 1), built about the year 1200, to Norham Gardens (right), with Lady Margaret's Hall (p. 238). The left branch, Woodstock Road, leads to the Roman Catholic *Church of St. Aloysius*, Somerville Hall (p. 238), and the *Radcliffe Infirmary* (Pl. 35; C, 1) and *Radcliffe Observatory*, both built at the end of last century with funds bequeathed by Dr. Radcliffe (comp. p. 230).

Beyond the observatory we turn to the W. into Observatory Street, from which Walton Street diverges to the left. In the latter stands the *University Press* (Pl. 44; B, 1), built in 1830. Farther on in the same street, opposite the end of Beaumont St., is **Worcester College** (Pl. 30; B, 2), erected in 1714 on the site of the Benedictine foundation of Gloucester College (1283; afterwards Gloucester Hall).

The chapel presents one of the richest Renaissance interiors in England, and the hall contains a few paintings. The Library has some valuable MSS. The shady **Gardens*, which contain a small lake, though less trim than some of the others, are very beautiful. Lovelace, De Quincey, and F. W. Newman studied at Worcester.

We now descend Beaumont Street, and at the church of St. Mary Magdalen turn to the right into *Cornmarket Street*. Here, to the left, stands **St. Michael's Church** (Pl. 8; C, 3), with a tower probably built by Robert d'Oily (11th cent.), as part of the town-wall; the rest of the church dates from various later periods. — To the right, a little way back from the street, are the rooms of the **Union Society** (Pl. B, 3), famous as a debating-society and undergraduates' club, founded in 1823.

Many of the most eminent of England's parliamentary speakers owe part of their success to their training in the debates of the 'Union'. Meetings for debate are held every Thurs. evening during term. The premises include reading, writing, smoking, and coffee rooms, a library, and a large hall in which the debates are held. The library is adorned with frescoes by Rossetti, Morris, and others. Visitors may be introduced for a few days by a member.

A little farther on, Cornmarket Street joins High Street at **Carfax** (Pl. B, 3), the name of which is supposed to be a corruption of *Quatre Faces* or *Quatre Voies*. The picturesque old conduit that formerly stood here was removed to Nuneham in 1787 (comp. p. 218). To the right is *St. Martin's Church*, with a tower of the 13th century.

Crossing Carfax, we follow *St. Aldate's Street* (pron. *St. Old's*), which forms a S. prolongation of Cornmarket Street. On the left stands the *Town Hall* (Pl. 41; B, C, 3), and on the right are the *Post Office* and the **Church of St. Aldate** (Pl. 5; B, 4), a Dec. edifice of the 14th century. The *Alms-Houses* to the S. of this church were founded by Card. Wolsey and endowed by Henry VIII., but were not completed till 1834. — To the W., behind the church, lies **Pembroke College** (Pl. 24; B, 4), founded in 1624, with a fine modern hall and a newly decorated chapel. This was the college of Dr. Samuel Johnson (rooms above the gateway), George Whitfield, Sir Thomas Browne, Francis Beaumont, and the patriotic Pym.

From Carfax *Queen Street* leads W. to the remains of the old *Castle* (Pl. B, 3; in New Road), now consisting of little more than a Norman tower within the walls of the County Gaol. The Empress Matilda was besieged in this castle by Stephen in 1141, but escaped during the night and found refuge at Wallingford (p. 219).

At the end of Queen St. is New Inn Hall St., leading to the N. past **New Inn Hall** (Pl. B, 3), which has been a place of education, with short interruptions, since about 1350.

Oxford possesses three halls for ladies, the discipline and tuition of which are assimilated as closely as possible to those of the men's colleges. *Lady Margaret Hall* and *St. Hugh's Hall* are situated in Norham Gardens (Pl. C, D, 1); *Somerville Hall*, named in honour of Mrs. Somerville, the mathematician, is in Woodstock Road (Pl. C, 1). The scholarship of the lady-students is tested by the examination-papers of the University, but they have a separate class-list and are not allowed to take a degree.

Excursions from Oxford.

Perhaps the most popular is that to *Woodstock* and *Blenheim*, which may be reached either by railway (comp. R. 33) or by road (carr. and pair there and back 20*s.*). Choosing the second and pleasanter of these alternatives, we leave Oxford by St. Giles Road and drive to the N.W., viâ *Wolvercote* and *Begbrooke*, beyond which we skirt Blenheim Park, to (8 M.) **Woodstock** *(Bear)*, a small and ancient town with 7500 inhab. and manufactories of leather gloves. Woodstock Manor was an early residence of the English kings, but no trace now remains of the palace built by Henry I. Edward, the Black Prince, was born at Woodstock in 1330, and here Henry II. constructed the bower in which he concealed 'Fair Rosamond'. The Princess Elizabeth was confined in the gate-house for some time by her sister Queen Mary. Chaucer was at one time a resident in Woodstock, and its name is also connected with literature by means of the romance of Walter Scott. A little way beyond the church is the entrance to ***Blenheim Park**, with the magnificent palace of the Duke of Marlborough. Woodstock Manor was presented to the first Duke of Marlborough in recognition of his numerous victories, and parliament voted him a sum of 500,000*l.* to build a residence. The park is about 12 M. in circumference and is stocked with deer. The *Palace* was built by Vanbrugh, and is a good example of his heavy though imposing style ('Lie heavy on him, Earth, for he Laid many a heavy load on thee'), with a Corinthian portico in the centre and two projecting wings. The length of the façade is nearly 400 ft. The interior is richly adorned with tapestry and painted ceilings by Thornhill. The best works of the valuable collection of paintings have recently been sold, but there still remain interesting examples of *Reynolds*, *Gainsborough*, *Hudson*, and others. The *Gardens* are very extensive and attractive, and contain temples, cascades, and fountains in the taste of the period. The park is always open to pedestrians, and the house and gardens are shown on Mon., Wed., and Frid. from 11 to 1 or 2 (fee for each 1*s.*). Carriages must be accompanied by one of the lodge-keepers (fee 2*s.* 6*d.*).

About 3½-4 M. to the S. of Oxford, beyond *South Hinksey*, rises *Boar's Hill*, a favourite point for short walks. The walk may be continued to *Abingdon* (p. 216); or we may turn to the left at the end of *Bagley Wood*, cross the Thames at *Sandford Mill*, and return to Oxford by *Littlemore* (of which Newman was chaplain) and *Iffley* (p. 218). The last-named village, which affords a good view of Oxford, possesses an interesting Norman church. This is a round of 7-8 M.

About 6 M. to the W. of Oxford lies *Stanton Harcourt*, the ancient seat of the Harcourt family, reached by a pleasant walk passing *Cumnor* and (4 M.) *Bablockhythe*, where we cross the 'stripling Thames' by a ferry. The old manor-house was built in the reign of Edward IV. and contains a room in which Pope spent two summers. The curious old kitchen, which still remains, has been described as 'either a kitchen within a chimney or a kitchen without one'. Pope, who wrote most of his 'Iliad here, has given a playful and picturesque account of Stanton Harcourt in one of his letters. Near the village are three large stones known as the *Devil's Quoits*. — *Cumnor Hall* (destroyed) is known to all readers of Kenilworth and friends of the unfortunate Amy Robsart. The church contains the tomb of Anthony Forster, with a highly laudatory inscription!

Shotover Hill (600 ft.), 4 M. to the E., commands a fine view of Oxford and its environs. It was a favourite resort of the undergraduate Shelley. About 1½ M. farther is *Cuddesden* (p. 217), with the palace of the Bishop of Oxford and a large theological college.

A pleasant walk of 9-10 M. may be taken along the E. bank of the *Cherwell* to *Islip* (p. 217), *Oddington*, and *Charlton-on-Otmoor*. The church of the last-named contains a fine rood-screen of carved oak (ca. 1500). A detour may be made to include *Water Eaton*, on the W. bank, with a good Elizabethan manor-house.

Archæologists may pay a visit to the 'British Village', near *Standlake*, about 7 M. to the S.W. of Oxford. A little to the E. of Standlake, is *Gaunt House*, a moated dwelling-house of the 15th century.

Excursions may also be made from Oxford to *Dorchester* (p. 219), *Wantage* and the *Vale of the White Horse* (p. 107), *Wychwood Forest* (10-12 M. to the N.W.), etc.

Boating on the Thames is a very favourite recreation at Oxford, two of the favourite points for excursions being *Iffley* and *Nuneham* (see p. 218). Another river-resort is *Godstow Nunnery*, 2 M. above Oxford. The building dates from the 12th cent., but the ruins are very scanty, and their chief interest arises from the fact that Fair Rosamond was educated here. About 1 M. to the W. of Godstow is *Wytham Abbey*, an Elizabethan mansion on the site of an early religious house. Visitors to the country round Oxford should be familiar with Matthew Arnold's 'Thyrsis' and 'The Scholar Gypsy'.

The direct route from Oxford to *Cambridge* (77 M., in 3-4 hrs., fares 13*s.*, 8*s.* 2*d.*, 6*s.* 5*d.*) runs viâ *Bletchley* (see p. 250) and *Bedford* (p. 355). The trains, however, are often slow and their connection imperfect; so that it is almost as quick to go viâ London.

33. From Oxford to Leamington, Warwick, and Birmingham.

Kenilworth.

66 M. Great Western Railway in 1½-3¼ hrs. (fares 11*s.* 6*d.*, 8*s.* 8*d.*, 5*s.* 6*d.*). Through-trains from London to Birmingham by this route (129 M.) take 2¾-4 hrs. (fares 17*s.* 4*d.*, 13*s.* 6*d.*, 9*s.* 5*d.*).

After leaving Oxford the train makes its first halt at (5½ M.) *Woodstock Road*, the station for Woodstock and Blenheim (p. 238).

The park lies to the left. — 19 M. *King's Sutton*, with a fine church containing an ancient wooden pulpit (branch-line to *Cheltenham*, p. 181).

23 M. **Banbury** *(Red Lion; White Lion)*, an old town with 3600 inhab., on the *Cherwell*, famous for its cakes and ale. *Banbury Cross*, immortalised in nursery-rhyme, has recently been restored. Of the old castle nothing now remains but the moat and a fragment of the wall.

From Banbury branch-lines diverge to Blisworth (p. 251) and Buckingham (p. 217). — Among places of interest near Banbury are *Broughton Castle*, *Wroxton Abbey*, and *Compton Winyates.*

From ($31^1/_2$ M.) *Fenny Compton* lines diverge to Stratford (p. 245) on the left and to Towcester and Blisworth (p. 251) on the right.

The former passes near **Edgehill,** 5 M. from Fenny Compton and 2 M. from *Kineton* station, where the first battle between the Royalists and Parliamentarians took place in 1642. — About 3 M. to the S.W. of *Morton Pinkney*, on the line to Blisworth, is **Sulgrave,** the ancestral home of the Washington family. The manor-house was built by Lawrence Washington about the middle of the 16th cent. and bears the Washington coat-of-arms (comp. p. 187) on the porch. The distinguished American antiquary, Mr. Henry Waters, has almost conclusively proved George Washington's descent from the Sulgrave family.

To the left rise the *Burton Dasset Hills.*

42 M. **Leamington.** — **Hotels.** *Regent, in the Parade; Clarendon, Lansdowne Place; *Manor House, Avenue Road, near the stations, with a garden. — Crown; Bath; Great Western, High St.; Avenue, 'pens'. 7*s*.; Guernsey Temperance. — Numerous *Boarding Houses* and *Lodgings.*

Baths. **Royal Leamington Bath & Pump Rooms*, Lower Parade, with swimming basin and Turkish baths; *Hudson's Sulphur & Saline Springs*, High St.; *Old Spring Pump Room* (Earl of Aylesford's), Bath St.; *Oldham's Open-air Swimming Baths; Free Fountain* (saline), Bath St.

Cabs. Per mile 1-2 pers. 1*s*., 3-4 pers. 1*s*. 6*d*., each addit. $^1/_2$ M. 6*d*.; per hour 2*s*. 6*d*., for each addit. $^1/_2$ hr. 1*s*. Each article of luggage carried outside 2*d*. — **Tramway** to Milverton (2*d*.) and (2 M.) *Warwick* (3*d*.).

Leamington, or *Leamington Priors*, a well-built watering-place with 23,000 inhab., is situated on the *Leam*, a tributary of the Avon, which is here crossed by three bridges. The streets are wide and pleasantly interspersed with trees and gardens. At the end of last century Leamington was still a small village, and it owes its subsequent prosperity to the mineral springs discovered here in 1797. These are of three kinds, chalybeate, saline, and sulphureous, and are found efficacious for dyspepsia and affections of the liver. The *Royal Pump Room* (see above) is adjoined by the *Pump Room Garden* (free), opposite which are the tastefully laid out **Jephson Gardens* (adm. 3*d*.; band). Leamington is also noted for its schools, the chief of which is *Leamington College.*

The new *Municipal Offices*, a handsome Renaissance structure, with a campanile, are situated on the Parade, near the middle of the town. The **Church of All Saints* is a modern Perp. building, in the form of a Greek cross and of a somewhat foreign appearance. The well-proportioned interior contains a handsome reredos. The church stands near the *Victoria Bridge* (view), over the 'high-complexioned Leam'.

Among the best points for short walks are *Warwick Castle* (p. 242), $2^1/_2$ M. to the W.; *Guy's Cliff* (p. 243), 3 M. to the N.W.; and *Offchurch Bury*, with a fine park, 3 M. to the N.E. — The excursion to *Kenilworth* (p. 243), 5 M. to the N.W., may be made by railway (see p. 242), but is pleasanter by road. Guy's Cliff and *Stoneleigh Abbey* (p. 244) may be included in the round. — *Chesterton*, 5 M. to the S., has a Perp. church.

Excursions may also be made from Leamington to *Stratford-on-Avon* (p. 245), either by railway viâ Warwick and Hatton (p. 244), or by road (10 M.); to *Coventry* (p. 253), to *Hampton Lucy*, *Compton Winyates*, *Compton Verney*, etc. The student of English history will find the battle-fields of Evesham, Tewkesbury, Bosworth, Naseby, and Edgehill all within reach.

From Leamington to Coventry, 9 M., L. N. W. Railway in 25-30 min. (fares 1*s.* 6*d.*, 1*s.*, $8^1/_2$*d.*). The intermediate stations are (1 M.) *Milverton* and (5 M.) *Kenilworth* (see above). 9 M. *Coventry*, see p. 253.

From Leamington to *Rugby*, see p. 253.

Beyond Leamington the train crosses the *Avon*.

$44^1/_2$ M. **Warwick** (*Warwick Arms*, R. & A. 3*s.* 9*d.*; *Woolpack*), a quaint old town with 11,800 inhab., situated on a hill rising from the Avon. It is a place of great antiquity, having been originally a British settlement, afterwards occupied by the Romans. Legend goes back for its foundation to King Cymbeline and the year one! Its present name is Saxon. Many of the houses have retained their mediæval appearance, and two of the old gates, the *East* and *West Gate*, are still standing. The picturesque ivy-clad house at the bottom of the main street, near the station, formerly belonged to the Knights of St. John. From the station a footpath leads to the old *Priory of St. Sepulchre*, now a private residence.

In the centre of the town is the **Church of St. Mary** (open 10-1 and 2-4), a large Perp. edifice, rebuilt after a fire in 1694. The E. end escaped destruction. The exterior suffers from the poor tracery of the windows in the rebuilt portion, and from the incongruous parapet added to the roof. The tower has been restored.

The **Interior** makes a much more satisfactory impression, especially the *Chancel* (1394), which contains two fine recumbent effigies of the Beauchamp family (14th cent.) and some curious epitaphs on brasses in front of the altar. A mural monument was erected in 1888 to *Walter Savage Landor* (1775-1864), a native of Warwick. In the *Chapter House*, to the N. of the choir, is the tomb of Fulke, Lord Greville (d. 1628), the friend of Sir Philip Sidney. — Below the choir is an interesting Norman *Crypt*. — On the S. side of the choir is the chief glory of the church the **Beauchamp Chapel* (adm. 3*d.*), a florid Perp. structure of 1464, recalling the Chapel of Henry VII. at Westminster Abbey. Among the numerous interesting monuments are those of *Richard Beauchamp, Earl of Warwick* (d. 1499), the builder of the chapel; *Robert Dudley, Earl of Leicester* (d. 1588), the favourite of Queen Elizabeth, with his wife Lettice; *Ambrose Dudley, Earl of Warwick* (d. 1589), the brother of the last; and an infant son (the 'Noble Impe', says the inscription) of Lord Dudley. The beauty of the first of these monuments shows that there was at least one English sculptor of the time not unworthy of comparison with his contemporaries, Donatello and Ghiberti.

Above the Market Hall, not far from the church, is the *Museum*, containing collections of birds, fossils, and local antiquities (open 11 to 4 or 5; adm. 6*d.*, free on Mon. and Tues.).

At the W. end of the High St., beyond the Warwick Armse is the *Leycester Hospital*, established by Lord Dudley for twelv, poor brothers in 1571, in a quaint half-timbered building of earlier date (open till 7 p. m.; small fee to the Brother who acts as guide).

The quadrangle is very picturesque, and the building c ontains severa interesting relics, such as a Saxon chair, said to be 1000 years old, and a piece of needle-work by Amy Robsart. The Spanish cedar beams of the hall look as white and fresh as if set up last week. The Bear and the Ragged Staff, the cognizance of the Warwick earldom, is frequently repeated, as in the Beauchamp Chapel (p. 241), and indeed throughout the town. The chapel, built over the West Gate of the town (comp. p. 241), is also older than Lord Dudley's foundation.

On a commanding position overlooking the Avon, at the S.E. end of the town, rises ***Warwick Castle**, the ancient and stately home of the Earl of Warwick. The castle, which is one of the finest and most picturesque feudal residences in England, probably dates from Saxon times; but the oldest portion now standing is the huge Cæsar's Tower, nearly 150 ft. high, which seems to have been built soon after the Norman Conquest. The great bulk of the residential part belongs to the 14th and 15th centuries. The roofs of the Great Hall and several other rooms were restored in the old style after a destructive fire in 1871. The outstanding event in the history of the castle is its successful defence by the Parliamentarians during the Civil War. Visitors are admitted to the castle after 10 a.m. by tickets (1*s.* each) obtainable at a shop opposite the gate.

From the *Porter's Lodge* a short avenue cut in the solid rock leads to the *Outer Court*, with Cæsar's Tower (see above) to the left and *Guy's Tower* (128 ft.) to the right. The top of the latter affords an admirable *View; the dungeons below Cæsar's Tower are interesting. The double gateway between them leads to the beautiful **Inner Court*, with its velvety turf. Opposite us is the mound on which stood the original keep.

The **Interior** contains an interesting collection of paintings, old armour, and curiosities. In the *Great Hall* are the sword and other relics of the legendary Count Guy of Warwick (comp. p. 243), the mace of Warwick the 'King-Maker', the helmet of Cromwell, and the armour in which Lord Brooke was killed at Lichfield. The windows of this and many of the other rooms afford fine views of the Avon. Among the paintings are a portrait of Ignatius Loyola by *Rubens* (in the *Gilt Drawing Room*); Charles I. by *Van Dyck* (in the *Passage*); and several other portraits by the same masters. In the *Cedar Drawing Room* is a fine Venetian mirror, and in the *Gilt Drawing Room* an inlaid table of great value.

On issuing from the interior we are conducted by another commissionnaire to the *Conservatory*, which contains the famous *Warwick Vase, found in Hadrian's Villa at Tivoli. The beautiful **Park* contains magnificent cedars and other trees.

An admirable *View of the castle is obtained from the bridge over the Avon, a little way from the lodge. 'We can scarcely think the scene real', says Hawthorne, 'so completely do those machicolated towers, the long line of battlements, the massive buttresses, the high-windowed walls, shape out our indistinct ideas of the antique time'. — The view is perhaps even better from an old mill, reached by the road descending from the lodge to the river.

Warwick is a good centre for excursions, the most popular of which are those to Kenilworth and Stratford, both reached either by road or railway. Route to *Stratford*, see p. 244. — To reach *Kenilworth* by railway we join the L.N.W. line at Milverton or Leamington (see p. 240); the railway-station at Kenilworth is 3/4 M. from the castle. The pleasant road-route is described below.

From Warwick to Kenilworth, by road, 5 M.; carr. with one horse there and back 9*s.* 6*d.*, with two horses 20*s.*, including the driver's fee. A pleasant round may be made by returning viâ Stoneleigh Abbey and Leamington (carr. for the round 15*s.*, with two horses 25*s.*). — The road leads to the N., and soon reaches (1 1/4 M.) ***Guy's Cliff**, the seat of Miss Bertie Percy, to which visitors are admitted in the absence of the family. The name is derived from Guy, Earl of Warwick, whose feats in slaying the Dun Cow (comp. p. 242) and other monsters form part of English legendary lore. On the river, a little below the house, is a cave in which he is said to have lived as an anchorite after his return from the Holy Land, daily receiving alms from the Countess Felice, who did not recognize her husband in his disguise. At his death, however, he revealed himself to her, and the two were buried together in the cave in Guy's Cliff. Near the cave is a small chapel. The house contains some interesting paintings, including several by *Bertie Greatheed*, son of a former owner of Guy's Cliff, a highly-gifted young artist who died in 1804 at the age of 22. Mrs. Siddons lived at Guy's Cliff for some time before her marriage, as companion to the Mrs. Greatheed of the time. — A few yards down the road which diverges to the right a little beyond the above-mentioned glade, by a picturesque old mill said to be of Saxon date, a beautiful view of Guy's Cliff House is obtained. — About 1/4 M. farther on, to the left, is *Blacklow Hill*, on which is a monument to *Piers Gaveston*, the unfortunate favourite of Edward II., who was slain here in 1312. — In 1/2 M. more we have a pretty view, to the left, of *Wootton Court*. We soon reach (1/2 M.) the village of *Leek Wootton*.

About 1 1/2 M. farther on are the first houses of *Kenilworth* (King's Arms Inn, see below; Abbey; Castle, opposite the castle, indifferent), a small straggling town with 4150 inhabitants. The castle is about 1 M. farther on. The King's Arms Inn contains the room in which Walter Scott made his first sketch of 'Kenilworth'. ***Kenilworth Castle**, one of the finest and most extensive baronial ruins in England, was originally founded by Geoffrey de Clinton, chamberlain of Henry I., about 1120. In the 13th cent. it passed into the hands of Simon de Montfort, and was maintained for six months by his son against the royal forces (1266). In 1362 Kenilworth came by marriage to John of Gaunt, who added largely to it. The castle afterwards became royal property, and in 1563 was presented by Queen Elizabeth to her favourite, the Earl of Leicester. Leicester spent enormous sums of money in enlarging and improving the building, and in 1575 entertained his royal patroness here in the magnificent style immortalised by Scott. Cromwell gave the castle to some of his officers, who demolished the stately pile for the sake of its materials and scattered its costly collections. After the Restoration it passed into the hands of the Earls of Clarendon, who still retain it. Perhaps no other English castle has had more varied points of contact with English history, from the stormy and semi-barbarous times of Simon de Montfort, down through the pompous and courtly luxury of the Elizabethan period, to the iconoclastic days of the Protectorate; while under the touch of the 'Magician of the North' it has renewed its youth in our own era, and, ruin though it be, is more familiar and present to contemporary thought than almost any occupied mansion in the country.

We enter (adm. 3*d.*) by a small gate to the N.W. of *Leicester's Gatehouse* (now occupied as a private dwelling), and passing along the wall turn to the right and obtain a view of the main part of the building. The part nearest us (to the right) is the *Norman Keep* or *Caesar's Tower*, which seems to have had three or four stories; the walls are 15-16 ft. thick. Beyond this, to the W., is a vacant space formerly occupied by the *Kitchen*, crossing which we reach (at the N.W. angle) the *Strong* or *Mervyn's Tower*, built by John of Gaunt (ca. 1392); the 'small octangular chamber' on the second floor is that assigned by Walter Scott to Amy Robsart. The *Pleasance*, of which it 'commanded a delightful view', is

For a plan of Kenilworth Castle see page 548

now an orchard and vegetable garden. The grotto in which Amy was discovered by the Queen adjoined the *Swan Tower*, at the apex of the Pleasance. At right angles to Mervyn's Tower is the **Banqueting Hall*, also built by 'time-honoured Lancaster', with two fine oriels at its S. end. The three apartments next in order, on the S. side of the quadrangle, are known as the *White Hall*, the *Presence Chamber*, and the *Privy Chamber*, and also date from the Lancastrian period. The large pile at the end, with Tudor windows, was erected by the Earl of Leicester, and in spite of its comparative youth needs support which the Norman keep disdains. The buildings just described form the Inner Court; and the outer line of defence, with the *Swan*, *Lunn's*, *Water*, and *Mortimer Towers*, may also be traced. The *Great Lake* lay to the W. and S. of the outer wall; and the *Tilt-Yard* lay outside Mortimer's Tower, at the S.E. angle of the enclosure. The *Chapels*, those of the original Norman building and of John of Gaunt, have disappeared. Comp. the Plan.

If time permit, we may, before leaving Kenilworth, visit the *Parish Church*, with some Norman details, and the adjacent fragmentary ruins of *Kenilworth Priory*, founded by Geoffrey de Clinton (p. 243).

About 3 M. to the E. of Kenilworth is **Stoneleigh Abbey**, the seat of Lord Leigh, a large mansion erected last century. It occupies the site of a Cistercian abbey, of which a gateway (16th cent.) remains, and contains a good collection of paintings and some fine wainscoting (state rooms shown to visitors). Fine oaks in the park. — About 6 M. to the N.W. of Warwick, 4 M. from Kenilworth and 2½ M. from Kingswood (see below), is *Wroxhall*, a modern mansion, incorporating some remains of a priory of the 12th century. The church is also interesting.

Excursions may also be made from Warwick to *Leamington* (p. 240), *Edgehill* (p. 240), *Coventry* (p. 253), etc.

Beyond Warwick the train quits the valley of the Avon. — 49 M. *Hatton*, the junction of a line to Stratford-on-Avon (see below). — 53 M. *Kingswood*; 55½ M. *Knowle*, with an Idiot Asylum and a handsome church; 58½ M. *Solihull* (George), a prettily situated village with an interesting restored church, in the Dec. and Perp. styles. The train then passes two or three other small stations and traverses the manufacturing suburbs of Birmingham.

66 M. **Birmingham** (Snow Hill Station), see p. 254.

34. From Warwick to Stratford-on-Avon.

14½ M. Railway in ½ hr. (fares 2*s*. 6*d*., 1*s*. 9*d*., 1*s*. 1½ *d*.). Carriages are changed at *Hatton*. — Warwick is 8 M. from Stratford by the direct road on the right bank of the Avon, and 10 M. by the pleasanter road on the left bank. Carriage with one horse 8-10*s*., with two horses 15-20*s*.

Stratford may also be reached by railway from *Fenny Compton* (p. 240), *Honeybourne* (p. 187), and *Broom Junction* (p. 188)

a. By Railway.

From Warwick to (4½ M.) *Hatton*, see above. — Our train here diverges to the left (S.) from the main G. W. R. line to Birmingham. — 6½ M. *Claverdon;* 10 M. *Bearley*, the junction of a line to (7 M.) *Alcester* (p. 188); 11½ M. *Wilmcote*, the birthplace of Mary Arden, Shakespeare's mother.

14½ M. *Stratford-on-Avon*, see below. Beyond Stratford the railway is continued to *Honeybourne* (p. 187).

For a coloured map of The Environs of Stratford-on-Avon and Warwick see page 573

b. By Road.

We leave Warwick by the road leading past the Leycester Hospital (p. 241), and at first follow the right bank of the *Avon.* At the fork we keep to the left, soon seeing to the right the spire of the fine new church of *Sherborne.* At (2 M.) *Barford* we cross the river, and about $1^1/_2$ M. farther on we pass the village of *Wasperton* (to the right), with a restored church. — About $^1/_2$ M. beyond Wasperton our road diverges to the right from the high-road, and reaches (1 M.) *Charlecote* and the N. extremity of *Charlecote Park* (see p. 247; view of the house to the right). The road now skirts the E. side of the park and then ($^3/_4$ M.) turns to the right and skirts its S. side. After $^3/_4$ M. we pass the lodge-gate at the S.W. angle of Charlecote Park. The pretty village of *Alveston* lies among trees to the right, $1^1/_2$ M. farther on, in a loop of the river, of which the road forms the chord. $^3/_4$ M. *Tiddington*, with some quaint old houses. After $1^1/_4$ M. more we reach the bridge leading across the Avon to Stratford. — The direct route from Warwick to Stratford (8 M.) follows the right bank of the Avon, but at some distance from the river.

Stratford-on-Avon (*Red Horse*, see p. 247; *Shakespeare Hotel*, with rooms named after Shakespeare's plays, R. & A. 4*s.* 6*d.*, table d'hôte 5*s.*; *Temperance*, next door to the Red Horse; *Falcon*, unpretending; *Rail. Refreshmt. Rooms*) is a clean and well-built little country-town of about 8200 inhab., with wide and pleasant streets containing numerous quaint half-timbered houses. It is a place of some antiquity, and is mentioned in a Saxon charter of the 8th century. Though not without importance as an agricultural centre, it owes its prosperity chiefly to the memory of the great dramatist born here in 1564, whose name and form have been imported, in one shape or another, into the trade-mark of almost every saleable article in the town †. It is a singular fact that the annual number of pilgrims to Stratford-on-Avon does not exceed 13,000 or 14,000 (mainly Americans), while over 30,000 annually visit the birthplace of Burns (comp. p. 481). Visitors are recommended to purchase the map of the town (price 2*d.*), published at 'Ye Five Gables', Chapel St.

***Shakespeare's House**, in which the poet was born on April 23rd, 1564, is in Henley St.; it is now national property, and is kept in scrupulously good order. It is open to visitors from 9 a.m. to 8 p.m. in summer, and till dusk in winter (adm. 6*d.*;

† 'I am sure, sir', said a worthy Stratfordian to Mr. J. W. Hales, 'we ought to be very much obliged to Mr. Shakespeare for being born here, for I don't know what we should have done without him'. — To write about Stratford is to write about Shakespeare, and the day has long gone by when it was possible to confine the poet, as Dugdale the antiquary did, to three lines at the end of a long article: 'One thing more in reference to this ancient town is observable, that it gave birth and sepulture to our late famous poet, Will Shakespeare'.

museum 6*d.* extra). The house has undergone various vicissitudes since Shakespeare's day, but the timber framework remains substantially unaltered, and the recent restoration has been directed towards a reproduction of the building at it stood in 1564.

Interior. The small chamber facing the street, on the first floor, has been consecrated by tradition as that in which the poet was born. Formerly the walls of all the rooms were covered with the inscribed names of visitors; but these were concealed with whitewash during the renovation of the building in 1864. An exception, however, was made in favour of the birth-room, where the signatures of Walter Scott (scratched on the window), Byron, Thackeray, Tennyson, Kean, and Dickens are pointed out. No new names are now allowed to be added. The back-room on the upper floor contains a very interesting old portrait of Shakespeare (the 'Stratford Portrait'), formerly in the possession of the Clopton family (see below), and showing the poet in the same dress as in the bust at the church (p. 247). Below the *Kitchen*, on the ground-floor, is a dark *Cellar*, probably the only room in the building that has not been changed since the poet's boyhood. — The rooms to the right on the ground-floor are fitted up as a *Shakespeare Museum*, and contain a most interesting collection of portraits, early editions, and other relics of the great dramatist, including his school-desk and signet-ring. — The *Garden* at the back of the house contains a selection of the trees and flowers mentioned in Shakespeare's plays.

From Henley St. we may now pass through *High Street*, where, on the right, is a picturesque half-timbered house, bearing the date 1596, and said to have been the home of the Harvard family, of which the founder of the famous American university was a scion. At the corner of *Chapel Street*, to the left, is the *Town Hall*, on the outside of which is a statue of Shakespeare; inside are portraits of Shakespeare by *Wilson* and Garrick by *Gainsborough* (small fee).

At the other end of Chapel St., also to the left, is **New Place**, the site of the house in which Shakespeare resided on his return to Stratford in later life, and where he died on April 23rd, 1616.

In the middle of last century, the house, said to have been built by Sir Hugh Clopton about 1530, came into the possession of the Rev. Francis Gastrell, who razed it to the ground owing to a quarrel about the rates, having previously cut down the poet's mulberry-tree to save himself from the importunities of visitors! The adjoining house (adm. 6*d.*) contains another but less interesting *Shakespeare Museum*, through which we obtain access to a small garden with the foundations of Shakespeare's house, an old well, and a thriving scion of the mulberry. — Behind (entr. from Chapel Lane) are the *New Place Public Gardens* (open all day, free; Sun. 2-6).

Opposite New Place, at the corner of Chapel Lane and Church St., stands the *Guild Chapel*, rebuilt by Sir Hugh Clopton (see above) and still, like the parish-church and the grammar-school, externally much the same as in the poet's days. It is adjoined by the old *Guild Hall*, where Shakespeare may often have seen the performances of strolling players; while the upper story, substantially unchanged, is the *Grammar School* in which he was educated, founded in the second half of the 15th century.

At the end of Church St. we turn to the left and follow the road named *Old Town* to the ***Church of the Holy Trinity,** a 15th cent. edifice, with a lofty spire, charmingly situated amid trees on the bank of the Avon. The church (adm. 6*d.*) has lately been restored.

The imposing ***Interior** contains many monuments of interest; but 'the mind refuses to dwell', as Washington Irving says in his well-known sketch, 'on anything that is not connected with Shakespeare. His idea pervades the place; the whole pile seems but as his mausoleum. The feelings, no longer checked and thwarted by doubt, here indulge in perfect confidence; other traces of him may be false or dubious, but here is palpable evidence and absolute certainty'. The *Grave* of the poet is on the N. side of the chancel, and is covered by a slab bearing an oft-quoted inscription, attributed to himself (of which 'rubbings' may be obtained in the town, price 1*s*.). On the wall above is the familiar *Bust*, executed soon after Shakespeare's death by Gerard Johnson. The original colouring has been reproduced. The stained-glass window above, representing the Seven Ages, was erected with the contributions of American visitors. — Close to Shakespeare's tomb are those of his wife, *Anne Hathaway* (d. 1623); his daughter, *Susan Hall* (d. 1649); his son-in-law, *Dr. Hall*; and *Thomas Nash*, the first husband of his granddaughter Elizabeth. — Among the other monuments are several of the *Clopton Family*, and the altar-tombs of *Dean Balsall*, the builder of the chancel, and *John Combe*, the money-lender. — Within the altar-rails is the font in which Shakespeare was christened.

The visitor should request the verger to show the registers containing the entries of Shakespeare's baptism and funeral, and also the autograph-book in which he has collected the signatures of the most eminent of recent visitors to the church.

The one jarring note in Stratford is the *Shakespeare Memorial Theatre* (6*d*.), a building, erected in 1879, in the spick-and-span red brick and terracotta style which is associated with industrial museums. It lies on the Avon a little above the church, at the end of Chapel Lane. Annual memorial performances are held here in April. The institute includes a gallery of Shakespearian paintings and a library of Shakespearian books. Visitors should ascend the tower for the *View of Stratford. — Higher up is the 'great and sumptuous *Bridge* upon the Avon', built by Sir Hugh Clopton (p. 246). It commands a charming *View up and down the Avon.

In Bridge Street, which leads from the bridge into the town, is the *Red Horse Hotel*, containing the room in which Washington Irving wrote his delightful paper on Stratford-on-Avon. The chair he sat in and the poker with which he meditatively poked the fire are still shown as 'Geoffrey Crayon's Throne and Sceptre'.

About 1 M. to the W. of Stratford is *Shottery*, which is best reached by a footpath, starting either from Evesham Place, or from a point near the G. W. R. Station. **Anne Hathaway's Cottage* is still standing here in substantially the same condition as when Shakespeare courted his future wife. It has now been divided into three dwellings, and the one nearest the road is still occupied by a descendant of the Hathaway family (Mrs. Baker). It contains an old settle, a carved bedstead, some 'ever-lasting linen sheets', and other relics of 300 years since. In front of the cottage is a small garden, gay with old-fashioned flowers. — From Shottery the walk may be continued to *Luddington*, where Shakespeare was married, 2 M. to the S.W. The church has, however, been rebuilt.

An excursion should also be made to **Charlecote**, the mansion where, according to the story, Shakespeare was brought up before Sir Thomas Lucy for deer-stealing, still occupied by a descendant and namesake (H. S. Lucy, Esq.) of that worthy 'Justice Shallow'. Visitors are freely admitted to the park, but a special permission (apply beforehand in writing) is required for the house. We cross the bridge over the Avon, turn to the left, pass through *Tiddington* and *Alveston* (comp. p. 245), and reach ($3^1/_2$ M.) the lodge-gate of Charlecote. Passing through the gate and crossing the park, which is still well-stocked with deer, we soon come in sight of the house, an extensive red brick building in the Elizabethan style, containing some good paintings. Visitors not provided with a special permit should not cross the small stream flowing past the house. To the left is visible the spire of *Hampton Lucy Church*, a handsome structure by Rickman and Scott, which may be reached by turning to the left on leaving the park at the other end. — *Charlecote Church* (comp. p. 245) contains several monuments of the Lucy family, including one to the wife of Sir Thomas Lucy (see p. 247), with a fine epitaph, ascribed to the knight himself, which should go far to prove that Shallow, if indeed meant for Sir Thomas, is a caricature of the original.

All lovers of Shakespeare will find much that is most suggestive and interesting in the quaint little villages around Stratford; and longer excursions may be made to *Warwick* (p. 241), *Leamington* (p. 240), *Kenilworth* (p. 243), *Evesham* (p. 187), *Edgehill* (p. 240), etc.

35. From London to Harrow, Rickmannsworth, and Chesham.

26 M. Railway from *Baker Street Station* in 1-$1^1/_4$ hr. (fares 3*s.* 10*d.*, 2*s.* 10*d.*, 1*s.* 11*d.*). This line is a recent extension of the St. John's Wood branch of the Metropolitan Railway.

Passing the suburban stations of *St. John's Wood*, *Marlborough Road*, *Swiss Cottage*, *Finchley Road*, *West Hampstead*, *Kilburn-Brondesbury*, and *Willesden Green*, the train quits London and enters a pleasant open country. To the N. of (6 M.) *Kingsbury-Neasden*, with the works of the Metropolitan Railway Co., lies the *Brent* or *Welsh Harp Reservoir*.

10 M. **Harrow-on-the-Hill** *(King's Head; Railway Hotel)*. The large *Public School* here, founded by John Lyon, yeoman, in 1572, is scarcely second to Eton, and has numbered Lord Byron, Sir Robert Peel, Sheridan, Spencer Perceval, Viscount Palmerston, and numerous other eminent men among its pupils. The older portion of the school is in the Tudor style. The chapel, library, and speech-room are all quite modern. The panels of the great school-room are covered with the names of the boys, including those of Byron, Peel, and Palmerston. The number of scholars is now about 500. *Harrow Church* has a lofty spire, which is a conspicuous object in the landscape for many miles round. The churchyard commands a most extensive *View. A flat tombstone, on which Byron used to lie when a boy, is still pointed out. — $12^1/_2$ M. *Pinner* (Queen's Head, a quaint 'Queen Anne' building), a prettily situated little town with 2500 inhabitants. A little to the W. lie *Ruislip Park* and *Reservoir*. — About 3 M. to the S.W. of ($14^1/_2$ M.) *Northwood* lies *Harefield*, the scene of Milton's 'Arcades'.

18 M. **Rickmansworth** *(Swan; Victoria)*, a small paper-making town (5500 inhab.) on the *Chess*, near its confluence with the *Colne*, is a good centre for excursions. Large quantities of water-cress are grown here for the London market. To the S.E., on the other side of the Colne, lies *Moor Park* (Lord Ebury), with its fine timber.

Walkers are advised to quit the railway here and proceed to ($9^1/_2$ M.) Chesham on foot through the ***Valley of the Chess.** We turn to the right on leaving the station, pass under the railway arch, follow a path to the left, cross the railway by a foot-bridge, and enter *Rickmansworth Park*, with its fine old trees. The walk across the park brings us in 25 min. to a road, which we cross obliquely to a meadow-path leading to (1/4 hr.) the high-road to Chenies, at a point near the village of *Chorley Wood* (1/2 M. from the station, see below). About 1 3/4 M. farther on we turn to the right (sign-post) for (1/2 M.) the picturesque and neatly built village of **Chenies** (**Bedford Inn*). The **Mortuary Chapel* attached to the church here contains the tombs of the Russells from 1556 to the present day, forming an almost unique instance in England of a family burial-place of this kind (admission only by order obtained at the Bedford Estate Office, Montague Street, Russell Square, London; key kept by Mr. White, whose house adjoins the above-mentioned sign-post). The finest monument is that of *Anne, Countess of Bedford (d. 1558), the builder of the chapel. Lord William Russell (beheaded in 1683) and Lord John Russell (d. 1878) are both buried here. Adjoining the church is a fragment of the old manor-house. — To reach Chesham we follow the lane between the church and the manor-house, and then turn to the left along a path through wood on the slope of the valley of the Chess. View of the Elizabethan mansion of *Latimers*, on the other side of the stream. After about 1/4 hr. we pass through two gates. 20 min. Lane, leading to the left to Chalfont Road station (see below). In 10 min. more we descend to the right to the road and follow it to the left to (2 M.) *Chesham* (see below).

A pleasant walk may also be taken from Rickmansworth to (5 M.) *Chalfont St. Giles* (see below).

20 M. *Chorley Wood* and (22 M.) *Chalfont Road* are each about 1 1/2 M. from *Chenies* (see above). They are also nearly equidistant (3-3 1/2 M.) from the charming little village of *Chalfont St. Giles*, containing the cottage in which Milton lived in 1665-68, finishing 'Paradise Lost' and beginning 'Paradise Regained'. It has been left unchanged since the poet's time and contains a few relics (adm. 6*d.*, a party 3*d.* each). About 3 M. to the S. of Chalfont St. Giles, on the way to *Beaconsfield* (see *Baedeker's London*), is *Jordans*, the burial-place of *William Penn* (d. 1718). — The present terminus of the railway is at (26 M.) **Chesham** (*Crown; George*), a quaint old town with 9000 inhab., mainly employed in the manufacture of furniture and other articles in beech-wood, cricket-bats, etc. Ducks and water-cress are also extensively produced. Fine view from the *Park*.

Amersham (*Griffin; Crown*), 3 M. to the S. of Chesham, with 2500 inhab., is another seat of the beechwood-chair industry.

36. From London to Birmingham
viâ Rugby and Coventry.

113 M. L. N. W. Railway (*Euston Station*) in 2 3/4-3 1/2 hrs. (fares 17*s.* 4*d.*, 13*s.* 6*d.*, 9*s.* 5*d.*). Luncheon-baskets may be obtained at Euston and the other chief stations. The country traversed is somewhat monotonous.

Beyond *Camden Town*, with the principal depôt of the North Western Railway, and *Chalk Farm*, the train threads the Primrose Hill Tunnel, 1160 yds. long. Near (3 M.) *Kilburn* is another tunnel, after which we see *Kensal Green Cemetery* (see *Baedeker's London*) on the left. — 5 1/2 M. **Willesden** (*Rail. Refreshmt. Rooms*), an important railway-junction, passed daily by 700 trains. Beyond (8 M.) *Sudbury* a view is obtained to the left of Harrow-on-the-Hill.

11 1/2 M. *Harrow*; the station is 1 M. from the town of *Harrow-*

on-the-Hill (p. 248). — Near (13½ M.) *Pinner* (p. 248), to the right, are the red brick buildings of the *Commercial Travellers' Schools.* Beyond Pinner we notice the ingenious arrangement by which the locomotives supply themselves with water, without slackening speed, from troughs laid down between the rails. — 16 M. *Bushey.* — 17½ M. **Watford** *(Clarendon; Maldon)* is pleasantly situated on the *Colne*, among the woods of *Cassiobury* (Earl of Essex) and the *Grove* (Earl of Clarendon). A pretty public walk crosses the park of the former, but neither house is shown. Watford is the junction of a line to (7 M.) *St. Albans* (see p. 357), and of another to (4 M.) *Rickmansworth* (p. 248). — We now pass through another tunnel, upwards of 1 M. long, and cross the Grand Junction Canal. — 24½ M. *Boxmoor*, the station for *Hemel Hempstead.* — 28 M. *Berkhampstead;* in the pretty valley to the left lies the town of *Great Berkhampstead* (King's Arms), birthplace of the poet Cowper (1731-1800), with the remains of a castle and a Dec. church. As the train approaches (32 M.) *Tring* (Rose & Crown), a small and ancient town with a handsome church, we obtain a view of the *Chiltern Hills*, which give name to the 'Stewardship of the Chiltern Hundreds', a nominal office conferred upon members of parliament wishing to resign their seats.

About 2½ M. to the W. of Tring is *Drayton Beauchamp*, where the 'Judicious Hooker' was rector (1585), when visited by Cranmer and Sandys, as narrated by Izaak Walton.

Beyond Tring the train traverses the Chiltern Hills by a deep cutting and enters Buckinghamshire. 36 M. *Cheddington* is the junction of a line to Aylesbury (p. 217). — 40½ M. *Leighton* is the station for *Leighton Buzzard* ('Beau Desert'; Swan), a small town ½ M. to the W., with an E. E. church and a market-cross.

About 3½ M. to the S. (1 M. from Cheddington) is *Mentmore*, a seat of Lady Rosebery (née Rothschild), containing a fine collection of paintings, tapestries, etc. (access sometimes obtainable on written application).

From Leighton to Dunstable and Luton, 11½ M., railway in ½-1 hr. (fares 1*s*. 10*d*., 1*s*. 6*d*., 11½*d*.). — 6 M. **Dunstable** *(Sugarloaf; Red Lion; Saracen's Head)*, a town with 4600 inhab. and manufactories of straw bonnets and baskets. Dunstable larks are sent in large quantities to London. The *Priory Church* (restored) is a fine Norman building, dating in part from the reign of Henry I. (1100-35). Charles I. slept at the Red Lion Inn here when on his way to Naseby. — 11½ M. **Luton**, see p. 357.

From Leighton an excursion may be made to *Woburn* (*Bedford Arms), 7 M. to the N., with an ivy-clad church. **Woburn Abbey**, the seat of the Duke of Bedford, built in 1747 on the site of a Cistercian abbey, contains a good collection of art (shown on Frid., 10-4, by order obtained at the Park Farm office). The large deer-park and pleasure-grounds are also very fine.

47 M. *Bletchley* (Rail. Rfmt. Rooms), the junction of lines to Oxford (p. 223) on the left, and to Bedford (p. 355) and Cambridge (p. 431) on the right. Woburn (see above) is about 5 M. to the E. of Bletchley. — 52 M. *Wolverton* (Victoria; Rail. Rfmt. Rooms), on the *Ouse*, with the carriage-building works of the L. N. W. R., is the junction for (4 M.) *Newport Pagnell* (Anchor; Swan), a small lace and paper-making town, with a large church.

A steam-tramway runs from Wolverton to (2 M.) *Stoney Stratford* and *Deanshanger*. The train then crosses *Wolverton Viaduct* and enters the well-wooded county of Northampton. At (60 M.) *Roade* the line forks, the old trunk-line running straight to Rugby, while a new loop-line runs to the right viâ Northampton, rejoining the main line just before Rugby.

The first station on the main line beyond Roade is (63 M.) *Blisworth* (Hotel), the junction of a line to *Towcester* and *Stratford-on-Avon* (comp. p. 240), of another to *Banbury* (p. 240), and of a short one to *Northampton* (see below). Beyond Blisworth the train crosses the Grand Junction Canal, and soon after threads a tunnel 500 yds. long. 70 M. *Weedon*, with extensive barracks, a powder-magazine, and a large military depôt, is the junction of a line to *Daventry*. The line here follows the direction of the old Roman road known as *Watling Street*. Beyond (76 M.) *Welton* is a tunnel 1$^1/_3$ M. long, on emerging from which the line enters Warwickshire and is rejoined by the loop-line above mentioned. Rugby (see p. 252) is reached almost immediately afterwards.

Leaving Roade (see above) by the loop-line, we pass through a cutting and a short tunnel and soon reach —

66 M. **Northampton.** — **Hotels.** George, Peacock, in the Market Place; Angel, Plough, Bridge St. — *Rail. Refreshmt. Rooms.*

Cabs. From the railway-stations into the town, with luggage, 1-2 pers. 1*s*., 3 pers. 1*s*. 6*d*., 4 pers. 2*s*.; beyond the borough, 1*s*. per mile.

Railway Stations. *Castle Station*, on the S.W. side of the town, for the L. N. W. trains; *Bridge St. Station* (L. N. W.), for trains to Peterborough; *Midland*, near the centre of the town, for trains to Bedford.

Northampton, the capital of the shire of that name, is a well-built town with 57,555 inhab., situated on the N. bank of the *Nene*, and widely known for its manufactures of boots and shoes. It is a place of considerable antiquity, and was the seat of numerous parliaments in the 12th, 13th, and 14th centuries. In 1460 the Lancastrians were defeated near Northampton, and Henry VI. taken prisoner by the Earl of Warwick.

The busiest parts of Northampton are the *Drapery* and the large *Market Square*. Among the buildings adjoining the latter are the Gothic *Town Hall*, built in 1864; the *Corn Exchange;* and the church of *All Saints*, with a tower of the 14th cent. and containing a statue, by Chantrey, of Spencer Perceval, who was assassinated in the lobby of the House of Commons in 1812. *St. Peter's Church*, restored by Sir G. G. Scott, is an interesting Norman structure (p. xxxix). The remains of the old *Castle*, built in the 11th cent., are scanty. The Castle Hill Chapel contains a tablet to *Dr. Doddridge*, the Nonconformist theologian, who ministered here for 22 years. The old *Hospital of St. John* also deserves attention.

The most interesting building in Northampton is, however, the **Church of St. Sepulchre*, supposed to have been built by Simon de

Liz at the beginning of the 12th cent., and one of the few round churches of England, (comp. pp. 437, 442). This church, which lies to the N. of the town, contains numerous E.E. additions, including a fine spire, and has been restored by Scott.

About 1 M. to the S. of Northampton is **Queen Eleanor's Cross*, the best survivor of those which Edward I. erected at every point where the body of his wife rested on its way to interment in Westminster. Not far off is *Delapré Abbey*, on the site of an old Cluniac religious house. — **Althorp**, the seat of Earl Spencer, 5 M. to the N.W. of Northampton, contains some good pictures (including a fine series of family-portraits by *Reynolds*, *Van Dyck*, *Kneller*, *Lely*, etc.) and a magnificient and celebrated collection of rare and curious books, including many incunabula. Near Althorp is *Barleston*, an interesting experiment in co-operative farming. — Excursions may also be made to *Earl's Barton* and *Castle Ashby* (see below).

From Northampton to Market Harborough, 18 M., railway in $^1/_2$-$^3/_4$ hr. (fares 2*s.* 9*d.*, 1*s.* 11*d.*, 1*s.* 5$^1/_2$*d.*). The kennels of the celebrated Pytchley Hunt are at (8 M.) *Brixworth*, which possesses a large church, perhaps formed out of a Roman building (p. xxxv). — 18 M. *Market Harborough*, see p. 354.

From Northampton to Peterborough, 42 M., railway in 1$^1/_4$-1$^1/_2$ hr. (fares 6*s.* 10*d.*, 4*s.* 5*d.*, 3*s.* 6$^1/_2$*d.*). — About 2 M. to the S. of (6 M.) *Ashby* is *Castle Ashby*, the seat of the Marquis of Northampton, the gardens of which are open on Tues. and Thurs. (house on Tues.). *Yardley Chase*, the park belonging to it, has a circumference of 7 M. Ashby is also the station for (1$^1/_4$ M.) *Earl's Barton*, famous for its church with a pre-Norman tower (p. xxxvi). *Whiston*, near Ashby, has an interesting church (see p. lii). — 10 M. *Wellingborough*, see p. 355. — 14 M. *Higham Ferrers* (Green Dragon), 1 M. from the station, was the birthplace of *Abp. Chichele* (1362-1443) and contains a handsome church, a school, a college, and other buildings erected by him. — 21 M. *Thrapstow*, the junction of lines to Huntingdon and Kettering (p. 354). — 26 M. *Oundle* (Talbot), a small town on the *Nene*, with an E.E., Dec., and Perp. church. At *Fotheringay*, 3$^1/_2$ M. to the N., Mary, Queen of Scots, was tried and executed. The castle was destroyed by James I., but the interesting Perp. church remains. *Warmington*, 2 M. to the S. E. of Fotheringay, has a good EE. church (p. xlv). — 42 M. *Peterborough*, see p. 362.

From Northampton to *Bedford*, see p. 355.

Beyond Northampton the Rugby train passes stat. *Althorp Park* (see above). To the left is *Great Brington Church*, containing some brasses of the Washington family (comp. p. 240). Beyond *Kilsby* we rejoin the main line (comp. p. 251).

---

83 M. **Rugby** (*Royal George; Horseshoes; Laurence Sheriffe's; Rail. Refreshmt. Rooms;* cab to the town, 1-2 pers. 1*s.*, each addit, pers. 6*d.*), a town with 9890 inhab., 1 M. from the station, is an important railway-junction (the 'Mugby Junction' of Dickens). It appears in Domesday Book as 'Rocheberrie' and in Elizabeth's time as 'Rokebie'. The famous *School*, founded by Laurence Sheriffe in 1567, and provided with endowments which now bring in 7000*l.* a year, is attended by 60 foundationers and 350-400 other boys. Its most interesting associations cluster round the name of Dr. Thomas Arnold, who was head-master here from 1828 to 1842 and is buried in the chapel. The scene of 'Tom Brown's School Days' is laid at Rugby. *St. Andrew's* is a 14th cent. building, restored by Mr. Butterfield. Rugby is a good hunting-centre. — About 1$^1/_2$ M. to the E. of Rugby is *Bilton Hall*, where Addison long resided; an avenue in the garden is known as Addison's Walk.

FROM RUGBY TO LEAMINGTON, 15 M., railway in $^1/_2$ hr. (fares 2*s*. 6*d*., 1*s*. 9*d*., 1*s*. 3*d*.). The intermediate stations are *Dunchurch*, *Birdingbury*, and *Marton*. — 15 M. *Leamington*, and thence to *Warwick*, see pp. 240, 241.

From Rugby to *Nuneaton* and *Stafford*, see R. 44a. This line forms part of the through-route of the L.N.W.R. from London to Liverpool.

FROM RUGBY TO MARKET HARBOROUGH, $17^1/_2$ M., railway in $^1/_2$-$^3/_4$ hr. (fares 3*s*. 2*d*., 1*s*. 11*d*., 1*s*. $5^1/_2$*d*.). — About 4 M. to the E. of stat. *Yelvertoft* is the field of *Naseby*, where Charles I. was defeated by Cromwell in 1645. — $17^1/_2$ M. *Market Harborough*, see p. 354.

FROM RUGBY TO LEICESTER, 20 M., railway in $^3/_4$ hr. (fares 2*s*. 8*d*., 1*s*. 8*d*.). 8 M. *Ullesthorpe*, see p. 354. — *Leicester*, see p. 352.

At Rugby our line diverges to the left from the main through-route of the North Western Railway from London to Liverpool (see R. 44a). After passing (89 M.) *Brandon & Wolston*, we soon see the three graceful spires of Coventry.

94 M. **Coventry** *(Queen's; King's Head; Craven Arms)*, an ancient city with 47,370 inhab., possesses extensive manufactories of ribbons and watches, and is famous for its artistic work in metal. It is also the headquarters of the manufacture of bicycles and tricycles, an industry that has now attained important dimensions.

The early history of Coventry is rather obscure, but a religious house of some kind seems to have existed here in the time of Canute. According to the well-known legend (versified by Tennyson) Coventry received its municipal independence in the 11th cent. from Leofric, Earl of Mercia, through the self-sacrifice of his wife, Lady Godiva ('I, Lurichi, for the love of thee, doe make Coventre tol-free'). Her memory is kept green by a periodical procession and by a statue in St. Mary's Hall (see below), while 'Peeping Tom' is pilloried in a bust at the corner of Hertford Street. At a later date Coventry was the meeting-place of several parliaments, and it became for a time (1102-85) a bishop's see, the beautiful cathedral-church of which was destroyed by Henry VIII. The 'Coventry Plays' are a valuable collection of miracle-plays and mysteries performed here in olden times. The phrase 'to send to Coventry' has never been quite satisfactorily explained. No reminder is needed of the march through Coventry of Falstaff and his ragged regiment.

Coventry contains many quaint old buildings and much to interest the student of architecture and archæology. Chief among these are the churches of St. Michael and Holy Trinity, adjoining each other on the E. side of the Cross Cheaping. **St. Michael's Church*, an edifice of red sandstone, is a noble specimen of the Perp. style, with a spire, 300 ft. high, considered one of the finest in Europe it was re-opened in 1890 after an extensive restoration. The interior is of great breadth, being provided with double aisles, and is adorned with numerous stained-glass windows, most of which are modern. — *Trinity* or the *Priory Church*, another fine Perp. structure, also has a lofty spire (237 ft.). It contains an interesting stone pulpit of the 15th cent. and a curious old fresco. — The third of the 'three tall spires' of Coventry is that of the old Grey Friars Monastery, to which the modern *Christchurch* has been attached. — The *Church of St. John*, on the W. side of the town, is an interesting 14th cent. building, restored.

Among secular buildings the place of honour belongs to **St. Mary's Guildhall*, to the S. of St. Michael's, a singularly interesting specimen of English municipal architecture in the middle ages (14-15th cent.). The great Hall (with its oaken roof and tapestry), the Mayoress's Parlour, and the Kitchen are among the most noteworthy rooms. — Near St. John's is *Bablake Hospital*, and in Grey Friars Lane is *Ford's Hospital*, two interesting examples of the domestic style of the 16th century. — Many of the narrow old streets, which reminded Hawthorne of Boston, contain picturesque houses with the upper stories jutting over the street. — Near the station is a statue of *Sir Thomas White*.

In the Foleshill road, to the N. of Coventry, is the house in which *George Eliot* (*Mary Anne Evans;* 1820-80) lived with her father before his death; and *Rosehill*, where she frequently visited Mr. and Mrs. Bray, is also close to the town. *Arbury Farm*, where she was born, and *Griff*, where she spent the first twenty years of her life, are between Coventry and Nuneaton. — The *Coventry Canal* connects Coventry with Oxford on the one side, and with the Mersey and Trent on the other.

Among the interesting points in the neighbourhood of Coventry are *Whitley Abbey*, 1½ M. to the E.; *Stoneleigh Abbey* (p. 244), 5 M. to the S; *Kenilworth* (see p. 243), 5 M. to the S.W. (a beautiful road); the Norman church of *Wyken*, 3½ M. to the N.E.; and *Combe Abbey*, the seat of Lord Craven, 4 M. to the E., where Elizabeth, daughter of James I., spent part of her girlhood, and to which she retired after the death of her husband, the Elector Frederick (King of Bohemia).

From Coventry to *Leamington* and *Warwick*, see p. 241.

From Coventry to Nuneaton, 9½ M., railway in 20-30 min. (fares 1*s*. 8*d*., 1*s*. 3*d*., 9½*d*.). The only intermediate station of any note is (6½ M.) *Bedworth*, a small town with 5180 inhab. At (9½ M.) *Nuneaton* (see p. 349) the line joins the main route from London to Liverpool.

Beyond Coventry the view is much interrupted by numerous deep cuttings. Beyond (99½ M.) *Berkswell*, the church of which has a Norman crypt, the train crosses the *Blythe* by a fine viaduct. Picturesque old bridge to the left. 103 M. *Hampton* is the junction of a line to *Tamworth* (p. 188). At (109 M.) *Stechford* the direct line to *Walsall* (p. 259) and *Wolverhampton* (p. 260) diverges to the right. Soon afterwards the train enters the spacious New St. Station at (113 M.) *Birmingham*.

Birmingham. — **Railway Stations.** The *Central* or *New Street Station* (Pl. D, 3, 4), New Street, is one of the largest railway-stations in the world (11 acres), with a fine iron and glass roof, 1100 ft. long, and good refreshment-rooms. It is used by the L. N. W. trains for London (viâ Coventry and Rugby), to Stafford, Crewe, Liverpool, and the North, to Wolverhampton, Lichfield, Derby, etc., and also for the Midland trains to London (viâ Leicester), Sheffield, Derby, Worcester, Gloucester, Bath, Bristol, etc. — The *Snow Hill Station* (Pl. F, 1) of the G. W. Railway, also with good refreshment-rooms, lies about ⅓ M. to the N., and serves for trains to London (viâ Warwick and Oxford), Worcester, Malvern, and South Wales. — There are also several suburban stations.

Hotels *Queen's (Pl. a; D, 4), at the New St. Station; Great Western (Pl. b; F, 2), at Snow Hill Station, R. & A. 5*s*., D. 5*s*.; Grand (Pl. c; E, 2), Colmore Row; *Plough & Harrow, 135 Hagley Road, old-fashioned, moderate charges; Colonnade (Pl. f; D, 3), New St.; Cobden (Pl. d; E, 3), at the corner of Corporation St. and Cherry St., a large temperance house, R. & A. 2*s*. 6*d*. 'ordinary' at 1.15 p.m. 2*s*.; Midland (Pl. e; D, 3), New St., commercial, R. & A. from 4*s*.; Stork (Pl. g; F, 3), Corporation St.; White Horse (Pl. i; C, 1), at the corner of Congreve St. and Great Charles St., unpretending; Swan (Pl. h; E, 4), at the corner of New St. and High St., commercial; Acorn, Temple St. (Pl. D, 3), small.

For a coloured street plan of Birmingham see pages 576 & 577

Restaurants. *Birmingham Restaurant*, 101 New St. (Pl. D, 3, E, 4); *Lissiter & Miller*, 20 Bennett's Hill (Pl. D, 2, 3); *Bryan*, 62 New St.; *Pattison*, 7 New St. and 54 High St.; *Nock*, Union Passage; *Garden Restaurant*, with vegetarian dinners, 25 Paradise St. (Pl. C, 2); *Arcadian*, 18 North West Arcade (Pl. F, 3), Corporation St. (fish-dinners); *Refreshment Rooms*, at the Central and Snow Hill Stations; also at most of the hotels.

Cabs. For 1-2 pers., $1^1/_2$ M., 1*s*.; per hour 2*s*. 6*d*., each addit. $^1/_4$ hr. 6*d*. Double fare 12-6 a.m. For each package carried outside, 2*d*.

Tramways. *Steam Tramways*, *Horse Tramways*, and *Omnibuses* traverse most of the principal streets and ply to points in the environs. The chief starting-points are *Old Square* (Pl. F, 3), *John Bright Street* (Pl. C, 3), *Albert Street* (Pl. F, 4), and *Suffolk Street* (Pl. B, 4). — A *Cable Tramway* runs from Colmore Row to *New Inn*. — *Electric Tramway* from Wellington Road to *Bournbrook*. — Fares 1-6*d*.

Coaches generally ply in summer to *Berkswell* (p. 259) and other places of local interest, starting from the Grand Hotel (p. 254).

Theatres. *Theatre Royal* (Pl. D, 3), New St.; *Prince of Wales* (Pl. A, 1), Broad St.; *Grand* (Pl. G, 3), Corporation St.; *Queen's* (Pl. F, 1), Snow Hill. — *Gaiety Concert Hall*, Coleshill St.; *Day's Music Hall*, Smallbrook St. (Pl. C, 5); *Canterbury Music Hall*, Digbeth (Pl. E, 5).

Post and Telegraph Office (Pl. C, 2), Paradise St., opposite the Town Hall; numerous branch-offices and pillar letter-boxes.

United States Consul, *John Jarrett, Esq.*, 53 Union Passage; vice-consul, *F. M. Burton, Esq.*

Public Baths, all with first and second class swimming-baths and hot and cold private baths: *Kent Street Baths*, with Turkish and vapour baths; *Woodcock Street Baths; Monument Road Baths*, with Turkish and vapour baths; *Northwood Street Baths*. Turkish bath 1*s*., first-class swimming or warm bath 6*d*., second-class 3*d*. — There are also *Turkish and Warm Baths* in Broad St., High St. and the Crescent.

Birmingham (450 ft. above the sea), the fourth town of England in size and population, and the see of a Roman Catholic bishop, stands on a series of gentle hills in the N.W. corner of Warwickshire. At the census of 1881 it contained 400,000 inhab., now about 450,000. In plan it is irregular, and many of its older streets are narrow and crooked; but much has been done to improve it within the last 20-30 years by the erection of handsome buildings and the formation of new and spacious thoroughfares. It is the chief centre in England, if not in the world, of the manufacture of brass, iron, and other metallic wares of all kinds, and it is the most important industrial town in England after Manchester. In spite of its numerous tall chimneys and often smoky atmosphere, Birmingham has the reputation of being healthier than most large manufacturing towns.

In the social and political sphere Birmingham has always, with the exception of the unhappy lapse of 1791 (p. 258), been distinguished as a centre of liberality and freedom of thought. It claims to be 'the most open and hospitable to ideas, to be regarded as the most fully developed example of the English city of the future — in a word as the city wherein the spirit of the new time is most widely, variously, energetically assuming visible form and shape' (Macdonald). Nowhere has the system of municipal government been more fully developed, and nowhere has a municipality been more distinguished for enlightened promotion of popular culture. Trades Unions were very powerful in Birmingham and managed to a great extent to prevent the introduction of machinery. Hence 'the manufactures of Birmingham are to this day in a great degree confined to those branches of industry which require comparatively a much greater amount of manual labour than machinery' *(Fawcett)*. About 200 separate trades are carried on by its 'small masters'.

The early history of Birmingham is very shadowy, but it is not improbable that it occupies the site of a small Roman station on the Icknield Way (p. 349). The name, which appears in Domesday Book as 'Bermingeha', is supposed to be derived from 'Berm' or 'Beorm', the name of some Saxon tribe. During the middle ages it appears under the protection of the De Berminghams, whose connection with it ceases in 1545. In 1538 it is described by Leland as a good market town with many smiths 'that use to make knives and all mannour of cuttinge tooles and many loriners that make bittes and a great many naylors'. In 1643 Birmingham was taken and partly burned by Prince Rupert. Under Charles II. it advanced rapidly, and its manufactures of firearms became considerable. Birmingham owes its modern importance chiefly to the improvements in steam-machinery carried out here by Watt and Boulton at the end of last century, and to the use it was thus enabled to make of the adjacent fields of coal and iron. In 1700 it contained only 15,000 inhab.; in 1801, 73,670; in 1841, 182,892; and in 1861, 296,076. Its main interest to tourists is centred in a visit to some of its large industrial establishments, most of which are willingly shown on previous application, especially to anyone provided with an introduction. The industries of Birmingham employ in all about 100,000 work-people and produce goods to the annual value of 4 or 5 millions sterling. About 10,000 are engaged in the manufacture of guns and rifles, producing upwards of 600,000 gun-barrels yearly. No fewer than 4 million military rifles were proved here in 1855-64 (including the period of the Crimean War), and 770,000 guns were sent from Birmingham to the United States during the Civil War. Among the most interesting manufactories are the steel-pen works of Gillott & Son, Graham St., and those of Messrs. Perry, 36 Lancaster St.; the 'Regent Works' of Manton, Shakespeare, & Co., Clissold St., for making buttons; the electro-plate manufactory of Elkington & Co., Newhall St. (Pl. B, 1); the glass and crystal works of Osler, Broad St. (Pl. A, 1); the lighthouse lens and plate-glass works of Chance Brothers & Co., Smethwick; Hardman's stained-glass works in Newhall Hill; the Gun-Barrel Proof-House, Banbury St.; the bronze-foundry and art metal-works of Winfield & Co., Cambridge St. (Pl. B, 1); the papier-mâché works of McCallum & Hodson, Summer Row (Pl. C, 1); and the Birmingham Small Arms Factory at Smallheath. Other important branches of industry represented in Birmingham are the rolling and stamping of iron and other metals, the manufacture of iron roofs and girders, the making of steam-engines, machinery, tools, bolts, screws, rivets, wire, pins, and small steel goods of all descriptions, jewellery, and the production of chemicals. At Heaton's Mint and Metal Works, in Icknield St., a great part of the bronze and copper money of England and many other countries is coined. The same firm manufactures seamless copper tubes.

A lively account of Birmingham and its industries is given in *Elihu Burrit's* 'Walks in the Black Country'. — 'The Arab sheikh eats his pillau with a Birmingham spoon, the Egyptian pasha takes from a Birmingham tray his bowl of sherbet, or illuminates his harem with glittering candelabra made of Birmingham glass, or decorates his yacht with cunningly devised pictures painted by Birmingham workmen on Birmingham *papier-mâché*. The American Indian provides himself with food, or defends himself in war, by the unerring use of a Birmingham rifle; the luxurious Hindoo loads his table with Birmingham plate, and hangs in his saloon a handsome Birmingham lamp; the swift horsemen who scour the plains of South America urge on their steeds with Birmingham spurs, and deck their gaudy jackets with Birmingham buttons; the negro labourer hacks down the sugar-cane with Birmingham hatchets, and presses the luscious juice into Birmingham vats and coolers; the dreamy German strikes a light for his everlasting pipe with a Birmingham steel and tinder, carried in a Birmingham box; the emigrant cooks his frugal dinner in a Birmingham saucepan, over a Birmingham stove, and carries his little luxuries in tins stamped with the name of a Birmingham maker'.

The only public building in Birmingham that has any claim to antiquity is the ***Church of St. Martin** (Pl. E, 5), an imposing Dec. edifice, in the Bull Ring, originally dating from the 13th, but rebuilt in the present century. It contains the tombs of some of the De Berminghams, the original lords of the manor (see p. 256). The interior contains a fine stained-glass window by *Burne Jones*, a native of Birmingham. In the Bull Ring, to the N. of the church, is a monument to *Nelson*.

From St. Martin's the High St. leads to the N., passing the large *Market Hall* on the left. Farther on, to the left, diverges New Street (Pl. E, 4, D, 3), the principal business-street of the town, with most of the best shops. In it, immediately to the left, is the handsome modern Tudor building, by Barry, in which the *Grammar School* (Pl. E, 4), founded by Edward VI. in 1552, is now installed. Its endowments yield upwards of 26,000*l.* yearly, and several branch-schools have been opened. Adjacent, also to the left, is the *Exchange*, at the corner of Stephenson Place, a short street leading to the *Central Station* (p. 254). Opposite diverges Corporation St. (p. 258). New Street, farther on, passes the *Theatre Royal* (p. 255), the *Colonnade Hotel* (p. 254), the *Masonic Hall*, and the *Society of Artists* (right), and ends in an open space (Pl. C, 2), round which are grouped the most handsome modern buildings in Birmingham. Immediately opposite the end of New St. is the —

***Town Hall** (Pl. C, 2), a large and imposing building in the Corinthian style, erected in 1832-50 in imitation of the temple of Jupiter Stator at Rome, and somewhat recalling the Madeleine at Paris and Girard College at Philadelphia, which were built after the same model. It stands on a rusticated basement, 22 ft. high, pierced with round-headed arches. The large hall in the interior, 145 ft. long, contains a fine organ with 4000 pipes and four manuals. A recital is usually given on Sat., at 3 p.m. (adm. 3*d.*). The Triennial Musical Festival is celebrated here. — To the W. of the Town Hall is the **Birmingham and Midland Institute**, in the Italian style, containing lecture and reading rooms, and natural history and industrial collections. The metallurgical school is especially important, and the penny lectures are a characteristic feature. It is adjoined by the *Central Free Library*, which contains 104,000 vols., including a splendid collection of Shakespearian books (8600 vols.). In Paradise Street, opposite the Town Hall, is the *General Post Office*, containing a statue of Sir Rowland Hill, who spent part of his boyhood at Birmingham. To the W. of the post-office, opposite the Midland Institute, is *Queen's College*, a school of medicine and theology.

The imposing edfice to the N.E. of the Town Hall, at the end of Colmore Row, is the new **Council House**, in the Grecian style, completed in 1878 at a cost of 250,000*l.* There is a fine mosaic by *Salviati* above the entrance. The back part of this pile (entr. from the side) contains the **Corporation Art Gallery and Museum** (open free; on Mon., Tues., Thurs., & Sat. 10-9, Sun. 2-5, Wed. and Frid. 10-4 in winter and 10-6 in summer), among the chief contents of which are a series of paintings by *David Cox* (1783-1859; a native of Birmingham), a large collection of weapons, and a collection of Wedgwood ware.

The small square at the back of the Town Hall is embellished with a *Monumental Fountain*, erected in honour of the *Right Hon. Joseph Chamberlain*, and statues of *George Dawson* (d. 1876), the essayist and lecturer, and *Sir Josiah Mason* (see below). In Ratcliff Place is a statue of *James Watt* (Pl. C, 2; d. 1819), and at the end of New St. one of *Sir Robert Peel* (d. 1850). In front of the Council House is a statue of *Joseph Priestley* (1733-1804), the theologian and chemist, who was pastor of a Unitarian Church in Birmingham for some years. In the 'Church and King Riot' of 1791 his house, containing his valuable apparatus and MSS., was burned down and he narrowly escaped with his life.

In Edmund St., on the N. side of the small square just mentioned, is the **Mason College** (Pl. C, 1, 2), a tasteful red brick edifice, built by Sir Josiah Mason in 1875-80 at a cost of 60,000*l.* and endowed by him with 140,000*l.* more. It is now attended by 500-600 students, and is completely equipped with Faculties of Arts and Science, a series of excellent laboratories, and a library of 18,000 vols. In the same street, farther to the E., at the corner of Margaret St., is the new *School of Art* (Pl. D, 1), built in 1884-85, and the first municipal school of art in England.

Colmore Row (Pl. D, E, 2), which leads to the E. from the Town Hall to Snow Hill, with the Great Western Hotel and Station, is perhaps the best-built street in the town. It contains numerous substantial insurance-offices and banks, the *Union Club*, and the *Grand Hotel* (p. 254). — To the S. of it, in a small open space, is *St. Philip's* (Pl. E, 2), a church of the Queen Anne period, occupying the highest ground in Birmingham. One of the stained glass windows is by Burne Jones (p. 257). In the churchyard is an obelisk in memory of *Col. Burnaby*, erected in 1885.

Another handsome modern thoroughfare is Corporation Street (Pl. E, F, G, 3), which contains the *New Grand Theatre* (Pl. G, 3), and the new *Victoria Law Courts* (Pl. G, 2). On the *Stork Hotel* (Pl. g; F, 3) is a tablet commemorating a visit of Dr. Johnson to his friend Hector. The Rom. Cath. **Cathedral of St. Chad* (Pl. F, 1), in Bath St., is a good specimen of Pugin's work and is in the Dec. style. It contains an oaken pulpit of the 16th cent., from Louvain, and stalls, throne, and lectern of the 15th cent., from St. Maria in Capitolio at Cologne. — The *Oratory of St. Philip Neri*, Hagley Road, is interesting as the home of Card. Newman; the church is Italian in style.

Among the n merous valuable private collections in Birmingham, perhaps the most generally interesting is the *Dickens Collection of *Mr. W. R. Hughes*, City Treasurer, numbering more than 3000 items, including all the original editions, extra illustrations, portraits, biographies, criticisms, books from Dickens's library, letters, autographs, prints, proof-sheets, etc. Mr. Hughes also possesses *George Eliot* and *Herbert Spencer* collections.

Birmingham possesses several public parks, the largest of which are *Cannon Hill Park* to the S., *Smallheath Park* to the S.W., and *Aston Park* to the N.E. A chief attraction of the last is ***Aston Hall** (open from 10, on Sun from 2, to dusk), a fine old Jacobean mansion, now containing collections of various kinds. The *Aston Lower Grounds* contain an aquarium, a large assembly-hall, running-tracks, gardens, etc. — The *Botanic Gardens* (adm. 6*d*., Mon. 2*d*.) are at *Edgbaston*, the fashionable west-end suburb of Birmingham, which also contains a public park with a small lake. *Highgate Park*, to the S., commands an excellent view of the town.

On the N. Birmingham is adjoined by the manufacturing suburb of *Handsworth*, in which stood the *Soho Works* of Watt and Boulton (p. 256), dismantled in 1850. Large engine-works, however, are still carried on by a grandson of the former at *Smethwick* (farther to the W.), under the style of *James Watt & Co.* Watt's house is still standing at *Heathfield* (tramway), and contains some interesting relics. Both Watt and Boulton are buried in the parish-church of Handsworth, where they are commemorated by monuments by Chantrey and Flaxman. — The old *Crown House*, at Deritend (beyond Pl. G, 5), is an interesting half-timbered edifice.

Environs. Among the most interesting points within easy reach of Birmingham are (7 M.) *Sutton Park* (see below), reached by railway in 1/2 hr.; *Packwood House*, with its interesting garden, near *Knowle* (p. 244); *Berkswell* (p. 254); *Halesowen Church*, with the grave of the poet Shenstone (d. 1763) in the churchyard, and the ruins of an abbey; the *Clent Hills; Dudley Castle*, 8 1/2 M. to the N.W.; *Bourneville*, to the W., with the extensive cocoa and chocolate manufactory of Cadbury Brothers; *Tamworth Castle*, etc. — Longer excursions (1-2 hrs. by rail) may be made to *Lichfield* (see below), *Warwick*, *Stratford-on-Avon*, *Kenilworth*, etc.

From Birmingham to Lichfield, 16 M., L. N. W. Railway in 1/2-1 hr. — Leaving the Central Station (p. 254), the train passes the suburban stations of *Vauxhall* and (2 1/2 M.) *Aston* (see above). A little to the W. of (5 M.) *Erdington* is the *Oscott Roman Catholic College*, which contains some fine old paintings. — 8 M. **Sutton Coldfield** (*Royal Hotel; Swan*), a small town with an old church. *Sutton Park*, famous for its hollies, is a favourite resort of picnic parties from Birmingham. — 16 M. *Lichfield*, see p. 347.

From Birmingham to Walsall, 17 M., Midland Railway in 3/4 hr. — 5 1/2 M. *Castle Bromwich;* 11 1/2 M. *Sutton Coldfield* (see above); 12 1/2 M. *Sutton Park*. — 17 M. **Walsall** (*George; Rail. Refreshmt. Rooms*), a town of 60,000 inhab., containing large manufactories of saddlers' ironmongery, and the centre of an important coal-district. This was the scene of the labours of '*Sister Dora*', who is commemorated by a statue (1886) and by a stained-glass window in the large *Church of St. Matthew*. — Walsall is the junction of lines to Wolverhampton, Lichfield, etc.

From Birmingham to *Wolverhampton*, see R. 37; to *Warwick* and *Oxford*, see R. 33; to *Worcester*, see R. 23; to *Derby*, see R. 23.

37. From Birmingham to Shrewsbury viâ Wolverhampton and Wellington.

42 M. Great Western Railway in 1 1/2-2 hrs. (fares 8*s*. 3*d*., 6*s*., 3*s*. 6*d*.).

Leaving the Snow Hill Station, the train passes *Hockley*, *Soho* (see above), and *Handsworth*, where a line to Stourbridge (p. 260) diverges to the left. — 6 M. **West Bromwich** (*Dartmouth; Great Western*), a busy iron-manufacturing town of recent origin, with about 50,000 inhab., possesses a large park, commanding a beautiful view. — 7 M. *Swan Village*, the junction of a line to Dudley (p. 260). The large *Gas Works* here, built at a cost of 120,000*l*., supply all the towns within a radius of 10 miles. — 8 1/2 M. **Wed-**

nesbury *(Anchor; Dartmouth Arms)* is an ancient town with 25,000 inhab. and large manufactories of railway axles and tires and other iron goods. The Perp. *Church* contains some good carving. — The next stations are (10 M.) *Bradley*, (11 M.) *Bilston* (24,000 inhab.), and (12 M.) *Priestfield*, all busy places with manufactures of iron and steel, beyond which we soon reach Wolverhampton.

Wolverhampton may also be reached from Birmingham by the L. N. W. Railway and by the Midland Railway from New Street. For the Midland route, see p. 259. The chief stations on the L. N. W. route (13 M., in 1/2-1 hr.) are: 4 M. *Spon Lane;* 5 1/2 M. *Oldbury*, a growing manufacturing town with 12,000 inhabitants. — 7 M. *Dudley Port* is the junction of a line to (3 1/2 M.) **Dudley** *(Castle; Dudley Arms)*, one of the largest and most important towns in the 'Black Country', with an extensive iron-trade, manufactures of anvils and vices, and 46,235 inhabitants. The picturesque ruins of **Dudley Castle*, belonging to the Earl of Dudley, crown a wooded hill rising above the station and date mainly from the 16th cent.; the keep is of the 13th century. They afford an excellent survey of the great coal and iron district of England, including numerous large manufacturing towns; the view is perhaps most impressive by night, when the flames issuing from the chimneys and furnaces envelope the scene in a curious lurid glare. The caves below the castle, formed by quarrying for limestone, are interesting (guide necessary). In the market-place is a Renaissance *Fountain*, presented to the town by the late Earl of Dudley, of whom a marble statue was erected in 1888. The *Geological Museum* contains specimens of the minerals of the district. [From Dudley a line runs S. to (5 1/2 M.) *Stourbridge* (Talbot), a glass-making town with 10,000 inhab., and (12 M.) **Kidderminster** *(Lion; Black Horse)*, a town of 27,600 inhab., famed for its manufactures of Brussels and other carpets. Kidderminster was the scene of the labours of *Richard Baxter* (1615-91), to whom a statue has been erected in the Bull Ring. His pulpit is in the vestry of the New Meeting House.]

13 M. **Wolverhampton.** — **Hotels.** Star & Garter, Victoria St.; Peacock, Snow Hill; Talbot; Coach & Horses. — *Rail. Rfmt. Rooms.*

Cabs. Per mile 1*s.*, each addit. 1/2 M. 6*d.*; per 1/2 hr. 1*s.*, each addit. 1/4 hr. 6*d.*

Tramways run from Queen Square, in the centre of the town, to *Tettenhall* (p. 261), *Bilston*, *Willenhall* (every 20 min.), and *Sedgley*. — **Omnibus** to *Penn*, five times daily.

Theatre, at the corner of Garrick St. and Cleveland Road. Theatrical performances are also given in the *Exchange*.

Railway Stations. *North Western & Midland*, at the foot of Lichfield St.; *Great Western*, in Sun St., near the other. The former station is known as the high-level, the latter as the low-level station.

Wolverhampton, the largest town in Staffordshire, with 85,000 inhab., derives its name from Wulfruna, sister of Ethelred II., who founded a college here in 996. It is the capital of the '*Black Country*', an extensive coal and iron mining district, in which vegetation is almost entirely replaced by heaps of slag and cinders. It lies, however, on the verge of this district, and the country to the N. and W. are of the normal and pleasanter green hue. The special manufactures of Wolverhampton are locks (370,000 a week), tin-plate, and japanned goods. The well-known lock-manufactory of the *Messrs. Chubb* is open to visitors daily, except Sat., 10-1 and 2-6. Wolverhampton is also an important agricultural market.

The most interesting building in Wolverhampton is the venerable ***Church of St. Peter,** in the market-place, a handsome Gothic structure of the 13-15th cent., occupying the site of a church of the 10th cent. and recently restored. It was formerly a collegiate establishment. Bishop Hall (d. 1656) was one of its prebendaries.

The INTERIOR contains a stone pulpit of the 15th cent., an ancient font, and several old monuments, including that of Col. Lane, who helped Charles II. to escape after the battle of Worcester (1651) and shared his hiding-place in the royal oak at Boscobel (see below), and a bronze statue of Admiral Leveson (temp. Charles I.), by *Le Sueur*. The stained-glass windows are modern — In the *Churchyard* is a rudely-carved cross or pillar, the origin of which is obscure. The *Tower* commands an extensive view of the Black Country, the blazing furnaces of which present a most weird spectacle after dark.

The *Town Hall*, in North Street, is a large and handsome modern building in the Italian style, with a Mansard roof; the *Free Library* and *Exchange* also deserve notice. In Lichfield Street is the *Art Gallery*, containing the fine Cartwright Collection of Pictures and other objects of art. The *Blue Coat School* dates from the 18th century. The *Orphan Asylum* is a handsome Elizabethan structure (250 children). Near the *Agricultural Hall* is a Statue of the *Right Hon. C. P. Villiers*, one of the leaders of the anti-corn-law agitation, who has represented Wolverhampton in parliament since 1838. Queen Square is adorned with a bronze equestrian *Statue of Prince Albert*, by Thornycroft. There is also a *Public Park*.

The elder *Edwin Booth*, the tragedian, was originally an artisan in Wolverhampton, working in the 'Old Hall Tin Factory'.

Environs. About 2 M. to the N. W., on the road to Shifnal (see below), is the pretty village of *Tettenhall*, the church of which contains a curious stained-glass window. In the churchyard are some fine yews. — *Boscobel*, where Charles II. lay in hiding after the battle of Worcester, under the care of 'Unparalleled Pendrell', is 8 M. to the N.W. of Wolverhampton and 2 M. to the N. of *Albrighton* (see below). The royal oak has now disappeared, but a hiding-place in the floor is shown in which the king was concealed. — Longer excursions may be made to (10 M.) *Enville*, with its beautiful gardens, *Bridgenorth*, and *Hagley*.

FROM WOLVERHAMPTON TO STAFFORD, 15 M., L. N. W. Railway in 1/2 hr. (fares 2*s.* 9*d.*, 2*s.*, 1*s.* 3 1/2 *d.*). Beyond (3 M.) *Four Ashes* the railway intersects the old Roman *Watling Street*. — 7 M. *Penkridge*, with a handsome red church (right). At (15 M.) *Stafford* we reach the main L.N.W. line (see p. 346).

Beyond Wolverhampton the train passes *Codsall*, *Albrighton*, and (25 M.) *Shifnal* (Jerningham Arms), a picturesque little town with half-timbered houses and a fine church. To the E. is **Tong Church*, a singularly pure example of early Perp. (1401-11).

32 M. **Wellington** *(Wrekin Hotel)*, a nail-making town of 6200 inhab., lies 2 1/2 M. from the N. base of the *Wrekin* (1320 ft.), a solitary hill of trap rock, which has for some time been conspicuous to the left. The top, on which are some fortified remains, commands an extensive *View.

FROM WELLINGTON TO MARKET DRAYTON, 29 M., railway in 1/2-3/4 hr. (fares 3*s.* 6*d.*, 2*s.* 6*d.*, 1*s.* 4 1/2 *d.*). Unimportant stations. From *Market Drayton* (Corbet Arms) lines go on to Crewe (p. 345) and Stoke (p. 346).

Wellington is also connected by railway with *Coalbrookdale*, Much Wenlock (p. 181), and Craven Arms (p. 180).

Farther on the train crosses the *Severn*.

42 M. **Shrewsbury** (*Raven*, Castle St., R. & A. 4*s.*, table d'hôte 4*s.*; *Lion*, Wyle Cop; *George; Crown; Clarendon*), the county-town of *Shropshire* or *Salop*, an ancient place of 26,480 inhab., with narrow steep streets and quaint old houses, picturesquely situated on a hill surrounded on three sides by the Severn. Its name is derived from *Scrobbesbyrig*, an appellation meaning wooded hill (comp. 'shrub', 'scrub'), assigned to the British town found by the Saxons on this spot. As an important position on the Welsh march, it was formerly surrounded with walls, of which few traces remain. The Severn is crossed here by two bridges, the Welsh and the English. Shrewsbury is celebrated for its cakes, and visitors may still enjoy 'a Shrewsbury cake of Pailin's own make' ('*Ingoldsby Legends*'). Not more than half-a-day need be devoted to Shrewsbury.

Above us, to the left as we quit the station, rises the **Castle**, originally founded by a vassal of William the Conqueror (entrance by a gate on the left, just beyond the *Presbyterian Church*).

On reaching the fine inner gate we obtain a view of the mansion formed out of the ancient keep. Visitors are not admitted to the interior, but may follow the path to the right, leading to a modern *Watch Tower*, which commands a fine view of the Severn and the country round Shrewsbury. — The walk outside the N. wall of the castle-enclosure leads to a covered bridge communicating with the station.

To the right, opposite the church, is the *Free Library*, with antiquities from Wroxeter, etc. — A little farther on, a street diverging from Castle St. leads to the ***Church of St. Mary**, with its lofty spire, which we enter by the porch on the N. side. The architecture is of various periods, ranging from Norman to late-Perpendicular.

The ***Interior**, with its fine stained glass, is more pleasing than the exterior. The *Nave* is late-Norman, the *Transept* E. E., and the *Trinity Chapel* (to the S. of the choir) Perp. (15th cent.). The last contains a monument of the 14th cent. and a memorial to *Bishop Samuel Butler* (d. 1840; see p. 263); and in the *Chantry Chapel*, on the N. side of the chancel, is the tomb of *Admiral Benbow* (d. 1702). The ceiling is of oak. The Jesse Window, at the E. end, dates from the 14th century.

On leaving St. Mary's we pass the *Salopian Infirmary* and the churches of *St. Alkmund* and *St. Julian*, and then descend to the S. (left), through the steep *Wyle Cop*, to the *English Bridge* over the Severn. Beyond the bridge we follow the road in a straight direction, passing under the railway, to the ***Abbey Church**, which is in part a Norman structure and belonged to a monastery built by the founder of the castle. Among its chief features are the fine W. window (Perp.) and the recessed Norman doorway. The interior contains some interesting monuments. In front of the church is the *Holy Cross*, and to the S. of it, in a coal-yard, is the fine *Stone Pulpit* of the Refectory, almost the only relic of the monastic buildings.

On recrossing the bridge we turn to the left (Beeches Lane) and follow the line of the *Town Walls*, passing the only remaining tower and the handsome *Eye & Ear Hospital*, to *St. Chad's Church*, a large circular building of the end of last century. Opposite is the **Quarry*, a park on the Severn, with fine lime-trees.

We may follow the walk along the river to the *Welsh Bridge*, on the N. side of the town, and return through the Mardol to the centre of the town. — The *Market Hall*, in a square off the High St., is an Elizabethan edifice of 1595; opposite to it is a statue of *Lord Clive* (d. 1774), by Marochetti. At the beginning of the High St. are two interesting half-timbered houses, one bearing the date 1591. At the end of the street, to the left, diverges **Butcher's Row*, an admirable example of the street-architecture of the 15th century. Many of the other private houses of Shrewsbury preserve their mediæval aspect substantially unchanged.

The *Grammar School* of Shrewsbury, founded by Edward VI., ranks among the best public schools of England. Bishop Samuel Butler was at one time head-master here, and Sir Philip Sidney, Wycherley, and Judge Jeffreys were pupils. The handsome new buildings of the school are in the suburb of *Kingsland*, on the right bank of the Severn, opposite the Quarry (p. 263). Farquhar wrote his comedy of 'The Recruiting Officer' at the Raven Hotel (p. 262).

Environs. *Battlefield Church*, 3½ M. to the N. of Shrewsbury, marks the scene of the battle in which Henry IV. overthrew Hotspur and his allies in 1403. It was on this occasion that Sir John Falstaff fought 'a long hour by Shrewsbury clock'. About 1¾ M. to the W. of the town is *Shelton Oak*, a fine but now decayed tree, 45 ft. in girth, from which Owen Glendower is said to have watched the progress of the contest. — The ruins of *Haughmond Abbey*, 4 M. to the N. E., founded about 1100, deserve a visit. They are in a mixed Norman and Pointed style; the nave of the church has an oaken roof. *Haughmond Hill* affords a fine view of Shrewsbury. — About 5 M. to the S. E. lies **Wroxeter**, with the interesting remains of the Roman city of *Uriconium*, a 'British Pompeii', forming an enclosure with a circumference of about 3 M. It is believed to have been burned by the West Saxons in the 6th cent., and the skeletons of three persons overtaken by the flames have been discovered among the ruins. Many of the antiquities found here are now in the Shrewsbury Museum (p. 262). — At *Acton Burnell*, 8 M. to the S. E., is an old castle in which Edward I. held a parliament in 1283. The church, restored in 1890, is a good specimen of E.E. work, inclining to Decorated. The road to Acton Burnell passes (5 M.) *Pitchford Hall*, a quaint half-timbered mansion of the 15th century. — Excursions may also be made to *Condover Hall*, *Buildwas Abbey* (12 M.), the *Wrekin* (p. 261), *Stokesay Castle* (p. 181), etc.

From Shrewsbury to *Hereford*, see p. 180; to *Chester*, see R. 39. — Shrewsbury is a convenient starting-point for a visit to Central Wales, see R. 38.

38. From Shrewsbury to Aberystwith. Central Wales.

81 M. Cambrian Railway in 3½-4 hrs. (fares 15*s.* 5*d.*, 10*s.* 5*d.*, 6*s.* 9½*d.*). This line crosses the centre of Wales, and has direct connection from various points with the Southern Welsh places described in RR. 24-29 and the Northern Welsh places of R. 40.

On leaving Shrewsbury the train crosses the *Severn* and runs almost due west. From (5 M.) *Hanwood* a branch-line diverges on the left to *Minsterley*. Near (15 M.) *Middletown* we skirt the base of the *Breidden Hills* (to the right; p. 264). At (17 M.) *Buttington Junction* we join the main Cambrian line.

20 M. **Welshpool** *(Royal Oak; Rail. Refreshmt. Rooms)*, a small town with 5000 inhab., situated near the Severn, which here be-

comes navigable for barges. It contains the *Powysland Museum* (10-4, 3*d.*; Sat., 1-4, free), and carries on a considerable trade in flannel. Fine view from the churchyard.

About 1 M. to the S. of Welshpool stands ***Powys Castle** (shown in the absence of the family), the venerable seat of the Earl of Powis, called by the Welsh *Castell Goch* (*i. e.* Red Castle) from the colour of the sandstone of which it is built. It was founded in the 12th cent., but has been much added to and modernised. The fine gateway is flanked by two massive round towers. The castle contains some good portraits and tapestry and a valuable collection of Indian curiosities brought home by Lord Clive, an ancestor of the Earl. The state-bedroom is still kept exactly as it was when once occupied by Charles II. The beautiful *Park* is open to the public (entrance in the main street of Welshpool); fine view from the terraces in front of the castle.

Among the other excursions that may be made from Welshpool are those to *Guilsfield*, 3 M. to the N., with a fine old church; to the waterfall of the *Rhiw*, near *Berriew*, $4^1/_2$ M. to the S., and on to (3 M.) *Montgomery* (see below); and to the N.E. to (4 M.) the **Breidden Hills**, the highest summit of which, *Moel-y-Golfa*, attains a height of 1300 ft. On *Breidden Hill* (1200 ft.) is a pillar commemorating Rodney's victory over the French in 1782 (view). Nearly all the hills near Welshpool are surmounted with remains of ancient fortifications.

From Welshpool to Oswestry and Gobowen, $19^1/_2$ M., railway in $^3/_4$-$1^1/_4$ hr. (fares 3*s.* 6*d.*, 2*s.* *d.*, 1*s.* $7^1/_2$*d.*). This line passes through a pretty district, which would repay the pedestrian, who, however, should make a detour through the glen of the *Tanat.* From (10 M.) *Llanymynech* a branch-line diverges to (9 M.) *Llanfyllin* (Wynnstay Arms), celebrated for its ales and sweet bells. It is the nearest station to (10 M.) **Pistyll Rhaiadr*, the highest waterfall in Wales, the route to which passes through (6 M.) *Llanrhaiadr-yn-Mochnant* (Wynnstay Arms). — 16 M. **Oswestry** (*Wynnstay Arms; Queen's; Rail. Refreshmt. Rooms*), an interesting old town with 8000 inhab. and a picturesque church-tower. At Old Oswestry is a British Camp. Oswestry is a convenient starting-point for an excursion to *Pistyll Rhaiadr* (see above); a brake runs twice weekly (Wed. & Sat.) in summer to (14 M.) *Llanrhaiadr* (see above; fare 2*s.*, return 3*s.*). — At ($19^1/_2$ M.) *Gobowen* we reach the railway from Shrewsbury to Chester (see R. 39).

26 M. *Montgomery.* The small town of **Montgomery** (*Green Dragon*), which lies 2 M. to the S. E. of the station, is interesting for the finely-situated ruins of the old **Castle*, dating from the 11th century. An extensive *British Camp* on an adjoining hill commands a fine view. The *Church* contains some old monuments.

Offa's Dyke, a boundary-wall erected by King Offa of Mercia (8th cent.), and extending from Flintshire to the mouth of the Wye (p. 174), passes within a mile or two of Montgomery (to the E.) and may be conveniently visited thence.

From (30 M.) *Abermule* a short branch-line diverges on the left to *Kerry*, with an interesting, partly Norman church. — 34 M. *Newtown* (Boar's Head), a flannel-manufacturing town with 7170 inhabitants. The new church contains a fine screen removed from the old church. *Robert Owen* (1771-1858), the Socialist, was born, died, and is buried here. — About 1 M. to the S., on the road to Builth, is a fine waterfall, 75 ft. high.

$38^1/_2$ M. *Moat Lane* (Rail. Refreshmt. Rooms), the junction of the line to Llanidloes, Builth, Brecon, and Merthyr Tydvil (see p. 203). — From (40 M.) *Caersws* a mineral line runs to the once celebrated *Van Lead Mines.* The line now quits the Severn and enters the pretty wooded valley of the *Carno*. About 1½ M. to the N.E. of (45 M.) *Carno* lie three picturesque little lakes. We now cross the highest point of the line (690 ft.). — 52 M. *Llanbrynmair;* 5 M. to the S. is the beautiful *Waterfall of the *Twymyn*, 140 ft. high. — From (56½ M.) *Cemmes Road* (Dovey Hotel) a short branch-line runs through the pretty valley of the *Dovey* to (7 M.) *Dinas Mawddwy* (Buckley Arms).

About 1½ M. to the S. E. of Dinas Mawddwy is *Mallwyd* (Peniarth Arms), a charmingly-situated village, with some fine yews in the churchyard. Walkers may go on from Dinas Mawddwy to (7 M.) the *Cross Foxes Inn* (p. 298) and (1 ½ M.) *Dolgelley* (p. 297); or they may cross the *Bwlch-y-Groes Pass* to (1 M.) *Llanuwchllyn* (p. 302).

61½ M. **Machynlleth** *(Lion*, R. & A. 4*s*.; *Queen's*, near the station; *Rail. Refreshment Rooms)*, pronounced *Machúnthleth*, a small town with 2000 inhab., believed to be the Roman *Maglona*, is prettily situated on the *Dovey*, at the foot of the *Arran-y-Gessel* (2225 ft.). It affords convenient headquarters for excursions, owing to its central situation and extensive railway-communications; but the want of a good hotel is a drawback. The fishing in the neighbourhood is good. The Welsh seat of the Marquis of Londonderry, *Plas Machynlleth*, adjoins the town on the S.

Among the favourite points within easy reach are Barmouth (p. 294), Dolgelley (p. 298), Cader Idris (p. 301), Mallwyd (see above), Llyfnant Glen (p. 266), Llanidloes (p. 203), Plinlimmon (see below), and Aberystwith (p. 267). The finest short excursion is to take the train to Glandovey (p. 266), and walk back to (9 M.) Machynlleth (see below).

From Machynlleth a short railway threads a pretty valley to **Corris** or *Abercorris* (*Braich Goch Inn*, rustic), whence a pleasant walk may be taken to (11 M.) Dolgelley. The first part of the road, as we ascend to the col (660 ft.), whence Cader Idris is well seen, is flanked with slate-quarries. When the Tal-y-Llyn valley is reached we turn to the right. The road skirts the E. cliffs of Cader Idris, and beyond another col reaches the *Cross Foxes Inn*. Thence to (3½ M.) *Dolgelley*, see p. 298. [A public conveyance plies from Corris to *Tal-y-Llyn* (p. 266).]

The road from Machynlleth to (20 M.) *Llanidloes* (p. 203) is pretty at each end, but dull in the middle. The only house of entertainment is the (12 M.) *Stay-a-Little Inn*.

The ascent of **Plinlimmon** (2460 ft.), which lies about 10 M. to the S. of Machynlleth, may be made from the head of the Llyfnant valley. The view is disappointing, and the mountain has been described as 'sodden dreariness'. *Duffryn Castell Inn* is 3½ M. to the S. of the summit, on the high-road between Llanidloes and Devil's Bridge.

The road from Machynlleth to (18 M.) *Aberystwith* (p. 267) is not of great interest, but walkers will be repaid by going as far as Llanfihangel (p. 266), with digressions to the *Llyfnant Valley* (see p. 266) and *Bedd Taliesin* (p. 266), the grave of the Welsh Homer (in all about 8 M.). The route recommended is as follows. We follow the hill-road to (3 M.) *Glas-Pwll* (see p. 266), but just before reaching it diverge to the left to (1 M.) *Gallt-y-Bladur Farm* (p. 266) for a view of *Pistyll-y-Llyn* (p. 266). From the farm we descend into the valley at the **Rhaiadr Gorge*, and follow the track leading down the stream to the (4 M.) main road, at the entrance of the valley. We then follow the road to the left, passing *Glandovey Station*, *Glandovey Castle*, and (2 M.) *Eglwys Fach*. At *Furnace*, ⅓ M. farther on, we leave the high-road and proceed through the main valley (left), in a due S. direction, to (3 M.) *Bedd Taliesin* (p. 266). Thence we may either proceed to the right to (1 M.) *Tre Taliesin* (Inn), on the main road, or continue in a straight direction to (2 M.) *Tal-y-Bont* (Hotel), which also lies on the main road, 3 M. to the N. of *Llanfihangel* (p. 266).

The train now descends the green valley of the *Dyfi* or *Dovey*. At ($65^1/_2$ M.) *Glandovey Junction* (Rail. Refreshment Rooms) the line forks, the left branch going to Aberystwith, and the right branch running N. to Barmouth (p. 294).

From Glandovey Junction to Barmouth, 22 M., railway in 1 hr. (fares 4*s.* 2*d.*, 2*s.* 10*d.*, 1*s.* $9^1/_2$*d.*). This beautiful line skirts the coast nearly the whole way. The view, to the left, of the estuary of the *Dovey* is fine at high-tide. — 6 M. **Aberdovey** (*Dovey; Raven; Britannia*), a small watering-place at the mouth of the Dovey, with good sands and a mild climate. The line here turns to the N. — 10 M. **Towyn** (*Corbet Arms; Cambrian*), a popular sea-bathing resort, with an ancient church, which has been partly rebuilt. It contains 'St. Cadfan's Stone', a time-worn relic, with an inscription that has never been satisfactorily deciphered. [A short railway, starting from the *Pendre Station*, 1 M. to the E. of the Cambrian station, runs from Towyn to (7 M.) *Abergynolwyn*, about $3^1/_2$ M. beyond which is *Tal-y-Llyn Hotel*, a favourite resort of anglers, on a lake at the S. base of Cader Idris, which may be ascended hence by active climbers in $2^1/_2$ hrs. The route follows a small valley to *Llyn-y-Cae* (p. 301), whence a steep climb brings us direct to the top.] — Beyond Towyn *Cader Idris* soon comes into view to the right. $16^1/_2$ M. *Llwyngwril*. — 20 M. *Barmouth Junction*, and thence (to 22 M.) *Barmouth*, see p. 294.

From Glandovey Junction the Aberystwith train descends the left bank of the Dovey to ($66^1/_2$ M.) *Glandovey*. Above the station is the pretty little *Glandovey Castle*.

*From Glandovey to Machynlleth by the Llyfnant Glen and Pistyll-y-Llyn, 9 M. This walk (comp. p. 265) is especially beautiful in autumn. From the station we follow the high-road to Machynlleth for $^1/_2$ M., and then ascend the lane to the right (sign-post, 'Llyfnant Valley'). At the ($^1/_3$ M.) fork we keep to the right. The track ascends through a beautifully wooded valley, and then descends to ($2^1/_2$ M.) *Glas-Pwll*, a small house embosomed among trees. At Glas-Pwll we cross a foot-bridge over a tributary brook and immediately reach another bridge over the main stream. The fall of *Cwm Rhaiadr* lies to our right, about $^3/_4$ M. up this stream, the best route ascending on the right bank (*i. e.* to our left as we ascend). The gorge with the fall is very picturesque. Instead of returning to the road at Glas-Pwll we may scramble up the high side of the gorge and so reach the road on the N. side of the valley, by which we proceed to the right to ($^1/_2$ M.) *Gallt-y-Bladur Farm*. [If we return to the road at Glas-Pwll, we follow it for 150 yds., and then turn to the right to reach the farm.] Near this farm we obtain the best view of the fall of *Pistyll-y-Llyn*, which lies about $1^1/_2$ M. to the S.; it is unnecessary to go nearer. We now return to the (1 M.) Machynlleth road, which leads to the N. of Glas-Pwll. After about $1^1/_4$ M., at the foot of a descent, we cross a stream and ascend the middle track, avoiding those which lead to the right and left through gates. After 5 min. we pass some cottages on the right and soon obtain a view of the Dovey valley to the left. The road then dips once more, but re-ascends to the ($^3/_4$ M.) point from which we make our final descent to the high-road through the Dovey valley. Machynlleth soon comes into sight; and a well-marked footpath to the right, at a cottage, cuts off a corner. — 1 M. *Machynlleth*, see p. 265.

The train now skirts the S. side of the *Dovey Estuary*, the attractions of which vary with the state of the tide. — 73 M. *Borth* (Borth Hotel), a small watering-place, with a good sandy beach. A walk may be taken from Borth to (5 M.) *Bedd Taliesin* (p. 265), with the burial cairn of Taliesin, the greatest of the Welsh bards (6th cent.). — $75^1/_2$ M. *Llanfihangel* (p. 265), a pretty little spot; 77 M. *Bow Street*. The train now makes a wide sweep to the left and enters (81 M.) *Aberystwith* from the S.E.

Aberystwith (**Queen's*; *Bellevue*, both facing the sea, R. & A. 4*s.*, table d'hôte 4*s.* 6*d.*; **Lion* or *Gogerddan Arms*, an old-fashioned house; *Talbot*, these two in the town; *Lodging Houses)*, situated at the confluence of the *Ystwith* and *Rheidol*, which here unite just before entering the sea, is a watering-place with 6650 inhabitants. The beach, which is well adapted for bathing and yields cornelians, agates, and other pebbles, is flanked by a *Marine Promenade*, ending at a pier. To the S.W., on a rocky promontory descending abruptly to the sea, are the ruins of an old *Castle*, erected by Gilbert de Strongbow at the beginning of the 12th cent., and finally destroyed by Cromwell. The grounds afford an admirable view of the Welsh mountains, including (in clear weather) Snowdon. Adjoining the castle grounds stands the *University College of Wales* (150 students), opened in 1872, burned down in 1885, and since rebuilt. It is an imposing though somewhat irregular building with large laboratories, etc. The churchyard contains some old tombs with quaint epitaphs. At the N. end of the bay rises the *Pen Glais* or *Constitution Hill* (450 ft.), and 1 M. to the S. of the town is *Pen Dinas* (400 ft.), two good points of view. The column on the top of the latter is to the memory of the Duke of Wellington. Most of the lead mines in the neighbourhood are closed owing to the low price of lead.

The country round Aberystwith is unattractive, but walks may be taken to (2¼ M.) *Allt-Wen* and (5 M.) *Twll Twrw*, or the *Monk's Cave*, both on the coast to the S.; to *Llanbadr-Fawr*, with its fine church, 1 M. inland; and to *Nant Eos*, 4 M. to the S.E. A railway-excursion may also be made to *Strata Florida* (p. 208).

No one should miss the excursion to (12 M.) the *Devil's Bridge*, to which brakes ply daily in summer (return-fare 4*s.*), returning (15 M.) *viâ* Pont Erwyd. The direct road follows the ridge on the S. side of the valley of the Rheidol, affording pleasant views. The brakes stop at the *Hafod Arms Hotel* (R., A., & B. 5*s.*; cold luncheon 2*s.*), close to the bridge. The ***Pont-y-Mynach**, or **Devil's Bridge**, is a small bridge constucted by the monks of Strata Florida in the 11th or 12th cent. over the deep gorge of the *Mynach*, at its junction with the wooded valley of the *Rheidol*. Both rivers form beautiful waterfalls near the junction. The old bridge is now surmounted by another added in 1753, but is well seen from below. Most of the best view-points are within the grounds of the hotel, for admission to which a fee of 1*s.* is charged. Walkers should visit the **Parson's Bridge*, which spans the Rheidol gorge 1½ M. farther up (to the N.). On the road just above (on the left bank) is the church of *Yspytty Cynfyn*, which the excursion-brakes pass on their return to Aberystwith; and 1½ M. farther on is *Pont Erwyd* (Inn), in front of which the river flows through a rocky 'gut', forming falls of some size after rain. The rest of the road to Aberystwith is through a somewhat bleak district, disfigured by numerous lead-mines. — About 4 M. to the S.E. of the Devil's Bridge is *Hafod*, a large mansion in a well-wooded park. Near it is the church of *Eglwys-Newydd*, containing a fine monument by Chantrey. From Hafod we may descend the valley of the *Ystwith*, passing *Pont Rhyd-y-Groes* (Inn), to (7½ M.) *Trawscoed*, whence we may return to Aberystwith by train. — *Strata Florida* (p. 208) is 6 M. to the S. of Hafod.

A mail-cart runs daily from Aberystwith to (16 M.) *Aberayron* (p. 208).
From Aberystwith to *Carnarvon*, comp. RR. 40b and 40c.

39. From Shrewsbury to Chester.

a. *Viâ Whitchurch.*

43 M. L. N. W. Railway in 1¼-2¼ hrs. (fares 6*s.* 10*d.*, 5*s.* 2*d.*, 3*s.* 2½*d.*).

The first stations are *Hadnall*, *Yorton*, and (12 M.) *Wem*. The notorious Judge Jeffreys (1643-89) was created Baron Wem by James II. — 21½ M. **Whitchurch** (*Victoria; Swan*), a town with 4000 inhab., is the junction of the Cambrian Railway to Whittington and Oswestry (p. 264) and of the L. N. W. line to Crewe (p. 346). The church contains a monument of Talbot, first Earl of Shrewsbury, killed at Bordeaux in 1453. About 4 M. to the N. E. is *Combermere Abbey*, the seat of Viscount Combermere, with a fine park (open to visitors) and a large lake or mere, the pike-fishing in which is famous. — The following stations are unimportant. — 43 M. *Chester*, see p. 269.

b. *Viâ Ruabon.*

42 M. Railway (*Great Western*) in 1-2 hrs. (fares 6*s.* 10*d.*, 5*s.* 2*d.*, 3*s.* 2½*d.*). This line, skirting the eastern margin of North Wales, is more attractive than the one above described, especially in the Dee valley.

The train leaves the *Severn* to the left and crosses the battle-field of Shrewsbury (p. 263). Beyond (7¼ M.) *Baschurch*, a village with remains of a British hill-fort, we traverse a flat and marshy district. The Breidden Hills are visible in the distance, with Rodney's monument (p. 264). — From (16 M.) *Whittington*, a prettily-situated village, with the ruins of an old castle, a pleasant excursion may be made to *Ellesmere*, 8 M. to the N., with a small lake.

Near (18 M.) *Gobowen*, the junction for the line to Oswestry and Welshpool (see p. 264), we cross *Watt's Dyke*, an embankment resembling Offa's Dyke, and supposed like it to have been erected by the Mercian Saxons to defend themselves against the Britons. Near (20 M.) *Preesgweene* the train crosses the charming valley of the *Ceiriog*, here the boundary between Shropshire and Wales, by a viaduct 100 ft. high. — 21¼ M. *Chirk* (*Hand Hotel), a prettily-situated village near the left bank of the Ceiriog.

To reach *Chirk Castle* (p. 306) from the hotel we follow the main street and turn to the right at the post-office, avoiding the descent to the left. We then pass a new road to the right, and, after again avoiding a descent to the left, soon come in sight of the park-gate. To the left of the road we have a view of the fine aqueduct and viaduct crossing the valley of the Ceiriog (see p. 307). There is also a footpath from Chirk to the Castle, which is nearly ½ M. shorter than the road. — About 1 M. to the S.E. of Chirk, overlooking the valley of the *Ceiriog*, is *Brynkinalt*, the seat of Lord Trevor, partly built by Inigo Jones. The Duke of Wellington spent many of his holidays here when a boy (adm. to grounds by order obtained at the Hand Hotel). — Tramway from Chirk to *Glyn Ceiriog*, see p. 307.

Beyond (23½ M.) *Cefn* the train crosses the valley of the *Dee* by a viaduct 145 ft. high and 1450 ft. long, commanding an exquisite *View in both directions. To the left is *Pont Cysylltau* (p. 307), in the distance are the *Berwyn Mts.* On the right we skirt *Wynnstay Park* (see p. 306), with its fine old oaks.

25 M. **Ruabon** *(Wynnstay Arms; Rail. Refreshmt. Rooms)*, near which are some important iron and coal mines, is the junction of the railway to Llangollen, Corwen, and Dolgelley (see R. 40c). The church contains several monuments of the Wynn family. The valley of the Dee and other environs afford numerous charming walks.

The line now runs parallel with Offa's Dyke and Watt's Dyke, through a district abounding in coal and iron. To the right, near Wrexham, is *Erddig Hall*, picturesquely situated on a hill.

30 M. **Wrexham** *(Wynnstay Arms)*, a well-built market-town with 11,000 inhab., sometimes called the metropolis of North Wales. The handsome **Church*, built in 1472 on the site of an earlier building, contains a monument by Roubiliac; the tower, added in 1506, is adorned with numerous figures of saints.

From Wrexham an alternative line to Chester, opened in 1890, runs viâ *Hope*, *Buckley*, and *Hawarden* (p. 276), crossing the *Dee* by a swing-bridge 527 ft. long.

33 M. *Gresford*, the birthplace of Samuel Warren (1807-77), author of 'Ten Thousand a Year', with a fine church. The line runs nearly parallel with the *Dee*, a short way from its left bank. To the left, in the distance, rise the *Clwyd Hills* (p. 280). 40 M. *Saltney*, with extensive works. The train now crosses the Dee by a huge cast-iron bridge, and passes through a short tunnel.

42 M. **Chester.** — **Railway Stations.** *General Station* (Pl. F, G, 1) an extensive and handsome building, used in common by the L. N. W. R. and the G. W. R., 1/2 M. from the centre of the town (to the N. E.); *Northgate Station* (Pl. D, 1), Victoria Road, for the 'Cheshire Lines'. — The hotel-omnibuses meet the trains.

Hotels. *Grosvenor (Pl. a; D, 3), Eastgate, a modern building in the old timbered style, R. from 2*s.* 6*d.*, A. 1*s.* 6*d.*; *Queen (Pl. b; F, 1), connected by a covered way with the General Station, R. & A. 4*s.*; Blossoms, just outside the East Gate (Pl. E, 3), commercial, R. & A. 3*s.*; Hop Pole, Green Dragon, Westminster Temperance, unpretending. — *Railway Refreshment Rooms; Bolland*, confectioner, Eastgate Row.

Cabs. For 1-2 pers. 1*s.* per mile; 6*d.* for each 1/2 M. additional; 3-5 pers. 1*s.* 6*d.* and 6*d.*; per hour 2*s.* 6*d.*; each addit. 1/4 hr. 6*d.* Fare and a half between midnight and 6 a. m. No charge for ordinary luggage.

Tramway from the General Station through the town to *Grosvenor Bridge*, *Eaton Park* (fares 3*d.* inside, 2*d.* outside), and *Saltney*.

Steamers (small), starting near the Suspension Bridge, ply up the Dee in summer to (3 M.) *Eccleston Ferry* (4d.), *Eaton Bridge* (6*d.*, return 9*d.*), and *Farndon*.

Boats on the Dee 6*d.* to 3*s.* per hour, 4-20*s.* per day, according to the size; charges doubled on Bank Holidays. — **Swimming Baths**, in the Dee, near the Suspension Bridge. — **Horse Races** on the Roodee (p. 271) in May. — **Post Office** (Pl. E, 3), St. John Street. — **Booksellers**, *Phillipson & Golder*, Eastgate Row (also photographs, etc.).

Chester, the capital of Cheshire and the seat of a bishop, with 36,788 inhab., is pleasantly situated on the right bank of the *Dee*, a few miles above its estuary, and is perhaps the most quaint and mediæval-looking town in England. Strangers arriving in Liverpool should unquestionably devote a day to this most interesting little city, even though unable to extend their tour into North Wales, of which Chester forms the usual portal. Every

For a coloured street plan of Chester see pages 578 & 579

effort has been made to carry out modern improvements in such a way as to interfere as little as possible with the characteristic features of the place. Chester formerly carried on a considerable shipping trade, most of which has been lost through the silting up of the Dee. Monthly markets are held for the sale of Cheshire cheese in the *Cheese Market* (Pl. D, 3), behind the Town Hall.

History. Whether or not a settlement of the early Britons occupied the place of modern Chester is uncertain, but the Romans at once recognised the importance of the position, and for four centuries, beginning about A. D. 60, *Deva*, or the camp upon the Dee, was the headquarters of the famous XXth Legion. Its claim to rank as a *colonia* has not been established, but its very name, a softened form of the Saxon *ceaster*, meaning the camp (Latin *castra*), proves its importance as a military post. The original Saxon name in its full form was, however, *Laegeceaster*, which like *Leinster* and the Welsh *Caerleon*, was a translation of the later Roman name, *Castra* or *Civitas Legionum*. Innumerable Roman remains have been found in different parts of the city, and are now preserved in the Grosvenor Museum (p. 275). After the departure of the Romans Chester was possessed in turn by the Welsh, the Saxons, and the Danes. In 607 it was destroyed by *Æthelfrith* of Northumbria, who on the same occasion massacred the 1200 monks of Bangor Isycoed, 'the last great victory of English heathendom over British Christianity.' It may then, according to one view, have lain desolate for nearly three centuries, till the Danes found refuge in it in 894 and maintained it for a year against King Alfred. Sixteen years later it was rebuilt by *Æthelred* of Mercia and his wife *Æthelflaed*, who extended the walls so as to embrace the site of the castle. Chester was the last English city to yield (in 1070) to William the Conqueror, who created his nephew, Hugh Lupus, Palatine Earl of Chester, and entrusted him with the task of curbing his Welsh neighbours. The earldom reverted to the crown under Henry III. (1237), and still furnishes a title to the heir-apparent of the throne. In the Great Civil War the citizens held out stoutly for Charles I. for two years (1644-46), but were finally starved into surrender. The modern history of the town has been uneventful, and it has not shared in the growth of most English towns of similar size. The present bishopric of Chester dates from the reign of Henry VIII. (1541), though the see of Lichfield was transferred to Chester for a few years in the 11th cent. (1075-1085), and all through the middle ages the bishops of Lichfield were as often as not called bishops of Chester.

Chester still bears distinct traces of its origin in a Roman castrum, and the older part of it forms an oblong, intersected by two main streets at right angles to each other and surrounded by walls, a walk round which forms the best introduction to the city. The present ***Walls,** constructed of red sandstone, are not older than the 14th cent, and it is doubtful whether even the foundations contain any work of an earlier period. On three sides, however, the line of the Roman walls is followed, while the S. wall has been pushed considerably forward. The circuit of the walls is nearly 2 M., and the paved footway on the top, 4-6 ft. in width, affords a delightful walk, commanding admirable views of the city and its surroundings. The gates are modern.

Walk round the Walls. Leaving the *General Railway Station* (Pl. F, G, 1), we pass through City Road and Foregate Street, and reach the walls at (1/2 M.) the East Gate (Pl. E, 3). Here we ascend the steps to the right and follow the walls towards the N. (right), obtaining almost at once a splendid view of the Cathedral (p. 272). At the N. E. angle of the walls is the *Phoenix Tower* (Pl. D, 2), the most interesting of those still remaining, with an inscription recording that Charles I. hence witnessed the defeat of his troops on Rowton Moor in 1645. The view from the top includes the ruined castle of Beeston (p. 276), on a hill 10 M. to the S. E. Along the N. wall, part of which seems of earlier workmanship than the rest (possibly Norman), runs the Shropshire Union Canal, taking the place of the ancient moat. After crossing the *North Gate* (Pl. C, 2) we reach a watch-tower called *Morgan's Mount* (Pl. C, 2; *View from the platform, including Moel Fammau and Flint Castle), and then, a little further on, *Pemberton's Parlour*, a semicircular tower, with an inscription recording repairs made on the walls in 1701. Beyond Pemberton's Parlour an opening has been made in the wall for the railway, close to *Bonwaldesthorne's Tower* (Pl. B, 2), at the N. W. angle of the old city. This is connected with an out-lying tower named the *Water Tower*, to which ships used to be moored in the days when the tidal waters of the Dee washed the walls of Chester. It is now used as a museum (adm. 6*d.*); and there are also some interesting Roman remains (hypocaust, columns, etc.) in the little garden at its foot. From the top of the Water Tower an admirable view is obtained of the estuary of the Dee and the Welsh Mts. Proceeding towards to the S., we again cross the railway, and, after passing over the *Water Gate* (Pl. B, 4), observe below us (right) the *Roodee* or *Roodeye* (Pl. A, B, 4, 5), a picturesque race-course (see p. 269). The name is said to be derived from a cross erected to mark the spot where an image of the Virgin was found, which had been thrown into the Dee by the sacrilegious natives of Hawarden. In front is *Grosvenor Bridge*, crossing the Dee in a single bold span of 200 ft., one of the largest stone arches in Europe. Within the walls, at their S.W. angle, is the *Castle* (see p. 275). The wall now skirts the Dee, and at *Bridge Gate* (Pl. D, 5) we pass the picturesque *Old Bridge*, of the 13th cent., and the huge *Mills of Dee*, which have existed here in one form or another for 800 years. On the left we get a good view, from the Bridge Gate, of the Bear and Billet Inn (p. 272). On the opposite side of the river is *King Edgar's Field*, containing the so-called *Edgar's Cave*, with a rude Roman sculpture. The story goes that in 971 King Edgar of Mercia was rowed from this point to St. John's Church by six subject kings or chieftains. Farther up, the Dee is crossed by a *Suspension Bridge* (Pl. F, 4). At the point where the wall again turns to the N. we ascend the *Wishing Steps*, as to which tradition declares that he who can rush up and down these steps seven times without taking breath may very deservedly count upon the fulfilment of any wish he may form. From the next part of the wall, the only part where the houses of the city are built against it, we have a view to the right of St. John's Church (p. 275) and the Bishop's Palace. Crossing the *New Gate* (Pl. E, 4), we now regain the East Gate, where we started.

The most characteristic and indeed the unique feature of Chester consists in the ***Rows**, found in the four main streets converging at the market-cross. In the Eastgate, Bridge, and Watergate Streets (Pl. C, D, 3) the Rows appear as continuous galleries or arcades occupying the place of the front rooms of the first floors of the houses lining the streets, the ceiling of the ground-floor forming the footpath, while the upper stories form the roof. These covered passages are approached from the street by flights of steps and contain a second row of shops, those in Eastgate Row being the most attractive in the city. In Northgate (Pl. C, 2, D, 2, 3) the rows occupy the ground-floor and recall the arcades of Bern and Thun. The most interesting parts of the Rows are in Eastgate and Bridge Street, the most quaint of all being the *Scotch Row* on the W. side of the latter. The Watergate Rows are somewhat less interesting, but the street contains the three finest specimens of the old timber-built houses, in the number of which Chester excels all other English cities. *God's*

Providence House (Pl. D, 3), to the left (S.), is so called from the inscription it bears, which is said to be a grateful commemoration of immunity from the plague in the 17th century. The house was originally built in 1652, and in 1862 it was carefully reconstructed in the old style and as far as possible with the old materials. Farther on, on the same side, is *Bishop Lloyd's House* (Pl. C, 3; 1615), with a richly carved and pargeted front. Passing the end of Nicholas St. and turning down a small entry on the left, we reach the **Stanley House* or *Palace* (Pl. C, 4; 1591), the oldest timber house of importance in Chester, originally the town-residence of the Stanleys (now divided into small tenements). The *Yacht Inn* (Pl. C, 4), where Swift once lodged, is also in Watergate St. On the opposite side of the street stands *Trinity Church* (Pl. C, 3), containing the tombs of *Matthew Henry* (d. 1714), the commentator, and *Thomas Parnell* (d. 1718), the poet.

The *Bear & Billet Inn*, at the foot of Bridge St. (Pl. D, 5), was formerly the town-mansion of the Shrewsbury family. The *Falcon Inn*, in Bridge St., has recently been to a great extent rebuilt. The antiquarian should visit the vaulted crypts in the basements of houses in Eastgate St. (No. 34), Watergate St. (Nos. 11 & 13), and Bridge St. (No. 12). They belonged to old religious houses formerly on the same sites, and apparently date from the 13th century. At No. 39, Bridge St., the remains of a Roman hypocaust are still *in situ*.

The ***Cathedral** (Pl. D, 3), which lies near the centre of the city, and is approached by Northgate St. and Werburgh St., is built of new red sandstone, with a massive central tower, and embraces details of various styles of architecture, from Norman to late-Perpendicular. A careful restoration of the entire edifice was recently carried out under the superintendence of Sir G. G. Scott and Mr. Blomfield. The dimensions of the cathedral are as follows: length 355 ft., width 75 ft., across the transepts 200 ft., height 78 ft., tower 127 ft. The nave and transepts are open to visitors daily till 5 or 6 p. m. according to the season; adm. to the choir, lady chapel, and chapter-house 6*d.* each, or 2*s.* 6*d.* for a party of 5-15; to the Norman crypt 6*d.* each; to the tower 1*s.* each, or 2*s.* 6*d.* for 5. The daily services are at 10. 15 a. m. and 4.15 p. m.; on Sun. at 3.30 (no sermon) and 6.30 p. m. also. Organ recital on Sun. after the evening service.

The site of Chester Cathedral seems to have been already occupied by a Christian church in the Roman period, and afterwards by a Saxon church and a convent dedicated to SS. Oswald and Werburgh. The relics of the latter saint, who was an abbess of Ely in the 8th cent., were brought hither by Elfreda, daughter of King Alfred, in the year 875. The convent was transformed into a Benedictine abbey by Hugh Lupus (p. 276), with the aid of monks from Bec in Normandy, at the head of whom was Anselm, afterwards Archbishop of Canterbury. The extensive abbey was not completed till nearly 200 years after the death of Lupus (d. 1101), and the Norman church which he founded does not seem to have stood more than a century before its re-erection in the Gothic style was undertaken. Parts of the Norman building still exist, however, in the present cathedral (see below). The next oldest portions of the existing church are the E. E. Lady Chapel and Chapter House (1200-1270). The greater part of the choir is of the early-Dec. period, with geometrical tracery; while the central

For a plan of Chester Cathedral see page 549

tower, the W. front, and the upper parts of the nave and S. transept are late-Perp. (ca. 1485-90). The abbey-church of St. Werburgh became the cathedral of Chester in 1541 (comp. p. 272). Considerable remains of the secular buildings of the abbey still exist (see post), and afford a good opportunity for studying monastic arrangements.

Perhaps the best general view of the exterior of the cathedral is obtained from the city-wall to the E., whence an interesting historical study may be made of the different forms of tracery in the windows, from the E.E. of the Lady Chapel to the late-Perp. of the clerestory of the S. transept. The W. front contains a fine Perp. window, but its general effect is somewhat poverty-stricken, and it is besides partly masked by its structural connection with the *King's School*, a fine modern building by Blomfield on the site of the old episcopal palace, which itself replaced the abbot's lodging. Among the other notable points of the exterior are the Tudor S. W. Porch with its parvise, the flying buttresses, the curious insertion of a doorway in the structure of one of the windows of the N. choir-aisle, the singular dip of the mouldings of two of the adjoining windows, the apsidal termination of the S. choir-aisle, and the fine toothed ornamentation on the cornice of the Lady Chapel.

Interior. Entering by the *S. Doorway*, we find ourselves at the W. end of the Nave, which is raised by a few steps above the level of the rest of the church. This is the best point for a general view of the interior, the rich warm colour of the stone producing a very pleasing effect. The elevated W. part of the nave is late-Perp., while the rest of the bays of the nave and also the S. aisle and the S. transept are in the Dec. style. The wall of the N. aisle is Norman, and at its W. extremity is an interesting fragment of the Norman church, restored as a baptistery. At the other end of the aisle is a Norman doorway, leading to the cloisters. The fan-vaulting of the nave is of oak, and was designed by Sir G. G. Scott. The large boss in the centre bears the arms of the Prince of Wales (Earl of Chester). At the W. end of the S. aisle is the *Consistory Court*, with Jacobean fittings. Two flags suspended at the W. end of the S. wall of the nave were present at the battle of Bunker's Hill. — The N. Transept, which we enter by passing under the handsome modern organ-screen, is of great interest for the examples it contains of early and late Norman workmanship, the lower and earlier portion showing much smaller stones and much wider joints. The windows and the flat roof are Perp. additions. This transept contains the monument of *Bishop Pearson* (d. 1686), the learned author of the 'Exposition of the Creed'. The stained windows are modern. A memorial to *Randolph Caldecott* (1846-86), the artist, was placed here in 1888. — The South Transept, as large as the choir and four times as large as the N. transept, is a curious result of the disputes between monastic and secular clergy which formerly played so large a part in the ecclesiastical history of England. The monks of St. Werburgh, anxious to extend their church, were unable to build towards the N. on account of the monastery-buildings, and could do so towards the S. only by annexing the neighbouring parish-church of St. Oswald. To effect this scheme they gave the parishioners a new church in another part of the town, and ultimately in the 14-15th cent. built the present S. transept, on the site formerly occupied by St. Oswald's. Towards the end of the 15th cent., however, the monks were compelled to re-admit the parishioners to their old place of worship; and down to 1880 the S. transept was separated by a partition from the rest of the cathedral and used as a parish-church. Another church (St. Thomas's) has now again been erected for parochial use, the partition has been removed, and the transept has been restored.

*Choir. The early-Dec. architecture of the choir is richer and finer than that of the nave. The triforium, only indicated in the nave, is here a distinct feature. The **Stalls* (15th cent.) are perhaps the finest specimen of wood-carving of the kind in England, equalled if anywhere by those at Lincoln alone. The *Episcopal Throne*, the *Pulpit*, the rich marble flooring, and the painted oak vaulting are all modern. The *Altar* is constructed of olive, oak, and cedar-wood from Palestine, and the tesselated border in the floor in front of it is composed of fragments from the Temple enclosure at Jerusalem. Most of the metal work in the choir is by Skidmore of Coventry. The large candelabra by the altar are of Italian cinquecento work. — The *N. Aisle* of the choir still contains a few relics of the original Norman building, such as the base of an old pier at the W. end; and the point where the Norman apse ended is indicated by a line of dark marble in the floor. The present E. end of the aisle is late-Perp. (ca. 1500). The interesting little *Canons' Vestry*, now entered from this aisle, but originally from the N. transept, is partly E. E., partly Norman (W. side). The *S. Aisle* now again terminates in an apse, restored as a memorial of Mr. Thomas Brassey, the railway-contractor, and reproducing the original form of the E. E. choir. In the middle of this aisle is a tomb, which an absurd tradition describes as that of Emp. Henry IV. of Germany (d. 1106), who is really interred in the Cathedral of Spires; it is probably the resting-place of an abbot.

The *Lady Chapel, now entered from the N. aisle by a doorway occupying the place of one of the original windows (comp. p. 273), is a good specimen of pure E. E., restored in the original style. The chapel to the N. of the Lady Chapel formerly sheltered the shrine and relics of St. Werburgh, and now contains the canopied tomb of Bishop Graham (d. 1865).

The Tower, the lower part which seems to be of the 14th cent., while the upper part is Perp., commands a good view (fee 1*s.*; see p. 272).

The *Chapter House and its vestibule, entered either from the N. transept or from the cloisters, are also in the E. E. style, and are somewhat earlier than the Lady Chapel, with which they vie in beauty. In the vestibule we should notice the graceful way in which the mouldings of the pillars run continuously up to the vaulting, without the interposition of capitals. The Chapter House, which like other early chapter-houses is rectangular, contains the cathedral-library. The modern stained glass in the fine E. window, depicting the history of St. Werburgh, is the best in the cathedral. The side-windows have double mullions.

Cloisters and Refectory. The conventual buildings of St. Werburgh lie to the N. of the church, instead of occupying the more usual position to the S., a fact which is probably due to the want of space on that side between the church and the boundary of St. Oswald's parish. From the cathedral we enter the *Cloisters* by the Norman door at the E. end of the N. aisle. The style of architecture is Perp., and on the S. and part of the W. side the arcades are double. In the S. cloister, which has been lately rebuilt, we see the Norman work in the N. wall of the nave; and at its W. end diverges a Norman passage leading to the N. W. front of the cathedral. A narrow vaulted chamber in the early-Norman style extends along the W. cloister from N. to S. The E. cloister is bounded by the *Fratry* (lately restored), the *Maiden Aisle* (a passage leading to the old infirmary), and the vestibule of the chapter-house (see above). Near the N. E. corner is the staircase leading to the *Dormitory*, which formed the second story of this part of the building. Several of the early abbots were buried in the S. cloister, as is *Dean Howson* (d. 1885), one of the authors of a well-known 'Life of St. Paul'. — To the N. of the cloisters stands the **Refectory*, an interesting E.E. structure, part of which has been cut off by a passage made from the cloisters to Abbey Square. It contains a very fine E. E. *Lector's Pulpit, with a staircase in the wall (near the S.E. corner), an arrangement seldom met with elsewhere in England.

In Market Square, to the W. of the cathedral, stands the new *Town Hall* (Pl. D, 3), a building in the Italian style with a tower 160 ft. high. Nearly opposite, to the N. of the King's School (p. 273), is the *Abbey Gateway* (14th cent.), leading into Abbey Square.

We now follow Foregate St., as far as Park Road, leading to *Grosvenor Park* (Pl. F, 3, 4), presented to the town by the late Marquis of Westminster, to whom a statue, by Thornycroft, has been erected. A good view of the river is obtained from the S. side of the Park. The path leading to the W. from the statue leads straight to St. John's. Near the church is the *'Anchorite's Cell'*, in which, according to a curious legend, King Harold lived as a hermit after the battle of Hastings, where he had been wounded, but not slain.

The ***Church of St. John** (Pl. E, 4), finely situated above the Dee, dates from the close of the 11th cent., and occupies the site of an earlier Saxon church. It was here that Peter de Leia, Bishop of Lichfield, set up his throne when he transferred the seat of his diocese to Chester in 1076 (p. 270), and thus St. John's may claim to rank as the second cathedral in the city. The present building, however, is a mere torso, consisting of little more than part of the nave of the original collegiate church, which was perhaps a finer edifice than St. Werburgh's itself. The choir and chancel, now in picturesque ruin, were crushed by the falling of the central tower in 1470; the W. front was destroyed by a similar accident a century later; and the massive detached tower on the N. W. also fell in 1881.

We enter by the N. porch, which has been admirably restored; above it is the ancient and battered effigy of an ecclesiastic. The *Interior is an excellent example of simple yet stately Norman architecture. The beautiful triforium is in the Transition style and dates from about a century later than the bays below; the clerestory is E. E. On the S. side of the chancel is an E. E. crypt or 'chapter-house', containing four interesting Saxon crosses of the 9-10th centuries. The ruins of the choir exhibit some very fine late or transitional Norman details (key kept by the sexton, who is to be found either in the church or at No. 1, Lumley Place, a little to the N.). According to two singularly parallel and baseless legends, Henry V. of Germany and Harold, the Saxon king, both spent their last years in seclusion at Chester and were buried in St. John's (see p. 274 and above). — Near St. John's is the *Episcopal Palace*.

From the middle of Bridge St. (p. 272), Grosvenor St. leads direct towards the S.W. to the entrance of the castle, passing on the left the *Grosvenor Museum and School of Science and Ar* (Pl. D, 4; daily, adm. 3*d*.). The museum contains Roman altars, coins, and inscribed stones found in the city, and other objects of local interest. On the right is an *Obelisk* to the memory of Matthew Henry (p. 272). The equestrian statue in front of the castle is that of *Field-Marshal Viscount Combermere* (d. 1865), in bronze, by Marochetti. To the right, opposite the castle, are the *Militia Barracks*. The **Castle** (Pl. D, 5), originally built by the first Norman Earl of Chester, now consists of a series of modern buildings, used as assize-courts, gaol, and barracks. The only relic of the Norman period is *Julius Caesar's Tower*, on the side next the river (S. W.), a square keep used as a powder-magazine. This tower has been recased with red stone, and has thus lost its venerable appearance.

The ancient history of the city is centred in that of its castle, upon which a flash of historical interest was also cast in modern times by the abortive attempt of the Fenians to capture it in 1867. — In the upper story of the tower is a beautiful little E. E. *Chapel*, which is most unjustifiably used as a storehouse.

The *Church of St. Mary* (Pl. D, 5), a good Perp. building adjoining the castle on the E., contains a few old monuments.

The *King's Arms Kitchen*, a small inn close to the East Gate (reached by the narrow passage to the N., inside the gate), is the meeting-place of a mimic corporation, said to have been established by Charles I. The room in which the society meets has been fitted up in the old-fashioned style, with a tiled floor; its walls are covered with wooden panels bearing the names of the officers of the corporation for the last 200 years. The chair of the 'Mayor' is a handsome piece of oak-carving, above which are hung the mace and sword of state.

Excursions from Chester.

Eaton Hall, an example of an English aristocratic mansion, adorned with all the resources of modern art and fitted up with lavish expenditure, is the seat of the Duke of Westminster, a descendant of Hugh Lupus (p. 270). It is finely situated on the Dee, $3^1/_2$ M. to the S. of Chester, and may be reached either by road or by river (steamer or small boat, see p. 269); in summer a public brake leaves Chester daily for Eaton Hall at 2 p.m., returning at 5 p.m. (fare 1*s.*, return 1*s.* 6*d.*). Visitors to the hall pay a fee of 1*s.* at the door, and tickets of admission to the gardens (also 1*s.*) may be obtained at the Grosvenor Hotel, from the Chester booksellers, or at the garden-gate; the proceeds are devoted to charitable objects. In approaching by steamer we may alight either at *Eccleston Ferry* (4*d.*), about $1^1/_2$ M. below the hall, and walk through the park, or at *Eaton Bridge* (fare 6*d.*) just above it. The stable-yard entrance by which visitors are admitted is at the N. end of the building. The present house, the fourth on the same site, is a magnificent Gothic pile erected by *Waterhouse* in 1870-82. In front of it is a bronze *Statue of Hugh Lupus*, by G. F. Watts. The interior is most sumptuously fitted up, and contains numerous modern paintings, including several family-portraits by *Millais* and a few works of *Rubens*. To reach the *Gardens*, with their extensive greenhouses and fine terraces, we turn to the right on leaving the house. Visitors are allowed to inspect the house and wander about the gardens without an attendant, and no gratuities are expected. The *Stud Farm* (a group of red buildings, visible from the garden-lodge, to the right of the avenue to Eccleston) contains several race-horses of renown. Those who wish to return to Chester by the steamer should make enquiries beforehand as to when and where they can meet it; for the convenience of visitors to Eaton Hall it often puts in at the bank at the end of the park, $^1/_2$ M. above Eccleston Ferry. The return-route may be varied by following the avenue that leads N. W. from the fine iron gates at the front of the house to ($2^1/_2$ M.) the *Overleigh Lodge*, a few hundred yards from the Grosvenor Bridge (tramway, see p. 269).

Hawarden. About 6 M. to the E. of Chester lies ***Hawarden** (pronounced *Harden*), the residence of the Right Hon. W. E. Gladstone, a station on the new railway to Wrexham (from Northgate or Liverpool Road station; comp. p. 269). The house stands in a picturesque park, containing the ruins of an old castle. Visitors are admitted to the park and to the old castle from sunrise to sunset; the modern mansion is not shown. The ruins of the ***Old Castle** consist mainly of a massive circular keep, the top of which commands a good view of the Dee valley; it probably dates from the end of the 13th cent., and contains a chapel. *Hawarden Church*, in which Mr. Gladstone often reads the Lessons, is an E. E. building, restored, after a destructive fire in 1857, by Sir G. G. Scott. — About 2 M. to the N. W. of Hawarden ($2^1/_2$ M. from Queen's Ferry, p. 278), are the romantic ruins of *Ewloe Castle* (13th cent.), in the woods near which Henry II. was defeated by Owen Gwynedd.

Beeston Castle. A visit may also be paid to **Beeston Castle** (open on Mon., Wed., Frid., and Sat.), commandingly situated on a lofty rock, 10 M. to the S. E. of Chester and $^3/_4$ M. from Beeston Castle station (p. 345). The castle belongs to Lord Tollemache, whose park of *Peckforton* is adjacent and may be visited on application at the lodge.

From Chester to Mold and Denbigh, $29^1/_2$ M., railway (L. N. W.) in $1^1/_3$ hr. (fares 5*s.*, 4*s.*, 2*s.* $5^1/_2$*d.*). 5 M. *Broughton Hall*; 9 M. *Hope*, both within easy reach of Hawarden (see p. 274). At (10 M.) *Hope Junction* we cross a line running N. to Connah's Quay (p. 278) and S. to Wrexham (p. 269). — 13½ M. **Mold** *(Black Lion)*, a busy little coal-mining town, with a good 15th cent. church, containing some fine painted windows. About 1½ M., to the S. is *Tower*, the curious seat of the Wynnes, with a lofty square tower of the 15th century. About 1 M. to the W. is *Maes Garmon*, where a column erected in 1736 marks the scene of the 'Alleluia Victory', said to have been gained by the Christian Britons over the Saxon and Pictish pagans in 420. Pedestrians may walk from Mold to Ruthin (p. 280), either direct (9 M.), or over the top of *Moel Fammau* (p. 280), the highest of the Clwydian hills (*View of the Vale of Clwyd, etc.). — At (29½ M.) *Denbigh* we reach the railway from Rhyl to Corwen.

From Chester to Manchester viâ Warrington, 31 M., railway (L. N. W.) in 1¼-2¼ hrs. (fares 6*s*., 4*s*. 6*d*., 2*s*. 10*d*.). — From (7 M.) *Helsby* a branch diverges to *Hooton* (p. 322). 9 M. *Frodsham*, with a Norman church close by, is the junction of a line to *Runcorn* (p. 345). — At (16 M.) *Warrington* we join the Liverpool and Manchester railway (p. 332).

From Chester to Manchester viâ Northwich, 34 M., railway ('Cheshire Lines') in 1½-1¾ hr. (fares 6*s*., 4*s*. 6*d*., 2*s*. 10*d*.). — This line traverses a rich salt-district. Most of the stations are uninteresting. Near (13 M.) *Hartford* it crosses the main L. N. W. line (comp. p. 340). — 15 M. **Northwich** *(Angel; Crown)*, the principal town of the salt-district, with 12,300 inhab. and several salt-mines and brine-springs. An interesting visit may be paid to the *Marston Mine*, 300 ft. deep, with a roof supported by huge pillars of salt. Nearly two million tons of salt are annually obtained within a radius of 7 M. from Northwich. The frequent subsidence of the earth, owing to the pumping out of the brine, gives a singular appearance to many parts of the town. — 21 M. *Knutsford* (Angel), a small town with 3600 inhabitants. The train now passes *Tatton Park*, on the left, an extensive domain belonging to Lord Egerton. — The train traverses the pretty valley of the *Bollin*. 28 M. *Altrincham*, with 11,250 inhab., contains numerous villas of Manchester merchants. — 34 M. *Manchester*, see p. 333.

From Chester to *Liverpool*, see R. 41; to *Bangor* and *Carnarvon*, see R. 40a; to *Crewe*, see p. 345.

40. North Wales.

The district usually included under the name of **North Wales** consists of that part of the principality lying to the N. of a line drawn from Aberystwith to Shrewsbury. It contains some of the finest mountain, coast, and valley scenery in the kingdom; and few districts of similar size can vie with 'Snowdonia' in the amount and variety of its natural attractions. From three to six weeks, or longer, are necessary for any approach to an exhaustive tour, but a flying visit to some of the finest points may be made in a few days. Numerous circular tours, varying in length from a few days to several weeks, have been arranged by the L. N. W. and G. W. railways, which, along with the Cambrian Railway, afford the chief means of communication in the N. and S. halves of the district respectively. The tours may be begun at Chester, Shrewsbury, Llandudno, and many other points, and the utmost facility is given for breaking the journey, adopting alternative routes, and the like. The visitor to Chester who cannot devote more than three days to N. Wales may apportion his time as follows. 1st Day. Proceed by early train to *Bangor*, visit the *Menai Bridges*, go on by train to *Carnarvon*, visit the castle, and take an evening train to *Llanberis*. 2nd Day. Ascend *Snowdon*, making an early start, and take the afternoon coach through the *Pass of Llanberis* to *Bettws-y-Coed*. 3rd Day. Proceed by railway to *Blaenau Ffestiniog;* then by the 'Toy Railway' to *Port Madoc;* by railway to *Chester* (or *Shrewsbury*) viâ *Barmouth* and *Dolgelley*, stopping for the night, if time permit, at the latter. Alternative routes for 2nd and 3rd days: 2nd Day.

Ascend *Snowdon* and descend to *Beddgelert;* visit *Pont Aberglaslyn;* drive through *Nant Gwynant* to *Capel Curig* and (if there be time), to *Bettws-y-Coed.* 3RD DAY. Visit the waterfalls, etc., near Bettws, and return through the *Vale of Conway* (taking the steamer, if the hour suit, at *Trefriw*) to *Conway* and *Chester.* It is needless to say that either of these arrangements involves a good deal of hurry and fatigue, while the walk over Snowdon to Beddgelert should not be attempted except by fairly robust pedestrians. — A more leisurely tour of a week, for moderate walkers, may be laid out as follows. 1ST DAY. Early train to *Llandudno;* walk or drive round the *Great Orme's Head;* in the afternoon by train to *Bettws* (*Conway Castle* may be included if time allows). 2ND DAY. *Fairy Glen* and *Falls of the Conway* (5 M.); walk or drive through the *Pass of Llanberis* to *Llanberis* (15½ M.). 3RD DAY. Ascend *Snowdon* and descend to *Beddgelert.* 4TH DAY. Walk or drive from Beddgelert to *Ffestiniog* by the old road (13 M.). *Cynfael Falls.* 5TH DAY. Railway (or on foot) to (3½ M.) *Duffws*; 'Toy Railway' to *Port Madoc;* railway to *Barmouth* and *Dolgelley* (or walk from Barmouth to Dolgelley, 10 M.). 6TH DAY. Ascent of *Cader Idris* (up and down 3½-5 hrs.); *Torrent Walk* (5 M); *Precipice Walk* (6-7 M., if time and strength permit). 7TH DAY. Railway from Dolgelley to *Chester*, stopping at *Llangollen* if desired, to visit *Dinas Bran* and *Plas Newydd.* — Tourists who wish to see as much as possible of N. Wales in a single day will, perhaps, best effect their purpose by joining the coach-route No. 5 (p. 281) from *Llandudno.* Or they may go to Carnarvon and take the coach, starting about 11 a. m., which makes the round of Snowdon viâ the *Snowdon Ranger*, *Beddgelert*, *Pen-y-Gwryd*, and *Llanberis* (35 M., in 7 hrs.). In summer a train (L. N. W. R.) runs from Chester to *Llanberis* direct, stopping at *Rhyl* and following stations, and returning in the evening. As the coaches run in connection with the trains, this route affords opportunity for a great variety of day-excursions in Snowdonia.

Tourists will find a slight knowledge of the pronunciation of Welsh names desirable, and they should therefore make acquaintance with the chief peculiarities of the Welsh alphabet (see Introd.).

Of the following tours, grouped under the general heading of 'North Wales', the sub-routes a., b., and c. draw a cordon round the district described, while the others deal with the interior of the circle. To Snowdon, as the great focus of attraction, a separate section has been allotted. *Aberystwith* and *Machynlleth*, frequently included for touring purposes in N. Wales, are described in R. 38 ('Central Wales'). Those who wish to combine S. Wales in one general tour with N. Wales will find no difficulty in joining this route to RR. 24-29, either from Aberystwith or Shrewsbury.

For other general remarks on Wales, see the Introduction.

a. From Chester to Bangor and Carnarvon. Llandudno. Anglesey.

Comp. Maps, pp. 307, 318.

68½ M. RAILWAY (L. N. W.) in 2¼-3½ hrs. (fares 12*s.* 8*d.*, 10*s.*, 5*s.* 8½*d.*). To *Bangor*, 60 M., in 1¾-2½ hrs. (fares 11*s.* 2*d.*, 8*s.* 9*d.*, 6*s.* 3*d.*); to *Llandudno*, 48 M., in 1⅓-2¼ hrs. (fares 9*s.*, 7*s.*, 5*s.*). — This is the line traversed by the Irish Mail to Holyhead (p. 290). The railway skirts the sea nearly the whole way, while on the other side (left) we have more or less distant views of the mountains.

On quitting the station the train traverses a tunnel, passes through the city-wall, and crosses the *Shropshire Union Canal* and the *Dee.* To the left lies the *Roodee* (p. 271), with the castle beyond it. The line skirts the Dee. Before reaching (6 M.) *Sandycroft* we cross a small brook and enter Flintshire and Wales. 7 M. *Queen's Ferry*, near Hawarden (p. 276); 9 M. *Connah's Quay* (p. 276). We now skirt for several miles the desolate and sandy estuary of the Dee (the 'Sands of Dee'). 13 M. *Flint* (Royal Oak), the county-town of Flintshire, is a smoky little town with 5130 inhab. and some chemical works. To the right are the 'rude ribs' of the old *Castle*, the scene of the meeting between Richard II. and Bolingbroke ('Richard II', III. 3); it is said to have been built by Edward I. On the Cheshire coast, on the other side of the estuary, are the small watering-places of *Parkgate* and *West Kirby* (p. 331).

Beyond (16 M.) *Bagillt*, on a wooded knoll to the left, are the ruins of *Basingwerk Abbey*, a Cistercian house founded by the Earl of Chester towards the end of the 12th century. $15^1/_2$ M. *Holywell;* the little town (King's Head) lies $1^1/_2$ M. to the S. of the station and takes its name from the sacred *Well of St. Winifrid* (adm. 2*d.*).

This well was formerly held in great veneration, ranking as one of the 'Seven Wonders of Wales', and still attracts Roman Catholic pilgrims. It was believed to have risen on the spot where the head of St. Winifrid fell to the ground, cut off by a pagan prince whose advances she had rejected. The red vegetable growth on the stones is believed by the vulgar to be the stains of St. Winifrid's blood. The Perp. chapel built over the well is attributed to Margaret, mother of Henry VII.

Near (21 M.) *Mostyn* is *Mostyn Hall*, the seat of the ancient family of that name, where the 'King's Window' is shown as that through which the Earl of Richmond, afterwards Henry VII., escaped from the soldiers of Richard III. The hall contains a collection of Welsh antiquities and some rare old MSS.

Downing Hall, 1 M. from Mostyn, was the birthplace (1762) of *Pennant* (b. 1762), author of the 'Tour in Wales'. It now belongs to the Earl of Denbigh and contains the 'Pennant Collection' of MSS. and antiquities.

The scenery now improves, and a row of wooded hills rises to the left. To the right we soon come in sight of the lighthouse on *Air Point*, the N.W. extremity of the Dee estuary, and of *Hoylake* (p. 331), at the N.E. end. Near (27 M.) *Prestatyn* we obtain a good view of Moel Fammau (p. 280) and the other Clwydian hills to the left, while the Great Orme (p. 282) may be descried on our right, in front.

30 M. **Rhyl** (**Westminster*, *Belvoir*, *Queen's*, facing the sea, $^1/_3$ M. from the station; *Royal*, *Mostyn Arms*, in the town; *Alexandra*, *Bee*, near the station; *Hydropathic; Rail. Rfmt. Rooms)*, a frequented sea-bathing resort, with a fine expanse of firm sandy beach, an esplanade, and a pier (adm. 2*d.*) 700 yds. long. Rhyl possesses little attraction for the tourist except as a convenient starting-point for excursions in the *Vale of Clwyd*, at the mouth of which it lies. The end of the pier affords a fair though distant view of Penmaenmawr, Carnedd Llewelyn, and other Snowdonian mountains. In summer a steamboat usually plies to Liverpool (2*s.* 6*d.*), Llandudno (2*s.*), and the Menai Straits (comp. p. 281; 3*s.*).

About $3^1/_2$ M. to the S. E. of Rhyl lie the ruins of *Dyserth Castle*, the direct and uninteresting road to which crosses the new Gladstone Bridge. A pleasanter way is to take the train to Rhuddlan (p. 280) and walk thence to (3 M.) Dyserth. The castle, which is of early Norman origin, is strikingly situated on a lofty rock (view). The walk may be prolonged towards the N.E. to ($2^1/_2$ M.) *Newmarket*, close to which is the extensive tumulus known as the 'Cop'; and from Newmarket we may go on either to (3 M.) Prestatyn (see above) or to (4 M.) Mostyn (see above). On the way to the former we pass the extensive *Talargoch Lead Mine*. — A public conveyance runs daily from Rhyl to *Bodelwyddan*, 5 M. to the S.W., the beautiful modern church of which, with its lofty spire, was erected by Lady Willoughby de Broke in memory of her husband. It is in the Dec. style of the 14th cent., and the interior is elaborately adorned with marble, carved oak, and stained glass. Bodelwyddan is 3 M. from St. Asaph (see below).

From Rhyl to Corwen, 30 M., railway (L. N. W.) in 1¾-2¼ hrs. (fares 6*s*., 4*s*. 6*d*., 2*s*. 5½*d*.). This line traverses the *Vale of Clwyd*, a pretty and fertile valley (20 M. long), with no pretension to scenic grandeur.

3 M. *Rhuddlan*, with a ruined castle of the 12th cent. (adm. 2*d*.).

6 M. **St. Asaph** (**Plough*; *Kinmel Arms*), a quiet little episcopal seat situated on an eminence between the Clwyd and the *Elwy*. The *Cathedral, which is the smallest in the kingdom, being only 182 ft. in length, (not one-third of the length of Winchester), is in its present form mainly a Dec. building of the 15th cent., though part of the nave and aisles date from the second half of the 13th century. It was recently restored by *Scott*. The exterior is very plain, the most conspicuous feature being the massive square tower, 100 ft. in height (small charge for ascending). The interior contains carved oak stalls, some good modern stained glass, and a few monuments, the most interesting of which are those of a bishop of the 14th cent. (S. transept) and of *Mrs. Hemans*, the poetess (d. 1835). The see of St. Asaph was founded by St. Kentigern about the middle of the 6th cent., and derives its name from his successor (d. 596). The church is closed except during divine service (on week-days, 8.15 a.m. and 3.15 in summer; the latter at 5 p. m. in winter), and the keys are kept by Mr. Robinson, lower down in the same street. — About 3½ M. to the S.W. of St. Asaph, in the pretty valley of the Elwy, are the *Cefn Caves*, in which numerous organic remains were found. The caves are only 2¼ M. from *Trefnant*, the station beyond St. Asaph.

11 M. **Denbigh** (*Crown; Bull*), the capital of the county of the same name, with 6500 inhab., picturesquely situated on the Clwyd and commanded by a ruined castle. The latter (adm. 2*d*.), dating from the reign of Edward I., commands an extensive view. In 1563 it was granted by Queen Elizabeth to Dudley, Earl of Leicester, who afterwards entertained the Virgin Queen here with great magnificence. The castle afforded shelter to Charles I. after the battle of Rowton (p. 270), but was dismantled at the Restoration. It has recently been partly restored, and the interior is used as a recreation-ground. The ancient church of *St. Hilary* (supposed to have been the garrison-chapel), the extensive remains of another large church begun by the Earl of Leicester but never finished, and the old parish-church at *Whitchurch* (1 M. to the E.) are all interesting. Henry M. Stanley is a native of Denbigh. Denbigh is the junction of a line to Mold and Chester (see p. 276).

14½ M. *Llanrhaiadr*. The church, ¾ M. to the W., contains a fine 'Jesse' window, said to have been purchased with the contributions of pilgrims to the adjoining sacred well of *Ffynnon Dyfnog*.

18 M. **Ruthin** (*Castle; Wynnstay Arms*), a quaint little Welsh town of 3000 inhab., contains an interesting church, recently restored, with a fine oaken ceiling in the N. aisle and a modern spire. The *Castle* shared the fate of many Welsh strongholds in being captured by the Parliamentarian general Mytton and was dismantled after the Restoration. A handsome modern mansion has been erected on part of the site. Ruthin is a good starting-point for an ascent of *Moel Fammau* (1823 ft.), the highest of the Clwydian range, which lies 4½ M. to the N.W. The *View includes the entire Clwyd valley, Snowdon, Chester, Liverpool, etc. — 25 M. *Derwen*, with a church containing a fine rood-loft of the 15th century. — At (30 M.) *Corwen* we join the line from Chester to Dolgelley (see p. 303).

On leaving Rhyl the train crosses the estuary of the Clwyd. affording a view, to the left, of Rhuddlan Castle, the tower of St. Asaph cathedral, and the spire of Bodelwyddan church. 34½ M *Abergele & Pensarn* (Hesketh Arms, Bee, at Abergele; Cambrian, near the station), the former 1 M. inland, the latter a small sea-bathing resort adjoining the station.

Beyond Abergele, on the heights to the left, is the imposing turreted mansion of *Gwrych*, 400 yds. long, with a central tower 100 ft. high; like Châtelherault (p. 480), it consists to a great extent merely of frontage, built for effect. Immediately beyond Gwrych, the huge but shallow cave of *Cefn Ogo* is conspicuous in the cliffs to the left. — 39½ M. *Old Colwyn* (Marine Hotel). — 41 M. **Colwyn Bay** (**Pwllychrochan Hotel*, with fine grounds; *Colwyn Bay Hotel*; *Coed Pella Hotel*; *Imperial*, near the station; *Hydropathic*), a rising watering-place, with good bathing, and numerous pleasant walks among the wooded hills and valleys to landward. To the W. is the village of *Llandrillo* (Rhos Abbey Hotel), now joined to Colwyn, with a curious fishing-weir, in which large catches are sometimes made, and the small and ancient *Capel St. Trillo*, built over a spring.

The train now crosses the neck of the promontory ending in the Great Orme and Little Orme, while the fine estuary of the *Conway* comes into view in front, backed by the mountains of the Snowdon range. From (45½ M.) *Llandudno Junction* (Junction Hotel; Ferry Farm Hotel; Rail. Rfmt. Rooms) a short branch-line diverges to Llandudno, 3 M. to the N. This is also the point of divergence of the railway to Bettws-y-Coed and Ffestiniog (R. 40*d*.).

Llandudno (comp. Map, p. 307). — **Hotels.** Imperial, Queen's, Adelphi, St. George's, all well situated on the Esplanade, with view of the sea; R. & A. about 4*s*. 6*d*., D. 4-4*s*. 6*d*., 'pens'. 11-13*s*. per day, 3½-4 gs. per week. Royal, Church Walks; Tudno Castle, near the station, D. 3*s*. 6*d*., R. & A. from 3*s*. 6*d*., 'pens'. 8*s*. 6*d*. (except in July and Aug.); Prince of Wales, Lloyd St., R. & A. 3*s*., table d'hôte 3*s*.; Alexandra, Clonmel St. — Numerous Boarding Houses (7-10*s*. a day). — Hydropathic Establishments, on the Esplanade (patients 4*l*. per week in summer, 3*l*. 5*s*. in winter; visitors 3*l*. 10*s*. and 3*l*.) and under the Little Orme's Head.

Cabs. 1. By distance: Carriage with two horses 1*s*. 6*d*. per mile, one horse or two ponies 1s., one pony or two donkeys 9*d*., one donkey or 1-2 goats 6*d*.; each. addit. ½ M. 9*d*., 6*d*., 4*d*., 3*d*. — 2. By time: per hour 5*s*., 3*s*., 2*s*., 1*s*. 6*d*.; each addit. ¼ hr. 1*s*. 3*d*., 9*d*., 6*d*., 4*d*. — 3. Special fares for the 'Marine Drive' round the Great Orme's Head: 8*s*., 5*s*., 4*s*., 2*s*. — Bath-chairs 1*s*. per hr., and 3*d*. for each addit. ¼ hr.

Horses 2*s*. per hr., ponies 1*s*. 6*d*., donkeys or mules 6*d*.

Coaches. 1. Public brakes ply round the *Great Orme's Head* at frequent intervals (fare 1*s*.). 2. To the *Little Orme's Head*, and back by the *Gloddaeth Woods* (1*s*.), also several times a day. 3. *Colwyn Bay* (see above), going by the *Vale of Mochdre* and returning by *Llandudno Junction* (fare 2*s*. 6*d*.). 4. To *Conway*, the *Sychnant Pass*, *Dwygyfylchi*, *Penmaenmawr*, and back. 5. Circular tour to *Conway*, *Trefriw*, *Llanrwst*, *Bettws-y-Coed*, *Capel Curig*, *Llyn Ogwen*, *Pass of Nant Ffrancon*, *Bethesda* (allowing time for a visit to the quarries), *Penrhyn Castle*, *Penmaenmawr*, *Conway*, and *Llandudno*, starting at 8 a.m. and returning at 7.30 p.m. (fare for the whole distance of 56 M., 12*s*.; intermediate distances in proportion).

Steamers. The vessels of the Liverpool, Llandudno, and Welsh Coast Steamboat Co. ply twice daily each way between *Liverpool* and *Menai Bridge*, calling at *Llandudno*, *Beaumaris*, and *Bangor*. The voyage from Llandudno to Liverpool takes 2¾ hrs. (1st class 4*s*. 6*d*., 2nd class 2*s*. 6*d*.; return 7*s*., 4*s*. 6*d*.), that from Llandudno to Menai Bridge 1½ hr. (2*s*., return 3*s*.) Special excursion-steamers also make frequent trips in summer to *Beaumaris*, *Bangor*, and *Menai Bridge*, and back (4-6 hrs.; fare 2*s*., return 3*s.*; to ***Carnarvon*** 3*s.*), to ***Rhyl*** and back (4½ hrs.; fare 2*s.*, return 2*s.* 6*d.*). — A small steamer also plies in summer from ***Deganwy*** (p. 284), 2 M. to the S. of Llandudno, up the river Conway to ***Conway*** and ***Trefriw*** (1½ hr.; fares 1*s.* 6*d.*, 1*s.*; return 2*s.* 6d., 1*s.* 6*d.*); the time of starting depends on the tide.

Boats. Sailing-boats 3*s.*, Rowing-boats 2*s.* per hour.

The *Llandudno Promenade Band* plays daily in the season from 11 to 1 at the end of the pier, and from 7 to 9.30 p.m. on the Esplanade.

Llandudno, the most fashionable of Welsh watering-places, is delightfully situated on the narrow peninsula between Conway Bay and Orme's Bay, facing the latter, the graceful swell of which is finely bounded by the bold limestone headlands called the *Great* and the *Little Orme.* Of late the town has extended to the S.E., across nearly the whole width of the flat neck of the peninsula, and there are now several houses on Conway Bay also. On this side, however, the beach is wet and somewhat muddy, contrasting unfavourably with the smooth and firm sands of Orme's Bay, while on the other hand it affords a fine view of the Welsh mountains, to which the houses on the N. bay turn their backs. The population of Llandudno in 1881 was 4838, and in the season it is frequented by about 20,000 visitors.

The climate of Llandudno is bracing in summer and comparatively mild in spring and autumn. The annual temperature is 50.5° Fahr. Llandudno is a good starting-point for many of the finest excursions in North Wales, and the two Orme's Heads afford several pleasant walks and drives in the vicinity of the town. The bathing is good and safe. Like Brighton, however, Llandudno lacks shade.

After a walk to the end of the **Pier** (adm. 2*d.*), which is 1250 ft. long and commands a capital view of the town and bay, the visitor should lose no time in exploring the ***Great Orme's Head**. This huge rocky promontory, rising precipitously to a height of 700 ft. above the sea, shields Llandudno most effectually from the keen N.W. winds and forms a grand feature in almost every view of the town.

The ***Marine Drive,** 5½ M. long, which has been constructed round the face of the cliffs, is one of the finest drives in Great Britain. We enter it at a toll-house (1*d.*, carriages 6*d.*) a little to the N. of the pier. The road ascends steadily, with nearly vertical walls of rock above and below, to (½ M.) *Pentrwyn*, the N.E. angle of the promontory, where we obtain a good view of the coast to the E. of Llandudno, with the Clwyd hills in the background. On an exceptionally clear day the Isle of Man, the hills of Cumberland, and the coast of Lancashire may be seen to the right. In ½ M. more we pass a footpath on the left, leading up to a farm-house ('Old Farm Refreshments'), and ¼ M. farther on is another, diverging at the foot of a bluff crowned with a flag-staff, and ascending to the (5 min.) old church of St. Tudno (p. 283). At the extreme N. point of the promontory, ¾ M. farther on, is a *Lighthouse* (visitors admitted), below which is the *Hornby Cave*, where the brig 'Hornby' was wrecked in 1824. After passing the lighthouse we gradually obtain a splendid *View of Anglesey, Puffin Island, the coast of N. Wales from Bangor to Conway, the Conway estuary, and the mountains of Snowdonia. Among the nearest and most conspicuous of the last are (named from right to left) Moel Wnion, the rounded top of Y Foel Fras, Penmaenmawr (on the coast), Tal-y-Fan, Penmaenbach, and Conway Mountain (the last two in the foreground, near Conway). Farther back, to the right of Y Foel Fras, is Carnedd Llewelyn, beyond and to the right of which the peaked summit of Snowdon itself may be descried on a clear day. We now descend along the S. side of the headland, passing (1½ M. from the lighthouse) the scanty remains of *Gogarth Abbey*. Conway Castle (p. 284) is well seen almost straight ahead. On reaching the toll-house at the other end of the drive we turn to the left, leaving Conway Bay on the right, and return to Llandudno by Abbey Road. The direction just described is the preferable one in which to make the circuit of the Great Orme.

Walkers should not omit to ascend to the top of the Great Orme, either direct, by a steep road ascending from Church Walks, at the N. end of the town, or by the path ascending to St. Tudno's Church from the Marine Drive (see p. 282). In the former case we pass Kendrick's Cave and Camera Obscura and enjoy fine views of Llandudno as we ascend. Near the top, where the road forks, we keep to the right, and in 4 min. more we reach a gate where a placard points out the path to the old church. [The other branch of the road leads to the *Telegraph Station*, now an inn.] We pass the 'Farm Refreshments' on the left, cross a field, and soon come in sight of the church.

St. Tudno's Church is a small building of a most primitive and unpretending character, dating from the 15th cent. (restored in 1855), but occupying the site of an older structure (12th cent.). It is said to mark the site of the cell of St. Tudno, a hermit of the 7th cent., who has bequeathed his name to the modern watering-place (Llandudno, *i.e.* church or village of Tudno). The interior contains an ancient font and two incised coffin lids of the 13th century. The church of St. Tudno is much frequented on Sun. evenings in summer, and the service is sometimes held in the open air. From the church we may continue our walk to the lighthouse (p. 282) or the signal-station, enjoying extensive views of land and sea. — The old copper mines, above the Happy Valley, are believed to have been worked by the Romans and ancient Britons.

The ***Little Orme's Head** looks much less rugged than its big brother, but a closer acquaintance will show that its cliffs are fully as picturesque and imposing.

To reach them we follow the road along the shore towards the E., which begins to ascend about 1¼ M. from the town. About ½ M. beyond the house at the foot of the ascent there is a break in the wall to the left, where we leave the road and ascend across turf to a small gate. On passing through the gate we may ascend to the left, direct to the top of the headland, or make the entire circuit of it by following the path to the right, soon passing through another gate in an iron fence. The summit is marked by a cairn, from which a most extensive and beautiful view is obtained, including Llandudno and Snowdonia (comp. p. 283) on the W., and the Clwydian hills and vale on the E. The seaward edge of the headland, with its cliffs descending sheer into the sea from a height of 300-400 ft., is also very fine.

On regaining the high-road we may continue our walk to (¼ M.) a point where four roads meet. That to the left leads to (2½ M.) Llandrillo (p. 281) and (1 M.) Colwyn Bay, passing near the old farm-house of *Penrhyn*, to which two curious legends attach. Either of the roads to the right will bring us, more or less directly, to the (1 M.) pleasant wooded grounds of *Gloddaeth House*, the seat of the Mostyn family. The curious tower of Llandrillo Church, with double-stepped battlements, is seen in the distance, to the left. The direct route from Llandudno to (2 M.) Gloddaeth diverges from the shore-road beyond Craig-y-Don Terrace.

The low wooded hills to the S. of the Little Orme's Head afford many pleasant rambles. The best point of view is ***Pabo Hill**, which rises about 2 M. to the S. of the Little Orme, and about 3 M., in a direct line, to the S.E. of Llandudno. We may either reach it by the Gloddaeth woods (see above), or follow the Conway road to a point ½ M. beyond the village of (1¾ M.) *Eglwys Rhos*, with its pretty church, and then diverge to the left. By the latter route we pass the old mansion of (2¼ M.) *Bodyscallen*, the grounds of which are open on Tues. and Thurs., 2-5 p.m. — The favourite boating-excursions (comp. p. 282) are to the caves in the cliffs of the Great and Little Orme, which can only be reached by water. In fine weather both these excursions are very enjoyable, and the sheer precipices of the two headlands are seen to great advantage from below. Perhaps the most interesting cave is the ***Llech***, in the Great Orme, which is said to have been fitted up as a marine summer-house by a far-back member of the Mostyn family. Good deep-sea fishing may also be had.

Conway (see below), with its picturesque castle, is within 4 M. of Llandudno, and may be easily reached by road, by river, or by rail. In the last case the traveller should alight at Llandudno Junction and walk across the Suspension Bridge. About halfway between Llandudno and Conway lies *Deganwy* (Deganwy Castle Hotel), commanded by a small hill (250 ft.; view), which is crowned with the scanty ruins of a castle built by Hugh Lupus (p. 270). Deganwy is the starting-point of the small steamer which ascends the Conway to Trefriw (comp. pp. 283, 307). The small pier lies a little below (to the N. of) the railway station. At Conway the steamboat-pier is just above the bridges.

From Llandudno Junction to ***Bettws-y-Coed*** and ***Ffestiniog***, see R. 40*d*.

Beyond Llandudno Junction the train crosses the wide mouth of the *Conway* by an iron *Tubular Bridge*, 410 ft. long and 18 ft. above high-water mark, constructed by Robert Stephenson and Fairbairn in 1846-48, and similar to that over the Menai Strait, though on a smaller scale (see p. 288). The road crosses the river by a graceful suspension-bridge (1/2*d.*) by Telford, close to the railway.

45 1/2 M. **Conway** (*Castle*; *Erskine Arms*; *Castle View*), also called *Aberconway*, is an ancient and picturesque little town on the left bank of the *Conway*, formerly strongly fortified, and still surrounded with walls, which are pierced by four Moorish-looking gates built at the time of the Crusades. Among the few remaining mediæval buildings is the *Plas Mawr*, a timber house dating from 1584, and said to have been once occupied by Queen Elizabeth and the Earl of Leicester; it stands in a lane leaving the High St. nearly opposite the Castle Hotel. The *Church of St. Mary*, mainly in the Dec. style, contains a fine rood-loft and the monument of Nicholas Hooker, the 41st child of his father and himself the father of 27 children.

*Conway Castle is finely situated on a rock rising above the river, and as seen from the E. (*e. g.* from the suspension bridge) is perhaps the most beautiful ruin in Wales. It was built by Edward I. in 1284, to hold the Welsh in check, and was designed by Henry de Elreton, the gifted architect to whom we also owe the castles of Carnarvon and Beaumaris.

In shape the castle is an irregular oblong, the walls of which, 12-15 ft. in thickness, are strengthened by eight massive, circular towers. Each of the towers was formerly surmounted by a graceful turret, as at Carnarvon, but only four of these now remain. We enter (adm. 3*d.*), at the N.W. angle, by a flight of steps ascending to the W. front. From the terrace at the top we pass, to the left, through a portcullised gateway, into the *Great Court*. To the right is the ***Banqueting Hall***, 130 ft. long and 32 ft. wide; the roof and floor are gone, but the level of the latter may be traced by the fireplaces. The ***Chapel*** was at the E. end of the hall. Near the E. end of the court is the old well, beyond which we pass into the ***Inner Court***, enclosed by the dwelling-rooms of the castle. The N.E. or ***Queen's Tower*** contains Queen Eleanor's private oratory, with a beautiful oriel window. The tower opposite (S.E.), called the ***King's Tower***, has a dungeon below it. The so-called '***Broken Tower***', to the W. of the last, lost much of its picturesqueness by reconstruction. The terrace at the

E. end of the castle, where there was formerly an entrance from the river, affords a good view of the Conway. For a view of the town of Conway visitors should ascend to the top of the walls.

Edward I. himself was besieged by the Welsh in this castle, and is said to have been in imminent danger until the subsidence of 'Conway's foaming flood' allowed reinforcements to reach him. In the Great Civil War it was held for the king, first by Archbp. Williams, a native of Conway, and then by Prince Rupert, but had to yield to the Parliamentarians.

On leaving the castle, visitors may take a pleasant stroll along the wooded knoll of *Bodlondeb*, rising from the Conway just to the N. of the town. The walk may be extended (W.) to (2 M.) *Conway Mount* (807ft.), or the *Town Hill*, on the top of which are traces of a fortified camp (fine view). We may follow the ridge westwards to *Allt Wen*, and descend into the *Sychnant Pass* (550 ft.), whence we may either return to (2½ M.) Conway by the main road, or go on to (1 M.) Dwygyfylchi (see below), Penmaenmawr (2 M.; see below), or the (¾ M.) Fairy Glen (see below).

As the train leaves Conway we have a view of Llandudno and the Great Orme to the right, and of Conway Mount to the left. We pass under *Penmaenbach* by a tunnel, beyond which Anglesey and Puffin Island come in sight on our right, in front. To the left are Dwygyfylchi (see below) and *Foel Llys* (1180 ft.). — 50 M. **Penmaenmawr** *(Penmaenmawr Hotel; Mountain View)*, a pleasant little marine resort, is delightfully situated at the foot of the hill of the same name ('great head of the rock'; 1550 ft.), a huge mass of crystalline rock descending almost vertically to the sea and forming the northernmost buttress of the Snowdon range.

A pleasant and easy walk may be taken to the pretty little *Fairy Glen* (adm. 4*d.*), either direct (1¾ M.), or viâ the village of *Dwygyfylchi* (Doo-i-gi-vulchy) and the *Sychnant Pass* ('dry valley'; 2½ M.). The top of Penmaenmawr Hill (ascent 1 hr.), with its numerous granite quarries, is crowned with the remains of an ancient fort and commands a view ranging from Snowdon on the S. to the Isle of Man on the N. Good walkers may follow the semicircular ridge, of which Penmaenmawr forms the N.W. horn, to (2 hrs.) *Foel Llys* (1180 ft.), and descend thence to their starting-point. On a hill about halfway round the semicircle are the *Meini-Hirion* ('long stones'), a circle of standing stones of doubtful origin. The direct route from Penmaenmawr to the (2 M.) Meini-Hirion is through the 'Green Gorge'.

52½ M. *Llanfairfechan* (Queen's), a small watering-place. — 55 M. **Aber** *(Bulkeley Arms)*, a village situated ½ M. from the coast, at the mouth of a lovely glen. Aber lies immediately opposite Beaumaris in Anglesey, and it was once possible to cross the sands at low water; several persons, however, were drowned in the attempt in 1817. In the middle of the village is a mound called the *Mwd*, said to have been the site of a castle where Llewelyn received the summons of Edward I. to surrender his principality.

The ***Glen of the Aber**, the entrance to which is flanked by *Maes-y-gaer* (753 ft.; view) on the E. and *Fridd-du* on the W., is one of the prettiest of the smaller valleys in Wales. About ½ M. from Aber the road crosses the graceful *Pont Newydd*, but the path to the head of the glen and the (1½ M.) **Aber Falls* keeps to the right and soon crosses a foot-bridge. The larger fall ('Rhaiadr Mawr') descends in a series of leaps, with a total height of 180 ft., and after rain is of considerable volume. The smaller fall, ½ M. to the W., lies on the way to *Moel Wnion* (1905 ft.; 'Oonion'), the ridge of which offers a pleasant route for returning to Aber (1-1½ hr.). — Aber and Llanfairfechan are starting-points for the ascent of *Carnedd Llewelyn* (p. 288; 4-4½ hrs.), viâ *Y Foel Fras* (3091 ft.).

Beyond Aber, Penrhyn Castle (p. 288) is a prominent object on the right, rising from the woods. The train crosses the valley of the *Ogwen* and threads two tunnels, between which the short branch-line to Bethesda (p. 287) diverges to the left.

60 M. **Bangor.** — **Arrival.** The *Railway Station* lies at the S.W. extremity of the town, 1/2 M. from the cathedral; the principal trains are met by hotel-omnibuses and cabs. The *Steamboat Pier* is at the other end of the town, 1 1/4 M. from the station.

Hotels. The *George, a large and finely-situated house, commanding a view of the Menai Strait and Bridges, lies outside Bangor, 1 1/4 M. to the W. of Bangor station, and 1/4 M. from the Menai Bridge station; R. & A. from 4*s.* 6*d.*, table d'hôte D. 4*s.* 6*d.* — *British, near the railway-station, R. & A. from 4*s.*; *Castle, near the cathedral, similar charges; Railway, Williams's Temperance, near the station. — In Upper Bangor, 3/4 M. from the station, Bellevue, pleasantly situated, but not so convenient for a short stay, R. & A. 3*s.* — *Railway Refreshment Rooms.*

Cabs. Per hour 2*s.* 6*d.*, each addit. 1/4 hr. 8*d.* — From the railway station to any part of the town 1*s.*; to the George Hotel 1*s.* 6*d.*; to Menai Bridge 2*s.*; to Penrhyn Castle 2*s.* 6*d.*; to Bethesda 5*s.* 6*d.*; to Penrhyn Quarries 6*s.* 6*d.*; to Beaumaris 7*s.* Carriage and pair about one-half more. Driver's fees and moderate luggage included.

Coaches. Coach daily through the *Pass of Nant Ffrancon* to *Llyn Ogwen*, *Capel Curig*, and *Bettws-y-Coed* (21 M. in 5 hrs.; 6*s.*). Omnibus to *Beaumaris* viâ the Suspension Bridge several times a day (7 M.; 1*s.* 6*d.*).

Steamers. To *Llandudno* and *Liverpool* daily in summer, fares 5*s.*, 3*s.*, return 8*s.*, 5*s.* (comp. p. 281); sometimes also up the Menai Strait to *Carnarvon.* Small steamer to *Beaumaris* several times daily from Garth Point (in 20 min.; fare 6*d.*). — *Garth Ferry* (steam-launch) across the strait, 2*d.*

Boats. Sailing-boats 3*s.* per hr., 1*s.* for each addit. 1/2 hr.; rowing boats 2*s.* and 1*s.* Boat to *Menai Bridge* 4*s.*, *Britannia Tubular Bridge* 5*s.*, *Puffin Island* 10*s.*, *Carnarvon* 12*s.* 6*d.* Return-fares one-half more.

Bangor ('high choir'), the seat of a bishop, is a brisk little town with 11,370 inhabitants. *Lower Bangor*, containing the railway-station and the business-portions of the town, occupies the lower part and the mouth of a narrow valley, and consists mainly of one long and irregular street. *Upper Bangor*, the pleasantest residential quarter, is beautifully placed on the ridge separating this valley from the Menai Straits. The town is an excellent centre for excursions in N. Wales, but lacks the bathing and other attractions of a seaside place. *Port Penrhyn*, the harbour of Bangor, lies to the E. of the lower town, and carries on a busy traffic in slates.

The Cathedral, in a low-lying situation near the middle of the town, is among the smallest and plainest of English minsters, but possesses some architectural interest. The original church on this site seems to have been erected in the 6th century, and was followed by three others, the first of which was destroyed in 1071, the second during the Welsh wars of Edward I. (ca. 1282), and the third by Owen Glendower in 1404. The choir was rebuilt about 1496, and the rest of the building early in the 16th century. A complete restoration was undertaken in 1870, under the superintendence of Sir Gilbert Scott. In style it affords examples of E. E., Dec., and Perpendicular. The central tower has not yet been completed.

Interior. The interior of the church is plain but harmonious. The nave and aisles have flat timber roofs, while the choir has good vaulting. The nave, the presbytery, and the choir-windows are Perpendicular. The rest of the choir, the transepts, and the S. aisle-windows are Decorated. In the S. transept is the tomb of Owen Gwynedd, Prince of Wales (d. 1169). — The Sun. services are held at 8, 11.30, and 4, week-day services at 8 and 5 (3 in winter).

The *Bishop's Palace* and the *Deanery*, adjoining the Cathedral, are unpretending buildings.

Bangor is the seat of the UNIVERSITY COLLEGE OF NORTH WALES, which is established in a large and plain building at the E. end of the town. The college, founded in 1883, has 130 students, numerous open scholarships, and excellent biological and other laboratories. Visitors should apply at the university-building.

In the High St., between the Cathedral and the station, is a *Museum*, containing a small ethnological collection. The steep slope of the gorse-clad hill forming the S. boundary of the valley in which the town lies has been laid out as *Recreation Grounds*, affording admirable views to seaward, including the Great Orme's Head. A wall at the top shuts out the view of the Snowdon region, but the visitor may see it by extending his walk to *Felin Esgob*, or the Bishop's Mill, 1/2 M. to the S. — The *Menai Park* in Upper Bangor commands fine views of the Menai Strait and Bridges.

PENRHYN CASTLE AND QUARRIES. Tourists who do not walk or drive the whole way may take the train to (6 M.) Bethesda (1*s*., 9*d*., 6*d*.), visit the (1 M.) Slate Quarries, and walk back to Bangor viâ the Castle (6 M.). Public waggonettes also ply between Bangor and Bethesda (fare 6*d*.). The milestones count from the E. end of Bangor, 1 M. from the station.

Bethesda (*Douglas Arms*, *Victoria*, *Waterloo*, all second class), now a busy and ugly little quarrymen's town with about 10,000 inhab., was formerly a small and pretty village named Glan Ogwen. Most of the quarrymen are Methodists. — To reach the quarries we cross the bridge 1/2 M. to the S. of the centre of the town and ascend to the left to (1/2 M.) the entrance, where we meet the guide. No charge is made for admission, but the guide expects a small fee. The interesting blasting operations take place at 25 min. past each hour; the dinner-hour (11.30 to 12.30) should be avoided.

The PENRHYN SLATE QUARRIES, the largest in the world, employ upwards of 3000 quarrymen and produce about 360 tons of slate per day. The general appearance of the quarry is that of a huge amphitheatre, the successive steps or terraces of which are each about 50 ft. in height. At present the quarry is about 1000 ft. deep, and it is calculated that there are still 1800 ft. of slate to exhaust before the underlying Cambrian grit is reached. Small tramway-lines traverse each terrace to convey the slate to the hydraulic lifts, which raise it to the surface, whence it is dispatched to Port Penrhyn by a small narrow-gauge railway. The quarrymen, who (in good times) earn 25-30*s*. a week, work in gangs of four, two devoting themselves to the actual quarrying of the slate, and the other two splitting and dressing it. The latter operations are interesting to watch, and the visitor may try his hand at splitting, a feat by no means so easy as it looks. Only about 10-15 per cent of the slate quarried is of any commercial value. Four different kinds of slate — red, blue, green, and gray — are found in this one quarry. The dressed slates are classed in different sizes, named queens, duchesses, countesses, and ladies. Each size must be of a certain thickness; thus if a 'queen' is found thinner than the standard she must be cut down to a 'duchess'. — Various little objects carved in slate may be purchased at the entrance.

In returning from Bethesda to Bangor by road we enjoy a fine view of the sea, Anglesey, the Great Orme, and Penmaenmawr, while behind us are the **Mts.** enclosing the pass of Nant Ffrancon (p. 310). — Penrhyn Castle is also prominent. We reach the entrance to the park at the model-village of *Llandegai*, with its pretty church (containing the tomb of Archbp. Williams, p. 285), 3 **M.** from Bethesda and **1 M.** from Bangor. — Instead of keeping to the high-road all the way, we may descend from the bridge leading to the quarry (see p. 287) by a cart-track on the W. side of the stream, which rejoins the road at a bridge about 1 M. to the N. of Bethesda.

Penrhyn Castle (adm. on Tues. and Thurs., 2-5, by tickets obtainable at the Bangor hotels; 1 pers. 2*s.*, each addit. pers. 1*s.*, no gratuities), the seat of Lord Penrhyn, owner of the quarries, is a large and handsome building, in which the difficulty of accommodating the Norman style of architecture to modern domestic requirements has been skilfully grappled with. The keep is an imitation of Rochester Castle. The interior (visitors ring at the entrance in the keep) contains fine carvings in oak, ebony, slate, and Anglesey marble, a '*Hirlas Horn*' (an heirloom of the Elizabethan period), and a few good pictures. *View from the towers. On leaving the house we should walk through the shady park to Port Penrhyn (p. 286).

Bethesda is a good starting-point for ascending *Carnedd Dafydd* (3430 ft.) and *Carnedd Llewelyn* (3482 ft.), twin-peaks, inferior in height to Snowdon alone among Welsh mountains. The ascent of the former takes 2-3 hrs., and the top of Carnedd Llewelyn, with which it is connected by a narrow saddle, flanked on the W. by fine precipitous cliffs, may be reached in 1 hr. more. The *View from these summits is very similar, embracing the sea, Anglesey, and the Ormes to the N.; the Conway valley to the E.; Moel Siabod and Cader Idris (in the distance) to the S.; the pyramidal Tryfan and the Glyders, with Snowdon in the background, to the S.W.; and Elidyr Fawr to the W. — The descent may be made to Capel Curig (p. 316), Aber (p. 285), or Tal-y-Cafn (p. 307). — A coach runs daily in summer from Bethesda to *Llyn Ogwen* (return-fare 2*s.* 6*d.*).

The drive from Bangor to *Bettws-y-Coed*, through Nant Ffrancon, is described in the reverse direction at p. 310. — The ascent of *Snowdon* may be made from Bangor in one day with the aid of the train to *Llanberis* viâ *Carnarvon*.

The two magnificent bridges, crossing the Menai Strait and connecting the mainland with the island of Anglesey, form the great centre of interest in the neighbourhood of Bangor. The ***Suspension Bridge**, 2 M. to the W. of the town, was constructed by Telford in 1819-26, and is a marvel of strength and elegance. To reach the still more wonderful ***Britannia Tubular Bridge, 1** M. to the S., we cross the Suspension Bridge (1*d.*) and follow the road to the left on the Anglesey bank.

The Suspension Bridge is 580 ft. long from pier to pier, and 1000 ft. over all; and the roadway is 100 ft. above the level of the water at high tide. Each of the 16 chains by which it is supported is 1735 ft. in length and is passed through 60 ft. of solid rock at each end. By applying at the cottage at the Anglesey end of the bridge, the traveller may be conducted underground to the place where the chains are fastened. The Menai Bridge is still the longest suspension-bridge in England; but it is not so long as the suspension-bridge over the Danube at Budapest, that over the Hudson at New York, and some others. The bridge commands a fine view of the Menai Strait, the Tubular Bridge, etc.

The Tubular Bridge, which was built by Robert Stephenson in 1846-50, consists of two parallel rectangular tubes or tunnels, formed by the combination of innumerable small tubes, firmly rivetted together. The material is wrought iron, in plates of 1/2-1 inch in thickness. The tubes rest upon five piers, one on the shore at each end and three in the water. The central tower, resting on the Britannia rock which gives name to the bridge, is 230 ft. high, and the line of rails is 104 ft. above the water

The entire bridge is 1840 ft. in length; each of the two central spans is 460 ft. long, each of the side-spans 230 ft. The total weight of iron in the bridge is upwards of 11,000 tons. In the construction of the bridge the chief difficulty was found in floating the large central sections of the tube, each weighing 1600 tons, into their site with the aid of pontoons, and then elevating them and placing them on the towers by huge hydraulic engines. Allowance has been made, by the use of movable rollers, for the expansion of the metal by the summer-heat, which sometimes increases the length of the structure by nearly a foot. On buttresses at each end of the bridge are colossal stone figures of lions couchant, 12 ft. high and 25 ft. long. To the inexperienced eye this bridge may at first appear somewhat insignificant, but a closer inspection, especially from below, soon produces a more adequate appreciation of its enormous proportions. To examine the interior a pass from the engineer at Bangor Station is required. To reach the beach below the bridge we follow a footpath diverging to the right (N.) at the Anglesey end.

The excursion from Bangor to the Bridges may be made in many ways. Menai Bridge station (p. 290) is not far from the Suspension Bridge, and Treborth (p. 291) is near the Britannia Bridge. The Beaumaris omnibus (p. 286) crosses the Suspension Bridge. Pedestrians may walk from Bangor to the Bridges, cross the Suspension Bridge, follow the Anglesey shore to Beaumaris ($4^1/_2$ M.), and return thence by steamer (in all about 12 M. of walking). The Bridges may also be visited by boat (p. 286).

The **Island of Anglesey** ('Isle of the English') or **Mona** (Môn, derivation uncertain), which is about 300 sq. M. in extent and contains 51,416 inhab., offers few picturesque features beyond Beaumaris Castle, the walk along the Menai Strait, Penmon Priory, Red Wharf Bay, and the island of Holyhead. It contains, however, numerous cromlechs, menhirs, and other antiquities.

On a knoll adjoining the Holyhead road, $^1/_4$ M. from the Tubular Bridge, rises the *Anglesey Column*, erected in 1816 in memory of the Marquis of Anglesey, second in command at Waterloo. The top (90 ft.; adm. 3*d.*) commands a splendid *Panorama of Anglesey, the Menai Straits, and the Carnarvonshire Mts. — *Plas Newydd*, seat of the Marquis of Anglesey, lies $1^1/_4$ M. to the S.; the grounds, containing two cromlechs, are open to the public in the absence of the family.

Beaumaris (*Williams-Bulkeley Arms*, opposite the pier, R. & A. from 4*s.*, D. 4*s.* 6*d.*, 'pens'. 10*s.* 6*d.*; *Liverpool Arms*), is a quiet little watering-place, the chief charm of which is the fine view it commands of the opposite coast, with the Snowdonian mountains in the background. The *Church* dates from the 13th cent., with a choir of the 16th century. The name Beaumaris, locally pronounced 'Bewmorris', is derived from its low-lying site ('beau marais'). — Routes from Bangor, see p. 286. The Liverpool steamers also call here in summer (comp. p. 281).

***Beaumaris Castle** (adm. 2*d.*), to the N. of the town, is another of the Welsh fortresses due to the vigour of Edward I. and the genius of Henry de Elreton (comp. pp. 284, 291). It is an extensive ruin, and in ground-plan is not very dissimilar to the castles of Carnarvon and Conway; but it cannot compete with either of these ruins in external picturesqueness. The castle proper is surrounded by an outer line of circumvallation, also strengthened with circular towers. The interior of the large central court is, however, very beautiful. We enter the quadrangle on the S. side, and see before us, at the N. end, the remains of the *Great Hall*, 70 ft. long and 24 ft. broad, lighted by five beautifully-traceried windows and draped with luxuriant ivy. On the E. side of the court, on the first floor, is the *Chapel*, an E. E. room with a Dec. arcade round it and four squints at the W. end. The various remains of the domestic apartments are also interesting. At the S. end of the court are the bases of large circular towers and other indications that apartments similar to those at the N. end once stood here. Fine views may be obtained from the top of the walls. The history of the castle is uninteresting, if we except the fact that it held out for Charles I., but had to yield to the inevitable General Mytton (p. 280).

The grounds of *Baron Hill*, the seat of the Bulkeley family, on the hill behind Beaumaris, are open to the public on Thurs. and Sun. afternoons. The lofty *Obelisk*, prominent in most views of Beaumaris, is a memorial to Sir Rich. Bulkeley (d. 1875). — *Henllys*, the seat of Col. Lewis, 1 M. to the N.W. of Beaumaris, contains a few paintings, and in the garden of the lodge next the town ('Curiosity Lodge') is a collection of old stone fonts and querns.

From Beaumaris to the Tubular Bridge, 6 M. The well-shaded road skirts the shore nearly all the way to the (4$^1/_2$ M.) Suspension Bridge and commands various fine views of the Strait and the opposite mainland. At low tide the strait contracts to the width of a fair-sized river, exposing large tracts of sand on each side; and it is then not difficult to realise that it was formerly fordable at the time of ebb (comp. p. 285). After 2 M. we pass the gates of a drive to Baron Hill, and beyond them reach the ferry to Bangor (2*d.*; Inn). After 2 M. more the road ascends to *Menai Bridge Village* (Victoria; Bulkeley Arms); the railway-station is on the other side (see below). About $^1/_3$ M. beyond the village we reach a gate on the left, from which a path leads through a fir-plantation and across a causeway to the curious little *Llandisilio Church*, romantically situated on an islet. Returning to the road and following it for 1 M. farther, we reach the Anglesey Column and the Tubular Bridge (see p. 289). Llanfair railway-station (see below) is $^1/_2$ M. beyond the Column.

From Beaumaris to Penmon Priory, 4 M. Passing the Castle and crossing the Green towards the N., we reach the road again at ($^1/_2$ M.) a modern house called the *Friars*. Here we take the branch to the right, and in a few hundred yards turn inland. If we keep to the road we pass near (2$^3/_4$ M.) *Castell Lleiniog*, a small Norman stronghold, dating from 1080. [A detour may be saved by following the shore all the way.] **Penmon Priory**, a Benedictine house, was originally founded in the 6th cent., but the Norman *Church*, restored in 1854, is the oldest part of the present buildings. (Key of church kept by the clerk, near the lighthouse, $^1/_2$ M. farther on.) To the S. of the church is the ruined *Refectory*, dating from the 13th cent.; the lintel of the window in the S.E. corner is formed of an ancient British cross. To the E. is a curious old *Dovecote*. Refreshments may be obtained in the house between the church and the refectory, on the site of the old prior's lodgings. Interesting old cross in the deer-park, to the W.

Puffin Island (*Priestholm*, *Ynys Seiriol*), separated from the N. E. point of Anglesey by a channel $^1/_2$ M. wide, contains the tower of a very ancient church, erected in connection with Penmon. The island is frequented in the breeding-season by great quantities of puffin-auks.

Red Wharf Bay, on the N. coast of Anglesey, 6 M. from Beaumaris (8 M. by road viâ *Pentraeth*), is a picturesque inlet, with smooth and firm sands. There is a small Hotel at the W. end, and at the E. end is the village of *Llanddona*, 1$^1/_2$ M. from which is *Bwrdd Arthur*, or Arthur's Table, a height affording the most extensive view in Anglesey.

From the Britannia Bridge (p. 289) the railway runs on, passing *Llanfair* (see above) to *Gaerwen*, the junction of a line to (18 M.) *Amlwch* (Dinorden Arms; *Bull Bay Hotel, 1$^3/_4$ M. to the N.W.), a small town and watering-place on the N. coast of Anglesey. The railway ends at (22 M.) **Holyhead** (*Marine Hotel; North Western*), the starting-point of the mail-steamers to Dublin (60 M., in 4 hrs.). The chief object of interest near Holyhead is the bold rocky scenery of the **North* and **South Stack* (lighthouse on the latter). Good view from *Holyhead Mountain* (720 ft.). The *Breakwater* is 1$^1/_2$ M. long.

Continuation of Railway to Carnarvon. Beyond Bangor the train passes through a long tunnel and stops at (61 M.) *Menai Bridge Station* (view of Suspension Bridge; comp. p. 288). Our line diverges here from the Dublin mail-route to Holyhead, which runs to the right through the Tubular Bridge (p. 290). Good views to the right of the Menai Strait and Bridges. 62 M. *Treborth;* 64½ M. *Port Dinorwic*, the port of the Llanberis slate-quarries.

68½ M. **Carnarvon.** — **Hotels.** *ROYAL, near the railway-station, old-fashioned, R. & A. 4*s.*; *ROYAL SPORTSMAN, Castle Street; CASTLE, Castle Sq.; QUEEN'S, PRINCE OF WALES, Bangor St., unpretending.

Coach daily round Snowdon, viâ Beddgelert and Llanberis, starting about 11 a.m. and regaining Carnarvon about 6 p.m. (a round of 35 M.).

Ferry Steamer from Victoria Pier, below the Castle, to Anglesey, several times daily (3*d.*).

Carnarvon or *Caernarvon* (*Caer-yn-ar-Fon*, the 'fort opposite Mona'), an ancient town with 10,170 inhab., is situated on the Menai Strait at the mouth of the river *Seiont*, near the site of the Roman *Segontium*. It is an old-fashioned place, with narrow and irregular streets, and a castle usually regarded as the finest in the kingdom. The central position of the town and its convenient railway-connections make it a good starting-point for excursions. The *Twt Hill* (190 ft.), behind the Royal Hotel (lane to the left, just beyond the hotel), commands a general view of the town and castle.

North Road and Bangor Street lead in an almost straight line from the station to the (½ M.) ***Castle,** which occupies the whole W. end of the town and is washed on two sides by the waters of the Seiont and the Menai Strait. It is one of the most imposing and extensive mediæval fortresses in Europe, and is built entirely of hewn stone. Before entering the castle the visitor should walk round it, or, better still, cross the Seiont and view it from the opposite shore. Carnarvon Castle was begun by Edward I. in 1283, and may be looked upon as the masterpiece of his architect, Henry de Elreton (comp. pp. 284, 289). It was not finished, however, till the reign of Edward II. The castle has recently undergone considerable restoration. Visitors are not admitted to the restored apartments. The principal *Gateway* (adm. 4*d.*), on the N. side, is surmounted by a mutilated figure of Edward I.

The ground-plan of the castle is an irregular oblong or oval, originally divided into two courts by a wall. The walls, 8-14 ft. in thickness, are strengthened by several polygonal towers, surmounted by graceful turrets. Iron standards bearing numbers have been placed in the interior to mark the site and shape of the different apartments formerly existing here, and lines are cut in the grass with the same object. Passing through the principal gateway, we enter the upper court close to the line of demarcation between it and the lower court. The most generally interesting part is the *Eagle's Tower*, at the W. end (to the right), in which Edward II., the first 'Prince of Wales', is said to have been born in 1284. Most authorities consider that this has been conclusively disproved; but Sir Llewelyn Turner, Deputy Constable of the Castle, maintains the accuracy of the popular tradition. The small chamber, which is pointed out as that in which the prince was born, measuring 12 ft. by 8 ft., is on the first floor of the tower, on a level with the gallery round the walls, and overlooking the Menai Strait. The turrets of the Eagle Tower, the name of which is derived from the eagles placed on one of them, command a fine view.. The interior of the *Queen's Tower* has been restored, and now contains a Masonic Lodge and the armoury of the Royal Naval Volunteers. — At the opposite end of the castle is the *Queen's Gate*, formerly approached by a drawbridge, but now closed. Tradition points out this gate as the place where the infant Edward was exhibited to the people as a 'prince of Wales who could speak no English'. There is also a postern in the base of the Eagle's Tower, from which a flight of steps descends to the river. — The 'shouldered arch' is sometimes called the Carnarvon arch from its general use in this castle.

The Town Walls of Carnarvon still exist, and visitors may walk round them in less than half-an-hour. On leaving the Castle we should turn to the right and pass round its river-front, where the quay is covered with slate from the quarries of Llanberis (p. 314). Beyond the Eagle Tower begins an *Esplanade*, which skirts the outside of the wall on this side, and forms a pleasant walk along the Menai Strait. The towers are now occupied by the County Gaol, the Royal Welsh Yacht Club, the North Wales Training College, and the vestry of St. Mary's Church (at the N.W. angle).

The site of **Segontium,** one of the most important Roman stations in Wales, lay about 1/2 M. to the E. of Carnarvon, on the road to Beddgelert, and traces of it may still be seen on the outskirts of the town and near the church of *Llanbeblig*, the mother-church of Carnarvon. From Llanbeblig we may walk across the fields to the *Park* on the S. bank of the Seiont, and return to the town by the Aber ferry (comp. p. 291).

From Carnarvon to *Llanberis*, see p. 314; to *Beddgelert*, see p. 317; to *Afon Wen*, *Port Madoc*, and *Barmouth*, see below.

b. From Carnarvon to Afon Wen, Port Madoc, and Barmouth.

451/2 M. Railway (L. N. W.) from Carnarvon to (18 M.) *Afon Wen* in 3/4-1 hr. (fares 3*s.* 4*d.*, 2*s.* 3*d.*, 1*s.* 6*d.*); from Afon Wen (Cambrian Railway) to (271/2 M.) *Barmouth* in 11/4-11/2 hr. (fares 5*s.* 2*d.*, 3*s.* 6*d.*, 2*s.* 31/2*d*).

The first part of this sub-route, completing the 'outer circle' of railway round North Wales, is comparatively little traversed by tourists, most of whom make their way from Carnarvon to Port Madoc viâ Snowdon and Beddgelert (comp. p. 317). — Comp. Map, p. 318.

As the train leaves Carnarvon we have a good retrospect of the castle to the right. It then crosses the Seiont. 31/4 M. *Dinas*, the junction of the narrow-gauge line to Snowdon Ranger and Rhyd-ddu (p. 317). — 7 M. *Pen-y-Groes*, the junction of a short line to (2 M.) *Nantlle* ('Nanthly'; Inn), a conglomeration of slate-quarries. Fine view to the left, up the valley, of Snowdon and the rocky hill called *Old Meredith*, resembling an upturned face.

The walk from Nantlle, through the pass, to the Carnarvon and Beddgelert valley, passes two or three small lakes and commands a still finer view of Snowdon. The distance to the Snowdon Ranger is about 6 M. — On the coast, 41/2 M. to the S.W. of Pen-y-Groes, is the village of *Clynnog* (Newborough Arms), with a large and handsome Perp. church 15-16th cent.), the holy well of St. Beuno, and a good cromlech.

11 M. *Pantglas* lies nearly opposite the *Rivals* ('Yr Eifl'; 1890 ft.), a graceful hill or group of hills to the right. On the E. peak are the remains of a British stronghold called *Tre'r Ceiri* (*View). — Moel Hebog (p. 319) also comes into view on the left.

18 M. *Afon Wen* (Rail. Rfmt. Rooms) is the point where the L.N.W.R. joins the Cambrian system (carriages changed). The station

(there is no village) lies on *Cardigan Bay*, and commands fine views both seaward and landward.

From Afon Wen to Pwllheli, 4 M., railway in 10 min. (fares 9*d.*, 6*d.*, 4*d.*). — **Pwllheli**, pron. *Poothlhely* (*Crown; Tower; Madryn Arms*), the terminus of the Cambrian Railway, is a small and quiet bathing-place, with perhaps the finest sandy beach in Wales and a new esplanade opened in 1890. Fine view from the *Carreg-y-Rimbill*, or *Gimlet Rock*, on the W. side of the harbour.

Pwllheli forms the most convenient headquarters from which to explore the **Lleyn Promontory**, a district little known and of comparatively small attraction. The inn-accommodation is of the scantiest. The principal excursions from Pwllheli are along the coast to (14 M.) *Aberdaron* (Ship Inn; omn. or mail-cart 2*s.*), and to the N.W. to (7½ M.) *Nevin* (Nanhoron Arms; omn. or mail-cart 1*s.*). Pwllheli may also be made the starting-point for the ascent of the *Rivals* (p. 292), which lie about 6 M. to the N. (better from Nevin). — Aberdaron is about 3 M. from *Braich-y-Pwll*, the 'Land's End' of N. Wales, and the walk thither reveals some fine coast-scenery. A conspicuous feature in the views is *Bardsey Isle*, which lies about 2 M. off the point and may in fine weather be reached from Aberdaron (boat about 1*l.*). The island was formerly a favourite burying-place, and contains according to tradition the graves of 20,000 saints. It also contains the scanty remains of a once famous abbey.

From Afon Wen the railway to Port Madoc runs to the E., along the N. coast of Cardigan Bay, to (22½ M.) **Criccieth** (*George IV.; White Lion*), a small sea-bathing resort, the chief attraction of which is its nearness to the finest part of Snowdonia. Its ruined *Castle* (adm. 1*d.*), on a hill between the station and the shore, was probably built by Edward I.; it commands a good view of the Mts. of Carnarvon and Meriónethshire, and of Harlech Castle (p. 294) on the other side of the bay. — Beyond Criccieth the train quits the coast for a short distance. Fine mountain-view to the left.

28 M. **Port Madoc** (*Sportsman; Queen's*, close to the station), the port for the Ffestiniog slate-quarries, is the starting-point of the 'toy-railway' to Ffestiniog (p. 313), and of the direct road to Beddgelert and Snowdon from the S. (Coach to Beddgelert, 8 M., several times daily; fare 2*s.* 6*d.*; comp. p. 319.)

About 1 M. to the N. of Port Madoc, on the road to Beddgelert, lies *Tremadoc*, a village at the foot of a picturesque line of cliffs. Both places take their name from a Mr. Madocks, M. P., who founded them at the beginning of this cent. and at the same time reclaimed the *Traeth-Mawr* (see Map, p. 318) by building a huge embankment across the mouth of the estuary. Shelley, who spent part of 1812-13 at *Tanyrallt*, Tremadoc, took a keen interest in the Faust-like undertaking of Mr. Madocks, and freely spent his energies and money in promoting it. *Moel-y-Gest* (750 ft.), the hill to the W. of Port Madoc, commands an extensive panorama.

Beyond Port Madoc the train crosses the above-mentioned embankment, or 'Cob', which affords a grand *View of Snowdon, rising at the head of the valley to the left, with Moel Hebog to the left of it, and the Glyders, Cynicht, and Moelwyn to its right.

30 M. *Mynffordd* is the junction for the Toy Railway to Ffestiniog (p. 314), which is here carried over the Cambrian line. — 31 M. *Penrhyndeudraeth*, a quarrymen's village, also a station of the Ffestiniog line (p. 313). Harlech Castle is visible to the right, in the distance. We now round the head of the estuary and turn

to the S. Beyond (33 M.) *Talsarnau* a series of fine retrospects (right) is obtained of Snowdonia, while the graduated hills of the Lleyn promontory are visible beyond Cardigan Bay. The line here runs across the *Morfa Harlech*, a level tract reclaimed from the sea.

36 M. **Harlech** *(*Castle; Lion)*, the old capital of Merionethshire, is a small place with only a few hundred inhabitants. Its *Castle* (adm. 4*d.*), one of the numerous buildings of Edward I., has been well described as 'the ideal castle of childhood — high-perched, foursquare, round-towered, and impressively massive'.

The well-known 'March of the Men of Harlech' commemorates the capture of the castle by the Yorkists in 1468. It was the last stronghold in N. Wales to hold out for Charles I. The castle commands a magnificent panorama of sea and mountain; and another very fine view of Snowdonia may be obtained from the top of *Moel-y-Senicl*, $1^1/_2$ M. to the E. From Moel-y-Senicl we may make our way to Cwm Bychan and the Rhinogs (more conveniently reached from Llanbedr; see below).

$38^1/_2$ M. *Llanbedr and Pensarn.* The village of *Llanbedr* (Victoria), situated on the *Afon Artro*, one of the best trout-streams in Wales, lies about $^3/_4$ M. to the S. of the station. The peninsula of *Mochras*, $1^1/_2$ M. from Llanbedr, is celebrated for its rare shells, and the neighbourhood abounds in cromlechs and other antiquities.

Llanbedr is the usual starting-point for a visit to Cwm Bychan, the Rhinogs, and the pass of Ardudwy, an excursion comprising the finest scenery in this part of Wales. Public conveyances ply in summer to and from ($5^1/_2$ M.) Cwm Bychan; but the best plan is to hire a carriage to Cwm Bychan, send it to meet us at Maes-y-Garnedd (see below), and walk round through the pass. This involves a drive of 12 M. and a walk of about 2 hrs. ***Cwm Bychan** is a lonely and romantic hollow, containing a small lake, and enclosed by the precipitous crags of the *Rhinog Fawr* (2345 ft.) on the S. and the *Craig Dwrg* (2100 ft.) on the N. A good echo may be awakened on the shore of the little llyn. The carriage-road ends here, but all who are able should go on to a point about 100 yds. beyond the lake, and then proceed to the right to the 'Roman Steps', a rude staircase of slabs of rocks, believed to have been formed either by the ancient Britons or the Romans. This leads to the (1 hr.) head of the pass named *Bwlch-y-Tyddiad*, whence the path descends to the N. to the village of (5 M.) Trawsfynydd (p. 303). We, however, soon diverge from the path and cross the valley to the right, skirting the E. side of the Rhinog Fawr, so as to reach the ***Bwlch Drws Ardudwy**, or pass of the 'Gate of Ardudwy', a well-marked depression between the Rhinog Fawr on the N. and the *Rhinog Fach* on the S. The scenery here is remarkably wild and sombre. Our route now leads nearly due W., and about 1 hr. after leaving the Bwlch-y-Tyddiad we reach the farm of *Maes-y-Garnedd*, whence we may drive back to ($6^1/_2$ M.) *Llanbedr.* — The **Rhinog Fawr**, which is most easily ascended (2 hrs.) from *Pen-y-Bont*, 2 M. from Llanbedr on the road to Cwm Bychan, commands a wide and interesting view, taking in Snowdon on the N. and Cader Idris on the S.

Beyond Llanbedr we have a view to the left of the Rhinogs, Llethr, and Diphwys, while the rounded green Moelfre rises in the foreground. $41^1/_2$ M. *Dyffryn*, another starting-point for a visit to the Ardudwy pass (see above). The ascent of *Moelfre* from Dyffryn takes 2 hrs. Between Dyffryn and Barmouth we pass on the left the woods of *Cors-y-Gedol* and the church of *Llanaber* (p. 296).

$45^1/_2$ M. **Barmouth.** — **Hotels**: Cors-y-Gedol, in the main street; Marine, well spoken of, on the Esplanade, facing the sea; Barmouth (R.

& A. 3*s*.), LION, unpretending, in the main street; TAL-Y-DON, a small private hotel, near the station. — **Lodgings** may also be easily procured (dear in Aug. and Sept.).

Boats on hire for fishing, and for excursions by sea or river. The usual charge for a boat to *Penmaen Pool*, at the head of the estuary, is 6*s*.

Barmouth, a corruption of the Welsh *Abérmaw* ('the mouth of the Mawddach'), a thriving watering-place, is situated at the N. entrance of the beautiful estuary of the *Mawddach*, on a narrow site between the sea and a barrier of rocky hills. It is within easy access of much of the grandest scenery in Mid-Wales, but in itself cannot vie as a marine residence with either Llandudno or Tenby. The sands are extensive and well adapted for bathing, but lack the charms of the curving outline and rocky boundaries of the bays at the places just mentioned, while another serious drawback is the fact that the railway has been carried between the town and the sea. The lofty railway-embankment has, however, the merit of protecting the place from the loose sand with which it used to be inundated; and the new *Esplanade*, to the N. of the station and on the seaward side of the railway, bears ample witness to the need of some such screen. The town is also destitute of a landward view.

About 1/2 M. to the S. of the station the railway crosses the estuary of the Mawddach by a fine ***Bridge**, or viaduct, 1/2 M. in length, including a footway, 8 ft. wide (toll 2*d*., weekly ticket 6*d*.). The *View up the Mawddach from this bridge, especially at high water, is charming. The wide expanse of the estuary resembles a large lake surrounded with wooded hills, which are backed by loftier and more rugged mountains, while the beauty of the scene is greatly enhanced by the delicacy and variety of the colouring.

On the left or N. side of the estuary the background is formed by the *Llawllech* range, culminating in the rounded *Diphwys*. To the right is the range of *Cader Idris* (p. 301), the most prominent peak being the *Tyrau Mawr*, to the left of which appears the true summit. In the minor ridge in front, farther to the E., is a hill known as the 'Giant's Head', from its resemblance to an upturned face. The most conspicuous hill at the head of the estuary, straight in front of us, is *Moel Offrwm* (1200 ft.). behind which, a little to the left, towers *Rhobell-Fawr* (2410 ft.). The prospect to seaward includes the *Lleyn* (p. 293) and *Bardsey Isle* (p. 293).

Excursions from Barmouth.

*PANORAMA WALK. At the end of Porkington Terrace, near the bridge, we quit the road and ascend the steep lane to the left. Where the lane forks (6 min.) we keep to the right; 4 min. gate; 8 min. another gate (sign-post), where the grassy track, ascending to the right, is to be avoided. In 3 min. more (sign-post) we trun to the right, bend back a little, and pass through a gap in the hill to the (4 min.) lodge, where we pay 1*d*. for admission to the ***Panorama Walk**, a path skirting the brow of the hill to the right, 200 ft. above the Mawddach estuary. The beautiful view is a 'bird's-eye edition' of that from the bridge (see above). The sloping summits of the *Arans* (p. 302), however, here form a more prominent feature in the background to the E. — We may now return to the lodge and descend to the Dolgelley road, which we may follow along the bank of the estuary to (2 M.) Barmouth. Or we may make our way back to the point where we quitted the lane (at the sign-post, beyond the second gate) and follow this lane for a few yards more. We then turn to the left and ascend the hill, passing (5 min.) the small farm of *Gwastadannes*. A short way beyond the farm the path forks; the branch to the right, uphill, leads to *Cell-Fawr* and *Llanaber* (see below), while that on the left descends to Barmouth.

Llanaber and Cors-y-Gedol, $5^1/_2$ M. About $1^3/_4$ M. to the N. of Barmouth, on the road to Harlech, is the interesting church of **Llanaber**, an E. E. building of the 13th cent., with a fine interior (key kept at an adjoining cottage). The solitary lancet window at the E. end is an unusual feature. The entrance-lodge to Cors-y-Gedol is $2^3/_4$ M. farther on, opposite the church of *Llanddwywe*. The drive thence to **Cors-y-Gedol**, formerly the seat of the ancient but now extinct family of the Vaughans, is nearly 1 M. long. The grounds contain some fine timber, and in the house, which is shown to visitors on previous written application to the owner (Mr. Ed. F. Coulson), are paintings by Rubens, Rembrandt, Hogarth ('Strolling Players rehearsing in a barn'), Reynolds, and Turner. About $^1/_2$ M. from the house (follow the cart-track to the right, beyond the farmyard) is a cromlech called *Arthur's Quoit*, said to have been hurled by that doughty monarch from the top of Moelfre (p. 294). — This excursion to Cors-y-Gedol scarcely repays the pedestrian, but should be made either by carriage or by train to *Dyffryn* ($1^3/_4$ M. from Cors-y-Gedol House). A pleasant round for walkers (about 7 M. in all) may be made as follows: From Barmouth to Llanaber, $1^3/_4$ M.; from Llanaber across the Llawllech range, passing the farm of Cell-Fawr (see above), to the Panorama View, $3^1/_4$ M.; back to Barmouth, either by the Dolgelley road or by the route above described, 2 M. This round may be increased to about 11 M. by extending the walk to Cors-y-Gedol and returning thence over the hills, while robust walkers may include the ascent of *Diphwys* (2467 ft.; View), which will add $2^1/_2$-3 hrs. to the excursion. The ascent is most often made from *Penmaenpool* (see below; $2^1/_2$-3 hrs.).

The *Road from Barmouth to Dolgelley, along the N. bank of the Mawddach, forms one of the finest drives in Wales, and is preferable to the railway. About 2 M. from Barmouth the road quits the Mawddach for a time. $2^1/_2$ M. *Pont-ddu* (Halfway House), pleasantly situated in a little wooded glen with a waterfall. Diphwys may be ascended hence in $1^1/_2$ hr. The road to the left ascends to some abandoned gold mines. Beyond Pont-ddu the road returns to the estuary and affords fine views of the opposite shore. $1^1/_2$ M. Bridge crossing to *Penmaenpool* (see above); $1^1/_2$ M. *Llanelltyd*. It then crosses the Mawddach, here an ordinary stream, and soon reaches (2 M.) *Dolgelley* (p. 297).

As the centre from which railways branch to the N., E., and S., Barmouth affords facilities for numerous longer excursions, such as those to *Llanbedr* and *Mochras* (p. 294); *Cwm Bychan* and *Drws Ardudwy* (p. 294); *Harlech* (p. 294); *Towyn* (p. 266); *Aberdovey* (p. 266); and *Machynlleth* (p. 265). — The ascent of *Cader Idris* (p. 297) is often made from Barmouth, occupying about 7-8 hrs. (there and back), but the actual starting-point is *Arthog* (p. 297), to which we proceed by train.

From Barmouth to *Aberystwith*, see p. 267.

c. From Barmouth to Dolgelley, Bala, Llangollen, and Chester.

71 M. Railway in $3^1/_2$-4 hrs. (fares 14*s.* 9*d.*, 10*s.* 2*d.*, 5*s.* 11*d.*); to *Dolgelley*, $9^1/_2$ M., in $^1/_2$ hr. (fares 3*s.* 6*d.*, 2*s.* 6*d.*, 1*s.*). The line from Barmouth to Dolgelley belongs to the Cambrian Co., but the G. W. R. Co., whose system we join at Dolgelley, has running powers as far as Barmouth.

On leaving Barmouth the train crosses the estuary of the *Mawddach* by the bridge mentioned at p. 295, commanding a magnificent view up the river to the left, and a survey of the *Lleyn* peninsula to the right. $1^3/_4$ M. *Barmouth Junction* (Rfmt. Rooms), at the S. end of the bridge, is the point where our line leaves the Cambrian route running S. to Aberdovey and Aberystwith (p. 267).

3 M. *Arthog* (Arthog Hall Hotel) is a small village at the foot of the spurs of the Cader Idris ridge. The *Arthog Lakes*, 1 M. to the E., are frequented by anglers (apply at the hotel). The 'Barmouth Ascent' of **Cader Idris** begins here (see below), and a guide (1*s.* per pers.; unnecessary) generally meets the morning-trains.

Ascent of Cader Idris from Arthog (Barmouth), 3 hrs. From the E. end of Arthog village, a few hundred yards to the S. of the station, we follow the lane ascending to the right. Beyond the trees we pass through a gate, and after ascending for a few min. more, turn to the left by a path leading to a stream (not to be crossed) which we follow to the farm-house of (25 min.) *Pant-y-Llan.* Beyond this the track (indistinct) crosses two fields and reaches the old Dolgelley and Towyn road, which we follow to the left (E.) as far as the farm of *Hafod-y-Fach.* Here we diverge to the right, through a gate, and follow a rough track, which soon brings us out on the open mountain-side. On gaining the (20 min.) top of the ridge, the summit of Cader Idris comes into view, and the rest of our course is plain-sailing, as we have simply to follow the ridge.

The direct route runs to the right of *Tyrau Mawr* (2000 ft.), on its S. slope, and those who do not care to make the whole ascent should at least climb to the top of this, the prominent W. peak of the Cader ridge ($1^1/_4$ hr. from Arthog), commanding a view not inferior to that from the highest point. We now follow the grassy ridge (fine views on both sides) and about 1 M. farther on, near a wall, our track is joined on the left by the bridle-path from Dolgelley (p. 300) and on the right by that from Towyn (p. 266). We now turn to the right and soon begin the final part of the ascent. Where two tracks are visible we should keep to the right. After about $^1/_2$ hr. we pass a good spring, a little beyond which is the point where the ponies are left and the Tal-y-Llyn route (p. 265) joins ours. A climb of 5 min. up a steep winding path now brings us to the summit (2925 ft.), which is marked by a cairn and a small stone hut (very dirty inside). The *View is described at p. 301. — Good walkers on their way to Dolgelley should descend by the 'Foxes' Path' (p. 300). Descent to Tal-y-Llyn and Towyn, see p. 266.

Beyond Arthog the train skirts the Mawddach estuary, affording fine views of the mountains on the opposite side. At ($7^1/_2$ M.) *Penmaenpool* (George Inn) the river is crossed by a bridge and ceases to be navigable. The line now bears to the right, and we obtain a view of the four peaks of Cader Idris (p. 301). As we cross the *Wnion* ('Oonion') we have a peep to the left of the *Ganllwyd* glen (p. 299), down which flows the *Mawddach*, uniting with the Wnion to form the estuary.

$9^1/_2$ M. **Dolgelley.** — **Hotels.** *Royal Ship, R. & A. 4*s.*; Golden Lion; Angel, all in the centre of town, about $^1/_4$ M. from the station and on the other side of the river. — *Lodgings*, moderate.

Brakes make the round of the Torrent and Precipice Walks (see p. 298) during summer.

Fishing. Trout abound in the Wnion, the Aran, and several lakes in the vicinity, permission to fish in which may be obtained at the hotels. The salmon-fishing in the Mawddach, at Tyn-y-Groes, is preserved.

Dolgelley (pron. *Dolgéthly*), the county-town of Meriónethshire, an irregularly-built little place with 2500 inhab., on the left bank of the *Wnion*, near the N. base of *Cader Idris*, is the centre of some of the finest scenery in Wales. The *Church*, recently restored, contains an effigy of a knight. Welsh woollen goods are made here.

Excursions from Dolgelley.

Torrent Walk, a round of 5$^1/_2$ M. The Torrent Walk itself is only 1 M. long, and visitors may drive to one end, and send the carriage round to meet them at the other. We quit the town by the Machynlleth road, which leads to the E., crossing the *Aran*. After 1$^1/_4$ M. we leave the road by a lane to the left, nearly opposite a small quarry, and soon reach ($^1/_2$ M.) a bridge, on this side of which, to the right, is the entrance to the 'Walk'. The *__Torrent Walk__ ascends along the side of an impetuous little mountain stream, and offers a perfect combination of rock, and wood, and water. The stream forms a continuous series of foaming rapids, cataracts, and waterfalls, with most picturesquely placed boulders hemming its course, while the narrow ravine is clothed from top to bottom with luxuriant trees, the branches of which extend from side to side of the torrent. At the upper end of the glen we cross a small foot-bridge into a road, where we turn to the right, pass the entrance-gates of *Caerynwch*, and soon regain the main (Machynlleth) road. Here we turn to the right and follow the road to (2$^1/_2$ M.) Dolgelley; or we may proceed to the left to (1 M.) the *Cross Foxes Inn*, whence the old road, commanding good views of Cader Idris, descends direct to (3 M.) Dolgelley.

Nannau and the Precipice Walk, 6-7 M. We cross the railway at the station, follow the Bala road (to the right) for about 250 yds., and then take the first turning to the left, a lane leading through a gate to a house. Behind the house we turn sharp to the right, along a wall (avoiding the path leading straight up the hill), and after a few yards ascend to the left through trees. In about 3 min. after leaving the cottage we emerge from the wood into the fields, and almost immediately cross a wall by a stile. Here we keep straight on, with first a low wall, then a hedge, and lastly a wood on our right. We then bear to the left, crossing the field diagonally, in the direction of a plantation, which we enter by another stile (4 min. from the last). Our path leads through the plantation to (3 min.) the small farm of *Tydden Bach*, round the front of which we pass into a lane and then turn to the right. 3 min. Gate, beyond which the lane forks. We keep to the left for 3 min. more; then turn to the right and follow a grassy lane to (13 min.) *Maes-y-Brynar Farm*. (Driving is practicable to this point, by another route.) At the farm we turn to the left and follow a rough cart-track (sign-post), which leads in 9 min., trending to the right, to the S. end of *Llyn Cynwch*. The hill to the right of this lake is called *Moel Offrwm* (1200 ft.; view), or the 'hill of offering'. At its foot lies **Nannau**, the old mansion of the Vaughans, finely situated in a beautiful park. — To reach the Precipice Walk, we pass through the gate at the S.W. (left) corner of Llyn Cynwch and climb a stile to the left. A few yards farther on (about 1 hr. from Dolgelley) we cross another stile and reach the *__Precipice Walk__, which runs round the steep slopes of *Moel Cynwch*. At first the walk is a mere green track along a grassy hillside, with rock cropping out, and has little that is precipitous about it. In 5 min. we reach a stile, where we have a fine view of Cader Idris and the estuary of the Mawddach. [Those who make the circuit of the Precipice Walk in the opposite direction may quit it here, and descend to Dolgelley or to Llanelltyd and Cymmer Abbey (p. 299).] 6 min. Another stile. This is the most precipitous bit of the walk; though nowhere sheer, the slope approaches the perpendicular so closely and the path is so narrow that a moderately steady head is desirable. The view of the Mawddach flowing in the narrow *Ganllwyd* glen below us is very fine. We reach another stile in 7-8 min., near the point where the path bends round the N.side of the hill.

[To reach *Tyn-y-Groes* we leave the Precipice Walk at a point about 5 min. beyond this stile. Just below is a wall running almost parallel with this section of the walk, and from this wall another descends at right angles towards the valley. Crossing the first wall and descending to the left of the second, we soon reach a wood, through which a steep and faintly-marked path descends to a cart-track on the left bank of the river. By following this to the right for 1 M. we reach the bridge crossing to *Tyn-y-Groes Inn* (see below). On our way we see the large wheels of a copper-mine to the right. This descent is scarcely adapted for ladies, but good walkers are advised to vary their homeward route by visiting Tyn-y-Groes and following the road to Llanelltyd (see below). They should, however, first follow the Precipice Walk far enough to get a view of Nannau.]

8 min. Stile. This is practically the end of the Precipice Walk. *Rhobell Fawr* (2409 ft.) is conspicuous to the left and Nannau House (p. 298) soon comes in sight. We then again reach Llyn Cynwch and pass along its W. side to the (12 min.) gate by which we entered.

The above is the preferable direction in which to make the circuit of the Precipice Walk, as the scenery improves as we proceed. The circuit from Maes-y-Brynar takes about 1 hr.

Tyn-y-Groes, Rhaiadr-Du, and Pistyll-y-Cain, 8 **M.** (there and back 16 **M.**). Crossing the railway, we turn to the left and follow the Barmouth road for about 1½ M. Here, a little short of Llanelltyd Bridge, a farm-road diverges on the right to (4 min.) *Cymmer Abbey*, a Cistercian foundation, the ruined church of which, dating from about 1200, is worth a visit. The key is kept at the adjoining farm, which incorporates the old 'Abbot's Hall'. (Route hence to Precipice Walk, see p. 298.) Returning to the road and crossing the bridge over the Mawddach we now reach (¼ M.) *Llanelltyd*, where we turn to the right and follow the road ascending the **Glen of Ganllwyd*. To the right, beyond the Mawddach, rises *Moel Cynwch* (p. 298), with the Precipice Walk. After 2 M. the road bends to the left, and the valley contracts and increases in picturesqueness.

¾ M. (4½ M. from Dolgelley) **Tyn-y-Groes Inn** (*Oakley Arms*, plain), a favourite little anglers' resort. We may vary our route in returning to Dolgelley from this point by crossing the bridge in front of the inn and proceeding to the right to the (¾ hr.) Precipice Walk (comp. above).

Beyond Tyn-y-Groes we pass the wooded grounds of *Dolmelynllyn* on the left, and reach a (½ M.) bridge over the *Camlan*. To reach the fall of (⅓ **M.**) ***Rhaiadr-Du** (a pleasant digression of ⅓-½ hr.) we cross the bridge and ascend to the left along the stream, at first by a cart-track and then by a path. The fall is not large, but its surroundings are picturesque.

About ¼ M. beyond the bridge the road forks, and we keep to the right, crossing another bridge over the *Eden*. We then pass through a gate (or over a stile) and enter the wooded glen of the upper Mawddach, which runs to our right, half hidden among the trees. About 12 min. after leaving the gate we see to our right a small foot-bridge, leading to a cottage on the other side of the stream. We, however, keep to the road on this side and in ¼ hr. more pass two new houses and reach the entrance to the *Gunpowder Works*, beyond which the ground is private, though visitors are admitted between sunrise and sunset. Driving is practicable to this point, and carriages may be left here while we go on to visit the Falls. No smoking is allowed on the premises, and matches and cigar-lights must be left at the entrance. A new path to the Falls has been made. The fall of Pistyll-y-Cain is on the *Afon Cain*, just above its junction with the Mawddach, a few yards from the new bridge (to the left); and the Rhaiadr Mawddach is reached by keeping straight on for 2 min. more. The ***Pistyll-y-Cain,** plunging from a height of 150 ft. into a deep rocky cauldron, is one of the most graceful waterfalls in Wales. The **Rhaiadr Mawddach** is wider, but neither so high nor so picturesque.

We may now return to Dolgelley, either by the route already traversed, or by crossing the Mawddach by the bridge a little above the fall and descending on its E. bank. If we select the latter route we turn to the left after about ¼ hr., and wind round the hillside to the (½ hr. valley of the *Afon-yr-Allt*, a feeder of the Mawddach, along which w may descend to the right, passing an old copper-mine, to the (½ hr.) track on the left bank of the Mawddach mentioned above. Thence we) either cross the bridge to Tyn-y-Groes (see above), or return to Dolgelley by the Precipice Walk (comp. p. 298).

The Torrent Walk, the Precipice Walk, and the Tyn-y-Groes and Pistyll-y-Cain excursion may all be included in one long day, somewhat as follows. Drive to one end of Torrent Walk ($^1/_4$ hr.); walk through it ($^1/_2$ hr.); drive from the other end to Maes-y-Brynar or Nannau ($^3/_4$ hr.); make the circuit of the Precipice Walk (1 hr.); drive from Maes-y-Brynar to the Gunpowder Works near Pistyll-y-Cain (3 hrs.); visit the three Falls (1 hr.); drive back to Dolgelley (2 hrs.). This makes $8^1/_2$ hrs., without including stoppages. Good walkers could do the entire round in the same time, descending directly from the Precipice Walk to Tyn-y-Groes (p. 299). The total distance would be 21 M., equivalent to 25-30 M. on a level road.

Ascent of Cader Idris. After that of Snowdon this is the most popular ascent in Wales, and the view from the top is considered by many to surpass that from the higher mountain. From Dolgelley there are three recognized routes to the top ($2^1/_4$-4 hrs.), but the third of those described below should be reserved for the descent, as the climb up the steep 'scree' known as the 'Foxes' Path' is very fatiguing. Mountaineers, however, who do not object to a scramble and who wish to make the descent to Barmouth, Towyn, or Tal-y-Llyn, may prefer the Foxes' Path as the shortest and in many ways the most interesting of the three routes. Guides (6*s.*) may be dispensed with in good weather by those who have had any experience in mountain-climbing. Ascent from *Arthog*, see p. 297; from *Tal-y-Llyn*, see p. 265.

1. *By the Bridle Path* ($2^1/_2$-3 hrs.; pony 6-7*s.*). We leave Dolgelley by the road leading S.W. from the church, and where it branches, just outside the village, at a letter-box, we keep up hill to the left. This is the old road to Towyn (p. 266), which ascends steadily for about $1^1/_2$ M. and then becomes more level. $^1/_2$ M. (2 M. from Dolgelley) *Llyn Gwernan*, a small lake on the right, with a cottage (formerly an inn) at its farther end, opposite which the Foxes' Path route begins. We, however, follow the road for $^1/_2$ M. more, cross a small bridge, and turn to the left, just on this side of a second bridge. The bridle-path crosses a stream, and ascends through a plantation, keeping the direction of the depression between the saddle of Cader and Tyrau Mawr (p. 297). In about 40 min. after leaving the road, the path reaches the top of the ridge and joins the route from Arthog at two stone posts. Thence, see p. 297.

2. *Along the Ridge viâ Mynydd Moel* (Aran route; $3^1/_2$-4 hrs.). As there is no regular path, this ascent should not be attempted in bad weather without a guide. Leaving the town by the Dinas Mawddwy road (S.E.) we cross the bridge over the *Aran* and turn down a lane to the right. After $^1/_2$ M., opposite *Pandy Mill*, we bend to the left, and a little farther on turn sharply to the right, through a gate. About $^3/_4$ M. beyond Pandy Mill the lane quits the Aran (which here turns to the right), passes some farm-steadings, and reaches the open side of a spur of Mynydd Moel, the easternmost summit of the Càder ridge. The direct route to the top of Mynydd Moel leads to the right, but it is better to keep somewhat to the left, in order to avoid the marshy hollow of the Aran, and to strike the ridge a little more to the E. To the right lies the little *Llyn Aran*, in which the stream takes its rise, The top of *Mynydd Moel* (2835 ft.; cairn) commands a very fine and extensive view, including Dolgelley, which is not visible from the Pen-y-Gader. The easy walk along the ridge from Mynydd Moel to the summit of Cader takes 15-20 minutes. Llyn-y-Gader and Llyn-y-Gafr (p. 301) soon come into view on the right. Good walkers may continue their walk along the ridge to *Tyrau Mawr* and (2 hrs.) *Arthog* (comp. p. 297), returning to Dolgelley by an evening-train.

3. *By the Foxes' Path* ($2^1/_4$-$2^3/_4$ hrs.). From Dolgelley to ($2^1/_4$ M.) the cottag at the S.W. end of Llyn Gwernan, see above. Here we leave the road by a wicket on the left, and follow a path over a grassy hill, with a little coppice. In 6-7 min. we cross a wall by a stile, and soon reach a point from which we have a fine view of the whole range of Cader; the steep stony slope to the left of the summit is the 'Foxes' Path'. We then descend to (3-4 min.) a gate, ascend along a wall, on the other side of which is a small wood, and soon reach the open hillside. After 5 min. we turn to the right through a gate at a sheepfold and go straight on, soon with a wall to our right. 5 min. Brook with a low wall and a small ladder, just beyond which we pass a soft piece of ground. 8 min. Gate

in a wall; 2 min. Stream crossed by stepping-stones; 3 min. *Llyn-y-Gafr*, a small lake, well stocked with trout. Beyond this point the path ceases, but the route can scarcely be missed. Crossing the stream issuing from Llyn-y-Gafr, we have a sharp climb of about 1/4 hr. to surmount the rock-strewn ridge intervening between Llyn-y-Gafr and *Llyn-y-Gader*, a somewhat larger lake finely situated below the wall of rock rising perpendicularly to the summit of the mountain. At the S. end of Llyn-y-Gader begins the steep slope of loose shingle, called the '*Foxes' Path*', which is about 900 ft. in height and inclined at an angle of 35°. Its ascent is extremely fatiguing, but there is no danger, though the hindmost members of a party should beware of falling stones. The usual time required to ascend this scree is 1/2-3/4 hr. At the top of the slope we turn to the right and pass over smooth turf to (5 min.) the cairn and the hut on the extreme summit.

[In descending, the 'Foxes' Path' (the top of which is indicated by a small cairn) is easy, as the loose shingle yields to our weight and carries us down with little exertion. We can scarcely go wrong after passing Llyn-y-Gafr, where the faintly-defined path begins and follows the general direction of the stream issuing from the Llyn. A little below the lake we cross the brook by the stepping-stones. At the gap in the wall, we keep to the right, on this side of the wall. Llyn Gwernan now soon comes into sight and determines our course.]

***Cader Idris** (2925 ft.), or the chair of the giant Idris, is one of the most beautifully shaped mountains in England, presenting a long row of wall-like precipices towards the estuary of the Mawddach on the N., while on the three other sides it sends off spurs towards the Arans, Plinlimmon, and Cardigan Bay. The total length of the Cader ridge from E. to W. is about 7 M.; above the general level of the ridge rise the four main summits (named from E. to W.) of *Mynydd Moel*, *Pen-y-Gader* (the top), *Cyfrwy*, or the 'Saddle', and *Tyrau Mawr*. The *View from the cairn on the summit is very extensive. On the N. is the beautiful estuary of the Mawddach, backed by the Llawllech range of hills, culminating in Diphwys (to the right), while beyond these again rise the Carnarvon Mts., visible in their entire extent from Bardsey Isle, at the end of the Lleyn promontory, on the left (S.W.), to Carnedd Llewelyn on the right (N.E.). The peak of Snowdon, rising above the Rhinog Fach, is easily distinguishable, and the other summits may be identified from the map (Moel Hebog and the Rivals to the left of Snowdon; Moel Siabod, the Glyders, etc., to the right). To the right, more in the foreground, is the rounded outline of Rhobell Fawr, to the left of which we have a view of the Ganllwyd glen and the Precipice Walk. The dark little tarn almost vertically below the summit on this side is the Llyn-y-Gader (see above). To the N.E. we have a fine view of the valley of the Wnion, extending to Bala Lake; Dolgelley, however, is hidden. The peaks to the left of Bala are the Arenigs, those to the right the Arans, while Moel Fammau, with its tower, rises in the extreme distance beyond the lake. More to the right are the Berwyns, and almost due E. are the three peaks of the Breidden Hills, near Shrewsbury. In exceptionally clear weather even the Wrekin (p. 261) is said to be visible in this direction. To the S. is the somewhat featureless expanse of rounded green hills, of which Plinlimmon is the highest point, while the Carmarthen Van may sometimes be descried in the extreme distance. To the W. we have Cardigan Bay and the coast as far S. as St. David's Head. Tal-y-Llyn is not visible, but we enjoy (S.W.) a pretty peep down the green valley of the *Dysynni*, with the Bird Rock. From the S. side of the summit-plateau, a short way from the cairn, we obtain a striking view of the **Llyn-y-Cae*, an ideal mountain tarn, situated in a wild rocky hollow at the foot of almost vertical crags. Those who do not wish to return to Dolgelley may descend either to Arthog (2 hrs., to Barmouth 3 hrs.; comp. p. 297), or to Tal-y-Llyn (1 1/2-2 1/2 hrs.; p. 265), or to Towyn (2 1/2-3 hrs. to Abergynolwyn, see p. 266).

Excursions may also be made from Dolgelley to *Towyn* (p. 266), by the coast-road 20 M., by the mountain-road 17 M.; to *Tal-y-Llyn* (p. 265), new road 9 1/2 M., old road 8 1/2 M.; to *Dinas Mawddwy* (p. 265), 10 1/2 M., old road 9 M.; to *Machynlleth* (p. 265), old road 14½ M., new road 16 M.. Visitors bound for Machynlleth may include Dinas Mawddwy or Tal-y-Llyn; from the former a railway runs to Machynlleth down the pretty valley of the *Dovey*, while a visit to the Llyn requires but a short digression from the Machynlleth road. At the highest point (860 ft.) of the road to Tal-y-Llyn lies the little *Llyn Trigraienyn*, or 'Lake of the Three Pebbles', named from three huge boulders, which Idris is said to have shaken out of his shoe. — From Dolgelley to (10 M.) *Barmouth* by road, see p. 296.

Continuation of Railway Journey. Beyond Dolgelley the train passes the mansion of *Dolserau*, near which is the Torrent Walk (p. 298). 12½ M. *Bont Newydd*, the nearest station for the ascents of Moel Offrwm (p. 298) and *Rhobell Fawr* (2409 ft.; 2¼ hrs., viâ *Llanfachreth*). On leaving Bont Newydd we enjoy a fine retrospect (right) of the complete outline of Cader Idris. The line ascends the charming valley of the *Wnion*, and the Arans (see below) soon come into sight on the right. — 16 M. *Drws-y-Nant.*

Drws-y-Nant is the starting-point for the shortest ascent (1¼-1½ hr.) of **Aran Mawddwy** (2972 ft.), the highest mountain in Mid-Wales. The twin-summit of *Aran Benllyn* (2902 ft.) is 70 ft. lower. Though 47 ft. higher than Cader Idris, Aran Mawddwy is not such an imposing mountain, nor is the view from the top so fine. Bala Lake (p. 303) is conspicuous. — The descent may be made viâ (½ hr.) Aran Benllyn to (1 hr.) *Llanuwchllyn* (see below), or on the S. side to (2 hrs.) *Dinas Mawddwy* (p. 265).

About 3 M. beyond Drws-y-Nant we reach the highest point of the line (760 ft.) and enter the bleak valley of the *Dwfrdwy*. — 22½ M. *Llanuwchllyn* (*Goat Inn, plain), another good starting-point for the ascent of the Arans (2 hrs.; see above). Good walkers may also start here for the ascent of *Arenig Fawr* (2800 ft.; 4 hrs.), descending to (1 hr.) *Arenig* station (p. 303). A fine walk leads over *Bwlch-y-Groes* ('Pass of the Cross'; 1950 ft.), and through the wooded valley of the *Dovey* to (12½ M.) Dinas Mawddwy (p. 265).

Llanuwchllyn is only 1 M. from the S. end of *Bala Lake* (600 ft.), the E. side of which the train skirts. To the left, beyond the lake, we see the Arenigs and the small church of *Llanycil.* To the right rise the Berwyns (p. 303). — 27 M. *Bala Junction*, at the N. end of the lake, is the station for a branch-line to (¾ M.) Bala and Ffestiniog (see p. 303). Between Bala Junction and the town a fine view is obtained to the left.

Bala (**White Lion*, 'pens'. in summer 3*l.* 3*s.* per week; *Plas Goch; Bull's Head)*, a small town with 1500 inhab., lies near the N. end of *Bala Lake*, or *Llyn Tegid*, the largest sheet of water in Wales (3½ M. long and ½ M. broad). The town itself is of little interest, but it may be made the starting-point of several pleasant excursions. The most prominent building is the *Calvinistic Methodist College.* The statue in front of the Methodist Chapel is that of the *Rev. Thomas Charles* (d. 1814), the originator of the British and Foreign Bible Society, who is buried in the churchyard of *Llanycil* (see above), the parish-church of Bala. The mound named the *Tomen-y-Bala* commands a good view of Bala Lake and the valley of the river *Dee*, which here issues from the lake.

The lake affords good perch and pike fishing, and trout-streams abound in the neighbourhood.

Excursions from Bala. Though the scenery of *Bala Lake* is not imposing, it is pleasant to walk or drive round it (11 M.). The walker may cut off 4 M. by taking the railway between Bala and Llanuwchllyn (p. 302). The two chief hotels keep boats for excursions on the lake. — Bala is one of the recognised starting-points for a visit to *Pistyll Rhaiadr* (p. 264), the highest waterfall in Wales. We take the train to (7 M.) *Llandrillo* (see below), and walk thence across the *Berwyn Hills* (c. 2500 ft.) to ($7^1/_2$ M.) the waterfall. Whether the traveller returns to Bala or goes on to *Oswestry* (see p. 264), this excursion requires a whole day. — The new *Liverpool Reservoir* ('Lake Fyrnwy'), in the *Valley of Llanwddyn*, 10 M. to the S. of Bala, is interesting, especially to engineers. When completed it will be 5 M. long and 15 M. in circumference, *i. e.* larger than Bala Lake. The direct route (a fair mountain-road) ascends the *Hirnant Valley*, passes *Moel-y-Geifr* (2055 ft.), to the right, at (7 M.) the head of the pass, and then descends to (3 M.) *Rhiwargor*, at the N. end of the reservoir. About 3 M. farther on is the village of *Llanwdden* (Inn), the site of which will be submerged, and 2 M. beyond it is the large embankment forming the S. end of the reservoir. Active pedestrians may combine this excursion with the last by sleeping at Llanrhaiadr (p. 264), 10 M. from Llanwdden (12 M. by high-road) and 4 M. from Pistyll Rhaiadr. — The ascent of the *Arans* and the walk by the *Bwlch-y-Groes* to *Dinas Mawddwy* are brought within easy reach of Bala by the railway to Llanuwchllyn (see p. 302). — The *Arenigs*, see below.

From Bala Junction to Blaenau Ffestiniog, $25^1/_2$ M., railway (G. W. R.) in 1 hr. 10 min. (fares 5*s.* 6*d.*, 3*s.* 8*d.*, 2*s.* 7*d*). As we leave the junction we see Bala Lake to the left. $^3/_4$ M. *Bala Town* (p. 302). The line now runs through the valley of the *Tryweryn*, and the Arenigs soon come into view on the left. Beyond ($3^1/_4$ M.) *Frongoch* the bare slopes of *Mynydd Nodal* rise on the left. — $8^1/_4$ M. *Arenig* (Rhyd-y-Fen Inn, at the foot of Arenig Fach, $^1/_2$ M. from the station), a small station situated between the two Arenigs. The ascent of *Arenig Fawr* (2800 ft.), to the S. of the station, takes 1-$1^1/_2$ hr. Extensive *View from the top, including Snowdon, Cader Idris, the Arans, and the sea. At the N.W. base of the mountain, $^3/_4$ M. from the station, lies the little *Llyn Arenig*. The descent may be made to *Llanuwchllyn* (comp. p. 302). The ascent of the *Arenig Fach* (2264 ft.) may be made from the inn in $^3/_4$ hr. — At *Llyn Tryweryn* the line reaches its highest point (1190 ft.) and begins the descent through the barren *Cwm Proesor*. The Rhinogs (p. 294), and soon afterwards Cader Idris (p. 301), are seen to the left. — From (17 M.) *Trawsfynydd* walkers may reach (14 M.) Llanbedr viâ the Bwlch Tyddiad and the Roman Steps (comp. p. 294). — The line here turns to the N. On the right is *Tomen-y-Mur* (p. 312); in front (left) the Moelwyns. — 20 M. *Maentwrog Road*, 2 M. from Maentwrog (p. 313). The train now sweeps round the valley of the *Cynfael*, commanding a fine view of the Ffestiniog mountains. 22 M. *Ffestiniog Village* (p. 311). — $25^1/_2$ M. *Blaenau Ffestiniog* (p. 311).

Beyond Bala the train passes through a short tunnel and descends the well-wooded valley of the *Dee.* On the right we pass the large mansion of *Palé* (occupied by the Queen in 1889), just before reaching (31 M.) *Llandderfel*, the church of which, also to the right, contains two curious wooden relics known as St. Derfel's horse (stag?) and crozier. — 34 M. *Llandrillo* (Dudley Arms, $^1/_2$ M. from the station) is the starting-point for the walk to (3 hrs.) *Pistyll Rhaiadr* (see above). *Cader Fronwen* (2573 ft.; view), the nearest of the Berwyns, may be ascended in $1^1/_2$ hr.

38 M. **Corwen** *(Owen Glyndwr*, $^1/_4$ M. to the E. of the station;

Rail. Refreshment Rooms), a small town with 2500 inhab., is a good centre for anglers (fishing in the Dee, Alwen, etc.). The church contains a curious monument to Iorwerth Sulien, one of its early vicars; and outside is the shaft of a cross ascribed to the 8th century. The rude cross on the lintel of the S. door is said to be the mark of Owen Glendower's dagger. It was at Corwen that this famous patriot assembled his forces before the battle of Shrewsbury, and most of the land round the town belonged to him. — Railway (L.N.W.) from Corwen to *Rhyl*, see p. 280.

Beyond (41 M.) *Carrog* we pass *Owen Glendower's Mound* on the left, while on the other side are the slopes of the Berwyns (*Moel Ferna*, 2070 ft.). — 43 M. *Glyndyfrdwy* (Inn), a small fishing station, from which Owen Glendower took his name. The river makes a long curve to the left, which the railway avoids by a tunnel 1/2 M. long. On emerging from the tunnel we have a charming glimpse, to the left, of the wooded valley, with *Moel-y-Gamelin* (1897 ft.) and *Moel Morfydd* (1804 ft.) in the background, while in front are the romantic church of *Llantysilio* and *Bryntisilio*, the summer-home of Sir Theodore and Lady Martin (Helen Faucit). 47 1/2 M. *Berwyn* (Chain Bridge Hotel; p. 305).

49 M. **Llangollen.** — **Hotels.** *HAND HOTEL, an old and comfortable house, close to the Dee, R. & A. 3*s.* 9*d.*, D. 4*s.* (harper in the hall); ROYAL HOTEL, well spoken of, similar charges. — GRAPES.

Fishing. Information may be obtained of Mr. Evans, chemist.

Llangollen (pron. Thlangóthlen), or the 'church of St. Collen', a neat little town with 3000 inhab., is delightfully situated on the river *Dee*, in a hollow surrounded with hills. Its Welsh flannel and beer have a reputation. The town is a favourite resort of anglers, who find good sport in the Dee and its tributaries. The fishermen of the Dee still use the 'coracle', or ancient British boat, made of skins (now-a-days tarpaulin) stretched over a slight framework of wood. The *Church*, a low Gothic building, near the centre of the town, contains a good oaken ceiling. In the churchyard is a monument to the Ladies of Llangollen and Mary Carryl (see p. 305). The *Bridge* over the Dee, a plain structure with four pointed arches, is reckoned for some inscrutable reason among the 'Seven Wonders of Wales'.

The ruins of **Dinas Bran,** or *Crow Castle* (1/2 hr.; donkey 1*s.*) surmount the boldly-formed hill (910 ft.) on the N. side of the **Vale of Llangollen.* We cross the bridge over the Dee, proceed a few paces to the right, and then ascend to the left to a bridge over the *Ellesmere Canal.* On the other side we find ourselves opposite a sign-post, pointing on the right to the Trevor Rocks, on the left to the Eglwyseg Rocks, and straight on to Dinas Bran. The path to the latter ascends through a few fields, crossing two cart-tracks, and reaches the open hillside at a gate just above a house where refreshments are sold. The ruins at the top are of very early origin, but are not so picturesque as they appear from below. The *View includes the finely shaped Eglwyseg Rocks on the N., the valley of the Dee on the E., Llangollen to the S., Moel-y-Geraint and the Berwyns to the S.W., and Moel-y-Gamelin to the N.W.

The view from ***Moel-y-Geraint** (1000 ft.; 1/2 hr.), or the *Barber's Hill*, on the other side of the river, is similar to that from Dinas Bran, but more extensive. The ascent begins by a steep lane near the Grapes Hotel. From the top we may descend to Berwyn (p. 309) and include a visit to Valle Crucis Abbey (see below) in our round.

Plas Newydd (*i.e.* 'New Place'), the residence of the celebrated 'Ladies of Llangollen', is situated about $^1/_3$ M. to the S. of the bridge. To reach it we turn to the left at the end of Castle Street and then ascend to the right of the Grapes Hotel. Where the road forks we keep to the left, and almost immediately reach a path with a railing on the left, which leads to the house. Admission 6*d.* — The 'Ladies of Llangollen' were two Irish damsels, Lady Eleanor Butler and the Hon. Sarah Ponsonby, who swore 'eternal friendship', devoted themselves to a life of celibacy, and secretly left their homes together in 1776. At first they settled at Denbigh, but afterwards removed to Llangollen, where they lived together for half-a-century. Their romantic story, and the half-masculine dress they affected, made them widely known, and they received visits from many eminent personages. Lady Eleanor Butler, who was 17 years older than her companion, died in 1829 at the age of 90, and Miss Ponsonby died two years later. Their faithful servant, Mary Carryl (see p. 304), who had bought for them with her savings the freehold of Plas Newydd, died in 1809. — The house now belongs to General Yorke, who has built an additional wing, which he occupies in summer. Both inside and out it is decorated with good carvings in oak; and it contains a few relics of the 'Ladies', curiosities, paintings, and the like.

We may now either return to Llangollen direct, or extend our walk round *Pen-y-Coed*, the hill to the S.E. of Plas Newydd. In the latter case we pass ($^1/_2$ M.) to the right of *Pengwern Hall*, now a farm-house, but originally (10th cent.) the residence of Tudor Trevor, the ancestor of the Mostyn family.

One of the pleasantest walks in the neighbourhood of Llangollen is the round of 5-6 M. to *Berwyn* ($1^3/_4$ M.; also reached by rail), the *Chain Bridge*, *Llantysilio Church*, and *Valle Crucis Abbey*. Good walkers may add the ascent of *Moel-y-Gamelin*. — Walkers cross the bridge and then follow (to the left) the well-shaded towing-path of the above-mentioned *Canal* (p. 304). After about 1 M. the canal turns to the left, while the shortest route to ($^1/_2$ M.) Valle Crucis (see below) leads across the bridge to the right. Continuing to follow the canal we soon reach ($^3/_4$ M.) the *Chain Bridge* (Inn), opposite *Berwyn* station, perhaps the most charming spot on the Dee. A little beyond the inn we pass a weir, where the canal issues from the Dee, and reach the romantically-situated little church of *Llantysilio* (service in English at 3.30 p.m.).

Behind Berwyn and Llantysilio rises the hill called *Braich-y-Gwynt*, and we may proceed from the latter to Valle Crucis (about 1 M.) round either side of this hill or over its top. If we keep to the N. side of the hill we turn to the right on reaching the high-road to Ruthin on the other side; if we choose the S. side we turn to the left. The abbey lies a little to the E. of the road (bell at the entrance; charge 6*d.*).

***Valle Crucis Abbey**, founded in the year 1200 by Madog ap Gruffydd Maelor of Dinas Bran, and dissolved in 1535, is the most important monastic ruin in N. Wales. It was a Cistercian establishment, dedicated to the Virgin Mary. The chief part of the ruin is the *Church*, in the E. E. style, which is 165 ft. long (transepts 98 ft.) and $67^1/_2$ ft. wide. The W. front (probably completed about 1250), with its three Dec. windows over the doorway and a rose-window above, is in good preservation. The E. end, which contains three lancet windows, seems to be the oldest part of the edifice. On the S. side the church is adjoined by some remains of the conventual buildings, including the chapter-house, with the dormitories above it. The juxtaposition of three different styles of doorway here (Norman, E. E., and Flamboyant) should be noticed.

We now return to the road and follow it (to the right) for about $^1/_4$ M. to the second milestone from Llangollen. Opposite this, in a field to the right, stands **Eliseg's Pillar**, erected by Concenn in the 8th or 9th cent. in memory of his great-grandfather Eliseg, Prince of Powys.

The present inscription dates from the renovation of the monument in 1779. The name of the valley is usually attributed to this 'cross', though some authorities explain it by the shape of the valley itself.

The ascent of **Moel-y-Gamelin** (1897 ft.; 1½ hr.) may be made either direct from Llantysilio or from the Oernant slate-quarries on the Ruthin road, about 2 M. beyond Eliseg's Pillar. The view is extensive, including Snowdon, the Arans, the vale of Clwyd, and the valley of the Dee.

Excursion to the Eglwyseg Rocks. We cross the railway and canal, and at the sign-post mentioned at p. 304 either turn to the left and proceed round the N. side of the Dinas Bran, or take the lane to the right, which leads round the other side of the same hill. In either case we reach the nearest point of the rocks not far from *Tan-y-Castell Farm*, 2 M. from Llangollen. The ***Eglwyseg Rocks**, the name of which (pron. *Eglooiseg*) is probably connected with Eliseg (see p. 305), are a line of bold limestone cliffs, beginning near Dinas Bran and sweeping round in a semicircle for a distance of about 4 M. They form the W. escarpment of a dreary upland plateau stretching towards the E. The breezy walk along their summit to the '*World's End*' (to which there is also a carriage-road), 5 M. from Llangollen, is very delightful in fine weather.

Chirk Castle. This excursion may be made either by railway to (11 M.) *Chirk* (changing carriages at Ruabon, p. 307; ¾ hr.), or by carriage (London and Holyhead road; 9 M.), or on foot (direct 4 M., viâ Pennant 6 M.) The direct walking-route, which is also practicable for riders, leads over the E. end of *Glyn Hill*. We follow the road to the left of the Grapes Hotel, cross the bridge, and where the road forks (¼ M.) keep uphill to the right. In 4-5 min. the road again forks, and we again keep to the right. We now skirt the wooded hill of *Pen-y-Coed* and pass (8 min.) the picturesque modern house of *Tyndwr*. At the (5 min.) cross-roads we keep straight on and ascend steeply, passing through a gate and avoiding two green tracks to the left (the second opposite a gate). After 8 min. our track bends to the left, while another leads to the right through a gate. In ¼ hr. we pass two large beeches and in 7 min. more join the road at the top of the hill. During the whole ascent we enjoy fine views over the valley of the Dee. At the (3 min.) cross-roads we keep straight on. We now descend, passing (7 min.) a cottage and soon reaching (5 min.) a farm where Chirk Castle is in full view. Our road keeps to the left, and in 7 min. reaches the park-gate and lodge, whence a drive of about ½ M. leads to the castle, passing a small lake on the left. *Offa's Dyke* (p. 264) crosses the park, but the swelling is scarcely distinguishable. At the castle we ring the bell at a postern on the right, at the top of a few steps (open on Mon. and Thurs., 11-1 and 2-5; adm. for 1-5 pers. 2*s*. 6*d*., each addit. pers. 6*d*.). ***Chirk Castle**, a rectangular structure with massive round towers at the angles, enclosing a large quadrangle, was erected by Roger Mortimer in the reign of Edward I. (1272-1307), on the site of an ancient fortress; but many of the details are of Elizabethan or later date. During the Civil War it was seized by the Royalists and besieged in vain by its owner, Sir Thomas Myddelton, at that time one of the Parliamentary leaders. The interior contains oak-carvings, family-portraits, and an ebony *Cabinet presented to Sir Thomas Myddelton by Charles II., the interior of which is adorned with silver plaques and a series of exquisitely coloured paintings on copper, ascribed to Rubens. The ramparts command a fine *View of the beautiful *Park* and the surrounding country. — The village of *Chirk* lies about 1½ M., and the station 1¼ M. to the E. of the castle (see p. 268).

Good walkers may combine the excursion to Chirk with a visit to **Wynnstay**, the seat of Sir Watkin Wynn, 6 M. to the E. of Llangollen, near Ruabon. The house is not shown, but visitors are admitted, on application, to the large *Park*, which contains some good timber and numerous deer. The three towers in the park afford extensive views.

A pleasant walk may be taken from Llangollen along the Dee to (10 M.) *Corwen*. The high-road on the S. bank commands the most open views, but the road on the N. bank is shadier and more picturesque.

Another pleasant walk may be taken to (3 M.) *Glyn Ceiriog* (New Inn Hotel), whence a tramway for slate and passengers runs to (6 M.) *Chirk.*

Continuation of Railway Journey. As we leave Llangollen the castle of Dinas Bran (p. 304) and the Eglwyseg Rocks (p. 306) are conspicuous to the left. Near (51$^1/_2$ M.) *Trevor* we have a view to the right of the *Dee Viaduct* of the Shrewsbury and Chester railway and of the imposing aqueduct of *Pont-y-Cysylltau*, constructed by Telford for the Ellesmere canal. 52$^1/_2$ M. *Acrefair* ('Akryvire'), with large iron-works. To the right is Wynnstay Park (p. 306).

54 M. **Ruabon** *(Rail. Refreshmt. Rooms)*, the junction of the Barmouth and Dolgelley branch with the main G. W. R. line from Chester to Shrewsbury (p. 262). Carriages often changed here. From Ruabon to (71 M.) *Chester* or (89 M.) *Shrewsbury*, see R. 39 a.

d. From Llandudno to Bettws-y-Coed and Ffestiniog.

30$^1/_2$ M. Railway (L. N. W. R.) to (18 M.) *Bettws-y-Coed* in $^3/_4$-1 hr. (fares 3*s.* 6*d*,, 2*s.* 8*d.*, 1*s.* 11*d.*); from Bettws to (12$^1/_2$ M.) *Blaenau Ffestiniog* in $^1/_2$-$^3/_4$ hr. (fares 2*s.* 6*d.*, 1*s.* 10*d.*, 1*s.* $^1/_2$*d.*). — In summer a small Steamer plies from Deganwy (p. 284) to *Trefriw* (see below) in 1$^1/_2$-2 hrs. (fares 1*s.* 6*d.*, 1*s.*), but the scenery up to this point is fairly well seen from the railway. — Pedestrians will find the walk along either side of the river (16-17 M.) repay them; the road on the W. side affords the best views.

From Llandudno to (3 M.) *Llandudno Junction*, see p. 281. Carriages are generally changed here. The line follows the winding course of the *Conway*, through the pretty valley of which it runs all the way to Bettws. Beyond (4$^1/_2$ M.) *Glan Conway* we have a view of the *Carnarvon Mts.* to the right, including Carnedd Llewelyn, Foel Fras, and the rounded Moel Eilio (in front). From (8$^3/_4$ M.) *Tal-y-Cafn*, walkers may pay a visit to the British earthworks at *Pen-y-Gaer* and the waterfalls of *Dolgarrog* (see Map), crossing the river by the ferry (1*d.*) and rejoining the railway at Llanrwst (in all, 3$^1/_2$-4 hrs.) The ascent of *Carnedd Llewelyn* (p. 288) from Tal-y-Cafn takes about 4 hrs. — About 1 M. beyond Tal-y-Cafn the small church of *Caerhun*, on the site of the Roman *Conovium*, is seen on the other side of the river; and, farther on, *Pen-y-Gaer* and the falls of *Porthlwyd* and *Dolgarrog* are also visible. The small village of *Trefriw* ('Trevrioo'; Bellevue Hotel), where the steamer stops, also lies on the right bank, about 1 M. from Llanrwst. Its chalybeate springs, the water of which may be seen coming down from the heights, are about 1$^1/_2$ M. to the N. In summer an omnibus for Trefriw meets the trains at Llanrwst.

14 M. **Llanrwst** *(Victoria*, on the river; *Eagles & Gwydir Arms)*, a small town with 2500 inhab., is picturesquely situated, $^1/_2$ M. from the station, on the right bank of the Conway, which is here crossed by a bridge ascribed to the Welsh architect Inigo Jones. The church contains the burial-chapel of the Gwydir family, a finely carved rood-loft, and the stone coffin of Llewelyn ap Jorwerth.

About $^1/_2$ M. from Llanrwst, on the other side of the Conway, is *Gwydir Castle*, long the seat of the Wynnes, but now the property of Ba-

For a coloured map of The Valley of The Conway see page 588

ron Willoughby de Eresby; the modern mansion contains some interesting tapestry and beautiful oak-carvings (visitors admitted).

The environs of Llanrwst are very picturesque; and pleasant walks may be taken to (2 M.) the old church of *Llanrhychwyn* ('Thlanrychooin'), to Trefriw and (4 M.) *Llyn Crafnant* (thence to Capel Curig 3 M.), and to Bettws-y-Coed viâ *Llyn-y-Parc* (6 M.; comp. Map).

The scenery between Llanrwst and Bettws is the best on the line. To the right the *Falcon Rock* rises above the Gwydir woods. The train crosses the Conway and then the *Llugwy*, affording a glimpse to the right of the Llugwy valley, with Moel Siabod in the background.

18 M. **Bettws-y-Coed.** — **Hotels.** Royal Oak, near the station (sign by David Cox, now kept indoors), R. & A. 4*s.* 6*d.*, D. 4*s.* 6*d.*; *Waterloo, 1/3 M. to the S.; Gwydir Arms; Glan Aber; Swan, Temperance, plain. — *Lodgings.*

Coaches run in summer to *Capel Curig* (5 1/2 M.; fare 2*s.*), *Llanberis* (16 M.; 4*s.*, return 6*s*), *Bangor* (20 1/2 M.; fare 6*s.*), *Beddgelert* (17 1/2 M.; 5*s.*, return 8*s.*), and *Port Madoc* (25 1/2 M.; 7*s.* 6*d.*). Brakes also run to the *Swallow Falls*, *Fairy Glen*, and other points.

Fishing. There is good fishing within easy reach of Bettws in the *Conway*, *Lledr*, *Llugwy*, etc. (particulars at the hotels).

Bettws-y-Coed (pron. Bettoosycoëd), or the Chapel in the Wood, is charmingly situated at the confluence of the *Conway* and the *Llugwy*, in a basin surrounded with luxuriantly-wooded cliffs and hills, and is perhaps the most popular resort in Wales for artists, anglers, and tourists. The Llugwy is crossed opposite the village by the *Pont-y-Pair*, a romantic structure of the 15th cent., below which the stream runs in a most picturesquely broken course, while about 3/4 M. to the S. is the *Waterloo Bridge*, crossing the Conway. Near the railway-station is the old *Church*, shaded with yew-trees and now used for interments only. Bettws is within 8 M. of the W. base of Snowdon, and only 4 M. from Moel Siabod, but no mountain is visible from its somewhat confined situation.

The Environs of Bettws, with their beautiful woods, streams, and waterfalls, are full of interest for walkers. A good introduction to the beauties of the neighbourhood is afforded by the general view obtained from Llyn Elsi or the hill above Capel Garmon. To reach the former, which lies about 1 3/4 M. to the S.W., we ascend to the left by a path behind the new church. At a direction-stone we keep to the right. Beyond a small farm the path leads across the moorland plateau to the S., in the direction of the valley of the Lledr, and turns to the right at a cairn, soon reaching the lonely little tarn of **Llyn Elsi.** The most conspicuous feature of the *View hence is the beautifully-formed *Moel Siabod* ('Shabod'; 2865 ft.). Behind Moel Siabod rises Snowdon; and the Glyders, Carnedd Dafydd, and Carnedd Llewelyn are also well seen.

The road to **Capel Garmon**, a small village 2 M. to the S.E., crosses Waterloo Bridge (see above) and turns to the left. If the view alone is the object, it is enough to ascend to the top of *Gallt-y-Foel* (800 ft.), the hill which here rises to the left (ascent in 3/4 hr. from Bettws); but a pleasant round may be made by going on to Capel Garmon and the *Cromlech*, 1 M. beyond it, and then returning to (3 1/2 M.) Bettws by the high-road.

The following Round of about 18 M. embraces most of the other favourite points near Bettws. Those who prefer driving will find public conveyances plying to the Swallow Falls, the Fairy Glen, and the Conway Falls. The walk across the hill from Pont-y-Gyfyng to Dolwyddelan, though not more than 4 M. in direct length, is rather rough and fatiguing (especially after rain) and takes 1 1/2-2 hrs.

We leave the village by the main Holyhead road, which runs to the W. from Pont-y-Pair. After 3/4 M. we reach a small gate on the right, which leads to the so-called ***Miner's Bridge***, a kind of ladder crossing the picturesque little Llugwy. We then return to the road, and 1 1/4 M. farther on reach the ***Swallow Falls Hotel***, opposite which is a gate leading to the ***Swallow Falls**, or *Rhaiadr-y-Wennol* (probably corrupted from 'Rhaiadr Ewynawl', *i. e.* the foaming cataract). These picturesque falls are three in number, and after rain are very fine. Visitors should follow the path to the foot of the middle fall and to the head of the uppermost fall.

Beyond the Swallow Falls the road bends a little to the left, still skirting the Llugwy, the placid and glassy surface of which above the falls affords a pleasing contrast to its broken and chafing course below. To the left we have a fine view of Moel Siabod, with Snowdon to the right in the distance. We cross the Llugwy, 3/4 M. above the falls, by the *Ty Hyll Bridge*, which is said to derive its name ('ugly cottage') from the primitive specimen of domestic architecture adjoining it. After 1 1/4 M. more, where the valley narrows and turns to the right, we reach another bridge, affording a view (to the left) of the *Pont-y-Gyfyng*, a picturesque bridge of one arch, below which the river forms a series of cascades. A few hundred yards farther on we pass the small *Tyn-y-Coed Hotel* and in about 3 min. more reach the *Tan-y-Bwlch Hotel* (well spoken of).

[**Moel Siabod** (2865 ft.; *View) may be ascended from this point in 1 1/4-1 3/4 hr. We cross the river by the wooden bridge opposite the hotel, pass to the right through a plantation, cross a wall, and turn to the left. We soon reach the open hillside, where our course is plain.]

We should follow the road for a few hundred yards beyond the Tan-y-Bwlch hotel, in order to obtain one of the best views of *Snowdon*, which rises before us in its full extent. The four peaks, named from left to right, are *Lliwedd*, *Y Wyddfa* (the summit), *Crib Goch* (in front), and *Crib-y-Dysgyl*. About 1 M. beyond Tan-y-Bwlch is *Capel Curig* (p. 316).

After our sight of Snowdon, however, we retrace our steps to the *Pont-y-Gyfyng*, cross it, and where the cart-track forks keep to the left, passing almost immediately afterwards a little church. At a school a little way farther on, we ascend to the right, and soon after, where the path again forks, near a cottage on the hillside, keep to the left. The track here is very rough and stony. In a few min. more (20-25 min. from Pont-y-Gyfyng) we pass through a gate and 10 min. later reach the top of the ridge, where the mountains on the other side come into sight. The path at the top, and in descending, is often very ill-defined, but by following the general direction of the water-course we cannot go far astray. Another gate is passed soon after we begin the descent, and in about 10 min. a ruined hut comes in sight, which serves as our next landmark. We keep to the left of the bed of the stream (generally dry). In 10 min. more we cross a stream by a slab-bridge and ascend straight to the above-mentioned hut. Beyond the hut we still follow the water-course, and in 1/2 hr. cross two streams. After the second of those we keep to the left, pass through (10 min.) a gate, and in 5 min. more reach *Dolwyddelan* (p. 310), on the high-road and railway from Bettws to Ffestiniog. The nearest inn is Elen's Castle, a few yards to the right. The station is on the other side of the river, beyond the bridge.

For Bettws we turn to the left and follow the road down the pretty **Valley of the Lledr*, with its varied colouring and picturesquely broken stream. 1 3/4 M. *Pont-y-Pant* (Hotel), at the prettiest part of the valley. After 1 1/2 M. more we pass under a railway-bridge. The track to the left leads straight to (2 1/2 M.) Bettws, but we follow the road and reach (1 1/4 M.) another bridge, which we leave to the right. About 1/2 M. farther on is yet another bridge, which we cross. The rough lane to the right (stile) leads to the Fairy Glen, which is entered by (1/4 M.) a small gate on the right (adm. 2*d*.). [The key of the glen is kept at a cottage on the left a little way up the lane, indicated by a notice-board; but in summer the custodian is generally to be found in the glen itself.]

The ***Fairy Glen** is a romantic little dell, with a charming combination of waterfall, rock, and wood. There is no path along the stream, and we have to return to the gate by which we quitted the lane. Here we turn to the right and soon cross another stile. Just before we reach the main Corwen road (view of Moel Siabod), a gate on the right (adm. 2*d.*) admits to the path descending to the **Conway Falls*, 50 ft. high.

We now return to the gate, enter the main road, follow it for 150-200 yds. to the right, then turn to the right, cross the bridge over the Conway, and follow the Penmachno road to (1/2 M.) the *Pant Bridge*. The self-styled 'janitor' in the old toll-house here keeps the key admitting to the so-called 'Roman Bridge', which spans the stream just below Pant Bridge (small gratuity). — We now descend by a cart-track near the left bank of the *Machno*, and soon reach *Pandy Mill*, a favourite 'bit' with artists. The **Machno Falls* are approached through the mill-garden (gratuity). Just below the falls the Machno joins the Conway, and our path (a stony cart-track) descends near the latter stream to a row of cottages. Beyond these, where the track forks, we keep to the right, and soon reach the Bettws and Dolwyddelan road at the bridge *before* the one we crossed (comp. p. 309), which is about 1 1/2 M. from Bettws. When we again reach the bridge which we crossed on our way to the Fairy Glen (see above) we may either cross it and follow the road to the left, or we may follow the cart-track on the other bank and cross by Pont-y-Pair.

From Bettws-y-Coed to Bangor, 20 1/2 M., coach in 4 1/2 hrs. (fare 6*s.*). This *Drive affords a great variety of scenery. — From Bettws to (5 1/2 M.) *Capel Curig*, see p. 309. (Ascent of Snowdon, see p. 321; drive through the vale of Llanberis, see pp. 315, 316.) The Bangor road turns to the N. and ascends through the bleak Llugwy valley. The three-peaked **Tryfan* (3000 ft.) soon comes into view on the left; on the central peak are the 'Shepherd and his Wife', two upright rocks resembling human figures (ascent, by the W. side, in 1-1 1/2 hr., recommended to good climbers). We pass the highest part of the road about 9 M. from Bettws, shortly before reaching *Llyn Ogwen*, a mountain-lake 1 M. long. The coach stops for about 1/2 hr. at the small Temperance Inn at the W. end of Llyn Ogwen, and this affords time for a flying visit to the gloomy and romantic little **Llyn Idwal*, which lies about 1/4 M. to the S. of the road and takes its name from a Welsh prince said to have been drowned here by his foster-father. High up on the rocks on its W. side is a curious cleft known as the Twll Du ('black cleft'), or the 'Devil's Kitchen', which extends back for about 500 ft. and is 200-300 ft. deep, while it is only about 6 ft. wide. After heavy rain the stream descends from the cleft in a fine cataract. The waters of Llyn Ogwen are discharged at its W. end in a series of cascades called the **Falls of Benglog*. These falls break through the rocky barrier at the head of ***Nant Ffrancon** (Vale of the Beavers), which, however, is seen to much greater advantage by those coming in the opposite direction. The mountain-background at the head of the pass (behind us) is formed by *Y Glyder Fawr* (3275 ft.) and *Y Glyder Fach* (3250 ft.). The road descends along the E. side of the valley, skirting the base of *Carnedd Dafydd* (p. 288). Near the foot of Nant Ffrancon the *Penrhyn Slate Quarries* (p. 287) come into view on the left, and we soon reach *Bethesda*, whence the route to *Bangor* is described at p. 286. Walkers may leave the coach at Bethesda and visit the Slate Quarries, as described at p. 287; the quarrymen, however, stop work at 5.30 p. m.

Pleasant excursions may also be made from Bettws to (6 M.) *Llanrwst* viâ *Llyn-y-Parc* (comp. p. 308), and to (6 1/2 M.) *Pentre Voelas*. The fine drives to *Beddgelert* and *Llanberis*, skirting respectively the E. and N. base of Snowdon, are described at pp. 318, 315. For those who start from Bettws the ascent of Snowdon begins at (10 1/2 M.) *Pen-y-Pass* (see p. 321), which is passed by the coaches between Bettws and Llanberis.

Continuation of Railway Journey. Beyond Bettws the train follows the Conway for about 1 M. more, and then turns to the right into the picturesque **Valley of the Lledr*. Fine view of Moel Siabod to the right. 22 1/2 M. *Pont-y-Pant* (Hotel), see p. 309. The peak of Snowdon soon comes into sight on the right. — 24 M. **Dolwyd-**

delan (*Benar View; Elen's Castle; Gwydir Arms*, all unpretending), pronounced 'Dolooithélan', is a quarrymen's village, at the foot of Moel Siabod. About 1 M. farther up the valley is *Dolwyddelan Castle*, the birthplace of Llewelyn the Great. The old Roman road, *Sarn Helen*, ascends the *Cwm Penamnaen*, to the S. of the station. The ascent of Moel Siabod takes about 2 hrs.; we leave the valley almost opposite the castle. Route across the E. spur of Moel Siabod to *Tan-y-Bwlch* (2 hrs.), see p. 309. — Passing Dolwyddelan Castle on the right, we next reach (26 M.) *Roman Bridge*, the name of which is unexplained. Good view of Snowdon, to the right. The train then turns to the left and quits the Lledr valley by a tunnel more than 2 M. long, emerging amid the slate-quarries and rubbish heaps of Blaenau Ffestiniog. Comp. the Map, p. 318.

$30^1/_2$ M. **Blaenau Ffestiniog** (*North Western Hotel*, close to the L. N. W. R. Station; *Queen's*, near the G. W. R. Station), a small town of recent origin, occupies a fine situation at the head of the valley of the *Dwyryd* ('Dooyrid'), surrounded by mountains, which are, however, greatly disfigured by slate-quarries. Pop. 10,000. The Palmerston Quarry is the most important. The workings here resemble mines more than the open-air quarries at Penrhyn (p. 287), and a visit to them is therefore less convenient. An extensive landslip occurred here in 1883, when it is estimated that five million tons of rock fell.

The terminus of the G. W. line to Bala (see p. 302) lies about $^1/_2$ M. to the E. of the L. N. W. Station. It is adjoined by the terminus of the 'Toy Railway' (p. 313), which, though called *Duffws*, lies really in Blaenau Ffestiniog. The Blaenau Station of the Toy Railway is close to the L. N. W. R. Station.

The tourist headquarters are at Ffestiniog Village, which lies $3^1/_2$ M. to the S., at the corner where the main valley is joined by the *Cynfael*. The easiest way to reach it is by the G. W. R. (p. 302). Walkers proceed to the left through the town, pass the termini of the G. W. and Toy railways, and follow the road down the E. side of the valley, generally near the railway.

Ffestiniog Village (**Pengwern Arms*, R. & A. from 3*s.* 9*d.*; *Abbey Arms*, well spoken of), a small place with a few hundred inhab., is charmingly situated on a projecting hill rising between the valleys of the *Dwyryd* and the *Cynfael*. The best point of view is the mound at the back of the church, reached by a track to the left of the churchyard-wall. To the left we look down the pretty vale of the Dwyryd to Cardigan Bay; opposite is *Moelwyn* (2529 ft.; ascended from Blaenau Ffestiniog in 2 hrs.), and to the right *Manod Mawr* (2171 ft.), rising above Blaenau. Fair trout and salmon fishing in the Dwyryd and in *Llyns Tecwyn* and *Garnedd*.

The first steps of the visitor to Ffestiniog are directed to the pretty **Falls of the Cynfael**. Opposite the Newborough Arms Inn, just beyond the church, we pass through the gate to the left, cross the farmyard, and follow the obvious path leading through the fields. After $^1/_2$ M. a grassy track descends on the right to the *Lower Fall*, which is chiefly interesting for its romantic setting. We then follow the path along the N. bank of the stream, which flows through a narrow wooded gorge, forming an uninterrupted series of rapids and cascades. A few yards above the lower fall is a singular rock known as 'Hugh Lloyd's Pulpit' from the tradition that a local sage and bard used to preach from its flat top. A little farther on, the path crosses the stream and continues to ascend on the S. bank. One of the best points of view is the so-called 'Goat's Bridge', a slab of rock spanning a narrow part of the stream. The *Higher Fall*, descending in two leaps, is reached a little farther on. Many visitors turn here, but the ravine is still very picturesque higher up, and the stream forms other little falls. The path passes under a railway-bridge, crosses a wall, traverses a plantation carpeted with heather, crosses another wall, and reaches a farm-road, which leads to the left after a few yards to the Ffestiniog and Trawsfynydd road. *Pont Newydd* (see below), $1^1/_4$ M. from Ffestiniog, lies a few paces to the left.

Crossing Pont Newydd, we may ascend the lane to the right for $^1/_4$ M. and then descend by a road to the right, which turns to the left on reaching the stream and leads along its N. bank. At the ($^1/_2$ M.) fork we ascend to the left, avoiding the descent to the stepping-stones. In 13 min. more we pass *Cym Cynfael*, a lonely farm-house, once the home of Hugh Lloyd (see above). The road here is a mere grassy track; farther on, it becomes very stony, and ascends to the left round a rocky knoll. At the top we come in sight of the **Rhaiadr Cwm*, a graceful but narrow fall, where the Cynfael is precipitated over a lofty barrier of rock. Just above the fall the track joins the high-road from Ffestiniog to Bala, at a point about $3^1/_4$ M. from Ffestiniog, for which we turn to the left. A good view of the fall is obtained from the road after we have gone a little way towards Ffestiniog. To the right, about $^1/_4$ M. from the road and not visible from it, lies *Llyn-y-Morwynion*, or the 'Lake of the Maidens', about $1^1/_4$ M. below which, and also $^1/_4$ M. from the road, is a spot called the *Beddau-Gwyr-Ardudwy*, or 'Graves of the Men of Ardudwy'. According to the legend, the men of Ardudwy had carried off a number of women from the vale of Clwyd, but were overtaken and slain here by the injured husbands and fathers. The women, however, rather than return to their homes, drowned themselves in the Llyn-y-Morwynion.

The road to ($1^1/_4$ M.) Pont Newydd diverges to the left about 1 M. from the point where we join the Bala road. In descending we have a view of Moelwyn and the mountains backing the estuary of the Dwyryd. The Bala road joins the Trawsfynydd road at the Ffestiniog station.

Tomen-y-Mur, Rhaiadr Du, and the Raven Fall. This excursion may be begun at *Maentwrog Road Station*, which is 2 M. from Ffestiniog, on the road to Trawsfynydd. From the station we follow the road to ($^1/_4$ M.) a small school, where it is joined by that leading to Maentwrog (see below). Here we turn to the left, and after a few hundred paces we leave the high-road by the second cart-track (very stony) to the left. This passes under the railway; and after about 12 min., just beyond a small cottage, we come in sight of **Tomen-y-Mur** (pron. 'Tommen-y-Meer') a circular mound about 30 ft. high, on the top of a grassy hill (reached from the path in 10 min.). It is supposed to mark the site of the Roman station *Heriri Mons*, from which the 'Sarn Helen' (p. 311) and other Roman roads diverged. It commands an extensive sea and mountain view. We now return to the school-house and descend towards Maentwrog for about $^1/_4$ M. We then turn to the left, opposite a private road leading to Maentwrog. After $^1/_2$ M. the lane turns to the right, opposite a gate; $^1/_4$ M. farther on, where it forks, we ascend to the left. We next reach an open spot commanding a good view of the Vale of Ffestiniog, and soon pass ($^1/_2$ M.) a cottage on the right, where we begin the descent to the lovely wooded glen of the *Prysor*. After 3 min. we descend to the left to a door in a wall. The path on the other side descends steeply to the track leading along the stream. Ascending this to the left, we soon come (3 min.) in sight of ***Rhaiadr Du** (pron. 'Dee'), or the 'Black Fall', most romantically placed. To reach the other fall, which is lower down, we return by the path to (5 min.) a wicket-gate and bear to the right to (3 min.) an old limekiln. Here we turn sharply to the left and descend for about 300 yds., when a small path on the right leads to the various points of view for the **Raven Fall.** Visitors should not go too near the brink. We now return to the limekiln, and 4-5 min. beyond it, at a gate, rejoin the main track from which we diverged to visit Rhaiadr Du. Our route now descends through a charming wooded glen to (1/2 M.) the high-road, which we follow to the right to (3/4 M.) Maentwrog (see below).

[In coming from Maentwrog we follow the Harlech road for 3/4 M. and leave it by a red gate on the left, just before a bridge. In a few paces more we pass another gate, beyond which there is a placard indicating the house of the guide to the falls. The track to the latter leads straight on, up the hill, and the guide may be dispensed with.]

Maentwrog *(Grapes Hotel)*, pron. '*Mántoorog*', is a small village on the S. side of the valley of the Dwyryd, at the foot of a low and partly wooded hill. It derives its name from the stone (maen) of St. Twrog, a rude uninscribed monument, 4 ft. high, at the W. end of the church. On the opposite side of the valley is *Tan-y-Bwlch* (p. 314). The mansion of *Plas* (p. 314) is also a conspicuous object. The distance by road from Maentwrog to Ffestiniog is 3 M. The road may be quitted at the (2 1/4 M.) foot of the last long hill up to the village, and the footpath through the vale of the Cynfael followed (stile to the right, at the bridge).

The above excursions may be accomplished in one day by tolerable walkers. Llyn Morwynion and the Graves of the Men of Ardudwy may be left out without much loss, and Tomen-y-Mur might also be omitted. The stages are as follows: From Ffestiniog to the Cynfael Falls and up the valley to Pont Newydd 1 1/2 M.; from Pont Newydd to the Rhaiadr Cwm 1 1/2 M.; back to Pont Newydd by the Bala road 2 1/4 M.; from Pont Newydd to Maentwrog Road 1 1/4 M.; thence to Tomen-y-Mur and back 2 M.; visit to Rhaiadr Du and the Raven Fall, and down to Maentwrog 4 M.; from Maentwrog to Ffestiniog 3 M. This makes in all 15-16 M., for which 6-7 hrs. should be allowed.

Excursions may also be made from Ffestiniog to (3 M.) *Tan-y-Bwlch* and (16 M.) *Beddgelert* (see p. 319), and viâ (5 M.) *Trawsfynydd* to the (5 M.) *Gate of Ardudwy* (p. 291) or *Pistyll-y-Cain* (p. 299). The ascent of the *Manods* (p. 311) does not repay the exertion, but *Moelwyn* (p. 311) or *Cynicht* (p. 319; 4 hrs.) may be climbed.

From Blaenau Ffestiniog to Port Madoc by the 'Narrow Gauge Railway', 13 M., in 1 hr. (fares 2*s.* 9*d.*, 2*s.* 2*d.*, 1*s.* 8*d.*; return-tickets 4*s.* 4*d.*, 3*s.* 6*d.*, 2*s.* 4*d.*).

This 'Toy Railway', in which the gauge is only 2 ft. and the carriages and locomotives correspondingly tiny, was originally a tram-line (made in 1836) for conveying slate, and was opened as a passenger-line in 1869. It runs along the N. side of the Dwyryd valley, of which it affords charming views. The engineering skill shown in the construction of the line is very great, and some of the curves are astonishingly abrupt. In approaching Tan-y-Bwlch station we sometimes see the train we here meet and pass steaming along the other side of the ravine in a direction parallel to our own. The open first-class carriages afford the best views (to the left in descending). Passengers should beware of putting their heads out of the windows, as the train runs within a hand's-breadth of the walls of the rocky cuttings. The railway is seen to greatest advantage in ascending.

The train starts from the terminus at *Duffws* (710 ft; see p. 311) and almost immediately stops again at *Blaenau Ffestiniog*. 2 1/2 M. *Tan-y-Grisiau* (630 ft.) is the best starting-place for the ascent of *Moelwyn* (1 1/2 hr.). We then pass through a tunnel, 3/4 M. long, beyond which we have a view of the valley, with the village of

Ffestiniog perched on a hill on the other side. We next thread another tunnel, pass a lake on the left, and a small waterfall on the right, and bend to the right round the glen of Tan-y-Bwlch. 6 M. *Tan-y-Bwlch* (400 ft.; *Tan-y-Bwlch Hotel, in the valley, 1 M. below), the crossing-station of the line, lies at the head of the most abrupt curve. Beyond Tan-y-Bwlch we see Maentwrog (p. 313) on the other side of the valley and the mansion of *Plas* immediately below us (visitors admitted to the grounds). Fine views of the estuary of the *Dwyryd.* 10 M. *Penrhyn*, a quarrymen's village. At (11 M.) *Mynffordd Junction* we cross the Cambrian railway (see p. 293). We then cross *Traeth Mawr* by a long embankment (view of Snowdon to the right) and reach (13 M.) *Port Madoc* (see p. 293).

e. From Carnarvon to Llanberis and Bettws-y-Coed.

Railway from Carnarvon to (9 M.) *Llanberis* in 1/2 hr. (fares 1*s.* 8*d.*, 1*s.* 3d., 11*d.*). Coach from Llanberis to (15 1/2 M.) *Bettws-y-Coed* in 2 3/4-3 hrs. (fare 4*s.*). The coaches run in connection with the morning-trains. A coach also leaves Carnarvon about 11 a. m. and makes the round of Snowdon viâ Beddgelert and Bettws, reaching Llanberis in the evening (in time for table d'hôte at the Victoria).

As the train quits Carnarvon station we see Twt Hill (p. 291) to the left, and after crossing the *Seiont* we obtain a good retrospect of the castle to the right. Our line then diverges to the left from the line to Afon Wen (p. 292) and ascends the wooded valley of the Seiont, crossing the stream several times. Beyond (7 M.) *Cwm-y-Glo* we pass through a tunnel (view of Snowdon to the right) and reach *Llyn Padarn* (2 M. long), the larger of the two Llanberis lakes, the beauty of which has been spoiled by slate-quarries.

9 M. **Llanberis.** — **Hotels.** *Victoria, a large house, finely situated just outside the village, 300 yds. from the station, with a garden, R. & A. 4*s.* 6*d.*, table d'hôte at 7 p.m. 4s.; Padarn Villa, well spoken of; Castle, Snowdon Valley, Vaenol Arms, an unpretending inn, at Old Llanberis. — *Lodgings* in the village.

Carriage to *Pen-y-Pass* 5s. 6*d.*, *Pen-y-Gwryd* 6*s.*, *Capel Curig* 10*s.*, *Beddgelert* 14*s.*, *Bettws-y-Coed* 16*s.*, and *Bangor* viâ Capel Curig 26*s.*

Guides and **Ponies** for the ascent of Snowdon, see p. 321.

Llanberis, the 'Chamonix of Wales', with about 2000 inhab., is situated at the head of Llyn Padarn, at the N.W. base of Snowdon, and near the foot of the celebrated Pass of Llanberis. The immediate neighbourhood is, however, becoming more and more disfigured by huge slate-quarries. The two *Lakes of Llanberis* are both surrounded by wild and barren hills, descending abruptly to the water's edge. *Llyn Peris* to the S.E., 1 1/4 M. long, is the more striking of the two, but is sadly encroached upon by the Dinorwic Slate Quarries. Behind the Victoria Hotel, at the lower end of Llyn Peris, is the picturesque *Dolbadarn Castle*, a solitary tower, whence there is a good view up the pass of Llanberis. The small village of *Old Llanberis* lies 2 M. to the S. E., at the beginning of the pass. Llanberis is the starting-point for the easiest ascent of Snowdon (see p. 321).

About 1/2 M. to the S. of the Victoria Hotel is the romantic waterfall of *Ceunant Mawr ('great chasm'). We follow the lane diverging from the road immediately opposite the approach to the hotel, turn to the right after 300 yds. (the Snowdon route leading straight on), cross the stream, and a little farther on turn to the left through a little gate and round the back of some cottages. The path then leads direct to the falls. From the village we may also ascend past the handsome new *Church* and join the above route at the cottages. The fall, which is 60 ft. high, makes a singular bend in the middle; after heavy rain it covers the whole face of the rock.

The *Dinorwic Slate Quarries*, rising tier over tier above Llyn Peris, are very productive and scarcely less imposing than those of Penrhyn. The blasting operations take place during the first few minutes of each hour; notice is given by a fog-horn, and the paths near the quarry are closed for the time being.

From Llanberis to the Snowdon Ranger, 4 M. (1 3/4 hr.). We ascend past the Ceunant Mawr waterfall (see above) and follow the cart-track along the right (W.) side of the valley. On the opposite side of the cwm is seen the Snowdon track. Beyond some cottages the cart-track narrows to a bridle-path. Soon afterwards it bends to the right and ascends through the lonely *Maes Cwm* to (1-1 1/4 hr.) *Bwlch-y-Maes-Cwm* (1100 ft.), the head of the pass, where a fine mountain-view breaks on our gaze, the most conspicuous summit at first being that of *Y Garn*. Snowdon is also well seen in our rear, and Llyn Cwellyn comes into sight as we descend. We pass through the small red gate to the left, and cross the field to (200 yds.) a similar red gate. Beyond this point the path is very ill-defined, but by bearing to the right we soon strike the Snowdon track (p. 322) and reach a gate with miry ground on both sides of it, whence a zigzag green track descends to a small farm just above the road and the railway. The *Snowdon Ranger* (see p. 317) lies a little way to the left and is reached in about 1/2 hr. (or less) from the time we left the top of the pass. Ascent of Snowdon from this point, see p. 322.

[In the reverse direction we cross the railway at the level crossing a little to the N. of the Snowdon Ranger and pass through the (5 min.) farm-yard. The path at first is scarcely marked, but the zigzag green track, ascending to (20 min.) the gate with wet ground on both sides, is distinctly visible. After passing through the gate we diverge to the left from the well-marked Snowdon track and ascend across the grassy slope, soon reaching the lower of the above-mentioned red gates. The ascent to the top of the pass from this side takes about 3/4 hr.]

The easy ascent of *Moel Eilio* (2300 ft.; *View), which rises to the S. of Llanberis, is worth making if time permit.

From Llanberis to Bethesda, 8 M. This mountain-walk is the shortest route from Llanberis to Nant Ffrancon and Bangor. We pass over the bridge between the lakes and then ascend to the left (see note as to the blasting, above). Farther on we cross a dreary moor, with a reservoir in the middle, pass a little to the left of the small hills *Drysgol Fawr* and *Moel-y-Ci*, and then descend by *St. Anne's Chapel* to *Bethesda* (p. 287). The route however, is intricate and requires the aid of a good map or guide. — With this walk may be combined (comp. Map) the ascent of the *Elidyr Fawr* (3033 ft.; 2 1/2 hrs. from Llanberis), which commands a good mountain-panorama, with Anglesey and the Menai Strait.

From Llanberis to Bettws-y-Coed. The coach runs along the W. side of *Llyn Peris*, passing a small castellated building on the left, descends to (2 M.) *Old Llanberis* (see above), and enters the ***Pass of Llanberis**, the wildest valley in N. Wales. The road now ascends pretty steeply, between the towering precipices of Snowdon on the right and Y Garn and the Glyders on the left.

A fine mountain-route (3-4 hrs.) leads from Old Llanberis across the range separating the Pass of Llanberis from Nant Ffrancon. We turn to the left a few yards beyond the *Church*, which possesses an interesting roof of the 15th cent., and follow a path up the hill. From the highest cottage we ascend steeply to the right of a wall, and when the wall turns we keep to the right by a streamlet. The path soon ends, but our route leads to the E., across the ridge to the S. of the summit of *Y Garn* (3107 ft.). Fine view of Snowdon to the right. Beyond the ridge we descend to *Llyn-y-Cwn* ('Lake of Dogs') and the head of the *Twll Du* or *Devil's Kitchen* (p. 310), where we obtain a splendid *View. From Llyn-y-Cwn it is a climb of about 3/4 hr. (3 hrs. from Old Llanberis) to the top of *Y Glyder Fawr* (3275 ft.; *View of Snowdon and the Pass of Llanberis). To reach *Llyn Ogwen* (p. 310) we descend to the right of the Devil's Kitchen (caution necessary in misty weather) to *Llyn Idwal.*

As we ascend, the valley rapidly grows narrower and wilder. Good retrospect of the Llanberis lakes and Dolbadarn Castle. To the right is the huge hollow of **Cwm Glas*, high up between the towering cliffs of Crib-Goch and Crib-y-Ddysgyl. Numerous traces of glacial action are visible on the rocks. About 1 1/2 M. from Old Llanberis we pass a small foot-bridge on the right, and soon after (1/4 M.) reach a huge fallen boulder (on the left), erroneously named the *Cromlech.* We then cross the *Pont-y-Gromlech*, and ascend to (1 1/2 M) *Gorphwysfa* or *Pen-y-Pass* (1200 ft.; Inn), the head of the pass, commanding a fine view in both directions. [Ascent of Snowdon, the summit of which is nowhere visible from the Pass of Llanberis, from this point, see p. 321.] About 1/2 M. beyond the inn the road turns sharply to the left, and we have a charming view down Nant Gwynant (p. 318) to the right, with Cynicht in the background. Moel Siabod (p. 309), seen to little advantage from this side, is prominent infront. At (1/2 M.) ***Pen-y-Gwryd Inn** ('Pen-y-Goorid'; 970 ft.), patronised by anglers and by tourists making the ascent of Snowdon from this side (comp. p. 321), the road through Nant Gwynant to Beddgelert diverges to the right (see p. 318).

The ascent of *Moel Siabod* (2865 ft.) from Pen-y-Gwryd takes about 2 hrs. (descent to Dolwyddelan, see p. 309, in 1-1 1/2 hr.). The shortest ascent of *Y Glyder Fawr* (see above; 1 1/2-2 hrs.) is also made from Pen-y-Gwyrd or Gorphwysfa. The route, which can scarcely be missed, leads straight up the ridge extending from Gorphwysfa (see Map).

Beyond Pen-y-Gwryd the road descends the somewhat uninteresting *Nant-y-Gwryd*, with a view of the Capel Curig lakes in the distance, to (4 M.) **Capel Curig** ('Kappel Kerrig'; **Royal; Bryntyrch*, plain), situated amid some of the finest scenery of N. Wales, and much frequented by mountaineers. It commands admirable views of Snowdon. Visitors to the Royal Hotel are entitled to fish in the *Llyniau Mymbyr*, two small lakes adjoining the village.

Among the ascents most frequently made from Capel Curig, after Snowdon (see p. 321), are those of *Moel Siabod* (p. 309; 1 1/2 hr.), *Carnedd Dafydd* (p. 288; 2 1/2-3 hrs.), *Carnedd Llewelyn* (p. 288; 2 1/2-3 hrs.), *Pen Llithrig* (2623 ft.; 1 1/4 hr.), and *Creigiau Gleision* (1 1/4 hr.), between Llyns Cwlyd and Crafnant. A pleasant walk may be taken to Trefriw (p. 307), either viâ (2 1/2 M.) *Llyn Cwlyd* (9 M.; 3 1/2-4 1/2 hrs.), or by *Llyn Crafnant* (6 3/4 M.; 2 1/2-3 hrs.), or by *Llyn Geirionydd* (7 1/2 M.; 3-4 hrs.).

From Capel Curig to (5 1/2 M.) *Bettws-y-Coed*, see p. 309.

f. From Carnarvon to the Snowdon Ranger, Rhyd-Ddu, and Beddgelert.

Railway to ($12^1/_2$ M.) *Rhyd-Ddu* in 1-2 hrs. (fares 2*s.* 2*d.*, 1*s.* 8*d.*, 1*s.* 3*d.*). Omnibus from Rhyd-Ddu to (4 M.) *Beddgelert* in $^3/_4$ hr. From Carnarvon we may also reach Beddgelert viâ *Llanberis*, whence a coach runs viâ Pen-y-Gwryd to ($14^1/_2$ M.) Beddgelert in $2^1/_2$ hrs. (fare 4*s.*); comp. R. 40e. Another coach, starting in the morning, runs all the way from Carnarvon to (13 M.) Beddgelert (fare 3*s.* 6*d.*; see p. 317).

From Carnarvon to ($3^1/_4$ M.) *Dinas*, see p. 292. We here leave the L. N. W. Railway and proceed by the narrow-gauge line of the Dinas and Snowdon District Railway, which diverges to the left. The line at once begins to ascend, commanding a view to the right of the Rivals (p. 292) and the Menai Strait. From ($5^1/_2$ M.) *Tryfan Junction* a short branch diverges on the right to (3 M.) *Bryngwyn*, on the slope of *Moel-y-Tryfan* (fine view). The train now follows the valley of the *Gwrfai* to (7 M.) *Waenfawr* and (8 M.) *Bettws Garmon.* The latter is the station for the picturesque *Nant Mill*, of which we have a view to the left a little farther on. To the left is *Moel Eilio*, and to the right, in front, is *Mynydd Mawr* (2295 ft.), with the precipitous *Craig Cwm Bychan*, at the foot of *Llyn Cwellyn.* The train now skirts the N. side of the lake, which is about 1 M. long, while in front we see the summit of Snowdon ('Y Wyddfa'), with the lower peak of *Yr Aran* (2264 ft.) to the right.

$10^1/_4$ M. **Snowdon Ranger Station** (**Inn*, unpretending), on the N. side of Llyn Cwellyn, is one of the regular starting-points for the ascent of Snowdon (see p. 322), and is frequented by anglers (trout and char) in Llyn Cwellyn. The top of *Mynydd Mawr* (see above), on the other side of the lake, commands a good view. From the Snowdon Ranger to (4 M.) *Llanberis*, see p. 315.

Beyond the Snowdon Ranger the train crosses a ravine, with a waterfall to the left, and ascends steadily. Fine views. Moel Hebog (p. 319) rises in front.

$12^1/_2$ M. **Rhyd-Ddu** (*Cwellyn Arms*, a rustic inn), pronounced 'Ruddthy', the terminus of the railway, is finely situated at the foot of Snowdon, which here presents a very imposing appearance. Rhyd-Ddu is only $3^1/_2$ M. from the summit (ascent, see p. 322). A road beginning opposite the inn ascends past *Llyn-y-Dywarchen* to *Bwlch-y-Felin* (750 ft.) and then descends between Mynydd Mawr and Y Garn to (6 M.) *Nantlle* (p. 292).

Rhyd-Ddu is 4 M. from Beddgelert (omn., see above). The road runs near the E. bank of *Llyn-y-Gader*, and soon reaches the highest point of the route (600 ft.). About 1 M. from Rhyd-Ddu we pass, on the right, *Pitt's Head*, a rock supposed to resemble that statesman; farther on is another rock inscribed *Llam Trwsgyll*, commemorating the step ('llam') made by the giant Trwsgyll from this point to the other side of the stream.

4 M. **Beddgelert.** — **Hotels.** *Royal Goat, a few hundred yards from the village, on the road to Port Madoc, R. & A. 4*s.*, table d'hôte 4*s.* 6*d.*; *Saracen's Head, *Prince Llewelyn, in the village. — *Lodgings.*

Coaches run from Beddgelert to *Port Madoc* (8 M.; fare 2*s.* 6*d.*), *Bettws-y-Coed* (17½ M.; 5*s.*, return 8*s.*), *Llanberis* (14½ M.; 4*s.*), *Pen-y-Gwryd* (8 M.), and *Capel Curig* (12 M.).

Fishing may be obtained in the *Colwyn*, the *Glaslyn*, and numerous lakes and tarns (particulars at the hotels).

Beddgelert, the 'gem of Welsh villages', is charmingly situated at the junction of the *Colwyn* and *Glaslyn*, near the S. base of Snowdon, and is in every respect one of the best centres for tourists in N. Wales. It is much less shut in than Bettws-y-Coed, and is surrounded by mountains instead of hills; its environs are not marred by slate-quarries like those of Llanberis; while its romantic situation has more individuality than that of Dolgelley. It derives its name, meaning 'Grave of Gelert', from the touching legend of Llewelyn's hound, of which this is said to have been the scene. The grave is marked by a few rude stones in a small shaded enclosure in the second field to the S. of the village.

We reach it either by a footpath beginning close to the wooden bridge at the confluence of the streams, or by passing through the shrubbery in front of the Goat Hotel and turning to the right. Wales, however, does not monopolize this pathetic story any more than Switzerland does that of William Tell; and similar legends have been current in Ireland, France, India, and Persia. Beddgelert is the principal scene of Southey's 'Madoc'.

About 1½ M. to the S. of the village, on the road to Port Madoc (see below), is the highly romantic ****Pass of Aberglaslyn**, enclosed by sheer walls of rock 800 ft. high, which barely leave room for the road and the little river *Glaslyn*, here crossed by the *Pont Aberglaslyn.* The richly-tinted rocks, the fine sky-line of the cliffs, the clear sea-green colour and picturesque brokenness of the river, the grouping of the trees, and the romantic ivy-draped bridge combine to make this one of the loveliest scenes in Wales. The best point of view is on the Port Madoc road, a little beyond the bridge. We may return to Beddgelert by the footpath on the E. side of the Glaslyn (rough, and very wet after rain), or along the top of the ridge, the *Craig-y-Llan*, on the same side of the stream.

From Beddgelert to Bettws-y-Coed, 17½ M., coach daily in 2½ hrs. (fares 5*s.*: to Capel Curig 3*s.* 6*d.*). This fine drive, through the picturesque ***Nant Gwynant,** completes the circuit of Snowdon, joining the Llanberis and Bettws road at (8 M.) Pen-y-Gwryd (p. 316). The road runs towards the N. E., at the foot of *Yr Aran* (p. 322), and soon reaches (2 M.) the pretty little *Llyn-y-Dinas.* About 1 M. farther on we have a view to the left, up *Cwm-y-Llan*, of the summit of Snowdon; to the right, in front, Moel Siabod (p. 309) is conspicuous. We then pass (1 M.) *Llyn Gwynant* and ascend steeply, following the course of the Gwynant, to (4 M.) *Pen-y-Gwryd* (p. 316). The mountains in front are the *Glyders* (p. 310). From Pen-y-Gwryd to (9½ M.) *Bettws-y-Coed*, see p. 314.

From Beddgelert to Port Madoc, 8 M., coach several times daily in 2 hrs. (fare 2*s.* 6*d.*). This road passes through (1½ M.) the beautiful **Pass of Aberglaslyn* (see above) and descends the expanding valley of the Glaslyn, skirting the slopes of *Moel-Ddu.* To the left rise the strikingly formed *Cynicht* (p. 319) and *Moelwyn* (p. 311). A fine retrospect of Snowdon also gradually opens out. Pedestrians may save about 1 M. by diverging to the left at (4½ M.) the *Glaslyn Inn* and following the tramway across the marsh. The road trends to the right and soon passes under a fine range of ivy-clad crags. In front rises *Moel-y-Gest* (p. 293). 7 M. *Tremadoc*, and (8 M.) *Port Madoc*, see p. 293.

From Beddgelert to Ffestiniog. The new road (16 M.) crosses the Pont Aberglaslyn (p. 318), turns to the right, and leads to the S. to (9 M.) *Penrhyndeudraeth* (p. 293). Here we turn to the left and ascend the valley of the *Dwyryd*, passing (4 M.) *Tan-y-Bwlch Hotel* (p. 314). — The old road (13 M.), shorter and more picturesque than the new one, but very rough for carriages, diverges to the left about ½ M. beyond an *Inn*, and 1½ M. on this side of Penrhyn. It leads over the *Bwlch-y-Maen Pass*, and descends, passing below the Toy Railway, to Tan-y-Bwlch. — The best route for walkers (11 M.) is the mountain-path, which branches to the left from the road, just beyond a small stream, ¼ M. past the Pont Aberglaslyn. We cross (1¼ M.) the small vale of *Nant-y-Mor* and (½ M.) the *Cwm Croesor* (slate-tramway). The track then runs along the W. slopes of the Moelwyns to (2½ M.) Tan-y-Bwlch. — The ascent of either Cynicht or Moelwyn may be combined with this route. The top of the fine conical ***Cynicht** (2370 ft.; pron. 'Cunnicht' or 'Cnicht'), which has been called the Welsh Matterhorn, is reached, by ascending the ridge on the hither side of Cwm Croesor (see above), in about 2½ hrs. after leaving Beddgelert. To reach the top of **Moelwyn** (2529 ft.; p. 311) we cross the Cwm Croesor and ascend to the left. Robust walkers, however, may easily ascend both summits (from Cynicht to Moelwyn 1 hr.) and descend to Ffestiniog (Tan-y-Grisiau or Tan-y-Bwlch, see p. 314) in about 7 hrs. — *Ffestiniog*, see p. 311.

Ascent of Moel Hebog, 1½-2 hrs. We may ascend by a path to the N. of the Goat Hotel, passing a small farm, and turning to the right beyond a gap in a wall; or we may follow the Carnarvon road for a short distance, cross the Colwyn by a small bridge, bend to the right, and ascend by the more northerly of the two spurs. The last part of the former route is rather steep. The top of **Moel Hebog** (2578 ft.) affords a charming bird's-eye view of Beddgelert, and the panorama includes Snowdon, the Glyders, Moel Siabod, Cader Idris, the Rivals, and Cardigan Bay.

Among other peaks which may be ascended from Beddgelert are those of *Yr Aran* (2800 ft.), the S. spur of Snowdon; *Mynydd Mawr* (2293 ft.; p. 317); and *Y Garnedd Goch* (2315 ft.).

g. Snowdon.

Snowdon (3571 ft.), Welsh *Eryri*, the highest mountain in England or Wales, but 835 ft. lower than Ben Nevis in Scotland (p. 495), deserves its rank as monarch of Welsh mountains as much for the grandeur of its form as for its height. It consists of a group of five distinct peaks: *Y Wyddfa* ('the conspicuous'), the central and highest; *Crib-y-Goch* ('red peak') and *Crib-y-Ddysgyl* ('Thusgil') on the N; *Lliwedd* ('triple-crested') to the S.E.; and *Yr Aran*, to the S. The best view of the entire group is that from Capel Curig (see p. 36), and the summit is, perhaps, best seen from the road near Port Madoc (see above) or from the Traeth Mawr embankment (p. 293). The view from the Nantlle valley (p. 292) is also celebrated. Notwithstanding its name, Snowdon is 800 ft. below the snow-line, and its summit is generally free from snow from April to the end of October. Snowdon, like nearly all the mountains of North Wales, belongs to the Cambrian and Silurian systems, and consists mainly of slate, grit, and porphyry, surmounted by felspathic lava.

For a coloured map of Snowdonia see pages 580 & 581

The four recognised ascents of Snowdon are those from *Llanberis* (p. 314), *Capel Curig* (*Pen-y-Gwryd* or *Gorphwysfa;* p. 320), *Beddgelert* (*Rhyd-Ddu;* p. 317), and the *Snowdon Ranger* (p. 317). None of these is attended with danger, if reasonable caution be observed; and travellers who have had any experience in mountaineering may dispense with guides in clear weather. The Llanberis track is particularly distinct and easy, while it is also the least interesting. Those who wish to see the mountain to greatest advantage are recommended to ascend from Capel Curig, the finest and steepest route, and descend to Beddgelert (or *vice versâ*). Travellers who begin and end their excursion at Llanberis should descend to *Pen-y-Pass*, and return through the fine Pass of Llanberis. Experts will find abundant opportunity of testing their skill and nerve, especially among the crags and precipices of Crib Goch and Cwm Glas (p. 316); but great caution is necessary when off the beaten track, and it should not be forgotten that Snowdon has a long list of victims.

At the top of Snowdon is the so-called *Snowdon Hotel*, consisting of two small huts where beds and refreshments may be obtained. A meal of ham and eggs, bread and butter, and tea or coffee, is furnished at a fixed charge of 2*s*.; and supper, bed, and breakfast cost 8*s*. Malt liquors and spirits are also provided at charges that cannot be called unreasonable.

Guides. The charges for guides are as given below, and travellers should not encourage their habit of asking for an additional douceur, unless they have had unusual trouble. The guides should carry light wraps, etc. Solitary travellers will generally find a companion at the hotels.

The **View from the top of Snowdon, though scarcely so wild and grand as some of the mountain-panoramas in Scotland (*e.g.* the mountains of Skye, p. 491), is very extensive and varied, including the greater part of North Wales, a wide expanse of sea, and upwards of twenty lakes and tarns. The view at sunrise or sunset is particularly fine (night-quarters, see above); but the summit is often swathed in mist for days at a time, and visitors should prepare themselves for a possible disappointment. The mist, however, is not always an unmixed evil, as some of the finest effects are produced by its surging or dispersal.

View. One of the most striking features is formed by the subsidiary ridges and huge hollows of Snowdon itself, which fill up the immediate foreground: to the N. and N.E. *Crib-Goch* and *Crib-y-Ddysgyl*, with the deep depression of *Cwm Glas;* to the S.W. and S. *Lliwedd* (with a memorial cross to a tourist killed in 1888) and *Yr Aran*, with the *Cwm-y-Llan* between them; to the W. and N.W. the less sharply-defined ridges of *Llechog* and *Clogwyn-du'r-Arddu*. To the N., beyond Crib Goch, the view extends to the *Sea*, *Anglesey*, the *Menai Strait* and *Bridges*, and, in the background, the *Isle of Man*. The lower end of *Llyn Padarn* at Llanberis is seen a little to the left of N., and to the right of it rises the pointed *Elidyr-Fawr*, next to which come the lofty *Carnedd Dafydd* and *Carnedd Llewelyn*. To the right of the latter, and somewhat nearer, are the *Glyders*, just behind which is the pyramidal *Tryfan*. To the N.E. stretch the *Clwydian Hills*, and due E. is *Moel Siabod*, with the *Capel Curig* lakes to the left of it. In the foreground are *Glaslyn* and *Llyn Llydaw*, with the green *Nant Gwynant* behind the latter. To the right of Siabod, in the background, are the *Berwyns*, and still farther to the right (S.E.) are the distant summits of the *Arenigs* and the *Arans*. Almost in the same direction, but much nearer, rise *Moelwyn* and the finely-shaped *Cynicht*. Almost due S. rises *Cader Idris*, with a bit of *Plinlimmon* behind it. To the right is *Cardigan Bay*, seen in its full extent from *St. David's Head* on the S. to the *Lleyn Promontory* on the N. To the S.W. rises *Moel Hebog*, to the right of which, and farther off, are the sharp peaks of the *Rivals*. The chief sheets of water visible to the S.W. and W. are the *Nantlle Lakes*, *Llyn-y-Gader*, and *Llyn Cwellyn*. To the N. (right)

For a Panorama from the top of Snowdon see pages 582 & 583

of the last rises *Moel Eilio*, beyond which the eye regains its starting-point. In clear weather the *Wicklow Mts.* (70 M. distant) are visible to the W. and the *Cumbrian Mts* to the N.E.; and it is said that even a part of Scotland may sometimes be distinguished. Comp. the Panorama.

Ascent of Snowdon from Llanberis (5 M., in 1¾-3½ hrs.; guide 5*s.*; with descent to Beddgelert, Snowdon Ranger, or Capel Curig 10*s.*; pony 5*s.*). There is a distinct and easy bridle-path all the way to the top. During the season the ascent is sometimes made by hundreds of persons in one day. Most walkers will easily outstrip the slow-moving ponies.

We leave the high-road by the lane opposite the Victoria Hotel (comp. p. 314), which ascends through wood to the left of the stream and the *Ceunant Mawr* (p. 315). Soon after quitting the wood, the path turns sharply to the left and ascends the ridge. The route beyond this can hardly be mistaken. On the other side of the valley we see the path leading to the Snowdon Ranger (see p. 315). In front the summit is seen towering to the right of Crib-y-Ddysgyl, while the retrospect includes the sea and the island of Anglesey. About 3 M. from Llanberis, at a height of about 2000 ft., we reach a *Refreshment Hut*. A few hundred yards to the right is the *Llyn Ddu'r Arddu*. Beyond the hut the path turns to the left and becomes steeper (fine views). It then ascends to the right, and beyond a ruined hut and spring of fresh water it is joined on the right by the Snowdon Ranger track and on the left (80 yds. farther on) by the path from Pen-y-Gwryd (p. 316). A stiff climb of ¼ hr. more brings us to the huts at the summit. If strength permit, the traveller should diverge to the left before reaching the spring and ascend to the top of *Crib-y-Ddysgyl* (p. 319), for the sake of the fine *View into the abysses of *Cwm Glas* (p. 316). View from the summit, see p. 320.

Ascent of Snowdon from Capel Curig, 9 M., in 3½-4½ hrs. (from Pen-y-Gwryd or Pen-y-Pass 2-3 hrs.). Ponies may be obtained at Capel Curig (10*s.*) or at (4 M.) Pen-y-Gwryd (5*s.*), guides at Pen-y-Gwryd or Pen-y-Pass (5*s.*). Tourists may also drive from Capel Curig to (5 M.) *Gorphwysfa* (*Pen-y-Pass;* 1200 ft.), where the actual ascent begins (see p. 316).

The track diverges to the left from the road a few yards on this side of the Pen-y-Pass Inn, and ascends gradually round an offshoot of Crib Goch. After about 1 M. we pass the tiny *Llyn Teyrn* on the left, with some deserted cottages, and ½ M. farther on reach *Llyn Llydaw* (1500 ft.), a fine sheet of water, upwards of 1 M. long, overhung by black and rugged cliffs. Our route crosses the lake by stepping-stones near its E. end (often under water in wet weather) and then runs to the left along the N. bank. [A footpath, diverging from the pony-track not far from the road, ascends rapidly at a higher level, under the peaks of Crib Goch and Crib-y-Ddysgyl, rejoining the pony-track at the upper part of the zigzag mentioned below.] In about 10 min. the track turns to the right and ascends through the *Cwm Dyli* (splendid view of Y Wyddfa in front) to the small tarn of **Glaslyn* (2000 ft.), lying at the foot of a precipice descending sheer from the summit of the mountain. From Glaslyn we ascend by a rough zigzag path, and after a stiff climb of ½-¾ hr. join the Llanberis route at the top of the ridge (see above). Hence to the top ¼ hr.

Ascent of Snowdon from Beddgelert, 6½ M., in 3-4 hrs.; guide 7*s.* 6*d.*, pony 7*s.* 6*d.*; from *Pont Rhyd-Ddu*, 3½ M., in 1½-2 hrs. (guide 5*s.*). These two routes unite very soon after leaving the high-road, and the best plan for visitors at Beddgelert is to drive to Pont Rhyd-Ddu (omn. daily) and begin the ascent there. The distant views of sea and lake and mountain are very fine.

From *Beddgelert* (p. 317) we follow the Carnarvon road to a point a few yards short of ($2^3/_4$ M.) *Pitt's Head* (p. 317), where we ascend to the right past a farm-house *(Ffridd-Uchaf)* and across a grassy slope with a hollow to the right. We join the Pont Rhyd-Ddu track about $^3/_4$ M. from the road. — From *Pont Rhyd-Ddu* (p. 317) we start from the road crossing the railway a little to the N. of the station, and follow a cart-track leading to a slate-quarry until it joins the ($^3/_4$ M.) Beddgelert route, where we ascend to the left. — After crossing the cart-track from Pont Rhyd-Ddu, the path, which is rather ill-defined at places, bends slightly to the right, crosses some rough ground, and passes through a wall near a sheepfold. We then go straight across the field and soon pass a small cairn, marking the spot where a tourist died from exhaustion in the snow. Fine view of Lake Cwellyn, Moel Hebog, Mynydd Mawr, the sea, Carnarvon, and Anglesey. A few yards farther on, the path leads through a wall, near a spring, bends round, and passes again through the wall. We are now on the shoulder of *Llechog*, from which we have a fine view into *Cwm y Clogwyn* (to the left), with its four small tarns. The Nantlle lakes (p. 292) are in sight to the W., between Mynydd Mawr and Y Garn, while the summit of Snowdon rises beyond the cwm. The path along the shoulders is well marked (fine views). Farther on, it bends to the left and ascends to the narrow ridge of **Bwlch-y-Maen*, from which the cliffs descend almost perpendicularly on either side; the fine hollow to the right is the *Cwm-y-Llan*. Persons subject to giddiness may find this part of the ascent a little trying, but the path is quite safe and is constantly traversed by ponies. A short but stiff climb now brings us to the top.

Ascent of Snowdon from the Snowdon Ranger (4 M., in $1^1/_2$-$2^1/_4$ hrs.; guide 7*s.* 6*d.*, pony 7*s.* 6*d.*).

From the Snowdon Ranger Inn to (20-25 min.) the point where the route to Llanberis diverges to the left, see p. 315. The Snowdon path leads straight on, and though it is sometimes indistinct, the general line towards the summit can scarcely be missed. By keeping well up the hill we avoid the marshy ground to the west. In about 1 hr. from the start we pass *Llyn Ffynnon-y-Gwas* on the right and begin the steep part of the ascent, which zigzags up the shoulder of *Clogwyn Du'r Arddu*, with the hollow of *Cwm Clogwyn* to the right. Farther up the path becomes very stony, and by diverging a few yards to the left we can look down upon the tiny *Llyn Du'r Arddu* (p. 321). The views from the latter part of the route, which joins the Llanberis track $^1/_4$ hr. from the summit, are very fine. Either this route or that from Pont Rhyd-Ddu is recommended as a descent for those who wish to reach Carnarvon.

Any of the above-described routes may be chosen for descending, and the directions given for the ascent will be found available for the descent. A good alternative descent to Beddgelert is the following. At the lower end of the Bwlch-y-Maen (see above), instead of turning to the right along the Llechog shoulder, we keep to the left in the direction of the summit of *Yr Aran* (2800 ft.), the S. outpost of Snowdon. From the *Bwlch-Cwm-y-Llan* we may now descend through the *Cwm-y-Llan* (see p. 320), passing some mines, to the road through Nant Gwynant (p. 318), which we reach $^1/_2$ M. to the S. of Llyn Gwynant. (To Pen-y-Gwryd, see p. 318.) Or we may proceed to the top of Yr Aran and descend on the other side direct to Beddgelert (p. 317).

41. From Chester to Birkenhead and Liverpool.

$16^1/_2$ M. Railway (joint L. N. W. and G. W. line) in $^3/_4$-1 hr., including the steam-ferry across the *Mersey* (fares 2*s.* 7*d.*, 2*s.* 1*d.*, 1*s.* 5*d.*).

The line traverses the peninsula between the estuaries of the *Dee* and the *Mersey*, commanding fine views of both. From (8 M.) *Hooton* branch-lines diverge on the one side to *Parkgate* and *West Kirby* (a sea-bathing resort on the Dee), and on the other to *Helsby* (for Warrington and Manchester). — $9^1/_2$ M. *Bromborough.* A little to the N. is *Eastham Ferry* (Ferry Hotel), whence steamers ply on the Mersey to Liverpool. The works of the *Manchester Ship Canal* (p. 339), which enters the Mersey here, include three large locks, 600, 450, and 150 ft. long. The outer gates weigh nearly 300 tons apiece. — $11^1/_2$ M. *Spital*, so named from an old hospital for lepers. 13 M. *Bebington*, with a church of the time of Henry VIII. The suburbs of Liverpool now come into sight beyond the Mersey. — 14 M. *Rock Ferry*, with frequent steamer-communication with Liverpool. — A little farther on, the train enters the spacious *Joint Station* at Birkenhead.

$15^1/_2$ M. **Birkenhead** *(Queen's; Woodside)*, a busy seaport of modern origin, with 83,324 inhab., on the left bank of the Mersey, which is here $^3/_4$ M. wide, practically forms an outlying part of Liverpool, and is connected with it by the Mersey Tunnel and several steam-ferries. At the beginning of this century the site of Birkenhead was occupied by a hamlet with scarcely 100 inhab., which had sprung up round the old *Priory of Byrkhed*, founded in the 11th cent.; the ruined priory-church of *St. Mary*, built in 1150, stands near the river, in the graveyard of the modern church.

The ***Docks** of Birkenhead cover an area of 170 acres, the largest being the *Great Float*, with a surface of 120 acres and a minimum depth of 20 ft. The two landing-stages are 800 ft. and 350 ft. long respectively, the *Quays* have a joint length of over 10 M.. and there are numerous large ship-building *Wharfs*. The celebrated *Alabama* was built here in 1862 by the *Messrs. Laird*, whose huge ship-building establishment contributes largely to the importance of the town. — Among the most prominent buildings are the *Town Hall;* the large *Market;* and *St. Aidan's College*, in the suburb of *Claughton*, for Anglican students. In the middle of the town is *Hamilton Square*, surrounded with handsome buildings and adorned with a *Statue of John Laird.* On the N.W. side of the town (tramway) is ***Birkenhead Park** (rail. stat., see p. 330), 180 acres in extent, laid out by Sir Joseph Paxton, the designer of the Crystal Palace at Sydenham, and adorned with several small lakes.

From Birkenhead to *New Brighton*, *Hoylake*, and *West Kirby*, see p. 330.

Through-passengers for Liverpool are carried by the train down to *Woodside Ferry*, whence a steamer conveys them across the Mersey to the *Landing Stage* (Pl. A, 3) in Liverpool. It is intended ultimately to run the train on to Liverpool through the Mersey Tunnel, which is at present used for local traffic only.

Liverpool. — **Railway Stations.** 1. *Lime Street Station* (Pl. D, 4), in the heart of the town, for the main L. N. W. service to London, Manchester, Edinburgh, Glasgow, etc. — 2. *Exchange Station* (Pl. B, 3), a handsome building, for trains to Manchester, Lancashire, Yorkshire, and Scotland. — 3. *Central* or *Ranelagh Street Station* (Pl. D, 5), for the Cheshire Lines, G. N. R., Midland, and Manchester, Sheffield, & Lincolnshire Co. (to Sheffield, London, Manchester, Derbyshire, Lincoln, etc.). — 4. *Woodside Station*, in Birkenhead (see above), for the G. W. and L. N. W. trains to Chester, Birmingham, Warwick, London, and Wales. — 5. *Mersey Tunnel Station* (Pl. B, 4), James St., for local trains to Birkenhead, New Brighton, Hoylake, and West Kirby. — *Cab* from the Lime St. or the Central Station to any of the undernoted hotels, 1*s*.

Hotels. *ADELPHI (Pl. a; D, 4), at the head of Ranelagh St., near the Central Station, R. & A. 4*s*.-7*s*. 6*d*., D. 3-6*s*.; *NORTH WESTERN HOTEL

For a coloured street plan of Liverpool see pages 584 & 585

(Pl. b; D, 4), at the Lime St. Station, R. & A. 4-6*s*., no table d'hôte; *LANCASHIRE AND YORKSHIRE HOTEL, at the Exchange Station (Pl. B, 3); *GRAND (Pl. c.; D, 4), IMPERIAL (Pl. d; D, 4), Lime St., opposite the station; *SHAFTESBURY TEMPERANCE (Pl. e; D, 5), Mount Pleasant, R. & A. from 3*s*.; *LAURENCE'S TEMPERANCE, 20 Clayton Sq. (Pl. C, 4); ALEXANDRA (Pl. f; B, 3), 51 Dale St.; COMPTON (Pl. g; C, 4), 39 Church St., commercial, R. & A. 5*s*.; ANGEL (Pl. j; B, 3), 22 Dale St., R. & A. 4*s*. 6*d*.

Restaurants. **Bear's Paw*, 53 Lord St.; *Wilson*, Castle St.; *Refreshment Rooms* at the Central, Lime St., and Exchange Stations, and at the Landing Stage (Pl. A, 3); also at the *North Western*, *Adelphi*, *Grand*, *Alexandra*, *Angel*, and other hotels (see above). — *Sainsbury's (Anderson's) Luncheon Rooms*, Exchange St. East, are crowded at midday by business men, and form one of the characteristic sights of Liverpool.

Cabs. For any distance not exceeding 1 M., 1*s*.; for each additional 1/2 M., 6*d*: By time, 6*d*. per 1/4 hr. These fares include 200*lbs*. of luggage on a four-wheeled cab, and 100*lbs*. on a hansom. Between midnight and 6 a.m. a fare and a half. Fares for two-horse cabs about double.

Tramways run through most of the principal streets and to the various suburbs. The chief starting-point is the *Pier Head* (Pl. A, 3). — *Omnibuses* along the Docks, see p. 329.

Steamers. A. RIVER STEAMERS, starting from the S. end of the *Landing Stage* (Pl. A, 3), ply to *Birkenhead* (Woodside; every few min.; fare 1*d*.; between midnight and 3.30 a.m., 6*d*.), *Egremont* (2*d*.), *Eastham* (p. 323; 4*d*.), *New Brighton* (p. 331; 3*d*.), *New Ferry* (2*d*.), *Rock Ferry* (p. 323; 2*d*.), *Seacombe* (1*d*.), *Tranmere* (1*d*.). The Birkenhead steam-ferries, before the opening of the tunnel, conveyed about 20 millions of passengers annually. — B. SEA-GOING STEAMERS ply to *Llandudno*, *Bangor*, and *Beaumaris*, daily in summer, in 4 hrs.; to *Penzance*, *Falmouth*, and *Plymouth*, at irregular intervals (fares 25*s*., 15*s*.); to *Milford* and *Bristol* in 28 hrs. (12*s*. 6*d*., 6*s*.); to the *Isle of Man*, see p. 340; to *Dublin*, daily (fare 8*s*.-13*s*. 6*d*.; deck 3-5*s*.); to *Glasgow* several times a week in 20 hrs. (12*s*. 6*d*, 6*s*.); and to various Continental ports. — The *American Liners*, or rather their tenders, also start chiefly from the N. end of the Landing Stage. Other steamers leave Liverpool at more or less regular intervals for Egypt, India, South America, and indeed for almost every part of the globe.

Shipping and Forwarding Agents. *United States Express Co. (Wheatley & Co.)*, 10 North John Street; *Pitt & Scott*, Corf's Buildings, Preeson's Row. See also p. 330. — **Steamer Chairs** may be obtained at *Bidston's*, Copperas Hill (opposite Adelphi Hotel) and 21 Lime St.; also from hawkers on board the steamers.

Theatres. *Shakespeare* (Pl. E, 3), Fraser St., London Road; *Court* (Pl. D, 4), Queen Sq.; *Alexandra* (Pl. D, 3, 4), Lime St.; *Prince of Wales* (Pl. C, 4), stalls 5*s*., dress circle 4*s*.; *Gaiety*, Camden St.; *Bijou* (Pl. D, 5), Bold St.; *Grand* (Pl. C, 4), Paradise St., stalls 2*s*.; *Rotunda*, Scotland Road; *Royal*, Argyle St., Birkenhead.

Music and Concert Halls. *Star Music Hall* (Pl. C, 4), Williamson Sq.; *Philharmonic Hall* (Pl. E, 6), Hope St., with room for 2500 persons; *St. James's Hall*, Lime St.; *Sefton Hall*, Park Road. — *Hengler's Circus*, West Derby Road. — *Organ Recitals* in St. George's Hall (p. 326), on Thurs. at 3 p.m. and on Sat. at 3 and 8 p.m. (adm. 6*d*.; on Sat. evening 1*d*.).

Baths. *George's Public Baths* (Pl. A, 4), belonging to the Corporation, adjoining the Landing Stage, with salt-water, swimming, and other baths; *Corporation Baths* also in Cornwallis St., Lodge Lane, Margaret St., and Steble St. (bath 6*d*.-1*s*.); *Turkish Baths*, Mulberry St., Duke St., and Werle St.

General Post Office (Pl. B, 5), in the Revenue Buildings.

United States Consul, *Thomas H. Sherman, Esq.*, 26 Chapel St.

Principal Attractions. The **Docks* (p. 329); *St. George's Hall* (p. 326); the *Exchange* and *Town Hall* (p. 327); *Revenue Buildings* (p. 327); *Prince's* and *Sefton Parks* (p. 328); a river-excursion to *Birkenhead* (p. 323) and *New Brighton* (p. 330), or upstream to *Eastham* (p. 323). — To gain some idea of the characteristic feature of the city the visitor is advised to drive from one end of the Docks to the other (6 1/2 M.; fare 2*d*.) on the top of an omnibus (p. 329), which affords the best views.

Liverpool, the second city and principal seaport of England, is situated on a sloping site on the right bank of the estuary of the *Mersey*, about 3 M. from the open sea, and in 1881 contained 552,425 inhab. (with the suburbs 740,000), including about 150,000 Roman Catholics and many Welsh and Irish. It is also the seat of a bishopric, created in 1880. Opposite Liverpool the Mersey is about 1 M. wide, but above the city it expands and forms a basin 3 M. across. Its mouth, which is strongly fortified, is partly closed by large sandbanks, leaving two channels, the Queen's and the Formby, for the entrance of vessels. The highest ground in the city is about 250 ft. above the sea. Owing mainly to its magnificent river and imposing series of docks, Liverpool makes a more pleasing impression than Manchester and many other large towns. The group of buildings round St. George's Hall has few equals in the country.

History. The name of Liverpool is popularly derived from an extinct bird, the Liver, which once haunted the Mersey and is still supposed to figure in the town-arms; but a more probable etymology connects it with the Welsh *Llyvrpwl*, 'the expanse of the pool'. The name of the manor of *Liverpul* first occurs in a charter (1207) of King John, who built a castle and founded a town here. The growth of the town during the following centuries was slow. For the siege of Calais in 1338 it furnished but one small bark with six men, and even in the reign of Elizabeth (1565) it possessed only 12 ships and contained only 138 householders. From 1588 to 1592 the borough of Liverpool was represented in Parliament by Sir Francis Bacon. In the Civil War Liverpool sided wiih the Parliamentarians, and with the aid of hastily thrown-up fortifications held out against Prince Rupert in 1644 for three weeks. The beginning of its commercial importance may be dated from the Restoration, and the first dock was constructed in 1709. At this time the little town contained about 5000 inhab., a number that increased to 12,000 in 1730, to 26,000 in 1760, and to 77,700 in 1801, while during the present century its growth has been extraordinarily rapid. In 1723 it already possessed a trading fleet of 131 vessels. The most lucrative occupation of the Liverpool shippers was long the nefarious traffic in negro slaves with the Spanish Main, in which it was the first English town to engage. With this was conjoined a smuggling trade in various English manufactures, and in the rum, sugar, and tobacco of the Spanish colonies. About 1840 regular steam-communication was opened between Liverpool and New York, and this may be said to have established the modern pre-eminence of Liverpool. The importation of raw cotton from the United States forms the great staple of its commerce, while it also carries on a large trade with Ireland (cattle, butter, and other provisions), Canada (timber), India, Africa, Australia (grain), China, the West Indies, and South America. The exports consist chiefly of manufactured articles, including a large quantity of the cotton goods made in the Manchester district, but the coal and salt of Wales and Cheshire also figure largely. The total value of the exports in 1889 was 115¾ millions sterling, of the imports 111 millions, as compared with 88 and 144¾ millions at London (see also p. 329). The commercial fleet of British vessels belonging to the port at the beginning of 1890 consisted of 935 steamers and 1378 sailing vessels, with a joint burden of 1,881,862 tons. This is larger than the registered tonnage of either London or Glasgow. The principal industries of Liverpool are ship-building, sugar-refining, iron and steel-working, rope-making, and the manufacture of chemicals. The distinguished natives of Liverpool include the *Right Hon. W.E. Gladstone* (b. 1809; see p. 328), whose father, Sir John Gladstone, was a prominent Liverpool merchant; *Mrs. Hemans* (1793-1835), *William Roscoe* (1753-1831), and *Mrs. Oliphant. Nathaniel Hawthorne* was U. S. consul at Liverpool from 1853 to 1857; his office was in Brunswick

St. (Pl. B, 4; comp. p. 328). Comp. *Sir J. A. Picton's* 'Memorials of Liverpool' (1875).

Immediately opposite Lime Street Station stands ***St. George's Hall** (Pl. D, 3, 4), the finest architectural feature of Liverpool, erected in 1838-54, at a cost of 300,000*l.*, from the designs of *H. Elmes*. It is in the form of a Græco-Roman temple, 600 ft. long and 170 ft. wide, and consists of a large central block with two wings. On the E. façade is a fine Corinthian colonnade with 16 columns, and at the S. end is a similar portico, the tympanum above which contains emblematical sculptures (commerce, art, etc.). The N. end is semicircular. The W. façade, with its pilasters and windows, is the least satisfactory of the four.

The **Great Hall*, 170 ft. long, 90 ft. wide, and 80 ft. high, is finely decorated and is used for public meetings, concerts, etc. The organ is one of the largest in the world (recitals, see p. 324). The hall contains several statues of local and other celebrities, and has a handsome mosaic pavement (boarded over). The arched roof is of stone. The wings to the N. and S. of the hall are occupied by the *Courts of Assize*. Over the N. vestibule is the *Small Concert Hall*, in elliptical form. The rest of the building is devoted to public offices.

Opposite the E. façade of St. George's Hall are equestrian statues of *Queen Victoria* and the late *Prince Consort*, by Thornycroft, between which is one of the *Earl of Beaconsfield*. To the N. of St. George's Hall, rises the *Wellington Monument*, a column 115 ft. high, surmounted by a colossal statue. Adjacent, to the N. of the Railway Station, is the *Alexandra Theatre* (Pl. D, 3, 4).

To the N. of St. George's Hall is an imposing group of buildings in the Grecian style (Pl. D, 3). The edifice to the right, with a Corinthian portico, is the *County Sessions House*. — This is adjoined by the **Walker Fine Art Gallery** (daily, 10 till dusk), erected in 1877 by Sir Andrew B. Walker, and containing a good collection of modern paintings, including *Dante's Dream, by Rossetti. Annual exhibitions of art are held here. — The circular building next the gallery is the **Picton Reading Room,** with a reference-library of 70,000 volumes. — To the left of the Picton Reading Room is the **Free Public Library and Museum,** erected in 1860 at the expense of Sir Wm. Brown.

It comprises a well-stocked *Library* of 80,000 vols. (10-10; on Frid. 10-2), spacious *Reading Rooms*, and a *Museum* (Mon., Wed., Thurs., & Sat., 10 till dusk). The chief attractions of the last are the zoological collection presented by the late Earl of Derby, and the Egyptian, Anglo-Saxon, and other antiquities given by Mr. Mayer.

At the back (W.) of St. George's Hall is *St. John's Church* (Pl. D, 3), a poor building which is to be replaced by the proposed cathedral.

From the N.W. corner of the square, Dale Street (Pl. B, C, 3), a well-built street with good shops and several important public buildings, leads to the S.W. towards the Docks. A little way down this street, on the left, are the **Municipal Offices** (Pl. C, 3), a huge edifice in a mixed style, erected in 1860 at a cost of 100,000*l.*, with a tower 210 ft. high. Opposite is the *Central Police Court* (Pl. C, 3).

At the back of the Municipal Offices, facing Victoria St., are the *County Court* and *Stamp Office* (Pl. C, 3).

Farther on are the *Conservative Club* (left), the *Junior Reform Club* (left), and the *Reform Club* (right). At the end of the street, to the right, rises the ***Town Hall** (Pl. B, 3), the oldest public building in Liverpool, erected in 1754 by Wood, the architect of the terraces at Bath. It is a rectangular structure in the Corinthian style, surmounted by a lofty dome. The portico was added about 1804. The building, which includes the official business and reception rooms of the Mayor, contains a statue of Canning, by *Chantrey*, and some portraits by *Lawrence*.

The Town Hall forms one side of a quadrangle, the other sides of which are occupied by the **Exchange** (Pl. B, 3), a large building in the French Renaissance style by *Wyatt*, erected in 1864 et seq. at a cost of 220,000*l*. The main front faces Tithebarn St.

The pediment in the centre of the N. side is adorned, on the face turned towards the quadrangle, with an allegorical group of sculpture; and on the parapet are statues of Columbus, Drake, Mercator, Raleigh, Cook, and Galileo. In the centre of the quadrangle is a bronze statue of Nelson. The fine *News Room* in the W. wing is 175 ft. long, 90 ft. wide, and 50 ft. high. The cotton-brokers, however, prefer to transact most of their business on the 'Flags' of the quadrangle instead of under cover. This is one of the 'sights' of Liverpool. The busiest hours are 12-1 and 2-4.

A little to the N. of the Exchange, in Tithebarn St., is the *Exchange Station* (Pl. B, 3; p. 323). — From the Exchange *Chapel Street* leads to the Docks (p. 329), passing the church of **St. Nicholas** (Pl. A, 3), the patron saint of mariners. This church was the first founded in Liverpool, of which it was the original parish-church; the present building, however, dates only from last cent., while the tower, with its lantern, was erected in 1815 on the fall of an older one.

From the town-hall, *Water Street* (Pl. B, 3), containing the offices of the Cunard and several other steamboat-companies, leads S.W. to the Docks, while the busy CASTLE STREET, the 'embodiment of Liverpool's character and the centre of its system', leads to the S.E., passing *St. George's Church* (Pl. B, 4), erected on the site of King John's castle (p. 325). Castle St. ends in CANNING PLACE, in which are the **Revenue Buildings** (Pl. B, 5), a huge and heavy pile in the Ionic style, with a central dome, occupying the site of the first Liverpool dock, and comprising the *Custom House*, *Post Office*, *Inland Revenue Office*, and *Dock Board*. In front of the N. side is a *Statue of Huskisson* (1770-1830), the free-trader, member of parliament for Liverpool (see p. 332). — Opposite the E. end of the custom-house is the *Sailors' Home* (Pl. B, 5), in an Elizabethan style.

A little to the N. of the Sailors' Home, in School Lane, is the *Bluecoat Hospital* (Pl. C, 4), erected in 1717, an institution similar to the well-known Christ's Hospital in London. Opposite the school is **St. Peter's Church** (Pl. C, 4), at present the pro-cathedral of the new diocese of Liverpool (services on Sun. at 3 p. m. and on week-days at 5 p. m.). — In Eliot Street, a little to the W. of the *Central Station* (Pl. D, 5; p. 323), is *St. John's Market* (Pl. C, D, 4), the chief provision-market of Liverpool, a huge covered structure 560 ft. long.

At the end of Hanover St., near the Sailors' Home (see above), begins *Duke Street* (Pl. C, 5), which we may now follow towards the S.E. It was in this street (No. 32) that Mrs. Hemans was born; and Hawthorne's 'Mrs. Blodgett' lived at No. 153. *Kent Street*, the fifth cross-street to the right, leads to an open space containing *St. Michael's Church* (Pl. C, 6), with a good Grecian portico and the highest spire in Liverpool. Opposite Kent St. diverges *Colquitt Street*, in which stands the **Royal Institution** (Pl. D, 6), founded mainly through the exertions of *William Roscoe* (d. 1831; p. 325), the author of the lives of Lorenzo de' Medici and Leo X. Opposite is a *Gallery of Art*, containing early Italian, Flemish, and German paintings, and casts of the Ægina marbles and other Greek sculptures.

Among the paintings, which are more interesting to the student of art than to the ordinary visitor, the following may be mentioned: *Filippo Lippi*, Birth of the Virgin; *Simone Memmi*, Christ with the Doctors of the Temple; *Roger van der Weyden*, Descent from the Cross; *Holbein*, Prodigal Son; cartoons by *Romney* and *Gibson* (Falling Angels); a striking sketch by *Tintoretto*. The statue of Roscoe is by *Chantrey*. — Adjoining is the *Royal Institution School*, the oldest school in Liverpool.

Colquitt Street ends at *Bold Street*, with many of the best shops. Here we may proceed to the left to Ranelagh Street and the Central Station (p. 323), passing at the foot of Bold Street, to the right, the *Lyceum* (Pl. C, 5), with a library of 70,000 vols. and a fine reading-room. If we turn to the right on reaching Bold St. we soon come to **St. Luke's Church** (Pl. D, 6), a handsome modern Gothic structure, built in 1811-31 and occupying a fine elevated site.

From this point *Renshaw St.* (Pl. D, 5) leads back to Lime St. (p. 326), passing the *Unitarian Chapel* in which *Roscoe* (d. 1831) is interred. Leece St. ascends to Rodney Street (Pl. D, 5, 6), at No. 62 in which *W. E. Gladstone* was born in 1809. — Following Hope Street towards the S., we pass a handsome *Unitarian Church* (Pl. E, 6) and the end of Mount Street, in which stands the **Liverpool Institute** (Pl. D, 6), originally established as a Mechanics' Institute, but now used as a high school. It is adjoined by the *Government School of Art*. — Hope St. ends at ***St. James's Cemetery** (Pl. D, 7), picturesquely laid out in an old quarry and containing the mausoleum of Huskisson (p. 327), with a statue by Gibson.

The S. end of St. James's Cemetery is skirted by Upper Parliament Street, from which, opposite Catharine St. (Pl. E, 7), diverges *Prince's Road*, a boulevard containing the *Greek Church* (in a Byzantine style), the *Church of St. Margaret* (with an elaborately-decorated interior), a *Synagogue* (in a Moorish style), and the *Welsh Presbyterian Church* (Gothic). Prince's Road ends at (1/2 M.) *Prince's Park*, 40 acres in extent.

At *Streatlam Towers*, between St. Margaret's and the Synagogue, is the ***Bowes Museum of Japanese Art**, formed by *Mr. J. L. Bowes*, Hon. Consul for Japan, and probably the most comprehensive and valuable collection of the kind in the world, Japan itself not excluded (Sat., 2.30 to 5.30 free; on other days, 2-4, by tickets obtained at the Japanese Consulate, 11 Dale St., 1*s.* each; proceeds devoted to charity). The contents include paintings (8-19th cent.), lacquer ware (10-19th cent.; *Cabinet by Tokugawa Shogun), wrought-iron work, bronzes, pottery, cloisonné enamels, wood and ivory carvings, embroideries, crystals, weapons, etc.

To the N.W. of Prince's Park is ***Sefton Park**, with an area of 400 acres, purchased and laid out by the Corporation at a cost of 410,000*l.* From the park we may return to the centre of the town by tramway. —

The *Church of SS. Matthew and James*, on Mossley Hill, overlooking Sefton Park, is a handsome red building, with a fine tower.

Starting again from Lime St. we may now follow the LONDON ROAD towards the E., passing the (4 min.) *Statue of George III.* (Pl. E, 4). On reaching Moss Street we follow it to the left (W.) to *Shaw Street*, which is perhaps the most regularly-built street in Liverpool. Immediately to the right rises **Liverpool College**, a large and handsome school for boys, in the Tudor style, by Elmes (p. 326). In Salisbury St., to the S. of Shaw St., is the large Roman Catholic *Church of St. Francis Xavier.*

From Moss St. (p. 328) Daulby Street and Pembroke Place, passing the *Royal Infirmary* (rebuilt at a cost of 75,000*l.*), lead S. to *Ashton Street*, which contains the old buildings of **Liverpool University College**, incorporated in 1881 and constituted one of the colleges of Victoria University (comp. p. 338) in 1884. The main part of the new Victoria Buildings of the college lie to the right, in Brownlow Hill, and consist of the Arts section and office, the Victoria Jubilee Tower (erected by the people of Liverpool in commemoration of Queen Victoria's jubilee), the library, and the engineering laboratories, built, fitted up, and presented to the town by Sir A. Walker. The chemical laboratories (abutting on Brownlow St.; Pl. E, 5) are excellently fitted up. To the W. is the *Medical School.* — We next enter MOUNT PLEASANT (Pl. E, 5), which brings us back with a semicircular sweep to Lime Street. On the right we pass the large *Workhouse* (Pl. E, 5; with room for 4000 inmates) and on the left the *Medical Institution*, the *Convent of Notre Dame*, and the *Young Men's Christian Association.*

The *Botanic Gardens* are in *Wavertree Park* (pron. 'Wartree'), 1/2 M. to the E. — To the N. extends the district of **Everton**, formerly a suburban village. It is largely inhabited by Welsh people. 'Everton Toffee' may still be purchased at one of the cottages near Everton Brow, where it was originally made.

To the N. E. of the city lies *Stanley Park* (reached by tramway, p. 324), laid out by the Corporation at a cost of 150,000*l.*, and commanding fine views of the Welsh and the Cumbrian Mts. — To the E. is *Newsham Park*, with the *Seamen's Orphanage* (tramway). Adjacent is the large *Cattle Market.* — The *Ancient Chapel of Toxteth Park*, on the S. side of the town, was the scene of the ministrations of Richard Mather, father of Increase Mather, and grandfather of Cotton Mather, of Massachusetts.

The most characteristic and interesting of the sights of Liverpool, however, consists in its ***Docks**, which flank the Mersey for a distance of 6-7 M. There are now in all upwards of 50 docks and basins, with a total water-area of 370 acres and 24 M. of quays.

The docks of Birkenhead (see p. 323) are under the same management (Mersey Docks and Harbour Board), and are reckoned as belonging to the harbour of Liverpool. The amount of dock-dues received in the year ending July 1st, 1890, was 1,110,057*l.*, paid by 23,633 vessels of 9,654,006 tons. — A. line of tram-omnibuses (p. 324; fare 2d.) traverses the whole of the streets skirting the Docks, affording easy access to any particular point.

The row of docks is interrupted near its centre by the principal ***Landing Stage** (Pl. A, 3) for steamers, consisting of a huge pontoon or floating quay, 2060 ft. long, connected with the shore by eight bridges. The predecessor of this stage was destroyed by fire in 1874, just when it was about to be opened, after an outlay of 400,000*l.*; but its reconstruction was begun at once and finished in 1878. Sea-going steamers start from the N. end of this pier, known as *Prince's*, while the river ferry-boats ply from *George's*, or the S. end. The open space opposite the principal approach to the Landing Stage is known as the Pier Head (Pl. A, 3), and is a busy terminus of numerous omnibus and tramway lines.

Cabin-passengers by the Transatlantic steamers are generally landed by tenders at the N. end of the Landing Stage, but sometimes at the Alexandra Dock. Their baggage is conveyed by machinery to a Customs Examining Hall on shore, where licensed porters are in waiting to carry it to the cabs (each trunk 6*d.*, smaller articles 3*d.*). Agents of the principal railway companies meet the steamers at the Dock or Landing Stage, and baggage may be 'checked' to any station on their systems at a charge of 2*s.* per package. Comp. p. 324 and p. xix.

The following are the principal docks, named from N. to S. The *Hornby Dock* was opened in 1885. Next to it is the *Alexandra Dock*, the largest of all, with a water-area of 44 acres. Most of the large Transatlantic 'liners' now dock here (apply to steward; fee), and it is also extensively used by grain-laden vessels. The ingenious arrangements for conveying the grain from the docks to the huge storehouses, 1/4 M. distant, by means of endless revolving belts in subways, are extremely interesting; as are also the similar contrivances for distributing the grain at the storehouses, which are on the 'silo' system. The visitor should apply for an order to see the warehouses at the office of the Liverpool Grain Storage & Transit Co., Fenwick St. (Pl. B, 3, 4). — The *Langton Dock* (21 acres) was constructed, like the Alexandra, to enable vessels of the largest size to enter without discharging cargo, as was formerly necessary at neap tides. The *Canada Dock*, used by vessels trading in timber, and the following three docks, *Huskisson* (timber), *Sandon* (with several graving-docks), and *Wellington*, are also on a large scale and can accommodate vessels of the largest size. A little farther up the river is *Salisbury Dock*, with a clock-tower, which is illuminated at night. The *Victoria Dock* (Pl. A, 1) is used by emigrant-ships. *Waterloo Dock* (Pl. A, 1) is partly surrounded with huge *Corn Warehouses*, holding 200,000 qrs. of grain. The arrangements for unloading resemble those at the Alexandra Dock (admission on application to the Dock Board). Behind *George's Dock* (Pl. A, 3, 4) are the *Goree Piazzas*, No. 1 in which was the scene of a commercial enterprise undertaken by Washington Irving. The experiment proved disastrous, and the shock threw Irving into a lethargic condition, one of the first signs of recovery from which was the composition of 'Rip van Winkle'. George's Dock is connected with *Canning Dock* (Pl. A, 4), the oldest now in existence, constructed in 1717. It lies opposite the Custom House (p. 327). The *Albert Dock* (Pl. A, 5), for E. Indiamen, differs from most of the Liverpool docks in being completely surrounded with warehouses (as in London). Adjoining *King's Dock* (Pl. A, 6) is the *Tobacco Warehouse*, in which about 20,000 hogsheads of tobacco generally lie in bond. The *Queen's* (Pl. A, 7; Russian vessels), *Coburg*, and *Brunswick Docks* are also fine large basins. The last is adjoined by extensive ship-building yards. The row of docks closes on the S. with the *Toxteth*, *Harrington*, and *Herculaneum Docks*, the name of the last embalming the memory of the once important Liverpool manufacture of pottery.

From Liverpool to Birkenhead, New Brighton, Hoylake, and West Kirby, 9 M., railway in 1/2 hr. This line passes under the river by the **Mersey Tunnel**, a huge structure resembling the Thames Tunnel in London, begun in 1880, and opened for traffic in 1886. It is about 1 M. in length, and is at present used for local traffic only, though ultimately to be connected with the main railway-systems on both banks of the

Mersey. The Liverpool Station is in *James St.* (Pl. B, 4). Lifts convey passengers between the streets and the platforms. Trains run to *Birkenhead* (Hamilton Square, with passenger lifts; 3-4 min.) at frequent intervals (fares 3*d.*, $2^1/_2$*d.*, 2*d.*). At Hamilton Square the line forks, the left branch leading to *Birkenhead Central* and *Green Lane* and to be prolonged to join the L. N. W. R. and G. W. R. joint line at *Rockferry* (p. 323). The right branch goes on to ($2^1/_2$ M.) *Birkenhead Park* (p. 323), where it emerges from the tunnel, and ($3^1/_4$ M.) *Birkenhead Docks*. Here the line again forks, one branch running to *Wallasey*, *Warren*, and ($6^1/_2$ M.) *New Brighton*, the other to (8 M.) *Hoylake* and (9 M.) *West Kirby* (see p. 322). — **New Brighton** (*Marine*; *Royal Ferry; New Brighton; Queen's*), a favourite resort of 'trippers', lies on the Cheshire side of the Mersey, 5 M. to the N.W. of Birkenhead. The *Pier* (Refreshmt. Rooms), 560 ft. long, affords a fine view of the shipping and docks of Liverpool, the Irish Sea, and the mountains of Wales. By the pier is a large *Palace & Winter Garden.* Near the end of the Promenade is the strongly-fortified *Rock Battery.* Frequent steamers to (4 M.) Liverpool (see p. 324); also to Birkenhead. — **Hoylake**, a small watering-place on the estuary of the Dee, is much frequented by golfers, its links being among the best in England.

Among the other attractive river-excursions that may be made from Liverpool are those to *Seacombe* (p. 324) and *Eastham Ferry* (p. 323). — The most interesting of the numerous manor-houses near Liverpool is **Knowsley**, the seat of the Earl of Derby, situated 5 M. to the N.E., in the midst of a large park. The house contains paintings by Rubens, Rembrandt, Teniers, Van de Velde, and Claude Lorrain, and a series of family-portraits, beginning with the first Earl of Derby, step-father of Henry VII. — *Childwall Hall*, 3 M. to the E., with remains of an old priory, belongs to the Marquis of Salisbury. — *Croxteth Hall*, the seat of the Earl of Sefton, lies $3^1/_2$ M. to the N.E. — *Speke Hall*, 7 M. to the S.E. of Liverpool, is another interesting old manor-house.

From Liverpool to Preston, $26^1/_2$ M., railway in $^3/_4$-$1^1/_4$ hr. (fares 4*s.* 6*d.*, 3*s.* 5*d.*, 2*s.* 5*d.*). We start from the Exchange Station. — The train crosses the Leeds and Liverpool Canal twice and reaches ($4^3/_4$ M.) *Aintree*, where the Liverpool race-meetings take place. — $11^1/_2$ M. **Ormskirk** (*Wheatsheaf*; *Talbot*), a busy market-town with 6650 inhab. The *Church, with its huge embattled tower and spire, contains the burial-vault of the Earls of Derby. In the vicinity are (3 M.) *Scarisbrick Hall*, (3 M.) *Lathom House* (Earl of Lathom), and (2 M. to the N.) the scanty ruins of *Burscough Priory*. — From (14 M.) *Burscough* lines diverge to Southport and Wigan (p. 373). — At ($26^1/_2$ M.) *Preston* we join the main L. N.W. line (p. 373).

From Liverpool to Southport, 18 M., railway in $^3/_4$-$1^1/_2$ hr. (fares 2*s.*, 1*s.* 8*d.*, 1*s.* 3*d.*). — We start from the Exchange Station. $2^1/_2$ M. *Bootle*, a borough with about 30,000 inhab., at the mouth of the Mersey, is practically a suburb of Liverpool. 5 M. *Waterloo* is also a suburb of Liverpool, with the villas of numerous Liverpool merchants. — 6 M. *Blundellsands & Crosby*. The little watering-place of *Crosby* (Blundell Arms) lies $1^1/_2$ M. to the W. of the station. In the neighbourhood is *Ince Hall*, with a large collection of paintings and sculptures. — Near (11 M.) *Formby* are *Altcar Flats*, where the 'Waterloo Coursing Meetings' are held. — 15 M. *Ainsdale*.

18 M. **Southport** (**Victoria; Prince of Wales; Royal; Queen's; Scarisbrick Arms; Pearjeant's Temperance; Palace; Hydropathic;* numerous lodging-houses) is a pleasant and handsomely-built modern watering-place with 32,000 inhab., frequented annually by many thousands of visitors from Liverpool, Manchester, and the manufacturing towns of Yorkshire. The broad sandy beach is fairly adapted for promenading and bathing, though a huge expanse of wet sand is exposed at low tide. The *Winter Garden* (concerts daily), which comprises a good *Aquarium* and a small *Theatre*, the long *Pier* (with tramway), *Kew Gardens*, and the **Botanic Gardens* (3 M. to the N.W.) attract numerous visitors. The *Esplanade* affords a fine view of the Welsh and the Cumberland hills, while the Isle of Man is also visible in clear weather. — Steamers ply regularly from Southport to *Lytham* (p. 373) and *Blackpool* (p. 373). The railway goes on to Preston (p. 373).

From Liverpool to *Manchester*, see R. 42; to *London*, see R. 44.

42. From Liverpool to Manchester.

a. *From Liverpool to Manchester viâ Newton-le-Willows.*

$31^1/_2$ M. L.N.W. Railway in $^3/_4$-$1^1/_2$ hr. (fares 5*s*. 6*d*., 4*s*., 2*s*. 6*d*.). This line, constructed in 1830 at a cost of 1,000,000*l*., is one of the oldest of existing railways. The crucial part of the undertaking was the filling up of *Chat Moss*, a huge and dangerous swamp, 12 sq.M. in extent and in places 30 ft. deep. The accomplishment of this task and the success of this railway were of the utmost importance in stimulating the extension of the railway-system. The manufacturing district traversed is uninteresting.

After leaving Lime St. Station (p. 323) the train stops at ($1^1/_4$ M.) *Edgehill*, near the Botanic Garden (p. 329). — From ($11^1/_2$ M.) *St. Helen's Junction* a branch-line leads N. to **St. Helen's** *(Raven)*, a town with 57,325 inhab., noted for its manufactures of plate-glass, and thence to Rainford (p. 333) and Ormskirk (p. 331), while another runs S. to *Widnes* and *Runcorn* (Royal Hotel), the latter a river-port with 15,000 inhab., situated on the Mersey, 12 M. above Liverpool. — 15 M. *Earlestown* is the junction of a line to Warrington (see below) and Chester (p. 269). — At (16 M.) *Newton-le-Willows* we cross the main line of the L.N.W. Railway from London to Carlisle and the North. At ($16^1/_2$ M.) *Parkside* Mr. Huskisson was killed at the opening of the railway (comp. p. 327). — $19^1/_2$ M. *Kenyon* is the junction of a line to *Bolton* (p. 339). Beyond (21 M.) *Glazebury & Bury Lane* the train crosses *Chat Moss* (see above). At ($26^1/_2$ M.) *Patricroft* is the Iron Foundry established by James Nasmyth, one of the largest in England. — $27^1/_2$ M. *Eccles* (Cross Keys), prettily situated on the *Irwell*, is a favourite residence of Manchestrians.

$31^1/_2$ M. *Manchester* (Exchange Station), see p. 333.

b. *From Liverpool to Manchester viâ Warrington and Glazebrook.*

34 M. 'Cheshire Lines' Railway in $^3/_4$-$1^3/_4$ hr. (fares 5*s*. 6*d*., 4*s*., 2*s*. 6*d*.). As far as (25 M.) Glazebrook (see p. 333) this line coincides with the main Liverpool and London line of the Midland Railway (see R. 44b).

We start from the Central Station in Ranelagh Street (p. 323). The train then stops at (1 M.) *St. James's* and ($2^1/_2$ M.) *St. Michael's*, crosses *Toxteth Park* (p. 329), and reaches ($3^1/_2$ M.) *Otterspool*. To the right a view is enjoyed of the *Mersey*. $5^1/_2$ M. *Garston* (p. 345); $12^1/_4$ M. *Farnworth*, the junction of a loop-line to *Widnes*.

$18^1/_4$ M. **Warrington** *(Patten Arms; Lion)*, a busy town on the right bank of the Mersey, with 35,260 inhab. and manufactories of cotton, iron, and glass. It is a place of considerable antiquity, and is believed to have been a Roman station. The *Parish Church*, a fine building in the Dec. style, has been restored. — From Warrington railways radiate to Wigan (p. 373), Bolton (p. 339), Chester (p. 269), etc.

Beyond Warrington the line runs nearly parallel with the celebrated Bridgewater Canal (35 M. long), one of the oldest in England, connecting Manchester and Liverpool.

The canal was constructed by Brindley for the Duke of Bridgewater in 1758-71. The Duke sank all his capital in the undertaking, but ultimately made a large fortune by the facilities it afforded for conveying the produce of his large coal-fields to Manchester and Liverpool.

At (25 M.) *Glazebrook* the direct line to London diverges to the right. — 34 M. *Manchester* (Central Station), see below.

c. *From Liverpool to Manchester viâ Atherton.*

37 M. Lancashire and Yorkshire Railway in 3/4-1 3/4 hr. (fares 5*s.* 6*d.*, 4*s.*, 2*s.* 6*d.*).

We start from the Exchange Station (p. 323). The district traversed is uninteresting and most of the stations unimportant. 11 M. *Rainford* is the junction of lines to *Ormskirk* (p. 331) and *St. Helen's* (p. 332). Near *Wigan* (p. 373), which the Manchester line avoids by a loop, we cross the main L.N.W. line. A little farther on the direct Manchester line diverges to the right from that to *Bolton* (p. 339). 26 M. *Atherton;* 29 M. *Walkden;* 34 M. *Pendleton;* 36 M. *Salford.* — 37 M. *Manchester* (Victoria Station), see below.

Manchester. — **Railway Stations.** 1. *Central Station* (Pl. E, 5), at the corner of Windmill St. and Lower Mosley St., for the trains of the Midland Railway and Cheshire Lines to London, Liverpool, Chester, Buxton, Matlock, Derby, etc. — 2. *London Road Station* (Pl. G, H, 5), for the L.N.W. trains to London, Stafford, Birmingham, etc., and also for the Sheffield & Lincolnshire Railway (in connection with the G.N.R.). — 3. *Exchange Station* (Pl. E, 2), on the N. side of the town, for the L.N.W. trains to Liverpool, Leeds, Chester, Wales, and Scotland, and G. W. R. trains to Chester and Wales. — 4. *Victoria Station* (Pl. F, 2), adjoining the last, for the Lancashire and Yorkshire lines to Liverpool, Bolton, Preston, Oldham, York, Leeds, Scarborough, etc. — 5. *Oxford Road Station* (Pl. F, 6), for trains to Altrincham, etc. — In addition to these stations, which are connected with each other by a loop-line, there are several secondary or suburban stations at which the trains generally stop before quitting Manchester. The chief of these is that at *Salford* (Pl. D, 3). — Single cab-fare (see below) from the stations to the hotels.

Hotels. *Queen's (Pl. a; G, 4), 2 Piccadilly, a long-established house near the London Road Station, R. & A. from 4*s.* 6*d.*; *Victoria (Pl. b; E, 3), Victoria St., R. & A. from 2*s.* 6*d.*, table d'hôte 3*s.* 6*d.*; *Grand (Pl. c; H, 4), Aytoun St., with lift, R. & A. 4*s.*-5*s.* 6*d.*, table d'hôte 4*s.* 6*d.*, 'pens'. 10*s.* 6*d.*-12*s.* 6*d.*; Grosvenor (Pl. d; E, 3), Deansgate, R. & A from 4*s.*; Albion (Pl. e; G, 3), 21 Piccadilly, R. & A. from 4*s.* 6*d.*; Clarence (Pl. f), Waterloo (Pl. g), in Piccadilly (6 & 8, Pl. G, 3, 4); Trevelyan Temperance (Pl. F, 3), 50 Corporation St., well spoken of, R. & A. 4*s.*; Royal (Pl. m; F, 3), 2 Mosley St.; the last six commercial.

Restaurants. *Atlantic*, 5 Cross St. (Pl. E, 3, 4; entr. from Newmarket), for men only; *Victoria*, at the above named hotel (Pl. E, 3); *Parker*, 18 St. Mary's Gate and 10 St. Ann's Sq. (Pl. E, 3); *Prince's Café*, opposite Prince's Theatre (Pl. E, 5); *Manchester Limited Restaurant Co.*, under the Exchange (Pl. E, 3); *Beresford's Luncheon Rooms*, Market Place and Chapel Walks; *Royalty Luncheon Rooms*, Princess St.; **Old Swan* (German), Pool St., Market St.; *Continental*, Peter Sq. — *Refreshment Rooms* at the stations.

Cabs. Per mile, 1-2 pers. 9*d.*, 3-4 pers. 1*s.*; for each additional third of a mile 3*d.* or 4*d.* By time, for each 1/4 hr. 6*d.* or 7 1/2*d.* For each article of luggage carried outside 2*d.* Double fares from midnight to 7 a.m. Complaints may be made at the Town Hall (p. 337).

Tramways. Manchester is covered with a network of tramways, traversing the main streets and extending to all the suburbs (fares 1*d.*-3*d.*).

Post and Telegraph Office (Pl. F, 3), corner of Market St. and Spring Gardens. Numerous branch-offices and pillar letter-boxes.

Theatres. *Royal* (Pl. E, 5), Peter St., stalls 6*s.*, dress circle 5*s.*, upper

For a coloured street plan of Manchester see pages 586 & 587 circle 2*s.* 6*d.*, pit 1*s.*; *Prince's* (Pl. E, 5), Oxford St.; *Comedy* (Pl. E, 4), Peter St., dress circle and stalls 5*s.*; *Queen's* (Pl. E, 4), Bridge St., dress circle 2*s.*, pit 6*d.*; *St. James's* (Pl. F, 5), Oxford St.

Concerts. *Concert Hall* (Pl. E, 5), Peter St.; *Hallé's Concerts*, Free Trade Hall (Pl. E, 4), every Thurs. in winter; *Manchester Vocal Society's Concerts; De Jongh's Concerts*, Free Trade Hall, every second Sat.

Popular Resorts. **Bellevue Gardens*, Longsight, to the S.E., with zoological collection, dancing-saloon, restaurant, fire-works, lake for boating, etc., much frequented by the lower classes. They may be reached by tram or by train from London Road to *Longsight*. — *Botanic Gardens*, Chester Road, Old Trafford, to the S.W. — *Circus*, Oxford St., and Peter St. — *Panorama* (Trafalgar), at the corner of Deansgate and Quay St. (Pl. E, 4; adm. 1*s.*).

Baths. *Herriott's*, 9 Stevenson Sq., near the Infirmary (Pl. G, 4); *Allison*, 40 Hyde Road; *Bartholomew*, 112 Stockport Road; *Constantine*, 21 Oxford St. — *Corporation Baths*, in Store St., Leaf St., Baker St., and Osborne St.

American Consul, *W. J. Grinnell, Esq.*

Manchester, the chief industrial town of England, and the great metropolis of the cotton-manufacture, is situated on the river *Irwell*, a tributary of the *Mersey*, in a gently undulating plain. Manchester proper lies on the left bank of the Irwell, which here receives two smaller streams, the *Medlock* and the *Irk;* but in ordinary speech the name is used to include *Salford*, on the opposite bank, which really forms one town with Manchester, though a distinct municipality, returning its own members to Parliament. In 1881 the population of the united city was 569,909 (Manchester, 393,676; Salford, 176,233), but Manchester alone, the municipal boundaries of which have been extended, now (1890) contains nearly as many. The population includes a large German element, whose influence may perhaps be traced in the zeal and success with which music is cultivated here. Besides cotton goods, Manchester also manufactures large quantities of silk, worsted, chemicals, and machinery. Its chief interest for the stranger lies in its huge manufactories and warehouses, and in the bustling traffic of its streets. Most of the streets of the older part of the town, centering in the Town Hall, are narrow, but many improvements have recently been effected. The suburbs on the other hand, such as *Cheetham Hill*, *Broughton*, *Old Trafford*, and *Fallowfield*, are generally well laid out and handsomely built. Many of the largest mills and factories are now in the villages around Manchester, and the town itself is becoming more of an emporium and less of an actual centre of manufacture. The rivers unfortunately do not add much to the attractions of the town, as their waters are black with mill-refuse. Since 1847 Manchester has been the seat of a bishop.

History. Manchester occupies the site of the *Mancunium* of the Romans, and the second half of the name represents the Saxon corruption of the Latin *Castrum* (comp. p. 270). In the 10th cent. we hear of Edward the Elder repairing and garrisoning the village of *Manigceaster*, and a line of Norman barons seems to have derived their title from this place. Towards the end of the 14th cent. it was already known as an industrial place of some importance, the manufacture of woollen and linen goods having, according to report, been introduced by Flemish immigrants in the time of Edward III. Under Henry VIII. (1509-1547) Manchester appears as the principal town of Lancashire, but its size cannot have been very great, as even in 1720 it did not contain 10,000 inhabitants. After the middle of the 18th cent. its progress began to be more rapid, and the population rose from 20,000 in 1760 to 94,000 in 1801. The first application of steam to machinery for spinning cotton was made here in 1789, and gave a great impetus to the cotton-manufacture. The advance was aided by the construction of the Bridgewater Canal (see p. 332), uniting Manchester and Liverpool; and in 1830 the Manchester and Liverpool railway (see p. 332) was opened. A 'Ship Canal', to connect Manchester with the sea, is now approaching completion (see p. 339). The increase of the city during the present century has been very rapid, and the population has multiplied sixfold within 80 years. Comp. *W. E. A. Axon's* 'Annals of Manchester' (1886).

The name **Manchester School** began to be used some 50 years ago to designate the political party that agitated for the repeal of the corn-laws and for the general recognition of the principles of free trade. The chief manufacturing town of England very naturally became the centre of the movement, and the head-office of the Anti-Corn-Law League was established in Newall Buildings, Market St. (comp. p. 338). Richard Cobden, the leader of the party, was a partner in a Manchester firm of cotton-printers, and in 1839 the Manchester Chamber of Commerce, at his instigation, opened the free-trade campaign by petitioning Parliament against the corn-laws. After the triumph of the principles of free trade, the name Manchester School stuck to the political party grouped round Cobden and Bright, though the city of Manchester was by no means invariably of the same mind as these politicians. The leading principles of Manchestrianism may be described as the development of complete freedom of trade and unrestricted competition, and the adhesion as far as practicable to a policy of non-intervention in foreign affairs. The expression has become domiciled in several Continental states, where it is sometimes used as a term of reproach for those who prefer peace and material welfare to the honour of their country.

No traveller should quit Manchester without having seen one at least of its great factories. A letter of introduction is desirable; but those who have none may send a written request to the head of the firm whose establishment they wish to inspect. Among the most interesting manufactories are the following: Birley's Cotton Spinning Mills at Chorlton-upon-Medlock; Dewhurst's Cotton Spinning Mills in Salford (with a chimney 245 ft. high); Wood & Westhead's Smallware Manufactory, Brook St.; Worthington's Umbrella Manufactory, Great Bridgewater St.; Fairbairn's Engineering Works, Ancoats; Hoyle's Print Works, Mayfield; Nasmyth's Bridgewater Foundry at Patricroft (p. 332).

We begin our walks through Manchester at the *London Road Station* (Pl. G, H, 5; p. 333), near which most of the principal hotels are situated. London Road is prolonged towards the N. by PICCADILLY (Pl. G, 4), one of the chief streets of the city. Here, to the left, rises the **Royal Infirmary** (Pl. G, 4), a large building founded in 1753, but since extensively altered and provided with a handsome Ionic portico. One wing was erected partly from the proceeds of a concert given by Jenny Lind. About 20,000 patients are annually treated here.

The pavement in front is adorned with four bronze statues. To the left is the *Duke of Wellington* (1769-1852), by Noble, surrounded by four allegorical figures. — In the centre are statues of *Dalton* (1766-1844), founder of the atomic theory, and *James Watt* (1736-1819), the inventor of the steam engine. — To the right is *Sir Robert Peel* (1788-1850), by Marshall.

Piccadilly is continued by MARKET STREET (Pl. E, F, 3), the main artery of traffic in Manchester. To the left, halfway down the street, is the new *Post Office* (Pl. F, 3). Market St. ends opposite the **Exchange** (Pl. E, 3), a massive structure in the classical style, erected in 1864-74 by *Mills* and *Murgatroyd*, with a Corinthian portico, and a campanile 180 ft. high.

The *Great Hall*, 200 ft. long and 190 ft. wide, is covered with a dome 80 ft. high. On cotton-market days (Tues. and Frid., 1-2) it is crowded with buyers and sellers from all parts of Lancashire, and presents a scene of great bustle and apparent confusion. Strangers are admitted to the galleries on application to the keeper. — In St. Ann's Square, adjoining the Exchange, is a *Statue of Cobden* (p. 335), by Wood.

We now turn to the right and proceed to the N. through Victoria Street to (5 min.) the **Cathedral** (Pl. E, 2), situated in an open space facing the Irwell. The building is in the Perp. style and dates mainly from the early half of the 14th cent., but restoration has given it a somewhat modern aspect. A new N. porch was added in 1889. It is the parish-church for the vast parish of Manchester and was made collegiate under a warden and fellow in the 15th century. It was raised to the dignity of a cathedral in 1847 and is one of the smallest of English cathedrals, being only 220 ft. long and 112 ft. broad. Its great comparative width is due to the fact that chapels have been added on both sides of the original church so as to form double aisles. The square tower, 140 ft. in height, was rebuilt in 1864-67. Part of the exterior is decorated with quaint carvings.

Interior (adm. free; services at 11 a.m. and 3.30 p.m.). The NAVE is impressive owing to its unusual width, but the CHOIR is the most interesting part of the interior. Both nave and choir have flat timber ceilings. The oaken *Choir Stalls*, dating from about 1505, are finely carved (quaint misereres). The stained glass is modern. Perhaps the most attractive chapel is the *Lady Chapel*, added about 1518. The outer N. aisle of the choir (rebuilt) is known as the *Derby Chapel*, and contains monuments to members of that family. Off this chapel opens the small *Ely Chapel*, with the monument of Bishop Stanley of Ely (d. 1515), who was Warden of Manchester Collegiate Church in 1485-1509 and built the beautiful clerestory of both nave and choir. At the E. end of the N. aisle of the choir is a *Statue of *Humphrey Chetham* (see below), by Theed. At the E. end of the S. choir-aisle is the small *Fraser Chapel*, erected in 1887 to the memory of *Bishop Fraser* (d. 1885), of whom it contains an effigy. To the S. of the choir is the octagonal *Chapter House*.

A little to the E. of the Cathedral, in Shudehill, is *Smithfield Market* (Pl. G, 2), which may be visited on Saturday evening, when the factory operatives lay in their supplies for the week. — To the S. of the Cathedral is a *Statue of Cromwell* (Pl. E, 3). — To the N. stands ***Chetham College** or **Hospital** (Pl. E, F, 2), with a Blue Coat School established by Humphrey Chetham in 1651, and a library of 40,000 vols. (open 10 to 4, 5, or 6).

The library is probably the oldest free library in Europe. The building itself (small gratuity to boy who acts as guide), enclosing a quadrangle, dates from the reign of Henry IV. (1422-1461) and is the most ancient and interesting in Manchester. It originally formed part of the collegiate buildings attached to the old church. The *Dining Hall* has a dais and screen. The *Library* (with a fine carved oak buffet and some old portraits), and the *Dormitories* are also interesting.

The large red building adjoining Chetham College is the *Grammar School*, of which De Quincey is the most famous alumnus (rebuilt since his time). Immediately to the N. are the *Exchange* and *Victoria Stations* (Pl. E, F, 2), the latter adjoined by the *Workhouse* (Pl. F, 1).

Passing the Victoria Station and crossing New Bridge Street, we now ascend Great Ducie Street to (6 min.) the ***Assize Courts** (Pl. E, 1), an imposing Gothic edifice, erected in 1864 from the designs of *Waterhouse*, at a cost of 100,000*l.*

The fine entrance, on the W. side, is adorned with the statues of eminent lawgivers, that of Moses crowning the apex of the gable. The capitals of the columns in the portico represent the judicial penalties of former times. The slender pointed tower rising from the centre of the building is 210 ft. high. The large central *Hall*, 100 ft. long, 48 ft. wide, and 75 ft. high, has a window (at the N. end), representing the signing of Magna Charta. — Behind the Assize Courts is the large *County Gaol.*

Deansgate (Pl. E, 3, 4, 5), one of the busiest thoroughfares in Manchester, begins to the S.W. of the Cathedral, and ends at *Knott Mill Station* (Pl. D, 6), in the district supposed to be the exact site of the Roman *Mancunium* (p. 334). To the left, at the corner of Lloyd St. (Pl. E, 4), are the new *School Board Offices. John Dalton Street*, the fifth cross-street on the left, leads to Albert Square (Pl. E, 4), which is embellished with statues of *Prince Albert* (d. 1861), by Noble, under a Gothic canopy by Northington, and *Bishop Fraser* (d. 1885), by Woolner. On the W. side of the square rises the ***New Town Hall** (Pl. E, 4), another enormous and imposing Gothic pile by *Waterhouse* (see above), erected in 1868-77 at a cost of 775,000*l.* The clock-tower is 286 ft. high (*View from the top); it contains a fine peal of bells and a carillon.

The **Interior** (adm. 6*d.*) contains 250 rooms. The great *Hall, 100 ft. in length, is adorned with frescoes of scenes from the history of Manchester by *Madox Brown*, and contains statues of Gladstone and Villiers. On the roof are the arms of English towns and counties.

In King St. (Pl. E, 3, F, 4), a little to the N., is the *Free Reference Library* (open 9-10, on Sun. 2-9), occupying the old Town Hall.

Adjoining the Town Hall is the *Memorial Hall* (Pl. E, 4), commemorating the ejection of the Nonconforming clergy in 1662.

Passing the N. side of the Town Hall, through Princess St., and crossing Cooper St., we reach Mosley St. (Pl. F, 4), another busy thoroughfare. Opposite us, at the corner of Princess St., is the **City Art Gallery** (formerly the *Royal Institution;* Pl. F, 4), a building in the Greek style by *Barry*, with an Ionic portico.

It contains a collection of pictures, casts of the Elgin Marbles in the British Museum, and a statue of Dalton (p. 335) by *Chantrey*. Annual exhibitions of art are held here. — Immediately to the N. of the Royal Institution is the *Athenaeum* (Pl. F, 4), a kind of club for young businessmen (quarterly subscription 6*s.* 6*d.*), with a good library.

If we turn to the right on reaching Mosley St. from Albert Square (see above), we soon reach *St. Peter's Church* (Pl. F, 5), containing an altar-piece after Carracci. In Peter Street, running hence to the W., stands the ***Free Trade Hall** (Pl. E, 4), in the Italian palatial style, by *Walters*, erected in 1856 on the site of the earlier edifice of the Anti-Corn-Law League (comp. p. 335).

The hall is 130 ft. long, 80 ft. wide, and 53 ft. high, and can accommodate 6000 persons.

The ground on which the original Free Trade Hall was erected was the property of Mr. Cobden, and was placed by him at the disposal of the League. On Aug. 16th, 1819, it was the scene of the 'Massacre of Peterloo', the name given in Manchester to a collision between the cavalry and yeomanry and the Manchester Reformers, when several lives were lost.

To the left of the Free Trade Hall are the *Royal Theatre* (p. 334) and the *Young Men's Christian Association*. Behind the Free Trade Hall is the large new *Central Station* (Pl. E, 5; p. 333).

From Mosley St., opposite Peter St., diverges *Oxford Street* (Pl. F, 5, 6), a long street leading S.E. to the suburban districts of *Rusholme*, *Fallowfield*, *Cheadle*, etc. — It contains the *Oxford Road Station* (Pl. F, 6; p. 333), *All Saints' Church* (Pl. F, 6), the *School of Art*, and the Rom. Cath. *Church of the Holy Name*, with an elaborate interior. — Farther out ($1^1/_4$ M. from the Town Hall) is the ***Owens College**, founded in 1845 by John Owens, who left 100,000*l.* for the purpose, and transferred to the present handsome Gothic edifice (by Waterhouse) in 1873. The buildings were extended in 1886-87.

The college was incorporated by Act of Parliament in 1874, and in 1880 it was constituted one of the colleges of Victoria University (see below). It is now attended by about 1200 students, taught by about 80 professors and lecturers, and includes a medical school and faculties of arts, law, and science. It possesses a good *Library*, well-furnished *Laboratories*, and a *Collection of Natural History*. *Mr. Stanley Jevons* (d. 1882) and *Sir Henry Roscoe* were professors at the Owens College.

Victoria University, incorporated by Royal Charter in 1880 and empowered to grant degrees, has its seat at Manchester and comprises at present the Owens College, Liverpool University College (p. 329), and the Yorkshire College (p. 403). In 1887 the University received an annual grant of 2000*l.* from the public funds.

The **Manchester Art Museum**, in *Ancoats* (to the E. of Pl. H, 4), opened in 1886, may be called the Bethnal Green Museum of Manchester (open free, week-days and Sundays). The objects exhibited are furnished with explanatory labels. Concerts, lectures, and classes are also held here for the people of the district.

Salford (p. 334), or Manchester on the right bank of the Irwell, contains little to interest the stranger, the greater part of it consisting of monotonous streets of warehouses and workmen's dwellings. The *Rom. Cath. Cathedral* (Pl. C, 2, 3), a good building by Pugin the Elder, with a spire 240 ft. high and a fine W. front, is much obscured by adjoining houses.

To the N.W., skirted by the Irwell, lies **Peel Park** (Pl. A, 2), a public park, prettily laid out, containing a museum and a library. The *Museum* is a large building in the Renaissance style, with a fair collection of antiquities and other objects of interest. The *Art Gallery* contains modern paintings and sculptures. The building also includes the *Salford Free Library*. The handsome wrought-iron gateway of the park commemorates the visit of Queen Victoria in 1857, and the park also contains statues of the Queen, Prince Albert, Cobden, and Sir Robert Peel. — The *Whitworth Park*, near Oxford St. (beyond Pl. F, 6), 24 acres in extent, a bequest of Sir Joseph Whitworth, was opened in June, 1890. The *Whitworth Institute*, in the park, with a picture gallery, a commercial museum, etc., has been founded for the promotion of the fine arts.

Manchester possesses several other public parks, some of them of considerable size. *Botanic Gardens*, see p. 334. — **Bellevue Gardens*, see

p. 334. The celebrated attempt to rescue Fenian prisoners in 1867 was made near the old *Bellevue Prison*, in the Hyde Road.

Those who wish to pay a visit to the works of the ***Manchester Ship Canal**, which none interested in inland navigation should omit, apply for an order at the Company's Offices in Deansgate. The canal, which is 35 M. long and 26 ft. deep, with a minimum bottom depth of 120 ft., is to be finished in 1892 at an estimated cost of 6,000,000*l*. It begins at Old Trafford (conveniently reached by tramway from Deansgate to the end of Trafford Road) and enters the Mersey at *Eastham* (p. 323). The docks at the Manchester end, on both sides of the Irwell, have an area of 114 acres, and the quay-frontage will be 5$^1/_4$ M. long. The locks and sluices at Trafford and other points of the canal are among the most important works of the kind ever executed. It is hoped that the canal will practically make Manchester one of the principal seaports in Great Britain. Comp. p. 323.

From Manchester to Bolton and Blackburn, 25 M., Lancashire and Yorkshire Railway in $^3/_4$-1$^1/_2$ hr. (fares 4*s*. 6*d*., 3*s*. 6*d*., 2*s*. 2$^1/_2$*d*.). — 10$^1/_2$ M. **Bolton-le-Moors** (*Swan; Victoria*), a prosperous town of 112,350 inhab., with large cotton-mills, bleaching and dye-works, engine factories, and iron-foundries. Crompton (1763-1827), the inventor of the spinning-mule, resided at Bolton and is commemorated by a statue in Nelson Square. In the vicinity are the (2 M.) *Hall-in-the-Wood*, an old timber house where Crompton perfected his invention, and (3 M.) *Smithills Hall*, an interesting old manor-house. — 25 M. **Blackburn** (*Old Bull*), a well-built industrial town of 116,850 inhab., the staple products of which are cottons, calico, and muslin. Hargreaves (d. 1788) the inventor of the spinning-jenny, was born here.

[From Blackburn branch-lines diverge on the left to *Preston* (p. 373) and on the right to *Hellifield* (p. 404). The latter passes *Whalley* (Whalley Arms), with a ruined abbey, and *Clitheroe* (Swan), with a ruined castle. About 5 M. to the N.W. of Whalley is the Jesuit college of *Stonyhurst* (250 pupils), containing a museum with some interesting historical relics, some fine illuminated MSS., a Roman altar, and a collection of paintings. From Clithero pleasant excursions may be made in the valley of the *Ribble* and to the *Hill of Pendle*, a famous haunt of Lancashire witches.]

From Manchester to Oldham and Rochdale, 10$^1/_2$ M., railway in $^3/_4$-1$^1/_2$ hr. (fares 2*s*., 1*s*. 6*d*., 10$^1/_2$*d*.). Departure from *Exchange* and *Victoria Stations* (p. 333). — 6$^1/_2$ M. **Ashton-under-Lyne** (*Boar's Head; Railway*), a busy cotton-spinning town with 43,490 inhabitants. Our line here diverges to the N. from that to Huddersfield and Leeds (see below). — 7$^1/_2$ M. **Oldham** (*Angel; Albion*), a busy town with 134,000 inhab., a museum, and extensive manufactories of cotton, hats, and machinery. — 10$^1/_2$ M. **Rochdale** (*Wellington; Duckworth's; Railway*), a town with 68,865 inhab., situated on the *Roche*, is one of the chief seats of the flannel and woollen industry, in which about 100 mills are here engaged. It possesses some interest in economical history as the place where the first impulse was given to the great movement of co-operation by the formation, in 1844, of the *Society of Equitable Pioneers*, which consisted of a few mill-hands, with a capital of 28*l*. The society now contains 11,340 members and possesses a capital of 353,470*l*. *John Bright* (d. 1889) lived and is buried at Rochdale.

From Manchester to Huddersfield and Leeds, 42$^1/_2$ M., railway in 1$^1/_2$-2$^1/_4$ hrs. (fares 7*s*., 5*s*. 3*d*., 3*s*. 7*d*.). To (6$^1/_2$ M.) *Ashton*, see above. Near (8 M.) *Stalybridge* (Castle), a cotton-spinning town with 40,000 inhab., the train enters a bleak moorland-district, and begins to cross the ridge of limestone hills stretching northwards from the vicinity of Derby (comp. p. 350) to the Lake District and the Scottish border. — Beyond (10$^1/_2$ M.) *Mossley* we enter Yorkshire. From (13 M.) *Greenfield* a short branch-line diverges to Oldham (see above). — 14 M. *Saddleworth* (Commercial), a manufacturing town with 20,000 inhab., in a bleak hollow at the foot of some picturesque rocks. The railway, the road, the *Huddersfield Canal*, and the river *Tame* here all run parallel through a deep valley. We penetrate the ridge by one of the longest tunnels in England (3 M.). — 26 M. **Huddersfield** (*George; Imperial; Queen; Rail. Refreshmt. Rooms*), one of the centres of the English cloth and woollen manufacture, is a well-built modern town of 90,000 inhab., situated on the *Colne*, on the W. margin of the limestone hills. The environs are pretty, and contain some Roman remains. — $30^1/_2$ M. *Mirfield* (Rail. Buffet) is the junction for Bradford (p. 404), and a little farther the line to Wakefield (p. 402) diverges to the right. $33^1/_2$ M. *Dewsbury* (Royal; Rail. Buffet), a manufacturing place with 30,000 inhab.; 35 M. *Batley.* — $42^1/_2$ M. *Leeds*, see p. 402.

From Manchester to London viâ Crewe, 189 M., railway in $4^1/_4$-$6^1/_2$ hrs. (fares 24*s.* 6*d.*, 20*s.*, 15*s.* $5^1/_2$*d.*; return 49*s.*, 40*s.*, 30*s.* 11*d.*). The remarks made at p. 345 as to sleeping-carriages, etc., apply also to Manchester trains. — The train starts from *London Road Station* (p. 333), and after passing several small suburban stations crosses a gigantic viaduct over the valley of the Mersey and part of the town of Stockport. — 6 M. **Stockport** *(George; Buckley Arms; Rail. Refreshmt. Rooms)*, a large cotton-manufacturing town on the Mersey, with 59,530 inhabitants. The huge *Union Sunday School* contains 80 class-rooms, with accommodation for 5000 children. — 8 M. *Cheadle Hulme* is the junction of the line to Macclesfield (see below). — 14 M. *Alderley Edge* (Queen's Hotel), with the house and park of Lord Stanley of Alderley, is a favourite residence of wealthy Manchestrians. — At (31 M.) *Crewe* we join the through-line of the L.N.W. Co. from Liverpool to London (see p. 345). — Other L.N.W. trains between Manchester and London leave this line at *Cheadle Hulme* (see above) and proceed through the *Potteries* (see p. 346) to rejoin the main line at *Norton Bridge* (p. 346) or *Colwich* (p. 347). The principal intermediate stations on this route are **Macclesfield** *(Macclesfield Arms; Queen's)*, an important centre of the silk industry, with 37,500 inhab.; *Stoke-upon-Trent* (p. 346); and *Stone.*

From Manchester to London viâ Derby, $191^1/_2$ M., railway in $4^1/_4$-$5^1/_2$ hrs. (fares 24*s.* 6*d.*, 15*s.* $5^1/_2$*d.*; returns 49*s.*, 30*s.* 11*d.*; comp. p. 349). The train starts from the Central Station (p. 333) and proceeds viâ several suburban stations to (9 M.) *Stockport (Tiviotale)*, where it unites with the route of the Midland Railway from Liverpool (see p. 349).

From Manchester to *Liverpool*, see R. 42; to *Chester*, see p. 277; to *London* viâ *Sheffield*, see R. 44c; to *Wigan* (also accessible by the L.N.W.R. from the Exchange Station), see p. 333.

43. The Isle of Man.

The usual routes to the Isle of Man are the following: —

From Liverpool to Douglas, 75 M., steamer daily in winter and twice daily (Sat. thrice) in summer (Sun. excepted), from the Prince's Landing Stage, in $3^1/_2$-$4^1/_2$ hrs. (fares 6*s.*, 3*s.*; return 10*s.* 6*d.*, 5*s.* 6*d.*).

From Barrow to Douglas, 46 M., steamer in 3 hrs., daily in summer and twice weekly in winter (fares as above).

From Fleetwood to Douglas, 54 M., steamer in summer daily, in 3 hrs., starting on the arrival of the 2 p.m. train (fares as above).

From Dublin to Douglas, 94 M., steamer in summer on Tuesdays and Fridays, according to tides (fares 6*s.*, 4*s.*; return 10*s.* 6*d.*, 7*s.* 6*d.*).

From Silloth to Douglas, 66 M., steamer twice weekly in summer (on the way to Dublin; comp. p. 376), calling at *Whitehaven* (fares 5*s.*, 3*s.*).

From Belfast to Douglas, 90 M., steamer once a week; oftener during July and August (fares 6*s.* 6*d.*, 4*s.*; return 10*s.*, 6*s.*, 5*s.* 6*d.*).

From Glasgow (Greenock) to Douglas, 140 M., steamer twice a week in summer, calling at *Ramsey* (fares 10*s.*, 5*s.*; return 15*s.*, 7*s.* 6*d.*).

From Liverpool to Ramsey, 85 M., steamer 5 times weekly in ummer, in 6 hrs. (fares 6*s.*, 3*s.*; return 10*s.* 6*d.*, 5*s.* 6*d*).

From Fleetwood to Ramsey, thrice weekly, via Douglas (see above).

From Whitehaven to Ramsey, 30 M., steamer fortnightly, in 2 hrs. (thrice weekly in July and Aug.; fare 6*s.*, 3*s.*; return 10*s.*, 5*s.*).

A Railway connects *Ramsey*, *Peel*, *Douglas*, and *Castletown*, and extends to *Port Erin* and *Port St. Mary*, giving access to most places of interest.

The **Isle of Man**, or **Mann**, is in the Irish Sea, between England, Scotland, and Ireland; hence its heraldic emblem (the three legs, or triune), and its Manx name, *Vannin* or *Mannin*, signifying 'middle'. The nearest point of the mainland (16 M.) is Burrow Head, Wigtonshire. The length of the island is about 32 M., its breadth about 12 M., its area 220 sq.M. More than half of the population (about 54,000) are in the four towns, Douglas, Ramsey, Castletown, and Peel. The central part of the island is mountainous and beautifully diversified; streams, flowing through narrow leafy glens, with precipitous sides, form numberless cascades. The whole island, however, has become practically one large playground for the operatives of Lancashire and Yorkshire; and their tastes have been so extensively catered for, by the erection of dancing saloons and the like at every point of interest, as to seriously interfere with the enjoyment of the scenery for its own sake. The hilly region ends with the valley of the *Sulby*, to the N. of which is a plain, unbroken except by low sand-hills, and including the *Curragh*, once a bog in which the fossil elk has been found. The highest point is *Snaefell* (2034 ft.), the top of which commands a view of England, Ireland, and Scotland. On the S. coast are many fine precipitous cliffs. The water is everywhere clear, and the smooth sandy shores afford safe and pleasant bathing. Good fishing is plentiful both in the rivers (trout) and the sea (mackarel, etc.).

History. The early history of the island is so mythical as to have little value, especially as there is no ancient Manx literature. Its hero, *Mannonan Mac-y-Lheir* (son of Lear), warrior, legislator, merchant, and magician, is said to have been slain by St. Patrick, who converted the Manx to Christianity (5th cent.). After this the island is supposed to have been under the sway of a long series of Welsh princes, and from the 10th to the 13th cent. it had Scandinavian rulers, many of the local names being evidently of Norse origin. In 1263 Alexander III. of Scotland subdued the island; but the Manx were so oppressed by the Scots, that by their desire Edward I. took it under his protection. Among the numerous subsequent rulers, or 'Kings', were William Montacute, Earl of Salisbury, Sir William Scroop, and Earl Percy (1399). In 1405 Henry IV. gave the kingdom to Sir John Stanley, and it remained with the Derby family till 1825, when the royal rights were purchased of the Duke of Athole, a descendant of the seventh earl, for 416,000*l.*

The political constitution of the island, said to be the oldest in Europe, is unique. The government is vested in the *Lieutenant Governor*, appointed by the Crown; the *Executive Council*, including the two 'Deemsters' (judges), the Clerk of the Rolls, the Receiver-General, the Bishop, the Archdeacon, and the Vicar-General; and the *House of Keys*, consisting of 24 members elected by male or female owners and male occupiers. These three together constitute the *Court of Tynwald* (see p. 343). Acts of the British Parliament do not extend to the Isle of Man, unless it is specially named; and it is exempt from all imperial taxation. The island is divided for civil jurisdiction into two districts, and each of these into three 'Sheadings'. The first part of the title of the Bishop of Sodor and Man is derived from the 'Sudreys' (the Hebrides), once included in the see. — The Manx language, resembling Gaelic, is fast dying out.

A good general view of the coast is afforded by a trip round the island in one of the large steamers which leave Douglas once or twice a week during the summer, calling at Ramsey and making the circuit of about 80 M. in 6 hours (fares 3*s.*, 2*s.*). — Living in the Isle of Man is cheap as compared with fashionable resorts in the S. The leading hotels at Douglas, Ramsey, etc., are good; but many of the so-called hotels at the smaller points of interest are merely wooden barracks adapted only for the refreshment of the passing traveller. — Man is famous for a breed of tailless cats. — The best guide to the island is *Brown's* (Isle of Man Times Office, Douglas).

Douglas. — **Hotels.** *Fort Anne, in a commanding situation at the S. end of the bay; Villiers, a large house close to the pier; Peveril, Grand, Granville, Regent (R. & A. 3*s.* 6*d.*), Athole, Central, all on the Esplanade; Castle Mona. — Innumerable *Boarding Houses* facing the sea (from 5*s.* per day).

Coach frequently in summer to *Port Erin* (return-fare 5*s.*). *Excursion Brakes* to *Laxey*, *Ramsey*, etc. — *Yachts* for sailing excursions. — Two *Theatres*. — *Bellevue Gardens*. — *Victoria Baths*. — *Tramway* round the bay (2*d.*).

Douglas, the capital of the island, with 18,000 inhab., lies on a fine bay, with a *Tower of Refuge* in the middle of it. Handsome new streets have displaced most of the old town, and a fine *Promenade* skirts the shore. The *Victoria Pier* is 1400 ft. long, the *Iron Pier* (adm. 1*d.*) 1000 ft., and the *Red Pier* 540 ft. The three huge *Dancing Pavilions* at Derby Castle, Falcon Cliff, and the Palace, of iron and glass, are conspicuous features. The *Castle Mona Hotel* was formerly the residence of the dukes of Athole (see p. 341). *Port Skillion*, at the foot of *Douglas Head*, reached by ferry across the harbour (1*d.*), has excellent open-air bathing for gentlemen. At *Government House* is a small *Collection of Local Antiquities.*

Walks. Among the most interesting points near Douglas are *Douglas Head* (view), the S. arm of the bay; the *Nunnery*, a modern but very picturesque mansion, on an ancient foundation (reached by crossing the bridge at the head of the harbour and turning to the right); *Port Soderick*, 3 M. to the S.; and ($1^1/_2$ M.) *Braddan*, with its old and new churches and Runic monuments.

Longer Excursions. A good glance at the inland scenery is obtained by driving along the 'Long Road' and the 'Short Road', together 40 M. in length (excursion-brakes, 2*s.* 6*d.*-4*s.* each pers.; 6-7 hrs.). The route leads by *Braddan* (see above), *St. Trinian's* ruined chapel, and *Greeba* to (8 M.) *Ballacraine*, where we turn to the right and ascend *Glen Mooar*, passing the entrance to (10 M.) *Glen Helen* (p. 344). To the left is the *Spooyt Vane Waterfall*. 15 M. *Kirk Michael* (p. 344); 16 M. *Bishopscourt* (the episcopal palace, mostly rebuilt by Bishop Wilson); 18 M. *Ballaugh* (p. 344); 21 M. *Sulby* (p. 344), beyond which, to the right, are *Lezayre Church* and *Ballakillingan* and *Milntown Parks*, at the foot of *Skyhill*. We then reach (24 M.) *Ramsey*, where a stay of 1-2 hrs. gives time for a visit to the (1 M.) *Albert Tower* (view). In returning by the 'Short Road', we skirt *Slieu Lewaigue* and pass (4 M.) *Ballaglass*, the (6 M.) *Dhoon Glens* (adm. 4*d.*), and ($8^1/_2$ M.) **Laxey**, a thriving mining-village with 2000 inhab., in a beautiful glen. Its 'Mining Wheel', $72^1/_2$ ft. in diameter (view from the top; fee 3*d.*), is one of the 'Lions' of the island. We then pass *Onchan*, with its curious church and monuments, and descend rapidly into (16 M.) Douglas. — Excursion-Brakes also ply direct to ($7^1/_2$ M.) *Laxey* (see above; fare 1*s.*, return-fare 1*s.* 6*d.*). — Perhaps the finest route from Douglas to Ramsey is by the so-called '*Mountains Drive*' (18 M.), crossing the shoulder of *Snaefell* (p. 341), an ascent of which may be combined with this route, and descending through *Sulby Glen* (p. 344) to *Sulby*, where it joins the above-mentioned route. — The following round is recommended to the moderate walker: walk from Douglas viâ *Braddan* (see above) to ($2^1/_2$ M.) *Union Mills* (p. 343); train to *St. John's* (p. 343); visit *Glen Helen* (p. 344; there and back 6 M.), and go on to (4 M.) *Glen Meay* (p. 344) and ($2^1/_2$ M.) *Peel* (p. 344). — Other excursions may be made to *Castletown* (see below), *Port Erin* (coach, see p. 342), etc.

From Douglas Port Erin, 16 M., railway in 1 hr. (fares 2*s.* 6*d.*, 1*s.* 4*d.*; no second class). — $3^1/_2$ M. *Port Soderick;* $6^1/_2$ M. *Santon;* 9 M. *Ballasalla* (Rushen Abbey Hotel), with the ruins of *Rushen Abbey*, founded in the 11th century. — $10^1/_2$ M. **Castletown** (*George*, *Union*, both unpretending) is the ancient capital and seat of government of the island. The chief attraction is *Castle Rushen*, formerly the palace of the Kings of Man, and until lately the prison of the island (adm. 4*d.*).

The present building occupies the site of a castle of the 10th cent., which was besieged and almost entirely destroyed by Robert Bruce in 1313. Many mysterious stories are connected with some of its unfrequented apartments. The keep, banqueting-hall, and chapel formed the royal residence; the late Rolls Office was occupied by the Derby family. The glacis was constructed by Card. Wolsey while he held the island as trustee for one of the Stanleys, then a minor. From the castle-tower, Snowdon, Anglesey, the Mourne Mountains, and parts of Cumberland are visible. The clock in the S. tower was given by Queen Elizabeth and is still going. — In the market-place are an antique *Sun Dial* and a monument to Governor Smelt (1833). *King William's College*, an excellent school of over 200 boys, contains a collection of local fossils. Near the college is *Hango Hill*, where William Christian (Illiam Dhone) was executed in 1602 as a traitor to the 6th Earl of Derby (then King of the Island). — Excursions may be made to *Derby Haven*, on the curious peninsula of *Langness;* to ($1^1/_2$ M.) *Malew Church*, with some curious relics; and to *Rushen Abbey* (see above).

$11^1/_2$ M. *Ballabeg;* 13 M. *Colby.* — 15 M. *Port St. Mary* (Cliff Hotel), a pleasant little seaport, now aspiring to be a seaside resort.

Walkers are advised to quit the train here and go by the *Chasms* to Port Erin (2-$2^1/_2$ hrs.). We follow the road (soon becoming a cart-track) which leads to the right, opposite the Cumberland Inn, near the harbour. 5 min. *Fistard.* At (7 min.) a gate the track bends to the right; 5 min. Gate; 4 min. Gate, beyond which is the house where we pay (2*d.*) for admission to the enclosure containing the ***Chasms**, fissures resembling those mentioned at p. 211. We now follow the cliffs as closely as possible to (1 M.) ***Spanish Head**, which commands a view of the *Calf of Man.* From Spanish Head we can either keep on round the coast, or shorten the walk by striking inland to *Cregneesh* and following a track across the *Mull Hills* to (1 M.) *Port Erin* (see below).

16 M. **Port Erin** (*Udall's; Falcon's Nest;* lodgings), a very picturesque little watering-place, at the head of a narrow and deep bay, the mouth of which is partly protected by the striking ruins of a huge breakwater, destroyed by a storm. The N. arm of the bay is formed by the lofty **Bradda Head*, surmounted by a view-tower.

Port Erin and Port St. Mary are good starting-points for visits by boat (experienced boatman necessary) to some of the grandest coast scenery, the *Calf of Man*, the *Chickens Lighthouse*, etc.

From Douglas to Peel, 12 M., railway in $^3/_4$ hr. (fares 1*s.* 10*d.*, 1*s.*). — $2^1/_2$ M. *Union Mills*, 1 M. from Braddan (p. 342); $5^1/_2$ M. *Crosby.* To the right, at the foot of *Greeba*, lies *St. Trinian's* (p. 342). — 9 M. *St. John's*, where our line diverges to the left from that to Ramsey (carriages sometimes changed). A little to the right (N.) of the station is the *Tynwald Hill*, a circular mound thrown up in very remote times for legislative meetings; and here all new Manx laws are promulgated on July 5th.

About 2 M. to the N. of St. John's (comp. p. 342) is the entrance (*Swiss Cottage Hotel*, D. 1*s*. 6*d*.) to *Glen Helen (adm. 6*d*.), one of the prettiest little valleys in the island, with the (1 M.) *Rhenass Falls*. — In the opposite direction lies (4 M.) *Glen Meay* (adm. 4*d*.), another small glen with a waterfall, opening to the sea, whence we may go on to (3 M.) *Peel* (comp. p. 342).

12 M. **Peel** (*Creg Malin*, on the shore; *Peel Castle)* is a small town at the mouth of the *Neb*, with 4000 inhab., engaged in fishing, boat-building, and net, sail, and rope-making.

Peel Castle (adm. 3*d*.), dating in its present form mainly from the 15th cent., is a picturesque ruin, to which much historic and legendary interest attaches. It lies on *St. Patrick's Isle*, connected with the mainland by a causeway (ferry across the harbour 1*d*.). 'Fenella's Tower' is pointed out as the scene of Fenella's escape in Scott's 'Peveril of the Peak'. The *Round Tower* (50 ft. high) in the centre of the enclosure is of uncertain origin. The oldest part of the ruined *Cathedral*, also within the castle enclosure, is the choir (1226-47).

On the *White Strand* (1 M. to the W.) fossil pebbles are found. On *Peet Hill* (450 ft.), a high tower, termed *Corrin's Folly*, was built by a Nonconformist of that name, as a burial-place; it affords a good general view of the town and castle.

From Douglas to Ramsey, 26 M., railway in 1½-1¾ hr. (fares 3*s*. 6*d*., 2*s*. 2*d*.). From Douglas to (9 M.) *St. John's*, see p. 343. 11 M. *Poortown;* 12 M. *St. Germains.* — 16 M. *Kirk Michael* (Mitre; Northern Railway), the churchyard of which contains several interesting Runic monuments. A little farther on *Bishopscourt* (p. 342) is passed on the right. — 19 M. *Ballaugh*, near the Curragh (p. 341). — 21 M. *Sulby Glen* (Hotel).

This is the best starting-point for a visit to *Sulby Glen, a wider and more open valley than most of the Manx glens, somewhat recalling parts of the Highlands. A walk of 3½ M. from the station along the road through the valley brings us to the *Tholt-e-Will Hotel*, in the grounds of which (adm. 4*d*.) are the *Alt* and the *Tholt-e-Will Falls* (the latter insignificant). Tholt-e-Will lies near the N.W. base of *Snaefell* (p. 341), which may be easily ascended hence. — From this point we may reach Ramsey viâ *Glen Auldyn*, to the N.E. of Snaefell.

22 M. *Sulby Bridge;* 24 M. *Lezayre.* — 26 M. **Ramsey** (*Queen's*, *Albert*, *Prince of Wales*, on the Esplanade; *Mitre*, in the town; *Old Swan*, unpretending; lodgings), a small town with 4500 inhab., is situated on the N.E. coast of the island, in the middle of a still finer bay than that of Douglas. The sandy beach affords excellent bathing, and there are a *Promenade* and a *Pier*, 2200 ft. long.

The environs are pretty, and pleasant walks may be taken to (1 M.) the *Albert Tower*, and to (1½ hr.) *North Barrule* (1850 ft.), and thence along the ridge to (4 M.) *Snaefell* (p. 341). To the S. of the town the shore is rocky, and at low tide we may follow it to *Port Lewaigue* (pronounced *league*) and other rocky little creeks at the foot of *Maughold Head*. On the hill is *Kirk Maughold*, with a very curious church and monuments. One of the favourite excursions is that to *Sulby Glen* (see above), with which may be combined *Glen Auldyn* (see above). — The *Ballaglass Falls* and *Ballure Glen* are also picturesque. — On a drive to (7½ M.) the *Point of Ayre*, the N. extremity of the island (fine sea view), we pass (4½ M.) *Kirk Bride*. The return may be made by *Andreas*, with a very lofty church-tower and some Runic monuments. About 1 M. to the S. of the village is the old fort of *Ballachurry*, a grassy mound of unknown date. — Beyond the Point of Ayre, the coast is lined with high sandy 'Broughs', which extend far down the W. side of the island.

44. From Liverpool to London.

The traveller from Liverpool to London has a choice of the lines of four different companies. The most direct route is by the *London & North Western Railway* to Euston Square, viâ Crewe and Rugby. The route of the *Midland Railway* (to St. Pancras) passes Matlock, Derby, Leicester, and Bedford, traversing the beautiful Derbyshire Peak (R. 45). The trains of the *Great Northern Railway*, to King's Cross, run by Manchester, Sheffield, Retford, Grantham, and Peterborough. The *Great Western Railway* to Paddington passes Chester, Shrewsbury, Birmingham, Warwick (Stratford-on-Avon), and Oxford. The fares are the same on all the lines (29*s.*, 21*s.* 9*d.*, 16*s.* 6*d.*; no second class on the Midland Railway). The time occupied by the fast trains (4½-5 hrs.) is about the same on each route. Drawing-room carriages are attached to the principal day-expresses (no extra charge), and sleeping-cars to the night-trains (berth 5-6*s.* extra). On arrival passengers need not leave the latter until convenient. — The journey may be broken at any of the intermediate stopping-places. Luncheon-baskets may be obtained at the London and other chief stations; and hot luncheons may be ordered in advance through the guard (charge 3*s.*, including wine or beer).

a. From Liverpool to London viâ Crewe and Rugby.

202 M. London & North Western Railway *(Euston Square)* in 4½-7 hrs. (fares, see above). Passengers leaving London by the 7.15 a.m. express reach Liverpool in time for the American steamers starting in the afternoon.

The train starts at Lime Street Station (p. 323) and passes through deep cuttings in the red sandstone. 1 M. *Edgehill*; 1½ M. *Wavertree*, with the lofty campanile of its church to the right. The large church at Sefton Park (p. 328) is visible on the same side. From (4 M.) *Allerton* a branch-line diverges to *Garston*, a town on the Mersey with 7840 inhabitants. Beyond (8½ M.) *Ditton*, junction of a line to Warrington (p. 332), the train crosses the *Mersey* by a long iron viaduct. 16 M. *Runcorn* (p. 332); 18 M. *Sutton Weaver*. We now cross the *Weaver*. From 22 M. *Acton Bridge*, on the main L.N.W. line, a branch diverges to (4½ M.) *Northwich* (p. 277).

We now traverse the fertile district which produces the famous Cheshire cheese. Beyond (32 M.) *Hartford* the line passes through the smiling *Vale Royal*, watered by the Weaver. To the right is the manor-house of *Vale Royal*, the seat of Lord Delamere. The hills of Wales are visible to the right.

43½ M. **Crewe** (**Crewe Arms*, connected with the station by a covered passage; *Royal; Railway Rfmt. Rooms)*, a town of 24,375 inhab., is the seat of the railway-works of the L.N.W.R., which employ 7000 men. A *Public Park* was opened in 1888. Crewe is also an important railway-junction, 500 trains passing through it daily.

Crewe Hall, a modern Elizabethan mansion, is a reproduction of the original building by Inigo Jones, which was burned down in 1866.

From Crewe to Chester, 31 M., railway in ½-1 hr. (fares 3*s.* 8*d.*, 3*s.*, 1*s.* 9*d.*). 9 M. *Beeston Castle* (Tollemache Arms), see p. 276. — 31 M. *Chester*, see p. 269.

From Crewe to Stoke-upon-Trent, 15 M., railway in ½-¾ hr. (fares 2*s.* 6*d.*, 1*s.* 11*d.*, 1*s.* 3*d.*). This line takes us into the heart of the **Potteries,** a busy manufacturing district in the N.W. of Staffordshire, where the celebrated English earthenware and porcelain are made. This district occupies the upper valley of the *Trent* for a distance of about 10 **M.**, and is rich in iron and coal; but most of the clay and other materials used in the manufacture of pottery is brought from a distance. The towns and villages it contains have gradually increased to such an extent that the district may now almost be described as one large and scattered town, with upwards of 300,000 inhabitants. In every direction rise chimneys, furnaces, warehouses, and drying-houses. The importance of this industry is in great measure owing to the enterprise of *Josiah Wedgwood* (1730-1795), a native of Burslem (see below), who established his works at the village of Etruria, 1½ M. to the S.W. of Stoke (see below). *Minton* and *Copeland* also did much to promote this industry.

Stoke-upon-Trent *(*Railway; Wheatsheaf; Rail. Refreshmt. Rooms)*, a town with 19,263 inhab., is the capital of the busy district known as the *Potteries* (see above). In front of the large station are statues of *Wedgwood* (d. 1795) and *Minton* (d. 1836; see above). A visit should be paid to the show-rooms of Minton or Copeland. — At *Burslem*, to the N. of Stoke, is the *Wedgwood Institute*, containing a school of art and a museum; it is elaborately adorned with porcelain plaques and friezes.

From Crewe to Whitchurch, 13 M., railway in 20-40 min. (2*s.* 6*d.*, 1*s.* 9*d.*, 1*s.* 2*d.*). — 9 M. *Nantwich* (7490 inhab.). 13 M. *Whitchurch*, see p. 268.

From Crewe to *Manchester*, see p. 340.

On leaving Crewe we have a view of the tower of *Crewe Hall* (p. 345), among trees, to the left. Beyond (52½ M.) *Madeley* we cross the line from Wellington to *Newcastle-under-Lyme*, a town with 16,000 inhab., in the Potteries (see above). — 63½ M. *Norton Bridge* (Railway Hotel), junction of a line to Stone and Stoke (comp. p. 340). — We now pass Stafford Castle (see below) on the right.

68½ M. **Stafford** *(North Western; Swan; Vine; Rail. Refreshmt. Rooms)*, the county-town of Staffordshire, with 19,980 inhab., situated on the *Sow*, 3 M. above its junction with the *Trent*. It carries on an extensive manufacture of boots and shoes. Near the station, but on the other side of the river, is *St. Mary's Church*, a handsome cruciform edifice, with an octangular tower and a late-Norman nave (1189). It contains a few old monuments. Close by, at the corner of Greengate, is the picturesque old *High House*. Nearly opposite the High House is *St. Chad's*, a restored Norman church. The *Museum*, in Eastgate, contains a collection of old books and MSS., presented by Mrs. Salt. *Izaak Walton* (1593-1683) was a native of Stafford, and a walk on the river-side, near the station, bears his name.

About 1½ M. to the N.W. of the town, on the Newport Road (passing the back of the station), is **Stafford Castle**, a square building with towers at the corners, finely situated on a hill commanding an extensive view. It belongs to Lord Stafford, but is now untenanted, except by the keeper (visitors admitted). Part of the old Norman keep is extant.

From Stafford to Shrewsbury, 29 M., railway in ¾-1¼ hr. (fares 5*s.* 2*d.*, 3*s.* 9*d.*, 2*s.* 5½*d.*). Near (11 M.) *Newport* (Shakespeare), with a fine 15th cent. church, are *Aqualate Hall*, with a small lake, and *Chetwynd Park*. — 19 M. *Wellington*, and thence to (29 M.) *Shrewsbury*, see p. 262.

From Stafford to Uttoxeter, 15 M., railway in ¾ hr. (fares 2*s.*, 1*s.* 8*d.*, 1*s.* 3*d.*). Near (5½ M.) *Ingestre* is *Ingestre Park*, the seat of the Earl of Shrewsbury. At (11 M.) *Chartley* are the ruins of an old castle of that name and another fine park. At *Chartley Hall* is shown a room in which Mary, Queen of Scots, was imprisoned for some time. — 15 M. **Uttoxeter** *(White Hart; Rail. Refreshmt. Rooms)*, pronounced *Uxeter*, is a pleasant little town of 4700 inhab., on the railway from Stoke (see above) to

Derby (p. 350). It was at Uttoxeter market that Dr. Samuel Johnson's father kept the book-stall, at which his son on one occasion refused to take his place. The penance he in after-life imposed upon himself for his disobedience is well known. Entering the market at the time of high business he stood for an hour in the rain, with his head bare, in front of the stall which had once been his father's. — Near *Alton*, on the railway to Macclesfield, 7$^1/_2$ M. to the N. of Uttoxeter, is ***Alton Towers,** the picturesque seat of the Earl of Shrewsbury. Its splendid collections have been to a great extent dispersed and the house is seldom shown; but the beautiful grounds (adm. 1*s.*) well deserve a visit. — *Leek* (George), another station on the same railway, has a fine church and an art-gallery. Near it are the ruins of *Dieulacresse Abbey*, incorporated in a farm-house.

From Stafford to Wolverhampton, 15 M., railway in 25-40 minutes. *Wolverhampton*, and thence to Birmingham, see pp. 259, 260.

Beyond Stafford the line turns to the left (E.). To the left lie *Ingestre Hall* and *Park* (p. 346). From (75 M.) *Colwich* (Stafford Arms), with a Dec. church (to the right), a line runs N.W. to *Stone*, where it unites with the line from Norton Bridge to Stoke (see p. 346). This is sometimes used as an alternative route by the Manchester express-trains. About 1 M. to the E. is *Shugborough Park*, the seat of the Earl of Lichfield and birthplace of Anson (1697-1762), the voyager. *Wolseley Hall* and *Park* are also visible to the right. The train follows the pretty valley of the *Trent*. — From (79 M.) *Rugeley Junction* a branch runs to *Rugeley* (Shrewsbury Arms), the square church-towers of which are seen to the right, and *Walsall* (p. 259). Near (81 M.) *Armitage* we leave the Trent, which here turns to the N. To the right are *Beaudesert Park*, the seat of the Marquis of Anglesey, and the hilly district called *Cannock Chase*, formerly a royal forest, and now an important mining region (coal and iron). As we approach Lichfield we have a view of its graceful cathedral-spires to the right. The L.N.W. Trent Valley Station is 1$^1/_2$ M. from the town (omn. 6*d.*).

86 M. **Lichfield** (**George*, the scene of Farquhar's 'Beaux' Stratagem', St. John St., R. & A. 4*s.*; *Swan; Anglesey*, unpretending), pleasantly situated on an arm of the *Trent*, is a small town with 8360 inhab., a fine cathedral, and many interesting associations with Dr. Samuel Johnson, who was born here in 1709.

The name of Lichfield is probably derived from the A. S. *leccian*, to irrigate, and refers to its well-watered situation. The chief industry of the town is brewing. According to Johnson the citizens of Lichfield 'are the most sober, decent people in England, are the genteelest in proportion to their wealth, and speak the purest English'.

The house in which Johnson was born is at the corner of the Market Place (reached from St. John St. by Bore Street, opposite the Clock Tower) and Sadler Street, and is recognisable by the three wooden pillars in front. Opposite is the *Church of St. Mary*, with a tall spire, the register of which contains an entry of Johnson's baptism. The market-place contains a colossal *Statue of Johnson*, erected in 1838, with bas-reliefs of scenes from his life on the pedestal. Johnson's father and mother are buried in the *Church of St. Michael*, to the E. of the town, where their tombs are marked by epitaphs composed by their son (in the central aisle). The free

Grammar School, attended by Johnson, Addison, and Garrick, was rebuilt about 1850. The old *Three Crowns Inn*, in the market-place, entertained Johnson and Boswell when they visited Lichfield in 1776, and it was the scene of the 'comfortable supper' after which the sage uttered the above encomium on his native place.

The * **Cathedral**, a building of red sandstone, dedicated to St. Chad (d. 672), the patron-saint of Lichfield, and situated in a small but picturesque close at the N. end of the main line of streets, dates mainly from the 13-14th centuries.

The diocese of Lichfield was formerly of immense size, having been at first conterminous with the kingdom of Mercia, and no fewer than twelve other modern sees once lay wholly or in part within its borders. At the end of the eighth century the bishop of Lichfield bore for a short time the archiepiscopal title. — The first cathedral, built in the 7th cent., was perhaps on the site of the present church of St. Chad (p. 349); but the earliest building on the present site was a Norman church dating from about 1100. The oldest part of the existing building is the lower part of the W. half of the choir, erected about 1200; the transepts followed in 1220-40; the nave dates from about 1250, and the W. front from about 1280; while the lady-chapel and presbytery belong to the beginning of the 14th century. The cathedral-close was formerly surrounded by a wall and moat, and in 1643 the cathedral was defended against the Puritans, who battered down the central tower and demolished many carvings monuments, and windows. It was, however, soon restored.

Lichfield Cathedral is sometimes styled the 'Queen of English Minsters', and though surpassed by other cathedrals in age, size, grandeur of site, and elaborate decoration, it has yet a good claim to the title in the exquisite symmetry, proportion, and picturesqueness of its general effect. The most conspicuous external features are the three beautiful spires and the fine W. façade. The central steeple (by Wren) is 260 ft., and those at the W. end each 190 ft. high. The **W. Façade*, dating from about 1280, is one of the most graceful and harmonious in England; and it has an advantage over such a front as that of Peterborough (p. 362) in its organic connection with the rest of the building. It is covered with niches for about 100 statues, now almost all filled with modern figures. The door of the N. transept is a fine piece of E.E. work. — The main dimensions of the cathedral are: length, 403 ft.; width of nave, 65 ft.; width across transepts, 149 ft.; height, 60 ft. The daily services are at 10 a.m. and 4 p.m. We enter by the W. portal.

The ***Interior** (adm. at any hour of the day; no fee) is worthy of the exterior; its proportions are very harmonious and pleasing, while the red hue of the stone gives an impression of great richness and warmth. The Nave is in the early-Dec. style, with a beautiful triforium. The aisles are unusually narrow. Most of the ancient monuments have been destroyed, but many of the modern ones are interesting, such as those of Lady Mary Wortley Montague, Johnson, and Garrick. The last is provided with an epitaph by Johnson. In the N. aisle is a monument erected by *Miss Seward* (d. 1809) to her parents, with an inscription by Sir Walter Scott referring to the poetess herself. The Transepts are E.E., with Perp. insertions.

The *Choir, which deflects palpably towards the N., was erected about 1200; but the E. half, forming the *Presbytery*, was rebuilt in 1325, while the clerestory of the W. part was also altered. The junction of the E.E. and Dec. styles is easily distinguishable. The reredos and stalls were designed by *Scott*. The floor, in Minton tiles, represents the early history of the diocese. At the E. end of the S. aisle is a celebrated monument, the **Sleeping Children* of Mrs. Robinson, by Chantrey; and at the corresponding place in the N. aisle is the kneeling figure of *Bp. Ryder* (d. 1836), also by Chantrey. — At the E. end of the choir is the Lady Chapel, built about 1300, and terminating in a polygonal apse (the only

For a plan of Lichfield Cathedral see page 550

Gothic apse in an English cathedral). The **Stained Glass Windows*, dating from 1530-44, were brought in 1802 from a convent near Liège. — A door in the N. aisle of the choir opens on a vestibule leading to the *Chapter House, an octagonal room, with a ribbed roof supported by a central shaft. A room above contains the diocesan *Library*, among the treasures of which are an illuminated MS. of 'Chaucer's Canterbury Tales' and a Saxon copy of the Gospels ('St. Chad's Gospels'; not later than 700) — In the Dean's Court, on the S. side of the cathedral, are busts of Dr. Johnson and Garrick, by *Westmacott.*

The *Episcopal Palace* is on the N. side of the close, and on the S. is a *Theological College*. — In Beacon St., opposite the *Minster Pool*, is the *Museum*, containing local antiquities and a few paintings. At the S. end of St. John St., 1/2 M. from the cathedral, is *St. John's Hospital*, a curious old structure, with eight large buttress-like chimneys and a chapel. Near this is the *City Station*, connected by a loop-line with the *Trent Valley Station* (see p. 347).

Environs. To the N.E. of Lichfield lies *Stowe Pool*, along which a pretty walk leads to *Stowe* and the ancient church of *St. Chad*, containing the tomb of Lucy Porter, Johnson's step-daughter. — *Wall*, the site of the Roman *Etocetum*, is situated 2 M. to the S., on Watling Street (p. 356). Remains of ancient earthworks are still visible. Another Roman road, named *Icknield Street*, leads from Lichfield towards the N.E.

From Lichfield to Walsall, 13 M., railway in 1/2-3/4 hr. (fares 2*s.* 3*d.*, 1*s.* 8*d.*, 1*s.* 1*d.*). This line traverses a busy coal-mining district. Stations uninteresting. 13 M. *Walsall*, see p. 259.

From Lichfield to Derby, 23 1/2 M., railway in 3/4 hr. — This railway, which is the N. prolongation of the line just described, follows the general direction of the Icknield Street (see above).

Beyond Lichfield the train passes between the parks of *Fisherwick* (left) and *Tamhorn* (right) and crosses the *Tame*. From (91 M.) *Tamworth* (p. 188), where our line intersects the Midland Railway from Birmingham to Derby (R. 23), the train follows the direction of the *Anker*. At (98 1/2 M.) *Atherstone* (Red Lion), in the Three Tuns Inn, Henry of Richmond passed the night before the Battle of Bosworth (1485), the field of which lies about 5 M. to the N.E.

104 M. **Nuneaton** *(Newdegate Arms; Bull; Rail. Refreshmt. Rooms)*, a ribbon-making town of 8465 inhab., with an old Gothic church and the remains of a nunnery, fitted up as a church.

120 M. *Rugby*, and thence to (202 M.) *London*, see pp. 252-249.

b. From Liverpool to London viâ Buxton and Derby.

220 M. Midland Railway in 5-6 1/2 hrs. (fares, etc., see p. 345). There are no second-class compartments on the Midland Railway, but the third-class carriages are well fitted up.

From Liverpool to (25 M.) *Glazebrook*, see p. 333. The London line here diverges to the right from that to Manchester. At (38 M.) *Tiviot Dale*, one of the stations of *Stockport* (p. 340), our line is joined by the direct line of the Midland railway from Manchester (Central Station) to London (comp. p. 340), while the trains from London Road come in at (41 M.) *Romilly*. Beyond (42 3/4 M.) *Marple* we enter Derbyshire, and the hills of the *Peak District* (R. 45) become visible to the left, at some distance.

We now traverse the valley of the *Goyt*, the beauties of which are marred by factories. At ($46^1/_4$ M.) *New Mills* we obtain, on the left, a distant view of Kinder Scout (p. 370), and farther on we pass the conical *Chinley Churn* (1490 ft.). The L.N.W. line from Manchester to Buxton here runs parallel with ours, on the right side of the valley. Beyond ($51^3/_4$ M.) *Chapel-en-le-Frith* (King's Arms), one of the starting-points for an exploration of the Peak (comp. p. 370), the line passes below the L.N.W. Railway, threads the *Doveholes Tunnel*, $1^1/_2$ M. long, and reaches its culminating point (985 ft.) at ($55^1/_2$ M.) *Peak Forest Station.* It then descends rapidly, through the *Great Rocks Dale*, to (60 M.) *Miller's Dale*, the junction of a short branch to *Buxton* (p. 370). We here enter the romantic **Valley of the Wye*, and the scenery between this point and Matlock is the most attractive on the line (best views to the left). Two tunnels. $62^3/_4$ M. *Monsal Dale*, exquisitely situated in a narrow part of the valley. Beyond the *Longstone Tunnel* the valley expands, and the train quits the bank of the river for a little. $66^1/_2$ M. *Bakewell* (p. 366). The train now penetrates a tunnel, passing Haddon Hall (not visible). 70 M. *Rowsley* (Peacock), the nearest station for Haddon Hall and Chatsworth (see p. 366; omnibuses 1*s.*). Beyond Rowsley the Wye flows into the *Derwent*, the broad valley of which, here called *Darley Dale*, we now follow. $72^1/_4$ M. *Darley.* Beyond ($74^1/_4$ M.) *Matlock Bridge* the train passes through the *High Tor Tunnel* and reaches ($75^1/_2$ M.) *Matlock Bath* (see p. 365).

Beyond Matlock the train threads another long tunnel. $76^1/_4$ M. *Cromford* (*Greyhound, plain, R. & A. 3*s.*), the 'cradle of the cotton manufacture'; the village and *Willersley Castle*, the seat of the Arkwright family, lie about $^1/_2$ M. to the right. It was here that Richard Arkwright (p. 373) built his first cotton-mill in 1770. — About $1^1/_2$ M. beyond Cromford our line is joined on the right by the *High Peak Railway*, for mineral traffic. — 79 M. *Whatstandwell Bridge;* 81 M. *Ambergate* (Hurt Arms), the junction of lines to Chesterfield (p. 402) and Sheffield (p. 359) and to Mansfield (p. 429). — 84 M. *Belper* (Lion), a small hosiery and cotton manufacturing town with 11,000 inhabitants. — 86 M. *Duffield*, with the remains of a fine Norman castle (11th cent.), is the junction of a line to ($8^1/_2$ M.) *Wirksworth.*

We now quit the hilly district and enter the wide plain of Central England. The town of Derby soons come into sight on the right, before entering the station of which we cross the Derwent Canal and the Derwent.

$91^1/_2$ M. **Derby.** — **Hotels.** *Midland, at the Midland Railway Station, 1 M. from the centre of the town; *St. James's, central, R. & A. 4*s.*; Royal; Bell; Wood's Temperance. — *Rail. Refreshmt. Rooms.*

Tramways run from the centre of the town through the principal streets to the *Midland Station* (fare 1*d.*) on the E., to the *Great Northern Station* on the N.W., and to various other points in the suburbs.

Cab 1*s.* per mile; from the Midland Station into the town 1*s.* 6*d.*

Derby, the county-town of Derbyshire, with about 95,000 inhab., lies on the *Derwent*, opposite the site of the Roman *Derventio.*

William the Conqueror presented the town and its environs to his natural son, 'Peveril of the Peak'; but the last relics of the castle erected by the latter are said to have disappeared in the reign of Queen Elizabeth. In 1745 Derby was the most southerly point reached by Charles Stuart and his Highlanders in their attempted march to London. The manufacture of silk, hosiery, elastic fabrics, cotton, iron, porcelain, and ornaments of Derbyshire spar is briskly prosecuted here. The extensive works of the Midland Railway cover 230 acres and employ 10,000 men.

Starting from Victoria St., in the centre of the town, we proceed to the W. through the Wardwick, which contains the new *Museum & Library* (adm. 10-4), to the FRIAR GATE, the broadest and best-built street in the town. Immediately to the right is *St. Werburgh's Church*, where we turn to the right and pass through Cheapside into *Sadler Gate*, leading to the MARKET PLACE, with the *Town Hall*. The *Iron Gate*, opposite the Town Hall, leads N. to **All Saints' Church**, with a fine Perp. Tower (175 ft. high) of the 16th cent., the architectural glory of the town, to which an incongruous body has been added.

The interior contains monuments by Roubiliac, Chantrey, and Nollekens; an almost unique wooden effigy of an abbot; a curious incised slab with the figure of an abbot; a fine iron chancel-screen; and the monument of *Bess of Hardwick* (p. 402; by the S. wall). Doles of bread are distributed here and at St. Werburgh's after the morning service.

A little farther to the N., at the end of *Queen St.*, is the lofty tapering spire of *St. Alkmund's* (205 ft.), a modern edifice, which is adjoined by the Rom. Cath. *Church of St. Mary*, by Pugin (good interior). — From this point we descend Bridge St. to the right to *St. Mary's Bridge*, with an interesting little chapel (14th cent.).

We now retrace our steps through Bridge St. and Queen St., and near the end of the latter, beyond the small church of *St. Michael*, we descend to the left for a glance at the *Old Silk Mill* (now a laundry), the first silk-mill in England, erected in 1718 on an island in the Derwent by John Lombe.

The *Arboretum*, a well laid out park, 1/2 M. to the S.W. of the Midland Station (tramway viâ Osmaston St.), contains a curious headless cross, said to have been used as a pay-table between the townsmen and peasants during the plague of 1665. On the way we pass the ivy-clad church of *St. Peter* (14th cent.). In Osmaston St. are the **Show Rooms of the Derby Crown Porcelain Co.* — *Derby Grammar School* was founded in 1160.

Samuel Richardson (1689-1761), the author of 'Clarissa Harlowe'; *Joseph Wright* (1734-1797; 'Wright of Derby'), the painter; and *Hutton* (d. 1815), the topographer, were natives of Derby. Dr. Erasmus Darwin wrote many of his works at Derby, and died here in 1802.

Derby is said to be the *Stoniton* of 'Adam Bede', and the *County Hall* in St. Mary's Gate the scene of poor Hetty's trial.

Derby is a very convenient starting-point for excursions to Chatsworth and the Peak (comp. R. 45). Among the most interesting points in the immediate neighbourhood are *Kedleston Hall*, 4 M. to the N.W., with a fine park and a collection of paintings; *Chaddesden*, 1 1/2 M. to the E.; *Elvaston Castle*, 4 M. to the S.E.; and *Duffield* (p. 350).

The two principal lines of the Midland Railway part company at Derby, the one running to the S.W. to Burton (p. 188), Birmingham (p. 254). Worcester (p. 183), and Gloucester (p. 170), while the other runs S.E, to Leicester, Bedford, and London (see below). — Alton Towers (p. 347) may be reached from Derby viâ Uttoxeter in 1 hr.

Beyond Derby the train follows the valley of the Derwent, and joins the London and Scotland trunk-line of the Midland Railway at (101 M.) *Trent Junction* (Rail. Refreshmt. Rooms), at the confluence of the *Soar* and the *Trent*, whence the branch-line to Nottingham diverges (p. 429). The line turns to the S., crosses the Trent and the Soar, and enters Leicestershire, celebrated for its short-horned cattle, its sheep, and its hunters. — $107^1/_2$ M. *Loughborough* (Bull's Head), a town with 14,735 inhab., who make lace and prepare yarn for hosiery. It contains a good cruciform church, restored by Scott, and a large bell-foundry, at which the 'Great Paul' of St. Paul's Cathedral was cast in 1882. To the right, in the distance, are the heights of *Charnwood Forest*, culminating in *Bardon Hill* (902 ft.). The train follows the valley of the *Soar*. About 1 M. to the S.W. (right) of ($109^1/_2$ M.) *Barrow-on-Soar* lies *Quorndon*, the headquarters of the well-known *Quorn Hunt*. Farther on, to the right, is *Mount Sorrel*, with granite-quarries. — 115 M. *Syston*.

Syston is the junction of a line to ($10^1/_2$ M.; to the E.) **Melton Mowbray** (*Harborough; George; Bell*), a small town with 5770 inhab., and the metropolis of fox-hunting in the Midlands, with numerous hunting-boxes and extensive stabling. In winter it is crowded with sportsmen. Melton Mowbray is also famous for its pork-pies and Stilton cheese. The parish-church is a fine E.E. edifice, with Dec. details. Beyond Melton Mowbray the line goes on to *Peterborough* (see p. 362). — About 3 M. to the N.W. of Syston is *Rothley Temple*, in which Lord Macaulay was born in 1800.

120 M. **Leicester.** — **Hotels.** Bell, Stag & Pheasant, Humberstone Gate; Royal; Wellington; White Hart; Blue Lion; Temperance.

Tramways (*1d.*, *2d.*) run from the Clock Tower (see below) through the principal streets to the various suburbs.

Railway Stations. *Joint Midland & L. N. W. Station*, near the centre of the town; *G. N. R. Station*, Belgrave Road, to the N.

Leicester, the county-town of Leicestershire, is an ancient place with 143,153 inhab., situated on the river *Soar*. It is one of the chief seats of the stocking-manufacture, and the making of boots and elastic fabrics is also extensively carried on.

Tradition ascribes the original foundation of Leicester to King Lear, and the present town occupies the site of the Roman *Ratae*, of which several interesting relics are preserved. Richard III. spent the night before the battle of Bosworth (p. 354) in the Blue Boar Inn at Leicester, now demolished, and his body was brought back here for burial. His stone coffin is said to have been afterwards used as a horse-trough for the inn. A building near the Bow Bridge (p. 353), bears the inscription: 'Near this spot lie the remains of Richard III., the last of the Plantagenets, 1485.' In the Civil War Leicester held out for the Parliament, and was taken in 1642 by Prince Rupert.

In the centre of the town, at the intersection of the five main streets, is a handsome *Memorial Cross* or *Clock Tower*, erected in 1868, with effigies of Simon de Montfort, Sir T. White, Ald. Newton, and William of Wyggestone, four benefactors of Leicester. Proceeding to the W., through High St., we pass the '*Brick Tower*', a quaint Elizabethan dwelling, and reach *St. Nicholas*, an ancient church, with some massive Norman masonry in the interior and thin Roman bricks in the clerestory. On the W. it is adjoined by the so-called *Jewry Wall*, the chief Roman relic in Leicester.

This wall derives its name from the fact that the Jews were formerly restricted to this part of the town. It is composed of rubble and Roman bricks, and is 75 ft. long and about 20 ft. high. On the E. side are four large archways; the W. side is concealed. — Farther to the W. is the *West Bridge* over the Soar, beyond which is *Bow Bridge* (see p. 352), over an arm of the river. Adjacent is an interesting Roman pavement.

To the S. of St. Nicholas, reached through Harvey Lane, is the site of the old **Castle** of Leicester, built soon after the Norman Conquest and afterwards occupied by Simon, Earl of Montfort, and the Dukes of Lancaster, of which nothing remains except the modernised *Great Hall*, now used for the county-assizes. Adjacent is a large earthwork called the *Mount* or *Castle View*, on which the castle-donjon or keep formerly stood; it commands a fine view of the town (entrance through the yard of a public-house). To the S. of the Mount is *Trinity Hospital*, founded in 1531. Close to the castle, of which it formed the chapel, is the **Church of St. Mary*, an interesting old building, exhibiting specimens of all the architectural styles from Norman to late-Perpendicular.

The archway to the S. leads to the Newark (*i.e.* the new work), originally an addition to the castle, from which another old gate (restored), adjoining the *Militia Barracks*, opens into Oxford St.

To the S. of the Memorial Tower is the Market Place, containing the *Market House*, with a curious outside-staircase in front. — In Horsefair St., to the S. of the market, are the new *Municipal Buildings*, with a clock-tower 145 ft. high. — At the end of Horsefair St. we turn to the left into Market St. and cross Belvoir St. into King St. To the left diverges the *New Walk*, leading to the *Municipal Museum*, which contains a good collection of Roman and other antiquities, etc. The *Art Gallery*, Hastings St., contains a fine work by *G. F. Watts* ('Fata Morgana').

Farther to the S., in De Montfort Sq., is a *Statue of Robert Hall* (1764-1831), the celebrated preacher, who lived at Leicester for many years.

From the Memorial Cross, Church Gate leads N. to *St. Margaret's Church*, with a Perp. tower.—The old *Town Hall* contains some fine carving (Mayor's Parlour). — *Wyggestone's Hospital* (p. 352), founded in 1513 for 25 men and women, now occupies buildings in the Hinckley Road; the charity also supports several schools.

About 3/4 M. to the N. of the town are the insignificant but picturesque ruins of **Leicester Abbey**, dedicated to 'St. Mary of the Meadows', where *Cardinal Wolsey* died in 1530. The abbey was erected in the 12th cent., but the remaining ruins, except the gateway in the E. wall, date only from the 16th century. (The entrance is on the N. side of the enclosure.) A house has been built with part of the old materials. The most convenient way to reach the abbey is to follow the Belgrave Road to the (3/4 M.) *G. N. R. Station* (tramway 1*d.*), whence the Abbey Park Road leads N. to the (1/2 M.) abbey-enclosure. To the left lies the **Abbey Park*, with its pretty flower-beds.

About 6 M. to the N.W. of Leicester is **Bradgate Park** (open to the public), the seat of the Earl of Stamford, with a fine avenue of chestnuts; the old house, now in ruins, was the birthplace of Lady Jane Grey (1535-54), whose father, the Duke of Suffolk, belonged to the family of the Barons Grey of Groby, a village in the neighbourhood. It was at Bradgate Park that Roger Ascham found his former pupil immersed in

Plato, while the rest of the family were hunting in Charnwood Forest. — Nearly 2 M. farther on are the picturesque ruins of *Ulverscroft Priory*. — An interesting excursion may be made from Leicester to Bardon Hill, 12 M. to the N.W., which is most easily reached by railway (see below). *__Bardon Hill__ (902 ft.) lies almost exactly in the centre of England and commands a very extensive prospect.

From Leicester to Burton, 30½ M., railway in 1-1½ hr. (fares 4*s.* 1*d.*, 2*s.* 6½*d.*). — 14½ M. *Bardon Station* lies 1 M. to the S.W. of Bardon Hill (see above). Adjacent, but rather nearer Coalville, the following station, is the Cistercian monastery of *Mount St. Bernard*, the only 'mitred abbey' in England, built by Pugin the Elder. From (16 M.) *Coalville* a branch diverges to Nuneaton (p. 349), passing *Market Bosworth*, near which, in 1485, Richard III. was defeated and slain by Henry, Earl of Richmond. — 21 M. **Ashby-de-la-Zouch** *(Royal; Queen's Head)*, a prosperous manufacturing town in the middle of an extensive coal-field. The old *Castle*, built in the time of Edward IV. (1461-83) and now in ruins, gave a night's lodging to Mary Stuart in 1569, but is, perhaps, more familiar from the rôle it plays in 'Ivanhoe'. The old *Church* contains the tomb of the *Countess of Huntington*, Wesley's friend, and a curious 'finger-pillory' for disturbers of divine service. The *Ivanhoe Mineral Baths* attract numerous patients. Near Ashby are the romantic ruins of *Grace Dieu Nunnery*. — 30½ M. *Burton*, see p. 188.

From (124 M.) *Wigston* branch-lines diverge to *Nuneaton* and *Birmingham* (p. 254), and to *Rugby* (p. 252).

About 3 M. to the S.E. of *Ullesthorpe*, on the latter line, is *Lutterworth*, where Wycliffe was rector from 1375 till his death in 1384; his alleged pulpit and other relics are preserved in the church.

136 M. **Market Harborough** *(Angel; Three Swans; Peacock)*, another great hunting-centre, is a small town with 5350 inhabitants.

The *Church* is a fine Perp. structure of the 14-15th cent., with a 'broach' spire (see Introd.). There are traces of a Roman camp in the vicinity, and the town itself is probably of Roman origin. Charles I. had his headquarters here before the battle of Naseby (1645), and the house in which he slept is still pointed out. *Naseby* lies 7 M. to the S.W. — From Market Harborough branch-lines radiate toStamford (p. 361), Rugby (p. 252), Peterborough (p. 362), Nottingham (p. 430), etc.

147 M. **Kettering** *(Royal; George)*, a town of 11,100 inhab., with an interesting late-Perp. church. In a house on the N. side of the town is the room in which the first missionary meeting in England was held in 1792 by Andrew Fuller and a few other Baptists.

From Kettering to Huntingdon and Cambridge, 48 M., railway in 2 hrs. (fares 7*s.* 2*d.*, 3*s.* 9½*d.*). — 9 M. *Thrapston*, from which a visit may be paid to the architecturally interesting churches of (½ M.) *Islip* and (2½ M.) *Lowick* (monuments and stained glass) and also to (1¾ M.) *Drayton*, a very fine specimen of a mediæval manor (15th cent.). At (17½ M.) *Kimbolton* is a fine old castle belonging to the Duke of Manchester, containing a collection of paintings; Catherine of Aragon died here in 1536. — 28 M. *Huntingdon*, and thence to (48 M.) *Cambridge*, see p. 352.

From Kettering to Oakham and Nottingham, 52 M., railway in 1-2½ hrs. (fares 6*s.* 10*d.*, 4*s.* 3½*d.*). This line forms an alternative route for some of the Midland expresses to the N. — 18 M. *Manton*, junction of a line to *Peterborough* (p. 362). *Uppingham*, 4 M. to the N. (omn.), has a well-known public school. — 22 M. **Oakham** *(George; Crown)*, the county-town of Rutland, with 3000 inhabitants. The walls of the Norman hall (now a court-room) of the old *Castle* (p. xxxix) are covered with horseshoes, given, in accordance with an ancient custom, by kings, queens, and peers who passed through the town. Among them are those given by Queen Elizabeth, Queen Victoria, and the Princess of Wales. — 33 M. *Melton Mowbray*, see p. 352. — 52 M. *Nottingham*, see p. 430. The line rejoins the main line at *Trowell*, near *Ilkeston* (p. 402).

The train follows the *Ise*, passing through beds of Northampton iron-stone. At (154½ M.) *Wellingborough* (Hind; Angel), a town with 13,796 inhab. and a tasteful church, we cross the L. N. W. line from Peterborough (p. 362) to Northampton (p. 251). *Ecton*, 3 M. from Wellingborough, was the birthplace of Benjamin Franklin's father. Benjamin Franklin visited the place and inspected the house in 1758. The train now intersects a range of hills and enters the valley of the winding *Ouse*, which we cross six times before reaching Bedford. Beyond (167 M.) *Oakley* diverges the Midland branch to Northampton (p. 251). To the left rises the Saxon tower of the church of *Clapham*.

170 M. **Bedford.** — **Hotels.** *Swan, on the river, at the S. end of High St., R. & A. 4*s.* 6*d.*; Red Lion, High St., well spoken of; George; Clarence, unpretending; Temperance, at the Midland Station.

Railway Stations. The station of the *Midland Railway* is on the W., the *L.N.W. Station* on the S.E. side of the town.

Bedford, the county-town of Bedfordshire and the place from which a suffragan of the Bishop of London takes his title, is a quiet agricultural town with 19,532 inhab., on the *Ouse*.

Now, as in the days of Camden, more than two centuries ago, Bedford is 'more eminent for the pleasantness of its situation and antiquity than anything of beauty or stateliness'. Its site seems to have been occupied before the Roman period, and it has been identified with the Saxon *Bedicanford*. In the 11th cent. a Norman castle was erected here to command the ford, and its important situation involved it in most of the internal struggles of England. The last siege it underwent was in 1224, when Henry III. captured the town and razed the castle.

From the *Midland Station*, near which are *Howard's Britannia Iron Works* (reaping-machines and other agricultural implements) the Midland Road leads in 10 min. to the *High Street*, the main street of the town. Near the bridge at its W. end is the site of the old *Castle* (no admission), marked by an artificial circular mound, 15 ft. high and 150 ft. in diameter. A pleasant walk may be taken on the Embankment.

To most visitors the chief interest of Bedford will probably centre in its reminiscences of *John Bunyan* (1628-88; see p. 356). The *Bunyan Meeting* occupies the site of the building in which he preached, and the vestry contains a chair which belonged to him and a door from Bedford Gaol.

The chapel was adorned in 1876 with a pair of handsome bronze doors, the gift of the Duke of Bedford, containing ten reliefs from the 'Pilgrim's Progress'. In the possession of the minister of the Meeting are Bunyan's cabinet, staff, jug, and will (in his own handwriting); also versions of the 'Pilgrim's Progress' in 70-80 languages and dialects. The *Literary & Scientific Institute*, in Harpur St., possesses Bunyan's copy of Foxe's Book of Martyrs. On St. Peter's Green, at the end of the High St., is a bronze *Statue of Bunyan*, by Boehm, presented to the town by the Duke of Bedford.

Bunyan was confined for 12 years (1660-72) in the old county-gaol, which stood on the now vacant space in High St., at the corner of Silver St., and was taken down in 1801. It was, however, during a subsequent imprisonment of six months in 1675-6 that he wrote the 'Pilgrim's Progress'. This was in the town-gaol on Bedford Bridge, which was removed in 1765. The offence for which he was imprisoned is described in his indictment as 'devilishly and perniciously abstaining from coming to church to hear divine service, and for being a common upholder of several unlawful meetings and conventicles, to the great disturbance and distraction of the good subjects of the kingdom, contrary to the laws of our Sovereign lord the king'. His treatment between the autumn assizes of 1661 and the spring assizes of 1662 was very lenient, but for the rest of the time his confinement was somewhat rigorous.

Among the churches of Bedford the most important is that of *St. Paul's*, a handsome Gothic structure, practically rebuilt in 1879. — The venerable church of *St. Peter*, at the E. end of High St., possesses a fine Norman doorway and some ancient stained-glass windows. The tower contains some Saxon work. — *St. Mary's* also has some Saxon work and a Norman tower.

Few towns of the size of Bedford can compete with it in the number and extent of its schools and charities, and with one-fourth of its population under tuition it may fairly be called the 'metropolis of schools'. This is mainly due to the liberality of Sir William Harpur (d. 1574), at one time Lord Mayor of London, who presented to his native town some land in Holborn, which has increased in value from 40*l.* to upwards of 15,000*l.* a year. The principal schools are **Bedford Grammar School**, one of the leading public schools of England (650 pupils), and the **Modern School** (550 pupils) adjoining it, both in Harpur St.

The *Ouse* is a capital river for boating (boats for hire at the Embankment), and Chetham, the well-known boat-builder, has his yard at Bedford. An illuminated *River Fête* is held here in summer.

Environs. About 1 M. to the S. of the town lies the village of **Elstow**, the birthplace of John Bunyan in 1628, still containing the cottage in which he lived after his marriage. To reach it we cross the bridge at the S. end of the High Street, and at the (1/2 M.) bridge over the railway turn to the right (road to Luton). Bunyan's cottage, indicated by a notice, is one of the first on the right. The church of Elstow is an interesting building, partly in the Norman and partly in the E. E. style, with a massive detached tower (Perp.). The keys are kept by the clerk (fee), next door to the Swan Inn. Bunyan was wont to practise the art of bell-ringing in the tower, and the sacristan does not hesitate to point out the very bell that he used to ring, showing the grooves worn by the rope in the stone archway under which Bunyan stood, in dread lest the bell should fall upon him. Two memorial-windows have been erected to Bunyan, with scenes from the 'Pilgrim's Progress' and the 'Holy War'. Even the unpretending village-green acquires interest when we remember Bunyan's account of the sudden awakening of his conscience while he was playing tip-cat here one Sunday afternoon. — John Howard, the philanthropist, lived at the village of *Cardington*, 2 1/2 M. to the S.E. of Bedford, from 1758 till his death in 1790.

From Bedford to Northampton, 21 M., Midland Railway in 40 min. (fares 2*s.* 11*d.*, 1*s.* 9*d.*). — 11 M. **Olney** *(Bull)*, where the poet Cowper resided with Mrs. Unwin in 1768-1800 and wrote many of his poems. The so-called 'Olney Hymns' were the joint production of Cowper and his friend John Newton, vicar of the parish. The house in which the poet lived, at the corner of the market-place, still exists. — 21 M. *Northampton*, see p. 252.

From Bedford to Cambridge, 29 M., L. N. W. R. in 1-1 1/4 hr. (fares 5*s.*, 3*s.* 1*d.*, 2*s.* 5 1/2*d.*). At (8 M.) *Sandy*, the Roman *Salinae*, this line intersects the main G. N. R. line (comp. p. 363). — 29 M. *Cambridge*, see p. 431.

From Bedford to Hitchin, 16 M., Midland Railway in 3/4 hr. (fares 2*s.* 2*d.*, 1*s.* 4*d.*). The first station on this line is (2 1/2 M.) *Cardington* (see above). At (16 M.) *Hitchin* we reach the main line of the G. N. R. (p. 363).

From Bedford to Bletchley, 16 M., L.N.W. railway in 1/2-3/4 hr. (2*s.* 6*d.*, 1*s.* 8*d.*, 1*s.* 4*d.*). This line runs for a time nearly due S., parallel with the Midland (p. 357), and then diverges off to the W. About 3 1/2 M. to the S.E. of (12 M.) *Woburn Sands* is *Woburn Abbey* (p. 250). — At (15 M.) *Fenny Stratford* the train crosses *Watling Street* (p. 349), the *Ouse*, and the *Grand Junction Canal.* At (16 M.) *Bletchley* we join the main line of the L. N. W. R. (p. 250).

Beyond Bedford the Midland Railway crosses the Ouse and continues to traverse a flat and fertile district. At (176 M.) *Ampthill* we pass a chain of low hills. The small town of **Ampthill** *(King's Arms; White Hart)*, from which Lord Ampthill (d. 1884), late ambassador in Berlin, derived his title, lies about $^3/_4$ M. to the E. of the station. Before reaching the station the line passes through a tunnel, below part of *Ampthill Park*, which is famous for its venerable oaks and its magnificent avenue of limes. *Ampthill House*, a seat of the Duke of Bedford, lies to the left, near the entrance of the tunnel. Close by is the site of the old castle where Catherine of Aragon resided during her trial (marked by a cross with an inscription by Hor. Walpole). The train now traverses a pretty, undulating country, while the section of the cuttings shows we are in a chalk district.

189 M. **Luton** *(George; Red Lion)*, a busy town of 24,000 inhab., on the *Lea* (Lea-town), famous for its manufacture of straw-hats. On Monday mornings the market in the *Straw-plait Halls* is sometimes attended by 2000 people. The parish-church, with its fine embattled tower, possesses a chapel founded in the reign of Henry VI. (1422-61) and contains a curious font.

From Luton a branch-line runs to (5 M.) *Dunstable* (p. 250) and (12 M.) *Leighton Buzzard* (p. 250). It is also connected by a short branch with *Hatfield*, on the main line of the Great Northern Railway (see p. 363).

Beyond Luton the Midland line runs for some distance parallel with the G. N. R. line to Hatfield (see p. 363). On the right is *Luton Hoo House*, a handsome mansion in a prettily-wooded park, with an artificial lake. Beyond (192 M.) *Chiltern Green* the line crosses the G. N. R. and passes into Hertfordshire.

199 M. **St. Albans** (*Peahen; George*, both near the Abbey, unpretending) lies a short distance to the E. of the site of *Verulamium*, the most important town in the S. of England during the Roman period, of which the fosse and fragments of the walls remain. Its name is derived from St. Alban, a Roman soldier, the proto-martyr of Christianity in our island, who was executed here in A.D. 304. Holmhurst Hill, near the town, is supposed to have been the scene of his death. The Roman town fell into ruins after the departure of the Romans, and the new town of St. Albans began to spring up after 795, when Offa II., King of Mercia, founded here, in memory of St. Alban, the magnificent abbey, of which the fine church and a large square gateway are now the only remains. Pop. (1881) 10,930.

The ***Abbey Church** is in the form of a cross, with a tower at the point of intersection, and is one of the largest churches in England. It was raised to the dignity of a cathedral in 1877, when the new episcopal see of St. Albans was created. It measures 550 ft. in length (being the second longest church in England, coming after Winchester), by 175 ft. in breadth across the transepts; the fine Norman *Tower* is 145 ft. high. The earliest parts of the existing building, in which Roman tiles from Verulamium were freely made use of, date from the 11th cent. (ca. 1080); the *Choir* was built in the 13th cent. and the *Lady Chapel* in the 14th century. An extensive restoration of the building, including a new E.E. *W. Front*, with a large Dec. window, has been accomplished. See Froude's 'Annals of an English Abbey'.

The fine **Interior** (adm. 6*d.*; tickets procured at the booksellers' in the town or from the verger) has recently been restored with great care. The Nave, the longest Gothic nave in the world, shows a curious intermixture of the Norman, E.E., and Dec. styles; and the change of the pitch of the vaulting in the S. aisle has a singular effect. The **Stained Glass Windows* in the N. aisle date from the 15th century. In the N. Transept some traces of old fresco-painting have been discovered, and the ceiling of the Choir is also coloured. The *Screen* behind the altar in the presbytery is of very fine mediæval workmanship, and has lately been restored and fitted with statues. Many of the chantries, or mortuary chapels of the abbots, and other monuments deserve attention. The splendid brass of *Abbot de la Mare* is best seen from the aisle to the S. of the Presbytery. In the *Saint's Chapel* are the tomb of Duke Humphrey of Gloucester (d. 1447), brother of Henry V., and the shrine of St. Alban. A door at the N. end of the transept leads to the *Tower*, the top of which commands a magnificent *View.

The *Gate*, the only remnant of the conventual buildings of the abbey, stands to the W. of the church. It is a good specimen of the Perp. style. It was formerly used as a gaol, and is now a school.

About 3/4 M. to the W. of the abbey stands the ancient *Church of St. Michael*, which is interesting as containing the tomb of the great Lord Bacon, Baron Verulam and Viscount St. Albans, who died at Gorhambury House here in 1626. The monument is by *Rysbrack*. To reach the church we turn to the left (W.) on leaving the cathedral and descend to the bridge over the *Ver*. The keys are kept by Mr. Monk, shoemaker (to the left, between the bridge and the church). The present *Gorhambury House*, the seat of the Earl of Verulam, 1 1/2 M. to the W. of St. Michael's, is situated in the midst of a beautiful park, and contains a good collection of portraits.

St. Albans was the scene of two of the numerous battles fought during the Wars of the Roses. The scene of the first, which ushered in the contest, and took place in 1455, is now called the *Key Field;* the other was fought in 1461 at *Barnard's Heath*, to the N. of the town, just beyond St. Peter's Church.

In summer a coach plies daily between St. Albans and London (fare 10*s.*).

For a notice of the remaining stations, the chief of which is (212 M.) *Hendon*, see *Baedeker's London*. The handsome station of *St. Pancras* in (220 M.) London is one of the finest in the world.

c. From Liverpool to London viâ Sheffield, Grantham, and Peterborough.

238 M. Railway in 6 hrs. (fares, etc., see p. 345). At first we travel by the *Manchester, Sheffield, & Lincolnshire Railway*, which runs in connection with the *Great Northern Railway* and joins it at Retford (see p. 361). Through-carriages run from Liverpool to London. — The express-trains from Manchester to (203 M.) London by this route perform the journey in 4 1/4 hrs. (fares 24*s.* 6*d.*, 20*s.*, 15*s.* 5 1/2*d.*).

From Liverpool to (25 M.) *Glazebrook*, see p. 332. 35 M. *Cheadle* (White Hart), with 6930 inhab.; 38 M. *Stockport*, see p. 340. At (43 M.) *Godley Junction* we join the *Manchester* line. The train now enters *Longdendale*, an elevated moorland district, flanked with hills.

Longdendale is filled with the huge reservoirs of the *Manchester Water Works*, with an aggregate capacity of 5,000,000,000 gallons. The largest is that at Woodhead (see below), holding 1,235,000,000 gallons.

48 M. *Dinting*, where the *Etherow* is crossed by a viaduct 136 ft. high, is the junction of a short line to (1 M.) *Glossop* (Norfolk Arms; Howard Arms), a town with 17,000 inhab., close to the N. margin of the *Peak* (R. 45). — Beyond ($55^1/_2$ M.) *Woodhead* we pass through a tunnel 3 M. long, one end of which is in Cheshire and the other in Yorkshire. At ($58^1/_2$ M.) *Dunford Bridge* the line enters the valley of the *Don*, which it follows to Sheffield.

64 M. **Penistone** *(Rose & Crown; Rail. Refreshmt. Rooms)*, a small town with 2255 inhab., is the junction of lines to Huddersfield (p. 339) and *Barnsley*. — Our line now turns to the S. Beyond (68 M.) *Wortley* we enter *Wharncliffe Chase*, a pretty, wooded district. The hill called the *Dragon's Den* takes its name from the tradition that the Dragon of Wantley was slain here. *Wharncliffe Lodge* (left) was the home of Lady Mary Wortley Montague.

76 M. **Sheffield.** — **Railway Stations.** *Victoria*, on the N.E. side of the town, close to the Don, for the G. N. R. and the Manchester, Sheffield, & Lincolnshire Railway. *Midland*, in Sheaf St., at the S.E. corner of the town, for the Mid. Railway. — Cab from either station into the town 1*s*.

Hotels. VICTORIA, connected with the Victoria Station; WHARNCLIFFE, King St.; MIDLAND, Midland Station; ROYAL, Waingate, opposite the Town Hall. — KING'S HEAD; CLARENCE; ANGEL; WAINWORTH TEMPERANCE.

Theatres. *Theatre Royal*, Tudor St.; *Alexandra Theatre*, Blonk St.

U. S. Consul, *Ben. Folsom, Esq.*, Bank Buildings, Bank St.

Sheffield, one of the principal manufacturing towns of England, with 316,288 inhab., lies in the district of *Hallamshire*, in the West Riding of Yorkshire, at the confluence of the *Don* and the *Sheaf*. Though itself unprepossessing and smoke-begrimed, it is pleasantly situated at the E. base of the range of hills forming the backbone of England, and its immediate environs are varied and picturesque. It was described by Horace Walpole as 'one of the foulest towns of England in the most charming situation'.

The history of Sheffield is comparatively uneventful, and the time of its foundation is doubtful. At the Norman Conquest it belonged to Earl Waltheof, the 'last of the Saxon barons', who forfeited his head by an unsuccessful rising against William the Conqueror. The manor finally came into the possession of the Howards, whose representative, the Duke of Norfolk, still owns a large part of the town. Mary, Queen of Scots, passed twelve years of her captivity here in the custody of the Earl of Shrewsbury, but the old castle in which part of that time was spent was demolished in the Civil War. Sheffield seems to have early acquired a reputation for its blades, and the Miller in the 'Canterbury Tales' is furnished with a 'Sheffield thwytel in his hose'. In 1736 its population was only 14,105, and even in 1801 it did not exceed 45,000. In the present century the history of Sheffield has been closely connected with that of Trades Unionism.

Sheffield enjoys a world-wide reputation for its *Cutlery*, *Files*, *Silver and Plated Wares*, *Armour Plates*, *Steel Guns*, *Shells*, and other heavy *Iron and Steel Goods.* The town itself is almost entirely given over to factories and business-premises, while the residential suburbs spread up the slopes of the hills on every side. Few visitors to Sheffield will fail to take some interest in the wonderful mechanical processes that may here be studied to perfection, such as file and saw grinding, electro-plating, plate-rolling, and the conversion of iron into steel by the Bessemer process.

Almost the only interesting public building is ***St. Peter's Church**, in a prominent situation in the centre of the town.

Originally dating from the 14th and 15th cent. (Dec. and Perp.), the church has undergone considerable alterations at various times; but the last restoration, in 1876-80, aimed at a return to the ancient plan. The *Shrewsbury Chapel* contains monuments of the Earls of Shrewsbury, including that of Queen Mary's gaoler (p. 359), with an epitaph by Foxe.

In Church St., to the S. of St. Peter's, is the **Cutlers' Hall**, in the Corinthian style, containing a few portraits and busts.

The *Cutlers' Company* was incorporated in 1624, and the office of Master Cutler is still the highest honorary dignity that the townspeople have to bestow. The annual banquet, held on the first Thurs. in Sept., is used, like the Lord Mayor's Feast, for a display of political oratory. The chief privilege of the company is the right of granting trade-marks.

High St., the E. prolongation of Church St., leads to the Market Place, with the Meat and Poultry Market. To the N. are the *Market Hall* and the *Corn Exchange.* Adjacent, at the corner of Castle St., is the *Town Hall.* — The *Firth College*, at the corner of Bow and Leopold St., is affiliated to Victoria University (p. 338).

On the W. side of the town, 1 M. from St. Peter's, is the *Weston Park*, which is embellished with a statue of *Ebenezer Elliot*, the 'Corn Law Rhymer', born near Sheffield in 1781. Here also is the *Public Museum* (open on Mon., Tues., & Sat. 10-9; on Wed. & Thurs. 10 till dusk), containing antiquities, objects illustrating the local manufactures, and a gallery of modern pictures. — *Meersbrook Hall*, acquired by the town in 1889, contains the *Ruskin Museum*, including paintings (one by Verrocchio), drawings (Turner, Ruskin), photographs, casts, minerals, coins, etc. The grounds are now a public park.

About 1½ M. to the S.E. of St. Peter's is the **Manor House** of the Earl of Shrewsbury, where Mary, Queen of Scots, spent much of her time during the 12 years she was in charge of the sixth Earl. — A little to the W. is *Norfolk Park*, from which we return to the centre of the town by the Norfolk Road, passing *Shrewsbury Hospital.* — Visits may also be paid to the *Botanical Gardens*, to the S.W. of the town (member's order necessary); and the *Cemetery*, with the grave of James Montgomery, the poet (also to the S.W.).

Among the interesting points in the environs of Sheffield are the ruins of *Beauchieff Abbey*, with the restored church, 4 M. to the S.; *Wharncliffe Woods* (p. 359), to the N.W.; *Worksop* and the *Dukeries* (see below), etc.

Sheffield may also be made a starting-point for a visit to the Derbyshire Peak (R. 45). Coaches run daily in summer to (12½ M.) *Baslow* (p. 368; for *Chatsworth*), to (11½ M.) *Ashopton* (p. 370), and to (17 M.) *Castleton* (p. 369). A good route for walkers ascends the valley of the *Rivelin* to (18 M.) the *Snake Inn*, and crosses thence into *Edale* (comp. p. 370).

Beyond Sheffield our line runs towards the E. — 80½ M. *Woodhouse* is the junction for *Rotherham* and Chesterfield (p. 402), and (89 M.) *Shireoaks* for *Mansfield.* — 92 M. **Worksop** (*Lion; Royal*), an agricultural town with 11,000 inhab., manufactures malt. The *Church*, a Norman building with later alterations, is a relic of an old priory.

The district round Worksop is known as the '**Dukeries**', from the number of ducal residences it contains. The most interesting is *Welbeck Abbey*, the seat of the Duke of Portland, which lies 4 M. to the S. W. It is approached by a tunnel 2 M. long, leading to a curious series of underground apartments, including a large library, a ball-room, a picture-gallery (with good paintings), and a riding-school. — *Worksop Manor*, adjoining the town on the S.W., has been sold by the Duchess of Norfolk to the Duke of Newcastle. — *Clumber Park*, the seat of the Duke of Newcastle, lies $2^1/_2$ M. to the S.E. It contains a good collection of portraits. — Other fine country-houses within access are *Thoresby*, the seat of Earl Manvers (formerly of the Duke of Kingston), and *Rufford Abbey*, belonging to Capt. Saville. All these mansions are surrounded with finely-wooded parks, open to the public. — About 10 M. to the S. is **Sherwood Forest**, the greenwood home of Robin Hood, still containing many fine trees. *Ollerton* (Hop Pole) affords good headquarters.

At (100 M.) *Retford* (White Hart) the train joins the main line of the G. N. railway and turns to the S.

Retford is also the junction of a line running N.E. to *Gainsborough*, *Hull* (p. 425), and *Grimsby* (p. 426).

The region now traversed is famous for its fruit-culture. — 118 M. **Newark-on-Trent** *(Clinton Arms; Midland; Saracen's Head; Rail. Rfmt. Rooms)*, an old town with 14,000 inhab. and large breweries.

The *Castle Grounds* were opened as a public garden in 1889.

The old *Castle*, dating from the 12th cent., was dismantled after sustaining three sieges in the Civil War. King John died here in 1216. The *Parish Church*, a Perp. edifice with a lofty spire, contains an unusually fine brass. — Newark is the junction of the Nottingham and Lincoln line (see R. 55) and of a line to Melton Mowbray (p. 352).

At (129 M.) *Barkstone* a branch-line diverges on the left to *Boston* (p. 429) and *Lincoln* (p. 426).

133 M. **Grantham** *(Angel*, well spoken of; *George*, both near the church, $^1/_2$ M. from the station; *Rail. Refreshmt. Rooms)* is a small and ancient town with 17,000 inhab. and large iron-works. Its principal attraction is its fine church, to reach which we turn to the left on leaving the station (on the side next the town). On the way we cross *St. Peter's Hill*, an open space adorned with a statue of *Sir Isaac Newton* (1642-1727), who was born at *Woolsthorpe*, 7 M. to the W., and educated at Grantham grammar-school. The **Ch rch of St. Wulfram* is a handsome structure, mainly in the E. E. style of the 13th century. It has a graceful spire, 280 ft. high, and contains some interesting monuments.

The *Angel Inn* is a quaint old building, formerly belonging to the Knights Templar and dating from the 13th cent., when King John is said to have held a court here (1213). It was here, too, that Richard III. signed the death-warrant of the Duke of Buckingham.

Grantham is the first stopping-place of the 'Flying Scotsman' express from London to Edinburgh, after an unbroken run of 105 M. Lines radiate hence to *Nottingham*, *Lincoln*, and *Boston* (viâ *Sleaford*).

About 3 M. to the N.E. is *Belton House*, the seat of Earl Brownlow, with some good paintings. — *Belvoir Castle*, the seat of the Duke of Rutland, 5 M. to the W., contains tapestry, armour, and pictures.

From (150 M.) *Essendine* a branch-line diverges on the left to *Spalding* and *Boston*, and another on the right to (4 M.) *Stamford*.

Stamford *(George; Stamford Arms)* is an ancient town, with four fine churches, two old gateways, and the scanty remains of a priory. The 'Stamford Mercury' was the earliest English newspaper (1712). About $1^1/_2$ M. to the S. is *Burghley House* (open 11-5), the seat of the Marquis of Exeter, a fine Renaissance building, with some good paintings, and carvings by Grinling Gibbons. — At *Bourn*, on the line to Sleaford, was the ancient Saxon camp, in which 'Hereward, the last of the English', made so determined a stand against the Conqueror.

162 M. **Peterborough** (**Great Northern Hotel*, at the G. N. R. station, R. & A. 4*s.*; *Angel*, *Bull*, in the town), an ancient city with 22,400 inhab., on the *Nene*. To reach its celebrated cathedral we walk straight from the station towards the E., passing the *Church of St. John* (lately restored), with a 15th cent. tower, and crossing the market-place.

The ***Cathedral** is one of the most important Norman churches left in England, though the first glance at the exterior does not seem to bear out this assertion. The elaborate and somewhat foreign-looking **West Façade*, with its recessed arches (81 ft. high), gables, parvise, and sculptures, is, however, a later addition (ca. 1220?), and forms, as it were, a screen in front of the original W. wall. The cathedral is 471 ft. long, 81 ft. wide, and 81 ft. high; the great transept is 202 ft. in length, and the N.W. tower 188 ft. high. The daily services are at 10 a.m. and 5.30 p.m. The building, now being restored, is open free of charge; adm. to the tower 6*d*.

The present building is the third church on this site. The first was founded by Peada, King of Mercia, in 656, as the church of the Benedictine monastery of *Medeshamstede*, which afterwards became one of the most important of English abbeys. This church was destroyed by the Danes in 870-3. The second was founded in 971 and burned down in 1116. The oldest part now standing is the choir, consecrated about 1140. The great transept dates from 1155-77, the late-Norman nave from 1177-93, and the W. transepts, in the Transition style, from 1193-1200 (see above). A series of uniform Dec. windows was added throughout the church in the 14th cent., and the retro-choir, or 'New Building', is a Perp. fan-vaulted structure of 1438-1528. The spires and pinnacles of the flanking turrets of the W. façade are of the Dec. and Perp. periods. The N.W. tower, behind that of the W. front, was added about 1265-70. The fine central tower, which was erected in the 14th cent. in place of the Norman lantern, was condemned as unsafe in 1883, and has been rebuilt by Mr Pearson. Peterborough was made a bishop's see in 1541.

From the market-place we enter the cathedral-precincts by the *Western Gateway*, dating originally from 1177-93; to the left is the chancel of the *Becket Chapel* (Dec.), now used as a museum of natural history. We then reach a spacious court in front of the W. façade of the cathedral, with two other old gateways, that on the right leading to the *Bishop's Palace*, that on the left to the *Deanery* (the old *Prior's House*).

The ***Interior** gives an impression of unusual lightness for Norman architecture. In 1643 it suffered very severely from the iconoclasm of the Puritans, who destroyed the reredos, the fine stained-glass windows, and most of the monuments and sculptural decoration. In the course of the recent restoration it was found that the apparently solid Norman piers were merely shells filled with rubble, and that their builders had strangely neglected to go down to the solid rock, here only 3-4 ft. below the original foundations. The clerestory and triforium of the NAVE are very important in size, and the effect produced is remarkably good. The painted wooden ceiling dates from the 12th century. The arches of the central tower were changed from circular to pointed at the close of the 14th century. To the N. of the W. door is a portrait of *Old Scarlett* (d. 1594), the sexton who buried Catherine of Aragon and Mary Stuart (see p. 363); to the S. is the ancient *Font*. — On the E. side of the N. TRANSEPT are two blocked-up arches, leading to the site of the *Lady Chapel* (1290), of which little remains. The timber roof of the transepts is probably the earliest of the kind in England. — The CHOIR or PRESBYTERY has an apsidal termination.

which is still *in situ*, standing within the 'new building'. The fine roof is of the Perp. period. In the N. choir-aisle is the grave of *Queen Catherine of Aragon* (d. 1548); and in the corresponding part of the S. aisle is a slab showing the former resting-place of *Mary, Queen of Scots* (d. 1587), whose remains are now in Westminster Abbey (see *Baedeker's London*). The monuments of both were destroyed by the Puritans.

On the S. side of the nave are the extensive remains of the *Cloisters*, the *Refectory*, and other monastic buildings.

About 2 M. to the W. of Peterborough is *Milton Park*. — The interesting ruined church of *Crowland Abbey (12-15th cent.; adm. 6*d*.), 9½ M. to the N. of Peterborough, may be reached by carriage, or by train to *Peakirk* or *Eye Green* (see below), each about 5 M. from the abbey. — Excursions may also be made from Peterborough to *Fotheringay* and *Warmington* (see p. 252).

From Peterborough to Sutton Bridge, 28 M., railway in 1¼ hr. (fares 3*s*. 10*d*., 2*s*. 1½*d*.). The first station is (6 M.) *Eye Green* (see above). 9 M. *Thorney*, with a ruined abbey. From (21 M.) **Wisbech** (*Rose & Crown*), a small town on the *Nene*, a line runs E. to *Watlington*. — 28 M. *Sutton Bridge*. Trains from Peterborough run through to (39 M.) *Lynn* (p. 441), where they join the lines for *Yarmouth*, *Norwich*, etc.

From Peterborough to *Northampton*, see p. 252; to *Boston*, see p. 429.

Leaving Peterborough, we obtain a good view of the cathedral to the left. We now traverse the flat district known as the *Fens*. From (169 M.) *Holme* a branch diverges to (6 M.) *Ramsey* (Anchor), with a few relics of a Benedictine abbey, and (11 M.) *Somersham*, on the line from Huntingdon to March. About 2 M. to the right of the line is *Stilton*, which has given its name to a well-known cheese.

178½ M. **Huntingdon** (*George; Fountain*), a small town on the *Ouse*, with 4230 inhab., was the birthplace of *Oliver Cromwell* (1599-1658), the entry of whose birth is preserved in the register of St. John's Church. The *Grammar School* in which the Protector was educated has been restored. The restored churches of *St. Mary* and *All Saints* are worthy of notice. The poet *Cowper* (1731-1800) lived at Huntingdon with the Unwins in 1765-67. To the right, near the station, is *Hinchingbrook*, the seat of the Earl of Sandwich.

From Huntingdon a joint line of the G.N.R. and G.E.R. runs E. to (6 M.) **St. Ives** (*Unicorn*), a place of great antiquity, believed to have been a Saxon settlement. Its foundation is ascribed to a Persian saint, St. Ivo. Lines radiate hence to *March*, *Ely* (p. 440; *Norwich*, *Yarmouth*), and *Cambridge* (p. 432).

186 M. *St. Neot's* (Cross Keys), with a good Perp. church. At (193½ M.) *Sandy* we cross the L.N.W. line from Oxford to Cambridge (p. 356). — 206 M. **Hitchin** (*Sun; Rail. Refresh. Rooms*), a thriving little country-town, with manufactories of lavender-water. It is the junction of lines to Cambridge and Bedford (comp. p. 356). — 213 M. *Knebworth*, with the seat of Lord Lytton. — 220 M. *Hatfield* (Red Lion; Rail. Refreshmt. Rooms), a small market-town on the *Lea*, with a large church.

Immediately to the E. of the town, in a beautiful park, is ***Hatfield House**, the seat of the Marquis of Salisbury, a stately Jacobean mansion (1611), containing interesting family-portraits and a valuable collection of historical MSS. (visitors admitted in the absence of the family). There are also a few remains of the original palace here, built in the 12th cent. by the Bishops of Ely, and afterwards a royal residence. It was in this older house that the Princess Elizabeth received the news of her accession to the throne; and a fine oak in the Park is pointed out as marking the limits of the walks allowed her while confined here. Charles I. was also imprisoned for a short time at Hatfield. The grounds are fine. — About 2½ M. to the N. of Hatfield is *Brocket Hall*, successively the residence of *Lord Melbourne* (d. 1848) and *Lord Palmerston* (d. 1865).

From Hatfield lines diverge to *St. Albans* (p. 357), *Luton* (p. 357), and **Hertford** *(Salisbury Arms;* comp. *Baedeker's London).*

231½ M. *New Southgate*, the station for *Colney Hatch Lunatic Asylum*, the extensive buildings of which lie to the right; 233 M. *Woodgreen*, the station for the *Alexandra Palace.*

238 M. **London** *(King's Cross)*, see *Baedeker's London.*

d. From Liverpool to London viâ Shrewsbury, Birmingham, and Oxford.

229 M. Great Western Railway in 6-8 hrs. (fares, see p. 345). Through-trains run daily by this route; the journey may be broken at Hatton (p. 244) for a visit to Stratford-on-Avon (p. 245).

The different sections of this route have been already described. From Liverpool to (16½ M.) *Chester*, see R. 41; from Chester to (42 M.) *Shrewsbury*, see R. 39; from Shrewsbury to (42 M.) *Birmingham*, see R. 37; from Birmingham to (66 M.) *Oxford*, see R. 33; from Oxford to (63 M.) **London** *(Paddington)*, see R. 30.

45. The Derbyshire Peak.

The hilly district generally known as the ***Peak** includes the highlands in the N.W. of Derbyshire and parts of the adjacent counties. It may be said, roughly, to extend from *Ashbourne* (p. 373) on the S. to *Glossop* (p. 359) on the N., and from *Buxton* (p. 370) on the W. to *Chesterfield* (p. 402) on the E., comprising an area 30 M. long and 22 M. broad. The district belongs partly to the gritstone, and partly to the limestone formation. The highest summits are *Kinderscout* (2080 ft.), on the N.; *Axe Edge* (1810 ft.), near Buxton; and *Mam Tor* (1710 ft.), near Castleton. In spite of the name, the hills have rounded and not pointed summits, and there is nothing in the scenery which can be called mountainous. The so-called High Peak, in the N. part of the district, consists mainly of a series of bleak moorland hills or plateaux, little diversified by wood or water. The chief centres of attraction are the rocky and wooded valleys, of the *Dove* (p. 372), the *Derwent* (at Matlock, p. 365), and the *Wye* (Buxton, p. 371); the ancient house of *Haddon* (p. 366); the modern mansion of *Chatsworth* (p. 367); and the *Castleton Caverns* (p. 369). All of these may be visited from Derby, though rather hurriedly, in 4 days. 1st Day: From Derby by train to *Cromford*, 16 M.; from Cromford by road to *Matlock*, 2 M.; from Matlock by train to *Rowsley*, 4½ M.; from Rowsley to *Haddon Hall* by road, 2 M.; from Haddon to *Chatsworth* by road, 5½ M.; from Chatsworth to *Edensor*, ½ M. [Or from Haddon to Edensor 5 M., leaving Chatsworth for the next morning.] — 2nd Day: From Edensor or Chatsworth to *Eyam* and *Castleton* by road, 16 M.; visit the *Caverns*; if time allows, ascend *Mam Tor*. — 3rd Day: From Castleton to *Chapel-en-le-Frith* by road, direct 7½ M. or through *Edale* 9-12 M.; from Chapel-en-le-Frith to *Buxton* by railway; from Buxton through *Cheedale* to *Miller's Dale* on foot, 6 M.; back to Buxton by train. [Or we may go on by train from Miller's Dale to *Bakewell*, and walk or drive thence to (11 M.) *Alstonefield.*] — 4th Day: From Buxton to *Alstonefield* by road, 14 M.; through *Dovedale* by footpath, 4 M.; from the lower end of Dovedale to *Ashbourne* by road, 4 M.; from Ashbourne to *Derby* by railway, 30 M. — The round may be equally well made in the opposite direction; and those staying in Manchester may begin it at Buxton (train from Man-

For a coloured map of The Derbyshire Peak District see page 589

chester to Buxton in 1-1½ hr.; fares 3*s.* 9*d.*, 2*s.* 9*d.*, 1*s.* 11½*d.*). The Peak may also be approached from *Sheffield* (comp. p. 360).

— Railway from Derby to (16 M.) *Cromford*, see R. 44b. Cromford lies at the lower (S.) end of the narrow part of the *Derwent Valley*, the picturesque limestone formations of which have made Matlock famous. The direct road to (1 M.) Matlock turns to the right, a few hundred yards from the station, beyond the bridge.

A pleasant round may be made by turning to the left and proceeding through the village and along the Wirksworth road to the (1½ M.) *Black Rocks*, a good point of view. We then follow the road to (½ M.) *Middleton Cross*, turn to the right, and at the (1½ M.) farther end of *Middleton* follow the road slanting down the hill to (½ M.) *Rider Point*. Here we turn to the right and descend the valley called the *Via Gellia* to (1 M.) the *Pig of Lead Inn*, whence we proceed to the left to (½ M.) *Bonsall* and (1½ M.) Matlock Bath.

Matlock. — **Hotels.** At *Matlock Bath:* *New Bath, with baths and a wonderful lime-tree in the garden, D. 4*s.* 6*d.*, R. & A. from 4*s.*, board 8*s.*; Royal, with baths; Temple; Terrace; these first-class, on the hill-side, with views. — Rutland Arms, Devonshire, Hodgkinson's, plain. — At *Matlock Bridge:* Old English; Crown; Brown's Temperance. — At *Matlock Bank:* Queen's Head; Wheatsheaf, both unpretending. Also Smedley's, Matlock House, Rockside, and several other hydropathics.

Excursion-Brakes in summer to *Haddon*, *Chatsworth*, *Dovedale*, etc.

As there are several Malverns (see p. 189), so there are also four Matlocks — *Matlock Bath*, *Matlock Bridge*, *Matlock Village*, and *Matlock Bank* — extending along the *Derwent* for about 2 M. and containing a joint population of about 6000. The first of these is situated in the very centre of the romantic gorge which the Derwent here forms, and is the best headquarters for tourists. Matlock Bridge lies in the floor of the valley, at the N. end of the gorge, and is the railway-station for Matlock Bank, situated on the hill-side above, and consisting to a great extent of hydropathic establishments, boarding-houses, and lodgings. Matlock Village lies on the N. side of the High Tor, opposite Matlock Bank. The tepid springs (68°), for bathing, are at Matlock Bath, and may be used at the New Bath Hotel, the Royal Hotel, and the *Fountain Baths.* — Directions for finding the way to points of interest in the vicinity are unnecessary, as the sign-posts and placards are only too conspicuous.

On the right (E.) side of the ravine, opposite Matlock Bath, is the ***High Tor**, an abrupt limestone rock, rising 400 ft. above the river and commanding a good *View of the valley (adm. 4*d.*). At the top, on the side farthest from the valley, is the so-called **Fern Cave* (adm. 1*d.*), a curious narrow fissure in the rock, 150 ft. deep. The *Roman Cave* is a similar but less striking crevice. The large house on the hill to the E. is *Riber Hall*, built by Mr. Smedley of the hydropathic establishment. A new carriage-drive leads from the top of the High Tor to *Matlock Bridge* and *Village.*

On the W. side of the valley rise the **Heights of Abraham,** (adm. 6*d.* *View), a buttress of the *Masson* (1110 ft.). Near the tower marking the Heights are the *Rutland Cavern* (adm. 6*d.*) and the *Old Roman Cave.*

On the side of the hill, at the back of the Matlock Bath hotels, are the ***Recreation Grounds** (adm. 6*d.*; *Views), containing a *Concert Pavilion* and the *Victoria* and *Speedwell Caverns.* — Of the other caverns at Matlock (very inferior to those of Castleton, p. 369) the best is the *Cumberland Cave* (adm. 6*d.*). — A visit may be paid to one of the *Petrifying Wells* (adm. 2*d.*). — The new **Promenades*, on both banks of the Derwent, are to be connected by an ornamental bridge.

Longer excursions may be made to *Bonsall*, *Cromford*, and the *Black Rocks;* to (6 M.) *Crich Stand* (view) and thence to ($2^1/_2$ M.) the ruins of *Wingfield Manor;* to the (9 M.) *Rowtor Rocks;* to (12 M.) *Chesterfield* (p. 402); to *Haddon* and *Chatsworth*; and to (9 M.) *Lathkill Dale.*

Railway from Matlock Bridge to ($4^1/_2$ M.) Rowsley, see R. 44b. — Darley Dale is the best station for a visit to the picturesque *Rowtor Rocks* (3 M. to the W.; entered through the Druid Inn).

Rowsley *(* Peacock Inn)*, a small village pleasantly situated at the confluence of the *Wye* and the Derwent, is the starting-point for a visit to ($1^1/_2$ M.) Haddon Hall. Excursion-brakes ply to Haddon (6*d.*) and Chatsworth (1*s.*).

The road to Haddon turns to the left at the station and passes under the bridge. At the 'Peacock' we follow the road to the extreme left and reach (1 M.) a bridge over the Wye. Here we leave the road by a stile to the right, on this side of the bridge, and follow a path (indistinct at first) along the river and through the park to (10 min.) Haddon Hall.

***Haddon Hall**, picturesquely situated on a slope rising from the Wye, is an almost ideal specimen of an old English baronial mansion, and, though unoccupied, is still in fair preservation (adm. free; gratuity to the custodian).

Held at an early period by the Avenel family, Haddon came in the 12th cent. into the hands of the Vernons, who retained possession of it for 400 years. By the marriage of the fair Dorothy Vernon (see below) it passed to the Rutland family, who still own it, though the Duke lives at Belvoir (p. 361). The building encloses two court-yards. The N.E. tower and part of the chapel are late-Norman; the great banqueting-hall, between the two courts, and most of the adjoining block date from the 14th, the E. range of buildings from the 15th, and the S. façade and the terraced gardens from the end of the 16th century.

Interior. The rooms are generally shown in the following order. The *Chaplain's Room*, containing a pair of jack-boots, a leathern doublet, etc.; the **Chapel*, with some fine Norman work and a stained-glass window of the 15th century; the *Kitchen*, with enormous fire-places; the **Banqueting Hall*, 35 ft. long and 25 ft. wide, with a dais, a minstrels' gallery, and some old paintings; the panelled *Dining Room*, with an oriel window overlooking the garden; the *Drawing Room*, hung with old tapestry; the *Earl's Dressing-Room* and *Bedroom*; the fine **Ball Room* or *Gallery*, 100 ft. long, with oaken wainscoting and floor; the *Ante-Room;* the *State Bedroom*, hung with tapestry, with a bed, dressing-table, and looking-glass said to have been used by Queen Elizabeth; the *Archers' Room*, in the oldest part of the building; and the *Eagle* or *Peveril's Tower*, the top of which commands a fine view. We then return to the Ante-Room (see above) and descend to the garden by a flight of steps, said to have been used by Dorothy Vernon when she eloped with Sir George Manners, son of the Earl of Rutland (16th cent.). The charming *View here of the S. façade, the terrace, and the old yew-trees is familiar from engravings and photographs.

To reach Chatsworth from Haddon by carriage (pedestrian route, see p. 367), without returning to Rowsley, we follow the road from the above-mentioned bridge to ($2^1/_2$ M.) **Bakewell** (*Rutland Arms*, frequented by anglers), the '*Badequelle*' of Domesday, a delightfully situated little town, with 2500 inhabitants. The large **Church*, with its lofty octagonal spire, has a Norman doorway, and contains an ancient font and the monument of Dorothy Vernon (d. 1584) and her husband (see above). A *Cross* in the churchyard is believed to date from the 8th or 9th century. The baths are unimportant.

About 1¾ M. to the N.W. of Bakewell is the village of *Ashford* (Devonshire Arms), with a pretty church. The walk may be continued to (1⅓ M.) *Monsal Dale* (p. 350).

At Bakewell we turn to the right and proceed by a circuitous route (direct path 1 M. shorter) to (3½ M.) *Edensor* (*Chatsworth Hotel), a model village, on the outskirts of Chatsworth Park. The church contains a memorial-window to *Lord Frederick Cavendish* (assassinated in 1882), who is buried in the churchyard.

Direct Walk from Haddon to Chatsworth, 3½ M. (1¼-1½ hr.). We ascend the flight of steps by the cottage opposite the entrance to Haddon and follow a footpath, which almost immediately joins a cart-track. The track passes to the left of an old bowling-green and ascends by a fence, and at the top, to the left, follows a wall, to (8-10 min.) a gate, opening on a lane. To the right is a farm-house. We pass through (2 min.) another gate and follow a green lane. At (9 min.) a gateway, with two stone posts but no gate, we keep to the left branch of the lane and cross a ridge between two valleys. At the end of the ridge we enter the wood by a (3 min.) gate and after 8 min. more ascend to the left. We then (1 min.) ascend to the right by a track skirting a drain. At (4 min.) the top of the wooded hill we proceed to the left along the wall for 180 yds. to a gate, passing through which we cross a field diagonally to (5 min.) another gate. This opens into a beech-plantation, on leaving which we emerge upon a sloping pasture. The path is now indistinct, but by bearing a little to the left, somewhat in the line of a dry water-course, we reach (7-8 min.) a stile in a wall, opposite a dam, which crosses a small pool to the left of a farm-house. In ascending the cart-road on the other side we keep to the right beyond the gate, and come to (5 min.) a broad green drive. Here we proceed to the right, towards the lodge, and at the end of the drive enter the wood by a (3 min.) stile adjoining a gate. The path crosses another green drive and enters Chatsworth Park by (5 min.) another stile. Chatsworth is now in sight; the way to the (¼ hr.) bridge is to the left.

***Chatsworth**, the magnificent seat of the Duke of Devonshire, is a striking contrast to Haddon, the one being as redolent of modern, as the other of mediæval state.

The huge Palladian residence of the Cavendishes, 560 ft. long, was built in 1687-1706, on the site of an earlier edifice, in which Mary Stuart was for a time a prisoner. The N. wing was added in 1820. The interior contains a large collection of paintings, drawings, and sculptures by eminent masters, exquisite wood-carvings ascribed to Grinling Gibbons, and historical and other curiosities. Visitors are admitted from 11 to 4, on Sat. 11-1 (gratuity to the attendant).

Interior. Passing through the handsome iron gates, we are conducted to the Sub-Hall, where we await the attendant. The Great Hall (60 ft. long), is adorned with frescoes by *Verrio* and *Laguerre*. The Chapel, with the altar at the W. end, is lavishly embellished with marble, Derbyshire spar, wood-carving, and paintings by *Verrio*. The State Apartments, in the third story, are adorned with wood-carvings, Derbyshire spar and marble, and paintings by *Verrio* and *Thornhill*. The State Dressing Room contains a piece of wood-carving in imitation of point-lace. In the Old State Bedroom, the walls of which are hung with stamped leather, are the coronation-chairs of George IV. and Queen Charlotte, and in the Music Room are those of William IV. and Queen Adelaide. Behind a half-open door is a clever piece of illusive painting by *Verrio* (a fiddle on the wall). The State Drawing-Room contains Gobelins tapestry from Raphael's cartoons. The State Dining-Room has some fine wood-carving. On the central table lies the rosary of Henry VIII. The Corridors of the third story form the *SKETCH GALLERY, containing upwards of 1000 original drawings by *Raphael*, *Leonardo da Vinci*, *Michael Angelo*, *Titian*, *Correggio*, *Rubens*, *Rembrandt*, *Dürer*, *Holbein*, *Claude Lorrain*, and other great masters (admirably lighted). — We now descend to the *PICTURE GALLERY, which contains works by *Van Eyck*, *Teniers*, *Titian*, *Tintoretto*, *Murillo*, *Holbein*, etc. It is adjoined by the BILLIARD ROOM, with well-known works by *Sir Edwin Landseer*. — The chief treasure of the LIBRARY is Claude's 'Liber Veritatis'.— The *SCULPTURE GALLERY, adjoined by the *ORANGERY, contains a Venus by *Thorvaldsen* (with a bracelet); Napoleon, Napoleon's Mother, and Endymion, by *Canova;* a Girl spinning by *Schadow*, etc.

From the Orangery we enter the *GARDENS (small fee to the gardener), which are fine but formal, with artificial cascades, fountains, surprise water-works, etc. The *Emperor Fountain* throws a jet 265 ft. high. The *Great Conservatory*, 280 ft. long, was erected from a design by Sir Joseph Paxton, the builder of the Crystal Palace, who was at the time head-gardener to the Duke of Devonshire. — On a height to the N.E. of the house is the *Hunting Tower* (90 ft. high), commanding an extensive view. *Queen Mary's Bower*, a low square tower surrounded by a moat, near the bridge over the Wye, is said to have been a frequent resort of Mary Stuart (see p. 367).

*CHATSWORTH PARK is 9 M. in circumference.

From Chatsworth or Edensor we now strike northwards towards (16 M.) CASTLETON by road (no public conveyance).

Those who prefer it may return to Bakewell (p. 366) and take the train thence to *Chapel-en-le-Frith* (p. 370), which is 8 M. from Castleton.

About 1/2 M. from the Chatsworth Hotel, at the fork, we take the right branch, which leads to (1 1/2 M.) *Baslow* (Peacock; Royal; *Hydropathic), a pleasant-lying village, from which coaches ply in summer to (12 1/2 M.) Sheffield (p. 360; fare 1*s*. 6*d*.). Beyond Baslow the road skirts the left bank of the *Derwent*, which it crosses near (1 1/2 M.) an *Inn*, where we turn to the left and pass the village of *Calver* (to the left). At (1/3 M.) another *Inn* the main road to Castleton viâ *Hathersage* (p. 369) diverges to the right. We go straight on and soon reach (2/3 M.) *Stoney Middleton* (Moon Inn), beyond which we enter the rocky *Middleton Dale*. After 3/4 M. the road to (1/2 M.) Eyam turns to the right.

The road ascending straight through the dale leads to (5 M.) Tideswell (*George; Cross Daggers*), a small town with a fine Dec. *Church. Tideswell is 5 M. due S. of Castleton, and 3 M. to the N. of Miller's Dale (p. 371).

Eyam *(Bull's Head)*, pron. '*Eem*', a prettily-situated village with 1000 inhab., is memorable for its terrible visitation by the plague in 1665-6, which carried off 260 out of its 350 inhabitants.

Thanks mainly to the heroic exertions of the rector, the *Rev. William Mompesson*, the village was strictly isolated from the rest of the country-side, and the plague thus prevented from spreading. The rector himself escaped, but he lost his wife. The victims of the disease were generally buried near the spot where they died, and the fields round Eyam are sprinkled with tombstones. The churchyard contains a *Saxon Cross*. Near the church is an arched rock, known as *Cucklet Church*, which Mr. Mompesson used as a pulpit during the plague. A pleasant path leads from Eyam across the moors to (5 M.) *Hathersage* (see p. 369).

To continue our route to Castleton viâ Hathersage we follow the road leading to the E. from Eyam, which affords a view of Midleton Dale and the tower of Stoney Middleton church to the right. After about 1 M. we turn to the left, and 3/4 M. farther on we rejoin the main road through the Derwent valley (comp. above). Beyond

($1/_2$ M.) *Grindleford Bridge* (Inn) the road runs through a narrow and finely-wooded part of the valley, which farther on again expands. 3 M. *Hathersage* (George, well spoken of; Ordnance Arms), a village which manufactures pins and needles.

The church, dating from the 14th cent., contains some good brasses. The grave of *Little John*, the lieutenant of Robin Hood, is pointed out in the churchyard. — About $1^1/_4$ M. to the W. are *Higgar Tor* and an interesting British fort named *Carl Wark*.

Our road now leads to the W. through *Hope Dale.* At (2 M.) *Mytham Bridge* (Inn) we leave the Derwent, which turns to the N. (to *Ashopton*, p. 370, 3 M.), and follow its affluent the *Noe.* At ($2^1/_2$ M.) *Hope* (Hall Inn) the road to Edale (p. 370) diverges to the right. — $1^1/_2$ M. **Castleton** *(Castle; Bull's Head)*, at the head of Hope Dale, is the centre for excursions in the wilder N. part of the Peak. Perched on a steep rocky height (260 ft.) above the village is *Peveril Castle*, a stronghold taking name from its first owner, the natural son of William the Conqueror (adm. 1*d.*; view). The *Church* contains a fine Norman archway between the nave and the chancel. The *Museum* contains Derbyshire spar, etc.

The three **Caverns** all lie near, and may be visited in half-a-day. Those who are pressed for time should at least view the entrance of the Peak Cavern and descend the Blue John Mine. The charge for admission to each cavern is 2*s.* for 1, 3*s.* 6*d.* for 2, 4*s.* 6*d.* for 3, 5*s.* for 4-5 pers., and 1*s.* for each pers. additional. Bengal lights extra. Guides are in attendance all day.

The **Peak Cavern**, at the foot of the castle-rock, extends for upwards of 2000 ft. into the hill. Its arched entrance (42 ft. high) is imposing; the other features of interest include a chamber 220 ft. square, a subterranean river known as the Styx, and several natural archways. The view of the landscape, framed in the entrance as we come out, is striking.

The **Speedwell Cavern** lies about $3/_4$ M. to the W., at the foot of the Winnats (see below). We descend by a rocky staircase to a subterranean canal $1/_2$ M. long, driven into the hill by miners in an unsuccessful search for lead-ore. We traverse this canal in a boat; and at the end of it reach a large **Cavern*, where the water is precipitated into an abyss of unknown depth. The height of the roof has not been gauged; but it is estimated that the floor is about 850 ft. below the surface of the hill. Nervous persons are advised to leave the Speedwell unvisited, as the passage of the canal is decidedly 'eerie'.

The ***Blue John Mine** lies about $1/_2$ M. to the W. of the Speedwell Mine. From the beautiful shape and loftiness of its chambers, the fine incrustations and crystallisations, and the great depth to which we descend by a natural vertical passage, this is perhaps the most interesting of the three. This gigantic chasm seems to have been formed by a convulsion of nature, not by water. The Blue John Mine is the only place where the beautiful spar of that name is found.

The best route from the Speedwell Mine to the Blue John Mine is through the ***Winnats** (*i.e.* Wind Gates), a turf-grown mountain-pass, 1 M. long, flanked with tall limestone rocks.

A little farther to the W. rises **Mam Tor** (1710 ft.), the top of which affords a good view of Hope Dale, Edale, Kinder Scout, and Eyam Moor. The name of 'Shivering Mountain' is given to this hill from the liability of its S. face to disintegration from frost. — A pleasant walk (2 hrs.) leads from Castleton to *Ashopton* (see p. 370) viâ *Win Hill* (1530 ft.).

Coach to Sheffield (fare 2*s.* 6*d.*), see p. 360. A public conveyance also runs in summer to *Buxton* ($11^1/_2$ M.; fare 2*s.*).

The Direct Route from Castleton to (8 M.) Chapel-en-le-

Frith leads to the W., passing the Blue John Mine and the S. side of Mam Tor. It is worth while, however, to make the detour through Edale (see below), which adds about 1½ M. to the distance for walkers and 5-6 M. for drivers; while those who keep to the direct route should diverge to the right by the road between Mam Tor and Lord's Seat in order to obtain a peep at the green Edale valley.

To reach Edale from Castleton by road, we retrace our steps to (1½ M.) *Hope* (p. 369), and then follow the road along the *Noe* to the left. 4 M. *Car House;* 1 M. *Lady Booth;* ¾ M. *Edale Mill*, beyond which a road leads to the right to *Oller Brook Booth.* About ½ M. farther on we reach another road to the right, ascending to (⅓ M.) the village of *Edale* (Inn). — Walkers, however, may proceed direct from Castleton to Edale by a footpath crossing the ridge between Mam Tor and *Back Tor*, reaching the road above described at a point a little short of (2½ M.) *Edale Mill.*

Edale is a sequestered and somewhat bleak little valley, watered by the Noe and enclosed by dusky green or moorland hills with great variety of outline. The hills to the N. belong to the plateau of **Kinder Scout** (2080 ft.), the highest part of the Peak; while to the S. are *Lose Hill* (1570 ft.), *Back Tor*, *Mam Tor* (see above), and *Lord's Seat* (1818 ft.). Those who have time should ascend *Grindslow*, at the back of Edale village, for the view; and they may prolong their walk thence across the plateau (no right of way) to the (4 M.) *Snake Inn*, in *Ashopdale*, 7 M. from *Glossop* (p. 359) and 6½ M. above *Ashopton* (p. 360).

Carriages continue from Edale village to follow the road on the floor of the valley to (1 M.) *Barber Booth*, where they turn to the left and ascend the steep hill leading to the gap between Mam Tor and Lord's Seat (comp. above) and to the (1¼ M.) high-road. Pedestrians save nearly 2 M. by a footpath ascending from Barber Booth to the S.W. towards the Stake Pass and joining the Chapel-en-le-Frith road a good deal lower down (a boy may be taken as a guide from Barber Booth). — The road going straight up the valley from Barber Booth ends in a path leading to (3M.) *Edale Cross* (1800 ft.) and (3½ M.) *Hayfield* (see below).

The road descending between Mam Tor and Lord's Seat to Edale (see above) is about 3½ M. from Castleton. The high-road continues to run towards the W. Roads diverge on the right for *Hayfield* (see above). After 4 M. we reach (7½ M. from Castleton) —

Chapel-en-le-Frith *(King's Arms; Bull's Head)*, a town with 3500 inhab. (comp. p. 350). The Midland Station (p. 349) is in the town; the L. N. W. Station, on the Manchester and Buxton branch, is ¾ M. to the S. By the latter line the railway-journey to Buxton takes about ¼ hr., by the former (viâ *Miller's Dale*, p. 372) about ½ hr. (fares 1*s.*, 8*d.*, 5½*d.*). The Mid. Railway passes under the L. N. W. Railway by the *Doveholes Tunnel* (p. 350).

Buxton. — **Hotels.** Palace, near the stations, R. & A. from 5*s.* 6*d.*, D. 5*s.*, B. 2*s.* 6*d.*, 'pens'. 14*s.* 6*d.*; St. Ann's, in the Crescent, R. & A. from 4*s.* 6*d.*, 'pens'. 13*s.* 6*d.*; Crescent, also in the Crescent, R. & A. from 4*s.*, 'pens'. 12*s.* 6*d.*; Royal, R. & A. from 4*s.*, 'pens'. in winter 10*s.* 6*d.*; *Old Hall, family hotel, facing the entrance to the Gardens, R. & A. from 4*s.* 6*d.*, 'pens'. 12*s.* — Lea Wood, on the Manchester Road; Burlington; George; Shakespeare, commercial; Eagle, in High Buxton, R. & A. from 3*s.* 6*d.* — At the Buxton hotels the prevailing custom is to have table-d'hôte meals and pay a fixed price per day. — Numerous *Boarding Houses* and *Lodgings*, and several small *Hydropathics.*

Cabs with one horse 1*s.* per mile, each addit. ½ M. 6*d.*; with two horses 1*s.* 6*d.* & 9*d.*; per hour 3*s.* & 4*s.*, each addit. ¼ hr. 9*d.* & 1*s.*

Buxton, one of the three chief inland watering-places in England and the highest town in the country (1000 ft. above the sea), contains a resident population of about 6000, which is doubled or trebled during the summer-season. It has a fine bracing climate, apt at times to be rather cold. The *Hot Springs* for which it is famous (Bath having the only other hot springs in England) seem to have been known to the Romans, and were several times visited by Mary Stuart when in the custody of the Earl of Shrewsbury (comp. p. 359). They rise from fissures in the limestone rock at a constant temperature of 82° Fahr., and are efficacious in rheumatism and other ailments. The *Tepid Baths* are at the W. end of the **Crescent,** the most prominent building in the town, and they are adjoined by the *Chalybeate Wells.* At the other end of the Crescent are the *Hot Baths.* In front of the Crescent is a grassy knoll known as the *Slopes*, and to the W. are the *Pleasure Gardens* (adm. 4*d.* or 6*d.*; music daily). The S. side of the Gardens is skirted by the Broad Walk, with its well-built villas. The large domed building, near the Palace Hotel, is the *Devonshire Hospital.*

The **Environs** of Buxton are rather bleak, but afford opportunities for a few delightful excursions.

Poole's Cavern, 1 M. At the end of the Broad Walk is a board indicating the path to this cave, which crosses two fields and passes Buxton College. At the road we turn to the right, and after 100 yds. reach the entrance to the cavern (adm. 1*s.*; for a party 6*d.* each). **Poole's Hole,** named after an outlaw who used it in the time of Henry IV. (ca. 1400), contains some fine stalactites, but is inferior to the Castleton Caves (p. 369), and has been vulgarised by being lighted with gas. The *Wye* rises here.

The **Duke's Drive** is a carriage-road about 1¼ M. long, constructed by the Duke of Devonshire in 1795, and connecting the lower road through Ashwood Dale with the higher one to Longnor. It begins and ends not much more than ½ M. from Buxton, so that the round is about 2½ M.

Excursion-brakes run daily (return-fare 1*s.* 6*d.*) to the (5 M.) *Cat & Fiddle Inn* (ca. 1700 ft.), on the road to Macclesfield, the highest inn in England (extensive view). — Walkers may combine with this excursion an ascent of **Axe Edge** (1810 ft.), the second summit of the Peak, which rises 2½ M. to the S. of Buxton. — Other favourite points are **Cheedale* (p. 372); the *Corbar Wood Walks*, ½ M. to the N.W.; the *Diamond Hill* (named from the quartz crystals found on it), 1½ M. to the S.; *Solomon's Temple*, ½ M. beyond Poole's Hole; the *Goyt Valley* (p. 349), to the N.W.; and the rocky chasm called *Lud's Church*, 9 M. to the S.W. — Coaches ply in summer to *Haddon* and *Chatsworth* (pp. 366, 367; return-fare 5*s.* 6*d.*).

From Buxton through Cheedale to Miller's Dale, 6 M. We leave Lower Buxton by Spring Gardens and follow the Bakewell road through *Ashwood Dale.* On the right we pass (1 M.) *Sherwood Dell* and the cliff called the *Lover's Leap.* At a point about 3¼ M. from Buxton, after passing under the Midland Railway 3-4 times, we diverge to the left by a well-marked track and cross the *Wye* by a bridge near the junction of the main line with the Buxton branch. We then follow closely the left bank of the river, keeping to the lower paths, and not crossing the flat wooden bridge a little lower down. After about ½ hr. the stream sweeps to the left and we cross it by a plank-bridge. We then again pass under the railway, recross the river, and reach the entrance to ***Cheedale,** a narrow valley flanked by fantastic and well-wooded walls of limestone rock. *Chee Tor* (fine view) rises boldly on the right to a height of 300 ft. [The path, which is rather rough and very miry after rain, is closed on Thursdays.] Farther on we pass through a small wood, cross a side-valley, and reach a wooden bridge, which we cross if we wish to climb Chee Tor. If not, we follow the left bank to ($^1/_4$ hr.) *Miller's Dale* (Inn; p. 350). — We now either return to Buxton, or go on to Bakewell (p. 366) by train.

From Buxton to (14 M.) Alstonefield, a pleasant drive (excursion-brakes in summer). The road runs S.E. from Higher Buxton. To the right, above us, is the *High Peak Railway* (p. 350). Beyond (5 M.) *Glutton Dale* we cross the *Dove.* — 2 M. **Longnor** *(Crewe Arms)*, a small market-town in a pleasant situation.

Good walkers may follow a footpath along the left bank of the Dove to (5 M.) **Hartington** *(*Charles Cotton Hotel)*, an angling-resort, and (5 M.) *Mill Dale* (see below), passing through the charming **Beresford Dale*, with the 'Fishing House' of Izaak Walton and his friend and biographer, Cotton. — On *Arbor Low*, 3 M. to the N.E. of Hartington, are some extensive 'Druidical' remains.

The road follows the valley of the *Manifold* for some time, and then strikes off towards the S.E. At (7 M.) **Alstonefield** *(George)* we leave the carriage and follow a footpath leading directly to ($^1/_2$ M.) *Mill Dale*, a hamlet at the head of Dovedale, though the prettiest part of the valley begins at *Dove Holes*, about 1 M. lower down. ***Dovedale** is a picturesque and narrow limestone valley, hemmed in by fantastic rocks, freely interspersed with woods.

Leaving the *Dove Hole Caverns*, we pass between two limestone crags and follow the left or Derbyshire bank of the Dove (the other being in Staffordshire). Various arbitrary names have been given to the rocks, few of which seem specially appropriate. The *Lion's Head*, one of the first we reach, is, however, an exception. Beyond (1 M.) *Reynard's Cave* (above, to the left) the vale slightly expands. Farther on, we have the *Tissington Spires* to the left and the *Church* and *Twelve Apostles* to the right. From *Sharplow Point* we have a fine view in both directions; to the S. rises *Thorpe Cloud* (900 ft.). At the foot of this hill we reach the stepping-stones, and a little farther on a foot-bridge, leading to the *Izaak Walton Hotel*, a favourite angling resort. A path to the left ascends to the *Peveril Hotel*, close to the village of *Thorpe*. This is the S. end of Dovedale proper. — Pedestrians bound for ($3^3/_4$ M.) Ashbourne (see p. 373) may continue to follow the right bank. At ($1^1/_2$ M.) a cross-road (bridge to the right) we climb a stile and cross a field (path not very distinct). $^1/_2$ M. Stone bridge, where a road to the right leads to Cheadle. We cross the road, pass a house near the river, and go through a gate. — $1^1/_2$ M. *Mappleton* (Oakover Arms). We cross the road and traverse two fields, reaching the road again a little farther on. In 4 min. more we follow the cart-track ascending to the left, passing a farm-house. At the top is a large field, where the path disappears; but by keeping in a straight direction we reach a stile on the other side of the field, beyond which the path is again clear. It descends through a park and past a large house to a gate near a bridge over an affluent of the Dove. From this point a path crosses a field to a lane leading to Ashbourne station.

[The road from the Peveril Hotel to (4 M.) Ashbourne passes (1 M.) the *Dog & Partridge Inn*, where a road to the left leads by the **Via Gellia* (fancifully named after the Gell family) to (12 M.) *Matlock* (p. 365).]

Ashbourne *(*Green Man*, an old-fashioned hostelry; *White Hart)* is a picturesque little town in a well-wooded valley. The **Church*, near the station, is in the E.E. and Dec. styles, with a lofty spire (212 ft.). Among the interesting monuments is a very touching one of little **Penelope Boothby* (d. 1791), by Banks.

About 4½ M. to the W. of Ashbourne is *Wootton Hall*, where Rousseau wrote the first part of his 'Confessions' (1766-7). — A pleasant walk may be taken by the *Weaver Hills* and *Alton Towers* to (10 M.) *Alton* (see below).

Railway from Ashbourne to Derby, 30 M., in 1¼-2 hrs. (fares 2*s.* 6*d.*, 2*s.*, 1*s.* 3*d.*). — 5 M. *Norbury*, with a highly interesting church (14-15th cent.; fine stained glass) and an ancient manor-house. — At (7 M.) **Rocester** *(Rail. Refreshmt. Rooms)* the pretty 'Churnet Valley Line' diverges to the right; the first station on it is (3½ M.) *Alton* (see p. 347). — 11 M. *Uttoxeter* (p. 346). 19 M. *Tutbury*, see p. 188. — 30 M. *Derby*, see p. 350.

46. From Liverpool or Manchester to Carlisle.

L. N. W. Railway in 3½-5½ hrs. (fares from Liverpool 18*s.* 11*d.*, 14*s.* 8*d.*, 9*s.* 11*d.*; from Manchester 18*s.*, 14*s.* 3*d.*, 10*s.* 1*d.*). The two lines unite at *Wigan* (see below; ½-1 hr.). The more frequented line from Manchester to Preston runs viâ Bolton (p. 339).

From Liverpool to (18½ M.) *Wigan*, see p. 331; from Manchester to (18 M.) *Wigan*, see p. 339. At **Wigan** *(Clarence; Victoria)*, an iron, brass, and cotton making town of 50,000 inhab., in an important coal-district, we join the trunk-line of the L. N. W. R. Beyond (28 M.) *Farington* we cross the *Ribble* (*View to the right).

29 M. **Preston** *(*Park Hotel; Victoria; Bull; Alexandra Temperance; Rail. Refreshmt. Rooms)*, an important centre of the cotton-manufacture, with 100,000 inhabitants. The principal buildings are the *Town Hall*, from a design by Sir G. G. Scott; the *Harris Free Library & Museum*, with good sculptures in the pediment by E. Roscoe Mullens; and the *Parish Church*, partly rebuilt in 1885. The town possesses three large *Public Parks*.

Preston is a place of considerable antiquity and was frequently the scene of contests between the English and the Scots. The Parliamentarians defeated the Royalists near Preston in 1648, and it was occupied by the Pretender in 1715. *Richard Arkwright*, the inventor, was born at Preston in 1732. Preston was the cradle of the temperance movement, and the first teetotal pledges were signed here by Joseph Livesey and his friends in 1833. — Preston is the 'dining station' of the Scottish expresses, which stop here for 20-30 minutes.

From Preston to Blackpool and Fleetwood, 21 M., railway in ¾-1 hr. (fares 3*s.* 3*d.*, 2*s.* 6*d.*, 1*s.* 8½*d.*). — From (8 M.) *Kirkham* a branch-line diverges to the left for the small watering-place of *Lytham* (Queen), whence it goes on to Blackpool (see below). — 14½ M. *Poulton* is the starting-point of the regular line to (18 M.) **Blackpool** *(Bailey's Hotel; Clifton Arms; County; Albion; Imperial Hydropathic)*, one of the most popular sea-bathing resorts in the North of England, with a fine esplanade, two piers, a winter garden, etc. — The direct line from Poulton goes on to (21 M.) **Fleetwood** *(Crown; Royal; Rail. Rfmt. Rooms)*, a small watering-place and seaport on the Irish Channel, with a good harbour. Mail-steamers ply hence daily to *Belfast*, and there is a summer-service to the Isle of Man (p. 340). About 3 M. to the S.W. is *Rossall School*, a large public school (400 boys).

50 M. **Lancaster** *(County; King's Arms; Rail. Refreshmt. Rooms)*, the county-town of Lancashire, with 21,000 inhab., lies near the mouth of the *Lune*. The *Castle*, to a great extent rebuilt,

but still retaining its ancient keep, is now the gaol. Adjoining it is the *Church of St. Mary* (15th cent.), containing good stained glass, some fine oak-carvings, and a few interesting brasses. *Ripley Hospital*, to the right of the line before Lancaster, was erected for orphan children at a cost of 100,000*l*.

Lancaster occupies the site of a Roman station. It was given by Edward III. to his son, 'Old John of Gaunt, time-honoured Lancaster', and the duchy of Lancaster is still attached to the Crown. Dr. Whewell and Sir Richard Owen, the comparative anatomist, were natives of Lancaster.

At Lancaster we cross the Midland branch from *Settle* (see p. 404), through the pretty valley of the *Lune*, to **Morecambe** *(Midland; Crown; West View; Imperial)*, another thriving watering-place, 3 M. to the W. of Lancaster, with a promenade, a pier, etc.

At (53 M.) *Hest Bank* diverges the L. N. W. branch to (3 M.) *Morecambe* (see above). View, to the left, of *Morecambe Bay*. — 56 M. **Carnforth** *(Station Hotel; Rail. Refreshmt. Rooms)* is the junction of the line to Ulverston, Lakeside (Windermere), and Whitehaven (see R. 47). — 69 M. *Oxenholme* (Rail. Rfmt. Rooms) is the junction of the branch to (3 M.) *Kendal* and (11 M.) *Windermere* (p. 378).

Kendal *(Commercial; King's Arms)*, the chief town of Westmorland (14,000 inhab.), is seen to the left as we proceed. It still carries on the manufacture of woollen cloth established by Flemish weavers in the 14th cent., but 'Kendal Green' is no longer made. On a hill to the E. of the town are the ruins of a *Castle*, in which Queen Catherine Parr was born.

The mountains of the Lake District are in sight on the left, and the scenery becomes more varied. From (78 M.) *Low Gill* (*View to the right) a line runs to the right to *Ingleton* (p. 405). 80 M. *Tebay* is the junction of the N.E. line to Darlington (p. 410) and Bishop Auckland (p. 414). — Beyond Tebay we reach the culminating point of the line (1000 ft.) and descend to (89 M.) *Shap* (Hotel; p. 391). Hawes Water (p. 391) is $5^1/_2$ M. to the W. of Shap; and Kidsty Pike, High St., and other summits of the Lake District are conspicuous to the left. Beyond (97 M.) *Clifton* we have a glimpse on the right of *Brougham Hall*, the home of Lord Brougham.

101 M. **Penrith** *(Crown; George)*, an ancient market-town, with 9300 inhab. and the remains of an old castle, is the junction of the line to Keswick and Cockermouth (see below). A small inn, named the *Gloucester Arms*, contains a room in which Richard III. once slept, and some good old oaken panelling. *Penrith Beacon*, crowning a wooded height to the N. E. of the town (25 min. from the station), commands a good view over Ullswater to the Helvellyn and High Street ranges (comp. p. 389).

About 4 M. to the N.E. of Penrith is **Eden Hall**, the ancient seat of the Musgraves, still containing the curious old glass goblet, the legend attached to which is celebrated in Uhland's well-known ballad, 'The Luck of Eden Hall' ('Das Glück von Edenhall'). — About 3 M. farther on is a Druidical circle known as *Long Meg and her Daughters*.

From Penrith to Keswick, Cockermouth, and Workington, 39 M., railway in $1^3/_4$ hr. (fares 7*s*. 2*d*., 5*s*. 1*d*., 3*s*. 3*d*.; to Keswick 2*s*. 11*d*., 1*s*. 10*d*., 1*s*. 2*d*.). As we start we have a view, to the left, of the heights around Ullswater. $9^1/_2$ M. *Troutbeck* (Inn) is one of the starting-points for a visit to Ullswater (see p. 397). The *Saddleback* (p. 399), seen on the right, may be ascended from ($14^1/_2$ M.) *Threlkeld* (see p. 399). To the left opens the

Vale of St. John (p. 396). Beyond Threlkeld the train passes through the charming valley of the winding *Greta*. — 18 M. *Keswick*, see p. 392. — The train now runs through the *Vale of Keswick* to (20 M.) *Braithwaite*, beyond which it turns to the N. and skirts the W. bank of *Bassenthwaite Lake* (p. 400). On the other side of the lake towers Skiddaw (p. 399). 25½ M. *Bassenthwaite Lake Station* (Pheasant Inn), near the N.W. end of the lake. — We now again turn to the W. — 30½ M. **Cockermouth** (*Globe; Reay's Temperance*), a small town with the relics of a Norman castle, was the birthplace of Wordsworth, who dedicated a well-known sonnet to his native place. His father is buried in the church. Lowes Water (p. 396) is 8 M. to the S. — 39 M. *Workington*, see p. 377. The trains go on to (7 M.) *Whitehaven* (p. 377).

From Penrith to *Pooley Bridge* (Ullswater), see p. 389.

119 M. **Carlisle.** — **Hotels.** *County Station Hotel, connected with the station by a covered passage, R. & A. 4-5*s.*; Central, Bush, near the station, similar charges; Viaduct; Crown & Mitre, commercial; Graham's Temperance. — *Rail. Refreshment Rooms.*

Carlisle, an ancient border-city with 36,000 inhab., is pleasantly situated on a gentle eminence at the confluence of three small rivers, the *Eden*, the *Caldew*, and the *Petteril*. It is the county-town of Cumberland, the see of a bishop, and an important railway-centre (comp. RR. 49, 51, 62a), and manufactures textile fabrics and iron.

Carlisle, the British *Caer Luel*, and the Roman *Luguvallium* or *Luguballia*, is the only purely English city which retains its ancient British name. At the time of the Saxon invasion it formed part of the kingdom of Strathclyde, and it withstood the invaders till the 7th century. It seems to have been destroyed by the Danes 200 years later, and to have remained almost deserted until William Rufus made it the defence of the English border and erected its castle. The bishopric was founded in 1133. At a later period it was an important border-fortress and city of refuge for the surrounding country. Carlisle submitted to the Young Pretender in 1745 and was taken by the Hanoverians. Comp. 'Carlisle', by *Canon Creighton* ('Historic Towns' series; 1889). — *Roman Wall*, see p. 376.

The *Citadel Railway Station* is a large structure covering 7 acres of ground, and used by eight different railway-companies. On issuing from it (on the N. side) we find ourselves in front of the two massive circular *Court Houses*, built on the site of the former citadel. To the left is the *Gaol*. Passing between the court-houses, we follow English St. to the Market Place, in which, to the right, is the *Town Hall*. Castle St., to the left, leads to the —

Cathedral, which was originally founded by William Rufus as the church of the Augustine Priory of St. Mary. This Norman church seems to have been almost wholly burned down some time before the middle of the 13th cent.; and the E. E. choir which replaced the old one was also destroyed by fire in 1292, and again rebuilt, in the Dec. style, in the following cent. (finished ca. 1400). The Central Tower (ca. 1410) is by no means imposing. The nave was never rebuilt, and still remains a fragment consisting of two Norman bays. The whole building was restored in 1853. The daily services are at 10 a.m. and 4 p.m. We enter by the N. door.

Interior. The Nave has a different axis from the choir. The fine Norman arches have been curiously crushed out of shape by the settling of the piers. The S. Transept contains an interesting Runic inscription (under glass) and a bust of *George Moore* (d. 1876), the philanthropist. To the E. it is adjoined by *St. Catharine's Chapel.*

The *Choir is entered by the central doorway to the N. of the organ, below the tabernacle-arch of the stalls. The lower arches are E.E., the triforium and clerestory Decorated. The glory of the choir is the late-Dec. or Flamboyant **E. Window*, one of the largest and finest in England, 50 ft. high and 30 ft. broad (glass modern). The wooden ceiling (14th cent.) has been repainted. The *Stalls* date from the 15th cent., and their backs are covered with rude paintings of legendary subjects. Among the monuments are those of *Dean Close* (d. 1882; S. choir-aisle) and *Archdeacon Paley* (d. 1805; behind the altar). At the N.E. angle of the N. choir-aisle is a door leading to the *Clerestory* and *Tower* (adm. 6*d.*; fine view). — Sir Walter Scott was married in Carlisle Cathedral in 1797. To the S. of the cathedral is the *Refectory* of St. Mary's Priory (see p. 375) and two dilapidated arches. The house with the square tower is the *Deanery*.

Castle St. ends at the **Castle**, which is now used as barracks and is open to visitors during the day. From the *Outer Bailey* we pass, to the right, into the *Inner Bailey*. Extensive view from the battlements. Visitors are not now admitted to the top of the *Norman Keep*, erected by Rufus, but the custodian (gratuity) shows the dungeons in which the prisoners of 1745 were confined, and some relics of Queen Mary's short captivity here in 1568.

A walk encircles the hill on which the castle stands, passing the only remains of the old *City Walls*, also constructed by William Rufus. — In Finkle St., near the Castle, is a small *Museum* (open 1-9; adm. 2*d*.).

Great Roman Wall. During the Roman occupation of Britain a *Vallum*, or earthen rampart, was constructed across the N. of England from the Solway Firth, a little to the W. of Carlisle, to a point on the North Sea near Newcastle. This was afterwards replaced (probably by Severus, ca. A.D. 208) by a *Stone Wall*, 8 ft. thick and 12 ft. high, which was guarded by 18 *Military Stations*, garrisoned by cohorts of Roman soldiers. At intervals of a mile were *Forts* (80 in all), containing 100 men each, and between each pair of forts were four watch-towers. Of this huge line of fortifications, however, the remains are remarkably meagre (see p. 418). Carlisle itself was not a station, but the suburb of *Stanwix (Axelodunum)*, on the other side of the Eden, reached by a handsome bridge, was one; and a few remains may be seen there.

Excursions may be made from Carlisle to *Corby* and *Wetheral* (p. 417); **Naworth* (p. 417); **Lanercost Priory*, 12½ M. to the N.E. (usually reached viâ Naworth); **Gilsland* (p. 417); *Eden Hall* (p. 374) and *Gretna* (p. 462); *Holme Cultram Abbey*, 18 M. to the W., near *Abbey*, on the Silloth Railway (see below); and *Netherby* (p. 455), 11 M. to the N.

From Carlisle to Maryport, 28 M., railway in 1-1¼ hr. (fares 3*s.* 10*d.*, 2*s.* 11*d.*, 2*s.* 4*d.*). — **Maryport** *(Senhouse Arms)* is a thriving little coaling-port. From Maryport to *Workington*, see p. 377.

From Carlisle to Silloth, 22½ M., railway in 1-1¼ hr. (fares 2*s.* 6*d.*, 2*s.*, 1*s.* 6*d.*). From (8½ M.) *Drumburgh* a branch-line diverges to (3½ M.) *Port Carlisle*. — **Silloth** *(Hotel)* is a seaport on the *Solway Firth*, with regular steam-communication with Douglas (p. 338), Dublin, and Belfast.

From Carlisle to *Newcastle*, see R. 51; to *Edinburgh* or *Glasgow*, see R. 62; to *Leeds* and *Sheffield*, see R. 49.

47. From Carnforth to Ulverston, Windermere *(Lake Side)*, Furness Abbey, and Whitehaven.

74 M. Railway in 3-3½ hrs. (fares 12*s.* 7*d.*, 8*s.* 5*d.*, 5*s.* 6½*d.*; fares to *Furness Abbey* 4*s.* 9*d.*, 3*s.* 2*d.*, 2*s.* ½*d.*).

Carnforth, see p. 374. The train skirts *Morecambe Bay*, passing *Silverdale* and *Arnside*, and crosses the estuary of the *Kent*. 9 M. *Grange-over-Sands* (*Grange Hotel), a pretty watering-place.

Cartmel Church, $2^1/_2$ M. to the W., is interesting (12th cent.). Near ($13^1/_2$ M.) *Cark* is *Holker Hall*. a seat of the Duke of Devonshire. We then cross the estuary of the *Leven;* the Coniston Old Man (p. 381) is conspicuous to the right.

19 M. **Ulverston** *(County; Sun)*, a market-town with 10,000 inhab., is supported mainly by its mines of hæmatite ore. *Conishead Priory*, 2 M. to the S.E. (branch-line, with one or two trains daily; also omn.), is now a popular hydropathic.

Ulverston is the junction of a short line ($9^1/_2$ M., in 25 min.) to *Lake Side*, at the foot of Windermere (comp. p. 379). The line skirts the *Leven*.

Beyond Ulverston we traverse the romantic 'Valley of Nightshade'. — 25 M. *Furness Abbey Station* (*Abbey Hotel, R. & A. from 4*s.*)

The ruins of ***Furness Abbey**, a Cistercian foundation of the 12th cent., are among the most extensive and picturesque in England. The Abbey was at one time exceedingly rich, and the Abbot exercised an almost regal sway over the surrounding country. The finest features of the ruins are the E.E. chapter-house and the triplet of grand Norman arches at the entrance to the cloisters. In the Abbot's Chapel are two effigies of Norman knights (12th cent.), said to be the only ones of the kind in England.

$26^1/_2$ M. *Roose* is the junction of a short branch to (2 M.) **Barrow-in-Furness** *(Imperial; Victoria)*, a thriving seaport, with 50,000 inhab., magnificent docks, handsome municipal buildings, and extensive iron-works. [Most of the trains, however, now run through Barrow.] Steamers ply hence to Douglas (p. 342) and Belfast.

40 M. *Foxfield* is the junction of the line to (1 M.) *Broughton* (p. 382) and *Coniston* (10 M., in 25 min.; see p. 381). — We now cross the estuary of the *Duddon* (p. 382). From ($57^1/_2$ M.) *Ravenglass* (Queen's Head) a branch runs to (7 M.) *Boot* (Mason's Arms; Woolpack), the nearest station to Wast Water (p. 400). — 59 M. *Drigg* (*Inn); 61 M. *Seascale* (see p. 401). — $69^1/_2$ M. **St. Bees** *(Sea Cote; Queen's)*, with an ancient church and a theological college. To the left is *St. Bees Head*, rising 300 ft. above the sea.

74 M. **Whitehaven** *(Grand; Globe; Black Lion)*, a seaport with 20,000 inhab. and a fine harbour. Steamers to Ramsey, see p. 344.

From Whitehaven the line is prolonged to (7 M.) **Workington** *(Railway Hotel)*, a seaport at the mouth of the *Derwent*, with large steel-works and important salmon-fisheries, and to (14 M.) *Maryport* (see p. 376).

48. The Lake District.

The picturesque mountainous region known as the ****English Lake District** is comprised within the counties of Westmorland and Cumberland, together with a small adjoining portion of Lancashire; and its boundaries may be roughly described as the Irish Sea and Morecambe Bay on the W. and S.; the railway from Lancaster to Carlisle on the E.; and a line drawn from Penrith to Workington on the N. Within these limits lies a wealth of charmingly diversified scenery; and though none of the mountains exceeds 3200 ft. in height, and the largest of the lakes is only $10^1/_2$ M. long, their picturesqueness and even wildness are far greater than their size would lead one to expect. There are in all about 16 lakes or meres (the largest being *Windermere*, *Ullswater*, *Coniston*, and *Derwentwater*), besides innumerable mountain-tarns. The highest summits are *Scafell Pike* (3210 ft.), *Scafell* (3160 ft.), *Helvellyn* (3120 ft.), and *Skiddaw* (3055 ft.).

For a coloured map of The Lake District see pages 590 & 591

The usual approaches to the Lake District are from Oxenholme (p. 374) to Windermere, from Carnforth (p. 374) to Lake Side (Windermere) or Coniston, and from Penrith (p. 374) to Keswick or Ullswater. Seascale (pp. 377, 401) is a convenient starting-point for the Wastwater district. The most common and perhaps the best plan is to begin with Windermere, as in this case we see the tamer scenery first. Those who can devote One Day only to the Lakes will see most by taking the coach from *Bowness (Windermere)* to *Ambleside*, *Grasmere*, *Thirlmere*, and *Keswick* (see p. 379); or they may make the circular tour from *Coniston* or *Ambleside*, mentioned at pp. 383, 385. A Second Day may be devoted to the *Buttermere* round described at pp. 394, 395, and a Third Day to *Ullswater*, in which case the Lake District is quitted viâ *Penrith* (see p. 389). — A week's walk may be planned thus: 1st Day. From *Windermere* to *Ambleside*, *Grasmere*, and *Dungeon Gill* (16 M.; steamer to Ambleside, see p. 379). — 2nd Day. From Dungeon Gill by *Rossett Gill* to *Wasdale Head*, 3-4 hrs., or including an ascent of *Scafell Pike*, 4 1/2-6 hrs. — 3rd Day. From *Wasdale Head* to *Angler's Inn*, *Ennerdale*, by the *Pillar* or by the *Black Sail Pass*, 6-7 hrs.; from Ennerdale to *Buttermere* viâ *Floutern Tarn* and *Scale Force*, 2 1/2-3 hrs. — 4th Day. From Buttermere to *Keswick* viâ *Honister Hause* and *Borrowdale*, 14 M. — 5th Day. From Keswick viâ *Helvellyn* to *Patterdale*, 5-6 hrs. — 6th Day. Sail on *Ullswater*, visit *Aira Force*, and go on to *Penrith*; or, from *Patterdale* to *Windermere* by the *Kirkstone Pass* and *Troutbeck*, 13 M. (digression to *Hawes Water*, 6 M.).

The following list of local names may be useful. *Beck*, brook; *Combe*, hollow (comp. p. 129); *Dodd*, a spur of a mountain; *Force* (Icelandic, 'Fors'; Norwegian 'Foss'), a waterfall; *Gill*, a gorge; *Hause*, the top of a pass, French 'col'; *Holme*, an island; *How*, a mound-like hill; *Nab* (A.S. *Nebbe*, nose), a projecting rock; *Pike*, a peak; *Raise*, the top of a ridge; *Scar*, a wall of rock; *Scree*, steep slope of loose stones; *Thwaite*, a clearing.

The *Hotels* in the Lake District are generally good and not exorbitant; while even the smallest inns, almost without exception, are laudably clean. *Guides* and *Ponies* may be procured at all the principal resorts.

Readers need scarcely be reminded of the *Lake School of Poetry*. Wordsworth in particular has made the district his own ('Wordsworthshire', as Lowell calls it), and few points of interest have been left unsung in his 'Excursion' or minor poems. Among interesting prose works relating to the Lakes may be mentioned *Harriet Martineau's* 'Guide to the Lake District' (4th ed., 1871), *Prof. Knight's* 'English Lake District as Interpreted in the Poems of Wordsworth' and 'Through the Wordsworth Country' (1887), *James Payn's* 'Leaves from Lakeland', *Wordsworth's* 'Guide to the Lake District' (5th ed., 1835; now out of print), *Gibson's* 'Folk-speech of Cumberland', and *Miss Alice Rea's* 'Beckside Boggle and other Lake Country Legends'. The botanist is referred to *Mr. J. G. Baker's* 'Flora of the Lake District' (1886).

The **Lake District Defence Society**, established in its present form in 1883, has for its praiseworthy object 'to offer a powerful and consolidated opposition to the introduction of unnecessary railways into the Lake District, and to all other speculative schemes which may appear likely to impair its beauty or destroy its present character'. Secretaries: *W. H. Hills, Esq.*, The Knoll, Ambleside; *Rev. H. D. Rawnsley*, Crosthwaite Vicarage, Keswick; *M. J. Baddeley, Esq.*, The Hollies, Windermere.

a. Windermere Section.

The village of **Windermere** (**Rigg's Windermere Hotel*, with view, R. & A. 4*s*., D. 4*s*.; *Queen's*, *Elleray*, unpretending; *Rail. Refreshmt. Rooms;* station, p. 377) lies about 300 ft. above the lake (450 ft. above the sea), from which it is distant 3/4 M. by the direct footpath and 1 1/2 M. by road. It is delightfully situated among trees at the foot of Orrest Head (see p. 379), affording fine views of the lake. Visitors may take up their quarters with almost equal advantage either here or at Bowness (see p. 379), on the shore of the lake, $1^1/_2$ M. to the S. (omn. from the station 6*d*.). There is now an almost continuous line of villas between the two places.

Those who reach the Lake at the *Lake Side Station* (see p. 377) may go on at once by steamer to (5 M.) the *Ferry* (p. 380) or (6 M.) *Bowness.*

Bowness. — **Hotels.** *Old England, close to the lake; *Royal Hotel; *Crown, on a height to the E. — *Ferry Hotel, see p. 380. — *Hydropathic Establishment, well situated on Biscay How. — *Lodgings.*

Coaches run daily in summer from Bowness and Windermere to ($12^1/_2$ M.) *Ullswater* (fare 6*s*., return 8*s*. 6*d*.); from Bowness across the ferry to (9 M.) *Coniston* (4*s*., return 6*s*.); and from Windermere station to *Ambleside* (5 M.; 1*s*. 6*d*.), *Grasmere* (9 M.; 2*s*. 6*d*.), and *Keswick* (21 M.; 6*s*. 6*d*.). — Omnibuses from the Bowness hotels and from (3 M.) *Low Wood Hotel* (p. 383) meet the trains at Windermere.

Steamers ply on Windermere at frequent intervals during the day, calling at several stations. Entire tour of the lake ($2^1/_2$ hrs.) 3*s*., 2*s*. 6*d*.; to *Lake Side* ($^3/_4$ hr.) 1*s*. 6*d*., 1*s*.; to *Waterhead* (for *Ambleside;* 1 hr.) 1*s*., 9*d*.

Boats on the lake 1*s*. per hour, 5*s*. per day; with boatman 1*s*. 6*d*. and 10*s*. They may be obtained either near the Bowness pier or at the Miller Ground Landing, the nearest point to the village of Windermere.

Bowness (135 ft. above the sea), with about 2000 inhab., the principal port of Windermere, is beautifully situated in a small bay on the E. side of the lake. The centre of the picturesque and irregularly-built little town is the old *Church of St. Martin*, the parish-church of Windermere, which has lately been restored and contains a good stained-glass window said to have been brought from Furness Abbey (p. 377). Bowness affords admirable headquarters for exploring the S. part of the Lake District, and in the height of the season is visited by thousands of tourists.

Visitors to Windermere and Bowness should first ascend *Orrest Head* or *Biscay How* (or both), to obtain a general view of the lake.

***Orrest Head** (784 ft.), the higher of the two, commands the more extensive view, and is ascended from Windermere in about 20 minutes. On issuing from the station we pass through the second of two gates on the right (a wooden one), adjoining the approach to the Windermere Hotel, and then ascend through the varied woods of Elleray by a path indicated by sign-posts. The **View comprises the entire S. half of the Lake District, the chief feature being, of course, the beautiful winding *Windermere* itself, with its clusters of islets and encircling mountains. The most prominent summits are the Langdale Pikes, rising to the N.W., near the head of Windermere. To the right of these is a wooded knoll called Loughrigg Fell, with Helm Crag rising behind, while still farther to the right are Fairfield, Wansfell Pike (with the village of Troutbeck), the conspicuous Red Screes, the ridge of High Street, and the fine cone of Ill Bell. To the E. is a long series of featureless hills extending to Ingleborough in Yorkshire, on the S.E. To the left (W.) of the Langdale Pikes rise the fine peak of Bow Fell, Scafell Pikes (in the distance), Pike o' Blisco and the three Crinkle Crags (in front), the rounded Weatherlam, and the Coniston Old Man, closing the mountain-screen in this direction. To the S. the view extends to Morecambe Bay. In descending we may keep more to the right and pass the cottage of *Elleray*, the former residence of Christopher North, shaded by the splendid sycamore of which he declared it were easier to suppose two Shakespeares than such another tree. Below it we reach the Ambleside road, where we may either turn to the left for ($^1/_3$ M.) Windermere, or to the right and then to the left (at the cross-roads) for ($1^3/_4$ M.) Bowness.

***Biscay How** rises immediately behind Bowness, and the way to the top (1/2 hr.) is obvious. The view is similar to that from Orrest Head, but less extensive. — Other good points of view are **Miller Brow*, 1 1/2 M. to the N. of Bowness, on the road to Ambleside, just on this side of the above-mentioned cross-roads, and **Brant Fell* (500 ft.), 1 M. to the S.E. The road to the latter ascends by the church and to the left of the Crown Hotel.

Windermere, or *Winandermere* (the 'winding lake', or, perhaps, 'Windar's lake'), is the largest lake in England, being 10 1/2 M. in length and 1/3-1 M. broad. It lies 134 ft. above the sea-level, and its greatest depth is 240 ft. Its banks are beautifully wooded and enlivened with numerous villas. The N. end of Windermere is enclosed by an amphitheatre of lofty mountains. At the S. end of the lake, 6 M. from Bowness (reached by crossing the *Ferry*, 3/4 M. below Bowness, and following the shady road on the W. bank), lies *Lake Side* (*Lake Side Hotel; Railway Refreshmt. Rooms), the terminus of the railway from Carnforth (see p. 376).

STEAMER ON WINDERMERE (see p. 379). Leaving Lake Side, the steamboat steers to the N., up the middle of the lake, which is here not wider than a river of moderate size. The banks are well wooded. To the right is *Gummer's How* (1054 ft.). We pass a few islets, and then the promontories called *Rawlinson Nab* (left) and *Storr's Point* (right), the latter with a small observatory. It was here that Scott, Wordsworth, Southey, Canning, and Wilson met in 1825 and witnessed a regatta held in honour of the first-named. Beyond *Ramp Holme* the steamer makes its first halt at the **Ferry Hotel*, charmingly situated on a small promontory jutting out from the W. bank (ferry, see below). It then steers across the lake towards Bowness, skirting the well-wooded *Belle Isle*, the largest island in the lake (1/2 M. long; landing forbidden). *Bowness*, see p. 379.

On leaving Bowness the steamer threads its way among several islets to the N. of Belle Isle and enters upon the most picturesque part of the voyage. The fine amphitheatre of mountains at the head of the lake becomes more and more distinct. Due N. is Fairfield; to the right of it, Red Screes, High Street, Froswick, and Ill Bell; to the left, the conspicuous Langdale Pikes. To the W. rise Weatherlam and the Coniston Old Man (comp. p. 382). To the right opens the little glen of the *Troutbeck*, which flows into the lake through the woods of *Calgarth*. On the shore to the left, a little farther on, is *Wray Castle*, a modern castellated mansion, rising above the trees. The steamer then stops on the E. side of the lake at the **Low Wood Hotel*, a large establishment close to the shore. High up on the same side is *Dove Nest*, once the temporary home of Mrs. Hemans. At the head of the lake open out the valleys of the *Brathay* (to the left) and the *Rothay*, which unite their waters just before entering the lake. To the left is *Pull Wyke Bay*. We then reach the pier of *Waterhead* (Hotel; Restaurant, with lodgings, at the pier), the station at the N. end of the lake. Omnibuses for (3/4 M.) *Ambleside* (p. 385) and (5 M.) *Grasmere* (p. 387) meet the steamers.

FROM BOWNESS TO ESTHWAITE WATER, HAWKSHEAD, AND CONISTON, 9 M. (coach, see p. 379). The road leads to the S. from Bowness to the (1 M.) *Nab Ferry*, which walkers may reach by a shorter footpath (3/4 M.) to the right. The lake here is only 1/4 M. wide, and the ferry-boat plies at short intervals during the day (fare 2*d*.; carr. 1*s*.-3*s*. 6*d*.). On the other side is the *Ferry Hotel* (see above).

From the Ferry Hotel the road ascends, skirting the *Claife Heights*, to (1 1/4 M.) *Far Sawrey* (Inn) and (1/2 M.) *Near Sawrey*, and then descends to the right to (1/2 M.) *Esthwaite Water* (217 ft.), a small lake, 1 3/4 M. long and 1/3 M. broad, well stocked with fish.

Our road skirts the E. side of the lake, passes a small pool called the 'Priest Pot' to the N. of it, and then turns to the left.

1¼ M. *Hawkshead* (Red Lion), a quaint and very irregular little town, with the grammar-school at which Wordsworth was educated. His name is cut on one of the oaken benches. The school was founded in 1585 by Abp. Sandys, a native of Hawkshead. The little height on which the church stands commands a good view.

The road leading straight on (to the N.) from Hawkshead leads to Ambleside. Our road turns to the left and ascends to (1½ M.) *High Cross* (600 ft.), the culminating point of the route, where it joins the road from Ambleside to Coniston (see p. 386). We now descend, facing the Old Man and Weatherlam, with the *Yewdale Crags* in front of them, and enjoying fine glimpses of Coniston Lake to the left, to (2 M.) the head of the lake, whence the road leads past the Waterhead Hotel to (1 M.) the village of Coniston.

Coniston (** Waterhead Hotel*, ½ M. from the village, near the pier; *Crown*, in the village; *Lodgings*), the terminus of a railway from Carnforth and Furness Abbey (see p. 377), is finely situated at the foot of the Old Man, ¾ M. from the lake, and is a pleasant centre for excursionists and anglers. — **Coniston Lake** (147 ft.), a 'miniature Windermere', is 5½ M. long, about ½ M. broad, and 260 ft. deep at the deepest part. The most picturesque part of it is the N. end, with the mountains rising above it, but the beautifully-wooded banks lower down have a charm of their own. The best view down the lake is obtained from Tarn Hows (see below). A small steamer plies up and down the lake (¾ hr. each way; fare 1*s.*, return 1*s.* 6*d.*). At the lower end is *Lake Bank Hotel*, which is 8½ M. from Ulverston (p. 377) and 5½ M. from *Greenodd*, a station on the Lake Side line (p. 377). As we descend the lake the distant tops of Helvellyn, Fairfield, and Red Screes come into sight on the N. and N.E. Among the houses on the E. bank are *Tent House* (opposite the Waterhead Hotel), where Tennyson once lived, and *Brantwood*, 1 M. lower down, the home of Ruskin.

The most attractive point for a short walk from Coniston is (2 M.) *Tarn Hows*, which pedestrians may easily include by a slight détour on their way from Bowness or Ambleside. We follow the Bowness (or Ambleside) road to a point about ¾ M. beyond the Waterhead Hotel, where we diverge to the left, nearly opposite the gate of Waterhead House, and ascend through the wooded dell to (¾ M.) *Tarn Hows Farm* (to the left). The high ground to the right, farther on, commands a beautiful *View. In returning we may descend by a steep path into *Yewdale* (p. 386), which we reach near the celebrated yew (p. 386), or take the opposite direction and descend to the Bowness road near High Cross (see above).

Ascent of the Coniston Old Man, 1½ hr. (ponies obtainable at the hotels). There are various ways of making this ascent, but if the summit is not concealed by mist the climber will not need much guidance. The slopes of the fell are covered with copper-mines and slate-quarries, and the interest of a visit to the former (apply to the manager) scarcely compensates for the disfigurement of the scenery. The regular pony-track ascends along a stream descending from the copper-mines, passes the mines, and then climbs to the left towards a conspicuous slate-quarry. near the *Low Water Tarn*. Hence we ascend to the S., passing another quarry, and soon reach the top. The summit of the ***Old Man** (2633 ft.), the name of which is a corruption of *Allt Maen* (*i.e.* 'steep rock'), commands a *View of great charm. To the N. is an expanse of rugged fells, culminating in the distant Skiddaw, to the right of which are ranged Helvellyn, High Street, and Ill Bell. To the E. we look over Coniston Water, Esthwaite Water, and parts of Windermere, with the Yorkshire hills in the background. To the S. are Morecambe Bay and Black Combe; and the summit of Snowdon is visible in clear weather beyond the expanse of sea. The view to the W. also includes the sea and the Isle of Man. The tarn high up among the fells is *Devoke Water.* To the N.W. tower Scafell and Scafell Pike. The immediate foreground is filled with the other members of the range of which the Old Man is the loftiest summit (Weatherlam, the Carrs, Dow Crag, etc.). Three small tarns, *Lever Water* and *Low Water* to the N., and *Blind Tarn* to the S.W., are visible; and by going a few yards to the W., we see a fourth, *Goats Water* (1646 ft.), at our feet. The descent may be varied in many ways. We may walk along the ridge connecting the summit with *Dow Crag* (2555 ft.) and descend by the *Walna Scar Pass* (2035 ft.); or we may descend to *Seathwaite Tarn* and follow the brook issuing from it down to the valley of the *Duddon* (see below), returning to Coniston by the Walna Scar road, or following the Duddon to *Broughton* and returning thence by train. Good walkers may make their way to the top of (2 hrs.) *Weatherlam* (2502 ft.; view) and descend thence either into the (1 hr.) *Tilberthwaite Glen* (see below), or by the N.E. side to (1 hr.) *Smithy Houses* (p. 386).

The Duddon Valley. The easiest way to visit this valley, immortalised by Wordsworth in his 'Sonnets to the Duddon', is to take the train to ($8^1/_2$ M.) *Broughton-in-Furness*, and drive or walk thence along the river. It may also be reached by the road over the *Walna Scar* (2035 ft.), to the S. of the Old Man, with the ascent of which it may be combined. The *Duddon* rises near the *Wrynose Pass* (see below), 14 M. above Broughton, where its sandy estuary begins, and forms the boundary between Cumberland (W.) and Lancashire (E.). There is a small inn at *Ulpha*, $5^1/_2$ M. above Broughton, where the route to *Dalegarth Force*, *Eskdale*, and *Wast Water* (p. 400) diverges to the left. About $2^1/_2$ M. farther on is *Seathwaite Church*, of which 'Wonderful Walker' was rector for 67 years (1735-1802), governing his parish with 'an entirely healthy and absolutely autocratic rule', leading the way in all manual labour as well as instructing his people in spiritual matters, bringing up and educating eight children, and leaving 2000*l.*, — all on an annual stipend of less than 50*l.*! He is buried in the churchyard. About $^1/_2$ M. beyond the church the road over the Walna Scar Pass (see above) diverges to the right (to Coniston 5 M.). From this point, too, we may ascend along the Seathwaite Beck to *Seathwaite Tarn*, and thence to the top of the *Old Man* (see above). It is, however, better to follow the Duddon to a point nearly opposite the head of Seathwaite Tarn, and then make for the tarn ($^1/_4$ M.) straight across country. From the head of the Duddon valley the *Wrynose Pass* (1270 ft.) leads past the 'Three Shire Stones', where Lancashire, Cumberland, and Westmorland meet, into *Little Langdale* (p. 386).

From Coniston to Dungeon Gill viâ Tilberthwaite and Fell Foot, 8 M. (rough road, barely passable for carriages). The road diverges to the left (N.) from the Bowness road near the Crown Hotel, and ascends through *Yewdale*, skirting the foot of *Yewdale Crag* (1050 ft.). At the ($1^1/_2$ M.) fork we ascend to the left through *Tilberthwaite Glen* and skirt the beck. To the right are the richly-tinted rocks of *Holme Fell* and *Raven Crag*. About 1 M. farther on we cross the beck. [To the left here opens **Tilberthwaite Gill*, a most romantic little gorge, which the path ascends by bridges, steps, and ladders. At the upper end is a pretty waterfall.] Beyond ($^1/_4$ M.) *High Tilberthwaite Farm* our track leads through the gate to the left (the right gate leading to *Smithy Houses*, p. 386). It first ascends past some slate-quarries, and then descends, keeping to the left, to the farm of ($1^1/_2$ M.) *Fell Foot*, which is surrounded by yew-trees. Ill Bell, Fairfield, Helvellyn, and the Langdale Pikes come into sight as we proceed. To the E. of Fell Foot lies the *Little Langdale Tarn* (340 ft.)

and to the W. rises the *Pike o' Blisco* (2304 ft.). The road to the *Wrynose Pass* (see p. 382) is seen ascending to the left. Just on this side of Fell Foot we cross the *Brathay* and turn to the right. After a few hundred yards we turn to the left, and follow the slope of *Lingmoor Fell*. We are now on the classic ground of Wordsworth's 'Excursion'. To the left is *Blea Tarn* (612 ft.), with the Solitary's cottage, while to the right the *Langdale Pikes* suddenly come into sight. About 1/2 M. beyond the tarn we reach the top of the pass (700 ft.) and begin the steep descent into *Great Langdale* (*View). We pass the *Wall End Farm*, and soon see the *Old Dungeon Gill Hotel*, at the base of the Langdale Pikes. The *New Dungeon Gill Hotel* is at *Millbeck*, 1 M. lower down, near the fall (comp. p. 386). The route hence to *Grasmere* is described at p. 387.

From Coniston to Ambleside, see route described in the reverse direction at p. 385. Coniston may also be made the starting-point for the combination circular tour there mentioned. — Those who wish to return from Coniston to Bowness may vary the above route by following the Ambleside road to (7 1/2 M.) *Waterhead* (p. 380), and going on thence by steamer. — Coniston is within easy reach by railway of *Furness Abbey* (p. 377).

From Windermere (and Bowness) to Ambleside, Grasmere, and Keswick, 21 M., coach several times daily in summer in 4 hrs. (fare 6*s*. 6*d*.; to Ambleside 1*s*. 6*d*., to Grasmere 3*s*.). This fine drive takes the traveller through the heart of the Lake District. It is, however, needless to say that all who can spare the time should stop at various points *en route*. The distances are calculated from Windermere station, whence the coach starts; from Bowness (p. 379) add 1 1/2 M.

From the station the road leads to the N.W., passing the grounds of *Elleray* (p. 379) on the right, and beyond the (3/4 M.) cross-roads (to Bowness on the left and Patterdale on the right) descends through trees to (1/2 M.) *Troutbeck Bridge* (Sun Inn). To the left are *Calgarth Hall* and *Park*. At (3 M.) *Low Wood Hotel* (p. 380) we reach the shore of the lake, which the road skirts to (1 M.) *Waterhead* (p. 380), passing below *Dove Nest* (p. 380; to the right). We now ascend the valley of the *Rothay* (to the left a road leading to Rothay Bridge) to (3/4 M.) *Ambleside* (p. 385).

Quitting Ambleside, we pass, on the left, the ivy-clad *Knoll*, the former residence of Harriet Martineau, and, across the Rothay, at the foot of Loughrigg Fell, *Fox Howe*, the home of Dr. Arnold. To the right opens the small valley of the *Scandale Beck*, and on the same side is the richly-wooded park of *Rydal Hall*. 1 1/4 M. **Rydal**, a small village near the E. end of *Rydal Water* (180 ft.), a pretty little lake, 3/4 M. long and 1/4 M. wide.

To reach *Rydal Mount*, the home of Wordsworth from 1817 till his death in 1850, we ascend the steep road to the right for 170 yds. A glimpse of the house, on a small hill behind the church, almost hidden by the trees, is got from the coach. It contains no relics of the poet and is not shown.

The pretty little *Falls of the Rydal* are within the grounds of *Rydal Hall*, the seat of the Le Flemings, and a guide must be obtained at a cottage below the church, to the left. The two falls are about 1/2 M. apart, and the upper one is about 3/4 M. from the high-road.

Walkers to Grasmere may leave the high-road at Rydal, take the first turning to the left beyond Rydal Mount, and follow a path along the W. slope of *Nab Scar* (views), which joins a narrow road at *White Moss* and reaches the high-road just beyond the Prince of Wales Hotel (see p. 384).

The coach-road † now skirts the N. bank of Rydal Water, passing *Nab Cottage*, where Hartley Coleridge (d. 1849) lived for many years. Silver Howe and Serjeant Man rise in front. Beyond Rydal Water the road turns sharply round a wooded knoll, and discloses a lovely *View of Grasmere lake and vale. The fells in front (left to right) are Helm Crag, Steel Fell, Seat Sandal, and Great Rigg. The coach skirts the lake for 1/2 M., and at the Prince of Wales Hotel turns to the left. (Walkers who do not call at the village may save 1/4 M. by keeping to the right here, rejoining the coach-road at the Swan Hotel.) — 9 M. (from Windermere) *Grasmere*, see p. 387.

About 1/2 M. beyond the village of Grasmere we pass the Swan Hotel, a little to the right, and soon begin the long ascent to the (3 M.) top of the *Dunmail Raise Pass* (780 ft.), between *Steel Fell* (1811 ft.) on the left and *Seat Sandal* (2415 ft.) on the right. The scenery becomes wilder. To the left we have a good view of *Helm Crag* (p. 387). The wall at the top of the pass is the boundary between Cumberland and Westmorland, and the small cairn is said to mark the grave of Dunmail, last king of Cumbria. We now obtain a view of Thirlmere, with Helvellyn to the right and Skiddaw in the distance. About 1 1/4 M. below the pass, and 1 M. from the S. end of Thirlmere, we reach *Wythburn* (Inn).

Thirlmere (533 ft.) is nearly 3 M. long, and nowhere more than 1/3 M. wide. Near the middle it contracts to a breadth of a few yards and is spanned by a small wooden bridge. Its greatest depth is 108 ft. In spite of strong opposition, a bill has passed through Parliament, allowing Manchester to supply itself with water from Thirlmere, and the requisite works have marred the beauty of the lovely mere. The W. side, opposite Helvellyn, is bordered with picturesque woods and crags.

The W. side is the preferable route for pedestrians, who may leave the road by a lane to the left, at the Wythburn Inn, and follow the cart-track, which rejoins the main road, 1/2 M. below the foot of the lake.

The road skirts the E. bank of the lake, at the base of Helvellyn, for about 1 M. It then ascends to the right and soon commands a fine view of the Vale of St. John, with Saddleback (or Blencathara) in the background. The wooded knoll to the left is *Great How* (1090 ft.). We pass (1 M.) the little King's Head Inn, at *Thirlspot;* 3/4 M. farther on, the road down the Vale of St. John diverges to the left. The Castle Rock of St. John, celebrated by Scott in 'The Bridal of Triermain', now rises on the right (1000 ft.). For the next 3 M. the scenery is less interesting, but when we reach the top of the ridge called *Castle Rigg*, we are repaid by a charming *View of the vale of Keswick, with the lakes of Derwentwater and Bassen-

---

† Dr. Arnold called the highest of the three roads between Rydal and Grasmere, 'Old Corruption'; the middle one, 'Bit-by-bit Reform'; and the lowest and most level, 'Radical Reform'.

thwaite. Skiddaw and Blencathara rise in front; to the W. are the fells round Newlands (p. 396) and Buttermere (p. 395). We have still a descent of about 1 M. to reach *Keswick* (see p. 392).

Foot-passengers may leave this route at *Armboth*, halfway down hde W. bank of Thirlmere, close to the little bridge (see p. 384), and procete to the W. by a bridle-path across the *Armboth Fell* (1588 ft.) to (1¼ hr.(*Watendlath*, 5 M. from Keswick (comp. p. 393).

Ambleside *(*Salutation; *Queen's; *White Lion; Waterhead Hotel*, on the lake, ¾ M. from the town; *Lodgings)*, a small town with about 2000 inhab., is beautifully situated in the valley of the *Rothay*, at the foot of *Wansfell Pike*, and ¾ M. from the head of Windermere. It is supposed to have been a Roman station, and fragments of tesselated pavements and other remains have been found in the neighbourhood. It is perhaps the best headquarters for excursions in the S. part of the Lake District, and has abundant omnibus and coach communication with Waterhead (p. 380), Grasmere, Windermere railway-station, Coniston, Keswick, and Patterdale. The *Church of St. Mary*, built by Sir G. G. Scott, contains a stained-glass window to the memory of Wordsworth.

Excursions from Ambleside. From the Salutation Hotel a road and path ascend by the stream to (½ M.) **Stock Gill Force*, a romantic little fall about 70 ft. high, with picturesque surroundings (adm. 3*d*.). — To the (2 M.) *Rydal Falls*, see p. 383. — A pleasant walk in the prettily-wooded valley of the *Rothay* may be taken by crossing the river near the church and ascending on the right bank, past *Fox Howe* (p. 383), to (1¾ M.) *Pelter Bridge*. Then back by the high-road (1 M.). — Another excellent view of Windermere is obtained from **Jenkin's Crag*, 1½ M. to the S. — Other short walks may be taken to *Skelwith Force* (p. 386), *Colwith Force* (p. 386), **Loughrigg Terrace* (see below), *Troutbeck* (p. 389), etc.

Ascents. The ascent of *Wansfell Pike* (1597 ft.), rising to the E. of Ambleside, takes ¾-1 hr. The best route is viâ Stock Gill Force, beyond which we bend to the right and follow the general direction of a wall running up the hill. The top affords a charming view of Windermere, Grasmere, and Rydal, with numerous mountains in the distance. The descent may be made on the S.E. to *Troutbeck* (p. 389) in 1½ hr., whence we return viâ (2 M.) Low Wood (p. 380) to (2 M.) Ambleside. — **Loughrigg Fell* (1100 ft.) may be ascended by several routes, and its long uneven top affords a variety of views. The easiest route (about 1 hr.) is by the path ascending from *Clappersgate* (p. 385), 1 M. to the S.W.; the shortest ascends from the bridge near St. Mary's Church (see above). — The *Fox Gill* ascent begins behind Fox Howe (see above). The descent (steep) may be made by Loughrigg Terrace and Red Bank to Grasmere (p. 387). — The top of *Nab Scar*, the southernmost spur of Fairfield, may be reached from Ambleside viâ Rydal in 1-1½ hr. We follow the road past Rydal Mount as far as it goes, and ascend a green slope between two walls. — *Fairfield* (2863 ft.) itself may be reached by following the ridge to the N. from Nab Scar (2-3 hrs. from Ambleside; fine views), but the usual ascent is by the bridle-path ascending from the Swan Inn near Grasmere (p. 384). — Ascent of the *Langdale Pikes*, see p. 386.

From Ambleside to Coniston by Barn Gates and back by Oxenfell (to Coniston 7½ M., back 8 M.). This round is made daily in summer by chars-a-banc (fare 5*s*.). Circular tour tickets are also issued at Ambleside for Coniston, Furness Abbey (train), Lake Side (train), Waterhead (steamer), and back to Ambleside by omnibus (fares 8*s*. 9*d*., 6*s*. 6*d*., 5*s*. 6*d*.; tickets available for a week). — The road leads to the S.W., crosses (½ M.) *Rothay Bridge*, and skirts the S. slopes of *Loughrigg Fell*. At (½ M.) the village of *Clappersgate* we diverge to the left from the road to the Langdales (see p. 386) and cross *Brathay Bridge*. We then traverse a well-wooded district at the head of *Pull Wyke Bay* (to the left, *Brathay Hall*), diverge to the right from the Hawkshead road, and ascend to (2 M.) *Barn Gates Inn*, where we obtain a good mountain view. At (2 M.) *High Cross* we join the route from Bowness, described at p. 380. $2^1/_2$ M. *Coniston*, see p. 381. — On the return-route we strike to the N. through *Yewdale*, turn to the right after $1^1/_2$ M., and ascend past *High Yewdale Farm*. The patriarchal yew for which the dale is celebrated is in a field to the left, near a group of cottages, $^1/_4$ M. beyond the farm. About this point the road turns to the left and ascends on the slope of *Oxenfell* to ($2^1/_2$ M.) the top of the pass (500 ft.; view). Farther on ($^3/_4$ M.) a road diverges on the left to *Colwith Force* (see below). To the left is *Elterwater Tarn*, near which is a small cottage-factory (St. Martin's), where Mr. Albert Fleming has resuscitated the old Lakeside industries of spinning and hand-loom weaving. Our road descends to the right to (1 M.) *Skelwith Bridge*, over the Brathay, which forms the small fall of *Skelwith Force* 300 yds. farther up. We then skirt the base of Loughrigg Fell to (2 M.) *Brathay Bridge* (see p. 385).

Tour of the Langdales, $19^1/_2$ M., coach daily in summer in 6 hrs. (fare 4*s*.). From Ambleside to (3 M.) *Skelwith Bridge*, see above. About 1 M. farther on we diverge to the right from the road to Coniston and descend to *Colwith Bridge*, just beyond which the road forks. [We may here stop to visit *Colwith Force*, a cascade in the pretty little valley to the right (key kept at a cottage by the fork; 3*d*.).] Our road ascends to the left, a little above the fall, through the vale of **Little Langdale**, which is separated from Great Langdale by *Lingmoor Fell* (to the right). Beyond the (1 M.) hamlet of *Smithy Houses* we pass *Little Langdale Tarn* (340 ft.) and a little farther on, near *Fell Foot*, join the route described at p. 383.

The coach stops at the *Old Dungeon Gill Hotel* (p. 383) for luncheon, and ample time is allowed for a visit to **Dungeon Gill Force*, romantically situated in a narrow gorge, hemmed in by vertical walls of rock and making a perpendicular descent of about 70 ft. Above the fall is a curious natural bridge formed by two rocks firmly wedged between the sides of the ravine. The fall is about the same distance ($^1/_2$ M.) from each hotel; those who have come from the Old Hotel may descend the hill to the New Hotel and there rejoin the coach.

[Dungeon Gill is the best starting-point for an ascent of the **Langdale Pikes** (*Harrison Stickle* 2400 ft.; *Pike o' Stickle* 2323 ft.), which takes $1^1/_2$-2 hrs. (pony and guide 10*s*.). We ascend in windings near the Dungeon Gill beck (with the stream to the right). As we approach the final part of the ascent the Pike o' Stickle rises to the left and the Harrison Stickle to the right, but to reach the latter we have to make a detour to the left round a spur. The view from the top is somewhat circumscribed, but commands Langdale and Windermere. The descent may be made by *Stickle Tarn* (1540 ft.), below Harrison Stickle. The route, which is unmistakable, passes between the *Pavey Ark Rocks* on the N. bank of the tarn, and then descends along the beck. — *Grasmere* may be reached in 2-$2^1/_2$ hrs. by keeping to the N. from Stickle Tarn and climbing the ridge in front, until a point is reached from which we look down upon Grasmere. In descending we keep to the right of *Codale Tarn* and *Easdale Tarn*. From the Pike o' Stickle we may descend on the N.W. to the *Stake Pass* (p. 396) and *Borrowdale* (see p. 394). — **Bowfell** (2960 ft.; *View) may be ascended from Old Dungeon Gill Hotel in 2-$2^1/_4$ hrs., viâ *Stool End Farm* and the shoulder called the *Band*.]

From Dungeon Gill our road runs to the E. through the green valley of **Great Langdale**, affording a fine retrospect of the Langdale Pikes. About 2 M. beyond Millbeck we reach *Langdale Church* and the village of *Chapel Stile*, on the fells near which are numerous slate-quarries. Here the road forks, and walkers who wish to return direct to (5 M.) Ambleside follow the branch to the right, passing *Elterwater* and *Loughrigg Tarn*. [A hill may be avoided by following the field-path leading from the Britannia Inn in the village of Elterwater along the N. bank of the *Elter Water* and rejoining the road at Skelwith Bridge.] The coach ascends the road to the left and soon reaches the top of the saddle between Silver

How and Loughrigg Fell, where we have a good retrospect of the Langdale Pikes, Bowfell, and other summits. As we descend, a fine *View of Grasmere is disclosed. To enjoy this to the full we diverge to the right a little farther on, pass through a gate marked 'private', and follow the drive to the so-called *Red Bank*, a bare spot on the N. side of Loughrigg Fell. We return by another 'private' drive (to the right), which brings us out on the road, 1¼ M. from the village of Grasmere. The road leads round the S.W. side of the lake. *Grasmere*, see below. From Grasmere to (4 M.) *Ambleside*, see pp. 383, 384.

Other excursions may be made from Ambleside to (8½ M.) *Patterdale* (coach daily, joining the route from Windermere at the Kirkstone Pass, reached from Ambleside by a steep ascent of 3 M. through the valley of the *Stock Gill Beck;* comp. p. 389); to *Wasdale Head* (p. 400), either by the *Wrynose Pass*, *Eskdale*, *Boot*, and *Burnmoor Tarn* (23¼ M.), or by *Dungeon Gill* (7½ M.) and by bridle-path over *Esk Hause* (2370 ft.; 3-3½ hrs.; comp. p. 398); and to *Keswick* viâ *Great Langdale* and the *Stake Pass* (road to Dungeon Gill 7½ M.; bridle-path over the pass 3-3½ hrs.; road from Rosthwaite to Keswick 6½ M.).

The village of **Grasmere** (**Prince of Wales*, on the lake, ½ M. from the village, R. & A. 4*s*., D. 4*s*. 6*d*.; **Rothay*, *Red Lion*, in the village; *Swan*, ½ M. to the N.; *Lodgings*) is charmingly situated near the N. end of the lake of the same name, a little to the W. of the main road from Ambleside to Keswick. Wordsworth (d. 1850) resided here for eight years, and is buried in the churchyard (comp. p. 383). Almost every point in the neighbourhood is celebrated in his poetry.

'Keep fresh the grass upon his grave,
'O Rotha, with thy living wave;
'Sing him thy best, for few or none
'Hear thy voice right, now he is gone' (*Matt. Arnold*).

***Grasmere** (208 ft.) is about 1 M. long and nearly ½ M. broad in the middle; its greatest depth is 180 ft. There is a solitary green island in the centre. Ferry near the Prince of Wales Hotel.

Helm Crag (1300 ft.; 1 hr.), rising to the N. of Grasmere, is a good point of view. We follow the Easdale road (see below) to a point about ⅓ M. beyond the slab-bridge, diverge to the right between two houses, pass through a gate to the right, and ascend by a wall. When the wall begins to descend we keep to the left. At the top are some curious crags, supposed to resemble, when seen from below, a lion and lamb, an 'Ancient Woman cowering beside her rifted cell', the 'astrologer, sage Sidrophel', etc. — The charming *View from (1½ M.) *Red Bank* has been mentioned above. We may return by the N. side of Grasmere (2½ M.), crossing the *Rothay* between Grasmere and Rydal lakes, or we may extend our walk to include a circuit of Rydal Water (6 M. in all). From Red Bank we may also ascend to the top of *Loughrigg Fell* (p. 385) in about ½ hr. — Perhaps the best short walk from Grasmere is that to (2½ M.) **Easdale Tarn.** There is a bridle-path all the way, and driving is practicable for 1¼ M. The route leads to the N.W., following the general course of the *Easdale Beck*. The turns to the right are to be avoided. About ⅓ M. from the village the road crosses the stream by a bridge, and a little farther on, walkers cross it again by a slab-bridge and ascend by its right bank. As we approach the tarn we pass *Sour Milk Force*, the milky water of which is conspicuous. Fine retrospect of Grasmere. The tarn lies in a secluded valley, 915 ft. above the sea and 700 ft. above Grasmere. The walk may be prolonged to *Dungeon Gill* (1½-2 hrs.) or to the *Langdale Pikes* (2-3 hrs.; comp. p. 386). The return to Grasmere may be varied by ascending *Silver How* (1345 ft.), which rises to the S. (see Map).

Ascent of Helvellyn (2¾-3½ hrs.; pony and guide 15*s*., both unnecessary for practised climbers). We follow the high-road to Keswick (see p. 384) for 1¼ M., to a bridge ¾ M. beyond the Swan Hotel. Here we pass through a gate on the right and ascend the rough track to the left of the stream. To the right is the charming little fall of ***Tongue Gill Force***, to which a digression should be made. Our track keeps to the left and can scarcely be missed, though some climbers have made the mistake of taking *Seat Sandal* (2415 ft.; to the left) for Helvellyn. Fine retrospects of Grasmere as we ascend. In about 1¾ hr. we reach the top of the *Grisedale Pass* (1930 ft.), between Seat Sandal and *Fairfield* (2863 ft.), where we pass through a gap in the wall. To the left lies *Grisedale Tarn* (1768 ft.). We now descend to the (12 min.) tarn, cross the stream issuing from it, and ascend by the steep zigzag track to the left to *Dollywaggon Pike* (2810 ft.), the S. and lowest extremity of the Helvellyn ridge. The ascent hence to the summit, reached in about 1-1¼ hr. from Grisedale Tarn, is comparatively easy. The *View from **Helvellyn** (3118 ft.; perhaps from 'El Velin', the hill of Veli or Baal), the second in height but most impressive in form of the Lake Mts., is very extensive, including all the main summits of the Lake District and the lakes of Windermere, Coniston, Esthwaite, and Ullswater. (Thirlmere is not visible from the highest point.) Immediately at our feet, on the E., is the *Red Tarn* (2356 ft.), between two spurs of Helvellyn, *Catchedicam* on the left and *Striding Edge* (2500 ft.) on the right. The Solway Firth and the hills of Dumfriesshire bound the view to the N., while the sea is the limit to the S. We may descend either to Grasmere, *Wythburn* (see p. 384), *Thirlspot* (see p. 384), or *Patterdale* (p. 391). The Wythburn path diverges to the right from the Grasmere route about 10 min. below the top. — Grasmere is also the starting-point for the easiest ascent of **Fairfield** (2863 ft.; 1½-2 hrs.). We turn to the right near the Swan Hotel and ascend by a well-marked bridle-path. Or we may diverge from the Helvellyn route near the top of Grisedale Pass (see above) and make straight for the summit.

From Grasmere to Patterdale (Ullswater) by the Grisedale Pass (8 M., in 3-4 hrs.; an easy and delightful excursion). From Grasmere to the (1½-2 hrs.) head of the **Grisedale Pass** (1930 ft.), see above. The descent beyond the tarn is steep at first. To the left towers Helvellyn, to the right *St. Sunday's Crag* (2756 ft.). Ullswater is generally hidden. Good walkers may ascend to the saddle between Fairfield and St. Sunday's Crag, and follow the ridge all the way to Patterdale (fine views). Beyond a shed, reached ½ hr. after leaving the tarn, we cross a small beck and keep to the left of the main stream. In ¼ hr. we pass through a gate and cross to the other side. From (10 min.) the farm of *Elm How* a good road leads to (1½ M.) *Patterdale* (see p. 390).

From Grasmere to Borrowdale viâ Easdale (to Rosthwaite 3-4 hrs.). We leave Grasmere by the Easdale Tarn route, follow the road for about ⅓ M. past the slab-bridge (p. 387), pass between the two houses (as on the ascent of Helm Crag, p. 387), and then follow the bridle-path to the left, which ascends *Far Easdale Gill*. About 1 M. from the point where we left the road we cross the beck at the *Stythwaite Steps*. The track ceases about 1 M. farther on, but we follow the course of the stream, and soon reach the (1 M.) head of the Easdale Valley. Beyond this we cross a depression (to the right the *Wythburn Valley*) and ascend again in the same general direction to (1 M.) *Greenup Edge* (2000 ft.), the highest part of the route, between *High Raise* (2500 ft.) on the left and *Ullscarf* (2370 ft.) on the right (*View). In descending we keep to the right, the direction being roughly indicated by heaps of stones. Lower down, the path reappears and descends on the right bank of the stream (view of Borrowdale). At the hamlet of *Stonethwaite*, about 2 M. below the top, we cross the stream by a stone bridge, and ½ M. farther on join the main Borrowdale road, ½ M. above *Rosthwaite* (p. 395). From Rosthwaite to (6½ M.) *Keswick*, see p. 395. — Walkers may also reach Keswick from Grasmere viâ *Dunmail Raise* (or *Armboth Fell*) and *Watendlath* (comp. p. 385).

From Windermere to Patterdale (Ullswater), 12½ M., coach daily in 1¾-2 hrs. (fare 5*s.*, return 7*s.* 6*d.*). Circular tour tickets, available for a week, are issued from Windermere to Keswick viâ Patterdale (coach, steamer, and train; fares 16*s.* 3*d.*, 14*s.* 3*d.*, 13*s.* 6*d.*). Our road diverges to the right from that to Ambleside, at a point 3/4 M. from Windermere station (p. 378), and ascends on the left side of the Troutbeck valley.

Another road leaves the Ambleside road at Troutbeck bridge, 3/4 M. farther, and ascends on the right bank of the beck; it is this road that passes through the long and picturesque village of **Troutbeck** and past the '*Mortal Man Inn*'. The two roads unite at the N. end of the village.

Our road soon quits the woods and commands charming views of Windermere. From (2 1/4 M.) *Troutbeck Church* a road leads to the left to the village of *Troutbeck* (see above), and 3/4 M. farther on our road unites with that leading through Troutbeck (see above). We now ascend steeply along the E. slope of *Wansfell* (p. 385) to the top of the **Kirkstone Pass** (1500 ft.), between *Red Screes* (2540 ft.) on the left and *Caudale Moor* (2500 ft.) on the right. About 200 yds. below the col we pass the *Traveller's Rest*, a small inn, which is sometimes wrongly described as the highest inhabited house in England (comp. p. 371). About as far on the other side of the col, to the left, is the stone that gives name to the pass; it is supposed to look like a 'kirk' from a point about halfway down. Brothers' Water comes into sight in front, with Place Fell, rising above Ullswater, in the distance. 2 1/2 M. *Brothers' Water Inn.* 1/2 M. *Brothers' Water* (520 ft.), 1/3 M. square, said to derive its name from the drowning of two brothers. Below Brothers' Water the road crosses the outlet of *Hayes Water*, turns to the left, and crosses (1/2 M.) the *Goldrill Beck.* We now descend through *Patterdale*, passing the mouth of *Deepdale*, between Fairfield and St. Sunday's Crag, on the left, and soon reach the hamlet of (1 3/4 M.) *Patterdale* (p. 390). *Ullswater Hotel* (p. 390) is about 1 M. farther on.

b. Ullswater Section.

Travellers who enter the Lake District on the Ullswater side leave the railway at *Penrith* (p. 374), whence several Coaches (fare 2*s.*) ply daily in summer to *Pooley Bridge* (5 1/2 M.; 1 hr.), situated at the lower end of the lake. The road leads to the S.W. and crosses (1 M.) *Eamont Bridge* (small inn with two old inscriptions). A little to the E. (left) are *Brougham Hall* and *Castle* (p. 374). A little farther on we diverge to the right from the road to Kendal and pass between *Mayburgh* (right) and *King Arthur's Round Table* (left), two circular enclosures of unknown origin (see Scott's 'Bridal of Triermain'). At (1 M.) *Yanwath* the road crosses the L. N.W. Railway. Farther on it passes (1 M.) *Tirril* and the old parish-church of *Barton.*

Walkers may turn to the S. at the station, without entering the town, and follow the left (W.) bank of the *Eamont.* The route passes (3 M.) *Dalemain Hall* and crosses *Dunmallet Hill* (view).

Pooley Bridge (*Sun) is a small village situated at the lower end of ***Ullswater** (477 ft.; 'Ulf's water'), the second in size of English lakes, measuring 9 M. in length and 1/4-3/4 M. in breadth.

Its greatest depth is 210 ft.. The scenery of the lake, which some prefer to that of Derwentwater and Windermere, increases in picturesqueness and grandeur as we approach the head. No general view of the lake is obtainable, as its bendings divide it into three reaches, each of which from some points seems a complete lake in itself. There is a good road along the whole of the W. side of the lake, but on the more precipitous E. bank the road stops at the entrance of Boredale (see p. 391). Boats may be hired at the hotels to fish in the lake; boat and man 5*s.* per day.

The small **Steamer** which plies on the lake (fares 2*s.*, 1*s.* 6*d.*; return 3*s.*, 2*s.*), taking 1 hr. to reach the upper end, starts from a small pier, 1/4 M. from Pooley Bridge. The scenery of the first reach, 3 M. in length, is rather tame. At the foot of the lake rises the wooded hill of *Dunmallet.* To the right is the *Brackenrigg Hotel*, 1 3/4 M. from Pooley Bridge. *Howtown* (p. 391), the only intermediate station, lies in a bay to the left. Opposite is the point of *Skelly Nab.* The middle reach, 4 M. long, extends to the islet of *House Holme.* To the left rise *Hallin Fell* (1270 ft.) and *Brick Fell* (1670 ft.), with *Boredale* and the hamlet of *Sandwick* between them. To the right are *Gowbarrow Fell* (1580 ft.), the finely-wooded *Gowbarrow Park* (forever associated with Wordsworth's 'Daffodils'), and *Lyulph's Tower* (see below). In front of us rises the stately Helvellyn. We now turn to the left into the upper reach, 2 M. long, which contains a few islets. The *View here is very grand. To the left *Place Fell* (2154 ft.) descends abruptly into the lake; opposite is the wood-clad *Stybarrow Crag.* At the head of the lake lies *Patterdale*, at the foot of *St. Sunday's Crag* (2756 ft.) The steamboat-pier is near the Ullswater Hotel, about 1/2 M. from the head of the lake.

Patterdale (*Patterdale Hotel*, well spoken of; *White Lion*, unpretending; *Lodgings)* is a small village, delightfully situated at the foot of the valley of that name and close to the head of Ullswater. It is a favourite centre for excursions in the N.E. part of the Lake District. About 1 M. to the N., on the E. bank of the lake, near the steamboat-pier, is the large **Ullswater Hotel* (table d'hôte 4*s*, R. & A. 4*s.*), with pleasant grounds. Near it is a *Temperance Hotel.* On the hillside above the Ullswater Hotel are the *Greenside Lead Mines*, which send a stream of polluted water into the lake.

The favourite short excursion from Patterdale is that to Aira Force (4 M.), which may be made either by land or by water. In the former case we follow the prettily-wooded road along the W. bank of the lake, passing (3 1/2 M.) the road to Troutbeck station (p. 397), to the beck just beyond it. We cross the beck and ascend by the path to the left to (1/2 M.) the fall. To the right is *Lyulph's Tower*, a square ivy-clad building, the name of which, like that of the lake itself, is said to commemorate a Baron de L'Ulf of Greystoke. A guide may be obtained here (unnecessary). For the water-route, which affords better views, small boats may be obtained either at the Patterdale or the Ullswater Hotel. The fall of ***Aira Force**, 70 ft. high, is very romantically situated in a rocky chasm with wooded sides. Two rustic bridges cross the stream above and below the fall and afford convenient points of view. The scenery of the glen above the fall is also picturesque, and another pretty little fall is formed higher up. A path leads along the left bank of the stream through Gowbarrow Park to (1 M.) *Dockray* (p. 397), but the gates are generally locked (comp p. 397). — The following is a fine round of 10-12 M. (4 hrs.) from Patterdale. We take the lane leading to the E. from the church and follow the track along the E. bank of the lake. (Visitors at the Ullswater Hotel may save 2 M. by ferrying across to *Bleawick.*) The higher of the two paths on the slope of *Place Fell* commands charming views of dale and fell. After 1 1/2 M. the path descends to the shore and rejoins the lower path, and after 1 M. more it turns to the right, away from the lake, and leads round a plantation. At (1 M.) *Sandwick*, a hamlet at the entrance to Martindale (view of High Street in the background), a road diverges to the right. Our path leads straight on through wood and along the base of *Hallin Fell* (1270 ft.), follows the line of the shore, bends to the right 1 M. farther on, and after 1/2 M. more joins the road about 1/4 M. short of **Howtown** (**Hotel*). From Howtown we at first follow the road, which ascends past the church and the hamlet of *Cowgarth*, to the (1 M.) saddle between Hallin Fell on the right and *Steel Knotts* (1190 ft.) on the left. It then descends, crosses a beck, and turns to the right towards Sandwick (see above). About 200-300 yds. from the bridge, however, we turn to the left and follow the road leading through **Boredale**. The road crosses (3/4 M.) the stream, and ends at the farm-house at (1 M.) *Boredale Head*. From this point we ascend by a steep bridle-path to (1¼ M.) *Boredale Hause* (1200 ft.; view). The descent on the other side to (3/4 M.) Patterdale is short and steep.

From Patterdale to Hawes Water. The easiest route is to take the steamer to *Howtown*, the land-journey to which has been described above, and ascend thence (2½-3 hrs.). Those who wish to drive must start from Pooley Bridge (to Mardale Green 15 M.). At Howtown we pass through a gate at the back of the hotel and ascend to the S. through the glen of *Fusedale*, at first on the left and then on the right bank of the beck. In about 1/2 hr. we bend to the left, up the fell, and soon cross a little stream (no path). Blencathara now appears in our rear and Helvellyn to the right, while High Street is visible to the S. On reaching the (1/2 hr.) top of the ridge (*Weather Hill*, 2174 ft.) we have a fine mountain view to the S. and W. In descending we bear to the left and cross the (3/4 M.) *Measand Beck* by a foot-bridge we saw from above. In 10 min. more we reach the road on the bank of the lake, which leads to the W. (right) to (2¼ M.) *Mardale Green* (see below). — The direct route from Patterdale to Hawes Water leads by Kidsty Pike (4-5 hrs.). We follow the Windermere road for about 2 M., and at the point where it turns to the right, just below Brothers' Water (see p. 389), we keep straight on through the hamlet of *Low Hartsop*. About 1/2 M. farther up our road (a cart-track) crosses the Hayes Water Beck, recrossing it in 1/2 M. more, and passing near the foot of *Hayes Water* (1343 ft.). We then ascend in zigzags to the (3/4-1 hr.) top of the ridge. From this point we may diverge to the right and ascend to the top of *High Street* (2663 ft.), which commands an extensive view. [The name of High Street is derived from an old Roman road that ran near the top of the ridge; some traces of it may be discerned near the summit of High Street.] *Kidsty Pike* (2560 ft.) rises in front, to the left. The direct route for Mardale Green keeps straight on through a gate in the wall at the top of the ridge, whence we have a steep and somewhat rough descent of about 1 hr.

Hawes Water (694 ft.), 2½ M. long and 1/3 M. wide, is a solitary little lake, embosomed among lofty mountains. Fair quarters may be obtained in the *Dun Bull Inn* at *Mardale Green*, 1 M. from the head of the lake. The lower end of the lake is 5½ M. from *Shap* (p. 374) by footpath and 7½ M. by road viâ *Bampton*. Good walkers may also go on to *Windermere* (12½ M.; 4½-5½ hrs.) by the *Nan Bield Pass* (2050 ft.), *Kentmere*, and the *Garbourn Pass* (1450 ft.; fine views in descending). Or they may ascend *High Street* (1½-2 hrs.; see above) and descend by the Troutbeck glen to *Windermere* (3-3½ hrs.).

Mountain Ascents from Patterdale. The ascent of **Place Fell** (2154 ft.; view) takes about 1-1½ hr. We ascend nearly to the top of *Boredale Hause* (see above), and then diverge to the left and climb the ridge. The descent may be made to the road through *Boredale* (see above). — To reach the top of **St. Sunday's Crag** (2756 ft.; 1½ hr.) we leave Patterdale by the bridle-path through *Grisedale* (comp. p. 388), and beyond (1½ M.) the farm of *Elm How* turn to the left and ascend a zigzag green path, on the right bank of a beck, to the (1/2 hr.) top of the ridge, where we turn to the right towards the (1/2 hr.) summit. The top commands a good view of Ullswater and Helvellyn. The descent may be made along the ridge and straight down to Patterdale. — **Helvellyn** (3118 ft.; p. 388) may be ascended either viâ *Glenridding* (3-4 hrs.) or by *Red Tarn* (2-2½ hrs.), the latter being the shorter but steeper route (pony and guide 12*s.*; on the second route the ponies must be left at the tarn, ½ M. from the top). By the Glenridding route we leave the high-road opposite the Ullswater Hotel and ascend the cart-track to (1½ M.) *Greenside Smelting Mill.* Here we avoid the track to the right, and follow the bridle-path in a straight direction. Near *Keppelcove Tarn* (1825 ft.) the path ascends in zigzags to the right, afterwards bending to the left, and soon reaching the top of the ridge, where we turn to the left (path no longer distinct), and reach the summit in ½ hr. more. Walkers may shorten the distance a little by ascending to the left of Keppelcove Tarn. For the more interesting Red Tarn route we follow the Grisedale path (p. 388) for about ½ M. and turn to the right, crossing the beck, at a sign-post. The pony-track from this point to a gateway about 2 M. farther is well marked, and beyond the gateway we come in sight of the *Red Tarn* (2356 ft.), the highest sheet of water in the Lake District. We keep to the right of the tarn and climb steeply to the top of the *Swirrel Edge*, along which a narrow path leads to the summit. Mountaineers may diverge to the left at the gateway and ascend by *Striding Edge.* Descent to *Wythburn* or *Thirlspot*, see p. 388; to *Grasmere*, see p. 388. — A good and easy *Mountain Walk* (5 hrs.), commanding excellent views, is the round by *Hart Crag* (2700 ft.; to the S.), *Fairfield* (p. 388), and *St. Sunday's Crag* (p. 388).

From Patterdale to *Keswick*, see p. 397 (various routes; for walkers the best is over Helvellyn and down to Thirlspot, 5-6 hrs.; the easiest and quickest route is by Troutbeck); to *Windermere* (and *Ambleside*) by the *Kirkstone Pass*, see p. 389; to *Grasmere* by the *Grisedale Pass*, see p. 388.

c. Keswick and Derwentwater Section.

Keswick. — **Hotels.** *KESWICK HOTEL, at the station, ¼ M. from the town, a large establishment with 200 beds; *QUEEN'S, in the main street, R. & A. 3-4*s.*; ROYAL OAK, at the corner of the road to the station; LAKE HOTEL, with a view of the lake, well spoken of, R. & A. 3*s.* 6*d.*; KING'S ARMS; *SKIDDAW TEMPERANCE, unpretending. — At *Portinscale*, 1½ M. from the station: *DERWENTWATER HOTEL. — *Lodgings* may also be obtained.

Coaches run daily from Keswick to *Borrowdale* (6*d.*, return 1*s.*), *Grasmere* (4*s.* 6*d.*; return 7*s.* 6*d.*), *Ambleside* (5*s.*, 7*s.* 6*d.*), *Buttermere* (there and back 5*s.*), and *Windermere* (6*s.* 6*d.*, 10*s.* 3*d.*). No fees. — *Hotel Omnibuses* from the station to the town 6*d.*

Boats on Derwentwater 1*s.* per hour, 5*s.* per day; with boatman 2*s.* for the first hr. and 1*s.* 6*d.* for each addit. hr.; 10*s.* per day.

Fishing. The lake contains trout, perch, pike, and eels, and some of the rivers in the neighbourhood are good trout-streams. Angler's ticket for the district 1*s.* per day, 2*s.* 6*d.* per month, 5*s.* for the season.

Railway from Penrith or Cockermouth to Keswick, see p. 374.

Keswick, a small market-town with 3300 inhab., is situated on the S. bank of the *Greta*, close to Derwentwater Lake and amid much fine mountain-scenery, of which, however, scarcely a glimpse is seen from the town itself. The interesting little *Crosthwaite Church*, ½ M. from the centre of the town, beyond the bridge over the Greta, at the lower end of the main street, contains a monument to Southey (inscription by Wordsworth). On an eminence to the right, on this side the bridge, is *Greta Hall*, the home of Southey in 1803-43. Shelley also lived at Keswick for a time after his marriage.

Near Greta Hall are two *Lead Pencil Manufactories*, to which strangers are admitted. The process of pencil-making is interesting; but the famous Borrowdale plumbago is now scarce, and the quality of the pencils usually offered for sale is not of a high class. — There is an interesting *Model of the Lake District* (3 in. to the mile) in the town-hall (adm. 6*d.*), and one on a larger scale (6 in. to the mile) in Mayson's book-shop, on the way to the lake (adm. 6*d.*).

***Derwentwater** (238 ft.), a lake 3 M. long, 1 M. wide, and 70 ft. deep at the deepest points, is perhaps the loveliest of the English lakes. Its compact form enables it to be taken in at one view. The picturesque variety of the steep wooded crags and green hills rising from its bank, and the grouping of its wooded islets are very beautiful. The best views of the lake include a fine mountain-background, with Skiddaw towering to the N. and Borrowdale opening to the S. The largest islands are *Derwent Isle* (with a house on it), *Lord Isle*, and *St. Herbert's Isle*; on the last is the ruined cell of a hermit of the 7th century. The 'Floating Island', which appears at intervals on the surface of the lake, consists of a mass of weeds made buoyant by the escape of gas from decayed vegetable matter.

The lake may be surveyed from several admirable points of view near Keswick. Perhaps the best is ***Castle Head**, or *Castlet*, a small wooded height (530 ft.), 1/2 M. to the S. of the town, on the left side of the Borrowdale road (see below). We leave the road by a wicket-gate and follow a winding path to the summit, where we overlook the whole expanse of the lake. At the S. end is the fine entrance to Borrowdale, apparently blocked by the conical *Castle Crag*. To the right of Castle Crag, in the distance, are *Great End* and the *Scafell Pikes*. At the S.W. corner of Derwentwater itself rises *Maiden Moor*, sloping rapidly downwards (to the N.) to *Cat Bells*. Behind these we see parts of *Hindscarth* and *Robinson*, and a little to the right and still farther back, *High Stile*, *Red Pike*, and other fells enclosing Buttermere (p. 395). To the N. of the gap beyond Cat Bells rise *Causey Pike*, with its curious hump, and *Grisedale Pike*; then come the fells above *Bassenthwaite Lake*, which is itself seen at full length. To the N. is *Skiddaw*. The view to the E. is limited, but *Helvellyn* peeps over the high ground in front. The wooded heights on the E. side of the lake are *Wallow Crag* and *Falcon Crag*. — A closer view of the lake, resembling that from Castle Head, is obtained from the **Friar's Crag*, a small rocky promontory jutting into the lake, about 3/4 M. from the town. To reach it we diverge to the right from the Borrowdale road, opposite the Lake Hotel. — What Southey described as the best general view of Derwentwater is obtained near Applethwaite, about 2 M. to the N. of Keswick. We cross the Greta by the bridge mentioned above, turn to the right, cross the railway, and take the (3/4 M.) lane to the right. Beyond (1/2 M.) *Ormathwaite* the lane bends round to the left and soon reaches (1/2 M.) *Applethwaite*. The point of view praised by Southey is between Applethwaite and (3/4 M.) *Millbeck*.

Circuit of Derwentwater by Road (10 M.; carr. about 10*s.*). This is a charming walk or drive, affording a series of varied and beautiful views. The best plan is to begin with the E. bank and return on the other side. We leave Keswick by the street which branches to the right (S.E.) behind the town-hall, and pass the *Church of St. John* and (1/2 M.) *Castle Head* (see above). For the next mile or so the road passes through the thickets at the base of *Wallow Crag* (see above), which is succeeded by the picturesque *Falcon Crag*. At a point about 2 M. from Keswick the road to *Watendlath* (p. 395) diverges to the left. Just beyond this is the lodge of Barrow House, where we may apply for permission to visit the *Barrow Falls*. These falls, about 125 ft. in total height, are among the least attractive in the district, but a digression to them takes a few minutes only.

Almost immediately after leaving Barrow we see in front of us, 1 M. off, the *Lodore Hotel*, with the **Lodore Falls** in the gorge to the left. The falls (reached from the hotel in a few minutes) are romantically framed with tall wooded crags; but as there is usually more rock than water, Southey's jingling verses are responsible for a good deal of disappointment. Those who have time should make their way up the beck to the **High Lodore*, another fall about 1/2 M. farther up, not far from the Watendlath road (more easily reached by a path near the Borrowdale Hotel). About 1/2 M. beyond the Lodore Hotel is the **Borrowdale Hotel*, which is conveniently situated for excursions in Borrowdale, but does not command so good a view of Derwentwater. At the (3/4 M.) village of *Grange* we diverge to the right from the road through Borrowdale (see below) and cross the *Derwent*. We pass through the village, turn to the right, and ascend to (3/4 M.) the farm of *Manesty*. Just beyond this the grass-grown old road diverges to the left, and as it affords better views than the modern road the pedestrian should follow it. The ridge to the left commands a good view of Newlands (p. 396). A lead-mine is passed on the right. At the end of the *Cat Bells* ridge, about 1 3/4 M. from Manesty, the two roads unite. About 1/4 M. farther on, our road is joined on the left by another road descending from *Skelgill*, and we turn sharply to the right, passing through a gate. Nearly opposite this gate, to the right, is a wicket, from which a footpath leads through the woods to Portinscale, rejoining the road 1/2 M. before reaching the village. After 1/2 M., at a finger-post, our road unites with that coming from Buttermere (comp. p. 396). 1 1/4 M. *Portinscale* (*Derwentwater Hotel, see p. 392; Lodgings) is a small village, pleasantly situated near the lake. The distance from Portinscale to Keswick by road is 1 1/4 M., but about 1/2 M. is saved by a footpath diverging to the right beyond the bridge.

*From Keswick to Buttermere by Borrowdale and Honister Hause, returning by Newlands, a round of 22 M. Public conveyances make this round daily (fare 5*s.*, driver 1*s.*), starting about 10 a.m., allowing time to visit the principal objects of interest on the way, and for luncheon at Buttermere, and reaching Keswick again about 6 p.m. This is perhaps the finest drive in the kingdom and should on no account be omitted. — The route as far as (4 1/4 M.) the entrance of Borrowdale has been described above. Instead of crossing the bridge at Grange we go straight on, and soon reach a (1/2 M.) slate-quarry, where a road diverging to the left ascends to (5 min.) the *Bowder Stone*. This is a huge mass of rock, estimated to weigh about 2000 tons, which has fallen from the neighbouring crags and settled in a wonderfully-balanced poise. The top of the stone (reached by a ladder; fee to cottager) affords an admirable view of the beautiful valley of ***Borrowdale,** with the richly-tinted rocks at its entrance, the wooded *Castle*

Crag opposite, and *Glaramara* (2360 ft.; due S.) and other summits forming its wider environment. Beyond the Bowder Stone the lane descends again to the high-road, which brings us to the ($1^1/_4$ M.) village of **Rosthwaite** (**Royal Oak*, **Scafell Hotel*, unpretending), prettily situated in the middle of the valley.

Walkers to Rosthwaite should vary their return to Keswick by following the bridle-track to (2 M.) the hamlet and tarn of *Watendlath*. The road thence to (5 M.) Keswick joins the above-described road near the Barrow Falls (comp. p. 394). This is an easy route, commanding exquisite views. — Routes over the *Stake Pass* and *Sty Head Pass*, see pp. 396, 397.

Beyond Rosthwaite the road to the Stake diverges to the left near the ($^1/_2$ M.) *Church;* and the path to the Sty Head Pass diverges on the same side $^3/_4$ M. farther on, near *Seatoller*, a hamlet with some lodging-houses. At Seatoller begins the steep and rough ascent to the ($1^1/_2$ M.) **Honister Hause** (1190 ft.). At the top of the pass we come in sight of the striking **Honister Crag* (1750 ft.), which rises almost perpendicularly to the left. Its face is seamed with slate-quarries. The descent on the other side is very steep at first. Buttermere and Crummock Water come into view as we descend. The fells rising above them (named from left to right) are High Crag, High Stile, Red Pike, Mellbreak, and Robinson. At the foot of the pass is the ($2^1/_2$ M.) farm-house of *Gatesgarth*, whence we see the *Scarf Gap Pass*, ascending to the left of High Crag. Beyond Gatesgarth we skirt the N. bank of Buttermere, passing the mansion of *Hasness*, and reach (7 M.) the village of **Buttermere** (*Victoria; Fish*), where the coach stops for 3 hrs.

Buttermere Lake (330 ft.), $1^1/_4$ M. long, $^1/_3$ M. wide, and 90 ft. deep, is connected by a short stream with ***Crummock Water** (320 ft.), $^3/_4$ M. to the N.W., which is $2^3/_4$ M. long, $^1/_3$-$^3/_4$ M. wide, and 130 ft. deep. The interval allowed by the coach is generally occupied with luncheon and a visit to ***Scale Force.** This waterfall, 160 ft. in height, one of the finest in Lakeland, is in a glen on the S. side of Crummock Water. It may be reached by a footpath (about 2 M.; often wet), crossing the stream between the lakes, but the usual route is to go by boat to the mouth of the glen (fare 1*s.* each, there and back) and walk thence to ($^3/_4$ M.) the force. — From Scale Force good walkers may cross the fells to the W. to ($1^3/_4$ M.) *Floutern Tarn* (1250 ft.; pronounced 'Flootern') and the ($2^1/_4$ M.) *Angler's Inn*, at the foot of *Ennerdale Water* (370 ft.). From Ennerdale Water they may ascend *Upper Ennerdale*, or the *Valley of the Liza*, and at the head of it follow either the *Scarf Gap Pass* to Buttermere on the left, or the *Black Sail Pass* to *Wasdale Head* on the right (p. 399). Or they may proceed direct to Wasdale Head over the *Pillar* or the *Steeple* (comp. p. 399).

Red Pike (2480 ft.), though not the highest peak in the neighbourhood, commands the best view. The ascent may be combined with a visit to Scale Force (2-3 hrs.), but the shortest route ($1^1/_4$-$1^3/_4$ hr.) is by the *Ruddy Beck*, the stream flowing into the S.W. angle of Crummock Water. The descent may be made by *Bleaberry Tarn* and *Sour Milk Gill*, the stream descending to Buttermere. The characteristic feature of the view is the large number of lakes and tarns. The large lake to the W. is *Ennerdale Water* (370 ft.), $2^1/_2$ M. long and $^1/_3$-$^2/_3$ M. broad. To the N.W. of Crummock Water is the lakelet called *Lowes Water*. — From Buttermere to *Wasdale Head viâ Scarf Gap & Black Sail Passes* (3-4 hrs.), see pp. 398, 399.

The road to the N., skirting the bank of Crummock Water, leads to (10 M.) *Cockermouth* (p. 375). Our road leads to the E. from the village of Buttermere, and ascends to the top of ($1^1/_4$ M.) *But-*

termere Hause (1100 ft.), between *Robinson* (2417 ft.) on the right and *Whiteless Pike* (2160 ft.) on the left. It then traverses the upland valley of *Keskadale* and descends through the somewhat uninteresting valley of *Newlands.* 3¼ M. *Newlands Hotel;* 1 M. *Stair;* ½ M. *Swinside* (Inn). About ¼ M. farther on we join the road round Derwentwater, at the finger-post mentioned at p. 394.

Another route from Keswick to (14 M.) Buttermere leads by the Whinlatter Pass. The road leads to the W. from (1¼ M.) *Portinscale* (p. 394) to (1½ M.) *Braithwaite* (Inn), beyond which the ascent to the top of the (2 M.) Whinlatter Pass (1040 ft.; *Inn*) begins. About 1¼ M. farther on we diverge to the left from the road to Cockermouth (p. 375) and proceed, past (2 M.) *Swinside*, to (3 M.) the *Scale Hill Hotel*, ½ M. from the foot of Crummock Water (p. 395). For walkers the distance hence to Buttermere village, by the road skirting the E. bank of Crummock Water, is about 3½ M. From the Scale Hill Hotel we may go on by *Lowes Water* to *Lamplugh* or to (11 M.) *Ennerdale Water* (Angler's Inn).

A fine route from Keswick to Buttermere, with splendid views, is afforded by the *Mountain Walk (6-7 hrs.) over *Cat Bells* (p. 394), *Maiden Moor*, *Dale Head*, and *Robinson* (see above).

From Keswick to Thirlmere by the Druids' Circle and Vale of St. John (7½ M.) We leave Keswick by the Penrith road, diverging to the right from the road to the station, and cross the railway twice, first passing under it and then over it. We then take the second turning to the right, and after about ½ M. (1 M. from Keswick) pass a lane on the right, just beyond which is a stile leading into the field with the *Druidical Stones*. Of these there are about forty, arranged in an irregular circle; the largest are about 7½ ft. high. The old Penrith road joins the new one ½ M. beyond the Druid Circle, just before it crosses the *Naddle Beck*. About ⅓ M. farther on, our road diverges to the right from the Penrith road, crosses (1 M.) *Wanthwaite Bridge*, and reaches the main road through the pretty **Vale of St. John**, ascending on the E. side of the *St. John's Beck*. To the left are the *Wanthwaite Crags*. At the head of the vale rises the *Castle Rock* (p. 384). *Thirlspot* (p. 384) is about 4½ M. from the bridge. *Thirlmere*, see p. 384. We may cross the lake by the foot-bridge and return along the E. bank to *Smaithwaite*, on the Windermere and Keswick road, where drivers may order their carriage to meet them.

From Keswick to Dungeon Gill by the Stake Pass (4½-5 hrs.; pony and guide from Rosthwaite 15*s*.). Driving is practicable as far as (6½ M.) *Rosthwaite*, see p. 395. Near the church, ½ M. beyond Rosthwaite, we diverge to the left from the Buttermere road and proceed to (⅓ M.) *Stonethwaite*, both before and after which we may take several short-cuts through the fields (to the left of the road). About ¾ M. beyond Stonethwaite we turn to the right, cross the *Langstrath Beck* (¼ M.) by a foot-bridge, and ascend by a rough path on its right bank. After crossing a tributary, 2 M. farther on, we leave the Langstrath Beck, the valley of which here bends to the right, and ascend in zigzags, in the direction we have hitherto been following, to (¾ M.) the top of the **Stake Pass** (1576 ft.), between Stickle Pike (p. 386) on the left and *Rossett Crag* on the right. We now cross a bleak upland plateau for about 1 M., and then descend, along the right side of the beck flowing through *Mickleden*, to ($2^1/_2$ M.) *Old Dungeon Gill Hotel* (see p. 386). To *Ambleside*, see p. 386.

From Keswick to Patterdale by the Sticks Pass, 11 M. (driving practicable for 5 M.). We follow the Ambleside road (see pp. 384, 385) for about 5 M., to the point where it is joined by the road through the Vale of St. John (p. 396). We follow the latter for a few yards, and then diverge to the right through a gate. The track passes the farm of *Stanah*, crosses a beck a little way beyond it, bends to the right, and ascends in zigzags. The top of the **Sticks Pass** (2450 ft.), marked by sticks inserted in the ground, forms part of the ridge of Helvellyn. Good retrospect of Skiddaw, the Buttermere fells, Scafell, etc. In front Ullswater, now comes into sight. In descending we pass the *Greenside Reservoir* and *Lead Mine*, and join the Glenridding ascent of Helvellyn at the *Greenside Smelting Mill*. Hence to Patterdale, see p. 392.

Good walkers in fine weather will do better to go from Keswick to Patterdale viâ the top of Helvellyn (3-4 hrs. from Thirlspot), for which sufficient directions will be found at pp. 388, 392, while others may prefer the approach viâ Troutbeck (see below).

From Keswick to Patterdale viâ Troutbeck, $16^1/_2$ M., by railway and coach (through-tickets 4*s.* 2*d.*, 3*s.* 6*d.*, 3*s.* 2*d.*; return 6*s.* 3*d.*, 5*s.* 3*d.*). Those who wish to drive the whole way must take this route. — Railway from Keswick to (9 M.) *Troutbeck* (not to be confounded with *Troutbeck* near Windermere), see p. 374. The first part of the route from Troutbeck to Ullswater is dreary. The road leads due S. from the station, and ascends to its culminating point (ca. 1100 ft.), to the W. (right) of the rounded ***Mell Fell*** (1760 ft.). We then descend to ($2^3/_4$ M. from Troutbeck) ***Matterdale End***, at the church of which, $^3/_4$ M. beyond the village, a road to the left leads to ***Greystoke***. At ($^1/_2$ M.) ***Dockray*** (Royal Hotel, plain), where the scenery improves, our road is joined on the right by a cart-track crossing the fells from Wanthwaite (see above). [Walkers should leave the road here and descend on the other side of the beck, through *Gowbarrow Park*. This is a private path, but a guide with keys to open the gates may be obtained at the inn. We pass through the farm-yard opposite the inn, and then follow a path skirting the slope of *Gowbarrow Fell*, on the left bank of the stream. We pass a picturesque old mill, the pretty little *High Force*, and a quaint little gully, and finally reach *Aira Force* (see p. 390). From Aira Force to *Patterdale*, see pp. 390, 391.]

From Dockray we descend between *Gowbarrow Fell* and *Park* on the left and the finely-wooded *Glencoin* on the right, and soon obtain a fine *View of the head of *Ullswater*, with Place Fell, St. Sunday's Crag, etc. We reach the bank of the lake $1^1/_2$ M. beyond Dockray. Thence to (2 M.) *Ullswater Hotel* and (1 M.) *Patterdale*, see p. 390.

From Keswick to Wasdale Head by the Sty Head Pass, 14 M. (5-6 hrs.). Driving is practicable to (9 M.) *Seathwaite*, and ponies can go the whole way (pony and guide from Rosthwaite 15*s.*). From Keswick to ($7^1/_2$ M.) *Seatoller*, see p. 395. Just before Seatoller we pass through a gate to the left and follow a lane, which skirts the *Derwent*, first on the left and then on the right bank.

By diverging to the right, before crossing the ($^3/_4$ M.) bridge, we may visit Wordsworth's 'fraternal four of Borrowdale' (a group of yews), and follow the path on the same side, past the *Plumbago Mine*, to Seathwaite.

About $^3/_4$ M. beyond the bridge we reach the hamlet of *Seathwaite*, said to be the rainiest place in England, the annual rain-fall averaging 150 inches. The *Plumbago Mine*, which formerly produced admirable lead for pencils (comp. p. 392), is almost exhausted. At Seathwaite the cart-track ceases, and we follow the path on the right bank of the stream. At the head of the valley *Great End* (see below) raises its perpendicular front; to the left rises *Glaramara* (2560 ft.), and to the right *Base Brown* (2120 ft.). At (1 M.) *Stockley Bridge* we cross the Derwent, pass through a gate, and ascend to the W. towards *Taylor's Gill Force*. After passing the fall we bend to the left, following the course of the beck, cross the stream, and reach the solitary ($1^1/_4$ M.) *Sty Head Tarn* (1430 ft.), situated amidst scenery of the wildest description. To the right are *Green Gable* and *Great Gable* (2950 ft.); in front *Lingmell* (2649 ft.), *Great End* (2984 ft.), and *Scafell Pikes* (3210 ft.). A few yards beyond the tarn the track leading past the *Sprinkling Tarn* (1960 ft.) and over *Esk Hause* (2370 ft.) to Dungeon Gill diverges to the left (comp. p. 387). Our path goes straight on, and very soon reaches the top of the **Sty Head Pass** (1600 ft.), where the green valley of *Wasdale* comes in sight below us. Wast Water is concealed by Lingmell. The descent is very steep and stony. (Those who have time and strength to spare may diverge to the left, visit *Greta Fall* and the romantic gorge of *Piers Gill*, and rejoin the regular track at the foot of the pass.) From ($1^3/_4$ M.) *Burnthwaite Farm*, now a temperance inn, a cart-track leads to the church, and a field-path to the right to ($^1/_2$ M.) *Wasdale Head Inn* (see p. 400).

From Keswick (or Buttermere) to Wasdale Head by Scarf Gap and Black Sail Passes (road to Gatesgarth; bridle-path thence $2^1/_2$-$3^1/_2$ hrs.). Pony and guide from Buttermere about 15*s*. From Keswick to *Gatesgarth*, either viâ Honister Hause or viâ Newlands, see pp. 394, 395. At Gatesgarth our route diverges to the S. from the road, passes through a gate, crosses ($^1/_4$ M.) a foot-bridge over a beck, and begins to ascend. In about $^1/_2$ hr. we reach the top of the **Scarf Gap** (1400 ft.), between *High Crag* (2443 ft.) on the right and *Haystacks* (1750 ft.) on the left. Fine retrospect of Buttermere. In front rises *Kirkfell* (2630 ft.), with *Great Gable* (see above) to its left and the *Pillar* to the right. On the slope of the latter rises the lofty *Pillar Rock*, the ascent of which is dangerous except for very expert cragsmen. We now descend into the lonely upper part of *Ennerdale*, through which flows the *Liza*. On reaching the ($^1/_4$ hr.) floor of the valley, the path ascends along the right bank of the stream for about $^1/_2$ M., and then crosses it by a small foot-bridge (sign-posts). It then ascends again, skirting a small mountain-torrent, to ($^1/_4$ hr.) ***Black Sail Pass** (1750 ft.), the depression between Kirkfell on the left and the Pillar on the right. [A mistake is sometimes made here, as the traveller is apt to believe that the Black Sail Pass must lead through the more inviting depression to the left of Kirkfell, between it and Great Gable. We must therefore take care to keep to the right of Kirkfell.] The scenery here is very wild and sombre. Looking back, we see (from right to left) Great Gable, Green Gable, Brandreth, Haystacks, and High Crag, with Fleetwith Pike rising behind Haystacks, and Robinson and Grasmoor in the distance. In front lies *Mosedale*, with *Red Pike* (2630 ft.; not to be confounded with the Red Pike at Buttermere) to the right and *Yewbarrow* (2058 ft.) to the left. In descending we bear to the left and obtain a sudden *View of Scafell (p. 401). The fell to the S.W. of the Pillar is called the *Steeple* (2746 ft.). *Wasdale Head* and *Wast Water*, see pp. 400, 401.

These two routes may be easily combined in one day's excursion from Keswick by making an early start. The necessary walking may be reduced to a very reasonable amount (4-6 hrs.) by driving to Seathwaite and ordering the carriage to wait at Gatesgarth; or the traveller may hire a pony (see p. 398) and avoid walking altogether. — Those who wish to go from Keswick to Wast Water without the fatigue of crossing any of the passes may drive viâ *Braithwaite*, *Whinlatter Pass*, *Scale Hill Hotel* (p. 396), *Lamplugh*, *Egremont*, and *Calder Bridge*, to (34 M.) *Strands* (p. 400), situated near the foot of the lake, 6 M. from Wasdale Head.

Mountain Ascents from Keswick. — **Skiddaw** (3058 ft.), the fourth highest summit in the Lake District, is probably the easiest mountain of its size to ascend in England (up and down 4-6 hrs.). Ponies (5*s.*) can go all the way to the top; guide, unnecessary, 6*s.* We pass below the railway, to the right (E.) of the station, turn to the left, and then take the (1/4 M.) second turning to the left (*Spoony Green Lane;* numerous guide-posts). This lane skirts the slope of *Latrigg* (1203 ft.; a spur of Skiddaw), the top of which is easily reached in about 1/2 hr. (by a railed-in path) and commands a charming view. The lane turns to the right round the N. side of Latrigg and passes through a (1 1/4 M.) gate into a road coming from Applethwaite. About 50 yds. farther on, this road ends at another gate, through which we pass on to the open fell. We then ascend to the left along a wall, through which we pass by a gate near a (3/4 M.) refreshment-hut. The ascent hence to (1/2 M.) another refreshment-hut is the steepest part of the climb (fine retrospects). Beyond the second hut the trackibends slightly to the left and soon becomes almost level. It keeps a little to the right of the top of the *Low Man* (2837 ft.), the S. buttress of the summit-ridge, which commands a better, because nearer, view of Lakeland than the 'High Man'. The distance hence to the top is about 1 M. The view to the S. includes a great part of the Lake District, but the fells are too distant to be seen to advantage. The Coniston Old Man is visible in the distance, and Helvellyn is conspicuous to the S.E. Immediately to the E., between Skiddaw and Blencathara, is the wild moorland tract called *Skiddaw Forest*. On the N. the view extends to the Solway Firth and the mountains of Kirkcudbright and Dumfries. To the W. is the sea. — The descent is usually made by the same route, but those who wish variety may descend by the N.W. side to *High Side*, 5 1/2 M. from Keswick and 4 M. from Bassenthwaite Lake Station (p. 375). Another descent leads by the *Carl Side* (2400 ft.) to *Millbeck* (p. 393). — The ascent of **Blencathara** or **Saddleback** (2847 ft.), with its fine 'Sharp Edge', is in many respects preferable to that of Skiddaw, though it is less easily accessible. The direct ascent and descent from the village of (3 1/2 M.) *Threlkeld* (see p. 374) take 3 1/2-4 hrs., but perhaps the best plan is to ascend by Scales Fell and follow the ridge of the mountain from E. to W. (a round from Threlkeld of 4-5 hrs; *Views). — The top of **Helvellyn** (3118 ft.) may be reached from Keswick either viâ (5 1/2 M.) *Thirlspot* (p. 384) or by (8 M.) *Wythburn* (p. 384). The actual ascent takes in the first case 1 3/4-2 1/4 hrs., in the second 1 1/4-1 3/4 hr. (pony and guide 10*s.*). At Thirlspot the pony-track, which can scarcely be missed, begins near the King's Head Inn and leads at first in a N.E. direction. Just before reaching *Fisher Gill* it turns to the right and ascends straight towards the summit. In about $1^1/_2$ hr. we reach the summit-ridge, where the pony track from Glenridding (p. 392) joins ours on the left. In $^1/_4$ hr. more we surmount the '*Low Man*' (3033 ft.), which is about 10 min. from the '*High Man*', or summit. The Wythburn ascent is the shortest and steepest. The bridle-path, also easily traced, leaves the road opposite the inn and ascends along the right bank of a small beck. Farther up it bends to the left, and about $^1/_2$ M. from the top it unites with the route from Grasmere (p. 388). View, see p. 388; descent to Patterdale, see p. 392. — Among the smaller hills near Keswick, *Latrigg* (see p. 399), *Swinside* (803 ft.; near Portinscale), and *Cat Bells* (1482 ft.; p. 393) are the best points of view. The ascents of *High Seat* (1996 ft.; from the Watendlath road) and *Glaramara* (2560 ft.; from Rosthwaite) are more fatiguing. — Active walkers will find the ascent of **Great Gable** (2950 ft.) one of the most repaying in the district. The view from the top is very fine, including Wast Water, Scafell and Scafell Pikes, Skiddaw, and Helvellyn. The ascent may be made either from the Sty Head Pass (p. 398; $^3/_4$-1 hr.) or from the Honister Pass (p. 395; 2-3 hrs.) viâ *Grey Knotts* (2287 ft.), *Brandreth* (2344 ft.), and *Green Gable* (2474 ft.). The descent may be made by Sty Head to Wasdale Head (p. 400).

Among other excursions from Keswick may be mentioned the *Walk to (5 M.) *Watendlath* (p. 394; charming views), returning viâ (2 M.) *Rosthwaite* and *Borrowdale* (in all $13^1/_2$ M.). — The easy way to visit **Bassenthwaite Lake** (226 ft.) is to take the train to (9 M.) Bassenthwaite station (p. 375) and hire a boat at the Pheasant Inn. The scenery of the lake, which is 4 M. long and $^3/_4$ M. broad, is rather tame.

From Keswick to *Thirlmere*, *Grasmere*, *Ambleside*, and *Windermere* by coach, see p. 383; to *Grasmere* viâ *Watendlath*, see p. 385.

d. Wast Water and Scafell Section.

***Wast Water** (204 ft.), 3 M. long and $^1/_2$ M. wide, is the deepest lake in the district, attaining in some places a depth of 270 ft. The scenery around it is wild and imposing. The head of the lake is enclosed by finely grouped mountains, including *Scafell*, *Lingmell*, *Great Gable*, *Kirk Fell*, and *Yewbarrow*. On the W. side of the lake the imposing cliffs of the *Screes*, culminating in *Illgill Head* (1980 ft.), rise sheer from the water's edge. The bank at the lower end of the lake is richly wooded.

The small but comfortable *Wasdale Head Inn* lies in a deep and romantic hollow, surrounded by lofty mountains, about 1 M. from the head of the lake. Ponies and guides may be obtained here for numerous excursions, including the ascent of Scafell Pike, which towers over the E. side of the little valley. — As the lake is not seen to advantage from this point, the traveller should hasten to visit its lower end, in order to enjoy the view of the grand mountain-amphitheatre at its head.

The best plan is perhaps to hire a boat, and go all the way by water (1*s.* per hr.; with boatman 2*s.* 6*d.* per hr.; to the foot of the lake and back 5*s.*). There is a road along the W. bank, and even the most hurried travellers should drive as far as *Bowderdale*, 1 M. from the head of the lake. Those who do not mind a little rough walking may make the round of the lake on foot, following the ridge of the Screes. There are two inns at *Strands*, a small village 1 M. from the S. end of the lake, on the road to *Gosforth* (with an ancient carved Cross, 15 ft. high).

The W. side of the Wasdale valley is bounded by the huge

Scafell or **Scawfell Group**, including its four principal summits: *Scafell Pike* (3210 ft.), *Scafell* (3162 ft.), *Great End* (2984 ft.), and *Lingmell* (2649 ft.). The first of these is the highest mountain in England, though surpassed by several peaks in Scotland and Wales, and is best ascended from Wasdale Head. Unlike that of Skiddaw, the ascent offers some genuine climbing; and though the ordinary routes are free from danger in good weather, it is better in doubtful weather not to attempt the ascent alone (pony and guide 15*s.*). Ponies go to within 20 min. of the top.

Ascent of **Scafell Pike**, 2-2½ hrs. The ordinary and easiest route from Wasdale Head ascends along the S. side of *Lingmell Gill*, which we reach by descending Wasdale for about 1 M. (to a point near Wast Water) and then turning to the left. We follow up the course of the stream for about ½ hr., and where it forks go straight up the green space between the arms. About 10 min. higher up, on more level ground, we bend to the left towards *Lingmell*, but turn again to the right, near a wall. The last part of the route is marked by cairns. Throughout this ascent Scafell, to the right, is more prominent than Scafell Pike. — A finer but steeper route leads viâ Lingmell Beck and Piers Gill. We proceed towards the N. to (½ M.) *Burnthwaite*, and then to the N.E. through the valley between *Great Gable* and *Lingmell*, with *Lingmell Beck* to the right. After about 10 min. the pony-track to the Sty Head Pass (p. 398) diverges to the left, and in ¼ hr. more we turn sharply to the right and ascend to the left of *Pier's Gill*. The path joins the one above described in the hollow between Lingmell and Scafell Pike. (The pony-track goes on to *Esk Hause* and then turns to the right.) — Scafell is also sometimes ascended from *Dungeon Gill* (p. 386; 3-4 hrs.; route marked by cairns), from *Rosthwaite* (p. 395; 3-4 hrs.; cairns; pony and guide 15*s.*), and from *Boot* (p. 377; 3-4 hrs.; path indistinct). — The **View* from the top is extensive and wild. It includes Skiddaw to the N., Helvellyn to the N.E., High Street to the E., a bit of Windermere and Ingleborough (p. 405; in the distance) to the S.E., the Coniston Hills to the S., and the Isle of Man and the sea to the S.W. and W. The view from *Great End*, the N.E. limb of the Scafell group, easily reached from the top of Scafell Pike in ¾ hr., is still finer. The top of *Scafell*, to the S., is somewhat less easy of approach, and the view it commands does not differ enough from that above described to repay the trouble.

From Strands (see p. 400) roads lead westward to the railway-stations of (7 M.) *Drigg* (Victoria Inn) and (8 M.) **Seascale** (*Scawfell Hotel*, 'pens'. 6*s.* 6*d.*), that to the latter passing an early *Cross*, 14 ft. high. Coaches run from Seascale to Wasdale Head (4*s.*) and to Ennerdale (4*s.*). — *Boot* (see p. 377) is reached from Wasdale Head by a pony-track (6½ M.) leading past *Burnmoor Tarn* (230 ft.), between Scafell on the left and *Illgill Head* (1980 ft.) on the right. In *Stanley Gill*, about 1 M. to the S. of Boot, is ***Dalegarth Force** (60 ft. high), which is, perhaps, the finest waterfall in the Lake District. The key to the fall is kept at a cottage, to which a sign-post directs; and a guide (advisable) may also be procured here. From Boot we may go on by the Wrynose Pass to Ambleside (comp. p. 387).

From Wasdale Head to *Keswick* by the *Sty Head Pass* or the *Black Sail Pass*, see pp. 398, 399.

49. From London to Sheffield, Leeds, and Carlisle.

308 M. Midland Railway in 7-10 hrs. (fares 40*s.* 6*d.*, 24*s.* 2½*d.*). — For the sections composing the *L. N. W. Route* from London to Carlisle (299 M., in 7¼-9 hrs.; fares 40*s.* 6*d.*, 32*s.*, 24*s.* 2½*d.*), see RR. 36, 44a, 46.

From London (St. Pancras) to (120 M.) *Trent Junction*, see R. 44 b. — The line follows the valley of the *Erewash*, now disfigured with iron-works. 126 M. *Ilkeston*, the junction of lines to *Derby* (p. 350) and to *Nottingham* and *Kettering* (see p. 354). Beyond (130 M.) *Langley Mill*, to the left, are the ruins of *Codnor Castle*.

146 M. **Chesterfield** *(*Angel; Station)*, a busy manufacturing town with 12,200 inhabitants. The curious twist of the spire of the *Parish Church* (14-15th cent.) is probably due to the warping of the wood-work below the leaden casing; local legend ascribes it to the devil. *George Stephenson* (d. 1848) is buried in *Trinity Church*.

About 7 M. to the S.E. of Chesterfield is **Hardwick Hall** (**Inn* at the entrance to the park), the seat of the Marquis of Hartington, an extensive Elizabethan mansion, with numerous windows, erected in 1590-97 by 'Bess of Hardwick', the building countess of Shrewsbury (p. 351), who was born here in a house which her own superseded. Mary, Queen of Scots, is said to have spent part of her captivity here. The *Picture Gallery* contains interesting portraits. — *Bolsover Castle*, 6 M. to the E., was also begun by 'Bess of Hardwick'.

Chesterfield may also be made the starting-point of a visit to the Peak (R. 45); it is 11-13 M. from Haddon and Chatsworth.

Beyond Chesterfield the loop-line by which the Scottish day-express trains run diverges to the right, rejoining our line at Masborough. — 154 M. *Beauchieff* is the station for *Beauchieff Abbey* (p. 360). — 158 M. **Sheffield** *(Rail Rfmt. Rooms)*, see p. 359.

163 M. *Masborough* (Prince of Wales) forms part of **Rotherham** *(Crown; Royal)*, a smoky iron-working town to the right, with 35,000 inhabitants. * *All Saints' Church* is a good Perp. edifice.

From (167 M.) *Swinton* branch-lines diverge to Doncaster (p. 405) and to Pontefract and York (p. 406). At (176 M.) *Cudworth* we cross the *Hull and Barnsley Railway*. — 181 M. *Sandal Walton* is the junction for (3 M.) **Wakefield** *(*Bull; Strafford Arms; Rail Refreshmt. Rooms)*, the capital of the West Riding of Yorkshire, with 31,000 inhab., a brisk trade in grain, wool, and cattle, and numerous mills and manufactories. The handsome **Parish Church* (14-15th cent.) has been carefully restored and is now the cathedral of the new bishopric of Wakefield (established in 1888). The *Chantry* on the bridge over the Calder is an interesting relic (14th cent.). — At (185 M.) **Normanton** *(Rail. Refreshment Rooms,* table d'hôte 2*s.* 6*d.)* the Scottish expresses stop ½ hr. for dinner. Lines radiate hence to York, Goole, Dewsbury, etc.

196 M. **Leeds.** — **Hotels.** *Queen's, at the Midland Station; Great Northern Station, well spoken of; Griffin, commercial; Bull & Mouth; Trevelyan Temperance, well spoken of. — *Refreshment Rooms* at the Midland, G. N. R., and Joint (N. E. and L. N. W.) stations.

Leeds, the great centre of the cloth-industry, the first town in Yorkshire, and the fifth in England, with 310,000 inhab., is situated on both banks of the *Aire.* It offers little to detain the tourist except a visit to some of its huge factories (introduction necessary). The history of the town, though dating back to Saxon times, is uneventful, and its principal buildings are modern. The chief streets are the ***Briggate***, containing the finest shops, and ***Wellington Street***, with the largest warehouses.

The *Town Hall*, in Park Lane, a large and ambitious structure in the Palladian style, with a Corinthian colonnade, contains a statue of Queen Anne presented to the town in 1712 (organ-recitals in the great hall twice weekly). In front of it is a *Statue of Wellington*, by Marochetti. The *Museum* (adm. 1*d.*) of the Philosophical Society, in Park Row, contains antiquarian, zoological, and geological collections. The *Municipal Offices*, the *Exchange*, the *Coliseum*, the *White Cloth Hall* (rebuilt), the *Mixed Cloth Hall*, the *Infirmary*, the *Mechanics' Institute*, and the *Unitarian Chapel* (Park Row) are also among the most prominent buildings. Most of the large *Factories* are near the river. At the *Red House*, in Guildford St., Charles I. was confined for a few days while being led captive to London. The *Yorkshire College*, at Beech Grove, is a member of Victoria University (p. 338).

The chief churches are *St. Peter's* (of which Dean Hook was vicar), *St. Saviour's*, *St. John's* (1634), and *All Souls*. Opposite the Post Office is *Mill Hill Chapel*, founded in 1672 and rebuilt in 1849, of which Dr. Priestley (p. 258) was minister for seven years.

The principal lungs of the town are *Woodhouse Moor*, to the N., and **Roundhay Park* (775 acres), to the N.E., the latter with two lakes and a manor-house, now used as a hotel and restaurant.

About 3½ M. to the N.W. of Leeds, in the valley of the Aire, reached either by tramway or railway (see p. 404), are the ruins of **Kirkstall Abbey** (adm. 2*d.*), second to Fountains (p. 423) alone among Yorkshire abbeys in extent and preservation. The surroundings, however, are now spoiled by iron-works. The abbey, a Cistercian house, was founded in the 12th cent., and most of the remains are in the late-Norman style. The tower is Perp. The abbey now belongs to the town of Leeds. — Excursions may also be made to (4½ M.) *Temple Newsam*, the birthplace of Lord Darnley; *Bolton Abbey* (see below); and *Harewood Castle* (p. 421). There is an interesting, partly Norman church at *Adel*, 5 M. to the N.N.W. of Leeds. The 'Shire Oak' at (2 M.) *Headingley* is 29 ft. in girth.

From Leeds to Ilkley, Bolton Abbey, and Skipton, 25 M., railway in 1½-1¾ hr.; to Otley (11 M., in ½-1 hr.). — The line diverges from the main line beyond Calverley (p. 404). — At (9 M.) *Menston Junction* a line diverges to the right to (2 M.) **Otley** (*White Horse*), a small town with 6800 inhab. and a partly Norman church. About 1½ M. to the N. is *Farnley Hall*, containing the sword and hat worn by Cromwell at Marston Moor, and other relics of the Civil War. Its celebrated collection of oil-paintings and water-colours by Turner was sold in June, 1890. — 12 M. *Ben Rhydding*, with a large and much-frequented Hydropathic Establishment, in a fine, breezy situation. — 13 M. **Ilkley** (*Crescent; *Middleton; Royal*), a popular watering-place, with numerous hydropathic establishments, is beautifully situated on the *Wharfe*. There are three curious Saxon crosses in the churchyard. Pleasant walks may be taken amid the heather-clad hills of the neighbourhood. Otley and Ilkley may also be reached from Leeds by the N. E. R. viâ *Holbeck* and *Arthington*. — 18 M.

Bolton Abbey Station (Devonshire Arms, 1/2 M. from the abbey). — ***Bolton Abbey**, an Augustine foundation of the 12th cent., is situated amid trees on the *Wharfe*. The chief part of the picturesque but not very extensive ruins is the *Church*, the E.E. and Dec. nave of which has been restored and is used for service. The Perp. W. front was added by Prior Moon in 1620. At the end of the single aisle is the Mauleverer Chantry, in the vault below which the Mauleverers and Claphams are said to have been interred in an upright posture, a tradition referred to by Wordsworth in the 'White Doe of Rylstone'. [*Rylstone* lies about 14 M. to the N.E.] To the W. of the Abbey is *Bolton Hall*, a modern residence of the Duke of Devonshire, incorporating the ancient gateway that figures in Landseer's well-known picture. The woods are open to visitors. On the Wharfe, 1 3/4 M. above Bolton Abbey, is the narrow rapid called the *Strid*, the story of which is told in Wordsworth's 'Force of Prayer'. — 25 M. *Skipton*, see below.

From Leeds to Bradford and Halifax, 17 1/2 M., railway in 1/2-3/4 hr. — 10 M. **Bradford** (*Victoria; Alexandra; Talbot; Rail. Rfmt. Rooms*), the headquarters of the worsted manufacture, is a bustling town with nearly 200,000 inhabitants. A statue of the Hon. W.E. Forster (d. 1886) was erected here in May, 1890. — 17 1/2 M. **Halifax** (*White Swan; Old Cock; Rail. Rfmt. Rooms*), with 75,000 inhab., is another important centre of the woollen cloth and cotton industry. — From Halifax the line goes on to Rochdale, Bolton, etc. (comp. pp. 339, 340).

From Leeds to Selby, 21 M., railway in 3/4-1 1/4 hr. (fares 2*s.* 10*d.*, 2*s.* 4*d.*, 1*s.* 8 1/2*d.*). 9 3/4 M. *Micklefield*. — *Selby*, see p. 405.

From Leeds to York, 25 1/2 M., railway in 3/4-1 hr. (fares 3*s.* 6*d.*, 2*s.* 11*d.*, 2*s.* 1 1/2*d.*). This line diverges to the left from that to Selby at *Micklefield* and runs towards the N.E. — 25 1/2 M. *York*, see p. 406.

From Leeds to *Harrogate*, *Ripon*, and *Thirsk*, see R. 53.

The Scottish expresses of the Midland Railway generally pass to the W. of Leeds without stopping.

Just beyond (199 M.) *Kirkstall* we have a view, to the right, of *Kirkstall Abbey* (p. 403). 199 1/2 M. *Kirkstall Forge*, with iron-works. — Beyond *Calverley* diverges the line to Otley and Ilkley (see p. 403). Beyond (203 1/2 M.) *Apperley* the train crosses the *Aire* and passes through a long tunnel. At (207 M.) *Shipley* (Sun) we cross the line from Bradford (see above) to Ilkley (p. 403). — 208 M. *Saltaire*, a woollen and worsted-making town, named from its founder Sir Titus Salt (d. 1876) and the river Aire. The factory of the Salt family (chiefly for alpaca) adjoins the line on the right.

213 M. *Keighley* (Devonshire Arms), pron. 'Keethley', a manufacturing town with 35,000 inhab., is the junction of a line to *Oxenhope*, which passes (4 M.) *Haworth*, the home of the Brontës. — 222 M. *Skipton* (Midland; Devonshire Arms; Rail. Rfmt. Rooms), the capital of the picturesque *Craven District*, with 10,000 inhab. and a late-Perp. church, is the junction of a line to *Bolton Abbey* and *Ilkley* (see p. 403). *Skipton Castle* (14-16th cent.), behind the church, was the seat of the Cliffords.

Near (229 M.) *Bell Busk*, where we leave the Aire, are **Gordale Scar*, a huge wall of cliffs (300 ft.), and *Malham Cove*, a fine rocky amphitheatre, nearly 285 ft. high. The '*Craven Fault*', of which Malham Cove is a part, is a curious dislocation of strata, well known by name to geologists. — From (232 M.) *Hellifield* a line runs to the S. to *Clitheroe* and *Preston* (p. 373).

Near (235 M.) *Settle* (Ashfield's; Lion) a line diverges on the W. to *Carnforth* and *Morecambe Bay* (p. 374), affording direct communication between the Midland Railway and the Lake District.

At (7¼ M.) *Clapham*, on the line to Carnforth, diverges a line running N.W. to (4¼ M.) *Ingleton*, (12 M.) *Kirkby Lonsdale*, and (24 M.) *Sedbergh*, joining the main L.N.W. line at *Low Gill Junction* (p. 374). — **Ingleton** (*Ingleborough Hotel; Wheatsheaf*), near the S.W. base of *Ingleborough* (2375 ft.; see below), is frequently visited for the sake of the picturesque caves and waterfalls in the vicinity.

Beyond Settle the construction of the railway was attended with great difficulty and necessitated numerous tunnels and viaducts. Fine view down *Dent Dale*, to the left. We ascend the valley of the *Ribble*, with *Ingleborough* (see above) and *Whernside* (2415 ft.) to the left and *Pen-y-Ghent* (2270 ft.) to the right. The country now becomes very bleak. Beyond (247½ M.) *Ribblehead* we cross *Batty Moss* by a viaduct, 1330 ft. long and at one point 165 ft. high, and then traverse a tunnel, 1½ M. long, to the right of Whernside (see above). After passing (257 M.) *Hawes Junction*, the junction of a branch to *Hawes* and Northallerton (p. 410), we reach the highest point of the line (1170 ft.). Soon after, we leave the bleak Yorkshire fells and enter the green valley of the *Eden*, in Westmorland. Before entering *Birkett Tunnel* (¼ M.) we see, to the right, *Pendragon Castle*, said to have been built by Pendragon, father of King Arthur, and beyond it, on the same side, is *Lammas Castle*. 267 M. *Kirkby Stephen*. — 278 M. *Appleby* (King's Head), on the Eden. *Appleby Castle*, to the left, was rebuilt in 1686. — The blue hills of the Lake District now bound the view on the W. — 308 M. **Carlisle**, see p. 375.

50. From London to York, Durham, Newcastle, and Berwick.

335½ M. Great Northern and North Eastern Railways in 7-9 hrs. (47*s*., 37*s*. 8*d*., 28*s*. 2½*d*.); to (188 M.) *York* in 3¾-4½ hrs. (27*s*., 21*s*., 15*s*. 8*d*.).

From London (King's Cross) to (138 M.) *Retford*, see R. 44c. 156 M. **Doncaster** (*Angel; Reindeer; Rail. Rfmt. Rooms*), a prosperous agricultural town on the *Don*, with 21,000 inhab., the works of the G.N.R., and a handsome modern Dec. church by Sir G. G. Scott, the tower of which is conspicuous to the right of the railway. The name is widely known in racing circles from the fact that the *St. Leger* (established in 1778) is run here in September.

Lines run from Doncaster to Sheffield, Manchester and Liverpool, Wakefield and Leeds, Pontefract and York, Goole and Hull, and Gainsborough and Lincoln. — *Conisborough Castle*, 5 M. to the S.W., is described in 'Ivanhoe'.

174½ M. **Selby** (*Londesborough Arms; Rail. Rfmt. Rooms*), a small agricultural town with 6000 inhab., on the *Ouse*, is the traditional birthplace of Henry I. Near the station is the Benedictine **Abbey Church* (p. xxxix), one of the finest monastic churches in England, though lacking the S. transept and in need of restoration.

The church (306 ft. long) was originally erected in the 12th cent., and part of the nave and transepts is in the Norman style. The E. part of the nave and the upper part of the W. front are E.E.; the choir and lady-chapel are Dec.; and some of the windows Perp. Among the points of special interest in the interior are the coloured ceiling of the nave; the slender detached columns reaching from the arches to the roof on the S. side of the nave; the tombs of the abbots in the lady chapel; some curious figures in the N. transept; and the grand E. window.

The handsome *Roman Catholic Church* and the new *Church of St. James* may also be visited.

From Selby branch-lines run to *Hull* (a continuation of the line from Leeds, p. 404) and to *Market Weighton* (p. 424). The former line passes (7 M.) *Howden* (Bowman's), with the fine *Church of St. Cuthbert (E.E., Dec., & Perp.), formerly belonging to the bishops of Durham (comp. p. liv).

Near (185 M.) *Naburn*, York Minster appears on the right.

188 M. **York.** — **Hotels.** *STATION, a large and well-equipped house, with a fine view of the city from the coffee-room, R. & A. 4*s.* 6*d.*, table d'hôte B. 2*s.* 6*d.*, D. 5*s.* (rooms near the electric bell boards should be avoided). *HARKER'S YORK, in a central situation; BLACK SWAN, R. & A. 3*s.* 6*d.*; SCAWIN'S; NORTH EASTERN; THOMAS'S; CLARENCE, plain. — *Rail. Rfmt. Rooms;* table d'hôte, served on arrival of the Scottish expresses, 2*s.* 6*d.*

York, the *Eboracum* of the Romans, situated on the *Ouse*, is now a quiet provincial town with 60,000 inhab. and few signs of industry or recent growth. As at Chester, the ancient walls are still standing and enclose the greater part of the city. Many of the streets are crooked and narrow, and there are not a few quaint old houses with overhanging upper stories. York is the seat of an archbishop, who bears the title of Primate of England. His province embraces the dioceses of Durham, Chester, Carlisle, Newcastle, Ripon, Sodor and Man, Liverpool, Manchester, and Southwell.

York, originally the British *Caer Evrauc*, comes into prominence about the middle of the second cent. of the Christian era, as the Roman *Eboracum*, the chief station in the province of Britain, the headquarters of the 6th Legion, and the frequent residence of the emperors. Severus died and was buried at York in 311, and Constantine the Great was proclaimed emperor here in 306.† York retained its importance in the Saxon period, and was the centre from which Christianity spread through northern England. It also became an important Danish colony. William the Conqueror built two castles here (see p. 409); and the name of York is connected with many other monarchs and innumerable important events in English history. The title of Duke of York is reserved for members of the royal family; and the mayor of York shares with those of London and Dublin the right of prefixing Lord to his official title.

The RAILWAY STATION, though without architectural pretention, is very spacious, and the long curving vistas of the interior produce a good effect. To reach the town we proceed to the left, passing *Leeman's Statue*, and cross the *Lendal Bridge* (toll $^1/_2$*d.*; view), just beyond which, to the right, is the *Yorkshire Club*. To the left is the entrance to the *Philosophical Society's Gardens* (adm. 1*s.*, or by a member's introduction), which contain a *Museum* (Roman antiquities, etc.) and some interesting ruins.

To the right of the entrance are the remains of *St. Leonard's Hospital*, originally founded in the Saxon era and rebuilt by King Stephen (1137). Beyond it is the so-called *Multangular Tower*, the lower part of which is

† The tradition that Constantine was born at York is unfounded.

Roman. Nearer the N. side of the gardens are the picturesque ruins of *St. **Mary's Abbey**, which are mainly of early-Dec. date, with some Norman features. — To the E. of the Gardens (entr. from St. Leonard's Place) is the picturesque ivy-clad **Manor House**, built by Henry VIII., now a *School for the Blind* (concert on Thurs., at 2.30 p.m.; adm. 6*d.*).

Following the street in a straight direction we soon reach —

***York Minster**, one of the largest and grandest cathedrals in England (525 ft. long, 100 ft. high, 110 ft. wide across the nave, 222 ft. across the transepts). The earliest church on this site was a small wooden one, hastily built for the baptism of King Edwin by Paulinus (627), the first Archbishop of York, and soon replaced by a stone basilica, which was burned down in the 8th century. A third church was burned down in 1069 by William the Conqueror, and a fourth was built in its place by the first Norman bishop. The choir was rebuilt by Archbishop Roger (1154-81); the S. transept by Archbishop Gray in 1215-55, and the N. transept about the same time; while the Norman nave was gradually replaced by the present one between 1290 and 1345. The Lady Chapel and presbytery were added in 1360-73, and the present choir was substituted for Archbp. Roger's before 1400. The towers date from the 15th cent., and the edifice as thus rebuilt was reconsecrated in 1472. In its present form, therefore, the part of the minster above ground shows examples of the E. E., Dec., and early and late Perp. styles. The most striking features of the exterior are the noble **W. Façade* (Dec.; towers, 201 ft. high, Perp.), the E.E. *Transepts*, the imposing *Central Tower* (216 ft.; Perp.), the external triforium of the *Presbytery*, the *Chapter House* (Dec.), with its flying buttresses, and the great *E. Window* (Perp.). The numerous fantastic gargoyles are also conspicuous. The best general view is obtained from the city-walls (see p. 409). The daily services are at 10 a. m. and 4.30 p. m. Adm. to the choir, chapter-house, and crypt 6*d.*; to see the bell, 'Big Peter', 6*d.* We enter by the door in the S. transept (fine view across transepts).

Interior. The *Nave, according to Rickman, is the finest example of the Dec. style in England, from the grandeur and perspicuity of its design; 'ornament is nowhere spared, yet there is a simplicity which is peculiarly pleasing'. The triforium does not form a distinct division, but appears part of the clerestory design. The roof is of timber, restored after a fire in 1840, and painted to resemble stone. In original stained glass York Minster excels all other English cathedrals, and this adds greatly to the richness of the interior. The oldest is the 'Jesse Window' in the clerestory of the N. side (2nd from the W. end), dating from about 1200; that of the beautiful W. *Window, with its graceful flowing tracery, is also very fine (1338). The aisles are unusually wide (30 ft.).

The Transepts, in a pure E.E. style, with clustered piers and pointed arcades, are the oldest part of the existing structure (see above). The five beautiful lancet-windows (50 ft. high) in the N. transept are known as the 'Five Sisters' and still retain their original glazing. In this transept are the monuments of *Abp. Greenfield* (1306-15) and *Thomas Haxey* (d. 1824; with a cadaver). In the S. transept is a good marigold window, filled with poor modern glass. The monument of *Abp. Grey* (1215-55), in its E. aisle, is considered the best in the cathedral. The piers supporting the *Central Tower* have a Norman core.

For a plan of York Minster see page 551

The majestic *Choir (Perp.) is separated from the nave by an elaborate *Rood Screen* (15th cent.), with rich tabernacle-work and statues of English kings. The general architectural arrangements of the choir resemble those of the nave; the E. part, including the *Presbytery* and the *Lady Chapel*, is the earliest. The so-called *E. Transept* does not project beyond the walls of the choir-aisles, but is indicated by a bay on each side running up to the roof without the interposition of a triforium or clerestory. The choir was set on fire by a madman in 1829, and the timber vaulting of the roof and the stalls were destroyed (since restored). The altar-screen is also a reproduction of the old one. The great **E. Window*, which is second in size (78 ft. × 33 ft.) to that at Gloucester alone (see p. 172), retains its original fine glazing. The glass in the clerestory and in the E. transepts is also old. The shrine of St. William of York, a 12th cent. saint, whose renown for sanctity brought great wealth to the cathedral, is supposed to have been in front of the present reredos. The military and other modern monuments in the choir are somewhat incongruous. Among the older ones are those of *William of Hatfield* (d. 1344), second son of Edward III. (N. aisle); *Abp. Savage* (1501-7; N. aisle); *Abp. Scrope* (beheaded in 1405; presbytery); *Abp. Bowet* (1407-23; presbytery).

From the E. aisle of the N. transept we enter the vestibule of the chapter-house, noticing near the door the Latin inscription: 'Ut rosa flos florum, Sic est domus ista domorum'. This motto scarcely exaggerates the merits of the *Chapter House (Dec.), which is generally considered the most beautiful in England. It is octagonal in form, and has no central pillar. Each bay is occupied by a large and handsome window, with geometrical tracery. The grotesque and other carvings below are also excellent.

The Crypt, entered from the choir-aisle, is of late-Norman date (12th cent.), though containing some earlier work, including a piece of herring-bone masonry, which may go back to theSaxon era (comp. pp. 406, xxxiv).

To the S. of the choir are the *Record Room*, *Vestry* (with the 'Horn of Ulphus' and other interesting relics), and *Treasury*. There are no cloisters; and in spite of the name minster, the church was never attached to a monastic establishment. — To the N. of the Minster are the *Deanery* and the *Cathedral Library*, with some valuable printed books and MSS. The latter is supposed to have been the chapel of the old *Archiepiscopal Palace*. The present palace is at *Bishopthorpe*, 2¾ M. to the S. of York.

In front of the W. end of the Minster is the Roman Catholic *Church of St. Wilfrid*, a tasteful French Gothic edifice, which, however, does not show to advantage in such close proximity to the Minster. Just to the E. of the cathedral is a Perp. gateway leading to *St. William's College*, a Jacobean block of buildings now divided into small houses. From the W. end of the Minster the Bootham leads N.W. to the *Fine Art Industrial Institution*, which contains a collection of ancient and modern paintings and of natural history objects (adm. 6*d*.). — A visit may also be paid to the *Guildhall*, an interesting Perp. building (15th cent.) on the river, approached by an archway through the *Mansion House*, in Coney St. The windows are filled with modern stained glass of scenes from the history of York.

Of the other churches in York the most interesting are *All Saints'*, North St., with fine old stained glass; *St. Martin-cum-Gregory*, Micklegate; *St. Mary the Younger*, Bishophill, with a Saxon tower; *St. Mary*, Castlegate, with a Perp. tower; *St. Margaret's*, Walmgate, with a rich Norman doorway; *St. Crux*, Pavement (partly dismantled), with a fine panelled wooden door (Perp.); *St. Helen's*, Stonegate; and *St. Martin's*, Coney St. (late-Perp.).

Perhaps the first thing a visitor should do at York is to make a circuit ($2^3/_4$ M.) of the **City Walls**, which were built about the middle of the 14th century, partly on the line of the Roman walls.

Beginning at the steps by the arch near the Leeman statue (p. 406), we ascend to the top of the wall, turn to the right (S.), pass round the S.W. corner, cross (5 min.) the railway, and soon reach (3 min.) *Micklegate Bar*, one of the six gateways. Beyond the Bar we have a good view of St. Mary's (see p. 408) and, farther on, of the Minster. In 7 min. more we pass the *Baile Hill*, or Norman Mound, the site of William the Conqueror's second castle, and cross the *Ouse* by an iron bridge ($^1/_2$*d.*). To the left, beyond the river, is the **Castle**, now used as a prison; the oldest part is *Clifford's Tower* (13th cent.), which occupies the site of William the Conqueror's original keep (see p. 406). It was here that the infamous massacre of 500 Jews took place in the reign of Richard I. (1189-99). — We cross the canal and regain the wall at (5 min.) *Fishergate*. 7 min. *Walmgate*, with a barbican, or outwork, and portcullis. At the (3 min.) *Red Tower* the wall again disappears, and we follow the river to (5 min.) *Layerthorpe Bridge*, where it begins again. 8 min. *Monk Bar*, with a portcullis. Beyond this point we have to leave the top of the wall and follow the *Lord Mayor's Walk* at its base to (8 min.) *Bootham Bar*. This is close to the Minster and within 5 min. of Lendal Bridge (p. 406).

From York to Harrogate, 20 M., N.E. Railway in $^3/_4$-1 hr. (fares 2*s.* 10*d.*, 2*s.* 4*d.*, 1*s.* $8^1/_2$*d.*). — About $^1/_2$ M. to the left of (6 M.) *Marston* is the field of *Marston Moor*, the scene of Cromwell's victory over the Royalists in 1644. — 9 M. *Kirkhammerton*, with a church partly of Saxon date. — $16^1/_2$ M. **Knaresborough** (*Elephant*), a small town with 5000 inhab., finely situated on the *Nidd*, which here runs through a deep ravine. The ruins of the ancient *Castle* (14th cent.) are of no great importance (adm. 6*d.*), but command a fine view. The *Church* contains some interesting monuments. The other attractions of Knaresborough comprise a *Dropping Well* (adm. 6*d.*), with petrifying properties, and *St. Robert's Chapel* (adm. 6*d.*), a cave in the limestone rock, with a rudely-carved figure of an armed man. About 1 M. down the river is *St. Robert's Cave*, where Eugene Aram concealed the body of his victim. — 20 M. *Harrogate*, see p. 422.

From York to *Whitby* and *Scarborough*, see R. 52; to *Beverley* and *Hull*, see R. 54.

To the right of the railway, 4 M. from York, lies *Skelton*, with an interesting E. E. church (p. xlv). From (204 M.) *Pilmoor* branch-lines diverge to Malton (p. 419) and Knaresborough (see above).

The Malton line passes (5 M.) *Coxwold*, with the ruins of *Byland Abbey*, 4 M. to the S. of Rievaulx Abbey (see below), and ($9^1/_2$ M.) *Gilling*, whence a branch diverges to (18 M.) *Pickering* (p. 419) viâ ($6^1/_2$ M.) *Helmsley* (Black Swan), with an interesting castle, the station for ($2^1/_2$ M.; or through *Duncombe Park*, $3^1/_2$ M.) ***Rievaulx** or **Rivers Abbey**, a Cistercian foundation of 1131. The picturesque ruins (adm. 1*s.*), in the Norman and E. E. styles, consist chiefly of the choir and transepts of the church (which lay nearly N. and S.), the gatehouse, and the refectory. Beautiful *View from the terrace above, embracing the pretty valley of the *Rye*. Hence a road leads viâ (5 M.) *Whitstone Cliff* (*View; Hambleton Hotel) to (11 M.) *Thirsk*. — The Knaresborough line passes ($5^1/_2$ M.) *Boroughbridge*, $^1/_2$ M. to the S. of which is *Aldborough*, on the site of the Roman city of *Isurium*, with a museum and numerous highly interesting remains.

$210^1/_2$ M. **Thirsk** *(Fleece; Rail. Rfmt. Rooms)*, a small country-town with 6300 inhab. and a good Perp. church, is the junction of a branch to Harrogate and Leeds (see R. 53). The *Hambleton Hills*, with their fine cliffs, are 5 M. to the W.

218 M. **Northallerton** *(Golden Lion)*, a busy railway-centre (4000 inhab.), 3 M. to the S. of the scene of the Battle of the Standard (1138).

From Northallerton to Stockton and Hartlepool, 32 M., N.E.

Railway in 1¼-1¾ hr. (fares *4s. 3d.*, *3s. 7d.*, *2s. 7½d.*). — 10 M. *Picton* is the junction of a branch to Whitby (p. 420). — 14 M. *Eaglescliffe* (Rail. Rfmt. Rooms) is the junction of lines from Darlington (see below) and to (6 M.) **Middlesborough** (*Queen's; Talbot; Rail. Rfmt. Rooms*), the capital of the Cleveland iron district, and the seat of a R. C. bishop, with 75,000 inhab., on the estuary of the *Tees*. Fine harbour of refuge. — 17 M. **Stockton-on-Tees** (*Black Lion; Vane Arms*), a thriving seaport with 41,000 inhabitants. — 29 M. **West Hartlepool** (*Royal; Rail. Rfmt. Rooms*), a modern seaport on *Tees Bay*, with 12,000 inhab., and a large trade in coal. — 32 M. **East Hartlepool** (*Railway; King's Head*), another seaport (18,000 inhab.), of ancient origin but modern prosperity.

From Northallerton to Leyburn and Hawes, 34 M., railway in 1½-1¾ hr. (fares *4s. 6d.*, *3s. 9d.*, *2s. 10d.*). This line traverses ***Wensleydale,** the upper valley of the *Ure*, a picturesque district, especially attractive to the pedestrian. — 8 M. *Bedale* (Black Swan), with a Dec. and Perp. church containing some fine monuments, at the entrance to Wensleydale, is also near the Roman Road running up *Swaledale*. *Hornby Castle*, 5 M. to the N.W., the seat of the Duke of Leeds, contains some good pictures. — 11 M. *Jervaulx* (pron. Jarvis), about 3½ M. to the N.E. of **Jervaulx Abbey**, built by Cistercians in 1156. — 18 M. **Leyburn** (*Bolton Arms; Golden Lion*), one of the best headquarters for excursions in Wensleydale. Fine *View from the *Shawl*, a rocky ridge ½ M. to the W. of the town. *Middleham* (White Swan), 2 M. to the S.E., contains several racing-stables and the massive ruins of an old castle (key in the village), which belonged to Warwick, the King-Maker, and was frequently visited by Richard III. Thence the excursion may be continued to (6 M. from Leyburn) *Jervaulx Abbey* (see above), (10½ M.) *Masham* (p. 424), (13 M.) *Hackfall Woods* (p. 424), and (21 M.) *Ripon* (p. 422). Excursions may also be made from Leyburn to (5½ M.) *Bolton Castle* and (8½ M.) *Aysgarth Force* (see below); to (9 M.) *Richmond* (see below), etc. — 19½ M. *Wensley*, with an interesting church (E.E. and Perp.). To the right of the line lies the picturesquely situated village of *Preston Scar*. — About 1 M. to the N.W. of (22½ M.) *Redmire* is ***Bolton Castle** (14th cent.), the stronghold of the Scrope family, and the prison of Mary Stuart in 1568-9. The castle-chapel is used as a village church. — 25 M. **Aysgarth** (*Miner's Arms*), with a church, rebuilt in 1866, containing a fine rood-screen from Jervaulx Abbey. **Aysgarth Force*, a fall on the Ure, ½ M. below the bridge, is one of the chief lions of Wensleydale. A road runs hence to the S. through *Bishopdale* to *Buckden* and (15 M.) *Kettlewell*, at the head of Wharfedale, which may also be reached through *Waldendale*. — From (29 M.) *Askrigg* (King's Arms), a small town once noted for clock-making, excursions may be made to (½ M.) *Mill Gill Force*, (2½ M.) *Whitfield Gill Force* and (3 M.) *Seamer Water*, a lake 100 acres in area, etc. — 34 M. **Hawes** (*White Hart*) is a good centre for excursions to (1½ M.) **Hardraw Force*, (7 M.) *Muker*, in Swaledale, etc. — Beyond Hawes the line goes on to join the Midland Railway at (6 M.) *Hawes Junction* (p. 405).

From Northallerton to *Leeds*, see R. 53.

From (227 M.) *Dalton* a branch runs to (10 M.) **Richmond** (*King's Head*), picturesquely situated on the *Swale*, with 5400 inhab., a good centre for excursions in *Swaledale*. **Richmond Castle*, with its grand Norman keep on a lofty crag sheer above the river, formerly belonged to the Dukes of Brittany. The handsome parish-church has been practically rebuilt.

Among the most attractive short walks from Richmond are those to *Easby Abbey* (1¼ M. to the E., on the N. bank of the Swale), to the *Race Course* (845 ft.; *View), to *St. Martin's Priory*, on the S. bank of the Swale (1 M.), and to *Aske Hall* (Earl of Zetland; 2 M. to the N.).

229½ M. *Croft Spa* (Spa Hotel), with a mineral spring.

233 M. **Darlington** (*King's Head; Fleece; Rail. Rfmt. Rooms*), a busy town with 35,000 inhab., is an important seat of the man-

ufacture of woollens and carpets. Its name is intimately associated with the birth of the railway-system in Great Britain. The 'Stockton and Darlington Railway', opened in 1825, was the first passenger-line in the country; and it was started mainly through the enterprise of *Mr. Edward Pease*, a member of a well-known Quaker family of Darlington. The first locomotive used on the line is set up as a memorial near the North Road Station. The *Church of St. Cuthbert* is a very handsome edifice, restored by Scott.

From Darlington a branch-line runs to ($15^1/_2$ M.) *Barnard Castle* (King's Head; Raby), with a picturesque ruined *Castle* (adm. *2d.*), on a crag overlooking the Tees, and the handsome *Bowes Museum;* ($21^1/_2$ M.) *Bowes* (Unicorn), with the reputed original of *Dotheboys Hall*, and 5 M. to the W. of *Rokeby;* ($38^1/_2$ M.) *Kirkby Stephen*, junction of a line to Appleby and Penrith (p. 374); and ($50^1/_2$ M.) *Tebay* (p. 374). This railway, which is carried over the *Stainmoor Fells*, opens up some fine scenery and at one point reaches a height of 1378 ft. above the sea.

Barnard Castle is the junction of the Tees Valley Line to ($8^1/_4$ M.) *Middleton-in-Teesdale*, $5^1/_2$ M. beyond which (coach) is **High Force** *(Hotel)*, one of the highest (60ft.) and finest waterfalls in England. Coaches also ply from Barnard Castle direct to High Force ($16^1/_2$ M.), passing through the most beautiful part of the *Tees Valley*.

Branch-lines also run from Darlington to *Bishop Auckland* (p. 414), *Middlesborough* (see p. 410), and *Stockton* (see p. 410).

256 M. **Durham.** — **Hotels.** *Three Tuns, New Elvet, an old-fashioned but comfortable house, R. & A. *4s.*; *County, Old Elvet, first-class. — Rose & Crown; Waterloo, unpretending. — *Rail. Rfmt. Rooms.*

Durham, the county-town of the shire of that name, and the see of a bishop (representing the old bishops of Lindisfarne, p. 417), is an ancient town with 15,000 inhab., finely situated on the *Wear*. The older and more important part of the town, including the cathedral and castle, occupies an elevated tongue of land almost entirely surrounded by a horseshoe loop of the river, but the more modern quarters lie on the flatter banks to the E. and W.

Durham may very likely have been originally a British station; but little is known of its history until 995, when the relics of St. Cuthbert were brought hither by Bishop Ealdhun, who also removed his see from Chester-le-Street to Durham (comp. pp. 414, 417). Walchĕr, the first bishop after the Conquest, was created Earl of Northumberland; and he and his successors for the next four centuries exercised an almost entirely independent sway over the Palatinate of Durham. 'The Prelate of Durham became one, and the more important, of the only two English prelates whose worldly franchises invested them with some faint shadow of the sovereign powers enjoyed by the princely churchmen of the Empire. The Bishop of Ely in his island, the Bishop of Durham in his hill-fortress, possessed powers which no other English ecclesiastic was allowed to share' (Freeman). At a later period Durham suffered severely from the inroads of the Scottish borderers.

The pleasantest way to reach the cathedral from the hotels is to follow the New Elvet and Church St. to (5 min.) *St. Oswald's Church*, cross the churchyard to the right of the church, and follow the pretty wooded walk called the 'Banks' to (8 min.) the *Prebend's Bridge.* After crossing the bridge we turn to the left, pass below the W. front of the cathedral, and then ascend to the right.

***Durham Cathedral**, dedicated to St. Andrew, and locally known as the *Abbey*, is one of the most important and most grandly

For a plan of Durham Cathedral see page 552

situated of English cathedrals. The general effect, however, has been impaired by the chipping away of the stone during Wyatt's restoration (see below). The distant views are the best. The cathedral is 510 ft. long, 80 ft. wide, 170 ft. across the transepts, and 70 ft. high. The *Central Tower*, the top of which commands a most extensive view, is 214 ft. high; the *W. Towers*, 138 ft.

When the monks of Lindisfarne, attracted probably by its capability of defence, fixed upon Durham as a resting-place for St. Cuthbert's remains (see above), they built a church here for the reception of the relics, and this edifice was consecrated in 999. To replace this, *Bishop William of St. Calais*, the second bishop after the Norman Conquest, began a new and larger church, and seems to have completed the *Choir* (1093-95). The *Transepts*, *Nave*, and *Chapter House*, also in the Norman style, were all finished by 1143; the Transitional *Lady Chapel* by 1195; the *E. Transept* or '*Nine Altars*' (E.E.), replacing the Norman apse, by 1230. The *Cloisters*, *Library*, and the upper part of the *Central Tower* are Perp. (1400-80). A destructive restoration was carried out by *Wyatt* (comp. pp. 99, 178) in 1778-1800, sweeping away many ancient details, and spoiling the exterior by scraping. Recently the entire building has been restored by Scott.

***Interior.** We enter the Cathedral by the *N. Portal*, consisting of five recessed arches in the late-Norman style, surmounted by incongruous (modern) pinnacles. To the door is affixed an ancient grotesque knocker, which was sounded by malefactors seeking sanctuary at the shrine of St. Cuthbert. The nave is open throughout the day, but application must be made to the verger for admission to the choir, Galilee, etc. On entering the *Nave, we at once realise the strength of the claim that is made for Durham as the grandest Norman building in the country (comp. p. xxxviii). The effect produced is one of great solemnity; Dr. Johnson describes it as making on him an impression of 'rocky solidity and indeterminate duration'. The full length of the building is seen in an unbroken view. The arches of the nave are borne alternately by massive circular piers, adorned with deep incised lines forming zigzag and lattice-work patterns, and by square piers, with subordinate shafts. The vaulting seems to be late-Norman work. The various portals should also be noticed. On the pavement, between the second pair of piers (beginning from the W. end), is a blue marble cross, marking the limit beyond which women were not allowed to pass. Among the few monuments in the nave the most interesting are those of the *Nevilles*, now in a very dilapidated condition, on the S. side, near the E. end. — The *W. Doorway* of the nave, formerly the main entrance to the Cathedral, now leads to the *Galilee † or Lady Chapel, a fine example of Transition Norman (ca. 1175), with later alterations, including the windows. Its effect, as has often been said, is almost Saracenic (comp. p. xxxix). To the S. of the main entrance are traces of the *Shrine of the Venerable Bede* (d. 735), whose remains are believed to lie below the slab in front, with the inscription: 'Hâc sunt in fossâ Bædæ venerabilis ossa'. On the other side was an altar to 'Our Lady of Pity', in a recess adorned with frescoes, which still remains. Bishop Langley (1406-37) blocked up the main door and erected an *Altar to the Blessed Virgin* in front of it, below which is his own tomb.

The Great Transepts were erected shortly before the nave, which they resemble; the large windows are of later insertion. The E. aisles were each occupied by three altars. In the S. arm is a *Statue of Bp. Barrington* (d. 1826), by Chantrey. — The Central Tower is borne by four huge clustered piers; round the interior of the lantern runs an open parapet resting on grotesque corbels. The staircase to the top is reached from the S. Transept.

The *Choir is separated from the nave by a screen designed by Scott. In general aspect it is like the nave, though there are numerous variations in detail, such as the spiral grooves round the circular piers and the

† So called from an allusion to 'Galilee of the Gentiles', as being less sacred than the rest of the church; comp. pp. 428, 440.

disposition of the clerestory. The vaulting dates from about 1300. The *Altar Screen* was erected in 1380, and the *Stalls* in 1660-72. The **Episcopal Throne* was erected by Bishop Hatfield (1345-81), to serve also as a tomb for himself. Behind the reredos is the *Feretory of St. Cuthbert*, on which his shrine stood. His remains still lie below it. The Norman choir originally ended in an apse, the place of which has been taken by the so-called 'NINE ALTARS', or E. TRANSEPT, a graceful erection of about 1230-80, showing the transition from E.E. to geometrical Decorated. The way in which this elaborate Gothic work is united with the massive Norman of the choir is marked by great constructive ingenuity and artistic sense. The nine altars were ranged along the E. wall. The arcade beneath the windows, and indeed all the details, deserve careful inspection. The poor tracery and glass of the rose-window are modern. At the N. end is a *Statue of Bishop Mildert* (d. 1831), by Gibson. The modern sculpture of a cow, on the outside (N.) of this transept, commemorates the legend that the monks of Lindisfarne were led to the site of the cathedral by a dun cow.

The CHAPTER HOUSE, which was undoubtedly the finest Norman room (1135-40) of the kind in England, was destroyed by Wyatt (p. 412). The present chamber, reached from the end of the S. transept, occupies the W. part of the old one and incorporates some of its details. — Through the **Prior's Door* (late-Norman) at the E. end of the S. aisle of the nave, we enter the CLOISTERS, which were begun in 1368 and finished in 1498. The window-tracery was renewed last century. The N. walk still retains its 'carrels', or study-recesses. In the centre of the cloister-garth is the *Monks' Lavatory*.

The DOMESTIC BUILDINGS of the Benedictine Monastery still remain in excellent order. To the S.E. of the cloisters is the *Priory* (now the *Deanery*). On the W. the cloisters are adjoined by the *Dormitory* (ca. 1400), now the *New Library*, a magnificent room, almost in its original condition. To the S. of the cloisters is the *Refectory*, now known as the *Old Library*, which contains several valuable MSS. and the interesting relics found in the coffin of St. Cuthbert (p. 411) in 1827. The early-Norman *Crypt* below this room is older than any part of the Cathedral itself. The *Monks' Kitchen*, adjoining the S.E. corner of the Dormitory, is a fine octagonal structure of the 14th century. The *Great Gateway*, on the E. side of the Abbey Yard, dates from about 1500.

To the N. of the Cathedral, on the other side of the *Palace Green* and on the neck of the peninsula, rises the **Castle** (adm. 1*s.*), originally erected by William the Conqueror in 1072, rebuilt by Bishop Hugh of Puiset about a century later, and subsequently added to and altered. It was long the seat of the bishops, and is now occupied by *Durham University*, established in 1833.

The most interesting part of the interior is the Norman work of Hugh of Puiset, including a fine arcade and a *Doorway resembling the Prior's Door in the Cathedral (see above). These are now seen in a gallery built in front of Hugh's work in the 16th century. Visitors should also ask to see the '*Norman Gallery*' on the upper floor, close to the students' dormitory. On the ground-floor of the *Keep* (14th cent.), the top of which commands a fine view, is the '*Norman Chapel*'. The *Dining Hall* (14th cent.) and the *Black Staircase* of carved oak (17th cent.) are also noticeable.

Most of the other buildings round Palace Green also belong to the University. On the W. side are the *Exchequer and Bishop Cosin's Library*. — Besides University College, with its seat in the Castle, the University comprises *Hatfield Hall*, in the North Bailey.

In the South Bailey, near the Cathedral, is the curious little church of *St. Mary the Less* (12th cent.), lately almost entirely rebuilt. Following the same street towards the S., we reach the *Water Gate* and a fragment of the old *City Wall*. — In the Market Place, to the N. of the Castle, are the *Town Hall*, the modern

Church of St. Nicholas, and a *Statue of the Marquis of Londonderry.* From this point Silver St. leads to the S. to *Framwellgate Bridge* (rebuilt in the 15th cent.), which affords a fine view of the Cathedral and Castle. Beyond the bridge are King Street and North Road, ascending to the station. In the latter, to the left, is the *Durham Miners' Hall*, with a statue of the late Alex. Macdonald, Esq., M.P., the miners' representative in Parliament.

Environs. A pleasant short excursion may be made to *Finchale Priory*, 3½ M. to the N. Starting from the market-place, we cross the Framwellgate Bridge and follow the Framwellgate to the right. At the (¼ M.) end of this street we bend to the right and take the road along or near the river, which soon becomes a green lane and finally a field-path. After about ½ M. we see to the right, on the other side of the river, the red-tiled *Kepier Hospital* (12th cent.), with its picturesque gateway. After ¼ M. more we turn to the left, ascending towards a farm, which we leave to our left, passing through a wicket-gate. We then cross a (7½ min.) stile into a lane, leading to (7 min.) a row of cottages, just beyond which we cross the railway, at the *Brasside Brick & Tile Works.* We then follow the road, which bends to the left, to the (½ M.) cross-roads, where a sign-post indicates the way to (1 M.) **Finchale Priory.* The ruins are charmingly situated on the bank of the *Wear* and are in the Dec. style (13th cent.). — We may return to Durham either by train from *Leamside*, which is 1 M. to the E. of the priory, or by the high-road (3½ M. from the above-mentioned cross-roads). In the latter case a slight detour may be made to include *Neville's Cross* (¾ M. to the S.W. of Durham), erected by Lord Neville to commemorate his defeat and capture of David II. of Scotland in 1346.

In the opposite direction (4½ M. to the S.W.) lies **Brancepeth Castle**, the ancient seat of the Nevilles. Adjacent is the curious old *Church of St. Brandon*. The direct road passes Neville's Cross (see above). — To the S. lie the *Maiden Castle* (a Roman or Saxon earthwork), *Mountjoy* (where the monks of Lindisfarne first halted), the manor-house of *Houghall*, visited by Oliver Cromwell, and the (3 M.) *Moated Grange of Butterby.* — Other points of interest are *Sherburn Hospital* (1181), 2½ M. to the E.; *Ushaw Rom. Cath. College*, 3½ M. to the W.; and *Langley Hall*. Longer excursions may be made to *Raby Castle* (see below), *Chester-le-Street*, etc.

From Durham to Sunderland, 14 M., N.E. Railway in ½-1 hr. (fares 2*s*., 1*s*. 6*d*., 1*s*. 3*d*.). — The first station is (4 M.) *Leamside*, near Finchale Priory (see above). — 14 M. **Sunderland** (*Queen's; Walton's; Empress; Rail. Rfmt. Rooms*), a busy seaport and outlet for a large coal-district, lies at the mouth of the *Wear* and contains 120,000 inhabitants. Its iron ship-building yards are important. Sunderland is also connected by railway with Newcastle, South Shields, Hartlepool, etc.

From Durham to Bishop Auckland, 10½ M., N.E. Railway in ½ hr. (fares 1*s*. 7*d*., 1*s*. 4*d*., 11*d*.). — 4½ M. *Brancepeth*, see above. — 10½ M. **Bishop Auckland** (*Talbot; Rail. Rfmt. Rooms*), an ancient town on the *Wear*, with 12,000 inhab., has its name from *Auckland Castle*, the large palace of the Bishops of Durham, with an extensive park (open). The stained-glass windows of the bishop's chapel contain portraits of Bishop Westcott, Abp. Benson, etc. — *Raby Castle*, 7 M. to the S.W., a fine building of the 14th cent., once belonged to the Nevilles and now to the Duke of Cleveland. — About 1½ M. to the N.W. of Bishop's Auckland is the interesting church of *Escomb* (see p. xxxv).

Soon after leaving Durham we reach (262 M.) **Chester-le-Street** (*Lambton Arms*), an ancient town (6650 inhab.), probably on the site of the Roman *Condercum.* After the flight from Lindisfarne (see pp. 417, 411), Chester-le-Street was the seat of the bishop of Bernicia for upwards of a century (883-995). About ¾ M. to the E. is *Lumley Castle*, the seat of the Earl of Scarborough. — Near (263½ M.) *Lamesley* is *Ravensworth Castle*, a fine baronial mansion be l ing to the Earl of Ravensworth.

267½ M. *Gateshead* is a large and uninteresting manufacturing town (70,000 inhab.), on the S. bank of the Tyne, practically forming part of Newcastle. — We now cross the river by the *High Level Bridge* (see below) and reach Newcastle.

268½ M. **Newcastle.** — **Hotels.** Station Hotel; Central Exchange, Grey St.; Douglas, County, Grainger St. West; Turk's Head, 69 Grey St. — Turf, R. & A. 3*s.* 6*d.*; Alexandra; Royal Exchange; Tyne Temperance. — *Rail. Refreshmt. Rooms.*

Tramways run through the chief streets, to *Gateshead* (see above), *Jesmond* (p. 416), etc. — **Cab** from the station to the town 1*s.*; omn. 6*d.*

U. S. Consul, *Horace C. Pugh, Esq.*

Newcastle-on-Tyne, a busy and somewhat dingy town, with 150,000 inhab., lies on the left bank of the *Tyne*, 9 M., from its mouth, in an extensive coal-field, which has made it one of the chief coal-exporting ports of Great Britain. It has also large ship-building yards and manufactories of locomotives and iron goods.

Newcastle, which occupies the site of the Roman *Pons Ælii*, was in the Saxon period named *Monk Chester*, from the number of its monastic institutions. It was also visited by numerous pilgrims to the Holy Well of Jesus Mount (Jesmond, see p. 416). The present name came into use after the erection of the castle by Robert Curthose (see below). Since 1882 Newcastle has been the see of a bishop.

On issuing from the *Central Station* we see in front of us, to the left, *St. Mary's Roman Catholic Cathedral*, a handsome modern building. We turn to the right, pass the *Statue of George Stephenson* (d. 1848), and proceed through Collingwood St. At the end of this street, to the left, are the *Municipal Buildings*. To the right stands the **Church of St. Nicholas** (14th cent.), with a fine lantern-tower (194 ft.).

St. Nicholas was raised to cathedral rank in 1882 (daily services at 10 and 5). — Among the monuments in the interior are those of a *Crusader* (14th cent.; in a small chapel off the S. aisle), *Sir Matthew Ridley* (by Flaxman; N.W. pier at cross), and *Admiral Collingwood* (S.W. pier at cross). The altar-piece is ascribed to *Tintoretto*. *John Knox* and *George Wishart* were both for a time afternoon lecturers at this church. — No. 27 St. Nicholas Churchyard was the workshop of *Thomas Bewick* (tablet; comp. p. 416).

On leaving the church we turn to the left and follow St. Nicholas Buildings to the *Black Gate*, built in 1248, and originally one of the gates in the wall surrounding the Castle; the upper story contains a collection of antiquities. The ***Castle** was founded in the 11th cent. by Robert Curthose (p. 193), but the *Keep*, the only part remaining, dates from 1172-77 (adm. 6*d.*).

The Keep is 85 ft. high (to the top of the turret 107 ft.), and its walls are 12-18 ft. thick. We reach the interior by ascending an outside staircase. The finest room is the Norman **Chapel*, on the first floor; but the *Great Hall* (in which Balliol swore fealty to Edward I.) and other chambers are also interesting. The roof affords a good *View of Newcastle.

We may now cross the river by the ***High Level Bridge** (toll ½ *d.*), a triumph of engineering skill, designed by Robert Stephenson, of which Newcastle is justly proud. The upper level, 112 ft. above high-water mark, is used by the railway, and from it is hung the roadway. The bridge cost nearly 500,000*l.* On the top of one end of the bridge is 'Stephenson's No. 1 Engine'.

Recrossing the Tyne by the *Swing Bridge*, just below the High Level Bridge, we proceed through the *Sandhill*, in which, to the right, stands the old *Guildhall*, now used as a commercial exchange.

Above No. 41 (tablet), on the other side, is a window, marked by a blue pane, through which Miss Surtees escaped in 1772, to elope with her lover, John Scott Eldon, afterwards Lord Chancellor of England.

From the end of the Sandhill we ascend to the left, through the *Side*, the picturesqueness of which is being modernized out of existence (No. 84, the birthplace of *Adm. Collingwood* in 1748), and pass through Dean St. (to the right) to Grey Street, one of the chief thoroughfares of Newcastle. To the right is the *Theatre Royal*, and to the left the *Bank of England*. At the top of the street are the *Central Exchange* (containing an art-collection) and a *Monument to Earl Grey* (d. 1845).

A tablet at No. 53 Grainger St., leading hence back to the station, commemorates visits of *Garibaldi* (1864), *Kossuth* (1856), and *William Lloyd Garrison* (1876).

Crossing Blackett St., we now proceed by Northumberland St. and Barras Bridge to the (1/2 M.) **Museum**, containing good cabinets of birds and fossils of the coal-measures, and a complete collection of the prints of the Northumbrian *Bewick* (d. 1828).

In Bath Road, diverging to the right from Northumberland St., is the *Medical School of Durham University*. — A road leading to the left at the beginning of Barras Bridge contains the *College of Science*. At 33 Eldon Place, the next opening on the left, George and Robert Stephenson lived in 1824-25 (tablet).

In *Elswick Hall*, in *Elswick Park*, 1 M. to the W. of the station, is an interesting collection of models of works by *Lough* and *Noble* (catalogue 3*d.*).

Those whose time allows should go on through the Jesmond Road (tramway, see p. 415) to (1 M.) *Jesmond Dene, a prettily wooded little glen, now laid out as a public park. The remains of the *Pilgrimage Chapel* (p. 415) stand on the edge of the valley. We may return across the *Town Moor*. — A visit may be paid (after previous application) to the Ordnance Works, Steel Works, and Shipbuilding Yard of Lord Armstrong, at *Elswick*, 2 M. to the W. of Newcastle (rail. stat.), which employ 16,000 workpeople. — A *Rowing Regatta* on the Tyne should be seen if possible.

A steamboat-trip (fare 6*d.*) may be taken down the Tyne to *Tynemouth*. In spite of the colour of the water, Tyne salmon have a great reputation for delicacy of flavour. Among the stopping-places are *Wallsend*, so-called from its position at the end of the Roman Wall (p. 376) and famous for its coal; *Jarrow*, with a few fragments of the monastery of the Venerable Bede; *North Shields;* and **South Shields** (*Royal; Golden Lion;* 57,000 inhab.), two important seaports. — **Tynemouth** (*Grand; Bath; Royal*) is frequented for sea-bathing (44,000 inhab.). The ruins of the *Priory* are interesting. — The return to Newcastle may be made by railway. — We may also make an excursion up the river to *Hexham* (p. 418) and *Gilsland* (p. 418).

From Newcastle to *Carlisle*, see R. 51. A railway also runs from Newcastle to *Sunderland* (p. 414).

At (275 M.) *Killingworth* George Stephenson made his first locomotive (see above). — 285 M. **Morpeth** *(Queen's Head; Black Bull)*, a small town (4600 inhab.), with the scanty ruins of a Norman castle and a curious clock-tower, is the junction for *Reedsmouth*, *Rothbury*, and *Blyth.* Beyond this point the sea is generally visible to the right. About 1$^1/_4$ M. to the right of (305 M.) *Warkworth* (Sun) is ***Warkworth Castle**, an excellently-preserved feudal fortress (12-14th cent.), near the mouth of the *Coquet.* *Warkworth Hermitage* figures in the Percy Reliques. — From (310 M.) *Bilton Junction* a branch diverges, on the left, to *Alnwick*, *Wooler*, and *Coldstream* (p. 456).

Alnwick *(White Swan)* is a town of 7500 inhab., on the *Alne.* ***Alnwick Castle**, the seat of the Duke of Northumberland, one of the finest feudal piles in England, has been restored, and contains interesting paintings and antiquities. The oldest part is the Norman gateway (12th cent.). — At the mouth of the *Alne*, 1 M. from Bilton and 4$^1/_2$ M. from Alnwick, is *Alnmouth*, a pleasant watering-place with golfing-links.

About 3 M. to the E. of (316 M.) *Christon Bank* are the ruins of *Dunstanburgh Castle.* — 323 M. *Lucker* is the nearest station for a visit to the *Farne Isles* (boat about 10*s.*).

The largest of these islands was St. Cuthbert's home for nine years. The *Long Stone Lighthouse*, on the easternmost isle, was the scene of *Grace Darling's* heroism in 1838. — On the mainland, opposite the Farne Isles (2$^1/_2$ M. from Lucker), is **Bamborough Castle**, on the site of a Saxon stronghold, which perhaps replaced a Roman station. The castle now belongs to a charity, and contains a surgery, a dispensary, and schools. Bamborough churchyard contains a memorial of Grace Darling. — About 6 M. to the S.W. of Lucker is *Chillingham*, the seat of Earl Tankerville; the park contains a herd of wild white cattle like those at Hamilton (p. 480).

330 M. *Beal* is the station for **Lindisfarne,** or *Holy Island (Inns)*, which is 1$^1/_2$ M. from the mainland by boat at high-water, and may also be reached on foot by crossing the sands at low water (3$^1/_2$ M.).

Lindisfarne Abbey was originally founded in the 7th cent. by *St. Aidan.* *St. Cuthbert* afterwards became Bishop of Lindisfarne and died here in 687. In 883 the monks of Lindisfarne left the island, through fear of the Danes, taking with them the relics of the saint, which found a final resting-place at Durham (comp. pp. 411, 414). Visitors will remember the description of Lindisfarne in 'Marmion and the fate of the nun Constance. The ruins belong to the *Priory Church*, which was erected towards the close of the 11th cent., on the site of the ancient church and in imitation of Durham Cathedral. The ruined *Castle* dates from about 1500.

333$^1/_2$ M. *Scremerston;* 335 M. *Tweedmouth Junction* (Union Hotel), on the S. bank of the *Tweed.* The train then crosses the Tweed by a fine viaduct, 720 yds. long and 126 ft. above the water.

335$^1/_2$ M. **Berwick-on-Tweed** *(King's Arms; Red Lion; Lyle's Temperance; Rail. Refreshmt. Rooms)*, an old town with 14,000 inhab., at the mouth of the *Tweed*, was for ages a constant object of contention between England and Scotland, while it is still regarded as a neutral county, belonging officially to neither of these countries. Parts of the old walls, with a tower and gateways, still remain.

The suburb of *Spittal* (Roxburgh) is frequented for sea-bathing. — The Tweed, like the Tyne (p. 416), is famous for its salmon, and about 150 tons of this fish are annually sent off to London and elsewhere.

From Berwick to *Edinburgh*, see R. 62b. — Branch-lines also run from Berwick to *Jedburgh* (p. 456), *Kelso* (p. 456), and *Melrose* (p. 457).

51. From Carlisle to Newcastle.

66 M. Railway in 2¼-2¾ hrs. (fares 8*s.* 1*d.*, 6*s.* 9*d.*, 5*s.*).

Carlisle, see p. 375. — 5 M. *Wetheral*, in the valley of the *Eden*, with a ruined priory. Opposite (bridge ½*d.*; ferry 1*d.*) is *Corby Hall*, a modernized baronial mansion, containing a fine art-collection. The beautiful walks in *Corby Woods*, praised by David Hume, are open to visitors on Wed. — 15½ M. *Naworth* (Inn).

***Naworth Castle**, the fine baronial residence of the Howards, about ½ M. to the N., most intimately associated with the name of 'Belted Will Howard', Lord Warden of the Marches in the first half of the 17th cent., who is described in Scott's 'Lay of the Last Minstrel'. The castle contains ancient armour, tapestry, and portraits (visitors usually admitted, 10-1 or 2-5). — About 1 M. to the N. of Naworth Castle are the picturesque ruins of **Lanercost Priory**, an Augustine foundation of the 12th century. The nave of the priory-church has been restored, and is used as the parish-church.

20½ M. *Gilsland* (Station Inn, plain), or *Rosehill*, is the station for **Gilsland Spa** (*Shaws Hotel*, 'pens'. 4*s.*-8*s.* 6*d.*; *Orchard House*, between the village and the Spa), pleasantly situated 1¼ M. to the N. (omn. 6*d.*). Its sulphur-springs and the pretty scenery attract visitors in search of a quiet watering-place. It was at Gilsland Spa that Sir Walter Scott met his future wife, Mlle. Charpentier, and he has immortalized the district in 'Guy Mannering'.

A cottage in the village is said to occupy the spot of the *Mumps Ha'*, in which Dandie Dinmont met Meg Merrilies. — In the wooded **Valley of the Irthing*, in which the sulphur-well lies, are pointed out the 'Popping Stone', where Sir Walter Scott is said to have proposed to Miss Charpentier, and the 'Kissing Bush', where he sealed the compact!

At *Birdoswald*, 2 M. to the S.W. of the Spa, are abundant remains of a station on the *Roman Wall*, which ran across the N. of England (see p. 376). The walk may be extended to (2 M.) *Coome Crags*. The archæologist will also find much to interest him in following the line of the Roman wall from this point eastwards to (17 M.) *Chollerford* (*George). — A four-horse coach plies frequently from the Shaws Hotel to *Lanercost Priory* (6½ M.; see above), *Naworth Castle* (see above; 7½ M.), the *Northumberland Lakes* (12 M.), the Roman station at *Housesteads* (13 M.), and various other points in this interesting but comparatively unfrequented district.

26 M. *Haltwhistle* (Crown), a small town with 1500 inhab., is the junction of a line to (13 M.) *Alston* (960 ft.), on the slopes of the Pennine Hills, said to be the highest market-town in England. It lies in an extensive lead-mining district.

Featherstonehaugh, *Blenkinsop Tower*, and *Thirlwall Castle* may be visited from Haltwhistle.

31 M. *Bardon Mill* is the nearest station to the pretty little *Northumberland Lakes*, 3½ M. to the N.

35 M. *Haydon Bridge* lies 6 M. to the S. of *Housesteads*, with the most complete remains of the Roman Wall (comp. above & p. 376).

42 M. **Hexham** *(Royal; Grey Bull; Tynedale Hydropathic)*, an ancient town with 6000 inhab. and see of a R. C. bishop, on the S. bank of the *Tyne*, is chiefly of interest for its fine **Abbey Church*, an excellent example of E.E., dating from the 12th century.

The first church on this site was built by *St. Wilfrid* in 676, and from 680 to 821 Hexham was the seat of a bishopric, afterwards united with Lindisfarne, and now included in the see of Durham (comp. p. 411).

The nave of the present church was destroyed at the end of the 13th cent., and the Saxon **Crypt* of St. Wilfrid has been discovered below its site. The **Choir* is separated from the *Transept* by a carved *Rood Screen* of about 1500. The *Shrine of Prior Richard* and other monuments deserve attention. — The *Refectory* and a *Norman Gateway* are also preserved.

In 1464 the Yorkists defeated the Lancastrians in an important battle at Hexham. — Branch-lines run from Hexham to *Allendale* on the S. and to *Chollerford* (see p. 418) and *Reedsmouth* (Riccarton, Rothbury, Morpeth) on the N.

Near (45 M.) *Corbridge* are the ruins of *Dilston Castle*. The train now follows closely the course of the *Tyne*. To the left, at ($52^1/_2$ M.) *Prudhoe*, are the ivy-clad ruins of its castle. At (55 M.) *Wylam* George Stephenson was born in 1781, and here the first working locomotive was constructed by William Hedley in 1812. As we near Newcastle the signs of industry increase. 63 M. *Scotswood*, so named from the camp of the Scottish army in the Civil War.

66 M. *Newcastle*, see p. 415.

52. From York to Scarborough and Whitby.

North Eastern Railway to (42 M.) *Scarborough* in 1-$1^1/_2$ hr. (fares 5*s.* 7*d.*, 4*s.* 8*d.*, 3*s.* 6*d.*); to (56 M.) *Whitby* in 2-$2^3/_4$ hrs. (7*s.* 6*d.*, 6*s.* 3*d.*, 4*s.* 8*d.*).

York, see p. 406. The first stations are unimportant. Near (15 M.) *Kirkham Abbey*, with its ivy-clad ruins, we reach the *Derwent*, the pretty, well-wooded valley of which we follow nearly all the way to Scarborough. — About 3 M. to the N.W. of (16 M.) *Castle Howard* (Hotel, $^3/_4$ M. from the park) is **Castle Howard**, the palatial seat of the Earl of Carlisle, containing a beautiful chapel and a fine collection of paintings (Velazquez, Titian, Rubens, Mabuse, Carracci, Reynolds, Clouet), sculptures, bronzes, tapestry, and old glass and china. The house and the **Park* are open daily.

21 M. **Malton** *(Talbot; Sun; Rail. Rfmt. Rooms)*, an ancient town of 9000 inhab., with large racing-stables and an old priory, is the junction of the direct line to *Whitby* (p. 420), which runs viâ *Pickering*. Another line runs S. to *Driffield* (p. 425).

42 M. **Scarborough.** — **Hotels.** On the South Cliff: Grand, with 300 beds; Crown, Esplanade, above the Spa Grounds; Prince of Wales; Cambridge, near the Valley Bridge, at some distance from the sea, 'pens'. 9*s.* — On the North Cliff (less expensive): Queen; Alexandra, 'pens'. 10*s.*; Albion, near the Castle. — In the Town: Pavilion, adjoining the station, R. & A. 3*s.* 6*d.*, 'pens'. 10*s.* 6*d.*-12*s.*; Royal, corner of St. Nicholas St.; Victoria, 'pens'. 7*s.* 6*d.*; Station, small. — Several of the hotels are closed in winter, and the rates of the others are lowered. — *Private Hotels* (7-10*s.* a day), *Boarding Houses*, and *Lodgings* abound.

Cab for 1-3 pers. 1*s.* per mile, 2*s.* 6*d.* per hr.; with two horses 1*s.* 6*d.* and 3*s.* 9*d.*; double fares between 11.30 p.m. and 6 a. m.; for each package carried outside 2*d.* — **Steamers** ply during summer to *Filey*, *Bridlington*, *Whitby*, etc. — **Boats** for 1-3 pers. 1*s.* 6*d.* per hr., each addit. pers. 6*d.*

Scarborough, the most popular marine resort in the N. of England, with a resident population of about 40,000, is finely situated, in the form of an amphitheatre, on slopes rising from the sea and terminated on the N. and S. by abrupt cliffs. The air is bracing and the beaches are good for bathing, but the older streets are narrow and dirty, and the fashionable quarters dull and formal. In the season Scarborough is very crowded.

The most prominent object is the lofty promontory (300 ft.), rising above the harbour and surmounted by the ruins of a *Castle* (12th cent.; fine view, extending on the S. to Flamborough Head). Near it is the old *Church of St. Mary*, consisting of the nave of an original late-Norman and E.E. building, the ruins of which still exist. The N. Cliff begins near the castle. New gardens and a promenade, protected by a sea-wall, were opened on the N. Bay in June, 1890. The *Promenade Pier* here is 1000 ft. long.

The old town of Scarborough is separated from the fashionable quarters of the S. Cliff by the *Ramsdale Valley*, a deep ravine laid out as a park and spanned by two bridges. The *Cliff Bridge* (toll 1/2*d.*), nearest the sea, is 414 ft. long and leads to the *Spa Gardens* (adm. 6*d.*), occupying the side of the cliffs and containing two mineral springs. The Spa Buildings, erected at a cost of 77,000*l.*, contain a theatre, a concert-hall, a fine-art gallery (adm. 6*d.*), a restaurant, etc. (band 11-1 and 7-9). Close to and partly below the Cliff Bridge is the **Aquarium* (adm. 1*s.*). Adjacent is a *Museum* (adm. 3*d.*). The beaches, both of the N. and S. bays, are connected with the top of the cliffs by inclined tramways.

At the back of the S. Cliff rises **Oliver's Mt.** (600 ft.), affording a good view of Scarborough and its environs. We cross the Valley Bridge (above the Cliff Bridge; 1/2*d.*), turn to the right, and follow the road bending round to the right, which reaches the top circuitously in 1/2 hr. Or we may cross the stile to the left and ascend straight to the top (steep) in 1/4 hr.

About 8 M. to the S. of Scarborough is the small sea-bathing place **Filey** *(Crescent; Crown)*, which may be reached by train. — The railway is prolonged thence to (11 M.) *Bridlington* (Black Lion) and **Bridlington Quay** *(Alexandra; Britannia)*, another popular watering-place. The **Parish Church* of Bridlington consists of the nave of a fine Augustine priory-church founded early in the 12th cent. (E.E. to Perp.); fine W. window. About 5 M. to the N.E. of Bridlington is **Flamborough Head**, a bold promontory, with perpendicular cliffs, 450 ft. high. In summer a coach plies between Scarborough and Bridlington (fares 5*s.*, return 8*s.*; to Filey 3*s.* and 5*s.*). — Other favourite points are *Everley*, *Hackness*, *Forge Valley*, *Ayton*, *Wykeham*, and *Hayburn Wyke*, to all of which public conveyances ply daily in the season (fares 1*s.* 6*d.*-3*s.*). A good cliff-walk may also be taken to (15 3/4 M.) *Robin Hood's Bay* and (6 M.) *Whitby* (comp. below).

From Scarborough to Whitby, 22 M., N.E. Railway in 1 1/4 hr. (fares 5*s.*, 4*s.*, 3*s.*). The line skirts the coast, affording views of the sea to the right. 7 M. *Hayburn Wyke*, a favourite point for excursions from Scarborough; 10 M. *Peak*, near *Peak Beacon*, 600 ft. above the sea. — A little farther on we obtain a fine view of ***Robin Hood's Bay,** with its lofty cliffs, far below us to the right. — 15 1/4 M. *Robin Hood's Bay* (Robin Hood's Bay Hotel; King's Head). — We then reach the (22 M.) *West Cliff Station* at Whitby, 1/2 M. from the Royal Hotel. This is the terminus of this line, but we may change carriages and take the short but circuitous branch-line (2 M.) to *Whitby Town Station.*

Whitby. — **Hotels.** *Royal, West Cliff, with sea-view, R. & A. from 5*s.*, 'pens'. 4*l.* 4*s.* to 4*l.* 10*s.* per week; Crown, Flowergate; Angel, near the Town Station, commercial; RAILWAY STATION HOTEL, commercial, R. & A. 2*s.* 9*d.*; JOBLING'S TEMPERANCE, opposite the station, unpretending.

Cab with one horse 1*s.* per mile, with two horses 1*s.* 6*d.*; for the first 1/4 hr. 1*s.*, each addit. 1/4 hr. 6*d.*, with two horses 1*s.* 6*d.* and 9*d.*

Boat 1-2*s.* per hr., according to size.

Whitby, a small town and watering-place, is situated on both banks of the *Esk*, the valley of which is here bordered by lofty cliffs. As seen from either the E. or W. cliff, the town looks very picturesque, with its crowd of red-tiled houses, clustering on both sides of the river and climbing the sides of the cliff.

Whitby originated in a priory founded here by St. Hilda in the 7th cent., and its development was aided in Elizabethan days by the discovery of alum-mines in the neighbourhood. Ship-building was also carried on here with great success for a time, and Capt. Cook, who was a Whitby apprentice, made one of his voyages round the globe in a Whitby vessel. His house in Church St. is still standing. At present the main industries are the manufacture of *Jet Ornaments* and the *Herring Fishery*.

The river is crossed by a *Swing Bridge*, and is formed into a kind of harbour by two *Piers*. On the W. Pier, which commands a good view of the town and abbey, is a ***Museum*** (adm. 6*d.*), containing a model of Cook's ship (see above) and other interesting relics.

We now cross the bridge and proceed to the left through Church St., from the end of which a flight of 199 steps ascends to *St. Mary's Church*, where some traces of the original Norman work may still be distinguished. — A little to the right lie the picturesque ruins of ***Whitby Abbey**, originally founded in the 7th cent., but dating in its present form from the 12-14th cent. (adm. 3*d.*). The poet Caedmon was a monk in Whitby Abbey. To the S.W., on the site of the abbot's lodging, is *Whitby Manor House*, with a hall of the 17th cent. (dismantled); the rest of the building has been restored.

On the W. Cliff, in front of the Royal Hotel, are the WEST CLIFF GROUNDS (adm. 6*d.*; *View), with a *Pavilion*, containing a theatre, restaurant, etc. A band plays here in the forenoon and evening.

The **Environs** of Whitby afford many pleasant excursions. Among the favourite points are *Robin Hood's Bay* (p. 420; fine walk along the cliffs); *Cockshot Mill*, 2 M. to the W.; *Sandsend*, 3 M. to the N. (by the sands); and *Mulgrave Castle* (5 M. to the W.), the seat of the Marquis of Normanby, with fine grounds and the remains of an old castle. — Whitby Abbey is visible from almost every point in the nearer environs.

Beyond Whitby the coast-railway from Scarborough is prolonged to (23 M.) **Saltburn** (*Zetland; Alexandra; Gilberton's Temperance*), a fashionable seaside resort, which has direct railway-communication with Stockton and Darlington (see p. 410).

From Whitby to *Picton*, see p. 410; to *Malton*, see p. 419.

53. From Leeds to Harrogate, Ripon, and Thirsk.

NORTH EASTERN RAILWAY to (18 M.) *Harrogate* in 3/4-1 hr. (fares 2*s.* 6*d.*, 2*s.*, 1*s.* 6*d.*); to (30 M.) *Ripon* in 1-1 3/4 hr. (fares 4*s.*, 3*s.* 4*d.*, 2*s.* 5 1/2*d.*); to (39 M.) *Thirsk* in 1 1/4-2 1/4 hrs. (fares 5*s.* 2*d.*, 4*s.* 4*d.*, 3*s.* 2 1/2*d.*).

Leeds, see p. 402. Passing some small stations, we reach (9 1/2 M.) *Arthington Junction*, whence a branch diverges on the left to *Otley* and *Ilkley* (p. 403). About 4 M. to the E. is *Harewood House*, the seat of the Earl of Harewood, containing a picture-gallery and a valuable collection of china (open on Thurs.). The church at Harewood contains the tomb of Chief Justice Gascoigne, who is said to have committed Prince Hal to prison.

18 M. **Harrogate.** — **Hotels.** — In High Harrogate: *Queen, Granby, Prince of Wales, three large houses facing the Stray, board 9*s.* 6*d.*, R. &. A. extra; Royal, Empress, also facing the Stray, somewhat less expensive; Clarendon; Gascoigne's, commercial. — In Low Harrogate (near the springs): Prospect Hotel, well situated, near the station, 'pens'. 11*s.* 6*d.*; Crown, 'pens'. 12*s.*; White Hart, similar charges; Wellington; Adelphi; George; Alexandra, 'pens'. 8*s.*; Somerset House, 'pens'. from 7*s.*; Commercial, 'pens'. 7*s.* 6*d.*; North Eastern Station, convenient for passing travellers; Claremont Temperance. — Hydropathic, near the wells. — Passing travellers, especially at the larger hotels, should come to distinct understanding beforehand as to prices, otherwise no allowance may be made for meals taken outside the hotel. The custom of dressing for dinner prevails at some of the most fashionable hotels. — *Boarding Houses* and *Lodgings* abound.

Cab from the station to any of the hotels, 1-2 pers. 1*s.*, 3-4 pers. 1*s.* 6*d.*

Harrogate (450 ft. above the sea), in a high and bracing situation among the Yorkshire moors, ranks with Bath and Buxton among the three chief inland watering-places of England. It consists of two parts, High and Low Harrogate, the former to the left (E.) of the station, the latter to the right. It is perhaps the most aristocratic of all the great English spas, and the one least exposed to the inroads of excursionists. The High Harrogate hotels face the *Stray*, a common 200 acres in extent. The **Wells** for which Harrogate is visited are in the lower part of the town, and have been known for nearly 300 years.

They include the chief sulphur-springs of England, and also chalybeate springs not unlike those of Kissingen and Homburg, though less pleasant to drink owing to the absence of carbonic acid. The *Sulphur Springs*, of which there are two strong (*Old* and *Montpellier*) and seventeen mild, are efficacious in most affections of the liver, jaundice, gout, rheumatism, and diseases of the skin. The six *Chalybeate Springs* are tonic and stimulant. The so-called *Bog Springs*, 16 in number, rise in a small piece of boggy ground, a little to the W. of the sulphur-springs, and though close together no two are exactly alike. Near the springs are various *Pump Rooms*, *Baths*, and other adjuncts of a fashionable spa. — Smollett gives an account of Harrogate a century ago in 'Humphrey Clinker'.

About 1 M. to the W. is *Harlow Hill* (600 ft.), with its tower (view). Other favourite points for excursions are *Knaresborough* (p. 409), 3 M. to the N.E. of High Harrogate; *Harewood* (p. 421), 8 M. to the S.; *Plumpton Park* (adm. 6*d.*), 4 M. to the E.; *Almes Cliff*, 5½ M. to the S.W.; *Ripon* and *Fountains Abbey* (see p. 423); and *Bolton Abbey* (p. 403), 16 M. to the W. — A line runs from Harrogate to (14½ M.) *Pateley Bridge* (King's Arms), near the picturesque *Brimham Crags*. — From Harrogate to *York*, see p. 409.

30 M. **Ripon** (**Unicorn*, old-fashioned, R. & A. 4*s.*; *Crown; Black Bull; Royal Oak)*, a quaint little country-town with 7500 inhab., pleasantly situated on the *Ure*, ¾ M. from the station (omn. 6*d.*). It celebrated its millenary in 1886, though it is doubtful whether any buildings except those connected with the monastery (see below), were in existence here in the 9th century.

A monastery was founded at Ripon in the 7th cent., and was rebuilt by St. Wilfrid about 670. In 678 the see of a bishop was fixed here, but it lapsed with the death of its first holder and was not revived till

1836. From time immemorial a horn has been sounded nightly, at 9 o'clock, before the house of the 'Wakeman', or Mayor, and at the market-cross.

The **Cathedral**, which does not occupy the same site as the church of St. Wilfrid (see p. 422), is approached from the market-place by the Kirk Gate. It dates in its present form from the 12-15th centuries. The transepts and part of the choir are in the Transition style (1154-81), the *W. Front* is E.E. (1215-55), the E. end of the choir is Dec. (1288-1300), and the nave, part of the S. side of the choir, and the *Central Tower* are Perp. (1460-1520). The *Saxon Crypt* is supposed to have belonged to a second church ascribed to St. Wilfrid. The whole church has been restored by Scott. It is one of the smaller English cathedrals, being only 270 ft. in length; but it is 87 wide across the nave and aisles. The daily services are at 10 a.m. and 4.15 p.m. Adm. to the choir and crypt 6*d*.

The Nave, which has no triforium, is Perp., except the E.E. bays opening into the W. Towers. Two of the original arches (E. and S.) below the central tower have been changed from Norman to Perp., but the other two are still circular, though the lofty shafting run up at the W. arch shows that the intention was to change them all. — The Transepts retain much of the Transition work of Archbishop Roger, the founder of the church. — The Choir, in which the Transition Norman, the Dec., and the Perp. portions are readily distinguishable, is separated from the nave by a good Perp. *Screen*. The triforium-openings have been glazed, so that there are three rows of windows at different levels. The Dec. E. window is fine, though its modern glass is poor. The beautiful carving on the stalls is of the 15th century.

To the S. of the choir are the Chapter House and Vestry, which are believed to have together formed a small Norman church. Below them is a Norman crypt. Above them is the Lady Loft, a chapel of the Dec. period, built against the outside wall of the cathedral.

From the N.E. angle of the Nave we descend to the *Crypt, which is one of the only two Saxon crypts in England, both built in the 7th cent. by St. Wilfrid (comp. p. 413). A long narrow passage leads to a small vaulted chamber, with a curious opening or hole called 'St. Wilfrid's Needle', which was used, it is said, as a test of chastity, the pure only being able to be drawn through it.

In Stammergate is the interesting ***Hospital of St. Mary Magdalene***, founded in the 12th cent. for lepers; in High St. is the ***Maison Dieu***, a hospital of the 15th cent.; and in Bondgate is *St. John's Chapel*. The ***Museum*** (adm. 2*d*.), in Park St., chiefly contains objects of natural history.

From Ripon to Fountains Abbey, 3 M. (carr. 3*s*.). Walkers leave the town by the Westgate, opposite the Unicorn Hotel, and after a few yards diverge to the left through Park St., passing the **Museum**. At the fork (finger-post) we again keep to the left. After about 1 M. we cross a bridge over the *Laver*, and take the road most to the right. About 3 min. farther on, a wicket on the left opens on a field-path, which cuts off 1/3 M. and emerges in the middle of *Studley Village*, where we turn to the left, soon reaching the outer gates of **Studley Royal**, the seat of the Marquis of Ripon. Passing through the gates we ascend the long avenue, at the end of which is a conspicuous ***Church***, built by the Marquis of Ripon in 1876. After about 3/4 M., before reaching the church, we turn to the left, under the beech-trees (Spanish chestnuts and other timber also fine), pass a lake, and arrive at the (1/4 M.) gate of the pleasure-grounds (1*s*.). The grounds, through which runs the *Skell*, are elaborately laid out, with trimmed hedges, parterres, ponds, statuary, and small temples. After passing various 'Views' (sign-posts) we cross the stream by a rustic bridge, bend back along the *Crescent* and *Moon Ponds*, and ascend to the *Octagon Tower*. We then turn to the right and proceed in the original direction to '*Anne Boleyn's Seat*', an arbour affording a sudden *View of Fountains Abbey, which lies below, on the opposite bank of the Skell. On the way down to it we pass *Robin Hood's Well*, where the 'Curtal Friar' soundly thrashed that noble outlaw and threw him into the river. — ***Fountains Abbey**, a Cistercian foundation of the 14th cent., is at once the most extensive and the most picturesque monastic ruin in England; and nowhere else in the country can the plan of the secular buildings be so clearly traced. The **Church* is in the Transition Norman and E.E. styles, with a Perp. Tower and an additional transept at the E. end resembling the 'Nine Altars' of Durham (p. 413). The Monastic Buildings lie to the S., and include the *Great Cloister* (300 ft. long), the *Chapter House*, the *Refectory*, the *Buttery*, the *Fratry*, and the *Kitchen*. A little to the E. of these are the remains of the *Infirmary* (?) and the foundations of the *Abbot's House*. — A little to the W. (beyond the bridge and the gate) is *Fountains Hall*, an interesting Jacobean mansion. We then return by the drive along the left bank of the Skell.

Other points of interest are *Maikenfield Hall*, 3½ M. to the S.W.; *Hackfall Woods* (adm. 6*d*.), 7 M. to the N.W.; and the *Brimham Rocks* (p. 422).

From (33 M.) *Melmerby* branch-lines diverge to (11 M.) *Northallerton* (p. 409) and (7½ M.) *Masham* (4½ M. from Jervaulx Abbey, p. 410). — 39 M. *Thirsk* (p. 409).

54. From York to Beverley and Hull.

North Eastern Railway to (34 M.) *Beverley* in 1¼-1½ hr. (4*s*. 6*d*., 3*s*. 9*d*., 2*s*. 9½*d*.); to (41½ M.) *Hull* in 1½-1¾ hr. (5*s*. 7*d*., 4*s*. 8*d*., 3*s*. 6*d*.).

York, see p. 406. To the left runs the Scarborough line (R. 52). 9 M. *Stamford Bridge* was the scene of the defeat of Hardrada of Norway by Harold in 1066. — 16 M. *Pocklington* (Feathers), a small town, with an E.E. church with a Perp. tower. — 23 M. *Market Weighton* (Londesborough Arms) is the junction of lines to Selby (see p. 405) and to (14 M.) Driffield (see p. 425). We now enter the undulating chalk-district known as the *Wolds*.

34 M. **Beverley** (**Beverley Arms*; *King's Arms*; *King's Head*; *Rail. Rfmt. Rooms*), a quiet town, the see of a R. C. bishop, with 11,500 inhab., surpasses all English towns of its size in possessing two fine churches of all but the first rank. The short Railway Street leads to a triangular space with a large lamp in the centre, where we turn to the left to reach the Minster, and to the right to the Market Place, St. Mary's, and the Bar

*Beverley Minster (334 ft. long, 64 ft. wide), which occupies the site of a much earlier church, dates mainly from the 13-14th centuries. The Perp. *West Façade* resembles that of York Minster.

Interior. Among the most noticeable points in the Nave, which is in the late-Dec. style (ca. 1350), are the triforium-arcade, the musical angels on the piers, the tabernacle-work below the W. window, and the 'Maiden's Tomb' (below the 15th bay from the W. on the S. side). — The E.E. Choir is separated from the nave by a good modern screen, and contains some fine old stalls. Between the choir and the N.E. Transept is the beautiful **Percy Shrine* (1365), a good view of which is obtained from the top of the reredos. The details of the choir repay close inspection. — The top of the *W. Towers* (200 ft.) affords an extensive view.

*St. Mary's Church, a little beyond the market-place, is an-

other unusually fine cruciform church, mainly in the Dec. and Perp. styles, though possessing features of earlier date.

Among the special points of interest are the *W. *Front*, the *S. Porch* (with a Norman arch on the inside), the *Flemish Chapel* (with flamboyant tracery), the panelled *Ceiling* of the chancel, and the *Sculptural Decoration* throughout the church.

A short way beyond St. Mary's is the *North Bar*, dating from the 14th cent., and formerly one of the gates of the town. Just outside it is a picturesque half-timbered house. — About 1/3 M. to the E. of the Minster is the handsome modern *Church of St. Nicholas*.

At Beverley the line from York joins the line from Hull to Scarborough, which runs northwards viâ (11 M.) *Driffield* (Red Lion), an agricultural town with 6000 inhab., *Bridlington* (p. 420), and *Filey* (p. 420).

38 1/2 M. *Cottingham*, a favourite residence of Hull merchants.

41 1/2 M. **Hull.** — **Hotels.** Imperial, near the N.E. Station; N.E. Station Hotel, R. & A. 4*s.*; Cross Keys; Vittoria, at the Pier; George; Royal; Central Temperance. — *Railway Refreshmt. Rooms.*

Railway Stations. Besides the *Paragon Station* of the N.E.R., near the centre of the town, there is a *Booking Office* of the Manchester, Sheffield, & Lincolnshire Railway at the Corporation Pier, whence a Steam Ferry conveys passengers to the Railway Terminus in *New Holland*, on the other side of the Humber.

Steamers ply regularly from Hull to *Bergen*, *Christiania*, *Copenhagen*, *Antwerp*, *Rotterdam*, *Hamburg*, *Bremen*, *New York*, *Rouen*, *Aberdeen*, *Dundee*, *Leith*, *Grimsby*, *London*, and numerous other British and foreign ports.

Tramways and Omnibuses traverse the main streets, running to the *Corporation Pier* and various suburbs (fares 1*d.*, 2*d.*).

Hull or *Kingston-upon-Hull*, a town on the *Humber* estuary with 155,000 inhab., is the chief emporium of the trade between England and Northern Europe, and the headquarters of a deep-sea fishing fleet of 500 boats. Though a place of considerable antiquity, it possesses few old buildings and offers little to detain the tourist.

The following walk (2-3 hrs.) passes most of the points of interest. Leaving the Paragon Station, we walk through Paragon St. and Waterworks St., pass the *Dock Office* and the *Wilberforce Column*, and cross the *Whitefriargate Bridge*, which affords a view (right) of the *Docks*. At the end of Whitefriargate, Trinity House Lane, with the *Trinity House* (established in 1369), leads to the right to ***Trinity Church,** a large Dec. and Perp. edifice, restored by Scott (see p. liii).

Passing round to the Market Place, in front of the church, we descend to the right through Queen St. to the Corporation Pier, which affords a good view of the traffic in the Humber and of the flat coast of Lincolnshire on the opposite side (ferry, see above).

We now retrace our steps to Humber St., turn to the right, and soon reach the quaint High St. In the latter, immediately to the right, is the old *De la Pole Residence*, with curious carvings. Near the middle of the street, to the left, is the *King's Head*, an old inn with an overhanging story; and at the end of the street, to the right (No. 25), is the red brick house in which *William Wilberforce* was born in 1759. Salthouse Lane, nearly opposite, leads to the large *Queen's Dock*. Here we turn sharply to the left into Lowgate, in which, to the right, stands the Town Hall, in the Italian style.

Opposite is the *Church of St. Mary*, a Perp. edifice, restored by Scott, with the side-walk running below the tower (good interior). — Silver St., at the end of Lowgate, leads back to Whitefriargate (see above).

From Hull to *Gainsborough*, see p. 361; to *Lincoln*, see R. 55. — Branch-lines also run from Hull to (15½ M.) **Hornsea** *(Marine; New)* and to (18 M.) *Withernsea* (Queen's), two small watering-places on the German Ocean.

55. From Hull to Lincoln and Nottingham.

75 M. Railway in 3¾-6 hrs. (fares 13*s.* 5*d.*, 6*s.* 6½*d.*). We travel by the Manchester, Sheffield, & Lincolnshire Railway to (42 M.) *Lincoln* and thence to (33 M.) *Nottingham* by the Midland Railway. Through-carriages are attached to some trains.

Hull, see p. 425. Taking our tickets at the booking-office on the *Corporation Pier* (comp. p. 425), we cross the Humber by a steam ferry to (2 M.) *New Holland*, the starting-point of the railway. The line traverses the flat and featureless county of Lincoln. At (6 M.) *Thornton Abbey*, to the right, is a picturesque old abbey. — 8½ M. *Ulceby*, junction of a line to Great Grimsby and Cleethorpes.

Great Grimsby *(Royal; Yarborough; Rail. Refreshmt. Rooms)* is a prosperous seaport and fishing-town on the S. bank of the Humber, with 30,000 inhabitants. — **Cleethorpes** *(Dolphin; Cliff; Victoria; Rail. Refreshmt. Rooms)*, with 3000 inhab., is a rising watering-place.

From Great Grimsby a line runs to the S. to *Boston* (p. 429).

13 M. *Barnetby* is the junction of lines to *Gainsborough* and *Doncaster* (p. 405). — 38 M. *Market Rasen* (White Hart).

42 M. **Lincoln.** — **Railway Stations.** The *G. N.* and the *Midland Railway Stations*, near each other, adjoin the High St. — **Hotels.** Great Northern Station Hotel, R. & A. 5*s.*; *White Hart, near the Cathedral; Saracen's Head; Albion; Spread Eagle. — *Rail. Refreshment Rooms.*

Lincoln, the county-town of Lincolnshire and the see of a bishop, with about 40,000 inhab., is finely situated on a hill rising from the *Witham*, in the midst of the low fen district.

Lincoln, the British *Lindcoit* and the *Lindum Colonia* (one of nine privileged Coloniæ) of the Romans, is one of the most ancient towns in Great Britain, and rivals Chester in the interest of its memorials of the past. In the 9th cent. Lincoln and Lincolnshire were occupied by the Danes, who have left traces of their settlement in the ending *by*, so common in local names in this shire. Lincoln was accounted the fourth city of the realm at the time of the Norman Conquest, and William I. selected it as the site of one of his castles. The chief external events in the subsequent history of the town are the captures of the Castle by King Stephen in 1140, by the Barons in 1216, and by the Parliamentarians in 1644. Christianity was first introduced here by Paulinus (p. 427) in the 7th cent.; but the bishopric was not established till 1073, when the Mercian see was transferred hither from Dorchester (comp. p. 219). The chief industry of Lincoln is the manufacture of agricultural implements, and it carries on a considerable trade with the Midlands by means of the Fossdyke Canal, which joins the Witham and the Trent.

The following round includes most of the principal objects of interest in Lincoln, though the archæologist and student of architecture will find material here to occupy him for many days. Leaving the *Midland Railway Station*, we proceed to the N. along High Street, passing the modern church of *St. Mark* on the left. On the opposite side (No. 333) is an interesting half-timbered house, which should be viewed from the court-yard. We then cross the G. N. Railway and reach *St. Mary-le-Wigford*, the tower of which is a good example of the pre-Norman style, though built shortly after the Conquest. The E.E. nave and chancel date from about 1225, and the S. aisle is modern. In front of the church stands *St. Mary's Conduit*, constructed in the time of Henry VIII. (1509-47) with fragments of an old monastery. To the left, farther on, are the ivy-clad remains of *St. Benedict's Church.*

We may here diverge, through the archway, to see *Brayford Pool* (boats for hire), the S. bank of which affords a good view of the Cathedral.

We now reach the **High Bridge*, an ancient structure, with a row of buildings on its W. side (quaint, Dutch-like view of their backs by descending the steps to the left). In front is the ***Stonebow,** a 15th cent. gate-house, the upper part used as the *Guildhall.*

Just beyond the Stonebow, at the church of *St. Peter-at-Arches* (18th cent.), we may diverge to the right, through Silver St., to visit *St. Swithin's Church*, which contains a Roman altar, discovered in 1884.

At the head of High St., we follow the narrow Strait, to the right. At the end of this, to the left, is the **Jew's House*, one of the most ancient specimens of domestic architecture in England (early 12th cent.; comp. p. xl). — The Strait is continued by the Steep Hill, halfway up which is a platform known as the *Mayor's Chair*. Near the top of the hill, to the right, is the *House of Aaron the Jew*, with a Norman window. Opposite is the *Bishop's Hostel*, connected with the Lincoln Theological School. To the right, farther on, is the *Exchequer Gate* of the Minster Yard (p. 429). In the meantime, however, we turn to the left and enter the **Castle** (adm. 2*d.*).

The Castle Walls enclose an area of 6½ acres, laid out as a garden, and contain the *Assize Courts* and the old *County Prison* (disused). To reach the *Keep* (12th cent.) we turn to the left on entering and pass through a gateway. View from the top of *Cobb's Hall*, the round tower to the S. of the entrance. Just inside the entrance-gateway, to the right, is a fine *Oriel Window*, brought from John of Gaunt's Palace (p. 429).

We now continue in a straight direction through the Bailgate, in which, in the cellar of Mr. Allis's House (No. 27, to the left; adm. 1*s.*), are the highly-interesting remains of a *Roman Basilica.*

In the Westgate, which diverges to the left from the Bailgate, is *St. Paul's Church*, occupying the site of the church of St. Paulinus (p. 426).

Bailgate ends at the *Newport Arch, one of the gates of Lindum Colonia and a unique specimen of a Roman city-gate in England. Its date is placed between B.C. 50 and A.D. 50. — We may now turn to the right and pass along the East Bight into the Minster Yard (see p. 429), which we reach on its N. side.

***Lincoln Cathedral,** splendidly crowning the hill on which the city is built, may perhaps claim to be the finest church in Great Britain. Other cathedrals may equal or surpass it in certain points, but in the combination of size, delicacy of detail, effectiveness of both interior and exterior, good preservation, and grandeur of position, it has probably no rival. The building is 480 ft. long (in-

For a plan of Lincoln Cathedral see page 553

ternal measurement), 80 ft. wide, 220 ft. across the W. transepts, and 82 ft. high. Daily services, 10 a.m. and 4 p.m. Adm. to the choir and cloisters 6*d*., to the tower 6*d*.

History. Of the original cathedral, built at the end of the 11th cent., there remains the lower portion of the W. front and part of the first bay of the nave. The Norman cathedral was injured by an earthquake in 1185, and its restoration was at once undertaken by Bishop Hugh ('St. Hugh of Lincoln'; 1186-1200), who finished the *Choir* and the *E. Transepts*, the earliest piece of E.E. work of known date (p. xlii). The *W. Transepts* and *Chapter House* were completed soon after, and the *Nave*, including the W. front, by about 1250. The *Presbytery* and *Cloisters* followed in the same cent., and the upper story of the *Central Tower*, the lower part of which dates from about 1240-50, was added between 1300 and 1320. The upper parts of the W. towers are late-Dec. (ca. 1380). The *Chapels* attached to the Presbytery are Perp. (15-16th cent.).

Exterior. Among the most noteworthy external features of the Cathedral are its fine **Central* and *W. Towers* (262 ft. & 200 ft. high); the **W. Façade*, which is imposing in spite of its mixture of styles (p. xxxix) and the fact that it is in some degree a mere screen; the *E. Front*, somewhat marred by the aisle-gables; the *Galilee Porch*, adjoining the S.W. Transept; the *S.E. Portal;* and the *Chapter House*, with its flying buttresses.

Interior. The usual entrance is by one of the W. doors. The NAVE is harmonious and imposing, though the vaulting is rather low and the bays too wide. At its W. end are two chapels, of somewhat later date. The Norman font stands under the second arch to the S. The stained glass is modern, and the monuments are of little interest. The way in which the E.E. work is accommodated to the pre-existing Norman front is interesting. — The CENTRAL TOWER is supported by four fine and lofty arches, with massive stone piers, contrasting with the slender piers of the nave. In the lantern hangs 'Great Tom', a bell weighing 5½ tons. — The GREAT TRANSEPTS contain two bays of St. Hugh's work, while the rest is a little later. The most interesting features are the two circular windows, that in the S. transept being called the **Bishop's Eye* (ca. 1325), and that in the N. the **Dean's Eye* (ca. 1225). The glass in both is old. The E. aisles of the transepts contain chapels, separated from the transepts by carved screens. The beautiful *Doorways* leading into the choir-aisles are of the latest E.E. period.

The *CHOIR, the oldest known example of the E.E. or pure Gothic style, is separated from the nave by a Dec. *Screen* (1320), surmounted by the organ. The lowness of the vaulting is felt here even more than in the nave. The five easternmost bays of the choir, beyond the E. TRANSEPTS, form the **PRESBYTERY or ANGEL CHOIR, 'one of the loveliest of human works', added in 1255-80. Its proportions and its details are alike admirable. The **Choir Stalls*, dating from the late-Dec. period (1360-80), are unsurpassed in England (comp. p. 273). Among other noticeable points in the choir are the **E. Window*; the *Easter Sepulchre*, to the left of the high-altar; the monuments of Catherine Swynford, third wife of John of Gaunt, and their daughter, the Countess of Westmorland, to the right of the altar; the site of the shrine of *Little St. Hugh of Lincoln*, a child alleged to have been crucified by the Jews; the unique *Piers* at the angles of the choir and E. transept, with their crocketed and detached shafts; the modern *Pulpit*; the monument of *Bp. Wordsworth* (d. 1885); the sculptured *Angels* in the Angel Choir; and the *Diapered Screen* of the *Choristers' Vestry*. Most of the stained glass is modern and bad.

From the N.E. Transept we enter a vestibule leading to the CLOISTERS, on the floor of which is a slab marking the grave of '*Mrs. Markham*' *(Elizabeth Penrose)*, the guide of our earliest historical studies. The Cloisters were erected towards the end of the 13th century. The N. Walk, rebuilt by Wren, affords one of the best views of the Cathedral. — In the E. Walk is the entrance to the *CHAPTER HOUSE, a decagonal building of the 13th cent., with vaulting borne by a central shaft. — The CHAPTER LIBRARY, above the N. Cloister, contains 5000 vols. and valuable MSS.

Many of the houses surrounding the CLOSE, or MINSTER YARD, are picturesque and interesting. Among these are the *Chancery* (14-15th cent.), at the N.E. angle; the *Cantilupe Chantry*; the house known as the *Priory*; and the quaint little *Vicars' Court* (14-15th cent.), opposite the S. Transept. The remains of the *Old Episcopal Palace* to the S., the oldest parts dating from early in the 12th cent., are also of great interest; they include *Bishop Alnwick's Tower* (now fitted up for the Theological School) and *Dining Room*, and *St. Hugh's Hall*. A new *Palace* has been erected by the side of the ruins of the earlier one, a part of which has been restored as the Bishop's Domestic Chapel. The *Deanery*, to the N. of the Cathedral, is modern; the *Sub-Deanery* (with a good oriel) and the *Precentory* have been modernized. — The main entrance to the Close is by the *Exchequer Gate* (see p. 427), a large three-arched gateway of the early 14th century. *Potter Gate*, at the S. E. corner, is of the same date.

Among other points of interest in Lincoln are the *Arboretum*, on the E. side of the city; the small ruin of *Monks' Abbey*; *St. Anne's Bede-Houses*; the large *County Hospital:* and the new *Science & Art School*. — In the High St., to the S. of our starting-point at the Midland Railway (see p. 426), is *St. Mary's Guild*, an interesting range of 12th cent. buildings, popularly known as John of Gaunt's Stables (to the left; near St. Peter's). On the opposite side (Nos. 122, 123) is *John of Gaunt's Palace* (much altered). The old church of *St. Peter-at-Gowts*, on the other side of the street, has a pre-Norman tower like that of St. Mary's (p. 427). The High St. ends at the *Bargate Bridge*, over an arm of the Witham.

The immediate environs of Lincoln contain few attractions for the ordinary traveller, but the ecclesiologist will find much to interest him in Lincolnshire churches.

From Lincoln to *Grantham*, see p. 361. — A line also runs from Lincoln to *Gainsborough* (p. 361). — The usual routes from London to Lincoln are the G. N. R. from *King's Cross* or the G. E. R. from *Liverpool St.* (3-4 hrs.; fares 18*s*. 10*d*., 14*s*. 3*d*., 10*s*. 9*d*.); it may also be reached from *St. Pancras* viâ Nottingham, or from *Euston* viâ Rugby and Trent.

FROM LINCOLN TO BOSTON, 30 M., G. N. R. in $1^1/_4$ hr. (fares 4*s*. 2*d*., 2*s*. $6^1/_2$*d*.). This line runs through the fen-country, following the lower course of the *Witham*. From ($8^1/_2$ M.) *Bardney* a branch-line runs N. to *Louth*, with a fine church-spire, 294 ft. high. — At ($14^1/_2$ M.) *Kirkstead*, with the remains of a Cistercian abbey (12th cent.), a line diverges to *Horncastle*, passing *Woodhall Spa*, with springs strongly impregnated with iodine. — To the left, near ($18^1/_2$ M.) *Tattershall*, is the keep of an old *Castle* (16th cent.).

30 M. **Boston**, *i.e. St. Botolph's Town (Peacock; Red Lion; Rail. Rfmt. Rooms)*, an ancient seaport at the mouth of the *Witham*, with 19,000 inhab., is perhaps chiefly interesting from its association with its famous namesake on the other side of the Atlantic. The **Church of St. Botolph* is a large Dec. building, with a lofty Perp. tower ('Boston Stump') crowned with an octagonal lantern (300 ft.). — Boston is a railway-centre of some importance, lines running N. to *Skegness* (a rising watering-place), *Willoughby* (with a branch to *Sutton-on-Sea* and *Mablethorpe*), *Louth* (see above), and *Grimsby* (p. 426); W. to *Sleaford* (p. 361) and *Barkstone* (p. 361); and S. to *Spalding* (*Lynn*, *Peterborough*, etc.). Many of the finest churches in Lincolnshire and Norfolk lie on the railway between Boston and Lynn (p. 441).

Beyond Lincoln the train continues to run through the fenny district, the meres and marshes of which have, however, been mostly converted into rich pasture and fertile corn-land. — At ($57^1/_2$ M.) *Newark* (p. 361) we cross the main line of the G.N.R.

$61^1/_2$ M. *Rolleston* is the junction of a line to ($7^1/_2$ M.) *Southwell* and ($14^1/_2$ M.) *Mansfield* (p. 350).

Southwell *(Saracen's Head)*, a small town with 3000 inhab., is often visited for the sake of its fine **Minster* (306 ft. long), formerly a collegiate church, and lately raised to the rank of a cathedral. It is one of the few great English churches of an early period that retain their three towers. The *Nave*, *Transepts*, and *Towers* are Norman, dating from the beginning of the 12th cent.; and the massive *Interior is very imposing. The *Choir*, with its ingeniously combined triforium and clerestory, is E.E., dating from 1230-50. The *Chapter House*, erected in 1285-1300, is adorned with exquisite *Stone-carvings. The fine *Screen* separating the choir and nave is Dec. (14th cent.). — To the S. of the cathedral are the ruins of an old *Palace* of the Archbishops of York and the *New Palace* by Bodley.

At (65 M.) *Thurgarton* is *Thurgarton Priory*, on the site of a Benedictine convent. The *Priory Church* is now the parish-church.

75 M. **Nottingham** *(George; Clarendon; Flying Horse; Maypole; Lion; Caledonian Temperance)*, the metropolis of the lace and hosiery manufacture of England, is pleasantly situated on the steep slope of a sandstone hill, near the junction of the small river *Leen* with the Trent. The population is now about 230,000.

Nottingham, the *Snodengahame* of the Saxons, is one of the most ancient towns in England, and probably occupies the site of an early British settlement. The castle (see below) was occupied by several of the English kings and is frequently heard of in English history. At the beginning of the present century Nottingham was a centre of the 'Luddite' riots, in which the stocking-makers endeavoured to improve their miserable position by concerted action against the masters, chiefly by the destruction of machinery. It was not till upwards of 1000 stocking-frames had been demolished and several rioters put to death that order was finally restored.

The Market Place of Nottingham, $5^1/_2$ acres in extent, is said to be the largest in England. It was formerly divided into two portions by a breast-high wall, which was erected when the town consisted of two distinct boroughs, English and Norman. The second stories of the houses round it project over the pavement and are supported by pillars, forming a kind of arcade. The **University College*, a handsome Gothic building, contains a free public library, a natural history museum, well-equipped laboratories, etc. The *Church of St. Mary* is a fine cruciform edifice of the 15th cent., with a tower and chancel of later date; it possesses a fine picture ascribed to Fra Bartolommeo. The *Rom. Cath. Cathedral* is a good example of Pugin's revived Gothic. The *School of Art* and the *Arboretum* may also be mentioned.

The ***Castle,** which occupies a commanding position on the W. side of the town, 150 ft. above the Leen, is, in its present form, a palatial building in the Renaissance style, containing the **Midland Counties Art Museum*.

The original castle, built by the Conqueror, soon came to be regarded as the key of the Midlands, and was a frequent object of contest. Mortimer, the guilty favourite of Queen Isabella, was surprised here in 1330 by Edward III., who gained entrance by a secret passage now known as 'Mortimer's Hole'; Owen Glendower was imprisoned within its walls; and David II. of Scotland was lodged here on his way to London. In 1642 Charles I. unfurled his standard and mustered his troops at Nottingham Castle, but in the following year it fell into the hands of the Parliament. It was then entrusted to the care of Col. Hutchinson, whose wife has left us in her well-known memoirs a charming account of various episodes of the Civil War. During the Commonwealth the old castle was demolished.

The modern one founded in 1674 by the conspicuous Royalist, William Cavendish, Duke of Newcastle, was burned down by the mob in 1831 in consequence of the then Duke's opposition to the Reform Bill, and was afterwards acquired by the Corporation and restored as a public museum. See Mr. T. C. Hine's interesting monograph.

The tourist should visit one of the large *Lace* and *Hosiery Factories*, in which the ingenuity and rapidity of the machines will interest the most unprofessional observer. The manufacture of machine-made lace was begun here upwards of a century ago and is now scarcely second in importance to the hosiery industry. Among the largest establishments are the hosiery-works of *Messrs. I & R. Morley* (6000 workpeople); the hosiery and lace factories of the *Nottingham Manufacturing Co.*; and the machine-works of the *Messrs. Blackburn*. The largest depot of lace in the town is that of *Messrs. Thomas Adams & Co.*

Henry Kirke White (1785-1806), the poet, was the son of a butcher here, and *Col. Hutchinson* (see p. 430; 1615-64) was also a native of Nottingham.

About 8 M. to the N.W. is *Newstead Abbey* (reached by train to *Newstead* or *Linby*), the seat of Lord Byron, who is buried in the church of *Hucknall Torkard*, 3 M. nearer Nottingham. A little to the S. of Newstead is *Annesley*, the married home of Mrs. Musters, the 'Mary Chaworth' of Byron's youthful poems. About 2 M. to the W. of Nottingham is *Wollaton Hall*, the seat of Lord Middleton, a fine Elizabethan mansion, said to have been designed by John of Padua; in the park is a famous double avenue of limes. — Excursions may also be made from Nottingham to the *Dukeries* (p. 360), *Sherwood Forest* (p. 361), and *Southwell* (p. 430).

56. From London to Cambridge.

56 M. Great Eastern Railway from *Liverpool Street Station* or *St. Pancras* in $1^1/_4$-$2^1/_2$ hrs. (fares 8*s.* 9*d.*, 6*s.* 9*d.*, 4*s.* $7^1/_2$*d.*). — Cambridge may also be reached by the G.N.R. viâ *Hitchin* (same times and fares), or by the L.N.W.R. viâ *Bedford.*

The trains starting from *Liverpool Street* and *St. Pancras* traverse the N.E. suburbs of London and unite at (6 M.) *Tottenham.* Beyond (8 M.) *Angel Road* the wooded heights of *Epping Forest* (see *Baedeker's Handbook to London)* are visible to the right. — 13 M. *Waltham Cross* (Four Swans), with Waltham Abbey and Cross (see *Baedeker's London).* At (14 M.) *Cheshunt*, famous for its rose-gardens, is the house where Richard Cromwell died. — 17 M. *Broxbourne* is the junction of lines to *Rye House* and *Hertford* (see p. 364 and *Baedeker's London*), and to *Widford* and *Buntingford.* Charles Lamb used to frequent Widford church in his boyhood. — We now cross the *Lea* and enter Essex. — From ($30^1/_2$ M.) **Bishop's Stortford** (*George;* 7000 inhab.) a branch runs to (9 M.) *Dunmow* (Saracen's Head), *Braintree* (18 M.), and (30 M.) *Witham* (p. 442).

Near Dunmow are the ruins of the *Priory*, where it was the custom (recently revived) to present a flitch of bacon to any married couple who had not repented of their marriage during a year and a day.

Near (42 M.) *Audley End* is the fine seat of Lord Braybrooke (park open to visitors).

About 2 M. to the N.E. is **Saffron Walden** *(Rose & Crown)*, a small town (6100 inhab.), with a large Perp. church, a ruined castle, a museum, and several quaint timbered houses.

46 M. *Great Chesterford;* 53 M. *Shelford.* Farther on, the low *Gogmagog Hills* are visible to the right. The red buildings on the same side as we enter the station are Cavendish College (p. 439).

58 M. **Cambridge.** — **Hotels.** Bull (Pl. a; B, 4), Trumpington St., R. & A. 4*s.* 6*d.*; University Arms, Regent St. (Pl. D, 4); Red Lion (Pl. c; C, 3), Petty Cury; *Old Castle, opposite Emmanuel College (Pl. D, 4); Hoop (Pl. d; C, 2), Bridge St.; Prince of Wales (Pl. e; C, 3), Sidney St., with restaurant; Bird Bolt Temperance (Pl. f; C, 4), St. Andrew's St., plain.

Restaurants. *Moyes*, Benet St.; *Prince of Wales Hotel*, see above; *Webb*, Market Passage, Market St.; *Rail. Refreshmt. Rooms.* — Ices at *Thurston's*, Market St.

Photographs. *R. H. Lord*, Market Place; *Stearn*, Bridge St.; *Hills & Saunders*, 15 King's Parade.

Baths. *Flack*, 25 St. Andrew's St. — *River Baths* at the University Sheds (not open to strangers) and on Sheep's Green.

Post and Telegraph Office (Pl. 13; C, 4), St. Andrew's St.

The **Railway Station** (beyond Pl. D, 6) lies $1^1/_2$ M. from the centre of the town; cab 1*s.* 6*d.* (each pers. beyond one, 6*d.* extra).

Tramways run from the Station through Hills Road, Regent St., and St. Andrew's St. to the *Post Office* (Pl. 13; C, 4) and through Lensfield Road and Trumpington St. to the *Market Place* (Pl. B, C, 3). Fares 1*d.*, 2*d.*

Principal Attractions. *Fitzwilliam Museum* (p. 433); *Peterhouse* (p. 433); *Queens' College* (p. 434); *King's College* (p. 435), with its grounds and chapel; *Clare College* (p. 436); Exterior of the *University Library* and *Senate House* (p. 435); *Trinity College* (p. 436), and grounds; *St. John's College* (p. 437), with grounds; the *Round Church* (p. 437); *Magdalene College* (p. 438); *Jesus College* (p. 438); *Gonville and Caius College* (p. 436). A college-service should be attended in the chapel of King's, Trinity, St. John's, or Jesus. A walk or a row along the **Backs* should on no account be omitted.

Boats may be hired on the *Lower River*, the *Upper River*, or the *Backs*, three reaches of the *Cam*, at different levels, separated by locks. Visitors who merely wish a short row should take a boat either at the Mill Pool (Pl. B, 5) or at Garret Hostel Bridge (Pl. A, 3), adjoining Trinity, and skirt the *College Backs* (see below). — The *Inter-Collegiate Boat Races* (comp. p. 227; chiefly in June) are rowed on the Lower River (p. 438), and here also all the necessary practice is performed. The *Procession of the Boats* at Commencement (p. 227) takes place at the Backs. The pretty but narrow Upper River is resigned to non-racing boats.

Cambridge, a town with about 40,000 inhab., situated on the *Cam*, in a somewhat flat but not unpleasing district, is interesting as the seat of one of the two great English Universities. Though on the whole less picturesque than Oxford, especially as regards general views, Cambridge contains several collegiate buildings which are at least equal in interest to those of the sister-university, while in certain points, such as the 'Backs', *i.e.* the beautiful lawns and avenues behind the colleges, it possesses charms peculiar to itself.

History. Though its authenticated pre-Academic epoch is longer, the history of Cambridge is identified, even more than is the case at Oxford, with the growth of its university. It is believed to occupy the site of the British *Caer Graunth* and the Roman *Camboritum*, situated on the N. (left) bank of the *Cam* or *Granta.* The name appears in the Anglo-Saxon Chronicle as *Grantebrycge*, and later as *Cantebrigge* (14-15th cent.). The town was ravaged several times by the Danes, and William the Conqueror built a castle here, of which almost nothing now remains (comp. p. 438).

In regard to the University, legend has been no less daring at Cambridge than at Oxford, ascribing the establishment of the first seat of learning here to a Spanish prince named *Cantaber*, 300 years before the Christian era! In both cases, however, the first establishment of teaching bodies seems to have taken place in the 12th cent., while their documentary history begins in the 13th. The earliest recognition of Cambridge University occurs in a writ of the second year of Henry III. (1217); the first college was founded in 1284; and in 1318 the University was recognised as a *studium generale* by Pope John XXII. The manner of its early development

For a coloured street plan of Cambridge see pages 592 & 593

was similar to that of Oxford, and has already been indicated at p. 224. Of the numerous disputes between the University and the Town, the most serious was that of 1381, when the townsmen stormed the colleges and destroyed most of their charters. In the Civil War many of the colleges sent their plate to the king, but the town acquiesced without resistance in the rule of the Commonwealth. Cambridge contains 17 colleges and 2 public hostels, attended by about 3000 students.

Comp. *Willis & Clark's* 'Architectural History of Cambridge' (4 quarto vols.; 1886), *J. Bass Mullinger's* admirable 'History of the University of Cambridge' (1873-84) and his shorter work in the 'Epochs of Church History' series (1888), *J. W. Clark's* 'Cambridge' (1890), the *University Calendar*, and the *Cambridge Student's Handbook*. See also pp. 224, 225 for a general sketch of the customs and organisation of the University.

At the (3 min.) end of Station Road we turn to the right and follow the tramway-line, passing the red *Church of St. Paul*, and Harvey Road, leading to the *University Cricket Ground*. A few hundred yards farther on, at the large *Roman Catholic Church*, we turn to the left into *Lensfield Road*, a broad thoroughfare passing the grounds of Downing College (on the right; p. 439) to the (1/4 M.) S. end of *Trumpington Street*. Here is situated *Hobson's Conduit* (Pl. C, 6), constructed in 1614, partly at the cost of *Thomas Hobson*, carrier and livery stable-keeper, whose rule of strict rotation in letting out his horses gave rise to the phrase 'Hobson's Choice'. His memory has been immortalised by Milton.

Following Trumpington St. towards the N., we pass *Addenbrooke's Hospital* (Pl. 1; C, 5) and reach the ***Fitzwilliam Museum** (Pl. C, 5; open daily, 10-6 in summer and 10-4 in winter; on Frid. to visitors accompanied by a member of the University in academic gown), a handsome building in a Grecian style, containing the important collections bequeathed by Viscount Fitzwilliam in 1816 and acquisitions of later date.

Interior. Passing through the beautiful ENTRANCE HALL, and ascending the STAIRCASE, we enter the large WEST GALLERY, containing pictures by *Holbein*, *Dürer*, *Rembrandt* (Officer), *Titian*, *Paolo Veronese*, *Dow*, *Hogarth* and others (catalogues provided). — To the right is the NORTH DOME ROOM, with paintings by British masters, and this is adjoined by the NORTH GALLERY, containing works of less interest. — The SOUTH DOME ROOM contains minor Italian works, and the SOUTH GALLERY works of the French, Flemish, and German schools. A collection of 25 Drawings by *Turner* is also shown. — In the BASEMENT ROOM are ancient sculptures, Greek vases, models of buildings, bronzes, Oriental curiosities, etc. — The fine LIBRARY, with one of the richest collections of prints in Europe, is shown to graduates and their friends only, or to undergraduates with an order.

The *Archaeological Museum*, an annexe to the Fitzwilliam Museum be hind St. Mary the Less (p. 434), contains upwards of 600 casts from the antique (open daily, except Frid., 10 to 4 or 6; catalogue by Dr. Waldstein).

On the same side, just beyond the Museum, is **St. Peter's College** (Pl. B, C, 5), or *Peterhouse*, the oldest college in Cambridge, founded by Hugh de Balsham, Bishop of Ely, in 1284. It possesses two courts, the first of which is divided into two parts by the *Chapel*, built in 1632 in an Italian Gothic style. The only parts of the original building are on the left side of the first court (visible from the W.). The new *Combination Room*, on the S. side of the second court, contains some beautiful stained glass by Burne Jones and Morris.

The most famous member of Peterhouse is the poet Gray, who occupied rooms on the N. side of the first court. They are recognisable by the iron bars at the window (on the outside wall, facing St. Mary the Less), which are said to have been placed there by Gray to facilitate the use of a rope-ladder in case of fire. — To the W., reached from either court, are the pleasant *College Grounds*.

Adjoining Peterhouse is the *Church of St. Mary the Less* (Pl. 8), which for 350 years served as the college-chapel. It is in the Dec. style of the 14th cent., but has been spoiled by alterations.

Opposite St. Mary's is **Pembroke College** (Pl. B, C, 5), founded by the Countess of Pembroke in 1347, but almost entirely rebuilt. The *Chapel* was built by Sir Christopher Wren in 1663-65; the *Hall*, *Library*, and *Master's Lodge* are recent erections by Waterhouse, the rest of the new buildings are by the younger Scott.

The room to the left of the entrance, formerly the chapel, contains a fine ceiling. The cloister leading to the chapel is also interesting. The pretty * *Gardens* contain a mulberry-tree associated with the memory of Edmund Spenser, who was a member of this college. Other eminent alumni are Ridley, Grindal, Andrews, Gray (who removed to Pembroke from Peterhouse), William Pitt, and Richard Crashaw.

To the left, at the corner of Mill Lane, stands the **Pitt Press** (Pl. B, 5), a large ecclesiastical-looking edifice, containing the *University Printing Office* and the *Registry*. It is nicknamed the 'Freshmen's Church'. To the right is *St. Botolph's Church* (Pl. 5).

Following Silver St. to the left, we reach ***Queens' College** (Pl. B, 4), founded in 1448 by Queen Margaret of Anjou, wife of Henry VI., and completed by Queen Elizabeth Woodville, wife of Edward IV.

We pass through the handsome vaulted *Gateway*, with its four turrets, and enter the Great Court, with the *Hall*, *Library*, and **Chapel*. On the wall of the latter (adm. 6*d*.), which has been judiciouly restored, is a large sun-dial. The passage adjoining the Hall leads into the picturesque *Cloister Court*, from which an old wooden bridge crosses the Cam to the **College Grounds*. To the S. of the Cloister Court is the *Erasmus Court*, with the *Erasmus Tower*, in which Erasmus lodged. On the N. side of the principal court is the *Walnut Tree Court*. A new court has been built still farther to the N. Thomas Füller was a member of Queens'.

By continuing to follow Silver St., crossing the Cam, and going through a lane in a straight direction, we reach *Ridley Hall*, a modern theological seminary. Farther on, beyond Corpus Cricket Ground, is **Selwyn College**, founded in 1882, and intended, like Keble College (p. 232), to provide an economical university training for members of the Church of England. — To the S. of Selwyn is **Newnham College**, one of the two women's colleges at Cambridge, established in 1875. It accommodates 100 students.

Leaving Queens' by the main gateway and turning to the left, we reach *St. Catharine's College* (Pl. B, 4), founded in 1475. Archbishop Sandys was Master of St. Catharine's. — Passing through this college, we again reach Trumpington St., opposite —

Corpus Christi College (Pl. B, 4), established in 1352 by the amalgamation of the 'Gilda Corporis Christi' and the 'Gilda Beatæ Mariæ Virginis'. The W. front and the first court are modern, but the picturesque *Old Court* (entered from the N.E. angle of the first court) belongs to the original building. The *Library* (to the right on entering) contains a very valuable collection of MSS., bequeathed by Archbishop Parker, and the *Buttery* possesses some fine old plate.

Archbishops Tenison and Parker, Marlowe, Fletcher, Richard Boyle, and Samuel Wesley are among the names on the college-books.

Behind Corpus, between Downing St. and Free School Lane, are the *Science Schools* and *Museums* (see p. 439).

In Benet Street, to the N. of Corpus, is *St. Benedict's Church* (Pl. 4), generally called *St. Benet's*, the tower of which is one of the best specimens of pre-Norman architecture in England. In the interior the arch opening into the tower is noticeable; the rest of the building has been modernized (key at 3 King's Parade).

The continuation of Trumpington St. is named the *King's Parade*, and here, in an open and central position, is ***King's College** (Pl. B, 4), founded in 1440 by Henry VI., and finished by Henry VII. and Henry VIII. The *Great Court* is separated from the street by a modern open-work stone screen. On the W. side are the Library and the Provost's Lodge, from which a fine lawn slopes to the river.

On the N. side of the principal court is the ****Chapel**, the glory of King's College and of Cambridge, built in 1446-1515, and one of the finest Perp. interiors in England (p. liii; open, free, 11-1 and 3-5). It is 290 ft. long and 85 ft. wide. The beautiful **Stained Glass Windows* date from the 16th cent., except that at the W. end, which is a modern imitation of the others. The fan-vaulted *Ceiling*, the carved *Stalls*, and the *Organ Screen* all demand notice. The altar-piece is a Descent from the Cross by *Daniele da Volterra*. The Tudor portcullis and rose are here, as elsewhere in Cambridge, freely used in the decoration. Visitors may ascend to the roof, which commands an extensive view, reaching on the N.E., to Ely Cathedral (p. 440); but they are not now admitted to the space between the stone vaulting and the upper roof of wood.

The other buildings of the college were built in the 18-19th cent. and have no particular architectural merit. The Fountain was erected in 1877. The bridge over the Cam affords a fine view. — Among the chief members of King's were Archbp. Sumner, Bp. Pearson, Sir Richard Temple, Sir Robert Walpole, Horace Walpole, and Lord Stratford de Redcliffe.

Visitors who do not intend to walk all along the Backs (p. 432) may obtain a view of them, at perhaps their prettiest point, by crossing King's College bridge and entering Clare (see p. 436) from behind.

The *Pythagoras School* (origin of name unknown), adjoining the Backs, near St. John's College, is an interesting late-Norman house (p. xli).

A little farther on, to the left and standing back from the street, is the *Schools Quadrangle*, now nearly absorbed by the **University Library** (Pl. 17; B, 3; open 10-4, on Sat. 9-1, to visitors accompanied by a graduate).

The original buildings of this Quadrangle were finished in the 15th century. Considerable additions were made about 1715, and the present façade was added in 1754-8. Other additions and alterations have been carried out during the present cent.; and most of the rooms formerly used as Examination Schools have been gradually absorbed by the Library.

The *Library*, which is surpassed in size in England by the British Museum and Bodleian alone, contains 450,000 vols. and 3000 MSS. Among the latter, many of which are of immense value, are the Beza MS. of the New Testament (6th cent.; presented by Theodore de Beza in 1581), a copy on vellum of Wycliffe's Bible, and a Persian MS. of 1388. There are also numerous incunabula and a folio of sketches by Rembrandt. — The *Public Schools* form part of the same block of buildings.

The Library is adjoined by the **Senate House** (Pl. 14), built by Gibbs in the Corinthian style in 1730. The interior contains statues of Pitt, by *Nollekens*, the Duke of Somerset, by *Rysbrack*, etc.

The graduation ceremonials and other great public functions of the University are held here. — Opposite the Library is **St. Mary's the Great** (Pl. 7), the University Church, a Perp. edifice of 1478-1519 (university service at 2 p.m. on Sun.).

We now go down Senate House Passage to **Trinity Hall** (Pl. B, 3), founded in 1350, and principally frequented by students of law.

The *Garden Court* is picturesque, and the small *Fellows' Garden* is also pretty. The book-cases in the *Library* still retain the iron bars to which the books used to be chained. Among the alumni of Trinity Hall are Hollinshed, Lord Howard of Effingham, Bishop Gardiner,, Lord Chesterfield, Lord Lytton, Lord Chief Justice Cockburn, and John Sterling.

To the S. of Trinity Hall lies **Clare College** (Pl. B, 3), the second oldest in Cambridge, founded in 1326; the present buildings, which enclose a large court on the bank of the Cam, are of later date.

At the back is a bridge leading across the Cam (view) to the beautiful **Fellows' Garden* and a fine avenue of limes. Archbishop Tillotson and Cudworth are, perhaps, the two most eminent names associated with Clare.

Opposite Clare is the handsome new W. façade of the Schools Quadrangle (comp. p. 435), incorporating and completing the old King's College Gateway. To the left of the gateway is the *Geological Museum* (open 10-4), containing a very extensive collection of fossils (Plesiosaurus, a skeleton of the Irish elk, etc.).

We now return to Senate House Passage and pass through the picturesque *Gate of Honour* into **Gonville and Caius College** (Pl. B, 3), shortly styled Caius ('Keys'), founded in 1348 by Edmund de Gonville, and refounded in 1558 by the erudite Dr. Caius, body-physician to Queen Mary. The principal entrance (modern) is at the corner of Senate House Passage and King's Parade.

The *Caius Court*, which we enter by the Gate of Honour, communicates with the first or main court by the *Gate of Virtue*, and is the work of Dr. Caius. The inner or *Gonville Court*, to the right, was refaced last century. Among former students of Caius are Harvey (discoverer of the circulation of the blood), Jeremy Taylor, Judge Jeffreys, and Lord Chancellor Thurlow. This college is affected by medical students.

In Trinity St., opposite Caius College, stands *St. Michael's Church* (Pl. 9; B, 3), a Dec. building restored by Scott. — To the left, beyond Caius, is the beautiful *King's Gateway* of ***Trinity College** (Pl. B, 3), the largest college in England, formed by Henry VIII. in 1546 by the amalgamation of several earlier foundations.

The lower part of the King's Gateway dates from the time of Edward IV., and the upper from that of Henry VIII., with a statue of whom it is adorned. On the inner face are figures of James I., Queen Anne of Denmark, and Charles I. The **Great Court*, which is not quite rectangular, is 325-345 ft. long and 255-285 ft. wide. On the N. side is the *Chapel* (open 11-12 and 2-3), built in the Tudor period; it contains good carved woodwork and numerous statues and busts, the finest of which is that of *Sir Isaac Newton by Roubiliac. The windows are modern. To the W. of the chapel is *King Edward's Tower*, with a statue of Edward III. The passage below this tower leads to the smaller *Fellows' Garden*. On the W. side of the court is the *Hall*, a handsome room, containing portraits of Newton, Bacon, Dryden, and other eminent alumni, and a fine portrait of the Duke of Gloucester (aged six) by Reynolds. To the S. of the Hall are the two *Combination Rooms*, corresponding to the Common Rooms at Oxford, and below these is the huge *Kitchen*, in which dinner is cooked daily for 700 persons. — The passage between the hall and the kitchen leads into the *Cloister* or *Neville's Court*, surrounded on three sides by covered arcades. On the W. side is the **Library*, built by Wren in 1676 (open 2-3) and containing 80,000 books and 2000 MSS. The interior is admirably fitted up, and the oaken book-cases are adorned with carvings by Gibbons. At the S. end is a fine *Statue of Lord Byron by *Thorvaldsen*, and round the rooms are busts of other famous members of the college. The MSS. of several of Milton's poems are exhibited in a glass-case. The *Vestibule* (entr. in the N.W. corner of the court) contains Roman antiquities found in England. — To the S. of the Cloister Court is the *New* or *King's Court*, the W. gateway of which leads to a bridge over the Cam (*View of the Backs and of St. John's) and to a stately **Avenue of Limes*. — On the other side of Trinity St., opposite the Entrance Gateway, are two other small courts belonging to Trinity, built by *Dr. Whewell* (d. 1862) and known as the *Master's Courts*.

Bentley and Whewell were Masters of Trinity, and the long list of its famous members includes the names of Newton, Bacon, Porson, Pearson, Dryden, Cowley, Herbert, Macaulay, Byron, Thackeray, and Tennyson. The first-floor rooms on the N. side of the King's Gateway were Newton's, and those below were Thackeray's. The ground-floor rooms next the chapel were occupied by Macaulay, and Byron had rooms on the N. side of the Cloister Court (first floor, central staircase). Tennyson lived out of college.

To the N. Trinity is adjoined by ***St. John's College** (Pl. B, 2), the second in size of the Cambridge colleges, founded in 1511 by Lady Margaret Beaufort, mother of Henry VII. It, however, represents a foundation even earlier than that of Peterhouse, having succeeded St. John's Hospital, established on this site in the 12th century.

St. John's consists of four courts. We enter the First Court by a handsome *Gateway*, with a statue of St. John. On the N. is the **Chapel*, a modern Dec. building by Scott (12-1 and 2-3). The interior is elaborately adorned with carving and coloured marbles, and contains several monuments removed from the old chapel. The **Hall*, on the W. side of this court, is a long oak-panelled room, with a fine roof and numerous portraits, including Wordsworth and Prof. Palmer (in Arabic costume; comp. p. 20). — The *Second Court (1595-1620), the brick of which has assumed a beautiful plum-red hue, has been pronounced by Mr. Ruskin the most perfect in the University. The long *Combination Room* is on the N. side, where also is a doorway leading to the gardens of the *Master's Lodge*. The passage at the N.W. angle of this court leads to the *Chapel Court*. — The *Library* (12-3), which is on the S. side of the Third Court, contains over 35,000 printed books (many incunabula) and 400 MSS; among its treasures are a vellum copy of Coverdale's Bible and an Irish Psalter. From the W. side of this court a covered bridge (Bridge of Sighs) leads across the river to the New Court, which is of stone. — From either the third or the fourth court we may enter the well-kept **College Grounds*. The *Fellows' Garden* is planted with trees in the form of a cathedral. — The roll of fame at St. John's, almost as long as that of Trinity, comprises the names of Roger Ascham, Lord Burleigh, Ben Jonson, Abp. Sandys, Gilbert, Stillingfleet, Herrick, Lord Strafford, Lord Falkland, Matthew Prior, Bentley, Erasmus Darwin, Kirke White, Henry Martyn, Rowland Hill, Horne Tooke, Wordsworth, William Wilberforce, and Lord Palmerston.

The red building opposite St. John's, in English Gothic style, contains the new *Divinity and Literary Schools*, opened in 1879. Adjacent is *All Saints Memorial Cross*, marking tbe site of Old All Saints Church, in the graveyard of which Kirke White was buried.

Turning to the left, we soon reach Bridge St. and the ***Round Church** (*St. Sepulchre's*; Pl. 10), an early-Norman building of 1101, the oldest of the four extant round churches of England (comp. pp. 252, 442; keys at 58 Park St.). — Behind the Round Church is the *Union* (see p. 226), containing a fine debating-hall, reading, writing, and smoking rooms, and a library of 20,000 vols.

Following Bridge St. towards the left, we pass *St. Clement's Church* (Pl. 6; B, 2) and cross a bridge affording a view of St. John's College. To the right, beyond the bridge, is **Magdalene College** (Pl. B, 1, 2; pron. Maudlin), founded in 1542 on the site of a Benedictine hostel or school for monks.

The chief interest of this college is the ***Pepysian Building** in the Second Court. It contains the valuable library bequeathed by Samuel Pepys, including the cypher MS. of his famous 'Diary', the key to which was discovered by Lord Grenville in 1825 (visitors not admitted unless accompanied by a fellow). Many of the other MSS. and early printed works are also of great interest. — Among the most distinguished members of Magdalene are Archbishops Grindal, Ussher, and Cranmer, and Samuel Pepys.

Beyond Magdalene are the churches of *St. Giles* (Pl. B, 1) and *St. Peter* (Pl. A, 1). A little farther on are the *County Court* (Pl. 12; A, 1) and *County Gaol*, adjoining the **Castle Mound**, a singular artificial elevation, on which stood the keep, the only relic of the castle founded by William the Conqueror. — About 3/4 M. to the W. is the *University Observatory*.

We may now return by Bridge St., passing St. Sepulchre's, and turning to the left into Jesus Lane, which leads to ***Jesus College** (Pl. D, 2), founded in 1497 on the site of a Benedictine nunnery. [Or we may follow Chesterton Lane, to the right, beyond Magdalene, cross the *Cam*, not far from the *University Boat Houses* (p. 432), and take the footpath across *Jesus Green* to the grounds of Jesus College, which in this case we enter from the back.]

This picturesque and extensive college is surrounded on all sides by its own **Grounds*. The most interesting of its buildings is the **Chapel* (open 11-12 and 3-4), on the S. side of the second or Cloister Court, which was originally the church of the nunnery, though now shorn of two-thirds of its nave. The transepts contain some late-Norman work; the rest of the building is E.E., with Perp. additions. The stained-glass windows in the transepts are by Morris and Burne Jones. Among eminent alumni are Sir Thomas Elyot, Cranmer, Sterne, and Coleridge.

By turning to the left on leaving Jesus College we soon reach *Midsummer Common*, to the N. of which, on the Cam, are the *University Boat-Houses*. — About 3/4 M. to the E., on the road to Newmarket, are the ruins of *Barnwell Abbey*, dating from the E.E. period.

From Jesus College, opposite which is the modern church of *All Saints*, we retrace our steps to the end of Jesus Lane and turn to the left. **Sidney Sussex College** (Pl. C, 3), which we thus reach, was founded by the Countess of Sussex, daughter of Sir William Sidney, in 1596, on the site of a suppressed Franciscan monastery.

The *Library* contains a bust of Oliver Cromwell, who was a student here; and there is an excellent contemporary portrait of him, in crayon, in the *Master's Lodge*. The pleasant *Gardens* are reached from the N.W. corner of the left court. Thomas Fuller was also a student at this college.

Sidney St. ends at MARKET STREET (Pl. C, 3) and *Holy Trinity Church* (Pl. 11), with its lofty Dec. spire. Farther on, Hobson Street, named after the carrier (p. 433), diverges to the left. To the right is *St. Andrew's Church* (Pl. 3; C, 3), opposite the entrance to **Christ's College** (Pl. C, 3), founded in 1506 by Margaret, Countess of Richmond (p. 437), mother of Henry VII., but completely modernized in the 18th century. The Tudor arms are above the gateway.

The buildings of this college are uninteresting, but the **Gardens* are among the prettiest in Cambridge. They contain a mulberry-tree said to have been planted by Milton in 1632. The poet's rooms were on the left (N.) side of the main court, on the first floor of the staircase next the entrance to the chapel. The college possesses some very fine old plate. Besides Milton, it has on its books the names of Sir Philip Sidney, Leland (the antiquary), Hugh Latimer, Cudworth, Francis Quarles, Paley, and Charles Darwin. Portraits of several of these hang in the Hall.

Farther on in the same street, also to the left, is **Emmanuel College** (Pl. D, 4), founded by Sir Walter Mildmay in 1584, and intended for the maintenance of Puritanical principles. Only a small part of the original buildings remain.

The *Chapel*, entered from the cloister opposite the entrance, was built by Sir Christopher Wren in 1678-88, and contains a fine altar-piece by *Amiconi*. Above the cloister is a *Picture Gallery*, containing some good portraits. The *Library* possesses a few rare MSS., and the college also boasts of a silver goblet, the 'Founder's Cup', ascribed to *Benvenuto Cellini*. The *Gardens* contain a large pond. Bishop Hall, Archbishop Sancroft, John Harvard (founder of Harvard College), Cudworth, Sir William Temple, and also several of the Pilgrim Fathers were students of Emmanuel.

Emmanuel faces the end of Downing St., in which, to the right, is the group of buildings belonging to the scientific and medical department of the University, generally known as the **New Museums** (Pl. 16; C, 4), and comprising laboratories, lecture-rooms, and collections of various kinds. Among the most prominent members of the group are the admirably equipped *Cavendish Laboratory*, abutting on Free School Lane, behind St. Benet's Church, and the new *Chemical Laboratory*, in Pembroke St. (Pl. C, 4). — The iron gate in Downing Street, opposite the *Anatomical Museum* (Pl. 2; C, 4), opens on a pleasant shady avenue, leading to (1/4 M.) **Downing College** (Pl. D, 5), which was founded by Sir George Downing in 1800 and consists of a group of uninteresting modern buildings in a fine park. From Downing College we may now return through Fitzwilliam St. (Pl. C, 5) to Trumpington St. (p. 433).

In Hills Road, beyond the Railway Bridge (beyond Pl. D, 6), is **Cavendish College,** founded in 1873 to afford a university education at an earlier age and at a smaller cost than at the ordinary colleges. It ranks in the University as a public hostel.

On the Huntingdon Road (beyond Pl. A, 1), 2 M. to the N.W. of the centre of the town, is **Girton College**, established in 1869 for the higher education of women. Women who have fulfilled the requisite conditions as to residence (at Newnham or Girton), etc., incumbent upon members of the University are now admitted to the Previous Examination and the Triposes, but not to the examinations for the ordinary degree (comp. p. 225).

On the Trumpington Road, to the S., are the *Botanic Gardens*.

The immediate environs of Cambridge have little claim on the traveller's attention, but no one should omit a visit to *Ely* (p. 440), which is reached by railway in 1/3-1/2 hr. — About 2 1/2 M. to the S.W. of Cambridge lies the village of *Grantchester*, which is believed by some authorities to be the real representative of Grantabrycge (p. 432). On the river here is 'Byron's Pool', 40 ft. deep. *Madingley* and *Cherry Hinton* are other favourite points for the 'constitutionals' of university men.

From Cambridge to *Huntingdon*, see p. 363.

57. From Cambridge to Ely and Hunstanton.

Great Eastern Railway to ($14^1/_2$ M.) *Ely* in 20-26 min. (2*s.* 9*d.*, 2*s.* 1*d.*, 1*s.* 3*d.*); to (56 M.) *Hunstanton* in 2-$2^1/_2$ hrs. (10*s.* 6*d.*, 8*s.*, 4*s.* $8^1/_2$*d.*).

Cambridge, see R. 56. As we leave the town we have a view, to the left, of the *Cam*, alive in term-time with the College Eights. The line traverses the unattractive *Fen District*. — $5^1/_2$ M. *Waterbeach*.

$14^1/_2$ M. **Ely** (*Lamb*, well spoken of; *Bell; Angel*, at the station; *Rail. Refreshmt. Rooms*), a small city with 8200 inhab., is situated on a slight eminence rising above the fens and formerly surrounded by water. Its name is said to be taken from the eels in the river. The only attraction is the cathedral, which is $^1/_2$ M. from the station.

The Isle of Ely is memorable as the last stronghold of the Saxons, who maintained themselves here, under the leadership of Hereward, the 'Last of the English', from 1066 to 1071.

As we approach the cathedral we pass the *Great Gateway* of the old monastery, now used by the King's School.

The ***Cathedral of Ely,** 'one of the very largest and most imposing, one of the most individual, and distinctly the most varied, in England' (*Mrs. Van Rensselaer*), occupies the site of an abbey founded here by St. Etheldreda in 673. The chief internal dimensions are: length 520 ft., breadth 77 ft., length of transepts $178^1/_2$ ft., height of nave 62 ft., height of choir 70 ft. The doors are open 9-1 and 2-6 (2-4 in winter); adm. to the choir 6*d.*, to the W. tower 6*d.* Daily services at 8.30 and 10 a.m. and 4 p.m.

The existing building was begun in 1083 by the first Norman abbot; and the E. half at least was complete in its original form when the see of Ely was created in 1109. The W. part of the nave, including the W. Tower, was finished about 1180, and the Galilee, or W. Porch, was added before 1215. Bishop Northwold (1229-54) pulled down the E. end of the church and added the present Presbytery. The Central Tower, which belonged to the original church, fell in 1322, and advantage was taken of this opportunity to construct the beautiful Dec. Octagon (1322-8). The Lady Chapel dates from 1321-49, and the Perp. Chantries adjoining the retro-choir were added between 1486 and 1550. A new spire was erected on the W. tower at the end of the 14th cent., the weight of which may have caused the collapse of the N.W. transept, though some authorities think the latter was never finished. The whole building has been restored since 1847 under the superintendence of Sir G. G. Scott.

Exterior. The most striking feature is the castellated *W. Tower*, which is unlike any other cathedral-tower in England, and to some extent suggests military rather than ecclesiastical architecture. The greater part of it is Transition Norman (1174-89), but the octagonal top and turrets were added in the Decorated period. The want of its N. wing destroys the symmetry of the W. front (comp. above). The effect of the *Central Octagon* (see p. xlix) is good from all points of view. The *E. End* is fine E.E.

Interior. We enter by the E.E. **Galilee*, or *W. Porch*, and find ourselves below the *W. Tower*. To the right is the S.W. Transept (Transition Norman), the Baptistery, with the apsidal chapel of *St. Catharine*, opening from its E. aisle. The N.W. Transept is wanting (see above).

The *Nave (208 ft. long) is a fine specimen of the late-Norman style. The roof, originally flat, was raised to the present angle on the construction of the Octagon, and has been painted by Mr. L'Estrange and Mr. Gambier Parry (comp. p. 172). In the S. aisle, near the *Prior's Doorway*, is a *Saxon Cross*, in memory of Ovinus, Etheldreda's steward. The *S. Doorway*, at the E. end of this aisle, was originally the monks' entrance from the cloisters. The stained glass is modern.

For a plan of Ely Cathedral see page 554

The nave ends at the **Octagon, a unique and very beautiful feature of Ely Cathedral. It is due to the genius of *Alan de Walsingham* (1322-28), who seems to have been the first to conceive the possibility of such a noble substitute as this for the usual narrow and lofty opening of a central tower. The lantern above is a clever piece of timber-work, 142 ft. above the flooring. The polychrome decoration is by Mr. Gambier Parry, and the stained-glass windows are also modern. The roof forms 'the only Gothic dome in existence'. — The Great Transepts, to the N. and S. of the Octagon, contain the only remains of the earliest Norman church (see p. 440), mainly on the ground-floor. The E. aisle of the S. arm is occupied by the *Chapter Library*.

The *Choir is separated from the Octagon by a modern oaken screen. The E. half of the choir is the older, dating from 1252 (E.E.), while the three elaborate W. bays are a century later (Dec.). The upper row of stalls dates from the 14th cent., but the carved panels and the lower stalls are modern, as are also the reredos, altar, and stained glass. There is no Episcopal Throne, the bishop occupying the stall usually assigned to the dean. Among the most interesting monuments are those of *Bishops de Luda* (1290-98), *Barnet* (1366-73), *Northwold* (1229-54), *Redman* (1501-6), and *Hotham* (1316-37). At the E. end of the N. aisle is the *Chantry of Bishop Alcock* (1486-1500), founder of Jesus College, Cambridge (p. 438); and at the E. end of the S. aisle is that of *Bishop West* (1515-34). In the S. aisle is the monument of *Professor Selwyn* (d. 1873) and in the retro-choir that of *Card. de Luxembourg* (1431-43). On the floor of the S. aisle is a curious piece of ancient (early-Norman?) sculpture.

From the N.E. angle of the N. Transept we enter the Lady Chapel, an elaborate specimen of the Dec. style (1321-49), now used as the parish-church of Holy Trinity. — Extensive view from the top of the *W. Tower*. — The remains of the Cloisters, to the S. of the nave, are scanty.

The remains of the Monastic Buildings, now in great part occupied as private dwellings, include the *Guesten Hall* (now the Deanery), the *Prior's Lodge* (with a Norman crypt), *Prior Crawden's Chapel*, and part of the late-Norman *Infirmary*. The *Bishop's Palace*, to the W. of the Cathedral, dates from the 15-16th centuries.

The cathedral-precincts are adjoined by a pleasant, well-wooded *Park*.

From Ely to Thetford and Norwich, 54 M., railway in 1³/₄ hr. (fares 8*s.* 8*d.*, 7*s.* 3*d.*, 4*s.* 4¹/₂*d.*). Beyond (16 M.) *Brandon*, which gives name to the Dukes of Hamilton and Brandon, the line traverses heath and plantations of fir. — 23 M. **Thetford** *(Bell)*, an ancient town with 4000 inhab., was formerly the seat of the kings and bishops of E. Anglia. The *Castle Hill*, a huge artificial mound, 100 ft. high and 1000 ft. round, is supposed to be a Roman or British fortification. There are also scanty ruins of a *Priory*. Thomas Paine, author of 'The Age of Reason', was born at Thetford in 1737. — From (27¹/₂ M.) *Roudham* a line runs N. to *Swaffham* (with a picturesque ruined priory), passing *Watton*, near which is *Wayland Wood*, said to be the scene of the 'Babes in the Wood'. — 38 M. *Attleborough* (Royal) has an interesting church. — At (43¹/₂ M.) **Wymondham** *(King's Head)* is one of the finest churches in Norfolk, belonging to an old *Priory*. A line runs hence to *Dereham* (King's Arms), the fine church of which contains the tomb of the poet Cowper (d. 1800). From Dereham lines run to Fakenham (p. 447) and Swaffham (see above). — 54 M. *Norwich*, see p. 444.

Branch-lines also run from Ely to *Newmarket* (p. 449) and to *March* (for Wisbech, Spalding, Lincoln, Doncaster, Peterborough, etc.).

As the train leaves Ely we see the cathedral to the left. — 41 M. **Lynn or King's Lynn** *(Globe; Crown; Cozen's Temperance)*, an ancient town with 18,500 inhab., lies near the mouth of the *Ouse*, and is connected with the sea by a waterway called the *King's Cut*. Among the chief points of interest are *St. Margaret's Church* (1091-1119; partly restored), containing two of the largest and finest brasses in England; the *Red Mount Chapel* (Perp.), supposed to have been a wayside chapel for pilgrims to Walsingham; the Elizabethan *Guildhall;* and the *Greyfriars' Tower.*

From Lynn branch-lines run W. to *Spalding* (p. 429) and E. to *Swaffham* and *Dereham* (see p. 441). The former passes ($6^1/_2$ M.) *Terrington* and ($8^1/_2$ M.) *Walpole St. Peter's*, both with fine Perp. churches. — From Lynn to *Fakenham* and *Norwich*, see p. 447.

44 M. *North Wootton* is the station for ($1^3/_4$ M.) **Castle Rising*, an important mediæval fortress, with a Norman keep, surrounded by earthworks of Roman or British origin. The interesting *Church* dates from the 12th cent. (late-Norman). — About $2^1/_2$ M. to the E. of (47 M.) *Wolferton* is *Sandringham Hall*, the country-house of the Prince of Wales. The 'Norwich Gates', at the main entrance of the *Park* (open in the absence of the family), are fine specimens of modern ornamental iron-work. — $49^1/_2$ M. *Dersingham* (Alexandra) and (51 M.) *Snettisham* (Royal) have interesting churches. — 54 M. *Heacham* is the junction of a line to Wells (see below).

56 M. **Hunstanton St. Edmunds** *(Sandringham; Golden Lion; Rail. Refreshmt. Rooms)* is a rising watering-place, with good bathing, a pier, and a promenade. Near *Old Hunstanton* (L'Estrange Arms), which lies 1 M. to the N., is *Hunstanton Hall*, which has been in the possession of the L'Estrange family for 800 years. The *Church* of Old Hunstanton is also interesting.

From Hunstanton to Wells, 20 M., railway in 1-$1^1/_2$ hr. (fares 3*s.* 11*d.*, 3*s.*, 1*s.* $8^1/_2$*d.*). The train diverges at (2 M.) *Heacham* (see above) from the Cambridge line. Near (18 M.) *Holkham* (Victoria) is *Holkham Park*, the seat of the Earl of Leicester. — 20 M. **Wells** *(Globe; Crown)* is a small seaport, of little interest to the tourist. From Wells to *Fakenham*, see p. 447.

58. From London to Colchester, Ipswich, and Norwich.

Great Eastern Railway to (52 M.) *Colchester* in $1^1/_4$-$2^1/_4$ hrs. (fares 9*s.* 9*d.*, 7*s.* 6*d.*, 4*s.* $4^1/_2$*d.*); to (69 M.) *Ipswich* in $1^1/_2$-3 hrs. (fares 13*s.*, 9*s.* 10*d.*, 5*s.* $9^1/_2$*d.*); to (114 M.) *Norwich* in 3-4 hrs. (fares 20*s.* 6*d.*, 15*s.* 9*d.*, 9*s.* $5^1/_2$*d.*). — Norwich may also be reached viâ Cambridge and Ely in $3^1/_2$-5 hrs. (comp. RR. 55, 56; fares as above).

The run from *Liverpool Street Station* to ($12^1/_2$ M.) *Romford* (White Hart), a small town (9000 inhab.) noted for its ale, is uninteresting. Farther on, the district is wooded and at places pretty. 18 M. *Brentwood.* 21 M. *Shenfield* is the junction of lines to *Wickford* and *Southend* (p. 450) and to *Woodham Ferris, Southminster, Burnham*, and *Maldon.* — 30 M. **Chelmsford** *(Saracen's Head)*, with 10,000 inhab., is the county-town of Essex. The church contains a curious double arch (N. wall of chancel). — From (39 M.) *Witham* lines diverge to *Braintree, Dunmow*, and *Bishop's Stortford* (see p. 431), and to *Maldon* (see above). — 42 M. *Kelvedon*, the birthplace of Spurgeon. — From (47 M.) *Mark's Tey* branch-lines run to *Haverhill* and *Bury St. Edmunds* (p. 450).

About $2^1/_2$ M. from *Halstead*, on the line to Haverhill, is *Little Maplestead*, with one of the four round churches of England (comp. pp. 252, 437). At ($9^1/_2$ M.) *Castle Hedingham* is a fine Norman castle.

On the line to Bury St. Edmunds we pass (12 M.) **Sudbury** *(Rose & Crown)*, a small town with three fine churches (the birthplace of Gainsborough, 1727-88), and (15 M.) *Long Melford.*

52 M. **Colchester** (*The Cups*; *George; Red Lion; Rail. Rfmt. Rooms*), an ancient place on the *Colne*, with 28,400 inhab., is the largest town in Essex and contains many interesting remains.

Colchester (A. S. *Colneceaster*) has been identified with the Roman *Camulodunum*, which had already been a place of importance with the Britons, and was made the first Roman colony in the island (A.D. 60). Two years later it was destroyed by the Iceni, but after the defeat of Boadicea it was rebuilt and surrounded with walls. Under the Normans it was also an important stronghold, as is evidenced by its castle, which was captured by Lewis the Dauphin in 1218 and by General Fairfax in 1648. Comp. 'Colchester', by *Rev. E. L. Cutts* (Historic Towns Series; 1888). — Colchester oysters have long been famous.

The station on the main line is 1 M. from the town, which we may reach either by road or by a loop-line to *St. Botolph's Station.* In the former case we pass through the **Roman Walls**, the line of which (2 M.), partly concealed by houses, is more complete than that of any other Roman city-walls in England.

To see the wall we should turn to the right at the cattle-market and follow it along the W. side, where stands the ruined *Balcon*, the principal Roman bastion, also called *King Cole's Castle*, from an association of Colchester with that hero of nursery rhyme. In this case we may make our way to the top of the High St. viâ the lofty *Water Tower*, which is the most conspicuous feature in Colchester.

The ***Castle**, the largest Norman keep in England, probably erected by the Conqueror, stands near the foot of the High St. (left; open free; small gratuity for seeing parts not generally open).

The keep measures 168 ft. by 126 ft. Its walls vary in thickness from 30 ft. to 11 ft. We enter by the S. side, and visit the *Vaults* and *Dungeons*. Fine view from the top of the walls. The herring-bone work of Roman tiles is striking. The *Chapel* is fitted up as a *Museum* (open 10-6), with interesting Roman antiquities found in or near Colchester.

From the foot of the High St. we follow Queen St. and St. Botolph St. to the right to reach *St. Botolph's Priory*, which stands a little to the left of the latter street, in the enclosure of St. Botolph's Church. The ruins are those of the priory church and are in the Norman style (ca. 1103); as in the castle, Roman bricks have been freely used. By turning to the right at the end of St. Botolph's Street we reach St. John's Green, with *St. John's Abbey Gate* (ca. 1500), the only relic of a large Benedictine monastery. — The pre-Norman tower of *Holy Trinity Church* is partly constructed of Roman bricks.

At *Lexden*, 1 M. to the W. of Colchester, are remains of Roman entrenchments and a public park, opened in 1890; 3/4 M. farther on is '*King Cole's Kitchen*', supposed to have been the Roman amphitheatre.

From Colchester a branch-railway runs to (19 M.) **Clacton-on-Sea** (*Royal; Osborne*) and (20 M.) **Walton-on-the-Naze** (*Marine; Clifton*), two frequented watering-places (also reached from London by steamer).

59 1/2 M. *Manningtree* is the junction of the line to (11 M.) **Harwich** (*Great Eastern*, *Pier*, at the harbour; *Three Cups*, in the town), a small seaport (7500 inhab.), with a good harbour, at the confluence of the *Stour* and the *Orwell*, well known as the starting-point of the G.E.R. steamers to Rotterdam and Antwerp (p. xix), which sail from *Parkeston Quay* (Great Eastern Hotel), on the N.

side of the estuary. *Dovercourt* (*Cliff; Phoenix), the S. suburb of Harwich, is a pleasant little sea-bathing place with a chalybeate spa (adm. 1*d.*). A steamer plies several times daily up the Orwell to (1 hr.) Ipswich (see below). — Beyond Manningtree we see the estuary of the *Stour* (right). After passing (63 M.) *Bentley* (junction of a line to *Hadleigh*) we come in sight of the estuary of the *Orwell.*

69 M. **Ipswich** (*White Horse*, Tavern St., celebrated in 'Pickwick'; *Crown & Anchor; Golden Lion; Temperance; Rail. Rfmt. Rooms*), the county-town of Suffolk, with 51,000 inhab., is situated at the head of the estuary of the *Orwell.* It was the birthplace of *Card. Wolsey* (1471-1530), who built a college here (see below).

From the station we proceed through Station Road and Princes Street (tramway 2*d.*) to Cornhill, an open space in the centre of the town, with the *Town Hall* and *Post Office.* Tavern St., with the *White Horse Hotel* (see above), runs hence to the right (S.), and parallel to it, on the W., is the Butter Market, containing *Sparrowe's House* or the *Ancient House* (now a bookseller's), a picturesque 16th cent. building (1567), with a pargeted façade, in which Charles II. is said to have lain concealed after the battle of Worcester. On the upper floor is the *Public Library* (interesting old room). — From the S. end of the Butter Market we proceed to the right through Upper Brook St., and then to the left through Tacket St. and Orwell Place, to *Fore Street*, containing several quaint old houses. — Proceeding to the N. (right) from Fore St., through Salhouse and Key St., we reach College St., containing *Wolsey's Gateway*, the only relic of the above-mentioned college.

In Tower St., leading to the E. from Tavern St., is the rebuilt church of *St. Mary-at-Tower*, with a graceful spire 176 ft. high. By turning to the right at the end of the street we reach *St. Margaret's Church* (restored). — The *Museum*, High St. (to the N.E. of Cornhill), contains local antiquities and fossils (adm. free).

The *Upper* and *Lower Arboretum* and *Christ's Church Park* are three pleasant parks; the first affords a good view of the town. A visit may also be paid to the agricultural implement works of *Ransomes, Sims, & Head.*

A branch-line runs from Ipswich to (16 M.) **Felixstowe** (*Bath; Pier; Ordnance*), a seaside resort, with golf-links, at the mouth of the Orwell, opposite Harwich. Circular tickets are issued allowing the journey in one direction to be made by water.

From Ipswich to *Yarmouth*, see R. 59.

81 M. *Stowmarket* (Fox) has manufactories of gun-cotton and a church with a curious wooden spire. — 83 M. *Haughley Road* is the junction of a line to *Bury St. Edmunds* (p. 450) and *Newmarket* (p. 449). From (100$^1/_2$ M.) *Tivetshall* a line diverges to *Bungay*, *Beccles* (p. 448), and *Lowestoft* (p. 448). Beyond (110 M.) *Swainsthorpe* we catch a glimpse, to the right, of the Roman camp at *Caistor.* We now enter the valley of the *Yare.*

114 M. **Norwich.** — **Hotels.** *Royal, in the Market Place; Maid's Head, near the Cathedral, R. & A. 4*s.* 6*d.*; Norfolk. — *Rail. Rfmt. Rooms.*

Railway Stations. The *Victoria* (London, Ipswich) and *Thorpe* (London, Yarmouth, Cromer, Wells) *Stations*, on the S. side of the city, belong to the G. E. R.; the *City Station*, to the N., is the terminus of the Eastern & Midlands Railway (Melton, Constable, Lynn). — *Cab* into the town 1*s*.

Steamers to *Yarmouth*, daily in summer, see p. 448.

Norwich, the capital of Norfolk and the see of a bishop, is a city with 90,000 inhab., situated on the *Wensum*. Most of the streets are narrow and tortuous, but in addition to the cathedral and castle they contain many interesting buildings. The town possesses large manufactories of mustard and starch (Colman's; 2000 hands), iron-works, and breweries.

Norwich is generally supposed to be the *Caergwent* of the Britons, and the Roman *Venta Icenorum*, though Caistor (p. 447) is a rival claimant. In 1003 the town was destroyed by the Danes, but it was rebuilt and furnished with a castle after the Norman Conquest. In 1094 the see of the bishop of E. Anglia was transferred from Thetford to Norwich. A fillip to its prosperity was given by the settlement of Flemish weavers here in the 14th cent., but the woollen industry has now almost deserted it.

The ***Cathedral** lies towards the E. side of the city, 1/2 M. to the N. of the Thorpe Station. It was begun in 1096, and has preserved its original Norman plan more closely than any other cathedral in England. The Close is entered by *St. Ethelbert's Gate* (ca. 1275; upper part modern) or by the *Erpingham Gate* (1420). The Cathedral is 407 ft. long, 72 ft. wide, 178 ft. across the transepts, and 70 (nave) to 83 1/2 ft. (choir) high. Nave open free; choir, transepts, and cloisters 11-1 and 2-4.30 (Sat. 2-2.45 and 4-6), 6*d.*; daily services at 10 a.m. and 5 (Sat. 3) p.m.

The building was begun by the first Bishop of Norwich, *Herbert de Losinga* (1091-1119), who completed the choir and transepts and began the nave (comp. p. xxxvii). The latter was finished by his successor (ca. 1140). The clerestory of the choir was rebuilt in 1356-69; and the vaulting of the nave and choir were added in the 15th century. In the same century the *W. Front* was altered (large Perp. window inserted) and the spire rebuilt. The cloisters were begun at the end of the 13th cent. and completed in 1430. The most prominent features are the fine Norman **Tower*, surmounted by a lofty *Spire* (315 ft.), and the apsidal termination of the *Choir*. The best general view is from the S.E.

Interior. The *NAVE (252 ft. long) is Norman throughout, except its fine lierne-vaulting (15th cent.) and the inserted Perp. windows. The large open arches of the triforium resemble those of Southwell Minster (p. 430). Two bays in the S. aisle were converted into a chantry by *Bishop Nix* (1501-36). In the N. aisle is the monument of *Sir Thomas Wyndham*. The stained glass is modern. — The two E. bays of the nave are shut off from the rest by the *Organ Screen* and form the ANTE-CHOIR, containing the **Stalls* (15th cent.); the misereres are very quaint. The CENTRAL TOWER, with its fine open lantern, is Norman, and rests on four tall circular arches. The curious and interesting carved bosses of the ceiling throughout the Cathedral deserve attention. — The TRANSEPTS resemble the nave in general character, and also have a fine vaulted ceiling (16th cent.). The N. Transept is adjoined on the E. by a small apsidal *Chapel*. In the S. Transept is a monument to *Bp. Bathurst* (d. 1837), by *Chantrey*. In the vestry adjoining this transept is an interesting *Altar-piece*, ascribed to an English painter of the 14th century.

The apsidal ending of the *CHOIR is as effective from within as from without, and recalls the churches of the Continent more than any other church of this size in England. The original ground-plan remains unaltered, but the clerestory has been rebuilt, the vaulting added, and the main arches changed from Norman to Perpendicular. Among the monuments are those of *Bishop Goldwell* (1472-79) and *Sir William Boleyn* (d. 1505), grandfather of Anne Boleyn. The stained glass is modern.

A fine view of the interior is obtained from the triforium. The choir-aisles end, on the E., in apsidal chapels: the *Jesus Chapel* on the N., and *St. Luke's Chapel* on the S. A *Lady Chapel*, forming the E. termination of the Cathedral, was built at the end of the apse in 1245-57 (E.E.) but was taken down in the time of Queen Elizabeth. The *Beauchamp Chapel*, opening off the S. aisle of the choir, is in the Dec. style. In the N. choir-aisle is a *Gallery*, supposed to have been used for exhibiting relics. — From the S. Transept we pass through the *Prior's Door* into the spacious *Cloisters (Dec.). In the W. walk are the Monks' Lavatories. The *Chapter House*, which stood to the E. of the cloisters, has long since perished.

To the N. of the Cathedral stands the *Bishop's Palace*, dating in great part from the beginning of the 14th cent., though since extensively altered and enlarged. — To the N.W., by the Erpingham Gate, is an old chapel, now used as a *Grammar School*. In front of the latter is a *Statue of Nelson*, who was a pupil here. — *Pull's Ferry*, a double arch at the end of the Lower Close, was formerly the water-gate to the cathedral precincts.

Leaving the Cathedral Close by the Erpingham Gate, we cross the Tombland obliquely to its S. W. corner, and follow Queen St. to the Castle, a Norman keep, 70 ft. high, situated on a lofty mound (adm. 3*d*.). It was refaced in 1839 and long used as the county-gaol, but has now been dismantled and is to be fitted up as a museum. *View of the town from the top of the keep. — To the W. is the Market-place, with the *Guild Hall*, the Council Chamber in which retains its fittings of the Tudor period and contains souvenirs of Nelson. In the S.W. corner of the market is **St. Peter Mancroft* (14th cent.), with a fine tower (good interior).

From the market-place Dove Lane and St. John St. lead N. to the *Free Library* and the *Norfolk Museum* (open free on Mon. & Sat., 10-4), containing fine collections of birds and fossils. — St. Andrew's St. leads hence to the right to *St. Andrew's Hall* (adm. 3*d*.), originally the nave of a Dominican Church (Perp.), and now used for the 'Norwich Triennial Musical Festival', etc.

Many of the other churches of Norwich show interesting specimens of the characteristic East Anglian 'flush-work', so called because faced flints are used to fill up flush the interstices of the freestone pattern (comp. p. li). A few remains of the *City Walls* still remain, including two or three of the forty towers with which it was strengthened. Quaint mediæval houses abound. — The *Roman Catholic Church* is a large edifice.

A good view of Norwich is obtained from *Mousehold Heath*, on the left bank of the *Wensum* (to the E.).

About 3 M. to the S. of Norwich is **Caistor St. Edmund**, with a large Roman camp, which many antiquarians believe to have been the true *Venta Icenorum*, while Norwich was merely an outlying fortress.

The Dolphin Inn at *Heigham*, 1½ M. to the N.W. of Norwich, is an interesting old house, parts of which probably date from the 14th century. Bishop Hall died here in 1656 and is buried in the parish-church.

From Norwich to Yarmouth, 18½ M., railway in ¾ hr. (fares 2*s*. 6*d*., 2*s*., 1*s*. 6*d*.). This line traverses the district of the 'Norfolk Broads' (see p. 449). The train starts from Thorpe Station (p. 444). 2 M. *Whitlingham*, see below. At (6 M.) *Brundall* the railway forks, the N. branch running direct to Yarmouth viâ *Lingwood* and *Acle* (King's Head; Queen's Head; a good centre for visiting the Broads, p. 449), while the S. branch makes a detour viâ *Reedham* (junction for Lowestoft, p. 448). Brundall is the station for *Surlingham Broad*. *Yarmouth*, see p. 448.

From Norwich to Cromer, 24 M., railway (from Thorpe Station) in 1 hr. (fares 4*s*., 2*s*. 9*d*., 2*s*.). At (2 M.) *Whitlingham* the line diverges to the N. (left) from that to Yarmouth. 9 M. *Wroxham*, with the 'Queen of the Norfolk Broads' (comp. p. 449), is the junction of a line to Aylsham and Dereham (p. 441). — 13 M. *Worstead* (New Inn) gave its name to worsted yarn, a colony of Flemish weavers having settled here in the 12th century. The church is interesting. — 16½ M. **North Walsham** *(Angel)*, with a large Perp. church, has also railway communication with Aylsham, Melton Constable, and Fakenham (see below), and with Caistor and Yarmouth viâ the Eastern & Midlands line. — Near (20 M.) *Gunton* is *Gunton Park*, the seat of Lord Suffield, open to the public on Thurs. during summer. — 24 M. **Cromer** *(Hôtel de Paris; Tucker's; Red Lion; Bellevue; Bath; Bond Street Restaurant)*, the 'English Etretat', perhaps the most charming spot in East Anglia, is a rising little water-place with admirably firm and smooth sands and cliffs 60-200 ft. high. The tower of the Perp. *Church* is a fine specimen of flint-work (p. li); chancel rebuilt in 1889. About 1 M. to the N.W. is *Cromer Beach*, the terminus of a line from Sherringham, Melton Constable, Fakenham, and Norwich. The *Lighthouse*, on a height to the E. (½ hr.), commands a fine view. Adjacent are fine golf-links. Excursions may be made to *Felbrigg Hall* (3 M. to the S.), *Mundesley* (sea-views; 8 M.), the *Roman Camp* (4 M.; *View), etc. The heaths round Cromer abound in 'pit-dwellings', which may have been primitive habitations.

From Norwich to Fakenham and Lynn, 50 M., railway in 2-2¼ hrs. (fares 6*s*. 6*d*., 3*s*. 3*d*.). This line (Midlands & Eastern) starts from the City Station (p. 445) and crosses the G.E.R. railway at *Reepham*. 22 M. *Melton Constable*, the junction of lines to *North Walsham* (see above; for Yarmouth) and to *Sherringham* (*Hotel) and *Cromer Beach* (see above). — From (29½ M.) *Fakenham* (Crown) a branch diverges to the N. for *Walsingham* (with the interesting ruins of an Augustine Priory; open on Wed., 10-5) and *Wells* (p. 442). Another runs S. to *Dereham* and *Wymondham* (comp. p. 441). Near (33½ M.) *Raynham Park Station* is *Raynham Park*, the seat of the Marquis of Townshend, with a fine collection of portraits and a master-piece (Belisarius) of Salvator Rosa. — 50 M. *Lynn*, see p. 441.

From Norwich to *Thetford* and *Ely*, see p. 441.

59. From London to Lowestoft and Yarmouth.

Great Eastern Railway to (117½ M.) *Lowestoft* in 3¼-5¼ hrs. (fares 22*s*., 16*s*. 8*d*., 9*s*. 10½*d*.); to (121½ M.) *Yarmouth* in 3¼-5¼ hrs. (fares 22*s*. 8*d*., 17*s*. 3*d*., 10*s*. 1*d*.). Cheap excursion-fares in summer.

As far as (69 M.) *Ipswich* this route coincides with R. 58. The first station beyond Ipswich is (72 M.) *Westerfield*, where a line diverges to Felixstowe (p. 444). — 84½ M. *Wickham Market* is the junction of a line to (6½ M.) **Framlingham** *(Crown & Horses)*, a small town (2500 inhab.), with a picturesque ruined castle and a fine church containing some interesting monuments (Earl of Surrey, the poet, etc.). — From (91 M.) *Saxmundham* a short branch-line runs to **Aldeburgh** *(White Lion; East Suffolk)*, a pleasant seaside resort with a golf-ground. The church contains some good brasses and a memorial of the poet Crabbe (1754-1832), a native of the parish. The town-hall or moot-hall is a half-timbered building of the 16th century. — 95½ M. *Darsham* (Stradbroke Arms) is the station for (5½ M.) *Dunwich* (Burne Arms), the earliest seat of the East Anglian bishopric (founded ca. 630) and once a town of some importance. Successive encroachments of the sea, however, have swept away its palaces and churches, and it is now a small village. — 101 M. *Halesworth* is the junction of a line to (3 M.) **Southwold** *(Centre Cliff; *Swan)*, another little watering-place, with a fine Perp. church, containing an interesting rood-screen. Excursions may be made to *Dunwich* (see above), *Coverhithe*, *Walberswick*, and *Blythburgh*, all with interesting churches. — 109 *Beccles* (King's Head) is the junction for *Bungay* and *Tivetshall* (p. 444) on the W., and for ($8^1/_2$ M.) *Lowestoft* on the E.

Lowestoft (**Royal; Harbour; Suffolk; Royal Oak*, at Kirkley) is a fashionable sea-bathing resort with 20,000 inhabitants. The old town, to the N. of the harbour, is an important fishing-station and contains a fine Perp. *Church*. The new town to the S., with its long *Esplanade*, is the watering-place proper. The *S. Pier* (adm. 1*d.*) is an agreeable promenade. Among the favourite resorts is (2 M.) **Oulton Broad** (*Wherry Hotel;* boats and stores from *James Bullen*), which affords amusement for boating and fishing parties, and may be reached by railway. *Somerleyton Hall*, the imposing residence of Sir Savile Crossley, 6 M. to the N.W., has a fine park to which visitors are admitted on Wednesday.

115 M. *St. Olave's* is the junction of lines to Lowestoft (see above) and *Reedham* (p. 446).

$121^1/_2$ M. **Yarmouth.** — **Hotels.** *Victoria, *Royal, Bath, Norfolk, Marine Parade; *Queen's, at the Britannia Pier, R. & A. 4*s.* 6*d*, D. 3*s.* 6*d.*; Star, an Elizabethan house, on the Quay; Angel, Market-place.

Railway Stations. *South Town Station*, on the left bank of the Yare (for London, Lowestoft, Cromer, Lynn, etc.); *Vauxhall Station*, on the N. side of Breydon Water (for Norwich, etc.); *Beach Station*, near the N. end of the town (for North Walsham and Lynn).

Tramway from the South Station to *Gorleston* (Tramway Hotel).

Steamers ply weekly to *Hull* and *Newcastle*, and in summer to *London*, *Cromer*, and *Lowestoft*. Small steamers also ply daily in summer up the *Yare* to *Norwich* and up the *Bure* to *Wroxham* (p. 446), affording a glimpse at the Broads (p. 449). Circular tickets are issued allowing the journey in one direction to be made by railway.

Yarmouth, the most important town and port on the E. Anglian coast, is situated at the mouth of the *Yare* and contains about 45,000 inhabitants. It is also a very popular watering-place, and in the height of summer is flooded almost daily with excursionists. Its attractions include firm and extensive sands for bathers, a marine parade, three piers, and an aquarium (theatrical performances, etc.). *Great Yarmouth*, the older part of the town, adjoining the river, contains numerous picturesque 'rows' or lanes, only 3-6 ft. wide. As Dickens puts it: 'Great Yarmouth is one vast gridiron, of which the bars are represented by the rows'. The church of *St. Nicholas*, the largest parish-church in England (230 ft. long, 112 ft. wide; area 23,265 sq. ft.), was originally founded in 1119, but the oldest part now standing is the Transitional nave (1190). Its library contains some interesting old books; the modern pulpit is handsome. In the chancel is a curious old *Revolving Book Desk.* Fine view from the tower. The old **Tolhouse* or *Gaol* (adm. 2*d.*), near the N. end of Middlegate St., is an interesting building of the 14th cent., now containing a public library (fine old hall). The *Town Hall*, on the South Quay, not far from the Tolhouse, is a large modern building. No. 4, South Quay, an Elizabethan house with a modern front, is said to have been the place in which the death of Charles I. was decided upon by Cromwell's supporters.

Parts of the old *Town Walls* are still standing, including the *S.E.* and *Blackfriars' Towers.* The *Nelson Column* (adm. 6*d.*), 144 ft. high, in the South Denes, commands a good view. The *Herring Fishery* is at its height in autumn, when 'Yarmouth Bloaters' may be seen in all stages of preparation. In 1887 about 250 million herrings were landed here. The *Fish Wharf* is near the mouth of the river. Off the coast are numerous sandbanks, between which and the land are *Yarmouth Roads.*

The district to the W. of Yarmouth is *par excellence* the country of the **Norfolk Broads**, large lagoons, generally connected with each other by sluggish rivers, and alternating with vast expanses of marsh and reed. There are in all 40-50 Broads, varying in size from 2 to 500 acres (in all 5000 acres), and connected by the *Bure*, the *Yare*, and the *Waveney* (in all 200 M. of navigable river), which all find their way into Breydon Water (see below). Most of them are on the Bure and its tributaries. The district affords admirable opportunities for boating, angling, and wild-fowl shooting. River-yachts for excursions on the Broads may be hired at Yarmouth, Norwich, Wroxham, or Oulton, at rates varying from 5*l.* to 10*l.* a week, according to the size and the number of the crew. The tourist who merely wishes to see the scenery may take a passage in one of the so-called *Wherries*, or trading barges, plying between Norwich and other inland places and the coast. Comp. 'Norfolk Broads and Rivers', by *G. C. Davies* (illus.; 1883), and the same writer's 'Handbook to the Rivers and Broads of Norfolk and Suffolk' (new ed., 1887).

The following round trip from Norwich, lasting 10-14 days, will include a visit to most of the principal Broads. — From Norwich to *Reedham* (p. 446) and *Yarmouth* (p. 448) by the *Yare*, including *Surlingham* and *Rockland Broads;* from *Yarmouth* to *Acle* (p. 446), *Wroxham* (p. 446), and *Coltishall* (rail. stat.) by the *Bure*, visiting *South Walsham*, *Ranworth*, *Hoveton*, *Wroxham*, and *Belaugh Broads;* back by the Bure to the mouth of the *Ant* (near which are the ruins of *St. Benet's Abbey*), 10 M. below Wroxham, and up this stream to *Barton* and *Stalham Broads;* then viâ the *Thurne* to *Heigham Bridge*, to visit *Heigham Sounds*, *Hickling* and *Somerton Broads*, and *Horsey Mere* (these for light-draught boats only); from Heigham Bridge back to Yarmouth viâ Acle. The chief Broads not included in this excursion are *Oulton* (p. 448); *Ormesby*, *Filby*, and *Rollesby*, easily reached by railway from Yarmouth to (5 M.) *Ormesby;* and *Fritton Decoy*, with its water-fowl decoys, 1 M. from *Haddiscoe*, on the railway from Yarmouth to Lowestoft. *Breydon Water*, see below.

Among points of interest in the neighbourhood of Yarmouth are (2 M.) *Gorleston* (tramway, see p. 448); *Burgh Castle* (4-5 M. to the S.W.), a well-preserved Roman fortification at the head of *Breydon Water* (estuary of the Yare); *Caistor Castle* (4 M.; to the N.); and *Lowestoft* (p. 448; 9 M.), by excursion-brake (1*s.* 6*d.*), railway, or steamer.

From Yarmouth to North Walsham by Eastern & Midlands Railway, 29 M., in 3/4-1 1/4 hr. (fares 4*s.*, 2*s.* 6*d.*, 2*s.*). 3 1/2 M. *Caistor* (see above); 6 1/2 M. *Ormesby* (see above); 22 M. *Stalham* (see above). — *North Walsham*, and thence to Cromer or Melton Constable, see p. 447.

From Yarmouth to *Norwich*, see p. 446.

60. From Cambridge to Newmarket and Bury St. Edmunds.

Great Eastern Railway to (14 M.) *Newmarket* in 1/2 hr. (2*s.* 7*d.*, 2*s.*, 1*s.* 2*d.*); to (28 M.) *Bury St. Edmunds* in 1-1 1/4 hr. (5*s.* 4*d.*, 4*s.* 1*d.*, 2*s.* 4*d.*).

Cambridge, see p. 432. The country traversed is flat. Near Newmarket we cross a singular earthwork known as the *Devil's Dyke.*

14 M. **Newmarket** *(Rutland Arms; White Hart)*, a small town

with 6000 inhab., is the metropolis of horse-racing. No fewer than seven race-meetings take place yearly, and about 400 race-horses are constantly in training here to meet their engagements.

The most important meetings are the *Craven* at Easter and the *Houghton* at the end of October. Beds and living rise to famine prices during the races and are sometimes almost unprocurable. The races are run at different parts of *Newmarket Heath* (comp. *Baedeker's London*). At other seasons the morning gallops of the 'youngsters' in training are a perennial source of interest to the betting world.

The old *Palace* in the High St., built by Charles II., who was a constant patron of Newmarket Races, is now occupied by the Duke of Rutland. The houses of 'Old Q' (the Duke of Queensberry), Nell Gwynne, and various other quondam visitors are also shown.

28 M. **Bury St. Edmunds** *(Angel; Suffolk; Bell)*, a bright and interesting little town with 16,000 inhab., first came into notice as the burial-place of St. Edmund, the last King of East Anglia, whose shrine here was long one of the chief resorts of English pilgrims. The abbey erected in the 11th cent. over his tomb soon attained great wealth and importance. See the characteristic account of Bury by *Carlyle*, in 'Past and Present'.

Opposite the Angel Hotel is the *Abbey Gateway*, a fine Dec. structure of 1337, leading to the *Botanic Gardens* (adm. 6*d*.), which contain the chief remains of the **Abbey**, including the ruins of the *Church* (within a railing, at the S.E. corner), the *Abbot's Palace*, and the *Abbot's Bridge* (N.E. corner). — Among other points of interest in Bury are *St. James's Church*, a Perp. edifice of the 15th cent.; a *Norman Tower* (ca. 1090); *St. Mary's Church*, with a fine timber ceiling (15th cent.); and *Moyses Hall*, a late-Norman building, supposed to have been a Jewish synagogue (now the police-office).

In the environs of Bury are (4 M.) *Hengrave Hall*, a fine Tudor mansion; *Ickworth House* (3 M.), the seat of the Marquis of Bristol, a large modern building; *Barton House* (2 M.), etc.

Beyond Bury the railway goes on to *Haughley Road Junction*, where it joins the line from Ipswich to Norwich (comp. p. 444). — Branch-lines also run from Bury to *Thetford* (p. 441) and *Mark's Tey* (p. 442).

61. From London to Tilbury and Southend.

Railway to (23 M.) *Tilbury* in 3/4-1 hr. (fares 2*s*. 6*d*., 1*s*. 11*d*., 1*s*. 4*d*.); to (42 M.) *Southend* in 1-1 3/4 hr. (fares 4*s*. 4*d*., 3*s*., 2*s*. 2*d*.). The above fares are from *Fenchurch Street Station;* for the fares from *Liverpool Street* to Tilbury, add 1*d*. in each case. From *Chalk Farm* the fares are slightly lower.

This line skirts the N. bank of the *Thames* and the Thames estuary. The stations as far as (23 M.) *Tilbury* are described in *Baedeker's London*. Beyond Tilbury the line turns to the N. — 28 M. *Stanford-le-Hope*, with an interesting church. To the left rises *Langdon Hill* (380 ft.), a good point of view. — Beyond (36 M.) *Benfleet* the ruins of *Hadleigh Castle* are seen to the left.

42 M. **Southend** *(Royal; Hope; Ship)*, a small watering-place (4600 inhab.) at the mouth of the Thames, is chiefly patronized by day-excursionists from London. It possesses an *Esplanade* and a wooden *Pier*, 2000 yds. long, traversed by a tramway. Excursion steamers ply to and from London in summer. — About 3 M. to the E. of Southend is **Shoeburyness** *(Cambridge Hotel)*, the government station for artillery practice, with a long gun-range.

SCOTLAND.

I. Travelling Expenses. Hotels.

Expenses. Travelling in the tourist-districts of Scotland has the reputation of being expensive; and as regards a few of the Highland hotels, which practically possess a monopoly of the traveller's custom, this reproach is perhaps deserved. A considerable improvement in this respect has, however, taken place of late years; and it may be questioned whether the average charges at Scottish hotels are higher than those in equally frequented districts of England (comp. p. xxiii). The competition of the steamboats and railways, and the extensive development of the system of *Circular Tours* (see below) have, on the other hand, made the expenses of locomotion very moderate. The ordinary tourist, frequenting the best hotels and availing himself of the usual means of locomotion, must be prepared to spend 25-30*s.* a day, but the pedestrian of modest requirements may reduce his expenditure to 10-12*s.* daily.

Hotels. The Highland hotels are generally good and comfortable, though their charges are high (see above) The average summer prices at houses of the first class are about as follows; R. & A. 4*s.*-5*s.* 6*d.*, plain breakfast or tea 1*s.* 6*d.*, D. 3*s.* 6*d.*-5*s.* The Scottish table d'hôte breakfasts, with their abundant choice of salmon, fresh herrings, chops, steaks, ham and eggs, preserves, cakes, and scones, are certainly not exorbitant at their usual rate of 2*s.* 6*d.*-3*s.*; and table d'hôte teas (7.30-8 p.m.) of a similar description are also sometimes provided for those who do not dine at table d'hôte (6 or 7 p.m.). Those who prefer it may order dinner in the middle of the day. The charges for luncheons and other light refreshments are often comparatively high. Wine in the Highland hotels is always dear and generally bad; but good whiskey — the *vin du pays* — which may be mixed with soda-water, may be obtained almost everywhere. In small quantities, diluted, it will be found a good drink for the pedestrian. The beds are usually good and clean; and the larger hotels contain comfortably fitted up drawing, reading, billiard, and smoking rooms. Gratuities need not be given except to the 'Boots', but it is usual to give a trifle to the waiter and chamber-maid if any stay be made (comp. p. xxiii).

Hotel Coupons (B., with meat and eggs, 2*s.* 6*d.*, L. 2*s.*, D. 3*s.* 6*d.*, plain tea 1*s.* 6*d.*, tea with meat 2*s.* 6*d.*, R. & A. 4*s.*) are issued by the Caledonian Railway Co. and by the tourist-agents (Cook, Gaze) in London; but at some places (*e.g.* Oban) these are not accepted at the leading hotels, nor are they available for the 'monopoly' hotels at the Trossachs, Tarbet, etc. *Temperance Hotels*, see p. xxiii. Ladies are advised to frequent first-class hotels only.

II. Railways, Coaches, and Steamers.

The general remarks made at p. xx on the railways of England apply also to those of Scotland. The principal Scottish railway-companies are the *North British* (1087 M.), the *Caledonian* (742½ M.), the *Highland* (425 M.), the *Glasgow and South Western* (454 M.), and the *Great North of Scotland* (312 M.).

The different railway-companies issue *Circular Tickets*, available by rail, coach, and steamer, in such variety of combination, that the traveller will find no difficulty in selecting a tour which includes exactly the points he wishes to visit. The Caledonian Co. alone has arranged upwards of 80 circular tours, embracing the whole of Scotland to the N. of Edinburgh and Glasgow; and the North British Railway has nearly as many. All, or almost all, the tours begin and end at Glasgow or Edinburgh; but many of them may also be begun at Perth, Stirling, Oban, Aberdeen, etc. Full information regarding these circular tours will be found in the Tourist Handbooks published by the railway-companies. The tickets are usually available for several weeks; and the utmost facilities are granted for breaking the journey. Most of the tickets are issued for 1st and 3rd class

See foldout Railway Map of Scotland at front of book

only. The latter, 15-30 per cent cheaper than the former, generally include equal privileges on steamers and coaches; but the Scottish third-class compartments are inferior to those of England. — The English railway-companies issue tourist tickets to Scotland at reduced rates, available for 1-2 months. — The Scottish 'Bradshaw' is *Murray's Time Tables* (monthly; 3*d*.).

Coaches. The Highland coaches are, as a rule, excellently horsed, and form a delightful means of seeing the country in fine weather. There is invariably a keen competition for the box-seats; and travellers, on reaching a point whence the journey is to be continued by coach, should send one of the party as quickly as possible to secure good places. The first coach, where there are more than one, suffers least from dust. The driver expects a gratuity of 6*d*.-1*s*. 6*d*. according to the length of the drive. — Posting, as in England (p. xxii).

Steamers. There is probably nowhere a better service of pleasure steamers than those which ply on the Clyde and along the W. coast of Scotland; and they are certainly much superior to the English river-steamers. Most of them belong to *Mr. David Macbrayne* (119 Hope St., Glasgow), who issues tickets for six days' sailing (3*l*.), available on any of his vessels (board included). The fares generally are very moderate, and the restaurants on board excellent. — A small but exasperating annoyance in steamboat travelling in Scotland is the constant demand for pier-dues (1-3*d*.) on landing or embarking, as the piers usually belong to private owners.

III. Plan of Tour.

The regular 'Season' for a tour in Scotland is July and August, when, however, the hotels are often over-crowded. June is in some respects one of the pleasantest months; but many of the circular tour tickets are not issued, and some of the coaches do not begin running, until July. The first half of July is generally less crowded than the following 4-6 weeks. The first half of September is also often a favourable season, but the days begin to be perceptibly shorter. — Sunday is practically a *dies non* in Highland travelling, and Sunday quarters should always be engaged in advance. Most of the trains, steamers, and coaches cease running on Sunday, and in some quarters it is even difficult to hire a private carriage.

As already stated, the possible combinations of tours in Scotland are so numerous that it is difficult to give advice in mapping out a journey. The following routes, however, will at least give an idea of the time required for a visit to the most attractive points.

a. Tour of 3-4 Weeks.

	Days
Edinburgh and Environs (*Roslin*, *Hawthornden*)	3-4
From Edinburgh to *Melrose* and *Dryburgh*, and back	1
From Edinburgh viâ *Callander*, the *Trossachs*, and *Loch Lomond* to *Glasgow* (Circular Tour)	1-2
Glasgow	1-2
Falls of Clyde and back	1/2-1
From Glasgow to *Ayr* (Burns Country) and back	1
From Glasgow to *Arran* (night-quarters) and back	2
From Glasgow to *Oban* by the *Crinan Canal*	1
Circular Tour from Oban to *Loch Awe* and back	1
From Oban to *Iona* and *Staffa*, and back	1
From Oban to *Ballachulish* and *Glencoe*	1
From Ballachulish to *Inverness*. *Caledonian Canal*. *Fall of Foyers*	1
From Inverness to *Loch Maree* and back	2
From Inverness to *Aberdeen* and in Aberdeen	1-1 1/2
From Aberdeen to *Braemar*	1
From Braemar through the *Spital of Glenshee* to *Perth*	1
From Perth to *Crieff*, *Comrie*, *Lochearnhead*, *Loch Tay*, *Kenmore*, *Aberfeldy*, and *Dunkeld*	1-2
From Dunkeld to *Pitlochry* and back to Perth	1
From Perth to Edinburgh or Glasgow	1/2
	22-27

Those who do not fear a short sea-voyage should undoubtedly add to this tour a visit to the island of *Skye*, which contains, perhaps, the grandest scenery in Scotland. The island is reached either from Oban or from Inverness (viâ Gairloch or Strome Ferry). These who dispense with a visit to Aberdeen may obtain a circular ticket from Edinburgh (Glasgow) for Perth, Dunkeld, Inverness, Dingwall, Achnasheen, Loch Maree, Gairloch, Portree (Skye), Oban, Crinan Canal, and Glasgow (or in the reverse direction). From Oban an excursion to Skye and back may be made by steamer in 2-3 days. The route viâ Dingwall and Strome Ferry (Dingwall & Skye Railway) offers the shortest sea-passage (Inverness to Skye and back in 2-3 days). — *Inveraray*, which is not included in the above itinerary, may be visited from Glasgow on a circular tour of 2-3 days.

b. A Week from Edinburgh or Glasgow.	Days
Edinburgh	1-2
From Edinburgh to *Inversnaid* as given in R. 67; thence by steamer to *Ardlui*, coach to *Crianlarich*, and railway to *Lochearnhead* (one long day from 6 or 7 a.m. to 7 p.m.)	1
Coach to *Crieff*, railway to *Perth*.	1
Railway to *Aberfeldy*, coach to *Kenmore*, steamer on *Loch Tay* to *Killin Pier*; railway to Edinburgh or Glasgow	1
[Or from Killin by railway to *Oban*, and on the following day by steamer or railway back to Edinburgh or Glasgow	2

c. A Week from Glasgow or Edinburgh.	
Glasgow	1
Railway to Greenock, steamer through *Loch Long* and *Loch Goil* to *Lochgoilhead*, coach to *St. Catherine's*, ferry to *Inveraray*, coach to *Tarbet*	1-2
Steamer to *Inversnaid*, and thence viâ the *Trossachs*, etc., as in R. 67, to Edinburgh or Glasgow	1-2

The remaining days may be filled up by excursions from Oban to *Staffa* and *Iona*; from Glasgow to *Arran*, *Ayr*, or the *Clyde*; from Edinburgh to *Melrose*, *Hawthornden*, etc.; or from *Perth* to *Dunkeld* or *Pitlochry*.

IV. Outline of Scottish History.

The first event in the history of Scotland to which a fixed date can be assigned is its invasion in A.D. 78 by *Julius Agricola*, who advanced as far as the Tay. *Antoninus Pius* (ca. 105) constructed an earthen rampart from the Clyde to the Forth, and *Severus* (208) carried the Roman arms to the Moray Firth; but practically the Romans made no permanent conquests beyond the Great Wall uniting the Solway and the Tyne (see p. 376). The earliest known inhabitants of the country were the three Celtic races: Britons, Picts, and Scots. The *Britons* extended as far as the Forth and Clyde and came partly under Roman influence. The *Picts* (Latin, 'Picti', painted) or *Cruithne* seem to have had their original settlements in the extreme N. of Scotland and Ireland. The *Scots*, who eventually gave their name to the whole country, came from Ireland and settled at first in Argyllshire. From an early period they united with the Picts in assaults on the Romans and Romanised Britons. The conversion of these three races to Christianity seems to have begun before the close of the 4th cent., and the three chief missionaries were *St. Ninian* (Galloway; 4-5th cent.), *St. Kentigern* or *Mungo* (p. 477; 5-6th cent.), and *St. Columba* (p. 490; 6-7tn cent.).

Down to the 9th cent. the history of the Picts, in the N. part of the country, and of the Scots, in their kingdom of *Dalriada* (Argyllshire) is somewhat confusing and uncertain. The Britons of South Scotland, the kingdom of *Strathclyde*, separated by the English from their S. kinsmen maintained their independence down to the 10th cent. (see p. 454).

844-860. *Kenneth Macalpine* unites the Picts and Scots in one kingdom, at first called *Albany* and afterwards (10-11th cent.) *Scotland*. Contests with the Britons of Strathclyde.

943-954. *Malcolm I.* extends his sway over Strathclyde (see p. 454).

1005-1034. *Malcolm II.* conquers Lothian.

1034-1040. *Duncan*, grandson of Malcolm II., is killed by —

1040-1057. *Macbeth*, who usurps the throne and proves himself an able ruler. He falls in battle against the son of Duncan —

1058-1093. *Malcolm III. Canmore*, who gives shelter to Edgar Atheling and marries his sister Margaret (1068). The English language, English customs, and English colonists begin to gain a footing in Scotland.

1107-1124. *Alexander I.* marries Sibylla, daughter of Henry I. of England.

1124-1153. *David I.*, the 'Scottish Alfred', does much to promote the civilisation of Scotland. He invades England, in support of Matilda, and is defeated at the Battle of the Standard (1138; see p. 409).

1154-1165. *Malcolm IV.*, the Maiden.

1165-1214. *William the Lion* is taken prisoner by Henry II. and has to acknowledge his supremacy, but afterwards re-establishes his independence. Alliance with France.

1214-1249. *Alexander II.* takes part with the English Barons against King John.

1249-1289. *Alexander III.*, a wise and good king, under whom Scotland enjoys peace and prosperity. After his death and that of his granddaughter and heiress, Margaret, the Maid of Norway (1290), the succession to the crown is disputed by Baliol and Bruce. Edward I. of England is appealed to and decides in favour of —

1292-1297. *John Baliol*, who, however, scarcely maintains a semblance of independence and after a short resistance to Edward's pretensions is carried prisoner to London (1297). *William Wallace*, the 'Man of the People', rises against the English, and defeats them at Stirling Bridge, but is finally captured by Edward I. and beheaded (1305).

1306-1329. *Robert Bruce*, however, succeeds as patriot-leader of the Scots, finally secures the independence of Scotland by his victory at Bannockburn (1314), and is recognised on all hands as king.

1329-1370. *David II.*, the weak son of a great father, carries on an unsuccessful war with England, is defeated at Neville's Cross (1346; p. 414), and is kept prisoner by Edward III. for 11 years.

1370-1390. *Robert II.*, son of Marjory, Bruce's daughter, is the first of the Stuarts. Battle of *Otterbourn* (1388).

1390-1406. *Robert III* also carries on war with England. Defeated at *Homildon Hill* (1402). His son and successor —

1406-1437. *James I.*, is taken prisoner by the English on his way to France in 1405 and spends the first 18 years of his reign in captivity. The Duke of Albany is appointed regent. Defeat of Donald, Lord of the Isles, at *Harlaw* (1412). James writes the 'King's Quhair' and other poems. His reforms are in advance of the age and he is assassinated by conspirators at Perth (see p. 498).

1437-1460. *James II.* stabs the Earl of Douglas, a dangerous and turbulent subject, at Stirling (1452; p. 485), and strengthens the royal authority. He is killed by the bursting of a gun at the siege of Roxburgh (p. 456).

1460-1488. *James III.* attempts to rule through favourites, who are put to death by Angus 'Bell the Cat' and other conspirators. A rebellion breaks out, and James is defeated by his nobles at Sauchieburn and slain.

1488-1513. *James IV.* marries Margaret, daughter of Henry VII., and is slain at the disastrous battle of *Flodden*.

1513-1542. *James V.* marries Mary of Guise. Represses the Border Freebooters. Is defeated at *Solway Moss* (1542) and dies of a broken heart.

1542-1567. *Mary Stuart* marries first the *Dauphin of France* (1558), then *Darnley* (1565), and lastly *Bothwell* (1567). Defeat of the English at *Ancrum Moor* (1544) and of the Scots at *Pinkie* (1547). Murder of *Rizzio* (1566). *Reformation* in Scotland (1560 et seq.); *John Knox*. Mary, while imprisoned in *Lochleven Castle*, abdicates in favour of her son (1567).

1567-1603. *James VI.* Defeat at *Langside* (1568) of Mary, who takes refuge in England. Regencies of *Moray* (1568), *Lennox* (1570), *Mar* (1571), and *Morton* (1572). *Raid of Ruthven* (1582). Queen Mary executed (1587). *Gowrie Conspiracy* (1600; see p. 498). James succeeds to the English throne.

V. Noest on the Gaelic Language.

The Gaelic of the Scottish Highlands is akin to the Welsh, and substantially identical with the Erse of Ireland. Owing to the numerous combinations of silent consonants and other causes, it is less easy, however, to indicate its pronunciation than that of Welsh. It may, however, be useful to bear in mind that the vowels have the Continental, not the English value (comp. p. xxxi); and that the frequently occurring aspiration of a consonant has the effect either of softening it or of effacing it altogether (thus *bh* = *v*, *dh* = *y*, *fh* mute, and *ch* guttural). The ordinary tourist will, however, find that English is always understood, though the enterprising pedestrian may occasionally stumble upon a Gael ignorant of all save his mother-tongue. The following is a short glossary of Gaelic roots of frequent recurrence in the names of places. *Aber*, mouth, confluence; *achadh (ach, auch)*, a field; *alt, ault* (genitive *uilt*), a brook; *an*, a diminutive termination; *ard*, high; *bal, baile*, a village or place; *ban*, white; *beag (beg)*, little; *beinn (ben)*, a mountain; *breac (vreck, vrackie)*, speckled; *cam, cambus*, crooked; *ceann (kin, ken)*, head; *clach*, a stone, *clachan* (dim.), a village; *dal*, a field; *dearg*, red; *dubh (dhû)*, black; *dùn*, a hill-fort; *eas (ess)*, waterfall; *fad, fada*, long; *fionn (fyne)*, white, shining; *garbh (garve)*, rough, rugged; *glas*, gray; *gorm*, blue; *innis (inch)*, island; *inbhir (inver)*, same as *aber; cil (kil)*, cell, church, parish; *coille (killie)*, wood; *caol (kyle)*, strait; *lag*, a hollow; *linn, linne*, a pool; *mam, meall*, a rounded hill; *mor (more)*, great; *muc* (gen. *muic*), a sow; *cuach, quoich*, a cup; *ross*, a point; *sruth, stru, struan*, running water; *tulloch (tilly, tully)*, a knoll; *tir (tyre)*, land; *uisge (esk)*, water (*usquebaugh*, water of life, hence *whiskey*).

62. From London to Edinburgh or Glasgow.

The traveller may choose between three different railway-routes for his journey to Scotland. The fast trains between London and Edinburgh take $8^1/_2$-10 hrs. Fares to *Edinburgh* 57*s.* 6*d.*, 44*s.* 9*d.*, 32*s.* 8*d.*; to *Glasgow* 58*s.*, 45*s.* 3*d.*, 33*s.*; reduced return-fares in summer. No second class on the Midland Railway. Pullman Drawing-room Cars are attached to the fast trains by day and Sleeping Cars (5*s.* extra) to the night-expresses. — The opening of the *Forth Bridge* (p. 495) has reduced the through-journey from London to *Aberdeen* (p. 504) to $12^1/_4$ (G.N.R.) -15 hrs. — *Steamers*, see p. 462.

a. Viâ Leicester, Leeds, and Carlisle.

Midland and North British Railways ('Waverley Route') from *St. Pancras Station* to (406 M.) *Edinburgh* in $9^1/_2$-$10^3/_4$ hrs.; to (423 M.) *Glasgow* in $9^3/_4$-$10^3/_4$ hrs. Half-an-hour is allowed for dinner at *Normanton* (p. 402) or *Leeds* (p. 402), and luncheon-baskets (2*s.* 6*d.*-3*s.*) may be obtained at St. Pancras and Leicester.

From London to (308 M.) *Carlisle*, see R. 49. A short way beyond Carlisle the line to Glasgow *(Glasgow and South Western Railway)*, described in R. 69, diverges to the left, while the Edinburgh trains follow the line of the *North British Co.*, running through the 'Waverley District'. From ($317^1/_2$ M.) *Longtown* a branch-line diverges to ($4^1/_2$ M) *Gretna Green* (p. 462). To the left lies *Solway Moss*, where the Scots were defeated by the English in 1542. To the right, near (320 M.) *Scotch Dyke*, is *Netherby Hall*, the scene of 'Young Lochinvar'. The train crosses the *Esk* and the *Liddel*, and ascends the valley of the latter, skirting the *Cheviots* (right). 322 M. *Riddings* is the junction of a line to *Canobie* and (7 M.) *Langholm*. The obelisk on the hill to the left commemorates *General Sir John Malcolm.* At (329 M.) *Kershope Foot* we cross the *Kershope Burn* and enter Scotland (Roxburghshire). — 332 M. *Newcastleton*, the centre of the district of *Liddesdale*, the home of 'Dandie Dinmont' (comp. p. 417). — 340 M. *Riccarton* is the junction of a line to Reedsmouth and Hexham (see p. 418). Farther on (left) rise the *Maiden Paps* (1675 ft.).

353½ M. **Hawick** *(Tower; Victoria)*, a woollen-making town with 17,000 inhab., contains little to detain the tourist. About 3 M. to the S. W. is *Branksome (Branxholme) Tower*, which still, as in the 'Lay of the Last Minstrel', belongs to the Buccleuch family.

Beyond Hawick we see to the right **Ruberslaw* (1390ft.), a finely-shaped hill commanding an extensive view. To the right of (358 M.) *Hassendean* are the picturesquely-wooded *Minto Crags* (720 ft.; *View), in the grounds of *Minto House*, seat of the Earl of Minto. — 366 M. *St. Boswells* is the nearest station to (1 M.) *Dryburgh Abbey* (p. 458); walkers may alight here, visit the abbey, and then go on to (4 M.) Melrose.

From St. Boswells to Kelso and Berwick, 35½ M. railway in 2 hrs. (fares 5*s*. 6*d*., 4*s*. 5*d*., 2*s*. 11*d*.). The line runs along the S. bank of the *Tweed*. To the right is the *Waterloo Monument*, on the top of *Penielheugh* (775 ft.); to the left is *Smailholm Tower*, the scene of Scott's 'Eve of St. John'. Adjoining the latter is the farm of *Sandyknowe*, where Scott, when a child, often visited his grandfather. — Beyond (9 M.) *Roxburgh*, the junction of the line to (7 M.) *Jedburgh* (see below), the train crosses the *Teviot*.

Floors Castle, the magnificent seat of the Duke of Roxburghe, is seen among the trees to the left (visitors admitted to the grounds on Wed.). Near Floors are the scanty remains of *Roxburgh Castle*.

11½ M. **Kelso** *(Cross Keys; Queen's Head)*, a prosperous little market-town with 4500 inhab., 1 M. from the station, is chiefly of interest for its ***Abbey**, a small but fine ruin in the Norman and E. E. styles, destroyed by the English in 1545. The *Museum* (open on Mon., Wed., & Frid., 12 3) contains objects of local interest. — At *Ednam*, 2 M. to the N.E., is a monument to *Thomson*, the poet, who was born there in 1699.

22 M. **Coldstream** *(Newcastle Arms)* gives its name to the Coldstream Guards, raised here by General Monk in 1660. About 6 M. to the S. is the field of *Flodden*, where the Scottish army, led by James IV., was defeated by the English in 1513. A branch-line runs from Coldstream to *Wooler* and *Bilton Junction* (p. 416). — At (25½ M.) *Twizell* we cross the *Till*. The Norman keep (12th cent.) of (27½ M.) *Norham* appears in the opening scene of 'Marmion'. — 34 M. *Tweedmouth*. — 35½ M. *Berwick-upon-Tweed*, see p. 417.

Another line runs from St. Boswells to *Duns* and (31 M.) *Reston Junction* (p. 459).

[**Jedburgh** *(Spread Eagle; Royal)*, a picturesque little border-town, with a stormy past, lies on the *Jed*, and contains about 3500 inhabitants. ***Jedburgh Abbey** (adm. 6*d*.), founded by David I. in 1118, is one of the largest and most beautiful ecclesiastical ruins in Scotland (late-Norman, with subsequent modifications). Several houses with historical associations are shown in Jedburgh: Queen Mary lodged in an old house in Queen Street, and Prince Charles Stuart at 9 Castlegate (after Prestonpans); Burns lived at 27 Canongate in 1787, Sir David Brewster (1781-1868) was born in the same street, and Scott visited Wordsworth at 5 Abbey Close (1805). 'Jeddart Justice', like Lydford Law (p. 135), is proverbial; and 'Jeddart Staves' were long unpleasantly familiar to the English Borderers. — Excursions may be made from Jedburgh to (2 M.) *Ferniherst Castle* (16th cent.), to (4 M.) the *Waterloo Monument* on *Penielheugh* (comp. above), and to (2 M.) *Dunion Hill* (1095 ft.; *View).]

The three hills, or rather triple-peaked hill, that have for some time been visible to the left are the **Eildons** (1385 ft.), which owe their present appearance, according to tradition, to the agency of the devil, working at the bidding of the wizard Michael Scott.

Thomas of Ercildoun, or '*Thomas the Rhymer*' (13th cent.) is said to have been carried off by the Queen of the Fairies, and detained for three years, like Tannhäuser in the Venusberg, in an enchanted land inside the hills.

As we approach Melrose we have a view of the abbey to the right.

369 M. **Melrose** (**Abbey; George; King's Arms; Waverley Temperance Hotel*, well spoken of, near the station; *Waverley Hydropathic*, 1/2 M. from the station), a small town with 1600 inhab., is prettily situated on the *Tweed*. The *Town Cross*, at the head of the High Street, dates from the 14th century.

***Melrose Abbey,** indisputably the finest ruin in Scotland, lies a few hundred yards to the N. of the railway-station (adm. 6*d.*). Originally founded in the 12th cent. by David I., that 'sair sanct for the crown', the abbey was afterwards almost wholly destroyed by Edward II. and rebuilt by Robert Bruce (14th cent.), and once more destroyed and rebuilt in the following century.

The principal part of the present remains is the **Choir*, a fine example of late-Gothic (ca. 1450), with slender shafts, richly-carved capitals, elaborate vaulting, and large and exquisitely-traceried windows (especially the *E. Window). The *Transept* crosses the choir near its E. end. Of the *Nave* there are comparatively few remains. The beautiful sculptures throughout the church were sadly defaced at the Reformation. On the N. side are two Norman arches. *Alexander II.* and the heart of *Robert Bruce* are interred at the E. end, near the site of the high-altar. The tomb of *Michael Scott* is pointed out in the chapel on the S. side of the choir (to the E. of the S. transept), and *Sir David Brewster* (d. 1868) is buried in the churchyard, close to the S. wall of the aisle.

On the right bank of the Tweed, 2 3/4 M. above Melrose, lies ***Abbotsford,** the picturesque home of Sir Walter Scott (open 10-5; adm. 1*s.*). The road to it (carr. 6*s.* 6*d.*) leads to the W. from Melrose, passing the *Waverley Hydropathic Establishment* and the village of *Darnick*, with its old 'peel' or Border tower.

In 1811 Scott bought the small farm of *Clarty Hole*, changing its name to Abbotsford, planting it with trees, and beginning the large and irregularly-built mansion which he occupied till his death in 1832. The rooms shown to visitors include the great novelist's *Study*, the *Library*, the *Drawing Room*, and the *Entrance Hall*. They contain numerous personal relics of Scott and also many historical curiosities. The *Dining Room*, in which Scott died, is not shown. — The house is now owned by the *Hon. Mrs. Maxwell Scott*, a great-grand-daughter of the novelist.

Next in interest to Abbotsford among places near Melrose is Dryburgh Abbey, where Sir Walter Scott is interred in the burial vault of his ancestors.

The pleasantest way to make this excursion is to walk or drive viâ the *Eildon Hills* (see above) and *St. Boswells* (p. 456; 4 1/2 M.) and return by *Bemerside* (6 M.; carr. for the round, with one horse 9-10, with two 13-15*s.*). Both routes afford charming views, the most extensive being that from *Bemerside Hill*. Bemerside has belonged to the family of Haig for seven centuries. Between Bemerside and Dryburgh is a huge and rude *Statue of William Wallace*. Abbotsford and Dryburgh can easily be included in one day's excursion from Melrose, even by the pedestrian (carr. and pair for the day 20-25*s.*).

The picturesque and extensive ruins of ***Dryburgh Abbey** (adm. 6*d.*) date from the 12-14th cent. and include parts of the church, the chapter house, the refectory, the cloisters, and the domestic buildings. *Scott* (d. 1832) is interred in *St. Mary's Aisle.* *John Gibson Lockhart* (d. 1854), Scott's son-in-law and biographer, is also buried here.

After leaving Melrose we have a glimpse of Abbotsford to the left, and cross the Tweed. — 373 M. **Galashiels** *(Commercial; Abbotsford Arms; Royal)*, a busy town of 16,000 inhab., is noted for its tweeds and tartans.

From Galashiels a short branch runs to (6 M.) *Selkirk*, passing (2½ M.) *Abbotsford Ferry*, the nearest station to (1 M.) Abbotsford (see p. 457). — **Selkirk** *(County; Fleece; Town Arms)*, another tweed-making town of 6100 inhab., with statues of *Sir Walter Scott* and *Mungo Park* (1771-1805), a native of Selkirkshire. A delightful excursion may be made hence through the lovely and much besung valley of the *Yarrow* to (15 M.) ***St. Mary's Loch.** The usual goal of the excursion, *Tibbie Shiels's Inn*, is at the S. end of the lake, 3 M. farther on. On the W. bank is the *Rodono Hotel* (D. 3*s.*). The district in which the loch lies is called *Ettrick Forest;* and a statue of *James Hogg* (1770-1835), the 'Ettrick Shepherd', has been erected near Tibbie Shiels's. — The excursion may be continued through *Moffat Dale*, passing the fine waterfall called the **Grey Mare's Tail*, to (16 M.) *Moffat* (comp. p. 461). Coaches ply thrice weekly from Selkirk to St. Mary's Loch (fare 3*s.*, return 5*s.*, driver 1*s.*), corresponding with the coaches to Moffat (p. 461).

From Galashiels to Peebles, 18½ M., railway in 1 hr. At (3½ M.) *Clovenfords*, above the junction of the *Gala* and *Tweed*, are *Thomson's Vineries*, which provide the London market with immense quantities of grapes. On the other side of the Tweed is *Ashiestiel*, where most of 'Marmion' and the 'Lay' was written. Beyond (6 M.) *Thornilee* we pass the ruined *Elibank Tower*, on the left. — 10 M. *Walkerburn.* — 12 M. Innerleithen *(St. Ronan's; Traquair Arms)*, a small watering-place with mineral springs, is the original of 'St. Ronan's Well'. — About 1 M. to the S. is *Traquair House*, supposed to be the 'Bradwardine' of 'Waverley', with a very ancient tower. — 15 M. *Cardrona.*

18½ M. **Peebles** *(Tontine; Cross Keys; Commercial; *Hydropathic Establishment*, 52*s.* 6*d.* per week), an ancient town with 6000 inhab., prettily situated on the Tweed. The old castle has disappeared, but the towers of two venerable churches still tand. Peebles was the native place of *William* (1800-83) and *Robert* (1802-71) *Chambers*, whose name is commemorated in the *Chambers Institute* (adm. 3*d.*), presented to the town by the elder brother. Part of it belongs to the old mansion of the Queensberry family and dates from the 16th century. The *Cross Keys* is believed to be the prototype of 'Meg Dods's Inn' in 'St. Ronan's Well'. — About 1 M. to the W. are the ruins of *Neidpath Castle*, finely situated on the Tweed (*View from the top). About 3½ M. farther on, on the S. side of the Tweed, near the farm of *Woodhouse*, is the '*Black Dwarf's Cottage*'. — Many other pleasant excursions may be made from Peebles, and the streams in the vicinity afford good fishing. — From Peebles we may go on to (27 M.) *Edinburgh* by train viâ *Leadburn* and *Eskbank* (see p. 459).

The train now ascends the valley of the *Gala Water.* From (379½ M.) *Stow* a coach runs to (6 M.) *Lauder*, where Archibald Douglas, Earl of Angus, surnamed 'Bell the Cat', seized and hanged Cochrane, favourite of James III. (1482). Beyond (390 M.) *Tynehead*, where we reach the highest point (900 ft.) of this part of the line, we pass the ruins of *Crichton Castle* (15th cent.) on the right and *Borthwick Castle* (1430; with room occupied by Queen Mary and Bothwell) on the left. — 393 M. *Fushiebridge.* — 394 M. *Gore-*

bridge. To the left are *Dalhousie Castle* and *Cockpen.* Near (397 M.) *Dalhousie* is *Newbattle Abbey*, the fine seat of the Marquis of Lothian; in the grounds is the largest beech in the kingdom, 33 ft. in girth. 398 M. *Eskbank*, the station for *Dalkeith* (p. 475). *Arthur's Seat* (p. 470) comes into sight on the left.

403 M. **Portobello** *(Brighton; Royal; Regent Temperance)*, the Margate of Edinburgh, with extensive sands and a promenade-pier (1*d.*; band on Sat. in summer). — We here join the East Coast Route (R. 62b), skirt the base of the *Calton Hill* (p. 471), with the castellated *Prison*, and enter the *Waverley Station* at —

406 M. **Edinburgh** (see R. 64).

b. Viâ York, Newcastle, and Berwick.

Great Northern, North Eastern, and North British Railways ('East Coast Route') from *King's Cross* to (393 M.) *Edinburgh* in 8½-10½ hrs.; to (444 M.) *Glasgow* in 9¾-11 hrs. The best train is the 'Flying Scotsman', starting at 10 a.m. Half-an-hour for dinner is allowed at York; and luncheon-baskets may also be obtained.

From London to (335½ M.) *Berwick*, see R. 50. — Beyond Berwick the line skirts the coast, turning inland at (341 M.) *Burnmouth*, a picturesque fishing-village. 343 M. *Ayton* is the station for *Eyemouth* (Cross Keys), a busy little fishing-town, with 3000 inhabitants. — 347 M. **Reston** *(Wheatsheaf)* is the junction of a line to *Duns* and *St. Boswells* (comp. p. 456).

Near the coast, 3½ M. to the N.E. of Reston (omn. 1*s.*), is the village of *Coldingham* (New Inn), with the Transition Norman ruins of a Benedictine priory, founded in 1098. From Coldingham we may proceed to the N. to (2½ M.) ***St. Abb's Head,** a bold rocky promontory, rising 300 ft. above the sea. On it are a *Lighthouse* and a ruined *Church.* — About 3½ M. farther up the coast are the scanty ruins of **Fast Castle*, perched upon a precipitous cliff that has been identified with the 'Wolf's Crag' of the 'Bride of Lammermoor'. Walkers who have come thus far may go on to rejoin the railway at (7 M.) *Cockburnspath* (see below).

Beyond Reston the train follows the course of the *Eye.* 352 M. *Grant's House.* At (356½ M.) *Cockburnspath* (Inn) we again reach the sea. 359½ M. *Innerwick.* Farther on we cross the *Broxburn*, where Cromwell defeated the Scots at the Battle of Dunbar (1650).

363½ M. **Dunbar** *(George; Royal)*, a small seaport and fishing-station, with 3500 inhab., formerly of more importance than at present. The ruins of the old *Castle*, which plays a prominent rôle in Scottish history, are very scanty; they stand on a crag immediately above the harbour, and command a fine view.

Beyond Dunbar we have a good view to the right of the Bass Rock (see p. 460) and North Berwick Law (see p. 460). About 3 M. to the N. E. of (370 M.) *East Linton* is *Tyninghame House*, the seat of the Earl of Haddington, surrounded by finely-wooded grounds, which are open to the public on Saturday.

375½ M. *Drem* is the junction of the short line to (5 M.) **North Berwick** *(*Marine*, facing the sea, R. & A. from 4*s.*, D. 4*s.* 6*d.*; *Royal*, at the station; numerous *Private Hotels* and *Lodgings)*, a very favourite seaside-resort, rivalling St. Andrews (p. 496). Its attractions include a good sandy beach, picturesquely interspersed with rocks, admirable golfing-links, and a neighbourhood which affords many pleasant excursions. At the back of the town rises *North Berwick Law* (612 ft.), the top of which commands a delightful view. Off the coast are numerous rocky islands, the most important of which is the *Bass Rock*. In a field near the station are the ruins of a *Cistercian Monastery* (1216). North Berwick is within 3/4 hr. of Edinburgh by quick through-trains, and excursion-steamers ply to and from Leith in summer.

Excursions. About 2 M. to the S.W. is *Dirleton*, one of the prettiest of Scottish villages, with a ruined *Castle* (open to visitors on Thurs.).

To the E. (2 1/2 M.) is *Canty Bay* (Hotel), the starting-point for a visit to the Bass Rock, which lies 1 1/2 M. from the shore (steam-launch 10*s*.; fishing-boat less). The ***Bass Rock**, which rises abruptly from the sea to a height of 350 ft., is the haunt of myriads of solan geese and other sea-birds. On it are the ruins of an old *Castle*, formerly used for the confinement of English prisoners and afterwards of Covenanters. The landing is difficult except in calm weather. — On the coast, about 1/2 M. beyond Canty Bay, is ***Tantallon Castle**, the romantic situation and appearance of which are most accurately described in 'Marmion'.

Tyninghame Woods (see p. 459) are 3 1/2 M. beyond Tantallon. — Excursion-steamers ply in summer to (10 M.) the *Isle of May*.

379 1/2 M. *Longniddry* is the junction of a line to (4 1/2 M.) **Haddington** *(George; Black Bull)*, a small town (4000 inhab.) on the *Tyne*, with an important grain-market. The *Knox Institute* commemorates the fact that John Knox was born in the suburb of Giffordgate in 1505. Samuel Smiles and Mrs. Carlyle (Jane Welsh; d. 1866) were also natives of Haddington; and the latter is commemorated by a tombstone in the churchyard.

Just before reaching (383 1/2 M.) *Prestonpans* we pass, to the right, the field of Prestonpans, where Prince Charles Stuart defeated the Royalists in 1745. The monument to the left, close to the line, is to the memory of Col. Gardiner, who fell in the battle. Prestonpans takes its name from its salt-pans, and has given name to a light table-beer. Prestonpans is also the station for *Tranent*, *Ormiston* (with an old cross), and the fishing-village of *Cockenzie*. — A little farther on we pass the scene of the battle of *Pinkie* (1547; to the left). 386 1/2 M. *Inveresk*. — 388 1/2 M. *New Hailes*.

New Hailes is the junction of a short line to (1 1/2 M.) **Musselburgh** *(Musselburgh Arms)*, a small seaport, much frequented by Edinburgh golfers. Near the station is a monument to *Dr. Moir* (1798-1851), the 'Delta' of Blackwood's Magazine. To the W. of Musselburgh is the fishing-village of *Fisherrow*, which extends nearly to *Joppa*, a suburb of Portobello (p. 459).

At (390 M.) *Portobello* we join the Waverley Route (R. 62a).

393 M. **Edinburgh**, see R. 64.

c. Viâ Crewe and Carlisle.

L.N.W. and Caledonian Railways ('West Coast Route') to (400 M.) *Edinburgh* in 8 1/2-12 1/2 hrs.; to (401 M.) *Glasgow* in 8 3/4-12 3/4 hrs. Dinner at *Preston* (25 min.).

From London to (299 M.) *Carlisle*, see R. 49. Soon after leaving

Carlisle the train passes under the line described at p. 455, and runs towards the N.W. Near (306 M.) *Floriston* it crosses the *Esk* and enters the 'Debatable Ground'. View to the left of the *Solway Firth.* 308$^1/_2$ M. *Gretna Junction* (comp. p. 462).

From Gretna Junction to *Dumfries* and *Stranraer*, see R. 63.

We now cross the *Sark* and enter Scotland. 313 M. *Kirkpatrick;* 317 M. *Kirtle Bridge*, the junction of a branch to (5$^1/_2$ M.) *Annan* (p. 462). — 320 M. **Ecclefechan** *(Inn*, plain), a small village in a somewhat bleak district, taking its name from the Irish St. Fechan (7th cent.), is now frequented by numerous pilgrims to the birth-house and grave of *Thomas Carlyle* (1795-1881).

About 3 M. to the N. is the hill of *Burnswark* or *Birrenswark* (920 ft.; view), with interesting Roman camps and British (?) forts.

326 M. **Lockerbie** *(King's Arms; Blue Bell)*, a small town with 7000 inhab., is the junction of a line to (14 M.) *Dumfries* (p. 462). Travellers by the fast trains, who wish to visit Burnswark and Ecclefechan, alight here. — Several small stations.

340 M. *Beattock* (Rail. Rfmt. Rooms) is the junction for (2 M.) **Moffat** *(Annandale Arms; Buccleuch Arms; *Hydropathic; Lodgings)*, a small town with 2000 inhab. (doubled in the season), on the *Annan*, and one of the chief inland watering-places of Scotland. Omnibuses ply daily (6*d.*) to the sulphureous-saline *Wells* (625 ft.), which lie 1$^1/_4$ M. from the town and about 300 ft. above it.

The **Environs** of Moffat are pretty and afford several pleasant excursions, among the most popular being those to (1 M.) *Gallow Hill*, the wooded height to the N. of the town; *Hartfell Spa*, 4$^1/_4$ M. to the N.E.; the *Devil's Beef Tub* (which figures in 'Redgauntlet'), 5 M. to the N.; *Beld Craig*, a wooded glen with a 'linn', or waterfall, 3$^1/_2$ M. to the S.E.; the (1$^1/_2$ M.) *Meeting of the Waters* (the *Annan*, the *Moffat*, and the *Evan*); and *Garpol Linn*, 3 M. to the S. — Coaches ply thrice weekly during the season (June-Sept.) to (11 M.) the **Grey Mare's Tail* and (15 M.) *St Mary's Loch* (comp. p. 458; fare 3*s.*, return 5*s.*, driver extra).

Beyond Beattock we reach the highest point of the line (1030 ft.) and begin to descend into *Clydesdale.* At (352$^1/_2$ M.) *Elvanfoot* we cross the infant *Clyde.* — From (366$^1/_2$ M.) *Symington*, the best station for an ascent of *Tinto Hill* (2300 ft.; view), a branch-line diverges to (3 M.) *Biggar* and (19 M.) *Peebles* (p. 458).

t (373$^1/_2$ M.) **Carstairs Junction** *(Rail. Rfmt. Rms.)* the Caledonian Railway forks, the W. branch going on to Glasgow, and the E. arm to Edinburgh. Those bound for the *Falls of Clyde* change carriages here for (4$^1/_2$ M.) *Lanark* (p. 480).

The chief stations on the Glasgow line, which traverses an iron and coal district, are (8$^1/_2$ M.) *Carluke*, (13$^1/_2$ M.) *Wishaw*, and (16 M.) *Motherwell* (Royal), the junction of lines to *Hamilton* (p. 480) and *Uddingston.* — 27 M. *Glasgow* (Central Station), see p. 476.

The Edinburgh line turns to the right (N.). 375 M. *Carnwath.* Beyond (379$^1/_2$ M.) *Auchengray* the train skirts the N. slopes of the *Pentland Hills.* To the right, at (383$^1/_2$ M.) *Cobbinshaw*, is the large reservoir of the Union Canal. At (391 M.) *Midcalder* we join the direct line from Glasgow to Edinburgh viâ *Holytown* (p. 476). Mineral oil-works abound in this district. 395$^1/_2$ M. *Currie Hill.*

Farther on, *Corstorphine Hill* (p. 474) comes into sight on the left, and *Arthur's Seat* (p. 470) on the right. $398^1/_2$ M. *Slateford.*

400 M. **Edinburgh** (Caledonian Station), see R. 64.

d. By Sea.

The steamers of the London & Edinburgh Shipping Company leave the *Hermitage Wharf, Wapping*, every Tues., Wed., and Sat. for *Leith;* those of the General Steam Navigation Co. leave *Irongate and St. Katherine's Wharf* twice weekly for *Granton.* Fares in each case 22*s.*, 16*s.* (food extra); duration of voyage about 30-36 hrs.

[There is also a bi-weekly service from the Carron and London and Continental Wharves to *Grangemouth* (22*s.*, 16*s.*), for *Glasgow* (26*s.*, 24*s.*, 17*s.*) and the West of Scotland. The steamers sail up the Forth and under the *Forth Bridge* (p. 504).]

This route, which may be recommended to the leisurely traveller in fine weather, affords a good view of the E. coast of England. Among the more prominent points are *Yarmouth* (p. 447), *Flamborough Head* (p. 420), *Scarborough* (p. 419), *Whitby* (p. 420), *Bamborough Castle* (p. 416), *Lindisfarne* (p. 417), *St. Abb's Head* (p. 459), *Tantallon Castle* and the *Bass Rock* (p. 460), and *Inchkeith* (p. 496). From *Leith* and *Granton* (see p. 474) trains run at frequent intervals to Edinburgh.

63. From Carlisle to Dumfries and Stranraer.

106 M. Railway in 5-$5^1/_4$ hrs. (17*s.* 8*d.*, 8*s.* 10*d.*; no 2nd cl.). Through sleeping-cars run from London (Euston and St. Pancras) to *Stranraer.*

From Carlisle to ($9^1/_2$ M.) *Gretna Junction*, see p. 461. Our line here turns to the left. $10^1/_2$ M. *Gretna Green*, formerly celebrated for its runaway marriages of couples from beyond the Border, the ceremony being generally performed by the village blacksmith. — 18 M. **Annan** *(Buck; Queensberry)*, a small town with 4500 inhab., was the birthplace of the *Rev. Edward Irving* (1792).

A line runs to the S. from Annan, across the *Solway*, to join the Carlisle and Maryport Railway (p. 376). — To *Kirtle Bridge*, see p. 461.

25 M. *Ruthwell.* About $1^3/_4$ M. to the S. of the station, in the manse-garden, is a famous **Runic Cross*, the inscription on which is said to be the earliest piece of written English extant.

33 M. **Dumfries** *(King's Arms; Queensberry; Commercial; *Station; Rail. Rfmt. Rooms)*, the chief town in S. W. Scotland, with 17,000 inhab., is situated on the *Nith.* A conspicuous building is *New Greyfriars Church*, occupying the site of the old castle. Close by lay the Greyfriars Monastery, in the church of which Bruce slew the Red Comyn (1306). Adjacent is the *Burns Monument*, erected in 1882. Burns's house in Bank St. is marked by an inscription. The house in which he died (21st July, 1796) is in Burns St., a lane leading out of St. Michael Street, next to the Industrial School, on which are a bust and inscription. His grave in the churchyard of *St. Michael's* is covered by a *Mausoleum* (adm. 3*d.*), in a tasteless classical style. The *Globe Inn* (entr. by 44 High St.), a favourite resort of the poet, contains his chair, his watch, and

lines cut by him with a diamond on the window. The *Statue of Burns*, in Church Place, is by Mrs. D. O. Hill. The *Old Bridge*, connecting the town with the suburb of *Maxwelltown*, dates from the 13th century. In Maxwelltown is the *Observatory* (adm. 6*d.*; view), containing a small museum; in the grounds is a statue of 'Old Mortality' (see below).

Environs. Crossing the bridge to Maxwelltown, taking the first turn to the right, and following the road to the N., we reach (1½ M.) **Lincluden Abbey**, prettily situated at the confluence of the *Cluden* and the *Nith*. The Abbey, a Benedictine house, was founded in the 12th cent., but the present remains are chiefly of a later date (14-15th cent.). The walk may be continued up the *Cluden* to (3 M.) *Irongray*, the churchyard of which contains the grave of Helen Walker, the original of 'Jeanie Deans', marked by an inscription by Sir Walter Scott. About ⅓ M. farther on is an interesting *Covenanters' Monument.* — On the *Solway*, 8 M. to the S. of Dumfries, is ***Caerlaverock Castle** (the 'Ellangowan' of 'Guy Mannering'), an ancient stronghold of the Maxwells (Earls of Nithdale), dating in its present form mainly from the 15th century. Caerlaverock churchyard contains the grave of 'Old Mortality' (R. Paterson). — Another charming excursion may be taken to (7½ M.) ***New or Sweetheart Abbey,** to the W. of the Nith estuary. The Abbey was founded in 1275 by Devorgilla Balliol, and derives its name *(douce coeur)* from the fact that she had the heart of her husband John Balliol (see p. 236) buried here in her own tomb. From Sweetheart Abbey walkers may go on to (3½ M.) the top of **Criffel** (1856 ft., *View).

From Dumfries to Glasgow, 92 M., railway in 2-3¾ hrs. (fares 13*s.* 9*d.*, 6*s.* 10*d.*; no 2nd cl.). — Soon after leaving Dumfries, we have a view of *Lincluden Abbey* (see above) to the left. To the right, 3-4 M. farther on, is the white farm-house of *Ellisland*, where Burns wrote 'Tam o' Shanter'. — 14½ M. *Thornhill* (Buccleuch Arms) is the starting-point for visits to (3½ M.) *Drumlanrig Castle* (gardens and park open on Tues. & Frid.) and (3 M.) *Crickhope Linn.* Near *Moniaive*, 7 M. to the S.W., lies *Craigenputtock*, for many years the home of Thomas Carlyle, who wrote 'Sartor Resartus' here. — 26½ M. *Sanquhar;* 37 M. *New Cumnock;* 42½ M. *Old Cumnock*, the junction of branches to Ayr (p. 481) on the left, and *Muirkirk* and Lanark (p. 480) on the right. The train crosses a lofty viaduct over the *Lugar*, celebrated by Burns. 44½ M. *Auchinleck*, with the mansion of the Boswell family. — 49 M. **Mauchline** *(Loudoun Arms)*, where Burns married Jean Armour, is the junction of another line to Ayr. Burns spent several of the most important years of his life at Mauchline and at the farm of *Mossgiel*, 1½ M. to the N., and wrote here many of his best-known poems. The 'Braes of Ballochmyle' are 1½ M. to the S.E. of Mauchline.

58½ M. **Kilmarnock** *(George)*, a busy manufacturing town of 25,000 inhab., possesses an elaborate monument to Burns (adm. 2*d.*), with a museum of relics, including MSS. of several of the poet's best-known poems and all the editions of his works hitherto published. The first edition of Burns's poems issued from the press at Kilmarnock. A branch-line diverges here to *Troon*, *Ardrossan* (p. 481), and *Largs.* — The rest of the route to Glasgow calls for no comment. The expresses run by *Barrhead*, the slow trains by *Dalry.* — 92 M. **Glasgow** *(St. Enoch's Station)*, see p. 476.

Beyond Dumfries the Stranraer line runs towards the S. — 47½ M. *Dalbeattie* (Maxwell Arms), a pleasant little town (4000 inhab.), with large granite-quarries and works. 53 M. **Castle Douglas** *(Douglas Arms)*, the chief town of *Galloway*, with 2600 inhab., lies on the N. side of *Carlingwark Loch.* Excursions may be made to (1½ M.) *Threave Castle*, (8 M.) *Auchencairn*, etc.

A branch-line runs S. to (10 M.) **Kirkcudbright**, pron. *Kircoobry (Selkirk Arms; Royal)*, a clean little town (2600 inhab.), at the head of the estuary of the *Dee.* About ½ M. to the S. is *St. Mary's Isle* (*View), now a peninsula, with a heronry. About 6 M. to the S.E. is **Dundrennan Abbey.* A coach (1*s.* 6*d.*) plies daily from Kirkcudbright to (8½ M.) *Gatehouse of Fleet* (Murray Arms), a prettily-situated little town.

From (59½ M.) *Parton*, at the foot of *Loch Ken*, an omnibus runs to (9 M.) *Dalry*, a favourite angling-resort. — 62 M. *New Galloway;* the town lies 5 M. to the N. 72 M. *Dromore*, 6 M. from *Gatehouse of Fleet* (see above); 77 M. *Creetown*, on the E. shore of *Wigtown Bay.* — 82½ M. **Newtown Stewart** *(Galloway Arms; Grapes)*, with 3000 inhab., prettily situated on the *Cree*, is a convenient centre for excursions to (13 M.) **Loch Trool*, etc.

Newtown Stewart is the junction of a branch-line to (7 M.) *Wigtown* and (19 M.) *Whithorn.* — **Wigtown** *(Galloway Arms)* is a small town (2200 inhab.) on the E. bank of Wigtown Bay. On a commanding site at the entrance to the town is the *Martyrs' Memorial*, commemorating *Margaret MacLachlan* (aged 63) and *Margaret Wilson* (a girl of 18), two Covenanters who were tied to stakes on the beach and drowned by the rising tide of the Solway. They are buried in the parish-churchyard. — **Whithorn** *(Grapes)* possesses a ruined *Priory Church*, believed to occupy the site of the earliest Christian church in Scotland, built by St. Ninian (366-432).

Near (96 M.) *Glenluce* are the remains of *Luce Abbey* (12-13th cent.). View across *Luce Bay* to the *Mull of Galloway.* Farther on, the direct line from Stranraer to Ayr and Glasgow diverges to the right. 102½ M. *Castle Kennedy*, with *Loch Inch Castle*, the seat of the Earl of Stair, and the ruins of Castle Kennedy. The *Grounds of Castle Kennedy (open on Wed. & Sat.) are remarkable for their variety of coniferous trees and their 'Dutch Garden'.

106 M. **Stranraer** *(George; King's Arms)*, a thriving little seaport (7000 inhab.), at the head of *Loch Ryan*, the steamers from which afford the shortest sea-passage to Ireland (to Larne, 2½ hrs.). Pleasant excursions may be made in the *Rhinns of Galloway*, the peninsula on which Stranraer lies. The railway goes on to (7 M.) *Portpatrick* (Downshire Arms). — From Stranraer to *Girvan*, *Ayr*, and *Glasgow*, see p. 481.

64. Edinburgh.

Railway Stations. 1. *Waverley Station* (Pl. E, 4), of the North British Railway, near the E. end of Princes St., for trains to *London* (viâ *Newcastle* and *York*, or viâ *Carlisle* and *Leeds*), to *Glasgow*, and to the N. and E. of Scotland; also for the *Suburban Line* (see below). — 2. *Caledonian Station* (Pl. C, 4), at the W. end of Princes Street, for trains to *London* viâ *Carlisle* and *Crewe*, to *Liverpool* and *Manchester*, to *Glasgow* and *Greenock*, and to the S. and S.W. of Scotland. — 3. *Haymarket Station* (Pl. A, 5), a second station of the N.B.R., where almost all the trains to and from the W. stop. — All the principal hotels are within the 1*s.* cab-fare from the Waverley and Caledonian Stations. — The *Suburban Railway* runs from the Waverley Station to *Portobello*, *Duddingston*, *Newington*, *Blackford Hill*, *Morningside*, *Craiglockhart*, *Gorgie*, *Haymarket*, and (13 M.) Waverley.

Hotels. The best-situated are those in *Princes Street*, to the W. of the Waverley Station: — *Royal (Pl. a; D, 3), No. 53; *Balmoral (Pl. b; D, 4), No. 91; *Windsor (Pl. c; D, 4), No. 100; *Palace (Pl. g; C, 4), at the corner of Castle Street; Edinburgh (Pl. e; E, 3), No. 36; Clarendon (Pl. h; D, 4), No. 104; Alexandra, Central, between Charlotte St. and Castle St.; Rutland (Pl. m; C, 4), adjoining the Caledonian Station, second-class. Charges at most of these: R. & A. from 4*s.*, B. 2*s.* 6*d.*-3*s.*, D. 4*s.*-5*s.* 6*d.* — Those in *Princes Street* to the E. of the Waverley Station are somewhat cheaper: Royal British (Pl. v; E, 3), 22 Princes St., commercial; Dou-

For a coloured street plan of Edinburgh see pages 594 & 595

GLAS, at the corner of St. Andrew's St.; BRIDGE, 1 Princes St.; WATERLOO (Pl. k; E, 3), 24 Waterloo Place. — The following are first-class *Private Hotels* ('pens'. 10-12*s.*): BEDFORD, 83 Princes St. (Pl. D, 4); ROXBURGHE (Pl. n; C, 4), 38 Charlotte Sq., quiet; VEITCH (Pl. p; C, 3), 127 George St. — *Commercial Hotels:* IMPERIAL (Pl. l; E, 4), Market St., near the Waverley Station; *LONDON (Pl. f; E, 3), 2 St. Andrew's Sq.; HANOVER (Pl. x; D, 3), Hanover St.; GEORGE (Pl. u; D, 3), 21 George St.; MILNE (Pl. w; E, 3), 24 Greenside St.; SHIP (Pl. y; E, 3), 7 East Register St.; JOHN'S (Pl. z; E, 4), 307 High St.; these last unpretending, R. & A. 2*s.* 6*d.* — *Temperance Hotels:* *OLD WAVERLEY (Pl. q; E, 3), 42 Princes St.; COCKBURN (Pl. r; E, 4), close to the Waverley Station; NEW WAVERLEY (Pl. s; E, 3), DARLING'S REGENT (Pl. t; E, 3), both in Waterloo Pl.; R. & A. at these from 2*s.* 6*d.* — CRAIGLOCKHART HYDROPATHIC ESTABLISHMENT, 2½ M. to the S. W. of Edinburgh, terms 8*s.* 6*d.* per day, 52*s.* 6*d.* per week.

Restaurants. *Grieve*, 21 Princes St.; *Royal*, 54 Princes St.; *Albert*, 23 Hanover St.; **Littlejohn*, 31 Leith St.; *Blair*, 37 George St.; *Daish*, 3 St. Andrew St. (these last three also confectioners); **Edinburgh Café*, 70 Princes St. (no alcoholic liquors); *Spiers & Pond*, at the Waverley Station; *Rutherford*, 5 Leith St. (for gentlemen only); also at many of the above-named hotels. — *Beer* may be obtained at most of these. '*Edinburgh Ale*', now little drunk, is sweet and heavy. *Wine* is generally dear: best at the bar of the *Bodega Co.*, 7 South St. Andrew St.

Confectioners. **Littlejohn*, *Daish*, *Blair*, see above; **Mackie*, 108 Princes St.; **Aitchison*, 77 Queen St.; *M'Vitie*, 24 Queensferry St.; *Ritchie*, 24 Princes St. (shortbread and other Scottish cakes at all these; ices in summer). **Ferguson* ('Edinburgh Rock' and other sweetmeats), Melbourne Pl., at the corner of High St. (Pl. E, 4).

Baths. *Turkish Baths*, 90 Princes St. (2*s.* 6*d.*); *Pitt Street Baths* (Pl. D, 2), with a swimming-basin, on the N. side of the town; *Baths* at 12 Nicolson Sq. (Pl. F, 5; to the S.). *Salt-water Baths* at Trinity (p. 474).

Theatres. *Lyceum* (Pl. C, 5), Grindlay St., performances at 8 p. m.; *Royal* (Pl. E, 3), Leith Walk; *Prince's's* (Pl. F, 5), Nicolson St.

Cabs. For 1-2 pers, ½ M. 6*d.*, 1½ M. 1*s.*, each addit. ½ M. 6*d.*; luggage above 100 lbs. 6*d.* extra. By time: 2*s.* per hr.; drives in the environs 3*s.* per hr. Double fares at night (12 to 7). Fare and a half on Sun., if ordered at an office.

Tramways. The central point of the excellent *Tramway System* of Edinburgh is the *Register House* (Pl. E, 3), whence lines radiate to *Leith* (p. 473), *Portobello* (p. 459), *Newington* (Pl. F, 6), *Colinton Road*, *Morningside* (Pl. C, 6), *Coltbridge*, etc. (fares 1-4*d.*). — A circular line, starting from the Register House, runs round the S. half of the city viâ the *North* and *South Bridges*, *Newington*, *Morningside*, the *Lothian Road*, and *Princes St.* (fare for the round 6*d.*; good view of the city from the top of the cars). — *Cable Tramways* run from the *Mound* to *Inverleith Row* (fares 1-2*d.*; with connecting omnibuses to *Granton*, *Trinity*, and *Newhaven*) and from *Frederick Street* to *Stockbridge* (Pl. B, C, 2) and *Comely Bank*.

Omnibuses and **Coaches**, starting from or near the Register House, run to *Cramond*, *Forth Bridge*, and *Queensferry*, *Liberton* and *Loanhead*, *Dalkeith*, *Roslin*, etc.; and from *Coltbridge* (tramway-terminus, see above) to *Corstorphine*.

City Guides, with badges, 6*d.* per hr., 3-5*s.* per day (unnecessary).

Post & Telegraph Office (Pl. E, 3), at the E. end of Princes St.

Steamers from Leith to *Aberdeen* 4-6 times weekly in summer; to *Aberdour* 2-3 times daily; to *Amsterdam* weekly; to *Antwerp* weekly; to *Bremen* fortnightly; to *Christiansand* and *Copenhagen* weekly; to *Hamburg* twice weekly; to *Hull* every Wed.; to *Kirkwall* (Orkney) and *Lerwick* (Shetland) twice weekly; to *London* on Wed., Frid., and Sat. (comp. p. 462); to *Rotterdam* once or twice weekly; to *Stirling* daily; to *Thurso* weekly; to *Wick* twice weekly, etc. Also excursion-steamers in summer to *North Berwick*, the *Bass Rock*, the *Isle of May*, *Elie*, etc. — From Granton to *Bergen* every Wed.; to *Burntisland* (comp. p. 496) several times a day; to the *Faroe Isles* and *Iceland* once a month; to *London* on Wed. and Sat.

United States Consul, *Wallace Bruce, Esq.*, 8 York Buildings.

Principal Attractions. *Princes Street; Scott Monument; Castle; Lawnmarket, High St.*, and *Canongate; Holyrood; National Gallery; Calton Hill* (view); *St. Giles's; St. Mary's Episcopal Cathedral; Museum of Science & Art*; the *Queen's Drive*. These points may all be visited in one long day (9-10 hrs.), but those who wish to see Edinburgh to advantage must devote at least 2-3 days to the town itself and 4-5 days to its environs.

Edinburgh, the capital of Scotland, and one of the most romantically beautiful cities in Europe, is finely situated on a series of ridges, separated by ravines, about 2 M. to the S. of the *Firth of Forth* (5-6 M. wide), of which charming views are obtained from the higher parts of the town. Perhaps no fairer or more harmonious combination of art and nature is to be found among the cities of the world, and even the buildings of little or no beauty in themselves generally blend happily with the surrounding scenery. The population, excluding Leith, is about 250,000. Edinburgh is the seat of the administrative and judicial authorities of Scotland, and is renowned for its excellent university and schools. It is also a great centre of the printing, publishing, and book trades, but has few important manufactures. The stranger is advised to begin his acquaintance with the 'Modern Athens' by obtaining a general view of it from the Castle (best), the top of the Scott Monument, the Calton Hill, or Arthur's Seat (p. 470).

History. The authentic history of Edinburgh begins about 617, when *Edwin*, King of Northumbria, established a fortress on the castle-rock, round which sprang up the settlement of 'Edwin's Burgh'. In the 10th cent. the town came into the possession of the Scots (Celts), whose name for it, 'Dunedin' (*i.e.*, hill of Edwin), did not permanently dispossess the Saxon form. The early history of the town is practically the history of the castle, which was a frequent object of contention between the Scots and the English; and it was not till 1437 that Edinburgh became the capital of Scotland in place of Perth. The city then increased steadily in size and importance, but the work of ages was undone by its capture and destruction by the English in 1544, when the castle, however, made a successful resistance. The subsequent history of Edinburgh would be almost tantamount to a history of Scotland, but among the salient points may be named the scenes accompanying the struggle between Queen Mary and the Reformers (1555 et seq.); the defence of the castle by Kirkaldy of Grange and its capture by the English in 1573; the capture of the castle by Cromwell in 1650; the persecution of the Covenanters after the Restoration (1660); the removal of the Scottish Parliament to London in 1707; the Porteous Riot in 1736; and the occupation of the city by Prince Charles Edward in 1745.

At the close of last and the beginning of the present century Edinburgh was the residence of a literary circle of great brilliancy, some idea of which may be obtained from the mention of *David Hume* (d. 1776), *Adam Smith* (d. 1790), *Robertson*, the historian (d. 1793), *Playfair* (d. 1819), *Henry Mackenzie* (d. 1831), *Robert Burns* (d. 1796), *Dugald Stewart* (d. 1828), *Scott, Wilson, Lockhart, Brougham, Jeffrey, Cockburn*, and *Chalmers*. The 'Edinburgh Review' was established by Jeffrey, Sydney Smith, and others in 1802.

Edinburgh consists of the picturesque Old Town, familiar to all readers of Walter Scott, which was rebuilt in the middle of the 16th cent. after a great fire, and of the New Town, to the N., which dates its beginnings from 1768. The former, once the seat of the fashionable world, but now resigned to the poorer classes, is full of interesting old houses, some of which are remarkable for their immense height (10-12 stories). The nucleus of the New Town, which is distinguished for its massive style of building, consists of the three parallel thoroughfares: *PRINCES STREET (Pl. C, D, 4, E, 3), perhaps the finest street in Europe (with pleasant *Gardens*, open to the public); *George Street* (Pl. C, D, 3); and *Queen Street* (Pl. C, D, 3). — Numerous modern suburbs have also sprung up, particularly to the S. of the Old Town.

In *East Princes Street Gardens*, near the Waverley Station, rises the magnificent ***Scott Monument** (Pl. E, 3), erected in 1840 from the design of *Kemp*, and enclosing a marble statue of Scott (d. 1832) by *Steell*. Fine view from the top (adm. 2*d*.). To the E. of the Scott Monument is a statue of *Livingstone* (d. 1873), the African traveller; to the W. are statues of *Adam Black*, a prominent citizen, and *John Wilson* ('Christopher North'; d. 1854). Between the East and West Princes Street Gardens rises the *Mound* (Pl. D, 4), a huge embankment connecting the New Town with the Old, at the foot of which stand two handsome buildings in a classical style: the **Royal Institution** (Pl. D, 4) and the **National Gallery** (Pl. D, 4). The former contains an *Antiquarian Museum* (open daily, except Mon., 10-4, and on Sat. 7-9 also; 6*d*. on Thurs. & Frid.; free on the other days) and a *Statue Gallery*, with a collection of casts (Thurs. & Frid., 10-4, 6*d*.; other days, free). The National Gallery (Mon., Tues., & Wed., 10-5, and Sat., 10-5 and 7-9, free; Thurs. and Frid., 10-5, 6*d*.) contains a good collection of paintings of the Italian, Spanish, and British Schools, a statue of *Robert Burns* (d. 1796) by *Flaxman*, some wax models by *Michael Angelo*, and water-colours by *Williams* and others (catalogue 6*d*.). The annual *Exhibition of the Scottish Academy* is held here in spring (15th Feb. to 15th May; adm. 1*s*.). — At the corner of *West Princes Street Gardens* next the Mound is a statue of the Scottish poet *Allan Ramsay* (d. 1758), whose house stands on the Castle Hill, in a direct line with the statue and overlooking the gardens.

On the S. side of the valley occupied by the West Princes Street Gardens rises the ***Castle** (Pl. D, 4; 430 ft.), the ancient seat of the Scottish kings, grandly situated on the summit of a bold rock, sloping gradually to Holyrood on the E. but descending almost perpendicularly on the other three sides. From Princes St. we ascend the Mound (to the left the Bank of Scotland, p. 468) and follow the first street to the right, between the *Free Church College* and Princes Street Gardens. At the top of the hill we again turn to the right and cross the *Esplanade* to the castle-gate (adm. free; interior 10-4 or 11-3).

We enter by a drawbridge, crossing the old moat and passing under a portcullis, and follow the main road to the highest part of the enclosure, where stand the *Crown Room*, containing the Scottish Regalia; *Queen Mary's Room*, in which James I. of England was born in 1566; the *Old Parliament Hall* (recently restored); and *St. Margaret's Chapel*, the oldest building in Edinburgh (ca. 1100). In front of the chapel is '*Mons Meg*', a huge cannon, resembling the 'Dulle Griethe' at Ghent, formerly believed to have been cast at Mons in Belgium, but now ascribed to native skill (1455). The other buildings, chiefly modern barracks and military storehouses, are not shown. A magnificent *View of the city and the Firth of Forth, with the Highland hills in the background, is obtained from the Bomb Battery and other points. A time-gun is fired daily from the Half-Moon Battery, at 1 p. m., by electrical communication with the Observatory on Calton Hill. — The history of the Castle has been indicated at p. 466.

We now follow the series of quaint old streets *(Castle Hill, Lawnmarket, High Street,* and *Canongate)*, which descend in a straight line from the Castle to (1$^1/_4$ M.) Holyrood and give some idea of Old Edinburgh, though many of the most picturesque houses have lately been removed. The visitor should inspect one of the characteristic, narrow closes, or wynds, which diverge on either side (especially on the N.). To the right, at the end of the Esplanade, stands the *Assembly Hall* (Pl. D, 4), where the General Assembly of the Church of Scotland takes place in May. The *Free Church Assembly Hall* is on the opposite side of the street. Bank Street, to the left, descends past the **Bank of Scotland** (Pl. E, 4), a handsome Renaissance building, to Princes St. To the right is *Melbourne Place*, containing the *Sheriff Court Buildings*, and continued by *George IV. Bridge*, spanning the *Cowgate* (p. 471) and leading to the S. quarters of the town. In George IV. Bridge is the chief entrance to the new *Free Library*, which rises from the Cowgate; it was presented to the town by Mr. Andrew Carnegie.

A little farther on rises ***St. Giles's Church** (Pl. E, 4), the exterior of which has suffered from an unskilful restoration in 1829, while the interior is now of great interest. The chief feature of the exterior is the *Lantern Tower* (160 ft.; 14th cent.), an imitation of that of St. Nicholas at Newcastle (p. 415).

St. Giles's, the oldest parish-church in Edinburgh, now usually styled 'Cathedral', was erected in the 12th cent., on the site of a much earlier edifice. In 1385, however, the greater part of it was destroyed by fire, and the present Gothic church was built in 1385-1460. At the Reformation the interior of the church was defaced and robbed of its artistic adornments; after which it was divided by partitions into four separate churches. In this condition it remained until 1871-83, when, at the instance and mainly at the cost of Dr. William Chambers (d. 1883), the well-known publisher, the interior was carefully restored to its original appearance.

The Interior (open, 10-3, adm. 3*d*.; on Mon., free), 196 ft. in length, presents an imposing though somewhat cold and bare appearance. The characteristic Scottish barrel-vaulting should be noticed. The stained-glass windows are modern. On entering by the handsome new *W. Doorway*, we see to the left, enclosed by an iron screen, the *Albany Aisle*, erected by the Duke of Albany, son of Robert II., in 1402, in expiation of the murder of his nephew, the Duke of Rothesay. This chapel and the adjoining *Chapel of St. Eloi* have modern mosaic floors. Opposite, to the S., is the *Moray Aisle*, containing a handsome altar and a modern monument to the Regent Moray (assassinated in 1570; p. 475); the metal plate is from the original tomb. To the right of the entrance is the font, after Thorvaldsen. — The *Transept*, the oldest part of the church, contains four massive Norman piers, which support the tower, and may perhaps date from the original edifice of 1120. — The *Chancel* contains a tasteful modern pulpit and the royal pew (in carved oak). The last pillar to the left, with the arms of James II. and his wife, Mary of Cleves, is called the '*King's Pillar*'.

In the small adjoining chapel lies *Walter Chepman* (d. 1532), the first Scottish printer. The *Preston Aisle*, to the S. of the choir, is a good specimen of the Perp. style (15th cent.) The *Crypt*, below the S. transept, contains the remains of the *Marquis of Montrose* (d. 1661) and the *Regent Moray* (see p. 468).

When Charles I. attempted to re-establish the Scottish Episcopal Church, St. Giles's was made the cathedral of the bishopric of Edinburgh (1634), and it was here that Jenny Geddes threw her stool at Dean Hanna, who is commemorated by a brass tablet affixed to one of the pillars in the nave. [The stool is preserved in the Antiquarian Museum, p. 467.] The Solemn League and Covenant was signed here in 1643. John Knox often preached in St. Giles's. — The small shops or booths, which were erected between the buttresses about 1560, were called *Kraimes*, and the wares sold in them *Kraimery* (comp. German *Krämerei*).

Outside the church, to the N.E., is the shaft of the old *City Cross*, restored at the expense of Mr. Gladstone in 1885, and mounted on a new pedestal. — To the N.W. is a figure of a heart in the pavement, marking the site of the *Old Tolbooth*, or city prison, known as the 'Heart of Midlothian'. Close by is a *Statue of the Duke of Buccleuch* (d. 1884).

To the S. of St. Giles's is *Parliament Square*, an open space, formerly the churchyard, with an *Equestrian Statue of Charles II.* Adjacent is a stone inscribed '**I. K.** 1572', supposed to mark the grave of John Knox. On the S. side of the square (entr. in the W. corner) stands the extensive **Parliament House** (Pl. E, 4), formerly the place of meeting of the Scottish Parliament, and now the seat of the *Supreme Law Courts* of Scotland (open daily, 10-4).

We first enter the ***Great Hall**, where numerous 'Advocates' in wig and gown, 'Writers to the Signet', and solicitors may be seen in conference with their clients. The hall, which has a fine oaken roof, contains statues and paintings of celebrated Scottish jurists and statesmen. The large **Stained Glass Window*, executed at Munich from a design by Kaulbach, represents the foundation of the College of Justice by James V. in 1537.

At the S. end of the Hall is a *Corridor*, extending 300 ft. towards the E., from which the different *Courts* are entered. The door opposite the entrance to the hall leads to a staircase descending to the **Advocates' Library**, the largest library in Scotland, containing upwards of 300,000 vols., numerous valuable MSS., a sitting figure of Sir Walter Scott, the MS. of 'Waverley', a copy of the first printed Bible (Fust and Gutenberg), the Confession of Faith signed by James VI. in 1590, etc. (keeper, *Mr. James Clark*). — Adjacent is the *Signet Library*, a fine hall with 65,000 vols., belonging to the 'Writers to the Signet' (*i.e.* solicitors, originally clerks of the Secretary of State, who prepared writs passing under the King's signet).

The **Supreme Court of Scotland** consists of two Courts of Appeal, each with 3-4 judges, forming the 'Inner House', and five Courts of first instance, with one judge each, forming the 'Outer House'. There are in all 13 judges, at the head of whom are the Lord President and the Lord Justice Clerk, presiding over the First and Second Divisions respectively of the Inner House. The Civil Courts sit daily, 10-4, except Mon.; the Criminal Court for serious offences on Mon. only. The legal vacations last from 20th Mar. to 12th May, from 20th July to 15th Oct., and for about a fortnight at Christmas.

In the High St., at the corner of the busy South Bridge Street, rises the *Tron Church* (Pl. E, 4), so called from the old 'Tron', or town weighing-machine. A little farther on, beyond the street known as the 'Bridges' (p. 471), to the left, is *John Knox's House* (Pl. F, 4), where the famous preacher lived from 1560 to 1572, recognisable by its projecting front (daily, 10-4, adm. 6*d.*). — We now enter the Canongate, passing *Moray House* (now a training-college; Pl. F, 4) on the right, and the Canongate *Tolbooth* (comp. p. 469; 1591), with its clock, on the left. In the churchyard of *Canongate Church* (Pl. F, 4) lie *Adam Smith* (d. 1790), *Dugald Stewart* (d. 1828), and *Robert Ferguson* (d. 1790; headstone erected by Burns).

At the foot of the Canongate lies ***Holyrood Palace** (Pl. G, 3), the former residence of the Scottish kings, dating in its present form mainly from 1670-79 (open 11-6, in winter 11-4; adm. 6*d.*, free on Sat.).

The rooms of *Mary, Queen of Scots*, are still preserved, and contain some relics of that ill-fated princess. In the vestibule of the audience-chamber a stain on the floor is pointed out as the blood of *Rizzio*. The *Picture Gallery* consists of a long series of imaginary portraits of Scottish kings, remarkable for their strong family-likeness.

The palace occupies the site of *Holyrood Abbey*, founded in 1128 by David I. on the spot where he was saved from an infuriated stag by the interposition of a miraculous cross. The only relics of this edifice consist of the E.E. ruined church, now called **Holyrood Chapel*. The abbey-precincts were formerly an inviolable sanctuary for criminals, and its privileges were maintained in the case of debtors down to the abolition of imprisonment for debt in 1880.

To the S.E. of Holyrood Palace extends the treeless *Queen's Park* (Pl. H, 3, etc.), at the foot of **Arthur's Seat** (822 ft.; Pl. H, 5), which may be ascended thence in $^3/_4$-1 hr. The path passes the ruins of *St. Anthony's Chapel* (Pl. H, 4). In fine weather the top commands an admirable survey of the city, the Firth, the Highland Mts. to the N.W., and the Pentland Hills to the S.W.

A pleasant road, named the ***Queen's Drive**, encircles Arthur's Seat (3 M.), affording a series of changing views. Proceeding to the E. from Holyrood, we pass in succession ($^1/_2$ M.) *St. Margaret's Loch*, with *St. Anthony's Chapel* (see above) above it, and ($1^1/_4$ M.) *Dunsappie Loch*. A little beyond the latter we have a *View to the left, below us, of *Duddingston* and *Duddingston Loch;* to the E. are the sea and the conical *North Berwick Law* (p. 460); to the S. the *Pentland Hills* (p. 474).

The *Salisbury Crags* (Pl. G, 4, 5), the curious detached ridge on the W. side of Arthur's Seat, afford a good view of Edinburgh. Near their base lies *Dumbiedykes* (Pl. F, 5), the home of Jeanie Deans.

Instead of returning to Holyrood we may leave the Queen's Park by the S. gate, 1 M. beyond Duddingston, and proceed to ($^1/_2$ M.) the suburb of *Newington* (beyond Pl. F, G, 6), whence we may return to Princes St. by tramway, by the suburban railway (p. 464), or on foot through the *Meadows* (p. 472) and across *George IV. Bridge* (p. 468). Those who take the train may alight at *Blackford Hill* (p. 474), 1 M. to the W. of Newington, a public pleasure-ground, affording fine views.

Proceeding to the E. from the Scott Monument (comp. p. 467), we pass on the right, below the level of the street, the large *Waverley Market* (Pl. E, 3), the roof of which forms a promenade. At (3 min.) the E. end of Princes St. is the *Register House* (Pl. E, 3), containing the Scottish archives. In front of it is a *Statue of Wellington*, by Steell (1852; 'the Iron Duke, in bronze, by Steell'). Opposite stands the *Post Office*, an imposing Renaissance edifice, completed in 1865. *Waterloo Place*, with a viaduct crossing the street below, leads hence to the E., past the *Old Calton Burial*

Ground (with the *Martyrs' Monument*, the tomb of *David Hume*, d. 1776, etc.), to (4 min.) the handsome castellated *Prison* (Pl. F, 3). The steps opposite ascend to the **Calton Hill** (355 ft.; Pl. E, 3).

To the left, at the top of the steps, is a monument to the philosopher *Dugald Stewart* (d. 1828), and a little farther on are the *Old* and the *New Observatory*. On the summit of the hill rises the *Nelson Monument* (102 ft.; adm. 3*d.*; *View from the top); a ball falls here at 1 p.m., when the time-gun is fired from the castle. Adjoining this tower is the unfinished *National Monument*, erected to commemorate the Battle of Waterloo.

At the S.E. base of the Calton Hill, near the Prison, is the **High School** (Pl. F, 3), a handsome building in a Grecian style. [Opposite is a footpath descending direct to Holyrood.] Farther on, to the right, are *Burns's Monument* (adm. 2*d.*), with a statue of the poet (d. 1796), and the *New Calton Burial Ground* (Pl. G, 3).

To the S. of the Register House (p. 470), the *North Bridge* (Pl. E, 3, 4), 300 yds. long and 60 ft. high, crosses the hollow between the old and new towns, now occupied by the railway; the view of the city from the bridge at night, after the lamps are lit, is very striking. The North Bridge ends at the High St. (comp. p. 469), beyond which it is continued by the *South Bridge* (Pl. E, 4), crossing the quaint but uninviting *Cowgate*, one of the oldest streets in the town. To the right, a little farther on, is the **University** (Pl. E, 5), a massive building dating from the end of last century.

The University of Edinburgh was founded by James VI. in 1582, and in 1890 it numbered 41 professors, 10 lecturers, and 26 examiners, besides upwards of 50 assistants, and 3600 students. The medical faculty (ca. 2000 students) has long been renowned, and a handsome new ***Medical School** (Pl. E, 5), in a striking Renaissance style, has lately been erected in Teviot Row at a cost of about 240,000*l.* The *University Library* (open daily 10-4, in summer 10-3; adm. 6*d.*, for a party 1*s.*) contains 150,000 volumes. — To the E. of the Medical School are the *Music Class Room*, the *Students' Union*, and the new *McEwan Hall* (for graduation ceremonials, etc.).

Behind the University, entered from Chambers St., is the large ***Museum of Science and Art** (Pl. E, 5), founded in 1861, and containing valuable and extensive collections of natural history, industrial art, and technology (open on Mon., Tues., & Thurs., 10-4, 6*d.*; Wed. 10-4, and Frid. & Sat. 10-4 & 6-9, free). — Opposite the Museum is the *Watt Institute & School of Art*. — Chambers St. occupies the site of the College Wynd, in which Sir Walter Scott was born in 1771.

Lothian Street, on the S. side of the University, leads westward to the *University New Buildings* in Teviot Row (see above), and to *Lauriston Place* (Pl. D, E, 5), with the magnificent new **Infirmary** (Pl. E, 5), consisting of several detached buildings in the Scottish baronial style. It cost 350-400,000*l.*, and accommodates nearly 8000 patients yearly. To the right is ***Heriot's Hospital** (Pl. D, E, 5), founded for the maintenance and education of fatherless boys by *George Heriot* (d. 1624), goldsmith and banker to James VI. (see 'Fortunes of Nigel'). The handsome building, long attributed to Inigo Jones, was designed by Wm. Aytoun (adm. 11-3, daily, except Sat. & Sun.; tickets from the Treasurer, 21 St. Andrew's Sq.).

The *Heriot Schools*, in different parts of the city, founded with the surplus funds of the Hospital, are attended by about 6000 children. — Among other similar schools are *Gillespie's Hospital School* (Pl. C, 6),

Gilmore Place; *Stewart's Hospital*, Queensferry Road (Pl. A, 3); *Donaldson's Hospital* (p. 473); and the *Merchant Company's Schools* for boys and girls.

The *Meadow Walk* (Pl. E, 5, 6), running to the S. between the University New Buildings and the Infirmary, leads to the Meadows (Pl. D, E, 6), an extensive recreation-ground, where the International Exhibition of 1886 was held. — At No. 25 George Square (Pl. E, 5, 6) took place the only interview between Scott and Burns.

We may now return to High St. and Princes St. by George IV. Bridge (p. 468), at the beginning of which, to the left, is old *Greyfriars' Church* (Pl. E, 5), in the graveyard of which the 'Solemn League and Covenant' was signed in 1638.

Among the tombs in the churchyard are those of *George Buchanan* (d. 1582), *George Heriot* (d. 1624), *Allan Ramsay* (d. 1758), *Henry Mackenzie* (d. 1831; the 'Man of Feeling'), and *Robertson* (d. 1793), the historian of Charles V. The 1200 prisoners taken at the Battle of Bothwell Brig (1679; p. 480) were confined here, and suffered great privations.

On regaining Princes St., we turn to the left to visit the W. part of the town. Among the handsome buildings to the right are several hotels and club-houses. To the left, in *West Princes Street Gardens* (Pl. C, D, 4; band once a week in summer), which occupy the place of the old *Nor' Loch*, is a sitting figure of *Sir James Y. Simpson* (d. 1870), the discoverer of the properties of chloroform. At the end of the street, on the same side, is *St. John's Episcopal Church* (Pl. C, 4), adjoining which is an Iona cross to the memory of *Dean Ramsay* (d. 1876). In the hollow behind St. John's is *St. Cuthbert's* or the *West Church* (Pl. C, 4), the graveyard of which contains the last resting-place of *Thomas de Quincey* (d. 1859). — Opposite St. John's is the *Caledonian Railway Station* (p. 464).

From this point *Queensferry Street* leads to the right to (6 min.) the ***Dean Bridge** (Pl. B, 3; 105 ft. high), which crosses the *Water of Leith* and commands a fine view. Beyond the bridge we pass *Trinity Church* and several handsome terraces and follow the *Queensferry Road*, which soon bends to the left. To the right we have a fine view of the *Firth of Forth*, with the imposing pile of *Fettes College*, a high-class school for boys, in the foreground. About 300 yds. farther on a lane diverges on the left to the (3 min.) N.E. entrance of the ***Dean Cemetery** (Pl. A, 3), containing the graves of Jeffrey, Cockburn, Wilson, Alison, and other eminent Scotsmen. Passing through the cemetery, we leave it by the S. gate, beyond which we cross the bridge to the left, and return by the old Queensferry Road to (8 min.) Queensferry St. (see above).

Melville Street, the second cross-street on the right, leads from Queensferry St. to (5 min.) ***St. Mary's Cathedral** (Pl. B, 4), a fine E.E. edifice, 260 ft. long, generally considered the master-piece of *Sir G. G. Scott*. It belongs to the Scottish Episcopal Church, and was erected in 1874-79 at a cost of upwards of 110,000*l.* The **Interior* (services at 11 and 5) is specially imposing and challenges comparison with some of the older cathedrals. The *Central Spire* (295 ft. high) seems rather large in proportion to the rest of the building, but may lose this appearance when the W. Towers are erected. The church stands in the centre of the fashionable *West End District*, a handsome and substantially-built quarter.

About 1/2 M. to the W. of this point is *Donaldson's Hospital (adm. on Tues. & Frid., 2-4), erected and endowed for the maintenance and education of 300 children, one-third of whom are deaf and dumb, by *Alexander Donaldson* (d. 1830), a printer, who left 200,000*l*. for this purpose.

From Queensferry St. (see p. 472) a passage leads to the E., past the somewhat heavy *Church of St. George* (Pl. C, 4), into CHARLOTTE SQUARE, which is adorned with an equestrian **Statue of Prince Albert* (d. 1861), by Steell. From Charlotte Square we follow (to the E.) the wide and handsome GEORGE STREET, soon crossing (3 min.) *Castle Street* (Pl. C, 3, 4), at No. 39 in which (between George St. and Queen St., E. side) Sir Walter Scott lived from 1800 to 1826. At the intersection of the streets rises a statue of *Thomas Chalmers* (d. 1847), by Steell. Farther on in George St. are statues of *Pitt* and *George IV.* (by Chantrey), the *Union* and *Commercial Banks* and the *Music Hall* (on the right), and *St. Andrew's Church* (Pl. D, 3; on the left). The street ends at ST. ANDREW'S SQUARE (Pl. E, 3), with the *Melville Monument* and several handsome *Banks*, whence we return through St. Andrew's St. to Princes St.

At the E. end of QUEEN STREET (Pl. D, 3) is the new *Scottish National Portrait Gallery*, opened in 1888.

The gallery (adm. on Mon., Tues., & Frid. free; Thurs. & Sat. 6*d*.) now contains about 150 portraits, a collection of casts from the antique, engraved prints of Scottish historical characters and French engravings of the 17-18th cent. (from the bequest of the late Mr. W. F. Watson), and a series of drawings of Old Edinburgh by *James Drummond*. — The building, which cost 50,000*l*., was presented by Mr. John R. Findlay.

In *Inverleith Row*, on the N. side of the town, reached from Princes St. viâ Hanover St., Dundas St., and Pitt St. (cable tramway), lies the (1 1/2 M.) ***Botanic Garden** (Pl. C, 1; open daily, incl. Sun.), with a large palm-house. The garden commands an admirable *View of Edinburgh. Adjacent is the *Arboretum* (Pl. B, 1). Not far off is the *Warriston Cemetery* (beyond Pl. D, 1), where *Sir James Simpson* (p. 472) is buried. About 1/2 M. to the W. is *Fettes College* (p. 472). By turning to the left at the end of Inverleith Row, and then to the right, we reach (1 1/2 M. from the Botanic Garden) *Granton* (see p. 474).

Among other points of interest in Edinburgh are the *Grassmarket* (Pl. D, 5), the scene of the Porteous Riots in 1736; the GRANGE CEMETERY, to the S., with the graves of *Dr. Chalmers* (d. 1847), *Dr. Guthrie* (d. 1873), and *Hugh Miller* (d. 1856); and *Merchiston Castle*, to the S.W., the birthplace of *Napier* (d. 1617), the inventor of logarithms, now a boys' school. Near *Merchiston* station, on the Caledonian Railway, is the site of the *International Electrical Exhibition* of 1890 (also reached by the suburban railway, p. 464, or by tramway).

About 2 M. to the N. of Edinburgh, but now connected with it by continuous lines of street, lies its harbour **Leith** (beyond Pl. F, G, 1), a bustling seaport with 70,000 inhab. and extensive *Docks*. Its two **Piers*, each 3/4 M. long, afford a fine view of the *Firth of*

Forth, enlivened with shipping and bounded by the coast of Fife (ferry between the pier-heads 1*d.*). The *Trinity House*, erected in 1816 on the site of an older building, contains some models of ships, a large *Painting, by *David Scott*, of Vasco da Gama rounding the Cape of Good Hope, and an old portrait of Mary, Queen of Scots. — *Steamers* from Leith, see p. 465.

About 1¼ M. to the W. of Leith (tramway viâ Junction Road) is the quaint fishing-village of **Newhaven** (*Peacock Inn*, fish-dinner 2*s.* 6*d.*), inhabited by a fisher-folk of Scandinavian origin, who rarely marry out of their own circle and have preserved most of their ancient customs. The costume of the 'fish-wives' is very picturesque.

A little to the W. of Newhaven is **Trinity,** a colony of villas, with a *Chain Pier*, which is a favourite resort of swimmers (adm. 1*d.*, towel 1*d.*). Trinity is contiguous to **Granton**, a modern seaport, with three magnificent *Piers*, constructed by the Duke of Buccleuch at a cost of 150,000*l.* (fine *View from the E. pier). The traffic here, however, is very inferior to that of Leith. Steamers, see p. 465. A pleasant walk may be taken from Granton to the W. by a rough road skirting the coast; at the (1½ M.) point where the road ceases we may turn to the left and return to (4 M.) Edinburgh. Leith, Newhaven, Trinity, and Granton are all connected with Edinburgh by railway, tramway, or omnibus.

Excursions from Edinburgh.

1. On a hill 1½ M. to the S. of the suburb of Newington (p. 470) stand the ruins of **Craigmillar Castle**, built in 1437, a favourite residence of Mary, Queen of Scots.

2. About 3 M. to the W. of Edinburgh lies **Corstorphine**, reached by the street passing Haymarket Stat. (p. 464) and Donaldson's Hospital (p. 473; coach, see p. 465). At the beginning of the village we may turn to the right and cross **Corstorphine Hill* (475 ft.; views of the Forth and the Highland hills) to (2 M.) the *Queensferry Road* (p. 472), whence we return viâ the (3 M.) *Dean Bridge* (p. 472) to Edinburgh. — Walkers should diverge from the road, to the right, about ¼ M. above Corstorphine, and follow a footpath leading to (18 min.) the view-point *'*Rest and be Thankful*', which commands a charming view of Edinburgh and the Firth. — We then descend (views) to (8 min.) a carriage-road, which we follow to the right to (2 M.) the W. end of Princes St. (or, a pleasanter route, we follow the road to the left for a short way and then turn to the right, 2½ M.).

3. **Blackford Hill** (station on the Suburban Railway), adjoining the city on the S., to the W. of Newington, has recently been acquired as a public park. The *View from it is described in a well-known passage of 'Marmion'. (Comp. p. 470.)

4. The **Pentland Hills**, which extend to the S. W. of Edinburgh, afford numerous pleasant rambles. The highest summits are *Scald Law* (1898 ft.) and *Carnethy* (1890 ft.), two good points of view (see Map). The most convenient way to reach the Pentlands is to take the train (Caledonian Stat.) to (3½ M.) *Colinton*, (6 M.) *Currie*, or (7½ M.) *Balerno* (comp. Map); or they may be approached on foot or by carriage through *Morningside* (pp. 464, 465) and over the *Braid Hills* (700 ft.).

5. From Edinburgh to Hawthornden and Roslin (1 day). Train from Waverley Station (p. 464) to (11 M.) *Hawthornden* in ½ hr. — ***Hawthornden** (open daily in summer, 10-6; adm. 1*s.*), charmingly situated on the bank of the *North Esk*, was the home of the poet *Drummond*, the friend of Shakespeare and Ben Jonson. From the house we walk through a romantic wooded glen to (¾ hr.) *Roslin Castle* (adm. 6*d.*), the ancient seat

of the St. Clairs, celebrated in Scott's 'Rosabelle', an outside view of which may suffice. Close by is ***Roslin Chapel** (adm. 1*s.*; service on Sun. at noon and 6 p. m.), founded in 1446 as the choir of a collegiate church (which was never finished), and remarkable for its profuse decoration, the style of which is generally believed to be Spanish. The *'*Prentice Pillar*' owes its name to a legend not unknown elsewhere. — Near the chapel is the *Royal Hotel*. We may now return to Edinburgh by coach (7 M.; fare 1*s.*), generally starting about 3.30 or 4 p. m., or by train from *Roslin Station*. Those who prefer to make the round in the reverse direction may leave Edinburgh by the coach starting for Roslin at 10 a.m. The railway company issues circular tickets (fares 2*s.* 2*d.*, 1*s.* 9*d.*), which are available for the stations at *Roslin*, *Hawthornden*, *Rosslynlee*, *Rosslyn Castle*, and *Polton*. One of the coaches also makes a circular tour (2*s.* 6*d.*).

6. From Edinburgh to Dalkeith (6 M.; coach or railway, comp. p. 459). The small town of *Dalkeith* (6400 inhab.) is uninteresting. To the N. is ***Dalkeith Palace**, the seat of the Duke of Buccleuch, containing a valuable collection of portraits and other paintings. The house and **Park* are open to visitors on Wednesdays. — *Newbattle Abbey* (p. 459) is 1 M. to the S.

7. From Edinburgh to Queensferry, 9 M., railway from Waverley Station (to *Forth Bridge*) in 18-33 min. (fares 1*s.* 7*d.*, 9½*d.*). — **South Queensferry** (*Queensferry Arms*), with 1100 inhab., the starting-point of the gigantic *Forth Bridge* (p. 495), is said to derive its name from Margaret, consort of Malcolm Canmore (see below). — About 2½ M. to the W. is *Hopetoun House*, the seat of the Earl of Hopetoun, with a fine park (*Views), open to the public. The village of *Dalmeny*, 1¼ M. to the E. of Queensferry, possesses an ancient Norman church. It is adjoined by **Dalmeny Park* (open), belonging to the Earl of Rosebery, with *Dalmeny House* and *Barnbougle Castle*, the latter incorporating ancient remains (station, see below). — *Queensferry* may also be reached from Edinburgh by coach (see p. 465; fare 1*s.*; on Sun., return 3*s.*).

Among other points easily reached from Edinburgh in one day are *Melrose* and *Dryburgh* (comp. pp. 457, 458); *Burntisland* and *Aberdour* (p. 496); the *Trossachs* (see R. 66); *North Berwick* (p. 459); *Linlithgow* (see below); *Dunfermline* (p. 500); *Stirling* (p. 484).

65. From Edinburgh to Glasgow.

a. *North British Railway.*

47 M. Railway from *Waverley Station* in 1 hr. 10 min. to 2 hrs. (fares 5*s.* 6*d*, 2*s.* 6*d.*; return-fares 9*s.* 6*d.*, 4*s.*; express 6*s.* 6*d.*).

After leaving *Haymarket* (p. 464) the train passes (3½ M.) *Corstorphine* (p. 474) and (5 M.) *Gogar*. 8 M. *Ratho*, the junction of a line to *Kirkliston*, *Dalmeny* (see above), and *Forth Bridge*. — 12 M. *Winchburgh*, the junction of a new line to the *Forth Bridge* for the traffic to and from Glasgow and the West of Scotland. — 14½ M. *Philipstoun*.

17½ M. **Linlithgow** (*Star & Garter*), an old town with 4000 inhab., was long a favourite residence of the Scottish kings. The *Palace (adm. 10-5; fee), visible from the railway (to the right), dates in its present form from the 14-17th centuries. Queen Mary was born here in 1542, and the Regent Moray, who was shot in the streets of the town, died here in 1570. *St. Michael's Church*, adjoining the Palace, founded by David I. (12th cent.), is a large edifice of various periods, from Norman to Perpendicular.

22 M. *Polmont* is the junction of the line to *Stirling* (p. 484). — 25½ M. **Falkirk** (*Red Lion*), a busy town of 13,200 inhab., with iron-works and coal-pits. '*Falkirk Trysts*' are large cattle-fairs. Wallace was defeated by Edward I. at the battle of Falkirk

in 1298, and Prince Charles Stuart defeated the English here in 1746. — Beyond (45½ M.) *Cowlairs* we descend a steep gradient through a long tunnel and enter the (47 M.) *Queen Street Station* of **Glasgow** (see below).

b. *Caledonian Railway.*

46 M. Railway in 1 hr. 5 min. to 2 hrs. (fares, see p. 475).

This line passes through a busy iron-working district, the lights of which are imposing at night. Among the chief stations, which possess little interest for the tourist, are: 10 M. *Midcalder* (from which the Firth of Forth and the Highland hills may be seen on a clear day); 16 M. *West Calder*, the centre of an extensive paraffin oil industry; 33 M. *Holytown;* 41 M. *Cambuslang;* 43 M. *Rutherglen.* — At (46 M.) *Glasgow* (see below) the trains stop at *Eglinton Street* or *Bridge Street* before running into the *Central Station.*

Glasgow. — **Railway Stations.** 1. *North British* or *Queen Street Station* (Pl. F, 3), Dundas St., for trains to Edinburgh and the North, London (viâ York), Helensburgh, Loch Lomond, Hamilton, etc. — 2. *Caledonian Central Station* (Pl. E, 4), Gordon Str., for Edinburgh, London (viâ Carstairs and Carlisle), Paisley, Greenock, Hamilton, etc. — 3. *St. Enoch's* (Pl. F, 5), of the G. & S. W. R., St. Enoch's Sq., for Paisley, Greenock, Ayr, Carlisle and London viâ Dumfries, etc. — 4. *Buchanan Street* (Pl. F, 2, 3), the Caledonian terminus for trains to Oban, Perth, and the N. — 5, 6. *Bridge Street* (Pl. E, 5) and *Eglinton Street* (comp. Pl. E, 6) are secondary stations for the S. trains of the Caledonian Railway. — 7. *College Street* (Pl. G, 4), a secondary N. B. station. — 8. *Main Street* (comp. Pl. F, 6), Gorbals, for trains running S. from St. Enoch's. — The *Glasgow City & District Railway* (underground) runs E. and W. from Queen St. Station, affording rapid access to the Cathedral *(College Stat.)*, the University and West End Park *(Charing Cross Stat.)*, and the West End suburbs *(Hyndland Stat.)*.

Hotels. *Central (Pl. b; E, 4), at the Central Station; St. Enoch's (Pl. a; F, 5), at St. Enoch's Station; two large railway hotels, R. & A. from 4*s*., D. 4*s*. 6*d*. — *George (Pl. c; F, 4), George Sq., near the N. B. R. Terminus; *Maclean's (Pl. i; D, 3), 250 St. Vincent St.; Grand Hotel (Pl. k; C, D, 2), Charing Cross (W. end); R. & A. at these 4-5*s*., D. 3-5*s*. — Royal (Pl. d; F, 4), Crown (Pl. h; F, 4), George Sq.; Hanover, Hanover St. (Pl. F, 3); North British Imperial (Pl. g; F, 4), at the corner of George St. and George Sq.; Victoria, 15 West George St. (Pl. E, 3); Alexandra (Pl. l; E, 3), Bath (Pl. m; E, 3), Bath St.; Steel's (Pl r; F, 4), 5 Queen St.; Bridge Street Station (Pl. q; E, 5). — *Temperance Hotels:* Washington, Waverley (Pl. s; E, 3), Sauchiehall St.; Cockburn (Pl. t; E, 3), 141 Bath St.; R. at these 1*s*. 6*d*.-2*s*. 6*d*., A. 9*d*.-1*s*., D. 2*s*. 6*d*.

Restaurants. **Lang*, 73 Queen St.; **Ferguson & Forrester* (*Prince of Wales)*, 36 Buchanan St.; *Brown*, 83 St. Vincent St.; *Queen's*, 70 Buchanan St.; *Forrester*, 7 Gordon St.; *Watson & Blane*, West George St.; *Assafrey*, St. Vincent St. and 171 Sauchiehall St.; at the *Central* and *St. Enoch Hotels.*

Post & Telegraph Office (Pl. F, 4), George Sq. Numerous branch-offices.

Theatres. *Theatre Royal* (Pl. E, 3), Cowcaddens; *Royalty* (Pl. E, 3), *Gaiety* (Pl. F, 3), Sauchiehall St. (operettas and burlesques); *Grand* (Pl. E, 2), Cowcaddens (melodrama); *Princess's*, Main St., Gorbals (Pl. F, 6). — *St. Andrew's Music Hall*, Berkeley St. (classical concerts in winter); *Queen's Rooms*, at the W. end of Sauchiehall St. (concerts, balls, etc.). — *Hengler's Cirque*, Bothwell St., near the Central Station.

Exhibitions. An *Annual Exhibition of Modern Paintings* is held in the Institute of Fine Arts, Sauchiehall St. — *Corporation Galleries*, see p. 479.

Cabs. From one station to another, or into the town, 1*s*. for 1-3 pers., 112 lbs. of luggage included; each addit. pers. 6*d*. — By time: for the first ½ hr. 1*s*. 6*d*.; each ¼ hr. addit. 6*d*.

Tramways traverse most of the chief streets and run to the suburbs. — The **Omnibuses** are few in number and of little use to the stranger.

Steamers ply from Glasgow to all parts of Great Britain and Ireland, and indeed to all parts of the world. [The first 2 hrs. of the river-journey may be avoided by proceeding by train to *Greenock* or *Gourock* (comp. p. 487; 3/4-1 hr.). Those, however, who wish to make an acquaintance with the port of Glasgow and its long series of ship-building yards, with the deafening din of their hammers, should sail the whole way.] From Greenock to *Belfast* daily in 8 hrs. (12*s.* 6*d.*; comp. p. 482); to *Dublin* daily in 18 hrs. (15*s.*); to *Fort William* and *Inverness* daily in summer; to *Liverpool* 4-5 times weekly in 15 hrs. (12*s.* 6*d.*), etc. Innumerable river-steamers ply to the watering-places on the estuary of the *Clyde* and its ramifications (comp. p. 480).

Harbour Steamers (*'Cluthas'*), affording an excellent view of the harbour and quays, ply between *Victoria Bridge* and *Meadowside* (Partick) every 1/4 hr. from 8 a.m. to 8.12 p.m., on Sat. & holidays till 9.12 p.m. (1*d.*).

Principal Attractions: *Cathedral* (p. 478); *Broomielaw* (p. 478); Walk through *Buchanan St.* and *Argyle St.* (p. 479); *University* (p. 479).

Glasgow, the commercial and industrial capital of Scotland and the second city of the kingdom, with (1890) about 800,000 inhab. (including the suburbs), lies on the *Clyde*, on the site of an episcopal see founded by St. Mungo in 560, and rivals Liverpool in its shipping trade and Manchester in its manufactures.

Among the numerous industries of Glasgow the most characteristic and important is its *Iron and Steel Ship Building*, in which it is *facile princeps* among British towns. Two-thirds of all British steamers are built on the Clyde, or at least provided there with their engines. The largest sea-going steamers and fast river-boats are alike built here; and in 1889 about 250 iron and steel vessels, of about 335,200 tons burden, were launched from the Clyde ship-building yards. The first steam-engine was constructed at Glasgow by *James Watt*, a native of the town, in 1763; and the first steamer on this side of the Atlantic was placed on the Clyde by *Henry Bell* in 1812 and plied between Glasgow and Greenock. In 1888 Glasgow possessed a fleet of 945 steamers of 695,536 tons burden and 588 sailing-vessels of 483,164 tons. Among the chief industrial establishments in or near Glasgow are the *St. Rollox Chemical Works* (Pl. G, 2), occupying 15 acres of ground, with a chimney 435 ft. high (over-topped, however, by a neighbouring chimney of 455 ft., which is probably the highest in the world); the *Steel Co. of Scotland's Works* at Newton (railway from Central Station in 1/4 hr.) and at Blochairn; and the ship-building yards at Govan. The *Singer Manufacturing Co.* of New York has huge works at Kilbowie (20 min. by train from Queen St. Stat.). The other chief products and industries of Glasgow include iron, cotton, and woollen goods, chemicals, sewing-machines, thread, tubes and boilers, calico-printing, glass, pottery, bleaching, dyeing, and muslin-weaving. The coal-traffic is also immense.

Glasgow is one of the best governed cities in Great Britain; and in the *Century* for March, 1890, *Mr. Albert Shaw* praises it highly for its 'broad, bold, and enlightened policy as regards all things pertaining to the health, comfort, and advancement of the masses of the citizens'. The gas and water works, tramway lines, parks, etc., are under the management of the Corporation, which has also established model lodging-houses and public baths and wash-houses, and in other ways busied itself with the sanitary well-being of the city. — The admirable water-supply is derived from *Loch Katrine* (p. 487), 42 M. distant. Nearly 2 1/2 millions sterling have been expended upon the works, which are now being extended.

The ***Harbour** and **Docks** of Glasgow are always thronged with vessels from all the corners of the earth. About half-a-century ago the Clyde at Glasgow was only 180 ft. wide and 3 ft. deep; now, by continual dredging, it has been made 480 ft. wide and 24-28 ft.

deep, allowing the largest vessels to unload here. Between 1845 and 1889 upwards of 4,750,000*l.* have been spent on the harbour and dock works, and more than 35,000,000 cubic yards of material have been dredged from the river-bed. The water-area of the harbour (which extends along the river for $2^1/_2$ M.) and the docks is 160 acres; the total length of the quays is upwards of 6 M. In 1889 the port was entered by 16,900 vessels (chiefly steamers), with an aggregate burden of 3,410,591 tons. The customs dues amount to about 1,000,000*l.* Most of the river passenger-steamers start from the **Broomielaw* (Pl. D, E, 5), a quay 800 ft. long, on the N. side of the river, just below *Glasgow Bridge* (Pl. F, 5; *View of the harbour) and the bridge of the Caledonian Railway. A little to the S.E., adjoining the river, is the open space known as *Glasgow Green* (Pl. G, H, 6), with *Nelson's Monument.* — The *High Street* (Pl. G, 4, 5), leading to the Cathedral, was the chief thoroughfare of the old city of St. Mungo and has recently been much improved. The old *College* is now a goods-station. At the point where the street sweeps to the right, and begins to ascend, Wallace defeated a detachment of the English in 1300.

The ***Cathedral** (Pl. H, 3; open daily 10-6; on Tues. and Thurs. 2*d.*, other days free), situated on the N.E. side of the town, is a fine edifice, dating from the 12-15th cent. and mainly in the E.E. style. The Sunday services are at 11 a. m. and 2 p. m. The building is 320 ft. long, 70 ft. wide, and 90 ft. high; the tower is 220 ft. in height.

Interior (fine organ). The Nave (14th cent.) has a flat timber ceiling. The windows throughout the church have been filled with modern stained glass, chiefly from Munich, at a cost of 100,000*l.* The Choir, separated from the nave by a carved screen, is a good specimen of E.E., probably dating from early in the 13th century. Behind the choir are the *Lady Chapel* and *Chapter House.* Below the choir is the *Crypt, the chief glory of the Cathedral, a charmingly proportioned structure, with fine vaulting. Its 65 pillars are surmounted by exquisitely carved capitals. On the N. side is the tomb of *Edward Irving* (d. 1834), of whom a portrait appears, as John the Baptist, in the window above.

Glasgow Cathedral is frequently referred to in 'Rob Roy', and the classical description of it is undoubtedly that of Andrew Fairservice.

To the left of the Cathedral stands the *Royal Infirmary* (Pl. H, 3), In the vicinity, in front of the handsome *Barony Church* (Pl. H. 3, 4), is a statue of *Dr. Norman Macleod* (d. 1872), by Mossman.

On a height to the E. of the Cathedral is the ***Necropolis** (Pl. H, 4), the chief cemetery of the town, containing numerous substantial monuments, the most conspicuous of which is the column to the memory of *John Knox* (p. 469). Near it is the grave of *Sheridan Knowles* (d. 1862). Fine views.

From the Cathedral we proceed through High St. and *George St.* to George Square (Pl. F, 4), the finest open space in the city, surrounded by the new *Municipal Buildings* (E.), the *Post Office* (S.), the *Bank of Scotland*, the *Merchants' House* (W.), several *Hotels*, and other substantial buildings.

In the centre of the square rises a column 80 ft. high, surmounted by a statue of *Sir Walter Scott.* Adjacent are equestrian statues, by Marochetti, of *Queen Victoria* and *Prince Albert.* The other statues are those of *Sir John Moore* (d. 1809), by Flaxman; *Colin Campbell, Lord Clyde* (d. 1863), by Foley; *James Watt* (d. 1819), by Chantrey; *Sir Robert Peel* (d. 1850), by Mossman; *William Pitt* (d. 1806), by Flaxman; *Dr. Graham*, by Brodie; *Robert Burns* (d. 1796), by Ewing; *Thomas Campbell* (d. 1844), by Mossman; *James Oswald*, by Marochetti; and *Dr. Livingstone* (d. 1873), by Mossman.

In Queen St., to the S. of George Sq., stands the **Royal Exchange** (Pl. F, 4), in the Corinthian style. In front is an *Equestrian Statue of the Duke of Wellington*, by *Marochetti.* The *Mitchell Library*, in Ingram St. (Pl. F, 4), contains 70,000 volumes.

The busiest streets are *Argyle Street* (Pl. D, E, 4), *Buchanan Street* (Pl. F, 3, 4), *Union Street* (Pl. E, 4), and *Sauchiehall Street* (Pl. D, E, 3), which contain the most attractive shops. Argyle St. is continued towards the E. by the *Trongate*, with the *Tron Church* (Pl. G, 5; comp. p. 469), which ends at the *Cross* (Pl. G, 5). From the Cross the *Saltmarket*, the home of Bailie Nicol Jarvie, runs southwards to the river.

Sauchiehall St. is a long street joining the E. and W. quarters of the town. On the N. side of it (No. 270) are the ***Corporation Galleries** (Pl. E, 3), containing 500 pictures, including specimens of Rembrandt, Ruysdael, and Venetian masters (adm. free, 10 till dusk, on Sat. till 9). Among the statues is one of *Pitt*, by *Flaxman.*

From the W. end of Sauchiehall St. we may enter the pretty **West End Park** (Pl. B, 2), with its *Museum.* On the hill to the W. of the park, on the other side of the *Kelvin*, rises ***Glasgow University** (Pl. A, B, 1), founded in 1450 or 1451 and transferred in 1870 to its present magnificent quarters, designed by Sir G. G. Scott (E.E. domestic style, with Scoto-Flemish features of later date). The buildings form a huge rectangle, 530 ft. long and 295 ft. wide, divided into two by the handsome *Common Hall*, erected at the expense of the Marquis of Bute (p. 193). The *Central Tower*, 200 ft. high, is surmounted by a spire of 100 ft. more. The total cost was about 500,000*l.* The fine 17th cent. *Gateway* of the old college (p. 478) has been re-erected, in a slightly modified form, at the entrance to the University grounds. The University possesses a library of 120,000 vols., and contains the *Hunterian Museum* (11-4; 6*d.*), with its famous anatomical collection. The number of students is 2300; of professors, lecturers, and assistants 60. — A little to the W. is the huge *Western Infirmary* (Pl. A, 1), and a little to the N. are the *Botanic Gardens* (beyond Pl. B, 1; adm. 6*d.*), with a large circular conservatory. — The terraces and streets in this part of the town are very handsome and substantial.

The S. part of the town is a busy manufacturing district; the S. W. part is mainly residential, with the large *Queen's Park*, commanding a *View of the city, and the new *Victoria Infirmary.* Adjacent is *Langside*, where the Regent Moray defeated the forces of Queen Mary in 1568 (memorial). The ruins of *Cathcart Castle*, whence the Queen watched the fortunes of the battle, lie 1½ M.

to the S. — A pleasant walk through the suburbs may be taken by following the *Great Western Road* (Pl. C, D, 1) to *Anniesland Toll*, proceeding thence to *Canniesburn* and *Bearsden*, and returning by *Maryhill;* or we may go by the Queen's Park (p. 479) and *Mount Florida* to Cathcart (p. 479), returning by Langside and Shawlands.

*Excursions.

Glasgow stands almost unrivalled among the towns of Great Britain for the number, charm, and variety of the excursions that may be made from it. The estuary of the Clyde alone is an almost inexhaustible field (comp. p. 477), and most of the circular tours referred to at p. 451 may be begun at Glasgow.

1. To Hamilton (1 day), 11 M., railway from the *Central*, *Bridge St.*, or *Queen St. Station* in 1/2-3/4 hr. (fares 1*s*., 7 1/2*d*.). — **Hamilton** (*Royal; County; Douglas; Clydesdale*), a prosperous little town with 18,000 inhab., pleasantly situated near the confluence of the *Avon* and the *Clyde*, is a favourite summer-resort of the Glasgowegians. Close to the town on the N. is **Hamilton Palace** (adm. only by special permission), the magnificent seat of the Duke of Hamilton, which formerly contained (down to 1882) one of the finest art-collections in the kingdom. The large *Park* (open on Tues. and Frid.) contains the imposing ducal *Mausoleum*. — About 2 M. to the S.E. of Hamilton, on the left bank of the Avon, are the picturesque ruins of **Cadzow Castle**, the subject of a well-known ballad by Scott. *Cadzow Forest*, with its patriarchal oaks, contains a herd of wild white cattle, survivals of an ancient British race met with here and at Chillingham (p. 416) only. Opposite Cadzow Castle, on the other side of the Avon, is the summer-château of *Chatelherault*, built by the Duke of Hamilton in 1732 in imitation of the house from which he took his French title, but little more than a façade. About 2 M. to the N. of Hamilton is *Bothwell Brig*, where the Covenanters were defeated by the Royalists in 1679. The village of *Bothwell* (Clyde Hotel), with the villas of numerous Glasgow merchants, is 1/2 M. farther on (train from Hamilton). On the Clyde, 3/4 M. to the N.W. of the village, is the picturesque ruin of ***Bothwell Castle**, the home of the Earl of Bothwell, husband of Queen Mary (open on Tues. & Frid., 10-3). We may return by train from Bothwell to Glasgow in 35 min. — This excursion may be combined with the next (one night out) by proceeding by train from Hamilton to (9 1/2 M.) *Tillietudlem*, with the ruins of the castle (*Craignethan*) immortalised in Old Mortality, and going on thence to (6 M.) *Lanark* (see below), taking Stonebyres (see below) on the way; or we may go by coach direct to (14 1/2 M.) Lanark.

2. To the Falls of Clyde (one day). Railway from the Central Station to Lanark (26 M.) in 1 1/4-2 hrs. Circular tickets (7*s*. 3*d*., 4*s*. 9*d*.), available in either direction, are issued for a combination of this route with Tillietudlem (see above); train to *Lanark;* coach to *Crossford* viâ *Corehouse*, *Kirkfieldbank*, and *Stonebyres* (6 M.); footpath to (1 1/2 M.) *Tillietudlem*. — **Lanark** (*Black Bull; Clydesdale*), a small town with 5000 inhab., was the scene of the earliest exploits of William Wallace (13th cent.). From 1784 onwards it was the home of Robert Owen, the Socialist (p. 264), who owned the mills at New Lanark, in which he carried on several interesting socialistic experiments. In visiting the ***Falls of Clyde** from Lanark the following is perhaps the best plan. After leaving the station we take the first street to the left, and immediately afterwards turn to the right. Near the *Black Bull* we again turn to the left, and at the fork we keep to the right. The road now descends (road to right between two houses to be avoided) to the first lodge of *Bonnington House*, in the grounds of which (adm. 6*d*.) are the falls of (1/2 M.) **Cora Linn* (85 ft.) and (1/2 M.) *Bonnington Linn* (30 ft.). We then return to Lanark, pass through the town, and proceed to the W. At the (1/2 M.) fork we take the lower road to the left. At (1/2 M.) *Kirkfieldbank* we cross a bridge over the Clyde. [About 1/2 M. to the N., on the *Mouse Water*, are the

pretty **Cartland Crags*, best viewed from the viaduct over the ravine.] At the inn on the other side of the bridge we obtain a ticket for *Stonebyres* (3*d*.), 68 ft. high and with the greatest volume of water of the three falls, which lies 1$^1/_4$ M. farther on. Crossford (see p. 480) is 2 M. beyond Stonebyres. Travellers with circular-tickets (p. 480) visit Cora and Bonnington Linns from the W. or *Corehouse* side of the Clyde (adm. 3*d*.).

3. To Paisley, 7 M. Railway from the Central or St. Enoch's Station in $^1/_4$ hr. — **Paisley** *(George; County; Globe)*, a smoke-begrimed industrial town on the *Cart*, with 60,000 inhab. and large thread (Coats; Clark & Co.), shawl, and corn-flour (Brown & Polson) factories, possesses a fine **Abbey Church*, dating in its present form from the 14-15th centuries. The handsome *Town Hall* was built at a cost of about 100,000*l*.

4. To Ayr and the Land of Burns (one day). The railway (St. Enoch's Station) to Ayr (40 M.; fares 5*s*., 2*s*. 6*d*.) runs viâ *Paisley* (see above); *Kilwinning*, with a ruined priory of the 12th cent. (to the E., *Eglinton Castle*); and *Irvine*, with a busy trade in coal. It then skirts the sea, passing the watering-places of *Troon* and *Prestwick* (golf-links). — **Ayr** *(Station; King's Arms; Queen's)*, an ancient seaport with 20,000 inhab., is chiefly interesting as the centre of the 'Burns Country', which attracts more 'pious pilgrims' than even Stratford-on-Avon (see p. 245). The '*Auld Brig*', dating from 1250, is still standing; while the '*New Brig*' of the poem (1788) has been replaced by a still newer. The *Pier* affords a good view of the mountains of Arran (see below). The *Wallace Tower* (130 ft. high), was built in 1832 on the site of an old tower, in which the hero is said to have been imprisoned. The road to the S. leads to (2 M.) the *Cottage* in which Robert Burns was born in 1759, containing a few relics of the poet (adm. 2*d*.). The whole country-side is full of associations with his poems. About $^1/_3$ M. farther on is *Auld Alloway Kirk*, between which and the road is the grave of Burns's father. Just beyond the church are two bridges over the *Doon*, the old one being that over which Tam O'Shanter escaped with such difficulty. The gardens adjoining the bridges contain the *Burns Monument*, a pretentious and somewhat incongruous structure in the style of a Greek temple (view), containing figures of Tam O'Shanter and Souter Johnny. We may return to Ayr by the road on the left (W.) bank of the Doon. — Beyond Ayr the railway goes on to *Maybole*, *Girvan*, and (59 M.) *Stranraer* (comp. p. 464).

In regard to the following excursions on the *Clyde*, comp. pp. 451, 452, 486 (Circular Tours).

5. To Arrochar, a pleasant excursion for one day. Steamer from Greenock or Gourock (p. 486) to *Arrochar* in 2 hrs. (through-fare from Glasgow 2*s*., 1*s*. 6*d*.). — **Arrochar** *(Hotel)* lies at the head of the long and narrow **Loch Long** (p. 487). From Arrochar we may walk or drive (coach) across to (2$^1/_4$ M.) *Tarbet* on *Loch Lomond* (p. 483), returning by steamer to *Balloch* (p. 483) and thence to Glasgow by railway (fare for the round, including coach, 7*s*., 5*s*.). Or we may retrace our steps from Tarbet to Arrochar, and return to Glasgow by the steamer we came in.

6. To Gareloch Head (one day). We take the train viâ Dumbarton (p. 483) to (23 M. in 1 hr.; fares 1*s*. 9*d*., 1*s*.) **Helensburgh** *(Queen's; Imperial)*, at the mouth of the Gareloch, and proceed thence by steamer to ($^3/_4$ M.) *Gareloch Head* (Hotel), finely situated at the upper end of the loch. Steamers ply from Helensburgh to *Greenock*, *Gourock*, *Dunoon* (where passengers join the Oban steamer; comp. p. 487), *Rothesay*, etc.

7. To Rothesay (one day), see p. 487.

8. To the Island of Arran (two days). We may either go the whole way by steamer (5-6 hrs.; fares 2*s*. 6*d*., 1*s*. 6*d*.); or by train from Bridge Street to *Wemyss Bay* in 1 hr. and thence by steamer ('Ivanhoe') in 2$^1/_2$ hrs. (fares 3*s*. 8*d*., 2*s*. 11*d*., 2*s*. 6*d*.); or by train from St. Enoch's to *Ardrossan* in 1-1$^1/_2$ hr. and thence by steamer in 1-1$^1/_2$ hr. (fares 4*s*. 6*d*., 2*s*. 9*d*.). It is possible, but not advisable, to make this excursion in one day. The steamer passes *Largs* and the *Cumbrae Islands*, and calls at *Corrie* (*Hotel), **Brodick** *(Douglas Hotel)*, and *Lamlash* (Hotel), all on the E. coast of the mountainous **Isle of Arran**, which is about 20 M. long and 12-13 M. wide. The picturesque *Brodick Castle* and nearly the whole of the island belong

to the Duke of Hamilton. The best short excursion (6 hrs.) is to ascend from Brodick through *Glen Rosa* to (2-2½ hrs.) the top of ***Goatfell** (2866 ft.; *View), descend through the wild **Glen Sannox* (1-1½ hr.), and return along the coast viâ (1½ M.) Corrie to (4½ M.) Brodick. **Loch Ranza* (Inn), at the N. end of the island, 9 M. from Corrie, also deserves a visit.

9. To Inveraray (1-2 days). For this excursion there are five different routes, among which it is difficult to choose: *a.* By steamer ('Lord of the Isles', well equipped) from Glasgow, Greenock, or Gourock to Inveraray direct; *b.* By steamer from Greenock or Gourock to *Arrochar* (p. 481) and thence on foot or by coach through *Glencroe* (20 M.); *c.* From Greenock or Gourock by steamer to *Lochgoilhead* in 2 hrs., thence by coach or on foot to (9 M.) *St. Catherine's Ferry* (hilly road), and from St. Catherine's to Inveraray by small steamer in ¼ hr.; *d.* From Greenock or Gourock by steamer to *Dunoon*, by coach to *Loch Eck* (*Inverchapel;* 8 M.), by steamer to the N. end of this loch (6 M.), by coach to *Strachur* (5 M.), and by steamer to Inveraray (4 M.; in all, 5 hrs. from Greenock); *e.* Railway from Queen St. Station to *Balloch Pier* in 1 hr., steamer to Tarbet in 1¼ hr., and coach thence viâ Arrochar to Inveraray in 4 hrs. (24 M.; 8*s.*) — **Inveraray** *(Argyll Arms; George)*, the insignificant little county-town (1000 inhab.) of Argyllshire, is beautifully situated at the N.W. end of **Loch Fyne** (famous for its herrings), in a district noted for the beauty and variety of its trees. Adjacent is *Inveraray Castle*, the seat of the Duke of Argyll, in a finely wooded park. Fine view from *Duniquoich* (900 ft.; up and down 2 hrs.). — From Inveraray a coach runs by *Glen Aray* to (10 M.) *Cladich*, near the romantic ***Loch Awe** (30 M. long, 1½ M. wide), on which a whole day may be pleasantly spent (steamer). To the N. rises the finely-shaped *Ben Cruachan* (3610 ft.). The finest scenery is at the N. end of the loch, and may be well seen by taking a small boat to (1½ hr.) *Kilchurn Castle*. Or we may descend the loch by steamer to *Ford*, returning in the evening. Or we may cross to *Loch Awe Station* (*Hotel, R. & A. from 4*s.*), or go on by coach from Cladich to *Dalmally*, and take the train from either of these points to Oban (comp. p. 489). There is a ferry across the loch at *Port Sonachan* (Hotel), 3 M. to the S.W. of Cladich.

10. To Belfast, viâ steamer 'Adder' from Greenock (12½ hrs. there and back; return-fares 12*s.* 6*d.*, 6*s.*). We leave Glasgow (St. Enoch's) at 8 a.m. and have 1½ hr. on shore at Belfast.

66. From Glasgow to Edinburgh viâ Loch Lomond, Loch Katrine, and Stirling.

Railway to *Balloch* in 1-1¼ hr.; Steamer to *Inversnaid* in 2½ hrs.; Coach to *Loch Katrine* in 1 hr.; Steamboat to the *Trossachs* in ¾ hr.; Coach to *Callander* in 2¼ hrs. (including halt of ½ hr. at the Trossachs Hotel); Railway viâ *Stirling* to *Edinburgh* in 2-2½ hrs. (or from Stirling direct to *Glasgow* in 1½ hr.). This tour, which takes in all 11-12 hrs., is in favourable weather one of the most delightful in the United Kingdom. It is better to take two days for it, sleeping at *Rowardennan* and climbing *Ben Lomond* on the following morning. The *Circular Tour Tickets* are available for 7 days, and the journey may be broken at any point. Fares from Glasgow and back 20*s.* 4*d.*, 16*s.* 4*d.*; from Glasgow to Edinburgh (or vice versâ) 22*s.* 4*d.*, 19*s.* 10*d.*; from Edinburgh and back, including Glasgow, 26*s.* 4*d.*, 20*s.* 4*d.* — Carriage and pair from Inversnaid to Loch Katrine 10*s.*, gratuity 2*s.*; from the Trossachs to Callander 15*s.* and 3*s.* 6*d.*; from Inversnaid to Stronachlacher 7*s.* 6*d.*-10*s.* and 1*s.* 6*d.*-2*s.* 6*d.*

The Trossachs tour from Glasgow to Edinburgh may also be made viâ *Aberfoyle* (fares as above); see p. 486.

The train runs to the W. from *Queen Street Station* (Low Level), following at first the underground suburban railway, and beyond (10 M.) *Dalmuir* approaches the busy waterway of the *Clyde*. At (13 M.) *Bowling* begins the *Forth & Clyde Canal*. — 16 M. **Dum-**

barton *(Elephant)*, an industrial town with 14,000 inhab., is commanded by a *Castle*, strikingly situated on a precipitous rocky hill (280 ft.) and presenting a very picturesque appearance, especially when seen from the Clyde. Dumbarton Castle plays a prominent part in Scottish history, and was one of the four fortresses secured to Scotland at the time of the Union. The town lies at the mouth of the *Leven*, through which Loch Lomond discharges its waters. — The train now turns to the N., leaving the Helensburgh line (p. 481) to the left. A little to the S. of (18 M.) *Renton* is *Dalquharn*, the birthplace of Tobias Smollett (1721-71). — At (21 M.) **Balloch** *(Hotel)* the train runs on to the pier, alongside the steamer (with restaurant, D. 2*s.* 6*d.*). Balloch lies at the S. end of ***Loch Lomond**, the largest (25 M. long, 1-5 M. wide) and in some respects the most beautiful of the Scottish lakes. Its beauty is enhanced by the numerous wooded islands, among which the steamer threads its way. *Luss* (*Hotel), our first or second stopping-place, is charmingly situated on the W. bank of the lake, at the point where it begins to contract. The majestic ***Ben Lomond** (3192 ft.) forms the background to the right; those who wish to ascend it disembark at *Rowardennan* (*Hotel, R. & A. 3*s.*, D. 3*s.* 6*d.*).

The ascent of Ben Lomond takes 2-3 hrs. (descent 1½ hr.) and is easily accomplished, even by ladies; guide unnecessary, pony with guide 8-10*s.* The only point where it is possible to miss the path is a marshy track about halfway up; here we bear to the left and soon come in sight of the cairn which serves as a land-mark. The *View is very extensive, stretching on the S.E. over the Lowlands as far as Edinburgh; to the W. lies Loch Lomond, with the Cobbler, Ben Vane, Ben Voirlich, and other mountains surrounding it; more to the right are the twin-peaks of Ben Cruachan and the tent-shaped Ben More. — The descent may be made to Inversnaid (see below) or to *Aberfoyle* (p. 486), to the S.E.

From Rowardennan the steamer takes 20 min. to reach **Tarbet** (**Hotel*, R. & A. 4*s.* 6*d.*, B. 3*s.*), prettily situated on the W. bank, and commanding the best view of Ben Lomond. Many tourists walk or drive from Tarbet to (2¼ M.) *Arrochar* (p. 481) and return to Glasgow by the afternoon steamer on Loch Long. — Our steamboat-journey ends at **Inversnaid** *(Hotel)*, one of the finest points on Loch Lomond, affording splendid views of the mountains above Arrochar. Just before reaching the pier we pass a pretty waterfall.

Those who have time may prefer to go on by steamer to (½ hr.) *Ardlui* (Hotel), at the head of the loch, and return later to Inversnaid. About 2 M. to the N. of the pier is the prettily-situated **Inverarnan Hotel.* Coaches ply daily from the Head of the Loch to (8½ M.) *Crianlarich* (p. 491), whence we may proceed by railway to *Dalmally* (p. 491) or *Killin* (p. 492). — A small-boat excursion may be made from Inversnaid to *Rob Roy's Cave*, 1 M. to the N., with an almost invisible entrance.

At Inversnaid the steamer is met by a coach to take the passengers across the ridge between Loch Lomond and Loch Katrine, a distance of 5½ M. Those who prefer it have plenty of time (1½ hr.) to walk, but the ascent from this side is long and somewhat fatiguing. The road passes the ruins of an old castle and the small *Loch Arklet*. On reaching *Stronachlacher* (*Hotel), we embark in the small screw-steamer that plies on ***Loch Katrine**, a beautiful lake about $9^1/_2$ M. long. The finest scenery is at its E. end, where steep cliffs alternate with beautiful woods, in which the bright green foliage of the birch is predominant. Here, too, is the charming little **Ellen's Isle*, immortalised in the 'Lady of the Lake'. (The traveller need scarcely be reminded that Scott's poem renders all other guide-books almost superfluous for this part of Scotland.) To the right towers the noble form of *Ben Venue* (2393 ft.). Some traces of the apparatus for conveying the water of Loch Katrine to Glasgow (comp. p. 480) may be seen on the S. shore.

The ***Trossachs** ('bristling country'), a richly-wooded and romantic valley, begin immediately to the E. of Loch Katrine, and there are few more beautiful districts in Scotland than that between Ellen's Isle and the *Trossachs Hotel*, on the bank of the small **Loch Achray*. The coach waits $^1/_2$ hr. at the ($1^1/_2$ M.) hotel, and luncheon (2*s.* 6*d.*) is ready for the passengers. At the E. end of Loch Achray we pass ($1^1/_2$ M.) the *Brigg of Turk*, and 1 M. farther on we reach **Loch Vennachar*, along the N. side of which the road runs for 4 M. To the left rises *Ben Ledi* (2875 ft.). At the E. end of the loch is *Coilantogle Ford*, the scene of the combat between Fitzjames and Roderick Dhu. On the top of a hill to the left, shortly before we reach (2 M.) Callander, is a curiously perched boulder known as 'Samson's Putting Stone'.

Callander (**Dreadnought Hotel*, R. & A. 4*s.*, B. 3*s.* 6*d.*, D. 4*s.*; *Macgregor's; Hydropathic)*, a favourite centre of Highland tourists, is picturesquely situated on the *Teith*.

Those who have not time to take the tour mentioned at p. 491 should at least walk or drive (one-horse carr. there and back 6-7*s.*) through the picturesque *Pass of Leny* to ($3^1/_2$ M.) *Loch Lubnaig* (comp. p. 492). Tolerable walkers should extend this excursion to *Strathyre*, $5^1/_2$ M. farther on, beyond the head of the lake, and return thence by train.

About $1^1/_2$ M. to the N. of Callander are the **Falls of Bracklin**, in a romantic wooded gorge. On the way from the station to the village we take the first cross-road to the right and ascend by a rough cart-track to (1 min.) a small wood. The indistinct footpath skirts this to the right and leads along the hillside to (8 min.) a wall, which we cross. We continue in the same direction (E.) to (8 min.) a deep hollow, and then descend to (2-3 min.) the falls. We cross the little wooden bridge and explore the pretty points of view on the opposite bank. — Callander is the usual starting-point for an ascent of **Ben Ledi** (2875 ft.; $2^1/_2$-3 hrs.; *View).

From Callander we continue our journey by railway. To the right, at (8 M.) *Doune*, is a picturesque ruined castle. — 11 M. **Dunblane** *(Stirling Arms; *Hydropathic)* has an E.E. *Cathedral (13th cent.), with a Norman tower, the choir of which is used as the parish-church, while the rest is in ruins. Pleasant walk through *Kippenross Park* to Bridge-of-Allan. A little to the W. of Dunblane is the field of *Sheriffmuir* (battle 1715). — 13 M. **Bridge-of-Allan** *(Royal; Queen; Hydropathic)*, a favourite inland watering-place, with mineral springs, famed for the mildness of its climate.

16 M. **Stirling** (**Golden Lion*, at the station; **Royal; Temper-*

ance), an ancient town with 16,000 inhab., is situated on the *Forth*, 35 M. above Edinburgh, and was formerly a favourite residence of the Scottish sovereigns. The picturesque and venerable *Castle is situated upon a lofty height overlooking the town and resembling the castle-rock of Edinburgh.

Stirling Castle plays a prominent part in Scottish history. In 1304 it was taken by Edward I. of England after a siege of three months, but it was retaken by Bruce ten years later, after Bannockburn. James II. (1430) and James V. (1512) were born in the castle; and here, in 1452, James II. stabbed the rebellious Earl of Douglas.

We first enter the Lower Court (no charge; small gratuity to the guide), in which, to the left, stands the Gothic *Palace of James V.* (16th cent.). Thence we pass into the Upper Court, on the E. side of which stands the *Parliament House*, and on the N. the *Chapel Royal*. The passage to the left of the latter leads to the *Douglas Gardens*, whence a flight of steps ascends to the *Douglas Room*, the scene of the above-mentioned tragedy. The best point of view is the **Ladies' Look-Out*, an opening in the garden-wall behind the governor's house: to the extreme left (W.) Ben Lomond, then Ben Venue, Ben A'an, and Ben Ledi; to the N. and E. the Ochils; nearer, Bridge of Allan, the Abbey Craig and Wallace Monument, Cambuskenneth Abbey, and the 'Links of Forth'; to the S., Bannockburn. The view from *Queen Mary's Look-Out* is similar.

We now pass through the park-like *Cemetery*, with its handsome Martyrs' Memorial, to the ancient *Greyfriars' Church* (1494), the tower of which affords another fine view (adm. 2*d.*). Adjacent is *Cowane's Hospital* or *Guildhall*, with a small museum. — Among the interesting old houses of Stirling is *Argyle's Lodging*, in Broad St. (E. side of the Castle Wynd), built in the 16th cent., and now a military hospital.

Excursions from Stirling. About 1½ M. to the S. of Stirling lies the village of *St. Ninian* (omn. 2*d.*), and ½ M. farther on is the field of **Bannockburn**, where Robert Bruce defeated the army of Edward II., thrice as large as the Scottish army, in 1314. The '*Bore Stone*', on which the Scottish standard was planted, is still pointed out (view). — At *Sauchieburn*, 3 M. to the S.W. of Bannockburn, James III. was defeated by his insurgent nobles in 1488. *Beaton's Mill*, the house in which he was assassinated after the battle, still exists.

Cambuskenneth Abbey (adm. 2*d.*), on the left bank of the Forth, a little below Stirling, was founded by David I. in 1147 and became the wealthiest Augustine monastery in Scotland. James III. and his wife Margaret of Denmark are buried in the abbey. The best way of reaching it is to descend the right bank for 1 M. and then cross by the ferry (1*d.*).

Just above the new bridge the Forth is spanned by the interesting *Old Bridge*, of the 15th cent., on which Archbp. Hamilton, the last Roman Catholic prelate in Scotland, was hanged for participation in the murder of the Regent Moray (1570). The famous battle of Stirling, in which Wallace defeated the English in 1297, took place a little farther up, near an old wooden bridge, which has long since disappeared.

Tramway-cars ply hourly from Stirling to (3 M.) *Bridge of Allan* (see p. 484; fare 3*d.*), passing, on the right, the ***Abbey Craig** (362 ft.; *View), which is surmounted by the heavy-looking *Wallace Monument* (adm. 2*d.*).

About 12 M. to the E. of Stirling (railway, viâ *Alloa*, in ¾ hr.) lies **Dollar** (180 ft.; *Castle Campbell Hotel*), a small town with a good public school (5-600 pupils), near which is the finely situated **Castle Campbell* (view). Farther to the E., 4½ M. beyond Dollar, is the **Rumbling Bridge* (rail. stat.; Hotel), crossing the romantic gorge of the *Devon* (adm. to walks 6*d.*). Near the bridge is the *Devil's Mill Fall*, and 1 M. lower down is the **Cauldron Linn*. From Dollar we may ascend *Ben Cleuch* (2363 ft.), the highest of the *Ochils* (view). — The railway runs on to (20 min.) *Kin-*

ross (Kirkland's), a small town on **Loch Leven**, a lake 4 **M.** long and 2 **M.** wide, famed for its trout (boat, with boatman, 2*s.* 6*d.* per hr.). On an island in the loch is an old castle in which Queen Mary was imprisoned in 1567, making her escape in the following year (comp. Scott's 'Abbot'). — From *Kinross* we may return to Edinburgh in 1-1½ hr. by train viâ *Cowdenbeath*, *Dunfermline*, and the *Forth Bridge* (p. 495).

From Stirling to Aberfoyle, 21½ M., railway in 1-1¼ hr. — The line diverges to the left from the main line to Callander and runs along the S. side of the *Forth*. 6 **M.** *Gargunnock;* 9 **M.** *Kippen;* 13 **M.** *Port of Menteith*, 4 **M.** to the S. of the *Lake of Menteith* (see below). — 15½ **M.** *Buchlyvie*, and thence to *Aberfoyle*, see below. Beyond Buchlyvie the line goes on (28 **M.**) *Balloch* (p. 483).

From Stirling we may also return to Edinburgh by steamer on the *Forth* (3-3½ hrs.; comp. p. 465).

The railway from Stirling to Edinburgh joins the Edinburgh and Glasgow line at *Polmont Junction* (p. 475).

The stages on the alternative route viâ *Aberfoyle*, mentioned at p. 482, are as follows: — Railway from Glasgow to Buchlyvie and Aberfoyle, 34 **M.**, in 1¼-1¾ hr.; Coach from Aberfoyle to Loch Katrine Pier, 7 **M.**, in 1½ hr. (fare 4*s.* 6*d.*); thence as above. — The train starts at the *Queen St. Station* (p. 476) and diverges to the N. (left) from the Edinburgh line at (6½ **M.**) *Lenzie.* 8½ **M.** *Kirkintilloch.* Beyond (11 **M.**) *Lennoxtown* it traverses the pretty *Campsie Glen.* 20 **M.** *Killearn.* At (22½ **M.**) *Gartness* we join the Balloch-Stirling line and turn to the right. *Loch Lomond* (p. 483) lies about 4 **M.** to the W. At (24½ **M.**) *Balfron* the pipes of the Loch Katrine aqueduct (p. 480) cross the railway. 28 **M.** *Buchlyvie* (Hotel) is the junction of the short branch-line to (6 **M.**) **Aberfoyle** (*Bailie Nicol Jarvie Hotel*), which traverses a swampy moorland and passes 2 **M.** to the W. of the small *Lake of Menteith* (see Scott's 'Rob Roy'). The ascent of *Ben Lomond* may be made from Aberfoyle in 3½-4½ hrs. — The road from Aberfoyle to the Trossachs (7 **M.**) affords a good view of *Ben Ledi* (p. 484) and a glimpse of *Loch Vennachar* (p. 484). To the right lies the pretty *Loch Drunkie.* Finally we pass the W. end of *Loch Achray* (p. 484) and join the above described route at the *Trossachs Hotel* (p. 484).

67. From Glasgow to Oban and Inverness. Western Scotland.

From Glasgow to *Oban*, 120 **M.**, steamer daily in 9 hrs., starting at 7 a.m. As far as *Ardrishaig* (see p. 488) we travel by the admirably appointed 'Columba', probably the finest river-steamer in Europe, with an excellent restaurant (B. 2*s.*, D. 2*s.* 6*d.*), drawing-rooms, baths, post-office, etc. Travellers may leave Glasgow by rail (*St. Enoch's* or *Central Station*) at 8.15-8.30 a.m., or Edinburgh (*Caledonian Station*, p. 464) at 7-7.30 a.m., and join the steamer at *Greenock* or *Gourock* (comp. p. 476).

Travellers may go by this route as far as Oban and return thence by train in one long day, reaching Edinburgh again at 11.15 and Glasgow at 11.30 p.m. Circular tour fares; from Glasgow 21*s.*, 11*s.* 6*d.*; from Edinburgh 29*s.*, 15*s.* 6*d.* Holders of third-class tickets may travel in the cabin of the steamer on paying 4*s.* 6*d.* extra to the purser.

Those who prefer it may go to Oban all the way by steamer ('Claymore' or 'Clansman') in about 14 hrs., leaving Greenock at 4 p.m. on Mon. and Thurs. (fare 10*s.*). The route, a very fine one for good sailors, leads past *Arran* (see p. 482), round the *Mull of Cantyre* (often stormy), and then to the N. between the mainland and the islands of *Islay* and *Jura.* Beyond Oban the steamers go on to *Tobermory* (p. 489), *Broadford* (p. 491), *Portree* (p. 491), and *Stornoway* (p. 494; 40 hrs. from Glasgow).

Steamers ply from Oban daily in summer to *Staffa* and *Iona*, and through the Caledonian Canal to *Inverness;* also to *Skye* several times weekly.

This route may be conveniently combined with the next by proceed-

For a coloured map of Loch Lomond & The Trossachs see pages 600 & 601

ing by railway from Inverness to Aberdeen; and the three routes, Nos. 66, 67, 69, with a few excursions from the chief centres, include all the finest scenery in Scotland between Edinburgh and Glasgow on the S. and Inverness on the N. A Circular Tour combining RR. 67 & 69 has been arranged by the Caledonian Railway Co. (fares 77*s.* 4*d.*, 47*s.* 10*d.*). Ample opportunities are allowed for breaking the journey, and at least a fortnight should be devoted to the round. 1st Day: From *Glasgow* to *Oban* by the *Crinan Canal.* 2nd Day: Excursion to *Iona* and *Staffa.* 3rd Day: Excursion to *Loch Awe.* 4th Day: From *Oban* to *Inverness* through the *Caledonian Canal.* 5th Day: From Inverness to *Loch Maree.* 6th Day: Return to Inverness. 7th Day: From Inverness to *Aberdeen.* 8th Day: At *Aberdeen.* 9th Day: From Aberdeen to *Braemar.* 10th Day: From Braemar to *Perth.* 11th Day: From Perth to *Crieff*, *Comrie*, *Lochearnhead*, *Killin*, *Loch Tay*, *Kenmore*, and *Aberfeldy.* 12th Day: From Aberfeldy to *Pitlochry* and *Pass of Killiecrankie*, and then back to Perth by *Dunkeld.* 13th Day: From *Perth* to *Edinburgh* viâ *Stirling.* Those who have time should certainly add an excursion to the *Isle of Skye* (comp. p. 491).

The 'Columba' at first threads its way through the crowded shipping of the harbour, among which may usually be seen some of the Atlantic steamers of the Anchor, Allan, and State Lines. To the right is the extensive *Queen's Dock*, and numerous large ship-building yards are passed on both banks. The first stopping-place is *Partick*, opposite the busy suburban town of *Govan* (p. 477; to the left). Below (6 M.) *Renfrew* (left) is *Elderslie*, the birthplace of William Wallace. 12 M. (right) *Bowling* (p. 482). — 18 M. *Dumbarton* (p. 482). Ben Lomond is visible to the N. in clear weather. — 18$^1/_2$ M. *Port Glasgow* (left) formerly was what its name implies, but has lost its importance through the deepening of the Clyde at Glasgow. The second stoppage (2 hrs. from Glasgow) is at —

22 M. **Greenock** *(Tontine; White Hart; Royal; Buck's Head)*, a finely situated and flourishing seaport, with ample harbour accommodation, extensive sugar-refineries, and large ship-building yards, iron-foundries, and engineering works. Pop. (1881) 68,897. The '*Tail of the Bank*', part of a large sandbank off Greenock, affords the best anchorage in the Clyde. One or more men-of-war are generally to be seen here. Passengers coming over the Midland and G. S. W. Railways join the steamer at Greenock.

Beyond Greenock the river widens. To the left is the seaside resort of **Gourock** *(Ashton Hotel)*, where passengers over the Caledonian (Glasgow, Edinburgh, etc.) and L. N. W. Railways embark. The trains run alongside the steamer. To the right is the long and narrow *Loch Long* (p. 481). The steamer calls at *Kirn* (at the mouth of the *Holy Loch*), *Dunoon* (where it is joined by passengers coming over the G. N. R., N. E. R., and N. B. R. viâ *Helensburgh*, p. 481), and *Innellan*, three popular watering-places. Nearly opposite Dunoon is the *Cloch Lighthouse.* We then pass *Toward Point* and *Lighthouse* (right) and cross to —

40 M. **Rothesay** (*Queen's; Bute Arms; Victoria*, R. & A. at these from 4*s.*, D. from 3*s.*; *Glenburn Hydropathic;* boat 6*d.* per hr.), the capital (8300 inhab.) of the island of *Bute* and in some respects the 'Brighton' of the Clyde. The scene at Rothesay Pier, in the

height of the season, is one of great bustle and liveliness. The ruins of *Rothesay Castle* date from the 14th century. The eldest son of the reigning monarch of Great Britain bears the title of Duke of Rothesay. Good view from *Barone Hill* (530 ft.). *Mountstuart*, a fine building, the seat of the Marquis of Bute, is 5 M. to the S.E. About 2 M. to the N. of Rothesay lies the village of *Port Bannatyne* (tramway 2*d.*), where cheaper lodgings may be had. Above the village stands the *Kyles of Bute Hydropathic* (well spoken of).

The Columba now turns to the N.W. (while the Arran steamers continue their journey southwards; p. 481) and threads the picturesque **Kyles of Bute*, the narrow strait separating the N. end of Bute from the mainland. To the right stretch *Lochs Striven* and *Ridden*. Stations *Colintraive* and *Tighnabruaich*. Rounding *Ardlamont Point*, the steamer enters *Loch Fyne* (famous for its herrings) and calls at *Tarbert* (Tarbert Hotel). A fine view is obtained at this point of the Mts. of Arran to the S.; to the N., view of Loch Fyne, with the twin-peaks of Ben Cruachan in the distance.

From Tarbert a coach runs down the Mull of Cantyre to *Campbeltown* (35 M., fare 10*s.*). Another coach conveys passengers to (1 M.) the head of *West Loch Tarbert*, whence a steamer plies daily to *Port Askaig* (on Mon. to *Port Ellen*) on the island of **Islay** (through-fares from Glasgow 12*s.* 6*d.*, 5*s.*). *Bridgend* is a good centre from which to explore Islay. From Port Askaig a ferry plies to (1/2 M.) the island of **Jura**, the *Paps* of which (2400-2570 ft.) command good views.

Beyond Tarbert the vessel steams up a small arm of Loch Fyne called *Loch Gilp*, and at about 1 p. m. reaches —

80 M. **Ardrishaig** *(Ardrishaig Hotel; Albion)*, where the Columba is quitted for a small steamer on the Crinan Canal.

From Ardrishaig a coach starts in summer on the arrival of the steamers for (16 M.) *Ford*, whence a steamer sails up *Loch Awe* (see p. 490) to *Loch Awe Station* (p. 490), on the railway to Oban. This is an alternative route to Oban from Ardrishaig. — **Lochgilphead** *(Argyll; Star)*, 2 M. to the N. of Ardrishaig, is frequented by summer visitors. — For *Inveraray*, at the head of Loch Fyne, see p. 482.

The **Crinan Canal**, which saves the long and often stormy voyage (75 M.) round the *Mull of Cantyre*, is only 9 M. long; but as the steamer has to pass through 9 locks, it takes 2 hrs. to the passage. It is easy to walk from Ardrishaig and join the steamer at the last lock. *Lochgilphead* (see above) is passed on the right. The canal is pretty, and more like a river than a canal. At Crinan the '*Chevalier*' or '*Grenadier*' is in waiting, on board which dinner is served at once. The sail from Crinan to Oban takes about 2 1/4 hrs. Soon after leaving Crinan we pass between *Craignish Point* and the N. end of *Jura* (see above; ferry), which is separated from the little island of *Scarba* by the tumultuous *Strait of Corrievrechan*. The next part of the course is sheltered by several islands, but farther on we are exposed for a time to the full swell of the Atlantic Ocean. Finally, however, we come under the lee of *Mull* (p. 489) and enter the *Sound of Kerrĕra*.

120 M. **Oban.** — **Hotels.** Great Western, *Alexandra, to the N. of the pier, R. & A. 5*s.* 6*d.*, B. 3*s.*, D. 5*s.*; *Station, Caledonian, near the station, to the S. of the pier, R. & A. 4*s.* 6*d.*, D. 4-5*s.*; Grand, on the hill behind the town, with fine view; Columba, opposite the N. pier; King's Arms, Victoria Temperance, Imperial, *Argyll, unpretending. — *Lodgings.* — *Rail. Rfmt. Rooms.*

Oban, a growing town with 5000 inhab., is picturesquely situated in a lovely bay of the *Firth of Lorn*, which is almost land-locked by the island of *Kerrĕra* (ferry 4*d.*) and forms a fine harbour, generally full of yachts and steamers. Oban is the starting-point for so many excursions and the centre of so much traffic by train and steamer that it has been called the 'Charing Cross of the Highlands'. The obelisk on Kerrera is a memorial of *David Hutcheson*, the pionier of steamboat traffic in the Western Highlands. On a rocky promontory on the N. side of the bay, 1 M. from the pier, rises *Dunolly Castle*, the pretty grounds of which (open to the public on Mon., Wed., and Frid.) afford fine views. In the drive leading to the house is the *Clach-a-Choin*, or dog-stone, to which it is said Fingal used to tie his dog Bran.

Excursions from Oban.

Walks. To the top of the hill at the back of the town (1/2 hr.); fine view of Oban, Kerrera, and Mull. — To *Dunstaffnage Castle*, 3 1/2 M., coach daily (return-fare 1*s.* 6*d.*). We follow the road leading from Oban towards the N. for about 3 M., and then take a track to the left leading along the shore past *Dunstaffnage Farm.* **Dunstaffnage Castle** (adm. 6*d.*) is associated with very early Scottish history, and the 'Stone of Destiny', now forming part of the 'Coronation Chair' in Westminster Abbey (see *Baedeker's London*), was kept here before its removal to Scone in 842. In clear weather the castle affords a fine view of Loch Etive, the Mts. of Mull, etc. The lofty mountain to the E. is Ben Cruachan.

Longer Excursions. 1. **To Staffa and Iona* (steamer there and back, including 1 hr. on each of the islands, 9-10 hrs.; fare 15*s.*). In fine weather this is perhaps the most delightful excursion on the W. coast of Scotland. (On three days a week the tour is made in the reverse direction to that described below.) The steamer steers to the N.W., between *Dunolly Castle* (right) and the island of *Kérrera* (left). In 3/4 hr. we pass the island of *Lismore*, at the mouth of the large *Loch Linnhe*, on the right, long the seat of the Bishops of Argyle; the 'Dean of Lismore's Book' is a collection of early Gaelic poems in MS., made by Sir James M'Gregor, Dean of Lismore, at the beginning of the 16th century. To the left is *Duart*, at the entrance of the *Sound of Mull*, a strait 1-2 M. wide, separating the mountainous isle of **Mull** from the mainland. To the right rises *Ardtornish Castle*, picturesquely placed at the entrance to the pretty *Loch Aline.* To the left, *Aros Castle*, another ancient seat of the Lords of the Isles. l. **Tobermory** (*Western Islands Hotel; Royal*), the chief place in Mull. The steamer now turns to the W. and faces the Atlantic Ocean. To the left is *Ardmore Point*, to the right *Ardnamurchan Point.* In clear weather the islands of *Muck*, *Eigg*, and *Rum*, and the Mts. of *Skye*, are seen to the N.; to the W., *Coll* and *Tiree.* Steering to the S., we next pass the small and rocky *Treshinish Isles*, one of which is known from its shape as the *Dutchman's Cap.* To the left is *Gometray.* **Staffa** ('island of pillars'), 1 1/2 M. in circumference, is now reached, and the steamer stops to allow the passengers to visit (by small boat) the celebrated ****Fingal's Cave.** [In rough weather, it is impossible to enter the cave by boat, and the passengers are then landed at some distance rom it.] The imposing entrance to Fingal's Cave is formed by a series of basaltic columns, 20-40 ft. height, bearing an arch that rises to a height of 65 ft.

above the sea. The cave penetrates the island for a distance of over 200 ft. Its floor consists of the surging waves, which even on a calm day awaken thunderous echoes in its dim recesses. The *Clam Shell Cave* derives its name from its shape. Staffa possesses other caves of great interest, especially to the geologist; but the short halt of the steamer does not allow time to inspect them.

In about 3/4 hr. after leaving Staffa we reach **Iona** or *Icolmkill* (*St. Columba Hotel*, *Argyll*, unpretending), an island 3 1/2 M. long and 1 1/4 M. broad, separated from Mull by the narrow *Sound of Iona*. We again land by a small boat. The interest of the island arises from the fact that *St. Columba* landed here from Ireland in 563 and began his missionary labours in Scotland. The oldest buildings now existing, however, date from the 12th century. The guide, who meets us on landing, leads us to the *Cemetery of St. Oran*, containing a great number of ancient tombs, many of which are said to be those of Scottish, Irish, and Norwegian kings. The **Cathedral*, or *Church of St. Mary*, mainly in the Transition-Norman style, dates from the 13-16th centuries. Near it is *St. Martin's Cross*, and on the road is *Maclean's Cross*, the only survivors of the 360 Runic Crosses that the island is said to have once possessed, most of them having been destroyed by Puritan iconoclasts. Dr. Johnson visited Iona in 1773 and was deeply impressed by its associations: 'That man is little to be envied whose patriotism would not gain force upon the plain of Marathon, or whose piety would not grow warmer among the ruins of Iona'.

The steamer now threads the *Firth of Lorn*, along the S. coast of Mull, with its fine basaltic formations, and passes through Kerrera Sound into Oban Bay.

2. Circular Tour to Loch Awe and Melfort (8 hrs.; fares 1st. cl. 17*s.*, 3rd cl. 15*s.* 6*d.*; driver's fees 2*s.*). By coach to (32 M.) *Ford*, at the S. end of **Loch Awe** (p. 482); steamer on Loch Awe to (20 M.) *Loch Awe Station* (p. 482); train to (24 M.) *Oban*. This route may be made in the opposite direction, but Loch Awe is seen to greatest advantage from S. to N. Those who have come to Oban by railway (see p. 491), having skirted Loch Awe and passed through the Pass of Brander, may omit this route. They should, however, take the coach as far as (16 M.) *Kilmelfort* (*Culfail Hotel), walk on for about 2 M., to obtain a view of **Loch Melfort**, and return by the same route (fare about 10*s.*). The finest points on the route are the *Pass of Brander*, a narrow and gloomy ravine (traversed by railway) and the **Pass of Melfort*, a picturesque defile, the ruggedness of which is softened by its fine woods (pine, oak, birch, mountain-ash, hazel). The view of Loch Melfort from a lofty part of the road, about 2 M. beyond Kilmelfort, is also very fine. Refreshments may be obtained at Kilmelfort (see above), Ford, or on the steamer. Oban is reached in time for table-d'hôte.

3. *Circular Tour by Glen Etive, Loch Etive, and Glencoe to Ballachulish, and back by Loch Linnhe (1 day; 1st cl. and cabin 25*s.*). Railway to (9 M.) *Ach-na-Cloich;* steamer up **Loch** Etive to (15 M.) *Lochetive Head;* coach to (30 M.) *Ballachulish;* steamer to (26 M.) *Oban*. This tour which embraces some of the deepest recesses and grandest scenery in the Highlands, may be made in either direction, and takes 10-12 hrs., bringing passengers back to Oban in time for dinner. It may, however, be omitted by those who are going on through the Caledonian Canal to Inverness, as they may get a good view of Loch Etive from Dunstaffnage (see p. 489), and may visit Glencoe from Ballachulish (see p. 492). Refreshments at Kinghouse Inn, about halfway between Lochetive Head and Ballachulish; dinner is provided on the steamer from Ballachulish to Oban.

4. From Oban to Callander. The direct route is by railway (71 M., n 3 hrs.; see p. 491). A pleasant round may be made by taking the steamer to *Ballachulish* (see above) and going thence by coach, in 5 1/2 hrs., through *Glencoe* (p. 492) to *Loch Etive* and (35 M.) *Ach-na-Cloich*. From Ach-na-Cloich we proceed by railway to *Callander* (p. 484) in 2 1/2 hrs., viâ *Crianlarich* and *Killin* (p. 492). Coach from Killin to *Aberfeldy*, see p. 501.

5. From Oban to Loch Lomond. Either as above, or by railway (viâ Dalmally, p. 491) to *Crianlarich*, and thence by coach, in 3 hrs., to *Ardlui* (comp. p. 483).

6. **From Oban to the Isle of Skye (2-3 days). Steamers ply several times a week from Oban to *Broadford* (14-18*s.*) and *Portree* (16-20*s.*). Tourists usually disembark at Broadford, and, after visiting the island, return from Portree. Broadford, however, and the route thence to Loch Scavaig are comparatively uninteresting; and a better plan is to take the steamer which plies once weekly to *Loch Scavaig* (see below), having telegraphed the day before to the landlord of the Sligachan Hotel to send a guide (and ponies if required; advisable for ladies) to meet the steamer. Those who land at *Broadford* (*Hotel) should walk or drive (one-horse carr. 5*s.*) to (6 M.) *Torrin*, and proceed thence by boat (with 2 rowers 18*s.*, with 4 rowers 24*s.*) to the *Spar Cave* and ***Loch Scavaig**, a wild and romantic arm of the sea running deep into the island. At its inner end, separated from it by a narrow neck of land, is ***Loch Coruisk**, offering a scene of solitary and savage grandeur, perhaps not elsewhere paralleled in the kingdom. From Loch Coruisk we may walk to the N. across *Drumhain* (800 ft.) and through **Glen Sligachan* to the (7-8 M.) **Sligachan Hotel* (a rough walk of 3 hrs.; not to be attempted after dusk without a guide). Or we may cross Loch Scavaig by boat to *Camasunary* (better than by the walking route, on which a steady head is necessary at the point called the 'Bad Step'), and follow the track through Glen Sligachan the whole way to the hotel (3 hrs.). To the left rises the graceful **Scuir-na-Gillean** ('Peak of the Young Men'; 3167 ft.), and to the right is *Blaven* (3042 ft.), both summits of the grand ***Cuchullin Hills** (pron. 'Coolin'), the impressiveness of which is heightened by the dark colour of their rocks. From the Sligachan Hotel we may ascend the former in 3 hrs.; the route is steep and requires a steady head, but a guide (10-12*s.*) is unnecessary except in misty weather. Ladies should not attempt it, unless prepared for considerable fatigue. The *View from the top is very fine. — From Sligachan a coach plies daily to (10 M.) **Portree** *(*Portree Hotel; Royal; Caledonian)*, the capital of the island, and the best general centre for excursions. *Prince Charles's Cave*, in the rocky coast, 4½ M. to the N., has no other interest than that the Young Pretender lay there in hiding. Those who have time should not quit Portree without a visit (1-2 days) to the Storr Rock and the Quiraing, perhaps the most striking rock-scenery in Great Britain. [In summer excursion-brakes run daily from Portree to Uig (return-fare 8*s.*) and thence to the Quiraing (4*s.*); see below.] The **Storr Rock** (2340 ft.), about 7 M. to the N., commands a very fine and extensive view; the walk to the top takes at least 3 hrs. A walk thence of 4 hrs. more, over dreary moorland, brings us to the ***Quiraing**, a grassy plateau enclosed by lofty cliffs and pinnacles of the most fantastic form and disposition. Those who reach the Quiraing too late to go on to Uig may sleep at the *Steinscholl Inn*, 2 M. to the S., which we passed on our way. Next morning we walk across the island (2½ hrs.) to *Uig* (Inn) on the W. coast, and return thence by carriage (ordered beforehand at Portree) or by coach to (2¼ hrs.) Portree (on foot 4½ hrs.). Those whose time is limited should drive from Portree to Uig, walk (or drive) to the Quiraing and back, and drive back to Portree (in all 8-9 hrs.), leaving the Storr Rock unvisited. — The steamboat-journey from Portree to Oban takes 14 hrs.; or we may take the steamer from Portree to (4 hrs.) *Strome Ferry* (p. 494), and proceed thence by railway, viâ Dingwall, to Inverness (p. 493).

Steam Yachts leave Oban at intervals in the season for a week or two's excursion (apply at M'Gregor's Coach Office).

From Oban to Glasgow, 116 M., railway in 3½-4 hrs. (fares 14*s.*, 11*s.*, 8*s.*; to *Edinburgh*, 123 M., 18*s.* 6*d.*, 14*s.*, 9*s.* 10*d.*). This railway traverses much picturesque scenery, and affords a convenient return-route for those unable to go farther north. On leaving Oban the train sweeps round to the N., passes *Dunstaffnage* (p. 489) on the left, and skirts *Loch Etive* (p. 490). Beyond (13 M.) *Taynuilt* (Inn) it threads the wild *Pass of Awe* and the *Pass of Brander* (p. 490), at the foot of Ben Cruachan. — 22 M. *Loch Awe Station* (p. 490). — 25 M. **Dalmally** *(Hotel)*, at the entrance to the beautiful *Vale of Glenorchy*, 3 M. from the N.E. end of Loch Awe. From Dalmally we may walk or drive, viâ (6 M.) *Cladich* (p. 482), to (10 M.) *Inveraray* (see p. 482). — 38 M. *Tyndrum* (Royal Hotel). From (42 M.) *Crianlarich*

(Hotel) a coach runs daily, in 2 hrs., to *Ardlui*, at the upper end of *Loch Lomond* (p. 483); and those who have not yet visited that beautiful loch may complete their journey by this route. — 53 M. *Killin Junction* commands a fine view of *Loch Tay* (see p. 501). The train then descends the wild *Glen Ogle* and passes the head of *Loch Earn* (station; see p. 498). It next skirts **Loch Lubnaig*, a picturesque sheet of water, and threads the *Pass of Leny*, where *Ben Ledi* (p. 484) towers to the right. — 71 M. *Callander*, and thence to *Glasgow* (or *Edinburgh*), see R. 65.

From Oban to Inverness through the Caledonian Canal, 98 M., steamer daily in 12 hrs. (6 a.m. to 6 p.m.; if a later boat be taken, the night may be spent at Banavie or Fort William, see below). The steamer sails through *Loch Linnhe* to ($2^1/_2$ hrs.) **Ballachulish** *(*Ballachulish Hotel; Loch Leven)*, a charming excursion in fine weather. The village is grandly situated at the entrance of *Loch Leven*, an arm of the sea stretching towards the E.

At Ballachulish coaches meet the steamer to convey passengers to the wild **Glencoe**, the scene of the atrocious massacre of the unsuspecting and hospitable Macdonalds on 14th Feb., 1692, by English soldiers. The drive there and back, including a stay of $^1/_2$ hr. at *Ossian's Cave*, the finest part of the glen, takes 4 hrs. (fare 5*s.* 6*d.*).

The steamer now crosses Loch Linnhe, calls at *Ardgour*, and passes through the *Corran Narrows*. At the head of the loch (16 M. or $1^1/_2$ hr. from Ballachulish) lies —

Fort William (**Caledonian; Alexandra; Chevalier; *Ramsay's Temperance; Imperial; Ben Nevis*, well spoken of), formerly the key of the Highlands. A coach runs hence daily, passing the 'Parallel Roads' of *Glen Roy*, to (50 M.; $6^1/_2$ hrs.) *Kingussie*, a station of the Highland Railway, 36 M. to the N. of Blair Athole (p. 502). — Passengers for Inverness do not disembark at Fort William, but go on with the steamer to ($^1/_4$ hr.) *Corpach* (Hotel), whence a coach-drive of 10 min. brings them to **Banavie** *(Lochiel Arms)*, at the mouth of the canal. The **Caledonian Canal**, 60 M. long, admitting the passage of large vessels from the W. coast to Inverness, traverses the 'Great Glen of Scotland' and consists of a chain of lakes *(Lochs Lochy, Oich, Ness, and Dochfour)*, united by artificial channels.

Banavie lies at the foot of ***Ben Nevis** (4406 ft.), the highest mountain in the British Islands, which may be ascended hence in 3-$3^1/_2$ hrs. by a good new pony-track. Those who use this track, which begins at (2 M.) the farm of *Achintee*, at the entrance to *Glen Nevis*, are expected to purchase a guide-ticket (1*s.*; for pony 3*s.*), the proceeds of which go to keep the path in repair. Guide (unnecessary) 10*s.*; pony and attendant 21*s.* The *View from the top is fine, especially on the N.E., where there is a precipitous descent of 1450 ft. At the top are an *Observatory*, established in 1883, and a *Temperance Inn* (Tea, R., & B. 10*s.*, L. 3*s.*). — The ascent may also be made from Fort William (see above), which has telegraphic communication with the top.

A mail-conveyance plies daily (three times weekly before July) from Banavie to (36 M.) *Arisaig Inn*, the last 25 M. of the route through splendid scenery, passing *Loch Eil*, *Loch Shiel*, *Loch Rannoch* (or *Loch Eilt*), and *Loch na Nuagh*. About 3 M. farther on is *Arisaig Pier*, where the steamers from *Oban* to *Skye* call several times weekly.

As the canal-steamer leaves Banavie we have a good view, to the right, of Ben Nevis. After 8 M. we reach the first lock and enter the picturesque *Loch Lochy* (10 M.), which is almost immediately succeeded by the charming little **Loch Oich* (5 M.). To the left is the romantic *Invergarry Castle*, from which a fine route leads through *Glen Shiel* to the W. coast (to *Balmacara*, on *Loch Alsh*, called at by the Oban and Gairloch steamers, 50 M.; thence to *Kyle Akin Ferry*, for *Skye*, 4 M.; comp. p. 506). Between the lower end of Loch Oich and (5 M.) **Fort Augustus** *(Lovat Arms)* are several locks, which the steamer takes 1½ hr. to pass through, so that this part of the journey may be performed on foot. The fort has now given place to a modern *Benedictine Abbey*, in the E.E. style (adm. 1*s.*; fine view from the tower). Most of the locks are within 2 M. of Fort Augustus; and those who do not care to walk the whole 5 M. may disembark near Fort Augustus and visit the abbey while the steamer passes the locks.

Fort Augustus lies at the S. end of **Loch Ness** (24 M. long), the scenery of which is less varied than that of the lochs already passed. *Invermoristown* is another starting-point for the rout through *Glen Shiel*, uniting with the above-mentioned at (25 M.) *Clunie*. On the right bank, ¾ hr. from Fort Augustus, is *Foyers* (Hotel), where the steamer stops for ¾ hr. to allow a hurried visit to the ***Fall of Foyers**, 90 ft. in height, which is probably the finest waterfall in Great Britain (pier-toll 4*d.*; seat in a carr. to and from the fall 1*s.*). Higher up is another fall (30 ft. high), which the steamboat-passenger has not time to visit. Opposite Foyers rises *Mealvourvonie* (2285 ft.). — The steamer halts at *Muirtown*, 1¼ M. from Inverness, and is met by the hotel-omnibuses.

Inverness. — Hotels. *CALEDONIAN HOTEL, R. & A. from 4*s.*, D. 4*s.* 6*d.*; STATION (R. & A. 4*s.* 6*d.*), ROYAL, IMPERIAL, all close to the railway-station; VICTORIA, pleasantly situated on the river, R. & A. 3*s.* 6*d.*, D. 3*s.* 6*d.*; WAVERLEY TEMPERANCE; MUIRTOWN HOTEL, at the pier, see above.

Inverness, the 'Capital of the Highlands', an old town with 17,400 inhab., situated at the point where the *Ness* enters the *Beauly Firth*, is the great travellers' centre for the N. of Scotland, as Oban is for the W. coast. The chief points of interest are included in the following walk. Starting from the station, we pass through Union St. and Church St. to the (3 min.) *Town Hall*, a modern Gothic building, in front of which, under the fountain, is the *Clach-na-Cudden*, or 'stone of the tubs', regarded as the palladium of Inverness. We thence ascend to the (3 min.) *County Buildings and Prison*, a castellated building on a hill, on which stood the castle of Macbeth, supposed by some to have been the scene of King Duncan's murder (comp. pp. 494, 499). We leave the castle enclosure at the W. end, descend to the river, and walk along the bank to (25 min.) the *Islands*, a favourite promenade, resembling the Margaretheninsel at Buda-Pesth, and connected with both banks by bridges. We now cross to the left bank and return towards Inverness, passing (10 min.) the *Northern Infirmary* and (5 min.) the ***Cathedral of St. Andrew**, a handsome Dec. building, erected in 1866-69; the interior is adorned with monolithic granite columns and stained glass. We may here diverge to the left, soon again turning to the left, and visit (1/4 hr.) *Tomnahurich* ('hill of the fairies'), a hill laid out as a cemetery, and commanding a fine view of the 'rose-red' town of Inverness. From the cathedral we return, across the *Suspension Bridge*, to the (5 min.) station. Another walk may be taken in the opposite direction to *Cromwell's Fort*, built by Cromwell in 1652-7, near the mouth of the Ness, and affording a view of the Beauly and Moray Firths.

Excursions from Inverness.

To *Craig Phadrig*, a hill 2½ M. to the W., commanding a fine view (more extensive than from Tomnahurich), and with traces of a vitrified fort. — To *Culloden Moor*, 5 M. to the S.E. (one-horse carr. there and back 8-10*s.*), where Prince Charles Stuart, the Pretender, was defeated on 16th April, 1746. — The ***Fall of Foyers*** (p. 493) may also be visited by carriage from Inverness (18 M.; picturesque road; carr. and pair there and back ca. 30*s.*). — To ***Beauly*** and the ***Falls of Kilmorack***, see below.

To Loch Maree and Gairloch, 77 M., in 7 hrs. (fares 1st cl. 16*s.* 9*d.*, 3rd cl. 13*s.*). From Inverness viâ ***Dingwall*** to (47 M.) ***Achnasheen***, see p. 506. At Achnasheen we change from the railway (which goes to ***Strome Ferry*** on the W. coast, see below) to the coach. — The road to Loch Maree skirts the small *Loch Rosque* and traverses moorlands. 10 M. (1½ hr.'s drive) *Kinlochewe* (*Hotel), 2 M. from the S.E. extremity of the loch. A mail-cart plies from Kinlochewe to (12 M.) *Loch Torridon* (fare 3*s.*). ***Loch Maree** is a wild and romantic lake, 18 M. long, surrounded by lofty mountains. To the N. rises *Ben Slioch* (3216 ft.). A small steamer now plies on the loch, and travellers may leave the coach at *Rhu Nohar* and proceed by water to the other end. About halfway down the S. side of the loch is the (9 M.; 1½ hr.) **Loch Maree Hotel* (boats for hire). Another coach is in waiting at *Tollie*, at the W. end of the loch, and takes us to (5½ M.) *Gairloch* (Hotel), on the W. coast. — The excursion to Loch Maree may be made part of either of the following pleasant tours (2-3 days) from Inverness: 1. Train to ***Strome Ferry*** (p. 506) in 4 hrs.; steamer viâ Broadford, Plockton, and Raasay to (4 hrs.) ***Portree*** in Skye and back to (2 hrs.) ***Gairloch*** on the mainland; coach and steamer on Loch Maree to (4½ hrs.) ***Achnasheen;*** train to (2½ hrs.) Inverness (or in reverse direction). 2. By rail to Strome Ferry in 4 hrs.; steamer to ***Stornoway***, in the ***Isle of Lewis***, and thence to ***Ullapool*** (p. 509), on the W. coast, about 20 M. to the N. of Loch Maree; thence by coach to (33 M.) ***Garve*** (p. 506), on the railway. — **Stornoway** *(Imperial; Lews; Royal)*, the chief place in the ***Hebrides***, with about 3000 inhab., is, perhaps, scarcely so fascinating in reality as in the pages of William Black, but is worth visiting by those who enjoy steamboat-sailing and wild rocky scenery. It may also be reached by steamer from *Glasgow* (40 hrs.), ***Oban***, ***Portree***, ***Gairloch***, ***Poolewe***, ***Loch Inver***, etc.

From Inverness to Glasgow or Edinburgh, railway viâ Perth, in 7-12 hrs. (fares to Glasgow 34*s.* 6*d.*, 17*s.* 2½*d.*; to Edinburgh 33*s.* 6*d.*, 15*s.* 10½*d.*). The most picturesque part of the Highland Railway is described at pp. 500-502. From Perth to ***Edinburgh*** or ***Glasgow***, see RR. 68b, 69.

From Inverness to Aberdeen, 109 M., railway in 5 hrs. (fares 18*s.* 1*d.*, 9*s.* 1*d.*). After the coast is quitted, the scenery on this line is comparatively uninteresting. — On leaving Inverness a fine view is obtained, to the left, of the Moray Firth. 3 M. ***Culloden***, to the S. of which lies ***Culloden Moor*** (see above). — 15 M. **Nairn** *(*Marine*, large, facing the sea; ***Anderson's***), finely situated on the Moray Firth, much frequented as a sea-bathing resort, and for its dry, mild climate. — From Nairn a drive may be taken to (6 M.) *Cawdor Castle*, the supposed scene of the murder of Duncan in Macbeth. The Castle, however, dates only from the middle of the 15th century. — 25 M. **Forres** (*Royal Station; Charleson's*, in the town; *Cluny Hill Hydropathic*, finely situated on a hill 1 M. from the station), the junction of the Highland railway to *Grantown* (a favourite inland watering-place), *Kingussie*, *Blair Athole*, and *Perth* (comp. p. 502). — About 1 M. to the N.E. is *Sweno's Stone*, a pillar about 20 ft. high, supposed to have been erected about 1014 to commemorate the expulsion of the Danes, and covered with carvings of figures and other objects. A drive may be taken to **Findhorn Glen*. — About 3 M. beyond Forres we pass on the left the ruins of *Kinloss Abbey*, founded in 1150. From (32 M.) *Alves* a branch-line diverges to *Burghead*. — 37 M. **Elgin** (*Station Hotel*; *Gordon Arms*), a town of 9843 inhab., with a fine **Cathedral*, chiefly in the E.E. style, founded in 1224 and rebuilt after a fire in 1390. It is very richly decorated (exquisite tracery), but is to a great extent in ruins. The best-preserved parts are the chapter-house and the two W. towers. The central tower, 200 ft. high, fell in 1711. The ruins of the bishop's palace and the Grey-friars' Monastery are also interesting. An excursion may be made to (6 M.) *Pluscarden Abbey*, a Cistercian foundation of 1230. Elgin is the junction of railways to *Lossiemouth* and *Buckie* on the coast, and to *Rothes* and *Boat of Garten* (on the Highland Railway; p. 502). — 55 M. *Keith* (Gordon Arms), the junction of the Highland and North of Scotland Railways. 67 M. *Huntly;* 87 M. *Inveramsay Junction*, for *Turriff* and *Banff* (Fife Arms); 92 M. *Inverurie;* 102 M. *Dyce Junction*, for (2 hrs.) Peterhead and Fraserburgh.

[**Peterhead** (*Royal*), a town with 11,000 inhab., is an important port for the herring-fishery and possesses quarries of red granite. It was the birthplace of *Marshal Keith* (d. 1758), of whom a statue, presented by King William I. of Prussia in 1868, stands in front of the town-hall. — *Fraserburgh* is also an important fishing-station.]

109 M. *Aberdeen*, see p. 504.

68. From Edinburgh to Aberdeen by the Direct Railway Routes.

a. North British Railway, viâ the Forth Bridge.

131 M. Railway in 3½-4 hrs. (fares 21*s.*, 9*s.* 8*d.*). This is the shortest and most direct route from Edinburgh to Aberdeen. Comp., however, the remark at the head of R. 69.

Edinburgh (Waverley Station), see p. 464. 1⅓ M. *Haymarket*. The new Forth Bridge line diverges to the right from the line to Glasgow (R. 65) near (3½ M.) *Corstorphine*. — 9½ M. *Forth Bridge Station*, where the Glasgow trains join ours (see p. 475), is the station for *South Queensferry* (p. 475).

The train now crosses the ***Forth Bridge**, pronounced by M. Eiffel 'the greatest construction of the world' and undoubtedly the most striking feat yet achieved by engineering in bridge-building. Fine views up and down the river.

This wonderful bridge, the total length of which, including the approaches, is 2765 yds., was begun in 1883 and finished in March, 1890, at a cost of 2,500,000*l*. It is built on the 'cantilever and central girder system', the principle of which is that of 'stable equilibrium', its own weight helping to maintain it more firmly in position. Each of the main spans, 1700-1710 ft. in length (100 ft. longer than that of Brooklyn Bridge), is formed of two cantilevers, each 680 ft. long, united by a girder 350 ft.

long. The steel towers from which the cantilevers spring are 360 ft. high (not much lower than the dome of St. Paul's) and are supported on granite piers, that in the middle resting on the small island of *Inchgarvie*. The clear headway at high water is 151 ft.; the deepest foundations are 88 ft. below high water. The total weight of metal in the bridge is 50,000 tons, or five times as much as that of the Britannia Bridge (p. 288). The designers and constructors of the bridge were *Sir John Fowler* and *Sir Benjamin Baker*.

13¼ M. *Inverkeithing* (Hotel), at the N. end of the Forth Bridge, is the station for *North Queensferry* and the junction of lines to the N. to *Dunfermline* (for Perth, Stirling, etc.; see R. 69) and to the E. to *Burntisland*, *Kirkcaldy*, etc. The Aberdeen train follows the latter line, which skirts the N. bank of the estuary of the Forth. — 18 M. *Aberdour* (Greig's), a favourite little sea-bathing place, with an old castle and the ruins of a Norman church. Adjacent are the pleasant grounds of *Donibristle*, seat of the Earl of Moray. A boating-excursion may be made to the islet of *Inchcolm*. In summer steamers ply from Aberdour to *Leith* (p. 465). A pretty wooded walk leads hence along the shore to (3 M.) Burntisland (see below).

21 M. **Burntisland** *(Forth Hotel)*, a small seaport and watering-place, is connected with (5 M.) *Granton* (p. 474; frequent trains to the Waverley Station at Edinburgh, 4½ M.) by a steam-ferry (fares 10*d.*, 5*d.*), but has lost some of its importance since the main traffic of the N.B.R. with the North has been diverted to the Forth Bridge route. In the firth, about halfway to Granton (to the left), lies the fortified island of *Inchkeith*. — 23½ M. *Kinghorn*. — 26½ M. **Kirkcaldy** *(George)*, a straggling town of 24,000 inhab., extending along the shore for 2 M., with a school in which Thomas Carlyle and Edward Irving were once teachers. — Near (29 M.) *Dysart* the line turns to the N. and quits the Firth of Forth. — At (32 M.) *Thornton Junction* we cross the railway extending on the W. to *Dunfermline* and *Stirling* (comp. pp. 500, 484) and on the E. to *St. Andrews* (see below). — 35 M. *Markinch* is the junction of a line to *Leslie*. At the village of *Falkland* (Bruce Arms), 3 M. to the W. of (37½ M.) *Falkland Road*, is an old royal *Palace* (16th cent.), now used as a private dwelling-house. At (40½ M.) *Ladybank* lines diverge to *Perth* (p. 498) and *Kinross* (p. 500). — 46 M. **Cupar** *(Royal; Tontine)*, the county-town of Fifeshire, with 5000 inhabitants. — 52 M. *Leuchars* is the junction of a short line to (4½ M.) *St. Andrews*.

St. Andrews *(Royal; Cross Keys; Marine)*, an ancient town with 6500 inhab., long the ecclesiastical metropolis of Scotland, is the seat of one of the four Scottish universities (founded 1411), and is perhaps the most fashionable watering-place in the country. It is the 'Metropolis of Golf', and the chief Golf Meetings, in May and October, attract large gatherings of visitors. It is one of the most ancient towns of Scotland, and the see of St. Andrews dates back to the 8th century. Patrick Hamilton, one of the first (1527), and Walter Mill (1558), the last Scottish martyr of the Reformation, both suffered at St. Andrews. George Wishart was also burned here in 1545, and his execution led to the speedy death of the Archbishop, Cardinal Beaton, who was assassinated in his palace in 1546 by several of Wishart's friends. The ruins of the **Cathedral*, built between 1159 and 1318, show that it must have been a very fine and extensive edifice. Adjacent is the square *Tower of St. Regulus* (108 ft.; view) erected about 1130, but assigned by popular tradition to a Pictish monarch of the 4th cent., and said to have been built in honour of St. Regulus, a Greek saint, shipwrecked here with the bones of St. Andrew, who henceforth became the patron-saint of Scotland. It may, however, occupy the site of an original Culdee cell. Near the W. end of the Cathedral is the beautiful arcade known as the *Pends*. On a rock rising above the sea is the old *Castle* of the bishops. Opposite *Madras College*, a large school attended by about 900 boys, is a beautiful little fragment of a Dominican priory of the 13th century. The *University of St. Andrews* consists of the College of St. Mary (theological) and the United Colleges of SS. Salvator and Leonard. A visit should be paid to the fine *Golf Links*, alive during the season with hundreds of votaries of the Scottish national pastime. — Beyond St. Andrews the line goes on along the coast to *Crail*, *Anstruther*, *Elie*, *Largo*, *Leven* (all sea-bathing and golfing resorts), and *Thornton Junction* (see p. 496).

Leuchars is also the junction of a line to *Tayport*, opposite Broughty Ferry (see below).

The train now crosses the *Tay* by the substantial new *Tay Bridge*, 2 M. long, opened in 1887 and replacing an older railway bridge, which was swept away by a hurricane on 28th Dec., 1879, precipitating a passenger train into the river. We then enter the *Tay Bridge Station* at —

61 M. **Dundee** *(Queen's; Royal; Royal British; Lamb's Temperance)*, the third town of Scotland in size, with 145,000 inhab., a busy commercial and manufacturing place (linen, jute, etc.), but possessing little interest for the tourist. The **Old Steeple* (156 ft. high), in the Nethergate, dates from the 14th century, and is one of the finest church-towers in Scotland (adm. 2*d.*; view). Adjacent is the *Town Cross* (1586). The *Albert Institute*, with a museum and picture-gallery, is a modern Gothic edifice by Sir G.G. Scott. The *University College* was established in 1883, chiefly with Miss Baxter's bequest of 140,000*l.* The *Royal Infirmary* is an extensive building. Good views are obtained from the *Esplanade*, skirting the Tay, from the *Baxter Park*, and from *Dundee Law* (570 ft.) — From Dundee to *Perth*, see p. 499.

The train now turns to the E. and skirts the N. bank of the Tay estuary. 65 M. *Broughty Ferry*, a favourite residence of the citizens of Dundee, at the mouth of the Tay; 67 M. *Monifieth;* 71$^1/_2$ M. *Carnoustie*, a watering-place, with golf-links. The line skirts the coast, with views of the sea. — 78 M. **Arbroath** *(White Hart; George)*, an industrial town and seaport, with 22,000 inhab., possesses an interesting ruined **Abbey*, founded by William the Lion in 1178. The remains are mainly E.E. About 10 M. off the coast is the *Inchcape* or *Bell Rock Lighthouse.* — 92$^1/_2$ M. **Montrose** *(Star; Queen's)*, a clean little seaport at the mouth of the *South Esk*, with 14,800 inhabitants. Montrose is said to have been the birthplace of the Marquis of Montrose (in 1612), and it was the first place in Scotland where Greek was taught. A branch runs hence to the N. to (12 M.) *Bervie*.

At ($94\frac{1}{2}$ M.) *Hillside* our line unites with the Caledonian Railway (see below). Stations *Laurencekirk* and *Fordoun*. — 117 M. **Stonehaven** *(Royal; Urie)*, the county-town of Kincardine, visited for bathing (4000 inhab.). A little to the S. (to the left of the railway), perched upon a rock overhanging the sea, are the picturesque ruins of **Dunnottar Castle*, built in the 13th cent. and afterwards possessed by the Keiths, Earls Marischal of Scotland.

131 M. *Aberdeen*, see p. 504.

b. Caledonian Railway.

158 M. Railway in 5-6 hrs. (fares as above). Comp. p. 500.

From *Edinburgh* (Waverley) to (36 M.) *Stirling* and (40 M.) *Dunblane*, see R. 66. Here the line to *Callander* and *Oban* (comp. pp. 484, 489) diverges to the left, while the Perth line runs to the right (N.). 50 M. *Greenloaning*. — From ($57\frac{1}{2}$M.) *Crieff Junction* a short branch diverges to (9 M.) *Crieff*.

Crieff *(Royal Hotel; Drummond Arms; *Hydropathic)*, a town with 4500 inhab., situated on a hill in the midst of a finely-wooded district, is a good centre for excursions. In the neighbourhood are several well-preserved old castles: *Drummond Castle* (3 M. to the S.), the seat of Baron Willoughby de Eresby; *Ochtertyre*, $2\frac{1}{2}$ M. to the N.W.; *Monzie* (pron. *Monee*), 3 M. to the N.; etc. — A four-in-hand coach is in waiting at Crieff station to take passengers on to Lochearnhead (22 M., in 4 hrs.), a delightful drive. The road leads through a well-wooded country, past (7 M.) *Comrie* (Royal), noted for slight earthquakes, to (6 M.) *St. Fillans* (*Hotel), a lovely little village at the E. end of *Loch Earn*. From St. Fillans the road skirts the N. bank of the Loch all the way to (7 M.) *Lochearnhead Station* (p. 492). To the left rises *Ben Voirlich* (3224 ft.). The excursion may be prolonged to *Killin* and *Loch Tay* (comp. p. 501).

68 M. **Perth.** — **Hotels.** Royal George, on the Tay, $\frac{3}{4}$ M. from the station; Perth Station Hotel, new; Pople's British Hotel, at the station, R. & A. from 4*s*., D. 3*s*. 6*d*.; Queen's, also at the station, unpretending; McMaster's Temperance, St. John's St.; Salutation, in the town. — *Rail. Refreshmt. Rooms.*

Perth, picturesquely situated on the *Tay*, with 30,000 inhab., is an ancient town, claiming to be of Roman origin, and long the capital of the Scottish kings (comp. p. 466). Few traces of its antiquity are, however, left, as the 'rascal multitude' (as Knox called the Perth mob at the Reformation) and the municipal authorities then and later made a clean sweep of all the old religious houses. The principal church is *St. John's*, mainly of the Dec. period, with an earlier tower; in front of the high-altar Edward III. of England is said to have stabbed his brother, the Duke of Cornwall, in 1336. John Knox often preached here (ca. 1559). The *County Buildings* occupy the site of the house in which the Gowrie Conspiracy against James VI. was formed (1600). On the N. side of the town stood the *Dominican Convent*, where James I. was assassinated in 1436, in spite of the heroic action of Catherine Douglas, who made her arm do duty for the missing bar on the door. (This incident is finely described in Rossetti's ballad, the 'King's Tragedy'.) Adjoining the river are two open spaces of green sward, known as the *North* and *South Inch* (*i.e.* island). The former, which is the larger of the two, was the scene of the judicial combat between the Clan Chattan and the Clan Quhele, described by Scott in the 'Fair Maid of Perth'. The 'Fair's Maid House' (so called) is shown in Curfew Row, near the North Inch. Good view from the bridge over the Tay.

Those who have an hour or two to spare at Perth should ascend ***Kinnoul Hill** (730 ft.), which lies on the left bank of the Tay, and may be ascended from the railway-station in 3/4 hr. The *View is charming. — Another good view is afforded by *Moncrieff Hill* (725 ft.), 3½ M. to the S.E. — An excursion may also be made to (2½ M.) *Scone Palace* (special permission necessary), a modern mansion on the site of the Augustine abbey in which the early Scottish kings were crowned.

From Perth to Dundee, 20 M., railway in ½-1 hr. (fares 3*s*. 6*d*., 2*s*. 6*d*., 1*s*. 8*d*.). This line skirts the N. bank of the *Firth of Tay* and traverses the fertile *Carse of Gowrie*. To the left are *Dunsinane* and the other *Sidlaw Hills*. — *Dundee*, see p. 497.

Beyond Perth our line runs to the N. to (72 M.) *Luncarty* and (75 M.) *Stanley Junction*, where it diverges to the E. (right) from the Highland Railway (see p. 500). — 80½ M. *Coupar Angus* (Royal) is the junction of the line to *Blairgowrie* (p. 503). — About 5 M. to the N. of (85 M.) *Alyth Junction* is the small town of *Alyth* (Airlie Arms), whence a road ascends the rocky and wooded valley of the *Isla* to (11 M.) *Glenisla*. The Isla forms several small waterfalls, the finest of which is the *Reekie Linn*. Near *Forter Castle*, 4 M. to the N. of Glenisla, a road leads to the W. to *Glenshee* (p. 503). — At (92 M.) *Glamis* stands **Glamis Castle* (open on Frid.), a stately baronial hall in a fine park, said by tradition to be the ancestral home of Macbeth. The room in which the thane is said to have murdered Duncan in 1040 is still pointed out! It seems probable that Malcolm II. was really murdered here in 1033. The present mansion, with its numerous towers and turrets, dates mainly from 1578-1621. — 96½ M. **Forfar** *(County Arms; Royal)*, an ancient town with 13,000 inhab., once the seat of the Scottish kings, is the junction of a branch to *Broughty Ferry* (p. 497). — 105 M. *Guthrie Junction* is the starting-point of a line to (8 M.) *Arbroath* (p. 497). — From (112½ M.) *Bridge-of-Dun* a short branch diverges to (4 M.) **Brechin** *(Commercial; Crown)*, a town of 10,500 inhab., with an ancient *Cathedral*, founded by David I. about 1150, but utterly spoiled by restoration in 1807. Adjacent is an interesting *Round Tower* (100 ft. high), dating from the 11th cent., or perhaps earlier. Not far off is *Brechin Castle*, the seat of the Earl of Dalhousie, a modern mansion on the site of an old castle.

A pleasant excursion may be taken from Brechin through the valley of the *North Esk*. At *Edzell* (Inns), 6½ M. from Brechin, are the interesting ruins of a large *Castle*, belonging to the Earl of Dalhousie.

115 M. *Dubton* is the junction of a short line to *Montrose*. From (116½ M.) *Hillside*, where we join the N.B.R., to (155 M.) *Aberdeen*, see p. 504.

69. From Edinburgh to Aberdeen viâ Perth and Blair Athole.

To this excursion, the finest route to Aberdeen, 5-6 days should be devoted. 1st Day. Railway from Edinburgh to *Perth* (1$^1/_3$-3$^1/_3$ hrs.; fares 9*s.* 6*d.*, 3*s.* 10$^1/_2$*d.*); and thence by an evening train, in $^3/_4$ hr., to *Dunkeld.* — 2nd Day. Railway from Dunkeld to *Blair Athole* in 1 hr. — 3rd Day. From Blair Athole to *Braemar*, a walk of 9-10 hrs. (pony and guide about 30*s.*); two-thirds of the way may be driven. — 4th Day. From Braemar by coach, in 2$^1/_2$ hrs., to *Ballater;* and thence by railway, in 1$^3/_4$-2$^1/_4$ hrs., to *Aberdeen.* — Direct railway-route, see R. 68. — Steamer from Leith to Aberdeen (see p. 465), 7-8 hrs.

The Caledonian route to (68 M.) *Perth* has been given in R. 68; the following is a description of the new direct route of the N. B. R. viâ the Forth Bridge.

From *Edinburgh* (Waverley) to (13$^1/_4$ M.) *Inverkeithing*, the junction for the Dundee line, see R. 68. The Perth line runs to the N. and soon enters the *Lower Station* of (16$^3/_4$ M.) **Dunfermline** *(City Arms)*, a linen-manufacturing town with 17,000 inhab., of interest to tourists for its ***Abbey**, founded by Queen Margaret and Malcolm Canmore towards the end of the 11th century. Of their building nothing now remains; but the nave of the second church on this site, a fine Norman edifice of 1150, still exists in conjunction with a barbarous modern structure of 1870. Robert Bruce, whose grave is marked by a monumental brass erected in 1888, and other Scottish monarchs are buried here. The remains of *Dunfermline Palace* are scanty. — From Dunfermline (Upper Station) a line runs to (23 M.) *Stirling* (p. 484).

19 M. *Halbeath;* 20$^1/_2$ M. *Crossgates;* 21$^1/_2$ M. *Cowdenbeath*, the junction of a line to *Thornton Junction* (for St. Andrews, Dundee, etc.; see p. 497); 24$^1/_2$ M. *Kelty;* 26$^3/_4$ M. *Blairadam.* To the right lies *Loch Leven* (p. 492). 29$^1/_2$ M. *Loch Leven Station.* — 30$^1/_2$ M. *Kinross*, the junction of a line to *Alloa* (see p. 485). — At (34 M.) *Mawcarse* the new direct line diverges to the left from the old line to *Ladybank* (p. 496) and enters the romantic vale of **Glenfarg*, the engineering difficulties of which have necessitated two long tunnels, 22 bridges, and numerous cuttings. 37$^1/_2$ M. *Damhead.* At (44 M.) *Glenfarg Junction (Bridge of Earn)* our line unites with the old line from Ladybank.

47$^3/_4$ M. **Perth,** see p. 498.

Beyond Perth we continue our journey by the Highland Railway, one of the most beautiful lines in the three kingdoms. — 4 M. (from Perth) *Luncarty* (p. 499); 7 M. *Stanley Junction*, for the line to *Forfar* and *Aberdeen* (p. 504); 10$^1/_2$ M. *Murthly.* The train now skirts the base of *Birnam Hill* (1325 ft.; to the left), the woods of which marched to *Dunsinane* (p. 501), to the discomfiture of Macbeth.

16 M. **Dunkeld** (**Birnam*, finely situated at the station; *Athole Arms*, **Royal*, in the town; *Perth Arms*, unpretending), a small 'city' with 750 inhab., charmingly situated on the left bank of

the Tay, 1/2 M. from the station. The finest points in the neighbourhood are in the **Park of the Duke of Athole*, which we reach by crossing the bridge and going straight through the town; about 50 yds. beyond the end of the town, to the left, is the entrance to the park. Here we are met by a guide (adm. for 1 pers. 2*s*., 2 pers. 2*s*. 6*d*., each member of a party 1*s*.), who conducts us to the cathedral, the hermitage, and other points of interest (a walk of 1 1/2-2 hrs.).

The ***Cathedral**, charmingly situated on a grassy lawn, dates mainly from 1318-1477. The choir has been restored and is used as the parish-church of Dunkeld. Near the main door is the tombstone of the 'Wolf of Badenoch'. Gavin Douglas (d. 1522), translator of Virgil, was Bishop of Dunkeld. Close to the W. end of the cathedral are some of the oldest larches in Scotland. We then walk through the pretty grounds, skirting the Tay, to the ferry. Here we cross the river and ascend to the *Falls of the Braan* and the so-called *Hermitage*, whence we return to (3/4 hr.) Dunkeld along the opposite bank of the Braan. This is the ordinary round, but for a small additional fee the guide will conduct the party up the left bank of the Braan to the **Rumbling Bridge* (1/2 hr. from the Hermitage), in the park of Sir Douglas Stuart, with a romantic waterfall in a narrow gorge; then along the right bank of the Braan to Dunkeld (1 hr.).

Birnam Hill (see p. 500), which may be ascended from the station in 3/4 hr., commands a beautiful view. Two splendid trees (an oak and a sycamore), close to the river, behind the Birnam Hotel, are held to represent 'Birnam Wood which came to Dunsinane'. Other walks may be taken to *Craig-y-Barns*, the (3 M.) *Loch of the Lowes*, etc.

From Dunkeld to Aberfeldy (viâ Ballinluig, see below), 17 M., railway in 1 hr. (fares 2*s*. 10*d*., 2*s*. 1*d*., 1*s*. 5*d*.). Near **Aberfeldy** (*Breadalbane Arms*; *Weem Hotel*, on the other bank of the Tay, 1 M. from the station), a village at the junction of the *Moness* and the Tay, are the romantic *Falls of Moness* (adm. 6*d*.), in a pretty little glen, clothed with the rowans and larches that have displaced the 'Birks (birches) of Aberfeldy'.

From Aberfeldy to Loch Tay and Callander, a delightful and easily accomplished excursion. Coach in summer twice daily to *Killin Pier* (see below) in 3 1/2 hrs., and railway thence to *Callander* in 3/4-1 hr. Or we may ascend Loch Tay by steamer (from Kenmore to Killin). This excursion may be combined with R. 65, as follows (circular tickets): 1st Day. From Edinburgh by early train to *Dunkeld* (allowing 4-5 hrs. here), thence on to *Aberfeldy*, and by coach or carriage (6*s*. 6*d*.) to *Kenmore*. 2nd Day. To Killin, Callander, and (in the evening) the Trossachs. 3rd Day. Back to Edinburgh viâ Loch Katrine and Loch Lomond. — From Aberfeldy the coach runs through the picturesque valley of the *Tay* to (5 M.) *Kenmore* (*Breadalbane Hotel), situated at the point where the river flows out of ***Loch Tay** (15 M. long, 1/2-1 M. wide), one of the finest of the Highland lakes. Adjacent is *Taymouth Castle*, the seat of the Earl of Breadalbane, surrounded by finely wooded grounds, which are open to the public (10-4). Two good roads lead from Kenmore to Killin, the one (16 M.) along the N.W., the other (18 M.), passing near the (2 M.) *Falls of Acharn*, along the S.E. shore of Loch Tay. The coach follows the former, turning to the right at the hotel and crossing the river (fine view from the bridge). Further on we skirt the base of *Ben Lawers* (3985 ft.; Temperance Hotel, at the foot of the mountain), enjoying fine views of the loch. Towards the middle of the latter, the scenery becomes more monotonous and the verdure scanty, improving again as we near Killin. At *Killin Pier* (*Lochay Hotel; *Macpherson's Hotel) we reach the railway, which crosses the Lochay (*View; pretty falls higher up) and leads to (1 M.) the pretty village of Killin (*Killin Hotel*), situated on both banks of the *Dochart*, near its entrance into Loch Tay. Thence the line runs to (4 1/2 M.) *Killin Junction*, where we reach the railway to *Callander* (p. 484) and *Oban* (p. 489). In front towers *Ben More* (3845 ft.).

Continuing to follow the Highland Railway from Dunkeld, we

soon reach (24 M.) *Ballinluig*, the junction of the line to *Aberfeldy* (see above). — 28½ M. **Pitlochry** (*Fisher's Hotel*; *Scotland's*, small; **Hydropathic*), a favourite summer-resort, in the midst of pretty scenery. To the right rises *Ben Vrackie* (2755 ft.).

About 1½ M. to the W. are the romantic **Falls of the Tummel*, whence we may continue the walk to (5 M.) **Loch Tummel* (3 M. long). The finely-shaped mountain to the S.W. of this lake is *Schiehallion* (3545 ft.). The road ascending the Tummel, which flows through the loch of that name, goes on to (13 M.) *Kinloch Rannoch* (Bun Rannoch; Macdonald Arms), at the E. end of *Loch Rannoch*, which is 11 M. long. A post-gig (three seats) runs daily from Pitlochry to *Tummel Bridge Inn*, 7 M. from Kinloch Rannoch. — Another charming spot near Pitlochry is (3 M.) *Garry Bridge*, at the entrance to the Pass of Killiecrankie (see below) and near the confluence of the Tummel and the Garry. — A good walk may be taken from Pitlochry over the hills to (11 M.) *Aberfeldy* (see p. 501). — A pleasant excursion (27-30 M.), practicable for driving, may be made from Pitlochry to *Kenmore* (see p. 501), viâ *Loch Tummel* (see above).

Beyond Pitlochry the train passes through the wooded ***Pass of Killiecrankie**, where the troops of William III. were defeated in 1689 by the Jacobites under Viscount Dundee. The spot on which Dundee (Claverhouse) fell is still pointed out. — 33 M. *Killiecrankie*.

36 M. **Blair Athole** (**Athole Arms*; *Glen Tilt*, smaller), in a finely wooded district, with *Blair Castle*, the principal seat of the Duke of Athole. In the **Park* (adm. 1*s.*) are the *Falls of the Fender* (1¼ M. to the E.). To the W. are the **Falls of the Bruar*, to reach which we follow the road from the station to the W. for about 3 M. and then diverge to the right. — At Blair Athole we leave the Highland Railway, which runs hence to the N., viâ *Kingussie*, *Aviemore*, *Boat of Garten*, and *Grantown* (a favourite inland health-resort), to (168 M. from Edinburgh) *Forres* (p. 495).

Those who wish to avoid the somewhat fatiguing route through Glen Tilt (described below) may drive from Dunkeld to Braemar by a good road (47 M.; coach in 6½-7 hrs.) viâ *Blairgowrie* and *Glenshee* (comp. p. 503). [The coaching distance may be reduced to 35 M. by going by railway from Perth to Blairgowrie, viâ *Coupar Angus*.] It is also possible to drive all the way from Pitlochry to Braemar, by a somewhat roundabout route (46 M.).

From Blair Athole to Braemar through Glen Tilt, 30 M. This route is usually accomplished on foot or on horseback (guide and pony 30*s.*), as the middle part of it (10 M.) is not available for carriages. It is, however, possible to drive or ride to (8 M.) *Forest Lodge*, walk thence to (10 M.) *Bynack Lodge*, and drive or ride the rest of the way (12 M.) by carriage or pony ordered from Braemar by telegram. Walkers should start early and take luncheon with them, as no inns are passed on the way. — The route follows the *Tilt* closely for the larger half of the way, passing through the wild **Glen Tilt**, which contains numerous red deer. To the right rises *Ben-y-Gloe* (3770 ft.), the 'mountain of the mist'. Several small waterfalls are passed. The road ceases at (8 M.) *Forest Lodge*, a shooting-box of the Duke of Athole, beyond which we follow a rough footpath. A little beyond the (5¼ M.) *Ford of Tarff*, now crossed by a bridge, we reach the highest point of the route (1550 ft.). At (4½ M.) *Bynack Lodge* (Earl of Fife) the road re-appears, and *Ben Muich-Dhui* (4296 ft.) comes into sight in front. In 2½ M. more we reach and cross the *Dee*, and we then follow its left bank to the (3 M.) **Linn of Dee*, where the river dashes through a narrow rocky 'gut'. We here again cross the Dee. About 1½ M. further on we reach a path on the right (with a placard announcing that no carriages are allowed this way), which leads to (1½ M.) the *Colonel's Bed*, a narrow ledge above a deep pool, which is said to have furnished shelter to one of those who were 'out in the 45'; the rapids a little farther up are also fine. [Those who make this digression have to return by the same way to the road.] About 2 M. beyond this path, to the left, at a bridge, is a rustic gate leading to the small but picturesque **Corriemulzie Falls* (close to the road). Nearly opposite this gate is the entrance to *Mar Lodge*, seat of the Duke of Fife. Then, 3 M. —

Braemar, or *Castleton of Braemar* (1100 ft.; *Fife Arms*, *Invercauld Arms*, both overcrowded in the season; *Lodgings*), a pleasant spot for a stay of a few days, romantically situated on the Dee and surrounded by lofty mountains. The environs are finely wooded. The air is bracing and exhilarating.

To the S.W. rises *Morrone Hill* (2819 ft.), easily ascended in 1 hr. and affording a good view of Braemar, Ben Muich-Dhui, etc. — To the **Falls of Garawalt*, 3-4 hrs. We follow the road to Ballater (see p. 504) for 3 M., and then turn to the right through a gate, on this side of Invercauld Bridge (sign-posts). Fine view from an iron bridge above the falls. — Perhaps the most interesting drive is to the (6½ M.) *Linn of Dee* (as above), visiting the Corriemulzie Falls and Colonel's Bed on the way, and returning along the N. bank of the Dee to (9 M.) *Invercauld Bridge* (in all 18-19 M.).

Ben Muich-Dhui (4296 ft.), the highest mountain in Scotland after Ben Nevis (p. 492), rises to the W. of Braemar, from which it may be ascended in 10 hrs., there and back (guide 10*s.*, pony 10*s.*). The road to it crosses the Dee, near Mar Lodge (see above), and leads to (10 M.) *Derry Lodge*, up to which point driving is practicable. This reduces the necessary walking or riding (up and down) to 5½-6 hrs. The pony-track from Derry Lodge is easily traced. The *View from the top is very extensive. Those who wish to descend to Aviemore (p. 502) should follow the ridge to the N. to the (1 hr.) top of **Cairngorm** (4084 ft.; view) and descend thence through *Rothiemurchus Forest* (guide or good map and compass desirable; also plenty of daylight). To the right (E.) of the ridge between Ben Muich-Dhui and Cairngorm lies the solitary and deep-blue *Loch A'an*, surrounded by rocky walls, 900-1500 ft. high.

Another favourite ascent from Braemar is that of ***Lochnagar** (3770 ft.), which lies to the S.E. (4-5 hrs.; guide 7*s.* 6*d.*, pony 7*s.* 6*d.*). The route leads through *Glen Callater*, and carriages can go as far as (5½ M.) *Loch Callater*, whence the path to the summit is fairly defined. Below the N. shoulder lies the small lake of *Lochnagar*. Byron spent part of his boyhood in the farmhouse of *Ballatrich*, 5½ M. from Ballater, and has sung the praises of Lochnagar in a well-known passage. — The descent may be made (clearly marked tracks) to *Ballater* or *Balmoral* (see p. 504).

From Braemar to Blairgowrie, 35 M., coach (8 a. m.) daily in 6 hrs., through *Glen Clunie* and the wild *Glenshee*. Halts are made at the (15 M.) *Spital of Glenshee Hotel* and the (11 M.) *Persie Inn*. The highest point of the road (2200 ft.) is near the Spital; best views in descending. Passengers for Perth may dine in *Blairgowrie* at the Royal Hotel (D. 3*s.*, ready on arrival of the coach) and go on by afternoon train. To *Dunkeld*, see p. 502.

From Braemar a well-appointed four-horse coach runs daily to ($17^1/_2$ M.) *Ballater*, a *Drive of $2^1/_2$ hrs. (fares 5*s*., 4*s*.). The coach passes *Invercauld House* on the left, and crosses (3 M.) **Invercauld Bridge*, the finest point on the road, which follows the *Dee* the whole way. 6 M. (to the right) **Balmoral Castle**, the Highland home of Queen Victoria (shown, by special order, in the absence of the Queen). The cairns which crown most of the hills here are memorials of friends of Her Majesty. To the left, $^3/_4$ M. beyond Balmoral, is *Crathie Church*, where the Queen often attends divine service. Then ($1^1/_2$ M.), to the right, *Abergeldie Castle*, a shooting-box of the Prince of Wales. — $6^1/_2$ M. **Ballater** (750 ft.; *Invercauld Arms*), a small summer-resort, pleasantly situated at the foot of the wooded *Craigendarroch* (1250 ft.), which is frequently ascended for the sake of the views ($^1/_2$ hr.).

From Ballater excursions may be made to *Morven* (2880 ft.), the (6 M.) *Linn of Muick*, (2 M.) *Pannanich Wells*, ($6^1/_2$ M.) *Burn of the Vat*, etc. It is also one of the recognised starting-points for an ascent of *Lochnagar* (see p. 503; 4-5 hrs.).

Ballater is the terminus of the Deeside Railway, which runs hence along the Dee to ($43^1/_2$ M.) *Aberdeen* ($1^1/_4$-2 hrs.; fares 7*s*. 3*d*., 3*s*. $7^1/_2$*d*.). The chief intermediate stations are (11 M.) *Aboyne* (Huntly Arms), with the seat of the Marquis of Huntly, and ($26^1/_2$ M.) *Banchory*. Beyond ($38^1/_2$ M.) *Murtle*, the large *Deeside Hydropathic* is seen to the right.

$43^1/_2$ M. **Aberdeen** (**Imperial*, *Palace*, near the station, R. & A. 4*s*. 6*d*., D. 5*s*.; *Forsyth's Temperance; Douglas*, Market St., 5 min. from the station; *Bath Temperance*, R., A., & B. 3*s*. 6*d*.), which may be called the capital of the N. of Scotland, is a handsome town, chiefly built of granite, situated on the Dee, $^1/_2$ M. from its mouth. Pop. (1881) 105,003.

Aberdeen is one of the oldest towns in Scotland, though the time of its foundation is obscure. The earliest known municipal charter, afterwards extended by Robert Bruce, was granted by William the Lion in 1178. Its characteristic industry is the production of polished granite monuments, columns, etc., in which about 60 firms are engaged. The art of granite-polishing, which had been lost (as far, at least, as this country is concerned) since the days of the Pharaohs, was revived here about 70 years ago by Mr. Alexander Macdonald (Macdonald, Field, & Co.), and has become the chief source of the town's prosperity. Upwards of 80,000 tons of granite are annually quarried in Aberdeenshire. The visitor should not quit Aberdeen without going over one of the highly interesting granite-works. Ship-building is also extensively carried on, and 'Aberdeen Clippers' have long been celebrated; while paper-making and carpet-weaving are other important industries. The trade of the town is very important, the chief article of export being the granite monuments mentioned above. It has a fine harbour and docks.

Union Street, the chief thoroughfare of Aberdeen, $^3/_4$ M. long and 70 ft. wide, built entirely of granite and one of the handsomest streets in Europe, has been described ('The Land We Live In') as possessing 'all the stability, cleanliness, and architectural beauties of the London West End streets, with the gaiety and brilliancy of the Parisian atmosphere'. It contains the *East* and *West*

Churches (with a tower in common), statues of the *Queen* and the late *Prince Albert*, and numerous elaborate granite façades; while at its S. end stands the fine *Municipal Offices*, the lofty tower (210 ft.) of which commands an extensive *View. To the N. of Union St., behind the *Music Hall*, rises the imposing spire (200 ft.) of the *Roman Catholic Church*, the most beautiful of the numerous church-steeples that form so conspicuous a feature in every view of Aberdeen.

A little to the N. of the Municipal Offices is *Marischal College*, part of the *University of Aberdeen*, one of the four Universities of Scotland (850 students). At No. 64 Broad St., near the College, is the house where Lord Byron lived with his mother in his boyhood.

The chief objects of interest are, however, in *Old Aberdeen* (omn. from Union St.), the seat of a bishopric founded by David I. in 1158, which lies 1 M. to the N., at the mouth of the *Don*. The *Cathedral of St. Machar*, dating from 1366-1522, is said to be the only granite cathedral in Christendom. It consists of the nave only of the original edifice, and is still in use as a parish-church. A little to the S. of the cathedral is **King's College*, the other member of Aberdeen University (comp. above), founded in 1494. The only remaining part of the old buildings is the *Chapel*, surmounted by a fine lantern-tower and containing some beautiful wood-carving. — About 1/2 M. from Old Aberdeen is the picturesque *Brig o' Balgownie*, or *Old Bridge of Don*, erected in 1320.

Mrs. Macdonald, widow of the late Mr. Alex. Macdonald, son of the founder of the granite industry (see p. 504), possesses a good collection of modern pictures, including a unique series of portraits of eminent modern artists, mostly painted by themselves.

The Great North of Scotland Railway has arranged several pleasant circular tours from Aberdeen, taking in Dundee, Perth, Dunkeld, Inverness, the Trossachs, etc.

70. From Inverness to Thurso and Wick.

Highland Railway to *Thurso*, 153 M., in 6-7 3/4 hrs. (fares 25*s*. 6*d*., 19*s*. 3*d*., 12*s*.); to *Wick*, 161 M., in 6-8 hrs. (fares 26*s*. 9*d*., 20*s*. 2*d*., 12*s*.); only two through-trains daily. The picturesque district opened up by this route offers many attractions to the angler and the pedestrian.

Inverness, see p. 493. — The train crosses the *Ness* and (1 M.) the *Caledonian Canal* (p. 492), and beyond *Craig Phadrig* (p. 494), on the left, comes in sight of the *Beauly Firth*, which it skirts for about 6 M.

On the opposite side of the firth is the **Black Isle**, the name given to the peninsula between the Firths of Beauly and Cromarty. The chief towns are *Fortrose* (874 inhab.), 10 1/2 M. to the N.E. of Inverness (steamer), once the episcopal town of Ross, with the ruins of a cathedral, and (8 M. to the N.E.) *Cromarty* (1360 inhab.) the county-town of Cromartyshire, with a safe and commodious bay. Hugh Miller (1802-1856) was a native of Cromarty.

Opposite (6 M.) *Lentran* rise *Redcastle*, dating from 1179, in the Black Isle, and (3 M. to the W.) *Tarradale*, birthplace of Sir Roderick Murchison (1792-1871). Beyond (7 M.) *Clunes* we cross the *Beauly* by a viaduct, from which there is a view, to the left, of Beaufort Castle (1885), the imposing seat of Lord Lovat, chief of the Frasers.

10 M. **Beauly** (pron. 'Bewley'; *Beauly; Lovat Arms; Caledonian*). The village, 1/2 M. to the right, contains a ruined *Priory* of 1230.

A pleasant walk or drive may be taken hence to the (3 M.) *Falls of Kilmorack* and (10 M.) *Struy*. Good walkers may go on thence through *Glen Affric* to (52 M. from Beauly; mail-cart daily to *Invercannich*, 17 M.) *Glen Shiel*, on the W. coast, one of the grandest walks in Scotland; or through *Glen Strathfarrar* to (35 M.) *Strathcarron* (see below); or through *Glen Cannich* to (40 M.) *Loch Alsh* (p. 493). Inns are few and far between on these routes. The *Falls of the Glomach*, the highest and wildest in Scotland, may be visited from the Shiel Inn (10 M.), or from *Balmacara Hotel* (p. 493) on Loch Alsh (16 M.).

13 M. *Muir of Ord* (Tarradale Inn), famous for its sheep and cattle markets. Beyond (16 M.) *Conon* we come in sight of the Cromarty Firth and cross the *Conon*.

18 1/2 M. **Dingwall** *(National; Caledonian)*, the quiet but prosperous-looking county-town of Ross, at the head of the Cromarty Firth. Pop. 1917.

A branch-line (fares 9*d.*, 7*d.*, 4 1/2*d.*) runs hence in 10 min. to (4 3/4 M.) **Strathpeffer** (200 ft.; *Ben Wyvis; Spa; Strathpeffer*), a much visited Spa, with sulphur and chalybeate springs, to which omnibuses also ply from Dingwall station. Numerous excursions in the picturesque neighbourhood. *Ben Wyvis* (3429 ft.; guide and pony 20*s.*) is easily ascended hence in 8 hrs. (there and back).

From Dingwall to Strome Ferry, 53 M., railway in 2 1/2-3 hrs. (fares 8*s.* 10*d.*, 6*s.* 8*d.*, 4*s.* 5*d.*). This picturesque line traverses Scotland from E. to W. From (12 1/2 M.) *Garve* (Inn) a coach runs to (33 M.) *Ullapool* (p. 509). To the left we pass *Loch Luichart*. At (28 M.) *Achnasheen* diverges the coach-road to Loch Maree (p. 434) and (29 M.) Gairloch (p. 494). From (46 M.) *Strathcarron* a road runs to (4 M.) *Lochcarron*, whence *Loch Torridon* may be visited. — 53 M. *Strome Ferry*, see p. 494.

Beyond Dingwall the railway skirts Cromarty Firth on the right, with a view of Ben Wyvis (see above) on the left. At (25 M.) *Novar* the misnamed *Aultgraat* ('Ugly Burn') descends through the **Black Rock of Kiltearn*, a curious deep and narrow gorge. — 31 1/2 M. *Invergordon* (Commercial), a thriving little shipping-port, with 1119 inhab., and a ferry to the Black Isle (p. 505). On the opposite side of the firth appears Cromarty (p. 505). 40 M. *Fearn* gave name to an abbacy founded in 1230, of which Patrick Hamilton (burned 1527), the first martyr of the Reformed faith in Scotland, was titular abbot. To the right lies the circular *Loch Eye*. A little farther on we obtain a fine view over the flat *Fendom More*, terminating in *Tarbat Ness* on the N., and over *Dornoch Firth*, behind which rise the Sutherland hills.

44 M. **Tain** *(Royal; Balnagown Arms)*, a quiet little town, with 2221 inhab., on Dornoch Firth, contains an ancient *Tower*, now forming part of the *County Buildings*, and the Gothic *Church of St. Duthac* or *Duthus*, erected in the 14th cent., and restored in 1871-76.

About 4 M. to the N.W. is *Meikle Ferry*, where we may cross the Firth to *Skibo*, 5 M. to the N. of which is **Dornoch** *(Sutherland Arms)*, the clean and quiet county-town of Sutherland, with a 13th cent. *Cathedral*, now used as the parish-church, and one tower of a castle destroyed in 1570. Good sea-bathing and golfing. — The nearest station is *The Mound* (see below), 7 M. to the N. (mail-cart daily, 2*s.*), and no less than 34 M. from Tain by the circuitous route followed by the railway.

Beyond Tain the railway skirts the upper part of Dornoch Firth. — 57 M. *Bonar Bridge* (Rail. Rfmt. Rooms, the last before Thurso and Wick; Balnagown Arms, 1 M. to the S.). We next cross the *Carron Water* and shortly afterwards the *Kyle of Sutherland*, formed by the *Shin* and *Oykell*. Fine views to the left. From (61 M.) *Invershin* (Inn), the first station in Sutherland, the train ascends the precipitous valley of the Shin, high above the stream.

$66^3/_4$ M. **Lairg.** The village *(Sutherland Arms)* lies 2 M. from the station, at the foot of *Loch Shin* (17 M. long, 1-2 M. broad).

The highly picturesque country to the W. and N.W. is traversed by several mail-cart routes from Lairg: (1) To *Loch Inver* (p. 509), 49 M. in 8-9 hrs. (fare 12*s.*), viâ *Oykell Bridge* (Inn), *Ledmore*, *Inchnadamph* (*Inn), and *Loch Assynt*. (2) To *Scourie* (44 M.; 12*s.*; p. 509) and *Durness* (56 M.; 15*s.*; p. 510), viâ Loch Shin and *Overscaig Inn* to *Laxford Bridge*, where the routes separate; (3). To *Tongue* (38 M.; 7*s.* 6*d.*) viâ *Altnaharra* (Inn), on Tues., Thurs., and Sat., returning on the alternate days.

The railway now descends to the coast through *Strathfleet*. 78 M. *The Mound*, so called from a mound 1000 yds. long, constructed by Telford across *Loch Fleet* to afford a passage for the road. Mail-cart to Dornoch, see p. 506. — $82^1/_2$ M. *Golspie* (Sutherland Arms), a pleasant but somewhat dull village with 956 inhab., on the coast. About $^3/_4$ M. to the E. is *Dunrobin Castle*, the magnificent seat of the Duke of Sutherland, a modern edifice incorporating the remains of an ancient fortress dating from 1097 (visitors admitted).

We now cross the *Brora* to ($88^1/_2$ M.) *Brora* (Inns), with coal-mines. In this neighbourhood numerous Pictish remains have been found, including *Cinn Trolla*, a Pictish house, passed by the railway 3 M. farther on. At ($95^3/_4$ M.) *Loth* we pass *Glen Loth*, where the last wolf was killed in Scotland in 1680. $101^1/_2$ M. *Helmsdale* (MacLeod's; Commercial), a flourishing seat of the herring-fishery, with a ruined castle (15th cent.). The railway here abruptly leaves the coast to avoid the *Ord of Caithness*, and ascends the uninteresting *Strath Ullie*.

From Helmsdale a road runs along the coast to (38 M.) *Wick*, via ($9^1/_2$ M.) *Berriedale*, ($15^1/_2$ M.) *Dunbeath* (Inn), (19 M.) *Latheron* (Inn), (21 M.) *Forse* (Inn), and ($23^1/_2$ M.) *Lybster* (Portland Arms), an important fishing village.

The *Suisgill Burn*, on the right, beyond ($110^3/_4$ M.) *Kildonan*, was the scene of the 'Sutherland gold-diggings' in 1868-69. To the left lies *Loch Ruar*. From ($128^1/_2$ M.) *Forsinard* a road runs due N. up *Strath Halladale*, to (16 M.) *Melvich* (p. 510). The scenery improves. To the left are the two peaks of *Ben Grian* (1930 ft., 1900 ft.) and (farther off) *Ben Loyal* (2500 ft.) and *Ben Hope* (3040 ft); and in the distance to the right rise *Morven* (2313 ft.), the *Maiden Pap* (1587 ft.), and *Scaraven* (2054 ft.). $145^3/_4$ M. *Halkirk* is situated on the *Thurso River*, a famous salmon-stream. The ancient *Brawl Tower* is fitted up as an anglers' hotel.

At ($147^1/_4$ M.) *Georgemas Junction* the line to ($5^3/_4$ M.) Thurso diverges to the N.

Thurso (*Royal; Station, St. Clair, Commercial*, smaller), an irregularly built town with 4026 inhab., is situated on a bay commanding a fine view of Hoy (p. 511). Large quantities of Caithness flagstones are exported annually. The harbour is small, and all large vessels lie in *Scrabster Roads*, 2 M. to the N.W. To the E. rise *Thurso Castle*, a handsome modern residence, and *Harold's Tower*, over the tomb of Earl Harold (d. 1190), who ruled Caithness, Orkney, and Shetland. — Steamer from Scrabster to *Orkney* (p. 511) daily; to *Leith* once a week; coach from Thurso to *Wick* daily; mail-car to *Tongue* (p. 510), on Mon., Wed., and Friday. — *Dunnet Head* (346 ft.), about 14 M. by road from Thurso, is the most northerly point of Scotland.

Beyond Georgemas we pass *Loch Watten*, on the left.

161 M. **Wick** *(Station; Caledonian)*, the chief seat of an extensive and important fishery district, with a harbour recently improved at a cost of 100 000*l*. During the herring-season the ordinary population of about 8000 is nearly doubled. The view of the herring-fleet entering or leaving the harbour, and the operations of cleaning and packing the fish are characteristic. About $1^1/_4$ M. to the S. of the town is the *Auld Man o' Wick*, a square tower of the castle of Old Wick.

A coach runs daily to (16 M.) the site of *John o' Groat's House* (Hotel). John o' Groat, according to the legend, was a Dutchman, who built an octagonal house, with eight doors and containing an eight-sided table, in order to prevent disputes as to precedence in his family. — About $1^1/_2$ M. to the E. is *Duncansby Head* (210 ft.) with fine cliff-scenery and sea-view.

Steamers ply from Wick to *Aberdeen* and *Leith*, twice a week, and to *Kirkwall*, once a week in summer. Coach daily to (21 M.) *Thurso* (see above); and another to *Lybster* and *Dunbeath* (p. 507).

71. From Gairloch to Ullapool, Loch Inver, Durness, and Thurso.

206 M. Coast Road practicable all the way for carriages, which may be hired at the principal hotels *en route*. Various short-cuts for pedestrians. There is no public conveyance all the way, but *Mail-Carts* ply over certain stages: *e.g.* Gairloch to (14 M.) Aultbea; Scourie to (25 M.) Durness; Tongue to (43 M.) Thurso. The tourist may also avail himself of the steamers from Oban (Glasgow), calling weekly at Gairloch, Poolewe, Aultbea, Ullapool, and Loch Inver (on the northward journey only), to Stornoway, and thence to Thurso, direct. During the season the Thurso steamers also call occasionally at Inverpolly, Badcall, Loch Inchard, and Loch Eribol (see *MacBrayne's Monthly Sailing Bills*). Sailing or rowing-boats may be hired at various points. — Dundonnell, Ullapool, Loch Inver, etc., are convenient starting places for excursions into the interior of Ross and Sutherland; and at various points mail-cart routes diverge to the E. and S.E., connecting with R. 70 at Garve (p. 506), Lairg (p. 507), etc. It should be noted that after the beginning of August, when deer-stalking begins, the liberty of traversing the moors and ascending the mountains is much curtailed. Anglers will find numerous good streams in this district, about which information is supplied at the hotels.

From Gairloch to Ullapool, 42 M. *Gairloch*, see p. 494. The road leads to the N.E., viâ (3 M.) *Loch Tollie*, whence there is a fine *View of Loch Maree (p. 494), to (7 M.) *Poolewe*, at the head of *Loch Ewe*. 14 M. *Aultbea* (Inn) lies opposite the well-cultivated *Ewe Island*. The rough road hence to (21 M.) *Gruinard*, at the mouth of the river of the same name, may be avoided by ferrying from *Sand*, 3 M. from Aultbea, to *Monkcastle*. A little farther on we obtain a fine view of *Little Loch Broom*, between *Sailmor* (2508 ft.) on the S. and *Ben Goleach* (2082 ft.) on the N. At the head of the loch lies (30 M.) *Dundonnell* (Inn).

To the S. lies the mountainous *Dundonnell Forest*, culminating in *Challich* (*An Teallach;* 3483 ft.). — The road to (35 M.) *Garve* (p. 506) ascends the picturesque course of the *Strathbeg River*, which enters the loch at Dundonnell.

The road now surmounts the col to the N., and descends to *Loch Broom* ('Loch of the Showers') at (37 M.) *Aultnaharrie Ferry*, whence we cross to (1 M.) —

42 M. **Ullapool** *(Royal Hotel)*, a regularly built village, with 897 inhab. and a good harbour. Founded in 1788 by the British Fishery Society as a fishing-station, Ullapool has lost its importance with the decline of the herring-fishery.

Steamer daily to *Stornoway* (5*s*.); mail-cart (7*s*.) daily to (33 M.) *Garve* (p. 506).

From Ullapool to Loch Inver, 32 M. — We skirt Loch Broom for some miles, with a view of *Isle Martin* to the left, strike inland at the *Cainaird River*, and beyond the slopes of *Ben More* (2430 ft.) turn to the W. along the N. banks of *Loch Lurgan* and *Loch Baddegyle*, with *Coulbeg* and *Stack Polly* on our right. 23 M. *Inverpolly* lies a little beyond the river *Polly*. Crossing the *Kirkaig*, with a view, to the right, of Suilven and (farther off) Canisp (see below), we reach (31 M.) the *Culag Hotel*, about 1/2 M. from the hotel at Loch Inver.

32 M. **Loch Inver** *(Hotel)*, with good sea-bathing, is a tourist and summer resort of growing popularity.

Among the numerous excursions conveniently made hence are those to *Suilven* or the *Sugarloaf* (2399 ft.), *Canisp* (2779 ft.), **Loch Assynt*, *Quinag* (2653 ft.), etc. Mail-cart daily to *Lairg* (comp. p. 507); steamer weekly to *Stornoway* (p. 494).

From Loch Inver to Scourie, 30 M. The usual carriage route ascends the valley of the Inver and skirts the N. bank of **Loch Assynt* to (11 M.) *Skaig Bridge*, whence it runs to the N. between *Glasven* (2540 ft.; right) and *Quinag* (left). At (18 M.) *Kylesku Ferry* (Inn) we cross the strait between *Loch Cairnbawn* (on the left) and *Lochs Glencoul* and *Glendhu* (on the right). The road approaches the coast again at *Edrachillis Bay*, a few miles to the S. of Scourie.

A shorter route diverges to the W. from the above at Loch Inver, and runs round the coast to (15 M.) *Drumbeg*, whence we ferry (5*s*.) to (22 M.) *Badcall*, on Edrachillis Bay (see above). 24 M. *Scourie*. This route should be chosen by those who have already seen Loch Assynt.

30 M. **Scourie** (Inn) is a straggling village, with a view of the island of *Handa*, interesting to ornithologists.

Mail-car to (25 M.) *Durness*, see p. 510; to *Lairg*, see p. 507.

From Scourie to Durness, 26 M. — A steep ascent brings us to (7 M.) *Laxford Bridge* (p. 507). 12 M. *Rhiconich Inn*, at the head of *Loch Inchard*. To the right rises *Foinaven* (2980 ft.). — 25 M. *Durness* (Durine Inn), at the mouth of the *Kyle of Durness*, with a view of Hoy (p. 511).

About 13 M. to the N.W. (good road) is Cape Wrath, the N.W. extremity of Scotland, with majestic cliffs from 250 to 600 ft. high. On the cape is a lighthouse.

From Durness to Thurso, 76 M. The road runs along the extreme N. coast of Scotland. 1 M. **Smoo Cave*, consisting of several huge chambers in the limestone rock. Farther on the road encircles *Loch Eribol* (fine scenery), but pedestrians may save 10 M. by means of the ferry to (18 M.) *Heilim* on the E. bank. Carriages as well as pedestrians are next ferried over the (20 M.) *Hope River* and the (27 M.) *Kyle of Tongue* to (30 M.) *Tongue* (Hotel at the village of Kirkiboll). Thence we proceed over the *Borgie* to (43½ M.) *Bettyhill of Farr* (Inn), at the mouth of *Strathnaver*. From (54½ M.) *Strathy* a coach plies daily to Thurso (2*s.*). 58 M. *Melvich* (Inn; to Forsinard, see p. 507). Shortly before reaching (65 M.) *Reay* (Inn) we enter Caithness. We cross the *Forss Water*. — 76 M. Thurso (p. 508).

72. Orkney and Shetland Islands.

Steamer daily from *Scrabster* (p. 508) to *Scapa* and *Stromness* (fares 7*s.*, 4*s.*), touching at *Hoxa* (for St. Margaret's Hope) on the return voyage. — From *Leith*, viâ (12 hrs.) *Aberdeen*, twice weekly to (24 hrs.) *Kirkwall* (22*s.*, 10*s.*) and (ca. 34 hrs.) *Lerwick* (26*s.*, 10*s.* 6*d.*), touching on the alternate voyages at *Wick* and *St. Margaret's Hope;* and once weekly to (24 hrs.) *Stromness* (20*s.*, 9*s.*), *Scalloway* (26*s.*, 10*s.* 6*d.*) and *Hillswick*. Return-tickets, available for three months, on all these routes, at a fare and a half. In winter the steamers ply less frequently. — From Kirkwall the 'Orcadia' plies twice weekly to the N. of Orkney; and from Lerwick the 'Earl of Zetland' twice weekly to the N. of Shetland; apply for all information at the offices of the North of Scotland and Orkney and Shetland Steam Navigation Co. at Kirkwall, Lerwick, or Scalloway. — See 'The Orkneys and Shetland', by *John R. Tudor*, with maps and illustrations (1883; 21*s.*).

The Orkney Islands (375 sq. M.; pop. 32,044) are 67 in number, of which 28 are inhabited. *Pomona* or *Mainland* (pop. 17,165) is the largest. They are separated from the N. of Scotland by the tempestuous *Pentland Firth*, 6½-8 M. wide. The Shetland Islands (551 sq. M.; pop. 29,705), about 100 in number, 29 inhabited, lie 50 M. to the N.E. of the Orkneys, with which they are united to form a county. *Mainland* (pop. 20,821) is the largest.

The inhabitants of these northern archipelagoes, who pride themselves upon their Scandinavian origin, stoutly refusing to call themselves Scots, speak a dialect of English, with, especially in Shetland, an infusion of Norse words; and they still retain many peculiar manners and customs. The *Udallers*, or small landowners ('peerie lairds'), are the only real freeholders in Scotland. The chief occupations are agriculture and fishing, the latter of which has recently been largely developed, so that Shetland is now one of the chief seats of the Scottish herring-fishery. Shetland hand-knit shawls and hosiery, and Shetland ponies are also noted. The chief attractions of the islands are the magnificent coast-scenery, and the *brochs* or round towers and other prehistoric antiquities, most abundant in Orkney. Their historical interest also is not small, and Sir Walter Scott has made them classic ground by his 'Pirate'. Anglers find excellent fishing for sea-trout and brown trout.

The best time for visiting these islands is between the middle of

June and the end of August. A week will be found ample time by the ordinary tourist. Enquiries as to inns or night-quarters in the northern parts of the groups should be made beforehand.

1. The Orkney Islands.

The steamer from Scrabster (p. 508) to Stromness crosses the *Pentland Firth*, and stops first at (4-5 hrs.) *Scapa*, on Mainland, 2 M. to the S. of Kirkwall, whence carriages meet the boat.

Stromness *(Mason's Arms; Commercial)*, a picturesque and prosperous little seaport, with 1705 inhab., on a sheltered bay, was the birthplace of John Gow, the 'Cleveland' of Scott's 'Pirate', and of Geo. Stewart, the 'Torquil' of Byron's poem 'The Island'.

Excursions. To the island of ***Hoy** (*Ship Hotel*, at Longhope), about 1 day; boat 10*s*., to the 'Old Man' 15*s*. The chief points in Hoy are the fine cliffs on the N. and N.W. coast (including the *Old Man of Hoy*, an isolated and conspicuous column of sandstone, 450 ft. high), the *Dwarfie Stone*, and *Ward Hill* (1564 ft.), the highest point in the county. — To (12 M.) *Birsay*, viâ *Black Crag* (406 ft.), *Hole of Rowe*, and other fine points on the W. coast of Mainland. At Birsay are a ruined *Palace* (16th cent.), built by a natural son of James V., a broch, and two ruined churches. — To (14 M.) *Kirkwall*, see below.

Kirkwall, *i.e. 'Church Bay' (Kirkwall; Castle)*, the capital of Orkney, is a clean but dull town, with 3947 inhab. and a good harbour. The **Cathedral of St. Magnus* (Norm. and E. E.), founded in 1137 but not completed till 1540, is one of the three old Scottish cathedrals that are still in nearly complete preservation. The chancel has good rose-windows. Adjoining are the ruined *Bishop's Palace*, in which Haco of Norway died in 1263, and the *Earl's Palace*, built about 1600 by Earl Patrick Stewart, the hall of which is mentioned in the 'Pirate'. To the E. of the town are the remains of a fort built by Cromwell, known as *The Mount*.

Excursions. Coaches (fare 2*s*. 6*d*., return 4*s*.) ply daily to (14 M.) *Stromness*, affording an opportunity of visiting (9 M.) the *Tumulus of Maeshowe* and (10½ M.) the Standing Stones of Stenness. The former (adm. 6*d*.; guide's house to the left of the road), a chambered sepulchral mound, 36 ft. high and 300 ft. in circumference, was found in 1861 to contain various rude carvings and Runic inscriptions. The ***Stones of Stenness** comprize two stone-circles in a bleak and striking situation on two promontories in the *Loch of Stenness*, connected by a causeway known as the *Bridge of Brogar*. 14 M. *Stromness*, see above. — Other excursions may be made to *Wideford Hill* (726 ft.; view), 2 M. to the W. of Kirkwall; to *Deerness*, the easternmost part of Mainland; to (20 M.) *Birsay* (see above), its N.W. extremity, etc.

To Burray, with a fine broch, a ferry (2s.) plies from *St. Mary's*, 6 M. to the S. of Kirkwall. From the S. side of Burray another ferry (6*d*.) crosses to *St. Margaret's Hope* (Inn; steamer, see p. 510) on South Ronaldshay. *Hoxa* (steamer, see p. 510) lies 3 M. to the W. — To (4 M.) Shapinshay, on which is *Balfour Castle*, with fine grounds, a mail-boat plies daily. — To Rousay, a local steamer (p. 510) thrice weekly. The adjacent Eglishay is said to derive its name from *Ecclesia*, in honour of the old ruined *Church of St. Magnus*, remarkable for its round tower.

To the Northern Orkneys by the 'Orcadia', see p. 510. — Stronsay and Sanday both contain brochs, and Eday has numerous antiquities. In Westray is the ruined *Castle of Noltland*, begun in 1422. The scenery of *Noup Head* (250 ft.), 3 M. from

Pierowall, the chief village in Westray, is famous. North Ronaldshay is accessible only by boat from Sanday.

2. The Shetland Islands.

The weekly steamer from Stromness to Scalloway affords a good view of the cliff-scenery on the W. side of the Orkneys; but most tourists will find the route from Kirkwall to (8-9 hrs.) Lerwick more convenient. About halfway on the latter we pass the lonely *Fair Isle* (214 inhab.), famous for its hand-knit hosiery, with patterns said to have been introduced by the crew of a shipwrecked vessel of the Spanish Armada.

Lerwick, i.e. '*Clay Bay*' (*Grand; Queen's*; *Royal)*, capital of Shetland, a seaport with 4045 inhab., has a good pier and esplanade and a fine town-hall (adm. 6*d*.). The *Anderson Institute* is a school. At the N. end of the town is *Fort Charlotte*, originally built by Cromwell. The island of Bressay landlocks the harbour.

Excursions. To the *Noup of Noss* (600 ft.), either by boat (8-9 hrs.; 15-20*s*.) round Bressay or on foot (14 M. there and back), ferrying from Lerwick to Bressay, and from Bressay to Noss. Permission to land on Noss must be obtained from the factor on Bressay. The cliffs are best seen from the sea. The tiny *Holm of Noss* is separated from the S. end of Noss by a precipitous chasm only 60 ft. wide, formerly crossed by a 'cradle' working along two parallel ropes, now removed in consequence of accidents. — To *Scalloway* (see below) viâ *Tingwall*, returning viâ *Gulberwick*, 15 M. there and back. — To *Mousa and Fitful Head*, 28 M. The road runs to the S. from Gulberwick (see above) to (13 M.) *Sandlodge*, where permission is obtained to ferry to the (2 M.) island of *Mousa*, on which is the finest **Broch* or '*Pictish Tower*' in Scotland. — From Sandlodge the road continues to the S. to (25 M.) *Sumborough Head* (300 ft.), and thence runs to the N.W. to (28 M.) **Fitful Head* (928 ft.). There is a lighthouse on each promontory.

Scalloway *(Scalloway)*, with 648 inhab., is picturesquely situated at the head of *Cliff Sound*, 6 M. from Lerwick. The *Castle*, built in 1600 by Earl Patrick Stewart, is in tolerable preservation.

The steamer route from Scalloway to Hillswick (comp. p. 510) is one of the finest excursions in the islands, with views of magnificent cliff-scenery. To the W. as we leave Scalloway appears the distant island of *Foula* (267 inhab.), a famous haunt of sea-fowl. To the right is the parish of *Walls*, noted for its 'voes' (bays) and lochs. At *Brae*, where Mainland narrows to an isthmus, the *Mavis Grind* or *Gull's Bridge*, only 50 yds. wide, it is sometimes possible to catch the Lerwick steamer in the *Sullem Voe*. *Hillswick* (lodgings) is near some of the best cliff-scenery in the islands.

To the Northern Shetlands by the 'Earl of Zetland', see p. 510. The steamer on certain voyages visits the N.W. parts of Mainland. — Whalsay is the first island touched at. Yell, a bleak island, has numerous brochs and ruined chapels. Fetlar, to the N.E. is fertile and picturesque. The nothernmost island is Unst, at the S.W. end of which is the ruined *Muness Castle* (1598). *Balta Sound*, on the E. coast, is an important fishing-station; near it are three stone-circles. About 2 M. to the N. is *Haroldswick*, where Harold Haarfagr landed in 872 to begin the conquest of the islands.

INDEX.

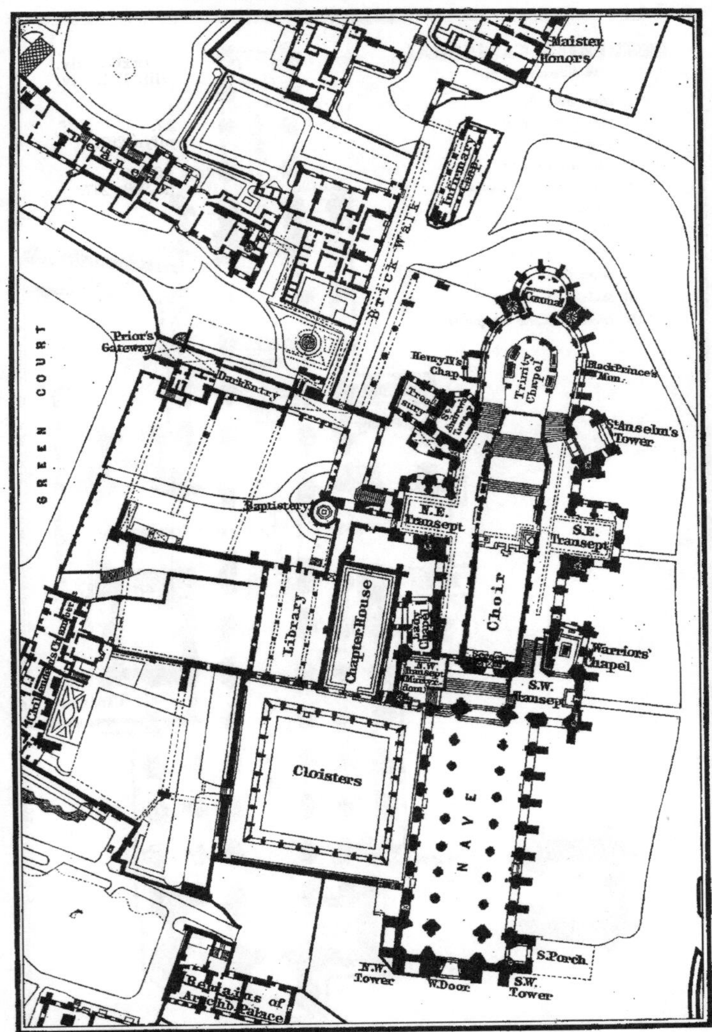
Maister Honors
Deanery
Infirmary Chap.
Brick Walk
Corona
Henry IV's Chap
Trinity Chapel
Black Prince's Mon.
Prior's Gateway
GREEN COURT
Dark Entry
Treasury
St. Andrew's Tower
St. Anselm's Tower
Baptistery
N.E. Transept
S.E. Transept
Library
Chapter House
Lady Chapel
Choir
Warriors' Chapel
N.W. Transept (Martyrdom)
S.W. Transept
Cloisters
NAVE
S. Porch
N.W. Tower
W. Door
S.W. Tower
Remains of Archb. Palace
Feet
Metres

See page 27

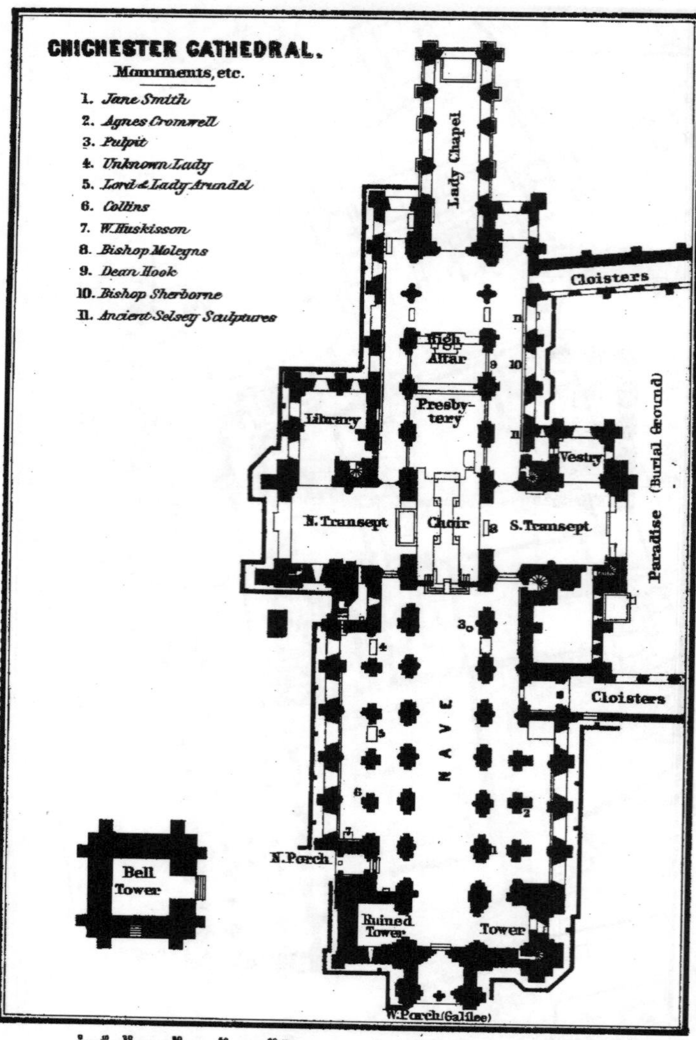
CHICHESTER CATHEDRAL.
Monuments, etc.
1. Jane Smith
2. Agnes Cromwell
3. Pulpit
4. Unknown Lady
5. Lord & Lady Arundel
6. Collins
7. W. Huskisson
8. Bishop Moleyns
9. Dean Hook
10. Bishop Sherborne
11. Ancient Selsey Sculptures
Lady Chapel
Cloisters
High Altar
Presbytery
Library
Vestry
N. Transept
Choir
S. Transept
Paradise (Burial Ground)
Cloisters
NAVE
N. Porch
Bell Tower
Ruined Tower
Tower
W. Porch (Galilee)
Feet
Metres

See page 54

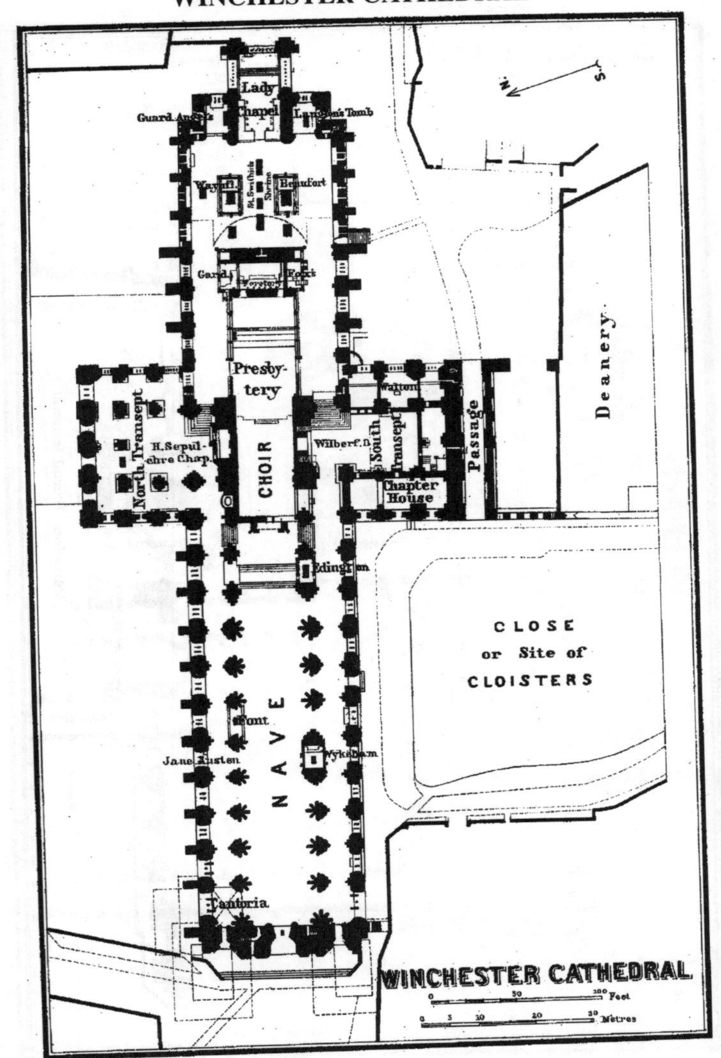
Lady Chapel
Guard. Angels
Langton's Tomb
N.
S.
Waynfl.
St. Swithin's Shrine
Beaufort
Gard.
Foxe
Presby-tery
Deanery
Walton
North Transept
H. Sepul-chre Chap.
CHOIR
Wilberf. D.
South Transept
Passage
Chapter House
Edington
CLOSE
or Site of
CLOISTERS
NAVE
Font
Jane Austen
Wykeham
Cantoria
WINCHESTER CATHEDRAL
0 50 100 Feet
0 5 10 20 30 Metres

See page 77

SALISBURY CATHEDRAL

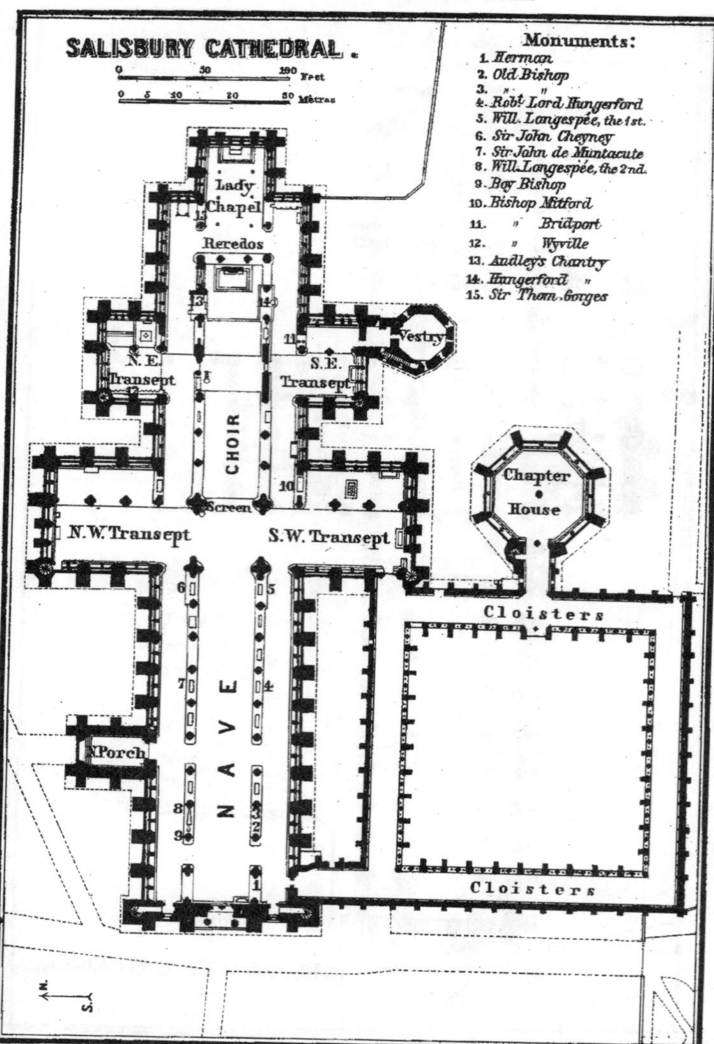
SALISBURY CATHEDRAL.
0 50 100 Feet
0 5 10 20 30 Mètres
Monuments:
1. Herman
2. Old Bishop
3. " "
4. Robt. Lord Hungerford
5. Will. Longespée, the 1st.
6. Sir John Cheyney
7. Sir John de Muntacute
8. Will. Longespée, the 2nd.
9. Boy Bishop
10. Bishop Mitford
11. " Bridport
12. " Wyville
13. Audley's Chantry
14. Hungerford "
15. Sir Thom. Gorges
Lady Chapel
Reredos
Vestry
N.E. Transept
S.E. Transept
CHOIR
Chapter House
Screen
N.W. Transept
S.W. Transept
Cloisters
NAVE
N. Porch
Cloisters
N.
S.

See page 99

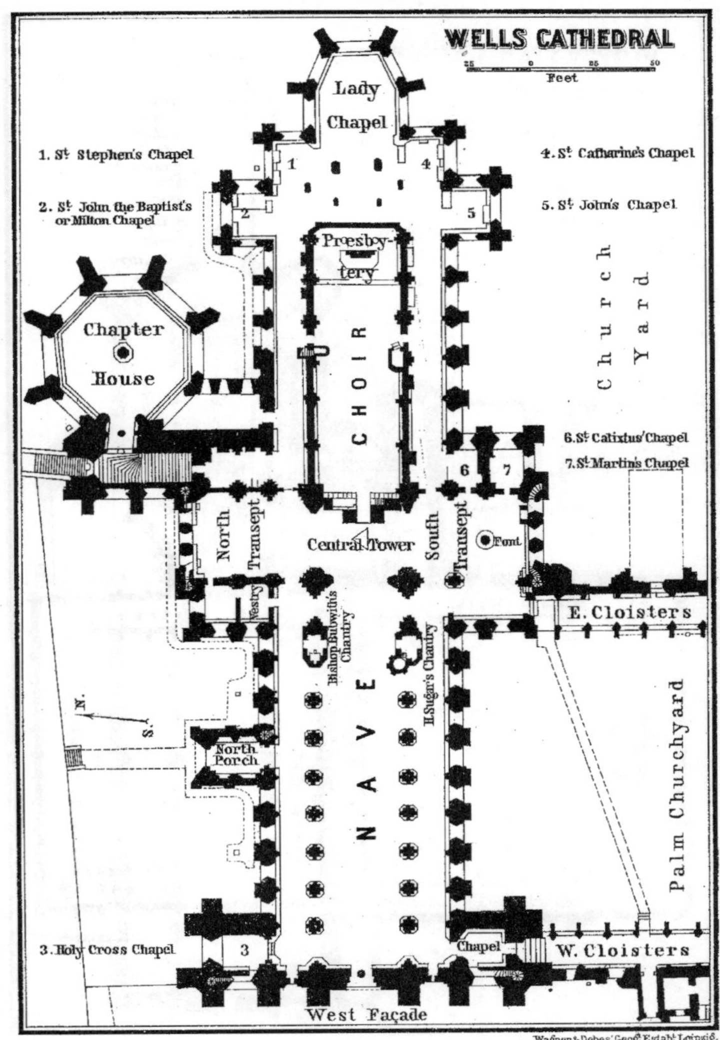
WELLS CATHEDRAL
25 0 25 50
Feet
Lady Chapel
1. St. Stephen's Chapel
2. St. John the Baptist's or Milton Chapel
4. St. Catharine's Chapel
5. St. John's Chapel
1
2
4
5
Presbytery
Chapter House
CHOIR
Church Yard
6. St. Calixtus' Chapel
7. St. Martin's Chapel
6
7
North Transept
Central Tower
South Transept
Font
Vestry
Bishop Bubwith's Chantry
H. Sugar's Chantry
E. Cloisters
NAVE
N.
S.
North Porch
Palm Churchyard
3. Holy Cross Chapel
3
Chapel
W. Cloisters
West Façade
Wagner & Debes' Geogr. Estabt. Leipzig.

See page 123

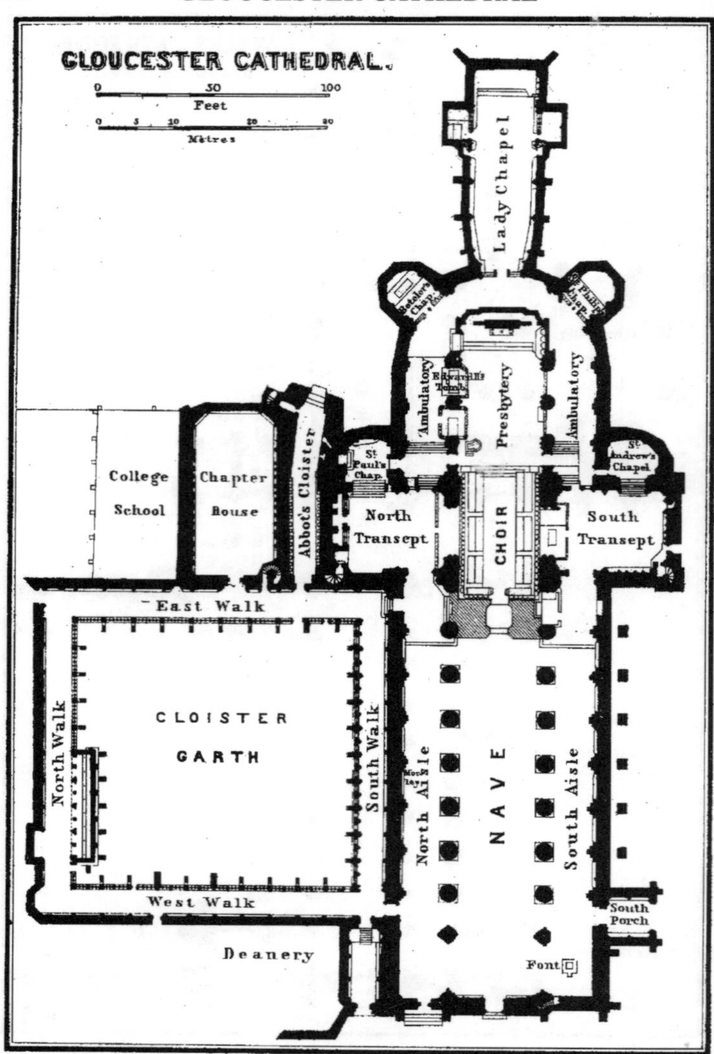

GLOUCESTER CATHEDRAL.
0 50 100
Feet
0 5 10 20 30
Metres
Lady Chapel
Boteler's Chap.
St Philip's Chap.
Ambulatory
Edward II's Tomb
Presbytery
Ambulatory
St Paul's Chap.
St Andrew's Chapel
College School
Chapter House
Abbot's Cloister
North Transept
CHOIR
South Transept
East Walk
CLOISTER
GARTH
North Walk
South Walk
North Aisle
NAVE
South Aisle
West Walk
South Porch
Deanery
Font

See page 171

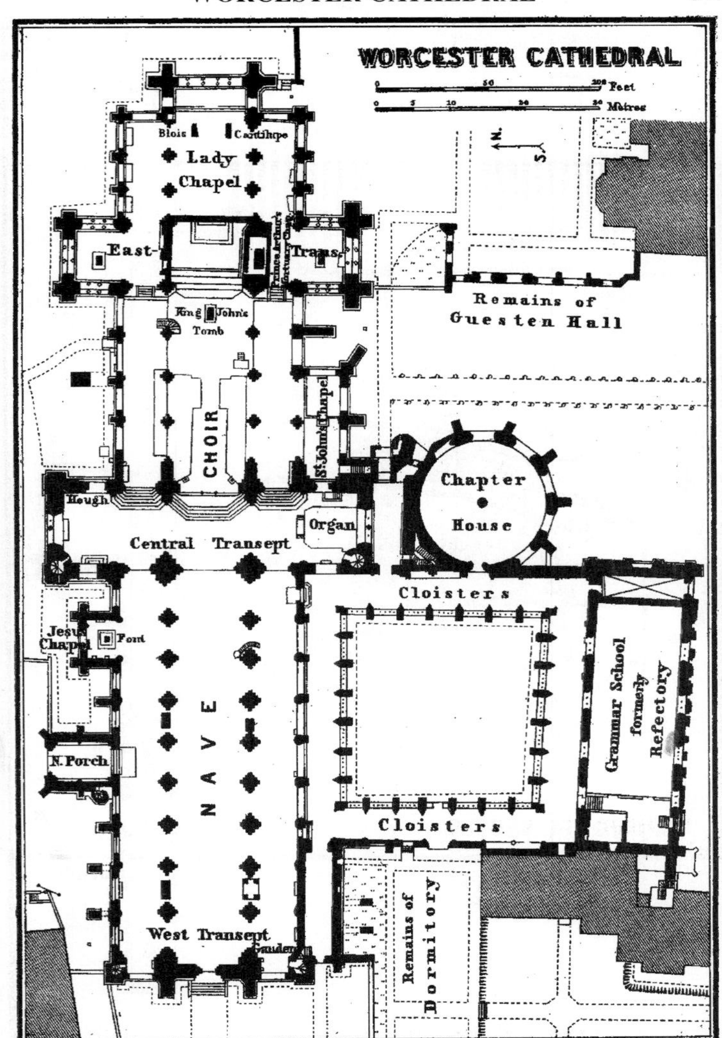
WORCESTER CATHEDRAL
0 50 200 Feet
0 5 10 20 30 Metres
N.
S.
Blois
Cantilupe
Lady Chapel
East- Trans.
Prince Arthur's Chantry Chap.
King John's Tomb
CHOIR
St. John's Chapel
Remains of Guesten Hall
Chapter House
Hough
Organ
Central Transept
Cloisters
Jesus Chapel
Font
Grammar School formerly Refectory
NAVE
N. Porch
Cloisters
West Transept
Sauden
Remains of Dormitory

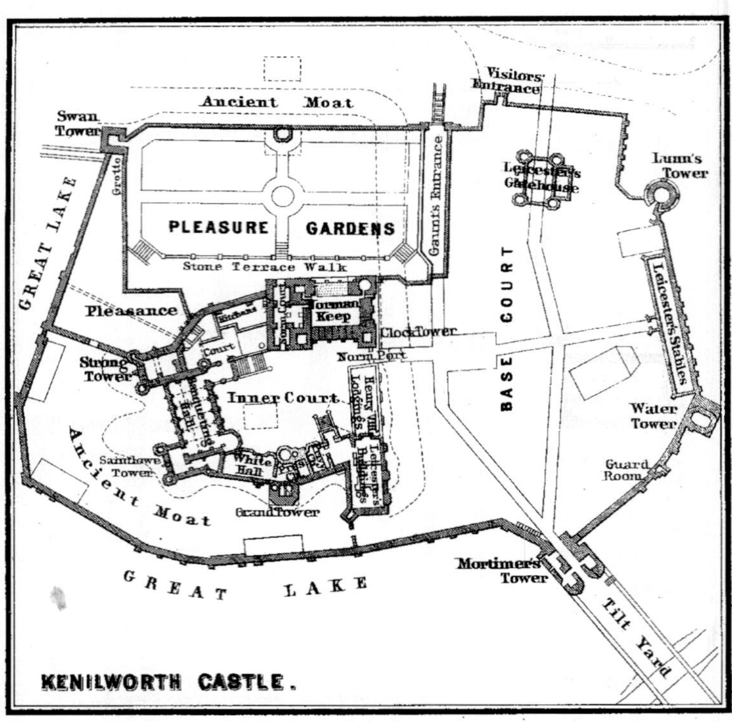
Visitors' Entrance
Ancient Moat
Swan Tower
Grotto
Gaunt's Entrance
Leicester's Gatehouse
Lunn's Tower
GREAT LAKE
PLEASURE GARDENS
Stone Terrace Walk
BASE COURT
Leicester's Stables
Pleasance
Kitchens
Norman Keep
Clock Tower
Court
Norm Port
Strong Tower
Inner Court
Henry VIII Lodgings
Water Tower
Banqueting Hall
Saintlowe Tower
White Hall
Leicester's Buildings
Guard Room
Ancient Moat
Grand Tower
Mortimer's Tower
GREAT LAKE
Tilt Yard
KENILWORTH CASTLE.

See page 243

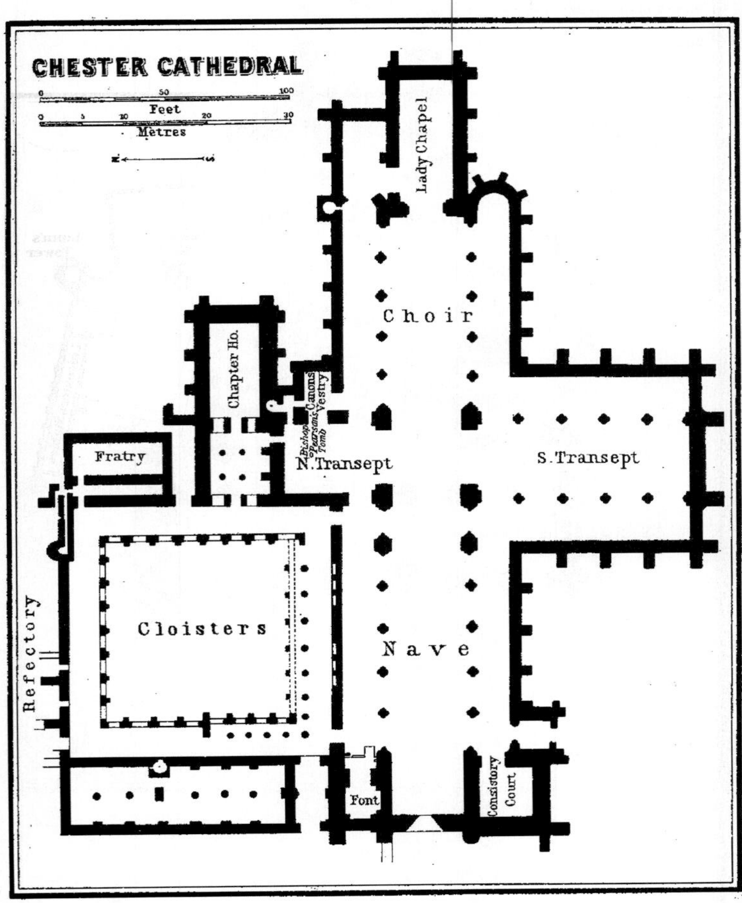
CHESTER CATHEDRAL
0 50 100
Feet
0 5 10 20 30
Metres
N S
Lady Chapel
Choir
Chapter Ho.
Canons Vestry
Bishop Pearson's Tomb
N. Transept
S. Transept
Fratry
Cloisters
Nave
Refectory
Font
Consistory Court

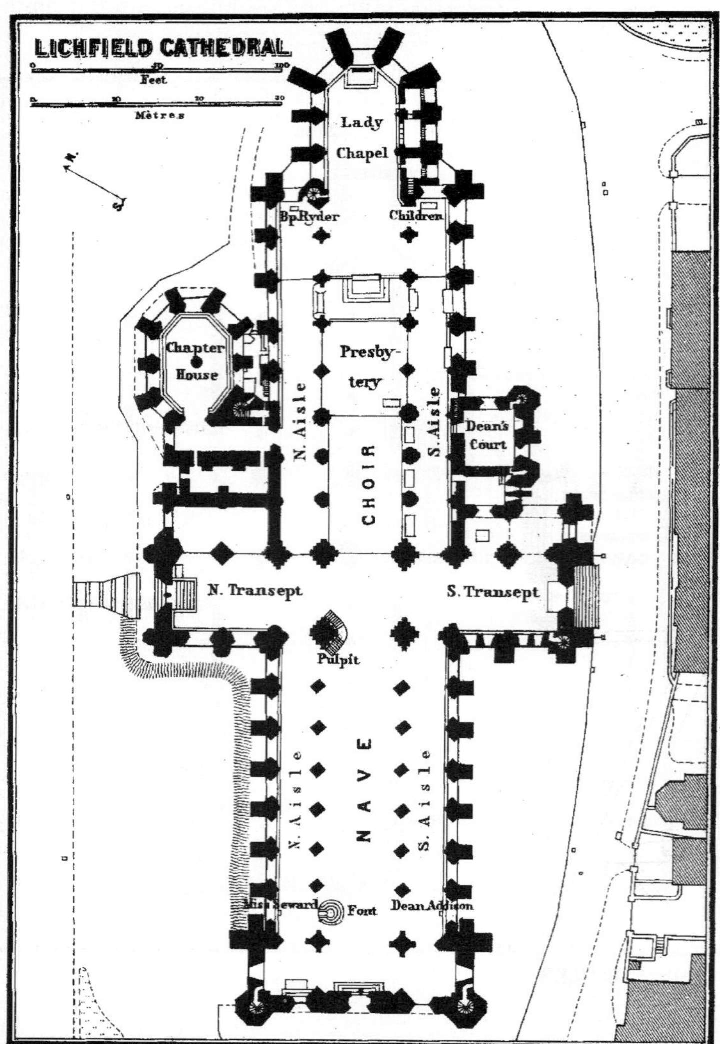
LICHFIELD CATHEDRAL
Feet
Mètres
N.
S.
Lady Chapel
Bp.Ryder
Children
Chapter House
Presbytery
N. Aisle
S. Aisle
CHOIR
Dean's Court
N. Transept
S. Transept
Pulpit
N. Aisle
NAVE
S. Aisle
Font
Dean Addison

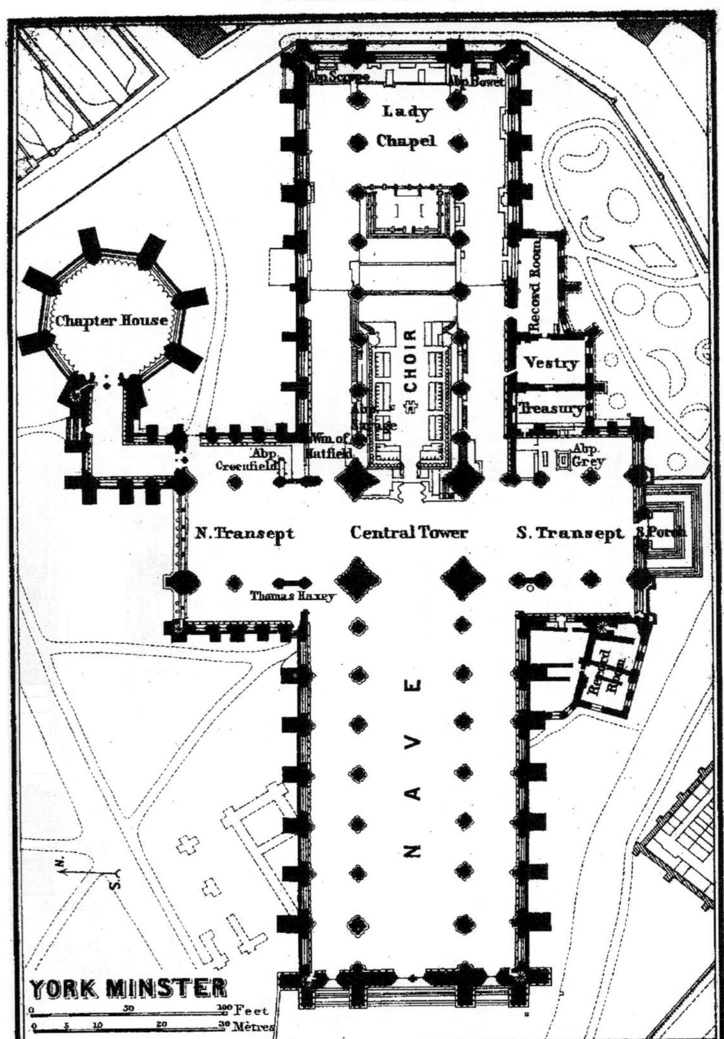
Abp. Scrope
Abp. Bowet
Lady Chapel
Record Room
Chapter House
CHOIR
Vestry
Treasury
Abp. Savage
Wm. of Hatfield
Abp. Greenfield
Abp. Grey
N. Transept
Central Tower
S. Transept
S. Porch
Thomas Haxey
Record Room
NAVE
N.
S.
YORK MINSTER
0 50 100 Feet
0 5 10 20 30 Mètres

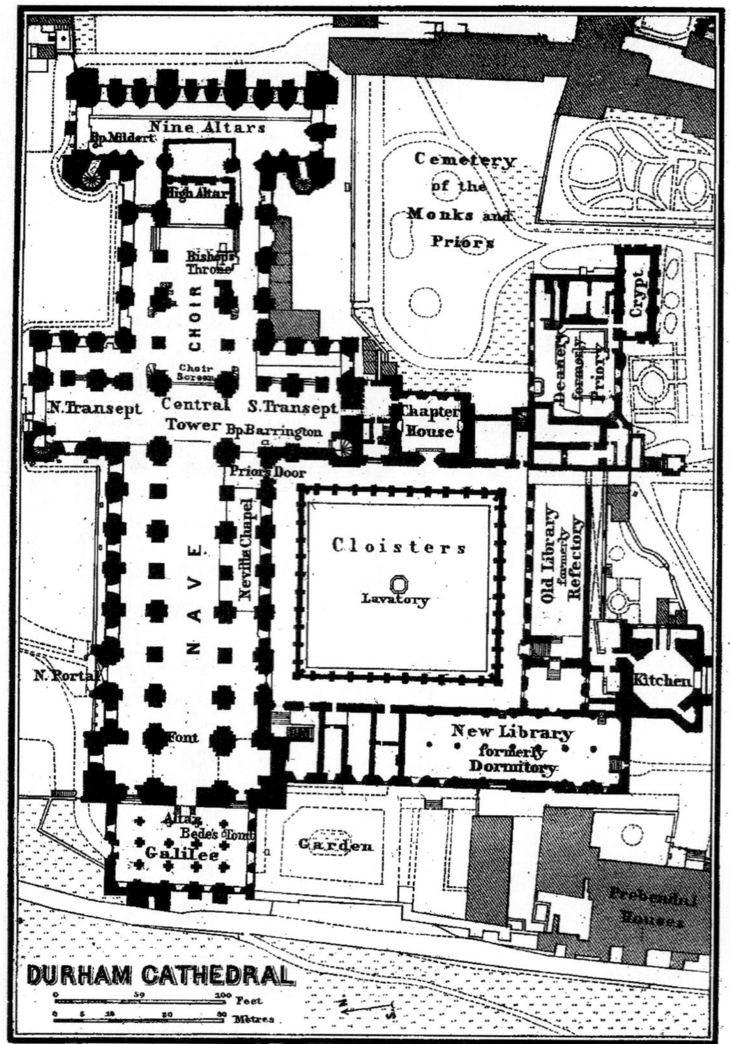
Nine Altars
Bp.Mildert
High Altar
Cemetery of the Monks and Priors
Bishops Throne
CHOIR
Crypt
Deanery formerly Priory
Choir Screen
N.Transept
Central Tower
S.Transept
Chapter House
Bp.Barrington
Priors Door
Nevills Chapel
Cloisters
Lavatory
NAVE
Old Library formerly Refectory
N. Portal
Kitchen
Font
New Library formerly Dormitory
Altar
Bede's Tomb
Galilee
Garden
Prebendal Houses
DURHAM CATHEDRAL
0 50 100 Feet
Metres

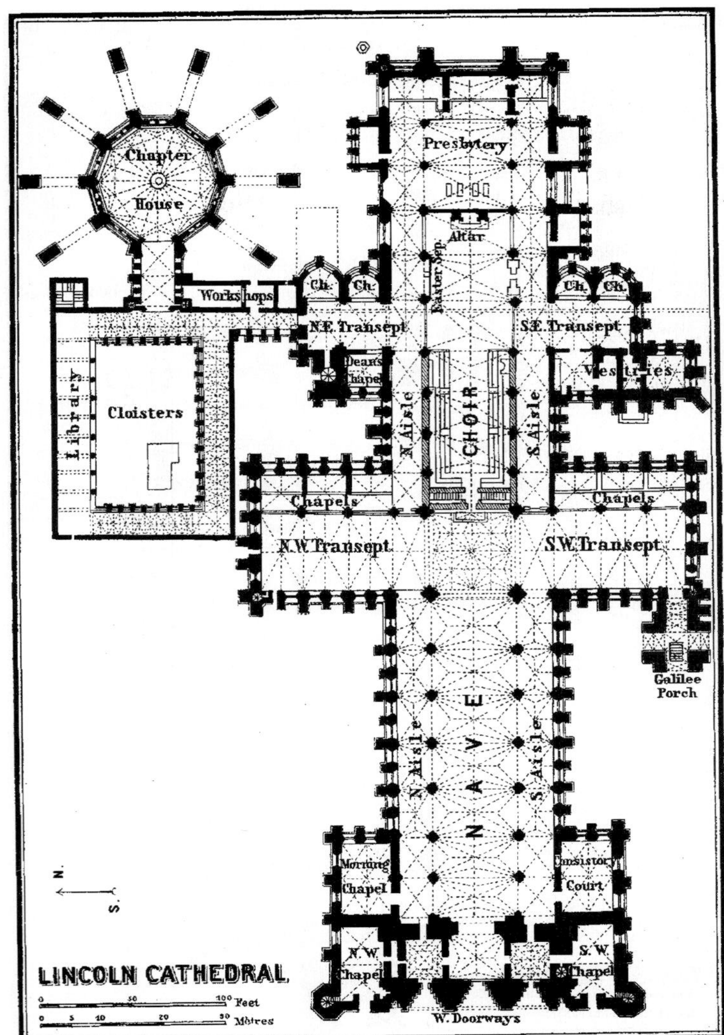
Chapter House
Workshops
Library
Cloisters
Ch.
Ch.
N.E. Transept
Deans Chapel
Presbytery
Altar
Easter Sep.
N. Aisle
CHOIR
S. Aisle
S.E. Transept
Vestries
Chapels
N.W. Transept
S.W. Transept
Galilee Porch
N. Aisle
NAVE
S. Aisle
Morning Chapel
Consistory Court
N.W. Chapel
S.W. Chapel
W. Doorways
N.
S.
LINCOLN CATHEDRAL
0 50 100 Feet
0 5 10 20 30 Mètres

See page 427

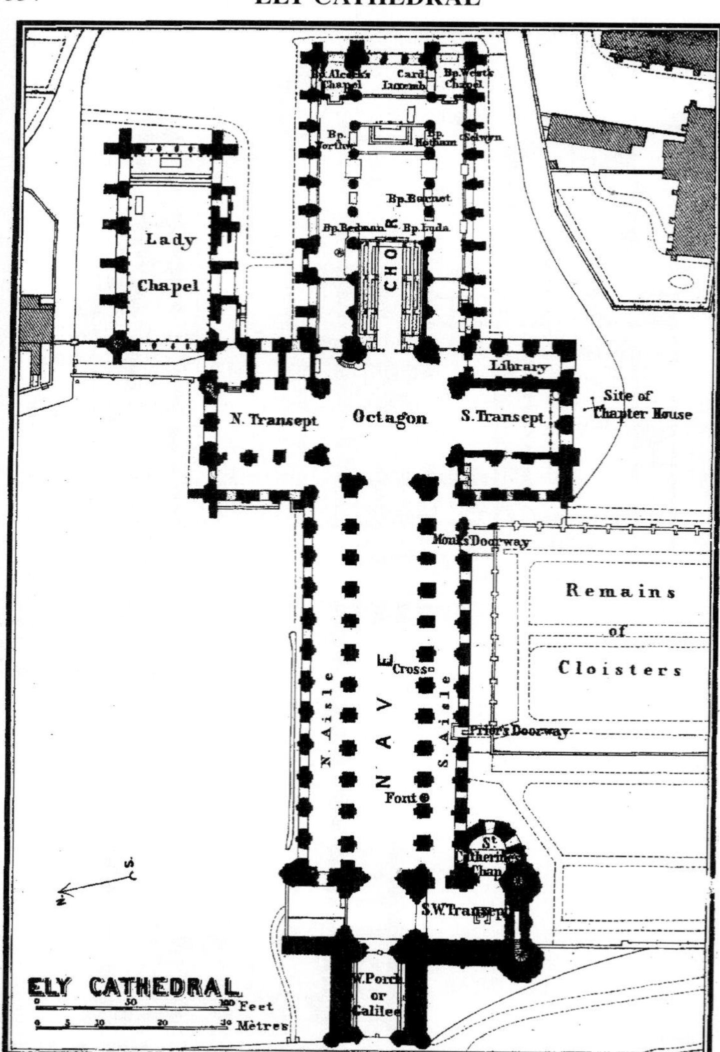
Bp. Alcock's Chapel
Card. Luxemb.
Bp. West's Chapel
Bp. Northw.
Bp. Hotham
Selwyn
Bp. Burnet
Bp. Redman
Bp. Luda
CHOIR
Lady Chapel
Library
Site of Chapter House
N. Transept
Octagon
S. Transept
Monks Doorway
Remains of Cloisters
Cross
N. Aisle
NAVE
S. Aisle
Prior's Doorway
Font
St. Catherine's Chap.
S.W. Transept
W. Porch or Galilee
ELY CATHEDRAL
0 50 100 Feet
0 5 10 20 30 Mètres
N.
S.

See page 440

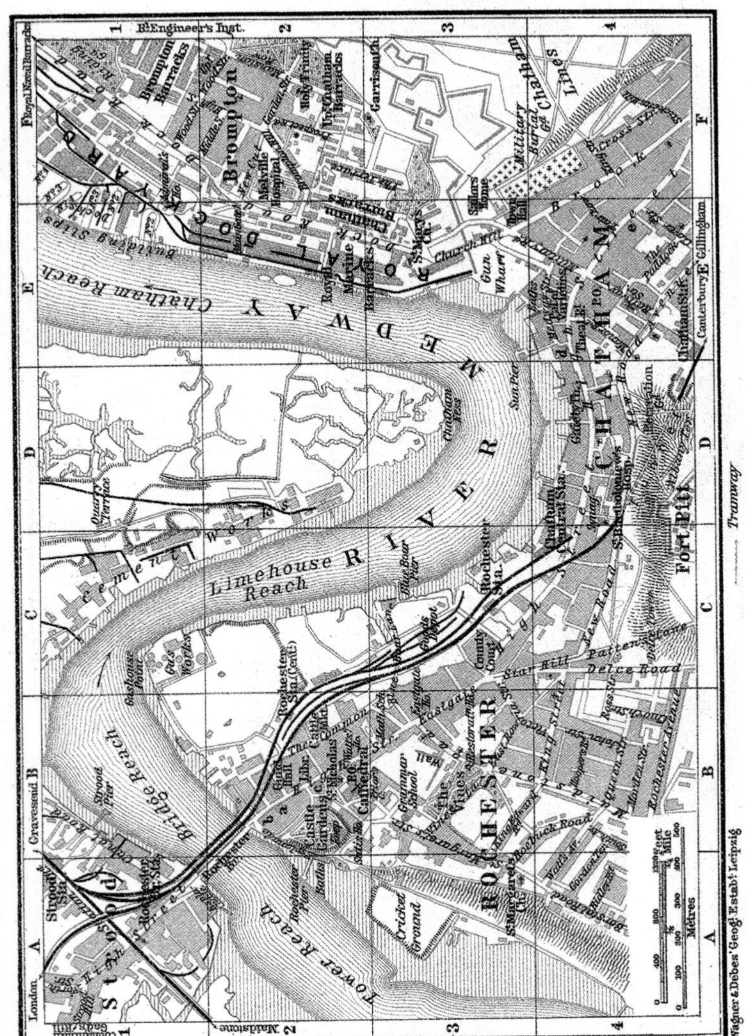
Rochester
Chatham
Strood
Brompton
River Medway
Limehouse Reach
Chatham Reach
Bridge Reach
Tower Reach
Royal Dockyard
Brompton Barracks
Chatham Barracks
Military Burial Gd.
Chatham Lines
Cement Works
Gas Works
Gashouse Point
Chatham Ness
Quarry Terrace
Sun Pier
Gun Wharf
Rochester Sta.
Chatham Central Sta.
Strood Sta.
Cathedral
Castle Gardens
Cricket Ground
Rochester Pier
Strood Pier
Star Hill
Delce Road
New Road
Fort Pitt
London
Gravesend
Maidstone
Canterbury
Gillingham
Metres
Tramway
Wagner & Debes' Geogl. Estabt. Leipzig

See page 18

RAILWAY PLAN OF LONDON

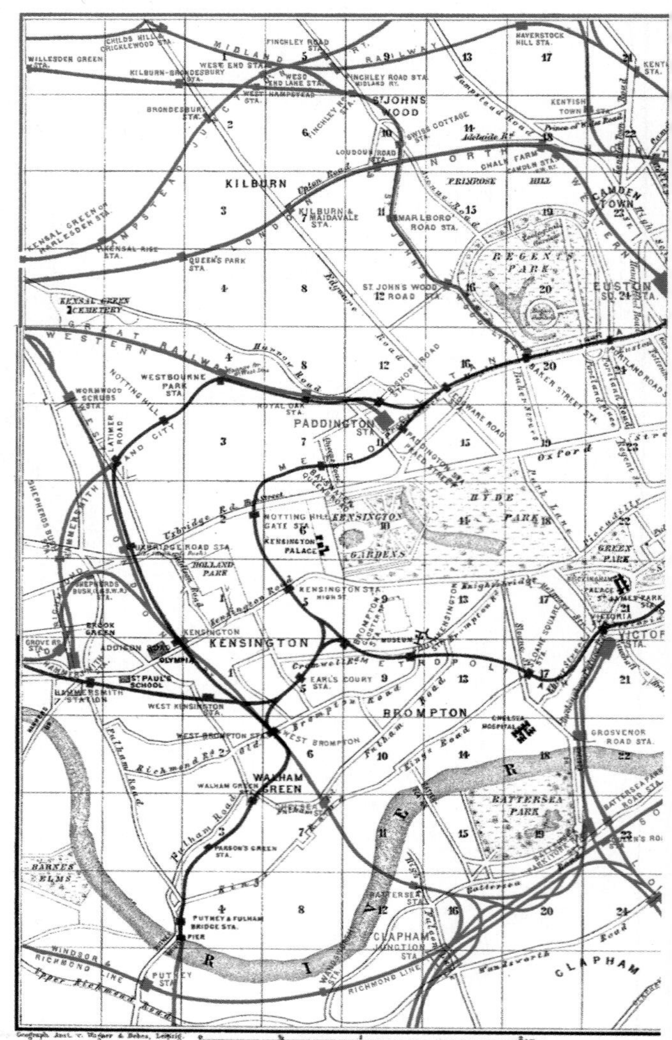

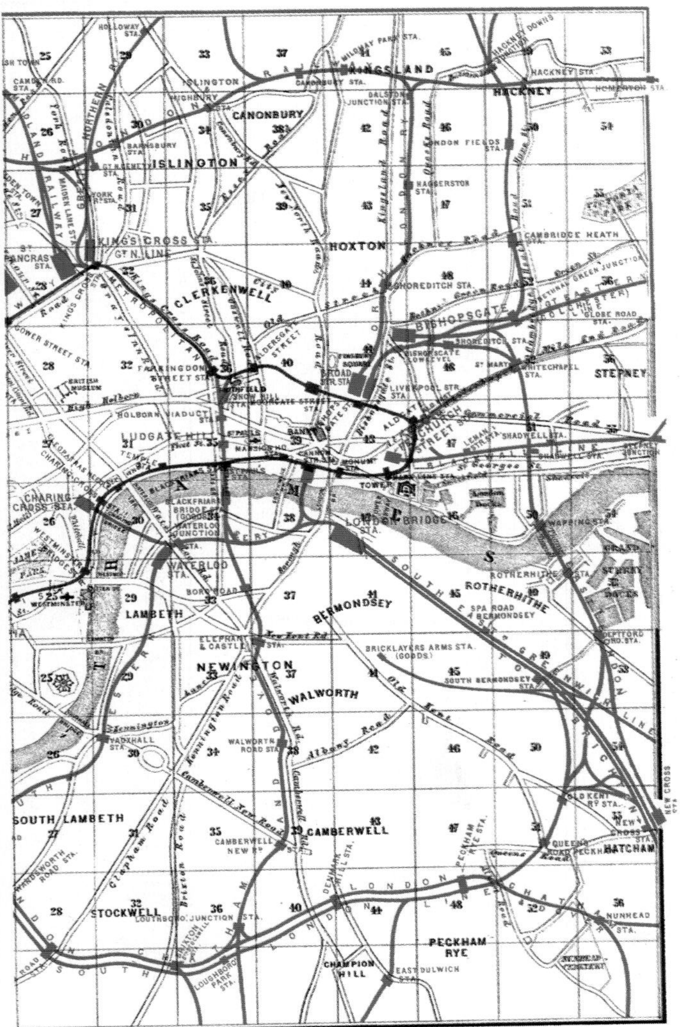
HOLLOWAY STA.
KINGSLAND
CANONBURY STA.
HACKNEY DOWNS
HACKNEY STA.
HACKNEY
HOMERTON STA.
ISLINGTON
HIGHBURY
DALSTON JUNCTION STA.
CANONBURY
LONDON FIELDS STA.
BARNSBURY STA.
ISLINGTON
HAGGERSTON STA.
KINGS CROSS STA.
GT. N. LINE
CAMBRIDGE HEATH
HOXTON
ST. PANCRAS STA.
SHOREDITCH STA.
CLERKENWELL
BISHOPSGATE
GLOBE ROAD STA.
GOWER STREET STA.
SHOREDITCH STA.
FARRINGDON STREET STA.
ALDERSGATE STREET
BISHOPSGATE LOW LEVEL
ST MARYS
WHITECHAPEL STA.
STEPNEY
BRITISH MUSEUM
BROAD STR. STA.
LIVERPOOL STR.
HOLBORN VIADUCT STA.
LUDGATE HILL
FENCHURCH STREET
LEMAN ST. STA.
SHADWELL STA.
TOWER
CHARING CROSS STA.
BLACKFRIARS BRIDGE (GOODS)
WATERLOO JUNCTION
LONDON BRIDGE
WAPPING STA.
WATERLOO STA.
ROTHERHITHE
ROTHERHITHE STA.
WESTMINSTER
LAMBETH
BERMONDSEY
SPA ROAD & BERMONDSEY
DEPTFORD ROAD STA.
ELEPHANT & CASTLE STA.
BRICKLAYERS ARMS STA. (GOODS)
NEWINGTON
WALWORTH
SOUTH BERMONDSEY STA.
VAUXHALL STA.
WALWORTH ROAD STA.
OLD KENT RD STA.
NEW CROSS STA.
SOUTH LAMBETH
CAMBERWELL
CAMBERWELL NEW RD STA.
QUEENS ROAD PECKHAM
HATCHAM
PECKHAM RYE STA.
DENMARK HILL STA.
STOCKWELL
NUNHEAD STA.
PECKHAM RYE
CHAMPION HILL
EAST DULWICH STA.
LOUGHBORO PARK STA.

See page 1

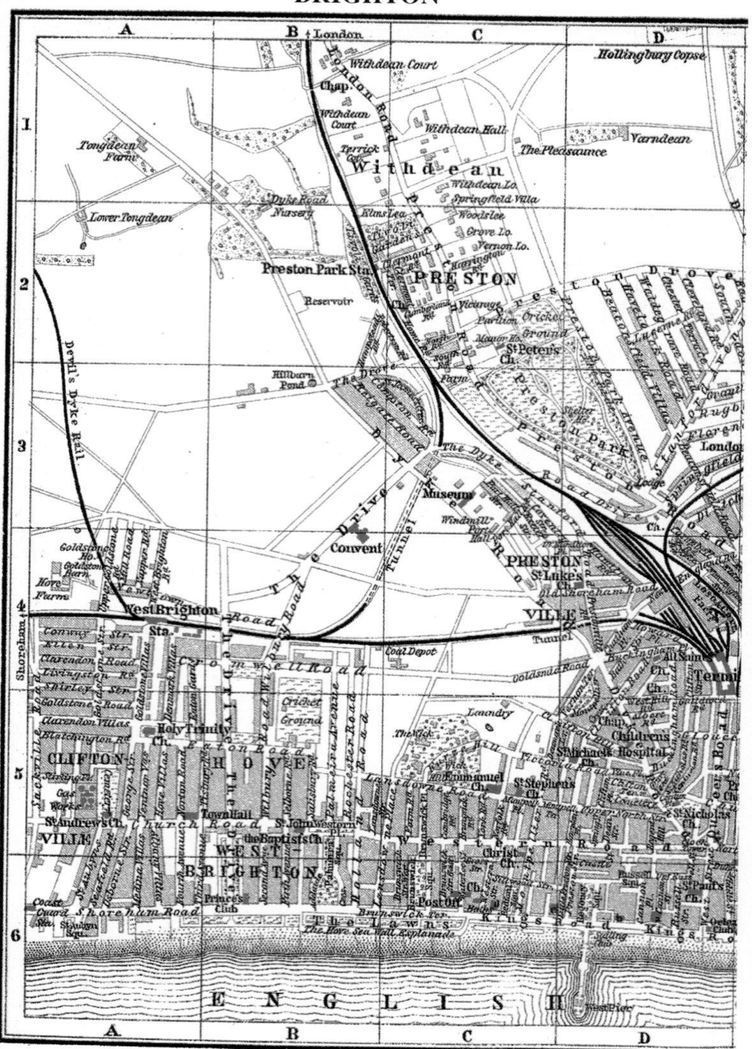
A
B
C
D
1
2
3
4
5
6
London
Withdean Court
Chap.
London Road
Withdean Hall
Hollingbury Copse
Varndean
The Pleasaunce
Tongdean Farm
Terrick Cot.
Withdean
Withdean Lo.
Springfield Villa
Dyke Road Nursery
Woodslee
Lower Tongdean
Elms Lea
Grove Lo.
Vernon Lo.
Preston Park Sta.
PRESTON
Preston Drove
Reservoir
Vicarage
Cricket Ground
Pavilion
Manor Ho.
St. Peter's Ch.
Devil's Dyke Rail
Hillburn Pond
The Drove
South Rd.
Farm
Preston Park
Shelter Ho.
Preston Park Avenue
Reigate Road
The Dyke Road
Lodge
London
Museum
Stanford Road
Windmill
The Drive
Convent
Tunnel
Goldstone Ho.
Goldstone Barn
Hove Farm
PRESTON
St. Luke's Ch.
Old Shoreham Road
West Brighton Sta.
Road
VILLE
Tunnel
Shoreham
Coal Depot
Conway Str.
Ellen Str.
Clarendon Road
Livingston Rd.
Shirley Str.
Goldstone Road
Clarendon Villas
Blatchington Rd.
Cromwell Road
Cricket Ground
Goldsmid Road
Laundry
All Saints Ch.
Termi
Holy Trinity Ch.
Eaton Road
The Wick
Chap.
Childrens Hospital
St. Michael's Ch.
CLIFTON
HOVE
Lansdowne Road
Emmanuel Ch.
St. Stephen's Ch.
Victoria Road
Gas Works
St. Andrews Ch.
Church Road
Town Hall
St. John
Western Pl.
St. Nicholas Ch.
VILLE
the Baptists Ch.
WEST BRIGHTON
Western Road
Christ Ch.
Ch.
Russell Sq.
St. Paul's Ch.
Prince's Club
Post Off.
Coast Guard Sta.
Shoreham Road
Brunswick Ter.
The Lawns
The Hove Sea Wall Esplanade
Kings Road
Sailing Club
ENGLISH
West Pier

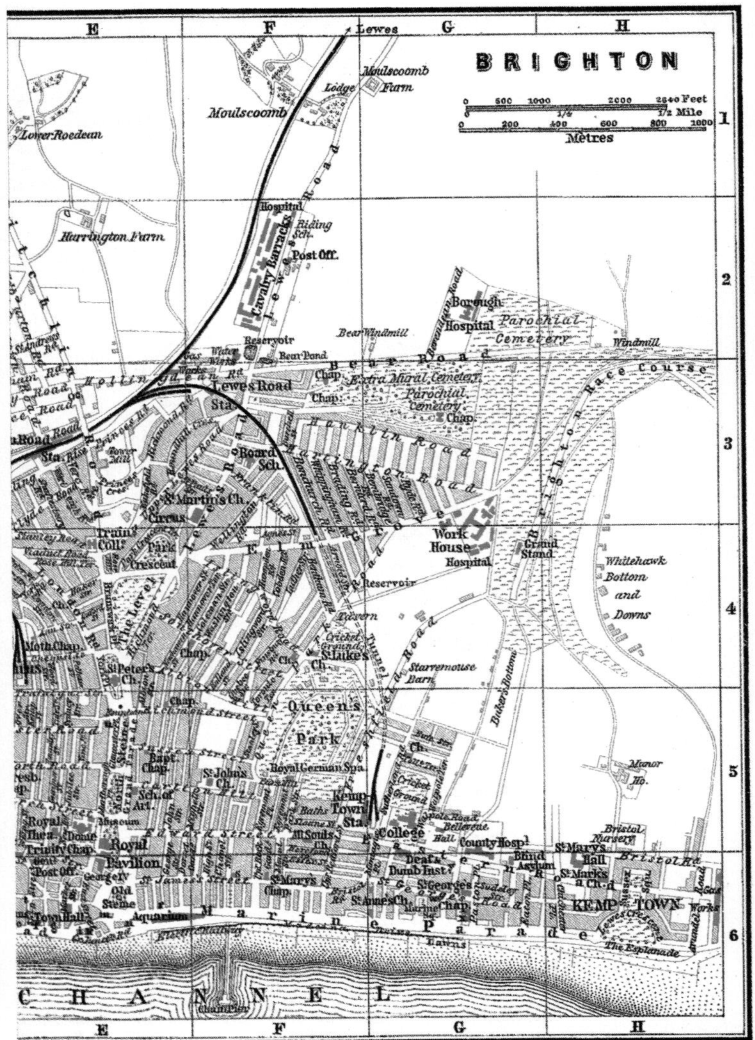
BRIGHTON
0 500 1000 2000 2640 Feet
1/2 Mile
0 200 400 600 800 1000
Mètres
E
F
G
H
1
2
3
4
5
6
Lewes
Moulscoomb
Moulscoomb Lodge
Farm
Lower Roedean
Harrington Farm
Hospital
Riding Sch.
Cavalry Barracks
Post Off.
Lewes Road
Borough Hospital
Parochial Cemetery
Bear Windmill
Windmill
Reservoir
Bear Pond
Bear Road
Race Course
Extra Mural Cemetery
Parochial Cemetery
Chap.
Lewes Road Sta.
Hanover Road
Board Sch.
St. Martin's Ch.
Circus
Train. Coll.
Park Crescent
The Level
Work House
Hospital
Grand Stand
Whitehawk Bottom and Downs
Reservoir
Tavern
Cricket Ground
St. Luke's Ch.
Starvemouse Barn
Baker's Bottom
St. Peter's Ch.
Queen's Park
Royal German Spa
St. John's Ch.
Bapt. Chap.
Sch. of Art.
Museum
Kemp Town Sta.
College
County Hosp.
Manor Ho.
Bristol Nursery
St. Mary's Hall
Royal Pavilion
Edward Street
St. James's Street
Dome
Trinity Chap.
Post Off.
Old Steine
Aquarium
Town Hall
St. Mary's Chap.
St. Anne's Ch.
Deaf & Dumb Inst.
Blind Asylum
St. George's Chap.
St. Mark's Ch.
Kemp Town
Lewes Crescent
The Esplanade
Gas Works
Marine Parade
Lawns
C H A N N E L
Chain Pier
Wagner & Debes' Geogl. Estabt., Leipsic.

see page 48

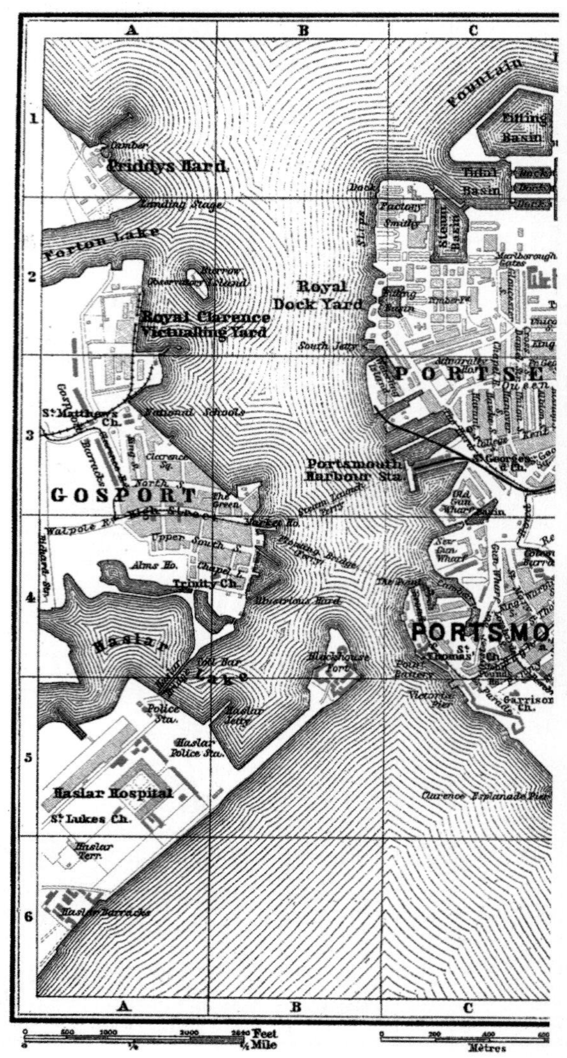

A
B
C
1
2
3
4
5
6
Fountain
Fitting Basin
Camber
Priddys Hard
Tidal Basin
Dock
Landing Stage
Factory
Smithy
Steam Basin
Forton Lake
Slips
Burrow
Observatory Island
Royal Dock Yard
Marlborough Gates
Royal Clarence Victualling Yard
South Jetty
Admiralty Rd.
P O R T S E
St. Matthews Ch.
National Schools
Barracks
Clarence Sq.
North S.
Portsmouth Harbour Sta.
St. Georges Ch.
G O S P O R T
The Green
Old Gun Wharf
Basin
Walpole Rd.
High Street
Market Ho.
Steam Launch Ferry
Upper South S.
Floating Bridge Ferry
New Gun Wharf
Alms Ho.
Chapel L.
Trinity Ch.
Illustrious Hard
PORTSMO
Haslar
Lake
Toll Bar
Blockhouse Fort
Point Battery
St. Thomas' Ch.
Victoria Pier
Garrison Ch.
Police Sta.
Haslar Jetty
Haslar Police Sta.
Haslar Hospital
Clarence Esplanade Pier
St. Lukes Ch.
Haslar Terr.
Haslar Barracks
Feet
Mile
Metres

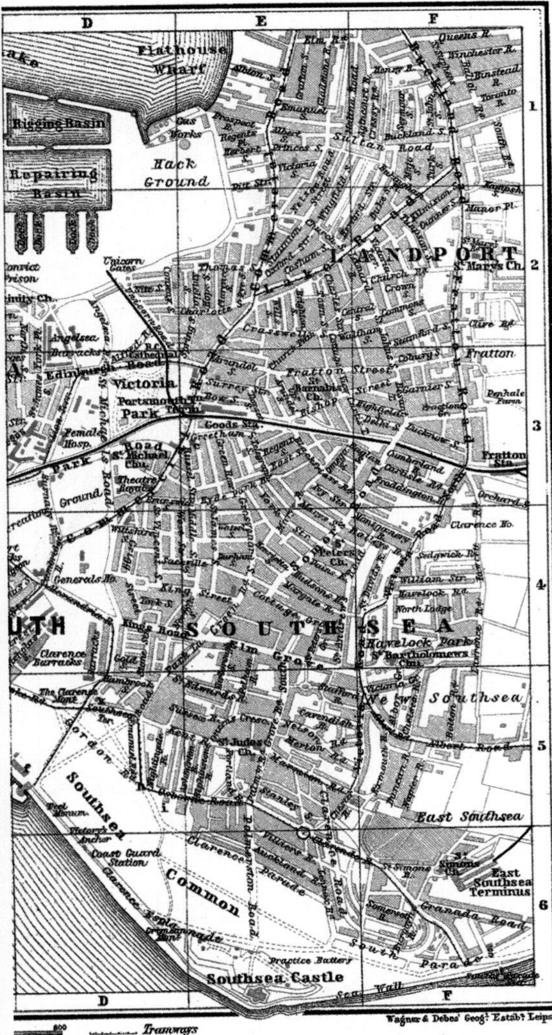
D
E
F
Flathouse Wharf
Rigging Basin
Repairing Basin
Hack Ground
Gas Works
Unicorn Gates
Convict Prison
LANDPORT
St. Marys Ch.
Fratton
Fratton Sta.
Victoria
Portsmouth Park
Goods Sta.
Angelsea Barracks
Edinburgh Road
Park Road
St. Michael Chu.
Theatre Royal
Female Hosp.
Sultan Road
Buckland S.
Arundel S.
Fratton Street
St. Barnabas Ch.
Bishop S.
Lucknow S.
Cumberland R.
Carlisle Rd.
Orchard S.
Clarence Ho.
Sedgwick Rd.
William Str.
Havelock Rd.
North Lodge
King Street
Kings Road
SOUTHSEA
Havelock Park
St. Bartholomews Chu.
Elm Grove
Clarence Barracks
Generals Ho.
New Southsea
Albert Road
East Southsea
St. Simons Ch.
East Southsea Terminus
Granada Road
South Parade
Southsea Common
Coast Guard Station
Clarence Esplanade
Practice Battery
Southsea Castle
Sea Wall
Osborne Road
Palmerston Road
Clarendon R.
Queens R.
Winchester R.
1
2
3
4
5
6
Wagner & Debes' Geogl. Establt. Leipsic.
Tramways

See page 56

Wagner & Debes' Geogr. Estabt. Leipsic.
Kilometres
DORKING
GUILDFORD
Mickleham
Little Bookham
Effingham
East Horsley
West Horsley
East Clandon
West Clandon
Merrow
Stoke
Wotton
Abinger
Shere
Albury
Shalford
Wonersh
Bramley

ISLE OF WIGHT

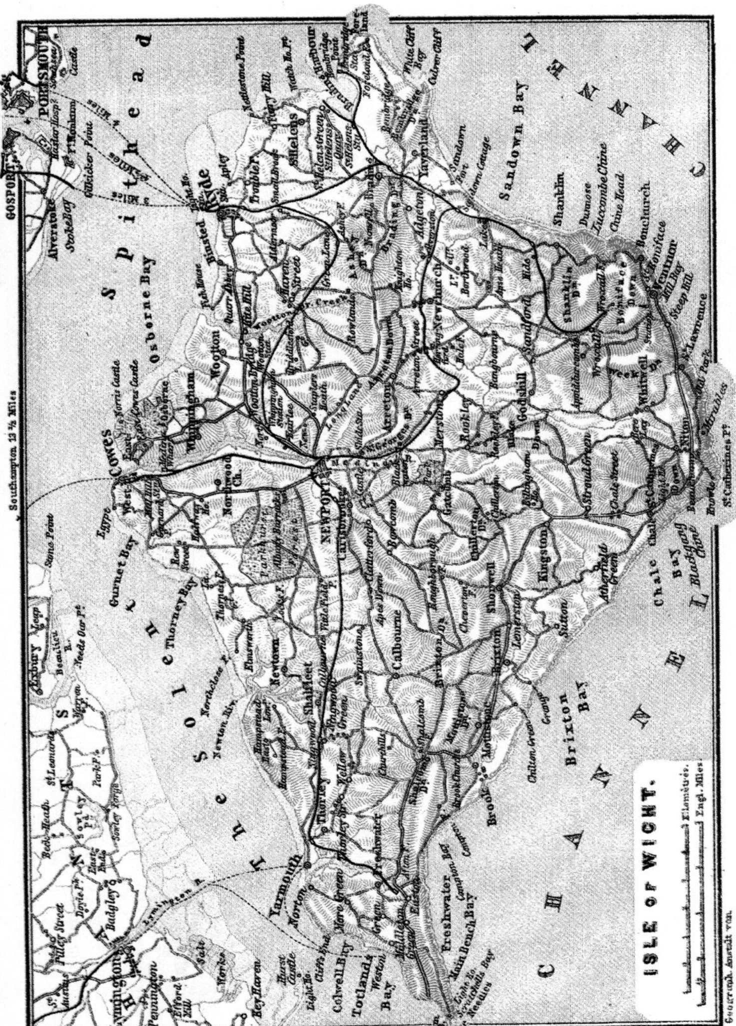

See page 67

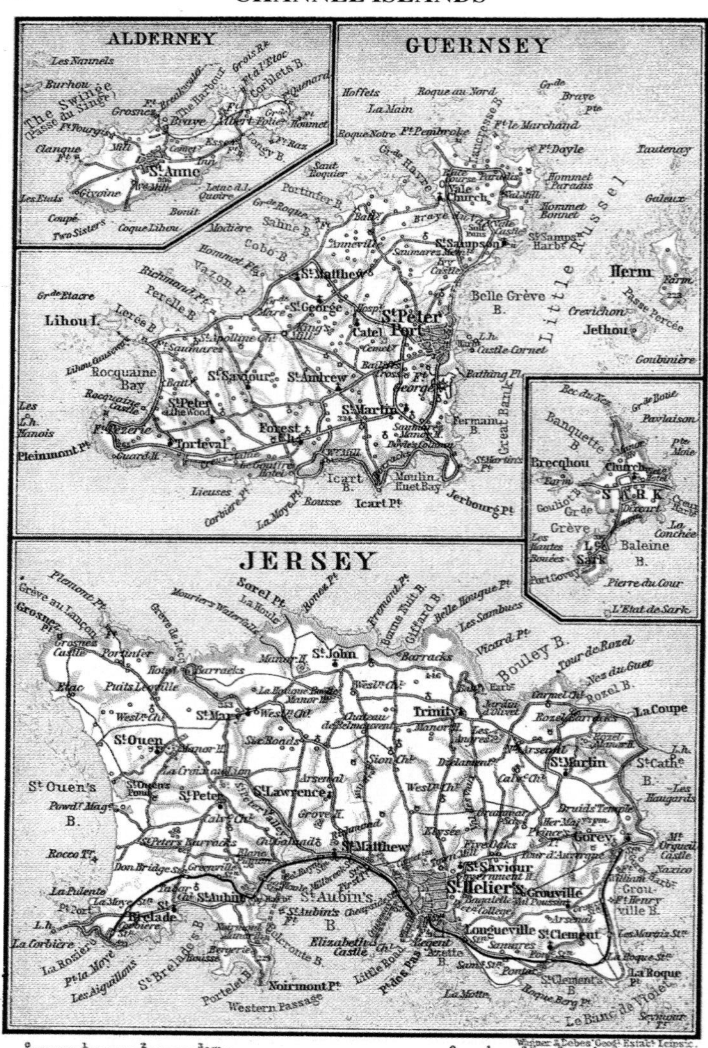
ALDERNEY
GUERNSEY
JERSEY
St. Anne
St. Peter Port
Herm
Jethou
Brecqhou
SARK
Little Sark
St. Helier's
St. John
Trinity
St. Mary
St. Ouen
St. Peter
St. Lawrence
St. Martin
St. Saviour
Grouville
St. Clement
Gorey
St. Aubin
St. Brelade
Lihou I.
Rocquaine Bay
St. Sampson
St. Saviour
St. Andrew
St. Matthew
St. George
Torteval
Forest
Icart Pt.
Jerbourg Pt.
Noirmont Pt.
Elizabeth Castle
St. Aubin's B.
St. Ouen's B.
Bouley B.
Wagner & Debes' Geogl. Estabt. Leipsic.
Miles
Kilomètres

See page 84

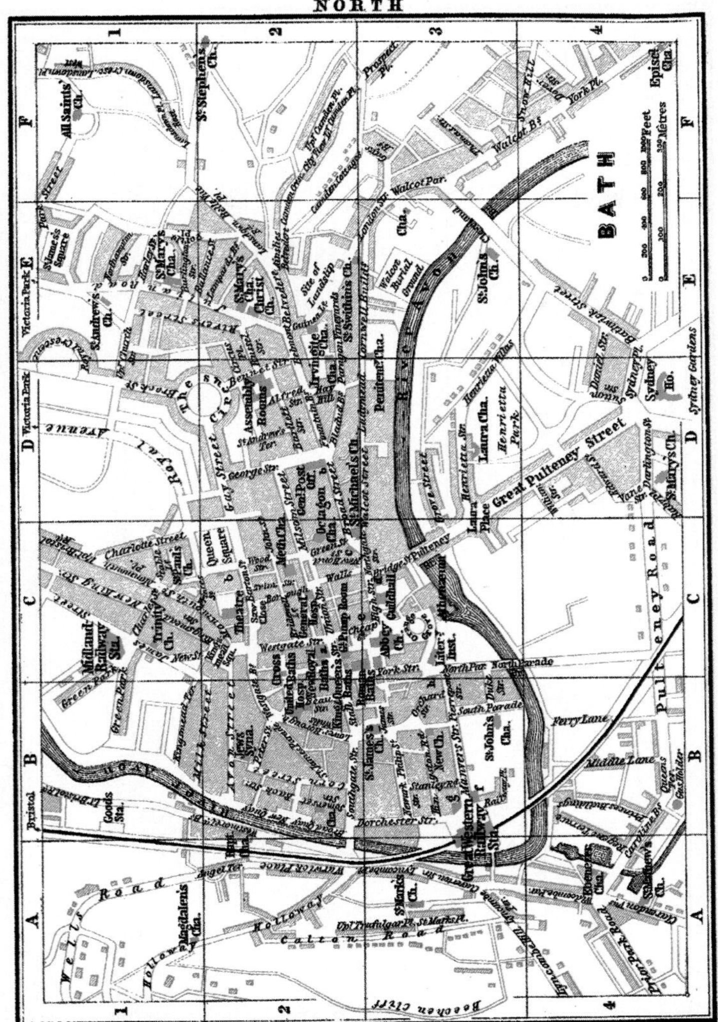
NORTH
SOUTH
BATH
Feet
Metres
Great Pulteney Street
River Avon
Pulteney Road
Great Western Railway Sta.
Midland Railway Sta.
Royal Avenue
The Circus
Queen Square
Assembly Rooms
Abbey Ch.
Guildhall
Pump Room
Milsom Street
Gay Street
Henrietta Park
Laura Place
Sydney Ho.
Sydney Gardens
Walcot Burial Ground
Victoria Park
Green Park
Theatre
Wells Road
Holloway
Beechen Cliff

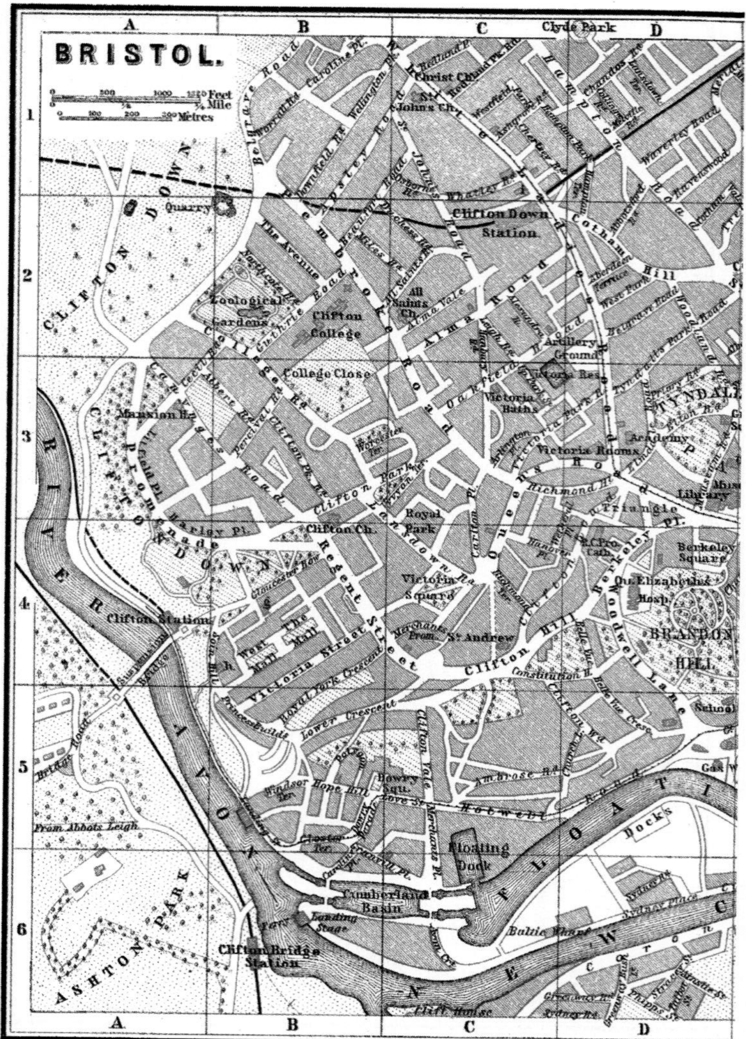
BRISTOL.
Feet
Mile
Metres
Clifton Down
Quarry
Clifton Down Station
Zoological Gardens
Clifton College
College Close
All Saints Ch.
Artillery Ground
Victoria Res.
Victoria Baths
Victoria Rooms
Tyndall's Park
Academy
Library
Triangle
Royal Park
Clifton Ch.
R.C. Pro Cath.
Berkeley Square
Qu. Elizabeth's Hosp.
Brandon Hill
Victoria Square
St. Andrew
Clifton Station
Suspension Bridge
River Avon
Floating Dock
Cumberland Basin
Landing Stage
Clifton Bridge Station
Ashton Park
From Abbots Leigh
Docks
Baltic Wharf
Cliff House
Clyde Park
Dowry Squ.
Hotwell Road
Clifton Hill
Regent Street
Victoria Street
Lower Crescent
Royal York Crescent
Whiteladies Road
Pembroke Road
Queens Road
Alma Road
Cotham Hill
Hampton Road
Gas W.
School

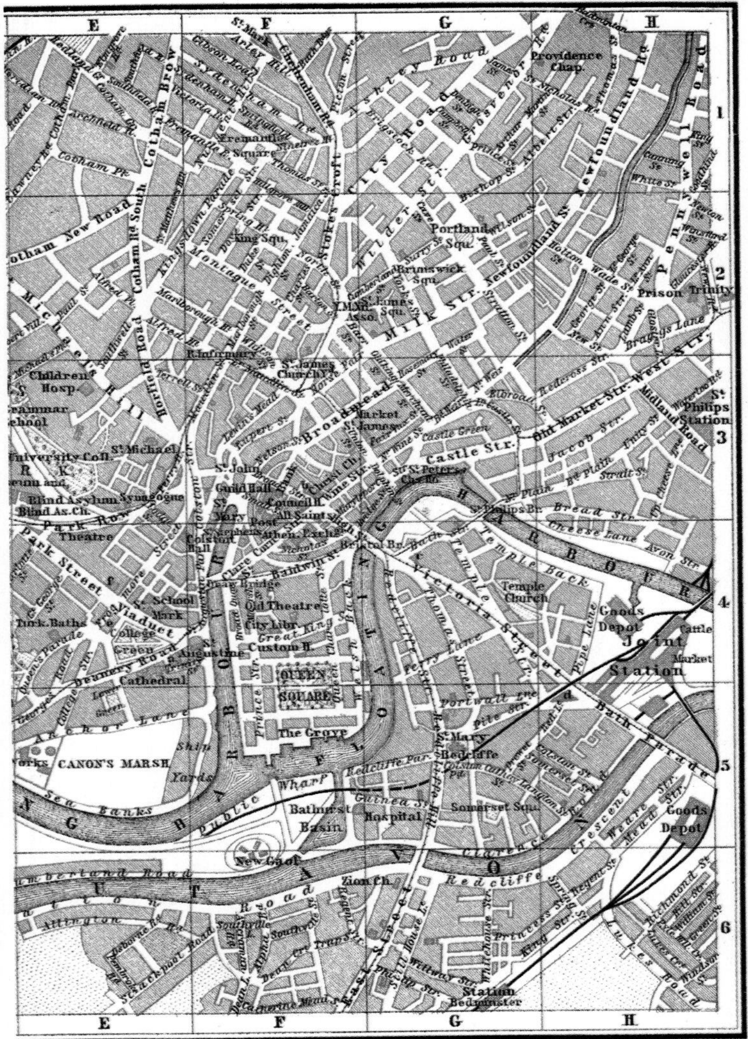
E
F
G
H
1
2
3
4
5
6
Providence Chap.
Ashley Road
Grosvenor Rd
Newfoundland Rd
Newfoundland St.
City Road
Stokes Croft
Cheltenham Rd.
Arley Hill
Cotham Brow
Cotham Rd South
Cotham New Road
Cotham Pk.
Fremantle Square
King Squ.
Montague Street
Portland Squ.
Brunswick Squ.
St James Squ.
Y.M.Xn. Asso.
Milk Str.
Wilder St.
Horfield Road
R. Infirmary
St James Church Y.
Children's Hosp.
Grammar School
University Coll.
St Michael
Broadmead
Market St James
Castle Green
Castle Str.
Old Market Str.
West Str.
St Philips Station
Midland Road
Jacob Str.
Prison
Trinity
St John
Guild Hall
Council H.
All Saints
Post
Athen.
Exch.
St Mary
Blind Asylum
Blind As. Ch.
Synagogue
Park Row
Theatre
Park Street
Colston Hall
Bristol Br.
Baldwin St.
Victoria Street
Temple Back
Temple Church
Temple St.
Goods Depot
Joint Station
Cattle Market
Drawbridge
Old Theatre
City Libr.
Custom H.
Queen Square
Prince Str.
St Augustine
Cathedral
College Green
Turk. Baths
St Mark
School
Viaduct
Deanery Road
Anchor Lane
Canon's Marsh
Ship Yards
The Grove
St Mary Redcliffe
Redcliffe Par.
Redcliff St.
Portwall Lne.
Pile Str.
Bath Parade
Somerset Squ.
Guinea Str.
Hospital
Bathurst Basin
Public Wharf
Sea Banks
New Gaol
Zion Ch.
Cumberland Road
Coronation Road
Redcliffe Crescent
Clarence Road
Goods Depot
Mead Str.
Princess Str.
East Street
Station Bedminster
Lukes Road
Richmond St.
Floating Harbour
River Avon

see page 113

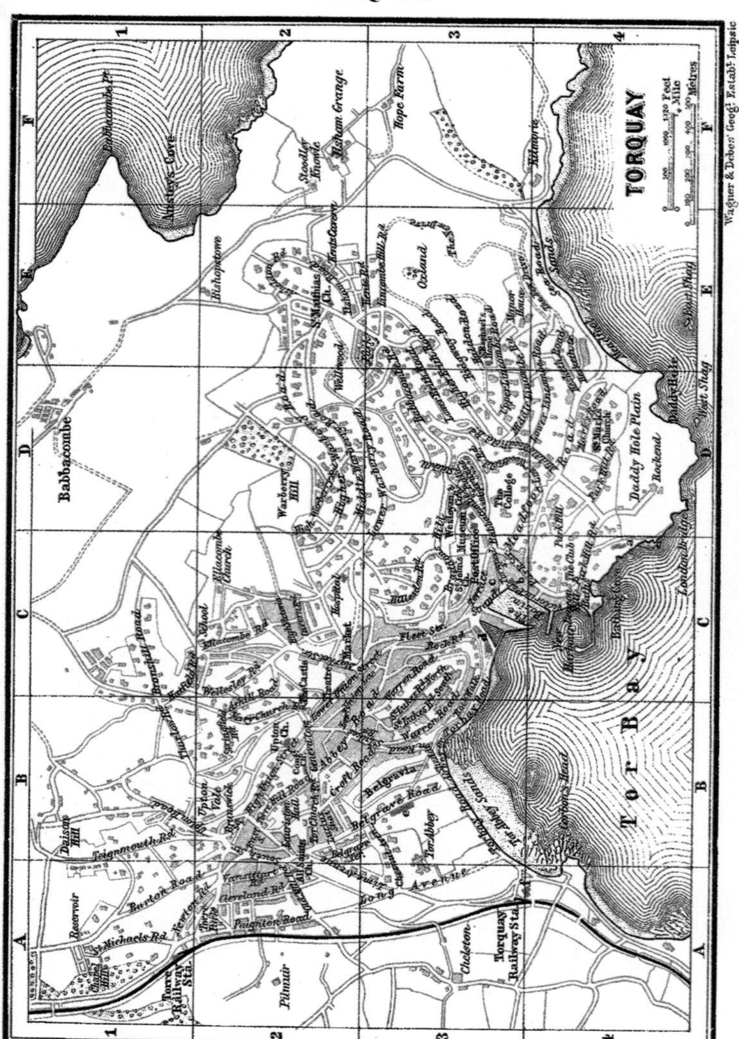
TORQUAY
TOR BAY
Babbacombe
Anstey's Cove
Torquay Railway Sta.
Torre Railway Sta.
Daddy Hole Plain
Warberry Hill
Torre Abbey
Wagner & Debes' Geog! Estab! Leipsic

See page 130

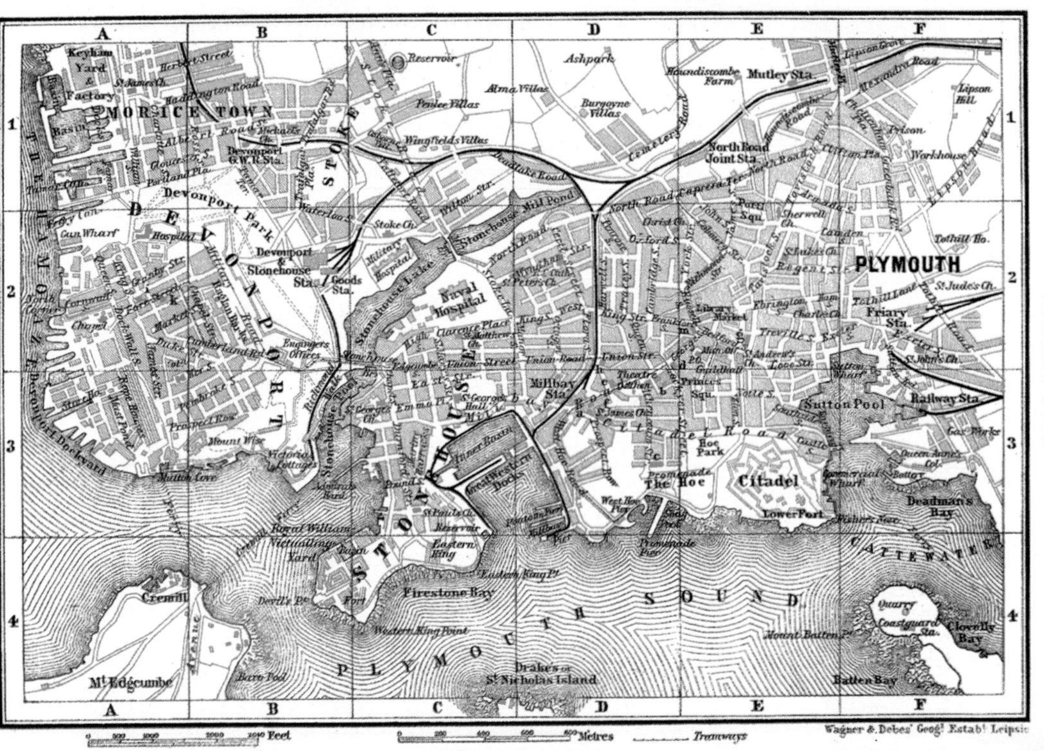

PLYMOUTH
DEVONPORT
STONEHOUSE
STOKE
MORICE TOWN
THE HAMOAZE
PLYMOUTH SOUND
CATTEWATER
Citadel
The Hoe
Hoe Park
Sutton Pool
Drake's or St. Nicholas Island
Mt. Edgcumbe
Cremill
Devonport Park
Naval Hospital
Millbay Sta.
North Road Joint Sta.
Mutley Sta.
Friary Sta.
Railway Sta.
Devonport Dockyard
Keyham Yard & Factory
Royal William Victualling Yard
Great Western Docks
Firestone Bay
Deadman's Bay
Batten Bay
Clovelly Bay
Stonehouse Lake
Stonehouse Mill Pond
Ashpark
Burgoyne Villas
Alma Villas
Reservoir
Military Road
Gun Wharf
Rope Houses
Mast Pond
Mount Wise
Prospect Row
Citadel Road
Union Street
Lower Fort
Feet
Metres
Tramways
Wagner & Debes' Geogl. Estabt. Leipsic

See page 139

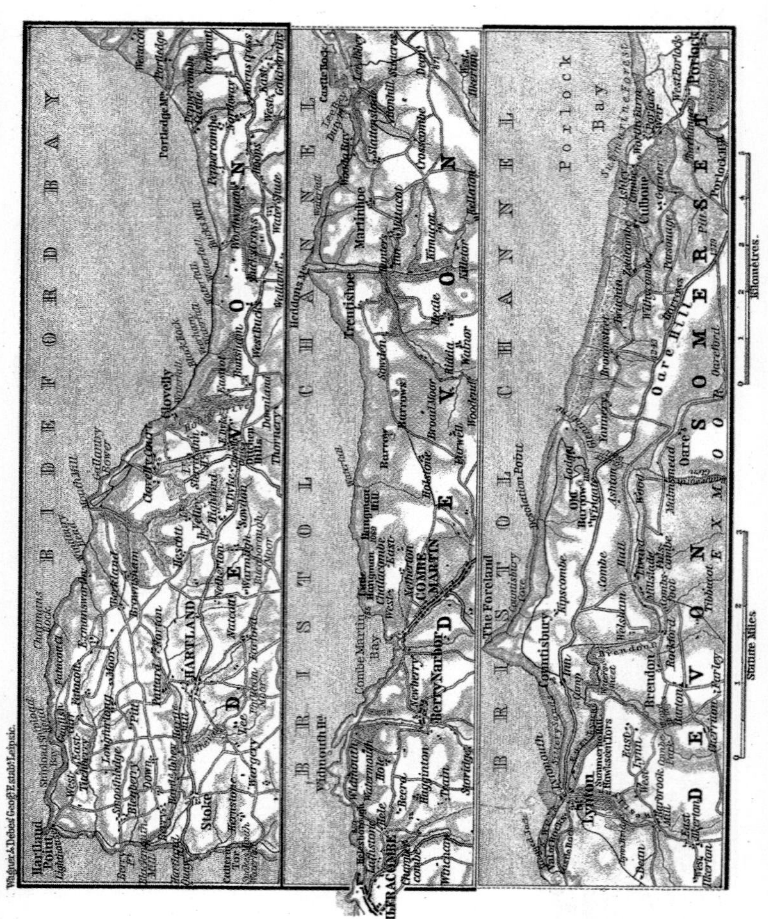
BIDEFORD BAY
BRISTOL CHANNEL
BRISTOL CHANNEL
Porlock Bay
DEVON
DEVON
DEVON
SOMERSET
EXMOOR
HARTLAND
Clovelly
COMBE MARTIN
Lynton
Porlock
Kilometres
Statute Miles
Wagner & Debes Geogr. Estab.t Leipsic.

See page 161

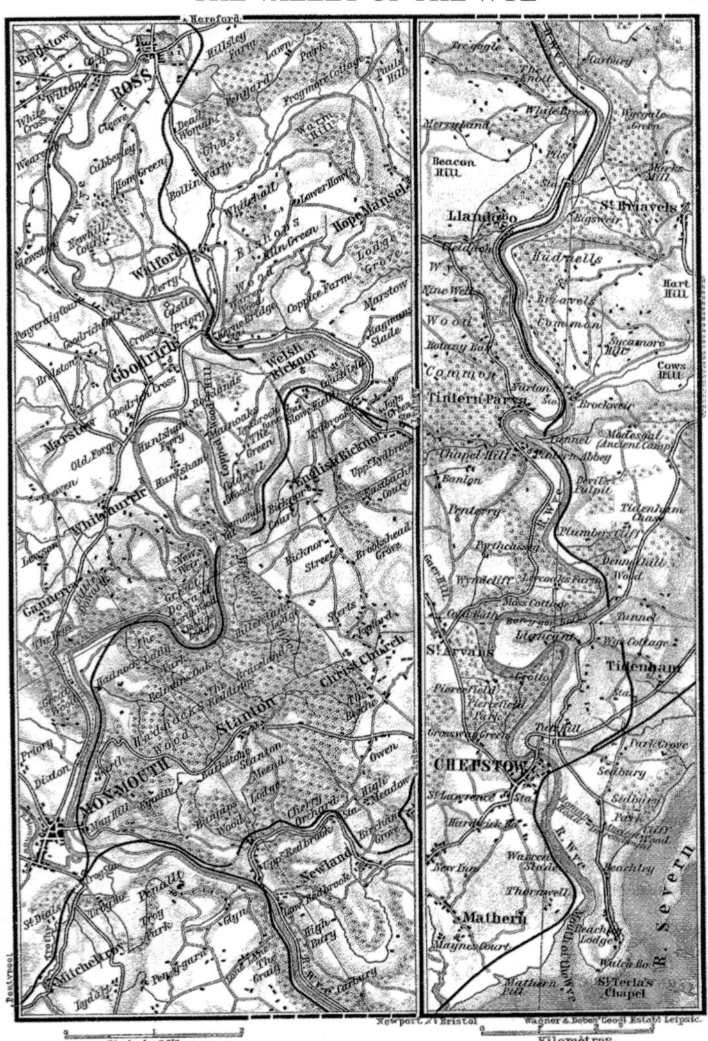
Hereford
ROSS
Wilton
Bridstow
White Cross
Weare
Cubberley
Hom Green
Dean Woman
Chase
Bollin Farm
Penyard
Hillsley Farm
Lawn
Park
Progmore Cottage
Pauls Hill
Warth Hill
Whitehall
Lower Howl
Bishops Wood
Kiln Green
Hope Mansel
Lodge Grove
Wilford
Ferry
Newhill Court
Glewstone
Castle
Priory
Goodrich
Goodrich Cross
Goodrich Court
Coppice Farm
Marstow
Bagmans Slade
Welsh Bicknor
Courtfield
Rocklands
Mainoaks
Coppet Hill
Huntsham Ferry
Huntsham
Old Forge
Marstow
Ganarew
Whitchurch
English Bicknor
Upp. Lydbrook
Eastbach Court
Coldwell
Symonds Yat
Bicknor Court
Bicknor Street
Brookshead Grove
New Weir
Great Doward
Little Doward
Hillersland
Christ Church
The Biche
Stanton
Hadnock
Beaulieu Wood
Braceland
Hadnock's Wood
Buckstone
Stanton Mead
Lodge
Bunjups Wood
Cherry Orchard
High Meadow
Owen
Birchan Grove
Priory
Dixon
MONMOUTH
Kymin
May Hill
Troy Sta.
Penallt
Trelleck
Troy Park
Newland
Upp. Redbrook
Low. Redbrook
Glyn
High Bury
St. Dials
Mitchel Troy
Pen y garn
Ivy Lane
The Graig
Llandogo
Pontypool
R. Wye
Carbury
Statute Miles
Newport
Bristol
Breygagle
The Knoll
Marbury
White Brook
Wyegale Green
Merryland
Beacon Hill
Pilis
Mocks Hill
St. Briavels
Bigsweir
Hudnells
Hart Hill
Nine Wells
St. Briavels Common
Wood
Botany Bay
Sycamore Hill
Common
Cows Hill
Tintern Parva
Brockweir
Tunnel
Madesgal (Ancient Camp)
Chapel Hill
Tintern Abbey
Devil's Pulpit
Penterry
Tidenham Chase
Plumbers Cliff
Porthcasseg
Dennel Hill Wood
Wyndcliff
Moss Cottage
Cold Bath
Tunnel
Llancaut
Wye Cottage
St. Arvans
Tidenham
Piercefield
Piercefield Park
Grotto
Tutshill
Park Grove
CHEPSTOW
Sedbury
St. Lawrence
Sedbury Park
Hardwick Ho.
New Inn
Warren Slade
Beachley
Thornwell
Mathern
Beachley Lodge
Maynes Court
Mathern Pill
St. Tecla's Chapel
Mouth of the Wye
R. Severn
Wagner & Debes' Geogl. Estabt. Leipsic.
Kilomètres

See page 175

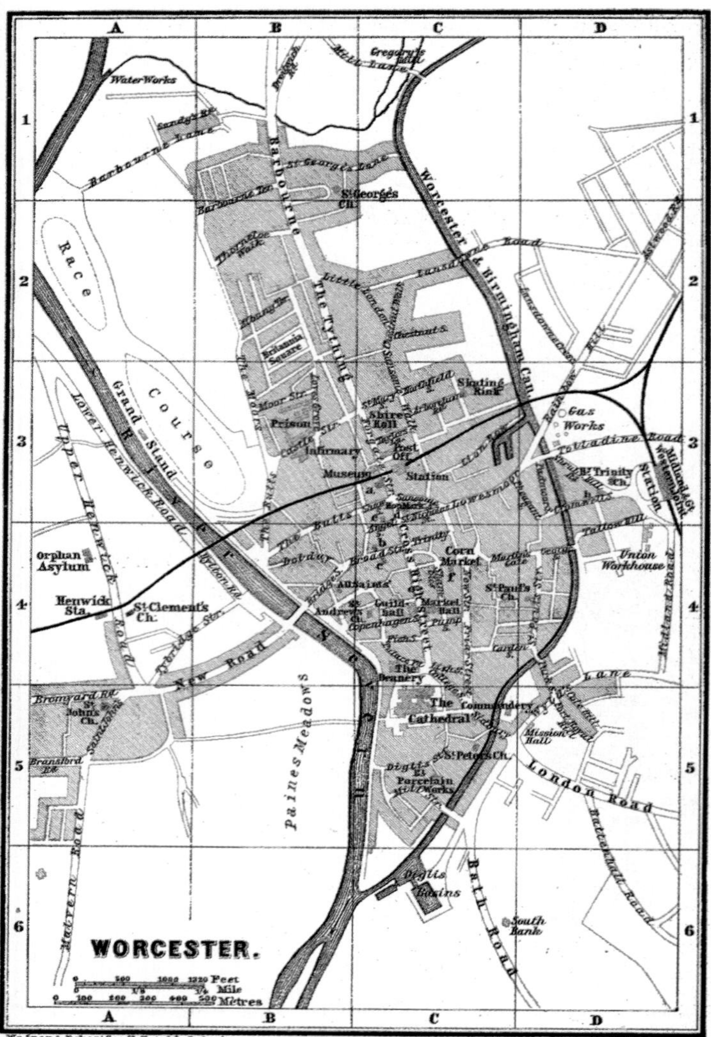

Wagner & Debes' Geogl. Estabt. Leipsic.

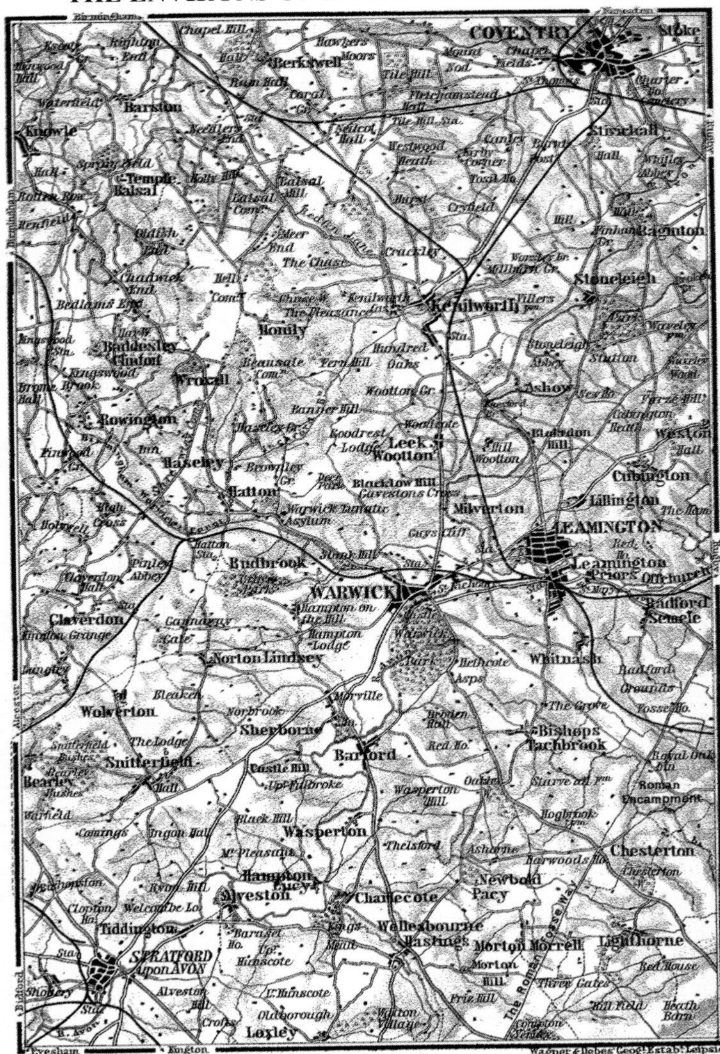
COVENTRY
Stoke
Chapel Hill
Berkswell
Mount Nod
Chapel Fields
Tile Hill
Barston
Knowle
Tile Hill Sta.
Stivichall
Canley
Westwood Heath
Temple Balsal
Balsal
Balsal Com.
Cryfield
Baginton
Meer End
The Chase
Crackley
Stoneleigh
Chadwick End
Bedlams End
Kenilworth
Honily
Baddesley Clinton
Wroxall
Hundred Oaks
Beausale Com.
Fern Hill
Stoneleigh Abbey
Ashow
Wootton Gr.
Rowington
Haseley
Leek Wootton
Hill Wootton
Blacklow Hill
Gavestons Cross
Hatton
Weston Hall
Cubbington
Lillington
Milverton
Warwick Lunatic Asylum
LEAMINGTON
Leamington Priors
Offchurch
Hatton Sta.
Budbrook
WARWICK
Radford Semele
Claverdon
Hampton on the Hill
Hampton Lodge
Norton Lindsey
Whitnash
Warwick Park
Bleaken
Wolverton
Norbrook
Sherborne
Bishops Tachbrook
Snitterfield
Barford
Bearley
Castle Hill
Roman Encampment
Wasperton Hill
Black Hill
Wasperton
Thelsford
Chesterton
Hampton Lucey
Alveston
Charlecote
Newbold Pacy
Clopton
Welcombe Lo.
Tiddington
Wellesbourne Hastings
Morton Morrell
Lighthorne
STRATFORD upon AVON
The Roman Fosse Way
Three Gates
Alveston Hill
Oldborough
Loxley
Walton Village
Heath Barn
R. Avon
Evesham
Wagner & Debes' Geogl. Estabt. Leipsic.

See page 244

OXFORD

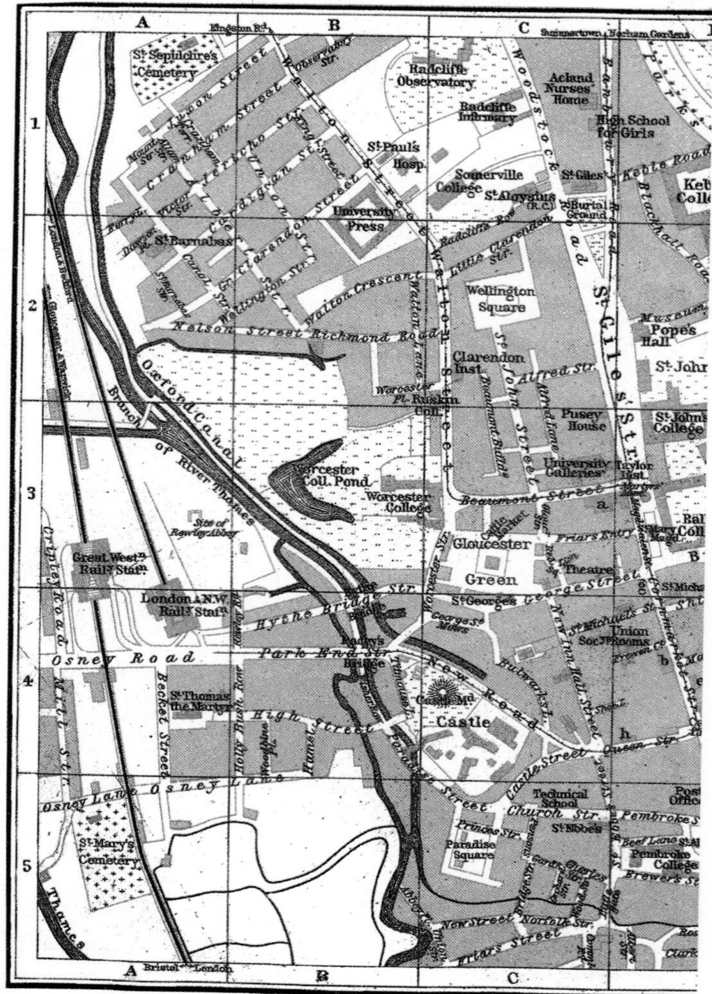

A
B
C
1
2
3
4
5
Kingston Rd.
Summertown, Norham Gardens
St. Sepulchre's Cemetery
Observatory Str.
Radcliffe Observatory
Acland Nurses' Home
Radcliffe Infirmary
High School for Girls
Jericho Str.
St. Paul's Hosp.
Somerville College
St. Aloysius (R.C.)
Burial Ground
St. Giles'
Keble Road
University Press
St. Barnabas
Radcliffe Row
Little Clarendon Str.
Wellington Square
Walton Crescent
Nelson Street
Richmond Road
Oxford Canal
Branch of River Thames
Clarendon Inst.
Alfred Str.
Ruskin Coll.
Pusey House
St. John's College
Beaumont Street
Worcester Coll. Pond
Worcester College
University Galleries
Taylor Inst.
Gloucester Green
Friars Entry
Theatre
George Street
Great West. Rail. Stat.
London & N.W. Rail. Stat.
Hythe Bridge Str.
St. Georges
Union Soc. Rooms
Osney Road
Park End Str.
New Road
Castle Md.
Castle
St. Thomas the Martyr
High Street
Becket Street
Holly Bush Row
Hamel Str.
Osney Lane
Castle Street
Queen Str.
Paradise Street
Technical School
Church Str.
Pembroke Str.
Post Office
St. Ebbe's
Princes Str.
Paradise Square
Pembroke College
Beef Lane
Brewer's Str.
St. Mary's Cemetery
Thames
New Street
Norfolk Str.
Friars Street
Bristol London

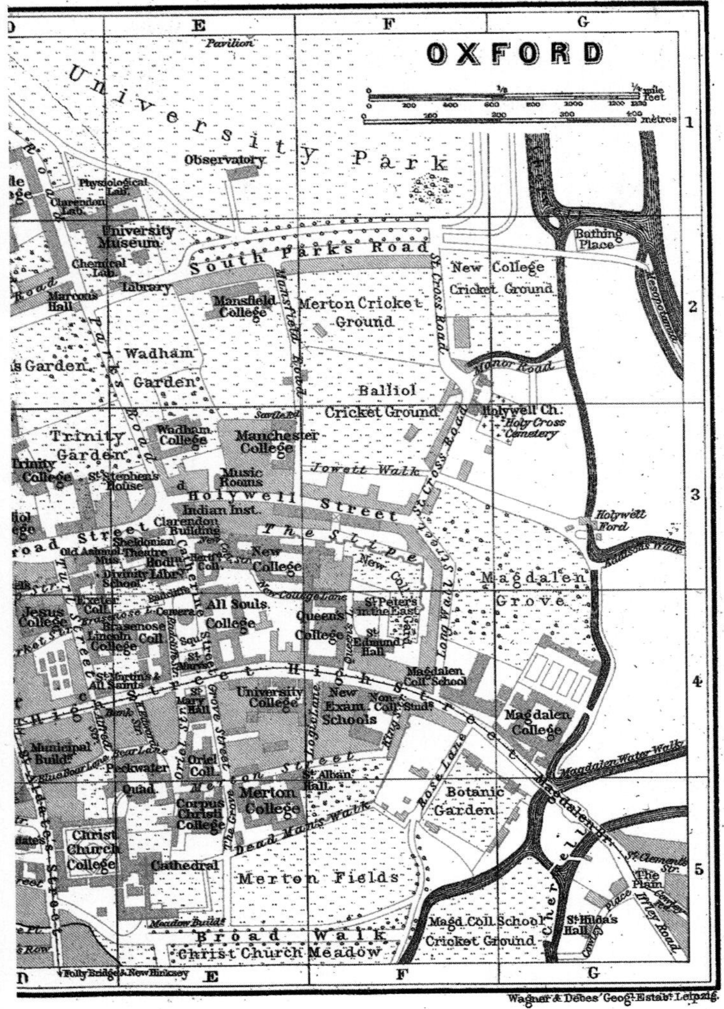

Wagner & Debes' Geogl. Estabt. Leipzig.

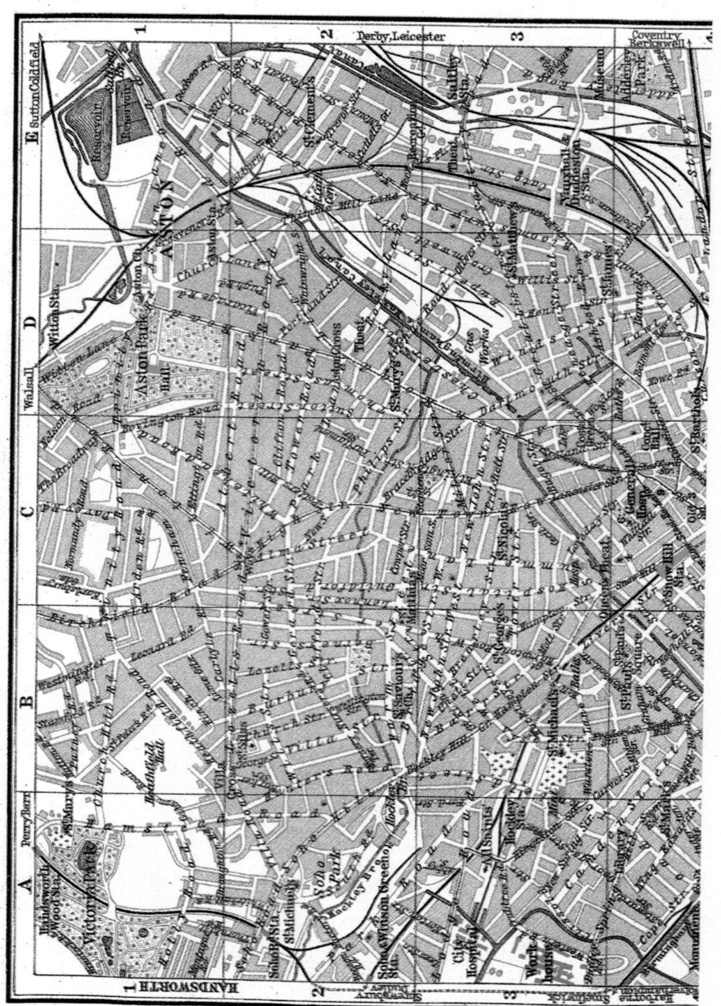
Sutton Coldfield
Walsall
Perry Barr
Derby, Leicester
Coventry
Berkswell
HANDSWORTH
Reservoir
Aston Park
Aston Hall
ASTON
Aston Sta.
Aston Ch.
Witton Sta.
Victoria Park
Handsworth Wood Sta.
Saltley Sta.
Museum
Adderley Park
Vauxhall & Duddeston Sta.
Gas Works
Soho Sta.
Soho
St. Michael's
Hockley Sta.
All Saints
City Hospital
Work-house
Snow Hill Sta.
St. Paul's Square
Queen's Theat.
Gen. Hosp.
Town Hall
A
B
C
D
E
1
2
3

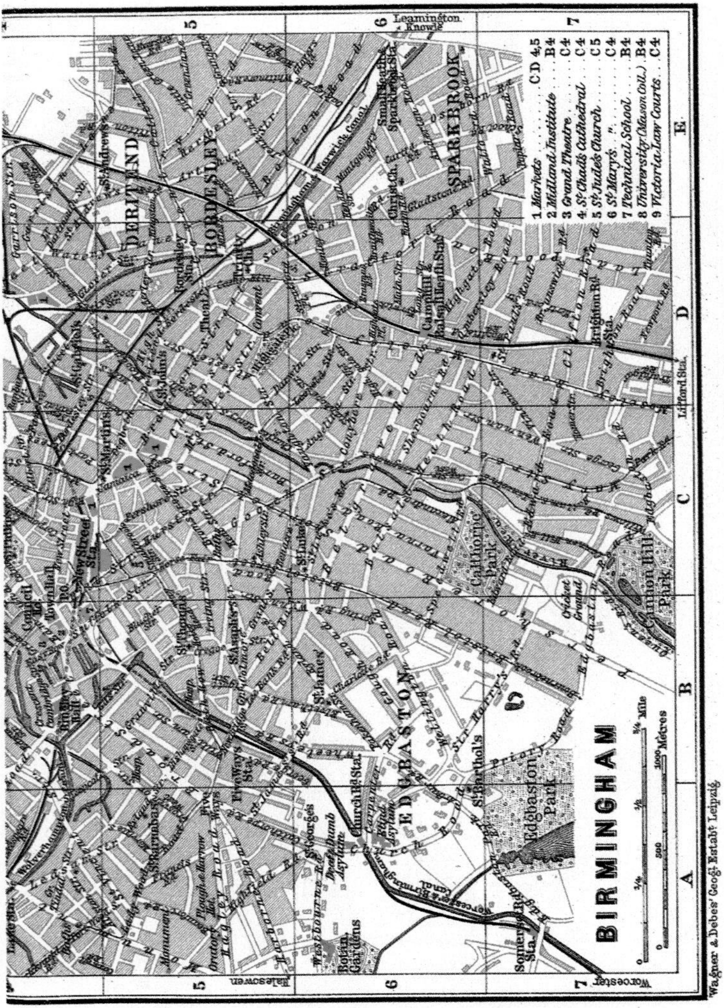

BIRMINGHAM
1 Markets . . . . C D 4,5
2 Midland Institute B4
3 Grand Theatre C4
4 St Chad's Cathedral . . . C4
5 St Jude's Church C5
6 St Mary's " C4
7 Technical School B4
8 University (Mason Coll.) . B4
9 Victoria Law Courts . . . C4
0 1/4 1/2 3/4 Mile
0 500 1000 Mètres
A B C D E
5 6 7
DERITEND
BORDESLEY
SPARKBROOK
EDGBASTON
Edgbaston Park
Calthorpe Park
Cannon Hill Park
Botan. Gardens
New Street Sta.
Council Ho.
Town Hall
Five Ways Sta.
Church Rd Sta.
Somerset Rd Sta.
Camphill & Balsall Heath Sta.
Small Heath & Sparkbrook Sta.
Brighton Rd Sta.
Lifford Sta.
Bordesley Sta.
Halesowen
Worcester
Leamington Knowle
Wagner & Debes' Geogr. Estabt. Leipzig

See page 254

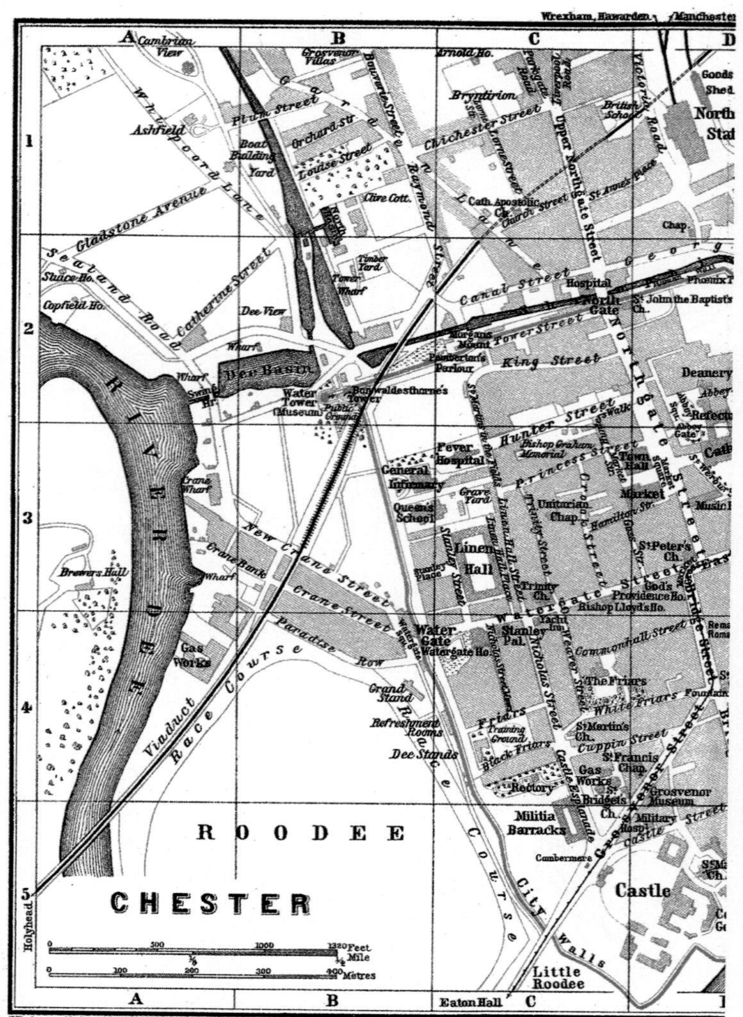

Wagner & Debes' Geogl. Establ. Leipsic.

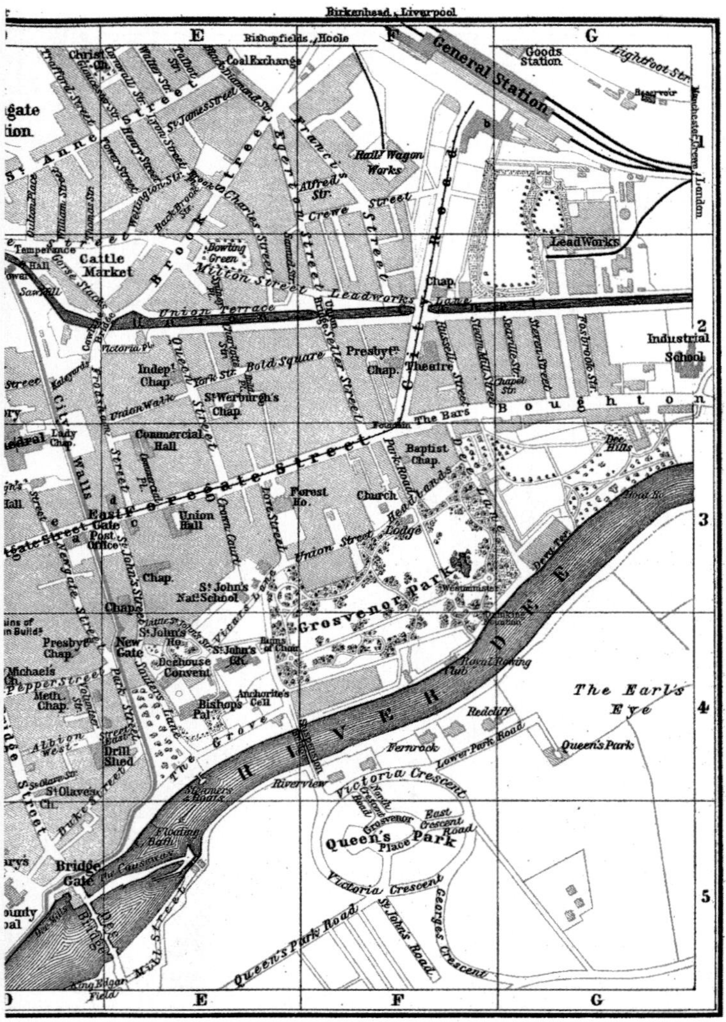
Birkenhead, Liverpool
Bishopfields, Hoole
General Station
Goods Station
Lightfoot Str.
Reservoir
Coal Exchange
Christ Ch.
Rail.y Wagon Works
Lead Works
Cattle Market
Temperance Hall
Bowling Green
Milton Street
Leadworks Lane
Union Terrace
Chap.
Industrial School
Presbyt.n Chap.
Theatre
Indep.t Chap.
Bold Square
St Werburgh's Chap.
Boughton
The Bars
Commercial Hall
Lady Chap.
Baptist Chap.
Dee Hills
Foregate Street
Eastgate
Forest Ho.
Church
Union Hall
Post Office
Union Street
Lodge
City Walls
Chap.
St John's Nat.l School
Grosvenor Park
Westminster
Presbyt.n Chap.
New Gate
St John's Ho.
St John's Ch.
Deehouse Convent
Royal Rowing Club
Meth. Chap.
Bishops Pal.
Anchorite's Cell
The Earl's Eye
Redcliff
Drill Shed
The Grove
River Dee
Fernrock
Lower Park Road
Queen's Park
Riverview
Victoria Crescent
St Olave's Ch.
Queen's Park
Grosvenor Place
Floating Bath
Bridge Gate
The Causeway
Dee Bridge
Victoria Crescent
Queen's Park Road
St John's Road
Georges Crescent
Mill Street
King Edgar Field
D E F G
1 2 3 4 5

See page 269

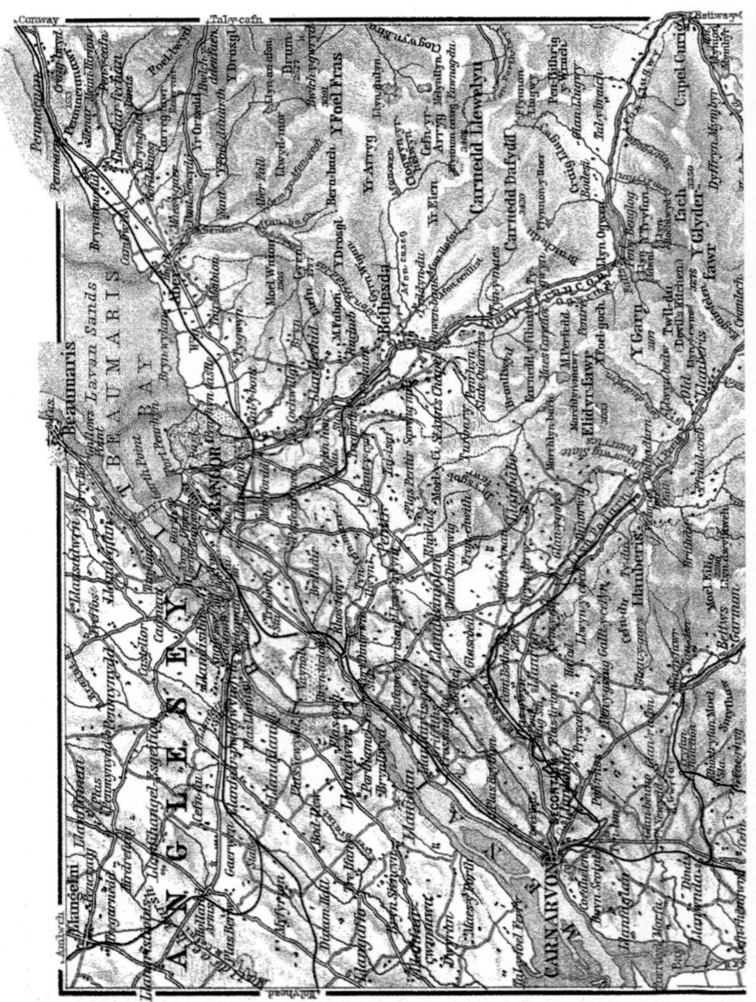
Conway
Tal-y-cafn
Bettws-y-Coed
Holyhead
Amlwch
ANGLESEY
BEAUMARIS BAY
Lavan Sands
Beaumaris
BANGOR
CARNARVON
Bethesda
Llanberis
Penmaenmawr
Y Foel Fras
Carnedd Llewelyn
Carnedd Dafydd
Capel Curig
Y Garn
Elidyr Fawr
Y Glyder fawr

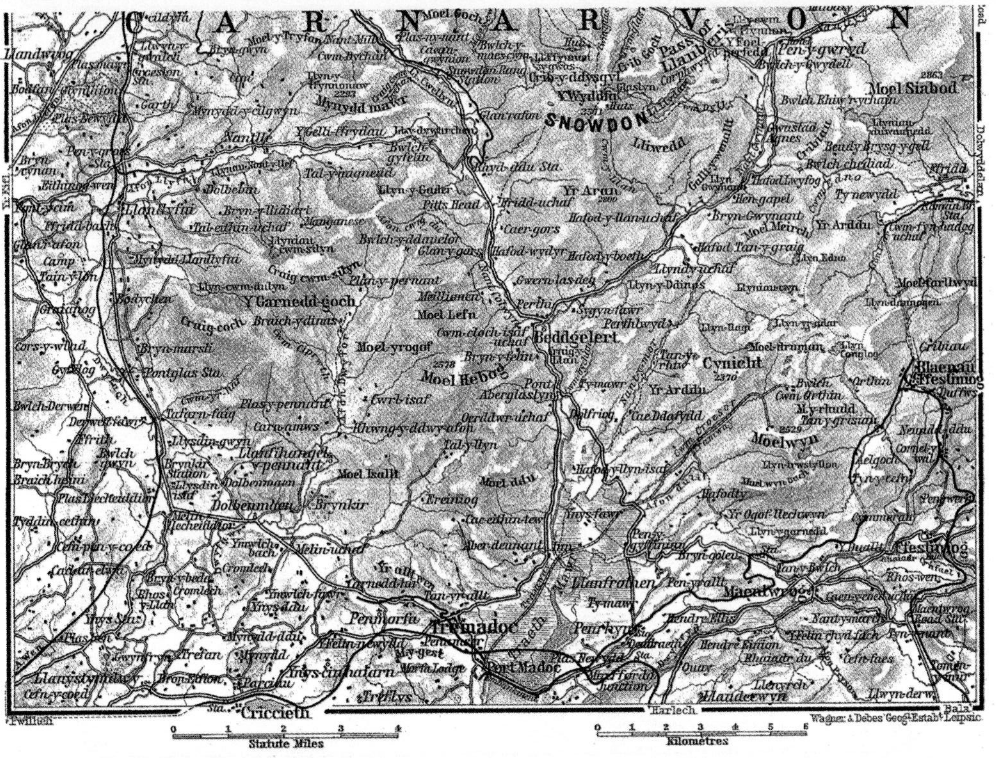
CARNARVON
SNOWDON
Y Wyddfa
Pass of Llanberis
Moel Siabod
Y Garnedd-goch
Moel Hebog
Moel Lefn
Cynicht
Moelwyn
Beddgelert
Nantlle
Llanllyfni
Dolbenmaen
Tremadoc
Port Madoc
Criccieth
Maentwrog
Ffestiniog
Blaenau Ffestiniog
Dolwyddelan
Harlech
Bala
Pwllheli
Statute Miles
Kilometres
Wagner & Debes' Geog! Estab! Leipsic

PANORAMA FROM THE TOP OF SNOWDON

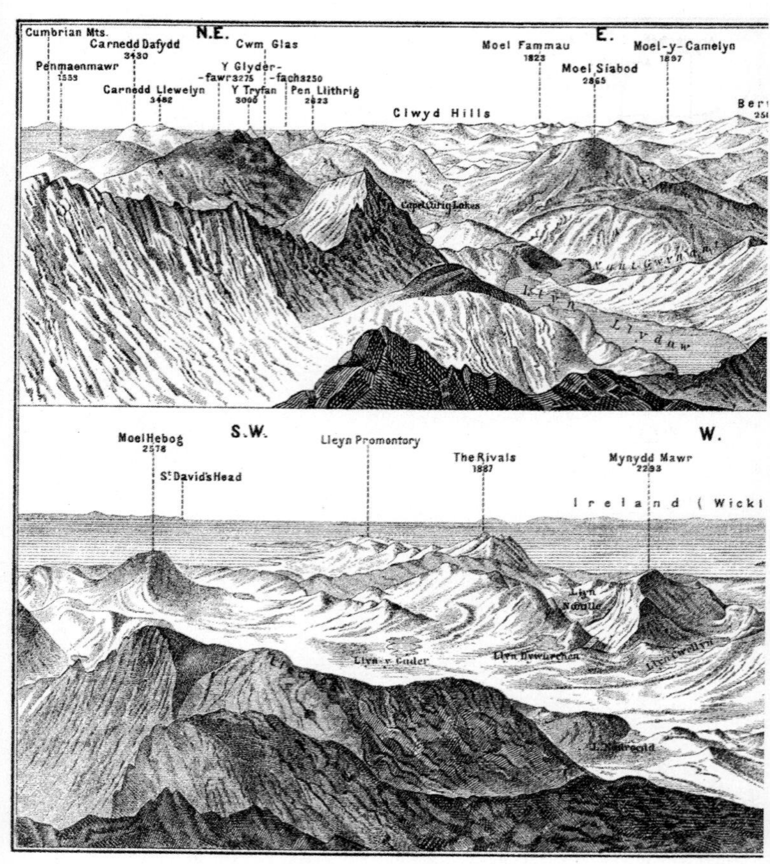

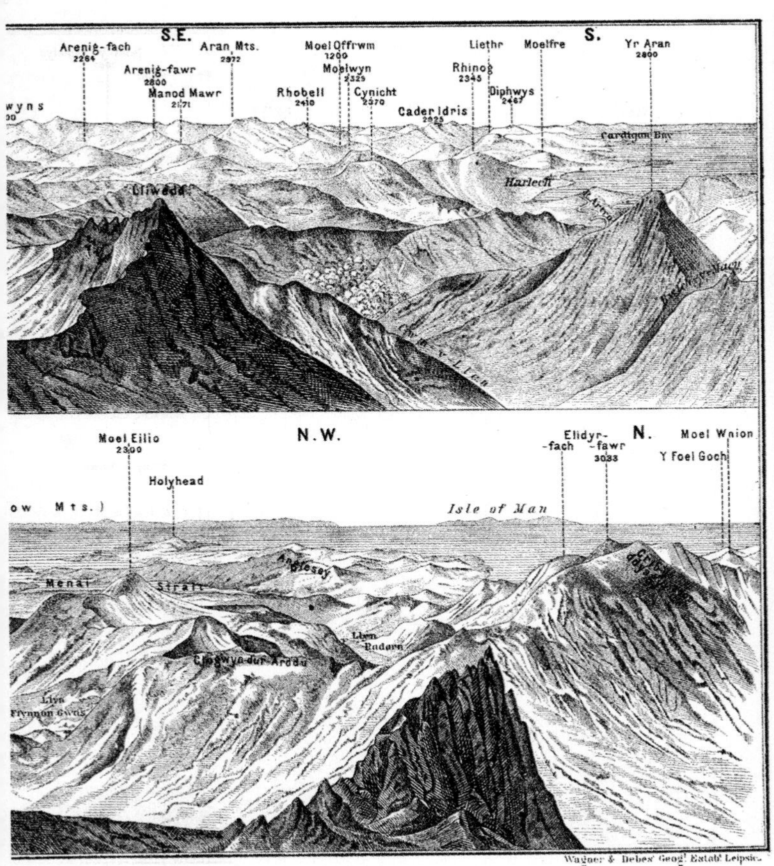
S.E.
Arenig-fach
2264
Arenig-fawr
2800
Aran Mts.
2972
Manod Mawr
2171
Moel Offrwm
1209
Moelwyn
2329
Rhobell
2410
Cynicht
2370
Cader Idris
2925
Liethr
Rhinog
2345
Moelfre
Diphwys
2467
S.
Yr Aran
2800
Cardigan Bay
Harlech
Lliwedd
N.W.
Moel Eilio
2300
Holyhead
Isle of Man
Elidyr-
-fach
-fawr
3033
N.
Moel Wnion
Y Foel Goch
Menai
Strait
Anglesey
Llyn
Padarn
Clogwyn dur Arddu
Llyn
Ffynnon Gwas
Wagner & Debes' Geogl. Estabt. Leipsic.

LIVERPOOL

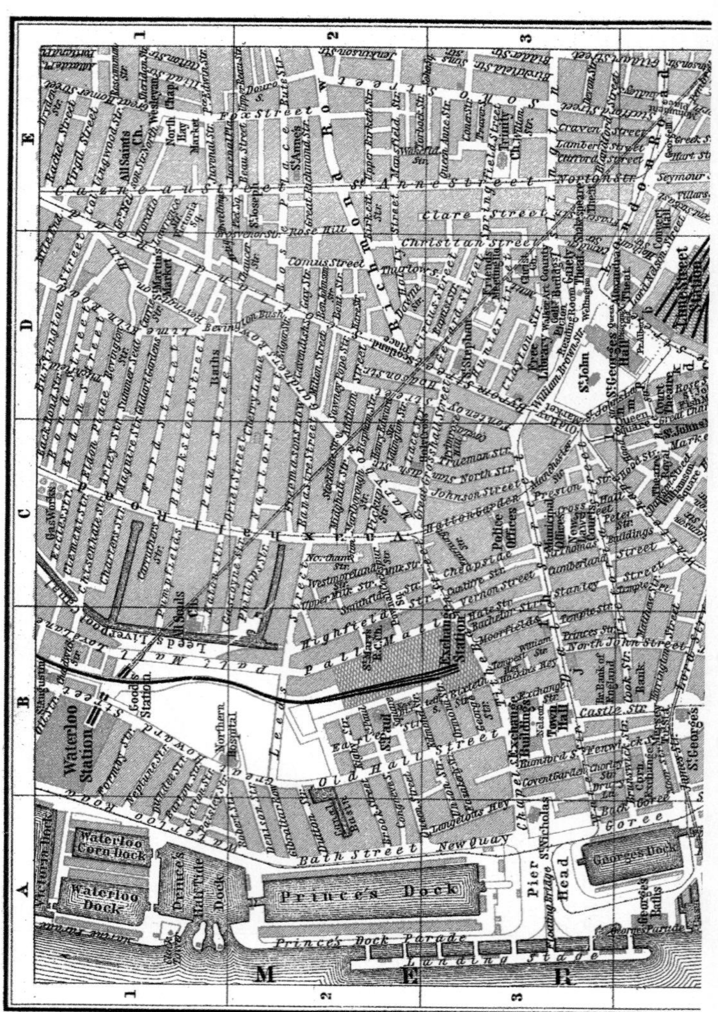

Wagner & Debes' Geog! Estab! Leipsic.

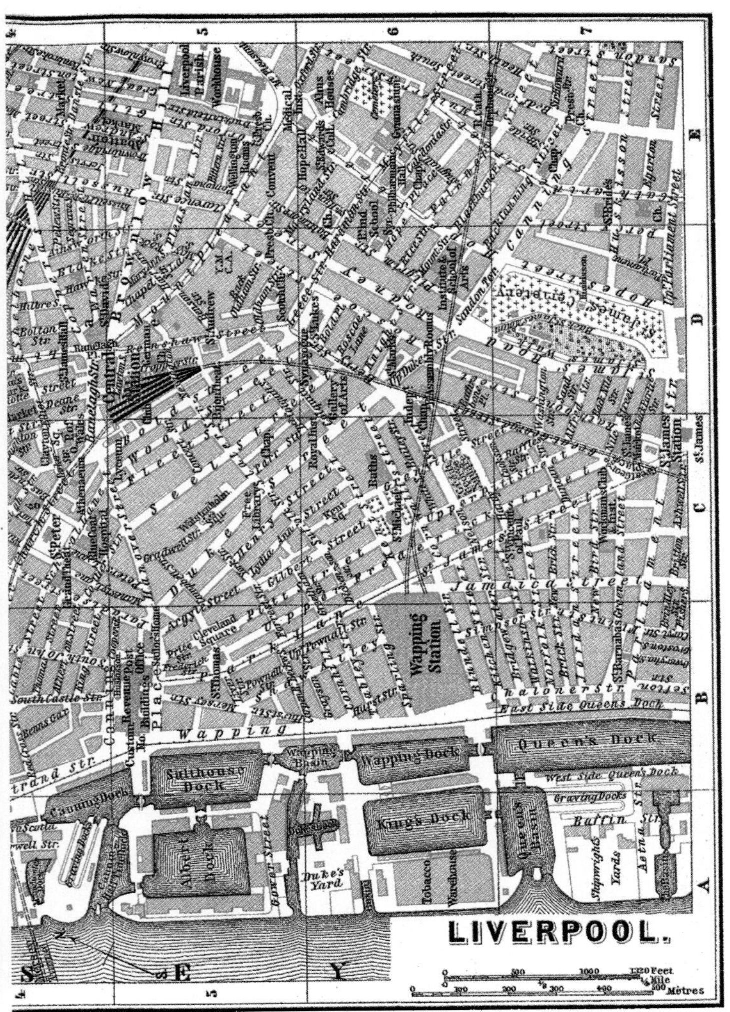

LIVERPOOL.
Queen's Dock
Wapping Dock
Wapping Basin
Salthouse Dock
Canning Dock
Albert Dock
King's Dock
Queens Basin
Duke's Yard
Tobacco Warehouse
Shipwrights Yards
Graving Docks
West Side Queen's Dock
East Side Queens Dock
Wapping
Wapping Station
Custom Ho.
Revenue Buildings
Post Office
Central Station
St. James Station
St. James Cemetery
Liverpool Parish Workhouse
Lyceum
Athenaeum
Wellington Rooms
Philharmonic
Gymnasium
Assembly Rooms
Institute & School of Arts
Gallery of Arts
Royal Inst.
Baths
Synagogue
Free Library
Jamaica Street
Duke Street
Seel Street
Wood Street
Bold Street
Canning Street
Hope Street
Rodney Street
Upper Parliament Street
S E Y
1320 Feet
¼ Mile
Mètres
A
B
C
D
E
5
6
7

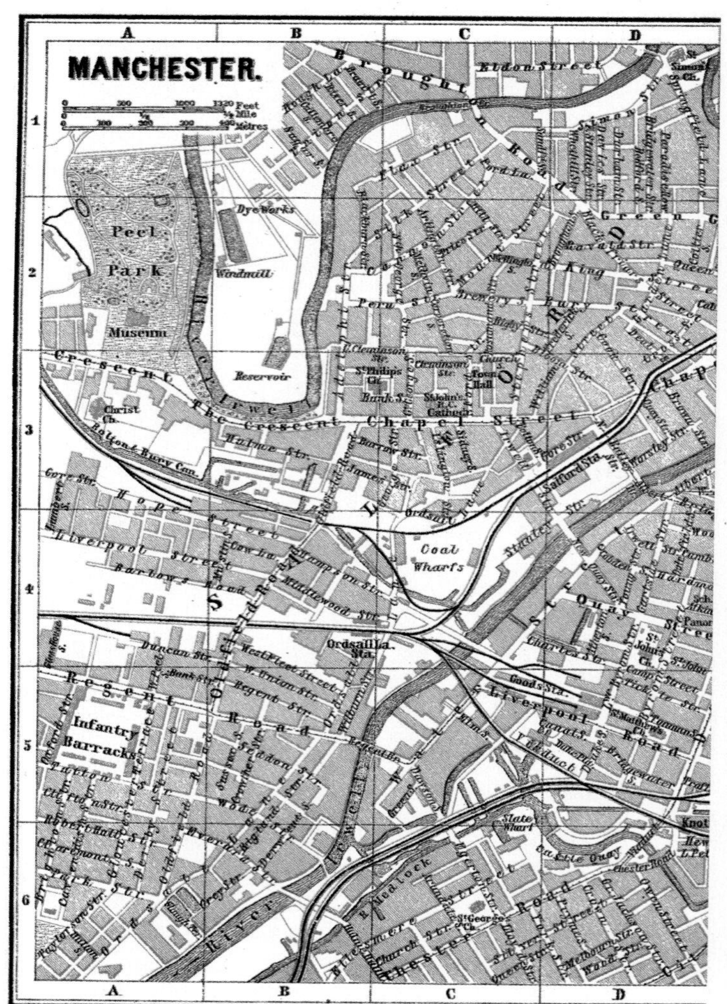

MANCHESTER.
Feet
½ Mile
Metres
A
B
C
D
1
2
3
4
5
6
Peel Park
Museum
Dye Works
Windmill
Reservoir
Christ Ch.
River Irwell
Crescent
The Crescent
Chapel Street
Bolton & Bury Can.
Hope Street
Liverpool Street
Barrows Road
Gore Str.
Hulme Str.
Barrow Str.
James Str.
Ordsall La.
Coal Wharfs
Salford Sta.
Stanley Str.
Quay Street
Charles Str.
Goods Sta.
Liverpool Road
Bridgewater
Viaduct
St. Philips Ch.
Bank S.
St. John's R.C. Cathedr.
Town Hall
Church
Bury Street
King Street
Greengate
Peru Str.
Brewery S.
Bigby Str.
Eldon Street
Broughton Road
St. Simon's Ch.
Springfield Lane
Durham Str.
Cleminson Str.
Cow La.
Hampson Str.
Middlewood Str.
Oldfield Road
Ordsall La. Sta.
Duncan Str.
West Fleet Street
W. Union Str.
Regent Str.
Regent Road
Infantry Barracks
Oxford Str.
Seddon Str.
Woden Str.
Slate Wharf
Castle Quay
R. Medlock
Ellesmere Str.
Church Str.
Chester Road
St. George's Ch.
River Irwell
St. John's Ch.
St. Matthew's Ch.
Camp Street
Albert Br.
Knott

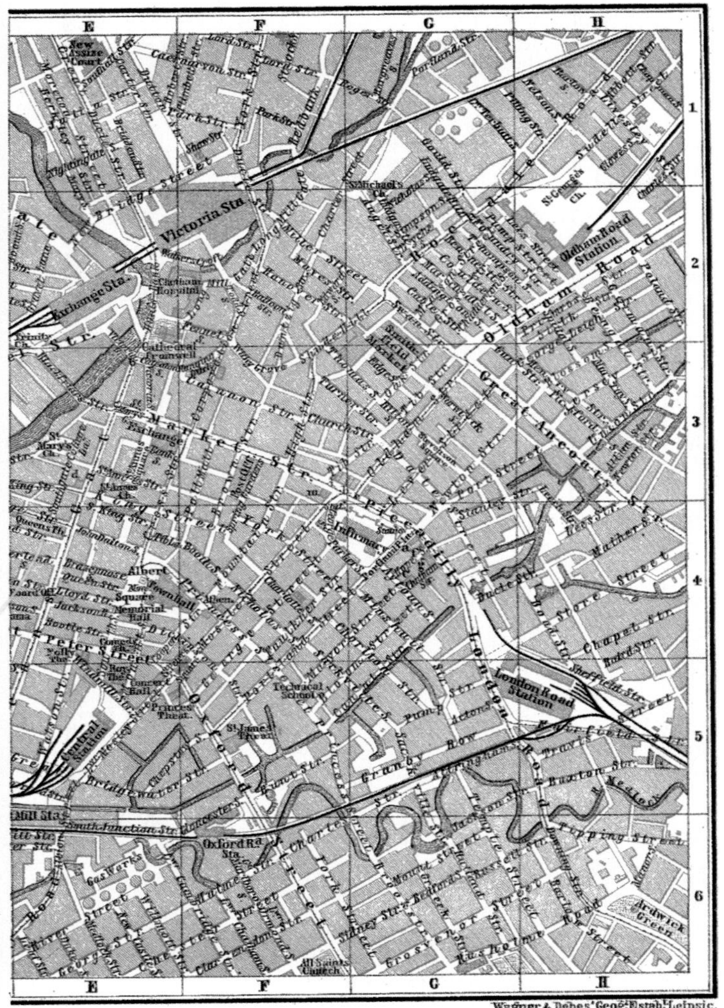

Wagner & Debes' Geogr. Estabt. Leipsic.

Wagner & Debes' Geog. Estabt. Leipsic.
Great Ormes Head
Light House
Llandudno
Ormes Bay
Little Ormes Head
Conway Sands
River Conway
Deganwy
Penmaenbach Point
Conway
Dwygyfylchi
Llansantffraid glan Conway
Colwyn Bay Sta.
Colwyn Sta.
Llandulas Sta.
Part of Carnarvon
Llysfaen
Rhos Hotel
Chapel St. Trillo
Moelfre
Tal-y-fan
Roe Wen
Llanbedr
Pen-y-Gader
Caerhun
Eglwys Bach
D E N B I G H
Llangerniew
Llanddoged
Llanrwst
Trefriw
Llanrhychwyn
Llyn Crafnant
Llyn Geirionydd
Gwytherin
Capel Curig
Swallow Falls
Bettws y Coed
Capel Garmon
Moel Siabod
Moel Suestog
Waterloo Bridge
Blaenau Ffestiniog
Bangor
Aber
Bethesda
Chester
Denbigh
C A R N A R V O N
Statute Miles
Kilomètres

Wagner & Debes' Geog! Estab! Leipsic.
Penistone
Manchester
Stockport
Sheffield
Nottingham
Macclesfield
Rocester
Derby
The Peak
Kinder Scout
Glossop
Hayfield
New Mills
Edale
Castleton
Hope
Hathersage
Chapel en le Frith
Peak Forest
Tideswell
Eyam
Buxton
Bakewell
Chatsworth
Great Longstone
Taddington
Monyash
Youlgreave
Hartington
Longnor
Winster
Matlock
Wirksworth
Dove Dale
Tissington
Ashbourne
Statute Miles
Kilomètres

THE LAKE DISTRICT

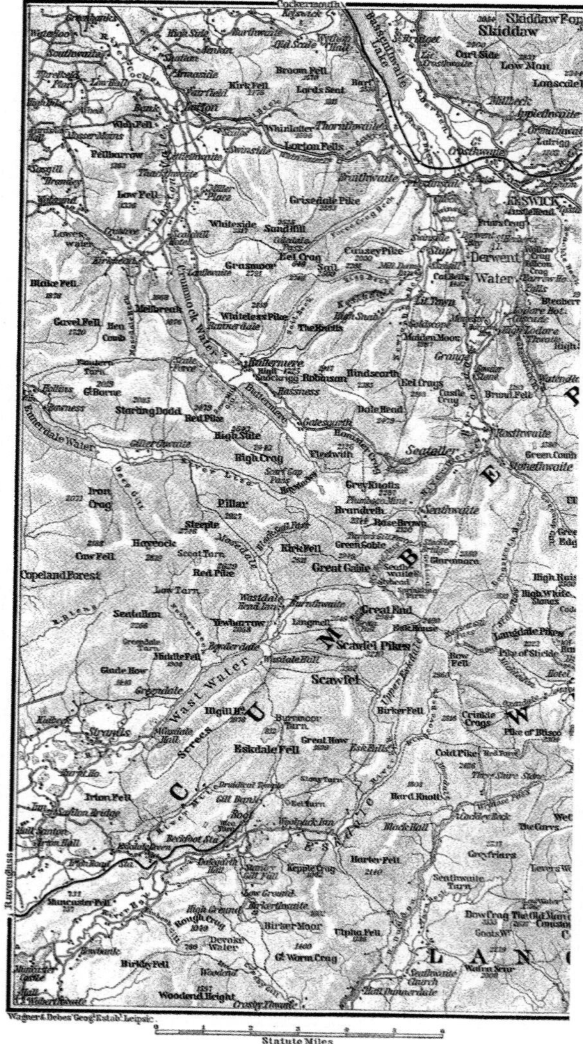

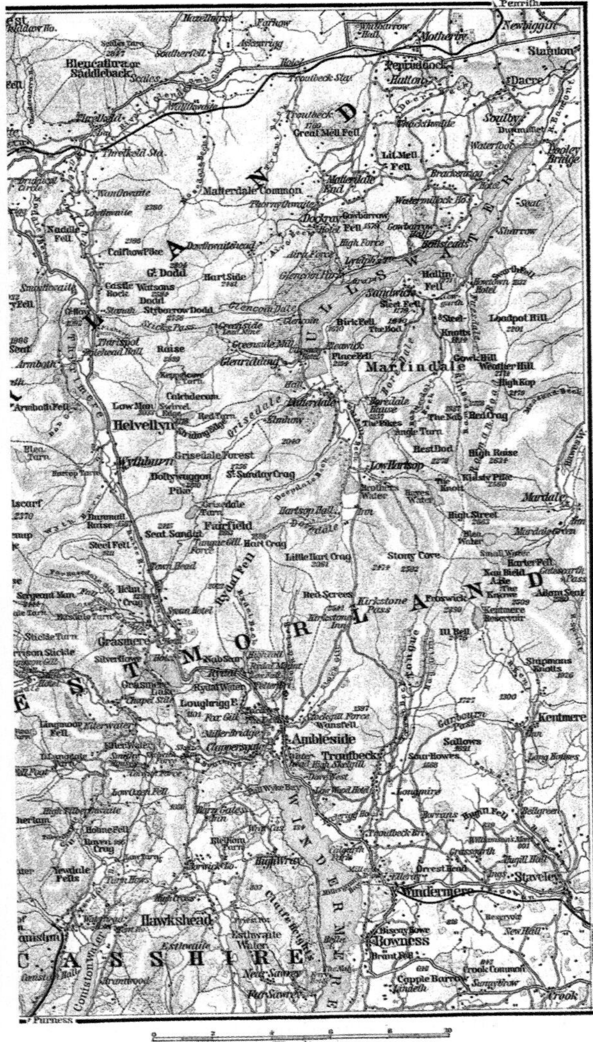
Penrith
Newbiggin
Stainton
Dacre
Motherby
Penruddock
Hutton
Troutbeck Sta.
Blencathra or Saddleback
Southerfell
Threlkeld Sta.
Great Mell Fell
Lit. Mell Fell
Soulby
Dunmallet
Waterfoot
Pooley Bridge
Matterdale Common
Matterdale End
Watermillock Ho.
Gowbarrow Fell
High Force
Aira Force
Sharrow
Nadale Fell
Calfhow Pike
Gt. Dodd
Hart Side
Castle Rock
Watsons Dodd
Styborrow Dodd
Stybarrow Dodd
Sticks Pass
Greenside
Glencoin
Birk Fell
The Bod
Hallin Fell
Sandwick
Steel Fell
Loadpot Hill
Raise
Place Fell
Martindale
Weather Hill
High Kop
Helvellyn
Red Tarn
Grisedale
Patterdale
Boredale Hause
The Pikes
Angle Tarn
The Nab
Red Crag
Rest Dod
High Raise
Grisedale Forest
Wythburn
Dollywaggon Pike
St. Sunday Crag
Low Hartsop
Kidsty Pike
Brothers Water
Hayes Water
Mardale
Grisedale Tarn
Fairfield
Hartsop Hall
High Street
Seat Sandal
Steel Fell
Hart Crag
Little Hart Crag
Stony Cove
Mardale Green
Small Water
Harter Fell
Nan Bield
Gatescarth Pass
Red Screes
Kirkstone Pass
Froswick
Kentmere Reservoir
Ill Bell
Sergeant Man
Helm Crag
Swan Hotel
Rydal Fell
Grasmere
Nab Scar
Rydal Water
Grasmere Lake
Loughrigg F.
Fox Gill
Wansfell
Ambleside
Troutbeck
Kentmere
Garburn Pass
Sallows
Sour Howes
Kirkstone Inn
Shipmans Knotts
Lingmoor Fell
Elterwater
Clappersgate
High Skelgill
Low Wood Hotel
Long Houses
Low Oxen Fell
Barn Gates Inn
Blelham Tarn
High Wray
Hugill Fell
Staveley
Windermere
Orrest Head
Ings
Hawkshead
Esthwaite Water
Bowness
Brant Fell
New Hall
Crook Common
Crook
Near Sawrey
Far Sawrey
Cunsey Beck
Claife Heights
Coniston Water
Furness
Kendal
C U M B E R L A N D
W E S T M O R L A N D
L A N C A S S H I R E
U L L S W A T E R
W I N D E R M E R E
Kilomètres
0 2 4 6 8 10

See page 377

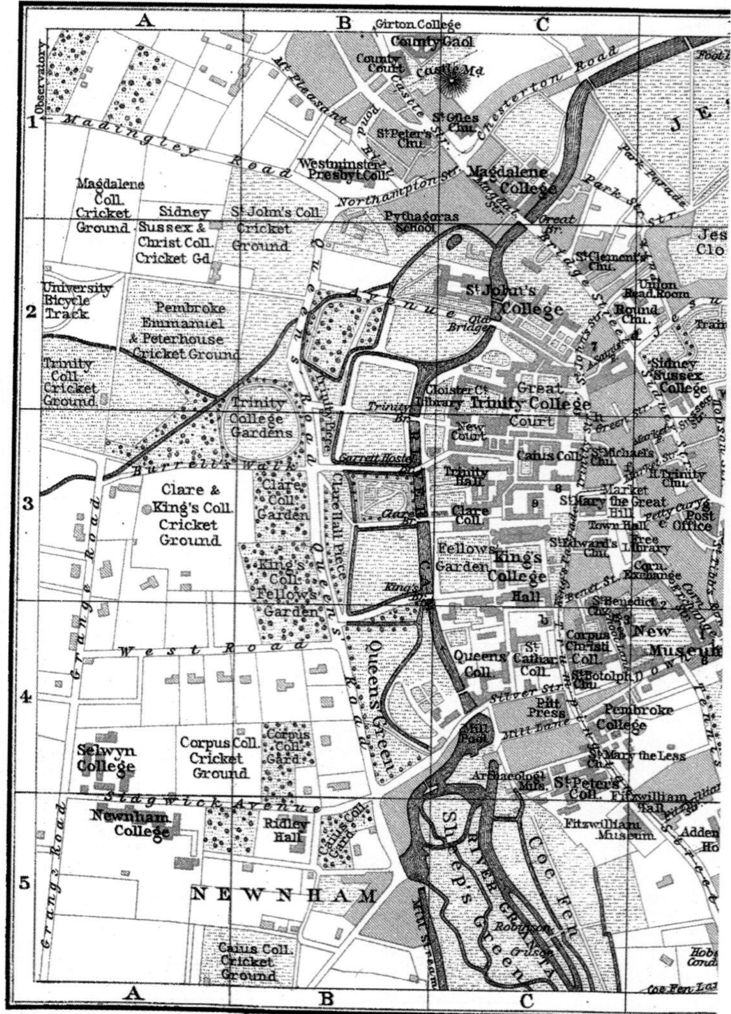
A
B
C
Girton College
County Gaol
County Court
Castle Md.
Madingley Road
Mt. Pleasant
Castle St.
St. Giles Chu.
St. Peter's Chu.
Chesterton Road
Westminster Presbyt. Coll.
Magdalene College
Northampton St.
Magdalene Coll. Cricket Ground
Sidney Sussex & Christ Coll. Cricket Gd.
St. John's Coll. Cricket Ground
Pythagoras School
Great Br.
Bridge Street
Park St.
Park Parade
St. Clement's Chu.
Union Road Room
University Bicycle Track
Pembroke Emmanuel & Peterhouse Cricket Ground
Avenue
St. John's College
Old Bridge
Round Chu.
Trinity Coll. Cricket Ground
Trinity College Gardens
Queen's Road
Trinity Br.
Cloister Ct.
Library
Great Court
Trinity College
New Court
Sidney Sussex College
Green St.
Caius Coll.
St. Michael's Chu.
Burrell's Walk
Garrett Hostel Br.
Trinity Hall
Clare & King's Coll. Cricket Ground
Clare Coll. Garden
Clare Hall Piece
Clare Br.
Clare Coll.
St. Mary the Great
Market Hill
H. Trinity Chu.
Post Office
Town Hall
Petty Cury
Free Library
St. Edward's Chu.
Fellows Garden
King's College
King's Coll. Fellows Garden
Corn Exchange
Hall
King's Br.
Benet St.
St. Benedict Chu.
New Museum
Corpus Christi Coll.
West Road
Queens' Coll.
St. Cathar. Coll.
Queens' Green
St. Botolph Chu.
Silver Str.
Pitt Press
Pembroke College
Mill Pool
Mill Lane
Selwyn College
Corpus Coll. Cricket Ground
Corpus Coll. Gard.
St. Mary the Less Chu.
Archaeolog. Mus.
St. Peter's Coll.
Fitzwilliam Hall
Sidgwick Avenue
Newnham College
Ridley Hall
Caius Coll. Gard.
Fitzwilliam Museum
Sheep's Green
River Granta
Coe Fen
NEWNHAM
Grange Road
Mill Stream
Robinson Crusoe
Caius Coll. Cricket Ground
Coe Fen Lane
Observatory
1
2
3
4
5

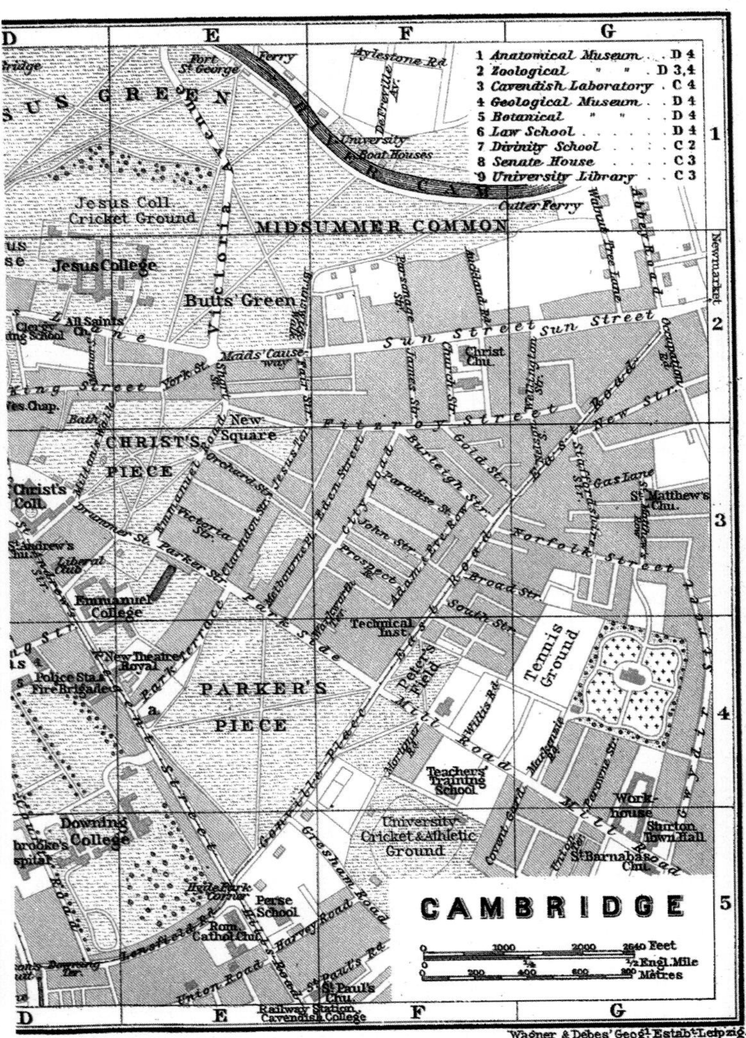
D
E
F
G
1 Anatomical Museum . . D 4
2 Zoological " " . D 3,4
3 Cavendish Laboratory . C 4
4 Geological Museum . . D 4
5 Botanical " " . . D 4
6 Law School . . . . D 4
7 Divinity School . . . C 2
8 Senate House . . . C 3
9 University Library . . C 3
1
2
3
4
5
Fort St George
Ferry
Aylestone Rd
De Freville Av.
University Boat Houses
River Cam
Cutter Ferry
Jesus Coll Cricket Ground
Jesus College
Midsummer Common
Butts' Green
Victoria Av.
All Saints' Ch.
Sun Street
Maids' Causeway
Christ Chu.
King Street
York St.
Wes. Chap.
Bath
New Square
Fitzroy Street
Christ's Piece
Christ's Coll.
Emmanuel Road
Orchard Str.
Victoria Str.
Clarendon Str.
Jesus Ter.
Eden Street
City Road
Burleigh Str.
Gold Str.
Paradise Str.
John Str.
Prospect Rd.
Adam & Eve Row
East Road
New Str.
Gas Lane
St Matthew's Chu.
Norfolk Street
Broad Str.
South Str.
Drummer St.
Parker Str.
Park Side
St Andrew's Chu.
Liberal Club
Emmanuel College
Technical Inst.
Peter's Field
Tennis Ground
Mill Road
New Theatre Royal
Police Sta. Fire Brigade
Park Terrace
Parker's Piece
Willis Rd
Mackenzie Rd
Perowne Str.
Teachers' Training School
Work-house
Sturton Town Hall
Covent Gard.
St Barnabas Chu.
Downing College
University Cricket & Athletic Ground
Gresham Road
Hyde Park Corner
Perse School
Rom. Cathol Chu.
Lensfield Rd.
Harvey Road
Union Road
St Paul's Rd
St Paul's Chu.
Downing Ter.
Railway Station, Cavendish College
CAMBRIDGE
1000
2000
2640 Feet
1/2 Engl. Mile
200
400
600
800 Mètres
Wagner & Debes' Geogl. Estabt. Leipzig.

See page 432

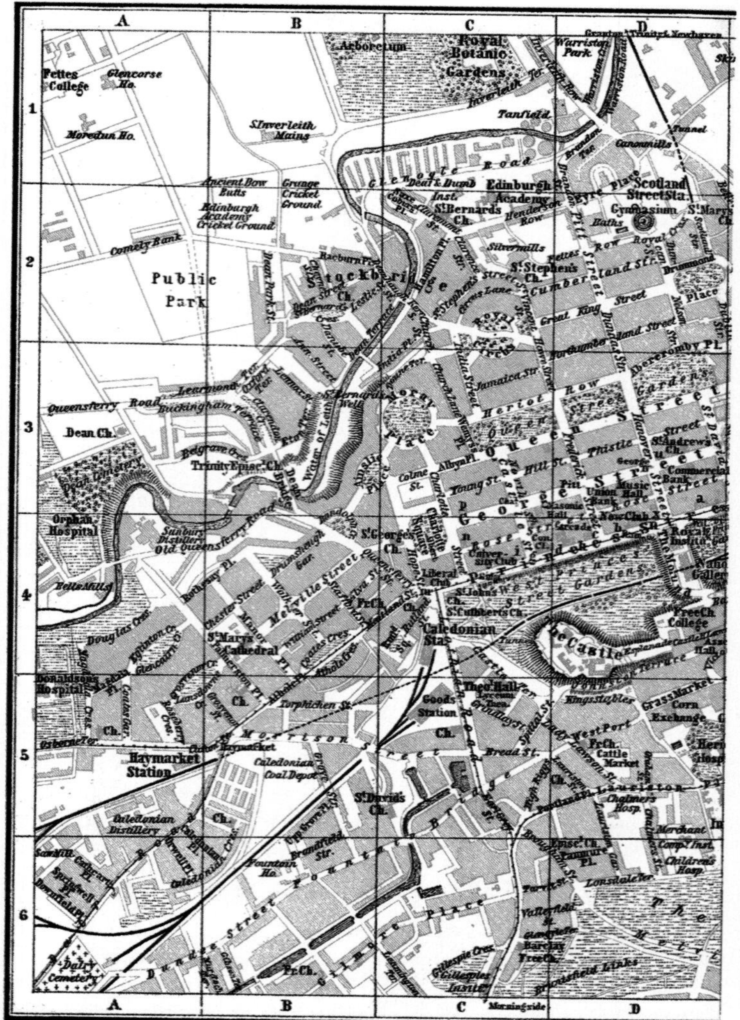
A
B
C
D
1
2
3
4
5
6
Arboretum
Royal Botanic Gardens
Fettes College
Glencorse Ho.
Moredun Ho.
St. Inverleith Mains
Warriston Park
Inverleith Ter.
Tanfield
Canonmills
Ancient Bow Butts
Grange Cricket Ground
Edinburgh Academy Cricket Ground
Comely Bank
Public Park
Deaf & Dumb Inst.
Edinburgh Academy
Scotland Street Sta.
Gymnasium
Henderson Row
St. Bernards Ch.
Silvermills
Raeburn Pl.
Stockbridge
St. Stephen's Ch.
Cumberland St.
Great King Street
Royal Circus
Northumberland Street
Abercromby Pl.
Learmonth Ter.
Queensferry Road
Buckingham Terrace
Dean Ch.
Belgrave Cres.
Trinity Episc. Ch.
Dean Cemetery
Water of Leith
St. Bernards Well
Moray Place
Jamaica St.
Heriot Row
Queen Street
Thistle Street
St. Andrews Ch.
Commercial Bank
George Street
Rose Street
Music Hall
Orphan Hospital
Sunbury Distillery
Old Queensferry Road
St. Georges Ch.
Charlotte Square
Princes Street
West Princes Street Gardens
Bells Mills
Melville Street
St. Marys Cathedral
Caledonian Sta.
St. Johns Ch.
St. Cuthberts Ch.
The Castle
Esplanade
Free Ch. College
Donaldsons Hospital
Torphichen St.
Goods Station
Grassmarket
Corn Exchange
Morrison Street
Haymarket Station
Caledonian Coal Depot
Bread St.
West Port
Cattle Market
St. Davids Ch.
Lauriston
Chalmers Hosp.
Caledonian Distillery
Merchant Comp. Inst.
Childrens Hosp.
Fountain Ho.
Brandfield Str.
Fountainbridge
Panmure Pl.
Lonsdale Ter.
Dundee Street
Gilmore Place
Dalry Cemetery
Gillespies Instit.
Bruntsfield Links
Barclay Free Ch.
Morningside

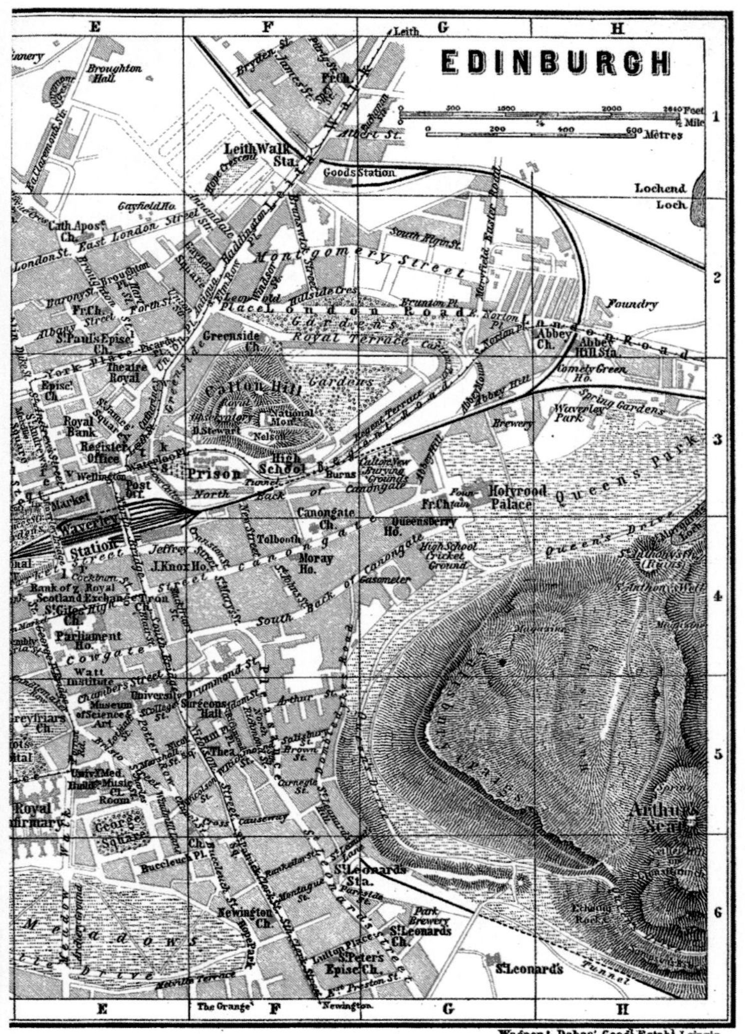

Wagner & Debes' Geogl. Estabt. Leipsic

See page 464

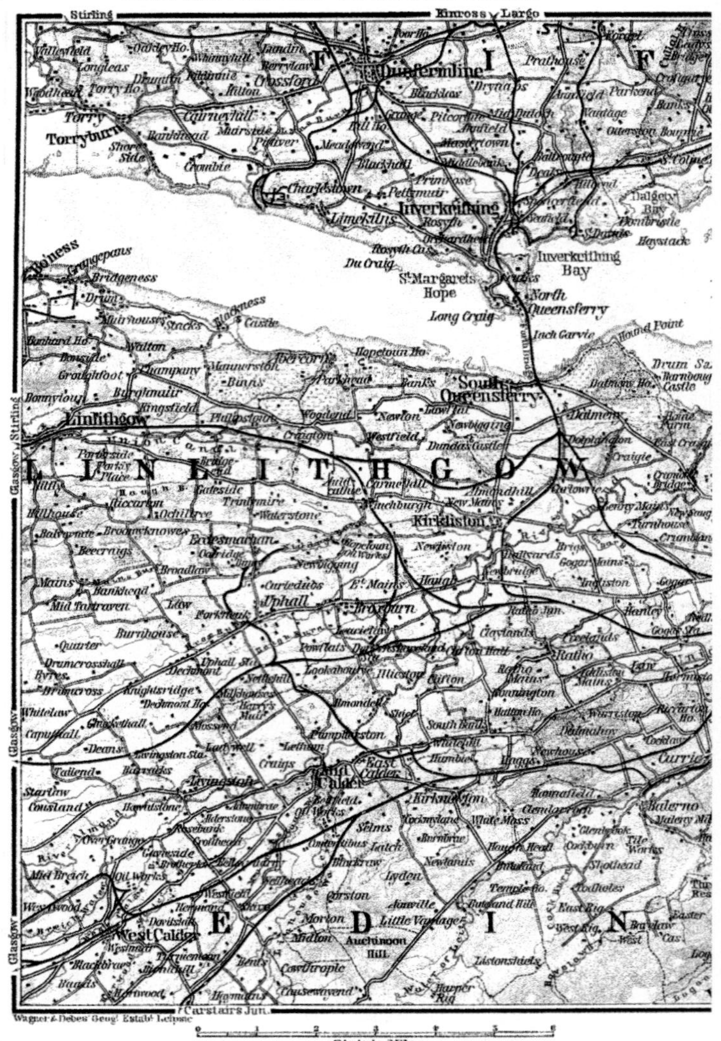
Stirling
Kinross
Largo
F
I
F
Dunfermline
Crossford
Torryburn
Torry
Charlestown
Limekilns
Rosyth
Inverkeithing
Pettymuir
Inverkeithing Bay
St. Margarets Hope
North Queensferry
Long Craig
Inch Garvie
Hound Point
Du Craig
Rosyth Cas.
Dalgety Bay
Haystack
Bo'ness
Grangepans
Bridgeness
Blackness Castle
Walton
Champany
Hopetoun Ho.
Abercorn
South Queensferry
Newton
Dalmeny
Linlithgow
Burghmuir
Kingsfield
Union Canal
Westfield
Dundas Castle
Newbigging
L I N L I T H G O W
Craigie
Winchburgh
Kirkliston
Ochiltree
Waterstone
Beecraigs
Broadlaw
Newliston
Ecclesmachan
Uphall
Broxburn
Ingliston
Gogar
Ratho
Claylands
Ratho Mains
Bonnington
Uphall Sta.
Lookaboutye
Clifton
Pumpherston
Almondell
Livingston Sta.
Livingston
Calder
East Calder
Humbie
Currie
Balerno
Kirknewton
Deans
Seafield
Whitelaw
Starlaw
Cousland
River Almond
Over Grange
Oil Works
Mid Breich
Westwood
West Calder
Blackbraes
Harwood
Morton
Midton
Harper Rig
Auchinoon Hill
Listonshiels
Little Vantage
Tile Works
Cockburn
Shothead
Glenbrook
E
D
I
N
Carstairs Jun.
Glasgow
Wagner & Debes' Geog! Estab! Leipsic
0
1
2
3
4
5
6
Statute Miles

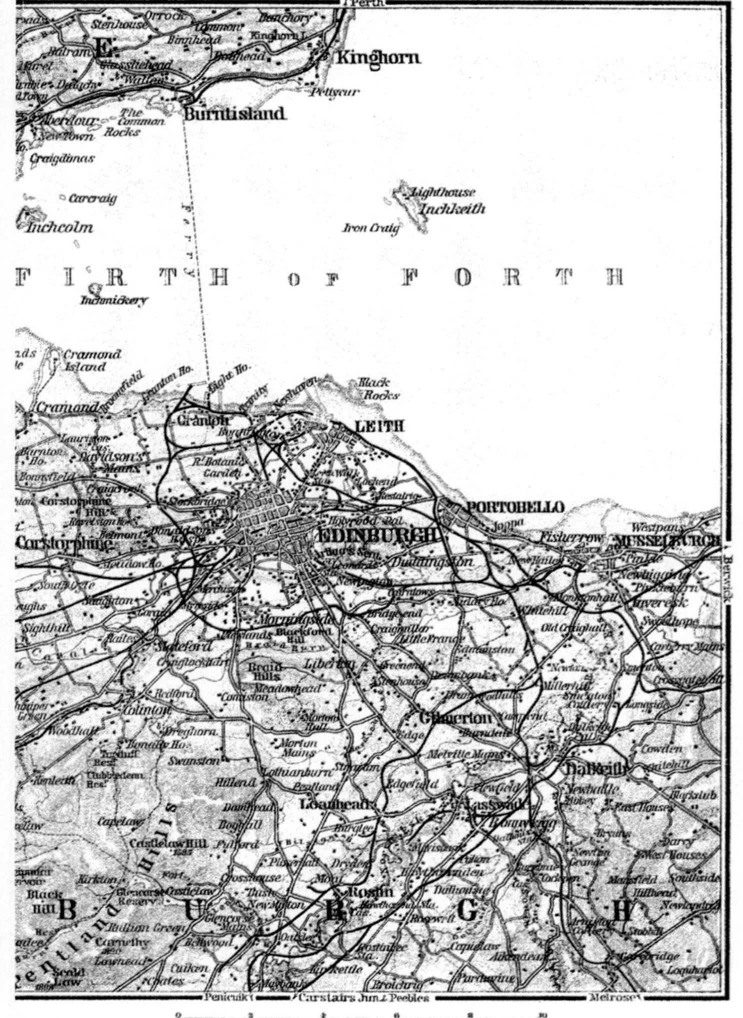
Perth
Kinghorn
Burntisland
Pettycur
Inchcolm
Inchkeith
Lighthouse
Iron Craig
FIRTH OF FORTH
Ferry
Cramond Island
Granton
LEITH
PORTOBELLO
EDINBURGH
Corstorphine
MUSSELBURGH
Fisherrow
Joppa
Duddingston
Newington
Morningside
Slateford
Liberton
Braid Hills
Colinton
Gilmerton
Dalkeith
Loanhead
Lasswade
Roslin
Inveresk
Pentland Hills
Castlelaw Hill
B U R G H
Penicuik
Carstairs Jun. & Peebles
Melrose
Berwick
Kilometres

GLASGOW.
A
B
C
D
1
2
3
4
5
6
Kelvinside
Maryhill
University
University Avenue
Western Infirmary
Partick
Museum
Park
Kelvin
River
North British & Caledonian Goods & Mineral Sta.
Queens Dock
North Basin
Centre Quay
South Basin
Stobcross Quay
Plantation Quay
Govan Road
Govan
Mavisbank Quay
Finnieston Quay
Lancefield Qu.
Anderston Quay
Broomie
Terminus Quay
Springfield Quay
Windmillcroft Quay
Kingston Dock
Caledonian & S.W. Goods Mine. Sta.
Sauchiehall Street
Berkeley Street
St. Andrews Hall
Kent Road
St. Vincent Crescent
Argyle Street
Stobcross Street
New City Road
Great George Str.
Scotland Street
Ibrox
Feet
Mile
Metres
Queen

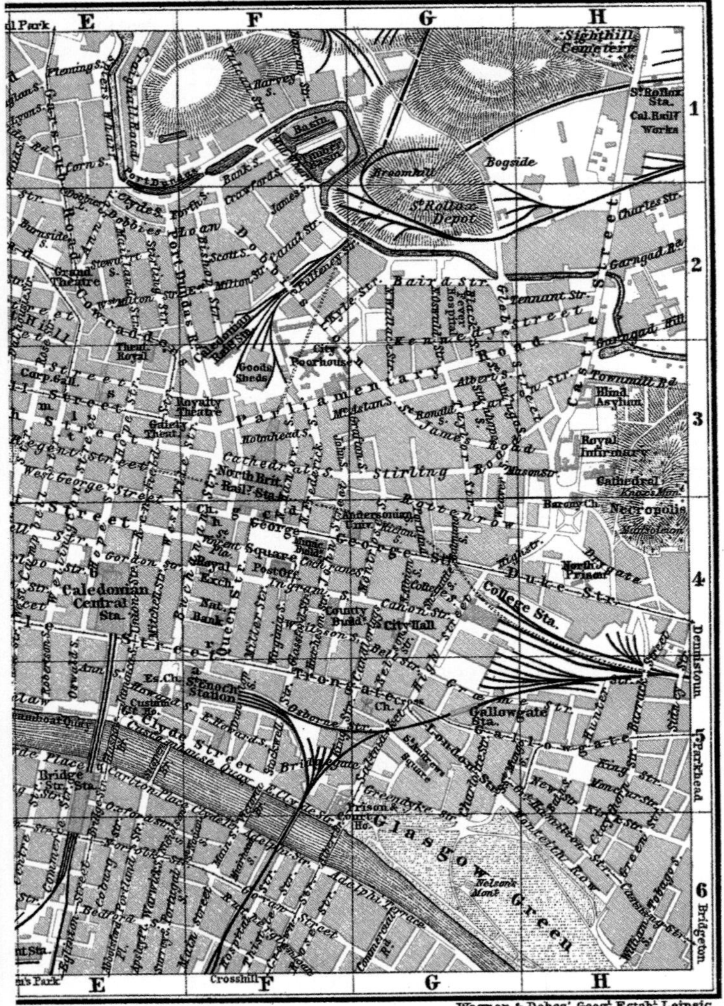
E
F
G
H
1
2
3
4
5
6
Sighthill Cemetery
St Rollox Sta.
Cal. Rail^y Works
Basin
Bogside
Broomhill
St Rollox Depot
Port Dundas
Charles Str.
Garngad Rd
Garngad Hill
Baird Str.
Tennant Str.
Kennedy Street
Parliamentary Road
Caledonian Rail^y Sta.
Goods Sheds
City Poorhouse
Grand Theatre
Theat. Royal
Royalty Theatre
Gaiety Theat.
Cowcaddens
Blind Asylum
Royal Infirmary
Cathedral
Necropolis
Barony Ch.
Stirling Road
Cathedral S.
North Brit. Rail^y Sta.
Rottenrow
George Square
Royal Exch.
Post Off.
Nat. Bank
County Build^s
City Hall
West George Street
Regent Street
Caledonian Central Sta.
Duke Str.
North Prison
College Sta.
High Street
Trongate
St Enoch Station
Custom Ho.
Clyde Street
Gallowgate Sta.
Gallowgate
London Str.
Bridgegate
Greendyke Str.
Prison & Court Ho.
Glasgow Green
Nelson's Mon^t
Bridge Str. Sta.
Carlton Place
Clyde Pl.
Adelphi Str.
Adelphi Terrace
Main Street
Monteith Row
Dennistoun
Parkhead
Bridgeton
Crosshill
Wagner & Debes' Geog^l Estab^t Leipsic.

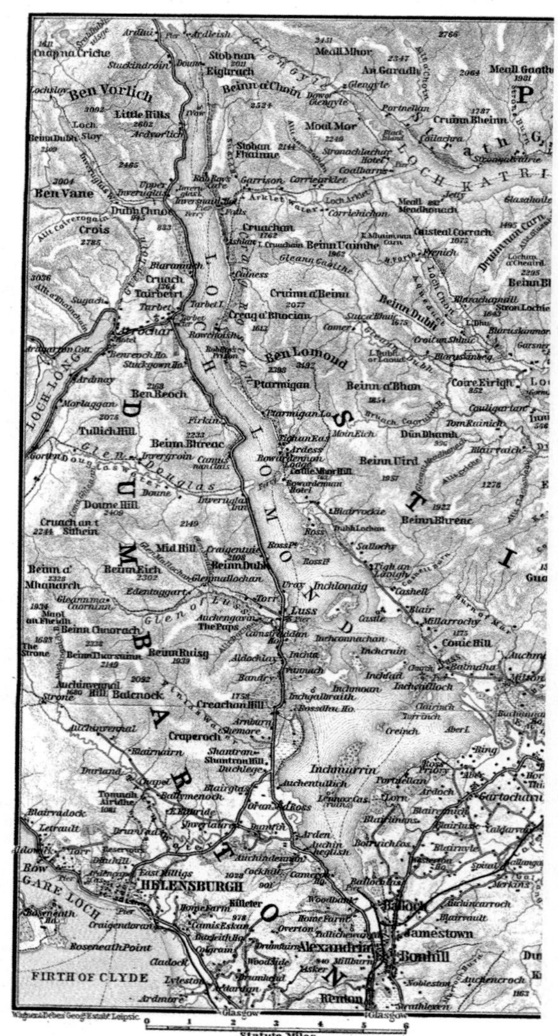

Ardlui
Ardleish
Cnap na Criche
Stuckindroin
Stob nan Eighrach
Glen Gyle
Meall Mhor
An Garadh
Meall Gaoth
Ben Vorlich
Beinn a'Choin
Glengyle
Little Hills
Loch Sloy
Ardvorlich
Portnellan
Cruinn Bheinn
Moal Mor
Stronachlachar Hotel
Strath Gartney
Loch Katrine
Stobhan Fhairne
Garrison
Corriearklet
Ben Vane
Upper Inveruglas
Inversnaid
Arklet Water
Loch Arklet
Corriehichon
Meall Meadhonach
Glasahoile
Dubh Chnoc
Crois
Cruachan
Beinn Uaimhe
Caisteal Corrach
Druimnan Carn
Gleann Gaoithe
Blarannich
Cruach Tairbeirt
Cruinn a'Beinn
Loch Chon
Beinn Dubh
Tarbet
Tarbet I.
Creag a'Bhocian
Arrochar
Rob Roy's Prison
Ben Lomond
Benreoch Ho.
Stuckgown Ho.
Loch Long
Ardnay
Ben Reoch
Ptarmigan
Beinn a'Bhan
Coire Eirigh
Morlaggan
Firkin
Tullich Hill
Beinn Bhreac
Tigh an Eas
Ardess
Moin Eich
Dun Dhamh
Glen Douglas
Douglas Water
Invergroin
Rowardennan Lodge
Rowardennan Hotel
Beinn Uird
Doune
Doune Hill
Inveruglas Inn
Blairvockie
Cruach an t Sithein
Mid Hill
Ross
Dubh Lochan
Beinn Bhreac
Sallochy
Craigentuie
Beinn Dubh
Ross Pt
Ross Pt
Beinn a' Mhanarch
Beinn Eich
Glenmallochan
Tigh an Lauigh
Inchlonaig
Edentaggart
Torr
Cashell
Glen of Luss
Luss
Blair
Auchengavin
The Paps
Castle
Millarrochy
Beinn Chaorach
Inchconnachan
Conic Hill
Beinn Ruisg
Inchtavannach
Inchcruin
The Strone
Balmaha
Aldochlay
Inchfad
Inchcailloch
Milton
Auchinvennal Hill
Balenock
Bandry
Inchmoan
Strone
Inchgalbraith
Creachan Hill
Rossdhu Ho.
Clairinch
Torrinch
Arnburn
Shemore
Creinch
Aber I.
Auchinvennal
Craperoch
Ring
Blairnairn
Shantron
Shantron Hill
Duchlage
Inchmurrin
Ross Priory
Durland
Chapel
Portnellan
Ardoch
Tomnah Airidhe
Ballymenoch
Blairglas
Auchentullich
Gartocharn
Lennox Cas. (ruins)
Blairvadock
Blairlinnans
Letrault
Arden
Caldarvan
Auchindennan
Auchin heglish
Blairnyle
Aldownick
Torr
Row
Gare Loch
East Millig
Helensburgh
Cameron
Balloch
Merkins
Woodbank
Balloch
Auchincarroch
Kilheter
Home Farm
Home Farm
Blairvault
Roseneath Hd.
Craigendoran
Camis Eskan
Overton
Tullichewan
Jamestown
Roseneath Point
Drumfairn
Alexandria
Bonhill
Cladock
Woodside
Millburn
Firth of Clyde
Tyleston
Drumhead
Auchencroch
Noblestone
Ardmore
Renton
Strathleven
Glasgow
Glasgow
Dumbarton
Stirling
Wagner & Debes' Geog! Estab! Leipsic.
Statute Miles
0 1 2 3 4 5 6

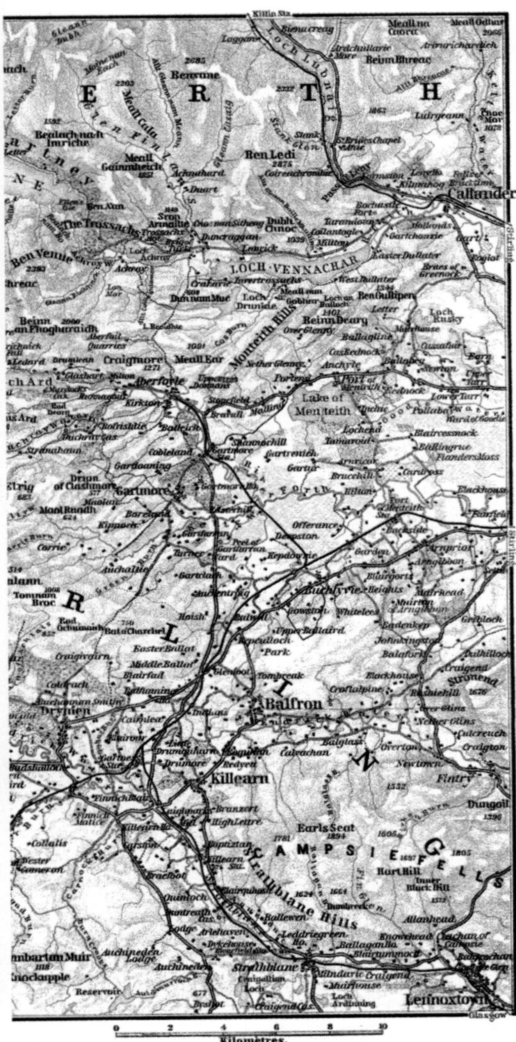
Killin Sta.
Loch Lubnaig
Benvane
2685
Ben Ledi
2875
Callander
The Trossachs
Ben Venue
Loch Vennachar
Ben Gullipen
Beinn Dearg
Loch Rusky
Menteith Hills
Craigmore
Meall Ear
Aberfoyle
Lake of Menteith
Port of Menteith
Gartmore
River Forth
Buchlyvie
Balfron
Killearn
Drymen
Fintry
Dungoil
Earls Seat
1894
Campsie Fells
Strathblane Hills
Strathblane
Lennoxtown
Glasgow
Stirling
Kilomètres
0
2
4
6
8
10

Victorian London Guide Books

Murray's Modern London 1860

An early guide for visitors to London a century and a half ago packed with beautifully written descriptions of pretty well everything an early tourist needed to know. So thorough is the research and depth of detail that it provides the modern day reader with a fascinating glimpse into the lives of Londoners in the first half of Victoria's long reign.

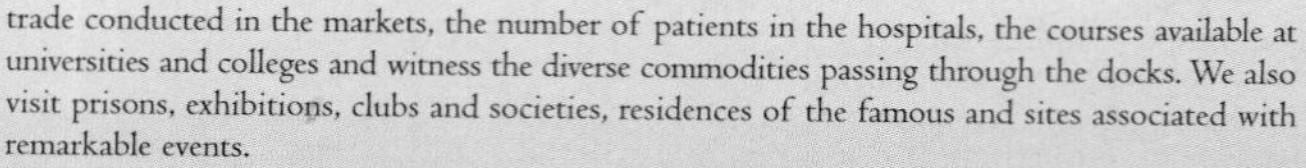

Packed with well researched facts and statistics we can wander around the streets, markets and fine buildings being told who lived where, what treasures were to be found within their houses, the volume of trade conducted in the markets, the number of patients in the hospitals, the courses available at universities and colleges and witness the diverse commodities passing through the docks. We also visit prisons, exhibitions, clubs and societies, residences of the famous and sites associated with remarkable events.

Much can also be learned about how daily life then differed from today. Some things were better such as the workings of the Post Office 'letters posted before 6 in the evening would be delivered the same evening within 3 miles'. But much was worse such as the appalling sewage arrangements. 'The daily discharge into the Thames would cover 36 acres to a depth of 6 feet' but already there was an understanding of pollution and sewage works were planned.

Hardback 376 pages, building plans and street guides, foldout colour map.

Baedeker's London and its Environs 1900

This book brings to life, in astonishing detail, a complete picture of all that a visitor might wish to know about the world's greatest city at the close of the Victorian era. All the major sites and attractions are mentioned, often with detailed plans of the buildings. There is copious advice on etiquette, security, accommodation, restaurants, pubs, travel to and within London, public baths and even recommended shops. There is also a history of London. There are 33 well described tours including The City, St Paul's, London Zoo and London Docks where visitors to the wine vaults 'should be on their guard against the insidious effects of the heavy vinous atmosphere. Ladies not admitted after 1pm'. Visitors are also guided on a dozen tours by steamer and train to London's environs such as The Crystal Palace, Windsor Castle and as far afield as Rochester and St Albans, each being packed with directions, historical facts, travel arrangements and costs.

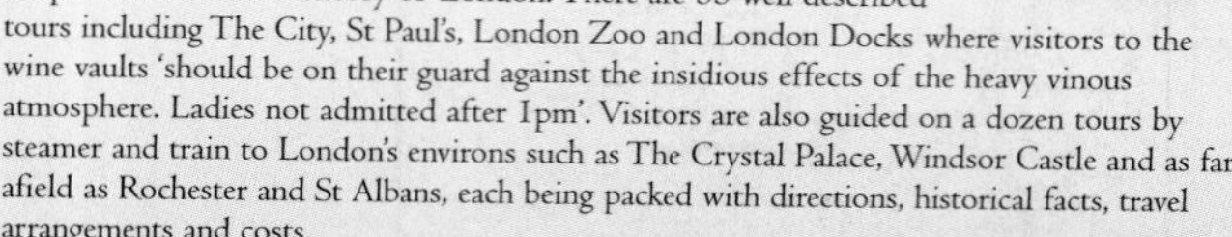

What better way to explore the past than to read a contemporary guidebook? Use it to research the lifestyle of your forebears and to find out just what London was like a century ago.

Hardback 512 pages including 31 pages of colour street maps, numerous building plans, foldout colour map of the home counties.

Dickens's Dictionaries

Dickens's Dictionary of London 1888

An unconventional Victorian guidebook which vividly captures the atmosphere and vitality of what was then the largest city in the world, the heart, not just of the nation, but also of a great empire.

Through a series of over 700 detailed entries contained in 272 pages printed facsimile from the original 1888 edition, we build up a living portrait of Victorian London, from the fashionable gentlemen's clubs of St James's to the markets and slums of the East End. The remarks on the principal buildings, the churches and the great railway stations, the banks, theatres and sporting facilities are informative and well observed, the comments of someone who obviously knew London like the back of his hand. Equally revealing and very entertaining are the wealth of tips on social behaviour. There is essential advice on everything from the hiring of servants (a parlour maid's recommended salary was £12 per annum), the benefits of cycling (most welcome in view of the saving of cruelty to horseflesh), how to cope with milk contaminated with diphtheria and typhoid, fogs (much appreciated by the predatory classes) through to avoiding the attention of carriage thieves.

This very detailed guidebook, and its companion volume *Dickens's Dictionary of the Thames* were published by Charles Dickens' son at the time of Queen Victoria's Golden Jubilee, provide a mine of information for all lovers of London and its past. *Hardback 272 pages*

Dickens's Dictionary of the Thames 1887

A fascinating portrait of the river at the height of its Victorian prosperity. On the upper Thames it was the carefree era of regattas and riverside picnics, while London's tideway and great docks were busy with the comings and goings of barges, steamers and sailing ships servicing the world's largest port and the Empire on which the sun never set. This treasure trove of a book has descriptions of the villages and towns along the river from its source near Cricklade to the Nore Lightship. It is packed with practical advice, maps of popular destinations, locations of angling and bathing spots. Riverside inns to accommodate oarsmen are listed with details of how to return boats by train at a time when an annual season ticket between Windsor and Paddington cost as little as £18.

This companion to *Dickens's Dictionary of London* describes the entire length of the Thames valley from its source to the sea with the exception of London. Detailed entries describe the carefree era of regattas and riverside picnics on the upper reaches of the Thames while London's tideway and great docks were busy with barges, steamers and sailing ships servicing the world's greatest port. There are descriptions of riverside towns as well as advice for fisherman and tourists at a time when The River Thames was the most popular tourist resort in the world.
Hardback 320 pages

Victorian and Edwardian Maps

A Street Map of London 1843

An early street map published over a century and a half ago so that passengers in Hansom cabs could check that they were being taken by the shortest route. It shows street names, prominent buildings, docks, factories, canals and the earliest railways in minute detail.

Beyond the built up area can be seen the orchards and market gardens of Chelsea and Southwark, the marshes of the Isle of Dogs and the outlying villages of Earls Court, Kentish Town and Bow.

The quality of life in 1843 was appalling and it was only in this year that it became illegal to employ children under the age of nine. Devastating cholera epidemics swept through the crowded city but plans for fresh water supplies and sewers were already being made.

Each map has a history of London in 1843. Use it to set the scene as you explore the capital of the young Queen Victoria and Oliver Twist or research the lives of your forebears.

Available folded in a protective wallet or in a gold-blocked hardback case and also rolled with a coloured printed 'mount' ready for framing.
Overall size with 'mount' 19 ½ x 30" (49.5 x 76 cms)

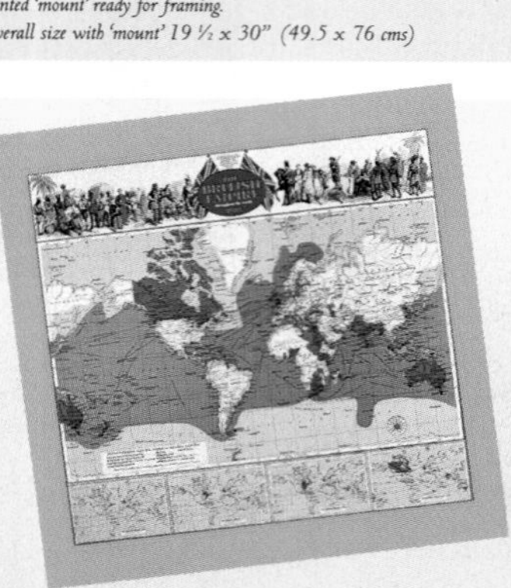

British Empire Map 1905

A ten-page gazetteer describes over 200 British possessions as well as 33 (including Normandy and the USA) which had been lost to the crown.

Available folded in a protective wallet and also rolled with a coloured printed 'mount' ready for framing.

Overall size with 'mount' 27 x 28" (69 x 71cm)

Victorian and Edwardian Maps

Bacon's up to date map of London 1902

A detailed street map published a century ago as the expansive Victorian era finally drew to a close. The development brought about by the industrial revolution of the nineteenth century is shown by the appearance of numerous docks and factories along the lower reaches of the Thames.

The railways serving other parts of the country were now well established and the new underground train system was already competing with the horse drawn trams for passengers within the capital.

Large areas that were orchards, market gardens and marshes only fifty years before are now well within the built up area, but many of today's suburbs are still shown as villages surrounded by open countryside.

Each map has an illustrated booklet produced to accompany the original edition. Together they provide a fascinating glimpse into life in London a century ago.

Available folded in a protective wallet or in a gold-blocked hardback case and also rolled with a coloured printed 'mount' ready for framing.
Overall size with 'mount' 26 x 31 ½" (66 x 80 cms)

British Empire Map 1905

As the twentieth century dawned the British Empire enjoyed its heyday. It spanned 11 ½ million square miles with 400 million inhabitants. This detailed colour reproduction of a contemporary world map shows details of global trade, including: the furs of fox, bear, seal and otter brought from the shores of Canada's Lake Athabasca by canoes in summer and dog sleds in winter; cochineal, indigo and vanilla from central America; teak and bamboo from Siam; cinnamon and pearls from Ceylon; tortoise shells and birds of paradise from New Guinea as well as minerals and foodstuffs from all over the world. In the Sahara we note that slaves were still traded. Coaling stations, telegraph cables, railways and caravan routes are all marked. Additional maps show the development of the Empire in the preceding three centuries.

The English and Englishness

London Stories 1910

These stories first appeared as magazine articles before the First World War. During the previous century travel had become the great occupation. Whether a Grand Tour of Europe's finest cities or a mere train journey out of London to the coast of Kent it was now possible for everyone and a plethora of guide books appeared. But they all concentrated on the places and not on the people. John O' London (a pen name which says it all!) recognised that nowhere was anywhere without the people who lived there and the extraordinary happenings, traditions and curiosities that coloured their lives.

He introduces us to The Duke of Wellington's outspoken boot maker, the 'apple woman' who annexed Hyde Park and the recluse who weighed the world. We read of the curious wanderings of Cromwell's head, the semaphore system which sent signals from the Admiralty to Deal in less than a minute and a fatal duel fought in Kensington for the most absurd reason. We hear of a fire at Drury Lane Theatre, military executions in Hyde Park, visit Dr Johnson's favourite pub and read a letter to The Times that prompted the building of Nelson's column. London Stories is a cornucopia of anecdotal gems that allow us to wander through the past and meet some of the people who helped define the character of the greatest city the world had ever seen.

Hardback 184 pages

'Vivid, alert, affectionate and cogent – a most entertaining book' Kingsley Amis

The English Companion

An idiosyncratic A-Z of England and Englishness
by *Sunday Times* columnist Godfrey Smith

In this witty and stylish companion to Englishness the author takes us on a leisurely but perceptive tour of all that he holds dear in England and the English. It is very much an informal ramble, as if in the company of an old friend. He treats us to a display of sparkling and knowledgeable comments on our national life from Churchill to Pubs, Elgar to Rugby, Bertie Wooster to George Orwell, British Beef to the National Lottery and from Fish and Chips to Evelyn Waugh.

'A mixture of eccentricity and scholarship, highly entertaining'. A.J.P. Taylor

'Godfrey Smith writes beautiful pithy English, he venerates the beauties of English towns and countryside, luxuriates in English freedoms, cherishes the riches of English civilisation, loves his country'. John Keegan

Hardback 288 pages, 24 illustrations

Life in Victorian Britain

Enquire Within Upon Everything 1890

In the wake of the Industrial Revolution the population swiftly developed a thirst for knowledge about the myriad of new goods and ideas that were becoming available. But before the days of television, newspaper advertising and junk mail how did people get to know about everything? Over a million people solved the problem by buying a copy of this book which caused a publishing sensation in Victorian Britain. Because it explained so much about so many different aspects of life then, it continues to provide a very enjoyable and informative peep into the lifestyle of our forebears for us over a century later.

In 2775 entries the enquiring Victorian learns to tell if food is fresh and when it is in season; how to dance; the difference between dialects; correcting grammar and spelling; the rules of games and puzzles; hints on etiquette; kitchen and household hints and recipes; cures for ailments including rheumatism and baldness; the origins of Christian names; first aid; employment and rental regulations; keeping fit; dressmaking and embroidery; births, marriages and deaths; personal conduct as well as scores of others. We know when and where the Victorians lived. This fascinating book explains much about how they lived.

Hardback 416 pages

The Confessions of a Poacher 1890

The tips and tricks of a true countryman who started dabbling in the fine art of poaching as soon as he was old enough to slip unseen through a copse at dusk or slither along the river bank to a trout filled pool.

These observations of nature are so well written that it is hard to imagine you are not out of doors when reading them. At first all is seen through the eyes of the trainee poacher and we feel the lure of the night as the young rustic watches his father's eventide preparations.

As our young man progresses he reveals the age old methods of inveigling the spoils of a night time's work from its roost to the security of the poacher's pocket without troubling the keeper with the loud report of a gun. There are chapters on poaching Partridges, Hares, Grouse, Pheasants, Rabbits, Salmon and Trout each packed with lore, experience and wisdom. But of all the wildlife to which we are so comprehensively introduced there is just one trouble making species that appears page after page - the squire's keeper. As much native cunning is employed to avoid him as is used to encounter the game. Even if you are not contemplating a life of rural misdeeds there is still much you could learn about the countryside from this delightful book, so also could the local squire, his keeper and the constabulary but let us hope that they do not pick up too many tips about preventing the fine art of poaching. *Hardback 176 pages*

Railways

Bradshaw's Railway Map 1907

This map shows lines in England, Scotland, Wales and Ireland with detailed enlargements of the major conurbations.
The great main lines with major stations and termini are marked as well as many small village halts on the humble country branch lines.

The map bears witness to the culmination of the gargantuan engineering feat which produced 23,000 route miles in the 82 years since the first 25 miles of railway was completed between Stockton and Darlington in 1825.

Compare that to the less than 11,000 miles we have a century later and use the map to explore the hundreds of routes, with their stations, which ran through so many parts of the country but survived for no more than a few generations before succumbing to the march of progress which favoured alternative means of transport.

Available folded in a protective wallet and also rolled with a coloured printed 'mount' ready for framing.
Overall size with 'mount' 37½ x 27¼" (95.6 x 69.4 cms)

Through the Window 1924

The Great Western Railway from Paddington to Penzance, 1924

From the age of steam and elegant travel. Enjoy the view from your GWR express train as you journey the 305 miles from Paddington to Penzance. A 1924 handbook for the railway traveller, enables you to do just that! It points out hundreds of interesting features which could be seen from the windows of the elegant carriages of God's Wonderful Railway, cross referenced to the accompanying maps and exquisite line drawings.

Paperback 144 pages

The River Thames

The Oarsman's and Angler's Map of the River Thames 1893

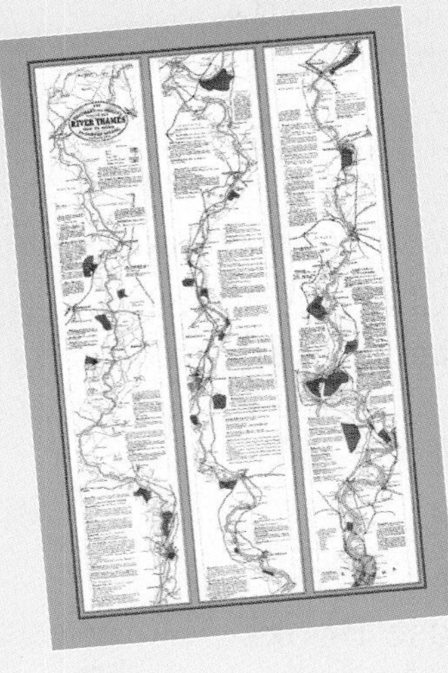

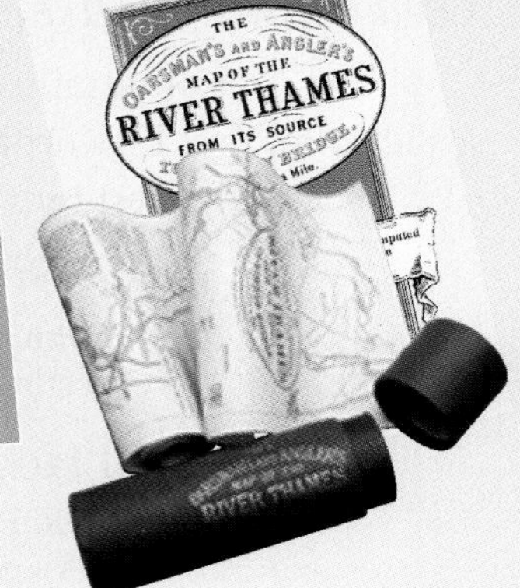

Explore Britain's best loved waterway with the map that must surely have been used by the *Three Men in a Boat.*

Very detailed, 1" to the mile and over 8 feet in length, it shows all 164 miles from the source to London. Riverside towns and villages are marked with historical information and details of the locks and how to operate them. For fishermen the best pools where trout, pike, perch and others were to be found. There are also details of toll charges and angling laws and a description of life on the river a century ago when the Thames was the nation's favourite place for recreation and sport.

8 foot 4 inches long and 6 inches wide. (255.5 x 15.5 cms).
Folded in a protective wallet or scrolled in a gold-blocked presentation tube.
Also available on one sheet (as above) in three sections with a coloured printed 'mount', rolled ready for framing.
Overall size with 'mount' 25" x 38½" (63.5 x 97.5 cms)

The first edition of this book
was published in 1890
by Karl Baedeker, Leipzig.
This facsimile edition was published in 2004 by
Old House Books
Printed and bound in India

ISBN 1 873590 32 6

Other titles published by Old House Books

For details of other facsimile
Victorian and Edwardian maps and guidebooks
published by Old House Books
see pages 601 - 608.

Further information is available by
requesting a catalogue

Old House Books
The Old Police Station
Pound Street
Moretonhampstead
Newton Abbot
Devon UK
TQ13 8PA

Tel: 01647 440707 Fax: 01647 440202
Email: info@OldHouseBooks.co.uk

or by visiting our website
www.OldHouseBooks.co.uk